EVIDENCE:
TEACHING MATERIALS FOR AN AGE OF SCIENCE AND STATUTES

Fifth Edition: 2002

Ronald L. Carlson
Fuller E. Callaway Professor of Law
University of Georgia

Edward J. Imwinkelried
Professor of Law
University of California at Davis

Edward J. Kionka
Professor of Law
Southern Illinois University

Kristine Strachan
(Retired) Dean and Professor of Law
University of San Diego

Library of Congress Control Number: 2001096164

ISBN#: 0-82055-313-1

Editorial Offices
744 Broad Street, Newark, NJ 07102 (973) 820-2000
201 Mission St., San Francisco, CA 94105-1831 (415) 908-3200
www.lexis.com

Dedications

Professor Carlson dedicates his work to Mary, Mike, and Andy.

Professor Imwinkelried dedicates his work to Cindy, Molly, Kenny, and Morgan; his parents, Mr. and Mrs. John Imwinkelried; and his parents–in–law, the late Mary Jane Clark and Lyman (Brownie) Clark.

Professor Kionka dedicates his work to his late parents, Antoinette H. Kionka and Edward F. Kionka.

Professor Strachan dedicates her work to Gordon, Lauren and Adam.

As a teacher, [Felix Frankfurter] . . . developed his threefold imperative to law students: (1) Read the statute; (2) read the statute; (3) read the statute!

—Henry J. Friendly, Benchmarks

Preface to the Fifth Edition

When we considered the title of our fourth edition, we selected a title highlighting our belief that evidence law has entered "AN AGE OF SCIENCE AND STATUTES." Developments since the release of that edition confirm our belief. In this new edition, we have attempted to refine our focus on issues relating to scientific evidence and legisprudence.

To begin with, the role of expert testimony, including scientific evidence, continues to grow–as does the controversy over this subject. The controversy swirls at two levels. At one level, the battle is between the proponents of *Daubert* and the advocates of *Frye*. Like the reports of Samuel Clemens' death, predictions of the demise of *Frye* have turned out to be "greatly exaggerated." Courts in many of the largest and most litigious states, including California, Florida, Illinois, and New York, have decided to adhere to some variation of the traditional general acceptance standard. At another level, in *Daubert* jurisdictions the battle is between the proponents of scientific testimony and the opponents. In some respects, *Daubert* appears to have toughened admissibility standards. In late 2000, the Federal Judicial Center released a study of the admissibility of expert testimony. In 1995, the center asked federal District Judges whether in their most recent trial, they had admitted all the proffered testimony. At that time, 75% of the judges answered in the affirmative. In the most recent study, that figure had fallen to 58%. In 1991, the center asked the judges whether they had ever excluded expert testimony. At that time, 25% of the judges answered yes. In the most recent study, that figure had risen to 41%.

Moreover, legisprudential issues loom ever larger. On December 1, 2000, a hefty set of amendments to the Rules took effect. Quite apart from the debates over the various amendments, there is a multi–faceted controversy over the legislative process. In a 1999 exchange, Professor Glen Weissenberger, one of the leading commentators on this subject, reiterated his view that the Federal Rules of Evidence should be neither conceived nor construed as statutes. Weissenberger, Evidence Myopia: The Failure to See the Federal Rules of Evidence as a Codification of the Common Law, 40 Wm. & M.L.Rev. 1539 (1999). In addition, Professor Paul Rice has been highly critical of the Advisory Committee process for revising the statutes. Rice, The Evidence Project–Proposed Revisions to the Federal Rules of Evidence, 171 F.R.D. 330, 335–36 (1997).

Last, in this new edition, we have introduced a pedagogical innovation. It is a commonplace observation among evidence teachers that our students struggle with such distinctions as the differences between substantive and credibility theories, character and non–character relevance, and hearsay and non–hearsay uses. Students frequently misunderstand these distinctions and err when they attempt to apply them, We have concluded that part of the reason for the confusion is that students do not appreciate what the judge will tell the jury about the evidence by way of instruction and what the lawyer may tell the jury about the evidence during closing argument. Accordingly, at various junctures in the credibility, character, and hearsay chapters, we have added material designed to force the students to think about the tenor of the relevant instructions and the permissible discussion of the evidence during summation. Our hope is that this new technique will help our students master the distinctions which they seem to struggle with year after year.

Ronald Carlson
Edward Imwinkelried
Edward Kionka
Kristine Strachan

Provenance: Notes from Earlier Prefaces

Fourth Edition

At the outset, we want to take this opportunity to welcome our new co-author, Dean Kristine Strachan. After three editions, the original authors unanimously concluded that we needed a fresh set of eyes to prepare the fourth edition. As an experienced evidence teacher, Dean Strachan provided the necessary, new perspective. In addition, she brought outstanding editorial skill to the project and kindly agreed to serve as general editor for this edition.

The *Devitt* casefile has undergone major surgery. In the prior editions, the complainant was an alleged rape victim. In most chapters of the new edition, there is a male victim of a battery. In the chapters discussing the evidentiary rules peculiar to sexual assault prosecutions, the facts are varied to include a rape charge.

The emphasis on scientific problems is evident at two levels. At one level, there are repeated reference to *Daubert* and its progeny. When the Court handed down *Daubert* in 1993, some commentators suggested that the Court had liberalized the standards for admitting purportedly scientific evidence. As the new edition explains, *Daubert* has proven to be a two–edged sword. Although the decision opens a window for admitting testimony about novel scientific theories, in other respects *Daubert* has toughened the standards. The lower courts are enforcing the new empirical validation standard with rigor.

At a second level, there is increasing resort to scientific research to critique the underlying assumptions of evidence law. Although *Daubert* has garnered the headlines, perhaps the most significant innovation since the release of our third edition has been the enactment of Federal Rules 413–415. There was certainly a political impetus for that legislation. However, another contributing factor was the reassessment of the empirical research into the validity of character as a predictor of conduct. A number of commentators, including David Bryden, David Crump, Susan Davies, Miguel Mendez, and Roger Park, have contributed to that reassessment. The fourth edition references their contributions.

Moreover, as in the prior editions, there is a heavy emphasis on statutory construction. If anything, that topic has heated up since the release of the third edition. At that time, the Justices of the Supreme Court seemed largely committed to a textualist approach to the interpretation of the Rules. Since that time, some Justices, notably Justices Breyer and Kennedy, have moved away from that approach. In addition, several scholars have endeavored to construct alternatives to textualism. Randolph Jonakait, Eileen Scallen, Andrew Taslitz, and Glen Weissenberger have been leaders in that endeavor. The fourth edition liberally cites to their works. Their articles have both enlivened and enriched the debate.

All four of us share a firm belief that in a modern evidence course, the teacher must do far more than review and critique evidentiary doctrine. As our new title indicates, this is an Age of Science and Statutes. Today a competent practitioner must be adept at working with materials generated by scientific researchers. Further, the practitioner must have sophisticated statutory interpretation skills. As a teaching tool, the fourth edition is designed to afford the student opportunities to work with scientific research material and to develop those interpretive skills. Admittedly, to ensure those opportunities, we have somewhat abbreviated our coverage of evidentiary doctrine. However, we hope that you will agree with us that the trade-off is in our students' best interest.

Prefaces to the Third and Second Editions

Two key reasons prompt the second and third editions: we wanted to place greater emphasis on developing students' statutory construction skills and we wanted to underscore the potential impact of science on evidence law.

Since the release of the second edition, statutory interpretation has become a "hot topic." The conventional wisdom has been that in interpreting statutes, judges should freely consult extrinsic legislative history material such as committee reports to identify the rational purpose inspiring the statute. Conservative jurists, notably Justices Rehnquist and Scalia and Judges Easterbrook and Posner, are now challenging that wisdom. Eskridge, *The New Textualism,* 37 U.C.L.A. L. Rev. 621, 624 (1990). Eskridge & Frickey, *Legislation Scholarship and Pedagogy in the Post–Legal Process Era,* 48 U. Pitt. L. Rev. 691 (1987). Liberal jurists, including Judge Patricia Wald, have rushed to the defense of the conventional practice. The dispute over the proper approach to statutory interpretation has surfaced in evidence decisions. Jonakait, *The Supreme Court, Plain Meaning, and the Changed Rules of Evidence,* 68 Tex. L. Rev. 745 (1990).

Moreover, the influence of science on evidentiary doctrine is becoming more evident. In some cases, commentators are citing empirical research to support calls for the reform of evidentiary doctrine. *E.g.,* Zacharias, *Rethinking Confidentiality,* 74 Iowa L. Rev. 351 (1989). In other cases, the battle over the admissibility of a novel type of evidence such as DNA typing is being fought over the scientific merit of the technique. Thompson & Ford, *DNA Typing: Acceptance and Weight of the New Genetic Identification Tests,* 75 Va. L. Rev. 45 (1989). These battles are making front–page headlines. San Francisco Chronicle, Jan. 29, 1990, at A1 ("Scientists Voice Doubts About DNA Tracking").

In light of these developments, we have made statutory interpretation and the impact of science pervasive themes in the third edition. To emphasize this focus on current developments in evidence law, we have renamed our course-book *Evidence in the Nineties.* The second edition acknowledged the contribution of Professors Richard Friedman and Dale Nance, whose perceptive criticisms and suggestions made that edition a better teaching tool.

Preface to the First Edition

In the preface to the first edition, we explained our reasons for wanting to publish a new evidence coursebook: providing a better analytical approach to the study of evidence; teaching through the problem method based on a civil and criminal case file; emphasis on the procedural context of evidence law; and enhanced focus on logical and legal relevance doctrine. This emphasis reflected our belief that in the courtroom, relevance is by far the most important evidentiary doctrine. Our litigation experience persuaded us that, for better or worse, few trials present really novel or thorny hearsay or privilege problems. However, in every trial, every attorney must deal with the logical relevance doctrine in establishing the materiality of the evidence and the authenticity of any exhibits offered; and problems of legal relevance are most pervasive. Moreover, a sound grasp of logical relevance—the ability to develop an imaginative alternative theory of relevance—is often the key to overcoming an objection based on one of the competence rules such as hearsay or the subsequent repair doctrine.

We also noted that the first edition was intended solely as a teaching device rather than a reference work. A relatively small number of cases and case extracts were used, based on our belief that evidence is not a good course in which to use the case method: it is simply too time–consuming. The all-important application of law to facts can best be learned through the use of problems and hypotheticals spun off the problems. Finally, we noted that some of our students commented that they could not understand evidence doctrine because they could not visualize applied use of the doctrine. Thus, we included at the end of every chapter a list of sample foundations in order to meld concrete application with conceptual theory.

Acknowledgments

The authors acknowledge their debt to the inspired writings on evidence by the late Mason Ladd, former dean at both the Iowa and Florida State law schools. Professor Carlson was privileged to serve as a casebook co–author with Dean Ladd. Portions of the Ladd and Carlson casebook were helpful in preparing this book, especially with regard to the hearsay rule.

Previous edition acknowledgments: Professor Imwinkelried's research assistants: Theodore Blumoff, Lucy Karl and Thomas Lammert; the Washington University Law School secretaries who prepared the first edition manuscript: Ilse Arndt, Barbara Aumer, Jane Bettlach, Dora Bradley, Susan Hutchings, Mary Ellen Powers, and especially Mary Schelling; and third edition research assistants: Joseph deUlloa and David Kornbluh. Professor Kionka acknowledged the Southern Illinois University School of Law, which provided research assistance and secretarial services.

The authors acknowledge their enormous debt and appreciation to Ms. Theresa Hrenchir of the University of San Diego School of Law for her extraordinary contribution to the preparation of the Fourth Edition. Successful completion of the project is in large part due to her outstanding legal ability, analytical skill and professionalism in producing the text, overseeing the work of three sets of research assistants, and coordinating the complexity of the communications and work product of the co–authors. Every group of law professors should be blessed with such a dedicated and meticulous editor. The authors are also grateful to their research assistants for their help on the Fourth Edition: Darren R. Beardsley, University of San Diego School of Law; Ryan Hall and Lynn Loschin, University of California at Davis, School of Law; Chandler Mason, Tripp Self, and Molly Kleiber, University of Georgia School of Law. Professor Carlson also acknowledges Mary Fielding of the University of Georgia staff for her assistance with manuscript preparation.

RLC
EJI
EJK
KS

We gratefully acknowledge the following sources of excerpts:

Belli, Demonstrative Evidence and the Adequate Award, 22 Miss. L. J. 284 (1951). Copyright 1951, Mississippi Law Journal, reprinted with permission.

C.D. Bowen, The Lion and the Throne 190-217, 414–16. Copyright 1956 by Catherine Drinker Bowen. First Published in Atlantic Monthly Press, Boston 1957.

Carlson, Impeaching Jury Verdicts, 2 Litigation, Fall 1975 at 31–33. Copyright 1983, American Bar Association, Section of Litigation, reprinted with permission.

Comment, The Husband-Wife Privileges of Testimonial Non–Disclosure, 56 Nw. U. L. Rev. 208, 220-22 (1961). Reprinted by special permission of Northwestern University School of Law, Law Review.

Cutler, Thigpen, Young & Mueller, The Evidentiary Value of Spectrographic Voice Identification, 63 J. of Crim. Law, Criminology and Police Science 343 (1972). Reprinted by special permission of Northwestern University, School of Law.

Davis, Judicial Notice, 55 Colum. L. Rev. 945, 952-53 (1955). Reprinted with permission.

Easterbrook, Statutes' Domains, 50 U. Chi. L. Rev. 533, 544-52 (1983). Reprinted with permission.

Garcia, Garbage In, Gospel Out: Criminal Discovery, Computer Reliability, and the Constitution, 38 U.C.L.A. L. Rev. 1043 (1991). Copyright 1991, The Regents of the University of California. All Rights Reserved. Reprinted with the permission of the U.C.L.A. Law Review and Wm. S. Hein & Co.

Gerard, The Usefulness of the Medical Model to the Mental Health Legal System, in Mental Health Law in the 1980's (1985), adapted version reprinted in Gerard, The Usefulness of the Medical Model to the Legal System, 39 Rutgers L. Rev. 377 (1987). Reprinted with permission.

Graham, Prior Consistent Statements: Rule 801(d)(1)(B) of the Federal Rules of Evidence, Critique and Proposal, 30 Hastings L. J. 575, 584 (1979). Copyright 1979 Hastings College of the Law, Univ. of California. Reprinted with permission.

R. Hastie, S. Penrod & N. Pennington, Inside the Jury 37-41 (1983). Copyright 1983 by the President and Fellows of Harvard College. Reprinted with permission of Harvard University Press.

Hutchins & Slesinger, Some Observations on the Law of Evidence, 28 Colum. L. Rev 432, 437-39 (1928). Reprinted with permission of the Columbia Law Review.

Imwinkelried, The "Bases" of Expert Testimony: The Syllogistic Structure of Scientific Testimony, 67 N.C. L. Rev. 1, 9 (1988). Reprinted with permission.

E. Imwinkelried, P. Giannelli, F. Gilligan & F. Lederer, Criminal Evidence 1089–1100 (3d ed. 1998). Copyright by The Michie Company. All Rights Reserved.

F. James & G. Hazard, Civil Procedure § 7.8 (3d ed. 1985). Reprinted with permission.

J. Jeans, Trial Advocacy § 8.13 (2d ed. 1993). Reprinted with permission of the West Group.

Kalven, The Jury, the Law, and the Personal Injury Damage Award, 19 Ohio St. L. J. 158, 170-72 (1958). Reprinted with permission of the Ohio State Law Journal.

Ladd, Some Observations on Credibility: Impeachment of Witnesses, 52 Cornell L. Q. 239, 245 (1967). Reprinted with permission. All Rights Reserved.

C. McCormick, Handbook of the Law of Evidence § 47 (West Publishing Co., Cleary ed. 1984). Reprinted with permission of the West Group.

C. McCormick, Evidence § 19, at 78-81 (4th ed. 1992). Reprinted from C. McCormick, Handbook of the Law of Evidence, with permission of the West Group.

McNaughton, Judicial Notice–Excerpts Relating to the Morgan–Wigmore Controversy, 14 Vand. L. Rev. 779 (1961). Reprinted with permission of Vanderbilt Law Review.

Margolis, Motion Pictures–An Effective Tool in the Presentation of the Personal Injury Claim, Trial Diplomacy J. 32 (Spring 1980).

Mendez, California's New Law on Character Evidence: Evidence Code Section 352 and the Impact of Recent Psychological Studies, 31 U.C.L.A. L. Rev. 1003, 1045-53 (1984). Copyright 1984, The Regents of the University of California. All Rights Reserved. Reprinted with the permission of U.C.L.A. Law Review and Wm. S. Hein & Co.

A. Morrill, Trial Diplomacy § 4.29 (2d ed. 1972).

J.E.B. Myers, Evidence in Child Abuse and Neglect Cases §§ 2.10-.11 (2d ed. 1992). Copyright 2001 Aspen Publishers, Inc. Reprinted with permission.

Note, Hearsay Bases of Psychiatric Opinion Testimony: A Critique of Federal Rule of Evidence 703, 51 Southern Cal. L. Rev. 129 (1977). Reprinted with permission of Southern California Law Review.

R. Posner, The Federal Courts: Challenge and Reform 286-93 (1988). Copyright 1985, 1996 by the President and Fellows of Harvard College. Reprinted by permission of Harvard University Press.

Professional Responsibility, Report of the Joint Conference, 44 A.B.A. J. 1159-61 (1958). Reprinted with permission.

Risinger, Denbeaux & Saks, Exorcism of Ignorance as a Proxy for Rational Knowledge: The Lessons of Handwriting Identification "Expertise," 137 U. Pa. L. Rev. 731 (1989). Copyright 1989. Reprinted with the permission of the University of Pennsylvania Law Review and Fred B. Rothman & Co.

Schmertz & Czapanskiy, Bias Impeachment and the Proposed Federal Rules of Evidence, 61 Georgetown L. J. 257, 265-69 (1972). Reprinted with permission.

Tribe, Triangulating Hearsay, 87 Harv. L. Rev. 957, 958-61 (1974). Copyright 1974 by the Harvard Law Review Association.

Walker, Thibaut & Andresli, Order of Presentation at Trial, 82 Yale L. J. 216-26 (1972). Reprinted by permission of The Yale Law Journal Company and Wm. S. Hein & Co.

Waltz & Huston, The Rules of Evidence in Settlement, 5 Litigation, Fall 1978, at 11. Copyright 1981. American Bar Association, Section of Litigation, reprinted with permission.

Waltz & Park, Evidence 82-83 (8th ed. 1995). Copyright 1995 Foundation Press, Inc. Reprinted with permission.

J. Weinstein & M. Berger, 2 Weinstein's Evidence ¶ 410[03] 410-36 to 37 (1986). Copyright by Matthew Bender & Co., Inc. All Rights Reserved.

J. Weinstein & M. Berger, 3 Weinstein's Evidence ¶ 607[04] (1995). Copyright by Matthew Bender & Co., Inc. All Rights Reserved.

J. Weinstein & M. Berger, 3 Weinstein's Evidence ¶ 601[03] at 601-20, 601-25 to 27, ¶ 607[06] (1981). Copyright 1990 by Matthew Bender & Co., Inc. All Rights Reserved.

2 Wigmore on Evidence §§ 411-12 (3d ed. 1940). Reprinted with permission of Aspen Publishers, Inc.

8 J. Wigmore, Evidence § 2285 (McNaughton rev. 1961). Reprinted with permission of Aspen Publishers, Inc.

J. Wigmore, A Student's Textbook of the Law of Evidence § 92 (1935). Reprinted with permission of Aspen Publishers, Inc.

Zacharias, Rethinking Confidentiality, 74 Iowa L. Rev. 351, 377-81, 383-86, 394-95, 409-11 (1989). Adapted and reprinted with permission.

Summary Table of Contents

Page

TABLE OF CONTENTS

Page

Chapter 14. Specialized Aspects of Legal Irrelevance: Character, Habit, Other Acts and Transactions
. . . .

313

Page

Part 1

BACKGROUND, FRAMEWORK AND
PROCEDURE

Chapter 1

THE PHILOSOPHY AND HISTORY OF AMERICAN EVIDENCE LAW

A. INTRODUCTION

A trial or hearing in a court or other tribunal is a dispute resolution mechanism. At the hearing, the judge, hearing officer, or jury makes findings of fact necessary to resolve the dispute. Public perception of the effectiveness of the hearing and the soundness of the result is critical. Unless there is widespread confidence that the dispute has been resolved fairly and efficiently, there is a danger that aggrieved parties will attempt to resolve their dispute or seek vindication privately in some socially unacceptable—perhaps violent—manner. *See, e.g.,* Nesson, *The Evidence or the Event? On Judicial Proof and the Acceptability of Verdicts,* 98 HARV. L. REV. 1357 (1985).

We could, of course, devise much simpler procedures and evidentiary rules for such hearings. There are not that many essential functions to perform in order to discover the truth: we must define the issues between the parties (the pleading function), gather information on the issues (the discovery function), and decide which information to consider in resolving the issues (the evidentiary function). We could choose to approach those tasks with relative informality and simplicity.

For reasons which will become apparent as you study this area of the law, we have chosen not to follow the simple approach. Quite to the contrary, we have developed complex procedures and evidentiary rules. In this chapter, we examine the philosophic and historic underpinnings of that development. Those underpinnings are reflected in our commitment to an adversary system; the use of lay jurors as fact finders; and the use of evidentiary rules to further other social policies. We must understand each of these aspects of the American legal system before we consider the specific procedures and evidentiary rules governing the process of proof at trial. As you analyze each aspect of the system, attempt to identify the assumptions of the current system and ask yourself whether those assumptions have been empirically validated.

B. THE ADVERSARY SYSTEM

The term "inquisitorial" has pejorative connotations in the Anglo–American legal system. The term conjures up images of the Star Chamber's secret hearings—trials presided over by oppressive judges and conducted by cruel interrogation methods. However, on the Continent, where inquisitorial procedures are common, the term has a different meaning. It connotes that a magistrate has primary responsibility for pretrial factual investigation and the presentation of evidence at trial. In the United States, partisan attorneys representing the opposing parties exercise primary control over the course of pretrial discovery and evidentiary presentation. In Europe, an independent, impartial magistrate exerts that control.

The differences between our adversary system and the Continental legal systems are most clearly reflected in procedure. During our pretrial stage, the discovery mechanisms ordinarily do not come into play until a party invokes them and specifically requests discovery by the other party. Rather than actively guiding the direction of pretrial discovery, the judge's role is passive. By and large, the judge merely rules on the propriety of the discovery requests and other discovery issues that cannot be informally resolved by the parties. Similarly, at trial, the parties shoulder most of the burden of presenting the case. As we shall see, trial judges have the power to call and question witnesses. However, most judges are reluctant to invoke that power. Schooled in the adversary system, they are usually content to let the attorneys "try their own case."

Although the adversary system is firmly entrenched in the United States, it has not gone without criticism. Langbein, *The German Advantage in Civil Procedure*, 52 U. CHI. L. REV. 823 (1985). Some commentators have called for the abolition of the system:

> The adversary system was born before the development of the scientific method and before the concept of objective truth. It is time that lawyers take themselves out of the Middle Ages of primitive intellectual and economic resources, out of the darkness that pitted hungry man against hungry man and away from the primal fear that taught that battle, cunning and evasion were the only ways to survive.

Greenfeld, *Abolish the Adversary System*, 1 CAL. LAW. 11, 12 (Dec. 1981). Undoubtedly the most famous call for the reform of the adversary system is Judge Frankel's article, *The Search for Truth: An Umpireal View*, 123 U. PA. L. REV. 1031 (1975). In the article, the judge notes that he has presided at trials at which it was evident that a "wily advocate . . . bested the facts and prevailed." *Id.* at 1034. In Judge Frankel's view, "[O]ur adversary system rates truth too low among the values that institutions of justice are meant to serve." *Id.* at 1032. He stressed that other countries and other disciplines "–history, geography, medicine, whatever–do not emulate our adversary system." *Id.* at 1036. Judge Frankel urged a relaxation of "our rigid insistence that the parties control the evidence until it is all 'prepared' and packaged for competitive manipulation at . . . trial." *Id.* at 1054.

Others–including most American trial lawyers and judges–vigorously defend the adversary system. M. FREEDMAN, LAWYERS' ETHICS IN AN ADVERSARY SYSTEM (1975); S. LANDSMAN, READINGS ON ADVERSARIAL JUSTICE: THE AMERICAN APPROACH TO ADJUDICATION (1988). The system's rationale is perhaps best stated in a 1958 Joint Conference Report of the American Bar Association and the Association of American Law Schools.

PROFESSIONAL RESPONSIBILITY: REPORT OF THE JOINT CONFERENCE, 44 American Bar Association Journal 1159, 1159–61 (1958)

The lawyer appearing as an advocate before a tribunal presents, as persuasively as he can, the facts and the law of the case as seen from the standpoint of his client's interest. It is essential that both the lawyer and the public understand clearly the nature of the role thus discharged. Such an understanding is required not only to appreciate the need for an adversary presentation of issues, but also in order to perceive truly the limits partisan advocacy must impose on itself if it is to remain wholesome and useful.

In a very real sense it may be said that the integrity of the adjudicative process itself depends upon the participation of the advocate. This becomes apparent when we contemplate the nature of the task assumed by any arbiter who attempts to decide a dispute without the aid of partisan advocacy.

Such an arbiter must undertake, not only the role of judge, but that of representative for both of the litigants. Each of these roles must be played to the full without being muted by qualifications derived from the others. When he is developing for each side the most effective statement of its case, the arbiter must put aside his neutrality and permit himself to be moved by a sympathetic identification sufficiently intense to draw from his mind all that it is capable of giving—in analysis, patience and creative power. When he resumes his neutral position, he must be able to view with distrust the fruits of this identification and be ready to reject the products of his own best mental efforts. The difficulties of this undertaking are obvious. If it is true that a man in his time must play many parts, it is scarcely given to him to play them all at once.

It is small wonder, then, that failure generally attends the attempt to dispense with the distinct roles traditionally implied in adjudication. What generally occurs in practice is that at some early point a familiar pattern will seem to emerge from the evidence; an accustomed label is waiting for the case and, without awaiting further proofs, this label is promptly assigned to it. It is a mistake to suppose that this premature cataloguing must necessarily result from impatience, prejudice or mental sloth. Often it proceeds from a very understandable desire to bring the hearing into some order and coherence, for without some tentative theory of the case there is no standard of relevance by which testimony may be measured. But what starts as a preliminary diagnosis designed to direct the inquiry tends, quickly and imperceptibly, to become a fixed conclusion, as all that confirms the diagnosis makes a strong imprint on the mind, while all that runs counter to it is received with diverted attention.

An adversary presentation seems the only effective means for combatting this natural human tendency to judge too swiftly in terms of the familiar that which is not yet fully known. The arguments of counsel hold the case, as it were, in suspension between two opposing interpretations of it. While the proper classification of the case is thus kept unresolved, there is time to explore all of its peculiarities and nuances.

The true significance of partisan advocacy touch[es] the integrity of the adjudicative process itself. It is only through the advocate's participation that the hearing may remain in fact what it purports to be in theory: a public trial of the facts and issues. Each advocate comes to the hearing prepared to present his proofs and arguments, knowing at the same time that his arguments may fail to persuade and that his proofs may be rejected and inadequate. It is a part of his role to absorb these possible disappointments. The deciding tribunal, on the other hand, comes to the hearing uncommitted.

The matter assumes a very different aspect when the deciding tribunal is compelled to take into its own hands the preparations that must precede the public hearing. In such a case the tribunal cannot truly be said to come to the hearing uncommitted, for it has itself appointed the channels along which the public inquiry is to run. The deciding tribunal is under a strong temptation to keep the hearing moving within the boundaries originally set for it. The result may be that the hearing loses its character as an open trial of the facts and issues, and becomes instead a ritual designed to provide public confirmation for what the tribunal considers it has already established in private. When this occurs adjudication acquires the taint affecting all institutions that become subject to manipulation, presenting one aspect to the public, another to knowing participants.

These, then, are the reasons for believing that partisan advocacy plays a vital and essential role in one of the most fundamental procedures of a democratic society. But if we were to put all of these detailed considerations to one side, we should still be confronted by the fact that, in whatever form adjudication may appear, the experienced judge or arbitrator desires and actively seeks to obtain an adversary presentation of the issues. Only when he has had the benefit of intelligent and vigorous advocacy on both sides can he feel fully confident of his decision.

Viewed in this light, the role of the lawyer as a partisan advocate appears not as a regrettable necessity, but as an indispensable part of a larger ordering of affairs. The institution of advocacy is not a concession to the frailties of human nature, but an expression of human insight in the design of a social framework within which man's capacity for impartial judgment can attain its fullest realization.

NOTES

1. The "intuitive hypothesis" of the Joint Conference Report has a plausible, common sense appeal. Thibaut, Walker & Lind, *Adversary Presentation and Bias in Legal Decisionmaking*, 86 HARV. L. REV. 386, 397 (1972). However, in scientific research, it can be a grave mistake to confuse the plausible and the proven.

To date, there has been little empirical research into the validity of the Joint Conference's hypothesis. Some research provides "empirical support for the general claim . . . that an adversary presentation significantly counteracts decisionmaker bias." *Id.* On the other hand, there are indications that "the adversary system does not provide a generally more vigorous search for facts . . . ." Lind, Thibaut & Walker, *Discovery and Presentation of Evidence in Adversary and Nonadversary Proceedings*, 71 MICH. L. REV. 1129, 1143 (1973). Additional empirical investigation is certainly in order.

2. The influence of adversary ideology is not limited to the procedural aspects in the American legal system. We shall see later that adversary theory accounts for several substantive evidentiary doctrines, including the admissions exception to the hearsay rule and the work product privilege.

C.   THE USE OF LAY JURORS

Continental legal systems differ from ours in another respect: juries are rare. In contrast, in America, juries are used frequently. Moreover, the Sixth and Seventh Amendments to the U.S. Constitution guarantee the right to a jury in certain instances. "More than ninety percent of the world's criminal jury trials, and nearly all of its civil jury trials, take place in the United States . . . ." Casper & Zeisel, *Lay Judges in the German Criminal Courts*, 1 J. LEGAL STUDIES 135 (1978).

The use of lay jurors as decisionmakers has affected both our procedures and the content of our evidentiary rules. Anglo–American jurists have long been skeptical of lay jurors' competence. Thayer remarked that our evidence law is a "product of the jury system . . . where ordinary untrained citizens are acting as judges of fact." J. THAYER, A PRELIMINARY TREATISE ON EVIDENCE AT THE COMMON LAW 509 (1898). Many of the rules which operate to exclude logically relevant evidence reflect doubts about the jurors' capabilities. Rather than risking the jurors' misevaluation of evidence of suspect reliability, the common law sometimes excludes the evidence altogether. For example, common law judges doubted that lay jurors were sophisticated enough to detect fraud or perjury. That doubt is one reason courts fashioned the authentication requirement, which requires that lay jurors not accept physical or documentary evidence at face value; before submitting such evidence to the jury, the proponent must present extrinsic evidence to prove that the exhibit is what the proponent claims it to be. In other words, before handing a letter to the jury, the proponent would call a witness to vouch that the letter is in the defendant's handwriting. The same doubts express themselves in the hearsay rule. Thayer proclaimed that the rule was a "child of the jury" system. THAYER, *id.* at 47. Restrictions on hearsay are thought to be necessary because jurors may be unduly impressed by an out–of–court statement or overlook the possible inherent weaknesses of declarant's perception, memory, narration, or sincerity. Morgan, *Hearsay Dangers and the Application of the Hearsay Concept*, 62 HARV. L. REV. 177 (1948).

In sum, much of evidentiary doctrine is calculated to enhance the reliability of the evidence ultimately presented to the jury. The law requires additional evidence of trustworthiness to compensate for the jurors' supposedly uncritical judgment.

Until the 1960's, there had been little serious empirical research into jury competence. However, the pioneering Chicago Jury Project gave us the first hard data on the subject. In H. KALVEN & H. ZEISEL, THE AMERICAN JURY, published in 1966, two University of Chicago law professors reported on their empirical studies of jury behavior:

> We begin our inquiry into what the jury makes of the evidence
> by establishing two basic propositions. The first is simply that,

contrary to an often voiced suspicion, the jury does by and large understand the facts and get the case straight. The second proposition is that the jury's decision by and large moves with the weight and direction of the evidence. . . .

The hypothesis that the jury does *not* understand the case has loomed large in the debate over the jury. It has not infrequently been charged that the modern jury is asked to perform heroic feats of attention and recall well beyond the capacities of ordinary men. A trial, it has been argued, presents to the jury a mass of material which it cannot possibly absorb, and presents it in an artificial sequence which aggravates the jury's intellectual problem. The upshot is said to be that the jury often does not get the case straight and, therefore, is deciding a case different from the one actually before it.

The authors go on to refute this hypothesis by comparing the extent to which the judge and jury agreed or disagreed in various trials, classified according to trial length, closeness of the case, and complexity. The authors found overwhelming evidence that jurors by and large do, in fact, understand the evidence as well as the judge, and that their decisions accurately follow the weight and direction of the evidence.

Some commentators assert that the data compiled since the Chicago Jury Project "virtually unanimously" support the hypothesis that lay jurors are capable of returning "well–reasoned" verdicts. Swanson, *Book Review*, 24 TRIAL, Sept. 1988, at 106 (reviewing J. GUINTHER, THE JURY IN AMERICA (1988)). The joint report recently released by the American Bar Association and the Brookings Institution concluded that "no case is inherently too complex for [lay] juries to decide . . . ." Shoop, *Report Sees Active Role for Civil Juries*, 29 TRIAL, March 1993, at 14. New research by Professor Neil Vidmar points to the same conclusion. Vidmar found that "juries . . . grasp the essentials of a case when they are carefully presented by lawyers and experts. 'Juries sometimes misunderstand cases, but so do judges and other professional dispute resolvers.'" *New Scholarly Study Refutes Myths About Runaway Juries*, 19 A.T.L.A. ADVOCATE 1 (Feb. 1993). In addition, although we commonly assume that lay jurors unquestioningly accept any expert's testimony, the most recent data indicate that lay jurors are much more independent and selective than originally supposed. Loftus, *Psychological Aspects of Courtroom Testimony*, in 347 ANNALS OF THE NEW YORK ACADEMY OF SCIENCES 27, 32–33 (1980).

On the other hand, some research indicates that jurors can be easily influenced by factors unrelated to the merits of the case. For example, the Duke Law and Language Project has found that the type of diction witnesses use during a trial can significantly affect the verdict. Parkinson & Parkinson, *Speech Tactics for Successful Trials*, 15 TRIAL, Sept. 1979, at 36. If the witness uses concrete nouns and verbs, the jury is more likely to convict; but if the witness employs abstract terms, the diction generates confusion that leads to doubts and acquittals.

One final caution: do not assume that every trial is a jury trial. Quite to the contrary, most trials are bench trials; the judge sits without a jury and serves as trier of fact as well as presiding judge. If we consider administrative hearings as well as judicial trials, it is clear that jury trials represent only a small percentage of the total number of hearings conducted each year in the United States. *See generally* Davis, *Hearsay in Nonjury Cases*, 83 HARV. L. REV. 1362 (1970).

D. EVIDENTIARY RULES BASED ON EXTERNAL SOCIAL POLICIES

At a bare minimum, any rational trial judge should regulate the presentation of evidence by excluding irrelevant evidence. It may also be defensible to exclude evidence which, although possibly relevant, is of suspect trustworthiness, such as some forms of hearsay. However, when evidence is relevant and reliable, it is quite another matter to exclude it based upon extrinsic social policies. Rather than enhancing the integrity of fact–finding, the exclusion of evidence for that purpose may distort the ultimate decision. When we deprive the trier of fact of relevant, reliable evidence, we increase the risk of a miscarriage of justice.

Yet, to a greater extent than any other legal system, the American legal system frequently excludes relevant, reliable evidence on the theory that the exclusion serves a social policy. The constitutional exclusionary rules epitomize the theory. For example, in *Mapp v. Ohio*, 367 U.S. 643 (1961), the Warren Court created the Fourth Amendment exclusionary rule, barring evidence seized in unreasonable searches. Writing for the majority, Justice Clark argued that the exclusionary rule would protect the right of privacy, a social policy prized in the United States. The rule can and does lead to the suppression of relevant, reliable physical evidence of guilt. Wright, *Must the Criminal Go Free if the Constable Blunders?*, 50 TEX. L. REV. 736 (1972); Friendly, *Is Innocence Irrelevant? Collateral Attack on Criminal Judgments*, 38 U. CHI. L. REV. 142 (1970).

It is remarkable enough that we exclude logically relevant evidence to effectuate social policies of constitutional stature. However, we have gone beyond that and exclude evidence to promote nonconstitutional policies, most notably in the privileges excluding communications between persons in confidential relationships (*e.g.*, husband and wife, attorney and client, psychotherapist and patient). We exclude privileged communications in the hope that the exclusion will facilitate a freer flow of information between the parties to the relationship. But here the trade–off is even more debatable: we exclude relevant evidence with the increased risk of miscarriage of justice in order to protect social policies which are not of constitutional dimension.

Moreover, there is a dearth of research to support the assumptions underlying the privileges. If the client or patient or spouse realized that there was no privilege, would his or her other motivations still prompt her to communicate the information accurately? If the abolition of the privilege would reduce the flow of reliable information, to what extent would it have that effect? These are questions that require empirical investigation rather than biased pronouncement. The available empirical research indicates that while the existence of the professional privileges is intended to "encourage client use of [professionals] and client forthrightness," the privileges do so to only a limited extent. Zacharias, *Rethinking Confidentiality*, 74 Iowa L. Rev. 351, 396 (1989).

In addition to the factors discussed above–the adversary system, the use of lay jurors, and external social policies–there are other considerations that underlie various rules of evidence. Rules of evidence (and related rules of trial procedure) can also have one or more of the following rationales:

- Saving time and money
- Minimizing the danger of unfair prejudice, or the danger of confusing or misleading the trier of fact
- Promoting fairness to witnesses
- Preserving the parties' right to test the credibility and trustworthiness of evidence

As we examine each rule of evidence, try to determine its underlying policy bases, its purposes, and the assumptions upon which it is premised. Knowing these things will not only help you to learn, understand, and remember the rule—it will also help you to construct arguments as an advocate or decide an evidentiary issue as a judge.

E. A RESEARCH AGENDA FOR THE FUTURE

Ever since the days of William James, American philosophy has had a distinctively empirical character. Sadly, the philosophizing about American evidence law has not lived up to that tradition. Whether the issue has been the adversary system, lay juries, or the exclusionary rule, all too often we have contented ourselves with untested assumptions. We have succumbed to the temptation to confuse the plausible and the proven. The assumptions of American evidence law require further empirical testing:

- Does the adversary model lead to a fuller record of facts at trial?
- What are the limits of lay jurors' competence?
- To what extent do we need to protect jurors from evidence that is unfairly prejudicial, or less than optimally reliable?
- To what extent would the abolition of a privilege interfere with the relationship it is intended to foster?

In one study of American jury behavior, R. Hastie, S. Penrod & N. Pennington, Inside the Jury (1983), the authors assert that given the availability of social science and statistical methods, it is no longer tolerable for legal policymakers to rely "on the vagaries of intuition and personal experience." In making that assertion, the authors echo one of the earliest and most insightful witness psychologists, Hugo Munsterberg. Munsterberg bemoaned the fact that the "lawyer and the judge and the juryman are sure that they do not need the experimental psychologist." H. Munsterberg, On the Witness Stand 9–10, 63 (1908). However, he was confident that "sooner or later" the legal profession would realize that it could no longer rely on "the primitive psychology of common sense." *Id.*; Munsterberg, *Nothing but the Truth*, 29 McClure's Mag. 532, 536 (1907). Before casting common sense aside, though, the reader must also understand some of the limitations of empirical techniques:

Two major methodological concerns face a researcher when designing a study, namely internal validity and external validity. Internal validity refers to the degree to which changes in the measured dependent variables can be attributed to the manipulated independent variables. External validity refers to the degree to which the findings or results of research in one setting, such as a laboratory experiment, can be generalized to another setting, such as an actual courtroom. Threats to internal validity generally arise when factors other than the independent variables may be the causes of observed changes in the dependent variables. Threats to external validity arise when differences between the two settings–the research setting and the target setting–are such that effects found in the research setting do not hold in the target setting.

There is a tension between the concerns of internal and external validity. The more control one has over an experimental environment, the more one can ensure that all variables other than the dependent variable are held constant, thereby decreasing or eliminating the possibility that these extraneous or confounding variables have a causal role in producing the observed effects. This means increased confidence in the internal validity of experimental findings. However, experimental control usually comes at the cost of increased artificiality of the research environment. This means decreased external validity or generalizability of any observed cause–and–effect relationships. In the other direction, the closer an experimental environment is to a real world setting, the more likely that any experimental result will be valid in the real world situation. But by drawing the complexities of the real world into an experiment, one usually sacrifices the control and simplicity of design that increase internal validity. For example, one field study identified a correlational relationship between the race of a defendant and the severity of sentence for interracial crimes. However, it would be difficult to conclude with any confidence that the race of the defendant alone caused the differences in sentencing. Any one of a number of other factors that may not have been measured and which certainly were not controlled could have contributed to the observed difference in sentencing. Indeed, subsequent research showed that the observed differences may have been attributable to the prior criminal history of the defendants rather than to racial factors. . . .

In jury research, field studies may be even more difficult to execute than in other areas of social research. Because of legal and ethical restrictions, a jury researcher can seldom, if ever, systematically manipulate the conditions under which an actual jury operates, such as jury size or decision rule, and can never directly observe many events of major interest, such as the content of jury deliberations. As a result, most jury research has used the mock–jury simulation method.

The main advantages of studying mock juries as opposed to real juries derive from the high internal validity of the controlled experiment. One of the most serious threats to internal validity is the possibility that the apparent cause in a cause–and–effect relationship is not the true cause. To be confident that a particular cause is actually producing an observed effect, it is desirable to hold all conditions besides the independent or causal variable constant. Thus, for example, to study the effect of the defendant's race on sentencing would require making sure that all variables other than race were the same in each group of cases. This is not possible in a natural setting, where each trial is different, each defendant is different, and a large set of variables besides race may differentiate two groups of cases which have been divided into categories by race. In a simulation, these potentially confounding variables may be controlled.

Social scientists often substitute statistical control for experimental control of confounding factors. Under some conditions statistical modeling methods can provide statistical control that allows a researcher to make causal inferences. In some cases, particularly where policy analysis is involved, statistical control may be more appropriate than experimental control. However, experimental or converging experimental and nonexperimental analyses are always preferable to statistical control alone in scientific research.

Extraneous differences in a real trial, such as the facts of the case or the characteristics of the defendant, are not the only possible sources of confounding of a relationship. Differences in the personal characteristics of members of a real jury can also confound a relationship. Here the advantage of a jury simulation is that the same stimulus trial may be shown to many sets of experimental juries. The performance of multiple replications removes the potentially confounding effect of individual differences, such as social class or gender. The method also permits study of a distribution of juror behavior, making it statistically possible to assess the replicability of observed differences.

The experimental control in a jury simulation which allows for increased confidence in observed effects also allows for systematic evaluation of an independent variable far beyond what could be done in a natural setting. One can ask mock jurors questions that the legal system would not usually ask real jurors. Mock jurors may be asked demographic questions, attitude questions, and questions concerning their feelings toward jury deliberation and verdicts or their assessments of other jurors. In addition to flexibility in the choice of measures, the jury simulation allows for observation of the mock jury's reactions to the trial and juror behavior during deliberations.

While methodological and practical reasons thus compel use of the simulation method for extensive jury research, the jury simulation entails drawbacks in the area of external validity. The seriousness of these drawbacks depends on the questions to be answered by the simulation and the way it is carried out. One problem has to do with the subject population. The vast majority of jury simulations have used students as mock jurors; only 12.5 percent have used subjects from an actual jury pool. But the use of student subjects is questionable. Because students differ as a group from actual jurors in terms of age, education, income, and ideology, students' behavior differs systematically from the behavior of real jurors. Students tend to be less likely to vote for conviction than typical jurors. Younger jurors and jurors with less jury experience are apt to show leniency, which may explain the leniency bias found among students. Since age and trial experience distinguish students from actual jurors, these two factors create a problem for generalizing from student mock jurors to real jurors. In general, evidence suggests that differences between students and real jurors pose a threat to the external validity of many conclusions from jury simulations that use only student subjects.

Still another important issue for jury simulations is the difference between the consequences of real jury and mock jury decisions. A real jury decides the fate of an actual defendant; a mock jury usually knows that its decision will have no such impact. Comparison of the verdicts of "alternate" jurors (subjects from the jury pool who observed as a group in the gallery of a courtroom) with real jurors in ten cases, revealed a greater tendency toward conviction among the alternate juries. In contrast, comparison of two groups of student jurors, half of whom were told they were actually deciding a student discipline case and half of whom were told they were mock jurors, found the mock juries more lenient. A similar study found no verdict differences between mock juries and real juries.

Excerpted from R. HASTIE, S. PENROD & N. PENNINGTON, INSIDE THE JURY 37–41 (1983) (citations omitted)

NOTES

Throughout this text, we shall refer to empirical studies questioning the underlying assumptions of evidentiary doctrines. However, just as we urge the reader to have a critical attitude toward evidentiary doctrine, we recommend that the reader review the studies with skepticism. As you read the various studies included in the text, keep these questions constantly in mind:

- Does the author of the study give us enough background information about the study to enable us independently to assess its internal and external validity?

- Did the researchers control all the variables that might explain their findings? Did the researchers rely on an incomplete model of human behavior?

- Can we confidently transfer the research findings to the real world? Was the data base large enough and representative enough? Was the study conducted under conditions that approximate real world situations?

F. THE HISTORY OF AMERICAN EVIDENCE LAW

1. INTRODUCTION

This is the Age of Statutes. G. CALABRESI, A COMMON LAW FOR THE AGE OF STATUTES (2000). American jurisprudence has common law origins, but statutes have become the dominant source of modern American law. Most major areas of American law are undergoing "statutization." Evidence law is no exception.

Until recently (*i.e.*, the 1970's), the law of evidence in both state and federal courts derived mostly from judicial decisions. Except in a few states, there were no evidence codes. The few statutes or court rules concerning evidence were very narrow, typically covering specific subjects such as the competency of witnesses, the admission of business records, and the privileges against being compelled to divulge the contents of certain confidential communications.

2. PRIOR TO THE FEDERAL RULES

In 1904, the massive body of American evidence case law that had developed to that time was synthesized in the first edition of Northwestern law professor John Henry Wigmore's monumental treatise. The influence of *Wigmore's Treatise* cannot be overstated; his work has remained the dominant authority in the field to this day. Perhaps this treatise was in part responsible for the fact that codification did not begin to take hold until the 1970's.

Among the earliest codification efforts was the *Field Code of Civil Procedure*, which you may have learned about in civil procedure. Only a few lawyers are aware that Field's code also contained rules of evidence. Although not adopted in Field's home state of New York, Oregon (1862) adopted all and California (1872) adopted substantially all of these evidence rules. In 1860, Georgia undertook to codify the common law, including its law of evidence. However, except for these states, statutory codification and reform of the law of evidence were limited to occasional enactments covering isolated rules until well into the twentieth century.

In 1920, a charitable foundation, the Commonwealth Fund, appropriated funds to encourage legal research. One of the first projects of its Legal Research Committee was to appoint an evidence law committee chaired by Professor Edmund M. Morgan of the Harvard Law School. *The Commonwealth Fund Report*, published in 1927, recommended five reforms. Four of its proposals had little or no effect on American evidence law, but the fifth–a modernized rule governing the foundation required for the admission of business records– became the basis for a federal statute and statutes or court rules in many states.

In 1939, the American Law Institute (which is responsible for the various Restatements of the Law) began work on the *Model Code of Evidence*. A major philosophic disagreement arose almost immediately concerning the scope of the proposed Model Code. Wigmore preferred a lengthy, detailed set of rules, like the evidence code he had drafted years earlier. In contrast, Judge Charles Clark, the drafter of the Federal Rules of Civil Procedure, wanted a condensed set of rules like the FRCP. Professor Morgan, the Reporter for the project, favored a middle ground. The Institute, faced with a choice between a "catalog, a creed and a code," adopted the Reporter's compromise position. As we shall see, later efforts to codify the law of evidence followed this approach.

The Model Code, published in 1942, was not merely a codification of the existing law of evidence; it contained many radical changes. While many of these reforms would be accepted in subsequent codifications, they were apparently too many too soon at the time. In addition, Morgan's vigorous advocacy of the Model Code may have gone further than necessary and unduly alarmed the bar. He characterized the Code as enhancing the trial judge's power at the expense of both the appellate courts and the adversary system. The Model Code was not adopted in any jurisdiction.

Since the futility of further efforts on behalf of the Model Code was apparent, the codification banner was taken up by the National Conference of Commissioners on Uniform State Laws. In 1953, the Conference unanimously approved the proposed *Uniform Rules of Evidence*. Several days later, they were endorsed by the American Bar Association. The 1953 Uniform Rules differed significantly from the Model Code. The Code had sought drastically to reform evidence law. The Uniform Rules were designed as a modest restatement of existing law to promote uniformity. The seventy–two Uniform Rules and their accompanying commentary required only fifty–seven pages. They were simpler and much less controversial than the Model Code. Even so, the 1953 Uniform Rules met with only slightly greater success than their predecessors. By 1971, the U.R.E. had been adopted only in 3 states: Kansas, New Jersey and Utah. The Uniform Rules were revised in 1974, but have still not attracted much of a following.

California decided not to adopt either the Model Code or the Uniform Rules, opting instead for its own Code of Evidence, effective January 1, 1967. The California rules are more detailed and comprehensive than other codifications and contain a number of well–drafted provisions that have been influential in other jurisdictions. (We shall cite a number of the California rules, *passim*).

3. THE FEDERAL RULES OF EVIDENCE

By far the most important event in the history of American evidence law was the advent of the Federal Rules of Evidence. It is impossible to overstate the impact of this development. The Federal Rules mark the beginning of a new era, the dawn of the Age of Statutes in evidence law; henceforth, they must be the central focus of any study of the law of evidence.

In 1961, Chief Justice Earl Warren appointed a Special Committee on Evidence to determine whether uniform rules of evidence for the federal courts were advisable and feasible. Nine months later, the committee reported in the affirmative. One of the perennial questions addressed was whether the Supreme Court's rulemaking power extends to the promulgation of rules of evidence. The committee concluded that it did and during the ensuing decade the work of the committee, comment by bench and bar, drafting and redrafting, all proceeded smoothly.

Suddenly, in 1971, organized opposition surfaced, notably from the United States Department of Justice. Conservative members of Congress were also upset, probably as much by the committee's exercise of what they saw as a legislative power as by their perception that the new Rules were too favorable to criminal defendants. After making revisions to meet some of these concerns, the Supreme Court approved the Rules on November 20, 1972, and authorized the Chief Justice to transmit them to Congress in accordance with the procedures of the Rules Enabling Act. Justice Douglas dissented. He thought that promulgating rules of evidence was beyond the Court's rulemaking power.

If Congress had done nothing, the Rules would have become effective in ninety days. But that was not to be. The Rules reached Congress at a time when many of its members sought to reclaim powers believed to have been lost by that branch to the Executive and Judiciary. In the aftermath of Watergate, Congress was jealous of its prerogatives vis–á–vis both the Executive and the Judiciary. The President had invoked evidentiary doctrines in an attempt to persuade the courts to block Congress' investigation into the Watergate break–in, and that attempt was probably fresh in Congress' memory when the Supreme Court transmitted the Federal Rules to Congress. Congress spent a great deal of time studying and rewriting the Rules. After a number of significant and controversial revisions were made by Congress, the Federal Rules of Evidence finally became law when the bill was signed by President Ford on January 2, 1975, to take effect on July 1, 1975.

To insure that it would continue to have effective supervisory power over the Rules, Congress added the following section (now 28 U.S.C. § 2074):

> (a) The Supreme Court shall transmit to the Congress not later than May 1 of the year in which a rule prescribed under section 2072 is to become effective a copy of the proposed rule. Such rule shall take effect no earlier than December 1 of the year in which such rule is so transmitted unless otherwise provided by law. The Supreme Court may fix the extent such rule shall apply to proceedings then pending, except that the Supreme Court shall not require the application of such rule to further proceedings then pending to the extent that, in the opinion of the court in which such proceedings are pending, the application of such rule in such proceedings would not be feasible or would work injustice, in which event the former rule applies.

> (b) Any such rule creating, abolishing, or modifying an evidentiary privilege shall have no force or effect unless approved by Congress.

One of the arguments used by the proponents of the Federal Rules was that their adoption would have a "domino" effect; that is, the states would tend to adopt evidence codes modeled after them. This prediction has proved to be correct. As of early 2001, forty–one states and several other U.S. jurisdictions– e.g., Puerto Rico (1979), Guam (1980), and the armed services (1980)–have adopted a version of the Rules:

Alabama (1996)	Nevada (1971)
Alaska (1979)	New Hampshire (1985)
Arizona (1977)	New Jersey (1993)
Arkansas (1976)	New Mexico (1973)
Colorado (1980)	North Carolina (1984)
Delaware (1980)	North Dakota (1977)
Florida (1979)	Ohio (1980)
Hawaii (1981)	Oklahoma (1978)
Idaho (1985)	Oregon (1982)
Indiana (1994)	Pennsylvania (1998)
Iowa (1983)	Rhode Island (1987)
Kentucky (1992)	South Carolina (1995)
Louisiana (1989)	South Dakota (1978)
Maine (1976)	Tennessee (1990)
Maryland (1994)	Texas (1983)

Michigan (1978)
Minnesota (1977)
Mississippi (1986)
Montana (1977)
Nebraska (1975)

Utah (1983)
Vermont (1983)
Washington (1979)
West Virginia (1985)
Wisconsin (1974)
Wyoming (1978)

California has had its own evidence code since 1967. In fact, the California Evidence Code served as a source or model for many provisions of the Federal Rules. From time to time, we will compare the California Evidence Code to the corresponding provision (or lack of provision) of the Federal Rules. Kansas has a code of evidence based on an earlier version of the Uniform Rules of Evidence.

The Connecticut Superior Court adopted a code of evidence effective January 1, 2000. Although purporting to codify Connecticut evidence law and not merely track the Federal Rules (*see* Borden, *The New Code of Evidence: A (Very) Brief Introduction and Overview*, 73 Conn. B.J. 1999), its structure directly parallels that of the Federal Rules, and its substance is, in very large part, either identical or quite similar.

Thus, as of this writing, only six states–Georgia, Illinois, Massachusetts, Missouri, New York, and Virginia–do not have codes of evidence. And of those that have codes, all but two are patterned after the Federal Rules.

Even in the states that have not adopted a code, the Rules are influential. The Federal Rules are sometimes treated as a restatement of the common law evidence rule or as persuasive authority. On occasion, a court will expressly incorporate a Federal Rule into its common law of evidence. *Wilson v. Clark*, 417 N.E.2d 1322, 1326–27 (Ill. 1981). The Federal Rules of Evidence are becoming the American law of evidence. Most states have largely "borrowed" their evidence law from the Federal Rules. The borrowed character of these state codes means not only that the wording of the codes is strikingly similar to that of the Federal Rules; in construing their own state codes, courts in the "borrowing" jurisdictions tend to adopt the gloss placed on the Federal Rules by the federal courts–stare de statute. W. ESKRIDGE & P. FRICKEY, CASES AND MATERIALS ON LEGISLATION: STATUTES AND THE CREATION OF PUBLIC POLICY 842 (2d ed. 1995).

G.   THE DEBATE OVER CODIFYING EVIDENCE LAW

As we have seen, most American jurisdictions have decided to codify their evidence law, either by statute or court rules. However, when Chief Justice Warren initially appointed the special committee in 1961, it was hardly a foregone conclusion that either federal or state evidence law would eventually be codified. In the ensuing years, legislators and jurists not only debated the wisdom of the specific provisions of the proposed Federal Rules, they also wrangled over the threshold question of whether or not it is desirable to codify evidence law.

This debate is but one example of the pervasive tensions in the law between specific and general rules of decision, and between (1) judge–made law, with its greater flexibility and relative ease of modification, and (2) codified law, with its greater certainty, predictability, and ease of determination. *See* Aronson, *The Federal Rules of Evidence: A Model for Improved Evidentiary Decisionmaking in Washington*, 54 WASH. L. REV. 31, 37–42 (1978); Powers, *Formalism and Nonformalism in Choice of Law Methodology*, 52 WASH. L. REV. 27, 28–37 (1976); Swift, *One Hundred Years of Evidence Law Reform: Thayer's Triumph*, 88 Cal. L. Rev. 2437 (2000). Professor Aronson describes the difference between "formal" and "nonformal" decisionmaking:

> One concept inherent in all decisionmaking has been described as the conflict between formal and nonformal decisionmaking. The former is characterized by well–defined, easily applied rules and by strict adherence to those rules. At the risk of oversimplification, such rules have the advantage of uniform and consistent application, and therefore predictability and stability; they have the disadvantage of inflexibility and inability to accommodate either unforeseen but relevant factors or scientific and socio–psychological advances. Nonformal decisionmaking, often appearing in legal decisions as a balancing test, permits the consideration of all relevant factors in each case, and thereby avoids unjust results due to the inflexibility of strictly applied rules. Nonformal decisionmaking, however, is time–consuming, subject to the biases of the judge in each case, and therefore less consistent or predictable. [citations omitted]

Note that formal rules are not necessarily codified rules. For example, even at common law, the hearsay rule was a simple, formal rule subject to a large number of judicially created formal exceptions. Conversely, a codified rule can be nonformal, such as the rule that allows a judge to exclude evidence if he or she determines that its probative value is outweighed by its tendency toward unfair prejudice (FED. R. EVID. 403).

NOTES

In general, which type of evidence law is preferable: statutory or decisional? It is arguable that certainty and predictability are more important in business law areas, such as contracts; for the economy to function efficiently, actors must be able to plan transactions on the basis of predictable legal principles. The argument runs that there is less need for predictability in litigation–related areas that come into play after the transaction is planned. On the other hand, an attorney cannot effectively plan and predict the legal consequences of a transaction unless the attorney knows which evidentiary rules the court will apply to proof of the transaction. Legal analysis is surrealistic. Suppose that you know that a certain event occurred, but that at trial, evidence law will preclude you from proving that the event occurred. Should you advise your client on the basis of the actual events or the provable events? In most cases, your advice will be based on the provable events.

Note Congress refused to adopt the specific rules governing evidentiary privileges that the Advisory Committee drafted for proposed Article V of the Federal Rules of Evidence. By default, Congress left responsibility for developing privilege law to the states and to the Judiciary. In part, this may have stemmed from concern for the *Erie* doctrine; the extrinsic social policies underlying many of the absolute privileges could be viewed as "substantive law" under some rationales. More generally, Congress' treatment of privileges may reflect the view that some areas of evidence law are more resistant to codification and therefore are good candidates for nonformal, judge–made rules.

Chapter 2

EVIDENCE: TYPES, SOURCES AND SUBSTITUTES

A. THE TYPES OF INFORMATION TO WHICH EVIDENTIARY RULES ARE APPLIED

The term "evidence" is quite broad. California Evidence Code § 140 defines the term as: "testimony, writings, material objects, or other things presented to the senses that are offered to prove the existence or nonexistence of a fact." To identify the various types of evidence, let us dissect this definition.

The statute first tells us that evidence includes "testimony." A witness may give oral testimony about his own perceptions or opinions. As we shall study later, a witness may testify on the basis of personal knowledge—that is, what he has seen, smelled, or heard firsthand. A police officer may testify about drugs he saw in the defendant's apartment, the odor of marijuana he smelled before breaking in the door, and the defendant's statements to him immediately after the arrest. If the officer had extensive experience in drug cases, the judge might even permit him to express an opinion about the street value of the drugs found in the defendant's apartment. *United States v. Kelly*, 679 F.2d 135 (8th Cir. 1982); *United States v. Golden*, 532 F.2d 1244 (9th Cir. 1976).

The statute next states that evidence includes "writings [and] material objects." The genus is physical objects, and the species is documentary evidence. Documents are very common evidence. However, they are only one illustration of the broader category of physical evidence. That category includes such items as pistols, knives, mufflers, and photographs. The category is not even limited to objects historically connected with the case (real or original physical evidence); for purposes of trial, the attorneys can prepare models and charts (demonstrative evidence). The introduction of physical evidence usually necessitates a witness' oral testimony; the witness "sponsors" the exhibit by testifying to its authenticity. However, physical evidence differs from oral testimony in an important respect: now the jurors themselves can observe the object and use their firsthand sense impressions to assess the witness' testimony about the object.

Given the breadth of the expression "material objects," the jurors are not even limited to situations in which a witness introduces them to physical evidence. In a jury view, a court official takes the jurors to a location outside the courtroom. Without the intervention of a sponsoring witness, the jurors make their own observations about the location. In the *O. J. Simpson* criminal trial, the trial judge allowed the jurors to visit the location where Nicole Brown Simpson and Ronald Goldman were murdered.

NOTES

1. Note the concluding reference in Evidence Code § 140 to "other things presented to the senses . . . ." While a witness is on the stand, she presents her demeanor to the senses of the trier of fact. Should demeanor be considered a species of evidence? The cases are divided over this question. *See* Imwinkelried, *Demeanor Impeachment: Law and Tactics*, 9 AM. J. TRIAL ADVOC. 183, 189–92 (1985).

On the one hand, there is a strong case against treating demeanor as evidence. The witness' behavior may not be a reliable indication of the witness' credibility. The witness' behavior may be idiosyncratic. Even if the behavior pattern is not peculiar to the witness, there may be causes for the conduct other than uncertainty or lying. For many witnesses, the courtroom is a new, unfamiliar environment. The novel environment may make the witness nervous or even afraid. W. PIERSON, THE DEFENSE ATTORNEY AND BASIC DEFENSE TACTICS § 90 (1956). Further, just as in the case of jury views, the trial court record cannot adequately reflect the witness' demeanor. To the extent that the trial court judgment rests on demeanor, the appellate court has lost the power to police the rationality of the judgment.

On the other hand, it seems unrealistic to deny demeanor evidentiary status. Communications experts commonly assert that when one person speaks to another, the speaker's nonverbal conduct accounts for more than 50% of the information communicated. J. KESTLER, QUESTIONING TECHNIQUES AND TACTICS § 2.50 (2d ed. 1992). If the speaker's statement is laden with emotion, more than 90% of the message can be communicated nonverbally. K. TAYLOR, R. BUCHANAN & D. STRAWN, COMMUNICATION STRATEGIES FOR TRIAL ATTORNEYS 49 (1984). Moreover, when the listener perceives a conflict between the speaker's statement and the accompanying nonverbal cues, the listener ordinarily disbelieves the statement, since "we trust actions more than . . . words." Peskin, *Non–Verbal Communication in the Courtroom*, 3 TRIAL DIPL. J. 8 (Winter 1980). In the Cleveland Jury Project conducted in the mid–1980's, the researchers found that when witnesses disagree, jurors often decide the case by focusing on the witnesses' demeanor. Austin, *Why Jurors Don't Heed the Trial*, NAT'L L.J., Aug. 12, 1985, at 18. Admittedly, much of this research is preliminary, but almost all of the studies point to the same conclusion.

B. THE SOURCES OF EVIDENCE LAW

1. CONSTITUTIONS

Especially in criminal practice, one of the most important sources of evidentiary rules is the Constitution. The key provisions are the Fourth Amendment prohibition of unreasonable searches and seizures, the Fifth Amendment privilege against self–incrimination, and the Sixth Amendment right to counsel. If the police gain evidence (a physical object or a confession) by violating one of these provisions, the Court has decreed that the evidence be excluded. The constitutional exclusionary rule is a judicial remedy for the violation of the constitutional right. *Stone v. Powell*, 428 U.S. 465 (1976);

United States v. Calandra, 414 U.S. 338 (1974). The police actions in question—searches, interrogations, and lineups—are evidence–gathering procedures, and the Court believed that excluding the evidence at trial would largely remove the incentive for police misconduct violative of the constitutional guarantees. *Mapp v. Ohio*, 367 U.S. 643 (1961).

The exclusionary rules based on the Fourth, Fifth, and Sixth Amendments are also enforceable against the states. The incorporation doctrine comes into play. *Malloy v. Hogan*, 378 U.S. 1 (1964). The Fourteenth Amendment's due process clause explicitly applies to the states, and the Court has held that Fourteenth Amendment due process incorporates many of the Bill of Rights guarantees, including the Fourth, Fifth, and Sixth Amendment exclusionary rules. *See, e.g., Griffin v. California*, 380 U.S. 609 (1965). Indeed, many of the leading criminal procedure precedents are cases originating in state court. *Mapp v. Ohio, supra* (the Fourth Amendment exclusionary rule); *Miranda v. Arizona*, 384 U.S. 436 (1966) (the Fifth Amendment requirement for warnings during custodial interrogation); *Gilbert v. California*, 388 U.S. 263 (1967) (the Sixth Amendment right to counsel at lineups).

State constitutions may also serve as a source of evidentiary rules. What is the relationship between a ruling based on a state constitution and one based on the federal Constitution? In *Harris v. New York*, 401 U.S. 222 (1971), the Supreme Court announced that if a defendant testifies in his own behalf, a prosecutor may use a voluntary but unwarned confession to impeach the defendant's credibility. But a state supreme court is free to adopt the view that under its state constitution, a prosecutor may not use an unwarned confession for any purpose. *Commonwealth v. Tripplett*, 462 Pa. 244, 341 A.2d 62, 64 (1975); Annot., 14 A.L.R.4th 676, 681 (1982). The provisions of the federal Constitution impose a floor but not a ceiling. *See State v. Jewitt*, 37 CRIM. L. REP. (BNA) 2409 (Vt. Sup. Ct. Aug. 9, 1985) ("Since 1970 there have been over 250 cases in which state appellate courts have viewed the scope of rights under state constitutions as broader than those secured by the federal Constitution as interpreted by the U.S. Supreme Court . . . . A lawyer today representing someone who claims some constitutional protection and who does not argue that the state constitution provides that protection is skating on the edge of malpractice."); Gest, *The Swing to the Left in State Courts*, 107 U.S. NEWS & WORLD REP., Oct. 23, 1989, at 32 (during the 1980's, there were over 400 state court decisions granting criminal accused more extensive protections than those guaranteed under the federal constitution).

2. STATUTES AND STATUTORY INTERPRETATION

Another important source of evidence law is statute. Congress has enacted the Federal Rules of Evidence, and 41 states (and other jurisdictions) have adopted evidence codes patterned after the Federal Rules. Since several states such as California had adopted codes before the promulgation of the Federal Rules, the vast majority of states now have a largely statutory body of evidence law. In these jurisdictions, in the final analysis, determining evidence law is an exercise in statutory interpretation. In fact, whether the evidence code was adopted by the legislature (statute) or by court rule (see section 3, below), similar issues of interpretation arise.

The proper methodology of statutory interpretation is now a point of dispute, and that dispute is surfacing in cases arising under the Federal Rules of Evidence. Until recently, the standard practice for judges construing statutes has been to resort liberally to extrinsic legislative history material such as committee reports. O. HETZEL, LEGISLATIVE LAW AND PROCESS: CASES AND MATERIALS 205 (3d ed. 2001). In Justice Frankfurter's words, "If the purpose of construction is the ascertainment of meaning, nothing that is logically relevant should be excluded." *Id.* at 175.

Professor Edward Cleary, the Reporter for the Advisory Committee that drafted the Federal Rules of Evidence, believed that because of the nature of the audience for the Federal Rules (lawyers and judges) and the history of evidence law in the United States (built on a large body of caselaw precedent), the meaning of the Rules cannot be divorced from their historical background and legislative history.

CLEARY, PRELIMINARY NOTES ON READING THE RULES OF EVIDENCE, 57 Nebraska Law Review 908 (1978) (citations omitted)

The legal background against which the Rules were enacted was a vast collection of common law precedents. True, occasional jurisdictions had enacted codes, and some parts of evidence law, *e.g.*, privilege and competency of witnesses, were largely statutory almost everywhere, but in the main the generalization held.

An initial question is whether the interpretive inquiry is properly directed to ascertaining the intent of the legislature or the meaning to its audience. Powerful arguments can be made in favor of meaning to the audience. However, the audience for the Rules of Evidence is a very specialized one of judges and lawyers, much given to downgrading the text of statutes and looking elsewhere for their meaning. Hence the saying in Washington, "You can write the bill, if you let me write the report." As a result, intent and meaning in this instance tend to come together, with meaning being arrived at in terms of materials also relevant to intent.

The well known and perhaps equally well criticized case of *Caminetti v. United States* [242 U.S. 470, 485 (1917)] gave voice to one oft quoted version of the so-called "plain meaning" rule:

> It is elementary that the meaning of a statute must, in the first instance, be sought in the language in which the act is framed, and if that is plain, and if the law is within the constitutional authority of the law-making body which passed it, the sole function of the courts is to enforce it according to its terms.

If what is meant is that meaning is to be ascertained by reading the statute with the aid only of a dictionary and such aphorisms of construction as *noscitur a sociis* and *ejusdem generis*, then it must be discarded as unrealistic. The slipperiness of meaning combines with the ingenuity and resourcefulness of the legal profession to render the evolution of a plain meaning by this approach unlikely in any disputed situation, and if one should appear the chance is greatly against its being acceptable. If, however, the plain meaning rule is read as mandating the text of the statute as the prime source of meaning, to be read in such context as may be relevant, then plain meaning becomes a useful tool.

If the Congress can speak only by passing bills, then a plausible argument can be made that as a matter of constitutional theory nothing said by the Congress in any other way has any force as law and ought to be disregarded. On policy grounds, the use of legislative history is criticized as inviting easy answers and drawing attention away from conveyed meaning, purpose, and general scheme. The British practice has been against referring to legislative history at all. But in the United States legislative history has proved irresistibly tempting, and it must be admitted that, in exploring nuances of meaning, the reasoning and thought processes of those involved may be helpful as a source of explication and illumination, without necessarily attributing to them the authority of law.

The principal considerations in the use of legislative history are its authoritativeness and its availability. Authoritativeness concerns the extent to which given materials reflect the thinking that actually went into the legislation. Availability is important for very practical reasons. In the public interest, how far should the profession and its menial diggers be expected, or even permitted, to excavate and sift for minute shards of legislative history? The components of legislative history [are] listed in a roughly descending order of importance as measured in terms of authoritativeness and availability.

1. *The Rules prescribed by the Supreme Court*. The Rules prescribed by the Court constituted the official document transmitted to the Congress. Moreover, they were the basis of the bills introduced in the Congress.

2. *The Advisory Committee's Notes.* The notes of the Advisory Committee served the purposes of both supporting and explaining the Rules. They accompanied the Rules through the successive stages of consideration by the Committee on Rules of Practice and Procedure, the Judicial Conference of the United States, and the Supreme Court. The Chief Justice transmitted them to the Congress with the Rules. They were carefully scrutinized by the involved congressional committees and subcommittees, and, except in those instances where superseding changes were made in the Rules by the Congress, must be taken to represent the thinking of that body as the equivalent of a committee report effectively serving as the basis of legislation.

3. *Congressional Materials.* The materials emanating from the Congress are of varying degrees of authority. Committee reports include those of the Subcommittee on Criminal Justice of the House Judiciary Committee, the House Committee on the Judiciary, the Senate Committee on the Judiciary, and the Conference Report. Some materials in the Congressional Record are of authority equivalent to a committee report, *e.g.*, statements by the committee chairman, sponsor of the bill, or sponsor of an amendment.

In principle, under the Federal Rules no common law of evidence remains. "All relevant evidence is admissible, except as otherwise provided." [FED. R. EVID. 402.] In reality, of course, the body of common law knowledge continues to exist, though in the somewhat altered form of a source of guidance in the exercise of delegated powers.

———

The practice of relying heavily on extrinsic materials—the so–called "legal process" approach—is currently under attack. Justice Scalia and Judge Easterbrook have emphasized the possible unreliability of legislative history material. Modern theories of literary and historical interpretation recognize the difficulty of reconstructing a person's earlier intent. The difficulty is compounded when the intent is that of 535 legislators rather than a single person. Finally, legislative history can be manipulated; a lobbyist may succeed in persuading a committee staff member to insert in a report language calculated to influence a court's subsequent interpretation of the statute. Justice Scalia and Judge Easterbrook realize that "committee members and lobbyists often write the [legislative] histories." Note, *Why Learned Hand Would Never Consult Legislative History Today*, 105 HARV. L. REV. 1005 (1992). Given these dangers, Judge Easterbrook advocates a new, strict constructionist approach to statutory interpretation.

EASTERBROOK, STATUTES' DOMAINS, 50 University of Chicago Law Review 533, 544–52 (1983)

Unless the statute plainly hands courts the power to create and revise a form of common law, the domain of the statute should be restricted to cases anticipated by its framers and expressly resolved in the legislative process. Unless the party relying on the statute could establish either express resolution or creation of the common law power of revision, the court would hold the matter in question outside the statute's domain. The statute would become irrelevant, the parties (and court) remitted to whatever other sources of law might be applicable. Because legislatures comprise many members, they do not have "intents" or "designs," hidden yet discoverable. Each member may or may not have a design. The body as a whole, however, has only outcomes. This follows from the discoveries of public choice theory. Although legislators have individual lists of desires, priorities, and preferences, it turns out to be difficult, sometimes impossible, to aggregate these lists into a coherent collective choice. Every system of voting has flaws. The one used by legislatures is particularly dependent on the order in which decisions are made. Legislatures customarily consider proposals one at a time and then vote them up or down. This method disregards third or fourth options and the intensity with which legislators prefer one option over another. Additional options can be considered only in sequence, and this makes the order of decision vital. It is fairly easy to show that someone with control of the agenda can manipulate the choice so that the legislature adopts proposals that only a minority support. The existence of agenda control makes it impossible for a court—even one that knows each legislator's complete table of preferences—to say what the whole body would have done with a proposal it did not consider in fact. Few of the best–intentioned, most humble, and most restrained among us have the skills necessary to learn the temper of times before our births, to assume the identity of people we have never met, and to know how 535 disparate characters from regions of great political and economic diversity would have answered questions that never occurred to them.

A principle that statutes are inapplicable unless they either plainly supply a rule of decision or delegate the power to create such a rule is consistent with the liberal principles underlying our political order. Those who wrote and approved the Constitution thought that most social relations would be governed by private agreements, customs, and understandings, not resolved in the halls of government. There is still at least a presumption that people's arrangements prevail unless expressly displaced by legal doctrine. All things are permitted unless there is some contrary rule. It is easier for an agency to justify the revocation of rules (or simple nonregulation) than the creation of new rules. A rule declaring statutes inapplicable unless they plainly resolve or delegate the solution of the matter respects this position.

In Judge Easterbrook's view, the unreliability of extrinsic legislative history material is a potent reason for placing greater stress on the text of the statute. After all, the text is "all that Congress enacts into'law' . . . ." Eskridge, *The New Textualism*, 37 U.C.L.A. L. Rev. 621, 648 (1990). Only the text has the force of law. *Id.* at 671. In Judge Posner's words, Congress "does not legislate by issuing committee reports." *American Hosp. Ass'n v. N.L.R.B.*, 899 F.2d 651, 657 (7th Cir. 1990). The textualists have resurrected Holmes' approach to statutory interpretation: "We do not inquire what the legislature meant; we ask only what the statute means." Holmes, *The Theory of Legal Interpretation*, 12 Harv. L. Rev. 417, 419 (1899).

While Judge Easterbrook has concentrated his criticism on routine reliance on extrinsic legislative history material, Judge Posner has attempted to redefine the question judges should ask while they search through legislative history. In the past, due in part to the writings of Professors Hart and Sacks, we tended to assume that the legislature is comprised of reasonable persons pursuing the public interest in good faith. W. Eskridge & P. Frickey, Cases and Materials on Legislation: Statutes and the Creation of Public Policy 49–66 (2d ed. 1995). On that assumption, each piece of legislation has a rational, organizing purpose; and the judge's task in reviewing the legislative history material is to identify that purpose. *Id.* at 481–511. However, law–and–economics theorists such as Judge Posner claim that this theory of legislation is unrealistic. They assert that a statute should be viewed as an arational deal between the legislature and interest groups. Eskridge & Frickey, *Legislation Scholarship and Pedagogy in the Post–Legal Process Era*, 48 U. Pitt. L. Rev. 691, 710, 718 (1987). Statutes "are the eventual product of strong competing political currents . . . ." *Woodland Joint U. School Dist. v. Comm'n*, 2 Cal. App. 4th 1429, 1452, 4 Cal. Rptr. 2d 227, 241 (1992). Under this view, the judge's task is to ascertain the nature of the compromise underlying the legislation and to implement that compromise. Judge Posner has elaborated on his view.

R. POSNER, THE FEDERAL COURTS: CHALLENGE AND REFORM 286–93 (1988)

I suggest a two–part approach. First, the judge should try to put himself in the shoes of the enacting legislators and figure out how they would have wanted the statute applied to the case before him. This is the method of imaginative reconstruction. If it fails, as occasionally it will, either because the necessary information is lacking or because the legislators had failed to agree on essential premises, then the judge must decide what attribution of meaning to the statute will yield the most reasonable result in the case at hand—always bearing in mind that what seems reasonable to the judge may not have seemed reasonable to the legislators, and that it is their conception of reasonableness, to the extent known, rather than the judge's, that should guide decision.

The judge who follows the suggested approach will not only consider the language, structure, and history of the statute, but also study the values and attitudes, as far as they can be known today, of the period when the legislation was enacted. It would be a mistake to ascribe to legislators of the 1930s or the 1960s and early 1970s the skepticism regarding the size of government and the efficiency of regulation that is widespread today, or to impute to the Congress of the 1920s current ideas of conflict of interest. The judge's job is not to keep a statute up to date in the sense of making it reflect contemporary values, but to imagine as best he can how the legislators who enacted the statute would have wanted it applied to situations they did not foresee.

Although the approach I have sketched has obvious affinities with the "attribution of purpose" approach of Professors Hart and Sacks, I want to stress one difference. They say that in construing a statute a court "should assume, unless the contrary unmistakably appears, that the legislature was made up of reasonable persons pursuing reasonable purposes reasonably." Coupled with an earlier statement that in trying to divine the legislative will the court should ignore "short–run currents of political expedience," Hart and Sacks appear to be suggesting that the judge should ignore interest groups, popular ignorance and prejudice, and anything else that deflects legislators from the single–minded pursuit of the public interest as the judge would conceive it. But this approach risks attributing to legislation not the purposes reasonably inferable from the legislation itself but the judge's own conception of the public interest. When Hart and Sacks were writing—in the wake of the New Deal—the legislative process was widely regarded as progressive and public–spirited. Today there is less agreement that the motives behind most legislation are benign, and this should make the judge wary about too readily assuming a congruence between his conception of the public interest and the latent purposes of the statutes he is called on to interpret.

A related characteristic of the passages from Hart and Sacks is a reluctance to recognize that statutes often are the product of compromise between opposing groups and that a compromise is unlikely to embody a single consistent purpose. Of course, as I pointed out earlier, it is hard for judges, limited as they are to the formal materials of the legislative process, to identify the existence of compromise. But where the lines of compromise are discernible, the judge's duty is to follow them, to implement not the purposes of one group of legislators but the compromise itself.

If the lines of compromise are not clear, if the judge's scrupulous search for the legislative will does not turn up anything, the second part of my approach ("reasonable result") comes into play—provided the case is at least within the statute's domain. If someone was shortchanged on the purchase of a bag of oranges and brought suit against the seller under the federal securities laws, arguing that the court should read "security" to include an orange because fraud is a bad thing, he would receive short shrift. The securities laws do not authorize the courts to deal with a sale of oranges. But if the case involves something that is or may be a security, and the judge is simply very uncertain whether the statute was meant to apply, he cannot just dismiss the case out of hand; it is within the scope of the legislative delegation to him. He must decide the case, even though on the basis of considerations that cannot be laid at Congress's door. These might be considerations of judicial administrability—what interpretation of the statute will provide greater predictability, require less judicial factfinding, and otherwise reduce the cost and frequency of litigation under the statute? Or they might be considerations drawn from some broadly based conception of the public interest. It is always possible, of course, to refer these considerations back to Congress—to say that Congress would have wanted the courts, in cases where they could not figure out what interpretation would advance the substantive objectives of the statute, to adopt the "better" one; or to say in the manner of Hart and Sacks that legislators should be presumed reasonable until shown otherwise. But these methods of imputing congressional intent are artificial; and it is not healthy for a judge to conceal from himself that he is being creative.

Recently, there has been a marked trend at the Supreme Court level to apply a textualist approach to construing the Federal Rules. Becker & Orenstein, *The Federal Rules of Evidence After Sixteen Years—The Effect of "Plain Meaning" Jurisprudence, the Need for an Advisory Committee on the Rules of Evidence, and Suggestions for Selective Revision of the Rules*, 60 GEO. WASH. L. REV. 857 (1992); Jonakait, *The Supreme Court, Plain Meaning, and the Changed Rules of Evidence*, 68 TEX. L. REV. 745 (1990).

However, there are differing schools of textualism. According to the strict view, the courts may resort to extrinsic legislative history material "only when a literal reading of the act compels an" absurd result or the text of the statute is ambiguous. *In re Brichard Securities Litigation*, 788 F. Supp. 1098, 1101 (N.D. Cal. 1992). Under this strict view, finding an ambiguity in the text is ordinarily a condition precedent to turning to extrinsic material. However, by and large, the Supreme Court Justices have embraced a more moderate version of textualism. "[R]ecent Supreme Court cases suggest that in all questions of statutory interpretation, a court may examine the legislative history in order to avoid an'unreflective' reading of a statute." *Id*. Moderate textualists are skeptical of legislative history and believe that the statute's apparent plain meaning should prevail unless a contrary legislative intention is "clearly expressed," (*Lever Bros. Co. v. United States*, 981 F.2d 1330 (D.C. Cir. 1993)); but they do not forbid the judge from consulting extrinsic material. In effect, moderate textualists entertain a "strong" but rebuttable "presumption" that a statute ought to be construed according to its plain meaning. *Gang v. United States*, 783 F. Supp. 376, 380 (N.D. Ill. 1992). *See, e.g.,* Jonakait,

Text, Texts or Ad Hoc Determinations: Interpretation of the Federal Rules of Evidence, 71 IND. L.J. 551 (1996).

There has been sharp criticism of the textualist approach to construing the Rules of Evidence. Professor Weissenberger notes that the Rules "originated in, and were designed by, the judicial branch and not the legislative branch." Weissenberger, *The Supreme Court and the Interpretation of the Federal Rules of Evidence*, 53 OHIO ST. L.J. 1307 (1992). He argues that the textualist approach represents a threat to judicial discretion in administering the Rules and that with few exceptions, Congress' only intent was to ratify the drafters' attempt to preserve and guide judicial discretion. *Id.* at 1310. He warns that a textualist construction of the Rules ignores "the common–law heritage of the Rules" and may undercut "the inherent discretionary powers of the federal trial judiciary." *Id.* at 1339. *See also* Weissenberger, *Are the Federal Rules of Evidence a Statute?*, 55 OHIO ST. L.J. 393 (1994). For a response to Professor Weissenberger's 1992 article, see Imwinkelried, *A Brief Defense of the Supreme Court's Approach to the Interpretation of the Federal Rules of Evidence*, 27 IND. L. REV. 267 (1993).

The interpretation debate continues. In addition to the articles cited above, *see, e.g.*, Taslitz, *Interpretive Method and the Federal Rules of Evidence: A Call for a Politically Realistic Hermeneutics*, 32 HARV. J. ON LEGIS. 329 (1995); Taslitz, Daubert's *Guide to the Federal Rules of Evidence: A Not–So–Plain Meaning Jurisprudence*, 32 HARV. J. ON LEGIS. 3 (1995); Scallen, *Classical Rhetoric, Practical Reasoning, and the Law of Evidence*, 44 AM. U.L. REV. 1717 (1995).

NOTES

1. In the following chapters, we shall encounter numerous questions of interpretation posed by the wording of the Federal Rules of Evidence. As you work through these questions, ask yourself whether it would make a difference if the court construing the statute followed the traditional practice rather than the heed of Judges Easterbrook and Posner.

2. Should the techniques for interpreting statutes be identical to those for construing a constitution? The courts tend to assume that the same "principles of construction" are "applicable to statutes and constitutional provisions alike" (*Mutual Life Ins. v. City of Los Angeles*, 267 Cal. Rptr. 589, 591 (Cal. 1990)), but this is not necessarily correct. Most modern statutes are detailed. In contrast, the phrasing of many constitutional provisions such as the due process guarantee is far more "general" and "open–textured." Chemerinsky, *Foreword: The Vanishing Constitution,* 103 HARV. L. REV. 43, 90 (1989). In addition, a statute can be amended more readily than the constitution. As Justice Brandeis remarked, a constitution is "a living organism . . . capable of . . . adaption to new condition." *Id.* at 92 n. 212. On this basis, one could insist on originalist statutory interpretation while permitting dynamic, evolutionary interpretation of the Constitution.

3. COURT RULES

In the process of promulgating the Federal Rules of Evidence, a dispute arose as to whether the Supreme Court had the authority to promulgate the

Rules. In an order dated November 20, 1972, the Court purported to exercise that authority. In a dissenting opinion, Justice Douglas cautioned that "[t]here are those who think that fashioning of rules of evidence is a task for the legislature, not for the judiciary." RULES OF EVIDENCE—COMMUNICATION FROM CHIEF JUSTICE OF THE UNITED STATES vi (1973). Congress intervened, blocked the Rules from taking effect, and made significant modifications. Congress ultimately adopted the Rules as an Act of Congress. In an amendment to 28 U.S.C. § 2076, Congress further provided that in the future, the Court could "prescribe amendments" to the Rules but that by resolution either house of Congress could disapprove the amendment.

A similar battle was fought in many of the states that considered adopting the Federal Rules. Giannelli, *The Proposed Ohio Rules of Evidence: The General Assembly, Evidence, and Rulemaking*, 29 CASE W. RES. L. REV. 16 (1978). The battle centered on the separation of powers doctrine. *Id.* at 27. If the legislature has already passed a statute granting the supreme court some rule–making authority, should the statute be construed as authorizing the promulgation of evidentiary rules? If not, should the state constitution itself be interpreted as empowering the court to adopt evidentiary rules? In some jurisdictions, the legislatures prevailed and adopted the Federal Rules by statute; in other states, the supreme court succeeded in promulgating the Rules as rules of court. *Id.* at 45–46.

NOTE

Which branch is better able to draft an evidentiary code? At first blush, the judiciary seems the more likely candidate. The courts work with the evidentiary rules on a daily basis and can see how the rules interface with other bodies of law such as civil and criminal procedure. What are the arguments on the other side? If additional empirical investigation of the assumptions underlying the rules is critically needed (as we suggest), which branch is better equipped to conduct that investigation?

4. THE COMMON LAW

Absent a controlling statute or court rule, the judge deciding an evidentiary issue can fall back on a vast body of common law. The staggering size of the common law of evidence led to the publication of some of the most influential American treatises, including James Bradley Thayer's A PRELIMINARY TREATISE ON EVIDENCE AT THE COMMON LAW (1898) and the various editions of Wigmore's monumental work, A TREATISE ON THE ANGLO–AMERICAN SYSTEM OF EVIDENCE IN TRIALS AT COMMON LAW in this century.

Although the volume of decisional evidence law dwarfs the statutory and constitutional law on evidence, constitutional and statutory law have higher places in the hierarchy of evidence law. Thus, if a statute conflicts with a constitutional provision, the latter prevails. *State v. Jalo,* 27 Or. App. 845, 557 P.2d 1359 (1976). *A fortiori,* when decisional law is at odds with a statute, the statute invalidates the case law. For example, before the adoption of the Federal Rules of Evidence, many jurisdictions held that expert witnesses could base their opinions only on data that was independently admissible; if an evidentiary rule such as the hearsay doctrine barred the admission of the evidence as substantive proof, the expert could not rely upon the data as part of the basis of her opinion. *Equitable Life Assur. Soc'y v. Kazee*, 257 Ky. 803, 79 S.W.2d 208 (1935). However, Federal Rule of Evidence 703 overturned that holding by allowing the expert to base an opinion on any data customarily employed in his specialty even if "the facts or data [are] . . . not . . . [independently] admissible in evidence." FED. R. EVID. 703. The statute compels the courts to follow its lead and abandon the prior common law view. Note, *Hearsay Bases of Psychiatric Opinion Testimony: A Critique of Federal Rule of Evidence 703*, 51 S. CAL. L. REV. 129 (1977).

NOTES

1. The resolution is relatively easy when a decisional rule conflicts with a statutory rule. The resolution is more troublesome, however, when a comprehensive evidence code is simply silent on a point covered by the prior common law. The experience of the California Evidence Code is illustrative. When the Code was enacted in the mid–1960's, the California Law Revision Commission manifested an intent to "wipe out all court–created exclusionary rules of evidence not based on a statutory or constitutional provision." 1 B. JEFFERSON, CALIFORNIA EVIDENCE BENCHBOOK § 21.1 (2d ed. 1982). Like Federal Rule of Evidence 402, California Evidence Code § 351 proclaims that "[e]xcept as otherwise provided by statute, all relevant evidence is admissible." In *People v. Starr*, 11 Cal. App. 3d 574, 583, 89 Cal. Rptr. 906, 912 (1970), the court grappled with the question of whether the corroboration requirements for accomplice testimony survived the adoption of the California Evidence Code. Although the requirements were of common law origin, the court refused to hold that the Code impliedly abolished them; the court announced that more explicit language was needed to repeal "such a firmly established and fundamental rule." Do you agree?

2. Professors Wright and Graham assert that "[v]irtually all of the witnesses in Congressional hearings assumed that the effect of the adoption of the Evidence Rules would be to foreclose courts from changing rules of evidence by decision." 22 C. WRIGHT & K. GRAHAM, FEDERAL PRACTICE AND PROCEDURE: EVIDENCE § 5199, at 222 n.17 (1978). For example, one witness expressed the opinion that after the adoption of the Rules, the judicial creation of exclusionary rules "will in all probability be prevented." *Id.* And, remember Professor Cleary's statement: "In principle, under the Federal Rules no common law of evidence remains." In a 1984 decision, the Supreme Court approvingly quoted that passage from Professor Cleary's article. *United States v. Abel*, 469 U.S. 45, 46–49 (1984). The Court did so again in *Daubert v. Merrell Dow Pharmaceuticals, Inc.*, 509 U.S. 579 (1993).

On the other hand, other commentators believe that uncodified, common law evidentiary rules have survived the enactment of the Federal Rules. Langum, *The Hidden Rules of Evidence: Michigan's Uncodified Evidence Law*, 61 MICH. B.J. 320 (1982). Which side is right? Is it possible that both are?

C. SUBSTITUTES FOR EVIDENCE: OTHER METHODS OF ESTABLISHING FACTS

In addition to proving facts through the admission of evidence at trial, there are several other ways in which facts can be established. These include (1) judicial notice, (2) stipulation, (3) judicial admission, and (4) preclusion.

1. JUDICIAL NOTICE

Read Federal Rule of Evidence 201.

A commonly invoked technique of establishing a fact is judicial notice. The judge notes the existence of a fact and instructs the jury that the fact exists. Judicial notice expedites the trial by dispensing with formal proof of the fact.

Professor Kenneth Culp Davis has long called upon the courts to employ a more "full–bodied factual technique" to investigate the assumptions underlying rules of law. K. DAVIS, ADMINISTRATIVE LAW TEXT § 15.03 (3d ed. 1972); *see also* K. DAVIS & R. PIERCE, ADMINISTRATIVE LAW TREATISE § 10.5 (3d ed. 1994). The courts can use judicial notice to feed more empirical information into the decision–making process. The modern extension of judicial notice to scientific "verifiable certainties" is in part a response to Professor Davis' urging. Congress recognized that extension in Federal Rule of Evidence 201.

a. Judicial Notice of Fact

To understand the scope of judicial notice of facts, we must consider the seminal work of Professor Kenneth Davis. Davis articulated the critical distinction between adjudicative and legislative facts. The Federal Rules reflect Davis' influence. By its terms, Federal Rule of Evidence 201, governing judicial notice, is limited to judicial notice of "adjudicative" data. FED. R. EVID. 201(a). The distinction is important because subsections (d) through (g) contain detailed procedures for taking judicial notice which are expressly inapplicable to the input of legislative facts.

DAVIS, JUDICIAL NOTICE, 55 Columbia Law Review 945, 952–53 (1955) (citations omitted)

Legislative and Adjudicative Facts

The judicial notice provisions of the Model Code and of the Uniform Rules seem unsound in failing to recognize a cardinal distinction which governs the use of extra–record facts by courts and agencies. This is the distinction between legislative and adjudicative facts.

When a court or an agency finds facts concerning the immediate parties—who did what, where, when, how, and with what motive or intent—the court or agency is performing an adjudicative function, and the facts so determined are conveniently called adjudicative facts. When a court or an agency develops law or policy, it is acting legislatively; the courts have created the common law through judicial legislation, and the facts which inform the tribunal's legislative judgment are called legislative facts.

Stated in other terms, the adjudicative facts are those to which the law is applied in the process of adjudication. They are the facts that normally go to the jury in a jury case. They relate to the parties, their activities, their properties, their businesses. Legislative facts are those which help the tribunal to determine the content of law and policy and to exercise its judgment or discretion in determining what course of action to take. Legislative facts are ordinarily general and do not concern the immediate parties. In the great mass of cases decided by courts and by agencies, the legislative element is either absent, unimportant, or interstitial, because in most cases the applicable law and policy have been previously established. But whenever a tribunal is engaged in the creation of law or of policy, it may need to resort to legislative facts, whether or not those facts have been developed on the record.

The formulation of law and policy, both in the judicial process and in the administrative process, obviously gains strength to the extent that information replaces guesswork or ignorance or intuition or general impressions. Questions of law and policy often yield to comprehensive factual study, as the magnificent leadership of Justice Brandeis in that direction so eloquently testifies. But the present development of the social sciences unfortunately brings us no more than to the threshold of ability to solve our basic problems of law and policy through a full–bodied factual technique. The result is an uneven mixture of *a priori* conjectures and partially informed guesses, with occasional factual investigations of varying depth.

The Advisory Committee addressed the same distinction between adjudicative and legislative facts in its Note to Rule 201(a):

> The omission of any treatment of legislative facts results from fundamental differences between adjudicative facts and legislative facts. Adjudicative facts are simply the facts of the particular case. Legislative facts, on the other hand, are those which have relevance to legal reasoning and the lawmaking process, whether in the formulation of a legal principle or ruling by a judge or court or in the enactment of a legislative body. The terminology was coined by Professor Kenneth Davis in his article *An Approach to Problems of Evidence in the Administrative Process*, 55 HARV. L. REV. 364, 404–407 (1942). The following discussion draws extensively upon his writings. . . .
>
> The usual method of establishing adjudicative facts is through the introduction of evidence, ordinarily consisting of the testimony of witnesses. If particular facts are outside the area of reasonable controversy, this process is dispensed with as unnecessary. A high degree of indisputability is the essential prerequisite.
>
> Legislative facts are quite different. As Professor Davis says:

"My opinion is that judge–made law would stop growing if judges, in thinking about questions of law and policy, were forbidden to take into account the facts they believe, as distinguished from facts which are 'clearly . . . within the domain of the indisputable.' Facts most needed in thinking about difficult problems of law and policy have a way of being outside the domain of the clearly indisputable." *A System of Judicial Notice Based on Fairness and Convenience*, PERSPECTIVES OF LAW 82 (1964).

An illustration is *Hawkins v. United States*, 358 U.S. 74 (1958), in which the Court refused to discard the common law rule that one spouse could not testify against the other; saying, "Adverse testimony given in criminal proceedings would, we think, be likely to destroy almost any marriage." This conclusion has a large intermixture of fact, but the factual aspect is scarcely "indisputable." *See* Hutchins and Slesinger, *Some Observations on the Law of Evidence: Family Relations*, 13 MINN. L. REV. 675 (1929). If the destructive effect of the giving of adverse testimony by a spouse is not indisputable, should the Court have refrained from considering it in the absence of supporting evidence?

"If the Model Code or the Uniform Rules had been applicable, the Court would have been barred from thinking about the essential factual ingredient of the problems before it, and such a result would be obviously intolerable. What the law needs at its growing points is more, not less, judicial thinking about the factual ingredients of problems of what the law ought to be, and the needed facts are seldom 'clearly' indisputable." Davis, *supra,* at 83.

Professor Morgan gave the following description of the methodology of determining domestic law:

"In determining the content or applicability of a rule of domestic law, the judge is unrestricted in his investigation and conclusion. He may reject the propositions of either party or of both parties. He may consult the sources of pertinent data to which they refer, or he may refuse to do so. He may make an independent search for persuasive data or rest content with what he has or what the parties present. . . . [T]he parties do no more than to assist; they control no part of the process." Morgan, *Judicial Notice*, 57 HARV. L. REV. 269, 270–271 (1944).

This is the view which should govern judicial access to legislative facts. It renders inappropriate any limitation in the form of indisputability, any formal requirements of notice other than those already inherent in affording opportunity to hear and be heard and exchanging briefs, and any requirement of formal findings at any level. It should, however, leave open the possibility of introducing evidence through regular channels in appropriate situations. *See Borden's Farm Prods. Co. v. Baldwin*, 293 U.S. 194 (1934), where the cause was remanded for the taking of evidence as to the economic conditions and trade practices underlying the New York Milk Control Law.

Similar considerations govern the judicial use of non–adjudicative facts in ways other than formulating laws and rules. Thayer described them as a part of the judicial reasoning process.

"In conducting a process of judicial reasoning, as of other reasoning, not a step can be taken without assuming something which has not been proven; and the capacity to do this with competent judgment and efficiency, is imputed to judges and juries as part of their necessary mental outfit." Thayer, PRELIMINARY TREATISE ON EVIDENCE 279–280 (1898).

As Professor Davis points out, *A System of Judicial Notice Based on Fairness and Convenience*, in PERSPECTIVES OF LAW 69, 73 (1964), every case involves the use of hundreds or thousands of non–evidence facts. When a witness in an automobile accident case says "car," everyone, judge and jury included, furnishes, from non–evidence sources within himself, the supplementing information that the "car" is an automobile, not a railroad car, that it is self–propelled, probably by an internal combustion engine, that it may be assumed to have four wheels with pneumatic rubber tires, and so on. The judicial process cannot construct every case from scratch, like Descartes creating a world based on the postulate *Cogito, ergo sum*. These items could not possibly be introduced into evidence, and no one suggests that they be. Nor are they appropriate subjects for any formalized treatment of judicial notice of facts. *See* Levin and Levy, *Persuading the Jury with Facts Not in Evidence: The Fiction–Science Spectrum*, 105 U. PA. L. REV. 139 (1956).

Another aspect of what Thayer had in mind is the use of non–evidence facts to appraise or assess the adjudicative facts of the case. Pairs of cases from two jurisdictions illustrate this use and also the difference between non–evidence facts thus used and adjudicative facts. In *People v. Strook*, 347 Ill. 460, 179 N.E. 821 (1932), venue in Cook County had been held not established by testimony that the crime was committed at 7956 South Chicago Avenue, since judicial notice would not be taken that the address was in Chicago. However, the same court subsequently ruled that venue in Cook County was established by testimony that a crime occurred at 8900 South Anthony Avenue, since notice would be taken of the common practice of omitting the name of the city when speaking of local addresses, and the witness was testifying in Chicago. *People v. Pride*, 16 Ill. 2d 82, 156 N.E.2d 551 (1951). And in *Hughes v. Vestal*, 264 N.C. 500, 142 S.E.2d 361 (1965), the Supreme Court of North Carolina disapproved the trial judge's admission in evidence of a state–published table of automobile stopping distances on the basis of judicial notice, though the court itself had referred to the same table in an earlier case in a "rhetorical and illustrative" way in determining that the defendant could not have stopped her car in time to avoid striking a child who suddenly appeared in the highway and that a nonsuit was properly granted. . . . It is apparent that this use of non–evidence facts in evaluating the adjudicative facts of the case is not an appropriate subject for a formalized judicial notice treatment. In view of these considerations, the regulation of judicial notice of facts by the present rule extends only to adjudicative facts.

NOTES

1. Note Professor Davis' reference in his article to Justice Brandeis. As a counsel before the Supreme Court, Brandeis developed the type of brief now named after him—a Brandeis brief, including economic, political, and sociological data. J. MAGUIRE, EVIDENCE: COMMON SENSE AND COMMON LAW 172–74 (1947). Perhaps the best example of such a brief is the brief filed by thirty–five social scientists in *Brown v. Board of Educ.*, 347 U.S. 483 (1954). The brief contained legislative data on the psychological effects of segregation on black children. Much of that data surfaced in footnote 11 of Chief Justice Warren's opinion. Legislative data plays a pivotal role in modern appellate advocacy; a good brief is a social impact statement, showing the court how a current or proposed rule of law affects society.

2. Professor Davis' writings greatly influenced the Advisory Committee. The committee explicitly cites several of his works in the Note to Rule 201. However, it would be an understatement to say that Professor Davis is displeased with the final draft of Rule 201. He faults the Committee for being too narrow: "the effect of Rule 201 is almost the equivalent of zero, because the vast majority of cases of judicial notice involve legislative facts, to which Rule 201 does not apply." 3 K. DAVIS & R. PIERCE, ADMINISTRATIVE LAW TREATISE § 10.6, at 157 (3d ed. 1994). He faults the courts for compounding the problem by misconstruing Rule 201, charging that almost all facts noticed under Rule 201 are legislative facts, not adjudicative facts. *Id.* at 153–58. A number of cases are cited as examples, such as *E.E.O.C. v. Delta Air Lines*, 485 F. Supp. 1004, 1009 (N.D. Ga. 1980). There the court referred to Rule 201 as a basis for noticing the proposition that "only females become pregnant." "The fact is obviously not adjudicative, and Rule 201 by its terms did not apply." DAVIS & PIERCE, *supra*, at 157.

3. If the procedures of Rule 201 are only applicable to taking judicial notice of adjudicative fact, what is the procedure for noticing legislative fact. Should parties at least be given the opportunity to challenge extra–record legislative fact prior to the court's decision to take judicial notice? *Cf.* FED. R. EVID. 201(e).

Defining "adjudicative fact" is only half the problem. The question remains: which types of adjudicative facts should be judicially noticed? When should we dispense with formal evidence? The courts and commentators are in agreement on two categories of data—and in disagreement over a third.

Matters of common knowledge. At early common law, the only type of noticeable fact was a matter of common knowledge. Federal Rule of Evidence 201(b)(1) codifies the doctrine by permitting notice of facts "generally known within the territorial jurisdiction of the trial court . . . ." Conrad gives a particularly colorful rationale for the doctrine: "Courts . . . cannot be presumed to be ignorant. Courts should at least know what everybody else knows." 2 E. CONRAD, MODERN TRIAL EVIDENCE § 983 (1956). If a fact is generally known in the vicinity, it is foolish to waste court time by requiring formal evidence to prove the fact. If a reasonable person of average knowledge and intelligence would be familiar with the fact, the judge may dispense with formal evidence.

This basis for judicial notice permits notice of a wide variety of facts. The court may notice the local town's population (*Solomon v. Miami Woman's*

Club, 359 F. Supp. 41 (S.D. Fla. 1973)), county boundaries (*Donie State Bank v. Knight*, 620 S.W.2d 698 (Tex. Civ. App. 1981)), and the location of a street address within a political subdivision. Annot., 86 A.L.R.3d 484 (1978). The judge may also note facts that hold true nationwide, such as inflationary conditions, *Johnson v. Penrod Drilling Co.*, 510 F.2d 234 (5th Cir. 1975); and the date of Father's Day in a particular year, *Allen v. Allen*, 518 F. Supp. 1234 (E.D. Pa. 1981). The judge may even take notice of well–known international events such as domestic turmoil in Iran, *Itek Corp. v. First Nat'l Bank*, 511 F. Supp. 1341 (D. Mass. 1981); and civil war in El Salvador, *Orantes–Hernandez v. Smith*, 541 F. Supp. 351 (C.D. Cal. 1982).

NOTES AND PROBLEMS

1. Problem 2–1. A Morena statute provides that the speed limit in the business district of any incorporated town is twenty–five miles per hour. At trial, Ms. Hill requests judicial notice that (a) El Dorado is an incorporated town; and (b) the corner where the collision occurred is in El Dorado's business district. As trial judge, would you grant the request? *Varcoe v. Lee*, 180 Cal. 338, 342–47, 181 P. 223, 224–27 (1919).

2. Problem 2–2. In the *Devitt* case, the prosecutor seeks to rebut evidence that the day before the occurrence, Paterson had been drinking in a bar. A Morena statute provides that no alcoholic beverages may be sold on Sunday. May the court judicially notice that March 14, 19YR, was a Sunday? *Pack v. Proffitt*, 463 F. Supp. 761, 761 (E.D. Tenn. 1976).

Verifiable certainty. Although common knowledge is the more familiar basis for judicial notice, the growth principle for the doctrine has been the alternative basis, verifiable certainty. Even if an adjudicative fact is not a matter of common knowledge, the judge may notice it if it is "capable of accurate and ready determination by resort to sources whose accuracy cannot reasonably be questioned." FED. R. EVID. 201(b)(2); *St. Louis Baptist Temple, Inc. v. Fed. Deposit Ins. Corp.*, 605 F.2d 1169 (10th Cir. 1979); *In re Marquam Inv. Corp.*, 942 F.2d 1462 (9th Cir. 1991) ("unquestionable" sources); *Assembly of State of Cal. v. United States Dept. of Commerce*, 797 F. Supp. 1554 (E.D. Cal. 1992) ("authoritative" sources). Thus, judicial notice is an important means of allowing the law to capitalize on the advances in scientific research. For example, if the judge can ascertain a scientific fact by consulting learned treatises, it makes sense to notice the fact "without resort to [the] cumbersome method" of formally introducing evidence. *Melong v. Micronesian Claims Comm'n*, 643 F.2d 10, 12 n.5 (D.C. Cir. 1980).

The courts have been willing, if not eager, to invoke this basis for judicial notice. For other instances of judicial notice of scientific facts, see annotations, 28 A.L.R.2d 1119 (judicial notice of reliability of fingerprint identification); 84 A.L.R.2d 979 (judicial notice of stopping distances of automobiles and driver reaction times); *Oesterle v. Couch*, 10 Wis. 2d 293, 102 N.W.2d 763 (1969) (the jury could use common knowledge of the scientific fact that a sufficiently great and rapid change in the temperature of glass will cause it to crack); *Alexander v. Fireman's Ins. Co.*, 317 S.W.2d 752 (Tex. Civ. App. 1958), *aff'd*, 328 S.W.2d 350 (Tex. Civ. App. 1959) (when an airplane exceeds the speed of sound, a report commonly called a sonic boom is heard and some concussion of air pressure accompanies it); *Winterberg v. Thomas*, 126 Colo. 60, 246 P.2d 1058 (1952) (court took judicial notice of unquestioned laws of mathematics to reverse lower court); *Linkhart v. Savely*, 190 Or. 484, 227 P.2d 187 (1951) (court took notice that accurate and scientific tests are available by which condition of eyes may be generally ascertained); *Application of Norris*, 179 F.2d 970 (C.C.P.A. 1950) (judicial notice taken of quotations from chemical textbook authorities); *Carter Oil Co. v. Dees*, 340 Ill. App. 449, 92 N.E.2d 519 (1950) (court took notice of scientific method of restoring pressure in abandoned oil wells so that they can again go into production); *Roy v. Smith*, 131 Cal. App. 148, 151, 21 P.2d 151, 153 (1933) (carbon dioxide has a specific gravity of 1.53 as compared with ordinary air); *City of Phoenix v. Breuninger*, 50 Ariz. 372, 380, 72 P.2d 580, 583 (1937) (the process usually called pasteurization is almost certain to destroy any form of dangerous bacteria that infects milk); *National Ice & Fuel Co. v. Industrial Comm'n*, 387 Ill. 31, 35, 55 N.E.2d 91, 93 (1944) (when the hand is exposed to cold steel, the steel draws the moisture and warmth from the hand so rapidly that the circulation is stopped, and what is known as a circulatory crisis is created); *Markulics v. Maico Co.*, 74 Cal. App. 2d 66, 69, 168 P.2d 35, 36 (1946) (a B battery used in a hearing aid is incapable of developing fire). On judicial notice of the reliability of radar speed detection devices, breath–intoxication devices, lie detection devices, and psychiatric evidence, see Boyce, *Judicial Recognition of Scientific Evidence in Criminal Cases*, 8 UTAH L. REV. 313 (1964); Note, *Judicial Notice of Medical Facts*, 16 MICH. ST. B.J. 221 (1937).

NOTES AND PROBLEMS

1. We commonly refer to this basis for judicial notice as "verifiable certainty." What does "certainty" mean in this context? How high must the likelihood be? As the director for the Center for Modern Technologies has pointed out, "with monotonous regularity, apparently competent men have laid down the law about what is technically possible and impossible—and have been proved utterly wrong, sometimes while the ink was scarcely dry from their pens." A. CLARKE, PROFILES OF THE FUTURE: AN INQUIRY INTO THE LIMITS OF THE POSSIBLE (1984). In 1878, while Edison neared the perfection of his invention of the electric light bulb, a special British Parliamentary committee announced that the concept was "unworthy of the attention of practical and scientific men." A year before the Soviet Union launched *Sputnik I,* the Astronomer Royal, Dr. Richard van der Riet Woolley, stated that proposals for space travel were "utter bilge." Even if a proposition qualifies as a verifiable scientific "certainty" today, the proposition may be discredited in a decade. In *Daubert v. Merrell Dow Pharmaceuticals, Inc.,* 509 U.S. 579 (1993), the majority opinion, authored by Justice Blackmun, observed that "arguably, there are no certainties in science."

2. Problem 2–4. In *Hill,* the plaintiff wants to prove that Mr. Worker had the time to notice the imminent danger, brake, and avoid the collision. Her attorney hands the judge a document entitled, "Table of Stopping Distances— Morena Highway Patrol." The attorney then says, "Your Honor, we'd like you to notice these correlations. For example, that at thirty miles an hour, the total stopping distance is eighty–eight feet." As trial judge, how would you rule? Recent Case, 38 Mo. L. REV. 678 (1973). Would it make a difference if Ms. Hill's attorney had said, "For example, that at thirty miles an hour under normal conditions, the average stopping distance is eighty–eight feet." Why?

***

Highly probable facts. Almost all courts limit the substantive scope of the judicial notice doctrine to matters of common knowledge and verifiable certainties. If the fact falls within either category, it is virtually indisputable. Requiring formal evidence to prove such a fact would be a waste of time. However, some commentators have urged the extension of the doctrine beyond these parameters to highly probable facts. In *Judicial Notice—Excerpts Relating to the Morgan–Wigmore Controversy*, 14 VAND. L. REV. 779 (1961), Professor McNaughton succinctly described the controversy:

> Professor Morgan and Dean Wigmore do not differ with respect to the application of the doctrine to "law." Their difference relates to judicial notice of "facts." Here Wigmore, following Thayer, insists that judicial notice is solely to save time where dispute is unlikely and that a matter judicially noticed is therefore only "prima facie," or rebuttable, if the opponent elects to dispute it. It is express in Thayer and implicit in Wigmore that (perhaps because the matter is rebuttable) judicial notice may be applied not only to indisputable matters but also to matters of lesser certainty. Morgan on the other hand defines judicial notice more narrowly, and his consequences follow from his definition. He limits judicial notice of fact to matters patently indisputable. And his position is that matters judicially noticed are not rebuttable. He asserts that it is wasteful to permit patently indisputable matters to be litigated by way of formal proof and furthermore that it would be absurd to permit a party to woo a jury to an obviously erroneous finding contrary to the noticed fact. Also, he objects to the Wigmorean conception on the ground that it is really a "presumption" of sorts attempting to pass under a misleading name. It is, according to Morgan, a presumption with no recognized rules as to how the presumption works—what activates it and who has the burden of doing how much to rebut it.

Wigmore and Thayer argue that the orthodox categories, common knowledge and verifiable certainty, do not exhaust the potential of the judicial notice doctrine. If the doctrine is designed to expedite trials and secondarily to regulate the rationality of verdicts, why not permit the judge to notice disputable facts that nevertheless have a high degree of likelihood? Or is the indisputability standard a more appropriate dividing line between judicial notice and formal evidence? Once we allow the opponent to attack the judicially noticed fact, judicial notice seems to become a sort of "glorified presumption." E. MORGAN, BASIC PROBLEMS OF EVIDENCE 10 (1963).

b. Judicial Notice of Law

The courts traditionally invoked judicial notice as the vehicle for feeding legal authorities into the decisionmaking process. E. MORGAN, BASIC PROBLEMS

OF EVIDENCE 1 (1963). In state court, the trial judge may notice "the common law and public statutes in force in the state . . . ." *Id.* The expression "public statutes" includes "the public Acts of Congress and the provisions of the Constitution of the United States and of the state . . . ." *Id.* In federal district court, the judge may notice "the common and statutory laws of every state in the Union." *Id.* 44 U.S.C. § 1507 states that "the contents of the Federal Register shall be judicially noticed," and it is arguable that this federal statute requires state courts to notice the federal laws published in the Register.

At common law, the courts were reluctant to extend the judicial notice doctrine beyond these types of authorities. Some jurisdictions still hold that municipal ordinances are not judicially noticeable. *Lange v. State*, 639 S.W.2d 304 (Tex. Crim. App. 1982); Case Comment, 25 U. FLA. L. REV. 811, 812 (1973). Similarly, some courts balk at noticing administrative regulations. *Campbell v. Mincey*, 413 F. Supp. 16 (N.D. Miss. 1975).

Moreover, the view was very strongly held that judicial notice should not extend to the legal authorities of other states or foreign countries. E. MORGAN, BASIC PROBLEMS IN EVIDENCE 2–3 (1963). Most jurisdictions have now adopted the Uniform Judicial Notice of Foreign Law Act; but in the context of the Act, "foreign" refers to another state rather than another country. *Id.* at 4. In a jurisdiction adhering to the traditional view, the person relying upon foreign law must still plead and prove the tenor of the law. Annot., 75 A.L.R.3d 177 (1977). There is authority that the traditional view still obtains in federal practice. *Munsell v. La Brasserie Molson Du Quebec Limitee*, 623 F. Supp. 100 (E.D.N.Y. 1985).

NOTES

1. Federal Rule of Civil Procedure 44.1 and Rule of Criminal Procedure 26.1 both govern the determination of foreign law. The last sentence of each rule reads: "The court's determination shall be treated as a ruling on a question of law." What is the significance of the statement that a particular determination "shall be treated as a ruling on a question of law"?

2. Do the Federal Rules treat the determination of law as an aspect of judicial notice? *See* FED. R. EVID. 201(a). Nonetheless, courts not only judicially notice legal doctrines embodied in constitutional provisions, statutes, and cases, but also notice legal events, such as the entry of judgments and orders. If we are going to use judicial notice as the theory for the input of legal authorities, should we limit the theory to judicial decisions and legislative enactments? Why not extend the doctrine to ordinances and regulations? At one time, the limitation could be defended on the ground that there was less ready access to written materials setting forth the ordinances and regulations. Does that ground have merit today?

2. OTHER METHODS OF ESTABLISHING FACTS

There are other substitutes for evidence–alternative methods by which facts can be established in litigation. Typically, these other methods are more appropriate to courses in civil and criminal procedure, but they will be mentioned briefly here because they are alternatives to formal proof of facts.

Stipulation. It is not uncommon for parties to stipulate to a fact. Although it can be done by a formal document, more often a stipulation is oral, made during trial or a pre–trial hearing or conference. A stipulation is simply an agreement between the parties or a commitment by one party not to contest the existence of a particular fact. For example, counsel may state, on the record, "Your Honor, we will stipulate that the traffic light was red when the truck entered the intersection." Such a stipulation, if otherwise agreeable or "accepted" by the other parties and the court (or required to be accepted by the court) is binding, and obviates the need for proof of that fact. *See* 22 C. WRIGHT & K. GRAHAM, FEDERAL PRACTICE AND PROCEDURE: EVIDENCE § 5194 (1978).

Judicial admission. There are two types of formal judicial admissions that can preclude proof of a fact. First, before trial in a civil case, a party can formally request that another party admit a fact. The procedure for doing so is spelled out in Federal Rule of Civil Procedure 36; every state has a comparable rule. Rule 36(a) provides that the request can be to admit the truth of "any matters within the scope of Rule 26(b)(1) set forth in the request that relate to statements or opinions of fact or of the application of law to fact, including the genuineness of any documents described in the request." Each matter so described is deemed admitted unless, within 30 days, the party to whom the request was made serves a written answer or objection. The answer may admit or deny the fact, or may state that the party cannot truthfully admit or deny the fact, and why. The answer may be qualified or admitted in part and denied in part. Lack of information or knowledge may not be given as a reason for denial unless the party has made a reasonable effort to obtain the information or knowledge. Rule 36(b) provides that "[a]ny matter admitted under this rule is conclusively established unless the court on motion permits withdrawal or amendment of the admission." Properly used, this device can obviate proof of undisputed or indisputable facts. For example, it is often used to eliminate the need to lay a foundation for the authentication of documents.

Another type of judicial admission occurs when a party, on the record, unequivocally alleges a fact under circumstances where the court will treat the allegation as binding on that party. For example, a party may plead that he is a citizen of Morena. As a general rule, the court will treat that allegation as binding and incontrovertible, obviating the need for proof of that fact, and in some cases that party will be precluded from later disclaiming or withdrawing that factual allegation. *See, e.g.*, Note, *Judicial Admissions*, 64 COLUM. L. REV. 1121 (1964). In addition, a failure to deny a fact in the appropriate pleading constitutes an admission, obviating the need for proof of the fact alleged. *See* 5 C. WRIGHT & A. MILLER, FEDERAL PRACTICE AND PROCEDURE: CIVIL 2D § 1279 (1990).

Binding judicial admissions must be distinguished from "mere" evidentiary admissions. As a general rule, any relevant statement a party has ever made can be admitted if offered against that party by another party. *See* FED. R. EVID. 801(d)(2). Although admissible, such "admissions" are not conclusive against the party making them and may be controverted.

Preclusive Prior Fact Determinations. Sometimes a fact issue will be deemed to have been conclusively decided in another proceeding, and therefore must be taken as decided and cannot be relitigated. No doubt you encountered this doctrine in the course in civil procedure, under the topic referred to as "issue preclusion" or "collateral estoppel." *See* 18 C. WRIGHT, A. MILLER & E. COOPER, FEDERAL PRACTICE AND PROCEDURE: JURISDICTION §§ 4416–4426 (1981). To the extent that this doctrine applies, it can also preclude the need for proof of facts.

Chapter 3
CHRONOLOGY OF A TRIAL

This chapter gives the reader a brief, simplistic overview of the way in which a trial is organized. For the most part, the chapter reviews the current prevailing practices. In addition to reviewing this material, the student would be well advised to visit a local courthouse and spend a day or so observing a jury trial, something many law students have never done. Or, if you have access to the Court TV channel, watch a real jury trial on television. Observing a trial and this background reading will give you a much better understanding of the manner in which a trial proceeds.

A. THE ORGANIZATION OF THE TRIAL

1. JURY SELECTION

At the outset of a jury trial, the judge and attorneys participate in the jury selection process. First, the judge introduces the attorneys and parties to the prospective jurors and describes in general terms the nature of the case. Then comes the *voir dire* examination of the prospective jurors: The judge (and, in some cases, the attorneys) question the prospective jurors to determine whether they are qualified to sit as jurors.

In all jurisdictions permitting attorneys to personally question during *voir dire*, the attorney has a right to ask questions logically relevant to grounds for challenge for cause. A number of jurisdictions also grant the attorney the right to question to "intelligently" exercise peremptory challenges. *People v. Williams*, 29 Cal. 3d 392, 628 P.2d 869, 174 Cal. Rptr. 317 (1981); *see also* Illinois Supreme Court Rule 234. However, it is no secret among experienced litigators that if the judge permits, *voir dire* examination can be used for two other important purposes.

One of these purposes is factual indoctrination: The trial attorney exposes the jury to key items of evidence that will be introduced during trial. Surprisingly, the conventional wisdom has it that the best factual indoctrination is exposing the jury to the items of evidence that are most harmful to your case. Suppose that in the *Devitt* case, the defense attorney knows that Devitt has several prior convictions. The defense attorney is positive that when Devitt takes the witness stand, the prosecutor will attempt to impeach Devitt with the convictions. To preempt the prosecutor, the defense attorney might state during *voir dire* examination: "Now, Mr. Grant, the evidence will show that my client, Mr. Devitt, has two prior criminal convictions. If he takes the stand and testifies, will you reject his testimony simply because of those convictions?" The reasoning underlying the "expose your weaknesses" strategy is simple: The impact of the evidence will be less damaging to your case if you mention the evidence first. If you let the opponent be the first to mention the evidence to the jury, the evidence would sound more damning, and some jurors might suspect that you were attempting to conceal the truth from them.

The other purpose of *voir dire* examination is legal indoctrination: The attorney teaches the jury about the legal doctrines most helpful to the attorney's case. Those doctrines are often evidentiary rules. For example, in the *Devitt* case, if the judge permitted, the defense attorney might devote some *voir dire* questioning to the prosecution's burden of proof and the presumption of innocence:

Q: Ms. Martinez, if you had to vote in this case right now, before hearing any evidence, what would your verdict be?

A: I guess "not guilty."

Q: So you understand that the defendant is presumed innocent?

A: Yes.

Q: You realize, don't you, that the prosecution has the burden of proving Mr. Devitt's guilt beyond any reasonable doubt?

A: Yes.

At the conclusion of the *voir dire* examination, the attorneys exercise their challenges. A challenge may be either for cause or peremptory. The accepted grounds for challenge for cause are usually specified by statute. If the challenge is for cause, the attorney claims that there is some reason, such as bias, why the venireperson is disqualified from serving as a juror. The judge rules on the challenge. In contrast, a peremptory challenge gives the attorney an absolute right to strike the prospective juror from the panel. The attorney ordinarily need not state any justification for exercising a peremptory challenge, except in those cases in which the challenge may be constitutionally impermissible. *See, e.g., Batson v. Kentucky*, 476 U.S. 79 (1986). Each attorney has a limited number of peremptory challenges. The number is usually specified in a local statute or court rule.

In some courts, attorneys are not permitted to conduct *voir dire* examination; all questioning is done by the judge alone. The purpose of this approach is to save time and prevent abusive indoctrination of the prospective jurors. However, the attorney may still suggest *voir dire* questions to the judge. *Turner v. Murray*, 476 U.S. 28, 37 (1986).

2. OPENING STATEMENT

After the jury has been selected, the attorneys present their opening statements. The plaintiff or prosecutor goes first. In most jurisdictions, the defense attorney may either present an opening immediately after the plaintiff's or prosecutor's, or reserve opening until the beginning of the defense's case–in–chief. (Usually, except in certain criminal cases, it is not a good idea to reserve opening statement.)

The function of the opening statement is to preview the admissible evidence for the jury. The attorney customarily tells the jury, "The evidence will show . . . ." Unless the attorney delivering the opening statement has analyzed the evidentiary problems likely to arise during the trial, the attorney can easily commit error—error that may even necessitate a mistrial—during the opening statement. The error may not only abort the trial, it might also lead to disciplinary sanctions against the attorney. The American Bar Association's Model Rules of Professional Conduct (1999 edition), Rule 3.4(e), specifically states that a lawyer shall not "allude to any matter that the lawyer does not reasonably believe is relevant or that will not be supported by admissible evidence."

The most common objection to the content of an opening statement, that an attorney is being "argumentative," illustrates this rule. As Professor Jeans explains, to avoid this objection the attorney must understand evidence law, especially the norms limiting the admission of opinion testimony:

> Opening statements should not be an argument—a tool of persuasion yes—but not an argument. It is objectionable, for instance, for your opponent to state that "the evidence will show that the defendant negligentlydrove at an excessive rate of speed" or "the poor plaintiff has suffered a most grievous injury that will severely affect her for the rest of her life." How best to recognize an objectionable argument? As you listen to your opponent's opening statement, ask yourself, "Will a witness testify in such fashion?" Relating to the examples, who will testify that "the defendant was negligent and drove at an excessive rate of speed"? These are conclusions and as such inadmissible. The testimony will relate to "tearing down the road at seventy miles an hour" and this should be the verbiage employed in opening statement. Or who will testify that "plaintiff suffered grievous injuries"? This too is conclusionary, thus inadmissible as evidence and consequently improper in opening statement. The lawyer should avoid these argumentative, conclusionary statements, not only because they are objectionable but because they are usually less effective than a detailed recitation of the facts on which those conclusions or arguments are based.

J. JEANS, TRIAL ADVOCACY § 8.13 (2d ed. 1993). Hence, in *Devitt,* it would be objectionable if the prosecutor stated during opening, "Now I'm going to explain to you why you should believe Ms. Paterson's testimony rather than the defendant's." Or, in the *Hill* case, the plaintiff could not state, "This is why you should infer that . . . ." The opinion rules would prohibit a witness from making those statements from the stand, and consequently the attorney cannot make them during opening. Evidentiary law dominates the opening just as it plays a significant role during *voir dire.*

3. THE PLAINTIFF'S OR PROSECUTOR'S CASE–IN–CHIEF

Evidence law recognizes several different methods of establishing the existence of a fact. These include the formal introduction of evidence by a party, a stipulation between the parties, judicial notice by the judge, judicial admissions, and certain prior fact determinations in another proceeding. Although the other methods are often used, in almost all cases the parties will have to present evidence to prove up the facts in the case. One of the fundamental principles of the adversary system is that the parties should generally control the presentation of evidence. S. LANDSMAN, READINGS ON ADVERSARIAL JUSTICE: THE AMERICAN APPROACH TO ADJUDICATION 2 (1988). As the Joint Conference Report, excerpted in Chapter 1, indicated, "This principle insulates the adjudicator from involvement in the contest. It also encourages the adversaries to find and present their most persuasive evidence." *Id.* at 3. The Anglo–American norm is that evidence is presented one witness at a time, and that one party presents his or her evidence before the other party offers contrary proof. The rationale is that this structure is more orderly and increases juror comprehension, each party having an opportunity to present his or her version of the facts in a relatively uninterrupted fashion.

The plaintiff and prosecutor have the first opportunity to present evidence to the jury. This portion of the trial is usually called the prosecutor's or plaintiff's case–in–chief. The plaintiff and prosecutor have the first opportunity to present evidence to the jury because they have the ultimate burden of proof on most of the factual issues in the case. During the case–in–chief, they have the right to present any evidence logically relevant to any factual issue on which they have the burden of proof. Indeed, in many jurisdictions, the scope is even broader; they have the right to present any evidence logically relevant to any factual issue in the case. In these jurisdictions, they not only can present evidence about factual issues on which they have the burden of proof; they also can anticipate defenses and offer evidence rebutting them. *United States v. Conley*, 523 F.2d 650 (8th Cir. 1975). Thus if, in our torts case, Polecat Motors had pleaded the statute of limitations in its answer, in her case Ms. Hill could have anticipated that defense and introduced evidence showing that the statute was tolled.

The plaintiff and prosecutor have discretion as to which witnesses they will call during the case–in–chief. They may even call adverse parties. For example, in the *Hill* case, Ms. Hill could call Polecat Motors' president as a witness during the plaintiff's case–in–chief. It is common practice in medical malpractice actions to call the defendant doctor during the plaintiff's case. Of course, the Fifth Amendment's privilege against self–incrimination precludes the prosecutor from calling the defendant as a witness during the prosecution case–in–chief. At the other extreme, there are a few instances in which a party is formally required to call a particular witness. For example, in some jurisdictions, the prosecutor must call all eyewitnesses to the crime during the case–in–chief. 4 WHARTON'S CRIMINAL EVIDENCE § 659 (15th ed. 1997). However, in most jurisdictions, the plaintiff and prosecutor can choose which witnesses to call during the case. If they decide not to call a witness during the case, the only possible penalty is that the judge may not permit them to call the witness later during rebuttal.

As the preceding paragraphs suggest, typically the only witnesses testifying during this case–in–chief are witnesses called by the plaintiff or prosecutor. However, the judge has discretion to permit a witness to be called "out of turn." If live testimony by a defense witness is essential and the witness can appear only while the plaintiff's or prosecutor's case–in–chief is in progress, the judge may allow the defense to call the witness during that case. *Loinaz v. EG & G, Inc.*, 910 F.2d 1, 5 (1st Cir. 1990). The trial judge has substantial discretion to make such "courtroom management" decisions. *Elgabri v. Lekas*, 964 F.2d 1255, 1260 (1st Cir. 1992).

4. DEFENSE MOTION FOR NONSUIT OR DIRECTED VERDICT

At the close of the plaintiff's or prosecutor's case, the plaintiff or prosecution will announce that it "rests." That announcement is the trigger for defense motions challenging the legal sufficiency of the plaintiff's or prosecutor's evidence. If the defense counsel believes that the evidence is legally insufficient to sustain the plaintiff's or prosecutor's burden (that is, even if the jury believes all the evidence, the evidence lacks sufficient cumulative probative value to permit the trier of fact to find all the facts on which the plaintiff or prosecutor has the burden), the defense counsel makes a motion at this point. The motion is variously called a motion for a nonsuit, judgment of acquittal, finding of not guilty, directed verdict, or judgment as a matter or law (FED. R. CIV. P. 50). Whatever its title, the motion challenges the legal sufficiency of the evidence. If the judge agrees with the defense counsel, the judge grants the motion and terminates the trial. If the judge disagrees, the trial proceeds to the defendant's evidence.

In ruling on the defense motion, the judge decides whether the plaintiff or prosecutor has sustained the initial burden of going forward or production. We shall analyze the burden in depth later. At this stage, there are three possibilities. The plaintiff or prosecutor could have presented such persuasive evidence of a fact that there is a true presumption or mandatory inference of the fact's existence—if the jurors believe the evidence, they must conclude that the fact exists. Or the evidence may be sufficient to sustain a bare permissive inference of the fact's existence—if the jurors decide to accept the evidence, they may conclude that the fact exists. If the judge believes that the plaintiff or prosecutor has created either type of inference, the judge will deny the defense motion; either inference usually suffices to satisfy the initial burden. However, the third possibility is that the evidence is so weak that it will not even support a permissive inference. If the judge believes the evidence is that weak, the judge will grant the motion.

NOTES

1. Why permit the judge to grant a nonsuit motion and take the case away from the jury before all the evidence is in? We ordinarily say that the judge decides questions of law while the jury decides questions of fact. Is this a question of fact or one of law? Is the jury as competent to rule on this question as the judge?

2. In deciding whether to grant the motion, should the judge use the same standard in civil and in criminal cases? In the typical civil action, the ultimate burden of proof is a preponderance of the evidence. In a criminal case, the corresponding burden is proof beyond a reasonable doubt. Should that difference affect the test determining whether to grant a directed verdict? *See Jackson v. Virginia*, 443 U.S. 307, 324 (1979).

5. THE DEFENSE'S CASE–IN–CHIEF OR THE CASE IN DEFENSE

The next major component of the trial is the defense's case–in–chief. The rules governing the defense case are markedly similar to the rules governing the opening case. The scope of the defense case includes evidence logically relevant to any fact in issue in the case. As is true of the plaintiff's or prosecutor's case, the defendant may call adverse witnesses. Hence, in our torts case, Polecat Motors could call Ms. Hill during the defense case–in–chief.

The formal sequence is that the defense case follows the plaintiff's or prosecutor's case. There have been some scientific studies to determine whether this formal sequence makes psychological sense. Consider the following excerpts from a report of the Human Behavior and Legal Process Project, funded by the National Science Foundation.

WALKER, THIBAUT & ANDRESLI, ORDER OF PRESENTATION AT TRIAL, 82 Yale Law Journal 216, 216–26 (1972)

The order of evidence in an adversary proceeding has an important effect upon the final determination of guilt or innocence. This effect is complicated by the fact that the adversary process is ordered in two distinct ways: a "gross order" of presentation by each party; and, within this gross order, an "internal order" for the presentation of each party's case.

Gross order is determined by statute and judicial decision for the three parts of the traditional adversary process: opening statements, presentations of evidence, and closing arguments. The prosecution or plaintiff usually has the right to make the first opening statement, present evidence first, and make both the first and the final closing arguments. The usual justification for this ordering is that the party with the burden of proof should have the advantage of making the first and last presentation.

The results of this experiment suggest that in a legal setting the impact of the final bits of evidence, in both gross order and internal order, is pervasive: In gross order, the side going second is strongly advantaged; internal order favors strong evidence occurring toward the end of the presentation except when the defense presents first.

In seeking to account for the gross order results, it is important to examine why facts presented *first* have less impact in a legal setting than elsewhere. First impressions normally have strong impact when individuals receive information about relatively stable characteristics of others, such as attitudinal and personality dispositions and abilities. However, the determination of whether another person has performed an unlawful act entails judgments not on permanent characteristics but rather on specific events. Thus the legal inquiry may reduce the natural impact of this type of early information. Another circumstance thought to strengthen early impressions is a finding of an inconsistency between earlier and later information. Once an early impression is formed, later inconsistent information is often "discounted" because the recipient of the information has relied on the first impression. However, the recipient of the information presented by each party in an adversary process knows that such information has been screened by the advocate and is thus plainly incomplete. Luchins has shown that by forewarning subjects of the imminence of additional information, the impact of early information is suppressed. Thus, when fact–finders know that early information is imperfect and that contrary information will follow, first impressions are not so strong that later information will be discounted. Similarly, early information presented in a legal setting is not likely to produce the strong bias that may in other settings lead to the "assimilation" of subsequent information. Moreover, even if fact–finders enter the case with a strong bias toward the side presenting first, the adversary system is designed to counter such biases.

Indeed, it appears that in legal settings it is the material presented first which is discounted. Sears has demonstrated that fact–finders exposed only to one side of a case (as compared with those exposed to both sides) made less extreme judgments on the relative merits of the presentation. This suggests that after having heard only the first presentation, decision–makers in a legal setting will reserve judgment until they have heard the remaining evidence. Moreover, Sears found that, where subjects who had heard both sides of the case were approximately equally interested in hearing additional information favoring one or the other party, those who had heard only one side were not as interested in receiving further information supporting that side but rather preferred to hear information favoring the opposition. It is this posture of legal fact–finders, with their suspension of commitment and heightened receptivity to the subsequent presentation, that may favor the party going second. Such effects are further promoted, of course, by a sharpened recall of the more recently presented evidence.

The results of this experiment suggest: (1) it makes a difference whether one goes first or second in the adversary presentation of legal materials, and the second position is the more advantageous; (2) the ordering of weak and strong elements within presentations also produces a difference in results, and the weak to strong (climactic) order is the more effective. But this second finding is true regardless of gross order only for the plaintiff or prosecution; the climactic order is advantageous for the defense only within second presentations and there only to a relatively minor degree.

Assuming that the ideal order for adversary fact–finding is a sequence of evidence which eliminates any advantage gained solely because of order, these two findings suggest an optimal sequence for an adversary system: The advocate asserting guilt or fault should go first and present his case in a climactic order; the advocate defending should follow and also present his case in a climactic order. Both advocates are thus given effective resources: This sequence gives a gross order advantage to the defense, offset by the climactic order advantage given to the preceding prosecution or plaintiff presentation. One of the groups in the experiment heard the hypothetical case in this sequence, and a high degree of balance was achieved. This result suggests the value of the traditional adversary system in generating balanced judgments by affording both parties fair access to their most effective resources.

The system, with its traditional gross order for opening statements and the presentation of evidence (prosecution or plaintiff first) provides the ideal order as long as both advocates follow their self–interest and present their evidence in a climactic order. The traditional adversary trial thus appears remarkably well arranged to neutralize the effects of order and thus maintain the fact–finding process relatively free of this powerful yet legally irrelevant influence.

6. PLAINTIFF'S MOTION FOR DIRECTED VERDICT

Like a civil or criminal defendant, a civil plaintiff may move for a directed verdict. The civil plaintiff may make the motion when the defense announces that it rests. As previously stated, when the defense moves for a directed verdict, the defense in effect asserts that the plaintiff's or prosecutor's evidence is so weak that it is legally insufficient—even if the jury believes all the evidence, the evidence has insufficient probative value to support a plaintiff's judgment or conviction. In contrast, when the plaintiff moves for a directed verdict, the plaintiff in effect claims that the plaintiff's evidence is so overwhelming that no rational juror could return a defense verdict in the case. As you might expect, defense motions are granted far more frequently than plaintiff's motions. It is the rare case in which the plaintiff's evidence is that overpowering. To gain a directed verdict, the plaintiff must do more than create a permissive or mandatory inference of the fact's existence. In those situations, the judge rules only that *if* the jury believes the evidence, they may or must infer the fact's existence. In this situation, the plaintiff claims that his or her evidence is so convincing that the jurors *must* believe the evidence. The plaintiff's evidence sustains the initial burden of going forward to the extent that the judge takes the case away from the jury and proclaims the plaintiff's victory on the issue.

7. THE PLAINTIFF'S OR PROSECUTOR'S REBUTTAL

After the defense's case–in–chief, the plaintiff and prosecutor can present rebuttal evidence. As the title "rebuttal" suggests, this part of the trial has a limited scope. The trial judge can limit the plaintiff or prosecutor to testimony that "is precisely directed to rebutting new matter or new theories presented by the defendant's case–in–chief." *Bowman v. General Motors Corp.*, 427 F. Supp. 234, 240 (E.D. Pa. 1977). However, the judge has wide discretion to broaden the scope to permit the plaintiff or prosecutor to introduce evidence mistakenly omitted during the case–in–chief. *United States v. Nussen*, 531 F.2d 15 (2d Cir. 1976). The appellate court will reverse the trial judge's ruling only when there has been a clear abuse of discretion. *United States v. Walton*, 552 F.2d 1354, 1366 (10th Cir. 1977).

8. THE DEFENSE SURREBUTTAL OR REJOINDER

The norms applicable to the surrebuttal are strikingly similar to those for rebuttal. The defendant has a right to surrebuttal only when new ground was covered during the rebuttal. *United States v. Wilson*, 490 F. Supp. 713 (E.D. Mich. 1980), *aff'd*, 639 F.2d 314 (6th Cir. 1981). Here, too, the judge has broad discretion, and the appellate courts ordinarily uphold the judge's decision to preclude surrebuttal. *United States v. Pino*, 608 F.2d 1001 (4th Cir. 1979). It is a rare occurrence when a trial proceeds to this stage. However, in a rare case, a denial of surrebuttal can constitute both error and a violation of due process. *United States v. One Single Family Residence Located at 15526 69th Drive N.*, 778 F. Supp. 1215 (S.D. Fla. 1991).

9.　WITNESSES CALLED BY THE TRIAL JUDGE

The trial judge need not be content with the witnesses the parties call. The judge may decide that the interests of justice require that other witnesses be called to testify. Annot., 16 A.L.R.4th 352 (1982); Annot., 53 A.L.R. Fed. 498 (1981). Federal Rule of Evidence 614 specifically states:

> The court may, on its own motion or at the suggestion of a party, call witnesses, and all parties are entitled to cross–examine the witnesses thus called.

This problem frequently arises in practice. A person may possess highly relevant knowledge but have such an unsavory background and be so easily impeached that neither party wants to call him as a witness. They both may fear that if the jury associates them with that witness, the jury's suspicions about the witness will spill over and impair the credibility of their other witnesses. In such cases, one of the parties will ask the judge to call the witness.

In addition, occasionally the trial court itself may want to call a witness in the interests of justice. There may be a person not called by any party whom the judge believes has relevant knowledge. Although this power may be more readily exercised in a bench trial, it is available and used in jury trials as well.

The judge has the power to call his or her own witnesses during one of the party's case–in–chief. As a matter of courtroom etiquette, the judge often waits until the completion of the parties' cases before calling the court's own witness. That restriction on the judge's power is purely self–imposed. However, there are some external restraints on the power.

In a criminal case, the trial court cannot call a witness where the government's case would be insufficient as a matter of law without the court's witness. *United States v. Karnes*, 531 F.2d 214 (4th Cir. 1976).

In addition, the trial court should instruct the jury that a witness is not entitled to any greater credibility because he or she was called by the court. *Id.*

In general, the power of the judge to call witnesses is and should be used sparingly. Excessive intervention by the judge runs counter to our traditional adversary practice, undermines the role of the judge as an impartial arbiter, and can result in prejudice to a party. *See generally* 4 J. WEINSTEIN & M. BERGER, WEINSTEIN'S FEDERAL EVIDENCE ¶ 614[01]–[05] (J. McLaughlin ed., 2d ed. 1997).

10.　WITNESSES REQUESTED BY THE JURORS

The judge has the power to call other witnesses, but the jurors may only request that the judge do so. The jurors cannot order that a person appear as a witness. When they make a request, the judge reviews it and decides whether the interests of justice necessitate the presentation of that person's testimony. Such requests are rare. Few jurors realize that they have this power, and most trial judges never inform the jury of their right to make a request.

11. CLOSING ARGUMENT OR SUMMATION

As we have seen, the attorneys may not mention inferences during the opening statement, and evidence law also restricts their ability to elicit opinions from witnesses, especially witnesses who do not qualify as experts. However, when all the evidence has been presented, the law permits counsel to argue inferences from it. The opportunity to argue is the closing argument or summation. The plaintiff or prosecutor ordinarily opens, the defense attorney then speaks, and the plaintiff or prosecutor closes. As the party with the burden of proof, the plaintiff or prosecutor usually has the privilege of both opening and closing.

There are several types of inferences the attorneys may properly argue during closing. First, the attorneys may argue credibility, namely, why the jurors should believe their witnesses and disbelieve the opponent's. Suppose that in the *Devitt* prosecution, during cross–examination, the defendant had admitted that he had a previous conviction for perjury. The prosecutor could argue: "Now, ladies and gentlemen, I'm going to tell you why you should disbelieve the defendant and reject his testimony. During his testimony, you heard him admit that he has previously been convicted of perjury. This man, Devitt, is a convicted perjurer, ladies and gentlemen. He took the stand in another courtroom. He took the oath in another courtroom. And he lied—just as he's lying today."

Next, the attorneys may argue historical inferences from the circumstantial evidence. Assume that in our torts case there was a dispute over the point of impact between Ms. Hill's and Mr. Roe's cars. Mr. Roe's attorney might argue, "It's true that Ms. Hill says that Mr. Worker struck the rear of her car while her car was still in the intersection. But, ladies and gentlemen, look at the physical evidence in this case. The policeman, Patrolman Officer, gave us a very detailed description of the accident scene. Most of the debris, including the broken glass, was found 100 feet from the intersection. And our expert testified that that glass matched Mr. Worker's headlight glass. When you consider all the circumstances, ladies and gentlemen, it's clear that the only reasonable inference is that the point of impact was not in the intersection, as the plaintiff claimed, but rather well down the street, as Mr. Worker testified."

Finally, the attorneys may argue that the jury should apply the law to the facts in a particular fashion. In our products liability case, one issue is whether the Polecat's fuel tank is an unreasonably dangerous product. "Unreasonably dangerous" is the substantive legal standard. However, that standard is inherently ambiguous, and its very ambiguity gives the jury a good deal of discretion in deciding whether to characterize the fuel tank as the sort of product that should give rise to strict products liability. To persuade the jury that they should do so, the plaintiff's attorney might argue: "Ladies and gentlemen, in a few moments his Honor is going to instruct you on the definition of an unreasonably dangerous product. Unfortunately, that definition is a bit vague. That vagueness is very important, ladies and gentlemen; it really means that you have to set the safety standard for this community. It's up to you to decide whether that sort of fuel tank is acceptable to the citizens of Morena. You've heard the evidence that the design of that tank greatly increased the likelihood of an explosion and fire. You listened to the testimony that for a few dollars more per car, the defendant could have easily changed that design and dramatically decreased the chances that this tragedy would have ever occurred. It's up to you, ladies and gentlemen, to tell auto manufacturers like this defendant that you consider this type of fuel tank unreasonably dangerous and that we don't want cars with such unsafe fuel tanks on the streets and highways of Morena."

Although the law permits the attorneys to argue inferences and conclusions during summation, the inferences must be conclusions from the evidence formally introduced at the trial. The American Bar Association's Model Rules of Professional Conduct (1999 edition), Rule 3.4(e), specifically states that a lawyer shall not:

> (e) in trial, allude to any matter that the lawyer does not reasonably believe is relevant or that will not be supported by admissible evidence, assert personal knowledge of facts in issue except when testifying as a witness, or state a personal opinion as to the justness of a cause, the credibility of a witness, the culpability of a civil litigant or the guilt or innocence of an accused; . . . .

12. THE JUDGE'S INSTRUCTIONS OR CHARGE TO THE JURY

In some jurisdictions, the attorneys argue after the judge gives the jurors their final instructions, but the prevailing practice is that the judge instructs after the closing arguments. In the final jury charge, the judge explains the substantive law, describes any pertinent evidentiary rules, and mentions the voting procedures the jury must use.

The evidentiary instructions are of most immediate concern to us. The final charge can include six different types of evidentiary instructions.

Admissibility instructions. In most cases, the judge decides whether an individual item of evidence is admissible, and the jurors' only task is to decide how much weight to ascribe to the item. However, in a few cases, the jurors must decide the admissibility of evidence. For instance, in some jurisdictions, the jurors must decide the admissibility of dying declarations and confessions challenged on voluntariness grounds. The judge initially instructs the jury on the test to be used to determine the admissibility of the evidence. The judge adds that the jurors may consider the evidence during their deliberations only if they decide that the evidence is admissible; if they decide that the evidence is inadmissible, they must disregard it and give it no weight during their deliberations.

Corroboration instructions. In some civil law countries on the Continent, there are special corroboration requirements. For example, to make out a submissible case, the proponent may have to present the testimony of two eyewitnesses or the testimony of one eyewitness and documentary corroboration. Corroboration requirements are rare in common law countries such as the United States. In the United States, the admissible testimony of one witness to a fact is usually sufficient evidence to support a jury finding that the fact exists.

However, even in the United States, an attorney occasionally encounters special corroboration requirements. As a case in point, a handful of jurisdictions require the corroboration of the testimony of an infant complainant in child sex abuse prosecutions. Other states require corroboration for an accomplice's testimony. Since an accomplice may be prosecuted and has an incentive to curry the prosecution's favor, the courts are wary of the testimony of accomplices called by the prosecution. In these jurisdictions, the final jury charge instructs the jury that they cannot convict the defendant on the accomplice's testimony standing alone. Rather, before returning a guilty verdict, the jurors must be satisfied that there is other credible evidence that "tends to connect the defendant with the commission of the offense." To an extent, a corroboration instruction formally limits the jurors' discretion in evaluating the weight of an accomplice's testimony.

Cautionary instructions. This sort of instruction directs the jury to be wary in evaluating the weight of particular testimony. For example, many jurisdictions use a cautionary instruction about the testimony of accomplices who appear as prosecution witnesses. As previously stated, the accomplice frequently has an interest in currying favor with the prosecution. For that reason, the judge instructs the jury to be skeptical in evaluating the accomplice's testimony. Other jurisdictions employ cautionary instructions for eyewitness testimony, and inform the jury that in stressful situations even a purported eyewitness can make a mistaken identification. Both *United States v. Telfaire*, 469 F.2d 552 (D.C. Cir. 1972), and *People v. Guzman*, 47 Cal. App. 3d 380, 121 Cal. Rptr. 69 (1975), set out model cautionary instructions for eyewitness testimony. Still other jurisdictions have developed a cautionary instruction about testimony by drug addicts. *United States v. Ochoa–Sanchez*, 676 F.2d 1283, 1289 (9th Cir. 1982).

In most cases, the need for a cautionary instruction is premised on the type of witness who is the source of the testimony: an accomplice, an eyewitness, or a drug addict. However, in some cases, the need arises because of weaknesses in the inferences underlying the theory of logical relevance for the testimony.

For example, in *Miller v. United States*, 320 F.2d 767 (D.C. Cir. 1963) (Bazelon, J.), a D.C. bus passenger, Watson, discovered that his wallet was missing. As a result of conversations with fellow passengers, he got off the bus and went into an alley where he saw four or five men, including Miller, looking through his wallet. Watson yelled, "Hey, that's my wallet. Give it back to me," and chased Miller, who ran away still holding the wallet. The chase lasted a number of blocks. Suddenly Miller stopped and came back towards Watson. Watson asked Miller for his wallet and Miller replied, "here, man, take this dollar and my ring and I will go back and get your wallet." Watson took the dollar and about that time a police officer appeared and took Miller into custody. During the ensuing excitement an unknown citizen returned Watson's wallet to him. Watson testified he did not see anyone take his wallet or see anyone throw it away.

Miller was convicted of robbery. There was no direct evidence; no one saw Miller pick Watson's pocket (if his pocket was indeed picked); no one identified him as being on or near the bus at the time of the alleged offense; and no one identified him as one of the persons who got off the bus and was "running down Fifth Avenue." The government's case rested heavily on the inference of guilt it claimed arose from Miller's flight. On appeal, Miller successfully argued that the jury should have been given a cautionary instruction to the effect that flight does not necessarily imply guilty knowledge:

> When evidence of flight has been introduced into a case, in my opinion the trial court should, if requested, explain to the jury, in appropriate language, that flight does not necessarily reflect feelings of guilt, and that feelings of guilt, which are present in many innocent people, do not necessarily reflect actual guilt. This explanation may help the jury to understand and follow the instruction which should then be given, that they are not to presume guilt from flight; that they may, but need not, consider flight as one circumstance tending to show feelings of guilt; and that they may, but need not, consider feelings of guilt as evidence tending to show actual guilt.

The appellate court identified the two factual assumptions that underlie the claimed relationship between flight and guilt: (1) that one who flees shortly after a criminal act is committed or when he is accused of committing it does so because he feels some guilt concerning that act; and (2) that one who feels some guilt concerning an act has committed that act.

The court noted that the first assumption—that one who flees shortly after a criminal act is committed or when he is accused of committing it does so because he feels some guilt concerning that act—has been criticized on the ground that common experience does not support it. It cited several 19th century cases that depreciated the evidentiary value of flight, including *Hickory v. United States*, 160 U.S. 408 (1896) and *Alberty v. United States*, 162 U.S. 499, 511 (1896), where the Court reversed convictions because the jury was wrongly instructed on flight. It noted that:

> it is not universally true that a man who is conscious that he has done wrong, "will pursue a certain course not in harmony with the conduct of a man who is conscious of having done an act which is innocent, right and proper;" since it is a matter of common knowledge that men who are entirely innocent do sometimes fly from the scene of a crime through fear of being apprehended as the guilty parties, or from an unwillingness to appear as witnesses. Nor is it true as an accepted axiom of criminal law that "the wicked flee when no man pursueth, but the righteous are as bold as a lion." Innocent men sometimes hesitate to confront a jury—not necessarily because they fear that the jury will not protect them, but because they do not wish their names to appear in connection with criminal acts, are humiliated at being obliged to incur the popular odium of an arrest and trial, or because

they do not wish to be put to the annoyance or expense of defending themselves.

The court went on to attack the second assumption, quoting none other than Sigmund Freud:

> You may be led astray . . . by a neurotic who reacts as though he were guilty even though he is innocent—because a lurking sense of guilt already in him assimilates the accusation made against him on this particular occasion. You must not regard this possibility as an idle one; you have only to think of the nursery, where you can often observe it. It sometimes happens that a child who has been accused of a misdeed denied the accusation, but at the same time weeps like a sinner who has been caught. You might think that the child lies, even while it asserts its innocence; but this need not be so. The child is really not guilty of the specific misdeed of which he is being accused, but he is guilty of a similar misdemeanor of which you know nothing and of which you do not accuse him. He therefore quite truly denies his guilt in the one case, but in doing so betrays his sense of guilt with regard to the other. The adult neurotic behaves in this and in many other ways just as the child does. People of this kind are often to be met, and it is indeed a question whether your technique will succeed in distinguishing such self–accused persons from those who are really guilty. [*]

Limiting instructions. If an item of evidence is admissible for one purpose but inadmissible for another, that item is not necessarily damned to exclusion. Federal Evidence Rule 105 codifies the common law rule:

> When evidence which is admissible as to one party or for one purpose but not admissible as to another party or for another purpose is admitted, the court, upon request, shall restrict the evidence to its proper scope and instruct the jury accordingly.

For instance, assume that in the *Devitt* case, the trial judge admitted proof of the defendant's prior convictions solely to impeach the defendant. The judge might give the jury this limiting instruction: "Ladies and gentlemen, during this trial you heard evidence that the defendant has a previous conviction in state court. You are not to consider that as evidence that the defendant is a bad man, and for that reason probably committed the assault he is charged with. You may consider that evidence for only one purpose, namely, determining his credibility. You may consider the fact of the conviction in deciding

---

[*] Freud, *Psychoanalysis and the Ascertaining of Truth in Courts of Law* (1906), in COLLECTED PAPERS (1959), Vol. 2, p. 13. Freud subsequently observed that a "sense of guilt" may derive from "criminal intentions" rather than from an actual past misdeed, and in so–called "normal" as well as neurotic individuals. *See, e.g., Freud, Criminality From a Sense of Guilt* (1915), in COLLECTED PAPERS (1959), Vol. 4, p. 342; Freud, *The Ego and the Id* (1923), in COMPLETE PSYCHOLOGICAL WORKS (1961), Vol. XIX, p. 48 ff.

Freud was, of course, not the first to notice this phenomenon. *See, e.g.,* DOSTOEVSKI, BROTHERS KARAMAZOV (Mod. Lib. 1950) 757–70, wherein the author describes how Ivan—the brother who had desired the death of the father but had not perpetrated the act—manifests all the traditional symptoms of guilt described by Wigmore, whereas the actual murderer reacts in a cool dispassionate way, consistent—according to Wigmore—with innocence.

whether the defendant is an honest, trustworthy person and worthy of belief." As in this illustration, a limiting instruction specifies for the jury the permissible and impermissible uses of the item of evidence.

Curative instructions. A curative instruction directs the jurors to disregard something they have already heard. For example, assume that a police officer is testifying in the *Devitt* case and unexpectedly blurts out the fact that the defendant has been arrested on twelve prior occasions. The evidence of the arrest is inadmissible, but the jury has already heard the testimony. To cure the error, the trial judge would instruct the jury: "Now, ladies and gentlemen, you just heard Officer Monroe refer to some previous arrests of the defendant. I instruct you to disregard that statement. You should not consider that statement at all in your deliberations on the defendant's guilt or innocence. You must strike that statement from your minds." A curative instruction will sometimes prove ineffective. If the statement is highly prejudicial and the judge realistically concludes that the jury will be unable to disregard the statement, he will grant a mistrial.

Sufficiency instructions. Like the judge, the jurors evaluate the sufficiency of the evidence. However, while the judge passes only on the legal sufficiency of the evidence, the jurors determine its factual sufficiency. For example, they decide whether to believe particular witnesses and ultimately whether a fact existed or an event occurred. To guide the jurors' decision, the judge instructs them on the ultimate burden of proof on the facts. Just as the judge decides whether the party has sustained the initial burden of going forward, the jurors decide whether the party has satisfied the ultimate burden of proof. The judge's instruction deals with the allocation and the measure of the burden.

In allocating the burden, the judge tells the jurors which party has the burden of proof on particular issues in the case. If the jurors cannot decide whether a fact exists, the burdened party must lose. In the *Hill* case, the trial judge would undoubtedly assign the plaintiff the burden on the question of whether Worker was driving negligently. Similarly, in the *Devitt* prosecution, the government will have the burden of establishing that there was an assault.

In addition to allocating the burden, the judge must inform the jury of the measure of the burden. On the negligence issue in *Hill,* the plaintiff's burden will probably be a preponderance of the evidence. The evidence must make it more probable than not that Worker drove carelessly. However, Count Five of the *Hill* complaint alleges misrepresentation. If the count alleged knowing misrepresentation—fraud, many jurisdictions would require the plaintiff to establish the fraud by a higher standard, namely, clear and convincing evidence. Finally, in *Devitt,* the prosecution must prove its case by the familiar standard of beyond a reasonable doubt.

In some jurisdictions, the judge is not limited to instructions on the law governing the allocation and measure of the burden; the judge may also comment on the sufficiency of particular items of evidence to satisfy the burden. In doing so, the judge must make it clear to the jurors that his or her comments do not bind them. In other jurisdictions, the judge may sum up the relevant evidence but may not expressly comment on its sufficiency.

In still other states, the judge may neither sum up nor comment; the judge may only instruct on the pertinent law.

NOTES

1. To what extent are jurors capable of carrying out the above types of instructions? Which of the six types places the greatest strain on the jurors' capacity? At one time, the courts routinely assumed that the jury was capable of following a limiting or curative instruction. However, the early empirical research of the Chicago Jury Project resulted in a more realistic assessment of the jury's capabilities. H. KALVEN & H. ZEISEL, THE AMERICAN JURY (1966). The Supreme Court itself has indicated that there are limits to its belief in the jury's capacity. *See Bruton v. United States*, 391 U.S. 123, 129 (1968) ("The naive assumption that prejudicial effects can be overcome by instructions to the jury . . . all practicing lawyers know to be unmitigated fiction").

Several empirical studies raise substantial doubts about the jury's ability to follow curative instructions. The most recent American Bar Foundation study calls that ability into question. Marcotte, *"The Jury Will Disregard . . .,"* 73 A.B.A. J. 34 (Nov. 1, 1987); Allen, *When Jurors Are Ordered to Ignore Testimony, They Ignore the Order*, WALL ST. J., Jan. 25, 1988, Sec. 2, p. 33. In a similar study, psychologist John Carroll of M.I.T. discovered that curative instructions sometimes "make matters worse. [T]he jurors tend to think,'The evidence must be even more important if they have to tell me to ignore it.' " Cope, *Can Jurors Ignore Inadmissible Evidence*, 24 TRIAL, Sept. 1988, at 80, 81.

2. To what extent will jurors be unwilling to perform these mental gymnastics? Consider, in particular, admissibility instructions on confessions and curative instructions to disregard. Can you conceive of situations in which a juror would understand such an instruction but nevertheless be inclined to disregard it? Why would a juror do so?

3. To what extent are these attacks on evidentiary instructions in reality attacks on the jury system? To be sure, the opponents of the jury system have advanced other arguments for eliminating the jury. For example, in an age of crowded court calendars, one appealing argument is that bench trials will expedite trials; by eliminating the jury, we also obviate the necessity for such time–consuming procedures as jury selection and instructions. However, doubts about the effectiveness of evidentiary instructions serve as another potent argument for the abolition of the jury, at least in civil cases. We said at the beginning of this chapter that the student cannot understand evidence law until he or she understands the procedural framework in which evidence law operates. The student must also understand that so profound a change in that framework as the abolition of the jury would undoubtedly have a dramatic impact on the complexion of American evidence law. In Britain, the radical simplification of the hearsay doctrine has coincided with the virtual abolition of the jury. If we were to curtail the use of the jury in the United States, that step might pave the way for a dramatic relaxation of evidentiary standards. Thus, the ongoing empirical research into the jurors' capability may determine not only the survival of the jury as an institution but also the future evolution of American evidentiary doctrine.

Chapter 4

THE EXAMINATION OF A WITNESS

Read Federal Rules of Evidence 106, 611, 614 and 615.

A. THE ORDER OF THE EXAMINATION OF A WITNESS

1. SEQUESTRATION OR EXCLUSION OF WITNESSES

When a judge "sequesters" a prospective witness, the judge orders that witness excluded from the courtroom. The judge may sequester witnesses before the trial begins. In some jurisdictions, judges automatically sequester most witnesses; in others, judges must do so on the motion of either party; and in still others, judges have discretion whether or not to sequester. The governing Federal Rule of Evidence is Rule 615:

> Federal Rule of Evidence 615. Exclusion of Witnesses. At the request of a party the court shall order witnesses excluded so that they cannot hear the testimony of other witnesses, and it may make the order of its own motion. This rule does not authorize exclusion of (1) a party who is a natural person, or (2) an officer or employee of a party which is not a natural person designated as its representative by its attorney, or (3) a person whose presence is shown by a party to be essential to the presentation of the party's case.

The judge may simply order the prospective witnesses from the courtroom or place the witnesses in the custody of an officer of the court. *Archer v. State*, 703 S.W.2d 664 (Tex. Crim. 1986). In addition to sequestering the witness, the judge customarily places the witness "under the rule," by ordering the witness not to discuss his or her testimony with other witnesses in the case. As the court remarked in *United States v. Sepulveda*, 15 F.3d 1161, 1176 (1st Cir. 1993), "such non–discussion orders are generally thought to be a standard concomitant of basic sequestration fare . . . ."

If a prospective witness violates a sequestration order, in some jurisdictions the judge may penalize the violation by ruling the person incompetent as a witness. However, even in those jurisdictions, the prospective witness' disqualification is not automatic. *Holder v. United States*, 150 U.S. 91 (1893); *United States v. English*, 92 F.3d 909, 913 (9th Cir. 1996). Automatic disqualification would be too Draconian a sanction. *United States v. Warren*, 578 F.2d 1058 (5th Cir. 1978). The judge has the discretion to decide whether disqualification is the most appropriate sanction. In exercising that discretion, the judge considers such factors as whether the witness' violation was inadvertent (*Barnard v. Henderson*, 514 F.2d 744 (5th Cir. 1975)) or willful (*United States v. English*, *supra*), whether the party or counsel cooperated and colluded in the violation (*United States v. Gibson*, 675 F.2d 825 (6th Cir. 1982); *Miller v. Universal City Studios, Inc.*, 460 F. Supp. 984 (S.D. Fla. 1978), *rev'd on other grounds*, 650 F.2d 1365, and how important the prospective witness' testimony is. *Barnard v. Henderson, supra*. Even if the judge decides against disqualifying the prospective witness, he or she can take some remedial action. For example, in the final charge to the jury, he or she may comment on the witness' violation of the sequestration order and give the jury a cautionary instruction about that witness' testimony. *United States v. Eastwood*, 489 F.2d 818 (5th Cir. 1973). The judge also has the options of mistrying the case, and holding the witness in contempt. *United States v. Miller*, 499 F.2d 736 (10th Cir. 1974).

NOTES AND PROBLEMS

1. What purpose is served by sequestering a prospective witness? How does sequestration contribute to the reliability of the witness' testimony at trial? What risks exist if the judge permits a witness to remain in the courtroom while other witnesses testify? First assume bad faith on the part of the witnesses. Then assume good faith.

2. The cases which first announced that the judge may disqualify a witness for violation of a sequestration order antedate the adoption of the Federal Rules of Evidence. By disqualifying the person, the judge in effect renders the person incompetent as a witness. Are those cases still good law after the adoption of Federal Rule of Evidence 601? Rule 615 does not expressly authorize disqualifying prospective witnesses who violate sequestration orders. However, if the judge disqualifies a prospective witness to enforce Rule 615, is it arguable that the disqualification is "provided [for] in these rules"?

3. Problem 4–1. In the *Devitt* case, at the very beginning of the trial Devitt is disruptive and boisterous. The judge warns Devitt once, but within a few minutes Devitt interrupts again. The prosecutor requests that the trial judge sequester Devitt. What result under Federal Rule 615(1)? Also consider *Illinois v. Allen*, 397 U.S. 337, 343 (1970).

4. Problem 4–2. To assist her during the trial, the prosecutor wants the detective in charge of the investigation at the counsel table. Under Rule 615, could the judge exempt the detective from the sequestration order? For that matter, does the prosecutor have an absolute right to have the detective exempted from the order? Is this problem governed by Rule 615(3) or Rule 615(2)?

5. Problem 4–3. In our torts case, the defense intends to present the testimony of an accident reconstruction expert. During the defense case–in–chief, the defense contemplates asking the expert a hypothetical question based on the testimony about the damage to the vehicles, the location of the debris, and other physical facts. Should the accident reconstruction expert be exempted from any sequestration order under Rule 615? Suppose alternatively that the plaintiff will also present an accident reconstruction expert's testimony. Now the defense wants its expert present in the courtroom to help the defense attorney follow and understand the plaintiff's expert testimony. Does the defense have a right to an "elbow expert"? *See People v. Valdez*, 177 Cal. App. 3d 680, 687–88, 223 Cal. Rptr. 149, 152–54 (1986). Does it suffice to show that the witness in question is critical to the proponent's case? *Opus 3 Ltd. v. Heritage Park, Inc.*, 91 F.3d 625, 629 n. 2 (4th Cir. 1996).

2. DIRECT, CROSS, REDIRECT, AND RECROSS EXAMINATIONS

When the attorney wants to present a prospective witness' testimony, the attorney calls that person as the next witness. In our adversary system, the attorneys representing the opposing parties dominate the questioning of the witnesses. S. LANDSMAN, READINGS ON ADVERSARIAL JUSTICE: THE AMERICAN APPROACH TO ADJUDICATION 3–4 (1988). A court official such as the reporter or bailiff then administers the oath to the witness or, if the witness has conscientious scruples against an oath, permits the witness to affirm under penalty of perjury. The witness takes the stand, and the questioning attorneys progress through the direct, cross, redirect, and recross stages of examination, which the California Evidence Code describes in this fashion:

§ 772. Phases of examination.

(a) The examination of a witness shall proceed in the following phases: direct examination, cross–examination, redirect examination, and recross–examination, and continuing thereafter by redirect and recross–examination.

(b) Unless for good cause the court otherwise directs, each phase of the examination of a witness must be concluded before the succeeding phase begins.

(c) Subject to subdivision (d), a party may, in the discretion of the court, interrupt his cross–examination, redirect examination, or recross–examination of a witness, in order to examine the witness upon a matter not within the scope of a previous examination of the witness.

(d) If the witness is the defendant in a criminal action, the witness may not, without his consent, be examined under direct examination by another party.

§ 760. Direct examination.

"Direct examination" is the first examination of a witness upon a matter that is not within the scope of a previous examination of the witness.

§ 761. Cross–examination.

"Cross–examination" is the examination of a witness by a party other than the direct examiner upon a matter that is within the scope of the direct examination of the witness.

§ 762. Redirect examination.

"Redirect examination" is an examination of a witness by the direct examiner subsequent to the cross–examination of the witness.

§ 763. Recross–examination.

"Recross–examination" is an examination of a witness by a cross–examiner subsequent to a redirect examination of the witness.

NOTES

1. Note the language of § 760. Is the statutory definition formal or functional? Under that definition, when would a technical cross–examination become direct examination? As we shall see later in this chapter, when that occurs, the form rules for direct examination apply to the technical cross–examination.

2. Both § 762 and § 763 use the article "an" rather than "the," as in § 760 and § 761. Why? May the judge permit the proponent of the witness to question the witness after a recross? If so, what is the title of that stage of examination? Or assume that the judge allows the opponent to question the witness after the proponent's third crack at the witness. What would that examination be termed?

3. QUESTIONS BY THE TRIAL JUDGE

Not only is the trial judge permitted to call witnesses on his or her own motion, the judge can also question witnesses called by the parties.

> Federal Rule of Evidence 614. Calling and Interrogation of Witnesses by Court.
>
> (b) *Interrogation by court.* The court may interrogate witnesses, whether called by itself or by a party.
>
> (c) *Objections.* Objections to the calling of witnesses by the court or to inter-rogation by it may be made at the time or at the next available opportunity when the jury is not present.

Even in an adversary system, the trial judge is not required to be a mere umpire or passive moderator at the trial. *United States v. Montas*, 41 F.3d 775 (1st Cir. 1994), *cert. denied sub nom. Felix–Montas v. United States*, 115 S. Ct. 1986, 131 L. Ed. 2d 873 (1995). The judge may certainly question actively to clarify the testimony elicited by the attorneys. *Dixon v. Maritime Overseas Corp.*, 490 F. Supp. 1191 (S.D.N.Y. 1980). Nonetheless, the philoso-phy underlying our adversary litigation system places some restrictions on the judge's right to call and question witnesses. Ordinarily, there must be an extremely high level of interference by the judge before judicial intervention crosses the line. *Ralph v. Nagy*, 950 F.2d 326 (6th Cir. 1991). The following case is illustrative.

UNITED STATES v. HICKMAN

592 F.2d 931 (6th Cir. 1979)

Keith, Circuit Judge.

Appellants Hickman and Head were jointly tried in the United States District Court for the Western District of Kentucky. Both defendants were found guilty of being convicted felons in possession of a sawed–off 12 gauge shotgun and of a 32 caliber revolver, in violation of 18 U.S.C. App., § 1202(a)(1). In addition, appellant Head was found guilty of possession of marijuana for one's own use in violation of 21 U.S.C. § 844(a). The jury was unable to agree on charges against both men on possession of marijuana with intent to distribute. We are sufficiently troubled by the conduct of the district judge to reverse and remand for a new trial.

The facts are relatively straightforward. Acting pursuant to a search warrant, Louisville, Kentucky Police searched defendants' apartment and found *inter alia,* a shotgun, a pistol and approximately four pounds of marijuana. Shortly thereafter, the two men were arrested as they were returning to the apartment. Appellant Head's conviction of possession of marijuana stemmed from the discovery of a small amount of the drug which he allegedly dropped on the ground just before being arrested. This was a one day trial which presented the principal question of whether the two men were guilty of constructive possession of the weapons and drugs found in the apartment. Simply stated, this was a non–complex, routine case.

Although this case is routine, the conduct of the trial judge was not. Appellants charge that the district court's conduct of the trial rendered a fair verdict impossible. Appellant Head, in his brief, asserts that the district court voluntarily interjected itself in the proceedings over 250 times. Our examination of the entire record of the case bears out the truth of this allegation. Although this bare figure, by itself, is not dispositive, it serves to emphasize the serious problems we have concerning the way this trial was handled.

The law in this area is as easy to state as it is difficult to apply. The proper role of a federal trial judge was best summarized by the Supreme Court in the following oft–quoted words:

> In a trial by jury in a federal court, the judge is not a mere moderator, but is the governor of the trial for the purpose of assuring its proper conduct and of determining questions of law.

Quercia v. United States, 289 U.S. 466, 469 (1933). Thus, the mere asking of questions is not at all improper:

> The trial judge in the federal court is more than a mere arbitrator to rule upon objections and to instruct the jury. It is his function to conduct the trial in an orderly way with a view to eliciting the truth and to attaining justice between the parties. It is his duty to see that the issues are not obscured and that the testimony is not misunderstood. He has the right to interrogate witnesses for this purpose.

United States v. Carabbia, 381 F.2d 133, 139 (6th Cir. 1967).

However, great care must be taken by a judge to "always be calmly judicial, dispassionate and impartial. He should sedulously avoid all appearances of advocacy as to those questions which are ultimately to be submitted to the jury." *Frantz v. United States*, 62 F.2d 737, 739 (6th Cir. 1933). As good a summary as any of the applicable law was recently stated by Judge Pierce Lively in *United States v. Frazier*, 584 F.2d 790, 794 (6th Cir. 1978): "The basic requirement is one of impartiality in demeanor as well as in actions."

The problem is that potential prejudice lurks behind every intrusion into a trial made by a presiding judge. The reason for this is that a trial judge's position before a jury is "overpowering." *United States v. Hoker*, 483 F.2d 359, 368 (5th Cir. 1973). His position makes "his slightest action of great weight with the jury." *United States v. Lanham*, 416 F.2d 1140, 1144 (5th Cir. 1969). For this reason, this Circuit has disapproved of extensive questioning of witnesses by a trial judge. *United States v. Ball*, 428 F.2d 26, 30 (6th Cir. 1970)

("It is not 'desirable practice' for him to interrupt the proceedings by questioning the witnesses.")

As is apparent, determining when a trial judge oversteps is difficult. Numerous factors need be considered. First, the nature of the issues at trial. In a lengthy, complex trial, intervention by the judge is often needed to clarify what is going on. *See United States v. Smith*, 561 F.2d 8, 13–14 (6th Cir.), *cert. denied*, 434 U.S. 958 (1977).

Second, the conduct of counsel. If the attorneys in a case are unprepared or obstreperous, judicial intervention is often called for. If the facts are becoming muddled and neither side is succeeding at attempts to clear them up, the judge performs an important duty by interposing clarificatory comments or questions. *See United States v. Frazier, supra* at 793.

Third, the conduct of witnesses. It is often impossible for counsel to deal with a difficult witness without judicial intervention. *See United States v. Burch, supra*. Similarly, a witness' testimony may be unbelievable and counsel may fail to adequately probe. *See United States v. Liddy*, 509 F.2d 428, 437–42 (1974), *cert. denied*, 420 U.S. 911 (1975). More commonly, judicial intervention will operate to clear up inadvertent witness confusion. *See United States v. McColgin*, 535 F.2d 471, 474–75 (8th Cir. 1976), *cert. denied*, 429 U.S. 853 (1976).

Assuming that a trial judge has good reason to interject himself into the trial, the manner in which he does so is crucial. Thus, an objective demeanor is important. Outright bias or belittling of counsel is ordinarily reversible error. *See United States v. Dellinger*, 472 F.2d 340, 385–91 (7th Cir. 1972), *cert. denied*, 410 U.S. 970 (1973).

More common is the appearance of partiality which can easily arise if the judge intervenes continually on the side of one of the parties. Our system of criminal jurisprudence hinges upon the advocacy role played by opposing counsel. Although a trial is a quest for the truth, and a federal trial judge is more than a neutral arbiter, interference with the presentations of counsel has the potential of making a mockery of a defendant's right to a fair trial, even in the absence of open hostility. *See United States v. Sheldon*, 544 F.2d 213, 216–19 (5th Cir. 1976); present is the danger that undue interference with cross–examination rights will result if a judge takes over examination by counsel. *Bursten v. United States*, 395 F.2d 976, 983 (5th Cir. 1968).

The presence of the presiding judge permeates this trial. Our examination of the entire record of this case leads us to conclude that this judge was not impartial and that these convictions cannot stand.

The nature and scope of the district judge's questions present problems. The destructive effects of the judge's intrusions are apparent from his handling of the defense's cross–examination of expert witness Stokes, the government chemist. The chemist testified that he performed three different tests for marijuana upon the substance that he was given to analyze. After defense counsel elicited the admission that the first test, the microscopic test, was not conclusive for marijuana, the judge interrupted and stated "He says it's not conclusive. That's why he made three tests." After defense counsel continued cross–examination as to the reliability of the second test performed by the chemist, the court interrupted once again:

By the Court: Well, I'll save time. Have you got any chemist that's going to show that this is not marijuana?

Mr. Kagin: No.

By the Court: You're just relying on your ability to satisfy the jury that this man doesn't know what he's talking about?

Mr. Kagin: That's right.

By the Court: Proceed. You haven't tested it?

Mr. Kagin: No, your Honor.

By the Court: You haven't tested.

Mr. Kagin: I want to see if he has—

By the Court: (Interrupting) Well, he says he has and there's no evidence to the contrary.

Counsel was then permitted to continue and amply cross–examine the witness further. Unfortunately, immediately after counsel had finished, the district judge stepped in at once and rehabilitated the witness' testimony. The entire sequence deserves reproduction:

Q: Is the thin layer chromatography test in and of itself conclusive for the presence of marijuana?

A: No, sir. It could have been hashish, it could have been Cannabin [sic], which is an active ingredient of marijuana.

Q: And it could have been something else that you've gotten here that's totally unrelated to marijuana and something that's not under control?

A: Well, if I hadn't done the microscopic test—

Q: (Interrupting) All right. Let's take that and say if you hadn't.

A: All right.

By the Court: Well, now, you're arguing with the gentleman. You remember he's the one that made the tests. You're not going to testify yourself. I'm not going to let you.

Q: Are you telling me that this test is not of itself conclusive, is that correct?

A: That is correct.

Q: So we have Test No. 1 that is not conclusive, Test No. 2 that is not conclusive, and Test No. 3 that's not conclusive. And from that you conclude it's marijuana, is that correct, sir?

A: That's correct.

Q: No further questions.

By the Court: Well, let's get this finished, and you can step down. Did you use the standard testing procedure that all United States chemists use in testing a substance to determine whether it is marijuana?

The Witness: I used three, the three.

By the Court: The standard ones that they use?

The Witness: Well, some people use two of them, but I used these three.

By the Court: I understand you used all three of them.

The Witness: That's correct.

By the Court: And in your professional opinion, the substance in each of the three samples is marijuana?

A. That's correct.

By the Court: Step down.

The district judge's brilliant redirect examination would have been entirely proper had it been done by the prosecutor. It was improper for the judge to have assumed the prosecutor's role under the circumstances.

The trial judge's attitude toward the testimony of defense witnesses was best summed up by a remark made by the Court just before the swearing in of the final defense witness, Beeler. The trial judge stated: "Is this witness in the same category?" The clear import of this statement was one of contemptuous disbelief. The trial judge was clearly telling the jury, albeit indirectly, that he did not believe the defense story.

On balance, this record fairly reveals constant interruptions which frustrated the defense at every turn and infringed upon defendants' rights of cross–examination. The only impression which could have been left in the mind of the jury was that the trial judge was a surrogate prosecutor.

When one combines the limitation on cross–examination, the anti–defendant tone of the trial judge's interruptions, the wholesale taking over of cross–examination of defense witnesses by the trial judge, one is left with the strong impression that these two defendants did not receive the fair and impartial trial which the Sixth Amendment to the Constitution guarantees them. We are convinced that judged as a whole, the conduct of the trial judge must have left the jury with a strong impression of the judge's belief of the defendant's probable guilt such that it was unable to freely perform its function of independent fact finder.

Our conclusion is reinforced because the judge's actions were so unnecessary. This was a one–day trial. The principal issue for the jury was whether it would impute possession of the contraband in the apartment to one or another defendant. Counsel for both sides were able, and at all times, conducted themselves properly. The testimony was relatively clear and any difficulties could easily have been handled by counsel had the judge restrained himself. There was no need for judicial intervention to assist the jury by clarifying the facts.

Given what occurred here we are persuaded that the district court's instructions to the jury could not offset the effects of his conduct. Nor do we hold the failure to object against defense counsel. We think that the following statement of the Seventh Circuit in *United States v. Hill*, 332 F.2d 105, 106–07 (7th Cir. 1964) is fully applicable here:

> Counsel for defendant in a criminal case is indeed in a difficult and hazardous predicament in finding it necessary to make frequent objections in the presence of a jury to questions propounded by the trial judge.

[W]e are convinced that the trial court's conduct amounted to plain error.

Reversed and remanded for a new trial.

NOTE

1. The empirical research by Harvard psychologist Robert Rosenthal bears out Judge Keith's observation that the judge's "slightest action" can be "of great weight with the jury." Note, *The Appearance of Justice: Judges' Verbal and Nonverbal Behavior in Criminal Jury Trials*, 38 STAN. L. REV. 89 (1985). The Note describes a research project funded by the National Science Foundation. The researchers attempted to determine: (1) whether a judge's knowledge of the defendant's criminal record affects the judge's attitude toward the defendant during a jury trial, and (2) if so, whether the judge's attitude is communicated nonverbally to the jury and influences the jury verdict. The researchers caution that their study is "preliminary." However, significantly, they found that, to some extent, a judge's belief in the defendant's guilt can be transmitted to the jury "through judges' subtle verbal and nonverbal behaviors," such as the way in which the judge reads the jury instructions. *Id.* at 92. These behaviors "leak" the judge's attitude to the jury and, at least in some cases, influence the jury's verdict. *Id.* at 150–51.

2. For another example of improper judicial intervention, *see Nationwide Mut. Fire Ins. Co. v. Ford Motor Co.* 174 F.3d 801 (6th Cir. 1999), where the same court that decided *Hickman* reversed a judgment because of judicial misconduct. The trial judge repeatedly interrupted plaintiff's opening statement, at one point telling counsel that two witnesses should not be called in his case–in–chief, repeatedly engaged in one–sided questioning of witnesses, and invited and even prompted objections by defense counsel. The court of appeals held that, although the standard of review is abuse of discretion, "the harmless error doctrine is inapplicable in cases where judicial bias and/or hostility is found to have been exhibited at any stage of a judicial proceeding." 174 F.3d at 808. Whether the judge was in fact biased against plaintiff was "irrelevant: His interruptions were so numerous and his questions so one sided, they must inevitably have left the jury with the impression that the judge believed Nationwide's actions were egregious and improper." *Id.*

4. QUESTIONS BY THE PETIT JURORS

Jurors may request that the judge call additional witnesses and also may request that questions be posed to any witness. Some commentators have urged that the jurors be encouraged to ask questions. Comment, *The Questioning of Witnesses by Jurors*, 27 AM. U. L. REV. 127 (1977). However, the commentators' pleas have generally fallen on deaf judicial ears. In most jurisdictions, even if the question is unobjectionable, the judge has discretion whether to put it to the witness. Only Kentucky seems to require that the judge pose the question if it is proper in form and substance. Most trial judges do not even tell the jury that they may suggest questions for the witness, and many appellate courts have made it clear to the trial bench that they do not want the jurors encouraged to ask questions. *E.g., United States v. Bush*, 47 F.3d 511, 515 (2d Cir. 1995). In recent years, some courts have gone to the length of absolutely forbidding questions by jurors. *State v. Zima*, 237 Neb. 952, 468 N.W.2d 377 (1991); *Morrison v. State*, 845 S.W.2d 882 (Tex. Ct. Crim. App. 1992).

NOTES AND PROBLEMS

1. The American Judicature Society and the State Justice Institute are funding research into the question of whether the jurors should take a more active role during the trial. The initial phase of the research was a study of 67 trials in Wisconsin. Maxwell, *Researching Jury Participation: Jurors in New Study Encouraged to Take Notes, Question Witnesses*, 75 A.B.A. J. 36 (Dec. 1989). The next phase will entail a study of 500 trials throughout the United States. The researchers' preliminary findings indicate that when jurors can take an active role, they tend to be more attentive to the trial testimony. Moreover, when jurors are permitted to ask questions which are troubling them, there is less risk that during final deliberation, the jurors will find a gap in the evidence; there is less likelihood that the jurors will base their verdict on sheer speculation about a factual proposition. Heuer & Penrod, *Trial Lawyers in the Box? Jurors Question Witness*, 13 THE DOCKET 4 (Fall 1989).

In 1998, the American Bar Association adopted 24 Civil Trial Practice Standards, developed by its Litigation Section. Among the standards (which include jury note–taking) is Standard 10 which recommends that the judge permit jurors to submit written questions for witnesses. After receiving a question, the judge should disclose it to the attorneys and give them the opportunity to object outside the presence of the jury. A cautionary instruction should explain, among other things, that some queries may be rejected or rewritten.

2. On the other hand, is there a danger that, as the title of the last article suggests, jurors will begin viewing themselves as trial lawyers—and develop biases during the trial? Is a juror likely to attach inordinate weight to an answer to a question which she posed to a witness? Judge Lay has raised these questions and observed that there are "no empirical studies [of] the effect of juror questions on [juror] neutrality . . . ." *United States v. Johnson*, 892 F.2d 707, 713 n.3 (8th Cir. 1989).

3. Problem 4–4. You are sitting as the trial judge in the *Devitt* case. Devitt is testifying. You notice that one of the jurors, Mrs. Lederer, is restive. You interrupt the case and ask, "Mrs. Lederer, is anything wrong?" She responds, "Well, Your Honor, I'd sort of like to ask a question." What do you do now? Should you permit her to state the question orally? What dangers arise if you do? What alternative do you have? *See United States v. Polowichak*, 783 F.2d 410, 413 (4th Cir. 1986).

5. EXCUSING THE WITNESS

When the questioning is completed, the witness is excused. There are two methods of excusing the witness. Typically, the witness is permanently excused. If the witness is permanently excused and an attorney later desires to elicit additional testimony from him, the attorney must seek leave of the court. In some cases, the witness will be excused subject to recall. In that case, the attorney has the right to recall him and elicit additional testimony. The difference between permanent excuse and excuse subject to recall can be critical—as we shall see later.

B. THE SCOPE OF THE EXAMINATION OF A WITNESS

1. DIRECT EXAMINATION

It is frequently said that the scope of direct examination includes any evidence logically relevant to any material fact of consequence in the case. That statement is somewhat imprecise. Stated more accurately, the scope of direct examination depends upon the segment of the case in which the direct examination occurs. For example, the scope of the plaintiff's case–in–chief is broader than the scope of the plaintiff's rebuttal. Hence, the scope of direct examination during the case–in–chief exceeds the scope of direct during rebuttal.

2. CROSS–EXAMINATION

a. The Split of Authority over the Proper Scope of Cross–Examination

It is frequently observed that there is a wide split of authority over the proper scope of cross–examination, and there is an element of truth in that observation. However, to avoid overstatement, we should first specify the points of agreement among the courts. All courts concur that the scope of cross–examination includes the witness' credibility. Consequently, during cross–examination, the questioner may attempt to impeach the witness' credibility. Further, most courts agree that the judge has discretion to broaden or narrow the normal scope of cross–examination on the historical merits of the case. The point of disagreement is the proper norm for cross–examination on the historical merits. There are three views.

Federal Rule 611(b) opts for the majority, restrictive view:

> (b) *Scope of cross–examination.* Cross–examination should be limited to the subject matter of the direct examination and matters affecting the credibility of the witness. The court may, in the exercise of discretion, permit inquiry into additional matters as if on direct examination.

This view is sometimes called the American rule. Under this view, the proper scope of cross is limited to the scope of direct. Thus the direct examiner may preclude the cross–examiner from probing an issue during cross by skirting the issue on direct. This view gives the direct examiner some control over the latitude of cross.

A second, minority view is that the scope of cross–examination should be wide open—the English rule. A number of states, including Tennessee, have adopted this position. *Ray v. Hutchison*, 17 Tenn. App. 477, 68 S.W.2d 948

(1933). The draft version of Rule 611(b) that the Supreme Court first transmitted to Congress incorporated this language:

> (b) A witness may be cross–examined on any matter relevant to any issue in the case, including credibility. In the interests of justice, the judge may limit cross–examination with respect to matters not testified to on direct examination.

Under this view, the direct examination does not limit the cross–examination. Depending on the segment of the case in which the cross–examination occurred, the cross–examiner could question to elicit any evidence logically relevant to any material fact of consequence in the case. Congress was more conservative about this than the Court and opted for the restrictive rule in the final version of Rule 611(b).

A third, distinct minority, compromise view is sometimes styled the Michigan rule. Comment, 36 U. Det. L.J. 162 (1958). This view is also known as the half–open door. Under this view, the cross–examiner may question about any fact on which the opponent has the ultimate burden of proof, but may not question about part of his or her own affirmative case unless the witness mentions that fact on direct.

NOTES AND PROBLEMS

1. Which of the views above is the soundest? Academic commentators in the main support the wide–open view, arguing that it promotes more expeditious examination; judicial economy favors eliciting all the witness' testimony at one time rather than recalling the witness later to give additional testimony. For their part, litigators ordinarily prefer the restrictive view, contending that it makes for a more orderly presentation of testimony to the jury. *See* Carlson, *Cross–Examination of the Accused*, 52 Cornell L.Q. 705, 706–07 (1967). It is also, coincidentally, the view which gives the litigators the greatest control over the content of their cases–in–chief. Which view promotes more accurate testimony? Do the contrasting views reflect different estimates of the jury's capacity to comprehend testimony?

2. Like most formulations of the American view, Rule 611 presents an obvious problem: how to define "the subject matter of the direct examination"? *See* Annot., 45 A.L.R. Fed. 639 (1979). Should we equate "the matters covered on direct examination" with the historical transactions mentioned on direct? Suppose that on direct, Devitt testified only about the circumstances surrounding his arrest ten hours after the alleged assault? Could the prosecutor then cross–examine Devitt about the offense itself? Or should we equate "the matters covered on direct" with the essential elements of the cause of action or crime mentioned on direct? Another possibility is to permit the cross–examiner to ask any questions that tend to rebut either express statements on direct or implications from the express statements made during direct. Which definition is most conducive to an orderly presentation of the evidence to the jury? Which definition would be the most manageable and predictable in application?

3. Problem 4–5. In the *Devitt* case, on direct examination Devitt simply denied hitting Paterson. Could the prosecutor cross–examine Devitt about whether Paterson consented to a fight with Devitt? There are occasional statements to the effect that consent is a defense to a battery charge at least when the battery results only in minor bodily injuries. LaFave & Scott, Criminal Law § 7.15(e), at 744 (3d ed. 2000).

4. Problem 4–6. Suppose that after the alleged battery, Paterson wrote a note to a close personal friend. The note's wording suggests that Paterson consented to a fight with Devitt due to an argument over how much Paterson owed Devitt for installing shelving in the kitchen. At trial, on direct examination he denies consent. On cross–examination, the defense attorney would not only like to question him about the note but also introduce the note into evidence. When the defense attorney attempts to do so, the prosecutor objects, "Beyond the proper scope of cross. The defense can't introduce exhibits during the cross–examination of a prosecution witness." Analyze this problem under Federal Rule 611(b). *Compare* A. Tanford, The Trial Process: Law, Tactics and Ethics 287 (2d ed. 1993) *with* R. Hunter, Federal Trial Handbook § 22.3 (3d ed. 1993).

b. The Consequences of Undue Restriction of the Scope of Cross–Examination

The judge has discretion to limit the extent to which the cross–examiner questions about a topic, even though that topic is within the proper scope. *United States v. Hernandez*, 995 F.2d 307, 312 (1st Cir.), *cert. denied sub nom. Sanchez v. United States*, 510 U.S. 954 (1993). It is a wholly different question if the trial judge completely forecloses cross–examination on such a topic. *United States v. Polk*, 550 F.2d 1265 (10th Cir. 1977). The Sixth Amendment right to confrontation guarantees a criminal defendant an opportunity for adequate cross–examination. *Davis v. Alaska*, 415 U.S. 308 (1974); *Smith v. Illinois*, 390 U.S. 129 (1968). The cross–examination guarantee is a right "of first magnitude," and the appellate court will carefully scrutinize any restriction on its scope.

If the witness testifies on direct examination but the witness or the judge restricts the scope of the cross–examination, the question arises whether all or part of the direct examination should be stricken. In deciding whether to strike, the courts consider two primary factors: the cause of the restriction and the importance of the subject on which cross–examination was foreclosed. The following is the best short treatment of the first factor.

1 C. McCormick, Evidence § 19, at 85–91 (5th ed. 1999)

What are the present consequences of a denial or failure of the right? There are several common situations. First, a party testifying on his own behalf may unjustifiably refuse to answer questions necessary to a complete cross–examination. Here it is generally agreed that the adversary is entitled to have the direct testimony stricken out, a result that seems warranted.

Second, a non–party witness may similarly refuse to be cross–examined, or to answer proper questions of the cross–examiner. Here the case is a little less clear, but the expressions of some judges and writers seem to sanction the same remedy of excluding the direct. This minimizes the temptation for the party to procure the witness' refusal, a collusion which is often hard to prove and protects the right of cross–examination strictly. There is also some authority for the view that the matter should be left to the judge's discretion. Finally, there is support for the notion that if the privilege against self–incrimination is invoked upon cross–examination to questions which go to the credibility of the witness and are otherwise immaterial, the testimony on direct examination should not be stricken, or at the least the judge should have an area of discretion in making his ruling on that matter.

Third, the witness may become, or purport to become, sick or otherwise physically or mentally incapacitated, before cross–examination is begun or completed. Many of such cases arouse suspicion of simulation, particularly when the witness is a party, and consequently the party's direct examination will often be excluded. In the case of the non–party witness, the same result is usually reached, but at least in civil cases, it is arguable that this result should be qualified so that the judge is directed to exclude unless he is clearly convinced that the incapacity is genuine, in which event he should let the direct testimony stand. He should then be authorized to explain to the jury the weakness of such uncross–examined evidence. Temporary incapacity may change this result, as indicated below.

The fourth situation is that of the death of the witness before the cross–examination. Here again it is usually said that the party thus deprived of cross–examination is entitled to have the direct testimony stricken, unless, presumably, the death occurred during a postponement of the cross–examination consented to or procured by him. In case of death there seems no adequate reason for excluding the direct testimony, except that exclusion may well be required if the witness is a state's witness in a criminal case. It has been suggested that exclusion of the direct should be discretionary but no matter how valuable cross–examination may be, common sense tells us that the half–loaf of direct testimony is better than no bread at all. To let the direct testimony stand was the accepted practice in equity. It is submitted that except for the testimony of the state's witnesses in criminal cases, the judge should let the direct testimony stand but should be required on request to instruct the jury in weighing its value to consider the lack of opportunity to cross–examine.

The above results may be modified in certain situations. It has been held that where the incapacity is temporary the cross–examiner may not insist upon immediate exclusion of the direct testimony, but must be content with the offer of a later opportunity to cross–examine even when this makes it necessary for him to submit to a mistrial.

PROBLEM

Problem 4–7. In *Devitt,* the complainant, Mr. Paterson, has just completed his direct examination. On cross–examination, he refuses to answer a question.

- In one variation of this problem, the question he refuses to answer is, "Isn't it true that two years ago you filed a false claim for welfare benefits?"

- In another variation of this problem, the question is, "Isn't it true that a year ago you filed a false assault charge against another man, a Mr. Johnson?"

- In a final variation of this problem, the question he refuses to answer is, "Isn't it true that the day after you reported this so–called battery to the police, you told your daughter that you had freely agreed to fight Mr. Devitt because of an argument over the price of his carpentry work?"

Assume that in all three variations of this problem, the question itself is unobjectionable and proper. In addition to considering the cause of the restriction of the scope of cross, the judge will analyze the importance of the topic on which cross was foreclosed. In which variation of the problem does the defense have the strongest case for striking the direct? In which the weakest case? Why? *See United States v. Cardillo*, 316 F.2d 606, 612–13 (2d Cir. 1963). Note the distinction the court draws between cross–examination that "would [develop] the general unsavory character of the witness" and "untruthfulness with respect to specific events of the crime charged." *Id.* at 613.

c. Expansion of the Scope of Cross–Examination

Suppose that the judge goes to the polar extreme. Rather than unduly restricting the scope of cross, the judge permits the cross–examiner to range beyond the normal scope. Assume that in our torts case, the jurisdiction normally limits cross–examination to the historical events mentioned on direct. As one of her witnesses, Ms. Hill calls her husband, Arthur Hill, who accompanied her to Jefferson Motor Car Co. when she bought the automobile. On direct examination, Arthur testifies only about the oral representations the salesman made to Ms. Hill. On cross–examination, the defense attorney begins questioning Arthur about his observation of the extent of the plaintiff's personal injuries suffered in the accident. The plaintiff objects that the question is beyond the scope of the direct. The judge responds, "You're right, of course. But I think I'll exercise my discretion to allow this line of inquiry." The cross–examiner has thus exceeded the normal scope of cross with the judge's permission. In this situation, the traditional view is that the cross–examiner "adopts" the witness with respect to the matter beyond the scope of the direct.

The question is: what are the procedural consequences of adoption?

NOTES

1. Earlier in this chapter we quoted California Evidence Code § 760. How does the adoption doctrine relate to that statutory definition of direct examination?

2. As we shall see later in this chapter, the courts ordinarily ban leading questions on direct examination. Conversely, leading questions are usually allowable on cross. When the cross–examiner exceeds the normal scope of cross, should she forfeit the right to lead the witness with respect to the new matter?

3. REDIRECT EXAMINATION

The common law rule is that, as of right, the proponent of the witness may conduct redirect about topics the opponent broached for the first time during cross–examination. The California Evidence Code states the rule in a rather cryptic, circuitous fashion:

§ 774. Reexamination.

A witness once examined cannot be reexamined as to the same matter without leave of the court, but he may be reexamined as to any new matter upon which he has been examined by another party to the action. Leave may be granted or withheld in the court's discretion.

The judge has discretion to permit the proponent of the witness to exceed this scope and cover topics that could have been mentioned on direct.

PROBLEM

Problem 4–8. In our torts case, Ms. Hill's husband, Arthur, is on the stand. On direct examination, he testifies only about the signing of the written contract with Jefferson Motor Car Co. On cross–examination, the defense interrogates Arthur about what the salesman said at the time the parties signed the written contract. On redirect, Ms. Hill's attorney would like to elicit Arthur's testimony that Arthur and the plaintiff made it clear to the salesman that they were relying on his judgment in picking out a safe, suitable automobile. Does Ms. Hill have the right to elicit that testimony on redirect? In a broad sense does that testimony relate to a subject the plaintiff broached on direct? But did the testimony really focus on the parties' oral statements until the cross–examination?

4. RECROSS EXAMINATION

The guidelines for recross parallel those for redirect. As of right, the cross–examiner may question about topics mentioned for the first time on redirect. Here too the judge has discretion to broaden the normal scope. As a practical matter, the judge rarely deigns to exercise this discretion to expand the scope of recross. *United States v. Morris*, 485 F.2d 1385 (5th Cir. 1973).

5. THE RULE OF COMPLETENESS

The so–called rule of completeness decrees that if one counsel introduces part of an item of evidence such as a deposition during one stage of a witness' examination, the opponent has the right to introduce other parts relevant to the same subject matter during the next stage of the examination. The rule is a scope doctrine; the doctrine provides that if one party introduces a half–truth during an examination of the witness, the opposing party has the right to show the whole truth during the next examination. Consider two codifications of the rule. First, review the Federal Evidence Rule 106:

When a writing or recorded statement or part thereof is introduced by a party, an adverse party may require the introduction at that time of any other part or any other writing or recorded statement which ought in fairness to be considered contemporaneously with it.

Now consider California Evidence Code § 356. Partial act declaration, writing—Inquiry into whole—Detached act—Necessary additions:

> Where part of an act, declaration, conversation, or writing is given in evidence by one party, the whole on the same subject may be inquired into by an adverse party; when a letter is read, the answer may be given; and when a detached act, declaration, conversation, or writing is given in evidence, any other act, declaration, conversation, or writing which is necessary to make it understood may also be given in evidence.

NOTES AND PROBLEMS

1. How do the two statutes differ? To trigger Rule 106, is it sufficient to show that the other pages of the deposition transcript relate to the same topic? If not, what is the test? Does the California Evidence Code employ the same test?

Under the federal statute, is the second attorney's only right to introduce the pertinent parts of the item of evidence during his or her next examination of the witness? Does the attorney have the same rights under the California statute?

On its face, the federal statute is inapplicable to oral statements. *United States v. Collicott*, 92 F.3d 973, 983 (9th Cir. 1996); *United States v. Castro*, 813 F.2d 571, 576 (2d Cir.) ("in practice verbal precision cannot be expected when the source of evidence as to an utterance is the memory of a witness"), *cert. denied*, 484 U.S. 844 (1987). However, could a federal judge in effect expand the scope of Rule 106 by invoking her authority under Rule 611(a)? *United States v. Alvarado*, 882 F.2d 645, 650 n.5 (2d Cir. 1989), *cert. denied*, 493 U.S. 1071 (1990). On the common law completeness doctrine and Rule 106, *see generally*, Nance, *Verbal Completeness and Exclusionary Rules Under the Federal Rules of Evidence*, 75 TEX. L. REV. 51 (1996).

2. While the California statute basically codifies the common law rule of completeness, Rule 106 deviates from the common law. Does Rule 106 mean that parties to federal trials may not invoke the common law rule? Read Rule 106 in conjunction with Rules 402 and 611(a). The McCormick text asserts that the common law rule of completeness is not abrogated by Federal Rule of Evidence 106. 1 C. MCCORMICK, EVIDENCE § 56, at 249 (J. Strong ed., 5th ed. 1999). The Advisory Committee Note to Rule 106 states that "[t]he rule does not in any way circumscribe the right of the adversary to develop the matter on cross–examination or as part of his own case." Does that statement suffice as support for the assertion in the McCormick text? Absent that statement, would you concur with the assertion? Does Rule 402 sweep away uncodified procedural rules in the same way in which it seems to abolish uncodified substantive evidentiary rules? Less than a handful of provisions in the Federal Rules deal with purely procedural issues. Moreover, the Federal Rules of Civil and Criminal Procedure regulate procedural issues in detail. In *Beech Aircraft Corp. v. Rainey*, 488 U.S. 153 (1988), the Supreme Court asserted that Rule 106 "partially codified" the common law doctrine of completeness—implying that the uncodified aspect of the doctrine is still in effect in federal practice.

3. Problem 4–9. In our torts case, Ms. Hill's husband is unavailable at the time of trial. Rather than calling her husband to the witness stand, Ms. Hill's attorney introduces pages 17–22 of his deposition relating to the signing of the written contract. The defendant would now like to introduce pages 23–30. Those pages also relate to the signing of the contract, but the plaintiff has a sound hearsay objection to the material on page 28. Does the rule of completeness override the hearsay objection? *United States v. Boylan*, 898 F.2d 230, 257 n.16 (1st Cir. 1990).

C.   THE FORM OF THE EXAMINATION OF A WITNESS

1.   IN GENERAL

There are procedural restraints on the form of a witness' examination as well as the examination's sequence and scope. The trial judge has discretionary control over the form of the examination. Although the judge has wide discretion at common law, in some areas the rulings have become so standardized that norms have emerged. Although most of these norms are common sense propositions, it is critical that the trial attorney master them, since most of the objections voiced at trial relate to problems of form rather than the substantive evidentiary doctrines. Consider these notes and problems.

NOTES AND PROBLEMS

1. Federal Rule of Evidence 611(a) gives the trial judge general, discretionary control over the form of questions at trial.

(a) *Control by court.* The court shall exercise reasonable control over the mode and order of interrogating witnesses and presenting evidence so as to (1) make the interrogation and presentation effective for the ascertainment of the truth, (2) avoid needless consumption of time, and (3) protect witnesses from harassment or undue embarrassment.

In the view of some commentators, the common law form rules survived the adoption of the Federal Rules. Langum, *Uncodified Federal Evidence Rules Applicable to Civil Trials*, 19 WILLAMETTE L. REV. 513, 516 (1983). However, other commentators argue that, under statutory provisions such as Rule 611(a), the common law rules are now nonexistent. Graham, *California's "Restatement" of Evidence: Some Reflections on Appellate Repair of the Codification Fiasco*, 4 LOY. L.A. L. REV. 279, 281 (1971). Which view is sounder? If you are inclined toward the latter view, can you distinguish these form rules from the common law completeness rule which allegedly survived the adoption of Federal Rule 106?

2. Problem 4–10. In the *Devitt* case, during his case–in–chief the prosecutor was conducting the direct examination of Mr. Paterson. The prosecutor asks:

Q. When you first spoke with the police, did you say that there had been a battery, and did you then identify the defendant as the attacker?

What objection would you as defense counsel raise? What is the danger of this form of question? As trial judge, would you sustain the objection?

3. Problem 4–11. On redirect of Mr. Paterson, for purposes of emphasis, the prosecutor wants to reask questions he had posed on direct examination. Can you as defense counsel object? What is the relevance of California Evidence Code § 774, *supra*?

4. Problem 4–12. During the defense's case–in–chief, your client, Mr. Devitt, takes the stand. The prosecutor is now conducting cross–examination. Your client has a prior conviction that under the local law the prosecutor may use to impeach your client's credibility. Your client has also been arrested several times, but the arrests themselves are inadmissible for impeachment. On cross, the prosecutor asks:

> Q. What kind of trouble with the law have you had?

Can you object? On what ground? Do you evaluate the question from the witness' perspective or the attorney's perspective? If the judge sustains your objection, what should the prosecutor do? Should the prosecutor completely abandon this line of inquiry?

5. Problem 4–13. During the same cross–examination of your client, the prosecutor asks:

> Q. And isn't it a fact that you were in the victim's apartment that day?

Devitt responds:

> A. Yes, but it wasn't a battery. As I've said all along, we got into an argument over how much I was going to charge him, and he threw the first punch.

What should the prosecutor do at this point? What procedural device should the prosecutor use? If the prosecutor calls the judge's attention to the problem but the judge concludes that the defendant's answer is otherwise admissible, must the trial judge grant the prosecutor the requested relief? Suppose that the defense attorney did not want the defendant to add that statement. Could the defense attorney request the same relief? Is this a standing problem?

2.   LEADING QUESTIONS

The form problems above arise with some frequency during the trial. However, the three most important form problems are leading questions, narrative questions, and argumentative questions.

The definition of a "leading" question. California Evidence Code § 764 sets out one of the simplest—and best—definitions of a "leading" question:

> A "leading question" is a question that suggests to the witness the answer that the examining party desires.

Judges listen carefully to the way in which the attorney's question begins. If the question begins with words such as "who," "what," "which," "when," "where," "how," and "why," the judge usually assumes that the question is nonleading. These are natural interrogatory words, the way a layperson usually begins a question when he or she does not know what answer to expect. In contrast, questions that begin with words such as "is," "are," "were," "do," and "did" tend to be mildly leading. There are two ways of making a question brutally leading. The prosecutor could ask:

> Q. Isn't it a fact (Isn't it true) (Isn't it correct) (Won't you admit) (Won't you concede) that you were in his apartment that day?

Or, shifting to the very end of the question, the prosecutor could ask:

> Q. You were in his apartment that day. Isn't that true (Isn't that a fact) (Isn't that correct) (Won't you admit that) (Won't you concede that)?

The second query includes two sentences. The first sentence is a declarative assertion of a fact. The second sentence is a short question, sometimes referred to as a "tag."

NOTES AND PROBLEMS

1. Under § 764, is a question automatically leading simply because it can be answered categorically, yes or no? If not, phrase a question for the defense counsel to ask Devitt on direct that can be answered categorically but is not leading. Be prepared to explain why the question is not leading.

2. Problem 4–14. During the direct examination of Mr. Paterson, the prosecutor asks:

> Q. At the lineup, did you pick out the man on the extreme right or the defendant who was standing roughly in the middle and wearing a blue jacket and brown slacks?

The question cannot be answered categorically. But is the question leading? If so, why? Can you think of other ways to phrase a noncategorical question to make it leading? These subtly leading questions are the most difficult for the opponent to detect in the heat of battle at trial. The opponent must develop an "ear" for leading questions. A trial attorney has to be a good, intense listener.

Leading questions on direct examination. The psychological studies tend to show that testimony elicited by specific, leading questions is more complete—but less accurate—than testimony elicited by questions calling for narrative responses. Gardner, *The Perception and Memory of Witnesses*, 18 Cornell L.Q. 391, 404 (1933), citing Marston, *Studies in Testimony*, 15 J. Crim. L. & Criminology 1 (1924). That psychological finding lends support to the rule regarding leading questions on direct in Federal Evidence Rule 611(c):

> (c) *Leading questions.* Leading questions should not be used on the direct examination of a witness except as may be necessary to develop the witness' testimony. Ordinarily leading questions should be permitted on cross–examination. When a party calls a hostile witness, an

adverse party, or a witness identified with an adverse party, interrogation may be by leading questions.

The courts have voiced their fear that through leading questions, the attorney can furnish the witness with "a false memory." *United States v. Johnson*, 495 F.2d 1097, 1101 (5th Cir. 1974). The courts assume that the normal relationship between the direct examiner and witness will be friendly and that a friendly, cooperative witness is likely to respond to a suggestive question by the attorney.

In modern times, the courts and legislatures have relaxed the rigor of the prohibition against leading questions on direct:

> We find no reported case in the last fifty years in which a reversal resulted solely from failure to control leading in the questioning process, and only one in which it was a major factor in the decision to reverse.

Denbeaux & Risinger, *Questioning Questions: Objections to Form in the Interrogation of Witnesses*, 33 Ark. L. Rev. 439, 465 (1979). Moreover, there are numerous more or less settled exceptions to the norm. The following notes illustrate some of the more noteworthy exceptions.

NOTES

1. The direct examiner may use leading questions on "preliminary" matters. For example, when the examiner is questioning the witness about the witness' personal background, leading questions are usually permitted. What is the justification for that exception? How broadly should "preliminary" facts be defined?

2. The direct examiner may use leading questions to interrogate a hostile witness. At common law, the witness became "hostile" only after there was some reflection of hostility on the record such as a refusal to answer or evasion. Contrast the approach of the third sentence of Federal Rule of Evidence 611(c). How does this statute differ from the common law approach? When attorneys call adverse witnesses in jurisdictions with statutes such as Rule 611(c), they often announce, "Your Honor, I now call the defendant's wife as an adverse witness pursuant to Rule 611(c)."

3. The direct examiner may use leading questions to refresh the witness' memory when the witness' memory is "exhausted." How do you show on the record that the witness' memory is "exhausted"? Why does that justify deviating from the norm against leading questions on direct? If the direct examiner invokes this exception to the norm, should the judge require that the examiner first use mildly leading questions before resorting to leading questions of the "Isn't it true . . .?" variety?

4. The direct examiner may use leading questions to interrogate witnesses such as children, retarded persons, and persons who are not fluent in English. What characteristic do all these types of witnesses share? What is the common denominator between this exception and the last exception?

5. It is often said that the direct examiner may use leading questions in interrogating an expert witness. Why? *See Dunn v. Owens–Corning*

Fiberglass, 774 F. Supp. 929, 943 (D.V.I. 1991) ("complicated testimony"), *aff'd in part, vacated in part*, 1 F.3d 1362, 1371 (3d Cir. 1993).

Leading questions on cross–examination. In contrast with the norm for direct examination, the second sentence of Federal Evidence Rule 611(c) assumes that the normal relationship between the witness and the cross–examiner will be hostile. For that reason, the witness is much less likely to docilely follow the lead of a suggestive question. Of course, that danger can arise in the rare case in which the relationship between the witness and the cross–examiner is actually a friendly one. Consider the Advisory Committee's Note to Rule 611(c):

> The rule . . . conforms to tradition in making the use of leading questions on cross–examination a matter of right. The purpose of the qualification "ordinarily" is to furnish a basis for denying the use of leading questions when the cross–examination is cross–examination in form only and not in fact, as for example the "cross–examination" of a party by his own counsel after being called by the opponent (savoring more of re–direct) or of an insured defendant who proves to be friendly to the plaintiff.

3.   QUESTIONS CALLING FOR A NARRATIVE RESPONSE

If the attorney is convinced that the person is a good witness, a person who will project honesty and intelligence to the jury, the attorney usually prefers to elicit the witness' testimony by questions calling for a narrative. If the attorney were to conduct the examination by leading questions, the witness would be consistently answering only yes or no. However, if the witness gives a narrative, the witness is "displayed" to the maximum possible advantage; the jurors will have a substantial opportunity to observe and be impressed by the witness' sincerity and perception. The attorney makes the simple request, "In your own words, tell us what happened." The witness responds with a narrative and, ideally, proceeds to win over the jurors.

Even at common law in many jurisdictions, there is no absolute rule against narrative testimony. *State v. Hardin*, 581 S.W.2d 67 (Mo. Ct. App. 1979). The trial judge has considerable discretion in deciding whether to permit narrative testimony. *Frisella v. Reserve Life Ins. Co.*, 583 S.W.2d 728 (Mo. Ct. App. 1979). A case can certainly be made for narrative testimony. Remember the psychological studies indicating that testimony elicited in this fashion is more trustworthy than testimony elicited in response to specific questions. Moreover, as the preceding paragraph suggested, it is often tactically advantageous to elicit the testimony in narrative form. Researchers at Duke University have studied the effect of different questioning styles on jurors. Conley, *Language in the Courtroom*, 15 TRIAL, Sept. 1979, at 32. The researchers discovered that some jurors are acute enough to realize that a witness is being led rather than being asked to give a narrative response. Some of those jurors infer that the questioning attorney lacks faith in the witness being led. *Id.* at 35. They then adopt the same attitude toward the witness—they discount the witness' credibility.

NOTE

If there are so many advantages to narrative testimony, what can explain the trial judge's reluctance in many instances to permit a narrative? What practical problems arise when the witness testifies in narrative form? Do all lay witnesses have a good sense of chronological organization? If a lay witness testifies without the benefit of chronological guidance in the form of leading questions, what problem will arise? Moreover, lay witnesses know little about the technical evidentiary rules. What problem does that present?

4. ARGUMENTATIVE QUESTIONS

Leading and narrative questions are the form problems most frequently encountered on direct examination. On cross–examination, the most important form objection is that the question is "argumentative." We have already seen that statements during opening statement may not be "argumentative." As is often the case in the law, we must avoid the one word–one meaning syndrome; we must not assume that "argumentative" means the same thing here that it meant in the opening statement context. In fact, in this context, "argumentative" has another meaning.

Perhaps the best published explanation of that meaning is the following article written by a trial judge. The article, Goff, *Argumentative Questions: Counsel, Protect Your Witness!*, appears in 49 Cal. State Bar J. 140 (1974). In the article, the author synthesizes the case law and advances the thesis that argumentative questions tend to have two characteristics. Negatively, they are not designed to elicit new substantive testimony from the witness. Rather, affirmatively, they are calculated to challenge the witness with respect to an inference from testimony already in the record. Marshalling the cases, the author gives numerous examples of objectionable, argumentative questions, *inter alia*: "Do you mean that seriously? Well, now, can you reconcile the two statements? And you are telling us, are you, that when . . . [the sheriff] asked those questions and you gave those answers, you were telling the truth; is that right?" The author cautions, though, that in deciding whether a question is argumentative, the judge should consider not only the wording of the question but also the questioner's "voice, inflection, emphasis, and gestures accompanying the words." Obviously, since the trial transcript usually does not reflect those matters, the trial judge is in a much better position to regulate those matters than the appellate court.

PROBLEMS

1. Problem 4–15. Paterson is testifying in the *Devitt* case. The first part of this problem is an excerpt from his direct testimony. The second part is a section of his cross–examination. Identify all the possible objections to these questions.

The prosecutor has already elicited Paterson's testimony about the assault. Now the prosecutor turns to the identification of Devitt as the attacker:

Q: Mr. Paterson, you've just testified about the assault. Was the room where the attack occurred dark, or was it well lit with four 100–watt globes?

A: It was well lit. I think there were four or five 100–watt globes in the room.

Q: Then there was nothing obstructing your view?

A: No.

Q: Did you recognize the man who attacked you?

A: Yes.

Q: And wasn't that man the defendant at the defense table right there?

A: Yes.

Q: Had you ever had any difficulty with him before the day of the attack?

A: No.

Q: Did you give him any provocation on that day or any other prior day?

A: No.

Q: So he attacked you without any good reason. Isn't that true?

A: Yes.

Q: Thank you, Mr. Paterson. (Turning to the defense attorney.) Your witness.

Q: Mr. Paterson, I have a few questions I'd like to ask on cross–examination. Isn't it true that you told your daughter that you freely consented to have a fight with Mr. Devitt?

A: Maybe I did, but later I said positively that I didn't.

Q: Please don't try to evade the question. I asked you about what you told your daughter. Isn't that what you told her?

A: I guess so.

Q: All right. You told your daughter one thing. Now you tell us something different. Which story do you expect us to believe?

A: The one I'm telling now because it's the truth.

Q: Sure. Let's shift to another topic to see if you can answer these questions. What was the lighting in the room where the alleged attack occurred?

A: I already told you.

Q: I'm so interested that I'd love to hear it again.

A: I told you that it was well lit.

Q: Let's be specific. Were all the light bulbs working? How good is your eyesight?

A: Just fine.

2. Problem 4–16. Assume that the defense counsel is relatively unsuccessful in eliciting favorable responses from Paterson. The defense counsel becomes desperate and decides to reask a number of the questions posed on direct in the faint hope that Paterson will change his story and make a prior inconsistent statement. The defense counsel begins asking questions such as, "So you say that Devitt attacked you. Correct?" The prosecutor objects, "Asked and answered." As trial judge, how would you rule on the objection? *See United*

States v. Caudle, 606 F.2d 451, 456–58 (4th Cir. 1979). Is California Evidence Code § 774, reproduced *supra*, pertinent?

Chapter 5

THE ROLES OF JUDGE, JURY AND ATTORNEYS

Read Federal Rules of Evidence 103 and 104.

A. THE ROLE OF THE PROPONENT OF AN ITEM OF EVIDENCE

1. PRETRIAL

In our adversary system, the attorneys representing the opposing parties are the primary movers in the process of determining the admissibility of an item of evidence. As we shall see in the next section, the opponent can make a motion *in limine* to exclude evidence. The opponent usually makes the motion in the judge's chambers before the trial begins. So too the proponent can make a motion *in limine* to obtain an advance ruling admitting evidence.

A pretrial motion to admit can have attractive advantages for the proponent and the trial judge. First, it may enhance the possibility of settling the case before trial. Settlements occur when the parties' predictions of the outcome of the case reach a certain congruity. Reducing uncertainty, such as by knowing what evidence is or is not admissible, can thus bring the parties' predictions closer together.

In addition, an advance ruling to admit may greatly affect the proponent's trial strategy. It may affect the party's opening statement. If there is uncertainty about whether certain evidence will be admitted, it is quite risky to mention that evidence in opening statement. If it is ultimately excluded, a mistrial can result; or, even if there is no mistrial, the party may lose credibility in the eyes of the jury when the promised evidence is not forthcoming.

When evidence, particularly opinion testimony, will require a lengthy foundation, offering the evidence might also be quite risky. If after two hours of foundational testimony the judge rules the opinion inadmissible, the ruling may embarrass the proponent. Or the judge may conclude that the foundational testimony was so prejudicial that a curative instruction to disregard will be ineffective; the judge concludes that even if instructed to disregard the foundational testimony, the jurors will probably be unable to forget what they have heard. When the judge reaches that conclusion but the jury has already heard the evidence, the judge may have to mistry the case.

Although, as a general proposition, the trial judge has discretion whether to entertain a motion *in limine*, there are situations in which a judge arguably has a duty to decide a pretrial motion *to admit or exclude*. As a practical matter, some evidentiary issues have to be decided during the course of the trial; the admissibility of the item of evidence depends upon the posture of the rest of the record. However, other issues are "capable of determination without the trial of the general issue." *See United States v. Barletta*, 644 F.2d 50, 57–58 (1st Cir. 1981). And in cases involving motions to suppress on constitutional grounds, it may be necessary to hold a hearing and rule prior to trial.

2. TRIAL

Suppose that in our torts case, Ms. Hill's attorney wants to introduce a letter written by the Polecat Motors sales manager. The letter contains language that could arguably be construed as an express warranty. The sponsoring witness for the letter is a casual acquaintance of the sales manager; the witness is somewhat familiar with the manager's handwriting style.

The plaintiff's attorney should keep the letter out of the jurors' view until the time for its offer. At that point the plaintiff offers the letter in this fashion. The record of trial might reflect the following exchange:

Q1. (To the judge) I request that this be marked plaintiff's exhibit number one for identification.

J. It will be so marked.

Q2. (To the judge) Please let the record reflect that I am showing the exhibit to the opposing counsel.

J. It will so reflect.

Q3. (To the judge) I request permission to approach the witness.

J. Granted.

Q4. (To the witness) I now hand you plaintiff's exhibit number one for identification. What is it?

A. A letter from the defendant's sales manager.

Q5. How do you recognize it?

A. I know his handwriting style.

Q6. How did you become familiar with his handwriting style?

A. We're close friends and associates.

Q7. How long have you known him?

A. At least five years.

Q8. How often have you seen him sign his name?

A. Probably tens of times.

Q9. (To the judge) Your Honor, I now offer plaintiff's exhibit number one for identification into evidence as plaintiff's exhibit one.

J. The exhibit will be received.

Q10. (To the judge) Your Honor, I request permission to publish the exhibit to the jurors and allow them to inspect the exhibit at this time.

J. Permission granted.

We shall now dissect this line of questioning.

Marking the exhibit and showing it to the opponent and witness. (Questions 1 through 4). Note that the proponent described the letter only as "plaintiff's exhibit number one for identification." Some jurisdictions would permit the proponent to say, "the letter marked as plaintiff's exhibit number one for identification."

However, the proponent may not reveal the contents of the document prior to its admission. For example, the proponent may not refer to the document as "a letter signed by the defendant." If the proponent did so, in effect the proponent would be testifying even though the proponent is not under oath. There is also an administrative rationale for this practice. In a given trial, the proponent may introduce several letters, all signed by the same defendant. If the plaintiff's attorney consistently used the expression, "the letter signed by the defendant," the record of trial would be confusing. The record will make much more sense to the appellate court if the proponent uses the accepted expression, "plaintiff's exhibit number one for identification."

The foundation or predicate. (Questions 5 through 8). The expressions "foundation" and "predicate" refer to the testimony the proponent must introduce before offering the letter; it is the foundation or predicate in the sense that it is usually a condition precedent to the admission of the letter. The substantive evidentiary doctrines discussed in the remainder of this text dictate the content of the foundation. In our hypothetical, the only foundation the proponent is laying is authentication. As we shall see later, the logical relevance doctrine requires that we "authenticate" articles such as letters. We must prove that the article is what we claim it to be; if the plaintiff claims that the article is a letter written by the defendant, the plaintiff proponent lays the foundation by presenting the testimony of one of the defendant's acquaintances that the letter is written in the defendant's style.

The trial judge usually has discretion to vary the order of proof. Although the judge commonly insists that the proponent lay the foundation before offering the exhibit, the judge has discretion to admit the exhibit conditionally on the proponent's assurance that the necessary, foundational testimony will be introduced later.

When an exhibit is admitted conditionally, without a complete foundation, it sometimes happens that the proponent neglects to complete the foundation prior to resting. If that happens, the opponent should immediately move to strike the exhibit. Although the judge may permit the proponent to reopen his or her case to complete the foundation, the judge may not if intervening events have made that difficult or unjust. And without a key exhibit, the opponent may be in a position to move successfully for judgment as a matter of law (*i.e.*, a "directed verdict").

The formal tender or motion for admission. (Question 9). When the proponent believes that the foundation is complete, the proponent formally tenders the exhibit into evidence. In some jurisdictions, the proponent "move[s] the admission of plaintiff's exhibit number one for identification into evidence as plaintiff's exhibit one." The formal tender signals the opponent that now is the time to make any foundational objections such as hearsay or lack of authentication; the tender is the trigger for those objections.

The publication of the exhibit to the jury. (Question 10). If the court admits the exhibit, the attorney may want to get the exhibit into the jurors' hands immediately. Reading the exhibit may be essential to the jurors' understanding of the balance of the witness' testimony. In other cases, the attorney may want to defer publishing the exhibit until the end of the witness' testimony so as to avoid distracting the jury during the testimony.

If the court decides not to admit the exhibit, the next step can be critical.

The offer of proof. Federal Evidence Rule 103(a)(2) states:

> (a) Effect of erroneous ruling. Error may not be predicated upon a ruling which admits or excludes evidence unless a substantial right of the party is affected, and
>
> . . . .
>
> (2) Offer of proof. In case the ruling is one excluding evidence, the substance of the evidence was made known to the court by offer or was apparent from the context within which questions were asked.
>
> . . . .

This is the so-called offer of proof or avowal procedure. If the judge sustains an objection to the tender, the proponent generally must make an offer to preserve the issue for appeal. If the proponent fails to make an offer, any error is ordinarily waived. The proponent can lose the right to challenge the most important adverse ruling during the trial simply because the proponent neglected to comply with Rule 103(a)(2). In addition to this formal function, the offer of proof procedure serves a number of vital, practical objectives.

NOTES AND PROBLEMS

1. Why require offers of proof? First consider the question from the trial judge's perspective. Suppose that the trial judge at first did not see the logical relevance of the line of questioning and, for that reason, sustained the objection. When the proponent makes the offer of proof, the relevance finally dawns upon the judge. What could the judge do at that point? In what sense does the offer serve an "educational" function?

2. In addition, consider the question from the appellate court's perspective. Why would the appellate court want an offer? How would an offer help the court to determine whether there was error, whether the error was prejudicial, or whether the proper disposition is simply to remand or rather to immediately enter a final judgment for one of the parties?

3. Problem 5–1. In the *Hill* case, the defendant Polecat Motors wants to present evidence of a telephone conversation between the witness, Jenkins, and Ms. Hill. The foundation would be proof that Jenkins is familiar with Ms. Hill's voice. The tender is the question, "And what did Ms. Hill say during that telephone conversation?" If the plaintiff's counsel thought that the authentication foundation was inadequate, the plaintiff would object. If the judge agreed and sustained the objection, the proponent might use this procedure:

Q: Your Honor, may I approach the bench?

A: Yes.

Q: Your Honor, I would like to make an offer of proof for the record.

A: Very well. Proceed.

Q: If you had permitted the witness to answer the question, the witness would have testified that in this conversation, Ms. Hill stated that she had made a full recovery from her injuries. I would like to offer this evidence as an admission that her testimony in this case concerning her injuries is exaggerated. The witness is sufficiently familiar with Ms. Hill's voice to identify it; the witness has already testified that he's spoken face to face with Ms. Hill "on numerous occasions."

The last "Q" is the offer of proof. What is the distinction between the two sentences in this offer of proof? What does the first sentence tell the judge? What function does the second sentence serve? What about the third sentence?

4. Problem 5–2. In the last problem, why did the attorney request permission to approach the bench? Should the jurors hear the offer?

5. Problem 5–3. In the hypothetical of Problem 5–1, the judge accepted the attorney's representation about the witness' expected testimony. Must the judge do so? What if the representation struck the judge as outlandish? In that case, what procedure could the judge require the proponent to follow? Does Federal Evidence Rule 103 address this question?

B. THE ROLE OF THE OPPONENT OF AN ITEM OF EVIDENCE

1. PRETRIAL

Motion to suppress. *Mapp v. Ohio*, 367 U.S. 643 (1961), teaches us that if law enforcement agents seize evidence in violation of the defendant's Fourth Amendment's privacy rights, the evidence is inadmissible against the defendant. When the Fourth Amendment exclusionary rule first emerged, the attorneys usually litigated the search's legality at the trial. However, many jurisdictions have since adopted statutes patterned after the model of Federal Rule of Criminal Procedure 41:

(e) *Motion for Return of Property.* A person aggrieved by an unlawful search and seizure or by the deprivation of property may move the district court for the district in which the property was seized for the return of the property on the ground that such person is entitled to lawful possession of the property. The court shall receive evidence on any issue of fact necessary to the decision of the motion. If the motion is granted, the property shall be returned to the movant, although reasonable conditions may be imposed to protect access and use of the property in subsequent proceedings. If a motion for return of property is made or comes on for hearing in the district of trial after an indictment or information is filed, it shall be treated also as a motion to suppress under Rule 12.

(f) *Motion to Suppress.* A motion to suppress evidence may be made in the court of the district of trial as provided in Rule 12.

The opponent may file a suppression motion before the case is even assigned to a trial judge. The presiding judge of the court may designate a particular judge to sit to decide all pretrial motions.

You can see why it is necessary to separate the decision on the Fourth Amendment issue from the decision on the issues on the historical merits of the case. The judge decides the Fourth Amendment issues, while the jury decides the other issues on the historical merits of the case, and it would be extremely prejudicial to the defendant for the jury to hear the evidence concerning the Fourth Amendment issue.

By case law, many jurisdictions have extended the practice of pretrial resolution of constitutional suppression issues to Fifth and Sixth Amendment challenges. Thus, if Devitt wants to exclude a confession obtained in violation of *Miranda*'s warning requirements, in these jurisdictions the defendant could similarly file a pretrial motion to suppress. Or assume that Paterson had identified Devitt at a lineup at which Devitt had been denied counsel in violation of *United States v. Wade*, 388 U.S. 218 (1967). Devitt could similarly make a pretrial motion to suppress any testimony about the pretrial identification.

Motion in limine to exclude. Motions to suppress assert constitutional grounds for excluding evidence. If there is a nonconstitutional ground for excluding the evidence, the opponent must resort to a motion *in limine*. R. CARLSON, SUCCESSFUL TECHNIQUES FOR CIVIL TRIALS, ch. 1 (2d ed. 1992). The attorneys make these motions in writing and notice them for hearing, or orally in the trial judge's chambers before the trial begins in open court.

For example, in civil cases in some jurisdictions, evidence that a person has consumed alcoholic beverages is not, by itself, admissible in an automobile accident case; there also must be evidence to show that the drinking resulted in intoxication. *Reuter v. Korb*, 248 Ill. App. 3d 142, 616 N.E.2d 1363 (1993). If the defendant's attorney suspected (or expected) that the plaintiff's attorney might attempt to insinuate that the defendant had been drinking just prior to the accident, but there was insufficient evidence of intoxication, the defense attorney could make a motion *in limine* to exclude any reference to the drinking.

In a criminal case, in many jurisdictions the judge can exclude evidence of prior convictions strikingly similar to the crime for which the defendant is now on trial. Suppose, for example, that Devitt had two prior battery convictions. If the prosecutor is allowed to introduce evidence of those convictions for the stated reason of impeaching Devitt's credibility, there is a serious risk that the jurors will misuse the evidence. Rather than limiting their consideration of the evidence to the evaluation of Devitt's credibility, the jurors may decide to convict Devitt simply to protect society, by imprisoning Devitt even if they are not convinced beyond a reasonable doubt that he is guilty of the crime charged. In this situation, Devitt's defense attorney might move *in limine* to prohibit any mention of the prior battery convictions at trial.

NOTES AND PROBLEMS

1. Problem 5–4. In *Devitt,* the defense counsel makes a motion *in limine* to exclude any reference to Devitt's prior convictions even if Devitt testifies at trial. As trial judge, you are inclined to think that the convictions will prove to be inadmissible, but you do not want to make a final decision until you can see how critical an issue Devitt's credibility becomes. You can conceive of a state of the record in which Devitt's credibility was the central issue and the prosecutor needed impeachment ammunition. How should you rule? Do you have any choices other than: refusing to hear the motion; denying the motion altogether; and absolutely forbidding any reference to the convictions at trial?

2. Suppose that in the last problem, the judge entertained the motion on the merits and denied the motion before trial. Must the defense attorney make an objection at trial to preserve the issue for appeal? Until recently, the answer was uncertain and the case law was in conflict. *See, e.g., Gill v. Thomas,* 83 F.3d 537 (1st Cir. 1996) (must be renewed at trial); *United States v. Wiman,* 77 F.3d 981 (7th Cir. 1996) (same); *United States v. Blum,* 65 F.3d 1436 (8th Cir.1995), *cert. denied,* 116 S. Ct. 824 (1996) (same); *Pandit v. American Honda Motor Co., Inc.,* 82 F.3d 376 (10th Cir. 1996) (need not be renewed at trial only if (1) matter was adequately presented to district court, (2) issue was of the type that can be finally decided prior to trial, and (3) court's ruling was definitive); *United States v. Williams,* 81 F.3d 1321 (4th Cir. 1996) (issue preserved if movant has clearly identified the ruling sought and trial court has ruled upon it); *Rosenfeld v. Basquiat,* 78 F.3d 84 (2d Cir. 1996) (issue preserved where pretrial ruling was explicit and definitive, no new circumstances arose that would have changed its resolution, and issue was essentially legal, not factual); *United States v. Birbal,* 62 F.3d 456 (2d Cir. 1995) (Rule 403 objections must be renewed at trial).

This issue has now been resolved by an amendment to Rule 103(a)(2) which became effective on December 1, 2000. The amended rule reads as follows (the new matter is underlined):

(a) Effect of erroneous ruling.—

* * *

(2) Offer of proof. In case the ruling is one excluding evidence, the substance of the evidence was made known to the court by offer or was apparent from the context within which the questions were asked.

Once the court makes a definitive ruling on the record admitting or excluding evidence, either at or before trial, a party need not renew an objection or offer of proof to preserve the claim of error for appeal.

The Advisory Committee Note accompanying the amendment explains the rule and its rationale and operation in some detail.

*   *   *

The amendment imposes the obligation on counsel to clarify whether an *in limine* or other evidentiary ruling is definitive when there is doubt on that point. *See, e.g., Walden v. Georgia–Pacific Corp.,* 126 F.3d 506, 520 (3d Cir. 1997) (although "the district court told plaintiff's counsel not to reargue every ruling, it did not countermand its clear opening statement that all of its rulings were tentative, and counsel never requested clarification, as he might have done.").

Even where the court's ruling is definitive, nothing in the amendment prohibits the court from revisiting its decision when the evidence is to be offered. If the court changes its initial ruling, or if the opposing party violates the terms of the initial ruling, objection must be made when the evidence is offered to preserve the claim of error for appeal. The error, if any, in such a situation occurs only when the evidence is offered and admitted. *United States Aviation Underwriters, Inc. v. Olympia Wings, Inc.*, 896 F. 2d 949, 956 (5th Cir. 1990) ("objection is required to preserve error when an opponent, or the court itself, violates a motion *in limine* that was granted"); *United States v. Roenigk*, 810 F.2d 809 (8th Cir. 1987) (claim of error was not preserved where the defendant failed to object at trial to secure the benefit of a favorable advance ruling).

A definitive advance ruling is reviewed in light of the facts and circumstances before the trial court at the time of the ruling. If the relevant facts and circumstances change materially after the advance ruling has been made, those facts and circumstances cannot be relied upon on appeal unless they have been brought to the attention of the trial court by way of a renewed, and timely, objection, offer of proof, or motion to strike. *See Old Chief v. United States*, 519 U.S. 172, 182 n.6 (1997) ("It is important that a reviewing court evaluate the trial court's decision from its perspective when it had to rule and not indulge in review by hindsight."). Similarly, if the court decides in an advance ruling that proffered evidence is admissible subject to the eventual introduction by the proponent of a foundation for the evidence, and that foundation is never provided, the opponent cannot claim error based on the failure to establish the foundation unless the opponent calls that failure to the court's attention by a timely motion to strike or other suitable motion. *See Huddleston v. United States*, 485 U.S. 681, 690, n.7 (1988) ("It is, of course, not the responsibility of the judge *sua sponte* to ensure that the foundation evidence is offered; the objector must move to strike the evidence if at the close of the trial the offeror has failed to satisfy the condition.")

* * *

2. TRIAL

If the opponent waits until trial, four questions arise.

What procedural device may the opponent use to assert the ground for excluding the evidence? The most common device is an objection. The opponent uses such phrasing as:

Objection, Your Honor. The question . . . .

Your Honor, I object to the question on the ground that . . . .

The opponent uses an objection to challenge the question itself; an objection can be used to raise the contention that the question's form is improper or that the question calls for substantively inadmissible matter.

The other common device is the motion to strike. While the objection ordinarily attacks the question, the opponent uses the motion to attack the witness' answer. For example, if the witness' answer unexpectedly refers to inadmissible hearsay, the opponent might use this language:

> Your Honor, I move to strike the last sentence on the ground that the sentence contains a reference to incompetent hearsay.

The opponent also resorts to the motion in two other situations: First, the opponent can move when the witness has already given some testimony and it later becomes apparent that the witness' prior testimony was inadmissible. For example, after three minutes of testimony the witness blurts out that she is testifying about an event on the basis of inadmissible hearsay rather than personal knowledge. Second, the witness may be quick on the trigger; the witness may begin the answer so quickly that the opponent does not have a fair opportunity to object to an improper question. In this situation, the opponent moves "for the purpose of interposing an objection to the question." Suppose that the judge grants the motion. What should the opponent request next? Remember that the jury has already heard the inadmissible matter.

When should the opponent assert the ground? The objection or motion must be "timely." If the ground the opponent is asserting challenges the question, the opponent should voice the objection before the witness begins the answer. If the ground challenges the answer, the opponent should ordinarily make the motion before the examiner poses the next question. Suppose that the witness is giving a long, narrative answer. In the situation, the opponent need not wait until the witness completes the answer to make the motion. The opponent may interrupt the witness, but the opponent should be very apologetic about doing so.

As the above paragraph indicates, an objection is not timely if it is voiced too late. However, an objection can also violate the timeliness requirement if it is premature. When the ground for the objection is the violation of a form rule, such as leading, the opposing attorney may state the objection as soon as the improper question is posed. However, when the ground is substantive, such as a violation of the hearsay doctrine, the opposing attorney must wait until the proponent of the item of evidence seeks to introduce the ultimate item of evidence. For example, the opposing attorney may not object when the proponent asks the witness: "Did the driver say anything?" The opposing attorney must wait until the proponent asks the question calling for the inadmissible hearsay: "What did he say?"

How should the opponent phrase the objection or motion? In addition to being "timely," an objection or motion must be "specific." The case law requires that the objection be specific in several respects.

The objection must specify the part of the question or answer the opponent is challenging. It is best to identify the very word, phrase, or sentence the opponent believes is improper. The requirement for specificity explains why it is so critical that the trial attorney be a good listener.

Further, the objection should specify the party on whose behalf the objection is being raised. Suppose that Devitt were being tried with an alleged conspirator. The conspirator had confessed; the confession would be admissible against the conspirator; but the confession might be inadmissible hearsay as against Devitt. You are representing both Devitt and his alleged conspirator. The prosecutor has just asked the question calling for the conspirator's confession. If you object, you should explicitly state that you are objecting "on behalf of the defendant Devitt" or that the confession is inadmissible "as against the defendant Devitt."

The basis or bases of the objection. Finally, the question must specify the reason for the objection, namely, the evidentiary rule being violated. Federal Evidence Rule 103(a)(1) provides:

Rule 103. Rulings on Evidence.

(a) *Effect of erroneous ruling.* —Error may not be predicated upon a ruling which admits evidence unless a substantial right of the party is affected, and

(1) Objection. In case the ruling is one admitting evidence, a timely objection or motion to strike appears of record, stating the specific ground of objection, if the specific ground was not apparent from the context . . . .

In most jurisdictions, a general objection such as "incompetent and inadmissible" does not preserve the error for appeal. However, the traditional view is that it is sufficient to name the generic evidentiary rule being violated:

Your Honor, I object to the introduction of that letter for lack of authentication.

Your Honor, I object to the introduction of that copy on the ground that it is not the best evidence.

Your Honor, I object to that question on the ground that it calls for incompetent hearsay.

It may be safer, however, to be more specific. There is a risk that a reviewing court may require greater specificity than the traditional view. For example, in *United States v. Fendley*, 522 F.2d 181 (5th Cir. 1975), defendant was convicted of tax evasion and filing a false tax return. On appeal, he claimed that the trial court had improperly admitted into evidence Government Exhibit 9–108, a computer printout, on the ground that the government had not complied with the business records exception to the hearsay rule. The court noted that business records are admissible under this exception if three conditions are met: (1) The records must be kept pursuant to some routine procedure designed to assure their accuracy; (2) they must be created for motives that would tend to assure accuracy (preparation for litigation, for example, is not such a motive); and (3) they must not themselves be mere accumulations of hearsay or uninformed opinion.

Defendant's objection in the trial court was worded as follows (*Id.* at 185):

"Then, Your Honor, we will renew our objection to Government's exhibit 9–108–B [sic] on the basis that there is no showing that the instrument is accurate as to the figures it reflects;

"And that the preparer was someone other than the witness here; that we cannot determine the accuracy of it, and therefore, it shouldn't be admitted;

"Because it would be hearsay and, again I cannot cross–examine the paper, obviously, without having the party assigned to compiling the figures on it before us.

"We object on that basis."

The Court of Appeals held that this amounted to little more than a hearsay objection, and that it was insufficient (*Id.* at 185, 186–87):

It appears to us that this loosely formulated and imprecise objection at most comes to this: (1) that the document was hearsay; (2) that the witness laying the foundation for its introduction was someone other than the preparer, and (3) that the witness laying the foundation was unable to personally attest to the accuracy of the figures contained in the document. There was no objection on the only grounds which would have permitted the trial court to have required that a fuller foundation be laid for the admission of the exhibit that the printout was made and kept in the regular course of business, for regular business purposes and relied upon by the business, and finally that it was not "mere accumulations of hearsay or uninformed opinion." . . .

The grounds asserted in the defendant's objection are clearly insubstantial. While obviously the document was hearsay, this in itself fails to state an objection as to whether the exhibit met the admissibility requirements of the Business Records Act. Similarly, nothing in the Business Records Act requires either that the foundation witness be able to personally attest to the accuracy of the information contained in the document, or that he have personally prepared the document. Both these requirements have been eliminated by 28 U.S.C. § 1732. . . .

[W]e do not find in the general objections made at trial any reference to the three–fold requirements set out in *United States v. Miller* for compliance with the foundation requirements of the Act; nor do we find in these objections any reference to the reliability of the method of preparation. To object as the defendant did that "the preparer is someone other than the witness here" and that consequently "there is no accuracy shown that the instrument is accurate as to the figures it reflects" in no way apprises the trial court that the defendant attacks the reliability of the method of preparation of the exhibit.

NOTES

1. Which view do you prefer, as a matter of policy, the traditional view or the *Fendley* view? First consider the question from the judge's point of view. Which view better enables you to make an intelligent ruling? Which view is more likely to save court time?

2. Now shift to the opponent's perspective. From that point of view, what is the danger of specific objections? Suppose that in *Fendley,* the opponent had said:

Your Honor, I object to the introduction of the exhibit on the ground that there is no showing that the exhibit was made and kept in the regular course of business.

On that ground, the judge sustains the objection. What should the proponent do next? Does a specific objection serve an educational function? Who is educating whom? Given our adversary litigation model, is it legitimate to force the opponent to teach the proponent?

Must the moving party testify at trial to preserve the issue for appeal? Assume that the party chooses the correct procedural device and that the objection is both timely and specific. If the judge overrules the objection, must the party testify to preserve the issue?

In *Luce v. United States*, 469 U.S. 38 (1984), the United States Supreme Court held that he must. Luce was convicted of conspiracy and possession of cocaine with intent to distribute. At trial, he moved *in limine* to bar his impeachment with a prior state conviction. (The admissibility of such prior convictions for purposes of impeachment is governed by Federal Rule of Evidence 609.) The trial court denied the motion. Defendant made no commitment to testify if the motion were granted, nor did he make an offer of proof as to what his testimony would be. In denying the motion, the trial court noted that the nature and scope of defendant's trial testimony could affect the court's evidentiary rulings; for example, the court was prepared to hold that the prior conviction would be excluded if defendant limited his testimony to explaining his attempt to flee from the arresting officers. However, if defendant took the stand and denied any prior involvement with drugs, he could then be impeached by the earlier conviction. Defendant did not testify, and the jury returned guilty verdicts.

The United States Supreme Court affirmed, stating, in part:

> It is clear, of course, that had petitioner testified and been impeached by evidence of a prior conviction, the District Court's decision to admit the impeachment evidence would have been reviewable on appeal along with any other claims of error. The Court of Appeals would then have had a complete record detailing the nature of petitioner's testimony, the scope of the cross–examination, and the possible impact of the impeachment on the jury's verdict.

> A reviewing court is handicapped in any effort to rule on subtle evidentiary questions outside a factual context.[4] This is particularly true under Rule 609(a)(1), which directs the court to weigh the probative value of a prior conviction against the prejudicial effect to the defendant. To perform this balancing, the court must know the precise nature of the defendant's testimony, which is unknowable when, as here, the defendant does not testify.[5]

> Any possible harm flowing from a district court's *in limine* ruling permitting impeachment by a prior conviction is wholly speculative.

---

[4] Although the Federal Rules of Evidence do not explicitly authorize *in limine* rulings, the practice has developed pursuant to the district court's inherent authority to manage the course of trials. *See generally* FED. RULE EVID. 103(c); *cf.* FED. RULE CRIM. PROC. 12(e).

[5] Requiring a defendant to make a proffer of testimony is no answer; his trial testimony could, for any number of reasons, differ from the proffer.

The ruling is subject to change when the case unfolds, particularly if the actual testimony differs from what was contained in the defendant's proffer. Indeed even if nothing unexpected happens at trial, the district judge is free, in the exercise of sound judicial discretion, to alter a previous *in limine* ruling. On a record such as here, it would be a matter of conjecture whether the District Court would have allowed the Government to attack petitioner's credibility at trial by means of the prior conviction.

When the defendant does not testify, the reviewing court also has no way of knowing whether the Government would have sought to impeach with the prior conviction. If, for example, the Government's case is strong, and the defendant is subject to impeachment by other means, a prosecutor might elect not to use an arguably inadmissible prior conviction.

Because an accused's decision whether to testify "seldom turns on the resolution of one factor," *New Jersey v. Portash*, 440 U.S. 450, 467 (1979) (Blackmun, J., dissenting), a reviewing court cannot assume that the adverse ruling motivated a defendant's decision not to testify. In support of his motion a defendant might make a commitment to testify if his motion is granted; but such a commitment is virtually risk free because of the difficulty of enforcing it.

Even if these difficulties could be surmounted, the reviewing court would still face the question of harmless error. *See generally United States v. Hasting*, 461 U.S. 499 (1983). Were *in limine* rulings under Rule 609(a) reviewable on appeal, almost any error would result in the windfall of automatic reversal; the appellate court could not logically term "harmless" an error that presumptively kept the defendant from testifying. Requiring that a defendant testify in order to preserve Rule 609(a) claims, will enable the reviewing court to determine the impact any erroneous impeachment may have had in light of the record as a whole; it will also tend to discourage making such motions solely to "plant" reversible error in the event of conviction. . . .

We hold that to raise and preserve for review the claim of improper impeachment with a prior conviction, a defendant must testify.

NOTE

If the trial court rules that the prosecutor may use the defendant's prior conviction for impeachment, and the defendant decides to testify, what are the Rule 103 consequences if defense counsel decides to blunt the impact of the impeachment by admitting the conviction on direct examination? In *Ohler v. United States*, 529 U.S. 753, (2000), a 5–4 decision of the United States Supreme Court, the Court held that by introducing her conviction on direct examination, defendant had waived any error in the ruling on the motion *in limine*. The Court's syllabus states as follows:

A defendant who preemptively introduces evidence of a prior conviction on direct examination may not challenge the admission of such evidence on appeal. Ohler attempts to avoid the well–established commonsense principle that a party introducing evidence cannot complain on appeal that the evidence was erroneously admitted by invoking the Federal Rules of Evidence 103 and 609. However, neither Rule addresses the question at issue here. She also argues that applying such a waiver rule in this situation would compel a defendant to forgo the tactical advantage of preemptively introducing the conviction in order to appeal the *in limine* ruling. But both the Government and the defendant in a criminal trial must make choices as the trial progresses. Ohler's submission would deny to the Government its usual right to choose, after she testifies, whether or not to use her prior conviction against her. She seeks to short–circuit that decisional process by offering the conviction herself (and thereby removing the sting) and still preserve its admission as a claim of error on appeal. But here she runs into the position taken by the Court in *Luce v. United States*, 469 U.S. 38, 41, 105 S.Ct. 460, 83 L.Ed.2d 443, that any possible harm flowing from a district court's *in limine* ruling permitting impeachment by a prior conviction is wholly speculative. Only when the Government exercises its option to elicit the testimony is an appellate court confronted with a case where, under normal trial rules, the defendant can claim the denial of a substantial right if in fact the district court's *in limine* ruling proved to be erroneous. Finally, applying this rule to Ohler's situation does not unconstitutionally burden her right to testify, because the rule does not prevent her from taking the stand and presenting any admissible testimony she chooses.

Do you agree with this result? Are there any better ways to further both the interests of the government and of the accused in this situation?

C. THE ROLE OF THE TRIAL JUDGE

It is a commonplace observation that during the trial, the judge resolves "questions of law" but the petit jurors decide the "questions of fact." Honesty demands that we admit at the outset that the distinction between law and fact is sometimes quite unclear. Some commentators have suggested that we entirely abandon the law–fact dichotomy and speak rather in terms of jury questions and judge questions. H. HART & A. SACKS, THE LEGAL PROCESS: BASIC PROBLEMS IN THE MAKING AND APPLICATION OF LAW 344–60 (Eskridge & Frickey, eds., 1994).

1. QUESTIONS OF LAW

The trial judge must decide pure questions of law. For example, assume that in our torts case, at trial, Polecat Motors moved for judgment on the pleadings. A motion for judgment on the pleadings challenges the legal sufficiency of the pleadings. In effect, the motion is a delayed demurrer and asserts that even if the plaintiff can prove all the facts alleged in the complaint, under the controlling substantive law the plaintiff is not entitled to recover damages from the defendant. Thus, the motion raises a question of law the judge must decide. Or assume that in the *Devitt* prosecution, the defense counsel requested a jury instruction and the prosecutor objected on the ground that the proposed instruction "misstates the law." The objection would raise a question of law allocated to the judge's decisionmaking power.

Depending on the jurisdiction and the type of case, sometimes judges also resolve questions of law that have a fact component. These are often referred to as mixed questions of law and fact. A judge sometimes excludes evidence on the ground that the accompanying probative dangers such as prejudice and undue time consumption outweigh the probative value of the evidence. Federal Rule of Evidence 403 authorizes the judge to balance the probative worth of the evidence against the incidental probative dangers. Since the judge must assess how probative the evidence is of the facts in the case, the balancing decision is not a pure question of law. However, since the judge is weighing intangibles, the question is not a pure issue of fact in the same sense as the jury's decision as to how fast Worker's vehicle was going when it struck Ms. Hill's car.

2. PRELIMINARY FACTS CONDITIONING THE ADMISSIBILITY OF EVIDENCE

The statement that the jurors decide the questions of fact during the trial is an oversimplification. The jurors resolve the questions of historical fact on the merits of dispute, but often the judge must also rule on questions of fact. It is well–settled that the judge rules on the admissibility of proffered items of evidence, and the ruling will often necessitate a decision on a question of fact. Federal Evidence Rule 104 addresses this subject:

(a) *Question of admissibility generally.* —Preliminary questions concerning the qualification of a person to be a witness, the existence of a privilege, or the admissibility of evidence shall be determined by the court, subject to the provisions of subdivision (b). In making its determination it is not bound by the rules of evidence except those with respect to privileges.

(b) *Relevancy conditioned on fact.* —When the relevancy of evidence depends upon the fulfillment of a condition of fact, the court shall admit it upon, or subject to, the introduction of evidence sufficient to support a finding of the fulfillment of the condition.

Thus, the face of Rule 104 suggests that there are two types of preliminary facts. One type, governed by (a), is finally decided by the court, that is, the judge. The second type, controlled by (b), is ultimately decided by the jurors; the trial judge makes only a preliminary determination that the proponent has introduced "evidence sufficient to support a [rational] finding" of the existence of the fact.

What is the basis for the distinction between the two types of facts? The distinction relates to our faith in the ability of lay jurors to decide evidentiary questions. Kaplan, *Of Mabrus and Zorgs—An Essay in Honor of David Louisell*, 66 CAL. L. REV. 987 (1978). The preliminary fact of a document's authenticity is an example of a Rule 104(b), conditional relevance question. Lay jurors are not only capable of deciding such a straightforward factual question; we can also be confident that when the jurors decide the document is a forgery, in most cases common sense will lead them to disregard the document during the final deliberations. Contrast the fact of a third party's presence at an attorney–client conversation, a fact that falls under Rule 104(a). If the third party was present to the knowledge of the attorney and client, the presence ordinarily negates the privacy needed for the attorney–client privilege to attach. On the one hand, lay jurors are certainly competent to decide whether a third party was physically present at the conversation. However, assume that the conversation contains a damaging admission by the client. Even if the jurors decide that no third party was present and that the conversation was consequently privileged, can we have the same confidence that the jurors will be able to forget about the damaging admission during deliberation?

In addition to deciding whether to draw a line such as the distinction between Rules 104(b) and (a), we must decide where to draw the line. Probably the most detailed and explicit treatment of this topic appears in the text and Assembly Committee Notes for California Evidence Code §§ 403 and 405:

> § 403. Procedure of determination of admissibility of proffered evidence.
>
> (a) The proponent of the proffered evidence has the burden of producing evidence as to the existence of the preliminary fact, and the proffered evidence is inadmissible unless the court finds that there is evidence sufficient to sustain a finding of the existence of the preliminary fact, when:
>
>> (1) The relevance of the proffered evidence depends on the existence of the preliminary fact;
>>
>> (2) The preliminary fact is the personal knowledge of a witness concerning the subject matter of his testimony;
>>
>> (3) The preliminary fact is the authenticity of a writing; or
>>
>> (4) The proffered evidence is of a statement or other conduct of a particular person and the preliminary fact is whether that person made the statement or so conducted himself.
>
> (b) Subject to Section 702, the court may admit conditionally the proffered evidence under this section, subject to evidence of the preliminary fact being supplied later in the course of the trial.
>
> (c) If the court admits the proffered evidence under this section, the court:
>
>> (1) May, and on request shall, instruct the jury to determine whether the preliminary fact exists and to disregard the proffered evidence unless the jury finds that the preliminary fact does exist.
>>
>> (2) Shall instruct the jury to disregard the proffered evidence if the court subsequently determines that a jury could not reasonably find that the preliminary fact exists.

> ### Comment
> ### Assembly Committee

Illustrative of the preliminary fact questions that should be decided under [this statute] are the following:

Relevancy. Under existing law, as under [this statute], if the relevancy of proffered evidence depends on the existence of some preliminary fact, the evidence is admissible if there is evidence sufficient to warrant a jury finding of the preliminary fact. *Reed v. Clark*, 47 Cal. 194 (1873). Thus, for example, if P sues D upon an alleged agreement, evidence of negotiations with A is inadmissible because irrelevant unless A is shown to be D's agent; but the evidence of the negotiations with A is admissible if there is evidence sufficient to sustain a finding of the agency. *Brown v. Spencer*, 163 Cal. 589, 126 P. 493 (1912). The same rule is applicable when a person is charged with criminal responsibility for the acts of another because they are conspirators. See discussion in *People v. Steccone*, 36 Cal. 2d 234, 223 P.2d 17 (1950).

Requirement of personal knowledge. Evidence sufficient to sustain a finding of a witness' personal knowledge seems to be sufficient under the existing California practice. *See, e.g., People v. Avery*, 35 Cal. 2d 487, 492, 218 P.2d 527, 530 (1950). ("Bolton testified that he observed the incident about which he testified. His testimony, therefore, was not incompetent.")

Identity of hearsay declarant. For most hearsay evidence, admissibility depends upon two preliminary determinations: (1) Did the declarant actually make the statement as claimed by the proponent of the evidence? (2) Does the statement meet certain standards of trustworthiness required by some exception to the hearsay rule?

The first determination involves the relevancy of the evidence. For example, if the issue is the state of mind of X, a person's statement as to his state of mind has no tendency to prove X's state of mind unless the declarant was X. Relevancy depends on the fact that X made the statement. Accordingly, if otherwise competent, a hearsay statement is admitted upon evidence sufficient to sustain a finding that the claimed declarant made the statement.

Authentication of writings. Under existing law, an otherwise competent writing is admissible upon the introduction of evidence sufficient to sustain a finding of the authenticity of the writing. *Verzan v. McGregor*, 23 Cal. 339 (1863). [This statute] retains this existing law.

§ 405. Other determinations.

With respect to preliminary fact determinations not governed by Section 403 or 404:

(a) When the existence of a preliminary fact is disputed, the court shall indicate which party has the burden of producing evidence and the burden of proof on the issue as implied by the rule of law under which the question arises. The court shall determine the existence or nonexistence of the preliminary fact and shall admit or exclude the proffered evidence as required by the rule of law under which the question arises.

(b) If a preliminary fact is also a fact in issue in the action:

(1) The jury shall not be informed of the court's determination as to the existence or nonexistence of the preliminary fact.

(2) If the proffered evidence is admitted, the jury shall not be instructed to disregard the evidence if its determination of the fact differs from the court's determination of the preliminary fact.

Comment
Assembly Committee

Illustrative of the preliminary fact questions that should be decided under [this statute] are the following:

Disqualification of a witness for lack of mental capacity. Under existing law, as under this code, the party objecting to a proffered witness has the burden of proving the witness' lack of capacity. *People v. Craig*, 111 Cal. 460, 44 P. 186 (1896).

Qualifications of an expert witness. Under Section 720, as under existing law, the proponent must persuade the judge that his expert is qualified, and it is error for the judge to submit the qualifications of the expert to the jury. *Eble v. Peluso*, 80 Cal. App. 2d 154, 181 P.2d 680 (1947).

Privileges. Under this code, as under existing law, the party claiming a privilege has the burden of proof on the preliminary facts. *San Diego Professional Ass'n v. Superior Court*, 58 Cal. 2d 194, 373 P.2d 448, 23 Cal. Rptr. 384 (1962). The proponent of the proffered evidence, however, has the burden of proof upon any preliminary fact necessary to show that an exception to the privilege is applicable.

Hearsay evidence. When hearsay evidence is offered, two preliminary fact questions may be raised. The first question relates to the authenticity of the proffered declaration—was the statement actually made by the person alleged to have made it? The second question relates to the existence of those circumstances that make the hearsay sufficiently trustworthy to be received in evidence—*e.g.*, was the declaration spontaneous, the confession voluntary, the business record trustworthy? Under this code, questions relating to the authenticity of the proffered declaration are decided under Section 403. But other preliminary fact questions are decided under Section 405.

For example, the court must decide whether a statement offered as a dying declaration was made under a sense of impending death, and the proponent of the evidence has the burden of proof on this issue. *People v. Keelin*, 136 Cal. App. 2d 860, 289 P.2d 520 (1955).

Best evidence rule. Under [this statute], as under existing law, the trial judge is required to determine the preliminary fact necessary to warrant reception of secondary evidence of a writing, and the burden of proof on the issue is on the proponent of the secondary evidence. *Cotton v. Hudson*, 42 Cal. App. 2d 812, 110 P.2d 70 (1941).

NOTES AND PROBLEMS

1. Some writers criticize the manner in which the Evidence Code drafters applied the distinction to various preliminary facts. Kaus, *All Power to the Jury—California's Democratic Evidence Code*, 4 Loy. L.A. L. Rev. 233 (1971).

California recognizes the hearsay exceptions for statements made by agents and co–conspirators. CAL. EVID. CODE §§ 1222–23. In a part of its Comment to Evidence Code § 403 we have not previously quoted, the Assembly Committee states: "[A]uthorized admissions [by an agent of a party] . . . are admitted upon the introduction of evidence sufficient to sustain a finding of the foundational fact. The admission of a co–conspirator is another form of an authorized admission. Hence, the proffered evidence is admissible upon the introduction of evidence sufficient to sustain a finding of the conspiracy." Many jurisdictions, including the federal courts, are contra and treat these preliminary issues as facts conditioning the competence of evidence rather than its logical relevance. Kaus, *supra*, at 237; *Bourjaily v. United States*, 483 U.S. 171 (1987) (excerpted *infra*).

2. There has also been criticism of the line drawn by the Supreme Court in *Huddleston v. United States*, 485 U.S. 681 (1988). In that case, under Federal Rule of Evidence 404(b), the prosecution intended to offer evidence of other crimes allegedly committed by the defendant. The question was whether the judge or the jury should decide the factual issue of the defendant's identity as the perpetrator of the other crimes. Prior to *Huddleston*, most jurisdictions assumed that the judge should resolve that question under 104(a). However, in *Huddleston*, the Court declared that the issue falls under Rule 104(b). Justice Rehnquist argued that if the jurors decide that the defendant did not commit the alleged crime, common sense will naturally lead the jurors to disregard the testimony about the crime. However, is there a risk that the jurors will suspect that "where there's smoke, there's fire"? Several commentators have called on Congress to amend Rule 104 to overrule *Huddleston*. Ordover, *Balancing the Presumptions of Guilt and Innocence: Rules 404(b), 608(b), and 609(a)*, 38 EMORY L.J. 135 (1989); Rothstein, *Needed: A Rewrite—Where the Federal Rules of Evidence Should Be Clarified*, 4 CRIM. JUST. J. 20 (Summer 1989).

A number of jurisdictions have refused to follow *Huddleston*. Minnesota amended its version of Rule 404(b) to reject *Huddleston* in criminal cases. *See also People v. Garner*, 806 P.2d 366 (Colo. 1991) (the judge should use the preponderance standard); *Phillips v. State*, 591 So. 2d 987 (Fla. Dist. Ct. App. 1991) (clear and convincing evidence); Adv. Comm'n. Comment, TENN. R. EVID. 404.

3. At this juncture, it is expected that you will find the Federal Rule 104(a)–(b) material difficult. You cannot master these materials until you understand the individual evidentiary doctrines conditioned by these preliminary facts. However, we shall use two simple problems to illustrate the procedures.

4. Problem 5–5. Assume that in the *Devitt* case, the defendant wants to introduce evidence that Paterson was grossly intoxicated at the relevant time. Assume that the hospital that treated him tested a blood sample, and that the test results show a high blood alcohol content. Defendant wants to introduce a hospital laboratory report stating that a lab technician, Peters, conducted a test on the blood sample and found a blood alcohol content of 0.19 percent. To lay the foundation, the defense attorney calls Ms. Imbau, the chief of the hospital's laboratory. On the stand, Ms. Imbau testifies that she can identify Peters' handwriting style. She says that the signature on the report "generally looks like her writing." The defendant then tenders the exhibit, but the prosecutor objects on the ground that "Your Honor, there clearly is insufficient authentication."

Is Ms. Imbau's testimony sufficient to satisfy Rule 104(b)? In other words, does the testimony have sufficient probative value to permit a rational juror to find that the document is genuine?

If it does, must the judge listen to controverting evidence from the government before admitting the exhibit? If not, when does the prosecutor present evidence attacking the document's authenticity such as testimony of a questioned document examiner that the report is forged?

Does the judge finally decide whether the document is genuine? Does the jury? If the jury makes the final decision, what should the judge tell the jury during the instructions about the authenticity of the exhibit? Word the instruction you think the judge should give.

5. Problem 5–6. Now the prosecutor objects that the report is hearsay (a statement prepared out of court by a person who is not on the witness stand now). The defendant attempts to qualify the report as a business entry. There is a recognized hearsay exception for business entries; business entries are regarded as so reliable that they are exceptionally admissible even though they fall within the definition of hearsay. One of the requirements of the business entry doctrine is that the report be prepared in the regular course of business "at or near the time" of the fact recorded. The witness, Ms. Imbau, testified to that effect; but the prosecutor has evidence from another witness, Mr. Elliot, that the lab technician who wrote the report was very inefficient and did not prepare the report until several months after the test.

Does the preliminary fact that the document was timely prepared in the regular course of business "at or near the time" of the fact recorded fall under Rule 104(a) or 104(b)?

If Rule 104(a) controls, does the judge consider only the defendant's evidence before deciding whether the document was so prepared? Assume that the witness who claims that the report was actually prepared months after the test, Mr. Elliot, is prepared to testify. Should the judge hear Mr. Elliot's testimony before ruling whether the exhibit qualifies as a business entry?

When the opponent believes that he or she has the right to present controverting evidence before the judge rules on a tender of evidence, opposing counsel asks permission to "take the witness on *voir dire* examination." We have already encountered the *voir dire* of prospective jurors. This is a second, different meaning of the expression "*voir dire*." If opposing counsel takes the witness on *voir dire*, functionally the opposing counsel conducts a cross–examination in the middle of the proponent's direct examination of the witness. Should the scope of the opposing counsel's *voir dire* be as broad as that of a normal cross–examination? If not, how would you define the proper scope?

Does the judge rule finally on this preliminary fact?

6. Problem 5–7. Remember that it is conceivable that a preliminary fact will coincide with a fact on the historical merits. For example, assume that a criminal defendant is charged with rape. Defendant claims that he was married to the complaining witness at the time of the alleged attack and, hence, under the law of his jurisdiction (Morena) he cannot be guilty of rape. Assume that under Morena's substantive criminal law, a husband cannot be convicted of raping his wife. Although the prosecutor has learned that defendant and the complaining witness went through a marriage ceremony, the prosecutor also discovered that defendant was previously married. The prosecutor believes that defendant's marriage to the complaining witness was bigamous and void. At trial, the prosecutor calls the complainant, wife number two. Defendant objects that as his wife she is incompetent to testify against him. The judge must rule on the admissibility of evidence, including the competency of witnesses. His decision turns on resolving the question of whether defendant is lawfully married to the second wife. Yet, is not that one of the very issues the jury is supposed to decide? It may be helpful to consider Federal Evidence Rule 104(c). That rule gives the judge the opportunity of ruling on the admissibility of evidence out of the jury's hearing. If the judge decided that defendant was not lawfully married to the second wife and, on that theory, permitted her to testify, should the judge inform the jury of the judge's finding of fact? Note the guidance in Cal. Evid. Code § 405(b).

7. In this section, we have suggested that the dividing line between conditional relevance facts and competence facts is our faith in the lay jurors: Can we be reasonably confident that if the jurors decide that the preliminary facts dictate the exclusion of the evidence, the jurors will be able to disregard the evidence during deliberation? Think back to the empirical studies of laypersons' ability to follow curative instructions, cited earlier. In those studies, a mock judge specifically ordered the subjects to disregard the inadmissible evidence, and the subjects still had difficulty putting the evidence out of their minds. However, are those studies apposite to this problem? In the studies, the judges directed the subjects to disregard relevant but technically inadmissible evidence such as hearsay or character testimony. In the fact situation we are now considering, the foundational fact is so fundamental that if the fact does not exist, the evidence is seemingly irrelevant.

D. THE ROLE OF THE PETIT JURORS

1. QUESTIONS OF LAW

Under early American law, jurors had power to decide questions of law. John Jay, the first Chief Justice of the United States, recognized the widespread practice of trial judges informing jurors that they had the power to ignore the judicial instructions on the law. The Jacksonian democrats supported that practice. However, since the decision in *Sparf v. United States*, 156 U.S. 51, 102 (1895), the marked trend has been toward depriving the jury of authority to decide issues of law. Thus, contemporary jurors have no formal power to decide questions of law. It is possible that in the secrecy of their deliberations they may decide to disregard the law; if they believe that the rule of law the judge described is unjust or silly, they can "nullify" the rule of law and decide the case on another basis. In some jurisdictions, nullification is misconduct and a ground for a new trial; but as we shall see, there is a shroud of secrecy which protects much of petit jury deliberations. Consequently, it is usually extremely difficult to prove that the jurors engaged in this misconduct. As a practical matter, nullification rarely occurs. Most trial judges never mention the possibility of nullification to the jurors, and they will forbid an attorney—sometimes under threat of contempt—from inviting the jury to nullify the controlling substantive law.

2. QUESTIONS OF FACT ON THE HISTORICAL MERITS

It is true that the primary role of the jury is to decide disputed questions of fact, although often juries also decide mixed questions of law and fact (*e.g.*, was the defendant negligent?). The term "fact" typically refers to the historical data relevant to adjudicating the merits of the dispute.

However, to provide an accurate picture, we must also hasten to point out that most adjudicative hearings in the United States are bench trials without a jury. In a bench hearing, the trial judge, magistrate, or administrative law judge also serves as the trier of fact.

Furthermore, juries only resolve disputed questions of fact. In some cases, the evidence on one side is so overwhelming that any rational juror would accept that evidence and enter a verdict accordingly. In these extreme cases, the facts are so clear and so one–sided that the judge may decide "as a matter of law." When she does so, the judge takes the case (or a factual issue in the case) away from the jury and announces the party's victory on the case as a whole or in part.

3. PRELIMINARY QUESTIONS OF FACT CONDITIONING ADMISSIBILITY

While the jurors' power over questions of law has waned, their power over preliminary questions of fact has increased. Today the extent of the jury's authority to resolve questions of foundational or preliminary facts turns on whether the factual issue falls under Rule 104(a) or Rule 104(b).

If the fact falls under Federal Rule 104(a), the judge's decision is normally final. In most jurisdictions, the jurors resolve only the types of factual issues falling under Federal Evidence Rule 104(b). With respect to those facts, the judge decides only whether the proponent's evidence is legally sufficient to support a finding that the fact exists. If it is, the judge admits the evidence; and the jury exercises ultimate fact–finding power to decide whether, for example, a letter was genuine. The items of evidence governed by this procedure are sometimes termed "conditionally relevant"; they are logically relevant only on the condition that they are genuine. Once the proponent fulfills the condition by presenting sufficient evidence of the letter's genuineness, the letter is admissible; and the jury can then make a final decision on the letter's authenticity.

NOTES AND PROBLEMS

1. Revisit the question we considered earlier: It is true that preliminary facts conditioning pure logical relevance are finally decided by the jurors. However, the judge must decide the preliminary facts conditioning almost all other evidentiary doctrines—the opinion rule, best evidence, hearsay, and privilege. If these issues are preliminary "facts," why allocate the decisionmaking authority to the judge? We earlier viewed the allocation as a reflection of our view of the jurors' limited capacity. Now consider another rationale, the related administrative problems. If the jury had to decide these preliminary questions, how would that affect the conduct of the trial? If the jurors reserved all their determinations of preliminary facts until the jury deliberations, how would that affect the complexity of the final jury deliberations? What "mental gymnastics" would the jurors have to engage in? Maguire & Epstein, *Preliminary Questions of Fact in Determining the Admissibility of Evidence*, 40 HARV. L. REV. 392 (1927).

2. Problem 5–8. In *Devitt,* the prosecutor has a signed confession by the defendant. In the confession, Devitt admits that he attacked Paterson with his knife. Morena procedure permits Devitt to delay his objection until the time of trial. Devitt does so. When the prosecutor attempts to elicit the confession from the interrogating officer, Devitt objects on voluntariness grounds. To support his objection, Devitt takes the stand and testifies that just before the interrogation he had experienced sharp abdominal pains; he had taken some sedatives to ease the pain; he was groggy when the questioning began; during the questioning, the police refused to let him go to the bathroom; and he finally gave the police the admissions they wanted after they threatened him with violence. The interrogating officer denies Devitt's charges. Who should decide the preliminary fact of the confession's voluntariness? In addition to analyzing this question under California Evidence Code §§ 403 and 405, consider the constitutional dimension of the problem. *See Jackson v. Denno*, 378 U.S. 368 (1964). When should the opponent's common law right to a decision by the judge on a preliminary fact be elevated to constitutional stature?

E.   PROOF OF FOUNDATIONAL FACTS

Note one final, peculiar provision in Rule 104(a). The last sentence reads: "In making its determination [the court] is not bound by the rules of evidence except those with respect to privilege." At first blush, it seems heretical and self–contradictory for an evidence code to dispense with compliance with evidentiary rules. What is the meaning of that sentence? The Supreme Court explored that question in the following case.

BOURJAILY v. UNITED STATES

483 U.S. 171 (1987)

CHIEF JUSTICE REHNQUIST delivered the opinion of the Court.

Federal Rule of Evidence 801(d)(2)(E) provides, "A statement is not hearsay if . . . [t]he statement is offered against a party and is . . . a statement by a coconspirator of a party during the course and in furtherance of the conspiracy." We granted certiorari to answer [two] questions regarding the admission of statements under Rule 801(d)(2)(E): (1) whether the court must determine by independent evidence that the conspiracy existed and that the defendant and the declarant were members of this conspiracy; [and] (2) the quantum of proof on which such determinations must be based.

In May 1984, Clarence Greathouse, an informant working for the Federal Bureau of Investigation, arranged to sell a kilogram of cocaine to Angelo Lonardo. Lonardo agreed that he would find individuals to distribute the drug. When the sale became imminent, Lonardo stated in a tape–recorded telephone conversation that he had a "gentleman friend" who had some questions to ask about the cocaine. In a subsequent telephone call, Greathouse spoke to the "friend" about the quality of the drug and the price. Greathouse then spoke again with Lonardo, and the two arranged the details of the purchase. They agreed that the sale would take place in a designated hotel parking lot, and Lonardo would transfer the drug from Greathouse's car to the "friend," who would be waiting in the parking lot in his own car. Greathouse proceeded with the transaction as planned, and FBI agents arrested Lonardo and petitioner immediately after Lonardo placed a kilogram of cocaine into petitioner's car in the hotel parking lot. In petitioner's car, the agents found over $20,000 in cash.

Petitioner was charged with conspiring to distribute cocaine, in violation of 21 U.S.C. § 846, and possession of cocaine with intent to distribute, a violation of 21 U.S.C. § 841(a)(1). The Government introduced, over petitioner's objection, Angelo Lonardo's telephone statements regarding the participation of the "friend" in the transaction. The District Court found that, considering the events in the parking lot and Lonardo's statements over the telephone, the Government had established by a preponderance of the evidence that a conspiracy involving Lonardo and petitioner existed, and that Lonardo's statements over the telephone had been made in the course of and in furtherance of the conspiracy. Accordingly, the trial court held that Lonardo's out–of–court statements satisfied Rule 801(d)(2)(E) and were not hearsay. Petitioner was convicted on both counts. The United States Court of Appeals for the Sixth Circuit affirmed.

Before admitting a co–conspirator's statement over an objection that it does not qualify under Rule 801(d)(2)(E), a court must be satisfied that the statement actually falls within the definition of the rule. There must be evidence that there was a conspiracy involving the declarant and the nonoffering party, and that the statement was made "in the course and in furtherance of the conspiracy." Federal Rule of Evidence 104(a) provides: "Preliminary questions concerning . . . the admissibility of evidence shall be determined by the court." Petitioner and respondent agree that the existence of a conspiracy and petitioner's involvement in it are preliminary questions of fact that, under Rule 104, must be resolved by the court. The Federal Rules, however, nowhere define the standard of proof the court must observe in resolving these questions.

We are therefore guided by our prior decisions regarding admissibility determinations that hinge on preliminary factual questions. We have traditionally required that these matters be established by a preponderance of proof. Evidence is placed before the jury when it satisfies the technical requirements of the evidentiary Rules, which embody certain legal and policy determinations. The inquiry made by a court concerned with these matters is not whether the proponent of the evidence wins or loses his case on the merits, but whether the evidentiary Rules have been satisfied. Thus, the evidentiary standard is unrelated to the burden of proof on the substantive issues, be it a criminal case, see *In re Winship,* 397 U.S. 358 (1970), or a civil case. The preponderance standard ensures that before admitting evidence, the court will have found it more likely than not that the technical issues and policy concerns addressed by the Federal Rules of Evidence have been afforded due consideration. We think that our previous decisions in this area resolve the matter. *See, e.g., Colorado v. Connelly,* 479 U.S. 157 (1986) (preliminary fact that custodial confessant waived rights must be proved by preponderance of the evidence); *Nix v. Williams,* 467 U.S. 431, 444, n.5 (1984) (inevitable discovery of illegally seized evidence must be shown to have been more likely than not); *United States v. Matlock,* 415 U.S. 164 (1974) (voluntariness of consent to search must be shown by preponderance of the evidence); *Lego v. Twomey,* 404 U.S. 477 (1972) (voluntariness of confession must be demonstrated by a preponderance of the evidence). Therefore, we hold that when the preliminary facts relevant to Rule 801(d)(2)(E) are disputed, the offering party must prove them by a preponderance of the evidence.

Even though petitioner agrees that the courts below applied the proper standard of proof with regard to the preliminary facts relevant to Rule 801(d)(2)(E), he nevertheless challenges the admission of Lonardo's statements. Petitioner argues that in determining whether a conspiracy exists and whether the defendant was a member of it, the court must look only to independent evidence—that is, evidence other than the statements sought to be admitted. Petitioner relies on *Glasser v. United States,* 315 U.S. 60 (1942), in which this Court first mentioned the so–called "bootstrapping rule." The relevant issue in *Glasser* was whether Glasser's counsel, who also represented another defendant, faced such a conflict of interest that Glasser received ineffective assistance. Glasser contended that conflicting loyalties led his lawyer not to object to statements made by one of Glasser's co–conspirators. The Government argued that any objection would have been fruitless because the statements were admissible. The Court rejected this proposition:

> "[S]uch declarations are admissible over the objection of an alleged co–conspirator, who was not present when they were made, only if there is proof *aliunde* that he is connected with the conspiracy . . . . Otherwise, hearsay would lift itself by its own bootstraps to the level of competent evidence." *Id.,* at 74–75.

The Court revisited the bootstrapping rule in *United States v. Nixon,* 418 U.S. 683 (1974), where again, in passing, the Court stated, "Declarations by one defendant may also be admissible against other defendants upon a sufficient showing, *by independent evidence,* of a conspiracy among one or more other defendants and the declarant and if the declarations at issue were in furtherance of that conspiracy." *Id.,* at 701, and n.14 (emphasis added) . . . . Read in the light most favorable to petitioner, *Glasser* could mean that a court should not consider hearsay statements at all in determining preliminary facts under Rule 801(d)(2)(E). Petitioner, of course, adopts this view of the bootstrapping rule. *Glasser*, however, could also mean that a court must have *some* proof *aliunde*, but may look at the hearsay statements themselves in light of this independent evidence to determine whether a conspiracy has been shown by a preponderance of the evidence. The Courts of Appeals have widely adopted the former view and held that in determining the preliminary facts relevant to co–conspirators' out–of–court statements, a court may not look at the hearsay statements themselves for their evidentiary value.

Both *Glasser* and *Nixon*, however, were decided before Congress enacted the Federal Rules of Evidence in 1975. These Rules now govern the treatment of evidentiary questions in federal courts. Rule 104(a) provides: "Preliminary questions concerning . . . the admissibility of evidence shall be determined by the court. . . . In making its determination it is not bound by the rules of evidence except those with respect to privileges." Similarly, Rule 1101(d)(1) states that the Rules of Evidence (other than with respect to privileges) shall not apply to "[t]he determination of questions of fact preliminary to admissibility of evidence when the issue is to be determined by the court under rule 104." The question thus presented is whether any aspect of *Glasser's* bootstrapping rule remains viable after the enactment of the Federal Rules of Evidence.

Petitioner concedes that Rule 104, on its face, appears to allow the court to make the preliminary factual determinations relevant to Rule 801(d)(2)(E) by considering any evidence it wishes, unhindered by considerations of admissibility. [However,] petitioner claims that Congress evidenced no intent to disturb the bootstrapping rule, which was embedded in the previous approach, and we should not find that Congress altered the rule without affirmative evidence so indicating. It would be extraordinary to require legislative history to *confirm* the plain meaning of Rule 104. The Rule on its face allows the trial judge to consider any evidence whatsoever, bound only by the rules of privilege. We think that the Rule is sufficiently clear that to the extent that it is inconsistent with petitioner's interpretation of *Glasser* and *Nixon,* the Rule prevails.[2]

We think that there is little doubt that a co–conspirator's statements could themselves be probative of the existence of a conspiracy and the participation of both the defendant and the declarant in the conspiracy. Petitioner's case presents a paradigm. The out–of–court statements of Lonardo indicated that Lonardo was involved in a conspiracy with a "friend." The statements indicated that the friend had agreed with Lonardo to buy a kilogram of cocaine

---

[2] The Advisory Committee Notes show that the Rule was not adopted in a fit of absent–mindedness. The Note to Rule 104 specifically addresses the process by which a federal court should make the factual determinations requisite to a finding of admissibility:

"'Should the exclusionary law of evidence, "the child of the jury system" in Thayer's phrase, be applied to this hearing before the judge? Sound sense backs the view that it should not, and that the judge should be empowered to hear *any relevant evidence,* such as affidavits or *other reliable hearsay.*'" 28 U.S.C. App., p. 681 (emphasis added).

The Advisory Committee further noted, "An item, offered and objected to, *may itself be considered in ruling on admissibility,* though not yet admitted in evidence." *Ibid.* (emphasis added). We think this language makes plain the drafters' intent to abolish any kind of bootstrapping rule. Silence is at best ambiguous, and we decline the invitation to rely on speculation to import ambiguity into what is otherwise a clear rule.

and to distribute it. The statements also revealed that the friend would be at the hotel parking lot, in his car, and would accept the cocaine from Greathouse's car after Greathouse gave Lonardo the keys. Each one of Lonardo's statements may itself be unreliable, but taken as a whole, the entire conversation between Lonardo and Greathouse was corroborated by independent evidence. The friend, who turned out to be petitioner, showed up at the prearranged spot at the prearranged time. He picked up the cocaine, and a significant sum of money was found in his car. On these facts, the trial court concluded, in our view correctly, that the Government had established the existence of a conspiracy and petitioner's participation in it.

We need not decide in this case whether the courts below could have relied solely upon Lonardo's hearsay statements to determine that a conspiracy had been established by a preponderance of the evidence. To the extent that *Glasser* meant that courts could not look to the hearsay statements themselves for any purpose, it has clearly been superseded by Rule 104(a). It is sufficient for today to hold that a court, in making a preliminary factual determination under Rule 801(d)(2)(E), may examine the hearsay statements sought to be admitted.

The judgment of the Court of Appeals is

Affirmed.

JUSTICE STEVENS filed a concurring opinion.

JUSTICE BLACKMUN, with whom JUSTICE BRENNAN and JUSTICE MARSHALL join, dissenting.

I disagree with the Court: I do not believe that the Federal Rules of Evidence changed the long–and well–settled law to the effect that the preliminary questions of fact, relating to admissibility of a nontestifying co–conspirator's statement, must be established by evidence independent of that statement itself. . . .

I agree that a federal rule's "plain meaning," when it appears, should not be lightly ignored or dismissed. The inclination to accept what seems to be the immediate reading of a federal rule, however, must be tempered with caution when, as in the case of a Federal Rule of Evidence, the rule's complex interrelations with other rules must be understood before one can resolve a particular interpretive problem. *See generally* Cleary, *Preliminary Notes on Reading the Rules of Evidence*, 57 NEB. L. REV. 908, 908 (1978) ("the answers to all questions that may arise under the Rules may not be found in specific terms in the Rules"). In addition, if the language of a rule plainly appears to address a specific problem, one *naturally* would expect legislative history (if it exists) to confirm this plain meaning. In this case, Rule 104(a) cannot be read apart from Rule 801(d)(2)(E), which was a codification of the common–law exemption of co–conspirator statements from the hearsay definition, an exemption that included the independent evidence requirement. An examination of the legislative history of Rule 801(d)(2)(E) reveals that neither the drafters nor Congress intended to transform this requirement in any way. In sum, the Court espouses an overly rigid interpretive approach; a more complete analysis casts significant and substantial doubt on the Court's "plain meaning" easy solution.

In order to understand why the Federal Rules of Evidence adopted without change the common–law co–conspirator exemption from hearsay, and why this adoption signified the Advisory Committee's intent to retain the exemption's independent–evidence requirement, it is useful to review briefly the contours of this exemption as it stood before enactment of the Rules. By all accounts, the exemption was based upon agency principles, the underlying concept being that a conspiracy is a common undertaking where the conspirators are all agents of each other and where the acts and statements of one can be attributed to all. *See* 4 J. WEINSTEIN & M. BERGER, WEINSTEIN'S EVIDENCE ¶ 801(d)(2)(E)[01], pp. 801–232 and–233 (1985) (Weinstein & Berger); Davenport, *The Confrontation Clause and the Co–Conspirator Exception in Criminal Prosecutions: A Functional Analysis*, 85 Harv. L. Rev. 1378, 1384 (1972) (Davenport).

Each of the components of this common–law exemption, in turn, had an agency justification. To fall within the exemption, the co–conspirator's statement had to be made "in furtherance of" the conspiracy, a requirement that arose from the agency rationale that an agent's acts or words could be attributed to his principal only so long as the agent was acting within the scope of his employment. *See* Levie, *Hearsay and Conspiracy: A Reexamination of the Co–Conspirators' Exception to the Hearsay Rule*, 52 MICH. L. REV. 1159, 1161 (1954) (Levie); 4 D. LOUISELL & C. MUELLER, FEDERAL EVIDENCE § 427, p. 348 (1980) (LOUISELL & MUELLER). The statement also had to be made "during the course of" the conspiracy. This feature necessarily accompanies the "in furtherance of" requirement, for there must be an employment or business relationship in effect between the agent and principal, in accordance with which the agent is acting, for the principal to be bound by his agent's deeds or words. *See* Levie, . . . at 1161; 4 LOUISELL & MUELLER, at 337.

The final feature of the co–conspirator exemption, the independent–evidence requirement, directly corresponds to the agency concept that an agent's statement cannot be used alone to prove the existence of the agency relationship.

> "Evidence of a statement by an agent concerning the existence or extent of his authority is not admissible against the principal to prove its existence or intent, unless it appears *by other evidence* that the making of such statement was within the authority of the agent or as to persons dealing with the agent, within the apparent authority or other power of the agent" (emphasis added). Restatement (Second) of Agency § 285 (1957).

See Levie, . . . at 1161.

Thus, unlike many common–law hearsay exceptions, the co–conspirator exemption from hearsay with its agency rationale was not based primarily upon any particular guarantees of reliability or trustworthiness that were intended to ensure the truthfulness of the admitted statement and to compensate for the fact that a party would not have the opportunity to test its veracity by cross–examining the declarant. *See* Davenport, . . . at 1384. As such, this exemption was considered to be a "vicarious admission." Although not an admission by a defendant himself, the vicarious admission was a statement imputed to the defendant from the co–conspirator on the basis of their agency relationship.

Although, under common law, the reliability of the co–conspirator's statement was never the primary ground justifying its admissibility, there was
some recognition that this exemption from the hearsay rule had certain
guarantees of trustworthiness, albeit limited ones. This justification for the
exemption has been explained:

> "Active conspirators are likely to know who the members of the
> conspiracy are and what they have done. When speaking to advance
> the conspiracy, they are unlikely to describe non–members as conspir-
> ators, and they usually will have no incentive to misdescribe the
> actions of their fellow members." R. LEMPERT & S. SALTZBURG, A
> MODERN APPROACH TO EVIDENCE 395 (2d ed. 1982).

See also 4 J. WIGMORE, EVIDENCE § 1080a, p. 199 (Chadbourn rev. 1972) ("the
general idea of receiving vicarious admissions, is that where the third person
was, at the time of speaking, in *circumstances that gave him substantially the
same interest* to know something about the matter in hand as had the now
opponent, and the *same motive* to make a statement about it, that person's
statements have approximately the same testimonial value as if the now
opponent had made them"). And the components of the exemption were
understood to contribute to this reliability. When making a statement "during
the course of" and "in furtherance of" a conspiracy, a conspirator could be
viewed as speaking from the perspective of all the conspirators in order to
achieve the common goals of the conspiracy, not from self–serving motives.
See Davenport, . . . at 1387. In particular, the requirement that a conspiracy
be established by independent evidence also is seen to contribute to the
reliability issue.

The Federal Rules of Evidence did not alter in any way this common–law
exemption to hearsay. The Rules essentially codify the components of this
exemption: Rule 801(d)(2)(E) provides that the co–conspirator's statement, to
be admissible against a party, must be "by a coconspirator of a party during
the course and in furtherance of the conspiracy." Moreover, the exemption was
placed within the category of "not hearsay," as an admission, in contrast to
the hearsay exceptions of Rules 803 and 804.

More importantly, by explicitly retaining the agency rationale for the
exemption, the Advisory Committee expressed its intention that the exemption would remain identical to the common–law rule and that it would not
be expanded in any way. The Advisory Committee . . . thought that the traditional exemption appropriately balanced the prosecution's need for a co–
conspirator's statements and the defendant's need for the protections against
unreliable statements, protections provided by the components of the common–law exemption. *See* 4 Weinstein & Berger, ¶ 801(d)(2)(E)[01], p. 801–
235. The Advisory Committee, however, expressed its doubts about the agency
rationale and, on the basis of these doubts, plainly stated that the exemption
should not be changed or extended: "the agency theory of conspiracy is at best
a fiction and ought not to serve as a basis for admissibility beyond that already
established." Advisory Committee's Notes on Fed. Rule Evid. 801, 28 U.S.C.
App., p. 718, 56 F.R.D., at 299. In light of this intention *not* to alter the
common–law exemption, the Advisory Committee's Notes thus make very

clear that Rule 801(d)(2)(E) was to include *all* the components of this exemption, including the independent–evidence requirement.

Accordingly, when Rule 801(d)(2)(E) and Rule 104(a) are considered together—an examination that the Court neglects to undertake—there appears to be a conflict between the fact that no change in the co–conspirator hearsay exemption was intended by Rule 801(d)(2)(E) and the freedom that Rule 104(a) gives a trial court to rely on hearsay in resolving preliminary factual questions. Although one must be somewhat of an interpretative funambulist to walk between the conflicting demands of these Rules in order to arrive at a resolution that will satisfy their respective concerns, this effort is far to be preferred over accepting the easily available safety "net" of Rule 104(a)'s "plain meaning." The purpose of *both* Rules can be achieved by considering the relevant preliminary factual question for Rule 104(a) analysis to be the following: "whether a conspiracy that included the declarant and the defendant against whom a statement is offered has been demonstrated to exist on the basis of evidence *independent of the declarant's hearsay statements*" (emphasis added). SALTZBURG & REDDEN, FEDERAL RULES OF EVIDENCE MANUAL 735 (4th ed. 1986). This resolution sufficiently answers Rule 104(a)'s concern with allowing a trial court to consider hearsay in determining preliminary factual questions, because the only hearsay not available for its consideration is the statement at issue. The exclusion of the statement from the preliminary analysis maintains the common–law exemption unchanged.

As the Court recognizes, in the more than 10 years since the enactment of the Federal Rules of Evidence, the Courts of Appeals, almost uniformly, have found no conflict between Rule 104(a) and the independent evidence requirement understood to adhere in Rule 801(d)(2)(E). Indeed, some courts have rejected the suggestion that Rule 104(a) has changed this component of the common law exemption, because, like the Advisory Committee, they recognize the incremental protection against unreliable statements that this requirement gives to defendants. *See, e.g., United States v. Bell*, 573 F.2d 1040, 1044 (CA8 1978). Yet the Court cavalierly disregards these years of interpretative experience, as well as the rich history of this exemption, and arrives at its conclusion solely on the basis of its "plain meaning" approach.

NOTES

1. At least a substantial minority of jurisdictions follow the contrary view that the technical exclusionary rules of evidence apply to foundational testimony. Some jurisdictions give the trial judge discretion as to whether to apply the technical exclusionary rules to foundational testimony. *Utah State Dep't. of Social Services v. Ruscetta*, 742 P.2d 114 (Utah. App. 1987).

2. Why dispense with compliance with the exclusionary rules under Rule 104(a)? Who makes the final ruling on questions of fact falling under Rule 104(a)—the judge or the jurors? Who makes the final ruling on questions of fact falling under Rule 104(b)?

Chapter 6

OVERVIEW: A CONCEPTUAL FRAMEWORK

Evidence law is a vast subject and it is easy to become lost in its mass of detail. For that reason, before beginning our study of specific evidentiary doctrines, we pause to consider the conceptual framework of evidence law. If the student can develop an overview of evidence law, the individual doctrines will make more sense and the student will better understand the application of evidence law.

Despite the enormous body of American evidence law, it is reducible to a simple analytic framework. First, is this individual item of evidence *admissible*? Second, considered cumulatively, are all the party's items of evidence *sufficient* to prove the fact in issue?

ADMISSIBILITY

Admissibility is the threshold question. To qualify for admission, an individual item of evidence must clear several hurdles. Initially, the item of evidence must originate from **a competent witness**. Even if the prospective witness' proposed testimony is otherwise unobjectionable, the judge may exclude all the proposed testimony on the ground that the person is incompetent to be a witness. The common law established certain moral and mental requirements for witnesses in the courtroom; some persons could not testify because they belonged to an excluded class of witnesses.

If the judge concludes that the prospective witness is competent, the next barrier is establishing the **logical relevance** of the item of evidence. We shift from the witness' personal qualifications to the content of the witness' proposed testimony. To be relevant, testimony must have probative value in two senses. First, on its face, the evidence must have some logical connection with the facts in dispute in the case. The item of evidence must have a tendency, in reason, to increase or decrease the probability that one of the disputed facts exists.

Second, the evidence must be shown to be authentic. Anglo-American evidentiary doctrine is imbued with a spirit of skepticism; rather than accepting evidence at face value, our evidentiary doctrine insists that the proponent (the person offering evidence) prove that it is what that person claims it to be. Thus, if a contract plaintiff claims that an exhibit is a letter written by the defendant, the plaintiff must ordinarily present some testimony to prove that the document is what its proponent claims it is.

Even if the evidence has logical relevance, the judge may exercise discretion to exclude the evidence on the ground that the evidence is **legally irrelevant**. While the logical relevance doctrine focuses on the evidence's probative value, the legal irrelevance doctrine analyzes the question of whether there are countervailing probative dangers that outweigh the bare probative value. The foremost probative danger is that the evidence is unfairly "prejudicial"; that is, the item of evidence may tempt the jury to decide the case on an improper basis. Our system of law is committed to the policy that the jury must decide the case on a proper basis. For example, in a criminal case, the jury may properly find the defendant guilty only if the jurors are convinced beyond a reasonable doubt that the defendant committed the specific crime alleged in the indictment or information. The underlying policy judgment is that it is illegitimate for the jury to convict simply because the jury believes that the defendant is a bad person from whom society should be protected. Given that policy, the judge may exclude evidence of the defendant's past criminal record as legally irrelevant. To be sure, the evidence is logically relevant in the case; there is a high rate of recidivism among criminals. However, the admission of the evidence can create an intolerable risk that the jury will misuse the evidence and return a guilty finding on an improper basis. Other probative dangers include the risks of distracting or confusing the jury or wasting the court's time. The legal irrelevance doctrine attempts to shield the trier of fact from evidence which may cause the trier to commit an inferential error in evaluating the testimony.

Another hurdle to admissibility is *a set of competence doctrines based on the supposed unreliability of certain types of evidence*. The evidentiary doctrine many laypersons are most familiar with is the hearsay rule. The rule sometimes excludes in-court testimony about out-of-court statements; the rule may prevent the witness on the stand from testifying about a statement that the witness or someone else made outside the courtroom. The rationale for the rule is our preference for evidence the reliability of which has been, or can be, subjected to the test of cross-examination. This set of doctrines, most notably, the best evidence rule, hearsay and opinion, restrict a witness' ability to paraphrase documents, relate statements made outside the courtroom, and express conclusions.

Extrinsic social policy can also lead to the exclusion of evidence. These policies have led to the development of rules such as the privilege for confidential communications between client and attorney. While the legal irrelevance doctrine focuses on the behavior of the trier of fact, privileges target the behavior of persons outside the courtroom. Privileged communications may be highly relevant and are usually quite reliable. When a judge excludes evidence on grounds of privilege, it is done to promote the extrinsic social policy of protecting the sanctity of certain relationships, such as attorney-client. Courts reason that society values this relationship and that the relationship needs an assurance of confidentiality to be effective. The attorney cannot represent the client effectively unless the client tells the attorney everything, and the client will be reluctant to be candid unless there is some assurance that what the client tells the attorney will remain secret. The exclusion of the relevant evidence is part of the social cost of the policy of protecting the relationship. In short, even if evidence passes muster under both the logical and legal relevance requirements, extrinsic social policy can render the evidence inadmissible.

SUFFICIENCY

Assume now that the individual item of evidence comes from a competent witness; is logically and legally relevant; and does not run afoul of any rules such as privilege or hearsay. If the proponent conquers all these hurdles, the procedural consequence is that the judge will admit the individual item of evidence. The case still may not go to the jury; the judge may grant a "directed verdict" or, as it is now called in federal procedure, judgment as a matter of law (FED. R. CIV. P. 50). Why? Because although the judge admits a party's individual items of evidence, the judge may conclude that when considered together, that party's items of evidence have *insufficient* probative value to support a judgment in that party's favor. For instance, assume that in a negligence action, the plaintiff presents admissible evidence that there was a collision between the plaintiff and defendant and that the plaintiff suffered personal injuries in the collision. The judge might admit every item of evidence the plaintiff offers. However, the judge could still enter judgment for the defendant before the case ever goes to the jury; if the plaintiff presents no evidence of the defendant's carelessness, the judge must take the case away from the jury and peremptorily announce the defendant's victory.

To determine whether a party has made out a submissible case for the jury, the judge asks this question: If the jury accepts all this evidence on face value, does the evidence have enough cumulative probative worth to sustain a rational verdict in that party's favor under the substantive law? A party cannot be content with offering admissible, individual items of evidence; the party must present evidence with sufficient cumulative probative value to get to the jury. There are admittedly other ways of proving facts; the judge can judicially notice some facts, and parties often stipulate that certain facts exist. However, in most instances, the party must prove the fact with evidence, and that evidence must satisfy the *sufficiency* rules as well as the *admissibility* standards.

ORGANIZATION

Learning the conceptual framework of a course is of enduring value. Long after the student forgets many of the specific, individual rules, the student will remember the framework — the analytical approach to evidentiary problems. This outline is both an overview of evidence law and a summary of the chapters of this text.

A CONCEPTUAL FRAMEWORK FOR THE COURSEBOOK

OVERVIEW

CASE FILES

ADMISSIBILITY

SUFFICIENCY

CONSTITUTIONAL QUESTIONS

Part 6: Constitutional Overrides to the Rules of Evidence

Part 2

CASE FILES

CIVIL CASE FILE—*HILL v. ROE &
POLECAT MOTORS*

CRIMINAL CASE FILE—*STATE v. DEVITT*

Civil Case File

CIVIL CASE FILE—*HILL v. ROE & POLECAT MOTORS*

TRAFFIC ACCIDENT REPORT — POLICE

POLICE ACCIDENT NO. A38771   INCIDENT NUMBER

716375

ON Number or Name of Highway or Street: MISSOURI ST.
COUNTY: EL DORADO   TOWNSHIP OR CITY: EL DORADO

At Intersection With: ILLINOIS
If Not At Intersection: ___ Feet ___ Miles N E S W of (Nearest Highway, Street, Bridge or Other Landmark)

DATE OF ACCIDENT MO. DAY YR. 9/15/YR
TIME OF ACCIDENT 4:00 PM
DAY OF THE WEEK M T W T(F)S S
TOTAL UNITS INVOLVED 2

TYPE OF REPORT (CIRCLE ONE OR MORE)
1 Conventional 2 Private Property 3 Animal 4 Hit and Run 5 Freeway or Expressway
Fatal / Property Damage / Arrest / Supplemental

PASSENGERS AND/OR WITNESSES
NAME: HILL, CINDY   INJ CODE
ADDRESS: 123 MEADOW LN.
CITY: JEFFERSON STATE: MOR.
AGE: 26 SEX: F   UNIT NO. 8 SEAT POS. 3 SAF. EQPT. TAKEN TO: COUNTY HOSP. TAKEN BY: AMBULANCE

NAME: SMITH, ROBERT   INJ CODE K
ADDRESS: 200 SO. ILLINOIS
CITY: JEFFERSON STATE: MOR.

Driver / Vehicle 3
DRIVER'S NAME: HILL, DEBRA
DATE OF BIRTH: 1/20/YR
ADDRESS: 123 MEADOW LN.
CITY/STATE/ZIP/PHONE: JEFFERSON, MORENA MOR. OP.
DRIVER'S LICENSE NO: K-521-2404-9039   CLASSIFICATION: OP.   RESTRICTIONS
VEHICLE TYPE: 4 DOOR SEDAN   MAKE: POLECAT   COLOR: L. BLUE   YEAR 19YR   MODEL: POLECAT
VEHICLE OWNER: ARTHUR/DEBRA HILL
OWNER'S ADDRESS: 123 MEADOW LN. JEFFERSON
VEHICLE REMOVED BY: ACME TOWING
TOTAL OCC. UNIT 1 Including Driver: 2
VEH. REGIST. STATE: MOR. TAG NO: K1001   YEAR: APRIL/YR
1. DRIVEN AWAY 2. TOWED AWAY
CIRCLE POINT OF CONTACT
APPROX. COST TO REPAIR OR REPLACE: UNDER $250 / OVER $250 / TOTAL
IF WITNESS, PLACE IN UNIT NO. BOX

Driver / Vehicle 6
DRIVER'S NAME: WORKER, RALPH   PEDESTRIAN
DATE OF BIRTH: 3/3/YR
ADDRESS: 456 STATE ST.
CITY/STATE/ZIP/PHONE: JEFFERSON, MORENA MOR. CH
DRIVER'S LICENSE NO: W-581-2606-4432   CLASSIFICATION: CH   RESTRICTIONS
VEHICLE TYPE: PICKUP   MAKE: FORD   COLOR: RED   YEAR 19YR   MODEL: WORKHORSE
VEHICLE OWNER: JACK ROE
OWNER'S ADDRESS: 789 CAPITOL AVE. EL DORADO, MORENA
VEHICLE REMOVED BY: ACME TOWING   OWNER
TOTAL OCC. UNIT 2 Including Driver: ONE
VEH. REGIST. STATE: MOR. TAG NO: B2003   YEAR: JUNE/YR
1. DRIVEN AWAY 2. TOWED AWAY
APPROX. COST TO REPAIR OR REPLACE

CODE FOR INJURY Use only most serious one in each space for injury.
X 0 No indication of injury
A ...
B ...
C ...

SEATING IN VEHICLE
1 2 3 / 4 5 6 / 7 8 9   STATION WAGON

SAFETY EQUIPMENT USE
0 - UNKNOWN, NOT STATED
1 - SAFETY BELTS USED
2 - SAFETY BELTS—NOT USED
3 - HELMET USED
4 - HELMET PRESENT—NOT USED
5 - CHILD RESTRAINT USED
6 - CHILD RESTRAINT USED—NOT BELTED
7 - CHILD RESTRAINT PRESENT—NOT USED
8 - AIR BAG ACTIVATED

DAMAGE TO PROPERTY OTHER THAN VEHICLE
NAME OF OWNER OF PROPERTY
ADDRESS OF OWNER
NATURE OF DAMAGE

TIME NOTIFIED OF ACCIDENT: 4:05 PM
ARRIVED AT SCENE: 4:08 PM
DATE NOTIFIED OF ACCIDENT: 5/15/YR
DATE REPORT COMPLETED: 5/17/YR

OFFICER (NAME)
REVIEWING OFFICER
TICKET NUMBER
SECTION NUMBER
BEAT/ZONE
ID NUMBER
COURT DATE

Sheet ___ of ___ Sheets
I.D.O.T. USE ONLY

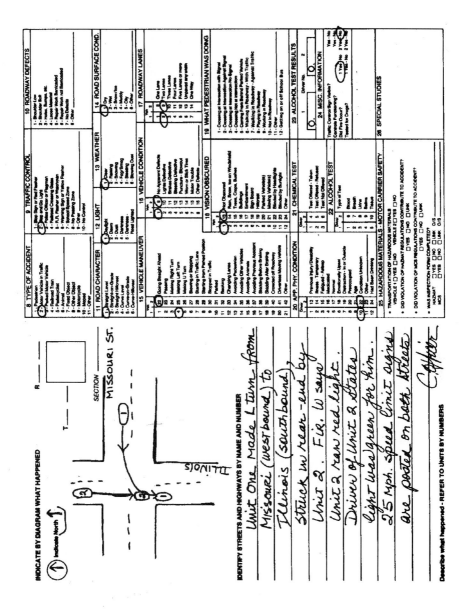

IN THE CIRCUIT COURT
FIRST JUDICIAL CIRCUIT
EL DORADO, MORENA

DEBRA HILL, individually and as Administrator of the Estate of Cindy Hill, Deceased, Plaintiff, vs. JACK ROE AND POLECAT MOTORS, INC., a corporation, Defendants.	Civil No. 12345

COMPLAINT

COUNT ONE

[Hill v. Roe]
[Negligence—Personal Injury]

DEBRA HILL, complaining of JACK ROE, alleges:

1. On May 15, 19YR, at approximately 4:00 p.m., Debra Hill was operating a 19YR Polecat automobile in a westerly direction on Missouri Street in the city of El Dorado, state of Morena.

2. Cindy Hill, then eight years of age and the daughter of Debra Hill, was a passenger in the automobile.

3. The Hill automobile entered the intersection of Missouri Street and Illinois Avenue and made a left turn from Missouri Street to the southbound lanes of Illinois Avenue.

4. At that same time and place, Ralph Worker was operating a truck in a southerly direction on Illinois Avenue.

5. At that time and place, Ralph Worker was an agent, servant, and employee of Jack Roe, d/b/a Roe Construction Company, and Ralph Worker was then and there acting in the course and scope of his employment.

6. At that time and place, and immediately prior thereto, Ralph Worker was negligent in one or more of the following ways:

a. He was operating his vehicle at a speed in excess of the posted speed limit and too fast for existing conditions, in violation of Morena Rev. Stat. c. 100, § 11–601;

b. He failed to obey a traffic control device, i.e., a red traffic light, in violation of Morena Rev. Stat. c. 100, § 11–305;

c. He failed to keep a proper lookout as he approached and entered the intersection.

7. As a direct and proximate result of one or more of the foregoing negligent acts, the truck being operated by Ralph Worker collided with great force with the Hill automobile immediately after the Hill automobile had completed its turn onto Illinois Avenue.

8. As a direct and proximate result of this collision, Debra Hill and Cindy Hill were thrown about the inside of the Hill automobile; and the fuel tank of the Hill automobile became distorted, disconnected, and ruptured; and gasoline and gasoline vapor entered the interior of the automobile and ignited.

9. As a direct and proximate result of the foregoing, Debra Hill was injured in the following ways:

a. She suffered a broken right arm;

b. She sustained numerous cuts, abrasions, and contusions;

c. She was severely burned over a large part of her body;

d. She has experienced severe physical and mental pain and suffering, and she will continue to experience severe physical and mental pain and suffering in the future;

e. She has been required to expend large sums for medical, doctor, and hospital bills and she will incur such expenses in the future;

f. She has lost earnings and will lose earnings in the future;

g. She has become disfigured and will remain disfigured;

h. She has been hospitalized for extended periods of time and has had to undergo surgery on several occasions;

i. She has been deprived of the ability to engage in the various activities of life, either entirely or to the extent she was able prior to her injuries.

WHEREFORE, DEBRA HILL prays judgment against JACK ROE in a sum which will fairly, adequately, and justly compensate her for her injuries, plus costs of this suit, and demands trial by jury.

COUNT TWO

[Debra Hill, Admr. of Est. of Cindy Hill v. Roe]
[Negligence—Wrongful Death]

DEBRA HILL, as Administrator of the Estate of Cindy Hill, Deceased, complaining of JACK ROE, alleges:

1. Plaintiff realleges paragraphs 1 through 8, inclusive, of Count One as similarly numbered paragraphs of this Count Two.

9. As a direct and proximate result of the foregoing, Cindy Hill was injured in the following ways:

a. She sustained numerous cuts, abrasions, and contusions;

b. She was severely burned over a large part of her body;

c. She experienced severe physical and mental pain and suffering;

d. She incurred medical, doctor, and hospital bills.

10. As a direct and proximate result of the foregoing, Cindy Hill died approximately 36 hours after the occurrence described.

11. Cindy Hill is survived by her mother, Debra Hill, and her father, Arthur Hill, as her next of kin.

12. As a direct and proximate result of the death of Cindy Hill, her next of kin:

a. Have been deprived of the support and services which Cindy Hill would have provided them but for her death;

b. Have been deprived of the society, companionship, love, and affection which Cindy Hill would have provided them but for her death;

c. Have incurred expense for the funeral and burial of the deceased.

WHEREFORE, DEBRA HILL, as Administrator of the Estate of Cindy Hill, Deceased, prays judgment against JACK ROE in a sum which will fairly, adequately, and justly compensate her estate and next of kin for the injuries and damages alleged, plus costs of this suit, and demands trial by jury.

COUNT THREE

[Hill v. Polecat Motors, Inc.]
[Strict Product Liability—Personal Injury]

DEBRA HILL, complaining of POLECAT MOTORS, INC., alleges:

1. On and for a long time prior to May 15, 19YR, Polecat Motors, Inc. was engaged in the business of designing, assembling, manufacturing, and marketing automobiles.

2. Some time prior to May 15, 19YR, Polecat Motors, Inc. designed, assembled, manufactured, and marketed a certain 19YR Polecat automobile, Vehicle No. 98765432, and placed that automobile into the stream of commerce by offering it for sale and selling it to its dealer, Jefferson Motor Car Co. of El Dorado, Morena.

3. On May 11, 19YR, Arthur and Debra Hill purchased the above–described 19YR Polecat automobile from Jefferson Motor Car Co.

4. On May 15, 19YR, the above-described 19YR Polecat automobile was in the same design condition as when it left the possession and control of Polecat Motors, Inc.

5. At the time the above–described 19YR Polecat automobile left the possession and control of Polecat Motors, Inc., and continuously thereafter until the occurrence described, that automobile was in a defective condition unreasonably dangerous to the user or consumer by reason of one or more of the following conditions:

a. Its fuel tank was located so as to be unnecessarily vulnerable to damage and leakage in the event of a rear-end collision;

b. Its fuel tank was designed and constructed of materials, and configured, so as to be vulnerable to damage and leakage in the event of a rear–end collision;

c. The filler pipe of its fuel tank was designed, constructed and located so that in the event of a rear–end collision, it would too readily become separated from the fuel tank and allow gasoline and gasoline vapor to escape into the interior of the automobile;

d. Its fuel tank did not have a collapsible plastic bladder;

e. There was no fire shield between the fuel tank and the interior of the automobile;

f. It did not come equipped with adequate warnings to the user or consumer of the foregoing design conditions and of the resulting fire danger.

6. On May15, 19YR, at approximately 4:00 p.m., Debra Hill was operating the above–described 19YR Polecat automobile in the vicinity of the intersection of Missouri Street and Illinois Avenue in the city of El Dorado, state of Morena, when it was struck in the rear end by a truck being operated by Ralph Worker.

7. As a direct and proximate result of one or more of the conditions described in paragraph 5, the fuel tank of the above–described 19YR Polecat automobile became distorted, disconnected, and ruptured and gasoline and gasoline vapor entered the interior of the automobile and ignited.

8. Plaintiff realleges paragraph 9 of Count One as paragraph 8 of this Count Three.

WHEREFORE, DEBRA HILL prays judgment against POLECAT MOTORS, INC., in a sum which will fairly, adequately, and justly compensate her for her injuries, plus costs of this suit, and demands trial by jury.

COUNT FOUR

[Debra Hill, Admr. of Est. of Cindy Hill v. Polecat Motors, Inc.]
[Strict Product Liability—Wrongful Death]

DEBRA HILL, as Administrator of the Estate of Cindy Hill, Deceased, complaining of POLECAT MOTORS, INC., alleges:

1. Plaintiff realleges paragraphs 1 through 7, inclusive, of Count Three as similarly numbered paragraphs of this Count Four.

8. Cindy Hill, then eight years of age and the daughter of Debra Hill, was a passenger in the automobile.

9. Plaintiff realleges paragraphs 9 through 12, inclusive, of Count Two as similarly numbered paragraphs of this Count Four.

WHEREFORE, DEBRA HILL, as Administrator of the Estate of Cindy Hill, Deceased, prays judgment against defendant POLECAT MOTORS, INC., in a sum which will fairly, adequately, and justly compensate her estate and next of kin for the injuries and damages alleged, plus costs of this suit, and demands trial by jury.

COUNT FIVE

[Hill v. Polecat Motors, Inc.]
[Misrepresentation—Rest. of Torts § 402B—Personal Injury]

DEBRA HILL, complaining of POLECAT MOTORS, INC., alleges:

1. Plaintiff realleges paragraphs 1, 2, and 3 of Count Three as similarly numbered paragraphs of this Count Five.

4. On and prior to May 10, 19YR, Jefferson Motor Car Co., acting as the agent of POLECAT MOTORS, INC., made certain representations of material facts concerning the above-described automobile to Arthur Hill, including one or more of the following:

a. The fuel tank and appurtenant structures were reasonably safe, and were not vulnerable to fire in the event of low–speed rear–end collisions.

b. The automobile, and especially the fuel system, was crashworthy.

c. The fuel tank would not rupture in the event of a rear-end collision at impact speeds lower than 45 miles per hour.

5. Arthur Hill purchased the above-described automobile in reliance upon these representations.

6. At the time the above–described 19YR Polecat automobile left the possession and control of Polecat Motors, Inc., and continuously thereafter until the occurrence described, those representations were false, in that:

a. Its fuel tank was located so as to be vulnerable to damage and leakage in the event of a rear–end collision;

b. Its fuel tank was designed and constructed of materials, and configured, so as to be vulnerable to damage and leakage in the event of a rear-end collision;

c. The filler pipe of its fuel tank was designed, constructed, and located so that in the event of a rear–end collision, it would readily become separated from the fuel tank and allow gasoline and gasoline vapor to escape into the interior of the automobile;

d. Its fuel tank did not have a collapsible plastic bladder;

e. There was no fire shield between the fuel tank and the interior of the automobile.

7. On May 15, 19YR, at approximately 4:00 p.m., Debra Hill was operating the above-described 19YR Polecat automobile in the vicinity of the intersection of Missouri Street and Illinois Avenue in the city of El Dorado, state of Morena, when it was struck in the rear end by a truck being operated by Ralph Worker at an impact speed of 25 miles per hour or less.

8. As a direct and proximate result of this collision, the fuel tank of the above–mentioned 19YR Polecat automobile became distorted, disconnected, and ruptured and gasoline and gasoline vapor entered the interior of the automobile and ignited.

9. Plaintiff realleges paragraph 9 of Count One as paragraph 9 of this Count Five.

WHEREFORE, DEBRA HILL prays judgment against POLECAT MO-TORS, INC., in a sum which will fairly and adequately compensate her for her injuries, plus costs of this suit, and demands trial by jury.

COUNT SIX

[Debra Hill, Admr. of Est. of Cindy Hill v. Polecat Motors, Inc.]
[Misrepresentation—Rest. of Torts § 402B—Personal Injury]

DEBRA HILL, as Administrator of the Estate of Cindy Hill, Deceased, complaining of Polecat Motors, Inc., alleges:

1. Plaintiff realleges paragraphs 1, 2, and 3 of Count Three as similarly numbered paragraphs of this Count Six.

4. Plaintiff realleges paragraphs 4, 5, 6, 7, and 8 of Count Five as similarly numbered paragraphs of this Count Six.

9. Plaintiff realleges paragraphs 9, 10, 11, and 12 of Count Two as similarly numbered paragraphs of this Count Six.

WHEREFORE, DEBRA HILL, as Administrator of the Estate of Cindy Hill, Deceased, prays judgment against POLECAT MOTORS, INC., in a sum which will fairly and adequately compensate her estate and next of kin for the injuries and demands alleged, plus costs of this suit, and demands trial by jury.

[Pleading requirements vary among jurisdictions. The degree of factual specificity as well as the elements of a cause of action or count also depend upon the jurisdiction and the approach of the attorney. Consequently, the foregoing example should not be taken as a model for use in all courts. In addition, in a real case, plaintiff would probably also sue the retailer and Worker, and might make additional allegations of negligence and perhaps reckless conduct against the auto manufacturer. Also, the wrongful death and survival claims might be pleaded in separate counts or even in different proceedings or different courts.]

CRIMINAL CASE FILE—*STATE v. DEVITT*

Criminal case files vary from one jurisdiction to the next, so we will not attempt to reproduce sample documents here. Assume the following facts.

Accused:	Daniel R. Devitt, age 31
Victim:	Patrick Paterson, age 49
Victim's Daughter:	Lynn Paterson, age 19
Location:	Aurora Apartments, El Dorado, Morena
Investigating Officers:	Karl Katz and George Hernandez

The police arrest record includes the following crime report, which was prepared by one of the investigating police officers, Officer Hernandez:

Crime Report

Victim, Patrick Paterson, is 49, a car salesman. He resides with his daughter, 19, a student at Smith Business College. They live in the Aurora Apartments in north El Dorado. The father hired suspect, Devitt, to do some carpentry at the apartment—building some shelves and doing some repair work in the kitchen. On morning of March 15, victim admitted suspect to apartment before leaving for work. He returned from work at approximately 1600 hours same day. Suspect was still in apartment. Victim noticed beer cans and a bottle, apparently of liquor. The victim noticed the suspect was going through drawers in a dresser in victim's bedroom. When victim told suspect to get out of the bedroom, suspect pulled knife and said, "Get out of my God damn way." Suspect then attempted to run by the victim toward the front door. When the victim endeavored to block the suspect's exit, the suspect first stabbed the victim and then hit him with his right fist. The victim then pretended to be unconscious. He thinks suspect remained another hour. When he was sure suspect had left, he ran to apartment of witness, Matilda Larson, 75–year–old widow living in same apartment complex. Witness tells this officer that victim came to door in disarray and bleeding slightly. Victim at first was incoherent. Witness gave him tea and calmed him. When victim told Larson what had happened, witness phoned north El Dorado police station. Call came in approximately 1830. This officer and Officer Katz immediately responded to scene.

[The case file also contains the following statement, signed by the accused:]

Statement of Arrested Person

I am a handyman carpenter. That's how I've made my living since getting out of the Marines. Last week this guy by the name of Paterson phones me and tells me that he wants some work done at his apartment. He tells me that he wants me to do some work like putting up shelves in the kitchen. I said that I could do it for $150. We agreed, and he told me to show up early Monday, March 15th. That's just what I did. When I got there, Paterson was gone; but his daughter let me in. She left for school, and I got right to work. I worked straight through the morning and almost finished. I took a lunch break and got some beer from the local 7–11. I had finished off a couple of beers and wrapped up the job when the old guy came home. By that time, it was late in the afternoon and real hot. He asked me if I wanted to share a beer, and I said sure. He must have had some booze already because he was acting pretty weird. We get to talking, and for no reason he starts cursing me. I tried to ignore him and get back to work. He wouldn't let me be. While I was trying to slice some tile with my linoleum knife, he walked up behind me and grabbed my arm real hard. He was saying something like, "Don't ignore me when I'm talking to you." I instinctively pulled my arm back, and the knife accidentally cut him. He goes ballistic and starts screaming and punching. I had enough of him. I just shoved him out of my way and left.

I left and went home. That same night, I was just sitting home when these two cops butt in. They didn't shove me around or nothing like that, but they tell me that Paterson had accused me of trying to steal from him and beating him up. I told the cop that the whole thing was the old guy's fault, but they wouldn't listen. So here I am sitting in jail on a frame-up.

/s/ Daniel R. Devitt

———————————

Assume that Devitt has been formally charged by an appropriate procedure — indictment or information — with (1) simple battery, (2) aggravated battery, and (3) attempted theft.

Morena statutes define the following crimes:

Battery (Morena Stat. 5/12-3). (a) A person commits battery if he or she intentionally or knowingly without legal justification and by any means, (1) causes bodily harm to an individual or (2) makes physical contact of an insulting or provoking nature with an individual. (b) Sentence. Battery is a Class A misdemeanor.

Aggravated Battery (Morena Stat. 5/12-4). (a) A person who, in committing a battery, intentionally or knowingly causes great bodily harm, or permanent disability or disfigurement commits aggravated battery. (b) In committing a battery, a person commits aggravated battery if he or she: (1) Uses a deadly weapon other than by the discharge of a firearm; . . . . (e) Sentence. Aggravated battery is a Class 3 felony.

Theft (Morena Stat. 5/16-1). (a) A person commits theft when he or she knowingly: (1) Obtains or exerts unauthorized control over property of the owner; or (2) Obtains, by deception, control over property of the owner; or (3) Obtains, by threat, control over property of the owner; . . . . (b) Sentence. (1) Theft of property, other than a firearm, not from the person and not exceeding $300 in value is a Class A misdemeanor.

Attempt (Morena Stat. 5/8-4). (a) Elements of the offense. A person commits an attempt when, with intent to commit a specific offense, he or she does any act which constitutes a substantial step toward the commission of that offense. (c) Sentence. A person convicted of an attempt may be fined or imprisoned or both not to exceed the maximum provided for the offense attempted but . . . (5) the sentence for attempt to commit any felony other than those specified in Subsections (1), (2), (3) and (4) hereof is the sentence for a Class A misdemeanor.

Part 3

ADMISSIBILITY OF EVIDENCE

Chapter 7

WITNESS COMPETENCY

Read Federal Rules of Evidence 601, 605 and 606.

A. INTRODUCTION

"Incompetent" is one of those ambiguous terms that must be used with care. It is occasionally employed to refer to the inadmissibility of a particular item of evidence by reason of one of the exclusionary rules. For example, in the *Devitt* case, the El Dorado Police Crime Report may be "incompetent" as evidence because it is inadmissible hearsay. This is the sense of the term in the inartful Perry Mason–type objection, "Your Honor, I object: that evidence is incompetent, irrelevant, and immaterial."

Similarly, it is sometimes said that a person is "incompetent" as a witness concerning a matter unless he or she has personal, "first hand" knowledge of that matter. The concept of "competency" need not be stretched this far. If a person has no personal knowledge, his testimony is either based on hearsay or a fabrication. We shall not use "competent" in this sense either in this chapter. The personal knowledge requirement is a logical relevancy concept that we shall cover later.

When we use the term "competent," we refer to the issue of whether a person called as a witness is eligible to testify. For the most part, the prospective witness' eligibility depends upon the person's status rather than the content of the person's proposed testimony. *United States v. Phibbs*, 999 F.2d 1053, 1069 (6th Cir. 1993), *cert. denied*, 114 S. Ct. 1071 (1994). These rules can have the dramatic procedural effect of keeping a person altogether off the witness stand. Manifestly, this is the threshold issue in analyzing the admissibility of evidence. Before we consider the content of any proposed testimony, we must ensure that the testimony comes from a proper source, a competent witness.

B. THE EARLY COMMON LAW COMPETENCY DOCTRINE

In a modern trial, almost all of the evidence consists of witnesses' testimony or tangible things for which a witness' testimony has laid the foundation. But it was not always so.

Historically, the modern witness does not appear as a main source of evidence to the jury until the 1600's. The jurors, originally, being taken from the neighborhood, were supposed to know something of the case; and they were free to make inquiry for themselves out of court. Moreover, the oath of a witness, in those earlier days, was an impressive, almost a decisive act; when sworn, it might impress the jury decisively; and its only proper place was in the other mode of trial, "wager of law," where the party's oath was decisive. Furthermore, the fear of being charged with "maintenance," *i.e.*, of influencing the jurors by persuasion in favor of one of the parties, kept possible witnesses away; and until Queen Elizabeth's period (say 1562) there was no regular compulsory process for them. Thus, when the jury developed and were no longer supposed or allowed to have knowledge of their own, and the ordinary witness became common and took oath, he was admitted only under strict limitations. He must be well qualified. Hence, [there are] many rules which lasted until modern time—for example, the rules excluding all parties in the case and other interested persons.

But with the development of the art of cross-examination in the 1700's and the spread of rationalism in the community, these traditional rules of limitation were gradually seen to be unwise and unpractical. By the middle of the 1800's a strong movement to abolish them took effect; and most of them are now gone. What remains has mostly some practical foundation.

J. Wigmore, A Student's Textbook of the Law of Evidence § 92 (1935).

At one time in the history of the common law, there were several categories of persons who were not permitted to be witnesses, including parties to the action and others interested in its outcome, spouses of parties, and persons convicted of certain crimes. The common law was virtually obsessed with the prevention of perjury, and it was thought that these categories of witnesses had too much incentive for false testimony.

C. THE PREVAILING MODERN DOCTRINE

Today the traditional blanket disqualifications have almost entirely disappeared. Nearly all jurisdictions have a statute similar to the federal or the California provision.

Federal Rule of Evidence 601. General Rule of Competency.

Every person is competent to be a witness except as otherwise provided in these rules.

California Evidence Code § 700.

General rule as to competency. Except as otherwise provided by statute, every person is qualified to be a witness and no person is disqualified to testify to any matter.

However, as we shall see, some vestiges of the former incompetencies persist.

1. GENERAL COMPETENCY REQUIREMENTS

Competency is structured around four concepts: moral capacity (sincerity) and the mental capacities to observe, remember, and narrate. On an appropriate objection, the trial judge must rule on the preliminary issue whether the prospective witness possesses these four capacities.

a. Moral Capacity: The Oath

When the law finally accepted the oath as a predicate for a witness' testimony (rather than as the testimony itself), it became a corollary that the witness was incompetent unless she believed in a Supreme Being who punished false testimony. A witness was incompetent unless she recognized a religious obligation to speak the truth.

That moral obligation has been replaced by a legal obligation to tell the truth, and the law's punishment for perjury has replaced a Supreme Being's retribution as the sanction that induces truthful testimony. The opponent may no longer challenge a witness' competency on the ground that the witness does not believe in a Supreme Being or divine punishment for perjury. In fact, a witness' beliefs or opinions on religious matters are inadmissible on the issue of credibility. FED. R. EVID. 610.

Although the prospective witness need not recognize a religious duty to testify truthfully, a witness cannot testify unless and until he takes an oath or affirms that he will tell the truth. *See* FED. R. EVID. 603. In a sense, this is a vestige of a competency rule. However, today it is more a rule of trial administration designed to subject the witness to the penalties for perjury and to signal to the witness the great importance of truthful testimony. If the witness refuses to make an appropriate oath or affirmation, he can be punished summarily for contempt of court, and he may not testify. *United States v. Fowler*, 605 F.2d 181 (5th Cir. 1979). No particular form of oath is required unless a form is set by statute or rule. *United States v. Thai*, 29 F.3d 785 (2d Cir.) *cert. denied*, 115 S. Ct. 456 (1994), *cert. denied*, 115 S. Ct. 1327 (1995). If the witness (for whatever reason) refuses to take an oath, she may "affirm" that her testimony will be the truth. Rule 603 states the general rule that the oath or affirmation be "administered in a form calculated to awaken his conscience and impress his mind with his duty to" testify truthfully. To require more is usually error. *United States v. Moore*, 217 F.2d 428 (7th Cir. 1954), *rev'd*, 348 U.S. 966 (1955). In *United States v. Ward*, 989 F.2d 1015 (9th Cir. 1992), the court ruled that the First Amendment free exercise clause entitled the accused to take an oath that he would speak with "fully integrated Honesty."

The proposed witness must have sufficient mental capacity to understand the oath's significance and his duty to tell the truth. For instance, California Evidence Code § 701(b) reads:

> A person is disqualified to be a witness if he is . . . incapable of understanding the duty of a witness to tell the truth.

Section 701 completes the evolution of the moral capacity requirement: what began as a religious test has become an essentially cognitive standard.

b. Mental Capacity to Observe

In addition to imposing the oath requirement, the common law allowed the judge to determine whether the prospective witness has the ability to observe. The term "observe" ordinarily connotes the sense of sight. However, in this context, the term has a broader meaning; a person can "observe" a fact or event through any sense organ. A deaf person can be a competent witness. *United States v. Barnes*, 30 F.3d 575, 577 (5th Cir. 1994).

At what time must the prospective witness possess this capacity? In *Devitt,* suppose that at the time of the alleged attack, Paterson could see but becomes blind before trial. At trial, could he still testify to the assailant's facial features he saw during the attack? Or, in *Hill,* assume that a witness heard Ms. Hill make an admission but becomes deaf before trial. Can the witness still testify about the statement?

c. Mental Capacity to Remember

In addition to having the capacity to observe the relevant fact or event, the prospective witness must be able to accurately recall the data at the time of trial. Suppose that, before trial, the witness has difficulty remembering relevant facts. Many psychologists now use hypnotic induction as a means of overcoming witnesses' memory blocks. Assume further that, under hypnosis, the witness purports to recall seemingly forgotten facts. Is the witness competent to testify to those facts at trial? What possible effects can hypnotic induction have on a person's ability to accurately recall? The following opinion addresses that question. In this case, the prosecution presented hypnotically enhanced testimony by Catherine, the alleged victim of a sexual assault. The opinion includes an in–depth review of the relevant scientific research and illustrates the central role which empirical research can play in the evolution of evidentiary doctrine.

PEOPLE v. SHIRLEY

31 Cal. 3d 18, 641 P.2d 775, 181 Cal. Rptr. 243, *cert. denied,* 459 U.S. 860 (1982)

Mosk, Justice.

The defense called Dr. Donald W. Schafer as an expert witness to testify on the subject of hypnosis. Dr. Schafer is a board-certified psychiatrist with 16 years of private practice and 10 years on the staff of the University of California at Irvine, where he is a clinical professor of psychiatry. He has had extensive training in hypnosis, and has used it in his practice for two decades. Dr. Schafer acknowledged that hypnosis has certain valid medical uses, such as pain control and relief from various psychosomatic symptoms. In appropriate cases it can also be used for the treatment of neuroses, *e.g.*, by assisting a patient to recover repressed memories of traumatic events, including rape.

Dr. Schafer warned, however, that there are grave risks in relying for other purposes on the accuracy of memories recalled under hypnosis. He explained that while no one knows exactly how the human mind stores information, it does *not* act like a videotape recorder, *i.e.*, a machine capable of "playing back" the exact images or impressions it has received. Rather, "there are many things that alter the storage of exact memory." There is therefore no assurance, the doctor testified, that a memory recalled in hypnosis is correct. On the contrary, a person under hypnosis can be mistaken in his recollection, or can hallucinate, or can "confabulate," *i.e.*, create a false or pseudomemory, or can even deliberately lie. Indeed, it may be easier to lie under hypnosis, because from the viewpoint of the person in the trance "the hypnosis would put the responsibility on the shoulders of the hypnotist."

Dr. Schafer made four additional important points. First, when a person is put under hypnosis and asked to recount an event, no one is able to determine whether he is telling the truth. Second, when a person has a subconscious motive to distort the truth, *e.g.*, in order to make himself look better in the eyes of others, that motive will usually operate even under hypnosis; indeed, "hypnosis would in a sense give [him] permission" to engage in such distortion. Third, the effect of hypnosis on a preexisting memory is usually additive, *i.e.*, it may permit the recall of additional details; if instead the person remembers the event differently under hypnosis, the discrepancy implies either that his statement describing the preexisting memory was a lie or that the memory under hypnosis was a confabulation. Fourth, when a person has been asked to recall an event while under hypnosis, and after hypnosis is asked to remember the same event, the effect of the prior hypnosis is to remove all doubt he may have had about the event; such persons would be "convinced that what they had said in hypnosis was the truth."

On cross-examination Dr. Schafer testified that although the hypnotic induction in the case at bar was excellent from the viewpoint of technique, the hypnotist did not take into consideration Catherine's possible motivation to distort the truth under hypnosis; one of the factors leading Dr. Schafer to question that motivation was the discrepancies in her testimony.

Summing up, Dr. Schafer had no doubt as to the unreliability of hypnosis for discovering the truth of a particular matter. He warned that "hypnosis in no way is a truth serum-like experience," and concluded "there is no way of assessing the reliability of something produced in hypnosis, as such."

The prosecution neither discredited Dr. Schafer's opinion on cross–examination, nor called any expert witness of its own.

The principal proponent of hypnotically aided recall is a police department psychologist, Martin Reiser, Ed.D.[35] According to his published writings, Dr. Reiser operates on the belief that human memory is like a videotape machine that (1) faithfully records, as if on film, every perception experienced by the witness, (2) permanently stores such recorded perceptions in the brain at a subconscious level, and (3) accurately "replays" them in their original form when the witness is placed under hypnosis and asked to remember them. (*See, e.g.*, REISER, HANDBOOK OF INVESTIGATIVE HYPNOSIS (1980), ch. 40.) . . . With minor variations, this belief—or assumption—is apparently shared by police psychologists and "hypnotechnicians" at all levels of law enforcement, and serves as the theory on which such personnel base their practice of hypnotizing potential witnesses to improve their recall of crime-related events.

The professional literature, however, rejects this belief: the scientists who work in the field generally agree that, as Dr. Schafer testified at trial, the memory does *not* act like a videotape recorder, but rather is subject to numerous influences that continuously alter its content. . . .

---

[35] Dr. Reiser is the director of behavioral science services of the Los Angeles Police Department. He is also the director of the Law Enforcement Hypnosis Institute, a proprietary school in Los Angeles that teaches courses in hypnotism to police and other law enforcement personnel.

[In rejecting] the "permanent memory" hypothesis, Professor Douglas L. Hintzman [examined one of the] phenomena most often cited as "evidence" for the permanent memory hypothesis. . . .

The second phenomenon often cited as evidence for permanent memory is "hypnotic age regression." This is the procedure by which, under hypnotic suggestion, a subject appears to regress in mental age until an earlier date in his life, then seems to "relive" the events he experienced on that date and their accompanying emotions. Again Professor Hintzman finds little persuasive value in such demonstrations, stressing that the subject's claim to recall specific individuals or events from his childhood is rarely if ever corroborated because of obvious difficulties in doing so. He also notes studies in which hypnotized subjects have instead undergone age "progression"—*i.e.*, have been made to believe they are living 10 or more years *in the future*—and have reported their future "memories" with equal conviction and verisimilitude. "Good hypnotic subjects," the author explains, "will go to great lengths to comply with the hypnotist's requests, and this apparently include constructing realistic scenarios and acting them out." Professor Hintzman concludes that while the permanent memory hypothesis is tantalizing in its simplicity, the evidence offered in its support is weak and the hypothesis is probably incorrect.

We turn, then, to the professional literature on the topic . . . and set forth its principal relevant conclusions.

1. Hypnosis is by its nature a process of suggestion, and one of its primary effects is that the person hypnotized becomes extremely receptive to suggestions that he perceives as emanating from the hypnotist. The effect is intensified by another characteristic of the hypnotic state, to wit, that the attention of the subject is wholly focused on and directed by the hypnotist. The suggestions may take the form of explicit requests or predictions by the hypnotist; or they may be inferred by the subject from information he acquired prior to or during the hypnotic session, or from such cues as the known purpose of that session, the form of questions asked or comments made by the hypnotist, or the hypnotist's demeanor and other nonverbal conduct. The suggestions can be entirely unintended—indeed, unperceived—by the hypnotist himself.[46]

2. The person under hypnosis experiences a compelling desire to please the hypnotist by reacting positively to these suggestions, and hence to produce the particular responses he believes are expected of him. Because of this compulsion, when asked to recall an event either while in "age regression" or under direct suggestion of heightened memory ("hyperamnesia"), he is unwilling to admit that he cannot do so or that his recollection is uncertain or

---

[46] Diamond, *Inherent Problems in the Use of Pretrial Hypnosis on a Prospective Witness* (1980) 68 CAL. L. REV. 313, 333; Orne, *Use and Misuse of Hypnosis in Court* (1979) INTERNAT. J. CLINICAL & EXPERIMENTAL HYPNOSIS 311, 322–327; Orne, *On the Simulating Subject as a Quasi–Control Group in Hypnosis Research: What, Why, and How*, in HYPNOSIS: RESEARCH DEVELOPMENTS AND PERSPECTIVES (Fromm & Schor edits. 1972) pages 400–403 [hereinafter cited as *Hypnosis Research*]; Orne, *The Nature of Hypnosis: Artifact and Essence* (1959) 58 J. ABNORN. & SOC. PSYCH. 277, 280–286, 297; *see generally* HILGARD, HYPNOTIC SUSCEPTIBILITY (1965); WEITZENHOFFER, HYPNOTISM: AN OBJECTIVE STUDY IN SUGGESTIBILITY (1953); HULL, HYPNOSIS AND SUGGESTIBILITY: AN EXPERIMENTAL APPROACH (1933).

incomplete. Instead, he will produce a "memory" of the event that may be compounded of (1) relevant actual facts, (2) irrelevant actual facts taken from an unrelated prior experience of the subject, (3) fantasized material ("confabulations") unconsciously invented to fill gaps in the story, and (4) conscious lies—all formulated in as realistic a fashion as he can. The likelihood of such self–deception is increased by another effect of hypnosis, *i.e.*, that it significantly impairs the subject's critical judgment and causes him to give credence to memories so vague and fragmentary that he would not have relied on them before being hypnotized.[48]

3. During the hypnotic session, neither the subject nor the hypnotist can distinguish between true memories and pseudomemories of various kinds in the reported recall; and when the subject repeats that recall in the waking state (*e.g.*, in a trial), neither an expert witness nor a lay observer (*e.g.*, the judge or jury) can make a similar distinction. In each instance, if the claimed memory is not or cannot be verified by wholly independent means, no one can reliably tell whether it is an accurate recollection or mere confabulation. Because of the foregoing pressures on the subject to present the hypnotist with a logically complete and satisfying memory of the prior event, neither the detail, coherence, nor plausibility of the resulting recall is any guarantee of its veracity.[49]

4. Nor is such guarantee furnished by the confidence with which the memory is initially reported or subsequently related: a witness who is uncertain of his recollections before being hypnotized will become convinced by that process that the story he told under hypnosis is true and correct in every respect. This effect is enhanced by two techniques commonly used by lay hypnotists: before being hypnotized the subject is told (or believes) that hypnosis will help him to "remember very clearly everything that happened" in the prior event, and/or during the trance he is given the suggestion that after he awakes he will "be able to remember" that event equally clearly and comprehensively.[50] Further enhancement of this effect often occurs when, after he returns to the waking state, the subject remembers the content of his new "memory" but forgets its source, *i.e.*, forgets that he acquired it during the hypnotic session ("posthypnotic source amnesia"); this phenomenon can arise spontaneously from the subject's expectations as to the nature and effects of hypnosis, or can be unwittingly suggested by the hypnotist's instructions. Finally, the effect not only persists, but the witness' conviction of the absolute truth of his hypnotically induced recollection grows stronger each time he is asked to repeat the story; by the time of trial, the resulting "memory" may be so fixed

---

[48] Diamond, *Inherent Problems*, pages 335, 337–338; Orne, *Use and Misuse*, pages 316–320; Putnam, *Hypnosis and Distortions in Eyewitness Testimony* (1979) 27 Internat. J. Clinical & Experimental Hypnosis 437, 446; Gibson, Hypnosis: Its Nature and Therapeutic Uses (1977) pages 58–59; Shor, *The Fundamental Problem in Hypnosis Research as Viewed From Historic Perspectives, in* Hypnosis Research, pages 37–39; Hilgard, Hypnotic Susceptibility (1965) page 9; Hull, Hypnosis and Suggestibility (1933) pages 111–115.

[49] Diamond, *Inherent Problems*, pages 333–335, 337–338, 340; Orne, *Use and Misuse*, pages 317–318, 320; Spiegel, *Hypnosis and Evidence: Help or Hindrance?* (1980) 347 Annals N.Y. Acad. Sci. 73, 79; Kroger & Douce, *Hypnosis in Criminal Investigation* (1979) 27 Internat. J. Clinical & Experimental Hypnosis 358, 365–367.

[50] Such suggestions are recommended by police hypnosis manuals (*e.g.*, Reiser, Handbook of Investigative Hypnosis (1980) ch. 40). . . .

in his mind that traditional legal techniques such as cross-examination may be largely ineffective to expose its unreliability.[51]

The professional literature thus fully supports the testimony of Dr. Schafer. It also demonstrates beyond any doubt that at the present time the use of hypnosis to restore the memory of a potential witness is *not* generally accepted as reliable by the relevant scientific community. Indeed, representative groups within that community are on record as expressly opposing this technique for many of the foregoing reasons, particularly when it is employed by law enforcement hypnotists.[52] We therefore hold that the testimony of a witness who has undergone hypnosis for the purpose of restoring his memory of the events in issue is inadmissible as to all matters relating to those events, from the time of the hypnotic session forward. It follows that the trial court erred in denying defendant's motion to exclude Catherine's testimony.

NOTES AND PROBLEMS

1. Most jurisdictions have rejected the *Shirley* approach to the competency of previously hypnotized witnesses. 1 P. GIANNELLI & E. IMWINKELRIED, SCIENTIFIC EVIDENCE § 12-4 (3d ed. 1999). In *Rock v. Arkansas*, 483 U.S. 44 (1987), the lower court judge applied the *Shirley* approach to a criminal accused's testimony. The accused underwent pretrial hypnosis to refresh her memory of the details of a shooting. Applying *Shirley*, the trial judge held that the accused was incompetent to testify about those details. Writing for the majority, Justice Blackmun held that the trial judge's ruling violated the

---

[51] Diamond, *Inherent Problems*, pages 339–340; Orne, *Use and Misuse*, pages 320, 327, 332; Cooper, Hypnotic Amnesia, in Hypnosis Research, pages 223–231; Cooper, *Spontaneous and Suggested Posthypnotic Source Amnesia* (1966) 14 INTERNAT. J. CLINICAL & EXPERIMENTAL HYPNOSIS 180; Evans & Thorn, *Two Types of Posthypnotic Amnesia: Recall Amnesia and Source Amnesia* (1966) 14 INTERNAT. J. CLINICAL & EXPERIMENTAL HYPNOSIS 162; HILGARD, HYPNOTIC SUSCEPTIBILITY (1965) pages 166, 182.

[52] Thus in October 1978 the Society for Clinical and Experimental Hypnosis adopted a resolution reading in part:

"The Society for Clinical and Experimental Hypnosis views with alarm the tendency for police officers with minimal training in hypnosis and without a broad professional background in the healing arts employing hypnosis to presumably facilitate recall of witnesses or victims privy to the occurrence of some crime. Because we recognize that hypnotically aided recall may produce either accurate memories or at times may facilitate the creation of pseudo memories, or fantasies that are accepted as real by subject and hypnotist alike, we are deeply troubled by the utilization of this technique among the police. It must be emphasized that there is no known way of distinguishing with certainty between actual recall and pseudo memories except by independent verification.

"Police officers typically have had limited technical training and lack the broad understanding of psychology and psychopathology. Their orientation is to obtain the information needed to solve a crime rather than a concern focusing on protecting the health of the subject who was either witness to, or victim of, a crime. Finally, police officers understandably have strong views as to who is likely to be guilty of a crime and may easily inadvertently bias the hypnotized subject's memories even without themselves being aware of their actions." (27 INTERNAT. J. CLINICAL & EXPERIMENTAL HYPNOSIS (1979) 452.)

In August 1979 an identical resolution was adopted by the International Society of Hypnosis. (*Id.* at p. 453.)

accused's constitutional right to present a defense. The justice conceded that "scientific understanding of the phenomenon and of the means to control the effects of hypnosis is still in its infancy." *Id.* at 61. However, he concluded that the available research has "not shown that hypnotically enhanced testimony is always . . . untrustworthy and . . . immune to the traditional means of evaluating credibility . . . ." *Id.*

2. In footnote 52, the *Shirley* majority quotes a resolution adopted by the Society for Clinical and Experimental Hypnosis. Note the second paragraph of the resolution, focusing on hypnotic induction by police officers. Is the Society's sole concern that police officers have little expertise in this area? Does the Society view a police officer using hypnosis as an impartial scientific investigator?

3. Refer back to our discussion of preliminary facts conditioning the admissibility of evidence. Should witness competency be finally determined by the judge (Rule 104(a)), or does the judge make only a preliminary determination that there is evidence sufficient to support a finding of competency by the jury (Rule 104(b))? Why?

4. Problem 7-1. In the *Hill* case, one of Ms. Hill's witnesses is Mr. Phipps, who claims to have seen the collision. Observing the collision was such a traumatic experience for Phipps that immediately after the accident, he began consulting a psychiatrist, Dr. McCoy. McCoy is convinced that Phipps is suffering from partial amnesia; the amnesia includes the date of the collision; and, hence, Phipps is lying when he claims to remember details of the collision. Polecat Motors challenges Phipps' competency. As trial judge, would you listen to McCoy's testimony before ruling on the competency objection? How does this problem relate to the preceding question? Weihofen, *Testimonial Competence and Credibility*, 34 Geo. Wash. L. Rev. 53, 55 (1965).

d. Mental Capacity to Narrate

The last required capacity is the witness' ability to narrate or relate what she remembers about the perceived event. California Evidence Code § 701(a) provides that:

> A person is disqualified to be a witness if he is incapable of expressing himself concerning the matter so as to be understood, either directly or through interpretation by one who can understand him . . . .

A witness is not incompetent by reason of the fact that she cannot communicate adequately (or at all) in the English language, provided she can do so through a qualified interpreter.

2. APPLICATIONS OF THE GENERAL REQUIREMENTS

a. Minors

Children who are too young to understand an oath's significance may nevertheless testify (if otherwise competent). The oath is excused. *State ex rel. R.R., a Juvenile,* 79 N.J. 97, 398 A.2d 76 (1979). In its place the trial judge conducts a *voir dire* examination of the child to determine if the child understands his obligation to tell the truth and the importance of doing so. Questions about the child's religious beliefs and practices are still common. When the judge is satisfied that the child understands and will probably testify truthfully, the judge declares that the child may testify. Ordinarily, counsel do not examine. The courts have been relatively liberal in admitting testimony by young children. By way of an example, in *In the Interest of J.R.*, 436 Pa. Super. 416, 648 A.2d 28 (1994), *appeal denied*, 655 A.2d 515 (Pa. 1995), the court found that a four–year–old child was competent to be a witness. However, there are limits. Thus, *Townsend v. State*, 613 So. 2d 534 (Fla. App. 1993) held a two–year–old incompetent. More surprisingly, in *In re Crystal*, 218 Cal. App. 3d 596, 267 Cal. Rptr. 105 (1990), a seven-year-old was ruled incompetent where the child repeatedly stated that he did not know the difference between the truth and a lie.

PROBLEM

Problem 7-2. Is the critical time the time of the event or the time of trial? Suppose that in *Hill,* a young child observed the collision. At that time, the child was only three, but by trial the child is eight. Polecat Motors objects to the child's competency as a witness. Does it matter whether Polecat is challenging the child's perceptual ability rather than the child's capacity to remember or relate? If so, why? Stafford, *The Child as a Witness*, 37 WASH. L. REV. 303, 306–07 (1962).

Remember that the substantive law of contracts and crimes recognized limitations on the competency of minors. The recognition of limitations on minors' competency as witnesses brings the law of Evidence into alignment. Is the recognition of these limitations also in line with the teachings of child psychology? One psychologist summarized the traditional view in this fashion:

> [One] school of thought views the child as passing through various developmental stages in each of which his thinking about causal matters differs from that of adults.
>
> The first stage, which precedes the time when the child has any clear idea of himself as a person, lasts until the age of 2 or 3 years. This is a time of pure autism, that is, of thoughts which are purely internal in the sense that they are preoccupied with needs and wants with no regard for the outside world. It is a time of dreams and day–dreams. . . . The causal ideas of the child at this time correspond to this magical mental state. He thinks that his wishes and desires have the ability to influence objects and that external things will be obedient to his wishes. At this period there is a great confusion between the self and the world.
>
> The second stage lasts from the end of the first to the age of 7 or 8. This is the period of egocentrism where the emotions and other subjective factors govern ideas of causality at the expense of a newly developing power of logical thinking. At this time the child often

confuses motive with cause. If a person had a strong motive for doing something then, in the child's mind, that was the person who did it. He also has a tendency to place together things that have some property in common, although they do not belong together. . . . The child knows that he is getting bigger so he says, "The moon gets bigger because we are getting bigger." Further, the child at this stage sees activity and life in even the inorganic substances about him and may say "That stone doesn't like me."

After the second stage comes the third great stage in which thinking about causal factors becomes deductive. It may be said that after eight the child thinks in the same way as adults, but that he is limited by lack of knowledge and the lack of development of other specialized abilities.

An important factor in causal thinking is the ability to pay attention. Without the ability to fixate accurately on some event it is not possible to remember it or to think about it. Up to the age of two years likes and dislikes govern the child's ability to pay attention, an ability which is very poor at this age level, the child being highly distractible. Up to the age of five, the child's attentive span increases slowly. . . .

From the age of five on, there is a marked increase in the ability to pay attention. (By the time the child is eight, his attentive ability is about half of what it will be at age 12.) Keeping his attention on an object for any length of time probably means, at least in the case of children of the later pre-school ages and above, the ability to see many qualities, relations, and characteristics in it to which he attends. So by about age five, ability at causal thinking and ability at paying attention are developmentally intertwined. . . . By age eight these abilities are fairly well developed.

The development of the concept of time also illustrates the developmental sequence laid down by causality and attention; the concept of time being an integral part of many types of causal analysis. Up to two years of age, the child's chief time word is "Now". He lives entirely in the present with the exception that he can learn to wait for brief periods of time. After two years the child knows "wait", "soon", and "this day" and by 30 months he can divide the day into "morning", "afternoon" and "night" and has the concepts of both "last night" and "tomorrow". The period of 30 months to 36 months shows rapid advances. The child learns to ask "what time?" and understands "all day" or "for two weeks". The child now talks as much about the future and the past as the present. By 42 months, both past and future tenses are used accurately. The child now knows "in the meantime" and "for a long time"—"for years", "it's almost time". By the age of four years, children have a good idea of when the events of the day take place in relation to each other. By five the child can tell what day it is, can name the days of the week in correct order, and can tell what day follows Sunday. He can also tell how old he will be by his next birthday. By six he understands the four seasons and has an increasing knowledge of durations. By seven, he can tell specific clock hours, including how many minutes of or past the hour, but he still doesn't understand the larger concept of what year it is. By the age of eight the child can handle well all of the extremes of time. . . .

Memory along with judgment and reasoning round out the factors involved in causal thinking. . . . If we ask adults to report all of the objects they see in a picture which they are to look at for one minute, they do about as well as the average child of seven or eight. If we look at the ability to recall visually or auditorally exposed numbers it is apparent that there is little improvement past 14½ years of age, and relatively little past 13½. Memory for various types of events, (numbers, words, pictures, etc.) of course varies with the nature of the events. However, a general rule may be stated: Memory is quite poor until after the fourth year after which it shows a rapid advance to years 11 or 12, after which there is a leveling off of ability. . . .

SINGER, PSYCHOLOGICAL INSIGHTS FOR LEGAL PROBLEMS: CAUSAL THINKING AND MEMORY IN CHILDREN (1956).

NOTE

The Singer excerpt discusses the traditional view that the cognitive development of the typical child progresses through various stages; and in the early stages, the child's cognitive ability is presumed to be minimal. In part due to increased concern about child abuse and the consequent need to rely on testimony by child witnesses, "[t]he 1980s [witnessed] a surge of research" in this area. Bessner, *The Competency of the Child Witness: A Critical Analysis of Bill C-15*, 31 CRIM. L.Q. 481, 500 (1989). The more recent research has called the traditional view into question. *Id.* at 503–06 (mentioning the pioneering research of psychologist Gail Goodman now of the University of California at Davis). In the words of one court, the modern empirical studies "have produced results indicating that most of the . . . traditional assumptions are . . . unfounded." *People v. Jones*, 51 Cal. 3d 294, 315, 792 P.2d 643, 655, 270 Cal. Rptr. 611, 623 (1990). To begin with, the contemporary research tends to undercut the assumption that the cognitive development of a child follows a neat, chronological progression. Furthermore, the studies suggest that the traditional assumption underestimates the ability of young children. The following excerpt summarizes some of the modern research. The author is a law professor who has frequently collaborated with Dr. Goodman.

1 J.E.B. MYERS, EVIDENCE IN CHILD ABUSE AND NEGLECT CASES §§ 2.10–.11 (2d ed. 1992)

[C]hildren's observational capacity develops rapidly during the first year of life. By the time children are one year old, their sense of sight, smell, touch, taste, and hearing is highly developed.

Adults sometimes assume that children notice less than adults. Psychological research discloses, however, that children are not less discerning observers than adults. In fact, young children sometimes notice events overlooked by adults. Johnson and Foley write:

[Y]oung children sometimes notice potentially interesting things that older children and adults miss. In a study on selective looking . . . , first graders, fourth graders, and adults were asked to watch a ball game on a TV screen and to press a key whenever a critical event took place. At one point, an irrelevant event occurred; a woman with an umbrella walked across the playing area and was in view for four seconds. When asked later about the woman in the film, adults had no idea that she had ever appeared. However, 22% of the fourth graders and 75% of the first graders remembered seeing the woman. . . .[A]s children get older, they increasingly . . . ignore nonrelevant information, such as what people wore or incidental pieces of conversation . . . .[Y]oung children may sometimes be better than adults at reporting events that are irrelevant to some ongoing activity. Such "irrelevant" events, though, potentially *are* relevant in the courtroom.[76]

It is time to discard the old bromide that children observe less than adults. Even young preschool children possess the observational capacity to testify. Furthermore, children remember what they observe. Thus, young children have the capacity to observe and recall events. Children's ability to interpret or explain what they observe is another matter, however. The ability to interpret and explain requires cognitive abilities that come with age and experience. Preschool children are not as adept as older children and adults at interpreting complex or ambiguous events. Young children have difficulty placing themselves in another person's shoes and understanding the other person's motives or feelings. Thus, a young child might provide a highly accurate description of *what* an adult did, but might not understand *why* the adult did it. Young children's difficulty interpreting events is a relative, rather than an absolute, deficit. The average three-year-old understands, for example, that adults are angry when they fight.

When considering testimonial competence, recall that children generally are asked to describe events they have experienced or witnessed. For the most part, these events are straightforward factual occurrences. . . . Children possess the observational capacity to describe what they experience. . . .

[B]y age three, children recall salient events quite well.[83] Children do not have a general memory deficit. Young children possess the memory skills to testify, especially when they are asked simple questions in a supportive atmosphere.[84]

---

[76] Johnson & Foley, *Differentiating Fact From Fantasy: The Reliability of Children's Memory*, 40 Soc. Issues. 33, 34 (1994). . . .

[83] Even infants have long-term memories for some events. Saywitz, Goodman & Myers, *Can Children Provide Accurate Eyewitness Reports?*, 1 Violence Update 1 (Sept. 1990).

Children remember significant events better than routine events. *See* Goodman, Rudy, Bottoms & Aman, *Children's Concerns and Memory: Issues of Ecological Validity in the Study of Children's Eyewitness Testimony*, in Knowing and Remembering in Young Children 249, 251 (R. Fivush & J. Hudson eds. 1990)) ("Cognitive research also supports the view that personally significant events are retained in memory better than less significant events"). . . .

[84] G. Melton, J. Petrila, N. Poythress & C. Slobogin, Psychological Evaluations for the Courts 102 (1987). *See also* Fivush & Hamond, *Autobiographical Memory across the Preschool Years: Toward Reconceptualizing Childhood Amnesia*, in Knowing and Remembering in Young Children 223 (R. Fivush & J. Hudson eds. 1990) ("children are capable of recalling accurate, organized information about events that have occurred in their past"). . . .

Children remember familiar as well as novel events. Children who participate in events generally remember more about the events than children who merely observe.[86] Traumatic and stressful events are remembered.[87] In several studies, researchers found that memory for stressful events was stronger than memory for nonstressful events.[88] Other research suggests that stress may impair memory.[89] In general, memory for the gist of events is more enduring than memory for details.

When considering children's memory, it is useful to consider two types of memory: free recall and recognition. Recognition memory is at work when cues trigger the child's memory for an event. . . . Thus, when a child picks a suspect from a lineup, the suspect triggers the child's recollection. Recognition memory develops very early in life.

A child relies on free recall when remembering an event without the assistance of memory cues. . . . Thus, a child uses free recall when asked, "What happened a week ago?" Free recall memory involves complex cognitive processes that develop gradually.

One of the most stable findings of research on children's memory is that when young children are asked open-ended questions like, "What happened?"—requiring free recall—they spontaneously recall less information than older children and adults. This is not to say that young children remember less, but that they are not as proficient at free recall as are older children and adults. Spencer and Flin summarize the psychological research:

> To date, research has shown clearly that the most salient and consistent age difference in witnessing is found when the memory test is free recall. This means that the subject is asked to recount everything he or she remembers without prompting, such as "Describe everything you saw." In response to this type of questioning, younger children typically report less information than older children and adults, but most significantly, the information they do recall is generally accurate.
>
> Thus there appear to be age differences in the *quantity* of freely recalled details but not in the *quality* (accuracy). . . .

---

[86] Goodman, Rudy, Bottoms & Aman at 258 ("There is reason to believe that participation leads to better memory in children"). . . .

[87] Pynoos & Eth, *The Child as Witness to Homicide*, 40 J. Soc. Issues 87 (1984) ("The dramatic nature of a parent's death causes multiple enduring effects on memory content and function. In our opinion, child witnesses to homicide remember certain details vividly"); . . . J. Spencer & R. Flin, The Evidence of Children 249 (1990) ("there is now increasing scientific evidence to suggest that if skillfully interviewed, children do remember a significant amount of information about traumatic events. Furthermore, there is no reason to suppose that their reactions to stress are essentially different to those of adult witnesses").

[88] *See* Goodman, Rudy, Bottoms & Aman at 272–73:

[T]here is reason to believe that high levels of stress will have a beneficial effect on memory. . . .[P]hysiological studies show that high levels of stress are associated with better memory. Psychological studies reveal that events of high emotionality and personal significance are retained better than events of low emotionality and little personal significance.

[89] *See* Peters, *The Influence of Stress and Arousal on the Child Witness*, *in* The Suggestibility of Children's Recollections 60 (J. Doris ed. 1990). . . .

In a typical forensic context, free recall and very general questions are of limited use and interviewers need to use more specific questions in order to elicit the maximum amount of information.[96]

As Spencer and Flin observe, the difficulty young children experience with free recall means such children often require memory cues to help them remember.[97] Whereas an adult or older child might be able to provide a detailed account in response to an open-ended question like "What happened?", young children often need specific questions to trigger "recognition memory."

Passage of time takes its toll on memory. Spencer and Flin write:

> Both adults' and children's memories are highly sensitive to the passage of time. Although some knowledge and experiences are stored for decades, a great deal of information is lost or becomes inaccessible due to decay or interference. . . .

[L]awyers generally assume that children's memories fade faster than adults'. "It is now widely accepted that children, including very young children, can be as reliable in their recollections of events as adults. However, it also seems to be generally accepted that a child's capacity for recall, especially on points of detail, may deteriorate more rapidly over time than would that of an adult. This seems to be particularly the case with young children."[99]

———

Modern psychological research on the capacity of children is not the only force shaping the law of competency. As Professor Myers stresses in his treatise, there has been growing realization of the widespread problem of child abuse in the United States. Galante, *New War on Child Abuse*, NAT'L L.J., June 25, 1984, at 1. In turn, the growing public consciousness of the problem has led to pressure on state legislatures to relax the competency standards for the young alleged victims in child abuse prosecutions. *Id.* at 26. In four states, the legislatures have enacted statutes providing that in certain types of child sex abuse prosecutions, the alleged victim is competent by law; the trial judge cannot find the alleged victim to be an incompetent witness. Ziegler, *The Child as Victim/Witness in Missouri*, 49 J. MO. BAR 303, 304 (July–Aug. 1993) ("automatic competency"); Comment, *The Competency Requirement for the Child Victim of Sexual Abuse: Must We Abandon It?*, 40 U. MIAMI L. REV. 245, 273 (1985) (citing statutes in Colorado, Connecticut, Missouri, and Utah).

---

[96] J. Spencer & R. Flin, THE EVIDENCE OF CHILDREN 240 (1990).

[97] Dent observes that "children's recall is facilitated by the increased cuing in specific questions but that the increase in suggestions created by posing more specific questions also has a detrimental effect on accuracy. . . .[G]reater care is needed when interviewing children than adults, but. . . .children are capable of as accurate recall as adults." Dent, *Experimental Studies of Interviewing Child Witnesses*, in THE SUGGESTIBILITY OF CHILDREN'S RECOLLECTIONS 138, 142, 145 (J. Doris ed. 1990).

[99] Spencer & Flin, THE EVIDENCE OF CHILDREN 249–50 (1990).

The advocates of these new statutes often cite the recent psychological research indicating that infants develop recognition memory at a very early age. However, can we be confident that the researchers have not been influenced by the growing consciousness of the problem of child abuse? Scientific researchers are human beings and have no immunity from the distorting influence of bias. *See generally* Black, *A Unified Theory of Scientific Evidence*, 56 FORDHAM L. REV. 595 (1988). The topic of child abuse is emotionally supercharged. Bias cannot only affect the technician applying a scientific technique, such as a police officer conducting a hypnotic session; it can also influence the scientist conducting the research to validate an hypothesis. Some commentators have charged that many researchers in the child abuse area have "a profound bias." Coleman, *Medical Examinations for Sexual Abuse: Have We Been Mislead?*, 13 THE CHAMPION 5, 10 (Nov. 1989).

b. Mentally Disordered Persons

Read the first sentence of Federal Rule of Evidence 601 again. In comparing this rule with the prevailing common law norms, in one of the early editions of their treatise Weinstein and Berger state:

> Under the early common law, insane persons, idiots, and inebriates were wholly disqualified because the testimony of such persons was considered totally untrustworthy. The testimony of children was likewise excluded, although perhaps on a different ground—their inability to understand the nature of the oath. This indiscriminate disqualification of certain classes of persons disappeared. Instead, judges conducted preliminary examinations to determine whether the particular defect or derangement of the potential witness rendered him untrustworthy "as to the specific subject of the testimony." The court's inquiry focused on whether the challenged witness had the capacity to observe at the time of the event, to recollect at the time of trial and to narrate so as to make himself understood.

> Eventually, observers noted that although courts continued to insist upon their right to exclude witnesses on the ground of mental incapacity, in practice virtually all witnesses were permitted to testify despite extreme youth or age or severe psychological and physiological infirmities. Recent codifications reflected this trend by eliminating the perception and recollection disqualifications; why the narration requirement was retained is somewhat difficult to understand in view of the actual practice in the courts. By the time Rule 601 was drafted, judges without expressly so stating had come around to Wigmore's view that a witness wholly without capacity is difficult to imagine and "that each witness' testimony be taken for what it seems to be worth."

> The Advisory Committee noting this development, decided that "frank recognition that the concept of mental capacity has small basis in reality, calls for its abandonment." Rule 601 accordingly contains no provision requiring any measure of mental capacity as a condition precedent to the giving of testimony.

3 WEINSTEIN'S EVIDENCE ¶ 601[03], at 601-25-27 (1981).

PROBLEMS

1. Problem 7-3. Assume that you are the trial judge in *Devitt.* The prosecutor calls Mr. Paterson as a witness. It is apparent from his answers to the first few questions that he is deeply mentally disturbed and not very coherent. You call counsel to the bench, and the prosecutor informs you that Paterson is suffering from a severe psychosis brought on by the attack upon him. Defendant moves for a psychiatric examination. How would you proceed? *See Ballard v. Superior Court,* 64 Cal. 2d 159, 176, 410 P.2d 838, 849, 49 Cal. Rptr. 302, 313 (1966) (*overruled by* CAL. PENAL CODE § 1112); *compare United States v. Raineri,* 91 F.R.D. 159, 164 (W.D. Wis. 1980); M. GRAHAM, HANDBOOK OF FEDERAL EVIDENCE § 601.2 (5th ed. 2001).

2. Problem 7-4. Assume that in the last problem, the judge ordered a psychiatric examination. During the examination, the psychiatrist concludes that although Paterson is generally well adjusted, he suffers from insane delusions about violent attacks. He often fantasizes such attacks. Do the delusions render him incompetent as a witness? Is it relevant how often he has fantasies? *People v. Jackson,* 273 Cal. App. 2d 248, 255, 78 Cal. Rptr. 20, 24–25 (1969).

3. Problem 7-5. Assume that in the last problem, the psychiatrist reached a different conclusion. In this variation of the problem, the psychiatrist concludes that Paterson is psychotic and suffering from a schizophrenic reaction. As trial judge, would you rule him to be an incompetent witness? Suppose that the psychiatrist added that Paterson's mental illness "might affect" the content of his testimony? Or assume that the psychiatrist testified that Paterson "is in poor contact with reality"? Would you sustain the objection now? *See Helge v. Carr,* 212 Va. 485, 488–91, 184 S.E.2d 794, 796–98 (1971).

D. THE FEDERAL RULES

The text of Rule 601 purports to abolish all non-statutory grounds for rendering prospective witnesses incompetent. The Advisory Committee's Note makes the intent even more explicit: "No mental or moral qualifications for testifying as a witness are specified. Standards of mental capacity have proved elusive in actual application. The question is one particularly suited to the jury as one of weight and credibility . . . ."

If we are to interpret Rule 601 and the accompanying Note literally, the Rule works a revolution. Rather than merely reforming the old moral and mental capacity requirements, the Rule overthrows and abandons them. The only remnant of the moral capacity requirement seems to be Rule 603 (the oath requirement), and the only vestiges of the mental capacity doctrine are Rule 602 (personal knowledge) and Rule 604 (interpreters).

As Professor John Schmertz has observed, although the legislative history of Rule 601 and its state counterparts almost conclusively demonstrates that a literal interpretation of the statute is the correct one, many courts continue to assume that the judge retains the common law power to bar a prospective witness by finding as a matter of fact that the witness lacks one of the capacities required at common law. *E.g., United States v. Whittington,* 26 F.3d 456,

466 n. 9 (4th Cir. 1994). Judges, schooled in the common law and comfortable with their ability to exercise discretion wisely, sometimes find it difficult to recognize the meaning of statutes intended to revolutionize the common law.

NOTES

1. If the trial judge under Rule 601 has no discretion to refuse to permit a witness to testify on grounds of mental incapacity or immaturity, is there any other basis on which the trial judge can properly exclude the testimony? Read Rules 402, 403, and 611(a).

2. Weinstein and Berger believe that under the statutory scheme of the Federal Rules, the trial judge may bar the witness' testimony if "no one could reasonably believe the witness could have observed, remembered, communicated or told the truth with respect to the event in question." 3 J. WEINSTEIN & M. BERGER, WEINSTEIN'S EVIDENCE ¶ 601[01], at 601–610 (1996); *United States v. Gutman*, 725 F.2d 417, 424–25 (7th Cir. 1984). Assume *arguendo* that that is the correct scope of the judge's remaining discretionary power to rule on "competency" issues. How does that power compare with the scope of the judge's power before the adoption of the Federal Rules? Think back to the discussion of preliminary fact-finding procedures under Rule 104(a). Before the adoption of the Federal Rules, did the judge rule on competency as a matter of fact or as one of law?

3. If all this ambiguity were not enough, the interpretation of Rule 601 has been further muddled in federal proceedings by recent legislation. In 1994, Congress enacted 18 U.S.C. § 3509(c) as part of a comprehensive crime bill designed in part to strengthen the national campaign against child abuse. Section 3509(c) reads:

> (c) Competency examinations.
>
> (1) Effect of Federal Rules of Evidence. Nothing in this subdivision shall be construed to abrogate rule 601 of the Federal Rules of Evidence.
>
> (2) Presumption. A child is presumed to be competent.
>
> (3) Requirement of written motion. A competency examination regarding a child witness may be conducted by the court only upon written motion and offer of proof of incompetency by a party.
>
> (4) Requirement of compelling reasons. A competency examination regarding a child may be conducted only if the court determines, on the record, that compelling reasons exist. A child's age alone is not a compelling reason.
>
> (5) Persons permitted to be present. The only persons who may be permitted to be present at a competency examination are–
>
> > (A) the judge;
> >
> > (B) the attorney for the government;
> >
> > (C) the attorney for the defendant;
> >
> > (D) a court reporter; and

(E) persons whose presence, in the opinion of the court, is necessary to the welfare and well-being of the child, including the child's attorney, guardian ad litem, or adult attendant.

(6) Not before jury. A competency examination regarding a child witness shall be conducted out of the sight and hearing of a jury.

(7) Direct examination of child. Examination of a child related to competency shall normally be conducted by the court on the basis of questions submitted by the attorney for the Government and the attorney for the defendant including a party acting as an attorney pro se. The court may permit an attorney but not a party acting as an attorney pro se to examine a child directly on competency if the court is satisfied that the child will not suffer emotional trauma as a result of the examination.

(8) Appropriate questions. The questions asked at the competency examination of a child shall be appropriate to the age and developmental level of the child, shall not be related to the issues at trial, and shall focus on determining the child's ability to understand and answer simple questions.

(9) Psychological and psychiatric examinations. Psychological and psychiatric examinations to assess the competency of a child witness shall not be ordered without a showing of compelling need.

What light, if any, does § 3509(c) shed on the proper interpretation of Rule 601? Note the disclaimer in § 3509(c)(1). Yet does § 3509(c)(2) make sense if Rule 601 sweeps away all competency requirements? Bear in mind the Supreme Court's oft–repeated caveat that "the views of a subsequent Congress form a hazardous basis for inferring the intent of an earlier one." *Consumer Products Safety Comm'n v. GTE Sylvania, Inc.*, 447 U.S. 102, 117–19 (1980). Consequently, in statutory construction, the views of a latter Congress are ordinarily deemed to be of little value. *Mitzelfelt v. Dept. of Air Force*, 903 F.2d 1293 (10th Cir. 1990).

E. SPECIALIZED ASPECTS OF COMPETENCY

1. DISQUALIFICATION FOR INTEREST: DEAD MAN'S ACTS

Judge Weinstein described the historical background of Dead Man's Acts: The common law disqualification for interest was based on the theory that certain classes of persons were so likely to testify falsely that total exclusion from the witness stand was needed as a safeguard. Originally applied to parties, defendants, codefendants, coindictees, and persons other than parties having an immediate legal interest in the action, this ground of incompetency is now virtually obsolete in all jurisdictions so that the first sentence of Rule 601 codifies previous practice— with one notable exception.

In the majority of American jurisdictions, a statutory exception "was carved out of the old disqualification and was allowed to perpetuate within a limited scope the principle of the discarded rule." Known generally as Dead Man's Acts, these statutory exceptions vary widely in their terms. Generally, they prohibit the party-witness and other interested persons from testifying to conversations, transactions, or other dealings with a decedent or incompetent when the decedent's estate or the incompetent's representative is an adverse party.

3 WEINSTEIN'S EVIDENCE ¶ 601.05[1][a], at 601–26 (J. McLaughlin ed., 2d ed. 1997).

At one time, Dead Man's Acts (also known as Survivor's Evidence Acts) were in force in about two thirds of U.S. jurisdictions and were enforced in the federal courts by virtue of Federal Rule of Civil Procedure 43(a). Ray, *Dead Man's Statutes*, 24 OHIO ST. L.J. 89 (1963). The statutes have proved remarkably difficult to overturn. However, the codification of rules of evidence in many jurisdictions has led to the abrogation of some of these acts. Since Professor Ray's article, fifteen states have abandoned their Dead Man's Acts in adopting evidence codes.[1] In four other states, the acts have been repealed outright.[2] But the acts remain in force in eighteen states,[3] including eleven states[4] that retain them despite adopting rules of evidence patterned after the Federal or Uniform Rules.

Although Dead Man's Acts vary greatly in wording and coverage (and can seem complex), the following working overview usually helps:

(1) To what kinds of actions does the statute apply?

(2) Whose testimony does the statute bar?

(3) What is the scope of the incompetence?

(4) What subjects is the witness precluded from testifying about?

(5) What exceptions are applicable?

(6) How can the statute be waived?

These six questions are usually the fundamental issues posed by such statutes, and can be used to dissect the statute into its component parts. Note the following general example of such statutes:

No person offered as a witness shall be excluded from giving evidence by reason of his interest in the action: *Provided, however,* that

(1) in an action where the adverse party sues or defends as executor, administrator or legal representative of any deceased person,

(2) a party in interest or to the record,

(3) shall not be admitted to testify in his own behalf

---

[1] Alabama, California, Delaware, Iowa, Kentucky, Maine, Michigan, Minnesota, Montana, Nebraska, North Dakota, Ohio, Oklahoma, South Dakota, and Utah.

[2] Georgia, Kansas, Mississippi, and Missouri.

[3] Alabama, Colorado, Florida, Idaho, Illinois, Indiana, Maryland, New York, North Carolina, Pennsylvania, South Carolina, Tennessee, Texas, Vermont, Washington, West Virginia, Wisconsin, and Wyoming.

[4] Colorado, Florida, Idaho, Indiana, Maryland, North Carolina, Tennessee, Texas, Washington, Wisconsin, and Wyoming.

(4) as to any transaction had by him with such deceased person.

Statutes from two populous states are instructive:

Illinois: 735 ILCS 5/8-201. Dead-Man's Act.

In the trial of any action in which any party sues or defends as the representative of a deceased person or person under a legal disability, no adverse party or person directly interested in the action shall be allowed to testify on his or her own behalf to any conversation with the deceased or person under legal disability or to any event which took place in the presence of the deceased or person under legal disability, except in the following instances:

(a) If any person testifies on behalf of the representative to any conversation with the deceased or person under legal disability or to any event which took place in the presence of the deceased or person under legal disability, any adverse party or interested person, if otherwise competent, may testify concerning the same conversation or event.

(b) If the deposition of the deceased or person under legal disability is admitted in evidence on behalf of the representative, any adverse party or interested person, if otherwise competent, may testify concerning the same matters admitted in evidence.

(c) Any testimony competent under Section 8–401 of this Act [relating to proof of account books and records], is not barred by this Section.

(d) No person shall be barred from testifying as to any fact relating to the heirship of a decedent.

As used in this Section:

(a) "Person under legal disability" means any person who is adjudged by the court in the pending civil action to be unable to testify by reason of mental illness, mental retardation or deterioration of mentality.

(b) "Representative" means any executor, administrator, heir, or legatee of a deceased person and any guardian or trustee of any such heir or legatee, or a guardian or guardian ad litem for a person under legal disability.

(c) "Person directly interested in the action" or "interested person" does not include a person who is interested solely as executor, trustee or in any other fiduciary capacity, whether or not he or she receives or expects to receive compensation for acting in that capacity.

N.Y. Civ. Prac. Law § 4519. Personal transaction or communication between witness and decedent or mentally ill person.

Upon the trial of an action or the hearing upon the merits of a special proceeding, a party or a person interested in the event, or a person from, through or under whom such a party or interested person derives his interest or title by assignment or otherwise, shall not be examined as a witness in his own behalf or interest, or in behalf of the party succeeding to his title or interest against the executor, administrator or survivor of a deceased person or the committee of a mentally ill person, or a person deriving his title or interest from, through or under a deceased person or mentally ill person, by assignment or otherwise, concerning a personal transaction or communication between the witness and the deceased person or mentally ill person, except where the executor, administrator, survivor, committee or person so deriving title or interest is examined in his own behalf, or the testimony of the mentally ill person or deceased person is given in evidence, concerning the same transaction or communication. A person shall not be deemed interested for the purposes of this section by reason of being a stockholder or officer of any banking corporation which is a party to the action or proceeding, or interested in the event thereof. No party or person interested in the event, who is otherwise competent to testify, shall be disqualified from testifying by the possible imposition of costs against him or the award of costs to him. A party or person interested in the event or a person from, through or under whom such a party or interested person derives his interest or title by assignment or otherwise, shall not be qualified for the purposes of this section, to testify in his own behalf or interest, or in behalf of the party succeeding to his title or interest, to personal transactions or communications with the donee of a power of appointment in an action or proceeding for the probate of a will, which exercises or attempts to exercise a power of appointment granted by the will of a donor of such power, or in an action or proceeding involving the construction of the will of the donee after its admission to probate.

Nothing contained in this section, however, shall render a person incompetent to testify as to the facts of an accident or the results therefrom where the proceeding, hearing, defense or cause of action involves a claim of negligence or contributory negligence in an action wherein one or more parties is the representative of a deceased or incompetent person based upon, or by reason of, the operation or ownership of a motor vehicle being operated upon the highways of the state, or the operation or ownership of aircraft being operated in the air space over the state, or the operation or ownership of a vessel on any of the lakes, rivers, streams, canals or other waters of this state, but this provision shall not be construed as permitting testimony as to conversations with the deceased.

a. Statutory Interpretation and Analysis

1) Types of Actions. The wording of the various statutes differs. To begin with, the statutes differ in identifying the protected party who may object and claim the benefit of the statute. Some statutes apply only to civil actions in which a decedent's or incompetent's personal representative (*e.g.*, executor or guardian) is a party; other statutes apply more broadly to any civil action in which a person claiming through the decedent or incompetent (heir, devisee, or successor in interest) is joined as a party. Furthermore, some statutes protect this party only when he or she is sued; other statutes more liberally allow the party to invoke the statute whether the party is suing or being sued.

2) Disqualified Witnesses. Whose testimony does the statute bar? The variations are (a) all parties who claim adversely to the protected party; or (b) all parties and other interested persons whose interests are adverse to the protected party. This is the more common form.

The definition of an "interested person" has produced much litigation. The expression has been held to include a party's partners, shareholders, and even his attorneys, spouse, and employees. Ordinarily a pecuniary interest is required. In most jurisdictions, one cannot remove his disqualification by assigning the interest to another. We shall refer to the person whose testimony is barred as the disqualified person.

3) Scope of the Incompetence. The variations are numerous. The most common statute prohibits the disqualified person from testifying to certain facts. A few statutes bar testimony by the disqualified person about all matters occurring before the death or incompetency.

The statute prohibits only testimony against the protected party. The statute does not prohibit the protected party from calling a disqualified person as a witness. Thus, the statutes operate more like privileges than full-fledged competency rules.

4) Subject Matter of the Incompetence. In most states the testimonial incompetence is not blanket; the statutes preclude only testimony that falls within one of these categories:

(a) A "transaction with or statement by" the decedent or incompetent person;

(b) A "personal transaction or communication" between the disqualified person and the decedent or incompetent;

(c) A "verbal statement of or transaction with" the decedent;

(d) A "conversation with or event which took place in the presence of" the deceased or incompetent person; and

(e) Oral communications between the decedent and the disqualified person.

Much litigation has centered on the question whether the events giving rise to a personal injury action, especially automobile accidents, are "transactions" with the decedent so as to bar a plaintiff's testimony about the accident when the alleged tortfeasor dies. The cases split, but many courts preclude such testimony. When we hear the expression "transaction," it usually connotes a consensual dealing such as a contract. A traffic accident is not a transaction in that sense. However, although the courts are generally hostile to these statutes, many have said that the expression "transaction" must be construed purposively. The purpose of the statute is to protect the estate from the injustice created by the unavailability of the decedent's testimony based on personal knowledge. Given that purpose, "transaction" should arguably be interpreted as including any fact or event which the decedent could have testified about on the basis of personal knowledge.

Some jurisdictions permit the disqualified person to testify for the limited purpose of authenticating business records. Although the party may not testify directly to the transactions, these courts permit the party to authenticate records that evidence the transactions.

5) Exceptions. Since Dead Man's Acts frequently defeat meritorious claims, there has been great hostility to the acts. Numerous exceptions to their operation have been recognized. Some are statutory; others are judicially created by artful statutory "construction." Most exceptions exempt parties standing in specified relationships from the act's operation. The relationships commonly exempted are employer–employee and partner–partner. These are important business relations. The fear is that if the act applied and precluded one party from testifying to normal business transactions, the interference with the relationship would be intolerable.

6) Waiver. If the Dead Man's Act is otherwise applicable and there is no exception, the party opposing the admission of the evidence should explicitly object. The party should use the following language: "[T]he witness is incompetent to answer the question asked because it calls for testimony of a personal transaction [or communication] with a person since deceased . . . , in violation of Section—of the state code." M. LADD & R. CARLSON, CASES AND MATERIALS ON EVIDENCE 295 (1972). Whenever the party opposing the evidence neglects to make such an express objection, he or she runs the risk that the court will find that the party waived the objection. Just as the skepticism about the acts' wisdom has led to several exceptions to the acts' scope, the hostility to the acts has made the courts receptive to waiver arguments. The courts have found—or strained to find—a waiver in a wide range of fact situations.

If the protected party calls a disqualified person as a witness, the incompetency is waived generally or at least as to the subjects on which the protected party examines the witness. All states recognize this exception.

There is similarly a waiver when evidence of the deceased or incompetent person's statement is introduced by the protected party. This will be in the form of a deposition or by virtue of a hearsay exception. The disqualified person may then testify about the same subject matter. This exception is also universal. There is a split, however, over whether the mere taking of the deposition effects a waiver, if the protected party does not offer it in evidence.

b. The Future of Dead Man's Acts

Dead Man's statutes have been under vigorous attack by legal writers and judges. Judge Weinstein described the reasons:

> Commentators have been virtually unanimous in their condemnation
> of the rules on the grounds that they:

"are fertile breeders of litigation, and most of them, while preventing the enforcement of many honest claims, are ineffective to prevent perjury by witnesses whose interest does not fall within the statutory ban."

3 WEINSTEIN'S EVIDENCE ¶ 601 [03], at 601-21(1992).

In discussing proposed Uniform Rule 601, Oklahoma's Evidence Subcommittee succinctly summarized the opposition:

The most beneficial effect in Oklahoma of this section would be the abolition of the Dead Man's statute. . . . This remnant of the general rule of disqualification for interest has no justification in logic or in a rational inquiry for truth in the trial of an issue of fact. Originally designed to balk the dishonest, it may defeat more legitimate claims than it will prevent dishonest claims since the statute does not disqualify a third party who might be suborned to perjury to manufacture a fraudulent claim whom the statute does not disqualify. A searching cross-examination should protect the estate from the fraudulent claims of unscrupulous survivors.

The reasoning of the drafters of the original acts was that since death had sealed the lips of one party to the transaction, fairness demands that the other party be silenced as well. The prevailing modern sentiment is that the risk that one party's death may create an evidentiary problem does not justify compounding the problem by depriving the finder of fact of other relevant evidence. *See also* Ray, *Dead Man's Statutes*, 24 OHIO ST. L.J. 89, 105–08 (1963); Ladd, *Witnesses*, 10 RUTGERS L. REV. 523, 526 (1956).

NOTES AND PROBLEMS

1. Should a Dead Man's Act apply to a will contest among the decedent's relatives? Can you distinguish a will contest from a lawsuit in which a stranger files a contract claim against the decedent's estate? Realistically, are the relatives claiming against the decedent?

2. Problem 7-6. In the *Hill* case, Worker's deposition was taken and filed. Shortly before trial, Worker died from causes unrelated to the accident, and his administrator was substituted as party defendant. What evidentiary problems would you anticipate in introducing the following items of evidence under the Dead Man's Acts of Illinois or New York; or the Dead Man's Act of your state, if any?

(a) Debra Hill's testimony about the accident;

(b) Debra Hill's testimony that Worker visited her at the hospital and what he told her during that visit;

(c) Testimony of Debra's husband, Arthur, about what he saw when he arrived at the accident scene; or

(d) Worker's deposition.

3. Several jurisdictions have developed an innovative solution. Instead of barring the survivor's testimony, they repealed or modified their Dead Man's Act so that declarations made by the decedent before her death (which otherwise would have been inadmissible hearsay) can be admitted into evidence.

Thus, both the survivor's testimony and the decedent's statements are placed before the trier of fact. *See, e.g.,* CAL. EVID. CODE §§ 1260–61; CONN. GEN. STAT. § 52-172; MO. ANN. STAT. § 491.010; UTAH RULES OF EVID. 601; VA. CODE ANN. § 8.01-397; WYO. STAT. ANN. § 1-12-102.

2. JUDGES, JURORS AND ATTORNEYS

a. Judges

A judge is a competent witness in a trial if the judge is not presiding over the trial. For instance, when a state prisoner files a federal habeas corpus action, the state judge can testify about the trial that resulted in the prisoner's conviction. But may the judge testify during a trial at which the judge is presiding? Perhaps it seems self–evident to you that the presiding judge should not take the witness stand and testify on behalf of a party. It will be extremely difficult for the jurors to resist the temptation to attach extraordinary weight to the judge's testimony. Moreover, the opposing attorney will find it awkward to cross–examine the judge. However, this is not a universal sentiment. *See, e.g.,* TENN. CODE ANN. § 24-1-205.

Almost all jurisdictions now disqualify the judge as a witness in the trial in which she is sitting. Federal Rule of Evidence 605 reads: "The judge presiding at the trial may not testify in that trial as a witness. No objection need be made in order to preserve the point." The Advisory Committee Note explains:

> In view of the mandate of 28 U.S.C. that a judge disqualify himself in "any case in which he . . . is or has been a material witness," the likelihood that the presiding judge in a federal court might be called to testify in the trial over which he is presiding is slight. Nevertheless, the possibility is not totally eliminated.
>
> The solution here presented is a broad rule of incompetency, rather than such alternatives as incompetency only as to material matters, leaving the matter to the discretion of the judge, or recognizing no incompetency. The choice is the result of the inability to evolve satisfactory answers to questions which arise when the judge abandons the bench for the witness stand. Who rules on objections? Who compels him to answer? Can he rule impartially on the weight and admissibility of his own testimony? Can he be impeached or cross-examined effectively? Can he, in a jury trial, avoid conferring his seal of approval on one side in the eyes of the jury? Can he, in a bench trial, avoid an involvement destructive of impartiality?
>
> The rule provides an "automatic" objection. To require an actual objection would confront an opponent with a choice between not objecting, with the result of allowing the testimony, and objecting, with the probable result of excluding the testimony but at the price of continuing the trial before a judge likely to feel that his integrity has been attacked by the objector.

PROBLEM

Problem 7-7. You represent defendant Devitt. The case is being tried without a jury. At the conclusion of the evidence, the judge announces her verdict — guilty. In giving the reasons for so finding, she states; "Now, I did not believe defendant's testimony. I visited the scene myself, and based on what I saw, I find that the events in question simply could not have unfolded the way he testified." Could you invoke Rule 605? *Lillie v. United States*, 953 F.2d 1188 (10th Cir. 1992).

b. Jurors

It may seem equally obvious that a juror should not step out of the jury box and onto the witness stand. The other jurors may be tempted to ascribe special significance to another juror's testimony. The problem should never arise. If the prospective jurors are properly questioned during *voir dire* examination, their personal knowledge of the case should be ascertained; ordinarily such knowledge will disqualify them as jurors. However, at early common law, when the problem arose, the courts permitted the juror to testify. Now read Federal Rule of Evidence 606(a).

> **606(a) At the trial.** A member of the jury may not testify as a witness before that jury in the trial of the case in which the juror is sitting. If the juror is called to testify, the opposing party shall be afforded an opportunity to object out of the presence of the jury.

The more practical issue is the extent to which a juror, after verdict, may testify about juror misconduct to impeach the verdict in support of the losing party's motion for a new trial. Read Federal Rule 606(b) and the Advisory Committee Note:

> **606(b) Inquiry into validity of verdict or indictment.** Upon an inquiry into the validity of a verdict or indictment, a juror may not testify as to any matter or statement occurring during the course of the jury's deliberations or to the effect of anything upon that or any other juror's mind or emotions as influencing the juror to assent to or dissent from the verdict or indictment or concerning the juror's mental processes in connection therewith, except that a juror may testify on the question whether extraneous prejudicial information was improperly brought to the jury's attention or whether any outside influence was improperly brought to bear upon any juror. Nor may a juror's affidavit or evidence of any statement by the juror concerning a matter about which the juror would be precluded from testifying be received for these purposes.

Advisory Committee Note:

> **Subdivision (b).** Whether testimony, affidavits, or statements of jurors should be received for the purpose of invalidating or supporting a verdict or indictment, and if so, under what circumstances, has given rise to substantial differences of opinion. The familiar rubric that a juror may not impeach his own verdict, dating from Lord Mansfield's time, is a gross oversimplification. The values sought to be promoted by excluding the evidence include freedom of deliberation, stability and finality of verdicts, and protection of jurors from annoyance and embarrassment. On the other hand, simply putting verdicts beyond effective reach can only promote irregularity and injustice. The rule offers an accommodation between these competing considerations.

The mental operations and emotional reactions of jurors in arriving at a given result would, if allowed as a subject of inquiry, place every verdict at the mercy of jurors and invite tampering and harassment. . . . As to matters other than mental operations and emotional reactions of jurors, substantial authority refuses to allow a juror to disclose irregularities which occur in the jury room, but allows his testimony as to irregularities occurring outside and allows outsiders to testify as to occurrences both inside and out. However, the door to the jury room is not necessarily a satisfactory dividing point . . . . Under the federal decisions the central focus has been upon insulation of the manner in which the jury reached its verdict, and this protection extends to each of the components of deliberation, including arguments, discussions, mental and emotional reactions, votes, and any other feature of the process. Thus testimony or affidavits of jurors have been held incompetent to show a [compromise verdict, quotient verdict, speculation as to insurance coverage, misinterpretation of instructions, mistake in returning verdict, and interpretation of guilty plea by one defendant as implicating others.] The policy does not, however, foreclose testimony of jurors as to prejudicial extraneous information or influences injected into or brought to bear upon the deliberative process. Thus a juror is recognized as competent to testify to statements by the bailiff or the introduction of a prejudicial newspaper account into the jury room. . . .

This rule does not purport to specify the substantive grounds for setting aside verdicts for irregularity; it deals only with the competency of jurors to testify concerning those grounds.

Carlson, *Impeaching Jury Verdicts*, 2 LITIGATION, Fall 1975, at 31–33, discusses this issue. Professor Carlson first poses a hypothetical in which a juror brings into the jury room an erroneous newspaper account of certain trial testimony that then serves as the basis for the verdict:

That the verdict was based upon an extraneous account which was inaccurate is clear. Now what? Can the party who lost get the verdict overturned? What if, in the course of a jury's deliberations, events take a slightly different turn? Instead of the jurors taking unsworn evidence from a newspaper, suppose they adopt an improper method of reaching a decision, such as drawing lots or using a quotient verdict to determine damages?

Newspaper clipping and quotient verdict problems seem to be more prevalent than other reported examples of jury "free enterprise." However, reported misconduct has ranged from unauthorized visits to a crime or accident scene by some jurors on their own, to the following situation: A defendant was being tried for illegal sale of alcoholic beverages. Exhibits in the case included three such bottles, all full, and these went with the jurors to the jury room when they retired to deliberate. Later, the bailiff was notified by the jurors that they had reached a verdict. The bailiff opened the door of the jury room and discovered that all three bottles had been opened and emptied. On review, the state supreme court ruled that "both parties have a right to the cool, dispassionate and unbiased judgment of each juror, and the rule seems to be well established that prejudice will be presumed if liquor is drunk after the jury has retired to consider the case." Whether jury misconduct is of the bizarre type as in the last example, or the more regularly encountered problem of the jury deciding the case on non-record information, the question remains—what may counsel do to remedy the situation?

State law is divided into the two competing positions. A strong minority view permits jurors to testify to objective misconduct—overt acts which can either be corroborated or disproved by the testimony of other jurors. Unauthorized trips by jurors to view the scene of a crime fall within this category, as do improper methods for arriving at a verdict. Under this view, deliberations do not lose all secrecy. Several items remain private. For example, a juror would be incompetent as a witness to report matters thought to "inhere in the verdict." Misconduct in this category is not objective misconduct and is not properly the subject of post–verdict attack. Examples include a juror's testimony that he misunderstood the judge's instructions, or one juror impugning another's reasoning in arriving at a verdict.

Sometimes, of course, it is not so much jury misconduct which taints a verdict as it is interference by outsiders. Opinions may be pressed upon jurors by others away from the trial as when parties or others talk or attempt to talk to jurors during a break in deliberations. Extraneous contact and opinions may come from several sources, as in *Parker v. Gladden*, 385 U.S. 363 (1966), where the bailiff made comments about the case to the jury during a break in deliberations.

This analysis, allowing attacks on verdicts marred by extraneous evidence or influence, basically follows the "Iowa Rule" formulated in 1866. A leading modern opinion embracing a similar approach is Chief Justice Traynor's decision in *People v. Hutchinson*, 455 P.2d 132 (Cal. 1969). *Hutchinson* involved a California trial court's rejection of a juror's affidavit. In the affidavit, the juror alleged that a bailiff came angrily into the jury deliberation room about dinner time and announced "This is it." Apparently wanting the jury to conclude deliberations quickly, the bailiff told the deliberating jurors, "If you knew what was going on out there, you would be shivering in your boots." A verdict convicting the defendant was returned. On a post-trial motion by the defendant, the trial judge refused to consider the juror's affidavit. The trial court followed the rule that juror testimony was incompetent to impeach a verdict. Citing the Iowa decision, *Wright v. Illinois & Mississippi Tel. Co.*, 20 Iowa 195 (1866), Chief Justice Traynor pointed out that admitting jurors' affidavits should have the "prophylactic effect of stripping from all prejudicial misconduct whatever veil of post-verdict secrecy is now reserved for the proper deliberations of the jury." When a verdict is improperly influenced, Chief Justice Traynor considered the wrong done to the individual on trial to be of paramount significance.

The competing, and still majority view, is known as the "Mansfield Rule." It came to dominate early American legal thought, and did so until cases such as *Wright* and *Hutchinson* appeared. The Mansfield Rule takes its name from Lord Mansfield's opinion in the old English case, *Vaise v.*

Delaval. Lord Mansfield ordained that jurors could not provide testimony as to their own misconduct in the jury room. However, an eavesdropper or spy could do so. Lord Mansfield appreciated the potential danger of juror misconduct, but provided for its exposure by stating that "in every such case the Court must derive their knowledge from some other source: such as from some person having seen the transaction through a window, or by some such other means."

Rule 606(b) of the new Federal Rules of Evidence provides a crisp, if partially disappointing, answer to the problem. Under the new rule, jury misconduct may be shown presumably either by live testimony or in juror affidavits supporting a motion for a new trial. Juror testimony attacking verdicts is allowed whenever "extraneous prejudicial information was improperly brought to the jury's attention" or when "outside influence was improperly brought to bear upon any juror." Thus, the jury's use of newspaper clippings may be exposed in a post-trial attack on the verdict. The clippings would constitute extraneous information which was improperly brought before the jury within the meaning of the federal rule. When a juror is approached by a party or another during a trial, the second provision of Rule 606(b) may be invoked to show that improper influence was brought to bear on any juror.

However, the rule insulates from attack a favorite ground for post-verdict complaint by defense lawyers in personal injury cases—the quotient verdict. Rule 606 as ultimately approved, provides that statements made during a jury's deliberations are not later reportable, except to show extraneous prejudicial information or improper outside influence.

PROBLEM

Problem 7-8. In *Hill,* which of the following could be shown by a juror's testimony:

(a) Most jurors misunderstood key instructions;

(b) Everyone ignored the judge's admonition not to be influenced by the fact that defendant could afford to pay a large judgment;

(c) A juror slept through the deliberations;

(d) The jurors agreed in advance that each would write a verdict amount on a slip of paper, they would add the amounts on the twelve slips, and they would be bound by the quotient of the sum divided by twelve;

(e) During the trial, a juror went to the public library and got some books on automobile design. She read excerpts aloud during the jury's deliberations;

(f) Several jurors read newspaper accounts of the trial;

(g) The jurors agreed to deliberate for a maximum of four hours;

(h) During deliberations, a juror related a similar personal experience with his automobile and that story influenced the verdict;

(i) During deliberations, several jurors made remarks clearly evidencing racial bias. (Ms. Hill is African-American.) *Shillcutt v. Gagnon*, 827 F.2d

1155 (7th Cir. 1987); *Dobbs v. Zant*, 720 F. Supp. 1566, 1571–79 (N.D. Ga. 1989), *aff'd*, 963 F.2d 1403 (11th Cir. 1991), *rev'd on other grounds*, 506 U.S. 357, 113 S.Ct. 835 (1993); *Powell v. Allstate Ins. Co.*, 652 So. 2d 354 (Fla. 1995);

(j) Throughout the trial several jurors consumed alcohol at lunch and tended to be sleepy in the afternoon sessions of the trial. *Tanner v. United States*, 483 U.S. 107 (1987); and

(k) At the beginning of the deliberations, the foreperson announced that she "strongly favored" a defense verdict and used "strong arm tactics" during deliberations to coerce other jurors to vote in favor of the defense. *United States v. Casamayor*, 837 F.2d 1509, 1515 (11th Cir. 1988), *cert. denied*, 488 U.S. 1017, 109 S. Ct. 813 (1989).

c. Attorneys

The American Bar Association's Model Rules of Professional Conduct (1999 edition), Rule 3.7(a) generally proscribes a lawyer's testimony in a case in which the lawyer is serving as an advocate unless (1) the testimony relates to an uncontested issue, (2) the testimony relates to the nature and value of legal services rendered in the case, or (3) disqualification of the lawyer would work a substantial hardship on the client. Most jurisdictions have a comparable rule. The former ABA Model Code of Professional Responsibility (DR 5-101(B)) contained a similar proscription. The Model Code, Ethical Consideration 5–9 articulates the rationale for the rule:

> If a lawyer is both counsel and witness, he becomes more easily impeachable for interest and thus may be a less effective witness. Conversely, the opposing counsel may be handicapped in challenging the credibility of the lawyer when the lawyer also appears as an advocate in the case. An advocate who becomes a witness is in the unseemly and ineffective position of arguing his own credibility. The roles of an advocate and of a witness are inconsistent; the function of an advocate is to advance or argue the cause of another, while that of a witness is to state facts objectively.

As a matter of policy, should the courts convert these ethical norms into competency rules and exclude testimony in violation of the professional responsibility rules? Although at one time an attorney was disqualified from testifying because of his financial interest, the modern trend has been to regard attorneys as competent. 3 J. WEINSTEIN & M. BERGER, WEINSTEIN'S EVIDENCE ¶ 601.04[3][a][1], at 601-20 (J. McLaughlin ed., 2d ed. 1997). However, playing the dual role of advocate and witness is viewed with disfavor. If an attorney expects to testify, he or she should not participate in the conduct of the trial. Although the court has discretion to exclude lawyer testimony, more often the testimony is permitted with conditions (such as requiring the lawyer to withdraw from active participation in the trial) or in some form other than direct and cross-examination (*e.g.*, narrative statement or stipulated testimony). *Id.* at 601–35 to 601–40. *See United States v. Johnston*, 690 F.2d 638, 642–43 n.10 (7th Cir. 1982) (collecting the cases); Note, *The Lawyer as a Witness for His Client*, 17 ALA. L. REV. 308 (1965).

NOTES

1. What danger arises if we permit the attorney to testify? The law ordinarily restricts witnesses to statements of observed fact; unless the witness qualifies as an expert, he or she may not draw conclusions or inferences. On the other hand, during closing argument, the attorney devotes most of her time to arguing inferences—conclusions as to whether the jury should believe a particular witness or whether the accident debris proves that the collision occurred in the northbound lane. How might the jury be confused if the attorney testifies as a witness?

2. Is there another reason to prohibit lawyer testimony if the lawyer is representing the client on a contingent fee basis? *See Anderson Producing, Inc. v. Koch Oil Co.*, 929 S.W.2d 416 (Tex. 1996). What about the prohibition against paying contingent compensation to a witness. *See* ABA Model Rule 3.4(b) and Comment [2], which states, in part, "The common law rule in most jurisdictions is that it is improper to pay an occurrence witness any fee for testifying and that it is improper to pay an expert witness a contingent fee."

3. The California Supreme Court has taken a step beyond Model Rule 3.7(a). In the California Rules of Professional Conduct, Rule 5-210 provides that the lawyer–advocate may testify before a jury if the lawyer "has the informed, written consent of the client." Advocates of the rule contend that the risk of jury confusion does not warrant barring the attorney's testimony. They point out that we sometimes permit the same witness to testify to both facts and opinions. For example, in a criminal case, an experienced police officer might both describe the defendant's conduct and opine that the conduct is consistent with the *modus operandi* of a particular type of crime. Bamberger, *The Dangerous Expert Witness*, 52 Brooklyn L. Rev. 855 (1986); *United States v. Thomas*, 896 F.2d 589 (D.C. Cir. 1990).

4. In light of the wording of Rule 601, does a federal judge have the authority to exclude an attorney's testimony? Although Rules 605 and 606 regulate the admissibility of testimony by judges and jurors, a provision on attorney's testimony is conspicuously absent from Article VI. However, remember Weinstein and Berger's thesis about the relationship between Rules 601 and 403.

5. In some cases, one party will seek to call an opposing party's attorney as a witness. What issues does this raise? *See Harter v. University of Indianapolis*, 5 F. Supp. 2d 657 (S.D. Ind. 1998).

3. THE CRIMINAL DEFENDANT

At one time, like all other parties to the litigation, the criminal defendant was incompetent as a witness by reason of his interest; he could not testify on his own behalf. That incompetency is now everywhere abolished.

Of course, the criminal defendant has a privilege not to take the stand. Moreover, criminal defendants, like any other witness, have a privilege not to be compelled to give incriminating testimony.

This privilege should be distinguished from the common law incompetency of persons convicted of certain crimes, based on their presumed lack of credibility. This incompetency is now abolished, except for a few state statutes making persons convicted of perjury incompetent. *E.g.*, MD. CODE ANN. CTS. & JUD. PROC. § 9-104 (1996). This incompetency may be unconstitutional, at least in criminal cases, if applied against a defense witness.

4. SPOUSES

At common law, spouses were not competent witnesses for or against each other. 2 J. WIGMORE, EVIDENCE § 600 (3d ed. 1940); 8 J. WIGMORE, EVIDENCE § 2227 (McNaughton rev. 1961). According to Wigmore, there were several historical bases for this rule: (1) *The common law unity of husband and wife.* Upon marriage, the wife lost her separate legal identity; and they became a legal unity, represented by the husband. Only he could sue or be sued. If the wife had an action, it had to be brought in the husband's name. Since parties were incompetent as witnesses, the husband could not testify. Therefore neither could his alter ego, his wife. (2) *The marital identity of interest.* Even apart from the spouses' legal identity, their interest in the outcome of any lawsuit would be the same. Hence, the rationale for the party's incompetency applied equally to the party's spouse. (3) *The assumed bias of affection.* Because of the spouses' intimate relationship and strong feelings for each other, their testimony was deemed incredible. (4) *Public policy.* There might be interference with marital harmony if the wife could be called to give unfavorable testimony against her husband. Even if the wife gave favorable testimony on direct examination, on cross–examination she may be required to give damaging testimony.

Wigmore and other commentators justifiably attacked the bases for the rule. Today the rule has been uniformly abolished by the statutes that make almost all persons competent. A spouse is now everywhere a competent witness for his or her spouse in criminal and civil cases. However, the special nature of the marital relationship and the strong public policy supporting that relationship militate against compelling a spouse to testify to marital confidences or to testify for the prosecution in a criminal case in which the other spouse is the defendant.

These considerations have led to two separate and distinct doctrines applicable to spousal testimony. Each has its own set of rules; they are quite different. In a given jurisdiction, one, some or all may be available. These doctrines, summarized here, are covered, *infra*, in the materials on privileges.

Husband–Wife (or Spousal) Disqualification. In most jurisdictions, a spouse may not be compelled, over objection, to testify against his or her spouse in a criminal case. In a few jurisdictions, the privilege extends to civil cases. Additionally, in some states, in a criminal proceeding the accused spouse can prevent the witness spouse from testifying against him. This rule has been analogized to a disqualification or competency rule, since it may prevent a spouse from giving any testimony at all. Some jurisdictions even extend the disqualification to bar the introduction of otherwise admissible hearsay statements by the witness spouse.

The Privilege for Confidential Marital Communications. The social policy promoting the privacy of the marital relationship supports creating a privilege to bar one spouse's testimony about confidential communications between the spouses during the marriage.

Chapter 8

LOGICAL RELEVANCE: PROBATIVE VALUE

Read Federal Rules of Evidence 401, 402, 602 and 901.

A. INTRODUCTION

In the preceding chapter we discussed the threshold admissibility question of whether a person is competent to serve as a witness. If a person does not qualify as a competent witness, that person cannot give any testimony at the trial. Assuming the competency hurdle can be overcome, there are several other hurdles that must be cleared to guarantee the testimony's admission. The next hurdle presented is the requirement of logical relevance.

The competency doctrine focuses on the prospective witness; we test the prospective witness' personal qualifications such as the ability to perceive and remember. However, the logical relevance doctrine shifts our focus to the substantive content of the witness' proposed testimony. Even if the person is qualified to give some testimony in the case, that conclusion does not guarantee the admissibility of everything to which the witness proposes to testify.

At the very least, to be admissible, evidence must have probative value. Federal Evidence Rule 402 states the principle succinctly: "Evidence which is not relevant is not admissible." The simplicity of the sentence in Rule 402 is deceiving. The evidentiary concept of logical relevance has several, subtle aspects. To grasp the concept, the student must master three basic distinctions covered in this chapter: (1) the distinction between pure logical relevance and materiality, (2) the distinction between direct and circumstantial logical relevance; and (3) the distinction between facial and underlying logical relevance. As we study this area, it will become increasingly clear that the Federal Rules of Evidence display a strong bias in favor of admitting logically relevant evidence.

B. THE DISTINCTION BETWEEN PURE LOGICAL RELEVANCE AND MATERIALITY

1. PURE LOGICAL RELEVANCE

Pure logical relevance is a matter of logic and experience, not a matter of law or policy. When we ask whether an item has "logical relevance," we are testing to see whether as a matter of logic and experience, the item tends to support a particular inference; we try to determine whether there is a rational nexus or connection between the item of evidence and the inference the item is offered to prove. To visualize the test, think of this diagram:

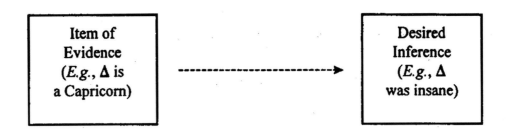

To draw the arrow, we must conclude that the item of evidence has some effect upon the balance of probabilities regarding the truth of the desired inference—either increasing or decreasing its probability. If the item increases or decreases the probability—no matter how slightly, the item has logical relevance. Do not be concerned with how greatly the item increases or decreases the probability; we shall turn to the matter of the quantum of probative value when we consider legal irrelevance. At this point we are interested only in whether there is bare logical relevance, that is, whether the item has any effect at all on the balance of probabilities.

PROBLEMS

1. Problem 8-1. In the *Devitt* case, the defense is attempting to prove that Devitt was insane at the time of the alleged battery. Which of the following items of evidence would be logically relevant? Why?

- Proof that there was a full moon the night of the alleged battery.

- Proof that Devitt is a Capricorn.

- Proof that Devitt was under psychiatric care twenty years ago.

- Testimony by a lay witness that she observed Devitt two hours before the alleged battery and that in her opinion, he was "acting a bit peculiar."

- Testimony of a licensed psychiatrist that Devitt is psychotic.

In answering these questions, pretend that you had never attended law school. Answer each question from the perspective of a logical and reasonably knowledgeable, adult layperson. Would such a layperson find a difference between proof of the full moon and evidence of Devitt's psychiatric treatment twenty years ago? If so, why?

2. Problem 8-2. In *Devitt,* the defense would like to offer evidence that the defendant took and passed a polygraph test. During the test, Devitt denied attacking Paterson. At trial, the defense calls Dr. Abrahams, the polygraphist who administered the test to Devitt. On the one hand, Dr. Abrahams testifies that the polygraph test is generally accurate 70-85% of the time. On the other hand, he concedes that as a scientist, he uses the rule of thumb that a scientific technique's validity is not proven until it attains an accuracy level of 90% or better. The prosecutor objects that Dr. Abraham's testimony is "absolutely irrelevant" given Abraham's admissions about the fallibility of the polygraph.

3. Problem 8-3. In our torts case, after the accident Ms. Hill files a claim for personal injury and property damage with her insurer, Midwest Mutual. Midwest Mutual denies the claim, and Ms. Hill later sues Midwest Mutual. She sues not only to recover the policy proceeds covering her losses but also for attorney's fees. The law of this jurisdiction allows an insured to recover attorney's fees in a suit against the insurer if the insurer denied the claim in bad faith. At the trial of her suit against Midwest Mutual, Ms. Hill offers evidence that she offered to submit a polygraph test administered by any examiner of Midwest Mutual's choosing. Midwest's attorney objects that the evidence is irrelevant. (Assume that polygraph evidence is generally inadmissible in this jurisdiction.) *See Criss v. Springfield Township*, 564 N.E.2d 440 (Ohio 1990); *Murphy v. Cincinnati Ins. Co.*, 772 F.2d 273, 277 (6th Cir. 1985).

4. Problem 8-4. In her lawsuit against Roe and Polecat, Ms. Hill offers evidence that before trial, Worker refused to submit to a polygraph test about the accident. The defense attorneys object that the evidence is irrelevant. *See* Comment, *The Courtroom Status of the Polygraph*, 14 AKRON L. REV. 133, 149 (1980). Suppose that Ms. Hill asked the judge to consider the following testimony from Dr. Miriam Laurens before ruling on the relevance objection: She operates a polygraph firm in town; Worker was formerly one of her employees; and she often heard Worker say that he considered the polygraph to be "highly reliable." (Once again, assume that polygraph evidence is ordinarily inadmissible in this jurisdiction.)

5. Problem 8-5. One month after the accident in the *Hill* case, Polecat redesigned the gas tank of the model of car involved in the accident. Polecat began marketing automobiles with the redesigned gas tank one year after the accident. At the trial, Ms. Hill's attorney offers evidence of the redesign. Polecat's attorney objects that "what we did later isn't at all relevant to whether we were at fault at the time of the accident. The only question is what happened then—not what might have occurred a whole year later."

6. Problem 8-6. In the *Hill* case, to show the defective nature of the gas tank Ms. Hill's attorney offers evidence of two accidents that occurred six years before the accident in *Hill*. In both of the prior accidents, the vehicles had gas tanks similar to the tank in Ms. Hill's car; the gas tanks exploded in the manner in which Ms. Hill's did; and the drivers suffered injuries similar to Ms. Hill's. However, neither injured party sued Polecat; and in this jurisdiction, there is a five-year statute of limitations on such claims. When Ms. Hill's attorney offers evidence of the prior accidents, Polecat's attorney objects that "those accidents can't be used against us now; since the period of limitations has passed, they're no longer actionable and, hence, irrelevant." *See Black Law Enforcement Officers Ass'n v. City of Akron*, 824 F.2d 475 (6th Cir. 1987).

7. Problem 8-7. In the *Devitt* case file, the pivotal question is whether Devitt attacked Paterson without provocation. Assume alternatively a prosecution in which the central issue is the assailant's identity. The victim, Paterson, testifies that during the fight, the assailant accidentally cut himself on his own knife so badly that the assailant bled on Paterson's shirt. The prosecutor lays a proper chain of custody for the shirt from the crime scene to Dr. Margolin at the crime laboratory. Dr. Margolin is prepared to testify that: She is an expert in blood identification; she analyzed the stain on the shirt and a sample of blood she drew from the defendant; both samples were type A blood; and approximately 42% of the world's population has type A blood. A. Moenssens, J. Starrs, C. Henderson & F. Inbau, Scientific Evidence in Civil and Criminal Cases § 13.10, at 778 (4th ed. 1995). The defense attorney objects that "so many persons have type A blood that this evidence has absolutely no probative value." *See People v. Sturdivant*, 91 Mich. App. 128, 134, 283 N.W.2d 669, 672 (1979). Do you agree?

8. Problem 8-8. In the *Devitt* case, suppose the victim testifies that the assailant kidnaped him and forced him to go to a nearby apartment. He testifies that the apartment in question had a moose head on one wall, a triangle-shaped mirror on another wall and a picture of the Empire State Building on a third wall. The prosecutor then calls the defendant's landlord to testify that the victim's description corresponds to objects on the walls in the defendant's apartment. The defense objects that "the testimony has nothing to do with this case." *See Bridges v. State*, 247 Wis. 350, 19 N.W.2d 529, 534–36 (1945). Suppose alternatively that the victim testifies only that the apartment contained a bed and a television. Once again the landlord is willing to testify that the defendant's apartment contains the items the victim described.

2. MATERIALITY

Suppose that in Morena, insanity is an affirmative defense in criminal cases. Further, Morena procedure requires that the defendant plead the defense at the time of arraignment. Devitt's attorney failed to do so. Nevertheless, Devitt's attorney offers the items of testimony in Problem 8–1 above at trial. In this situation, at common law, the prosecutor would have to object that the testimony was "immaterial" rather than "irrelevant": The testimony has logical relevance to prove insanity, but insanity is not properly at issue in the case. In other words, if Devitt's attorney had properly pleaded insanity, some of the items in 8–1 would be both logically relevant and material. However, because of the pleading error, such evidence is objectionable as immaterial. It still has pure logical relevance (*i.e.*, it is probative of insanity), but it lacks materiality (*i.e.*, insanity is not an issue in the case).

NOTES AND PROBLEMS

1. What factors do you consider in determining whether a proposition is material? Do you look only to the substantive law governing the case? How do the pleadings figure into your determination? Focus particularly on the defense's responsive pleading such as the answer. Can that pleading enlarge or contract the scope of "material fact"?

2. Problem 8-9. Now review the indictment in the *Devitt* case file. Be prepared to list all the ultimate facts in issue under the indictment.

3. Problem 8-10. In the *Devitt* case, the prosecutor offers evidence that the alleged battery occurred within the limits of the city and county of El Dorado. Is that evidence material? To what?

4. Problem 8-11. In our torts case, Ms. Hill prays for punitive damages and that prayer is still in the complaint when the case goes to trial. Could she introduce evidence of Polecat Motors' wealth? Would that be material? Why? *See* Annot., 79 A.L.R.3d 1138, 1139–40 (1977).

5. Problem 8-12. In the *Devitt* case, the state charges the defendant with both battery and first-degree assault. Under Morena law, first-degree assault is a specific *mens rea* crime. Could Devitt introduce evidence that he had been drinking heavily three hours before the alleged incident? To what would that evidence be material? What if the state charged Devitt with third-degree assault, a general *mens rea* crime?

We have already identified two factors we consider in deciding what is material: the substantive law and the pleadings. There is a third factor, namely, the evidence that has been introduced to date in the trial. That factor gives rise to the **curative admissibility** or "opening the door" doctrine. If one party injects inadmissible evidence in the case, should the judge permit the opponent to respond in kind to "cure" the prejudice caused by the inadmissible evidence?

At common law, there is a three-way split of authority over that doctrine. Comment, *Evidence — Curative Admissibility in Missouri*, 32 Mo. L. Rev. 505, 505–08 (1967). A minority of courts do not recognize the doctrine at all; unless the evidence is relevant to the substantive law and pleadings, the evidence is inadmissible. These courts reason that "the admission of incompetent evidence without objection never justifies a rebuttal in kind." Two wrongs do not make a right. In effect, these courts give the opponent only one option: objecting to exclude the inadmissible evidence.

The overwhelming majority of jurisdictions, however, have endorsed some version of the curative admissibility doctrine. Most subscribe to the view that the opposing attorney may resort to similar inadmissible evidence. This view is premised on a simple forfeiture rationale: Having introduced incompetent evidence, the first attorney has forfeited the protection of evidence law and consequently is in "no position to complain" when the opponent proffers technically inadmissible, responsive testimony. The opponent is entitled to "fight fire with fire."

Other courts have developed a more sophisticated version of the majority view. This view is sometimes dubbed the Massachusetts rule. According to this rule, the opponent may introduce incompetent, responsive testimony only when it is needed to remove unfair prejudice caused by the proponent's evidence. The linchpin of this view is a fairness rationale; the evidentiary rules yield when it would be unfair to permit the opponent to meet the proponent's evidence. However, when there is little or no resultant prejudice, the rules should remain in force.

NOTES AND PROBLEMS

1. Which view is soundest? The majority rule has the support of the weight of the authority, but does it really rest on legitimate evidentiary considerations? Or are we simply penalizing the other party for having violated the evidentiary rules? Is that a proper consideration in the formulation of relevance doctrine? If the evidence improperly admitted was otherwise irrelevant and we permit the party to meet that evidence, are we not running the risk that the jury will be diverted from the real issues in the case?

2. Problem 8-13. In the *Devitt* case, the prosecutor has inadmissible evidence that four years before the alleged battery, Devitt had made an unprovoked attack on a supervisor at work. The evidence would normally be inadmissible because of the character evidence rules that we shall discuss. However, add a fact: on direct examination by his own attorney, Devitt volunteers the statement that "I've never committed a battery or attacked anybody or done anything bad like that in my life." Would that statement "open the door" to rebuttal by otherwise inadmissible evidence?

3. Is the "curative admissibility" doctrine codified in the Federal Rules of Evidence? It is sometimes said that the "principle of completeness" codified in Federal Rule 106 is, in part, based on the concept of "opening the door." *See United States v. Corrigan*, 168 F.2d 641, 645 (2d Cir. 1948).

It is true that the Federal Rules do not expressly codify the doctrine. For that matter, no jurisdiction recognizing the doctrine has codified it. Why? The doctrine rests on well-recognized concepts of common law reasoning, namely, waiver and forfeiture. May a court consistently hold that (a) the Federal Rules impliedly abolish most uncodified evidentiary rules, but (b) the court may still employ fundamental tools of legal reasoning, such as the forfeiture concept, although the Rules make no mention of the concept? Waiver and forfeiture are not evidentiary rules; they are broader notions which are sometimes applied in an evidentiary context. In *United States v. Mezzanatto*, 513 U.S. 196, 115 S. Ct. 797, 130 L. Ed. 2d 697 (1995), speaking for the majority, Justice Thomas declared that "absent some affirmative indication of Congress' intent to preclude waiver, we have presumed that statutory provisions are subject to waiver . . . ."

3. MODERN STATUTORY TREATMENT OF LOGICAL RELEVANCE AND MATERIALITY

As we previously indicated, the early common law separated the doctrines of logical relevance and materiality. If the proponent's evidence did not prove what he or she offered it to prove, the opponent had to voice the objection that the evidence was "irrelevant." In contrast, if the desired inference was not within the range of dispute in the case, the opponent had to make the "immaterial" objection. The trial judge could overrule the objection if the opponent confused the two concepts.

Federal Evidence Rule 401 is typical of the modern statutory treatment of the two concepts:

"Relevant evidence" means evidence having any tendency to make the existence of any fact that is of consequence to the determination of the action more probable or less probable than it would be without the evidence.

This statute merges the two concepts. Given this definition of "relevant evidence," the opponent no longer has to differentiate between the "immaterial" objection and the "irrelevant" objection. To raise either contention, the opponent need only object that the evidence is "irrelevant."

Under this definition, determining the logical relevance of evidence is a two-step process. First, the proponent must identify all the material facts of consequence in the case. These facts can include preliminary facts such as venue, the historical facts on the merits such as an essential element of a crime, and collateral facts such as the credibility of all the witnesses who have already testified in the case. (In this respect, relevance as an evidentiary concept is narrower than relevance in the context of pretrial discovery. *Hofer v. Mack Trucks, Inc.*, 981 F.2d 377 (8th Cir. 1992). An item is discoverable before trial so long as it is logically relevant to an issue which the pleadings could be amended to include. *Oppenheimer Fund, Inc. v. Sanders*, 437 U.S. 340 (1978). In contrast, apart from the operation of the curative admissibility doctrine, for evidentiary purposes at trial the item must relate to an issue which has actually been pleaded.)

Second, the proponent must convince the judge that the item of evidence is logically relevant to one of the material facts. Notice the standard announced in Rule 401: "more probable or less probable than it would be without the evidence." As one court has remarked:

> [I]n determining whether evidence is relevant, the . . . court must not consider the weight or sufficiency of the evidence. Even if a . . . court believes the evidence is insufficient to prove the ultimate fact for which it is offered, it may not exclude the evidence [under Rule 401] if it has even the slightest probative worth.

Douglass v. Eaton Corp., 956 F.2d 1339, 1344 (6th Cir. 1992). Initially, the judge ascertains what the proponent *claims* that the item is; and under Rule 401, the judge inquires whether the item affects the balance of probabilities of the existence of a material fact *if* the item is what it is claimed to be.

NOTES

1. Notice what Rule 401 does <u>not</u> say.

2. California Evidence Code § 210 contains the following definition of "relevant evidence":

> "Relevant evidence" means evidence, including evidence relevant to the credibility of a witness or hearsay declarant, having any tendency in reason to prove or disprove any disputed fact that is of consequence to the determination of the action.

How does that language differ from the wording of Federal Evidence Rule 401? Suppose that, in its answer in our torts case, Polecat Motors admits that it manufactured the instrumentality or that Polecat later formally tenders a stipulation to that effect. Given the admission or stipulation, must Ms. Hill offer proof of manufacture to make out a submissible case? Even if Ms. Hill need not do so, may she do so under Rule 401? Under California Evidence Code § 210? The Advisory Committee Note to Rule 401 indicates that the drafters deliberately rejected Evidence Code § 210 as a possible model, and in the same paragraph the Note adds that "[t]he fact to which the evidence is directed need not be in dispute." Rule 401 commits the federal courts to the most liberal trial relevance standard in effect anywhere in the United States.

C.   THE DISTINCTION BETWEEN DIRECT AND CIRCUMSTANTIAL LOGICAL RELEVANCE

1.   DIRECTLY RELEVANT EVIDENCE

Even lay people have heard of the distinction between direct and circumstantial evidence. They have seen movies in which the criminal defense attorney attempted to persuade the jury by disparaging the prosecution's evidence as "circumstantial." There is an intuitive reaction that somehow direct evidence is more reliable than circumstantial proof. However, in truth, there is only one clear difference between the two types of evidence: primarily, they differ in the manner in which they are logically relevant to the material facts.

Evidence is directly "relevant" (as defined in Rule 401) if the immediate inference from the evidence is the existence or nonexistence of a material fact. Direct evidence is "[e]vidence, which if believed, proves [the] existence of [the] fact in issue without inference or presumption." *E.E.O.C. v. MCI Intern., Inc.*, 829 F. Supp. 1438, 1447 (D.N.J. 1993). One of the material facts in dispute in our torts case is whether Ms. Hill was in pain immediately after her collision with Worker; the pain is one of Ms. Hill's elements of damage. It would be direct evidence if Ms. Hill testifies that she was conscious after the collision and can distinctly recall suffering excruciating pain.

To visualize the definition, the evidence and the logical relevance are direct if we can draw an arrow in a straight, uninterrupted line from the item of evidence to the item in the box:

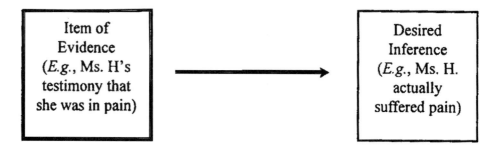

The only remaining question for the jurors is the witness' credibility, that is, whether the witness is believable. Other than that, the jury does not have to draw any intermediate inference between the testimony and the desired inference.

2. CIRCUMSTANTIALLY RELEVANT EVIDENCE

Assume now that the proffered item of evidence does not create an immediate inference that a material fact exists. The evidence can still be logically "relevant" as defined in Rule 401—but it would be circumstantially relevant. Again we must resort to logic and experience: Our experience tells us that the item of evidence can serve as a step in a process of logical reasoning toward the existence or nonexistence of a material fact. The jury must draw an intermediate inference, but the item can serve as a link in a chain of reasoning steps leading to the ultimate, desired inference. Visualize circumstantial evidence in this fashion:

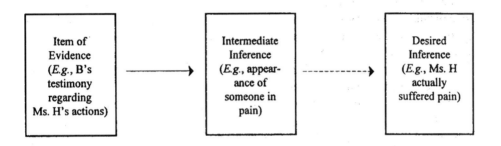

For example, in the *Hill* case, a bystander's testimony that he observed Ms. Hill bent over and holding her head would be circumstantial evidence that she was in pain. Even if the jurors decide that the bystander's testimony is credible, they must also decide to infer Ms. Hill's pain from the circumstances to which the bystander testified. The jury may decide to make the additional inference or decline to do so, drawing the contrary inference that Ms. Hill was merely slightly disoriented after the accident. Testimony by Ms. Hill that she was in pain would be direct evidence; the only step needed to get from Ms. Hill's testimony to the desired inference is whether the jury believes her testimony.

PROBLEMS

Are the following items of evidence direct or circumstantial? If they are circumstantial, lay out the entire line of reasoning leading from the item of evidence to the ultimate, desired inference:

1. Problem 8-14. As in Problem 8-7, the prosecutor offers testimony of a physician that the defendant's blood type is A. Assume that the following evidence has already been admitted: The victim Paterson testifies that during the fight the assailant accidentally cut himself on his own knife; Paterson thinks that the assailant bled a bit during the fight; the investigating police officer testified that he found red stains at the alleged crime scene and took them to the police laboratory. A laboratory serologist testifies that the stains were blood of type A. Remember that roughly forty two percent of the population has type A blood. *See People v. Vernon*, 89 Cal. App. 3d 853, 869, 152 Cal. Rptr. 765, 775 (1979).

2. Problem 8-15. In the battery prosecution, Paterson testifies that the assailant attacked him from behind and that consequently, he cannot recognize his face. However, he adds that the attacker did speak during the scuffle and that he can recognize the attacker's voice. He testifies that he heard the defendant testify at an earlier hearing in the case and that he can identify the defendant's voice as the assailant's voice. Assume a worst case scenario from the prosecution's perspective: an extreme case in which Paterson admits that to the best of his knowledge, before the alleged attack he had never met or spoken with the defendant. *See Patterson v. State*, 598 S.W.2d 265, 270 (Tex. Crim. App. 1980).

3. THE SIGNIFICANCE OF THE DISTINCTION BETWEEN DIRECT AND CIRCUMSTANTIAL EVIDENCE

In most respects, there is no distinction between the two types of relevant evidence. Some commentators have even charged that the distinction is of purely academic significance—still another thin distinction with which to torture law students. However, the distinction has some formal and practical significance. Rosenberg & Rosenberg, *"Perhaps What Ye Say Is Based Only on Conjecture"—Circumstantial Evidence Then and Now*, 31 Hous. L. Rev. 1371 (1995).

In some jurisdictions, when a party is relying primarily or exclusively upon circumstantial evidence, the trial judge must give the jury a special cautionary instruction. In Georgia, for example, the trial judge often gives the jury an instruction tracking the language of Ga. Code Ann. § 24-4-6 (1982): "To warrant a conviction on circumstantial evidence, the proved facts shall not only be consistent with the hypothesis of guilt, but shall exclude every other reasonable hypothesis save that of the guilt of the accused." There has been growing hostility to the practice. Even in the jurisdictions subscribing to that view, the courts are reluctant to give the instruction if there is "any" direct evidence of the fact. *Bates v. State*, 587 S.W.2d 121 (Tex. Crim. App. 1979); *Arney v. State*, 580 S.W.2d 836 (Tex. Crim. App. 1979). There has been a noticeable trend toward abandoning the special, circumstantial evidence instruction. *Galvan v. State*, 598 S.W.2d 624 (Tex. Crim. App. 1979) (collecting the authorities from the various jurisdictions and concluding that "Texas should join the growing list of jurisdictions who have abandoned the circumstantial evidence charge"). *See also Hankins v. State*, 646 S.W.2d 191 (Tex. Crim. App. 1983).

Characterizing an item of evidence as direct rather than circumstantial may also affect its admissibility. As we shall see *infra*, evidence must be *legally* as well as *logically* relevant. The judge can exclude the evidence as legally irrelevant if the judge concludes that there are dangers to admitting it which outweigh the probative worth of the evidence. One probative danger is the tendency of an item of evidence to distract the jurors from the central, historical issues in the case. By its very nature, circumstantial evidence usually has a greater tendency to generate collateral (possible distracting) issues.

Labeling evidence circumstantial rather than direct can also affect the availability of pretrial summary judgment in the case:

> Where the nonmoving party has come forward with direct evidence contrary to that offered by the movant, a credibility issue is raised. Credibility determinations are for the trier of fact and, therefore, are not appropriately resolved by summary judgment. However, when the only evidence offered in opposition to the motion for summary judgment is circumstantial . . ., . . . the court may inquire into the plausibility of inferences drawn from that evidence.

Travers v. Sullivan, 791 F. Supp. 1471, 1474 (E.D. Wash. 1992), *aff'd sub nom. Travers v. Shalala*, 20 F.3d 993 (9th Cir. 1994). Moreover, in some jurisdictions, when the prosecution relies solely or primarily on circumstantial evidence, the judge holds the prosecution to a more rigorous standard in passing on a defense motion for a judgment of acquittal as a matter of law. R. CARLSON, CRIMINAL LAW ADVOCACY—TRIAL PROOF ¶ 9.04, at 9-39-40 (1982).

Furthermore, some appellate courts have asserted that they exercise a broader scope of review of lower court findings when the findings rest on circumstantial evidence. Note, *Appellate Review of Circumstantial Evidence in Indiana Criminal Cases*, 7 IND. L. REV. 883 (1974). Hence, the distinction can make a difference at the appellate level. The circumstantial character of the case will cause the appellate court to use a more rigorous standard in evaluating the sufficiency of the proponent's evidence.

Aside from these formal distinctions between direct and circumstantial evidence, the fundamental question arises whether direct evidence is more trustworthy than circumstantial evidence. Eyewitness testimony is "direct" evidence; the only question the jury must answer is whether to believe the witness when he says that with his own eyes he saw the defendant commit the crime. Lay jurors are quite willing to rely on eyewitness testimony. A study by Dr. Elizabeth Loftus, a respected witness psychologist, shows that lay jurors are more willing to convict on the basis of eyewitness testimony than on the basis of high quality scientific proof such as fingerprints or questioned document analysis. N.Y. TIMES, March 17, 1981, at Y16.

Yet in this century, witness psychology has given us some disturbing insights into the reliability of purported eyewitness identifications. Levine & Tapp, *The Psychology of Criminal Identification: The Gap from* Wade *to* Kirby, 121 U. PA. L. REV. 1079 (1973). *United States v. Wade*, 388 U.S. 218 (1967) is the landmark decision in which the Court recognized the defendant's right to counsel at post-indictment lineups. Writing for the Court in *Wade*, Justice Brennan stated:

> The vagaries of eyewitness identification are well-known; the annals of criminal law are rife with instances of mistaken identification. Mr. Justice Frankfurter once said: "What is the worth of identification testimony even when uncontradicted? The identification of strangers is proverbially untrustworthy. The hazards of such testimony are established by a formidable number of instances in the records of English and American trials. These instances are recent—not due to

the brutalities of ancient criminal procedure." The Case of Sacco and Vanzetti 30 (1927). A major factor contributing to the high incidence of miscarriage of justice from mistaken identification has been the degree of suggestion inherent in the manner in which the prosecution presents the suspect to witnesses for pretrial identification. A commentator has observed that "[t]he influence of improper suggestion upon identifying witnesses probably accounts for more miscarriages of justice than any other single factor—perhaps it is responsible for more such errors than all other factors combined." Wall, Eye-Witness Identification in Criminal Cases 26. Suggestion can be created intentionally or unintentionally in many subtle ways. And the dangers for the suspect are particularly grave when the witness' opportunity for observation was insubstantial, and thus his susceptibility to suggestion the greatest.

Moreover, "[i]t is a matter of common experience that, once a witness has picked out the accused at the line-up, he is not likely to go back on his word later on, so that in practice the issue of identity may (in the absence of other relevant evidence) for all practical purposes be determined there and then, before the trial."

More recently, the Court of Appeals for the Second Circuit declared: "Eyewitness identification is the most direct evidence of criminal conduct available yet many believe it to be more than occasionally unreliable." *United States v. Sureff*, 15 F.3d 225, 229 (2d Cir. 1994).

Contrast direct eyewitness testimony with scientific evidence. In most cases, scientific evidence will be circumstantial. Suppose, for instance, that Devitt denied ever entering Paterson's bedroom but a fingerprint expert testifies that latent fingerprints found on a plastic comb in the bedroom belong to the defendant. That evidence is only circumstantial proof of guilt; but given Devitt's denial, the fingerprint evidence has great probative value.

Just as the lay assumption of the superiority of direct evidence is uncritical, it would be a mistake to leap to the conclusion that scientific circumstantial evidence is always reliable. Studies of the accuracy levels of analyses by crime laboratories suggest that errors are far from infrequent. In the middle of the last decade, the Law Enforcement Assistance Administration sponsored a Laboratory Proficiency Testing Program. The program began in the fall of 1974. Between 235 and 240 crime laboratories from throughout the United States participated. The Project Advisory Committee prepared samples and submitted them to the participating laboratories for analysis. The Committee had already determined the data that a proper forensic analysis of the samples would yield, and the Committee compared the participating laboratories' reports against that data. The results of the program were alarming. Test 3 concerned blood analysis. Only 60% of the laboratories testing for the MN system reached the correct conclusion. PROJECT ADVISORY COMMITTEE, LABORATORY PROFICIENCY TESTING PROGRAM, SUPPLEMENTARY REPORT-SAMPLES 1–5, at i (1975). Test 8 was another blood analysis. On this test, only 37.4% of the laboratories correctly concluded whether two bloodstains could have had a common origin. PROJECT ADVISORY COMMITTEE, LABORATORY PROFICIENCY TESTING PROGRAM, SUPPLEMENTARY REPORT-SAMPLES 6–10, at 3 (1976). In still later tests, over half of the participating laboratories misanalyzed hair samples. *Crime Labs' Credibility Questioned*, 14 TRIAL, Oct. 1978, at 9. Similarly, a study of toxicology laboratories in the early 1980's reported a "disappointingly low" level of proficiency. Peat, Finnigan & Finkle, *Proficiency Testing in Forensic Toxicology: A Feasibility Study*, 28 J. FORENSIC SCIENCES 139 (1983). In 1985, a government study pronounced the existence of a "crisis" in the quality of drug testing in American laboratories. Hansen, Caudill & Boone, *Crisis in Drug Testing: Results of CDC Blind Study*, 253 J.A.M.A. 2382 (1985) (study conducted by Center for Disease Control in conjunction with National Institute on Drug Abuse); Miike & Hewitt, *Accuracy and Reliability of Urine Drug Tests*, 36 U. KAN. L. REV. 641, 651–57 (1988) ("error rates continue to be high"). Proficiency tests of questioned document examiners also disclose shockingly high error rates. Risinger, Denbeaux & Saks, *Exorcism of Ignorance as a Proxy for Rational Knowledge: The Lessons of Handwriting Identification "Expertise,"* 137 U. PA. L. REV. 731, 738–51 (1989).

Perhaps the most intelligent position is the stance the Supreme Court took in *Holland v. United States*, 348 U.S. 121, 140 (1954): "Circumstantial evidence . . . is intrinsically no different from testimonial [direct] evidence." Most courts are persuaded of the wisdom of that position. That position leads us back to our starting point and explains why, in most respects, courts treat circumstantial evidence in the same fashion as direct evidence. In short, when the opposing attorney objects that your evidence is "irrelevant," you need not be able to characterize the challenged item of evidence as "direct." You only need to be creative enough on the facts of your case to find and articulate logical relevance on any theory.

D.   THE DISTINCTION BETWEEN FACIAL AND UNDERLYING LOGICAL RELEVANCE

1.   FACIAL LOGICAL RELEVANCE

To understand the concept of relevance under Rule 401, it is helpful to distinguish between "facial" and "underlying" logical relevance. In deciding the question of facial relevance, the question is whether the item of evidence— "on its face" —appears to be logically relevant to the material facts. The basic questions are: What does the proponent claim that the item is? If it is what it is claimed to be, is it "relevant" to the material facts (*i.e.*, will the item of evidence increase or decrease the probability of the existence of any material fact?) For example, a love letter from defendant to the victim, on its face, tends to suggest that defendant loved the victim. The true relevancy of this depends upon whether defendant actually wrote (or somehow adopted) the love letter.

2.   UNDERLYING LOGICAL RELEVANCE

To understand the concept of underlying logical relevance, one must understand that the common law was imbued with a spirit of skepticism. In everyday life, if we receive a letter purportedly signed by "Grant Hanson," we routinely assume that Grant Hanson wrote the letter. The common law obstinately refused to make that assumption.

More specifically, the common law refused to accept evidence at face value. The proponent must not only persuade the judge that the item is relevant under Rule 401 *if* the item is what it is claimed to be (facial relevance); the proponent must also prove that the item of evidence *is* what the proponent claims it to be (underlying relevance). This requirement for a showing of underlying relevance takes two forms.

Personal Knowledge. First, before a witness can testify to a fact or event the witness purportedly observed, there must be foundational proof of the witness' personal knowledge of the event. Federal Evidence Rule 602 states:

> A witness may not testify unless evidence is introduced sufficient to support a finding that he has personal knowledge of the matter. Evidence to prove personal knowledge may, but need not, consist of the testimony of the witness himself.

Even though the witness' testimony on its face would be logically relevant to the material facts in the case, the common law will not permit the witness to testify until there is proof that the witness will be testifying from firsthand knowledge—to the common law way of thinking, a necessary guarantee of the testimony's underlying probative value. Thus, the common law will not permit a witness to describe the way Ms. Hill and Mr. Worker's cars collided unless the witness was in a position to have observed the collision. The description is unquestionably relevant under Rule 401, but inadmissible until the proponent also complies with Rule 402.

Authentication. Second, in most cases, before the proponent formally introduces a physical exhibit such as a knife or letter, the proponent must introduce a sponsoring witness' testimony that the item is genuine or authentic. The generic term for the presentation of such testimony is "authentication." Rule 901 is in point. Rule 901 announces that the authentication or identification of physical evidence is "a condition precedent to admissibility." Again, although on its face the content of a letter was highly relevant to the material facts in the case, the common law will not allow the letter's introduction until there is an added guarantee of the letter's underlying probative value. Suppose that Polecat Motors had a letter, purportedly written by Ms. Hill, in which the writer acknowledged "full responsibility" for the collision. Again, on *its face* the letter is certainly relevant to the material facts of consequence in the case: the contents of the letter satisfy Rule 401. However, the defendant may not introduce the letter until the defendant satisfies Rule 901 with proof that Ms. Hill wrote the letter. The defendant claims that the exhibit is a letter written by Ms. Hill, and Rule 901 requires that the defendant establish the exhibit's genuineness and *underlying* relevance by proving that claim.

NOTES

1. The imposition of the personal knowledge and authentication requirements is an added guarantee of the reliability of the judicial fact-finding process. But is that incremental increase in reliability worth the trouble and expense the proponent must go through? Why not allocate the burden to the opponent to show lack of authenticity? After all, in the normal social and business intercourse, when we receive a letter in the mail we generally assume that it is genuine.

2. What is the pertinence of discovery procedures, especially the procedure for requests for admission? As discovery becomes more liberal, does the authentication requirement become more or less defensible? Why not assume that people are testifying from personal knowledge or that exhibits are genuine and force the opponent to prove the contrary—at least when the pretrial discovery rules would have permitted the opponent to depose the witness or inspect the exhibit?

Inroads have occurred at the local level. "Authenticity of all exhibits will be deemed established unless written objection is filed (either in a pretrial memorandum or by motion) at least five (5) days before trial." *See, e.g., McQueeney v. Wilmington Trust Co.*, 779 F.2d 916, 928 n.20 (3d Cir. 1985). See also the latest amendments to FED. R. CIV. P. 26, which have been adopted in about half of the local federal court rules. Subject to adoption or opt-out by local rule, Federal Rule of Civil Procedure 26(a)(3)(C) requires mandatory disclosure (even absent a request by the opposing party) of a list of "each document or other exhibit . . . which the party expects to offer" at trial. The concluding language of 26(a)(3)(C) reads:

> Unless otherwise directed by the court, these disclosures shall be made at least 30 days before trial. Within 14 days thereafter, unless a different time is specified by the court, a party may serve and file a list disclosing . . . any objection, including the grounds therefor, that may be made to the admissibility of materials identified under subparagraph (C). Objections not disclosed, other than objections under Rules 402 and 403 of the Federal Rules of Evidence, shall be deemed waived unless excused by the court for good cause shown.

a. Underlying Logical Relevance — Personal Knowledge

To ensure the underlying probative value of their oral testimony, lay witnesses must ordinarily base their testimony on personal observation. Proof of personal knowledge is thus part of the foundation for their testimony. As we have seen, the Federal Evidence Rules revolutionized the law of the competency of witnesses. In particular, Rule 601 junked most of the traditional mental qualifications for prospective witnesses. However, the Rules retained the personal knowledge requirement. Under Rule 602, as at common law, the courts generally apply the requirement to both in-court witnesses and out–of–court hearsay declarants. *United States v. Owens-El*, 889 F.2d 913 (9th Cir. 1989). The following case illustrates the continuing vitality of the personal knowledge doctrine.

ELIZARRARAS v. BANK OF EL PASO

631 F.2d 366 (5th Cir. 1980)

KRAVITCH, CIRCUIT JUDGE.

In a jury trial appellee Elizarraras was awarded damages of $89,800 due to appellant bank's failure to honor appellee's check. . . . [W]e reverse the judgment and remand for a new trial solely on the issue of damages.

On April 2, appellee, a citizen and resident of Mexico, issued a check for $12,000 to Joe Rey as partial payment for a tractor. The check was written on appellee's account at the Bank of El Paso, appellant herein. On April 5, Rey, also a depositor at the Bank of El Paso, presented the check for payment. The bank applied $1,115.07 to one note owed to the bank by Rey and $7,539.04 to another note which it marked "paid" and delivered to Rey. The balance, $3,345.89, was deposited by the bank in Rey's account. On the same day, the appellee delivered to the bank a stop payment order, on a form provided by appellant, which included an agreement by appellee to indemnify appellant for all expenses and costs resulting from appellant's honoring the stop payment order. On either April 5 or April 6, appellant reversed the entries it had made with respect to Rey. On April 6, appellee issued a check for $64,000, which he believed to be the amount he had on deposit in the Bank of El Paso, payable to Financiera Del Norte, S.A., a Mexican bank. On April 15, Rey filed suit against appellee and appellant, alleging that appellee wrongfully stopped payment on the check and that appellant wrongfully reversed the entries it had made. On April 26, Pedro Jurado, vice president of the Bank of El Paso "acting as commercial loan and regular installment loan officer," notified appellee that there was a shortage of $756.68. Appellee testified that he emphasized to Jurado that it was important that the $64,000 check not be returned for insufficient funds, since such a return would have serious repercussions in Mexico, including a penalty and loss of credit. According to appellee, Jurado assured him that there would be no problem covering the $64,000 check. On April 30, without giving notice to appellee, appellant returned the $64,000 check to the Mexican bank for insufficient funds and deposited $12,000 from appellee's account into the federal court in which Rey's suit was pending, interpleading Rey and appellee. When Rey's suit was subsequently dismissed for lack of subject matter jurisdiction and Rey sued in state court, the appellant interpled the money into state court.

Appellee subsequently filed suit in federal district court alleging that the wrongful dishonor of the $64,000 has damaged him in Mexico. Appellee prevailed in a jury trial. The jury awarded damages in the amount of $89,800: $75,000 for loss of credit and damage to reputation, $12,800 for the penalty the Mexican bank charged appellee, and $2,000 for interest on the $64,000 still owed to the Mexican bank.

The appellant contends that the trial court erred in several respects. Appellant contends that essential evidence to support the award of $12,800 penalty and $2,000 interest to the Mexican bank was wrongfully admitted.

At trial appellant objected to the following statement made by appellee: "I paid the $64,000; then $12,800 and twenty-three and something else." Under Fed. R. Evid. 602, a "witness may not testify to a matter unless evidence is introduced sufficient to support a finding that he has personal knowledge of the matter." The Advisory Committee on the Federal Rules, in its notes on Rule 602, points out that "[t]his rule would prevent [a witness] from testifying to the subject matter of [a] hearsay statement, as he has no personal knowledge of it." The problem in the instant case is that the appellee did not carry the burden Rule 602 puts on him of showing personal knowledge of the matter testified to (although appellant objected on hearsay grounds, not personal knowledge, we will not draw such a fine line). In context, it is clear that as to the penalty and interest appellee was not testifying to any act of payment he committed, but rather to the fact his account was charged $12,800 and $2,000; thus, this is not an instance where one can infer personal knowledge from the testimony itself.[21] The only basis appellee appeared to have for his testimony concerning the payment of the penalty and interest was the Mexican bank officers' oral assertions[22] and the Mexican bank notice appellant received; yet this evidence had been excluded as inadmissible hearsay.[23] Neither the conversation nor notice is in the record on appeal. Therefore, we do not rule on the admissibility of this evidence.

Nor can we agree that admission of the appellee's testimony was harmless error. The testimony was introduced to show that the appellee paid the Mexican bank a penalty of $12,800 and interest of $2,000 due to the return of the check. The only other evidence introduced with regard to these facts was expert testimony on whether Mexican law would have required a 20% penalty on the return of the check and authorized the interest charge, and appellee's testimony that the bank asserted that he owed it interest due to the return of the check. Although to reach its verdict the jury had to find that under Mexican law the Mexican bank was entitled to a penalty of $12,800 and interest of $2,000 from the appellee, and that the Mexican bank asserted there was an interest charge, the jury might very well have not found these facts alone without proof of payment sufficient to establish the disputed damages. *See Liner v. J.B. Talley & Co., Inc.*, 618 F.2d 327 (5th Cir.1980) (articulating harmless error standard). We therefore reverse the judgment insofar as it awards the appellee $12,800 and $2,000 and remand for a new trial on those issues.

NOTES AND PROBLEMS

1. How does the personal knowledge requirement differ from the former competency requirements? Is proof of the possession of the basic capacity to observe part of competency or personal knowledge? What about proof of the opportunity to observe? What about proof of actual observation?

2. In *Elizarraras,* the court alludes to both the personal knowledge and hearsay doctrines and mentions the "fine line" between the doctrines. What is the relation between the two doctrines? It is tempting to say that the distinction is this: The personal knowledge objection is available when it negatively appears that the testimony does not rest on personal knowledge while the hearsay objection is available when it affirmatively appears that the testimony rests on a third party's out–of–court statements.

---

[21] An example would be "I saw X in the room."

[22] On *voir dire*, appellee began to testify that the Mexican bank officials told him about the $12,800 penalty and the $2,000 interest (in context this seemed to be what he was about to say), but an objection to this as hearsay was sustained.

[23] If this testimony had been based on admissible hearsay, this would presumably satisfy Rule 602, though we do not decide the question.

3. Problem 8-16. In the *Devitt* case, the prosecutor calls Mr. Garrett, one of Paterson's neighbors, as a witness. Garrett is prepared to testify that soon after the time of the alleged battery, he saw Devitt fling open Paterson's apartment door, run out the door, leap into a car, and speed away. Before he begins this testimony, Devitt's attorney interrupts:

O. Your Honor, I object on the grounds that this witness has no personal knowledge.

Q. Your Honor, the witness has indicated that he saw all this happen.

O. Your Honor, may we approach the bench?

J. Yes.

O. (At sidebar) Your Honor, we have a witness, Mr. Michelson, who is prepared to swear that at this point in time, he and Garrett were drinking at a bar twenty miles from the apartment complex. I'd like you to listen to Mr. Michelson's testimony before you rule on my objection.

As trial judge, must you consider Michelson's testimony before ruling? Does this preliminary fact fall under Federal Rule 104(a) or 104(b)? Does the fact of personal knowledge condition the competence or the logical relevance of Garrett's testimony? *M.B.A.F.B. Federal Credit Union v. Cumis Ins. Soc'y*, 681 F.2d 930, 932–33 (4th Cir. 1982). Consider the first two sentences of Rule 602. How would you rule on the objection assuming that the only proof of Garrett's firsthand knowledge is Garrett's own testimony?

4. Problem 8-17. Under Rule 602, is the judge limited to inquiring whether the witness has some personal knowledge of the facts he or she is testifying to, or may the judge also assess the adequacy of the personal knowledge? *McCrary-El v. Shaw*, 992 F.2d 809, 810–11 (8th Cir. 1993). Pay special attention to the "unless" clause in the first sentence of Rule 602. In *Elizar-raras*, the court stated that the issue was whether it could "infer" personal knowledge. Suppose that in the last problem, Garrett admits that he did not have a frontal view of the person who fled from Paterson's apartment. Instead he saw part of the profile as the fugitive ran past some bushes; Garrett concedes that his identification of Devitt as the fugitive rests primarily on "the peculiar shape of the guy's nose that I happened to notice." Does Garrett's testimony satisfy Rule 602? (This problem draws on the fact situation in *United States v. Sears*, 332 F.2d 199 (7th Cir. 1964), a case which was argued on appeal by Professor Kenneth Broun, one of the authors of the current edition of the McCormick treatise.)

5. Problem 8-18. In the *Hill* case, the plaintiff calls a mechanic who worked on Roe's truck before the accident. The mechanic inspected the truck's brakes a few days before the accident. The mechanic testifies that he handed Roe a sheet of paper stating that the mechanic had found a number of specific deficiencies in the brakes. When the plaintiff attempts to elicit the mechanic's further testimony that he, the mechanic, "could tell" that after reading the sheet of paper, Roe "understood that the brakes were bad," the defense objects. Roe's attorney argues that the mechanic "can't have any personal knowledge of what's going on in another person's mind"? What ruling? *United States v. Kupau*, 781 F.2d 740, 745 (9th Cir. 1986) (citing Federal Rule of Evidence 602).

In Problem 8-18, when objecting, many defense attorneys would also have objected that the plaintiff's attorney's question called for "improper speculation." We shall revisit this issue, *infra*, when we cover the materials on lay opinion testimony. Should the mechanic at least be permitted to testify that Roe "appeared" or "seemed" to understand that the brakes were bad?

6. Commonly, courts do not capitalize on the available scientific method of investigation. Assume, for example, that the question is whether, under the circumstances at the time of the relevant event, the witness could actually have seen or heard what he or she claims. A witness may testify that although she was 70 feet away and there was only a crescent moon, she made out the letters and numbers on the license plate of a car that sped away from the crime scene. Witness psychologists point out that it is possible to conduct a visibility test—duplicating the conditions, including the witness' vision—to determine scientifically whether the witness could actually have observed those details. *See generally* A. TRANKELL, RELIABILITY OF EVIDENCE (1972); Levine & Tapp, *The Psychology of Criminal Identification: The Gap from* Wade *to* Kirby, 121 U. PA. L. REV. 1079 (1973). In testing claims of personal knowledge, the law has not fully exploited the available scientific techniques. To be sure, it would be unduly time-consuming to test every witness' personal knowledge claim in this fashion. However, when there is substantial doubt about the ability of an important witness to have perceived a pivotal fact in the case, it would seem worthwhile to resort to scientific testing. Note that in certain circumstances, Fed. R. Civ. P. 35 empowers the courts to order physical or mental examinations.

b. Underlying Logical Relevance—Authentication

As in the case of the personal knowledge requirement, the authentication requirement is satisfied by proof sufficient to support a rational jury finding that the document is authentic. If the proponent presents that quantum of foundational proof, the judge admits the exhibit; and during deliberations, the lay jurors finally resolve the question of the document's authenticity. In this respect Federal Rule of Evidence 901(a) prescribes the same fact-finding procedure as Rule 104(b). Can we trust lay jurors to resolve questions of personal knowledge and authenticity? Suppose that after considering the foundational testimony, the jurors decide that a particular exhibit is a forgery. Is the jurors' exposure to the exhibit likely to distort their deliberations?

With some types of evidence, fairly hard and fast norms on the manner of authentication of evidence have emerged. Some fact patterns have recurred so frequently and the courts have ruled so consistently that one can predictably conclude that an item of evidence can be authenticated in a particular fashion. We shall address most of the well-settled norms, *infra*, as we cover various specialized applications of the authentication doctrine. However, one must never lose sight of the fact that under Rule 901(a) the fundamental test is *not* whether the proponent has complied with a well-settled norm, but rather whether the proponent has marshalled sufficient surrounding circumstances to create a rational, permissive inference that the item of evidence is authentic. The only limits on the authentication doctrine itself are the rules of logic and the attorney's creativity, as illustrated by the following case.

UNITED STATES v. WILSON

532 F.2d 641 (8th Cir. 1976)

LAY, CIRCUIT JUDGE.

Defendants Gray (a/k/a Punkin), Wilson (a/k/a Big Man), and Brenda Brown appeal from their convictions for conspiracy to distribute heroin in violation of 21 U.S.C. § 846. The issue presented on appeal is whether the trial court erred in admitting two notebooks and their contents which a government witness read to the jury. We find no error and affirm the convictions.

The sufficiency of the evidence supporting the conspiracy conviction of each defendant is not challenged. However, a review of the facts is essential to the ruling on the controversial notebooks. The indictment recited nine overt acts involving drug sales and conversations with Drug Enforcement Agents and government informant McCoy (a/k/a Poor Boy). The overt acts alleged and proven were:

1. On November 1, 1974, unindicted co-conspirator Fleming, in a conversation with a Federal Narcotics Agent, agreed to contact Gray to arrange a purchase of two spoons of heroin by the Federal Narcotics Agent.

2. On November 1, 1974, Brenda Ann Brown had a conversation with an undercover Federal Narcotics Agent in which she agreed to contact Gray concerning the purchase of two spoons of heroin.

3. On November 1, 1974, Wilson had a conversation with an undercover Federal Narcotics Agent concerning the purchase of two spoons of heroin.

4. On November 1, 1974, Gray had a conversation with a confidential government informant concerning the purchase of two spoons of heroin.

5. On November 4, 1974, Fleming sold a quantity of heroin to an undercover Federal Narcotics Agent.

6. On November 5, 1974, Wilson had a conversation with an undercover Federal Narcotics Agent where he agreed to sell two spoons of heroin for $325.00.

7. On November 5, 1974, Fleming sold a quantity of heroin to an undercover Federal Narcotics Agent.

8. On November 7, 1974, Wilson had a conversation with an undercover Federal Narcotics Agent concerning the purchase of two spoons of heroin.

9. On November 7, 1974, Wilson had a conversation with Gray concerning the sale of heroin to the undercover Federal Narcotics Agent.

McCoy, the informant, testified that on various occasions he purchased heroin from each of the defendants and had sold heroin for them as well. McCoy described the defendants' operations, stating that he received heroin from each of the three defendants which he would sell at "a rate." He testified that the defendants ran their operation from various houses in St. Louis.[1]

---

[1] McCoy described in detail how a "house" was operated:

Q. Now, in the actual running of a house what would be the jobs of the individuals that were running the house?

These houses were on Elliott and St. Louis, Evans and Sarah, and Grand and Herbert in St. Louis. The money and heroin would be passed through a hole in the door and then, according to McCoy, the transactions were usually recorded in code in a book by either "Pauncho" (an unindicted co–conspirator) or Brenda. He stated heroin was sold either in "spoons" or in capsule form called "buttons." The "house" at Grand and Herbert was an apartment run by someone known to the informant as "Jimmy."

Detective Klier of the St. Louis Police Department went to the "house" at Grand and Herbert on April 30, 1975, on information that drugs were being sold there. Detective Klier found James Shelton in the apartment. The door had a two-inch hole in it and the apartment was practically vacant except for certain small items. Klier testified that he found numerous empty red capsules in one room and syringes and two notebooks in the bedroom.

Over defendants' objections, the government introduced the notebooks *and* their contents. The trial court overruled defendants' objections. Detective Klier was allowed to read all the contents of the notebooks to the jury. The notations specifically identified "Brenda" and "Punkin" (Gray's nickname) as taking drugs and money. Defendant Wilson was not mentioned in the notebook.[3]

A. Well, the first thing the job is you got to have a protection in a house so somebody would have to have something there to protect what you got in that house because, let's face it, people, you know, stick you up, highjack you, take your stuff. So once you get your protection set up in the house then it's a simple matter of dealing once people know where you're dealing from and if the stuff is there such where, you know, where when junkies will buy. Well, then it's easy to run a house. You just go to the house; they know you; you stick your money through the hole; they stick the stuff back out; and that's that.

Q. Did you ever open the door or was that a normal procedure?

A. Well, it's not a normal procedure unless you know a person real good, exceptionally good.

Q. But normally it would be sent through a hole, is that correct?

A. Right.

Q. How big would the hole be?

A. Just a small hole big enough to put a spoon through.

Q. What would be the purpose of putting a spoon through?

A. Well, you see, you stick your money through the hole and if you're getting say — let's say you're getting two or three things; well, you can put that on a spoon and stick it right back through the hole.

Q. And that way the door would never have to be opened?

A. No, it wouldn't have to be opened.

Q. Did you ever run any of these houses?

A. Well, no I wouldn't say run a house but I have been up in one of the houses.

Transcript at 96–97.

[3] Government Exhibit No. 3 contained the following entries:

On page one:

4-26-75

$112.00 cash and 21 in the bottle 24, and 60 in the plastic bags. So you started with 105, buttons.

S/ J.R.

On page two:

Left Nut

I started with 78 buttons. He brought 80, but gave me two for myself. Brenda picked up $133 Dollars for 19 buttons Brenda picked up $210 Dollars for 30 buttons, She has picked up the last $203 Dollars for 29 buttons. All total she has picked up $546 Dollars for 78 buttons.

The defendants presented no evidence, relying on their motions for acquittal at the end of the government's evidence. The jury returned verdicts of guilty. The defendants argue that no proper foundation has been laid for the notebooks, since the identity of the writer or writers was not shown. We find sufficient evidence to show *prima facie* authenticity or genuineness of the notebooks.

The entries in the notebooks are hand printed by one or more persons. The government represents that it does not know the identity of the author.

Rule 901 of the Federal Rules of Evidence provides:

> (a) General provision. The requirement of authentication or identification as a condition precedent to admissibility is satisfied by evidence sufficient to support a finding that the matter in question is what its proponent claims.

> (b) Illustrations. By way of illustration only, and not by way of limitation, the following are examples of authentication or identification conforming with the requirements of this rule:

> . . . .

>> (4) Distinctive characteristics and the like. Appearance, contents, substance, internal patterns, or other distinctive characteristics, taken in conjunction with circumstances.

Under this rule, the contents of a writing may be used to aid in determining the identity of the declarant. The primary concern in relying on the contents of an instrument to prove its authenticity is the danger of forgery or substitution of a fraudulent document. However, as has been authoritatively explained:

> For this principle to operate the [writing] must deal with a matter sufficiently obscure or particularly within the knowledge of the persons corresponding so that the contents of the [writing] were not a matter of common knowledge.

> The evidential hypothesis in the authentication step is this: only those who knew the details in the [writing] could have written it; if the purported writer can be shown to have probably known the details and if no other person is likely to have known them when the [writing] was written, it is likely that he wrote it. The force of the inference decreases as the number of people who know the details and may have written the [writing] increases. Moreover, if there is a serious question of forgery, the inference is subject to being rebutted by the possibility that the details were added by someone to give an air of verity to the document rather than by the purported author who obtained the information in the usual way. 5 J. WEINSTEIN & M. BERGER, WEINSTEIN'S EVIDENCE ¶ 901(b) (4) [01], at 46.

It is well settled that the genuineness of a writing can be established by circumstantial proof without resort to the handwriting or typewriting. Where

---

Brenda brought 74 buttons, gave Lesa two and Punkin 4 that 6 buttons counted for. All total Punkin took 8 buttons.

I'm leaving 54 buttons, and $84 Dollars. 12 buttons. [other pages to same effect. eds.]

the writings are such that only those persons acquainted with the particular transactions involved could have written them, the authenticity of the evidence is considered more reliable.

Under these principles, we find the contents of these notebooks refer to activities (in this case, drug trafficking) and are characterized by a code of which only someone connected with the transactions would have known. The writer uses nicknames of individuals and the code term "buttons" which the informant had testified were heroin capsules. The writer was obviously familiar with the procedures used by the defendants in their drug operations. Although the precise identity of the declarant is unknown, we think there was at least a *prima facie* showing that the declarant was a member of the drug conspiracy charged in the indictment.

Moreover, there is other evidence which corroborates the authenticity of the notebooks. The books were found in an apartment which the informant said both "Punkin" and Brenda frequented, and in which drugs were sold. The apartment had an unusual hole in its door fitting the informant's description and a known co-conspirator was found there at the time of the raid. The informant further testified that the defendants' drug transactions were recorded in notebooks. This evidence in our view provides a *prima facie* showing of authenticity of the notebooks. This showing could have been, but was not, countered by any evidence from defendants that the documents were forged or otherwise not what the government claimed.

Judgments are affirmed.

NOTES AND PROBLEMS

1. Federal Evidence Rule 901 contains a lengthy list of the accepted authentication techniques. Is that list exclusive, or as at common law may the proponent rely on any circumstantial inference of authenticity? Notice the initial clause of Rule 901(b).

2. Early chapters argued the generalized proposition that the Federal Rules of Evidence swept away uncodified, common law evidentiary doctrine. Rule 901(b) requires that we refine that generalization. To an extent, Rule 901(b) preserves common law process; judges may find adequate authentication of an item of evidence even if the proponent's foundational testimony does not satisfy one of the specific authentication techniques codified in Rules 901(b)(1)–(10). In effect, Rule 901(b) opens a window to the common law.

3. Do you agree with the result in *Wilson*? The evidence certainly supports the court's conclusion that the notebooks were connected with a drug trafficking conspiracy. But is that what the prosecution claimed that the notebooks were? If you had been the prosecutor, would you have laid a more complete foundation? What additional facts would you have established? As a practical matter, how do you prove that the information contained in a document is so "obscure or particularly within the knowledge" of the person claimed to be the author? You are essentially being asked to prove a negative.

4. Problem 8-19. In our torts case, Ms. Hill is testifying to authenticate the original contract of purchase. The unsigned contract was left in a room on a table; there was also a pen on the table. She saw her husband, Arthur, enter the only door to the room. A few moments later she saw Arthur emerge from the room; at the time, she noticed ink stains on his shirt. She walked into the room and saw the contract, still on the table. The contract bore Arthur's purported signature; the signature was in ink, and the ink was obviously still wet and fresh—the ink smudged a bit when she picked up the contract. On this foundation, the plaintiff's attorney offers the exhibit into evidence. The defense counsel objects:

> O. Your Honor, I must object. There's insufficient authentication for this exhibit. She's so much as admitted that she didn't see him sign, and there's no evidence yet that she's sufficiently familiar with his handwriting style.

As trial judge, how would you rule on the objection? *See* 7 J. WIGMORE, WIGMORE ON EVIDENCE § 2131, at 712 (Chadbourn rev. 1978). (authentication by "sundry circumstances"). *See also United States v. Natale*, 526 F.2d 1160, 1173 (2d Cir. 1975), *cert. denied*, 425 U.S. 950 (1976).

5. Problem 8-20. At trial Ms. Hill's attorney wants to use a model of the intersection to illustrate the witnesses' testimony about the collision. Does the authentication doctrine apply to the model in the same fashion that it applies to the contract in Problem 8–19? Does the doctrine apply at all? Go back to fundamentals; authentication consists in proving that an item is what you claim it to be. What does Ms. Hill's attorney claim that the model is? Does a model necessarily have to be "substantially similar" to the intersection to be helpful to the jury? Must the model at least be "similar"? *See* 2 McCORMICK, EVIDENCE § 213 (J. Strong ed., 5th ed. 1999). Dombroff, *Innovative Developments in Demonstrative Evidence Techniques and Associated Problems of Admissibility*, 45 J. AIR L. & COM. 139, 145–50 (1979).

E. CONCLUSION: LOGICAL RELEVANCE

We have seen that the proponent of evidence must demonstrate the logical relevance of the item of evidence in several respects. Rule 401 requires that the proponent persuade the judge that the item has "facial" logical relevance: that the item either increases or decreases the probability that one of the material facts of consequence exists. The relevance can be either direct or circumstantial. We also studied the final aspect of logical relevance: underlying relevance. Simply stated, the common law will not accept an item of evidence at face value. The proponent must prove that the item *is* what he or she claims it to be. Federal Evidence Rules 602 and 901 impose this requirement on the proponent. For example, if the proponent claims that a witness is testifying from personal knowledge, Rule 602 provides that the proponent must show the witness' personal knowledge. If the proponent claims that an item is the defendant's letter or pistol, Rule 901 mandates that the proponent authenticate the item as such.

In the material ahead, we will analyze the most common, specialized applications of the authentication doctrine: authentication of writings by identifying their author; identification of physical evidence; authentication of tape recordings by identifying the speaker; verification of the accuracy of photographs; and validation of scientific evidence.

Chapter 9

SPECIALIZED ASPECTS OF LOGICAL RELEVANCE: AUTHENTICATION OF WRITINGS

Read Federal Rules of Evidence 901 and 902.

A. INTRODUCTION

Wigmore observed that authentication ordinarily consists of proving the connection between an object and a person involved in the case. That observation holds true with writings. The authentication requirement ordinarily mandates that we identify the author of a document offered in the courtroom.

Before we turn to specific examples of authenticating documents, remember the procedural context and the procedures for offering a single item of evidence such as a letter, check, or invoice. The proponent first marks the exhibit for identification. After showing the exhibit to the opponent, the proponent hands the exhibit to the sponsoring witness. At this point, the proponent elicits the foundation for the exhibit's introduction. The foundation usually includes, *inter alia,* proof of the document's authenticity. The proponent may tender the exhibit into evidence only after complying with the doctrines outlined in the remaining sections of this chapter.

B. PRIVATE WRITINGS

Modern technology and business practices account for the emergence of the so-called "documents cases," complex commercial or antitrust law cases in which the attorneys spend years in pretrial discovery to sort through thousands or even millions of relevant documents. In the Washington Public Power Supply System Securities litigation (the *WPPSS* case), the parties exchanged more than 200 million pages of documents before settling. Sugarman, *Coordinating Complex Discovery,* 15 No. 1 Litigation, Fall 1988, at 41. However, even before the advent of the contemporary "documents case," attorneys frequently resorted to documentary evidence. Indeed, attorneys preferred to use this type of evidence because juries tend to find it more credible than testimony of potentially biased lay witnesses. For that reason, the common law developed several doctrines for authenticating private writings.

The California Evidence Code contains an excellent codification of most of the recognized doctrines:

§ 1411. Subscribing witness not required to authenticate.

Except as provided by statute, the testimony of a subscribing witness is not required to authenticate a writing.

§ 1412. Subscribing witness denying or does not recollect writing—Other evidence.

If the testimony of a subscribing witness is required by statute to authenticate a writing and the subscribing witness denies or does not recollect the execution of the writing, the writing may be authenticated by other evidence.

§ 1413. Observing witnesses.

A writing may be authenticated by anyone who saw the writing made or executed, including a subscribing witness.

§ 1414. Authentication by admission—Action as authentic by adverse party.

A writing may be authenticated by evidence that:

(a) The party against whom it is offered has at any time admitted its authenticity; or

(b) The writing has been acted upon as authentic by the party against whom it is offered.

§ 1415. Genuineness of handwriting.

A writing may be authenticated by evidence of the genuineness of the handwriting of the maker.

§ 1416. Authentication of handwriting by knowledgeable witness.

A witness who is not otherwise qualified to testify as an expert may state his opinion whether a writing is in the handwriting of a supposed writer if the court finds that he has personal knowledge of the handwriting of the supposed writer. Such personal knowledge may be acquired from:

(a) Having seen the supposed writer write;

(b) Having seen a writing purporting to be in the handwriting of the supposed writer and upon which the supposed writer has acted or been charged;

(c) Having received letters in the due course of mail purporting to be from the supposed writer in response to letters duly addressed and mailed by him to the supposed writer; or

(d) Any other means of obtaining personal knowledge of the handwriting of the supposed writer.

§ 1417. Authentication of handwriting by comparison by trier of fact.

The genuineness of handwriting, or the lack thereof, may be proved by a comparison made by the trier of fact with handwriting (a) which the court finds was admitted or treated as genuine by the party against whom the evidence is offered or (b) otherwise proved to be genuine to the satisfaction of the court.

§ 1418. Handwriting expert.

The genuineness of writing, or the lack thereof, may be proved by a comparison made by an expert witness with writing (a) which the court finds was admitted or treated as genuine by the party against whom the evidence is offered or (b) otherwise proved to be genuine to the satisfaction of the court.

§ 1419. Handwriting—Ancient writings.

Where a writing whose genuineness is sought to be proved is more than 30 years old, the comparison under Section 1417 or 1418 may be made with writing purporting to be genuine, and generally respected and acted upon as such, by persons having an interest in knowing whether it is genuine.

§ 1420. Authentication of handwriting by response to communication.

A writing may be authenticated by evidence that the writing was received in response to a communication sent to the person who is claimed by the proponent of the evidence to be the author of the writing.

§ 1421. Authentication of writing referring to matters unlikely to be known to persons other than author.

A writing may be authenticated by evidence that the writing refers to or states matters that are unlikely to be known to anyone other than the person who is claimed by the proponent of the evidence to be the author of the writing.

In routine cases, when the opponent insists on the authentication of a written exhibit, the proponent can usually rely on the opinion testimony of a layperson familiar with the author's handwriting style. Like the common law, § 1416 authorizes the receipt of such testimony. However, studies suggest that such lay testimony is highly unreliable. Inbau, *Lay Witness Identification of Handwriting*, 34 ILL. L. REV. 433 (1939). Professor Inbau, the Wigmore Professor Emeritus at Northwestern University School of Law, conducted an informal handwriting identification experiment. The subjects were his colleagues on the law faculty. He asked them to determine whether certain specimen writings had been authored by other colleagues—persons whose handwriting style the subjects were familiar with. The subjects' scores were so low that Inbau concluded that "[l]ay witness identifications . . . are too unreliable to be considered acceptable as legal evidence." *Id.* at 440.

Moreover, lay jurors do not find this type of testimony as impressive as testimony by an expert witness. In major cases, that is, felony prosecutions and civil actions involving substantial sums of money, the attorneys will rarely be satisfied with skilled lay observer testimony. They will ordinarily employ professional questioned document examiners to study the writings in question and venture their expert opinions as to the authorship of the writings. The examiner's opinion is based on a comparison of the questioned document with exemplars or standards. Exemplars can be either "request" or "nonrequest." An exemplar is request if the examiner asks the suspected author to provide a sample of his or her handwriting. The typical nonrequest exemplar is a preexisting document which the suspected author created for a purpose wholly unrelated to the litigation. A signature on an earlier check or letter would be a nonrequest exemplar. The examiner carefully compares the questioned document with the exemplars to determine whether they all exhibit the same individual characteristics—characteristics supposedly unique to the suspected author. To enhance the detail of the comparison, the examiner can resort to various scientific instruments such as microscopes. In the following article, the authors present some disturbing findings on the reliability of expert questioned document evidence.

RISINGER, DENBEAUX & SAKS, EXORCISM OF IGNORANCE AS A PROXY FOR RATIONAL KNOWLEDGE: THE LESSONS OF HANDWRITING IDENTIFICATION "EXPERTISE," 137 University of Pennsylvania Law Review 731 (1989)

[L]et us turn to the published FSF [Forensic Sciences Foundation] studies. Some preliminary observations are in order before describing the studies themselves. First, these tests were developed as proficiency tests for specialists by a group that assumed there was such a thing as competency. That is, while they were willing to believe there might be some incompetent practitioners, they assumed that there were competent practitioners whose results would be dependably valid, and who would always outperform you or me. Hence, the tests were not presented to control groups of non–"experts" to determine if the problems presented were too easy. Second, the people to whom the tests were given knew they were being tested, so the problem of special effort devoted to competency tests was present.

a. The 1975 test

In the 1975 test, researchers sent a letter composed of both type–writing and handwriting to the participating examiners along with four exemplars written by four different people. Examiners were asked to determine whether any of the "suspects" executed the handwriting on the questioned document. In actuality, one of the four "suspects" had written the letter. Of the seventy–four responding laboratories: 66 (89%) correctly identified the suspect who wrote the questioned letter; 1 (1%) reported partially correct and partially incorrect results; 4 (5%) said they could not make any conclusion from what had been submitted; 3 (4%) identified the wrong person.

b. The 1984 test

In the 1984 test, three handwritten letters containing bomb threats were said to have been received by the news media and followed by bombings by a terrorist organization. Forty-one participating laboratories employing document examiners were sent the three letters plus twelve pages of known handwriting samples (two pages for each of six suspects). Examiners were asked to determine whether all of the questioned letters were written by the same person, and whether any of the questioned letters were written by any of the authors of the known writings. Two of the letters were written by one person, whose writing was not submitted, and the third letter was written by one of the suspects whose exemplar was in his normal hand but who in writing the questioned letter attempted to simulate the writing in the other two letters. Only twenty-three of the forty-one laboratories submitted reports: 17 (74%) caught the different authorship of the third letter; 6 (26%) said erroneously that all the letters were written by the same person; 23 (100%) failed to recognize the author of one of the questioned letters among the known exemplars. Thus they were all correct concerning letters 1 and 2 and all wrong concerning letter 3. Every examiner failed to recognize the author of one of the questioned letters among the exemplars.

c. The 1985 test

Twelve checks all bearing a signature in the same name were sent to forty–two participating laboratories. They were asked to determine which if any of the signatures were made by the same person. In actuality, two of the twelve had been signed by the same person. A third was a freehand forgery by a person of no known skill or experience as a forger. A fourth was a tracing. The others were signed by different people in their own hands. Only thirty–two of the forty–two laboratories returned the 1985 test. Of those, 13 (41%) gave correct results; 2 (6%) of the responses were incorrect in attributing one of the forgeries to the real repeat signatory; 10 (31%) said they were unable to reach conclusions; 7 (22%) were substantially wrong.

d. The 1986 test

The scenario for this study was that police stopped a car with three known occupants. In the car they found incriminating evidence, including a hand–printed note used in the commission of the crime. Samples of printing were obtained from the three occupants of the car. The test materials included two samples taken from an actual case and written by the same author, one submitted as the "crime note" and one as an exemplar. Two other exemplars were added for the test, one in a document examiner's normal printing and one produced by a document examiner attempting to simulate the printing of the crime note. The subjects' task was to determine which, if any, of the writers of the exemplars wrote the crime note. The materials were requested by forty–eight laboratories. Thirty–one responded: 4 (13%) gave correct answers; 3 (9%) were partially correct in that they said none of the authors of the exemplars wrote the crime note, when in fact two had not, but one had; 10 (32%) were unable to reach conclusion; 14 (45%) gave incorrect answers, mostly by assigning authorship to the forger.

e. The 1987 test

Because of complaints from document examiners that prior tests were too difficult, the Proficiency Advisory Committee decided to make the 1987 test easy. According to the report, "[t]his test was designed to be a relatively easy and straightforward test, because of complaints about previous test design. All the writings in this test were natural and free of disguise." This test involved a single questioned extortion note written by one suspect. Both request and non–request known exemplars from four suspects were provided to the participants. After comparing the questioned and the known, examiners were to offer an opinion concerning which, if any, of the known exemplars was written by the same person who wrote the questioned note. Of fifty–five laboratories requesting materials, thirty–three returned reports: 17 (52%) gave correct answers; 1 (3%) incorrectly eliminated the correct suspect; 15 (45%) were unable to reach a conclusion.

NOTES AND PROBLEMS

1. The publication of the Risinger article prompted further empirical studies to investigate the premise that questioned document examination constitutes a genuine expertise qualifying for admission in court. In 1994, Kam, Wetstein, and Conn released a study entitled *Proficiency of Professional Document Examiners in Writer Identification*, 39 JOURNAL OF FORENSIC SCIENCES 5 (1994). They found that professional questioned document examiners were far more successful than laypersons in making authorship determinations:

> The hypothesis that professionals and nonprofessionals are equally proficient in performing writer identification was found . . . to have the probability of less than 0.001. These findings give indication that handwriting identification expertise indeed exists . . . .

2. *Infra*, we shall discuss the Supreme Court's 1993 decision in *Daubert v. Merrell Dow Pharmaceuticals, Inc.*, 509 U.S. 579 (1993). In *Daubert*, the Court announced a new test for the admissibility of scientific evidence. The Court ruled that to qualify for admission, proffered testimony must constitute "scientific . . . knowledge" within the intended meaning of that term in Fed. R. Evid. 702. The Court stated that to decide whether proffered testimony qualifies, the judge should consider many factors, including the error rate for the scientific technique. In a footnote, the Court indicated that this new test applies to both novel scientific techniques and conventional techniques that in the past have enjoyed judicial approval. Citing the Risinger article, *supra*, and *Daubert*, some commentators have argued that the courts should rethink the question of the admissibility of testimony by questioned document examiners. Jonakait, *Real Science and Forensic Science*, 1 SHEPARD'S EXP. AND SCI. EVID. Q. 435, 447 (1994). In *United States v. Starzecpyzel*, 880 F. Supp. 1027 (S.D.N.Y. 1995), the court approvingly cited the Risinger article. Although the court ultimately decided to allow testimony by forensic document examiners (FDE), the court added that "the jury will be instructed . . . that FDEs offer practical rather than scientific expertise."

3. As the language of Rule 901(b)(3) indicates, the questioned document examiner bases his or her testimony on an in-court comparison. The examiner compares the questioned document with other standards or exemplars of the suspected author's handwriting style. How does the proponent introduce the exemplars? At first glance, the issue of the exemplars' authenticity seems to be a preliminary fact conditioning the logical relevance of the exemplars. 5 J. WEINSTEIN & M. BERGER, WEINSTEIN'S FEDERAL EVIDENCE ¶ 901.02[4], at 901–18 (J. McLaughlin ed., 2d ed. 1997). If so, would not the trial judge let the jury ordinarily make the final decision on the exemplars' genuineness? If we apply the normal Rule 104(b) procedure to the fact of the exemplars' authenticity, do any peculiar administrative problems arise? On that assumption, how would the trial judge word the instruction to the jury? What mental gymnastic would the jury have to engage in? Is the jury capable of that gymnastic? *See* Wellborn, *Authentication and Identification Under Article IX of the Texas Rules of Evidence*, 16 ST. MARY'S L.J. 371, 378–79 (1985).

4. Which approach do the Federal Rules of Evidence take? Do they commit the final decision to the judge or the jury? Consider Rule 104(a)–(b), Rule 901(a), and Rule 901(b)(3). The federal version of Rule 901(b)(3) concludes "which have been authenticated." The Texas version of the same rule ends "which have been found by the court to be genuine." Wellborn, *supra*, at 378. Nonetheless, as a matter of statutory construction, early on most courts concluded that Federal Rule 901 commits the final decision to the jury; the judge decides only whether there is sufficient evidence for the jury to rationally find that the exemplar is authentic. 5 C. MUELLER & L. KIRKPATRICK, FEDERAL EVIDENCE § 513, at 8 (2d ed. 1994).

5. Problem 9–1. In our torts case, Polecat Motors denies that Jefferson's sales manager signed one of the letters which purports to describe a warranty by Polecat. To attack the signature's authenticity, the defense intends to call a questioned document examiner. The defense wants the expert to compare the exhibit with several samples of the sales manager's handwriting style. The sales manager prepared the samples a few days before trial. Should the trial judge permit the witness to use those samples in making a comparison on the witness stand? Is it significant that the sales manager prepared the exemplars so close in point of time to the trial? *See United States v. Lam Muk Chiu*, 522 F.2d 330, 331–32 (2d Cir. 1975).

Lam Muk Chiu antedates the Federal Rules of Evidence. In the opinion, the court cites common law authorities for the proposition that *post litem motam* exemplars are "inherently suspect." *Id.* Did that common law restriction survive the adoption of the Federal Rules? The restriction rests on a doubt about the credibility of exemplars prepared after litigation has arisen. May the judge factor the credibility of an item of evidence into a Rule 403 analysis? The overwhelming majority of courts have answered that question in the negative. Imwinkelried, *The Meaning of Probative Value and Prejudice in Federal Rule of Evidence 403: Can Rule 403 Be Used to Resurrect the Common Law of Evidence?*, 41 VAND. L. REV. 879, 886 (1988). If the courts construed the expression "probative value" in Rule 403 as subsuming the credibility of the source of the evidence, how would that construction affect Rule 104(b). *Id.* at 887–88. Just as we should attempt to harmonize Rules 402 and 403, we should endeavor to reconcile Rules 104(b) and 403.

6. Problem 9–2. In the *Devitt* case, Paterson testifies that a few days after the attack, he received an unsigned, handwritten letter. The letter related minute details about the attack—details that had not been mentioned in any of the newspaper articles about the attack. The letter's final sentence was, "I got you once, and if you don't stop blabbing to the police I'll be back to get you again." There is no witness prepared to testify that they saw Devitt write the letter. You are the prosecutor, and you want to introduce the letter against Devitt. What authentication techniques would you attempt to use? *See United States v. Beecroft*, 608 F.2d 753, 760–61 (9th Cir. 1979).

C.   BUSINESS WRITINGS

In criminal cases, the documentary evidence usually takes the form of private writings. However, both in white collar crime prosecutions and civil actions, the documents are usually business writings. We begin with the assumption that any technique available to authenticate a private writing is equally available to authenticate a business writing. However, there are additional, special techniques for authenticating business documents.

1. CUSTODY

When we refer to "custody," we mean the place where the document is found. There is a large body of case law endorsing the proposition that the proponent may authenticate a business writing simply by proving that the document came from the proper custody. The proponent elicits the sponsoring witness' testimony that the witness has personal knowledge of the filing system of the business in question; the witness went to the right file cabinet, drawer, and file; the witness removed the document from that file; and the witness recognizes the exhibit as the document he or she removed from the file.

NOTES

1. Why should proof of proper custody suffice to authenticate a business writing? What assumption is the court making about the procedures and routines of the typical business? Suppose that in a particular case, the opponent had evidence that the business in question was very sloppy in its records filing. Would that evidence preclude the admission of a record from that company, or would that evidence be admitted only to attack the weight of the record?

2. In most instances, the sponsoring witness will be an agent of the institution or business that generated the record. Carlson, *Policing the Bases of Modern Expert Testimony*, 39 VAND. L. REV. 577, 585 (1986). Must the sponsoring witness be an employee of the business? Suppose that witness were the bookkeeper of the parent corporation or of a company that had extensive dealings with the business. Would their testimony be satisfactory? Does the witness' status as the parent corporation's bookkeeper automatically qualify the witness to authenticate the record? If not, what additional foundational testimony would the proponent have to elicit before an accountant or book-keeper could qualify as the sponsoring witness? *See United States v. Blake*, 488 F.2d 101, 104–06 (5th Cir. 1973).

3. Does Rule 901 countenance authentication of a business writing by custody?

2. COMPUTER RECORDS

One of the major technological advances in data storage has been the emergence of the computer. Most businesses transfer data from documents to computer storage, and many feed data directly into the computer without generating an intermediate document. Thus, the computer printout has become a vital type of business document. Nevertheless, there are doubts about the reliability of computer-generated documents. Anyone who has seen the popular movie *War Games* knows why there is concern over unauthorized access to computer systems. The following article identifies a whole range of concerns.

GARCIA, "GARBAGE IN, GOSPEL OUT": CRIMINAL DISCOVERY, COMPUTER RELIABILITY, AND THE CONSTITUTION, 38 U.C.L.A. Law Review 1043 (1991)

[T]he various overlapping stages of computer processing . . . illustrate how reliability problems can creep in.

1. The Underlying Information

The information entered into a computer may be incomplete, incorrect, or misleading. The risk of error depends on the purpose for gathering the information, the motivation of the people who gather the information, and the amount of information involved. Information may be gathered for a routine business purpose, for general intelligence, for a specific investigation, or expressly for persuasive impact as evidence at trial.

For instance, while business records may have circumstantial guarantees of trustworthiness if a business routinely prepares and relies on them, the same is not necessarily true of government records, such as those involved in the Customs border crossing system. Customs agents who sit at border checkpoints and enter license plate numbers may have no motive to fabricate entries, but they may have little motivation and little opportunity to check their entries. No one routinely relies on the information for any purpose. No one has any reason to review the accuracy of the records on a regular basis.

2. Entering the Information

People may enter, leave out, modify, or erase information in a computer due to mistake, fraud, or bias. The risk of error again depends on a variety of factors, including the motivation and training of the people entering the data, the amount of information to be entered, and the quality controls placed on the process.

As personal computers have become ubiquitous, the distinctions between the people who gather the information, enter it into the computer and use the information have diminished. For example, the prosecutors in one case typed many of their own transcripts into the computer, rather than rely on government word processing pools.

The Los Angeles Police Department (LAPD) is studying the use of lap top computers to prepare police reports automatically. L.A. [police] currently spend fifteen to twenty percent of their time writing reports, and file a total of three million reports each year. A cop can type information directly into a computer in her squad car. The computer generates the necessary reports in the proper format and enters the information into a central database. Whether the cops have the opportunity or motivation to double check their work before it is entered into the central database remains an unanswered question.

3. Errors and Biases in the Program

The program that processes the information may contain errors, or may reflect the biases and assumptions of the developers. As a result, numbers may be miscalculated, names may not be sorted properly, information may not be saved or retrieved, and printouts may not accurately reflect what is stored in the computer. The risk of error varies depending on several factors, including the complexity of the program; whether the program is commercially available, custom–designed by computer professionals for a specific purpose, or home–brewed; and the sophistication of the programmers, and users.

On January 15, 1990, for example, the AT&T network, the largest long-distance telephone network in the nation, virtually collapsed because of a software error, preventing millions of people from making long-distance calls for nine hours. In 1985, faulty software altered 32,000 government securities transactions that were to be processed by the Bank of New York. By the time the software was fixed two days later, the bank was overdrawn with the Federal Reserve by over twenty-three billion dollars. The collapse of the AT&T telephone network was caused by one line in a program containing two million lines of instructions. That bug was introduced when programmers tried to fix an unrelated flaw.

The premises on which a program is based may be wrong, incomplete, misleading or biased. While all of these may not be considered programming errors, they nevertheless raise reliability concerns because of the potential for built–in errors or bias. For instance, animated computer simulations can be used to recreate . . . crime scenes. Ultimately, computer simulations are simplified models of reality that include only some of the variables that shaped an event. A simulation is only as good as its underlying assumptions. The simulation may exclude some relevant factors and include irrelevant ones. It may be necessary to examine the underlying program and the assumptions on which it is based in order to assess the reliability.

4. Inadequate Security

Some experts estimate that companies in the United States lose between three billion to five billion dollars each year to computer crime. Companies do not publicize these losses . . . because they want to maintain public confidence in the reliability of their computer systems. At the same time, only thirty-five percent of IBM mainframe computers used security software in late 1988.

Tight security can minimize the risk of error and fraud. Passwords help prevent access to those who are not familiar with the system, or who wish to manipulate the system by deleting, modifying, or adding information. Passwords also make it easier to detect error and fraud if it does occur. But security systems will not work if they are not enforced. Recent computer crimes have highlighted that computer systems are vulnerable, and that security issues are not taken seriously enough in assessing the reliability of computerized information.

For example, the IRS has concluded that the agency "does not provide adequate evaluation of the security and integrity of service computer-based information systems." [In addition, a] recent GAO report concluded that a lack of adequate security is endangering Justice Department computers that are used by ninety–four United States Attorneys' offices nationwide. These computers are used to store highly sensitive information . . . . Unauthorized users can enter and exit the system over the telephone without being detected.

National Security Adviser John Poindexter erased more than 5,000 messages he wrote or received on the White House electronic mail system after federal investigators started searching the National Security Council files for documents concerning the illegal sale of arms to Iran to finance United States aid to the Contras in Nicaragua. Oliver North deleted over 700 messages.

[5. Output]

The actual output of the information system is simply the product of all of the processes described above. The reliability of the output will vary depending on each of those factors. To insure accuracy, it is necessary to check the output against the underlying data, and to test the system that retrieved the information and produced the output.

It is easy to envision a system in which people who gather the information have no opportunity or motivation to check the accuracy of the information. The information is typed into computers by low–paid, poorly trained, overworked clerical workers who have no opportunity or motivation to check the accuracy of their input. The hardware is outdated. The software may contain undetected bugs. The computer is accessible over the telephone lines without adequate security. The information is not backed up. The organization that prepares and maintains the information does not rely on it in the ordinary course of business and has no reason to insure the accuracy of the information. There are not audits of the system to determine accuracy. The output, however sophisticated is may seem, is only as reliable as the input and processing. Garbage in, garbage out.

NOTES AND PROBLEMS

1. On reflection, does the tender of a computer printout present one or two authentication problems? The identification of the document as the very paper the computer printed out is the most obvious authentication issue, but in a sense is there another authentication problem lurking here?

2. Before the adoption of the Federal Rules of Evidence, some jurisdictions required detailed, comprehensive foundations for the admission of computerized records. Peritz, *Computer Data and Reliability: A Call for Authentication of Business Records Under the Federal Rules of Evidence*, 80 Nw. U.L. Rev. 956, 958 (1986). Since the adoption of the Rules, most courts have been more receptive to the admission of computerized data. *Id.* The courts tend to admit the evidence so long as the proponent shows that the business in question has relied on the computer system for a substantial period of time. *Id.* at 961. One commentator argues that the courts should return to their earlier, more skeptical attitude toward computerized data. "Because program changes or data manipulations can be accomplished without leaving any trace and without affecting the day–to–day operation of a computer system, both unintentional error and intentional fraud are difficult to discover behind a perfect-looking document." *Id.* at 960. Do you concur with the commentator? As a general proposition, the courts do not concur. *See United States v. Moore*,

923 F.2d 910, 915 (1st Cir. 1991) ("it is not required that computers be tested for programming errors before computer records can be admitted . . . ."); *United States v. Briscoe*, 896 F.2d 1476, 1494 (7th Cir.) (the proponent of computerized records need not show that the computer has been tested for internal programming errors), *cert. denied sub nom. Usman v. United States*, 498 U.S. 863 (1990).

3. Problem 9–3. In our torts case, the defense contends that Ms. Hill cannot sue on the contract because Mr. and Mrs. Hill defaulted in their installment payments before the accident in which she was injured. The defense wants to offer a printout from Jefferson Motor Cars' computer; the printout shows that the day before the accident, the plaintiff was two installments delinquent in her payments. The sponsoring witness is the head of Jefferson's accounting department. She helped design the computer system when it was installed eight years ago. Prepare the part of her direct examination in which she will authenticate the computer printout. Do not be content to satisfy the minimal evidentiary requirements; attempt to make the line of testimony as persuasive as possible. *See* Peritz, *supra*, at 973–75 (discussing the provisions of the Federal Judicial Center's MANUAL FOR COMPLEX LITIGATION relating to computerized data).

4. Problem 9–4. When you offer the computer printout into evidence, the plaintiff objects on a different ground:

> Your Honor, that printout was prepared specifically for purposes of this trial. The witness admitted only a few moments ago that she made this printout at the defense attorney's request only two days ago. I cite *Lam Muk Chiu*, 522 F.2d 330, 331–32 (2d Cir. 1975) as authority for my position.

Assume *arguendo* that the *post litem motam* restriction survived the adoption of the Federal Rules of Evidence. Can you distinguish the exemplars in the *Lam* case from the printout in this problem? What is the critical point in time—the date on which the printout is made or some earlier date? What earlier date? When is the computer "record" created?

5. Of course, computers represent only one of the new technologies to which the authentication doctrine must adapt. Other such technological advances include the FAX and e-mail. Some courts have already passed on the authentication of FAXed documents. *People v. Hagan*, 145 Ill.2d 287, 164 Ill.Dec. 578, 583 N.E.2d 494 (1991). The American Bar Association's Information Security Committee is at work on the draft of a set of guidelines for electronic commerce, including procedures for authentication by "cybernotaries." Slind-Flor, *Moving Into Cyberspace as Notaries: The Need to Authenticate Electronic Documents Is a New Frontier For Attorneys*, NAT'L L. J., Dec. 18, 1995, at A1.

3. SIMPLIFIED PROCEDURES FOR INTRODUCING BUSINESS RECORDS

There is a growing trend toward relaxing the procedures for introducing business documents. The following California statutory scheme is illustrative.

§ 1560. Business records—Copies—Transmittal procedure.

(a) As used in this article:

. . . .

(2) "Record" includes every kind of record maintained by a business.

(b) Except as provided in Section 1564, when a subpoena duces tecum is served upon the custodian of records or other qualified witness of a business in an action in which the business is neither a party nor the place where any cause of action is alleged to have arisen, and such subpoena requires the production of all or any part of the records of the business, it is sufficient compliance therewith if the custodian or other qualified witness, within five days after the receipt of such subpoena, delivers by mail or otherwise a true, legible, and durable copy of all the records described in such subpoena to the clerk of court or to the judge if there be no clerk, together with the affidavit described in Section 1561.

(c) The copy of the records shall be separately enclosed in an inner envelope or wrapper, sealed, with the title and number of the action, name of witness, and date of subpoena clearly inscribed thereon; the sealed envelope or wrapper shall then be enclosed in an outer envelope or wrapper, sealed, directed as follows:

(1) If the subpoena directs attendance in court, to the clerk of such court, or to the judge thereof if there be no clerk.

(2) If the subpoena directs attendance at a deposition, to the officer before whom the deposition is to be taken, at the place designated in the subpoena for the taking of the deposition or at his place of business.

(3) In other cases, to the officer, body, or tribunal conducting the hearing, at a like address.

(d) Unless the parties to the proceeding otherwise agree, or unless the sealed envelope or wrapper is returned to a witness who is to appear personally, the copy of the records shall remain sealed and shall be opened only at the time of trial, deposition, or other hearing, upon the direction of the judge, officer, body, or tribunal conducting the proceeding, in the presence of all parties who have appeared in person or by counsel at such trial, deposition, or hearing. Records which are not introduced in evidence or required as part of the record shall be returned to the person or entity from whom received.

§ 1561. Business records—Affidavit of custodian—Procedure.

(a) The records shall be accompanied by the affidavit of the custodian or other qualified witness, stating in substance each of the following:

(1) The affiant is the duly authorized custodian of the records or other qualified witness and has authority to certify the records.

(2) The copy is a true copy of all the records described in the subpoena.

(3) The records were prepared by the personnel of the business in the ordinary course of business at or near the time of the act, condition, or event.

(b) If the business has none of the records described, or only part thereof, the custodian or other qualified witness shall so state in the affidavit, and deliver the affidavit and such records as are available in the manner provided in Section 1560.

§ 1562. Copy of records—Affidavits—Presumptions.

The copy of the records is admissible in evidence to the same extent as though the original thereof were offered and the custodian had been present and testified to the matters stated in the affidavit. The affidavit is admissible as evidence of the matters stated therein pursuant to Section 1561 and the matters so stated are presumed true. When more than one person has knowledge of the facts, more than one affidavit may be made. The presumption established by this section is a presumption affecting the burden of producing evidence.

§ 1564. Personal attendance of custodian or witness—Production.

The personal attendance of the custodian or other qualified witness and the production of the original records is required if the subpoena duces tecum contains a clause which reads:

The personal attendance of the custodian or other qualified witness and the production of the original records is required by this subpoena. The procedure authorized pursuant to subdivision (b) of Section 1560, and Sections 1561 and 1562, of the Evidence Code will not be deemed sufficient compliance with this subpoena.

Although until recently the Federal Rules of Evidence did not incorporate a simplified procedure for authenticating business records, several states with codes patterned after the Rules have amended their version of Article IX to include a simplified procedure. *E.g.*, ALASKA R. EVID. 902(11); TEX. R. EVID. 902(10). For its part, in the Comprehensive Crime Control Act of 1984, Congress authorized the use of an attestation to authenticate foreign business records. 18 U.S.C. § 3505. Federal prosecutors frequently use the attestation procedure in drug smuggling prosecutions.

In 2000, though, the Federal Rules were amended to go beyond 18 U.S.C. § 3505. Effective December 1, 2000, subdivisions (11) and (12) were added to Rule 902. Rule 902(11) permits the authentication of domestic business records by certification while 902(12) similarly allows the authentication of foreign business records by certificate. A notice requirement is included to provide the opponent an opportunity to contest foundational adequacy

NOTES AND PROBLEMS

1. While some jurisdictions apply simplified procedures across the board to all business writings, other jurisdictions limit the special procedures to records of activities such as hospitals and banks. What is the justification for these special procedures? Do the operation of those entities implicate a public interest?

2. Assume that Morena has adopted a statutory scheme identical to Cal. Evid. Code §§ 1560–64. Suppose that in a particular case, the business' documents are critical to the case's outcome and a party suspects that the copies produced under the special procedure (1) may have been tampered with or (2) will not clearly show the fine detail in the original that the party's claim turns on. What recourse does the party have? What is the significance of § 1564? How should the party word the subpoena duces tecum?

3. Problem 9–5. Again, suppose that Morena adopted a statutory scheme identical to Cal. Evid. Code §§ 1560–1564. In our torts case, Ms. Hill moved for the production of Polecat Motors' safety test records for the two years preceding her accident. Could Polecat Motors respond by submitting copies and an affidavit complying with § 1561? Read § 1560 carefully.

D. OFFICIAL WRITINGS

Like businesses, government has become a more and more important source of documentary evidence. As government regulation becomes more pervasive, government file cabinets have grown to include more and more data, and attorneys have more occasion to use official records as evidence. Any technique for authenticating a private or business writing can be used to authenticate an official writing. Moreover, special statutes such as Federal Evidence Rule 902 are designed to facilitate the use of official records.

Rule 902 governs the admission of official records in federal trials. Under the full faith and credit clause of the Constitution, Congress has the power to dictate the circumstances under which the courts of one state must accept official records from another state. Congress exercised that power in enacting the following two provisions of Title 28, United States Code:

§ 1738. State and territorial statutes and judicial proceedings: full faith and credit.

The Acts of the legislature of any State, Territory, or Possession of the United States, or copies thereof, shall be authenticated by affixing the seal of such State, Territory or Possession thereto.

The records and judicial proceedings of any court of any such State, Territory or Possession, or copies thereof, shall be proved or admitted in other courts within the United States and its Territories and Possessions by the attestation of the clerk and seal of the court annexed, if a seal exists, together with a certificate of a judge of the court that the said attestation is in proper form.

Such Acts, records and judicial proceedings or copies thereof, so authenticated, shall have the same full faith and credit in every court within the United States and its Territories and Possessions as they have by law or usage in the courts of such State, Territory or Possession from which they are taken.

§ 1739. State and territorial nonjudicial records: full faith and credit.

All nonjudicial records or books kept in any public office of any State, Territory, or Possession of the United States, or copies thereof, shall be proved or admitted in any court or office in any other State, Territory, or Possession by the attestation of the custodian of such records or books, and the seal of his office annexed, if there be a seal, together with a certificate of a judge of a court of record of the county, parish, or district in which such office may be kept, or of the Governor, or secretary of state, the chancellor or keeper of the great seal, of the State, Territory, or Possession that the said attestation is in due form and by the proper officers.

If the certificate is given by a judge, it shall be further authenticated by the clerk or prothonotary of the court, who shall certify, under his hand and the seal of his office, that such judge is duly commissioned and qualified; or, if given by such Governor, secretary, chancellor, or keeper of the great seal, it shall be under the great seal of the State, Territory, or Possession in which it is made.

Such records or books, or copies thereof, so authenticated, shall have the same full faith and credit in every court and office within the United States and its Territories and Possessions as they have by law or usage in the courts or offices of the State, Territory, or Possession from which they are taken.

Under these Rules and statutes, official documents are self–authenticating, and the proponent need not present live, sponsoring testimony. The proponent marks the exhibit for identification, shows the judge the exhibit, and then tenders the exhibit into evidence. This is one area where the law of evidence seemingly abandons its skeptical attitude and accepts evidence at face value. The exhibit is admissible so long as there is an attached certificate or chain of certificates that complies with the controlling Rule or statute. The following is an example of the type of certificate that might be attached to a copy of an official record to make the copy self–authenticating:

No._____ Dept. _____

SUPERIOR COURT
STATE OF CALIFORNIA
COUNTY OF SAN DIEGO

AUTHENTICATED COPY OF

In above entitled matter.

STATE OF CALIFORNIA,
                                                     ss.
COUNTY OF SAN DIEGO,

I, JESSE OSUNA, Clerk of the County of San Diego and ex-officio Clerk of the Superior Court of the State of California for the County of San Diego, which is a court of record having a seal, do hereby certify that by law I have custody of the seal and all the records, books and documents of or pertaining to said court.

I further certify that the document or documents described below and annexed hereto contain a full, true and correct copy of the original document or documents of or pertaining to the Superior Court which is/are on file in my office.

WITNESS my hand and the seal of the court this __ day of _____, 19__

JESSE OSUNA, County Clerk and ex-officio Clerk of the Superior Court of the State of California for the County of San Diego

I, _____, Judge of the Superior Court of the State of California, for the County of San Diego, do hereby certify that JESSE OSUNA, whose signature is affixed to the above certificate, is the Clerk of the County of San Diego and ex-officio Clerk of the Superior Court of the State of California for said County. As such clerk, he is the proper certifying officer of the court, and by law has custody of the seal and all the records, books and documents of or pertaining to the court, and his certificate is in due form as used in this state.

IN WITNESS WHEREOF I have hereunto set my hand this __ day of _____, 19__

Judge of the Superior Court of the State of California, for the County of San Diego

STATE OF CALIFORNIA,
                                                     ss.
COUNTY OF SAN DIEGO,

I, JESSE OSUNA, Clerk of the County of San Diego, State of California, and ex-officio Clerk of the Superior Court thereof, which is a court of record having a seal, do hereby certify that the Honorable _____ whose name is subscribed to the above certificate of qualification, was at the date thereof a Judge of the Superior Court of the State of California, for the County of San Diego, duly appointed or elected and qualified and acting; that he is authorized to make such certificates; that full faith and credit are due to his official acts as such judge. I further certify that the signature subscribed on the certificate is genuine and that the certificate is executed according to the laws of the State of California.

WITNESS my hand and the seal of the Superior Court this __ day of _____, 19__

JESSE OSUNA, County Clerk and ex-officio Clerk of the Superior Court of the State of California, for the County of San Diego

NOTES AND PROBLEMS

1. Why single out official documents and treat them so differently than private and business writings? Does it reflect an underlying judgment about the reliability of official documents? What problems would arise if courts demanded live, sponsoring testimony to authenticate public records or if attorneys were entrusted with *original* official documents for use in the courtroom?

2. Under these special procedures, the key is ensuring that the copy of the official record bears a proper attesting or authenticating certificate. An attesting certificate usually states that the signatory is the custodian of the original official document and that the attached document is a true and accurate copy of the original. The court judicially notices or presumes the signature's authenticity. That step triggers a chain reaction. Consider the various steps in the chain. If the signature on the certificate is genuine, what effect does that have on the certificate? In turn, if the certificate is authentic, what effect does that have on the attached copy of the official record?

3. Most jurisdictions limit the presumption to the signature of relatively high-ranking local and state officials. If the custodian is a low-ranking official, the presumption is inapplicable. The proponent must then resort to an authenticating certificate. That type of certificate states that the signatory holds a particular government office (high enough to trigger the presumption); the signatory is familiar with the lower ranking official; and the signature on the attesting certificate is the genuine signature of that low–ranking official.

4. Problem 9–6. In the *Devitt* case, the prosecutor wants to impeach the defendant with evidence of a prior conviction for perjury. (a) What type of supporting documentation would the prosecutor have to offer in court if the judgment of conviction had been entered in Kansas; and when the prosecutor received the copy of the judgment of conviction from Abilene, the prosecutor noticed that the judgment itself bore a seal. What else would the prosecutor need then? (b) The conviction had been entered in New York; and when the copy of the judgment arrived in the mail, the prosecutor noticed that there was no seal on the copy. (c) What if the conviction had been entered in France.

5. Problem 9–7. The prosecutor wants to impeach Devitt with evidence of a Cambodian conviction. However, Cambodian officials inexplicably refused to cooperate with the local American consul. Consequently, the prosecutor could not obtain the necessary certification of the copy of the judgment of conviction. In some situations, lack of local cooperation is not unusual. May the prosecutor nevertheless introduce the conviction? Consider Evidence Rule 902(3). *See United States v. Leal*, 509 F.2d 122, 126 (9th Cir. 1975).

6. Unless the proponent can invoke *Leal*, under the current Federal Rules of Evidence the proponent must produce a final certification from an American official. However, the 1961 Hague Convention Abolishing the Requirement of Legalization for Foreign Public Documents would eliminate that requirement. Under the convention, the foreign official attaches a special certificate called an apostille and maintains a register showing the serial number of the apostille. An American court could then check the foreign register to verify the authenticity of the apostille. The convention came into force for the United States on October 15, 1981. T.I.A.S. 10072, U.N.T.S. 189; 67 A.B.A. J. 1705 (1981). In late 1984, an amendment to Fed. R. Civ. P. 44 was proposed:

The final certification shall be dispensed with whenever both the United States and the foreign country in which the official record is located are parties to a treaty or convention that abolishes or displaces that requirement, in which case the record shall be certified as provided in the treaty or convention.

A model apostille is annexed to the convention:

APOSTILLE

1. Country ....

This public document ....

2. has been signed by ....

3. acting in the capacity of ....

4. bears the seal/stamp of ....

....

Certified

5. at .... 6. the ....

7. by ....

8. No. ....

9. Seal/stamp: Signature:

....

---

7. The proposed amendment to Rule 44 was never adopted. May a proponent of evidence nevertheless use the apostille procedure in federal practice? The convention came into force after the effective date of the Federal Rules of Evidence. Does the convention supersede the Rules? Is it necessary to reach the supersession issue? Consider the language of Rule 902(10).

Chapter 10

SPECIALIZED ASPECTS OF LOGICAL RELEVANCE: IDENTIFICATION OF PHYSICAL EVIDENCE

Read Federal Rule of Evidence 901(b)(1) and (4).

A. INTRODUCTION

Previously, we dealt with the authentication of one type of physical object, namely, a document. Trial attorneys have occasion to introduce as evidence a variety of physical objects other than writings. Experienced litigators realize that visual aids make their case much more appealing to lay jurors. Psychological research indicates that we gather eighty-five percent of our data about the external world through the sense of sight and only ten percent exclusively through the sense of hearing. Perlman, *Preparation and Presentation of Medical Proof*, 2 TRIAL DIPL. J. 18 (Spring 1979). Moreover, according to other empirical studies, the respective long–term retention rates are twenty percent of what we hear, thirty percent of what we see, and fifty percent of what we both hear and see. Briggs, *Real and Demonstrative Evidence* 4 (unpublished article available in National College of District Attorneys Library, University of South Carolina).

Furthermore, physical exhibits can be important for reasons other than their intrinsic evidentiary value. The psychological phenomenon of associational logic enhances the importance of exhibits; the presence of the exhibits in the deliberation room helps the jury remember the testimony of the witnesses who laid the foundation for the exhibit. As of right or in the judge's discretion, the exhibits go into the deliberation room with the jurors. If an exhibit was admitted during a particular witness' testimony, the exhibit's presence in the deliberation room can serve as a constant visual reminder of the witness' testimony. Many experienced attorneys make it a practice to admit at least one exhibit during each key witness' testimony, clearly associate the witness with that exhibit in closing argument, and request that the exhibit be sent to the jury. If the exhibit is sitting on the table in the middle of the deliberation room, the exhibit will help the jurors remember the testimony of the associated witness.

The lesson is clear: if a trial attorney wants the jury to understand the evidence in the short term and remember it in the long term, the attorney should integrate physical evidence into the presentation. The display of the physical object will help the jurors visualize the proponent's theory of the case. When that second sense comes into play, the proponent's theory becomes much more plausible and believable.

The process of authenticating physical evidence is usually termed the "identification of the evidence." Federal Evidence Rule 901(b) expressly uses the term "identification." Before the attorney needs to resort to the physical evidence, the attorney should keep the object out of the jury's view. American Bar Association Prosecution Function Standard 3–5.6(c) declares:

> It is unprofessional conduct for a prosecutor to permit any tangible evidence to be displayed in view of the judge or jury which would tend to prejudice fair consideration by the judge or jury until such time as a good faith tender of such evidence is made.

Defense Function Standards 4–7.5(c) contain identical language.

When the proponent is ready to use the evidence, the proponent follows the usual procedures. The proponent first marks the exhibit for identification, shows it to the opposing counsel, and then hands the exhibit to the sponsoring witness. The witness next lays the foundation for identification—a line of testimony complying with one of the doctrines mentioned in this chapter. At that point, the proponent formally offers the exhibit into evidence. If the judge admits the evidence, to heighten the impact on the jurors, the proponent then usually requests permission to hand the exhibit to the jurors for their personal examination and inspection.

B. REAL OR ORIGINAL PHYSICAL EVIDENCE

Real or original physical evidence has an historical connection with the facts on the merits of the case. For example, in our torts case, Ms. Hill's attorney might want to show the jurors the gas tank of Ms. Hill's car. The gas tank would be real, original evidence. Or in the *Devitt* prosecution, a shirt with bloodstains on it would be original physical evidence if the prosecutor alleged that the exhibit was the shirt Mr. Paterson was wearing when he struggled with his attacker. To authenticate an item, the proponent must prove that it is what he or she claims that it is. Here, since the proponent claims that the object has an historical connection with the case, the authentication doctrine requires that the proponent establish the historical nexus. There are several techniques the proponent may use to prove that nexus. Giannelli, *Chain of Custody and the Handling of Real Evidence*, 20 AM.CRIM. L. REV. 527 (1983).

1. READY IDENTIFIABILITY

At first, the authentication of an item of physical evidence might seem to be difficult and time consuming. In truth, the foundation can be laid with surprising brevity. Suppose that in a prosecution for assault and battery, the police officer who responded to the scene is testifying. The prosecutor marks a pistol for identification and hands it to the witness:

Q: I now hand you state's exhibit one for identification. What is it?

A: It's the pistol I found at the crime scene.

Q: How can you recognize it?

A: I remember the serial number.

Q: What was that number?

A: 15273956.

Q: When did you first notice the serial number?

A: I carefully noted it when I first picked up the weapon at the scene of the alleged attack.

Q: How can you recognize that number now?

A: I've always had a great memory for numbers. There's no question in my mind. This is the pistol I picked up that afternoon.

Q: Your Honor, I now offer state's exhibit one for identification into evidence as state's exhibit one.

Wigmore described the theory underlying the ready identifiability doctrine:

> Where a certain circumstance, feature, or mark may commonly be found associated with a large number of objects, the presence of that feature or mark in two supposed objects is little indication of their identity because, on the general principle of Relevancy . . . , the other conceivable hypotheses are so numerous, i.e. the objects that possess that mark are numerous and therefore any two of them possessing it might well be different. But where the objects possessing the mark are only one or a few, and the mark is found in two supposed instances, the chances of the two being different are "nil" or are comparatively small. Hence, in the process of identification of two supposed objects by a common mark, the force of the inference depends on the degree of the necessariness of association of that mark with a single object. (I)n practice it rarely occurs that the evidential mark is a single circumstance. The evidencing feature is usually a group of circumstances, which as a whole constitute a feature capable of being associated with a single object. Rarely can one circumstance alone be inherently peculiar to a single object. It is by adding circumstance to circumstance that we obtain a composite feature or mark which as a whole cannot be supposed to be associated with more than a single object. The process of constructing an inference of Identity thus consists usually in adding together a number of circumstances, each of which by itself might be a feature of many objects, but all of which together make it more probable that they coexist in a single object only. A mark common to two supposed objects is receivable to show them to be identical whenever the mark does not in human experience occur with so many objects that the chances of the two supposed objects are too small to be appreciable. But it must be understood that this test applies to the total combination of circumstances offered as a mark, and not to any one circumstance going with others to make it up.

2 WIGMORE ON EVIDENCE §§ 411-412 (3d ed. 1940).

The courts have been quite liberal in treating objects as readily identifiable. When the witness was prepared to say that he or she recognized the exhibit as a particular object seen on an earlier, relevant occasion, on that basis, the courts admitted such objects as a screwdriver, *Lopez v. State*, 490 S.W.2d 565 (Tex. Crim. App. 1973); a pair of scissors, *Riggins v. State*, 490 S.W.2d 124 (Ark. 1973); a money bag, *Overton v. State*, 490 S.W.2d 556 (Tex. Crim. App. 1973); a bottle, *State v. Paladine*, 2 Conn. Cir. 457, 201 A.2d 667 (1964); a leather key case, *Raullerson v. People*, 157 Colo. 462, 404 P.2d 149 (1965); a piece of rope, *Burris v. American Chicle Co.*, 120 F.2d 218 (2d Cir. 1941); and a tire, *United States v. Pagerie*, 15 C.M.R. 864 (A.F.B.R. 1954).

NOTES AND PROBLEMS

1. Do the Federal Rules codify the ready identifiability doctrine? Be prepared to identify the controlling language. What is the test for determining whether an item should be treated as a readily identifiable article? *See Transclean Corp. v. Bridgewood Services, Inc.*, 77 F.Supp.2d 1045, 1074 (D.Minn.1999) (the test is whether the proponent has made "a prima facie showing. . . *See United States v. Kandiel*, 865 F.2d 967, 974 (8th Cir. 1979) ('Any question concerning the credibility of the identifying witness simply goes to the weight the jury accords this evidence, not to its admissibility'); *United States v. Reilly*, 33 F.3d 1396, 1409 (3rd Cir. 1994) ('contradictory evidence goes to the weight to be assigned by the trier of fact and not to admissibility'). In formulating the test, consider Federal Evidence Rule 901(b)(1) and (b)(4) as well as Rules 104(a)–(b). The judge must decide whether to *characterize* an object as readily identifiable. The question of whether a tire has a particular mark on it is obviously a preliminary "fact" within the meaning of that expression in Rule 104. However, is the characterization itself a "factual" issue? Do not fall into the trap of thinking that Rules 104(a)–(b) control every decision conditioning the admissibility of evidence.

2. Problem 10–1. In the *Devitt* case, the defendant challenges his identification as Paterson's assailant. Immediately after the alleged incident, Paterson gave the police a description of the clothing his attacker wore: green jeans, a blue shirt, and black cowboy boots. Could the police testify that when they arrested Devitt seven hours after the alleged battery, he was wearing green jeans, a blue shirt, and black cowboy boots? The police seized these articles of clothing when they booked Devitt. The prosecutor marks the articles of clothing as exhibits at trial. What is the materiality of introducing the clothing at trial? What testimony must Paterson and the police officers give before the judge will admit the articles of clothing into evidence? *See Banning v. United States*, 130 F.2d 330, 335 (6th Cir. 1942), *cert. denied*, 317 U.S. 695 (1943). Would it make a difference if the arrest occurred seven weeks later? Seven months later? *United States v. Robinson*, 560 F.2d 507, 512–13 (2d Cir. 1977).

3. Problem 10–2. In *Devitt*, Paterson claims that Devitt threatened him with a knife before fleeing from the apartment. When the police arrived at the scene, they found a knife laying by the bed. The knife had no distinctive natural markings; but following standard operating procedure in most police departments, the seizing officer scratched her initials and the date on the knife blade. Do those marks convert the object into a readily identifiable article? *See United States v. Madril*, 445 F.2d 827, 828 (9th Cir.), *vacated*, 404 U.S. 1010 (1971); *State v. Ross*, 275 N.C. 550, 553, 169 S.E.2d 875, 878 (1969).

2. CHAIN OF CUSTODY

Chain of custody is an alternative, well–settled technique for identifying physical evidence. As we shall see in the next Problem, the technique is of particular importance when the proponent contemplates introducing testimony about a scientific analysis of the physical object in question. This article gives you a straightforward overview of the issues raised by the chain of custody technique:

COMMENT, THE IDENTIFICATION OF ORIGINAL, REAL EVIDENCE, 61 Military Law Review 145 (1973)*

When must the proponent prove a chain of custody?

There are three situations in which the proponent ordinarily resorts to proof of a chain of custody.

The first situation is where the item is not readily identifiable. As previously stated, the courts are exceedingly liberal in deciding to treat articles as readily identifiable items. However, there are some items which even the most liberal court would not label readily identifiable. If the issue is the identity of a specimen of blood, urine, or drugs, the court will not admit the specimen solely on the basis of the witness' purported identification of the substance. To identify a fungible item, the proponent ordinarily must prove a chain of the item's custody.

The second situation is where by its nature the item is readily identifiable but the witness neglected to note the characteristics which make the item readily identifiable. For example, suppose that the item is a serially numbered pistol but the witness failed to note the serial number. If he had noted the number, the court would treat the item as readily identifiable; as long as the witness testified that he remembered the number, the pistol's identification would be complete. However, if the witness failed to note the number, the proponent could still identify the pistol by proving the chain of its custody. Where the witness fails to note the special identifying characteristics of a readily identifiable item, proof of the chain of its custody is "a more than adequate substitute."

The third situation is where the item is a delicate article and its condition at the time of seizure is a pivotal issue in the case. The chain of custody is a method of establishing both the item's identity and its condition at the time of seizure. McCormick takes the position that if the item is "susceptible to alteration by tampering or contamination, sound exercise of the trial court's discretion may require" proof of a chain of custody. He gives the example of chemical specimens. Another illustration would be a delicate part of the engine of a crashed aircraft. Suppose the instrument is serially numbered. Assume further that the setting of the instrument at the time of crash would determine the ultimate liability for the accident. . . . [P]laintiff's counsel attempts to offer the instrument in evidence. He calls as a witness a Federal Aviation

---

* The opinions and conclusions presented herein are those of the author and do not necessarily represent the views of the Department of Defense, the Department of the Army, The Judge Advocate General's School, or any other governmental agency.

Administration investigator. The investigator testifies that he found the instrument at the crash site. The plaintiff's counsel hands the instrument to the witness and asks him to identify it. The witness identifies it on the basis of the serial number. The plaintiff's attorney then offers the item in evidence. Would the trial judge be justified in requiring proof of a chain of the instrument's custody? The answer is probably yes. The witness' testimony proves the item's identity, but the critical question is whether the instrument was at the same setting at the time of crash as it is when offered in evidence. Since the item is a delicate instrument, the judge would be justified in exercising discretion to require proof of a chain of custody. If the item has been subject to careless or rough handling in the interim between seizure and trial, the handling might have jarred the instrument into a different setting. Even though the item is readily identifiable, the posture of the case warrants the requirement for proof of the chain of custody.

What is the length of the chain of custody? What period of time must the proponent account for?

. . . To answer this question, counsel should distinguish between two fact situations.

The first situation is where the item's logical relevance depends upon a witness' in-court identification of the item. The trial counsel wants to authenticate the knife by proving a chain of custody. In this situation, the chain must run from the time of seizure to the time the knife is offered in evidence. The proponent must prove an identity between the item seized and the item offered, and he must assume the burden of proving a chain running from the time of seizure to the time of offer.

The second situation is where the proponent is relying upon the real evidence as the basis for expert testimony of the evidence's chemical analysis.

. . . [T]he overwhelming, majority view is that the chain must run only from the time of seizure to the time of analysis or test. In *United States v. Singer*,[67] the court stated that the evidence of the analysis is admissible even if the sample analyzed is lost or destroyed after the test. In fact, it is "nowise customary to produce in court a specimen or part upon which an analysis has been made." The majority view is the better-reasoned rule. If the proponent is offering only the results of the analysis, he must prove identity between the substance seized and the substance analyzed. There is no rule of evidence or logic which compels him to offer the substance in evidence. In some jurisdictions, the party opponent is entitled to inspect the substance and subject it to an independent test; but it is specious to suggest that the proponent's duty to formally offer the substance into evidence is a necessary correlative of the opponent's right to discover and examine the substance.

Which persons comprise the links in the chain of custody?

. . . It is well–settled that persons who merely had access to the item do not constitute links in the chain and that the proponent need not make any affirmative showing of their conduct with respect to the item. Such persons have an opportunity to come in contact with the item; but unless there is some

---

[67] 43 F. Supp. 863 (E.D.N.Y. 1942).

indication that they in fact came into contact with the item, they do not constitute links in the chain of proof.

There is some authority that the proponent need not make any affirmative showing of the conduct of a person who handled the article but who (1) held the item for a very short time and (2) performed only mechanical functions with the item. In *Commonwealth v. Thomas*,[73] the court held that the proponent did not have to make any showing of the conduct of the laboratory technician who merely placed the brushings in question under a microscope. . . . [The court's] reasoning probably ran along these lines: Proof of a chain of custody is a method of negativing any probability that substitution or tampering occurred; a person should be held to be a link, whom the proponent must account for, only if the person had a substantial opportunity to substitute for or tamper with the item; and, finally, persons who handle the item momentarily to perform purely mechanical functions do not have a substantial opportunity for substitution or tampering. There is a strong counter-argument that in the case of fungible, malleable goods, even a person who possesses the article only momentarily has a substantial opportunity for substitution or tampering. To date, the counter-argument has prevailed and the *Thomas* doctrine remains a distinct minority view. . .

The most significant concession the courts have made is their rule that the proponent need not make any affirmative showing of postal employees' handling of mailed items. Here the courts apply presumptions that postal employees properly discharge their duties and that articles "regularly mailed are delivered in substantially the same condition in which they were sent." It is indisputable that the postal employees who handle a mailed article are custodians of the article. However, if the sender uses the mail, it is virtually impossible to identify all the postal employees who handled the article; and the courts are understandably reluctant to adopt a rule of evidence which, in practical effect, would prevent evidence custodians from using the mail to transmit articles.

What showing must the proponent make to prove the chain of custody?

The courts have expressed the proponent's burden in various ways. Some have said that he must prove the chain by a "clear preponderance" of the evidence. Others have said that he must establish a "reasonable certainty." Others say that he must prove the chain "unequivocally." Still others say that he must create a "clear assurance." The most definite and often used expression is that the proponent must prove a "reasonable probability."

What is the nature of the probability the proponent must establish? In the leading federal case, *United States v. S.B. Penick & Co.*,[82] the Court of Appeals attempted to define the content of the showing the proponent must make. Affirmatively, he must show it is probable that the item offered in evidence is the same item originally acquired in substantially the same condition it was in at the time of acquisition. Negatively, he must show that it is improbable that either substitution or tampering occurred. In making this determination, the judge must weigh three factors: the nature of the article, the circumstances

---

[73] 448 Pa. 42, 292 A.2d 352 (1972).

[82] 136 F.2d 413 (2d Cir. 1943).

surrounding its preservation and custody, and the likelihood of any tampering by intermeddlers.

With respect to each link in the chain, the proponent must demonstrate: (1) his receipt of the item; (2) his ultimate disposition of the item, *i.e.*, transfer, destruction, or retention; and (3) his safeguarding and handling of the item between receipt and ultimate disposition. The third element poses the most difficult problem of proof for the proponent.

The courts have held that proof that the article was kept in a sealed container in the interim is an adequate showing of safekeeping and handling. The very "nature of a sealed container" makes substitution or tampering unlikely. It is now the standing operating procedure of law enforcement agencies to place seized fungibles in locked, sealed envelopes. . . . A recent case, *State v. Simmons*,[89] demonstrates the probative value of sealed containers even more dramatically. In *Simmons*, a tissue sample taken from a girl's body was placed in the hospital's tissue laboratory refrigerator. The tissue sample was in a sealed bag. The evidence next indicated that a policeman picked the bag up at the hospital desk. There was no evidence of the bag's safekeeping in the interim between its deposit in the refrigerator and the time when the officer picked up the bag at the desk. There was no evidence identifying the person who transported the bag from the refrigerator to the desk. Nevertheless, the court held that the proof of the chain of custody was sufficient. The court emphasized that although there was a gap in the chain of proof . . . .[t]here was, however, testimony that each of the specimens had been sealed in a bag and that the seals were intact at all times and did not reveal evidence of tampering.

The courts have also held that proof that the article was kept in a secure area in the interim is an adequate showing of safekeeping. The courts have held that articles kept in the following areas were adequately safeguarded: a secured closet, a locked automobile, an evidence locker, a police safe, a police lock box, a locked evidence cabinet, a locked evidence file, a police department evidence room, and a locked narcotics cabinet.

Finally, even in the absence of other proof of safekeeping, the courts have upheld showings of chain of custody where (1) the proponent at least accounted for the article's whereabouts and (2) the whereabouts were places where it was unlikely that intermeddling would occur.

As a practical matter, the standard of proof in chain-of-custody cases is rather slight. The proponent need not negate every possibility of substitution or tampering. . . .

The courts have even gone so far as to sustain chains when there were glaring discrepancies in the proponent's evidence. In one case, the court sustained the chain even though the name written on the narcotics container was a name other than that of the government special employee who allegedly obtained the narcotics. In another case, the envelope containing the drug stated an analysis date which conflicted with the government chemist's testimony. Again the chain was sustained. In still another case, the police lost

---

[89] 203 N.W.2d 887 (Wis. 1973).

the knife before trial. The police found the knife after trial began. A government witness testified that he could identify the knife because of the brown envelope in which it was placed. Again the chain was upheld.

There are two types of cases in which the courts tend to impose a strict standard of proof.

The first type of case is one in which there is a strong possibility that the article has been confused with other, similar articles. In *Nichols v. McCoy*,[123] the item in question was a blood sample. The sample had been extracted from a body at the coroner's mortuary. The evidence indicated that bodies were customarily kept at the mortuary and that samples were ordinarily extracted there. The proponent did not make any affirmative showing that the body or blood sample had been segregated from the other bodies and blood samples at the mortuary. The evidence raised a serious question concerning the blood sample's identity, and the court held that the proof of the chain was insufficient.

The second type of case is one in which the article is delicate and malleable. The trial judge has discretion to determine the amount of evidence necessary to lay a proper foundation; and he can vary the standard of proof, depending upon the ease or difficulty with which the item can be altered. If, in a particular case, the judge has "more than a captious doubt about the authenticity of the exhibits," he may require "a very substantial foundation. . . ." Some courts frankly admit that they impose a higher standard of proof when the object is "easily alterable" or "easily susceptible to undetected alteration." In contrast, they apply a lower standard of proof if the article is a solid object.

Blood samples are malleable articles. One commentator remarked that blood samples are:

> easily susceptible to accidental alteration through carelessness in taking, storing, or testing, and to wilful tampering by intermeddling litigants. In addition, the mechanics of calculating alcoholic content will greatly magnify even a slight change in the condition of the specimen, whatever its cause.

For this reason, the courts tend to impose a stricter standard of proof for the chain of a blood sample's custody.

NOTES AND PROBLEMS

1. What are the limits of the *Thomas* doctrine mentioned in the excerpted article? Suppose that the laboratory technician had held the article for an hour. Three hours? Overnight? At what point does the technician become such an important custodian that the proponent must make an affirmative showing of his or her safekeeping? Is the time of possession the only relevant factor?

2. Prior to the adoption of the Federal Rules, some courts had held that the preliminary fact of an object's authenticity was for the trial judge rather than the jury. 1 P. GIANNELLI & E. IMWINKELRIED, SCIENTIFIC EVIDENCE § 7-4, at 352 (3d ed. 1999). What effect do the Federal Rules have on the

---

[123] 106 Cal. App. 2d (Adv. 661), 235 P.2d 412 (1951).

procedure for determining this preliminary fact? Consider Rules 104, 901(a), and 901(b)(1) and (4).

Do those Rules "do away with any chain of custody requirement"? In 2 S. SALTZBURG & M. MARTIN, FEDERAL RULES OF EVIDENCE MANUAL 478 (5th ed. 1990), the authors contend that the Rules are susceptible to that interpretation. Should any deficiencies in the chain go solely to the weight of the evidence and not its admissibility?

Or do the Rules retain the requirement but convert the preliminary fact into a conditional relevance issue for the trial judge under Rule 104(b)? 1 C. MUELLER & L. KIRKPATRICK, FEDERAL EVIDENCE § 35, at 191 (2d ed. 1994), citing *United States v. Chaplinski*, 579 F.2d 373, 374–75 (5th Cir. 1978).

3. Problem 10-3. In the *Devitt* case, Paterson told the police that he was certain that before leaving, the attacker rested his hand on a plastic jewelry box in the bedroom. The officer scratched her initials on the box and took it to the police laboratory. At the laboratory, she handed the box to a technician. In turn, the technician delivered the box to the head of the fingerprint division. The head of the division developed latent fingerprints on the box and is prepared to compare photographs of those prints with the defendant's fingerprints. Do the markings make the box readily identifiable? Do we need a chain of custody? If so, why? If the prosecutor wants to offer the fingerprint testimony, is the only predicate proof of the box's identity? What issue arises when the analyst attempts to testify to the results of a test of the box? *See Whaley v. Commonwealth*, 214 Va. 353, 355–358, 200 S.E.2d 556, 558–59 (1973).

4. Problem 10-4. In the last problem, the prosecutor calls three witnesses: the officer, the technician, and the head of the fingerprint division. At what point should the prosecutor first have the box marked for identification? When should the prosecutor formally offer the box into evidence? After the first link's testimony? After the second link's testimony? After the third link's testimony?

5. Problem 10-5. On cross-examination, the technician admits the following: The officer delivered the box to him just before the close of business on March 12th; for that reason, he did not analyze the box on the 12th; he left the box on his workbench overnight; only police and janitorial employees have keys to the work area; and when he came to work the morning of the 13th, his work area appeared undisturbed. The defense counsel now moves to strike the technician's testimony and exclude the box. As judge, would you grant the motion? *See Wright v. State*, 420 S.W.2d 411, 413 (Tex. Crim. App. 1967). What result if you believe that the judge should evaluate the sufficiency of the proof of the chain of custody under Rule 104(b)?

3. CIRCUMSTANTIAL IDENTIFICATION OF PHYSICAL EVIDENCE

Ready identifiability and chain of custody are long-accepted techniques of authenticating physical evidence. However, as we have repeatedly stressed, in the field of logical relevance the proponent is not limited to the well-settled doctrines. The proponent can be creative so long as the proponent can marshal sufficient circumstances to support a permissive inference of genuineness. The following case is notable for its brevity and creativity.

PEDEN v. UNITED STATES

223 F.2d 319 (D.C. Cir. 1955)

PRETTYMAN, CIRCUIT JUDGE.

Appellant was indicted, tried and convicted for narcotics violations.

Appellant urges error in the admission of an exhibit (the vial of narcotic tablets). He says the Government failed to establish an effective chain of control over the vial from him to the officers. In brief the evidence was that a female informer, in the presence of police officers, made a telephone call and received one. She was then searched by a policewoman and was given marked money, placed in a taxicab, and driven several blocks. The cab stopped; a man, identified as Peden, approached the cab; the rear door was opened for a few minutes; Peden leaned into the cab; the door was then closed and the driver drove off. The police officers had observed the transactions from a distance. They immediately took both the informer and Peden into custody. The informer had a vial of tablets, analyzed as dromoran hydrobromide, genetically related to morphine, and Peden had the marked money. At the trial the informer did not testify. Peden urges that without her testimony there was no proof of the sale of the drugs by him. We think the chain of evidence was ample. Reasonable men might well have been persuaded beyond a reasonable doubt, by the chain of events we have narrated, that Peden made the sale to the informer. The police cannot be expected to locate an observer close enough to transactions in this traffic to see the actual passage of the goods and the money. The informer in this case was an addict. An extensive search for her, under an attachment issued by the court, failed to locate her at the time of the trial.

NOTES

1. Is there an analogy between the result in *Peden* and the chain–of–custody cases dealing with locked, sealed envelopes? In what respects is the inference from the act of sealing the envelope similar to the inference from the initial search of the informer? Would a pat–down search of the informer suffice, or is a strip or cavity search necessary?

2. Is *Peden* still good law under the Federal Rules? How can you square the result in *Peden* with the statutory text of Rule 901?

3. In some cases, when the informant is a key witness to the facts determining the defendant's guilt or innocence, the government will have a due process obligation to produce the informant at the trial. *See United States v. Hart*, 546 F.2d 798, 799 (9th Cir. 1976), *cert. denied*, 429 U.S. 1120 (1977). In a fact situation such as *Peden*, it is conceivable that that due process duty would come into play even though the prosecutor could circumstantially identify the contraband without the informant's live testimony. Do not confuse the evidentiary issue, addressed in *Peden*, with the criminal procedure question, analyzed in *Hart*.

C. DEMONSTRATIVE PHYSICAL EVIDENCE

In addition to real or original evidence, there is another type of evidence—demonstrative evidence. There is no logical necessity for limiting the attorneys to objects historically connected with the case. A mannequin, model, replica or chart can be very helpful to the jury. Even if the aid is prepared specially for purposes of trial, the object can assist the jurors in visualizing and understanding the testimony. *State v. Holmes*, 609 S.W.2d 132 (Mo. 1980). In addition, a visual aid can be a powerful tool of advocacy. For years, the late Melvin Belli was one of the most innovative masters of demonstrative evidence. Mr. Belli's anecdote in the following article confirms the finding of psychological researchers that physical evidence can have a major impact on the outcome of a trial.

BELLI, DEMONSTRATIVE EVIDENCE AND THE ADEQUATE AWARD, 22 Mississippi Law Journal 284 (1951)

The Jeffers Case

To illustrate demonstrative evidence, I refer you to a case I tried against our Municipal Railway: Catherine Jeffers had suffered the traumatic amputation of her right limb below the knee as she was getting off a streetcar on Market Street at its regular stopping point in San Francisco.

At the first trial, the verdict was $65,000. At the first trial I employed all of my ability as a trial man, all of my attributes of sincerity and humility. I failed to use one thing. I didn't use *demonstrative evidence*. Perhaps I should say I did not use imagination. Imagination to me in the courtroom is merely another way of saying I did not think the case through clearly enough so that I could portray to others in the most dramatic fashion what was so obvious to me. I failed to realize that I was trained in the courtroom, I went to law school and had become a specialist, that jurors are chosen because they know nothing of law, know nothing of the procedure of the courtroom, nothing of medicines, and they are mystified as much as they are frightened at the thought of "going to law."

On motion for new trial, excessiveness of verdict, the trial judge set the verdict of $65,000 for a lost limb aside.

I reset the case for trial before another judge and another jury. On the next trial, the verdict was $100,000, and there was another motion for excessive damages. This time the verdict of $100,000 was sustained.

Why the difference? . . .

The first trial judge in my *Jeffers* case had never seen an artificial limb. When I came into court on the second trial it occurred to me, "I am asking this jury to give my client something. I must show them, if possible, just exactly what it is. I can't show them an intangible commodity: pain and suffering and tears."

As if to emphasize my thoughts, defendant's counsel had commented to me that he was going to prove that science has now progressed to the point that an amputee can be fitted with a prosthesis which is just as good as the amputated limb the Lord had given him. . . .—I drive cars, play bridge, dance, swim, eat, tie neckties, and do practically everything . . . a normal limb can do. . . . This is exactly the argument that the City Attorney made. I saw the jury impressed by this argument.

On the first day of trial, at the time of the opening argument, I had brought into court a large object wrapped in yellow butcher paper. I placed this down on the counsel table and left it there during the entire trial. Of course, the jury, the judge and opposing counsel were curious. I moved it from the side of the table to the back of the table to the front of the table, close to the jury. . . .

When it came time for me to argue the case, I took the object in the paper before the jury box. It took me about five minutes to unwrap it. When I did, I said, "This is what this young girl is going to have to wear for the rest of her life—this artificial limb, this marvelous scientific invention. You have seen the metal and the harness and the strapping and the brutality of an artificial limb no matter how adeptly made."

I took the artificial limb and I asked Number One Juror to handle it and then to pass it among the other jurors. I asked them to "feel the fine texture of the flesh, to feel the warm blood coursing through the veins, to move the noiseless joints, to compare them with the articulating parts of their own knees." I told them here was this great piece of scientific achievement my friend had spoken of and which anyone would gladly substitute for their own limb.

The jury passed the limb from juror to juror. All this time my plaintiff sat in the courtroom in plain view with only one natural leg! It took about a half an hour for them to pass it about. I could see the verdict sealed in the looks on their faces as this limb was being passed around. The jury was convinced; the trial judge was convinced. The jury was out thirty minutes!

NOTES AND PROBLEMS

1. As defense attorney in *Jeffers,* would you have objected to the manner in which Mr. Belli used the artificial limb during summation? If so, on what ground? Remember the Prosecution Function Standard cited in the introduction to this chapter. What if it were applied to criminal prosecutions?

2. It is easy to see how the authentication doctrine applies to real or original physical evidence. Does the doctrine apply as well to demonstrative evidence? What does the proponent claim that an item of demonstrative evidence is? What did Mr. Belli impliedly claim that the artificial limb was?

3. Judges ordinarily admit models only when the sponsoring witness testifies that the object is "substantially similar" to the object historically involved in the case. The trial judge has wide discretion in deciding whether the proponent has made a sufficient showing of similarity. Is the requirement of substantial similarity solely a corollary of authentication? Under Rule 105, when a judge admits an exhibit on the theory that it is demonstrative rather than original evidence, what sort of limiting instruction should the judge give the jury? Suppose that the police could not locate the very knife which Devitt allegedly used to threaten Paterson but that the judge allowed the prosecutor to use a similar knife during Paterson's direct examination to illustrate Paterson's testimony about the battery. In the instruction, what should the judge tell the jury about the knife displayed during Paterson's testimony? How would that instruction limit what the prosecutor could say about the knife during closing argument?

4. Problem 10-6. In *Devitt,* the prosecutor attempts to introduce the knife Devitt allegedly used to threaten Paterson during the battery. After the trial judge excluded the knife for insufficient identification as real evidence, the prosecutor asked, "If that's your decision, Your Honor, just allow me to use it as demonstrative evidence to illustrate his testimony." Defense counsel objects strenuously, "The prosecutor's been waving that exhibit around the courtroom for the last hour. The prosecutor wants to use the very knife that's been referred to as the one used in the alleged attack. That's too prejudicial." What ruling on defense counsel's objection? What is the risk if the judge permits the prosecutor to use the same exhibit as demonstrative evidence? *See* FED. R. EVID. 403; *Toledo v. State,* 651 S.W.2d 382, 384 (Tex. Ct. App. 1983).

5. Demonstrative evidence is handled differently by courts:

Some courts treat demonstrative exhibits exactly as they do substantive exhibits, that is, by formally admitting them into evidence and allowing the jury to view the exhibits during deliberations. Other courts admit demonstrative exhibits into a twilight zone reserved for "demonstrative purposes only," apparently indicating that such exhibits can be identified for the record but must be precluded from use by the jury during deliberations. Still other courts admit demonstrative exhibits "for limited purposes," but nevertheless permit the jury to view the exhibits during deliberations. Finally, some courts explicitly refuse to "admit" demonstrative exhibits into evidence at all, but allow witnesses to refer to them during testimony. . . .— some permitting the jury to view this unadmitted evidence during deliberations, while others do not.

Brain & Broderick, *The Derivative Relevance of Demonstrative Evidence: Charting Its Proper Evidentiary Status,* 25 U.C. DAVIS L. REV. 957, 965–66 (1992). *See also* MAINE RULE OF EVIDENCE 616 ("illustrative aids" "shall not accompany the jury during deliberations unless by consent of all parties or order of court on good cause shown"); *United States v. Wood,* 943 F.2d 1048, 1053 (9th Cir. 1991) ("such pedagogical devices should be used only as a testimonial aid and should not be admitted into evidence or otherwise be used by the jury during deliberations").

Chapter 11

SPECIALIZED ASPECTS OF LOGICAL RELEVANCE: IDENTIFICATION OF SPEAKERS AND VERIFICATION OF PHOTOGRAPHS AND CHARTS

Read Federal Rules of Evidence 901(a) and (b)(5)–(6).

A. THE IDENTIFICATION OF A SPEAKER

In the authentication of writings, the essential task is identifying the author. In the authentication of statements, the task is identifying the speaker. The techniques for authenticating statements and conversations largely parallel the techniques for authenticating documents. As in the case of authenticating documents, the proponent can rely on direct evidence: a witness may identify the speaker of a statement made in the witness' presence. A brief review of several of the techniques for circumstantially identifying the speaker will further demonstrate the parallel.

1. THE TELEPHONE DIRECTORY DOCTRINE

Federal Evidence Rule 901(b)(6) describes one authentication technique for an oral statement.

> (b) <u>Illustrations</u>. By way of illustration only, and not by way of limitation, the following are examples of authentication or identification conforming with the requirements of this rule:
>
> (6) <u>Telephone conversations</u>. —Telephone conversations, by evidence that a call was made to the number assigned at the time by the telephone company to a particular person or business, if (A) in the case of a person, circumstances, including self-identification, show the person answering to be the one called, or (B) in the case of a business, the call was made to a place of business and the conversation related to business reasonably transacted over the telephone.

This doctrine rests on the assumption that the telephone directory is reliable. That is certainly an assumption we readily make in our daily lives. This is one instance in which the law of evidence has been willing to accept an everyday assumption. Given that assumption, the doctrine tells us that the pattern of circumstances identified in Rule 901(b)(6) is sufficient to create a permissive inference of the speaker's identity.

2. IDENTIFICATION BASED ON THE CONTENT OF THE ORAL STATEMENT

Alternatively, a statement can be authenticated by proof that only a particular person is likely to know the data disclosed in the statement. *In the matter of R.J.W.*, 770 S.W.2d 103 (Tex. App. 1989). We examined a similar method of authenticating writings. If the proponent can establish that certain facts were disclosed in the oral statement and that only a particular person was likely to know those facts, we may conclude that the speaker was that person.

3. SKILLED LAY OBSERVER

One of the most frequently used techniques of authenticating oral statements is skilled lay observer testimony. Federal Evidence Rule 901(b)(5) codifies the technique:

> Identification of a voice, whether heard firsthand or through mechanical or electronic transmission or recording, by opinion based upon hearing the voice at any time under circumstances connecting it with the alleged speaker.

This technique is strikingly similar to the use of skilled lay observer testimony to identify a handwriting style. *United States v. Albergo*, 539 F.2d 860 (2d Cir.), *cert. denied*, 429 U.S. 1000 (1976). The foundation requires proof that the witness is sufficiently familiar with the person's voice. Annot., 79 A.L.R.3d 79 (1977). Some of the older decisions suggest that it suffices if the witness heard the alleged speaker talk on one prior occasion. Many modern opinions require that the witness have had more significant exposure to the alleged speaker's voice. In *Albergo, supra*, the witness certainly had the requisite exposure. The witness testified that "he had heard appellant's voice on tape some 500 different times and that he had on one occasion visited . . . [a] [b]ar and listened to appellant talking with a group of men at the [b]ar." 539 F.2d at 862. Thus, *Albergo* is an easy case to resolve even under the modern standard. However, the following problems are a bit more challenging.

NOTES AND PROBLEMS

1. Problem 11–1. In *Devitt*, the day before the incident, Paterson received an angry telephone call. At the time, he did not recognize the voice. Assume Devitt was not asked to speak at the lineup, and he elected not to testify at the preliminary hearing. Hence, while testifying during the prosecution case-in-chief, Paterson cannot and does not testify that he recognized Devitt's voice on the telephone. However, after testifying, he remains in the courtroom and is present to hear Devitt testify in his own defense. During the prosecution rebuttal, the prosecutor recalls Paterson as a witness. He is prepared to identify Devitt's voice on the basis of hearing him testify in court. The defense attorney objects that "the courtroom environment is too artificial a setting for any voice identification to be reliable." What ruling? *United States v. Duran*, 4 F.3d 800 (9th Cir. 1993).

2. Suppose Devitt never took the stand at trial. Courtroom voice identification can be aided in such situations by compelling the accused to provide a voice exemplar in the presence of the jury. Is such a process violative of the Fifth Amendment privilege against self-incrimination? No, says *Burnett v. Collins*, 982 F.2d 922 (5th Cir. 1993). Burnett was required to repeat the exact words of the armed robber, even though he chose not to testify during trial. "A voice exemplar does not violate one's Fifth Amendment privilege against self-incrimination because the exemplar is merely a source of physical evidence."

3. Problem 11–2. The police have a tape recording of a threatening call to Paterson, made after the incident. To identify the speaker as Devitt, the prosecutor calls John Roselle. Roselle has never met Devitt face to face, but he transacts business with him over the telephone several times a week. On the basis of those telephone conversations, he is prepared to say that he can identify Devitt's voice. Specifically, he is prepared to testify that the voice on the recording is Devitt's. Is Roselle's lack of personal contact with Devitt fatal to the admissibility of his testimony? *See United States v. Green*, 40 F.3d 1167 (11th Cir. 1994).

Most courts have adopted a liberal approach to voice identification, even though some psychologists claim that lay opinions identifying voices are unreliable. McGehee, *The Reliability of the Identification of the Human Voice*, 17 J. Gen. Psychology 249 (1937). In the McGehee study, there were 49 "readers" (31 male and 18 female) and 740 "auditors." In most of the experiments, five readers spoke behind a screen. The auditor had heard only one of the readers' voices before, and the auditor was asked to identify that reader. In some of these experiments, there was only a one day lapse between initially hearing the reader's voice and the screen test. The researchers retested the auditors at a longer period up to five months since the initial hearing. In the study, after five months, only 13% of the auditors correctly identified the reader they initially heard. The researchers concluded that the reliability of lay opinions routinely admitted in court is "relatively low." However, like Professor Inbau's study of lay opinions on handwriting and the proficiency studies of questioned document examiners, the studies of voice identification have not persuaded the courts to preclude or restrict the admissibility of lay opinion testimony on this topic.

4. EXPERT TESTIMONY BASED ON SOUND SPECTROGRAPHY

Just as an expert document examiner can authenticate a writing, an expert in sound spectrography may be willing to testify that the same voice produced two spectrograms. The following article describes the spectrography technique and some of the research conducted to determine the technique's efficacy.

CUTLER, THIGPEN, YOUNG, & MUELLER, THE EVIDENTIARY VALUE OF SPECTROGRAPHIC VOICE IDENTIFICATION, 63 Journal of Criminal Law, Criminology, and Police Science 343 (1972)

The Technique

Speaker recognition by spectrographic voice analysis is a seemingly simple, but fundamentally complex, method of personal identification. In making an identification by this method, the first step is to tape–record an exemplar of an individual's voice. The sound spectrum of his speech sample is then scanned electronically by a high–speed sound spectrograph which produces a spectrogram, a visible amplitude–frequency–time display of the speech sounds recorded. This visible portrayal of the frequency variations in an individual's voice can then be subjectively compared with spectrograms of phonetically identical sounds produced by "unknown" individuals. The sound patterns represented on the spectrogram are the product of the energy expelled during speech and are shaped and determined by the dynamic interplay between the individual's vocal mechanism and the coupling and placement of his articulators. The validity of the technique as a means of personal identification rests on the premise that the sound patterns produced in speech are unique to the individual and that the spectrogram accurately and sufficiently displays this uniqueness.

Kersta: Theory, Experiments, and Replication

Lawrence Kersta, an electrical engineer and physicist, has been the foremost advocate of the validity of personal identification by spectrographic voice analysis. His claim that the technique is accurate and reliable is founded on two propositions.

The theory of invariant speech is the cornerstone of his hypothesis that individuals can be identified by the spectral characteristics of their voices. The theory posits that the characteristic spectral patterns of phonetically identical utterances vary more between two individuals (interspeaker variability) than between two such utterances spoken by the same individual (intraspeaker variability). Although so far the theory has not been proven directly, Kersta has buttressed the theory by applying his own hybrid form of statistical probability to the acoustic theory of speech production. He argues that since both the dimensions of the vocal cavities and the coupling of the articulators, which define the spectrum for a given sound, are affected by heredity, sex, age, and socio–environmental factors, it is extremely unlikely that two individuals would develop spectrographically identical speech patterns. While a superficially attractive rationale for voice uniqueness, a proper application of probability theory demands substantially more precision than this.

[Kersta's initial experiments with spectrographic voice analysis demonstrated extremely low error rates. Kersta concluded that spectrograms of an individual's speech patterns for particular words are as unique in their identifying characteristics as fingerprints, thus rendering the technique a reliable method of personal identification when performed by a trained examiner. In addition, Kersta claimed that neither passage of time nor conscious efforts at mimicry could frustrate a system of identification based on spectrographic voice analysis. He further maintained that the relatively higher pitch of the female voice would not affect the accuracy of such an identification technique.

Other experimenters, all reputable scientists in speech, phonetics, or associated fields, were unable to duplicate Kersta's high accuracy rates. However a study completed in 1970 under the direction of Oscar Tosi at Michigan State University replicated Kersta's original experiments and confirmed his high accuracy rates.]

The Tosi Study: Format and Results

Since in the matching–to–sample tests conducted by Kersta and others a match for the "unknown" spectrogram always existed, the trial became merely a process of elimination. This type of trial has no relation to a forensic application of the technique, and the results obtained through such trials cannot be extrapolated to validate the technique as a means of identification. The format of the Tosi study, however, was designed to test varying conditions which could be expected to have a major impact on the reliability of the technique in a forensic setting.

[First, both open and closed trials were conducted. Second, the effect of a reduction in cue material on identification accuracy rates was tested. A third very important feature of the Tosi study was its use of both contemporary and non–contemporary matching spectrograms in testing speaker identification. A fourth variable tested was the effect of the context of the cue material and its mode of recording on the reliability of the technique.]

In selecting a speaker population of two hundred fifty males, drawn from a population of twenty-five thousand at the university, Tosi attempted to meet one of the requirements for validation of the technique: homogeneity of the speaker group. The speakers selected had no speech defects and utilized a standard American English dialect.

Each of the twenty–nine examiners used in the experiment was given one month of training in basic acoustic speech principles and in the interpretation of speech spectrograms. Moreover, the examiners were given several objective points of similarity to look for when making comparisons between spectrograms. This training was far more extensive than that given examiners in previous speaker recognition experiments utilizing spectrograms.

In each of the nearly thirty-five thousand random trials, aural comparison of the speech samples was prohibited. The examiner was forced to come to a positive conclusion, either rejecting or accepting one of the "known" spectrograms as identical with the "unknown", and an average time of only fifteen minutes was devoted to study of the spectrograms before a conclusion was demanded. These inhibiting factors, while necessary as a control in the experiment, would not be present in forensic application of the technique.

The statistical results of the open set trials, which tested the reliability of the technique in various forensic applications, indicate that overall accuracy levels of 82–85% are possible under the conditions tested. Although these figures indicate an error range of 15–18%, this gross error rate includes two types of error: <u>false elimination</u> (a match was present but the examiner failed to perceive it) and <u>false identification</u> (a match was not present but the examiner mistakenly thought there was one, or a match was present but the examiner chose the wrong one). Only the latter error, false identification, is particularly troublesome from a legal standpoint. Moreover, a breakdown of the gross error rate to reflect the differentiation between types of error reveals that the risk of false identification is only 5–6% while that of false identification is only 10–12%.

NOTES

Perhaps the primary lesson to be learned from the debate over the admissibility of sound spectrography is that the courts must not accept at face value an expert's assertion that "numerous experiments" have validated the hypothesis of the accuracy of a technique such as sound spectrography. In testing the assertion, courts should ask questions which check the internal and external validity of a process.

- What was the composition of the group of subjects in the experiment? The early sound spectrography experiments involved almost exclusively white male subjects. Suppose that the expert relied on sound spectrography as the basis for identifying a black female speaker. E. Imwinkelried, THE METHODS OF ATTACKING SCIENTIFIC EVIDENCE § 10–6(B), at 297 (3d ed. 1997).

- What were the test conditions? In the early sound spectrography experiments, the speakers made no attempt to disguise their voice. National Academy of Sciences, ON THE THEORY AND PRACTICE OF VOICE IDENTIFICATION 24 (1979). Assume that in a given case, the expert relied on the sound spectrography technique to attempt to identify the person who made a threatening call. It is obvious from the audiotape of the call that the speaker was attempting to disguise his voice. *People v. Law*, 40 Cal. App. 3d 69, 114 Cal. Rptr. 708 (1974).

There is currently a sharp split of authority over the admissibility of sound spectrography evidence. Many states exclude voiceprint evidence. *E.g.*, *State v. Gortarez*, 141 Ariz. 254, 686 P.2d 1224 (1984); *People v. Kelly*, 17 Cal. 3d 24, 549 P.2d 1240, 130 Cal. Rptr. 144 (1976); *Cornett v. State*, 450 N.E.2d 498 (Ind. 1983). One point of objection to this form of evidence in such courts involves the difficulty which spectrography proof has experienced in achieving general scientific acceptance. A Committee on Evaluation of Sound Spectrograms of the National Academy of Sciences has announced its position that the experimental verification of some of sound spectrography's underlying premises is inadequate. National Academy of Sciences, ON THE THEORY AND PRACTICE OF VOICE IDENTIFICATION (1979).

However, federal courts as well as some other states have been much more receptive to voiceprint evidence. *United States v. Smith*, 869 F.2d 348 (7th Cir. 1989); *United States v. Williams*, 583 F.2d 1194 (2d Cir. 1978); *United States v. Maivia*, 728 F. Supp. 1471 (D. Haw. 1990); *State v. Williams*, 4 Ohio St. 3d 53, 446 N.E.2d 444 (1983); *State v. Williams*, 388 A.2d 500 (Me. 1978). The decision in *Maivia* illustrates the reasoning of courts taking this view. An important piece of government evidence was a threatening tape recorded message of some 65 words left on the alleged victim's telephone answering machine. An expert in spectrographic voice identification was proffered by the defense. The court relied upon the Tosi study, *supra*, in deciding to allow the defense expert to give his opinion of the identity of the speaker on the tape. In this case, the court felt that the testimony of both the defense and government voice experts would be of "appreciable help" to the jury. The message on the phone machine was the primary evidence against the accused. The court observed: "[w]hile the federal courts heavily favor admissibility, state courts are more evenly split on the issue. . . ."

There is some prospect that the trend in federal courts may be accelerated by developments in the scientific evidence field. In a 1999 decision, citing *Daubert*, the Alaska Supreme Court ruled sound spectrography testimony admissible. *State v. Coon*, 974 P.2d 386 (Alaska 1999). The court did so even though the court acknowledged that the "scientific literature cited by the [defendant] permits a conclusion that there is significant disagreement among experts in the field of voice spectrographic analysis regarding the reliability of the technique." *Id.* at 402. You will need to revisit this when you review the next chapter and consider the impact of the *Daubert* case.

5.   TAPE RECORDINGS

Although many celebrated cases have focused public attention on the evidentiary importance of audiotapes, the traditional attitude of the courts toward sound recordings has been one of skepticism. The courts' fear of possible tampering with audiotapes led them to insist on a thorough foundation. The courts ordinarily demand a more complete foundation for the admission of a tape recording than they do in the case of a photograph. A recent decision illustrates the foundational steps, and the hazards of not complying with them.

McALINNEY v. MARION MERRELL DOW, INC.

992 F.2d 839 (8th Cir. 1993)

WOLLMAN, CIRCUIT JUDGE.

[A former employee brought suit against an employer. The employee alleged employment discrimination on the basis of national origin. McAlinney was born in Northern Ireland, where he attended medical school. Later, he was hired in the Kansas City area, and served as defendant's Associate Medical Director. When he concluded he was not receiving fair annual reviews as a result of ethnic discrimination based on his Irish ethnicity, he began recording numerous conversations with particular employees. He employed a microcassette recorder hidden in one of his socks.]

McAlinney makes four arguments attacking the propriety of the district court's evidentiary rulings at trial. We note initially that "[w]e give substantial deference to the district court's rulings on the admissibility of evidence, and we will not find error in the absence of a clear showing of abuse of discretion." *Freidus v. First National Bank*, 928 F.2d 793, 794 (8th Cir. 1991).

McAlinney first argues that the district court erred in refusing to permit him to offer tape recordings of conversations between McAlinney and various Marion management–level employees, particularly Dr. Flicker, during his case–in–chief.

As noted earlier, McAlinney had compiled numerous microcassette tapes of surreptitiously recorded conversations, mostly between himself and Dr. Flicker, recorded at work and from his home telephone. McAlinney re–recorded selected portions of these microcassette tapes onto eight cassette tapes. McAlinney then submitted these eight cassette tapes, containing approximately nine hours of conversations, to the district court prior to trial. Marion subsequently filed a motion in limine to exclude the tapes from evidence. After listening to all of the tapes, the district court observed that many of the cassettes were inaudible and that some of the cassettes were fairly audible, but that the conversations on them were difficult to track. The district court determined that although some of the tapes were potentially relevant, they had foundational problems and might confuse or mislead the jury. Accordingly, it excluded the tapes from McAlinney's case–in–chief.

We set forth the requirements for introducing tape recordings into evidence in *United States v. McMillan*, 508 F.2d 101, 104 (8th Cir. 1974), *cert. denied*, 421 U.S. 916, 95 S. Ct. 1577, 43 L. Ed. 2d 782 (1975). In order to be admissible, the proponent must establish that (1) the recording device was capable of taking the conversation offered into evidence; (2) the operator of the device was competent to operate the device; (3) the recording is authentic and correct; (4) changes, additions, or deletions have not been made; (5) the recording has been preserved in a manner that is shown to the court; (6) the speakers are identified; and (7) the conversation elicited was made voluntarily and in good faith, without any kind of inducement. Id. We have also held that "[r]elevant evidence may nevertheless be excluded if its probative value is substantially outweighed by a danger of confusion of the issues or of undue delay." *Hogan v. American Telephone & Telegraph Co.*, 812 F.2d 409, 411 (8th Cir. 1987); *see* Fed. R. Evid. 403.

A careful review of all nine hours of the tapes has confirmed the wisdom of the district court's decision to exclude them from McAlinney's case-in-chief. With the exception of three telephone conversations, only one of which is with Dr. Flicker, McAlinney recorded the balance of the conversations on a tiny microcassette recorder hidden in his sock. The resulting tapes are mostly garbled, often unintelligible, and suffer from an excess of background noise. Moreover, the tapes exhibit serious problems of continuity because, either through editing or recorder malfunction, there are numerous blank spots on each tape. Last, certain conversations appear twice on the tapes. Consequently, serious issues arise concerning whether changes, additions, or deletions have been made. *See McMillan*, 508 F.2d at 104. Indeed, McAlinney concedes that he edited the tapes. Moreover, McAlinney testified at great length concerning the statements allegedly made on the tapes. Accordingly, we find no error in the district court's refusal to permit McAlinney to use the tapes in his case–in–chief.

The *McAlinney* case involved a pretrial investigation wherein the district court painstakingly listened to all nine hours of the tapes. Sometimes the issue does not reach the judge until trial. At that point, a classic article in the field describes the process:

> The wire or tape recording should be marked and offered in evidence. Upon receiving such offer of proof, the wire or tape recording should be played before the judge, in the absence of the jury. Upon consideration of objections to the recording as a whole or parts thereof, the court should permit the recording or competent portions thereof to be played to the jury. While the tapes are being played, the court reporter should take down such recorded statements.

Conrad, *Magnetic Recordings in the Courts*, 40 VA. L. REV. 23, 35–36 (1954).

Some courts list the elements of the foundation in mechanical, checklist fashion. *E.g.*, *United States v. Stone*, 960 F.2d 426, 436 (5th Cir. 1992); *United States v. Branch*, 970 F.2d 1368, 1372 (4th Cir. 1992). The checklist ensures that the proponent lays the usual, strict foundation outlined in the *McAlinney* case. Sound recordings, see *State v. Cusmano*, 274 N.J. Super. 496, 644 A.2d 672 (App. Div. 1994); Comment, 48 RUTGERS L. REV. 263 (1995).

NOTES

1. In principle, is it always necessary to lay this lengthy foundation to authenticate a tape recording? Is the question of the recording's accuracy governed by Federal Rule 104(a) or (b)? If Rule 104(b) governs, is strict insistence on a traditional foundation justified? *Ricketts v. City of Hartford*, 74 F.3d 1397 (2d Cir. 1996); Imwinkelried, *Federal Rule of Evidence 402: The Second Revolution*, 6 REV. LITIGATION 129, 143 (1987) ("The traditional foundational requirements are . . . more onerous than the logical relevance doctrine demands. Since the Federal Rules do not codify the traditional requirements, Rule 402 overturns them.").

2. Modernly, there has been a trend in some courts to relax the strict foundation requirements for tape recordings. *United States v. Buchanan*, 70 F.3d 818 (5th Cir. 1995).

3. In a criminal case where the government proffers a tape recording of a drug transaction or an interrogation of a suspect, the government has the burden of demonstrating that the recording is an accurate reproduction of relevant sounds. *United States v. Buchanan*, *supra*. In several cases, police or other officers who had verbal contact with a defendant were allowed to make positive identification of a voice on a tape recording as belonging to the defendant. *United States v. Degaglia*, 913 F.2d 372 (7th Cir. 1990). *See Brown v. City of Hialeah*, 30 F.3d 1433 (11th Cir. 1994); *In the Matter of R.J.W.*, 770 S.W.2d 103 (Tex. App. 1989).

4. When tape recordings are used, the attorneys often prepare transcripts for the jurors to follow while the tape is being played. In *United States v. Stone*, 960 F.2d 426 (5th Cir. 1992), a DEA agent's conversation with a drug conspirator was recorded on audio tape. The agent testified he had worn a hidden transmitter, that the tape of the conversation had been kept in a secure place from the time it was made, and that no alterations had been made. A heavy thunderstorm during the conversation interfered with the recording and made portions of the tape hard to understand. As the tape was played the jury listened and at the same time reviewed a typed transcript of the tape. The defendant objected to the use of transcript. The court instructed the jury: "It [the transcript] is not evidence in this case. The tape is the evidence." On review, the court of appeals concluded the district court's handling of the situation was within its discretion.

5. The preferred practice is for the court not to submit transcripts of tape recordings to the jury unless the parties stipulate to their accuracy. If the parties cannot agree, the second method is for the court to determine the accuracy of the transcript by reading the transcript against the tapes. This review is accomplished *in camera*. *United States v. Scarborough*, 43 F.3d 1021 (6th Cir. 1994). Care must be exercised in performing this function, because when tapes are difficult to hear, a transcript intended as an aid to the jury inevitably becomes, in the minds of the jury, the evidence itself. *United States v. Segines*, 17 F.3d 847 (6th Cir. 1994).

6. Sometimes the jurors are allowed to take the transcripts into the jury room as they deliberate on the case. *United States v. Nixon*, 918 F.2d 895 (11th Cir. 1990). Judges who allow this practice seem to view the transcripts as evidence. Contrary to the jury charge in *United States v. Stone, supra*, the decision in *United States v. Valencia*, 957 F.2d 1189 (5th Cir. 1992), adopts the view that "transcripts may be used as substantive evidence to aid the jury in determining the real issue presented, the content and the meaning of the tape recordings. It is therefore incorrect to think of the transcripts as simply an 'aid' —as better lighting fixtures in the courtroom would be an 'aid' to the jury's vision of witnesses—and not as evidence of any kind. They are evidence and, like other evidence, may be admitted for a limited purpose only." Even in such courts, however, the tape recording controls if there is an inconsistency between tape and transcript: "When both a tape and a transcript are admitted, or a transcript is used by the jury as an aid when listening to the tape, the jury is generally given a limiting instruction that if it encounters a discrepancy between the tape and the transcript, the tape controls."

B.   THE VERIFICATION OF PHOTOGRAPHS

The widespread realization of the persuasive value of visual aids accounts for the frequent use of photographic evidence. Some students of photographic evidence estimate that photographs are used in roughly half the cases in the United States. 1 C. Scott, Photographic Evidence § 1 (2d ed. 1969). Photographic evidence adds "a touch of drama or exotica." Weissman, *Discovery: Auxiliary Exotic Evidence, and the Duty to Detail*, Trial, June 1980, at 28, 30.

Before examining the various techniques of authenticating photographs, we must pause to analyze the basic theory of admissibility. The proponent ordinarily introduces the photograph during the testimony of a sponsoring witness. The witness testifies about the object or scene and then adds that the photograph is a "true," "accurate," "fair," or "correct" depiction of the object or scene. On that foundation, the judge admits the photograph. The question is this: Once the photograph is admitted, to what evidentiary status is the photograph entitled?

BERGNER v. STATE

397 N.E.2d 1012 (Ind. Ct. App. 1979)

Chapman, Judge.

Indiana courts traditionally have stressed three requirements for the admission of photographic evidence. First, an adequate foundation must be laid. Our courts have consistently held this requires the testimony of a witness who can state the photograph is "a true and accurate representation of the things it is intended to depict." *Wilson v. State*, (1978) Ind., 374 N.E.2d 45. Relevancy is the second requirement for the admission of photographic evidence in Indiana. Like all evidence, a photograph must meet the usual relevancy standard, *i.e.*, it must tend to prove or disprove a material fact. Finally, some Indiana cases require the photographs aid juror's understanding of other evidence. *See Whitfield v. State* (1977) 266 Ind. 629, 366 N.E.2d 173.

Although all three requirements for the admission of photographic evidence are important, in this case we are singularly concerned with the foundation requirement. Indiana's approach to the admission of photographs, as guided by the current foundation requirement, falls within what has been characterized as the "pictorial testimony theory" of photographic evidence. 111 J. Wigmore, Evidence § 790 (Chadbourn rev. 1970). This theory categorizes photographs with maps, models and diagrams, and thus treats photographs purely as demonstrative evidence. As such, a photograph is not evidence in itself, but is used merely as a nonverbal method of expressing a witness' testimony and is admissible only when a witness can testify it is a true and accurate representation of a scene personally viewed by that witness.

The "silent witness theory" for the admission of photographic evidence permits the use of photographs at trial as substantive evidence, as opposed to merely demonstrative evidence. Thus, under the silent witness theory there is no need for a witness to testify a photograph accurately represents what he or she observed; the photograph "speaks for itself." III J. Wigmore, Evidence § 790 (Chadbourn rev. 1980)

One of the most frequent, and often unintentional, utilizations of the silent witness theory occurs when X-rays are admitted into evidence. Obviously, no witness can testify he or she saw what an X-ray depicts, thus rendering the pictorial testimony theory logically inapplicable. 3 C. Scott, Photographic Evidence § 1262 (1969). Nevertheless, every jurisdiction admits X-ray photographs as substantive evidence upon a sufficient showing of authentication.

In other words, these courts have not blindly followed the formal, traditional requirement of admitting photographs solely as demonstrative evidence. Instead, these jurisdictions have analyzed the theory behind the traditional requirements, and have recognized the probative potential of photographic evidence. As a result, these courts view photographic evidence in a modern, realistic light and admit photographs where their authenticity can be sufficiently established in view of the context in which the photographs are sought to be admitted. We think this creative analysis and refusal to follow traditional standards merely because such standards exist is laudable as the highest form of a progressive judiciary (*sic*). We hereby accept the State's invitation and adopt the silent witness theory for the admission of photographic evidence as the law in Indiana. In so doing, we cannot help but note the good company in which we find ourselves. *See e.g. U.S. v. Gray*, 531 F.2d 933 (CA 8 1976); *People v. Bowley*, 59 Cal. 2d 855, 31 Cal. Rptr. 471, 382 P.2d 591 (1963); *People v. Byrnes*, 33 N.Y.2d 343, 352 N.Y.S.2d 913, 308 N.E.2d 435 (1974); *Franklin v. State*, 69 Ga. 36 (1882).

We recognize our adoption of the silent witness theory permits the admission of photographs as substantive or demonstrative evidence. We stress we are not changing existing Indiana law; we are adding a second basis for the admissibility of photographic evidence. Thus, our holding in no way affects the use of photographs as demonstrative evidence; the traditional requirements for admissibility as laid down in numerous Indiana cases remain wholly effective.

The foundation requirements for the admission of photographs as substantive evidence under the silent witness theory are obviously vastly different from the foundation required for demonstrative evidence. However, we feel it would be wrong to lay down extensive, absolute foundation requirements. Every photograph, the context in which it was taken, and its use at trial will be different in some respect. We therefore hold only that a strong showing of the photograph's competency and authenticity must be established. Whether a sufficiently strong foundation has been laid is left to the sound discretion of the trial court, reviewable only for abuse.

Photography is not an exact science. The image a camera produces on film can be affected by a variety of things that may lead to distortion and misrepresentation. However, assuming any misleading qualities of a photograph are not so egregious as to result in an inadequate foundation, complaints concerning a photograph's distortion go on to the weight to which a photograph is entitled, not admissibility.

NOTES AND PROBLEMS

1. Which view do you prefer—the "pictorial testimony" theory or the "silent witness" theory? Which view better guarantees the underlying probative value of photographs admitted at trial? Advances in photographic technology have created the possibility of digitally retouching a photograph. At what point, however does the insistence on underlying probative value reach a point of diminishing returns? Given the impressive scientific evidence of the reliability of the photographic process, should not a photograph qualify as substantive evidence? Most commentators support the "silent witness" theory. In Gardner, *The Camera Goes to Court*, 24 N.C. L. REV. 233, 245 (1946), the author lambasts the "pictorial testimony" theory for its "baffling, Alice–in–Wonderland quality far removed from the realistic directness of the man-on-the-street." The author adds that only the "tortured" logic of the law, "wrought from centuries of philosophic inbreeding," could account for such a result. *Id.*

2. Problem 11–3. What is the practical importance of the difference between the two theories? In *Devitt*, one of Paterson's neighbors saw a green Mustang parked outside his apartment at the time of the alleged battery. Another prosecution witness, one of Devitt's neighbors, verifies a photograph of Devitt's green Mustang. Devitt's neighbor testifies that the photograph is a "true and accurate" depiction of Devitt's car. The photograph is in color and shows Devitt's car to be green; but the witness does not specifically describe Devitt's car as "green." During closing argument, could the prosecutor say, "One of Mr. Paterson's neighbors, Mrs. Nelson, said she saw a green Mustang parked right outside Mr. Paterson's apartment at that time. And we know that the defendant owns and drives a green Mustang." Does the propriety of making the remark depend on whether the court subscribes to the "pictorial testimony" or "silent witness" theory?

3. As we have seen, when a trial judge admits an item of evidence for a limited purpose, that purpose affects the content of both the proponent's closing argument and the trial judge's limiting instruction. Problem 11–3 illustrates the impact of the "pictorial testimony" theory on the proponent's closing argument. Suppose that you were the trial judge in Problem 11–3 and that the defense requested a limiting instruction based on the "pictorial testimony" theory. What would you tell the jury about the evidentiary status of the photograph?

1. VERIFICATION OF STILL PHOTOGRAPHS

Photography is a complex, technical field. For that reason, the courts could require a very detailed foundation as the predicate for admitting a photograph. Fischnaller, *Technical Preparation and Exclusion of Photographic Evidence*, 8 GONZ. L. REV. 292 (1973). In particular, since the lens has a profound impact on the quality of the end-product photograph, the courts could demand a showing of the type of lens used. M. HOUTS, PHOTOGRAPHIC MISREPRESENTA-TION §§ 5-46, 5-49 (1964). However, the courts have opted not to impose those foundational requirements. *United States v. Stearns*, 550 F.2d 1167 (9th Cir. 1977). It is not that the technical information is irrelevant; quite to the contrary, on cross–examination the opponent may attack the photograph's accuracy by questioning about the camera setting, film type, and development process. *Id.* However, those matters are not part of the foundation for admitting the photograph.

The courts have imposed very lax foundational requirements for admitting photographs. The witness ordinarily testifies that he or she is familiar with the object or scene depicted; explains how they acquired the familiarity; and lastly opines that the photograph is a "fair" depiction of the object or scene. *Banghart v. Origoverken*, 49 F.3d 1302 (8th Cir. 1995).

PROBLEM

Problem 11–4. In our torts case, Ms. Hill wants to introduce a photograph of the intersection where the collision occurred. Must the sponsoring witness be the photographer? Does Federal Rule 104(b) or 901(a) require the photographer? Does the familiarity requirement necessitate testimony by the photographer? *See United States v. Holmquist*, 36 F.3d 154 (1st Cir. 1994).

2. VERIFICATION OF AN X–RAY

The use of X–rays is critical in personal injury litigation. Proof of damages can often be the more important part of the battle, and X–rays can be the most persuasive evidence of injury. Since the "pictorial testimony" theory of verifying photographs cannot be applied to X–rays, courts have fashioned an adaptation to the authentication doctrine for proof of the accuracy of an X–ray.

SCOTT, X–RAY PICTURES AS EVIDENCE, 44 Michigan Law Review 773 (1946)

Before an X–ray can be admitted in evidence, someone who has knowledge of the fact must take the stand and verify the accuracy of the picture, for X–ray photographs are not admissible in evidence without preliminary proof of their accuracy. But this proof need only relate to the particular X–ray picture in question, for today the science of X–ray photography is too well founded and generally recognized to render it any longer necessary for a witness to testify to the reliability and trustworthiness of the X–ray process itself before X–ray pictures are admitted in evidence.

Since an X–ray picture purports to show only shadows of objects not otherwise visible to the eye, it is evident that a witness' verification of an X–ray photograph ordinarily must be based on the scientific fact that the properly taken X–ray photograph accurately pictures the shadows of internal objects as does the ordinary photograph picture an object's external surface. Therefore, in verifying an X–ray picture ordinarily the following requirements should be met, although it is not uncommon for X–rays to be admitted in evidence without one or more of them being satisfied.

1. The X–ray film should be identified as a picture of the person whose condition is in question. Since X–ray pictures usually are taken by technicians who make hundreds of pictures a week, usually the only practical way to identify a film as being a picture of the person in question is by the use of identification marks verified by some competent witness.

2. There should be proof that the physical condition of the subject at the time of being X–rayed was the same as at the time in issue. This requirement is usually satisfied by testimony of the injured party that after the time in question and before the X–ray pictures were taken he suffered no additional injury to the part of the body under consideration.

3. It should be shown that the X–ray apparatus used was dependable and in good working condition.

4. There should be testimony that the person who took the picture was qualified by training and experience to take accurate X–ray pictures of the human body.

5. The manner of taking the X–ray picture should be completely described, especially in such particulars as the distance from the X–ray tube to the

subject, the distance between subject and film, the angle from which the X–rays were directed through the body onto the film, and the length of exposure.

Whenever possible the authentication of an X–ray picture should be made by the physician, dentist or X–ray technician who took the picture. But it has been held that even though the X–ray photographer is not called as a witness, an X–ray film may be sufficiently identified by a physician, dentist or X–ray technician who was present when the picture was made and knows the conditions under which it was made, even though he did not take the picture himself. Authentication by a witness who did not see the picture taken is unsatisfactory and does not render the picture admissible according to the better reasoned cases, but there are decisions to the contrary.

3.　AUTOMATED PHOTOGRAPHIC SYSTEMS

Automated photographic systems are becoming increasingly common. For example, many retail stores now use check cashing cameras. When a person cashes a check at the store, the camera automatically takes a split-screen photograph; one half of the screen is the face of the person cashing the check, and the other half is the check being cashed. Banks also make extensive use of automated systems, particularly surveillance cameras.

Authentication is a simple matter when there are eyewitnesses who recall the event. Thus, if a surveillance camera takes a series of still photographs of a bank robbery, an eyewitness in the bank at the time can verify the film. *United States v. Neal*, 527 F.2d 63 (8th Cir. 1975), *cert. denied*, 429 U.S. 857 (1976). However, sometimes there are no eyewitnesses (as when a break-in occurs after hours) or the eyewitnesses were unobservant. Verifying the surveillance photographs in this situation is a much more challenging task.

NOTES AND PROBLEMS

1. Does the analogy to the process of authenticating X–rays suggest a technique to verify the surveillance photograph?

2. Problem 11-5. In *Devitt*, the defense is now alibi. Devitt wants to prove that he was shopping in another town at the time of the alleged assault. The defense attorney contacts the store, May Shoes, where Devitt says he was shopping. The store manager tells the defense attorney that their records show that Devitt purchased a pair of shoes and cashed a check in the store at the time the assault was allegedly occurring forty miles away. Better still, the store uses a Regiscope camera, which takes a split–screen photograph of the drawer and the check. There is such a photograph showing Devitt and his check. Unfortunately, no store employee remembers Devitt. How can the defense attorney verify the Regiscope photograph? Should the defense attorney call a representative from the Regiscope company? If so, what testimony should the attorney elicit from the representative? Should the attorney call the May Shoes employee who maintains the camera and has the film developed? *See Ferguson v. Commonwealth*, 212 Va. 745, 745–47, 187 S.E.2d 189, 190–91 (1972).

3. A body of law is developing which authorizes bank personnel familiar with the operation of automatic teller machine (ATM) cameras to authenticate

ATM photographs. *United States v. Fadayini*, 28 F.3d 1236 (D.C. Cir. 1994); *United States v. Rembert*, 863 F.2d 1023 (D.C. Cir. 1988) (silent witness theory). *See also Brooks v. Commonwealth*, 15 Va. App. 407, 424 S.E.2d 566 (1992).

4. VERIFICATION OF MOTION PICTURES, VIDEOTAPES AND ELECTRONIC IMAGERY

Motion pictures can have an even more dramatic impact than still photographs. They depict action and, for that reason, can easily capture the jurors' attention. Some attorneys have even filmed reenactments of accidents, acted by Hollywood stunt doubles. TRIAL, March 1982, at 14. In personal injury cases, the civil plaintiff often presents a "day-in-the-life" film. Margolis, *Motion Pictures—An Effective Tool in the Presentation of the Personal Injury Claim*, TRIAL DIPL. J. 32 (Spring 1980). In his article, Margolis outlines the content of a typical "day–in–the–life" film.

(1) Exterior Day. Establishing shot of where Client lives, to set stage for later shots of transportation difficulties in leaving home. Open on close-up of sign, "Handicapped Resident." Camera zooms out to show apartment building, and then zooms in to bedroom window of her upper story apartment.

(2) Interior. Low angle medium shot of client in bed, framed by bed rails in foreground. Bedside drainage bag will be visible here (although other more detailed shots of toilet activities should probably be omitted in the interests of good taste). Bed rails are lowered by Client's husband.

(3) Medium shot as Client's husband begins to sponge bathe her in bed.

(4) Wide shot as Client's husband begins to dress his wife in her bed. Some closer shots here will also be useful in showing need for assistance in getting hands in sleeves, handling buttons and other simple elements of getting dressed that we tend to take for granted.

* * *

(6) Series of medium close-ups show the nature of the net that will hold and lift her, and show Husband's activities as he attaches hooks, makes adjustments, sees to her comfort and begins to operate the lift.

(7) Wide shot. Client being moved from bed to wheel chair, as Husband operates lift. When transfer is complete, he sees to her comfort, disconnects lift (close-ups) and removes it. At this point, if her wheel chair has been made operational, she will move herself to her accustomed location in front of the television set. Otherwise, Husband returns and moves chair to that position.

(8) Another series of close-ups as he sees to her comfort. These shots will particularly emphasize the hand wrappings that keep her wrists stiff, the difficulty she has in sliding her hands to positions of comfort, and the adjustments that must be made to the chin brace holding her head upright.

(9) Medium shot. Low angle. Husband turns on television set, as an indication of the only kind of passive entertainment and activity she has available to her.

(10) <u>Wide shot</u> as Husband moves feeder device into place behind wheel chair.

* * *

(13) <u>Low angle medium shot</u> as she works at feeding herself. This may also include <u>close-ups</u> of hands as she tries to grip utensils and of Husband's hands as he assists her. We need only show the beginning of this eating process, keeping with it long enough to indicate the types of difficulties she has.

(14) <u>Fade in on wide shot</u> as visiting therapist enters.

(15) Series of <u>medium close-ups</u> indicate some of the activities and exercises she goes through with the therapist. Sequence ends with <u>fade to black</u>. . . .

* * *

(20) <u>Wide shot</u> as Husband and fire department representative enter and prepare to carry her for trip to hospital.

(21) <u>Close-ups</u> of preparation, including readying of two-man carry and movement to Client from wheel chair.

(22) <u>Wide shot</u> from hallway outside apartment, as they maneuver her through apartment and doorway.

(23) <u>Low angle and wide shot</u> looking up stairs from bottom, as they carry her down.

(24) <u>Exterior wide shot</u> as she is brought out of building, positioned on stretcher, and maneuvered into ambulance. Doors are closed, and vehicle drives away. <u>Fade out</u> to black.

———————

The emotional impact of such a film should be obvious. Nor has the persuasive power of motion pictures been lost on civil defendants. Like civil plaintiffs, they frequently resort to motion pictures. For instance, a defendant auto manufacturer such as Polecat Motors may use a film depicting safety tests of the model involved in the case; a film showing the model withstanding the very type of impact involved in the case can be impressive evidence of the car's crashworthiness. *E.g., Balian v. General Motors*, 121 N.J. Super. 118, 296 A.2d 317 (1972). A film can be especially potent evidence if the opponent prepared the film but the proponent obtained the film during pretrial discovery:

> In products liability cases, plaintiffs sometimes seek to secure and use test . . . . films made by the manufacturer. In the California case of *Richard Grimshaw v. Ford Motor Company*, the jury voted a verdict of several million dollars in damages against the defendant. Grimshaw was burned when the 1972 Pinto he was riding in was struck in the rear, and the gas tank ruptured and exploded. The trial proof featured a showing of Ford's own test film of a Pinto backed into a wall at 20 m.p.h. The gas tank ruptured. One juror commented: "In my mind, that film beat the Ford Motor Co."

R. Carlson, SUCCESSFUL TECHNIQUES FOR CIVIL TRIALS § 3:34, at 234 (2d ed. 1992).

The evolution of the courts' treatment of motion pictures is similar to the courts' approach to sound recordings. Just as the courts are gradually relaxing the foundational requirements for tape recordings, we are now witnessing a similar relaxation of the standards for admitting motion pictures. As in the case of the authentication of tape recordings, the courts are going back to fundamentals and realizing that in the final analysis, the relevant question is the test established by Federal Rule of Evidence 104(b): Has the proponent presented sufficient evidence to create a permissive inference that the motion picture is genuine? If the proponent's foundation satisfies that test, it is immaterial that the foundation does not fit neatly into one of the well-settled pigeonholes in the case law. Common law decisions, imposing more rigorous foundational requirements, are no longer good law under the Federal Rules.

In the past decade, there has been an explosion of interest in courtroom use and adaptation of videotape technology. The use of videotape technology to film out-of-court events is commonplace. For example, police can videotape an undercover drug transaction. *United States v. Roach*, 28 F.3d 729 (8th Cir. 1994). A defendant's confession can be videotaped—as graphic proof that the police administered the proper warnings and that the defendant was not coerced. *United States v. Benitez*, 34 F.3d 1489 (9th Cir. 1994); *Battle v. Delo*, 19 F.3d 1547 (8th Cir. 1994). With prior court authorization, a videotape machine can even be installed surreptitiously in a defendant dentist's office to record unlawful sexual assaults on unconscious or semiconscious patients. *People v. Teicher*, 90 Misc. 2d 638, 395 N.Y.S.2d 587 (Sup. Ct. 1977); *Recent Development*, 16 AM. CRIM. L. REV. 183 (1978).

Of course, before this evidence can be shown to the jury, it must be authenticated. Since the film has both sound and action, the bodies of law on authenticating sound recordings and films interface here. *Roy v. State*, 608 S.W.2d 645 (Tex. Crim. App. 1980) discusses the interface. *Roy* involved videotapes of transactions in which police posed as "fences" for stolen property. The court addressed the admissibility issue:

> Appellant contends that the trial court erred in permitting the video-tapes to be shown to the jury. Videotapes are a simultaneous audio and visual recording of events. As such, a predicate is required to establish their accuracy and reliability. This Court has unswervingly upheld the seven-pronged predicate for the admission of sound record-ings that was first set forth in *Edwards v. State*, 551 S.W.2d 731, 733 (Tex. Crim. App. 1977), as follows:
>
> "(1) a showing that the recording device was capable of taking testi-mony, (2) a showing that the operator of the device was competent, (3) establishment of the authenticity and correctness of the recording, (4) a showing that changes, additions, or deletions have not been made, (5) a showing of the manner of the preservation of the recording, (6) identification of the speakers and (7) a showing that the testimony elicited was voluntarily made without any kind of inducement. . . .
> [W]e also find that at least some of the requirements can be inferred

from the testimony and need not be shown with the same particularity required for admissions of other mechanically acquired evidence. . . ."

In a separate, but also frequently used, category are reenactments or simulations of historical events. In an airplane crash case, a litigator might use synchronized videotape simulations—one depicting the activity in the cockpit and the other a view of the plane's exterior, showing the plane's descent and maneuvers. Marcotte, *Putting Jury in Your Shoes*, 73 A.B.A. J. 20 (July 1, 1987). Videotaped animations or recreations have a dramatic impact. In *Robinson v. Missouri Pacific R. Co.*, 16 F.3d 1083 (10th Cir. 1994), an expert witness created a video by first making a scale model of the accident scene. He simulated an accident by using models of a passenger car and a train which resulted in a dramatic two-minute silent color video. The video depicted the plaintiff's theory of a railroad crossing collision. The court of appeals decision by Judge Bright approved the decision of the district court which permitted the animation to be shown at trial. The opinion added:

> Having determined that the district court did not abuse its discretion, we add some additional comment. Video animation adds a new and powerful evidentiary tool to the trial scene. McCormick's work on evidence observes that with respect to one party's staged reproduction of facts "not only is the danger that the jury may confuse art with reality particularly great, but the impressions generated by the evidence may prove particularly difficult to limit. . ." 2 McCormick on Evidence 19 (4th ed. 1992) (footnote omitted). Because of its dramatic power, trial judges should carefully and meticulously examine proposed animation evidence for proper foundation, relevancy and the potential for undue prejudice. Normally, the trial judge should review the video outside of the jury's hearing. . . . Courts in appropriate circumstances may permit demonstrative use of audio or visual presentations which may assist the jury. . . .

Reenactments can also emanate from the computer. Juries in modern trials have witnessed computer imaging technology recreating auto accidents, sewer explosions, airplane crashes, or other litigated incidents. Computer graphics evidence is analyzed in M. Bright & R. Carlson, Objections at Trial 45 (rev. ed. 1993). *See Commercial Union Ins. Co. v. Boston Edison Co.*, 412 Mass. 545, 591 N.E.2d 165 (1992) (computer simulation evidence admissible).

The line between reenactment of known historical fact and animation of forensic theory can be a blurry one, especially to the jury. A case approving computer-generated animation is *Datskow v. Teledyne Continental Motors Aircraft Prods.*, 826 F. Supp. 677 (W.D.N.Y. 1993) The district court held that a videotaped computer-generated animation illustrating an expert's theory of where a fire began inside an airplane engine and how it spread was admissible in a products liability action against the engine manufacturer. The trial judge rejected defendant's argument that the jury might view the animation as a re-creation of the airplane crash, and give the video undue weight. The court concluded that most jurors are fairly sophisticated in that they are exposed to television and motion pictures. The court observed that it had given a cautionary instruction that the animation was not a re-creation of the accident but a series of computer pictures to help the jury understand the expert's testimony.

Computer-generated animations (CGA) are now in vogue. There are good discussions of the evidentiary problems posed by CGA in Henke, *Admissibility of Computer-Generated Animated Reconstructions and Simulations*, 35 TRIAL LAWYER'S GUIDE 434 (1991), and Comment, *Admission of Computer Generated Visual Evidence: Should There Be Clear Standards?*, 6 SOFTWARE L. J. 325, 333–34 (1993). If the proponent is content to proffer the animation merely for demonstrative purposes, the requisite foundation is minimal. In that event, it suffices if the witness testifies that he or she has viewed the animation and that the animation fairly and accurately depicts the witness' version of the event. *People v. McHugh*, 124 Misc.2d 559, 476 N.Y.S.2d 721 (1984). However, a more elaborate foundation is necessary when the proponent wants to introduce the demonstrative evidence for substantive purposes. The foundation must include testimony about the computer hardware and software as well as the information input that generated the animation. *Comm. Union Ins. Co. v. Boston Edison Co.*, 412 Mass. 545, 591 N.E.2d 165 (1992).

For an overview of electronic imaging technology, see, Note, *A Picture is Worth a Thousand Lies: Electronic Imaging and the Future of the Admissibility of Photographs into Evidence*, 18 RUTGERS COMPUTER & TECH. L.J. 365 (1992). The author warns that computer manipulation is not only possible, but worse still, virtually undetectable. *Id.* at 374. The same observation and warning has been made with respect to computerized records: ". . . program changes or data manipulation can be accomplished without leaving any trace. . ." Peritz, *Computer Data and Reliability: A Call for Authentication of Business Records Under the Federal Rules of Evidence*, 80 Nw. U.L. REV. 956, 960 (1986).

PROBLEMS

1. Problem 11-6. In our torts case, Polecat Motors follows the lead of GM in the *Balian* case, *supra*, and films a safety test of its product. The defendant's vice–president in charge of industrial operations was present when the test was filmed. The defense attorney expected to use the photographer to verify the film, but unexpectedly the photographer becomes seriously ill on the trial day on which the attorney wants to use the film. Unlike the photographer, the vice–president knows nothing about the type of equipment or film used or even custody of the film since the day of the test. Does that preclude the vice-president from verifying the motion picture?

2. Problem 11-7. In the previous problem, does your analysis or answer change if it is a videotape? If it is a computer imaging technique, such as an electronic photograph? Some of these scan conventional film, some eliminate the need for film because of magnetic computer disks, and some do not involve the reproduction of any extant image. Image synthesis technology creates photographically realistic images through mathematics.

3. Problem 11-8. In the *Devitt* case, assume Paterson's apartment complex had an automated surveillance camera. The camera photographed Devitt entering and leaving the apartment complex. Devitt is still claiming alibi. As a prosecutor, how would you lay the foundation for the automated film? Which witnesses would you call? What testimony would you elicit from each witness? *See Brooks v. Commonwealth*, 15 Va. App. 407, 424 S.E.2d 566 (1992).

5. ENHANCED PHOTOGRAPHS

STATE v. HAYDEN

90 Wash. App. 100, 950 P.2d 1024 (1998)

KENNEDY, Acting Chief Judge.

Eric H. Hayden appeals his conviction of felony murder in the first degree, contending that the trial court erred in admitting enhanced–fingerprint evidence after conducting a *Frye* hearing. Finding no error, we affirm.

* * *

[Hayden was accused of the rape and murder of Dawn Fehring, who was found nude near the foot of her bed with her top bed sheet and T–shirt wrapped around her head and neck. Blood stains were found on the carpet near her body and bloody hand prints were visible on the fitted bed sheet covering the matress.]

During the ensuing investigation, police interviewed occupants of the other apartments in the building, one of whom was appellant Eric Hayden. Hayden became a suspect when he was unable to account for his whereabouts on the night of the murder and seemed nervous during a police interview. He told police that he had been drinking with friends on Friday evening but was unable to identify the friends. He told his girlfriend that he was too drunk that evening to remember where he had been.

The Kirkland Police Department took the fitted bed sheet to Daniel Holshue, a King County latent print examiner. Holshue cut out the five areas of the bed sheet that contained the most blood prints. He then treated the pieces of sheet with a dye stain called amido black that reacted with the protein in the blood, turning the sheet navy blue. Next, he rinsed the pieces of sheet in pure menthanol to lighten the background, leaving only the protein stains dark blue. Finally, he dipped the pieces in distilled water to set the prints. Still, after these chemical processes were completed, the contrast between the latent prints and the pieces of bed sheet was too subtle for Holshue to identify the minimum of eight points of comparison required to make a positive identification.

Holshue took the pieces of sheet to Erik Berg, an expert in enhanced digital imaging at the Tacoma Police Department, for computer enhancement. Berg took computer photographs, or digital images, of the pieces of sheet and then utilized computer software to filter out background patterns and colors to enhance the images so that the prints could be viewed without the background patterns and colors. Using the enhanced photographs of the latent prints, Holshue found twelve points of comparison on one of the fingerprints and more than forty on one of the palm prints. Thus, he concluded that the prints on the bed sheet belonged to Eric Hayden.

On June 5, 1995, the State charged Hayden by information with one count of felony murder in the first degree. Specifically, it alleged that Hayden committed the crime of rape against Fehring, causing her death in the course of, in furtherance, and in immediate flight from that crime. After an 8–day trial, a jury found Hayden guilty. Hayden appeals.

* * *

[T]he trial court held a *Frye* hearing to determine the admissibility of the prints identified by use of the enhanced digital imaging process. The State presented testimony from two experts, Holshue and Berg, who explained the steps they took to ultimately identify Hayden's palm and fingerprint from the fitted bed sheet. The State also provided the trial court with forensic literature regarding digital image enhancement. Hayden did not present any witnesses at the *Frye* hearing and presented no controverting literature. Based upon the testimony, the trial court found that the amido black chemical dipping process is generally accepted by forensic scientists and that the enhanced digital imaging process is not novel scientific evidence to which the *Frye* test applies. Nonetheless, the court also concluded that the enhanced digital imaging process passed the *Frye* test.

Hayden. . . argues that the enhanced digital imaging process has not obtained general acceptance in the relevant scientific community because its use for this purpose is recent and because the computer programs used to enhance the images were not designed for forensic science. He maintains that the procedure used to produce the enhanced prints did not satisfy the *Frye* standard and, therefore, that the trial court erred in admitting the evidence. . . .

A. Novel Scientific Evidence

In 1994, the enhanced digital imaging process was described by Berg, the State's digital imaging expert, as "a totally new process based upon research and development done in the late 1960's and early 1970's for the space program." E. Berg, Latent Image Processing—A Changing Technology, The Pacific Northwest International Association for Identification Examiner, Second Quarter 1994. This and other literature presented reflects that the technology used to enhance photographs of latent prints evolved from jet propulsion laboratories in the NASA space program to isolate galaxies and receive signals from satellites. The Tacoma Police Department began using digital imaging technology in forensics in January of 1995.

The State contends that because the underlying scientific theory behind enhanced digital imaging is not new, its application to forensic science does not constitute a novel process; it suggests that it was merely the high cost of the process that prevented law enforcement organizations from using it earlier. Yet, a 1987 article from the FBI Academy's International Symposium on Latent Prints observed:

Latent print examiners across the country react differently when image enhancement of latent prints is discussed. Often, the initial reaction is one of disapproval. The concern is that nonexistent detail is added to the latent print. Image enhancement techniques are not designed to create detail but to improve images for human interpretation.

A.L. McRoberts, Digital Image Processing as a Means of Enhancing Latent Fingerprints, Proceedings of the INternational Forensic Symposium on Latent Prints, FBI, July 7–10, 1987, at 166. Although this article may not be reflective of the current latent print examiner community because it was written 10 years ago, it indicates that skepticism, in addtion to high costs, may have contributed to the delay in the use of digital image enhancement in forensic science.

In support of its argument that the process is not novel, the State relies further upon *State v. Noltie*, 57 Wash.App. 21, 786 P.2d 332 (1990), *aff'd*, 116 Wash.2d 831, 809 P.2d 190 (1991). At issue in *Noltie* was the admissibility of enlarged views of a child abuse victim's sex organs obtained using a colposcope, a microscope developed and used to diagnose cancer. Id. at 28–29, 786 P.2d 332. This court concluded: "We find no basis for Noltie's contention that colposcopy constitutes a 'novel' field or scientific technique, even though its use in child abuse cases may be relatively recent." Id. at 29, 786 P.2d 332. It called the colposcope "a magnifying glass with a fancy name" and concluded that it was not subject to the *Frye* test. Id. at 29–30, 786 P.2d 332.

* * *

Certainly digital photography is not a novel process. Neither is the use of computer software to enhance images. It is only the forensic use of these tools that is relatively new. Although we find the State's argument that the process is not novel to be persuasive, because this is a question of first impression we analyze the admissibility of the evidence under the *Frye* standard.

B. The *Frye* Test

* * *

At trial and in his articles, Berg explained the process of enhanced digital imaging in detail. See also B.E. Dalrymple & T. Menzies, Computer Enhancement of Evidence Through Background Noise Suppression, 39 J. Forensic Sciences, Mar. 1994. The advantage of digital photographs, rather than analogue film photographs, is that digital photography can capture approximately 16 million different colors and can differentiate between 256 shades of gray. Digital photographs work with light sensitivity, just like film photographs, except the computer uses a chip and a hard drive in place of the camera's film. At trial, Berg testified that there is no subjectivity in this process.

The digital photographs are enhanced using software that improves sharpness and image contrast. In addition, pattern and color isolation filters remove interfering colors and background patterns. This is a subtractive process in which elements are removed or reduced; nothing is added. At trial, Berg testified that the software he used prevented him from adding to, changing, or destroying the original image. In contrast with "image restoration," a process in which things that are not there are added based on preconceived ideas about what the end result should look like, "image enhancement" merely makes what is there more usable. See William J. Watling, Using the FFT in Forensic Digital Image Enhancement, 43 J. Forensic Ident. 574 (1993).

On cross examination at trial, Berg admitted this was the first time he had ever taken a latent print off of a fabric. Still, nothing in the literature presented to the trial court and for this appeal indicates that the validity of the process depends upon the nature of the material upon which the print is found. We have examined the fabric and the digitally enhanced photographs in the course of our review. It is clear even to the untrained eye that the fabric contains a hand print and that nothing appears in the digitaly enhanced photograph that was not present on the fabric. Rather, the image of the hand print is merely enhanced by removing background detail unrelated to the points of identification by which the hand print was identified as Hayden's. The evidence in the record supports the trial court's unchallenged findings that the technique utilized by Berg has a reliability factor of 100 percent and a zero percent margin of error and that the results are visually verifiable and could be easily duplicated by another expert using his or her own digital camera and appropriate computer software.

The literature presented by the State indicates that digital image processing has been used as a means of enhancing latent fingerprints by the Los Angeles County Sheriff's Department since at least 1987. See A.L. McRoberts, Digital Image Processing as a Means of Enhancing Latent Fingerprints, Proceedings of the International Forensic Symposium on Latent Prints, July 7–10, 1987 at 165–66. Because there does not appear to be a significant dispute among qualified experts as to the validity of enhanced digital imaging performed by qualified experts using appropriate software, we conclude that the process is generally accepted in the relevant scientific community. Accordingly, we reject Hayden's contention that the trial court erred by admitting the challenged evidence and affirm his conviction.

NOTES AND QUESTIONS

1. To produce an enhanced image, researchers study the degradation produced when certain types of photographic equipment are used to produce images of particular types of objects. G. JOSEPH, MODERN VISUAL EVIDENCE § 8.04[2] (1999). The process of image enhancement reverses the degradation. The technique has been used in many contexts "including medicine, physics, meteorology, resource exploration, factory automation and robotics control." Id at 8–22. Before using the computer software which reverses the degradation, the expert converts the normal, analogue photograph into a digital image: "Digital images are composed of millions of tiny dots, referred to as 'pixels.'" Dolan v. State, 743 So.2d 544, 545 (Fla.Dist.Ct.App. 1999). The software manipulates the pixels to brighten certain areas and thereby improve the contrast with the details in the other areas of the photograph.

2. Distinguish an enhanced photograph from both enlarged and restored photographs. Enlargement is a multiplication process. That process has been in use for so long and is so widely accepted that its validity is judicially noticeable. The *Hayden* court mentions a third technology, image restoration. How does an enhanced image differ from a restored image?

3. What foundation would an enhanced photograph require in a *Frye* jurisdiction? What foundation is necessary in a *Daubert* jurisdiciton?

C. CHARTS, INCLUDING MAPS

The category of demonstrative evidence includes many varieties of evidence, for example, maps and charts. The technique for verifying a map or chart is strikingly similar to the method of authenticating a photograph. A witness familiar with the object or area depicted vouches that the chart is an "accurate," "fair," or "true" representation.

Although some of the techniques discussed in this chapter, such as sound spectrography and videotapes, are expensive high technology, rudimentary charts can be both effective and inexpensive. In traffic accidents such as *Hill*, one of the most difficult tasks for the jury is to visualize the respective positions of the automobiles at successive points in time: How were the cars situated with respect to each other 15 seconds before impact? Ten seconds before impact? It is virtually impossible for an attorney to clearly describe a traffic accident without using a chart. Better still, the attorney can use a series of simple charts:

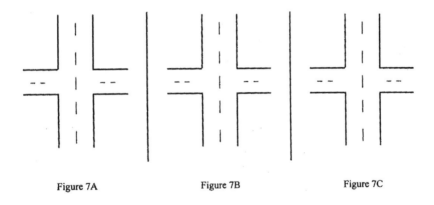

Figure 7A   Figure 7B   Figure 7C

Assume, for instance, that in a traffic accident case, the plaintiff's attorney has the chart on the extreme left marked Plaintiff's Exhibit 7A, the middle chart 7B, and the final chart 7C. During the plaintiff's direct examination, the attorney might ask the plaintiff to depict the position of the two cars 30 seconds before impact. The attorney could then invite the witness to mark the positions of the cars 10 seconds before the impact on 7B and just before impact on 7C. The use of multiple charts — sequential graphics — helps the jury visualize how the accident unfolded. Bieder, *How to Grab the Jury's Attention in a Medical Case*, TRIAL DIPL. J. 25 (Winter 1981).

Charts are not only helpful for presenting an attorney's version of the case; they are equally useful in attacking the opposition's theory. At Ms. Hill's deposition, Polecat's attorney might ask her to draw a diagram or series of diagrams indicating how she remembers the accident developing. At trial, the defense attorneys can use the diagrams as prior inconsistent statements. In one respect, the diagrams are more effective impeachment than oral inconsistent statements. In an oral statement, Ms. Hill might have used an ambiguous word that allows her to explain away the inconsistency at trial. It may be more difficult for her to find an ambiguity in a diagram, especially if the diagram was drawn to scale. Charts can also be used to set up contradictions between witnesses for the same side. Assume that in the *Hill* case, in addition to testifying herself, Ms. Hill calls an eyewitness, Mr. Coronado. Suppose further that at Polecat's request, Mr. Coronado was sequestered and excluded from the courtroom during Ms. Hill's testimony. During her cross–examination, the defense attorney forces Ms. Hill to draw a diagram of her version of the accident. Similarly, during the cross–examination of Mr. Coronado, the defense attorney directs him to prepare a chart. There is a high probability that there will be significant differences between the two depictions of the accident. During summation, the defense can hold up the charts, point to the differences, and argue "the plaintiff's witnesses don't even agree among themselves."

NOTES

1. Must a chart be drawn to scale to be admissible? In any event, will the "to scale" feature of a chart aid admissibility? What type of instruction should the judge give the jury when the chart is introduced? Consider FED. R. EVID. 105. *See* S. GOLDBERG, THE FIRST TRIAL: WHERE DO I SIT? WHAT DO I SAY? 152–53 (1982).

2. In addition to marking a demonstrative exhibit for identification, should the proponent of the exhibit formally offer the exhibit into evidence? Brain & Broderick, *The Derivative Relevance of Demonstrative Evidence: Charting Its Proper Evidentiary Status*, 25 U.C. DAVIS L. REV. 957, 965–67, 1021–22 (1992). In the case of a diagram, should the answer to the question depend on whether the diagram is to scale? S. GOLDBERG, *supra*.

Chapter 12

SPECIALIZED ASPECTS OF LOGICAL RELEVANCE: VALIDATION OF SCIENTIFIC EVIDENCE

Read Federal Rules of Evidence 702, 703, 704 and 705.

A. INTRODUCTION

In the 1940's and 1950's, the heavier reliance on demonstrative and photographic evidence changed the way in which cases were tried. Before the advent of these new types of evidence, trial attorneys had usually relied on purely testimonial evidence. These new types of evidence created a more visual style of trial advocacy, popularized by litigators such as Melvin Belli. The 1960's witnessed another major development, namely, the emergence of scientific evidence. It is now virtually impossible to try a major personal injury case without extensive medical evidence at least on the issues of causation and damages. In even a simple personal injury case like *Hill*, the plaintiff's attorney might have occasion to call an accident reconstruction expert. The same trend has swept into the criminal arena. In the early 1960's, the Warren Court began fashioning the exclusionary rules banning evidence obtained in violation of the Fourth, Fifth, and Sixth Amendments. In the minds of many prosecutors, those rules created a "void" in their cases–a void that they filled with scientific evidence. In the early 1970's, the Law Enforcement Assistance Administration accelerated the trend by funding research into the legal applications of scientific techniques. In the courtroom as well as the laboratory, we have entered an era of quickening scientific advance, "an age when one scientific advancement tumbles in rapid succession upon another . . . ." *Phillips v. Jackson*, 615 P.2d 1228, 1234 (Utah 1980). The prosecution of O.J. Simpson in California in 1995–96 showcased advances in genetic marker analysis.

The alarming fact is that at the same time that more and more scientific evidence is being offered in the courtroom, it is becoming apparent that there is a substantial possibility of error in scientific analysis. As noted earlier, in the mid–1970's the Law Enforcement Assistance Administration conducted the Laboratory Proficiency Testing Program to evaluate the accuracy of crime laboratories throughout the United States. That program unquestionably documented a very real possibility of error in the analysis conducted by forensic laboratories in the United States. Peter Huber of the Manhattan Institute also asserts that American courts were frequently permitting the introduction of "junk science" in civil actions. P. HUBER, GALILEO'S REVENGE: JUNK SCIENCE IN THE COURTROOM (1991).

Although the revelation of this incidence of error is unsettling, it is even more disturbing to realize that until very recently, few attorneys–or judges–took a close, critical look at scientific evidence. The judicial treatment of sound spectrography (voiceprint) is a case in point. At first, the courts seemed eager to admit voice identifications based on this technique. *See, e.g., United States v. Wright*, 17 C.M.A. 183, 37 C.M.R. 447 (1967). Later, after the courts realized the lack of experimental verification of some of the technique's premises, the trend turned markedly toward inadmissibility. *People v. Kelly*, 17 Cal. 3d 24, 549 P.2d 1240, 130 Cal. Rptr. 144 (1976). The explanation for the early cases admitting voiceprint was simple; as the court pointed out in *Hodo v. Superior Court*, 30 Cal. App. 3d 778, 106 Cal. Rptr. 547 (1973), in approximately eighty percent of the cases in which such expert opinion testimony was admitted, there was no opposing expert testimony on the issue of reliability and general acceptability by the scientific community. When a National Academy of Sciences committee studied the voiceprint issue, the committee found "the very large proportion (of cases) in which the only experts testifying were those called by the state" to be "striking." COMMITTEE ON EVALUATION OF SOUND SPECTROGRAMS, NATIONAL ACADEMY OF SCIENCES, ON THE THEORY AND PRACTICE OF VOICE IDENTIFICATION 49 (1979). In part because they were unfamiliar with the relevant scientific learning, the trial attorneys did not probe and challenge.

The same cycle was repeated with the DNA cases. All the early cases were receptive to DNA evidence. Harmon, *How Has DNA Evidence Fared? Beauty is in the Eye of the Beholder*, 1 EXPERT EVID. REP. 149 (Feb. 1990). As in the early voiceprint cases, the opposing counsel in the early DNA cases essentially accepted the experts' scientific claims at face value. Lewin, *DNA Typing on the Witness Stand*, 244 SCIENCE, June 2, 1989, at 1033. The tide turned only when opposing counsel took a more critical look at the manner in which the tests were conducted and began calling their own experts to critique DNA evidence. *State v. Schwartz*, 447 N.W.2d 422 (Minn. 1989); *People v. Castro*, 144 Misc. 2d 956, 545 N.Y.S.2d 985 (Sup. Ct. 1989).

Attorneys are understandably reluctant to probe and challenge; to do so effectively ordinarily requires mastering a formidable amount of scientific lore. It seems all too easy to become lost in a maze of atomic absorption, DNA, electrophoresis, scanning electron microscopes, and trace metal detection technique. To overcome this reluctance, the student must realize that the appearance is deceiving. Although many scientific techniques appear mystifying, laying the foundation for scientific evidence usually involves some simple, fundamental elements. Even in the most complex cases involving sophisticated instrumentation, the scientific testimony ordinarily follows a predictable pattern.

The proponent first calls an educating witness. This scientist teaches the jury about the underlying theory and any instrumentation used in the case. The proponent next calls a reporting witness. This scientist describes to the jury the manner in which the test was conducted in the case and states the test result. Finally, the proponent will call an interpreting witness. This scientist evaluates the test result and illuminates its significance for the jury. We shall use this schema to review the elements of a complete foundation for an offer of scientific evidence. As we review the foundational elements, we shall consider the impact of the adoption of the Federal Rules on the standards for admitting scientific testimony.

B. THE EDUCATING OR TEACHING WITNESS

The first witness teaches the jurors about the underlying scientific theory and the instrument implementing the theory. The proponent calls this expert to elicit the opinions that the theory is valid and that the instrumentation involved is reliable.

In some cases, live testimony on the theory and instrument will be unnecessary. When we studied judicial notice, if a scientific theory qualifies as "a readily verifiable certainty," the judge may judicially notice the theory's validity. Likewise, on occasion the judge may dispense with the need for proof of the reliability of an instrument. Courts routinely judicially notice the validity of the theories such as those underlying fingerprint identification and the reliability of instruments such as the stationary radar speedmeter. However, when judicial notice is unavailable, the proponent should elicit live testimony from the teaching witness about his or her qualifications, the theory's validity, and lastly the instrument's reliability.

1. QUALIFICATION OF THE WITNESS

Rule 702 announces that to qualify as an expert, the witness must possess "knowledge, skill, experience, training, or education." As we shall see in Chapter 23 on expert opinion testimony, the trial judge has wide discretion in deciding whether a person qualifies as a witness. Under statutes such as Federal Rule of Evidence 104(a), the judge's decision is final. The most important point to bear in mind is that the level of requisite expertise is relative to the subtlety and complexity of the subject–matter of the proposed testimony. The teaching witness testifies at a relatively high plane of abstraction about the validity of an underlying scientific theory and the reliability of an instrument implementing the theory. Consequently, this witness usually needs heavy academic credentials. In the words of the statute, the witness has "knowledge" gained through "education." In 1994, the Federal Judicial Center released a REFERENCE MANUAL ON SCIENTIFIC EVIDENCE. In one of the chapters in the manual, Professor Margaret Berger describes the process by which judges examine "whether the actual qualifications" of the expert will enable him or her to assist the trier of fact on the precise issue before the court. Berger, Evidentiary Framework, in MOORE'S FEDERAL PRACTICE, REFERENCE MANUAL ON SCIENTIFIC EVIDENCE, 37, 58–64 (1997).

There are signs that the courts are tightening the standards governing whether a witness qualifies as an expert. For instance, although the old bromide is that a witness need not be a specialist to qualify as an expert (*Wheeler v. John Deere Co.*, 935 F.2d 1090 (10th Cir. 1991)), in *Alexander v. Smith & Nephew, L.P.C.*, 90 F.Supp.2d 1226 (N.D.Okla.2000), the court ruled that a proffered witness was not an expert in part because the witness was not board certified in the relevant medical specialty.

2. THE VALIDITY OF THE UNDERLYING THEORY AND THE RELIABILITY OF THE INSTRUMENT IMPLEMENTING THE THEORY

At first, proof of these two elements of the foundation seems to be a question of pure logical relevance. The wording of the Federal Rules of Evidence supports that initial impression. The proponent of scientific evidence claims that the instrument or technique enables the expert to accurately make a particular determination. Given the nature of the claim, an offer of scientific evidence seems to fall within Federal Evidence Rule 901(b)(9):

> Process or system. Evidence describing a process or system used to produce a result and showing that the process produces an accurate result.

If scientific evidence falls within 901(b)(9), 901(a) governs and imposes the normal standard for authentication:

> The requirement of authentication or identification as a condition precedent to admissibility is satisfied by evidence sufficient to support a finding that the matter in question is what its proponent claims.

While logical relevance analysis and the language of the Federal Rules point to the treatment of scientific evidence as a simple question of authentication, all jurisdictions reject that approach to scientific evidence; they require more. Well into the 1970's, in forty–five states and most of the federal circuits, the courts demanded compliance with the *Frye* test. *Recent Developments*, 64 COR-NELL L. REV. 875, 878–79 (1979); Note, 40 OHIO ST. L.J. 757, 769 (1979).

Frye v. United States, 293 F. 1013 (D.C. Cir. 1923), is the landmark American decision, announcing a special standard for the admission of scientific evidence. In *Frye*, the defendant offered a forerunner of the modern polygraph, systolic blood pressure evidence. The defense witness was prepared to testify that by studying the defendant's blood pressure changes during questioning, the witness had determined that the defendant was telling the truth when he denied committing the crime. The witness vouched for the theory and his instrumentation. That testimony would ordinarily satisfy the authentication requirement. However, the trial judge excluded the evidence, and the appellate court affirmed. The appellate court found that the foundation was incomplete because the witness did not add that the technique had gained general acceptance within the relevant scientific fields, namely, psychology and physiology. Neither advancing a policy justification nor citing any precedent, the court simply announced:

> Just when a scientific principle or discovery crosses the line between the experimental and demonstrable stages is difficult to define. Somewhere in this twilight zone the evidential force of the principle must be recognized, and while the courts will go a long way in admitting expert testimony deduced from a well–recognized scientific principle or discovery, the thing from which the deduction is made must be sufficiently established to have gained general acceptance in the particular field in which it belongs. *Id.* at 1014.

Frye was a common law decision, and the common law has often demonstrated a remarkable capacity for *post hoc* rationalization. As previously stated, the *Frye* court itself neither articulated a policy rationale for its test nor marshalled any authority to support the test. However, in a 1976 decision authored by Justice Richardson in *People v. Kelly*, 17 Cal. 3d 24, 31–33, 549

P.2d 1240, 1244–45, 130 Cal. Rptr. 144, 148–49 (1976), the California Supreme Court made a spirited defense of the *Frye* doctrine:

> The test for determining the underlying reliability of a new scientific technique was described in the germinal case of *Frye v. United States* (1923) 293 F. 1013, 1014, involving the admissibility of polygraph tests.

> We have expressly adopted the *Frye* test and California courts, when faced with a novel method of proof, have required a preliminary showing of general acceptance of the new technique in the relevant scientific community. *Huntingdon v. Crowley* (1966) 64 Cal. 2d 647, 653–654, 51 Cal. Rptr. 254, 414 P.2d 382 [blood tests]. Some criticism has been directed at the *Frye* standard, primarily on the ground that the test is too conservative, often resulting in the prevention of the admission of relevant evidence. McCormick, Evidence (2d ed. 1972) § 203, pp. 490–491. As indicated below, we are satisfied that there is ample justification for the exercise of considerable judicial caution in the acceptance of evidence developed by new scientific techniques.

> Arguably, the admission of such evidence could be left, in the first instance, to the sound discretion of the trial court, in which event objections, if any, to the reliability of the evidence (or of the underlying scientific technique on which it is based) might lessen the weight of the evidence but would not necessarily prevent its admissibility. This has not been the direction taken by the California courts or by those of most states. *Frye,* and the decisions which have followed it, rather than turning to the trial judge have assigned the task of determining reliability of the evolving technique to members of the scientific community from which the new method emerges. As stated in a recent voiceprint case, *United States v. Addison*, 498 F.2d 741, 743–744: "The requirement of general acceptance in the scientific community assures that *those most qualified to assess the general validity of a scientific method will have the determinative voice.* Additionally, the *Frye* test protects prosecution and defense alike by assuring that a minimal reserve of experts exists who can critically examine the validity of a scientific determination in a particular case." (Italics added.)

> Moreover, a beneficial consequence of the *Frye* test is that it may well promote a degree of uniformity of decision. Individual judges whose particular conclusions may differ regarding the reliability of particular scientific evidence, may discover substantial agreement and consensus in the scientific community. (See Comment, *supra,* 35 Md. L. Rev. 267, at p. 290).

> The primary advantage, however, of the *Frye* test lies in its essentially conservative nature. For a variety of reasons, *Frye* was deliberately intended to interpose a substantial obstacle to the unrestrained admission of evidence based upon new scientific principles. "There has always existed a considerable lag between advances and discoveries in scientific fields and their acceptance

as evidence in a court proceeding." (*People v. Spigno*, 156 Cal. App. 2d at p. 289, 319 P.2d at p. 464.) Several reasons founded in logic and common sense support a posture of judicial caution in this area. Lay jurors tend to give considerable weight to "scientific" evidence when presented by "experts" with impressive credentials. We have acknowledged the existence of a ". . . misleading aura of certainty which often envelops a new scientific process, obscuring its currently experimental nature." (*Huntingdon v. Crowley*, 64 Cal. 2d at p. 656, 51 Cal. Rptr. at p. 262, 414 P.2d at p. 390.) As stated in *Addison*, in the course of rejecting the admissibility of voiceprint testimony, "scientific proof may in some instances assume a posture of mystic infallibility in the eyes of a jury . . . ." (*United States v. Addison*, 498 F.2d at p. 744.)

As of early 2000, *Frye* was still the controlling test in slightly fewer than 20 jurisdictions. 1 P. GIANNELLI & E. IMWINKELRIED, SCIENTIFIC EVIDENCE § 1–15 (3d ed. 1999). For example, in 1994, the California Supreme Court reaffirmed its adherence to *Frye*. *People v. Leahy*, 8 Cal. 4th 587, 882 P.2d 321, 34 Cal. Rptr. 2d 663 (1994). The courts in several other large states have decided to continue to adhere to *Frye*. *E.g.*, *Logerquist v. McVey*, 1 P.3d 113 (Ariz. 2000); *Murray v. State*, 692 So.2d 157 (Fla. 1997); *People v. Miller*, 173 Ill.2d 167, 670 N.E.2d 721 (1996), *cert.denied*, 520 U.S.1157 (1997); *People v. Wernick*, 89 N.Y.2d 111, 674 N.E.2d 322, 651 N.Y.S.2d 392 (1996); *Commonwealth v. Blasioli*, 552 Pa. 149, 713 A.2d 1117 (1998).

Perhaps the most obvious flaw in the general acceptance standard is that it misconceives the scientific process. It is true that to determine the scientific validity of a hypothesis, it is relevant to inquire whether the hypothesis is widely accepted. Black, *A Unified Theory of Scientific Evidence*, 56 FORDHAM L. REV. 595, 625 (1988). A scientist publishes his or her research methodology and findings to enable other scientists to replicate the experiment in order to double–check the findings. However, the extent of the acceptance of the technique by peers is not the substantive test of scientific validity; the degree of acceptance is merely circumstantial evidence that the hypothesis has been properly validated by experimentation. *Id.* at 625, 632. To validate an hypothesis, an expert must do more than ask for a show of hands at a scientific convention. As the Georgia Supreme Court observed in its opinion overruling *Frye*, under *Frye* the admissibility of scientific testimony turns on "counting heads." *Harper v. State*, 249 Ga. 519, 292 S.E.2d 389 (1982). To put the matter bluntly, the general acceptance test is a crude, indirect measure of the validity of the scientific theory or technique. From a scientific perspective, the more meaningful question is whether the theory rests on "solid empirical research." *State v. York*, 564 A.2d 389, 390–91 (Me. 1989).

Furthermore, the critics of *Frye* charged that the *Frye* test rests on unsubstantiated, elitist assumptions about the ability of lay jurors to evaluate scientific testimony. In *Kelly*, the California Supreme Court makes several, unflattering assertions about the capacity of laypersons to weigh scientific evidence. Those assertions are hardly self–evident propositions. More importantly, the assertions are at odds with the few empirical studies conducted of lay jurors' ability to evaluate scientific testimony. Chapter 1 excerpted THE

AMERICAN JURY, summarizing the Chicago Jury Project. As the excerpt indicated, the researchers generally found that the jurors were capable of understanding the evidence. Many of the cases studied in the Project involved scientific testimony. H. KALVEN & H. ZEISEL, THE AMERICAN JURY 137 (1966). A later phase of the Project, dealing with psychiatric testimony, confirmed the earlier finding. R. SIMON, THE JURY AND THE DEFENSE OF INSANITY (1967). In this phase, the researchers concluded that mock lay jurors understood the essence of psychiatric testimony presented to them. *Id.* at 217–18. Several studies of polygraph evidence, including both surveys of courtroom use and controlled experimental simulations, indicate that jurors are not overwhelmed by that species of scientific evidence. Imwinkelried, *The Standard for Admitting Scientific Evidence: A Critique from the Perspective of Juror Psychology*, 28 VILL. L. REV. 554, 567–68 (1983) (collecting the studies). After reviewing the studies, two commentators concluded that "[t]he image of a spellbound jury mesmerized by . . . a forensic expert is more likely to reflect . . . fantasies than the . . . realities of courtroom testimony." Rogers & Ewing, *Ultimate Opinion Proscriptions: A Cosmetic Fix and a Plea for Empiricism*, 13 LAW & HUM. BEHAV. 357, 363 (1989).

NOTES AND PROBLEMS

1. Assume that *Frye* is still governing in Morena. Should *Frye* apply only to instrumental techniques such as polygraph, or should it also extend to "software" techniques such as psychiatry? Compare *People v. Shirley*, 31 Cal. 3d 18, 52–53, 641 P.2d 775, 795, 181 Cal. Rptr. 243, 263–64 (1982) with *People v. McDonald*, 37 Cal. 3d 351, 373–74, 690 P.2d 709, 723–24, 208 Cal. Rptr. 236, 250–51 (1984). As we have seen, one of the rationales underlying *Frye* is the fear that scientific evidence will overawe the jury. Suppose that in the *Hill* case, as an element of damages, Ms. Hill claimed that the accident caused her to suffer post–traumatic stress disorder (PTSD). Does PTSD evidence pose that fear to the same extent as instrumental evidence? McCord, *Syndromes, Profiles and Other Mental Exotica: A New Approach to the Admissibility of Nontraditional Psychological Evidence in Criminal Cases*, 66 OR. L. REV. 19, 84–86 (1987). According to one commentator, in most *Frye* jurisdictions, the courts have refused to extend the general acceptance test to "soft" expert testimony. Hanson, *James Alphonzo Frye Is Sixty–Five Years Old; Should He Retire?*, 16 WEST. ST. U. L. REV. 357, 411 (1989).

2. Problem 12–1. In the battery prosecution, Devitt denies fighting with Paterson. The prosecutor wants to prove that there were fibers from Paterson's clothing on the defendant's clothing. The police removed certain fiber strands from the defendant's clothing and submitted them together with a sample of Paterson's clothing to the police laboratory. The laboratory conducted a scanning electron microscope examination of the two samples, and the microscopist is prepared to testify that under the SEM, the two samples were "indistinguishable–a match." Scanning electron microscope is a relatively new advancement in microscopy; it permits magnifications much more powerful than a conventional optical microscope. The SEM scans the sample with a beam of electrons. The scan triggers secondary electron emissions. The SEM instrument analyzes the emissions and converts them into a visual image of the surface on a cathode tube. At trial, the analyst testifies that SEM is "an established, well–known technique" in microscopy. On the other hand, he admits that he knows of no court cases admitting SEM evidence. Is that admission fatal? *People v. Palmer*, 80 Cal. App. 3d 239, 253–56, 145 Cal. Rptr. 466, 472–74 (1978).

3. Problem 12–2. In the *Hill* case, Polecat calls Mr. Chin, an accident reconstructionist and the president of Accident Analysis, Inc. Mr. Chin testifies that: He has advanced degrees in physics and has taken course work in photography and computers as well; he has developed a new technique for computer generation of videotape reconstruction of accidents; he programmed all the applicable rules of physics governing accident reconstruction into a computer; he connected the computer to a videotape machine; he further programmed the computer to generate a video reconstruction of the accident defined by the data fed into the computer; he fed all the data about Ms. Hill's accident into the computer; and his machine has generated a videotape indicating how the accident occurred. *People v. McHugh*, 476 N.Y.S.2d 721, 722–23 (Sup. Ct. 1984). When Polecat's attorney offers the videotape, Ms. Hill's attorney objects that Mr. Chin's new technology "does not satisfy *Frye*." Polecat's attorney responds that "*Frye* is limited to criminal cases." What ruling? *See In re "Agent Orange" Prod. Liab. Litig.*, 611 F. Supp. 1223, 1242 (E.D.N.Y. 1985). Remember that in *Frye*, it was the defense that offered the scientific evidence. In addition, consider the rationale for *Frye*. The proponents of *Frye* argue that lay jurors may overestimate the probative value of scientific testimony and decide the case improperly for that reason. A prosecutor and a civil plaintiff offer the very same item of scientific evidence–creating the same supposed risk of jury overvaluation. In which case, the prosecution or the civil action, is the admission of the item of evidence more likely to result in an erroneous verdict? As a later chapter notes, the ultimate burden of proof is higher in a prosecution than in a civil action.

4. Before the adoption of the Federal Rules of Evidence, all federal courts followed *Frye*. However, after their adoption, the question arose as to whether *Frye* had been impliedly overruled. Article VII, governing the admissibility of expert testimony, made no mention of any "general acceptance" test. Given the Supreme Court's commitment to a textualist philosophy of statutory interpretation, some commentators observed that there was a strong argument that *Frye* was no longer good law. Jonakait, *The Supreme Court, Plain Meaning, and the Changed Rules of Evidence*, 68 Tex. L. Rev. 745, 764 (1990). Thus, the stage was set for the Supreme Court's 1993 decision in the celebrated *Daubert* case.

DAUBERT v. MERRELL DOW PHARMACEUTICALS, INC.
509 U.S. 579 (1993)

JUSTICE BLACKMUN delivered the opinion of the Court.

In this case we are called upon to determine the standard for admitting expert testimony in a federal trial.

I

Petitioners Jason Daubert and Eric Schuller are minor children born with serious birth defects. They and their parents sued respondent in California state courts, alleging that the birth defects had been caused by the mothers' ingestion of Bendectin, a prescription anti–nausea drug marketed by respondent. Respondent removed the suits to federal court on diversity grounds.

After extensive discovery, respondent moved for summary judgment, contending that Bendectin does not cause birth defects in humans and that petitioners would be unable to come forward with any admissible evidence that it does. In support of its motion, respondent submitted an affidavit of Steven H. Lamm, physician and epidemiologist, who is a well–credentialed expert on the risks from exposure to various chemical substances. Doctor Lamm stated that he had reviewed all the literature on Bendectin and human birth defects—more than 30 published studies involving over 130,000 patients. No study had found Bendectin to be a human teratogen (*i.e.*, a substance capable of causing malformations in fetuses). On the basis of this review, Doctor Lamm concluded that maternal use of Bendectin during the first trimester of pregnancy has not been shown to be a risk factor for human birth defects.

Petitioners did not (and do not) contest this characterization of the published record regarding Bendectin. Instead, they responded to respondent's motion with the testimony of eight experts of their own, each of whom . . .. possessed impressive credentials. These experts had concluded that Bendectin can cause birth defects. Their conclusions were based upon "in vitro" (test tube) and "in vivo" (live) animal studies that found a link between Bendectin and malformations; pharmacological studies of the chemical structure of Bendectin that purported to show similarities between the structure of the drug and that of other substances known to cause birth defects; and the "reanalysis" of previously published epidemiological (human statistical) studies.

The District Court granted respondent's motion for summary judgment. The court stated that scientific evidence is admissible only if the principle upon which it is based is "sufficiently established to have general acceptance in the field to which it belongs." The court concluded that petitioners' evidence did not meet this standard. Given the vast body of epidemiological data concerning Bendectin, the court held, expert opinion which is not based on epidemiological evidence is not admissible to prove causation. Thus, the animal–cell studies, live–animal studies, and chemical–structure analyses on which petitioners had relied could not raise by themselves a reasonably disputable jury issue regarding causation. Petitioners' epidemiological analyses, based as they were on recalculations of data in previously published studies that had found no causal link between the drug and birth defects, were ruled to be inadmissible because they had not been published or subjected to peer review.

The United States Court of Appeals for the Ninth Circuit affirmed. Citing *Frye*. . ., the court stated that expert opinion based on a scientific technique is inadmissible unless the technique is "generally accepted" as reliable in the relevant scientific community. The court declared that expert opinion based on a methodology that diverges "significantly from the procedures accepted by recognized authorities in the field . . . cannot be shown to be 'generally accepted' as a reliable technique." Contending that reanalysis is generally accepted by the scientific community only when it is subjected to verification and scrutiny by others in the field, the Court of Appeals rejected petitioners' reanalyses as "unpublished, not subjected to the normal peer review process and generated solely for use in litigation." The court concluded that petitioners' evidence provided an insufficient foundation to allow admission of expert testimony that Bendectin caused their injuries and, accordingly, that petitioners could not satisfy their burden of proving causation at trial.

We granted certiorari, in light of sharp divisions among the courts regarding the proper standard for the admission of expert testimony.

II

A

In the 70 years since its formulation in the *Frye* case, the "general acceptance" test has been the dominant standard for determining the admissibility of novel scientific evidence at trial. Although under increasing attack of late, the rule continues to be followed by a majority of courts . . . .

The *Frye* test has its origin in a short and citation–free 1923 decision concerning the admissibility of evidence derived from a systolic blood pressure test, a crude precursor to the polygraph machine. In what has become a famous . . . passage, the then Court of Appeals for the District of Columbia . . . declared: "Just when a scientific principle or discovery crosses the line between the experimental and demonstrable stages is difficult to define. Somewhere in the twilight zone the evidential force of the principle must be recognized, and while courts will go a long way in admitting expert testimony deduced from a well–recognized scientific principle or discovery, the thing from which the deduction is made must be sufficiently established to have gained general acceptance in the particular field in which it belongs." Because the deception test had "not yet gained such standing and scientific recognition among physiological and psychological authorities . . . .," evidence of its results was ruled inadmissible.

The merits of the *Frye* test have been much debated . . . . Petitioners' primary attack, however, is not on the content but on the continuing authority of the rule. They contend that the *Frye* test was superseded by the adoption of the Federal rules of Evidence. We agree.

We interpret the legislatively–enacted Federal Rules of Evidence as we would any statute. *Beech Aircraft Corp. v. Rainey*, 488 U.S. 153, 163 (1988). Rule 402 provides the baseline: "All relevant evidence is admissible, except as otherwise provided by the Constitution of the United States, by Act of Congress, by these rules, or by other rules prescribed by the Supreme Court pursuant to statutory authority. Evidence which is not relevant is not admissible." "Relevant evidence" is defined as that which has "any tendency to make the existence of any fact that is of consequence to the determination of the action more probable or less probable than it would be without the evidence." Rule 401. The Rule's basic standard thus is a liberal one.

Frye, of course, predated the Rules by half a century. In *United States v. Abel*, 469 U.S. 45 (1984), we considered the pertinence of background common law in interpreting the Rules of Evidence. We noted that the Rules occupy the field but, quoting Professor Cleary, the Reporter, explained that the common law nevertheless could serve as an aid to their application: "In principle, under the Federal rules no common law of evidence remains. 'All relevant evidence is admissible except as otherwise provided . . . .' In reality, of course, the body of common law knowledge continues to exist, though in the somewhat altered form of a source of guidance in the exercise of delegated powers." We found the common–law precept at issue in the *Abel* case entirely consistent with Rule 402's general requirement of admissibility and considered it unlikely that the drafters had intended to change the rule. In *Bourjaily v. United States*, 483 U.S. 171 (1987), on the other hand, the Court was unable to find a particular common–law doctrine in the Rules, and so held it superseded.

Here there is a specific Rule that speaks to the contested issue. Rule 702, governing expert testimony, provides: "If scientific, technical, or other specialized knowledge will assist the trier of fact to understand the evidence or to determine a fact in issue, a witness qualified as an expert by knowledge, skill, experience, training, or education, may testify thereto in the form of an opinion or otherwise." Nothing in the text of this Rule establishes "general acceptance" as an absolute prerequisite to admissibility. The drafting history makes no mention of *Frye*, and a rigid "general acceptance" requirement would be at odds with the "liberal thrust" of the Federal Rules and their "general approach of relaxing the traditional barriers to 'opinion' testimony." *Beech Aircraft Corp. v. Rainey*, 488 U.S. at 169. Given the Rules' permissive backdrop and their inclusion of a specific rule on expert testimony that does not mention "general acceptance," the assertion that the Rules somehow assimilated *Frye* is unconvincing. *Frye* made "general acceptance" the exclusive test for admitting scientific testimony. That austere standard, absent from and incompatible with the Federal Rules of Evidence, should not be applied in federal trials.

B

That the *Frye* test was displaced by the Rules of Evidence does not mean, however, that the Rules themselves place no limits on the admissibility of purportedly scientific evidence. Nor is the trial judge disabled from screening such evidence. To the contrary, under the Rules the trial judge must ensure that any and all scientific testimony or evidence admitted is not only relevant, but reliable.

The primary locus of this obligation is Rule 702, which clearly contemplates some degree of regulation of the subjects and theories about which an expert may testify. "If scientific, technical, or other specialized knowledge will assist the trier of fact to understand the evidence or to determine a fact in issue" an expert "may testify thereto." The subject of an expert's testimony must be "scientific . . . knowledge."[7] The adjective "scientific" implies a grounding in

---

[7] Rule 702 also applies to "technical, or other specialized knowledge." Our discussion is limited to the scientific context because that is the nature of the expertise offered here.

the methods and procedures of science. Similarly, the word "knowledge" connotes more than subjective belief or unsupported speculation. The term "applies to any body of known facts or to any body of ideas inferred from such facts or accepted as truths on good grounds." Webster's Third New International Dictionary 1252 (1986). Of course, it would be unreasonable to conclude that the subject of scientific testimony must be "known" to a certainty; arguably, there are no certainties in science. *See, e.g.*, Brief for Nicolaas Bloembergen et al. as Amici Curiae 9 ("Indeed, scientists do not assert that they know what is immutably 'true' . . . ."); Brief for American Association for the Advancement of Science and the National Academy of Sciences as Amici Curiae 7–8 ("Science is not an encyclopedic body of knowledge about the universe. Instead, it represents a process for proposing and refining theoretical explanations about the world that are subject to further testing and refinement"). But, in order to qualify as "scientific knowledge," an inference or assertion must be derived by the scientific method. Proposed testimony must be supported by appropriate validation . . . . In short, the requirement that an expert's testimony pertain to "scientific knowledge" establishes a standard of evidentiary reliability.[8]

Rule 702 further requires that the evidence or testimony "assist the trier of fact to understand the evidence or to determine a fact in issue." This condition goes primarily to relevance. "Expert testimony which does not relate to any issue in the case is not relevant and, ergo, non–helpful." 3 Weinstein & Berger 702[02], p. 702–18. *See also United States v. Downing*, 753 F.2d 1224, 1241(CA3 1985) ("An additional consideration under Rule 702–and another aspect of relevancy–is whether expert testimony proffered in the case is sufficiently tied to the facts of the case that it will aid the jury in resolving a factual dispute"). The consideration has been aptly described by Judge Becker as one of "fit." *Ibid.* "Fit" is not always obvious, and scientific validity for one purpose is not necessarily scientific validity for other, unrelated purposes. The study of the phases of the moon, for example, may provide valid scientific "knowledge" about whether a certain night was dark, and if darkness is a fact in dispute, the knowledge will assist the trier of fact. However . . ., evidence that the moon was full on a certain night will not assist the trier of fact in determining whether an individual was unusually likely to have behaved irrationally on that night. Rule 702's "helpfulness" standard requires a valid scientific connection to the pertinent inquiry as a precondition to admissibility.

C

Faced with a proffer of expert scientific testimony, the trial judge must determine at the outset, pursuant to Rule 104(a), whether the expert is proposing to testify to (1) scientific knowledge that (2) will assist the trier of fact to understand or determine a fact in issue.[10] This entails a preliminary

---

[8] We note that scientists typically distinguish between "validity" (does the principle support what it purports to show?) and "reliability" (does application of the principle produce consistent results?). [O]ur reference here is to evidentiary reliability that is, its trustworthiness. In a case involving scientific evidence, evidentiary reliability–will be based upon scientific validity.

[10] Although the Frye decision itself focused exclusively on "novel" scientific techniques, we do

assessment of whether the reasoning or methodology underlying the testimony is scientifically valid and of whether that reasoning or methodology properly can be applied to the facts in issue. We are confident that federal judges possess the capacity to undertake this review. Many factors will bear on the inquiry, and we do not presume to set out a definitive checklist or test. But some general observations are appropriate.

Ordinarily, a key question to be answered in determining whether a theory or technique is scientific knowledge that will assist the trier of fact will be whether it can be (and has been) tested. "Scientific methodology . . . is based on generating hypotheses and testing them to see if they can be falsified; indeed, this methodology is what distinguishes science from other fields of human inquiry." *See also* C. Hempel, Philosophy of Natural Science 49 (1966) ("[T]he statements constituting a scientific explanation must be capable of empirical test"); K. Popper, Conjectures and Refutations: The Growth of Scientific Knowledge 37 (5th ed. 1989) ("[T]he criterion of the scientific status of a theory is its falsifiability, or refutability, or testability").

Another pertinent consideration is whether the theory or technique has been subjected to peer review and publication. Publication (which is but one element of peer review) is not a *sine qua non* of admissibility; it does not necessarily correlate with reliability . . ., and in some instances well–grounded but innovative theories will not have been published . . . . Some propositions, moreover, are too particular, too new, or of too limited interest to be published. But submission to the scrutiny of the scientific community is a component of "good science," in part because it increases the likelihood that substantive flaws in methodology will be detected. The fact of publication (or lack thereof) in a peer–reviewed journal thus will be a relevant, though not dispositive, consideration in assessing the scientific validity of a particular technique or methodology . . . .

Additionally, in the case of a particular scientific technique, the court ordinarily should consider the known or potential rate of error, *see*, *e.g.*, *United States v. Smith*, 869 F.2d 348, 353–54 (CA7 1989) (surveying studies of the error rate of spectrographic voice identification technique), and the existence and maintenance of standards controlling the technique's operation.

Finally, "general acceptance" can yet have a bearing on the inquiry. A "reliability assessment does not require, although it does permit, explicit identification of a relevant scientific community and an express determination of a particular degree of acceptance within that community." *United States v. Downing*, 753 F.2d at 1238. Widespread acceptance can be an important factor in ruling particular evidence admissible, and "a known technique that has been able to attract only minimal support within the community," *Downing*, at 1238, may properly be viewed with skepticism.

The inquiry envisioned by Rule 702 is, we emphasize, a flexible one. Its overarching subject is the scientific validity–and thus the evidentiary

---

not read the requirements of Rule 702 to apply specially or exclusively to unconventional evidence. Of course, well–established propositions are less likely to be challenged than those that are novel, and they are more handily defended. Indeed, theories that are so firmly established as to have attained the status of scientific law, such as the laws of thermodynamics, properly are subject to judicial notice under Fed. Rule Evid. 201.

relevance and reliability–of the principles that underlie a proposed submission. The focus, of course, must be solely on principles and methodology, not on the conclusions they generate.

Throughout, a judge assessing a proffer of expert scientific testimony under Rule 702 should also be mindful of other applicable rules. Rule 403 permits the exclusion of relevant evidence "if its probative value is substantially outweighed by the danger of unfair prejudice, confusion of the issues, or misleading the jury . . . ." Judge Weinstein has explained: "Expert evidence can be both powerful and quite misleading because of the difficulty in evaluating it. Because of this risk, the judge in weighing possible prejudice against probative force under Rule 403 . . . exercises more control over experts than over lay witnesses." 138 F.R.D., at 632.

We conclude by briefly addressing what appear to be [some] underlying concerns . . . Respondent expresses apprehension that abandonment of "general acceptance" as the exclusive requirement for admission will result in a "free–for–all" in which befuddled juries are confounded by absurd and irrational pseudoscientific assertions. In this regard respondent seems to be overly pessimistic about the capabilities of the jury, and of the adversary system generally. Vigorous cross–examination, presentation of contrary evidence, and careful instruction on the burden of proof are the traditional and appropriate means of attacking shaky but admissible evidence. Additionally, in the event the trial judge concludes that the scintilla of evidence presented supporting a position is insufficient to allow a reasonable juror to conclude that the position more likely than not is true, the court remains free to direct a judgment, Fed. Rule Civ. Proc. 50(a), and likewise to grant summary judgment, Fed. Rule Civ. Proc. 56. These conventional devices, rather than wholesale exclusion under an uncompromising "general acceptance" test, are the appropriate safeguards where the basis of scientific testimony meets the standards of Rule 702.

IV

To summarize: "general acceptance" is not a necessary precondition to the admissibility of scientific evidence under the Federal Rules of Evidence, but the Rules of Evidence–especially Rule 702–do assign to the trial judge the task of ensuring that an expert's testimony both rests on a reliable foundation and is relevant to the task at hand. Pertinent evidence based on scientifically valid principles will satisfy those demands.

The inquiries of the District Court and the Court of Appeals focused almost exclusively on "general acceptance" . . . . Accordingly, the judgment of the Court of Appeals is vacated and the case is remanded for further proceedings consistent with this opinion.

NOTES

1. On remand, the Ninth Circuit applied the new test but concluded that the plaintiffs' evidence was inadmissible. 43 F.3d 1311 (9th Cir. 1995). Writing for the Ninth Circuit, Judge Alex Kozinski (who *also* had written the earlier *Daubert* opinion) explained:

One very significant fact to be considered is whether the experts are proposing to testify about matters growing naturally and directly out of research they have conducted independent of the litigation, or whether they have developed their opinions expressly for purposes of testifying. That an expert testifies for money does not necessarily cast doubt on the reliability of his testimony, as few experts appear in court as an eleemosynary gesture. But in determining whether proposed expert testimony amounts to good science, we may not ignore the fact that a scientist's normal workplace is the lab or the field, not the courtroom or the lawyer's office. While plaintiffs' scientists are all experts in their respective fields, none claims to have studied the effect of Bendectin on limb reduction defects before being hired to testify in this or related cases. If the proffered expert testimony is not based on independent research, the party proffering it must come forward with other objective, verifiable evidence that the testimony is based on "scientifically valid principles."

Id. at 1317–18. Judge Kozinski added that he could not find any "other objective, verifiable" evidence supporting the plaintiffs' experts' opinions in the record. The Advisory Committee Note accompanying the December 1, 2000 amendment to Rule 702 approvingly cites Judge Kozinski's opinion.

2. How does a *Daubert* foundation compare with a *Frye* foundation? Which foundation is likely to be more elaborate?

3. As previously stated, many *Frye* jurisdictions exempted "soft" scientific evidence such as psychological and social science testimony from the general acceptance standard. Is there such an exemption under *Daubert*? The lower federal courts seem to assume that *Daubert* applies across the board to any purportedly scientific testimony. *E.g.*, *United States v. Amador–Galvan*, 9 F.3d 1414, 1417–18 (9th Cir. 1993) (psychological testimony about the supposed unreliability of eyewitness testimony). In this respect, which standard is more rigorous–*Daubert* or *Frye*?

4. Note footnote 10 to Justice Blackmun's opinion. Although the *Frye* test applied only to novel scientific techniques, the *Daubert* test applies to any scientific testimony. The footnote raises the possibility that the courts will have to rethink the admissibility of ". . . conventional" scientific techniques such as questioned document examination. Jonakait, *Real Science and Forensic Science*, 1 SHEPARD'S EXP. AND SCI. EVID. Q. 435 (1994). In *United States v. Starzecpyzel*, 880 F. Supp. 1027 (S.D.N.Y. 1995), the court cited footnote 10 and ruled that questioned document examiners "offer practical rather than scientific expertise."

There is now a growing body of literature on such questions as whether questioned document examinations qualify as admissible "scientific. . . knowledge." Risinger & Saks, *Science and Nonscience in the Courts:* Daubert *Meets Handwriting Identification Expertise*, 82 IOWA L.REV. 21 (1996); Moenssens, *Handwriting Identification Evidence in the Post–*Daubert *World: Identifying the Genuine Article and the Genuine Legal Issue: Broader Standards Needed for "Scientific Knowledge,"* 66 U.M.K.C.L.REV. 251 (1997); Risinger, Denbeaux & Saks, *Brave New "Post–*Daubert *World"–A Reply to Professor Moenssens,* 29 SETON HALL L. REV. 405 (1998). The steadily increasing number of cases and articles bears out Judge Nancy Gertner's observation that *Daubert* and its progeny "plainly invite a reexamination even of 'generally accepted' venerable, technical fields." *United States v. Hines*, 55 F.Supp.2d 62 (D.Mass. 1999).

C.   THE REPORTING WITNESS

After the teaching witness leaves the stand, the proponent calls the reporting witness. This witness is usually the laboratory technician who personally conducted the test. The witness will describe both the test and the test result. In the process of describing the test, this witness will venture the opinions that proper test procedures were used and that any equipment used was in good working order.

1.   THE QUALIFICATIONS TO CONDUCT THE TEST

The qualifications required of the person who conducts a test differ from those required of the first, teaching witness. Suppose that in *Devitt,* when the defendant is arrested, the police administer a breathalyzer test to him. They want to determine if he is intoxicated. The police may be qualified to conduct the test, but they are not necessarily qualified to explain the theory underlying the instrument or evaluate the significance of the test result. The tasks of maintaining and operating the equipment are essentially mechanical, and the technician can develop the skill to perform those tasks on the job. The extent of the requisite training can vary greatly; it obviously requires more sophistication to operate a research reactor than to use a breathalyzer. However, in both instances, in qualifying the witness, the emphasis will be on proof of mechanical skills rather than academic knowledge, as in the case of the teaching witness. In the words of Rule 702, the reporting witness could qualify as an expert by virtue of "skill" gained through "experience [and] training."

2.   PROOF THAT THE REPORTER RECEIVED THE OBJECT TO BE TESTED

To establish the logical relevance of the reporter's testimony, the proponent must show that the reporter tested the same object that was found at the crime or accident scene. This showing ordinarily necessitates proof of a chain of custody satisfying Federal Rule of Evidence 104(b); the proponent traces the chain from the time the object was originally found to the reporter's initial receipt of the object. Having identified the object to be tested, the proponent turns to the equipment used to conduct the test.

3.   PROOF THAT ANY INSTRUMENT INVOLVED WAS IN PROPER WORKING ORDER

In most jurisdictions, the proponent must affirmatively show that at the time of the test, any equipment used was in good, working order. There are often several methods of proving the equipment's operational condition. For example, in the case of the radar speedmeter, there are three satisfactory methods. First, the officers could testify to a road test; the officer ran a chase car through the speedmeter's operational zone, and the officers checked the speedmeter readout against the chase car's speedometer. Second, the officer may use a tuning fork to determine whether the speedmeter is correctly registering frequencies. Finally, the mechanic from the police motorpool could testify that she ran an internal electronic function test on the speedmeter shortly before the speedmeter was used to clock the defendant. The standard of proof is lax, and one or a combination of these methods would suffice to lay this element of the foundation.

Although the prevailing view in the United States requires an affirmative showing of the instrumentation's working order, a few jurisdictions have taken a different position with respect to the radar speedmeter. Their position is that the lack of evidence of the particular speedmeter's working order goes to the weight of the evidence rather than its admissibility. *People v. Dusing*, 5 N.Y.2d 126, 181 N.Y.S.2d 493, 155 N.E.2d 393 (1959); *People v. Abdallah*, 82 Ill. App. 2d 312, 226 N.E.2d 408 (1967) (dictum); *State v. Dantonio*, 18 N.J. 570, 115 A.2d 35 (1955) (dictum). Under the minority view, the prosecutor need not make any affirmative showing of the speedmeter's condition; and even if the defense has some evidence that the speedmeter was defective, the prosecutor at least gets to the jury.

NOTES AND PROBLEMS

1. Is the minority view justifiable? How likely is it that a police speedmeter is not in working order? Is that probability relevant to the question of who should have the burden of proof? If we allocate the burden to the defense, where does the defense go to find the information to meet the burden? Should the liberality of discovery in the jurisdiction be factored into the decision on the allocation of the burden of proof?

2. Does *Daubert* strengthen the case for the minority view? Does the statutory language of Article VII codify the majority view? If not, did the majority view survive the adoption of the Federal Rules?

3. Problem 12–3. Assume that Morena follows the majority view and allocates the burden to the proponent. In our torts case, the attending physician had an electroencephalogram conducted to determine whether Ms. Hill sustained any brain damage in her accident. To prove that the EEG was in working order, the plaintiff calls Mr. Furniss, a hospital employee. Furniss testifies that he and another employee, Graves, are responsible for the maintenance of the EEG equipment at the hospital; they work as a team, Furniss checking four functions of the equipment and Graves testing another four; they checked the EEG before the test of the plaintiff; and on that date, the EEG seemed to be in working order. As defense counsel, what objection might you raise to Furniss' testimony. Consider both Federal Evidence Rule 801 and Rule 104(a). Focus on the last sentence of Rule 104(a). *See State v. Cardone*, 146 N.J. Super. 23, 368 A.2d 952, 954–55 (1976). As you may recall, in the *Bourjaily* case excerpted *supra*, the Supreme Court had occasion to construe the last sentence in Rule 104(a).

4. PROOF THAT THE PROPER TEST PROCEDURES WERE USED

Like the prior element of the foundation, this topic has produced a split of authority among the courts. Harmon, *supra*, at 150–51. Some courts "have indicated that [this] question goes to the weight of the evidence, not the admissibility . . . ." *People v. Castro*, 144 Misc. 2d 956, 545 N.Y.S.2d 985, 987 (Sup. Ct. 1989).

However, at common law most jurisdictions require foundational proof that the witness used the proper test procedures on the occasion in question. The majority view is attractive; many of the proficiency studies of forensic laboratories point to improper test procedure as a common cause of erroneous test outcomes. The December 1, 2000 amendment to Federal Rule of Evidence 702 codified the majority view, adding a requirement that the proponent demonstrate that "the witness has applied the principles and methods reliably to the facts of the case." Even the courts subscribing to the majority view, though, usually accept rather conclusory testimony from the witness: "I followed the standing operating procedure in running the test." If the proponent wants to go into a bit more detail, the proponent can proceed in this fashion. The proponent initially spends a minute or two having the witness describe the various steps in the customary procedure for conducting the test. Then the proponent asks, "And on the occasion in question, what procedures did you use in conducting the test?" When the witness responds that he or she followed the customary procedure they previously described, the foundation is complete.

5. STATEMENT OF THE TEST RESULT

At the end of his or her testimony, the reporting witness describes the test result. This element of the foundation is an ideal opportunity for using physical evidence. For example, the proponent may use a photographic enlargement of a developed fingerprint or a polygram chart. Remember that validating the scientific evidence is itself a logical relevance problem. A second logical relevance issue, the authentication of the photograph, arises if the proponent attempts to use a photographic enlargement of the fingerprint. In effect, it is an authentication problem within an authentication problem.

D. THE INTERPRETING OR EVALUATING WITNESS

The reporting witness' testimony sets the stage for the third, interpreting witness. In some cases, the proponent will not need a third witness. For instance, sometimes the test result is self–explanatory; some breathalyzers register "Pass" or "Fail" rather than yielding a numerical blood alcohol concentration reading. Moreover, in part as a result of the national campaign against drunk drivers, in recent years forty–one states have enacted laws making it a crime to drive on the highways with a certain level of blood alcohol—so–called *per se* laws. Under these laws, proof of the blood alcohol level is sufficient to establish the crime. Or there may be a statutory presumption that obviates the necessity for a third witness. Thus, even in a driving under the influence prosecution in most jurisdictions, when a breathalyzer yields a numerical test result, the prosecutor does not need to call a toxicologist or physician to testify that a 0.08 BAC (blood alcohol concentration) level indicates intoxication; there will be a statutory presumption to that effect. *See* Tenth Annual Criminal Advocacy Institute (Practising Law Institute 1978) (collecting the state statutes). Finally, in many cases, the reporting witness will also have the qualifications to interpret the test result. The two sets of qualifications do not necessarily equate, but the reporting witness will often qualify to both conduct and evaluate the test. For example, in the case of polygraphy, the same person administers the test and evaluates the polygram chart.

However, when the proponent's evidence does not fall within one of the above situations, the proponent will need a third witness to complete the foundation. This witness will express an opinion, interpreting the test result and explaining its significance to the jurors. This witness' testimony is almost syllogistic in structure. After stating his or her qualifications, the witness states an interpretive standard (the major premise), applies the standard to the test result to which the reporter testified (the minor premise), and thereby derives an ultimate conclusion.

1. THE QUALIFICATIONS TO INTERPRET THE TEST RESULT

Once more, Federal Rule 702 comes into play. As we have seen, the teaching witness needs relatively heavy academic credentials. In contrast, the reporter's qualifications are usually experiential, normally on–the–job training. The ideal evaluating witness is a hybrid and has both academic and experiential qualifications. The jury tends to attach more weight to the witness' testimony if, for example, the expert testifying in a products liability case has not only advanced degrees in the field but also practical experience in the industry. Likewise, in addition to completing four or five years of graduate training, forensic pathologists have "observed or participated in 400–500 autopsies." 2 P. Giannelli & E. Imwinkelried, Scientific Evidence § 19–2, at 78 (3d ed. 1999).

2. INFORMING THE INTERPRETER OF THE TEST RESULT

The basic function of the interpreting witness is to evaluate the significance of the test result described by the reporting witness. The interpreting witness will base his or her opinion on that result. We shall study the bases for expert opinion later in detail. Briefly stated, in most jurisdictions, the expert may base an opinion on: (a) facts the expert has personally observed; (b) facts that are the type of data customarily considered by practitioners of the specialty; and (c) hypothetically assumed facts.

It is, of course, ideal if the interpreter was present when the reporter conducted the test. In that situation, the interpreter may testify to the test result from personal knowledge. However, even when the interpreter lacks personal knowledge, many jurisdictions now permit the interpreter to base an opinion on the test result so long as that is a widespread practice within the interpreter's scientific discipline. Lastly, if all else fails, the proponent may include the test result in a hypothetical question and invite the interpreter to base an opinion on the assumed facts in the hypothesis. The next question to arise is what standard the interpreter employs to evaluate the test result.

3.   THE INTERPRETIVE STANDARD USED TO EVALUATE THE TEST RESULT

If the test result is not self–explanatory, the witness must serve as an interpreter for the trier of fact. After describing his or her qualifications but before stating the final opinion, the witness states the interpretive standard that leads to the opinion. Evidence law does not formally require that the expert articulate the interpretive standards used to evaluate the test result; but in order to make the opinion understandable and appealing to the lay jurors, a competent proponent almost always asks the expert to do so. Suppose that Devitt wants to raise an insanity defense. He might call a psychiatrist to testify that at the time of the alleged battery, Devitt was suffering from a serious mental disorder, a psychosis, and that the disorder deprived him of criminal responsibility under the appropriate insanity test in Morena. To make the psychiatrist's opinion more appealing to the jurors, the defense attorney often forces the psychiatrist to articulate his or her interpretive standard before allowing the psychiatrist to state the opinion itself. In the case of psychiatric evidence, the interpretive standard is the symptomatology, the peculiar set of symptoms that characterizes that specific mental disorder.

Courts and commentators have often bemoaned the "softness" of symptomatology in psychiatry. *Smith v. Schlesinger*, 513 F.2d 462, 475 (D.C. Cir. 1975); Ennis & Litwack, *Psychiatry and the Presumption of Expertise: Flipping Coins in the Courtroom*, 62 CAL. L. REV. 693 (1974). In *Washington v. United States*, 390 F.2d 444 (D.C. Cir. 1967), Judge Bazelon wrote:

> [I]t may be that psychiatry and the other social and behavioral sciences cannot provide sufficient data relevant to a determination of criminal responsibility no matter what the rules of evidence are. If so, we may be forced to eliminate the insanity defense altogether or re–fashion it in a way which is not tied so tightly to the medical model. *Id.* at 457 n.33.

In the following article, one of the leading American commentators on the admissibility of such testimony addresses the same problem.

GERARD, THE USEFULNESS OF THE MEDICAL MODEL TO THE MENTAL HEALTH LEGAL SYSTEM, in Mental Health Law in the 1980s (1985), adapted version reprinted in Gerard, *The Usefulness of the Medical Model to the Legal System*, 39 Rutgers L. Rev. 377 (1987) (some citations omitted)

There are two obstacles to reliable diagnoses. The first is vague descriptions of symptoms. Suppose, for example, that "anxious expression" were listed as a symptom. No observer could know for certain what kind of expression he was supposed to be looking for. And it is unlikely that any two observers would agree upon whether a given expression was "anxious" or not. Vague descriptions conduce to conflicting and confusing diagnoses.

The second problem is "criterion variance," which means a disagreement about which symptoms are required for, or preclude, a given diagnosis. (Recall that a valid clinical description must distinguish this illness from others; that is why preclusive symptoms are listed.) If there is disagreement about the symptoms that are required to make a diagnosis, conflict and confusion are inevitable.

Vague descriptions. Critics of the mental health legal system have argued for years that psychiatry's descriptions of illnesses were vague, overlapping and confusing. They were essentially correct. Ironically, however, as Stone has pointed out, this criticism reached its peak at precisely the time psychiatry began to take steps to correct the problem.

The first edition of the DIAGNOSTIC AND STATISTICAL MANUAL OF MENTAL DISORDERS was published in 1952.[114] This marked the first attempt of the American Psychiatric Association to provide official descriptions of mental illnesses. Until then, the legal system had no official source from which to draw criteria for reliable diagnoses. The descriptions in the first two editions of *DSM,* although clear enough to be of some use had the legal system chosen to adopt them, still fell short of providing the kind of certainty the critics were right in demanding. In part, these failings were an inevitable by–product of the dominance in America of the [Freudian] psychoanalytic model, which viewed diagnosis as an irrelevance.

But psychiatrists who followed the medical model were insisting even then upon clear descriptions of symptoms.[116] They had to. In the medical model, diagnosis is the essential first step in the scientific investigation and treatment of mental illness. Diagnosis is difficult, if not impossible, without clear descriptions of symptoms. Followers of the medical model insisted that descriptions had to be stated in operational terms to be clear. An "operational term" is one that all observers can immediately apply, with a minimum of judgment, to an aspect of behavior. "Crying," for example, is an operational term; "anxious expression" is not. Operational terms are essential because

---

[114] AMERICAN PSYCHIATRIC ASS'N, DIAGNOSTIC AND STATISTICAL MANUAL OF MENTAL DISORDERS (3d ed. 1980) (hereafter cited *DSM–III*). It is conventional to designate the edition by Roman numerals. Thus the first edition of the MANUAL, published in 1952, is referred to as *DSM–I. DSM–II* was published in 1968.

[116] *See, e.g.,* S. GUZE, CRIMINALITY AND PSYCHIATRIC DISORDERS (1976). The article that has become the classical statement of the diagnostic criteria, now generally known as "The Feighner Criteria," for these illnesses is Feighner *et al., Diagnostic Criteria for Use in Psychiatric Research,* 26 ARCH. GEN. PSYCHIATRY 57 (1972). The Feighner Criteria cover fifteen illnesses: (1) Alcoholism; (2) Anorexia Nervosa; (3) Anti–Social Personality [Sociopathy]; (4) Anxiety Neurosis; (5) Drug Dependence; (6) Homosexuality; (7) Hysteria; (8) Mental Retardation; (9) Obsessive–Compulsive Neurosis; (10) Organic Brain Syndrome; (11) Phobic Neurosis; (12) Primary Affective [Manic-Depressive] Disorders; (13) Secondary Affective Disorders; (14) Schizophrenia; and (15) Transsexualism. In this discussion I have included secondary affective disorders with primary affective disorders and have ignored transsexualism as irrelevant to the topic. That accounts for the difference between the thirteen diseases mentioned in the text and the fifteen diseases covered by the Feighner Criteria.

There are differences between the Feighner Criteria and the diagnostic criteria in *DSM–III* for the same illnesses. The differences appear to be minor, however.

they maximize the chance that all observers will notice the same phenomena. Or, put the other way around, they lessen the chance that observers will disagree about the presence or absence of symptoms.

After years of losing all of the battles, the medical model won the war with the publication of *DSM–III* in 1980. Most of the disorders contained in it are accompanied by lists of symptoms that are stated in operational terms. As a result, conflicting diagnoses that are caused by vague descriptions of symptoms should be reduced substantially.

Criterion variance. The enormous differences between *DSM–III* and its two predecessors are immediately apparent upon even a casual comparison. Almost all of the *DSM–III* disorders are accompanied by elaborate diagnostic criteria and such other elements of the clinical description as are known. These descriptions stand in vivid contrast to the perfunctory descriptions of the earlier manuals. They represent the acceptance by a majority of mental health professionals of the medical model's historic insistence upon the importance of diagnosis.

Their significance for the legal system is obvious: they state the signs and symptoms that a consensus of mental health professionals have agreed must be present if a diagnosis is to be as reliable as possible. By requiring that these diagnostic criteria be satisfied before it accepts a diagnosis as reliable, the legal system could take a very long step indeed towards eliminating unreliable or inconsistent diagnoses. A jurisdiction might provide, for example, that an expert's testimony will be inadmissible unless the diagnosis he proffers satisfies all of the *DSM–III* criteria for that diagnosis.

Even minimal uncertainties will be unacceptable to some critics, who seem to believe that absolute precision is possible and therefore mandatory. But what process, legal or medical, they have in mind as a model is not readily apparent. For centuries the legal system has tried– and failed–to define crimes in terms precise enough to eliminate any doubt whether a given course of conduct is included or excluded. Yet, so far as I know, no one has ever argued that the law against theft should be abolished simply because it is hard to distinguish between the crimes of larceny, larceny by trick, and embezzlement, and sometimes even harder to decide whether given conduct falls within the description of any of them.

Nor is a better medical process immediately obvious. Recent evidence suggests that the emergency room diagnoses of physical illnesses of comparable seriousness are no more reliable than the diagnoses of mental illnesses.

NOTES

1. There is some hard evidence that the advent of improved diagnostic criteria such as the new standards discussed in Professor Gerard's article has increased the reliability of evaluations of criminal responsibility. Rogers, *Assessment of Criminal Responsibility: Empirical Advances and Unanswered Questions*, 15 J. PSYCHIATRY & LAW 73, 78, 80 (Spring 1987). In turn, that evidence led the American Psychiatric Association to incorporate even more empirically based diagnostic criteria into DSM IV (1994). In the process of preparing DSM IV, the drafters conducted 150 reviews of the relevant literature, reanalyzed 50 existing data sets, and held field trials involving more than 7,000 subjects at 88 universities and research institutions, Weitzel, *Diagnostic and Statistical Manual of Mental Disorders Fourth Edition (DSM–IV)*, THE ADVOCATE 25, 26 (Aug. 1994).

2. How much subjectivity can the law of evidence tolerate in these interpretive standards? At what point do the standards become so subjective that the opinion based on the standards is of no use to lay jurors? Note the reference to "assist" in Federal Rule of Evidence 702–a reference which the *Daubert* Court went to pains to emphasize.

3. Federal Rule of Evidence 702 was amended in 2000 in response to *Daubert*:

Rule 702. Testimony by Experts (revisions underlined)

If scientific, technical, or other specialized knowledge will assist the trier of fact to understand the evidence or to determine a fact in issue, a witness qualified as an expert by knowledge, skill, experience, training, or education, may testify thereto in the form of an opinion or otherwise, if (1) the testimony is based upon sufficient facts or data, (2) the testimony is the product of reliable principles and methods, and (3) the witness has applied the principles and methods reliably to the facts of the case.

The federal revision is similar to amended Ohio Rule 702(c) which reads:

To the extent that the testimony reports the result of a procedure, test, or experiment, the testimony is reliable [and admissible] only if: (1) the theory upon which the procedure, test, or experiment is based is objectively verifiable or is validly derived from widely accepted knowledge, facts, or principles; (2) the design of the procedure, test, or experiment, reliably implements the theory; and (3) the particular procedure, test, or experiment was conducted in a way that will yield an accurate result.

4.   THE STATEMENT OF THE ULTIMATE OPINION

This topic presents two main issues. First, some jurisdictions still insist that the expert vouch for the ultimate opinion to a "reasonable scientific (or medical) certainty." If the witness is not prepared to do so, the opinion is inadmissible as a matter of law. We examine this rule at greater length later in the material on expert opinion testimony.

The more difficult question is to what extent may the witness couch the opinion in terms of a statistical probability. One of the leading–and most notorious–cases on this subject is:

PEOPLE v. COLLINS
68 Cal. 2d 319, 438 P.2d 33, 66 Cal. Rptr. 497 (1968)

SULLIVAN, JUSTICE.

We deal here with the novel question whether evidence of mathematical probability has been properly introduced and used by the prosecution in a criminal case. While we discern no inherent incompatibility between the disciplines of law and mathematics and intend no general disapproval or disparagement of the latter as an auxiliary in the fact–finding processes of the former, we cannot uphold the technique employed in the instant case. As we explain in detail *infra,* the testimony as to mathematical probability infected the case with fatal error and distorted the jury's traditional role of determining guilt or innocence according to long–settled rules. Mathematics, a veritable sorcerer in our computerized society, while assisting the trier of fact in the search for truth, must not cast a spell over him. We conclude that on the record before us defendant should not have had his guilt determined by the odds and that he is entitled to a new trial. We reverse the judgment.

A jury found defendant Malcolm Collins and his wife defendant Janet Collins guilty of second degree robbery (Pen. Code, §§ 211, 211a, 1157). Malcolm appeals from the conviction.

On June 18, 1964, about 11:30 a.m. Mrs. Juanita Brooks, who had been shopping, was walking home along an alley in Los Angeles. She was pulling behind her a wicker basket carryall containing groceries and had her purse on top of the packages. She was using a cane. As she stooped down to pick up an empty carton, she was suddenly pushed to the ground by a person whom she neither saw nor heard approach. She was stunned by the fall. She managed to look up and saw a young woman running from the scene. According to Mrs. Brooks, the latter appeared to weigh about 145 pounds, was wearing "something dark," and had hair "between a dark blond and a light blond," but lighter than the color of defendant Janet Collins' hair as it appeared at trial. Immediately after the incident, Mrs. Brooks discovered that her purse, containing between $35 and $40, was missing.

About the same time as the robbery, John Bass, who lived on the street at the end of the alley, was in front of his house watering his lawn. His attention was attracted by "a lot of crying and screaming" coming from the alley. As he looked in that direction, he saw a woman run out of the alley and enter a yellow automobile parked across the street from him. He was unable to give the make of the car. The car started off immediately and pulled wide around another parked vehicle so that in the narrow street it passed within six feet of Bass. The latter then saw that it was being driven by a male Negro, wearing a mustache and beard. At the trial Bass identified defendant as the driver of the yellow automobile. However, an attempt was made to impeach his identification by his admission that at the preliminary hearing he testified to an uncertain identification at the police lineup shortly after the attack on Mrs. Brooks, when defendant was beardless.

In his testimony Bass described the woman who ran from the alley as a Caucasian, slightly over five feet tall, of ordinary build, with her hair in a dark blonde ponytail, and wearing dark clothing. He further testified that her ponytail was "just like" one which Janet had in a police photograph taken on June 22, 1964.

On the day of the robbery, Janet was employed as a housemaid in San Pedro. Her employer testified that she had arrived for work at 8:50 a.m. and that defendant had picked her up in a light yellow car about 11:30 a.m. On that day, according to the witness, Janet was wearing her hair in a blonde ponytail but lighter in color than it appeared at trial.

There was evidence from which it could be inferred that defendants had ample time to drive from Janet's place of employment and participate in the robbery. Defendants testified, however, that they went directly from her employer's house to the home of friends, where they remained for several hours.

In the morning of June 22, Los Angeles Police Officer Kinsey, who was investigating the robbery, went to defendants' home. He saw a yellow Lincoln automobile with an off–white top in front of the house. He talked with defendants. Janet, whose hair appeared to be a dark blonde, was wearing it in a ponytail. Malcolm did not have a beard. The officer explained to them that he was investigating a robbery specifying the time and place; that the victim had been knocked down and her purse snatched; and that the person responsible was a female Caucasian with blonde hair in a ponytail who had left the scene in a yellow car driven by a male Negro. He requested that the defendants accompany him to the police station and they did so.

At the trial the prosecution experienced some difficulty in establishing the identities of the perpetrators of the crime. The victim could not identify Janet and had never seen the defendant. The identification by the witness Bass, who observed the girl run out of the alley and get into the automobile, was incomplete as to Janet and may have been weakened as to defendant. There was also evidence that Janet had worn light–colored clothing on the day in question, but both the victim and Bass testified that the girl they observed had worn dark clothing.

In an attempt to bolster the identifications, the prosecutor called an instructor of mathematics at a state college. Through this witness he sought to establish that, assuming the robbery was committed by a Caucasian woman with a blond ponytail who left the scene accompanied by a Negro with a beard and mustache, there was an overwhelming probability that the crime was committed by any couple answering such distinctive characteristics. The witness testified, in substance, to the "product rule," which states that the probability of the joint occurrence of a number of *mutually independent* events is equal to the product of the individual probabilities that each of the events will occur.[8] *Without presenting any statistical evidence whatsoever in support of the probabilities for the factors selected,* the prosecutor then proceeded to have the witness *assume* probability factors for the various characteristics which he deemed to be shared by the guilty couple and all other couples answering to such distinctive characteristics.[10]

---

[8] In the example employed for illustrative purposes at the trial, the probability of rolling one die and coming up with a "2" is $\frac{1}{6}$, that is, any one of the six faces of a die has one chance in six of landing face up on any particular roll. The probability of rolling two "2's" in succession is $\frac{1}{6} \times \frac{1}{6}$, or $\frac{1}{36}$, that is, on only one occasion out of 36 double rolls (or the roll of two dice), will the selected number land face up on each roll or die.

[10] Although the prosecutor insisted that the factors he used were only for illustrative purposes to demonstrate how the probability of the occurrence of mutually independent factors affected the probability that they would occur together–he nevertheless attempted to use factors which he personally related to the distinctive characteristics of defendants. In his argument to the jury he invited the jurors to apply their own factors, and asked defense counsel to suggest what the latter would deem as reasonable. The prosecutor himself proposed the individual probabilities set out in the table below. Although the transcript of the examination of the mathematics instructor and the information volunteered by the prosecutor at that time create some uncertainty

Applying the product rule to his own factors the prosecutor arrived at a probability that there was but one chance in 12 million that any couple possessed the distinctive characteristics of the defendants. Accordingly, under this theory, it was to be inferred that there could be but one chance in 12 million that defendants were innocent and that another equally distinctive couple actually committed the robbery. Expanding on what he had thus purported to suggest as a hypothesis, the prosecutor offered the completely unfounded and improper testimonial assertion that, in his opinion, the factors he had assigned were "conservative estimates" and that, in reality "the chances of anyone else besides these defendants being there, . . . having every similarity, . . . is somewhat like one in a billion."

Objections were timely made to the mathematician's testimony on the grounds that it was immaterial, that it invaded the province of the jury, and that it was based on unfounded assumptions. The objections were "temporarily overruled" and the evidence admitted subject to a motion to strike. When that motion was made at the conclusion of the direct examination, the court denied it, stating that the testimony had been received only for the "purpose of illustrating the mathematical probabilities of various matters, the possibilities for them occurring or reoccurring."

Defendant (contends) that the introduction of evidence pertaining to the mathematical theory of probability and the use of the same by the prosecution during the trial was error prejudicial to defendant.

As we shall explain, the prosecution's introduction and use of mathematical probability statistics injected two fundamental prejudicial errors into the case: (1) The testimony itself lacked an adequate foundation both in evidence and in statistical theory; and (2) the testimony and the manner in which the prosecution used it distracted the jury from its proper and requisite function of weighing the evidence on the issue of guilt, encouraged the jurors to rely upon an engaging but logically irrelevant expert demonstration, foreclosed the possibility of an effective defense by an attorney apparently unschooled in mathematical refinements, and placed the jurors and defense counsel at a disadvantage in sifting relevant fact from inapplicable theory.

We initially consider the defects in the testimony itself. As we have indicated, the specific technique presented through the mathematician's testimony and advanced by the prosecutor to measure the probabilities in question suffered from two basic and pervasive defects–an inadequate evidentiary foundation and an inadequate proof of statistical independence. First, as to the foundation requirement, we find the record devoid of any evidence relating to any of the six individual probability factors used by the prosecutor

---

as to precisely which of the characteristics the prosecutor assigned to the individual probabilities, he restated in his argument to the jury that they should be as follows:

Characteristic	Individual Probability
A. Partly yellow automobile	1/10
B. Man with mustache	1/4
C. Girl with ponytail	1/10
D. Girl with blond hair	1/3
E. Negro man with beard	1/10
F. Interracial couple in car	1/1000

and ascribed by him to the six characteristics as we have set them out in footnote 10, *ante*. To put it another way, the prosecution produced no evidence whatsoever showing, or from which it could be in any way inferred, that only one out of every ten cars which might have been at the scene of the robbery was partly yellow, that only one out of every four men who might have been there wore a mustache, that only one out of every ten girls who might have been there wore a ponytail, or that any of the other individual probability factors listed were even roughly accurate.[12]

The bare, inescapable fact is that the prosecution made no attempt to offer any such evidence. Instead, through leading questions having perfunctorily elicited from the witness the response that the latter could not assign a probability factor for the characteristics involved,[13] the prosecutor himself suggested what the various probabilities should be and these became the basis of the witness' testimony (*see* fn. 10, *ante*). It is a curious circumstance of this adventure in proof that the prosecutor not only made his own assertions of these factors in the hope that they were "conservative" but also in later argument to the jury invited the jurors to substitute their "estimates" should they wish to do so. We can hardly conceive of a more fatal gap in the prosecution's scheme of proof. A foundation for the admissibility of the witness' testimony was never even attempted to be laid, let alone established. His testimony was neither made to rest on his own testimonial knowledge nor presented by proper hypothetical questions based upon valid data in the record. (*See generally:* 2 WIGMORE ON EVIDENCE (3d ed. 1940) §§ 478, 650–652, 657, 659, 672–684; *State v. Sneed*, (1966) 76 N.M. 349, 414 P.2d 858.) In the *Sneed* case, the court reversed a conviction based on probabilistic evidence, stating: "We hold that mathematical odds are not admissible as evidence to identify a defendant in a criminal proceeding *so long as the odds are based on estimates, the validity of which have* [sic] *not been demonstrated.*" (Italics added.) (414 P.2d at p. 862.)

But, as we have indicated, there was another glaring defect in the prosecution's technique, namely an inadequate proof of the statistical independence of the six factors. No proof was presented that the characteristics selected were mutually independent, even though the witness himself acknowledged that such condition was essential to the proper application of the "product rule" or "multiplication rule." (*See* Note, Duke L.J. 665, 669–670, fn. 25.)[14] To the

---

[12] We seriously doubt that such evidence could ever be compiled since no statistician could possibly determine after the fact which cars, or which individuals, "might" have been present at the scene of the robbery; certainly there is no reason to suppose that the human and automotive populations of (Los Angeles), include all potential culprits–or, conversely, that all members of these populations are proper candidates for inclusion. Thus the sample from which the relevant probabilities would have to be derived is itself undeterminable. (*See generally*, YAMAN, STATISTICS, AN INTRODUCTORY ANALYSIS (1964), ch I.)

[13] The prosecutor asked the mathematics instructor: "Now, let me see if you can be of some help to us with some independent factors, and you have some paper you may use. Your specialty does not equip you, I suppose, to give us some probability of such things as a yellow car as contrasted with any other kind of car, does it? I appreciate that you can't assign a probability for a car being yellow as contrasted to some other car, can you? A. No, I couldn't."

[14] It is there stated that "A trait is said to be independent of a second trait when the occurrence or non–occurrence of one does not affect the probability of the occurrence of the other trait. The multiplication rule cannot be used without some degree of error where the traits are not independent."

extent that the traits or characteristics were not mutually independent (e.g. Negroes with beards and men with mustaches obviously represent overlapping categories),[15] the "product rule" would inevitably yield a wholly erroneous and exaggerated result even if all of the individual components had been determined with precision. (Siegel, Nonparametric Statistics for the Behavioral Sciences (1956) 19.)

In the instant case, therefore, because of the aforementioned two defects–the inadequate evidentiary foundation and the inadequate proof of statistical independence–the technique employed by the prosecutor could only lead to wild conjecture without demonstrated relevancy to the issues presented. It acquired no redeeming quality from the prosecutor's statement that it was being used only "for illustrative purposes" since, as we shall point out, the prosecutor's subsequent utilization of the mathematical testimony was not confined within such limits.

We now turn to the second fundamental error caused by the probability testimony. Quite apart from our foregoing objections to the specific technique employed by the prosecution to estimate the probability in question, we think that the entire enterprise upon which the prosecution embarked, and which was directed to the objective of measuring the likelihood of a random couple possessing the characteristics allegedly distinguishing the robbers, was gravely misguided. At best, it might yield an estimate as to how infrequently bearded Negroes drive yellow cars in the company of blonde females with ponytails.

The prosecution's approach, however, could furnish the jury with absolutely no guidance on the crucial issue: *Of the admittedly few such couples, which one, if any, was guilty of committing this robbery?* Probability theory necessarily remains silent on that question, since no mathematical equation can prove beyond a reasonable doubt (1) that the guilty couple *in fact* possessed the characteristics described by the People's witnesses, or even (2) that only *one* couple possessing those distinctive characteristics could be found in the entire Los Angeles area.

As to the first inherent failing, we observe that the prosecution's theory of probability rested on the assumption that the witnesses called by the People had conclusively established that the guilty couple possessed the precise characteristics relied upon by the prosecution. But no mathematical formula could ever establish beyond a reasonable doubt that the prosecution's witnesses correctly observed and accurately described the distinctive features which were employed to link defendants to the crime. (*See* 2 WIGMORE ON EVIDENCE (3d ed. 1940) § 478.) Conceivably, for example, the guilty couple might have included a light–skinned Negress with bleached hair rather than a Caucasian blonde; or the driver of the car might have been wearing a false

---

[15] Assuming *arguendo* that factors B and E (see fn. 10, ante), were correctly estimated, nevertheless it is still arguable that most Negro men with beards *also* have mustaches (exhibit 3 herein, for instance, shows defendant with both a mustache and a beard, indeed in a hirsute continuum); if so, there is no basis for multiplying 1/4 by 1/10 to estimate the proportion of Negroes who wear beards *and* mustaches. Again, the prosecution's technique could never be meaningfully applied, since its accurate use would call for information as to the degree of interdependence among the six individual factors. Such information cannot be compiled, however, since the relevant sample necessarily remains unknown. (*See* fn. 10, *ante.*)

beard as a disguise; or the prosecution's witnesses might simply have been unreliable.[16]

The foregoing risks of error permeate the prosecution's circumstantial case. Traditionally, the jury weighs such risks in evaluating the credibility and probative value of trial testimony, but the likelihood of human error or of falsification obviously cannot be quantified; that likelihood must therefore be excluded from any effort to assign a *number* to the probability of guilt or innocence. Confronted with an equation which purports to yield a numerical index of probable guilt, few juries could resist the temptation to accord disproportionate weight to that index; only an exceptional juror, and indeed only a defense attorney schooled in mathematics, could successfully keep in mind the fact that the probability computed by the prosecution can represent, at best, the likelihood that a random couple would share the characteristics testified to by the People's witnesses–*not necessarily the characteristics of the actually guilty couple.*

As to the second inherent failing in the prosecution's approach, even assuming that the first failing could be discounted, the most a mathematical computation could *ever* yield would be a measure of the probability that a random couple would possess the distinctive features in question. In the present case, for example, the prosecution attempted to compute the probability that a random couple would include a bearded Negro, a blonde girl with a ponytail, and a partly yellow car; the prosecution urged that this probability was no more than one in 12 million. Even accepting this conclusion as arithmetically accurate, however, one still could not conclude that the Collinses were probably *the* guilty couple. On the contrary, as we explain in the Appendix, the prosecution's figures actually imply a likelihood of over 40 percent that the Collinses could be "duplicated" by at least *one other couple who might equally have committed the robbery.* Urging that the Collinses be convicted on the basis of evidence which logically establishes no more than this seems as indefensible as arguing for the conviction of X on the ground that a witness saw either X or X's twin commit the crime.

Again, few defense attorneys and certainly few jurors could be expected to comprehend this basic flaw in the prosecution's analysis. Conceivably even the prosecutor erroneously believed that his equation established a high probability that *no* other bearded Negro in the Los Angeles area drove a yellow car accompanied by a ponytailed blonde. In any event, although his technique could demonstrate no such thing, he solemnly told the jury that he had supplied mathematical proof of guilt.

Sensing the novelty of that notion, the prosecutor told the jurors that the traditional idea of proof beyond a reasonable doubt represented "the most hackneyed, stereotyped, trite, misunderstood concept in criminal law." He sought to reconcile the jury to the risk that, under his "new math" approach to criminal jurisprudence, "on some rare occasion . . . an innocent person may

---

[16] In the instant case, for instance, the victim could not state whether the girl had a ponytail, although the victim observed the girl as she ran away. The witness Bass, on the other hand, was sure that the girl whom he saw had a ponytail. The demonstration engaged in by the prosecutor also leaves no room for the possibility, although perhaps a small one, that the girl whom the victim and the witness observed was, in fact, the same girl.

be convicted." "Without taking that risk," the prosecution continued, "life would be intolerable . . . because . . . there would be immunity for the Collinses, for people who chose not to be employed, to go down and push old ladies down and take their money, and be immune because how could we ever be sure they are the ones who did it?"

In essence this argument of the prosecutor was calculated to persuade the jury to convict defendants whether or not they were convinced of their guilt to a moral certainty and beyond a reasonable doubt. Undoubtedly the jurors were unduly impressed by the mystique of the mathematical demonstration but were unable to assess its relevancy or value. Although we make no appraisal of the proper application of mathematical techniques in the proof of facts (Finkelstein, *The Application of Statistical Decision Theory to the Jury Discrimination Cases* (1966), 80 HARV. L. REV. 338, 338–340)), we have strong feelings that such applications, particularly in a criminal case, must be critically examined in view of the substantial unfairness to a defendant which may result from ill conceived techniques with which the trier of fact is not technically equipped to cope. We feel that the technique employed in the case before us falls into the latter category.

We conclude that the court erred in admitting over defendant's objection the evidence pertaining to the mathematical theory of probability and in denying defendant's motion to strike such evidence.

The judgment is reversed.

NOTES AND PROBLEMS

1. Perhaps the most frequently quoted sentence in *Collins* is the court's assertion that "[m]athematics, a veritable sorcerer in our computerized society, while assisting the trier of fact in the search for truth, must not cast a spell over him." The *Collins* court assumes that scientific evidence–in this case, statistical testimony–will overawe the jury. Once again, the assumption is dubious. There have been few studies of the effect of statistical testimony–on laypersons. However, some of the leading research studies have reported that the lay subjects in those studies tended to underutilize the statistical testimony; the subjects gave far less weight to the testimony than one might suppose. Kaye & Koehler, *Can Jurors Understand Probabilistic Evidence?*, 154 J. ROYAL STATIS.SOC. 74, 79–80 (1991)("[t]he clearest and most consistent finding" in the studies conducted to date); Faigman & Baglioni, *Bayes' Theorem in the Trial Process: Instructing Jurors on the Value of Statistical Evidence*, 12 LAW & HUM. BEHAV. 1, 13–16 (1988); Thompson & Schumann, *Interpretation of Statistical Evidence in Criminal Trials: The Prosecutor's Fallacy and the Defense Attorney's Fallacy*, 11 LAW & HUM. BEHAV. 167, 183 (1987) ("[F]inal judgments of guilt. . . tended to be significantly lower than a [statistical] analysis suggests they should have been.").

2. Since the rendition of the *Collins* decision, many courts have admitted statistical evidence. Statistical evidence is very common in discrimination cases; the plaintiffs rely on statistics as evidence to support the inference of discriminatory intent. Montlack, *Using Statistical Evidence to Enforce the Laws Against Discrimination*, 22 CLEV. ST. L. REV. 259 (1973). The evidence has also been admitted in criminal cases somewhat similar to *Collins*. One case, *People v. Gillespie*, 24 Ill. App. 3d 567, 321 N.E.2d 398 (1974), is particularly noteworthy. The court permitted the witness to use the multiplication rule. *Gillespie* was a burglary prosecution. An eyewitness testified that the burglar was a Black male. Bloodstains found near a broken window at the crime scene were determined to be type A with a positive rheumatoid arthritis factor. The medical expert testified "that approximately 27 percent of the Black population have type A blood. He also stated that from 5 to 10% of the population as a whole have a positive rheumatoid arthritic factor in their blood . . . ." By multiplying these figures, the witness testified that only 2.7% of the Black population would have type A blood with a positive rheumatoid arthritis factor. The witness cited preexisting data complications on the frequency of blood types within the various races, and it is generally believed that the blood grouping systems are independent.

3. At several points in its opinion, the *Collins* court stressed that the defense attorney was unschooled in mathematics. The court suggests that it was unfair to expect the defense counsel to detect the flaws in the prosecution's statistical evidence. Is that suggestion sound? In an adversary system of litigation, it is arguably the defense counsel's responsibility to learn enough about the proposed statistical evidence to effectively attack the evidence.

4. The *Collins* court finds several flaws in the prosecutor's use of statistical evidence. List separately each flaw that the court identified. Which flaws were the most important in the court's mind?

5. Problem 12–4. In *Devitt,* the defendant denies ever being at the scene of the battery. Paterson testifies that during the struggle, the attacker accidentally cut himself on his own knife and bled. The police laboratory technicians find blood stains at the apartment, and conventional red cell tests (ABO, MN, and Rh) exclude Paterson as the source of the stains. At trial, the prosecutor calls Dr. Paul Merton of the University of El Dorado Medical School. Dr. Merton is prepared to testify that his laboratory uses both ABO and white cell tests, so–called HLA (human leukocyte antigen) tests; he conducted comparative ABO and HLA tests of the bloodstains at the crime scene and a sample of Devitt's blood; the ABO test revealed that both samples belonged to a grouping including only 2% of the American population; the HLA test showed that both samples belonged to a grouping including a mere 0.5% of the population; and the two blood grouping systems are independent. Given these findings, what ultimate opinion is Dr. Merton permitted to testify to? How close does *Collins* come to announcing a categorical rule against phrasing the ultimate opinion in mathematical terms? Under *Collins,* when, if ever, may the witness do so?

6. Problem 12–5. In the last problem, Dr. Merton asserts that the ABO blood grouping includes only 2% of the American population and that the HLA population frequency was only 0.5% of the population. Certainly, in light of *Collins,* proof of these individual probabilities is a key to gaining the admission of the statistical evidence. As prosecutor, would you rely solely on Dr. Merton's assertion? If the defense challenged Dr. Merton's assertion, how would you prove the individual probabilities? Be prepared to list the types of evidence you would offer to corroborate Dr. Merton's assertion. Consider Federal Evidence Rules 104, 201, 703, and 803(18). How do these Rules interrelate?

7. In 1992, the National Research Council released its initial report, DNA TECHNOLOGY IN FORENSIC SCIENCE. The report discusses the use of the multiplication or product rule in DNA cases. DNA testimony presents some of the same problems as the statistical evidence in *Collins*.

To ensure the independence of the genetic markers, the report recommended the use of single–locus probes targeting sites on different chromosomes. Previously, many laboratories had used multi–locus probes. Multi–locus probes can target sites which are close together on the same chromosome. There is a risk that genetic markers proximate on the same chromosome will be transmitted together–the problem of linkage disequilibrium. If so, the markers are not independent; and the use of the product rule would therefore be inappropriate.

Moreover, there are concerns about the reliability of the population frequencies which are multiplied. The 1992 report acknowledged that although many of the laboratories employing the rule rely on population frequencies for broad categories (Caucasian, Hispanic, and Afro–American), there is a distinct possibility of substructuring within these groups. For instance, the frequencies of Hispanics of Cuban ancestry in Miami may differ from those for Hispanics of Mexican ancestry in Los Angeles. When there is an extraordinary degree of intermarriage within the subpopulation, the frequencies may no longer be in Hardy–Weinberg equilibrium.

In the long term, to compensate for the problem of substructuring, the report urged the laboratories to use a so–called "ceiling" principle. The prepublication draft stated: "To determine ceiling frequencies, the committee strongly recommends the following approach: (1) Draw random samples of 100 persons from each of 15–20 populations that represent groups relatively homogeneous genetically. (2) Take as the ceiling frequency the largest frequency of any of these populations or 5%, which is larger." Thus, even if the accused were Irish but the largest frequency for a particular marker occurred for Native Americans, the computation for the accused would use the frequency for Native Americans.

In the short term, before the new random samples are compiled, the report recommended that the laboratories apply a modified version of the ceiling principle to the existing data bases. The draft stated: "In applying the multiplication rule, the 95% upper confidence limit of the frequency of each allele should be calculated for separate U.S. "racial groups" and the highest of these values or 10% (whichever is higher) should be used. Data on at least three major races (*e.g.* Caucasians, blacks, Hispanics, Asians, and Native Americans) should be analyzed."

The case law reacting to the NRC report has progressed through several stages. Initially, several courts already approvingly cited the NRC report as a basis for excluding DNA testimony. 2 P. GIANNELLI & E. IMWINKELRIED, SCIENTIFIC EVIDENCE § 18–5(C) (2d ed. 1993). Particularly when the issue has arisen in *Frye* jurisdictions, the courts excluded testimony about computations that did not comply with the NRC guidelines. The courts reasoned that in light of the NRC report, it could not be said that the computational techniques used in the past are generally accepted. Next, the courts began to admit computations made in the more conservative fashion recommended by the NRC. *Id.*

at § 18–5(C) (1996 Supp.). The courts argued that such computations are generally accepted as, if anything, understatements of the improbability of a random match in DNA markers. However, the most recent empirical studies tend to show that the 1992 NRC overstated the risk of substructuring. Lander & Budowle, *DNA Fingerprinting Dispute Laid to Rest*, 371 NATURE, Oct. 27, 1994, at 735, 736. Given those studies, the cases are coming full circle. Even in some *Frye* jurisdictions, courts are once again admitting testimony based on the computational techniques earlier used by the F.B.I. and Lifecodes. *E.g.*, *People v. Wilds*, 31 Cal. App. 4th 636, 37 Cal. Rptr. 2d 351 (1995). The testimony is also being received in *Daubert* jurisdictions.

In mid–1996, the National Research Council released a new report, THE EVALUATION OF FORENSIC DNA EVIDENCE. That report noted the recent empirical studies indicating that substructuring is a less serious risk than the 1992 report assumed. At several points in its new report, the NRC explicitly stated that the new research has rendered it unnecessary to employ the ceiling or modified ceiling principle. In the report's words, "abundant data" now indicate that random match probabilities computed by the traditional product rule are appropriately conservative. The 1996 report has accelerated the judicial trend toward the admissibility of testimony about such probabilities. Random match probabilities, computed in the traditional fashion, are now almost universally accepted. 1 FAIGMAN, KAYE, SAKS & SANDERS, MODERN SCIENTIFIC EVIDENCE §15–4.0 (2000 Supp.); 2 GIANNELLI & IMWINKELRIED, SCIENTIFIC EVIDENCE § 18–5(c) (3d ed. 1999). *See generally*, MOORE'S FEDERAL PRACTICE, REFERENCE MANUAL ON SCIENTIFIC EVIDENCE, FEDERAL JUDICIAL CENTER (1994).

Chapter 13

LEGAL IRRELEVANCE: THE DISCRETION OF THE COURT TO EXCLUDE

Read Federal Rule of Evidence 403.

A. INTRODUCTION

An ideal model of jury behavior underlies and inspires the doctrine of legal irrelevance. Gold, *Limiting Judicial Discretion to Exclude Prejudicial Evidence*, 18 U.C. DAVIS L. REV. 59 (1984). Ideally, we want the jury to employ an item of evidence only to prove the facts that the item may legitimately be used to establish, ascribe the proper weight to the item of evidence, and concentrate on the key issues in dispute in the case. As a matter of internal trial administration policy, the courts favor these behaviors because they maximize the likelihood of an accurate decision. Dolan, *Rule 403: The Prejudice Rule in Evidence*, 49 S. CAL. L. REV. 220, 284 (1976). Realistically, the admission of some technically logically relevant evidence may create a risk that the jury will deviate from this model. We should not naively assume that presenting more logically relevant evidence to the jury always increases the probability of an accurate decision; the contrary may be true. Graham, *"There'll Always Be An England": The Instrumental Ideology of Evidence*, 85 MICH. L. REV. 1204, 1211 (1987). Drawing on his or her knowledge of jury psychology, the judge may fear that the jury will misuse the item as proof of another proposition, overvalue the weight of the item, or be distracted from the pivotal issues by the item. The common law legal irrelevance doctrine gives the judge discretion to exclude logically relevant evidence that realistically triggers these dangers.

Before proceeding, we must add a caveat. Throughout the balance of this text, we shall use the expression "legal irrelevance" to denote the judge's authority to exclude logically relevant evidence when the attendant probative dangers such as prejudice outweigh the probative value. The reader should realize, though, that many courts no longer use this expression. 1 C. McCORMICK, HANDBOOK OF THE LAW OF EVIDENCE § 185, at 648 n. 70 (5th ed. 1999). Some of the leading commentators oppose the use of the expression on the ground that the expression can be confusing and misleading. However, we have decided to continue to use "legal irrelevance." It is not only a traditional usage, but the student can still expect to occasionally encounter the term in practice. We want to emphasize that in this text, the expression is used in the narrow sense of a power of exclusion inspired by institutional trial administration policies.

B. THE MODERN DOCTRINE OF LEGAL IRRELEVANCE

There were numerous pre–Rules precedents, including Supreme Court decisions, recognizing a common law version of the legal irrelevance doctrine. *Eichel v. New York Cent. R. Co.*, 375 U.S. 253 (1963); *Tipton v. Socony Mobil Oil Co.*, 375 U.S. 34 (1963). Modernly though, Rule 403 is the starting point for any analysis of the modern legal irrelevance doctrine. Not only is Rule 403 significant in itself, but it also forms part of the context of virtually every provision in the Federal Rules. Rule 403 reflects a bias favoring the admission of logically relevant evidence, based upon the assumption that the trial judge can reliably forecast the impact of an item of evidence on lay jurors.

Under Rule 403, the court assesses the evidence's probative value, and then balances that against the trial concerns. Thus, in some cases, the fact that the evidence is logically relevant is not enough; it must also be legally relevant in the sense that its probative value offsets the countervailing factors. Although the statute's text is brief and seemingly straightforward, the statute presents several thorny issues of statutory construction.

C. APPLYING THE LEGAL IRRELEVANCE DOCTRINE

The doctrine of legal irrelevance is applied by a three–step analysis.

1. STEP ONE: DETERMINING THE PROBATIVE VALUE OF THE ITEM OF EVIDENCE

Federal Rules of Evidence 401 and 402 use the adjective "relevant." In contrast, Rule 403 employs the language "probative value." The expression is admittedly ambiguous, but the drafters' use of a different expression in Rule 403 suggests that they had in mind a concept broader than bare logical relevance. Dolan, *supra*, at 234. When a drafter uses different expressions in two similar statutory provisions, we ordinarily presume that the choice was advertent and that the drafter meant different things. *Interinsurance Exch. v. Spectrum Inv.*, 209 Cal. App. 3d 1243, 258 Cal. Rptr. 43, 51 (1989).

The courts and commentators agree that the concept of probative value allows the trial judge to consider at least four elements in balancing under Rule 403. *See generally*, Imwinkelried, *The Meaning of Probative Value and Prejudice in Federal Rule of Evidence 403: Can Rule 403 Be Used to Resurrect the Common Law of Evidence?*, 41 VAND. L. REV. 879 (1988). First, a judge may consider the apparent flaws, vagueness or uncertainty of the proposed testimony. When the weakness of the testimony is evident on its face, a judge certainly should be permitted to consider that flaw.

Next, the judge may consider the number of intermediate propositions between the item of evidence and the ultimate consequential fact that the item is offered to prove. The larger the number of intermediate inferences the jury must draw, the greater the probability that the jury will commit some inferential error. This element comes into play when the evidence is circumstantial rather than direct. How long is the chain of inferences connecting the item of evidence and the consequential fact under Rule 401? The longer the chain, the more possibilities for error.

In addition, there is consensus that the judge may consider the strength of the inference from the item to the consequential fact that it is offered to prove. Suppose that to prove Devitt's motive to attack Paterson, the prosecutor attempts to introduce a letter which Devitt wrote several years before the alleged attack; the letter indicates that at that time, Devitt took offense at something he thought Paterson had done. The remoteness in time lowers the probative value of the evidence. Remoteness in place can have the same effect. Whenever the item of evidence is removed in space or time from the events alleged in the pleadings, the removal creates the possibility of intervening events, such as Devitt's discovery that a third party—rather than Paterson—committed the act which offended Devitt, that could reduce the probative value of the evidence.

Finally, the Advisory Committee Note to Rule 403 states that "[t]he availability of other means of proof may be an appropriate factor." In our hypothetical, assume that the prosecutor has no evidence of Devitt's motive other than the somewhat dated letter. The unavailability of alternative evidence increases the prosecutor's need to resort to the letter as proof of Devitt's motive.

This final factor figured prominently in the Supreme Court's 1997 decision in *Old Chief v. United States*, 519 U.S. 172 (1997). There the defendant was charged with violating 18 U.S.C. § 922(g)(1), which prohibits persons with certain prior felony convictions from possessing a firearm. At trial, the prosecution proffered a copy of the defendant's order of judgment and commitment to prove the fact of his prior conviction. The document stated that in 1988, the defendant "did knowingly and unlawfully assault Rory Dean Fenner, said assault resulting in serious bodily injury . . . ." The defendant interposed a Rule 403 objection to the introduction of the document. In support of his objection, the defendant offered to stipulate to the prior conviction element of the charged offense. He argued that in light of his offer, the trial judge should bar the prosecution from informing the jury of the name and nature of his prior offense. The trial judge overruled the objection and refused to require the prosecution to accept the stipulation. The Supreme Court reversed. Justice Souter, writing for a 5–4 majority declared:

> [W]hat counts as to the Rule 403 "probative value" of evidence . . . may be calculated by comparing evidentiary alternatives. The Committee Notes to Rule 401 explicitly say that a party's concession is pertinent to the court's discretion to exclude evidence on the point conceded. Such a concession, according to the Notes, will sometimes "call for the exclusion of evidence offered to prove [the] point conceded by the opponent . . . ." The Notes to Rule 403 then take up the point by stating that when a court considers "whether to exclude on grounds of unfair prejudice," the "availability of other means of proof may be an appropriate factor." The point gets a reprise in the Notes to Rule 404(b), dealing with admissibility when a given evidentiary item has the dual nature of legitimate evidence of an element and illegitimate evidence of character: "No mechanical solution is offered. The determination must be made whether the danger of unfair prejudice outweighs the probative value of the evidence in view of the availability of other means of proof . . . ."

On the facts before the Court, Justice Souter noted that the defendant's stipulation would have given the prosecution "seemingly conclusive evidence of the element." Although he acknowledged that the prosecution ordinarily has the right to present a natural, coherent narrative, that consideration "has . . . virtually no application when the point at issue is a defendant's legal status, dependent on some judgment . . . wholly independent . . . of the concrete events of later criminal behavior charged against him." The majority concluded that the stipulation possessed substantially the same probative value as the judgment proffered by the prosecution and that Rule 403 compelled the acceptance of the tendered stipulation.

It would be a mistake, though, to read too much into *Old Chief*. The decision has not resulted in a large number of defense victories in the lower courts. The lower courts have found numerous bases for distinguishing and limiting *Old Chief*. E. IMWINKELRIED & D. SCHLUETER, FEDERAL EVIDENCE TACTICS § 4.03[5][b][ii], at 4–34.2–34.9 (rev.1998) (listing nine different bases for distinguishing the *Old Chief* decision). For example, in *Old Chief*, Justice Souter noted that the conviction was relevant "solely to prove the element of prior conviction" in the § 922 (b)(1) charge. In footnote 2, the justice indicated that the facts would have presented a different case if the conviction had also been relevant for impeachment under Rule 609. Furthermore, in *Old Chief* the defense tendered a full, unconditional stipulation to the fact which the evidence was offered to prove. If the stipulation had been incomplete or conditional, the prosecution might not have been required to accept the stipulation. Saltzburg, *Stipulations by the Defense to Remove Other Act Evidence* 9 CRIM.JUST. 35, 39 (Wint. 1995).

NOTES

1. The common denominator shared by the four factors is that the judge can evaluate them by considering the face of the evidence; the judge need not consider the credibility of the source of the evidence.

2. There is a split of authority over the question of whether the judge may consider credibility in assessing probative value under Rule 403. The minority view is that the judge may do so. For example, one commentator contends that a judge may consider whether the source of the evidence has been impeached. Sharpe, *Two–Step Balancing and the Admissibility of Other Crimes Evidence*, 59 NOTRE DAME L. REV. 556, 589 (1984). In the same vein, one court has indicated that the judge may consider whether the item of evidence has been corroborated. *United States v. Murzyn*, 631 F.2d 525, 529 (7th Cir. 1980), *cert. denied*, 450 U.S. 923 (1981). However, the prevailing view is to the contrary.

3. Consider the issue as a problem of statutory interpretation. In the American trial system, the jury traditionally evaluates credibility. The Sixth and Seventh Amendments secure a constitutional right to jury trial. Would empowering the judge to pass on credibility raise any doubts about the constitutionality of Rule 403? 22 C. WRIGHT & K. GRAHAM, FEDERAL PRACTICE AND PROCEDURE: EVIDENCE § 5214, at 266 (1978). There is a maxim of statutory interpretation that a court should prefer an interpretation of a statute that eliminates any substantial questions about its constitutionality. 3 N. SINGER, SUTHERLAND STATUTORY CONSTRUCTION § 57.24 (5th ed. 1992).

In addition, consider the broader statutory scheme of the Federal Rules. Specifically, reread Rules 104(b), 602, and 901(a). Those statutes make it clear that in certain contexts when the judge is passing on the admissibility of an item of evidence, the judge is supposed to accept the item at face value. What effect would authorizing the judge to pass on credibility under Rule 403 have on those statutes? As parts of the same statutory scheme, those statutes and Rule 403 should be harmonized.

2.   STEP TWO: IDENTIFYING THE COUNTERVAILING PROBATIVE DANGERS

After assigning a probative value to the item of evidence, the judge turns to the probative dangers cutting against the admission of the evidence. The probative dangers represent the risks that, in one respect or another, the jury will deviate from the ideal model of jury behavior. We can visualize the model, as depicted in the diagram below:

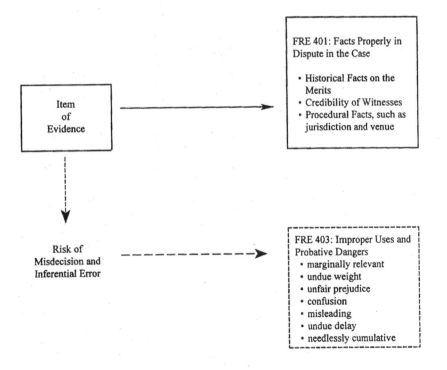

Again, we want the jury to use the item of evidence as proof only of the fact or facts the judge admits the item to prove. The solid arrow from the item of evidence should shoot to one of the facts in the Rule 401 box rather than outside the box. The jurors should concentrate on their principal task, which is to decide whether the historical events alleged in the pleadings occurred—and not become distracted by the irrelevant or influenced by the prejudicial.

Thus, the inferential process is imperiled when a judge admits an item of evidence that is likely to tempt the jury to decide the case on an improper basis cognizable under Rule 403, as suggested by the dotted line.

The philosopher Jeremy Bentham called this problem the risk of "misdecision." 6 J. BENTHAM, THE WORKS OF JEREMY BENTHAM 105–09 (J. Bowring ed. 1962). The Advisory Committee Note to Rule 403 states that the term "[u]nfair prejudice" means "an undue tendency to suggest decision on an improper basis, commonly, though not necessarily, an emotional one." Suppose, for example, that in the *Devitt* case, the trial judge admits testimony about another alleged battery committed by Devitt. On the one hand, this testimony may be relevant for a legitimate purpose. Devitt may have committed the prior attack with a *modus operandi* strikingly similar to the manner in which Paterson was attacked; and therefore testimony about the attack may be relevant to establish Devitt's identity as Paterson's assailant. On the other hand, the same testimony unquestionably gives rise to an inference that Devitt has a bad character and a propensity for committing violent acts—an improper basis for the jury to decide the case on. Even if the judge gives the jury a limiting instruction that forbids consideration of the testimony about the earlier battery as bad character evidence, the evidence may have an improper subconscious influence on the jury.

The jury might commit another type of inferential error, namely, by ascribing more weight to the item of evidence than it deserves or by concentrating too much of their attention on a minor or marginally important issue. Lempert, *Modeling Relevance*, 75 MICH. L. REV. 1021 (1977). The judge may fear that the jury will draw a stronger inference than is warranted from the evidence. Many courts assume that lay jurors overestimate the objectivity and certainty of scientific testimony. Suppose, by way of example, that in the *Devitt* case, the prosecutor attempts to introduce expert testimony about a new genetic marker, autoantibodies. The expert, who has just won the Nobel Prize, is prepared to testify that Devitt has the same autoantibody type as the bloodstains found at the crime scene. However, because the autoantibody marker system is so new, the expert cannot quantify the percentage of the population having that autoantibody type. The judge might exclude the expert testimony on the ground that the jury would overvalue the testimony about the match in autoantibody types.

Before excluding evidence under Rule 403, though, the judge must do more than conclude that the jury will probably attach a great deal of value to the testimony; rather, the judge must conclude that the jury will overvalue the testimony. In *Old Chief v. United States*, 519 U.S. 172 (1997), discussed *supra*, the dissenters stressed that the judge may not exclude relevant evidence simply because the evidence will "hurt" or "damage" the opposition. In an adversary system, the proponent has the right to do precisely that.

Suppose that a witness testified on a marginally important issue for only ten minutes, but because of the witness' celebrity status as a famous movie star, the opposing lawyer fears the jury will accept the testimony as absolute truth. Consequently, the lawyer wants to spend two hours of court time devoted to the witness' credibility. Admitting that much testimony on credibility might divert the jurors' attention from their most important task, deciding the historical merits of the case. The Federal Rules place significant restrictions on the admissibility of evidence logically relevant only to the witnesses' credibility in order to reduce the probative danger of diverting the jury's attention.

NOTES

1. Rule 403 expressly mentions several probative dangers: "unfair prejudice," "confusion of the issues," "misleading the jury," "undue delay," "waste of time," and the "needless presentation of cumulative evidence." At least one court has opined that "[a]s a general rule, evidence may not be excluded solely to avoid delay." *General Signal v. MCI Telecommunications Corp.*, 66 F.3d 1500, 1509 (9th Cir. 1995). However, the court conceded that "several courts have upheld exclusion of rebuttal testimony based on inability to conform to time limits . . . ." *Id.* at 1510.

2. Suppose that in the *Hill* case, Polecat's attorney offered into evidence an expert report that the plaintiff's attorney had not had an opportunity to inspect during discovery. May Ms. Hill's attorney object under Rule 403? Is the maxim *expressio unius est exclusio alterius* (the expression of one is the exclusion of the other) relevant here? 2A N. SINGER, SUTHERLAND STATUTORY CONSTRUCTION § 47.23 (5th ed. 1992.). At common law, it was unclear whether surprise was a ground for exclusion under the legal relevance doctrine. Is it a ground under Rule 403? Consider the Advisory Committee's Note to 403:

> The rule does not enumerate surprise as a ground for exclusion, in this respect following Wigmore's view of the common law. 6 Wigmore § 1849. *Cf.* McCormick § 152, p. 320, n. 29, listing unfair surprise as a ground for exclusion but stating that it is usually "coupled with the danger of prejudice and confusion of issues." While Uniform Rule 45 incorporates surprise as a ground and is followed in Kansas Code of Civil Procedure § 60–445, surprise is not included in California Evidence Code § 352 or New Jersey Rule 4, though both the latter otherwise substantially embody Uniform Rule 45. While it can scarcely be doubted that claims of unfair surprise may still be justified despite procedural requirements of notice and instrumentalities of discovery, the granting of a continuance is a more appropriate remedy than exclusion of the evidence. Tentative Recommendation and a Study Relating to the Uniform Rules of Evidence (Art. VI. Extrinsic Policies Affecting Admissibility), Cal. Law Revision Comm'n, Rep., Rec. &Studies, 612 (1964). Moreover, the impact of a rule excluding evidence on the ground of surprise would be difficult to estimate.

3. Suppose that the proponent offers a very expensive computer–generated animation (CGA). Assume further that the opponent objects under Rule 403 and asserts that the judge should consider the fact that the opponent lacks the financial resources to either hire an expert to thoroughly critique the CGA or prepare a CGA for the opponent. Is that argument cognizable under Rule 403? There is evidently no authority squarely holding that under Rule 403, a trial judge may consider a disparity in financial resources. Savikas & Silverman, *Making the Poverty Objection*, NAT'L L.J., July 26, 1999, at C1. In a survey of 15 federal District Court judges, "[e]ight. . .stated that a disparity in resources would not be considered at all." *Id*. at C6. The other seven judges indicated that they thought that it was proper to weigh a disarity in economic resources. "Virtually all [of those] judges stated that they would make 'appropriate' remarks to the jury if only one side was using the technology." *Id*. What remarks would be "appropriate" in those circumstances?

3. STEP THREE: WEIGHING THE BALANCE BETWEEN PROBATIVE VALUE AND PROBATIVE DANGERS

The last step in the process of applying the legal irrelevance doctrine is the trial judge's *ad hoc* determination of whether the probative dangers outweigh the probative value of the evidence. In effect, the judge must conduct a "cost/benefit" analysis. Consider the standard for making this determination. Evidence may not be excluded unless its probative value is "substantially outweighed" by the trial concerns. The passive voice of the sentence suggests that the opponent has the burden of demonstrating that the probative dangers outweigh the probative value of the evidence, and the adverb "substantially" indicates that the opponent's burden is a heavy one.

There is legislative history to support this interpretation. In the early hearings on the then proposed Federal Rules of Evidence before the House of Representatives, Albert Jenner, the chair of the Judicial Conference Advisory Committee on Federal Rules of Evidence, asserted that "the overall philosophy and thrust of the Rules" is to "place the burden upon he who seeks the exclusion of relevant evidence." *Quoted in* RULES OF EVIDENCE, HEARINGS BEFORE SPECIAL SUBCOMM. ON REFORM OF FEDERAL CRIMINAL LAWS OF THE HOUSE COMM. ON THE JUDICIARY, 93d Cong., 1st Sess. 77, 78. Moreover, a 1990 Advisory Committee Note to an amendment of Rule 609(a) comments that generally under Rule 403, the party opposing the admission of relevant evidence must be able to point to a real danger of prejudice that is sufficient to outweigh substantially the probative value of the evidence. That language has persuaded many lower courts that Rule 403 allocates the risk of non–persuasion to the party opposing the introduction of logically relevant evidence.

NOTES AND PROBLEMS

1. In striking the balance, the trial judge is said to have "discretion." What does that expression mean? Some commentators argue that there are two types of discretion: primary discretion to render a decision and secondary discretion, namely, a high degree of insulation from appellate scrutiny. Waltz, *Judicial Discretion in the Admission of Evidence Under the Federal Rules of Evidence*, 79 NW. U.L. REV. 1097, 1102 (1985). Does Rule 403 give the trial judge the power to formulate substantive evidentiary doctrine, or is the discretion simply a procedural byproduct of the appellate court's limited supervisory powers? *See* Leonard, *Power and Responsibility in Evidence Law*, 63 S. CAL. L. REV. 937, 977, 980 (1990) ("when trial courts apply evidentiary rules that call for the balancing of factors based on the circumstances of each case, they are exercising that weak form of discretion that simply connotes the use of judgment;" the judge does not exercise "strong" discretion "in the sense" that she is "not bound by standards established by a higher authority").

2. Does Rule 403 apply in bench trials? *Compare Gulf States Utils. Co. v. Econodyne Corp.*, 635 F.2d 517, 519 (5th Cir. 1981) *with* Dolan, *Rule 403: The Prejudice Rule in Evidence*, 49 S. CAL. L. REV. 220, 280–83 (1976). On its face, is Rule 403 limited to jury trials? On the one hand, considerations of "undue delay, waste of time, [and] needless presentation of cumulative evidence" can certainly arise in a bench trial. On the other hand, when the trier of fact is a trained judge, is there as great a risk of misuse of the evidence by the trier? *Schultz v. Butcher*, 24 F.3d 626 (4th Cir. 1994).

3. Problem 13–1. In the *Hill* case, be prepared to argue (a) against, and (b) in favor of the admission of a "day–in–the–life" film depicting Ms. Hill's personal injuries. *Bolstridge v. Central Me. Power Co.*, 621 F. Supp. 1202, 1203–04 (D. Me. 1985); Passanante, *The Use of Clinical and "Day–in–the–Life" Presentations in Personal Injury Litigation: A Rising Star in the American Courtroom*, 20 WAKE FOREST L. REV. 121 (1984).

4. Problem 13–2. In the *Devitt* case, the defendant proposes to call ten character witnesses to testify to their opinion of Devitt's good moral character. The defendant may introduce such evidence under Federal Rule of Evidence 404(a). The prosecutor objects and requests that the trial judge limit the defense to two witnesses. Under Rule 403, does the judge have the power to impose that limitation?

D.   RECURRING PROBLEMS OF LEGAL IRRELEVANCE

Most of the 400 and 600 series of the Federal Rules of Evidence are, in whole or in part, specific applications of the general principles of Rule 403. We shall study those specific rules in later chapters. But in several different recurring fact situations, there is a well–established body of case law supporting a "Rule 403" objection. These recurring situations include the following.

1.   TANGIBLE OBJECTS, PHOTOGRAPHS, AND OTHER VISUAL EVIDENCE

The most frequent objections are to tangible objects and photographs that may shock or "inflame" the jury. For example, in *United States v. Marino*, 658 F.2d 1120 (6th Cir. 1981), the defendant objected to the admission of several weapons found in a briefcase he was carrying at the time of arrest. The defendant was charged with conspiracy to import a large quantity of cocaine. The defendant, specifically invoking Rule 403, claimed that the evidence was prejudicial; the evidence tempted the jury to convict him on the ground that he had a bad character. However, the court found the weapons to be highly probative, commenting that dealers in large quantities of drugs need guns to protect their "assets." Like weapons, gruesome photographs are a common Rule 403 problem.

STATE v. ROWE
210 Neb. 419, 315 N.W.2d 250 (1982)

PER CURIAM.

The defendant, Paul J. Rowe, was charged in the District Court with having on May 1, 1980, committed murder in the first degree and arson in the first degree. The court submitted to the jury the issues of the defendant's guilt on a charge of murder in the second degree and arson in the second degree. The jury returned verdicts of guilty on these charges.

The defendant and his wife, Layne Rowe, resided in a farm residence near Alvo, Nebraska. The defendant was an independent trucker. The wife was employed by a Lincoln manufacturer. On the morning of May 1, 1980, passersby noticed smoke coming from the Rowe residence and noted the house was burning. The fire department was called. After the fire had been extinguished, the body of Layne Rowe was discovered, wrapped in a blanket and lying on a bed in one of the second floor bedrooms.

The defendant was not found at the residence, but later that day family members informed the "authorities" that the defendant was in a Lincoln hospital where he had earlier that day been admitted upon the request of a Lincoln psychiatrist, Dr. E. F. Whitla.

Mrs. Rowe's body, when discovered, was found to be mutilated in the following fashion: One breast had been removed with a sharp instrument. An incision with a sharp instrument had also been made in the torso from just below the sternum through the vaginal and rectal areas, exposing the viscera and other internal organs. A later autopsy disclosed that in addition to the mutilations above described, Mrs. Rowe had suffered a skull fracture in the area back of the left ear. The sternum was also fractured.

The pathologist who performed the autopsy testified that a skull fracture of such a nature would have ultimately resulted in death. However, the immediate cause of death was bleeding, a consequence of the mutilations in which the iliac artery to the right leg had been severed. In the pathologist's opinion, the skull fracture occurred before the mutilations. The basis for the opinion was that in order for the mutilations to have occurred, the victim would have had to have been unconscious because there were no signs of resistance as indicated by an absence of any defensive wounds or bruises on the arms. He further expressed the opinion that the victim was still alive when the incision was made and the artery severed. This conclusion was evidenced by the absence of blood in the heart and blood vessels, indicating that the heart was still beating when the cutting occurred.

The pathologist further testified that he believed the skull injury resulted from a moving object striking the skull. He explained the forensic medical reasons for this conclusion. The nature of the fracture was consistent with one which would result from a blow with the side of the head of a clawhammer found on a landing at the head of the stairs near the entrance to the bedrooms. He stated that the fracture could not have been caused by the head striking a flat object such as a floor. On cross–examination he indicated that it was possible, but unlikely, that the fracture could have resulted from the head striking the edge of the steps.

The defendant, through counsel and in open court, judicially admitted he made the cuts upon his wife's body.

The defense to the homicide charge had two aspects. First, the defendant denied he had struck his wife, and argued that the skull fracture must have occurred when she fell down a stairway. Secondly, he argued that when the cutting of his wife's body occurred, he was suffering from a "brief reactive psychosis," a consequence of the belief his wife was dead. It was also argued that he was in the psychotic state when he admittedly set the house afire.

The defendant took the stand in his own behalf. He testified that he did not strike his wife with any object. According to his version of events, he came home about 11 p.m. on the day before the fire. He had been at a bar, drinking beer and dancing. When he came home Layne was in bed. He had another beer and then went to bed in the room in which he and Layne habitually slept. Layne was sleeping in the guest bedroom. He assumed this was because she had to rise about 4:30 a.m. to be at work at 6 a.m. He fell asleep without disturbing her. Later he heard a noise and got up to investigate. He found Layne at the bottom of the steps, unconscious and bleeding from the nose. He attempted to revive her, using cardiopulmonary resuscitation, but his efforts failed. He felt she had left him. He wanted to join her and attempted to shoot himself, but the weapon did not fire. The earlier described mutilation then took place. His testimony surrounding the mutilation was similar to that he related to the defense psychiatrists, on the basis of which they rendered their opinion of "brief reactive psychosis," initiated by his wife's assumed death. The psychiatrists stated he did not know right from wrong nor appreciate the nature and quality of his act during the time of the mutilation. Their testimony was based upon the defendant's statements made to them during their examination of him. The testimony of the psychiatrist testifying for the prosecution contradicted that of the defense and was to the effect the defendant was legally sane at the time of the occurrence in question.

The defendant argues it was error for the court to receive in evidence over his objection four photographs, exhibits 30, 31, 32 and 33. The photographs were, respectively: (1) One picture of Layne Rowe's body in the condition it was delivered to the hospital for the autopsy, partially covered with a burned quilt. (2) One picture of the torso showing the mutilations. (3) Two photographs of the victim's skull taken during the autopsy. The objections to these exhibits are: (1) They are irrelevant because the defendant had stipulated he did the cutting. (2) The risk of unfair prejudice outweighs the marginal relevance the photographs might have. (3) Sufficient foundation was not established because it is not clear from the evidence when the skull photos were taken.

In objecting to these exhibits, the defendant relies upon the principles stated in Neb. Rev. Stat. § 27–403 (Reissue 1979) as follows: "Although relevant, evidence may be excluded if its probative value is substantially outweighed by the danger of unfair prejudice, confusion of the issues, or misleading the jury, or by considerations of undue delay, waste of time, or needless presentation of cumulative evidence."

The objection on the grounds of relevance is founded upon the defendant's stipulation that the defendant did the cutting and the pathologist described adequately his observations, what he did during the autopsy, and his conclusions. The objection on the basis of unfair prejudice is founded upon the proposition that the photographs are "grisly" and "gruesome." It must be conceded they are. The third objection is based upon the claim that the jury might have believed the photos of the skull showed injuries made by the defendant rather than wounds from the autopsy.

In *State v. Williams*, 205 Neb. 56, 67, 287 N.W.2d 18, 25 (1979), we said: "The admission of photographs of a gruesome nature rests largely within the sound discretion of the trial court, which must determine their relevancy and weigh their probative value against their possible prejudicial effect. Although it is true that the probative value of gruesome photographs should be weighed against the possible prejudicial effect before they are admitted, if a photograph illustrates or makes clear some controverted issue in a homicide case, a proper foundation having been laid, it may be received, even if it is gruesome. In a homicide case, photographs of the victim, upon proper foundation, may be received in evidence for purposes of identification, to show the condition of the body, the nature and extent of wounds or injuries, and to establish malice or intent."

The defendant's judicial admission covered only the fact that he mutilated his wife's body. He did not admit he caused the skull fracture. It is clear from the testimony that exhibits 32 and 33 were made during the autopsy; one photo being taken after the scalp had been laid back and the other after the skull had been opened. The testimony showed that the head wound which occurred when the skull was fractured was not evident from casual external examination, and there was no external bleeding from the wound. These two photographs show quite clearly the depth and, to some extent, the configuration of the fracture in a way that words cannot express. These photographs would assist the jury in determining the validity of the pathologist's testimony that the fracture occurred in the way he stated it did. One photograph in particular illustrates the severity of the impact which caused the fracture. These photographs would tend to lead a layman to the conclusion that such a fracture could not be caused by a fall on wooden steps. The court would have erred if it had refused the admission of these photographs, even though the State would have no recourse had they not been received.

The picture of the torso and the blanket–wrapped body fall into the category which we believe lies within a proper judicial discretion. The picture of the torso shows the nature of the major incision and would tend to cast doubt on the defendant's statement to the psychiatrists that a purpose of the cutting was to remove a baby, which defendant believed Layne might be carrying. This photo also tended to show either the defendant's insanity or, on the other hand, the extent of his rage. The photo of the blanket–covered body was marginally relevant, but would tend to support the contention that the purpose of the fire was to conceal the crime by burning, thus casting some doubt upon the defendant's claim that the fire was set to purge the house of the evil spirit he believed was present. The admission of these last two photographs on retrial will be at the discretion of the district judge.

NOTES AND PROBLEMS

1. What stipulation, if any, by Rowe would have blocked the admission of all four exhibits? How does a stipulation affect the analysis under Rule 403? Remember the *Old Chief* case discussed in section C.1 of this chapter.

2. The courts have been notoriously liberal in the admission of shocking photographs. In *United States v. Bowers*, 660 F.2d 527, 529–30 (5th Cir. 1981), the court sustained the admission of a color photograph of a two–and–one–half–year–old child's lacerated heart. Bowers was charged with cruelty to a child under a child abuse statute. She had stipulated to the cause of death, and the court acknowledged that the photograph "had the potential to inflame the jury."

3. Problem 13–3. In *Hill,* the plaintiff offers into evidence photographs of burn victims in twelve other crashes involving 19YR Polecat automobiles struck in the rear by another vehicle, similar to the occurrence here. Argue for and against admission.

4. Problem 13–4. In *Hill,* the plaintiff suffered burns over 70% of her body. In her prayer for relief, Ms. Hill asks both for medical expenses and damages for pain and suffering. During a two year period, she underwent ten complex operations. The plaintiff's attorney arranged to have photographs taken of the various stages of the plaintiff's treatment. At trial, the plaintiff's primary treating physician not only testifies about the operations, he also describes the pain which the plaintiff endured at each stage of her treatment. At the end of his direct examination, the plaintiff's attorney attempts to introduce 78 photographs depicting the various stages of the plaintiff's treatment and rehabilitation. The defense objects that the photographs are unduly gruesome and prejudicial. What result? *Washburn v. Beatt Equipment Co.*, 120 Wash.2d 246, 840 P.2d 860 (1992).

2. EXPERIMENTS AND TESTS

Oral testimony about out–of–court experiments and tests is often challenged on legal irrelevance grounds. As we saw in the last subsection, gruesome physical evidence is normally challenged on the ground of the probative danger of prejudice. Testimony about experiments is usually objected to on the ground of a different probative danger, namely, misleading the jury. To moot that danger, most courts require that the proponent of an out–of–court experiment prove that the test conditions were substantially similar to those obtaining at the time of the relevant event. Note, *Experimental Evidence— Similarity of Conditions*, 21 Def. L.J. 512 (1972). The courts are ordinarily lax in enforcing the substantial similarity requirement; the court is likely to admit the testimony so long as the witness can identify the differences and explain the significance of each difference to the jury. *See, e.g., Spraker v. Lankin*, 218 Kan. 609, 545 P.2d 352 (1976).

However, there are limits to the courts' tolerance. *Sansonetti v. Archer Laundry*, Inc., 44 Ill. App. 3d 789, 358 N.E.2d 1142 (1976). In *Jackson v. Fletcher*, 647 F.2d 1020 (10th Cir. 1981), the defendant's accident reconstruction expert testified about a test of a tractor's stopping distance. The court held that the admission of the testimony was error. The court found "vast" differences between the circumstances at the time of the test and those at the time of the collision. The court reversed on classical legal irrelevance grounds; the court stressed that the differences "cause concern that the jury could have been misled. . . ." *Id.* In *French v. City of Springfield*, 65 Ill. 2d 74, 81–82, 357 N.E.2d 438, 442 (1976), the court held that a "posed" movie showing the view out of the windshield of an automobile being driven past the accident scene was improperly admitted:

> This movie was taken 4 years after the incident. It was filmed in daylight, while the accident occurred at night. The City maintains that one of the wooden barricades involved in the accident was painted white and would reflect the headlights of an approaching vehicle. This effect was not shown in the film. The City also contends that flare pots, illuminated at night, would tend to make the barricades more visible than shown in the daylight.

NOTE

Assume that before Morena adopted the Federal Rules of Evidence, it was a well–settled, common law rule in that jurisdiction that the proponent of testimony about an out–of–court experiment must establish that the circumstances at the time of the experiment were substantially similar to those obtaining at the time of the relevant event. After the passage of the Federal Rules, may the trial judge still insist on a showing of substantial similarity as a categorical requirement? Consider the interplay between Rules 402 and 403.

3. EXHIBITIONS

a. Jury Views

With the judge's permission, a party may exhibit inanimate objects to the jury. However, suppose that one of Ms. Hill's experts is going to testify about a large machine used in the manufacture of Polecat automobiles. You are convinced that a purely oral description will be confusing if not incomprehensible; a two–dimensional photograph would not be much better, and a model would not impress the jury with the size and awkwardness of the machinery. Another option is to take the jury to visit the scene outside the courtroom. Such a visit is termed a "jury view." The rationale of the jury view doctrine is that if the object or scene cannot be brought into the courtroom, the jury can go to the object or scene.

A jury view implicates the legal irrelevance doctrine because it poses severe administrative problems for a judicial system geared to the receipt of testimony in the courtroom. These problems are usually more substantial than those incident to a simple in–court exhibition. The unanticipated might occur:

> In the celebrated "Twilight Zone" manslaughter trial, producer John Landis found himself defending allegedly dangerous conditions in an outdoor Vietnam battle set where Vic Morrow and two child actors were killed in a crashing helicopter. The jurors were taken to view

the actual scene of the accident. In the middle of the proceeding, a large helicopter made an unexpected fly–by. The defense moved for a mistrial, claiming that the unanticipated presence of the helicopter had a powerful emotional effect on the jurors.

Lipson, *"Real" Real Evidence*, 19 LITIGATION, Fall 1992, at 29, 32.

Many jurisdictions have statutes granting the condemnee a right to have the trier of fact view the parcel taken by eminent domain. *E.g.*, ILL. REV. STAT. ch. 110, § 7–118 (1982). Absent such a statute, the party must invoke the judge's discretion. In deciding whether to grant a jury view, the judge weighs the complexity of the proposed testimony; the more complex the testimony, the greater the likelihood is that the judge will authorize a view. The judge also considers the time lapse between the incident in question and the time of the request. The greater the time lapse, the greater the likelihood is that the object or scene has changed, and the less the likelihood that the judge will grant a view.

In an old decision, *Snyder v. Massachusetts*, 291 U.S. 97 (1934), the Supreme Court held that even in a criminal case, the defendant does not have a right to be present at the jury view. However, now by statute or custom in almost every jurisdiction, the parties accompany the jurors to the scene. The judge ordinarily designates some court official (such as a marshal or sheriff) to serve as "shower." At the scene, the shower makes brief, descriptive statements about the object or scene viewed. The jurors may not make their own measurements or inspection during the view. Nor may they converse at the scene with each other or with third parties. *See also* Hauck, *Jury View of Site—Help or Hindrance?*, 48 J. MO. BAR 362, 367 (July–Aug. 1992) ("Comments, discussions, or arguments by jurors . . . are improper. Jurors viewing the scene should be dissuaded from making notes, taking measurements, or drawing maps or diagrams"). The traditional practice precludes actual receipt of testimony at the scene of the jury view, but more and more jurisdictions permit even that. The judge, court reporter, witness, and counsel accompany the parties and jury to the scene. California Code of Civil Procedure § 651(b) provides that "[t]he court shall be in session throughout the view. The proceedings at the view shall be recorded to the same extent as the proceedings in the courtroom."

NOTES

1. What is the evidentiary status of a view? Suppose that in an eminent domain case, the government's expert witness testifies that the parcel is worth $100,000; the condemnee's expert testifies to a market value of $125,000. After viewing the parcel, the jury returns an award of $150,000. The traditional view is that the sense impressions the jurors gain at the jury view are not "evidence" at least absent a stipulation by the parties. *Noble v. Kertz & Sons Feed & Fuel Co.*, 72 Cal. App. 2d 153, 164 P.2d 257 (1945). On that premise, is the jury's verdict sustainable? Note the language of California Evidence Code § 140:

"Evidence" means testimony, writings, material objects, or other things presented to the senses that are offered to prove the existence or non–existence of a fact.

Does this statute codify the traditional view? Do the Federal Rules? If the Rules are silent on the question, may the courts themselves decide whether to treat a jury view as evidence? *See Lillie v. United States*, 953 F.2d 1188, 1190 (10th Cir. 1992).

2. Is it realistic to show the jury an object or scene during a view and then instruct the jury that the data gathered during the view is "not evidence"? On the other hand, what arguments can be made in favor of the traditional view? In a jurisdiction abandoning the traditional view, how could the appellate judges exercise control over the rationality of the jury's findings?

3. Suppose that the jurisdiction in question subscribes to the traditional view that the sense impressions which the jurors gain during a jury view are not evidence. If you were the trial judge and the two experts gave the testimony mentioned in Note 1, in your limiting instruction about the jury view what would you tell the jury? What would you permit the counsel to say about the jury view during their closing arguments?

b.   Displays of a Person or Parts of the Body

Exhibitions are not limited to inanimate objects. The judge may also permit the display of a person or a part of a person's body. Notwithstanding the potential dangers under Rule 403, courts have gone very far in permitting displays. One of the masters of the use of physical evidence was the late Melvin Belli. *See* MELVIN BELLI, MODERN TRIALS §§ 60.1, 60.9–.13 (2d ed. 1982). As Belli noted, a "Victorian sense of modesty and indecency" formerly made trial judges reluctant to permit displays of bodily parts. Today, however, the courts take "a far more practical approach" to such displays especially when they are relevant to "the determination of the injuries" in a case. In *Burnett v. Caho*, 7 Ill. App.3d 266, 285 N.E.2d 619 (1972), the plaintiff removed his artificial eye while on the witness stand. *Allen v. Seacoast Prods. Inc.*, 623 F.2d 355 (5th Cir. 1980) is in accord. In *Sullivan v. Minneapolis, St. Paul & S.S.M. Railroad*, 55 N.D. 353, 213 N.W. 841 (1927), the plaintiff displayed an injury to a genital organ to the jury. Citing *Darling v. Charleston Community Memorial Hosp.*, 50 Ill. App. 2d 253, 200 N.E.2d 149, 185 (1964), *aff'd*, 33 Ill. 2d 326, 211 N.E.2d 253, *cert. denied*, 383 U.S. 945, as an illustration, Belli asserted that there is ample authority for the proposition that "[i]t will usually be permissible to expose the bare stump of an amputated limb to the jury in any case involving an amputation."

An exhibition may also consist of a simple display of a person to the jury. Suppose that in a paternity case at the time of trial, the child is seven months old. In the plaintiff's mind, the child bears a striking resemblance to the putative father. As trial judge, would you permit the plaintiff to display the baby to the jury as evidence of the defendant's paternity? The courts are badly divided on this issue. Some courts routinely permit the display; others just as routinely forbid it. Perhaps the majority permit the display if the child is old enough to have "settled" facial features. Suppose that in a defense attorney's mind, there are obvious racial differences between the child and the putative father. In this situation, the courts are in general agreement that a display is allowable.

PROBLEM

Problem 13–5. Ms. Hill's attorney tells the judge, "Your Honor, I have a request. As you know, we're claiming damages in part for the disfigurement and disability of plaintiff's right hand, which has become hard and lifeless as a result of the fire. Her hand was burned so badly it's like a rock now. I ask permission to have the jurors individually touch and feel it." What additional dangers arise now? How would you rule? *See Curry v. American Enka, Inc.*, 452 F. Supp. 178, 180–82 (E.D. Tenn. 1977).

4. DEMONSTRATIONS

In an exhibition, the attorney passively displays the object to the jurors. In a demonstration, the attorney shows the jury some process in action. For instance, in our torts case, Ms. Hill's attorney might conclude that it would be helpful if the jury understood how a gas injection system functions. While an oral description of a complex object may be marginally adequate, a purely oral description of a complex, multistep process is almost always confusing to jurors. Hence, there may be a greater need for a demonstration than there is for an exhibition. In one medical malpractice case, using latex models of the colon, cecum, appendix, and peritoneum, the defendant doctor reenacted the appendectomy on a small platform before the jurors. O'Reilly, *Defending a Doctor Against All Odds*, 72 A.B.A. J. 44, 45 (1986).

As in the case of a request for an exhibition, a request for a demonstration is ordinarily committed to the judge's discretion, and the Rule 403 considerations apply. The judge will typically insist that the proponent demonstrate that the conditions for the in–court demonstration are substantially similar to those that prevailed at the time of the relevant event. *United States v. Torres*, 537 F.2d 1299 (5th Cir. 1976). A demonstration will ordinarily entail more difficulties than a mere display but fewer difficulties than a jury view. The following problem highlights some factors that the judge should consider in addition to the purely logistical difficulties.

PROBLEM

Problem 13–6. A demonstration involving persons entails even more problems than demonstrations involving machinery. In our torts case, Ms. Hill claims that as a result of the accident, she no longer has a full range of motion in her left arm. What would be the best way to show that injury to the jury? What objection should the defense attorney raise? When the proponent presents evidence on direct examination, what is the most obvious mechanism the opponent has to attack the weight of the evidence? How effective would that mechanism be in this context? What other methods of attack are available to Polecat Motors' attorney?

Chapter 14

SPECIALIZED ASPECTS OF LEGAL IRRELEVANCE: CHARACTER, HABIT, OTHER ACTS AND TRANSACTIONS

Read Federal Rules of Evidence 404, 405, 406, 412, 413, 414 and 415.

A. CHARACTER EVIDENCE

1. CHARACTER AS DIRECT EVIDENCE

In this section, we first encounter the two fundamental character evidence issues: (1) the proper use of character and (2) the methods of proof that may be used to establish character.

a. When Is Character Itself In Issue?

Earlier, we discussed the difference between direct and circumstantial evidence. We noted that an item of evidence is directly relevant when the immediate inference from the evidence is the existence or nonexistence of a material fact. In rare cases, the character of a party to a lawsuit will be one of those material facts under Rule 401. In such cases, proof of character is an end in itself.

Consider these civil cases: A newspaper publishes an editorial, charging that a lawyer is "an habitual liar and thief." The lawyer sues the newspaper for libel, and the newspaper raises the affirmative defense of truth. When the newspaper files its answer setting out that affirmative defense, the truth of the charge (the lawyer's character for honesty) is added to the range of issues in dispute in the case. Or assume that a truck strikes a pedestrian and the injured pedestrian sues both the employee driver and the employer. The complaint alleges that the employer is vicariously liable on a *respondeat superior* theory and that the employer was guilty of negligent entrustment. On the second count, the complaint alleges that the employee "is a careless driver," that the employer should have realized the employee was a careless driver, and that the employer was negligent in entrusting such a dangerous instrumentality as a large truck to a careless driver. The allegation in the second count that the employee "is a careless driver" makes the employee's character as a careless driver one of the material facts of consequence in the case.

NOTES

1. Suppose Mr. and Mrs. Hill were going through a divorce and fighting over custody of their children. Section 33 of the Morena Family Law Statutes

313

provides that in custody disputes, the judge must consider "the interests of the child" and award custody to "the party more fit to be a parent." Would Ms. Hill's character be an ultimate issue in the custody dispute?

2. Many of the "offenses" in juvenile court are "status" offenses such as the status of being a delinquent or a person in need of supervision (PINS). *In re Dennis J.*, 72 Cal. App. 3d 755, 761, 140 Cal. Rptr. 463, 466 (1977). When a juvenile is alleged to be a PINS, is the juvenile's character in issue? In what sense?

b.   If So, What Methods of Proof Are Admissible?

When character itself is in issue under Rule 401, three methods of proof are available: reputation, opinion, and specific instances of conduct. Federal Rule of Evidence 405 adopts this view. The Advisory Committee's Note adds that this view is the "conventional contemporary common law doctrine." When character itself is in issue, some jurisdictions even prefer specific instances of conduct as the method of proof.

In contrast, under the traditional view when character is used circumstantially, there are severe restrictions on the available methods of proof. When you have reviewed the next section of this chapter, ask yourself whether the difference between direct and circumstantial use of character justifies the disparity in methods of proof. Specifically, can the difference be justified in terms of the probative dangers listed in Federal Rule of Evidence 403?

2.   CHARACTER AS CIRCUMSTANTIAL EVIDENCE OF THE CONDUCT OF A PARTY

In the overwhelming majority of cases, character evidence is offered as circumstantial proof of the person's conduct. Proof of character is not an end in itself; rather, the end objective is proving conduct, and character is merely employed as a means to that end. In the words of Federal Rule of Evidence 404(a), the proponent proves character and then invites the jury to infer that on the occasion in question, the person "acted in conformity therewith."

In the leading Supreme Court precedent, *Michelson v. United States*, 335 U.S. 469 (1948), Justice Jackson explained this theory of circumstantial logical relevance: "[T]he defendant may introduce affirmative testimony that the general estimate of his character is so favorable that the jury may infer that he would not be likely to commit the offense charged." Simply stated, the proponent argues that the party is not the *type* of person who is likely to perform that *type* of act. In closing argument, the defense counsel might tell the jury: "Consider all the testimony showing what a peaceful person Mr. Devitt is. Ladies and gentlemen, he's simply not the type of person who would commit the brutal, violent crime that he's charged with."

Although the Supreme Court sanctioned it in *Michelson*, common law courts were notably reluctant to admit most character evidence. Federal Rule of Evidence 404(a) reflects the traditional hostility toward character evidence. A powerful case can be made for the traditional hostility.

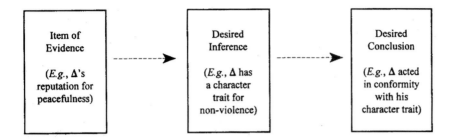

Consider the above diagram. When the proponent of character evidence uses the theory of logical relevance depicted in the diagram, she invites the jury to draw an inference: that given this particular character trait, the defendant acted consistently with the trait on the occasion in question. There is an obvious risk in inviting the jury to draw the inference. In deciding whether to draw the inference, the jury must consciously focus on the type of person the defendant is. This sword is sharply double–edged. When the defendant has a long criminal record or violent past, there is a grave risk that at the subconscious level (at least) the jurors will be tempted to penalize him for his antisocial past. In short, rather than decide whether or not he is guilty of the specific crime charged, they may punish him for his past or status—sometimes in violation of the Eighth Amendment. *See Robinson v. California*, 370 U.S. 660 (1962). There is also the further danger that the trier of fact will overestimate the probative value of character evidence. The following article defends the traditional hostility to character evidence by marshalling psychological studies documenting the dangers thereof.

MENDEZ, CALIFORNIA'S NEW LAW ON CHARACTER EVIDENCE: EVIDENCE CODE SECTION 352 AND THE IMPACT OF RECENT PSYCHOLOGICAL STUDIES, 31 U.C.L.A. L. Rev. 1003, 1045–53 (1984)
(some citations omitted)

. . . Psychologists have found that people give greater weight to unfavorable, unpleasant or socially derogatory information about a person than to information of equal intensity but of a positive dimension.[227] . . . . Thus, although both sides may introduce character evidence, the jury is likely to place more weight on the prosecution's evidence of bad conduct or untrustworthiness than on the accused's countervailing evidence. A prior conviction, for example, will be likely to impress the jury in a way that the accused cannot counteract by evidence of a pardon or of having led a blameless life since the conviction.

Perhaps the factor that most induces jurors to overestimate the probative value of character evidence is what psychologists term the "halo effect."[233]

---

[227] *See, e.g.,* Hamilton & Huffman, *Generality of Impression–Formation Processes for Evaluative and Nonevaluative Judgments,* 20 J. PERSONALITY & SOC. PSYCHOLOGY 200, 201, 204 (1971); Schneider, *supra* note 226, at 299. *But see* Weinstein & Crowdus, *supra* note 226, at 389 ("The basic hypothesis that negative information has greater saliency than positive information for person perception was generally not supported [by the study].").

[233] *See* G. ALLPORT, PERSONALITY—A PSYCHOLOGICAL INTERPRETATION 5521 (1937).

In the present context it might be more aptly called the "devil's horns effect." The term refers to the propensity of people to judge others on the basis of one outstanding "good" or "bad" quality. This propensity may stem from a tendency to overestimate the unity of personality to see others as consistent, simple beings whose behavior in a given situation is readily predictable.[235] Gustav Ichheiser has described the effects of this need to oversimplify

> [The mental processes] function so as to transcend in many ways and many directions the pure raw material and to construct out of this material a more or less well–organized and integrated image of the given personality.

This oversimplification, says Ichheiser, magnifies the impact of character evidence, even when the evidence is barely probative, if at all:

> A man is under suspicion of murder. During the investigation certain definite abnormalities of his sexual behavior come to light, even though there is no evidence that they are related in any way to the committed murder. Again, the frequent reaction in many people, if verbalized, would read something like this: "This man whose sexual life deviates so strangely from the norm can also be expected to deviate from other social norms in any other respect."

Early psychological theories supported the intuition that character evidence was predictive of behavior. Gordon Allport, in particular, helped formulate the theory that "traits" are "the fundamental dispositions of personality." "Trait theory" essentially holds that the behavior of a given individual is governed by personality traits that exert sufficient influence to produce generally consistent behavior in widely divergent situations.[264]

Subsequent empirical research, however, has not only failed to validate trait theory but has generally rejected it.[265]

Instead, the research shows that behavior is largely shaped by specific situational determinants that do not lend themselves easily to predictions about individual behavior. Mischel, a leading exponent of the new theory of specificity, explains:

> First, behavior depends on stimulus situations and is specific to the situation: response patterns even in highly similar situations often fail to be strongly related. Individuals show far less cross–situational consistency in their behavior than has been assumed by trait–state theories. The more dissimilar the evoking situations, the less likely they are to lead to similar or consistent responses from the *same* individual. *Even seemingly trivial situational differences may reduce correlations to zero.*[268]

---

[235] Ichheiser, *Misunderstandings in Human Relations—A Study in False Social Perception,* 55 AM. J. SOC. 27–28 (Supp. 1949).

[264] *See id.* at 289; H. EYSENCK, THE STRUCTURE OF HUMAN PERSONALITY 3 (1970); W. MISCHEL, PERSONALITY AND ASSESSMENT 6 (1968).

[265] Burton, *Generality of Honesty Reconsidered,* 70 PSYCHOLOGY REV. 481, 482 (1963).

[268] Mischel, *supra* n. 264, at 177 (emphasis added).

These findings threaten the basic assumptions about the probative value of character evidence. If even seeming trivial situational differences can render behavioral predictions totally invalid, then character evidence may possess little or no probative value. From this psychological perspective, evidence that a witness has been convicted of a felony involving dishonesty or has cheated on his taxes may or may not tell us anything about whether he was truthful on the stand.[269] Likewise, evidence that the accused was engaged in an altercation after a New Year's Eve party may tell us nothing about his behavior during a peace demonstration. As Mischel emphasizes, "The assessor who tries to predict the future without detailed information about the exact environmental conditions influencing the individual's criterion behavior may be more engaged in the process of hoping than of predicting."[270] Indeed, the work of Mischel and other psychologists, including Allport who acknowledged the weaknesses of his original theory,[271] has moved one legal commentator to conclude that "the theory of behavior that was so compatible with the [lay] notions about character [has] ceased to have *any* scientific recognition."[272]

NOTES

1. Although Professor Mendez defends the traditional hostility to character evidence, other commentators have criticized the orthodox view. It is clear, for example, that laypersons routinely rely on character reasoning in everyday decisionmaking. Uviller, *Evidence of Character to Prove Conduct: Illusion, Illogic, and Injustice in the Courtroom*, 130 U. Pa. L. Rev. 845, 883, 890 (1982).

[269] *See, e.g.,* the studies of Hugh Hartshorne and Mark May examining the propensity of school children to deceive. Although they concluded their research over fifty years ago, their findings were remarkably similar to Mischel's:

> What we actually observed is that the honesty or dishonesty of a child in one situation is related to his honesty or dishonesty in another situation mainly to the degree that the situations have factors in common. For example, a child may cheat on his arithmetic test and ten minutes later, in the same room, under the same examiner, under the same general conditions, be perfectly honest in a spelling test. In like manner, he may be dishonest in all classroom situations but be perfectly honest in his dealing with his fellow pupils in the playground or at party games. Indeed, the most striking thing about the conduct of children is the amount of *inconsistency* exhibited. If we call perfect consistency one hundred and perfect inconsistency zero, the average consistency score . . . is only twenty, and there are a great many more scores between twenty and zero, than there are between twenty and one hundred.

H. Hartshorne, Character in Human Relations 209 (1932) (emphasis added). Not surprisingly, they concluded by rejecting the validity of trait theory in these situations: "The results of these studies show that neither deceit nor its opposite, 'honesty,' are [sic] unified character traits, but rather specific functions of life situations . . . .. Lying, cheating, and stealing as measured by the test situations used in these studies are only *very loosely* related." H. Hartshorne & M. May, Studies in the Nature of Character–Studies in Deceit 411 (1928) (emphasis added). These studies, of course, involved children in school situations, not adults in the formalized surroundings of the courtroom, but the doubts raised are at least disturbing.

[270] W. Mischel, *supra* note 264, at 140.

[271] Allport, *Traits Revisited,* 21 Am. Psychologist 1, 9 (1966).

[272] Lawson, *Credibility and Character: A Different Look at an Interminable Problem*, 50 Notre Dame L. Rev. 758, 783 (1975) (emphasis in original).

2. Moreover, there has been a reassessment of the pertinent psychological literature. In *The Use of Character to Prove Conduct: Rationality and Catharsis in the Law of Evidence*, 58 U. COLO. L. REV. 1 (1986–87), Professor Leonard generally supports Professor Mendez' position. However, he concedes that the modern understanding is that, for some persons, character is an excellent predictor of conduct in specific situations. In *How Should We Treat Character Evidence Offered to Prove Conduct*, 58 U. COLO. L. REV. 279, 283 (1987), Professor Crump sharply disputes Professor Mendez' position. Professor Crump states that "social science is by no means monolithic in condemning trait theory. Modern textbooks for college courses teach Allport's view without categorically rejecting it, and they suggest that a modern trait theory might have considerable validity. Although the addition of situational factors may enhance the validity, the literature suggests an ambivalence toward both trait and situation theory." Likewise, Davies, *Evidence of Character to Prove Conduct: A Reassessment of Relevancy*, 27 CRIM. L. BULL. 504 (Nov.–Dec. 1991) challenges Professor Mendez' position. Ms. Davies points out that just as situationism supplanted trait theory, interactionism is now replacing situationism. Interactionists are of the view that given an adequate sample of a person's prior conduct in similar situations, a reliable prediction of the person's behavior in an analogous setting is possible.

The state of the commentary reflects the state of the law. Although Rule 404(a) continues the traditional prohibition against character evidence, there are exceptions to the prohibition. The following subsections address the exceptions.

a.   Circumstantial Character Evidence in Criminal Cases

1)   When Does the Defendant's Character Come into Issue?

The Traditional Approach—At the Defendant's Election

Under Federal Rule of Evidence 404(a)(1), the defendant's character generally comes into issue only when the defendant presents evidence dealing with his or her character. The choice is the defendant's. *United States v. Gilliland*, 586 F.2d 1384 (10th Cir. 1978). However, as we shall see later in this chapter, by virtue of a December 1, 2000 amendment to Rule 404(a)(1), the defendant now places one of his or her character traits in issue by introducing evidence of the same character trait of the alleged victim of the charged offense.

Customarily, the defendant "opens" the issue by calling a witness to give reputation or opinion testimony regarding the defendant's good character. The defendant could testify to his or her own good reputation within the community, but the defendant is such an obviously biased source for the testimony that the testimony is virtually self–impeaching. Hence, the accused usually calls third parties as defense witnesses to give the character testimony. The defendant may even place character in issue by attempting to elicit favorable evidence during the cross–examination of prosecution witnesses. *Franklin v. State*, 303 S.E.2d 22 (Ga. 1983).

Under Federal Rule of Evidence 404(a)(1), the third parties must testify to "a pertinent trait of his [the defendant's] character." This language seems to limit the defendant to testimony about specific character traits. In other jurisdictions such as California, the defendant can also choose the extent to which character will be placed in issue. California Evidence Code § 1102 permits the defendant to introduce evidence of specific relevant character traits or general, moral, law–abiding character.

NOTES AND PROBLEMS

1. If character evidence has as little probative value as Professor Mendez contends, why permit even the defense to introduce character evidence? Are the probative dangers of Rule 403 more likely to disadvantage the prosecution or the defense? If the defendant is the more likely victim of those risks, why not permit the defendant to waive the character evidence ban?

2. The defendant may present evidence of a pertinent character trait. In this context, what does "pertinent" mean? Annot., 49 A.L.R. Fed. 478, 480–81 (1980). What trait is pertinent in a battery prosecution such as the *Devitt* case? A larceny prosecution? A perjury prosecution? What if the defendant raises an entrapment defense?

3. Testimony about the defendant's general character would seem to be easier to find; but do not leap to the conclusion that it is always in a defendant's interest to open up general character as well as a specific trait. In what circumstances, under California Evidence Code § 1102, would you as a defense counsel place in issue a specific trait rather than general character? Suppose that although Devitt had never been arrested for a violent crime, he had previous convictions for drug offenses. Would it be to his advantage to place his general, law–abiding character in issue? Would it be safer to open only the narrower issue of character trait of peacefulness?

4. Problem 14–1. In *Devitt,* at the outset of his direct examination, the defendant testifies to these facts: He has always lived in El Dorado; he went to grammar and high school in El Dorado; immediately after graduating from high school, he went to work for Ganesh Fixit and Carpentry; he has worked there for seven years and now holds the title of assistant manager; he is married; and he and his wife have three children. Standing alone, each fact appears to be neutral background information. However, cumulatively, the facts create the impression that Devitt is a stable, responsible family person— the type of person who would be unlikely to commit an unprovoked battery. After this testimony, may the prosecutor attack Devitt's character? *United States v. Masino*, 275 F.2d 129, 133 (2d Cir. 1960) ("What a [witness] is permitted to say about himself by way of introduction"). *See also Wilson v. Vermont Castings*, 977 F. Supp. 691, 699 (M.D.Pa. 1997)("Information about a party or a witness' background, job and education is certainly appropriate and admissible in every action. Juries cannot make assessment of credibility in a vacuum. Such information gives background on the witness and a point of reference in assessing that individual's credibility. . ."), *aff'd*, 170 F.3d 391 (3d Cir. 1999).

5. Problem 14–2. In *Devitt*, on direct examination, the defendant goes on at length about his battlefield decorations during the Gulf war and his position with the local Episcopalian church. (As we shall see, even when the defendant places his or her character in issue, the defendant ordinarily may not introduce specific instances of good conduct. Hence, the prosecutor could have objected to this testimony.) After the defendant's testimony, may the prosecutor now attack the defendant's character? Think back to the concept of curative admissibility. *See United States v. McLister*, 608 F.2d 785, 790 (9th Cir. 1979); *State v. Bowers*, 218 Kan. 736, 545 P.2d 303, 305–07 (1976). Is this problem distinguishable from Problem 14–1?

The FRE Approach: Rules 413–14—The Abolition of the Defendant's Veto

Under the traditional view, in effect, the defendant has the power to veto the use of his or her character as circumstantial evidence of conduct at trial. Rules 413 and 414 are recent. They depart from the traditional view. Under these Rules, the prosecution may resort to evidence of a defendant's similar sexual assaults or child molestations to prove "any matter to which it is relevant." Under Rule 401, such acts are logically "relevant" as circumstantial proof to establish the defendant's commission of the charged *actus reus*. Under these rules, the prosecution has the choice whether to introduce the evidence. Thus, unlike Rule 404(a), this type of evidence can be admitted during the prosecution case–in–chief; the judge need not await the defense case–in–chief to determine whether the defense will open the door and deliberately or inadvertently place character in issue.

Federal Rule of Evidence 413. Evidence of Similar Crimes in Sexual Assault Cases.

(a) In a criminal case in which the defendant is accused of an offense of sexual assault, evidence of the defendant's commission of another offense or offenses of sexual assault is admissible, and may be considered for its bearing on any matter to which it is relevant. . . .

Federal Rule of Evidence 414. Evidence of Similar Crimes in Child Molestation Cases.

(a) In a criminal case in which the defendant is accused of an offense of child molestation, evidence of the defendant's commission of another offense or offenses of child molestation is admissible, and may be considered for its bearing on any matter to which it is relevant. . . .

Note the operative phrase in each subdivision (a): "is admissible." The wording raises the question of whether the judge can exercise Rule 403 discretion to exclude evidence that is otherwise admissible under Rule 413 or 414. In Rule 609(a)(2), when the drafters wanted to make it clear that certain types of convictions were automatically admissible for impeachment, they used the verb "shall." Under a strict textualist approach, "is" may be ambiguous enough to permit the court to resort to extrinsic legislative history material. Although the rules were approved by Congress during the Clinton Administration, the Justice Department originally submitted the proposed rules during the Bush Administration. When the department initially submitted the rules, the rules were accompanied by an Analysis Statement which explicitly stated that judges could continue to exercise their Rule 403 discretion under the proposed rules.

NOTES

1. Rules 413 and 414 single out prosecutions for sexual assault and child molestation. Is it defensible to divest defendants accused of those crimes of the protection of the traditional rules of character evidence? In a study by the Bureau of Justice Statistics released in 1984, the respondent citizens rated rape and child abuse as the second and third most serious — and potentially most repulsive — crimes. THE SEVERITY OF CRIME, BUREAU OF JUST. STATISTICS BULL. (Jan. 1984). In a 1989 study conducted by the Bureau of Justice Statistics, the recidivism rate for rape was the second lowest. Bryden & Park, *"Other Crimes" Evidence in Sex Offense Cases*, 78 MINN. L. REV. 529, 572 (1994). In short, the crimes chosen appear to present the probative dangers inspiring the character evidence rules to a greater degree than crimes still subject to the character evidence prohibition. Both the United States Judicial Conference and the A.B.A. House of Delegates went on record as opposing the promulgation of Rules 413–14.

2. On the other hand, it is arguable that the very gravity of these offenses makes them appropriate choices. Assuming that the character rules might give a recidivist pause before he or she commits another crime, we unquestionably should attempt to deter repeat rapists and child molesters. Prior to the adoption of the Federal Rules, many states recognized a "lustful disposition" exception to the character evidence prohibition. Reed, *Reading Gaol Revisited: Admission of Uncharged Misconduct Evidence in Sex Offender Cases*, 21 AM. J. CRIM. L. 127 (1993). Further, there is a particularly powerful argument for the admission of evidence of the defendant's character in date or acquaintance rape cases:

> If two other women . . . accuse [the defendant] of date rape, he may be able to raise . . . doubts about each of their individual accounts . . . . If one considers all three accusations together, however, and no reason exists to suspect collaboration among the accusers, each of the charges will corroborate the others' to a much greater degree than in cases involving eyewitness identifications derived from "mugshot books" of rapists. Although it remains conceivable that the defendant is innocent of the crime charged, the danger of an erroneous conviction appears to be less in this sort of case than in many ordinary criminal trials.

Bryden & Park, *supra*, at 577. Arizona, California, Illinois, Indiana, and Missouri have followed the lead of the federal drafters and carved out exceptions to the character evidence prohibition in child molest cases. *See e.g.*, CAL. EVID. CODE § 1108–09; IND. STAT. ANN.§ 35–37–4–15; MO. REV. STAT. § 566.025. Similar legislation is under serious consideration in other states.

With one exception, the courts have uniformly upheld the constitutionality of these new statutes. *United States v. Mound*, 149 F.3d 799 (8th Cir. 1998), *cert. denied*, 525 U.S. 1089 (1999); *People v. Brown*, 77 Cal.App.4th 1324, 92 Cal. Rptr.2d 433 (2000); *People v. Hoover*, 77 Cal.App.4th 1020, 92 Cal.Rptr.2d 208 (2000); *People v. Falsetta*, 21 Cal.4th 903, 983 P.2d 182, 89 Cal.Rptr.2d 847 (1999); *United States v. Wright*, 48 M.J. 896 (A.F.C.C.A. 1998). The solitary exception is *State v. Burns*, 978 S.W.2d 759 (Mo. 1998). There the court premised its decision on §§ 17 and 18(a) of Article I of the Missouri Constitution. In prior cases, the Missouri courts had held that those provisions forbade the receipt of testimony about uncharged crimes not "properly related to the cause on trial." However, even the *Burns* decision may be of limited precedential value. The *Burns* court emphasized that it read the state statute as providing for mandatory admission of propensity evidence; as the appellate court interpreted the statute, the trial judge had no discretion comparable to a federal judge's discretion under Rule 403. To date, the lower federal courts have ruled that trial judges retain their Rule 403 discretion to exclude evidence otherwise admissible under Rules 413–15. *United States v. Meacham*, 115 F.3d 1488, 1492 (10th Cir. 1997); *United States v. Larson*, 112 F.3d 600 (2d Cir. 1997); *United States v. Guardia*, 955 F.Supp. 115 (D.N.M. 1997), *aff'd*, 135 D.3d 1326 (10th Cir. 1998).

2) What Methods of Proof Are Permissible?

The Traditional View—Only Reputation and Opinion

Since the defendant has the election to open up the issue of his or her character under the traditional view, we shall initially consider defense character evidence and then turn to the restrictions on prosecution rebuttal.

Defense evidence. Consider the direct testimony by the defense character witness. In the inquest following the famous shootout at the O.K. Corral, Wyatt Earp filed an affidavit signed by several leading citizens of Dodge City. In part, the affidavit read:

> We, the undersigned citizens of Dodge City, . . . Kansas, . . . certify that we are personally acquainted with Wyatt Earp, late of this city; that he came here in 1876; that during the years of 1877, 1878, and 1879, he was Marshal of our city; that he left our place in the fall of 1879; that during his whole stay here he . . . was regarded and looked upon as a high–minded, honorable citizen; and while kind and courteous to all, he was brave, unflinching, and on all occasions proved himself the right man in the right place. Hearing that he is now under arrest, charged with . . . the killing of those men termed "Cow Boys," from our knowledge of him we do not believe that he would wantonly take the life of his fellow men, and that if he was implicated, he only took life in the discharge of his sacred trust to the people . . . .

The affidavit is mix of reputation and opinion. The affidavit was a product of the common law. The classic article analyzing the common law was written by Professor Carlson's late coauthor, Dean Mason Ladd. Ladd, *Techniques and Theory of Character Testimony*, 24 Iowa L. Rev. 498 (1939).

To begin with, Dean Ladd noted that when the proponent is using character as circumstantial proof of conduct on the historical merits of the case, the common law did not authorize the proponent to introduce specific acts proving the existence of character. The common law rationale was the fear that if "the law were to permit proof of the bad acts [and then] allow those be countered by showing the good deeds . . ., all trials would become burdened with confusion and be endlessly prolonged." That fear, of course, is a consideration cognizable under both the common law legal irrelevance doctrine and Federal Rule of Evidence 403.

Next, Dean Ladd pointed out that the traditional, common law view also excluded evidence of opinion as to the person's character or character traits. Dean Ladd joined Dean Wigmore in criticizing the exclusion of opinion evidence. Dean Ladd argued that while it could be highly probative of character, opinion testimony presented less risk of undue time consumption than evidence of specific acts. He contended that in many reported cases, opinion testimony had been admitted as thinly disguised reputation. He noted — and applauded — an incipient trend toward explicitly permitting the admission of opinion testimony about character.

Lastly, Dean Ladd acknowledged the common law rule that testimony about reputation within the community was the only permissible method of establishing character. He described reputation as "the general concurrence of a great number of people reflecting the sentiment" about a person. In his judgment, as aggregate hearsay, reputation was less trustworthy than opinion testimony. Dean Ladd did approve, though, of the expansion of the concept of "community." The original understanding was that the community was the local neighborhood. Dean Ladd documented the evolution of the concept to include churches, lodges, police departments, and businesses.

Dean Ladd's article was influential in the drafting of the Federal Rules of Evidence 404–05 governing character evidence. Cleary, *Mason Ladd*, 66 Iowa L. Rev. 701, 702–08 (1981). The traditional common law ban on specific instances of conduct remained firm in those provisions. According to the Advisory Committee's Note, Federal Rule 405 implicitly codifies the prohibition. Not only is a character witness forbidden from testifying directly to specific acts; a character witness testifying to an opinion may not even cite specific instances of conduct on direct examination for the limited purpose of showing the basis of the opinion. However, as Dean Ladd urged in his article, the restrictions on reputation and opinion were relaxed. For one thing, in the context of reputation evidence, the courts were permitted to continue expanding the meaning of "community." The courts have gradually broadened the meaning of the term to include any substantial social group in which the person is likely to have a settled reputation. *United States v. Mandel*, 591 F.2d 1347 (4th Cir. 1979) (a particular law office can constitute a community); *O'Bryan v. State*, 591 S.W.2d 464 (Tex. Crim. App. 1979) (community includes business circle); *Freeman v. State*, 132 Ga. App. 742, 209 S.E.2d 127, 130–31 (1974) (church congregation). Further, the clear majority of jurisdictions now admit opinion evidence.

NOTES AND PROBLEMS

1. Problem 14–3. In *Devitt*, the defendant is a student at a university and offers evidence of his campus reputation. Would that be admissible? *United*

States v. Oliver, 492 F.2d 943, 945–47 (8th Cir. 1973), *cert. denied*, 424 U.S. 973 (1976). What additional facts would you like to know? Would it be relevant that Devitt was a senior rather than a freshman? Would it be helpful to know the size of the student body?

2. Problem 14–4. Trial attorneys have refined laying the foundation for reputation testimony into a well–accepted ritual. Creech, *Adducing Proof of Character or Reputation: A Precise Methodology*, CASE & COM. 32 (July–August 1975). If you had a witness prepared to testify to Devitt's reputation for peacefulness in El Dorado, what foundational questions would you have to ask?

3. Problem 14–5. If you were going to present favorable opinion testimony about Devitt, what foundation would you have to lay? How does the reputation foundation differ from the opinion foundation? Does a reputation witness have to personally know the defendant? Must an opinion witness?

4. Should expert testimony regarding a person's character be admissible? *See People v. Stoll*, 49 Cal. 3d 1136, 783 P.2d 698, 265 Cal. Rptr. 111 (1989); Falknor & Steffen, *Evidence of Character: From the "Crucible of the Community" to the "Couch of the Psychiatrist,"* 102 U. PA. L. REV. 980, 987–90 (1954). *But see United States v. Webb*, 625 F.2d 709, 710–11 (5th Cir. 1980). If we concede the admissibility of lay opinion, does not logic compel that we admit expert testimony, as presumably more reliable? The Advisory Committee Note to Rule 405 alludes to "the opinion of [a] psychiatrist based upon examination and testing." However, the congressional hearings and committee reports do not reflect any realization that the adoption of Rule 405 would open the door to expert opinions or any appreciation of the special problems posed by expert opinions. 22 C. WRIGHT & K. GRAHAM, FEDERAL PRACTICE AND PROCEDURE: EVIDENCE § 5265, at 588–95 (1978).

5. Problem 14–6. Devitt himself testifies. On direct examination, the defense attorney attempts to elicit Devitt's testimony that he, Devitt, has never before been charged with or even arrested for a crime. The prosecutor objects that this "is an improper method of proving character." What ruling? *Compare Government of the Virgin Islands v. Grant*, 775 F.2d 508, 511–13 (3d Cir. 1985) *with United States v. Blackwell*, 853 F.2d 86, 87–88 (2d Cir. 1988). Is Devitt attempting to smuggle in evidence of specific good acts? *Grant* appears to be the prevailing view.

———

Prosecution evidence. After the defendant opens the issue, the prosecutor may rebut the defense evidence of good character. During the prosecution rebuttal, the prosecutor can respond in kind, that is, rebuttal testimony by adverse reputation and opinion witnesses. The courts generally apply the same rules to character evidence introduced during the prosecution rebuttal that they do to evidence admitted during the defense case–in–chief; prosecution reputation and opinion testimony must satisfy the same foundational requirements as defense evidence.

The slippery problem, though, is prosecution cross–examination of defense character witnesses. Even before calling bad character witnesses during its rebuttal, the prosecution can cross–examine the defense's good character witnesses during the defense case–in–chief. Until recently, the courts were preoccupied—some would say obsessed—with the form of the cross–examination questions. *Michelson, supra*, sanctioned "Have you heard . . . .?" cross–examination. For example, if Devitt's character witness testified on direct that Devitt had a good reputation for peacefulness, on cross–examination the prosecutor could ask about events inconsistent with such a reputation: "Have you heard that three years ago the defendant (committed a battery) (was arrested for a battery) (was indicted for a battery) (was convicted of a battery)?"

NOTES

1. What is the logical relevance of this inquiry? What is its impeachment value if the witness answers yes? How does that answer reflect on the soundness of the witness' standard for assessing good reputation? What is its impeachment value if the witness answers no? How does that answer reflect on the extent of the witness' knowledge of the defendant's reputation? What sort of limiting instruction should the judge give the jury? Who is being impeached—the defendant or the defense character witness?

As trial judge, would you permit the prosecutor to make the following closing argument if the character witness denied hearing the report?

> On cross–examination I asked Mr. Stacey, the defendant's character witness, whether he'd heard that three years ago the defendant was convicted of a battery. Mr. Stacey answered that he'd never heard such a report. Think about that answer. Mr. Stacey expects you to believe that he knows the defendant's reputation for peacefulness well, but he's never heard a report about a battery conviction three years ago. A battery is a violent crime. A battery is just plain inconsistent with the defendant's supposedly peaceful reputation. Yet Stacey claims that he never heard of the report. That answer tells you that Stacey really doesn't know the defendant's reputation. If he knew the defendant's reputation as well as he claims, he certainly would have heard that report.

Would you allow the following closing argument if the character witness admitted hearing the report?

> Think about that answer. On the one hand, Stacey testifies that the defendant has a good reputation for peacefulness, and he expects you to believe that he–Stacey–is a good judge of character. On the other hand, he admits that he's heard that the defendant was convicted of battery a mere three years ago. Ladies and gentlemen, Mr. Stacey must have a pretty strange standard for deciding whether someone has a good reputation for peacefulness. When a person is reported to have been convicted of a battery, most reasonable people would say that that person has a terrible reputation for peacefulness. But not Mr. Stacey. Either he has a weird standard for judging character, or he's simply a biased witness. In either case, you just can't trust Stacey's testimony.

2. At early common law, just as the courts uniformly sustained the "Have you heard . . .?" form of cross–examination, they almost unanimously condemned the "Do you know . . .?" form. At first blush, this might seem to be a nonsensical distinction. However, remember that these courts were beginning with a premise that the only proper form of direct examination was reputation testimony. Is the "Have you heard . . .?" form in some sense a corollary of the reputation form of direct examination? Modernly, as the courts have begun to accept opinion direct examination, they have also begun to sanction the "Do you know . . .?" form of cross–examination. Gaffney & Cohen, *The New Practice in Cross–Examination of a Character Witness Under Arizona Rule of Evidence 405(a)*, 1978 ARIZ. ST. L.J. 31.

3. What position do the Federal Rules take on the proper form of the prosecutor's questions on cross–examination? Consider both the last sentence in Rule 405(a) and this paragraph in the Advisory Committee's Note:

> According to the great majority of cases, on cross–examination inquiry is allowable as to whether the reputation witness has heard of particular instances of conduct pertinent to the trait in question. *Michelson v. United States*, 335 U.S. 469 (1948); Annot., 47 A.L.R.2d 1258. The theory is that, since the reputation witness relates what he has heard, the inquiry tends to shed light on the accuracy of his hearing and reporting. Accordingly, the opinion witness would be asked whether he knew, as well as whether he had heard. The fact is, of course, that these distinctions are of slight if any practical significance, and the second sentence of subdivision (a) eliminates them as a factor in formulating questions. This recognition of the propriety of inquiring into specific instances of conduct does not circumscribe inquiry otherwise into the bases of opinion and reputation testimony.

4. This line of inquiry can be so prejudicial that in addition to the form limitations, there are significant procedural restrictions on this type of cross–examination. The prosecutor must have a good faith basis in fact for asking the question. *State v. Johnson*, 389 So. 2d 372, 376 (La. 1980); *State v. Steensen*, 35 N.J. Super. 103, 113 A.2d 203, 205–06 (1955). For example, the prosecution might have a police report or eyewitness statement describing the act. The information constituting the basis for believing that the defendant committed the act need not be independently admissible under the technical rules of evidence. However, if the defense objects to the line of inquiry, at sidebar the prosecutor should be prepared to both describe the information and insert any pertinent documents into the record.

The FRE Approach: Rules 413–14—Specific Acts

As previously stated, in sexual assault and child molest cases, Rules 413–14 no longer accord the defendant the right to decide whether his or her character may be used as circumstantial proof of conduct. The rules depart from tradition in another respect. The preceding paragraphs point out that under the traditional view, both defense and prosecution are typically restricted to reputation and opinion testimony. Refer back to the language of subdivision

(a) of Rules 413 and 414 set forth above. Note that Rules 413–14 expressly permit the admission of testimony about specific acts.

NOTES

1. Do the rules also permit the admission of testimony about reputation and opinion? At the very least should Congress have amended Rule 405 at the same time it approved these rules?

2. Assume *arguendo* that the rules do not authorize the admission of either reputation or opinion. On that assumption, the rules introduce a peculiar asymmetry into character evidence law. When the defendant's character is being used as circumstantial proof of the commission of a sexual assault or a child molestation, the only permissible method of proof is evidence of specific acts. However, under Rules 404–05 when the defendant's character is employed as circumstantial evidence of the perpetration of any other type of crime, the only authorized means are reputation and opinion. Does that distinction make sense?

b. Circumstantial Character Evidence in Civil Cases

The Traditional View

Most courts ban the circumstantial use of character evidence in civil cases. However, a substantial minority of courts will admit character evidence in civil cases with criminal overtones such as assault actions. Annot., 91 A.L.R.3d 718 (1979). These courts reason that the position of a civil defendant who is alleged to have committed an assault is analogous to that of a criminal defendant and, for that reason, the civil defendant should similarly be allowed to use character as circumstantial proof of conduct. Can you justify the majority view? Why differentiate so markedly between criminal and civil cases? Does the probative value of the evidence mysteriously disappear simply because it is offered in a civil case? Is the danger of distraction greater in a civil case? Why give the criminal defendant, to use a common expression, "a special dispensation"?

NOTES

Most courts construe Federal Rules 404–05 as generally precluding the circumstantial use of character evidence in civil cases. *Ginter v. Northwestern Mut. Ins. Co.*, 576 F. Supp. 627, 628 (E.D. Ky. 1984). However, a handful of federal courts have taken the contrary view "when the central issue involved in a civil case is in nature criminal . . . ." *Perrin v. Anderson*, 784 F.2d 1040, 1044 (10th Cir. 1986); *Bolton v. Tesoro Petr. Corp.*, 871 F.2d 1266, 1277–78 (5th Cir.) (in a securities fraud action, a party offered character testimony by former President Gerald Ford; the court commented that "[s]uch evidence can be admissible in a civil trial raising quasi–criminal allegations against a defendant"), *cert. denied*, 110 S. Ct. 83 (1989). Consider the problem as a question of statutory construction. Read Rules 401, 402, and 404(a). Which interpretation of the Rules is sounder? Remember the *expressio unius* maxim of interpretation. Focus in particular on the phrasing of Rule 404(a)(1). That section refers to "an accused" rather than "a defendant." Which expression more clearly connotes a criminal proceeding, "an accused" or "a defendant"?

The FRE Approach: Rule 415

Federal Rule of Evidence 415. Evidence of Similar Acts in Civil Cases Concerning Sexual Assault or Child Molestation.

> (a) In a civil case in which a claim for damages or other relief is predicated on a party's alleged commission of conduct constituting an offense of sexual assault or child molestation, evidence of that party's commission of another offense or offenses of sexual assault or child molestation is admissible and may be considered as provided in Rule 413 and Rule 414 of these rules. . . .

Congress approved Rule 415 in the same bill which promulgated Federal Rules 413–14. How does Rule 415 change the state of the law? Under this statute, does either party have the power to "veto" the use of character reasoning? When the statute comes into play, are the parties restricted to reputation and opinion evidence? For that matter, would reputation or opinion even be admissible under Rule 415?

3. CHARACTER AS CIRCUMSTANTIAL EVIDENCE OF THE CONDUCT OF A NON–PARTY

Although mentioned in the indictment or information, the victim is not a formal party in a prosecution. In most instances, the common law prohibits the introduction of evidence regarding the character of non–parties. The only two recognized exceptions are the victims of violent offenses and sex crimes.

a. The Victims of Violent Crime

It is critical to realize that sometimes the defense can rationalize the introduction of evidence of the alleged victim's violent character without arguing that the evidence is circumstantial proof that the alleged victim in fact began the fight, that is, was the aggressor. Suppose that the defendant claims self–defense. The subjective element of self–defense is the defendant's reasonable belief that he or she is about to be attacked. Assume that the alleged victim not only had committed violent acts in the past but, moreover, the defendant knew of the acts before the fight between the two. The defendant need not offer evidence of the alleged victim's acts as circumstantial character evidence, that is, to increase the likelihood that the alleged victim threw the first punch. There is an entirely alternative theory of logical relevance. What is that theory? See Martinez v. Wainwright, 621 F.2d 184, 188 (5th Cir. 1980). However, if the defendant did not know of the acts before the encounter with the alleged victim, the defendant would then be forced to resort to a character theory. In reviewing that theory, think back to the two recurring questions: When is it legitimate to use character evidence, and how may you prove character?

1) When Is Proof of the Victim's Violent Character Admissible as Circumstantial Evidence of the Victim's Conduct?

When we decide that the only tenable theory of logical relevance is circumstantial evidence of conduct, we must reach this question. The rules are roughly parallel to the rules for the introduction of evidence of the defendant's own character. In both settings, the defendant may open the issue. Thus, Federal Rule of Evidence 404(a)(2) permits the defendant to attack the "character trait of peacefulness of the victim." Once the defendant has done so, the prosecution can rejoin with evidence of the victim's peacefulness. Moreover, under the December 1, 2000 amendment to Rule 404(a)(1), once the defendant has done so, the prosecution may introduce "evidence of the same trait of character of the accused. . ." The accompanying Advisory Committee Note states that "[t]he amendment makes clear that the accused cannot attack the alleged victim's character and yet remain unshielded from the disclosure of equally relevant evidence concerning the same character trait of the accused."

Furthermore, under Rule 404(a)(2), in a homicide case the prosecution need not wait until the defense first attacks the victim's character. Under that Rule, it is sufficient that the defense has offered any type of "evidence that the [alleged] victim was the first aggressor." It suffices that the defendant or any defense witness testifies that the alleged victim threw the first punch. Many states have taken a contrary view and admit prosecution character evidence only if the defense attacks the alleged victim's character.

2) What Methods of Proof Are Available?

Here the courts are badly divided. We have seen that there are three conceivable methods of proving character: reputation, opinion, and specific instances of conduct. Some courts permit the use of the same methods usable to prove the defendant's character. Depending on the jurisdiction's normal character rules, these courts permit the proponent to resort to only reputation or reputation and opinion. These courts forbid the use of specific instances of the victim's conduct. In contrast, other courts go to the extreme of permitting proof of specific instances of the victim's violent character. Still other courts will admit proof of specific prior violent acts only if they were directed at the defendant. *State v. Black*, 587 S.W.2d 865 (Mo. Ct. App. 1979). In the view of these courts, acts directed at the defendant have far greater probative value than acts committed against third parties.

NOTES

1. Why does this sort of evidence pose a legal irrelevance problem? How great is the risk that the jury will decide the case on an improper basis? If the jury hears enough evidence of the alleged victim's violent character, might they not subconsciously begin to think that the victim was such a vile person that "he deserved what he got"? The jury might be tempted to, in effect, nullify the substantive law of homicide.

2. Which position do you prefer: (1) the traditional view that the prosecutor may prove up the alleged victim's peaceful character only after the defendant makes a frontal assault on the victim's character, or (2) Rule 404(a)(2)'s provision allowing the prosecutor to introduce evidence of the victim's good character whenever in a homicide case the defense contends that the alleged victim began the affray? Is this evidence likely to bog the jury down on collateral issues? Why is the Rule limited to homicide cases? Does that limitation suggest any special need for the evidence?

b. The Victims of Sexual Crimes

When we study credibility evidence, we will see that some jurisdictions still admit evidence of a complainant's promiscuous conduct on the tenuous theory that such conduct impeaches the complainant's credibility. Our focus here is conceptually very different: here the defendant wants to introduce evidence of the complainant's past consensual intercourse in order to invite the inference that she consented to intercourse with the defendant. In effect, the defendant is attempting to use the complainant's character as circumstantial proof of her conduct on a particular occasion.

Until recently, many courts throughout the United States routinely permitted the defendant to introduce evidence of the complainant's reputation for unchastity and specific sexual acts. Annot., 95 A.L.R.3d 1181 (1979); Annot., 94 A.L.R.3d 257 (1979). Change the facts in the *Devitt* case; suppose that it was Mr. Paterson's daughter—rather than Paterson himself—who walked in on Devitt burglarizing the apartment. Ms. Paterson claims that after she confronted Devitt, he attacked and raped her. Devitt is now charged with raping Ms. Paterson rather than battering Mr. Paterson. In a rape prosecution, in the past courts might well have admitted a psychiatrist's testimony that Ms. Paterson is a nymphomaniac constantly fantasizing about sexual attacks. As originally written, Federal Rule 404(a)(2) seemed generally to sanction the continuation of the practice of liberal admission of evidence of unchastity.

However, with the advance of the feminist movement and the growing awareness of the seriousness of the problem of rape in the United States and the deterrent on victims to testify, more and more jurisdictions abandoned the old view. In some cases, the courts adopted restrictions on evidence of the complainant's specific sexual acts by decisional rule. *State v. Mastropetre*, 400 A.2d 276 (Conn. 1978). Similarly, by case law some courts limited the admissibility of evidence of the complainant's unchaste reputation. *McLean v. United States*, 377 A.2d 74 (D.C. Ct. App. 1977). These courts reason that since the rules liberally admitting the evidence were fashioned by case law, they can and should be changed by case law. In other jurisdictions, the legislatures pressed the reform and enacted so–called "rape shield" laws. The same reform movement led to the adoption of Federal Rule of Evidence 412:

Federal Rule of Evidence 412. Sex Offense Cases; Relevance of Alleged Victim's Past Sexual Behavior or Alleged Sexual Predisposition.

(a) Evidence generally inadmissible. The following evidence is not admissible in any civil or criminal proceeding involving alleged sexual misconduct except as provided in subdivisions (b) and (c):

(1) Evidence offered to prove that any alleged victim engaged in other sexual behavior;

(2) Evidence offered to prove any alleged victim's sexual predisposition.

(b) Exceptions.

(1) In a criminal case, the following evidence is admissible, if otherwise admissible under these rules:

(A) evidence of specific instances of sexual behavior by the alleged victim offered to prove that a person other than the accused was the source of semen, injury or other physical evidence;

(B) evidence of specific instances of sexual behavior by the alleged victim with respect to the person accused of the sexual misconduct offered by the accused to prove consent or by the prosecution; and

(C) evidence the exclusion of which would violate the constitutional rights of the defendant.

(2) In a civil case, evidence offered to prove the sexual behavior or sexual predisposition of any alleged victim is admissible if it is otherwise admissible under these rules and its probative value substantially outweighs the danger of harm to any victim and of unfair prejudice to any party. Evidence of an alleged victim's reputation is admissible only if it has been placed in controversy by the alleged victim. . . .

NOTES AND PROBLEMS

1. Realistically, does legal irrelevance analysis alone account for the enactment of rape shield laws within the past few years? Is this area of evidence law being transformed into one dominated by extrinsic social policy rather than legal irrelevance analysis? In late 1994, Congress approved the current version of Rule 412 in the same package of legislation which included new Rules 413–15. The current version extends Rule 412 to civil actions and more types of prosecutions. The approval of Rules 413–15 was driven in part by Congress' belief that the new rules would contribute to the national campaign against rape, and the inclusion of the expanded version of Rule 412 in the same bill suggests that the rape shield law is justified by similar policies.

2. Problem 14–7. In *Devitt,* the defense wants to offer evidence that three months before the alleged rape, the defendant and Ms. Paterson met at a disco in downtown Morena. The defendant is prepared to testify that they went to his apartment that night and had consensual intercourse there. Is that evidence admissible under Federal Rule of Evidence 412? Which provision controls?

3. Problem 14–8. Devitt offers the testimony of Mr. Bruce Langley. Langley is prepared to testify that he met Ms. Paterson at a party the night before the alleged rape. At the time, she told him that she was depressed because she had just broken up with her boyfriend; they went to his apartment and had consensual intercourse there. Again, which provision in Rule 412 governs?

4. Why does this type of evidence pose a legal irrelevance problem? Suppose that we liberally admit evidence of Ms. Paterson's nonmarital intercourse. As in the case of evidence of the violent character of alleged victims of forcible offenses, is the fear that the jury may acquit a rapist on an improper basis?

5. Rule 412(b)(2) prescribes a balancing test. How does that test compare to the test under Rule 403? *See Rodriguez–Hernandez v. Miranda–Velez*, 132 F.3d 848, 856 (1st Cir. 1998) ("Rule 412 . . . reverses the usual approach of the Federal Rules of Evidence on admissibility by requiring that the evidence's probative value 'substantially outweigh' its prejudicial effect").

B. HABIT OR ROUTINE PRACTICE

Proof of a person's habit can be used as direct or circumstantial evidence of the person's conduct. Direct use is rare, but in occasional cases a person's habit can become a material fact of consequence in the case under Rule 401. Evidence of the habit is then directly relevant. However, as in the case of character evidence, in most cases the proponent uses proof of a person's habit as circumstantial proof of the person's conduct on a particular occasion.

1. THE DIFFERENCE BETWEEN CHARACTER AND HABIT EVIDENCE

There are major differences between the concept of a habit and the concept of character—conceptual differences that in turn account for differences in the evidentiary rules governing habit and character. Character is a generalized concept; we are referring to character when we say that a person is "a good, moral, law–abiding individual," and even the description of the person as "a good driver" is a statement of a character trait. A habit is a different "beastie." Perhaps the most insightful exposition of the concept appears in the Advisory Committee's Note to Federal Rule of Evidence 406:

> An oft–quoted paragraph, MCCORMICK § 162, p. 340, describes habit in terms effectively contrasting it with character:
>
>> "Character and habit are close akin. Character is a generalized description of one's disposition, or of one's disposition in respect to a general trait, such as honesty, temperance, or peacefulness. "Habit," in modern usage, both lay and psychological, is more specific. It describes one's regular response to a repeated specific situation. If we speak of character for care, we think of the person's tendency to act prudently in all the varying situations of life, in business, in family life, in handling automobiles and in walking across the street. A habit, on the other hand, is the person's regular practice of meeting a particular kind of situation with a specific type of conduct, such as the habit of going down a

particular stairway two stairs at a time, or of giving the hand–signal for a left turn, or of alighting from railway cars while they are moving. The doing of the habitual acts may become semi–automatic."

Equivalent behavior on the part of a group is designated "routine practice of an organization" in the rule.

There is general agreement that habit evidence is highly persuasive as proof of conduct on a particular occasion. Again quoting McCor-mick § 152, p. 341:

> "Character may be thought of as the sum of one's habits though doubtless it is more than this. But unquestionably the uniformity of one's response to habit is far greater than the consistency with which one's conduct conforms to character or disposition. Even though character comes in only exceptionally as evidence of an act, surely any sensible man in investigating whether X did a particular act would be greatly helped in this inquiry by evidence as to whether he was in the habit of doing it."

In short, the proffered testimony would attain the status of habit only if the testimony relates to a specific, repeated behavioral pattern—only, for instance, if the witness were to testify that on numerous occasions the witness saw the person execute a right–hand turn in a particular fashion and the issue is whether the person, the defendant, executed a right–hand turn in that particular, careful fashion at the time in question. There must be a high reaction–to–situation ratio: On all or substantially all the occasions on which the person finds herself in the same situation, she follows the same, particul-ized behavioral pattern. *Mobil Exploration v. Cajun Const. Services*, 45 F.3d 96, 99–100 (5th Cir. 1995). Given the specificity and repetition of a behavioral pattern qualifying as a habit, habit has more probative value than character. On that assumption, the legal irrelevance limitations on habit evidence should be—and indeed are—laxer than the restrictions on character evidence.

This definition of "habit," requiring proof of only a repetitive, specific behavioral pattern, is sometimes termed the "probability theory." Mengler, *The Theory of Discretion in the Federal Rules of Evidence*, 74 Iowa L. Rev. 413, 417 (1989). The above quotation from the Advisory Committee Note to Rule 406 certainly lends support to that theory.

There is, however, a competing definition—the so–called "psychological theory." *Id.* Like the probability theory, this theory requires that the propo-nent of alleged habit evidence prove that the evidence relates to a frequently repeated, specific behavioral pattern. However, the psychological theory imposes a further restriction; this theory limits the definition to conduct which is "unconsciously mechanical—Pavlovian." *Id.* Mengler explains:

> [O]n this psychological theory, the routine practice of reading a novel before going to bed, while customary, could not be habitual because it is volitional. In contrast, the regular practice of turning the pages of the novel with one's left hand could be habitual because of its mechanical or automatic nature.

Id. This theory also finds support in the Advisory Committee Note to Rule 406 which cites *Levin v. United States*, 338 F.2d 265 (D.C. Cir. 1964), *cert. denied*, 379 U.S. 999 (1965). That case excluded testimony offered as habit for the stated reason that "the very volitional basis of the activity raises serious questions as to its invariable nature." *Id.* at 272. Many lower courts subscribe to this theory. *Becker v. ARCO Chemical Co.*, 207 F.3d 176, 204 (3d Cir. 2000) (semi–automatic, situation–specific); *Gamberdinger v. Schaefer,* 603 N.W.2d 590 (Iowa 1999) (invariable); *Washington St. Physicians Ins. v. Fisons Corp.*, 122 Wash.2d 299, 858 P.2d 1054 (1993) ("semi–automatic, almost involuntary and invariabl[y] specific responses to fairly specific stimuli").

NOTES

1. How can we explain the presence of passages supporting two, inconsistent definitions of "habit" in the Advisory Committee Note? Assume "the Note's facial incoherence was intended." Mengler, *supra*, at 423. The Committee disagreed over the definition of "habit," set out its disagreement in its Note, and invited the courts to resolve the issue.

The next question is which courts: the trial courts or the appellate courts? In a common law system, the answer would be the appellate courts. They would settle the definition as a question of law and then announce that rule as binding on the trial bench. However, Mengler argues forcefully that in the statutory scheme of the Federal Rules, the decision should be left to the trial courts on a case–by–case basis. Several factors support his argument. The habit provision rests largely on Rule 403 policy concerns. As we have seen, the trial judiciary exercises Rule 403 discretion on an ad hoc basis. Further-more, "a principal cause for the codification movement" was "skepticism about appellate decisionmaking." *Id.* at 423–24. Thus, like 403, Rule 406 may effect a shift in the balance of power between the trial and appellate courts.

2.   WHEN IS HABIT EVIDENCE ADMISSIBLE?

Federal Rule of Evidence 406 governs the admission of evidence of a person's habit (or an organization's routine practice). On its face, the Rule makes no distinction between criminal and civil cases. The prosecutor need not wait until the defendant places his or her habit in issue. Hence, there is a marked contrast between the habit norms announced in Rule 406 and the character norms we encountered in Rules 404 and 405. Rule 406 appears to authorize any litigant to use habit or routine practice as circumstantial proof of conduct. The proponent may simply argue that the existence of the habit or practice makes it more likely that the person acted consistently with the habit or routine on the occasion in question. *Hall v. Arthur*, 141 F. 3d 844 (8th Cir. 1998).

At common law, many jurisdictions admitting habit evidence imposed one of the following limitations on its admissibility. Some courts admit habit evi-dence only when corroborating evidence exists that the person acted consis-tently with the habit on the occasion in question. *State v. Wadsworth*, 210 So. 2d 4 (Fla. 1968). A second common restriction is that habit evidence is admissible only when there is an exceptional need for circumstantial evidence of conduct, namely, when there are no eyewitnesses. Snell, *Eyeing the Iowa No Eyewitness Rule*, 43 IOWA L. REV. 57 (1957). Does Rule 406 preserve those limitations?

3.   WHAT METHODS OF PROOF ARE ADMISSIBLE?

There are two recognized methods of proving the existence of a person's habit or an organization's custom: specific instances and opinion. The original draft of Federal Rule 406 set forth both methods: "Habit or routine practice may be proved by testimony in the form of an opinion or by specific instances of conduct sufficient in number to warrant a finding that the habit existed or that the practice was routine." DRAFT FED. R. EVID. 406(b). Congress ultimately deleted section (b), deciding to leave it up to the courts to deal with on a case–by–case basis.

NOTES AND PROBLEMS

1. Problem 14–9. In the *Hill* case, one count in the plaintiff's complaint alleges that Polecat Motors was guilty of negligent manufacture. Polecat wants to show that its quality control procedures would have caught the defect if it existed in the product at the time of manufacture. The head of quality control is prepared to testify that the safety checks include a check for leaks in the gas tank, one of the defects that allegedly caused the injury in this case; she trains all the defendant's quality control inspectors to conduct that test before the product leaves the assembly line; and she has personally seen the inspectors conduct that test "thousands of times." Will her testimony qualify as habit? Is it especially appropriate to rely on the probability theory when the issue is the conduct of an entity which can act only through natural persons? The courts tend to admit evidence of business customs more liberally than testimony about personal habits. "This may be because there is no confusion between character traits and business practices, as there is between character and [personal] habit, or it may reflect the belief that the need for regularity in business and the organizational sanctions which may exist when employees deviate from the established procedures give extra guarantees that the questioned activity followed the usual custom." 1 McCORMICK, EVIDENCE § 195, at 689 (5th ed. 1999).

2. Problem 14–10. Devitt wants to defend on an alibi theory. He is ready to testify that for the past "year or so, on Monday at 3:30 in the afternoon, I almost always stop by Ernie's Bar and Grill and hang around for about two hours." If he had done so, he would have been at the Bar and Grill rather than at the apartment when the battery occurred. Is the evidence of Devitt's customary visit to the bar admissible? *See Levin v. United States*, 338 F.2d 265, 272 (D.C. Cir. 1964), *cert. denied*, 379 U.S. 999 (1965).

C.   OTHER ACTS AND TRANSACTIONS

1.   INTRODUCTION

In the course of a criminal or civil action, it sometimes becomes logically relevant to prove an act by a party other than the acts giving rise to the claim or the crime charged. There is a substantial body of case and statutory law governing the admissibility of evidence of other acts.

In some respects, this body of law is remarkably similar to the character evidence law we just studied. The strongest common denominator is that the same legal irrelevance considerations underlie both bodies of law. Sometimes the other act the prosecutor wants to prove is another similar crime by the defendant. The introduction of proof of that act may convince some of the jurors that the defendant is an habitual criminal who deserves to be imprisoned, whether or not the defendant is guilty of the charged crime. Moreover, to the extent that we condone the proof of separate acts and events, we run the risk of distracting and confusing the jurors—another probative danger recognized in Rule 403.

Although there are important similarities, there are also radical differences between character evidence and evidence of other acts. Two differences should be underscored. First, unless Rule 413, 414, or 415 applies, other acts evidence must be offered on an entirely different theory of logical relevance than character evidence. While character evidence may sometimes be offered as circumstantial proof of the conduct of a person (*i.e.*, that the person acted in conformity with the character trait, disposition, or propensity), "other acts" evidence may *never* be offered on that theory of relevance (unless the facts trigger Rule 413, 414, or 415). In sum, other acts evidence must have "special" or "independent" logical relevance—other than a character theory. *United States v. Forgoine*, 487 F.2d 364, 366 (1st Cir. 1973), *cert. denied*, 415 U.S. 976 (1974), a pre–Federal Rules decision, refers to the "elementary" doctrine that other acts evidence must have "independent relevancy." Federal Rule of Evidence 404(b) codifies the doctrinal requirement for a showing of such *noncharacter* relevance.

Second, the method of proof of other acts evidence differs from the method of proof for character evidence. When the proponent of character evidence offers it as circumstantial proof of a party's conduct, the proponent is usually restricted to reputation or opinion. The proponent cannot introduce evidence of specific acts. The rules for other acts evidence are the mirror image. Affirmatively, the proponent of other acts evidence may and must prove a specific act, namely, the other act. Negatively, unless Rule 413, 414, or 415 applies, the proponent may not resort to reputation or opinion.

We turn now to a more detailed analysis of other acts evidence, first the common law in criminal prosecutions, next the law in civil actions, and finally a comparison between the two bodies of law. Throughout this chapter we shall encounter empirical evidence that other acts evidence can have a potent impact on the trier of fact. Common sense and empirical data suggest that the courts should be more cautious admitting evidence of other crimes in prosecutions than in admitting evidence of other non–criminal misconduct in civil actions. Yet a survey of the case law both at common law and under the Federal Rules demonstrates that the courts admit similar acts evidence more liberally in criminal cases. In attempting to determine whether that relative liberality is justified, we shall attempt to refine our understanding of the relationship between Rules 403 and 404.

2. OTHER ACTS EVIDENCE IN CRIMINAL CASES

Federal Evidence Rule 404(b) sets out the governing standard for criminal cases. While many of the cases and commentaries refer to this species of proof as "similar crimes" evidence, that title is inaccurate. The crime need not be similar to the crime charged to have independent logical relevance and be admissible under 404(b). For instance, many courts now admit proof of the defendant's narcotics addiction to prove the defendant's motive to commit a charged robbery. *United States v. Parker*, 549 F.2d 1217 (9th Cir. 1977), *cert. denied*, 430 U.S. 971; *United States v. Lee*, 509 F.2d 400 (D.C. Cir. 1974), *cert. denied*, 420 U.S. 1006 (1975).

Moreover, there is no necessity that the act be a crime at all. Consider this hypothetical. The defendant is charged with murdering his mistress' husband. The prosecution may offer evidence of the defendant's intercourse with the decedent's wife; the evidence is indisputably logically relevant to prove the defendant's motive to commit the murder. The evidence would be admissible whether or not adultery was a crime in the jurisdiction. The act is not admissible because it is a crime; the act is admissible because of its independent logical relevance and in spite of the fact that it is prejudicial evidence of a crime. *United States v. Beechum*, 555 F.2d 487 (5th Cir. 1977), *cert. denied*, 440 U.S. 920 (1979). In this text, we shall use the expression, "uncharged misconduct" to refer to any misconduct other than that for which the defendant is currently on trial.

This topic is of enormous importance. In many jurisdictions, alleged errors in the admission of uncharged misconduct are the most frequent ground for appeal in criminal cases. 22 C. WRIGHT & K. GRAHAM, FEDERAL PRACTICE AND PROCEDURE: EVIDENCE § 5239 (1978). Moreover, in some jurisdictions errors in the admission of such evidence are the most common ground for reversal. Casenote, 1978 ARIZ. ST. L.J. 153, 156. The Federal Rule of Evidence in point, Rule 404(b), has generated more reported cases than any other subsection of the rules. 2 J. WEINSTEIN & M. BERGER, WEINSTEIN'S EVIDENCE ¶404[08] (1995). There are so many reported cases because prosecutors offer uncharged misconduct evidence so frequently, and in turn they offer it so frequently because they appreciate how potent the evidence is.

a. The Independent Logical Relevance Requirement

As prefaced, unless Rule 413, 414, or 415 comes into play, the key task facing the proponent of uncharged misconduct evidence is articulating a noncharacter theory of logical relevance. The early American view was that uncharged misconduct evidence was admissible in criminal cases so long as it was logically relevant to some fact of consequence other than the defendant's bad character. Stone, *The Rule of Exclusion of Similar Fact Evidence: America*, 51 HARV. L. REV. 988 (1938). However, in the 1840's the courts began developing the exclusionary doctrine that the evidence was admissible only if it was logically relevant on such well–recognized theories as motive, identity, and intent. *Id.*; *United States v. Long*, 574 F.2d 761 (3d Cir. 1978), *cert. denied*, 439 U.S. 985. The courts announced a rigid rule excluding uncharged misconduct evidence and treated such theories as motive and identity as pigeonhole "exceptions" to the norm. Note, *Developments in*

Evidence of Other Crimes, 7 U. MICH. J.L. REFORM 535, 536 (1974). These traditionalist courts conceived of the doctrine as an exclusionary norm with pigeonholed exceptions. Some even reduced the doctrine to a mnemonic: MIMIC ((M)otive—(I)ntent–negating—(M)istake or accident—(I)dentity—(C)ommon plan or scheme). Comment, 9 U. BALT. L. REV. 245, 266 (1980).

However, the exclusionary approach in criminal cases was subjected to withering criticism. Professor Amsterdam has written:

> It is often stated as a general rule of evidence that proof of a defendant's prior record and unrelated crimes is inadmissible; then a number of "exceptions" to the rule—use of other offenses to show identity, motive, common scheme, and so forth—are defined. This may be well and good if the trial judge believes it, but there is no such general rule. Prior record and unrelated crimes are inadmissible, like other facts, unless they are relevant. If relevant, they are admissible, and the so–called exceptions simply state several grounds of relevancy. The actual evidentiary principle . . . involved here [is that t]here is one specific purpose for which prior crime evidence may not be used; that is, to show that the defendant is an evil or a vicious person, as a basis for the further inference that s/he therefore is guilty of the present charge.

3 A. AMSTERDAM, TRIAL MANUAL FOR THE DEFENSE OF CRIMINAL CASES § 368, at 123 (5th ed. 1988). Professor Amsterdam's position is often termed "the inclusionary approach" to the admissibility of uncharged misconduct evidence. In part due to the widespread adoption of Federal Rule 404(b) and in part due to the influence of the *Woods* case, excerpted *infra*, the inclusionary approach is now the majority view in both state and federal court.

Under the inclusionary approach, the prosecutor may offer evidence of a defendant's uncharged crimes for any logically relevant purpose other than the purpose explicitly forbidden by the first sentence of Rule 404(b): "to prove the character of [the defendant] in order to show action in conformity therewith." Hence, if the facts support a theory of logical relevance other than the "verboten" one, the prosecutor may use the uncharged misconduct evidence to show the defendant's identity as the perpetrator of the charged crime or to prove the defendant's possession of the requisite *mens rea*.

By way of example, the following are some of the most commonly employed theories invoked by prosecutors to introduce uncharged misconduct to prove the defendant's identity:

> ***Modus operandi.*** One identity technique is to establish that the defendant committed another crime and that both that crime and the charged crime share a very distinctive *modus operandi*. The similarities between the crimes must be so great that they support an inference that the charged crime was the defendant's handiwork. *United States v. Park*, 525 F.2d 1279 (5th Cir. 1976). The *modus operandi* must be so unique that it serves as the defendant's "signature." *People v. Alvarez*, 44 Cal. App. 3d 375, 118 Cal. Rptr. 602 (1975).

> If the prosecution relied on this theory, the trial judge might give the jury the following limiting instruction: "Evidence has been

introduced for the purpose of showing that the defendant committed a crime other than the offense for which he is on trial. Even if you believe this evidence, you may not treat it as proof that the defendant is a person of bad character or that he has a disposition to commit crimes. You may consider the evidence only for the limited purpose of determining if it tends to show the identity of the person who committed the crime of which the defendant is accused."

If the judge gave the above limiting instruction, during closing agument the prosecutor would initially marshal the testimony indicating that the defendant perpetrated the uncharged crime. The prosecutor would then highlight all the points of similarity between the charged and uncharged offenses. Next, the prosecutor would tell the jury that the modus operandi of the two offenses was so distinctive that "common sense tells you that the same man committed both crimes." At this point the prosecutor would probably quote the judge's limiting instruction. The prosecutor could conclude by stating: Ladies and gentlemen, the same man commited the other robbery. Therefore, according to her Honor's instruction, you're entitled to conclude that the same man–this defendant–perpetrated the charged offense."

Consciousness of guilt. The defendant's post–arrest attempt to break jail or bribe a prosecution witness evinces a consciousness of guilt on the defendant's part. *United States v. Myers*, 550 F.2d 1036 (5th Cir. 1977).

The witness' prior familiarity with the defendant. If the witness identifies the defendant as the perpetrator, the witness' prior familiarity with the defendant shows that the identification is reliable. The prior observations of the defendant are admissible even when they were observations of the defendant committing other crimes. *United States v. Matthews*, 346 F. Supp. 861 (E.D. Pa. 1972).

Identity. The prosecution may prove another act of misconduct putting the defendant in possession of an instrument linked to the crime the defendant is now being tried for. For example, it would be relevant to show that the defendant stole the getaway car used in the charged bank robbery. *United States v. Waldron*, 568 F.2d 185 (10th Cir. 1977), *cert. denied*, 434 U.S. 1080 (1978).

Motive. Proof of the defendant's involvement in the Watergate break–in of a psychiatrist's office supplied the motive for his participation in the Watergate conspiracy. *United States v. Haldeman*, 559 F.2d 31 (D.C. Cir. 1976). Similarly, as previously stated, evidence of the defendant's addiction to expensive narcotics can supply the motive for the charged robbery. *United States v. Lee*, 509 F.2d 400 (D.C. Cir. 1974).

Plan. If the charged crime and other crimes appear to be part of a common plan, proof of the plan is admissible at the trial for the charged crime. Note, *Admissibility of Evidence Under Indiana's "Common Scheme or Plan" Exception*, 53 IND. L.J. 805 (1978). Suppose, for instance, that the defendant, one of the heirs to Greenacre, decides to gain title to Greenacre by murdering all the other heirs. The overall objective, gaining Greenacre, necessitates the commission of a number of crimes, all inspired by the objective. Proof of the overall plan tends to establish the defendant's guilt of the killing of any one of the other heirs.

There was substantial case authority for each of these theories at common law, and each theory remains tenable under Rule 404(b) as a means of proving the defendant's identity as the perpetrator.

Similarly, the prosecutor may offer uncharged misconduct evidence on noncharacter theories of logical relevance to establish the *mens rea* element required for the charged offense. Assume, for example, that the defendant is charged with knowing receipt of stolen goods. The court may allow the prosecutor to introduce evidence of the defendant's earlier receipt of other stolen property from the same transferor to strengthen the inference of guilty knowledge. *Lanier v. State*, 172 Tex. Crim. 238, 356 S.W.2d 671 (1962). A prior transaction with the same transferor under suspicious circumstances might put the defendant on notice that the transferor is a "fence," and that notice might lead the defendant to suspect that the other goods the same transferor later gave the defendant were stolen.

May the prosecutor employ uncharged misconduct evidence to establish that there was an *actus reus*? The court grapples with that question in the following case. The defendant was charged with infanticide. The defendant's foster son, Paul, died as a result of cyanosis, a condition caused by lack of oxygen. The defendant claimed that the death was an accident. The prosecution offered evidence that nine children in the defendant's custody had suffered a minimum of 20 cases of cyanosis. The prosecution offered the evidence to prove a corpus delicti, namely, that the death was due to an *actus reus* rather than natural accident. The trial judge admitted the evidence over objection; and on appeal the defendant correctly noted that this jurisdiction, the Fourth Circuit, had not previously approved of that use of uncharged misconduct evidence. Thus, the prosecution could not "pigeonhole" the evidence within a theory already recognized by the case law. (Note that the author of the opinion is Judge Winter, the former chair of the Advisory Committee on the Federal Rules of Evidence.)

UNITED STATES v. WOODS
484 F.2d 127 (4th Cir. 1973), *cert. denied*, 415 U.S. 979 (1974)

WINTER, CIRCUIT JUDGE.

The evidence of what happened to the other children was not, strictly speaking, evidence of other crimes. There was no evidence that defendant was an accused with respect to the deaths or respiratory difficulties of the other children, except for Judy. Simultaneously with her trial for crimes alleged against Paul, defendant was being tried for crimes alleged against Judy, but there was no direct proof of defendant's guilt and the district court ruled that the circumstantial evidence was insufficient for the government to have proved its case. Thus, with regard to no single child was there any legally sufficient proof that defendant had done any act which the law forbids. Only when all of the evidence concerning the nine other children and Paul is considered collectively is the conclusion impelled that the probability that some or all of the other deaths, cyanotic seizures, and respiratory deficiencies were accidental or attributable to natural causes was so remote, the truth must be that Paul and some or all of the other children died at the hands of the defendant. We think also that when the crime is one of infanticide or child abuse, evidence of repeated incidents is especially relevant because it may be the only evidence to prove the crime. A child of the age of Paul and of the others about whom evidence was received is a helpless, defenseless unit of human life. Such a child is too young, if he survives, to relate the facts concerning the attempt on his life, and too young, if he does not survive, to have exerted enough resistance that the marks of his cause of death will survive him. Absent the fortuitous presence of an eyewitness, infanticide or child abuse by suffocation would largely go unpunished. *See Minnesota v. Loss*, 295 Minn. 271, 204 N.W.2d 404 (1973).

Admissibility of Evidence Generally. The government and the defendant agree that evidence of other crimes is not admissible to prove that an accused is a bad person and therefore likely to have committed the crime in question. Indeed, the rule is beyond dispute: *Michelson v. United States*, 335 U.S. 469, 475–476, 69 S. Ct. 213, 93 L. Ed. 168 (1948). Defendant argues that while there are certain recognized exceptions to this rule, the instant case cannot be fitted into any of them, emphasizing that corpus delicti is not an exception. McCormick on Evidence § 190 (Cleary Ed. 1972). The government, in meeting this approach, contends that the evidence was admissible on the theory that it tended to prove (a) the existence of a continuing plan,[7] (b) the handiwork or signature exception,[8] (c) that the acts alleged in the indictment were not inadvertent, accidental, or unintentional, and (d) the defendant's identity as the perpetrator of the crime. We are inclined to agree with the defendant that the evidence was not admissible under the scheme or continuing plan exception because there was no evidence that defendant engaged in any scheme or plan, or, if so, the objective or motive. The evidence may have been admissible under the lack of accident exception, although ordinarily that exception is invoked only where an accused admits that he did the acts charged but denies the intent necessary to constitute a crime, or contends that he did the acts accidentally. McCormick, p. 450. However, in *State v. Lapage*, 57 N.H. 245, 294 (1876), there was dictum that under certain circumstances where several children of the same mother had died, evidence of the previous deaths ought to be admissible because of the unlikelihood of such deaths being accidental. Finally, the identity exception is not really an exception in its own right, but rather is spoken of as a supplementary purpose of another exception. McCormick, p. 451.

---

[7] *Makin v. Attorney General of New South Wales*, [1894] A.C. 57 (P.C. 1893) (N.S. Wales) and *Regina v. Roden*, 12 Cox Cr. 630 (1874) support this view. Makin was a prosecution for infanticide by a professional foster parent. Evidence that the bodies of twelve other infants, who had been entrusted to him with inadequate payment for their support, was held admissible. In *Roden*, a prosecution for infanticide by suffocation, evidence that three of defendant's other children died in her lap, was held admissible.

[8] *Rex v. George Joseph Smith*, [1914–15] All E.R. Rep. 262 ("Brides of Bath" case) and *People v. Peete*, 26 Cal. 2d 306, 169 P. 2d 924 (1946) permitted proof of unique methods of previous homicides to establish guilt of the accused.

The handiwork or signature exception is the one which appears most applicable, although defendant's argument that cyanosis among infants is too common to constitute an unusual and distinctive device unerringly pointing to guilt on her part would not be without force, were it not for the fact that so many children at defendant's mercy experienced this condition. In the defendant's case, the "commonness" of the condition is outweighed by its frequency under circumstances where only defendant could have been the precipitating factor.

While we conclude that the evidence was admissible generally under the accident and signature exceptions, we prefer to place our decision upon a broader ground. Simply fitting evidence of this nature into an exception heretofore recognized is, to our minds, too mechanistic an approach.

McCormick, in listing the instances in which evidence of other crimes may be admissible, cautions "that the list is not complete, for the range of relevancy outside the ban is almost infinite. . . ." *Id.* 448. And then, McCormick states:

> [S]ome of the wiser opinions (especially recent ones) recognize that the problem is not merely one of pigeonholing, but one of balancing, on the one side, the actual need for the other crimes evidence in the light of the issues and the other evidence available to the prosecution, the convincingness of the evidence that the other crimes were committed and that the accused was the actor, and the strength or weakness of the other crimes evidence in supporting the issue, and on the other, the degree to which the jury will probably be roused by the evidence to overmastering hostility.

Id. p. 453. This approach is one which finds support in *Dirring v. United States*, 328 F.2d 512 (1 Cir. 1964), *cert. denied*, 377 U.S. 1003, 84 S. Ct. 1939, 12 L. Ed. 2d 1052 (1964); and *United States v. Hines*, 470 F.2d 225 (3 Cir. 1972), *cert. denied*, 410 U.S. 968, 93 S. Ct. 1452, 35 L. Ed. 2d 703 (1973).These cases stand for the proposition that evidence of other offenses may be received, if relevant, for any purpose other than to show a mere propensity or disposition on the part of the defendant to commit the crime, provided that the trial judge may exclude the evidence if its probative value is outweighed by the risk that its admission will create a substantial danger of undue prejudice to the accused.

We think that the evidence would prove that a crime had been committed because of the remoteness of the possibility that so many infants in the care and custody of defendant would suffer cyanotic episodes and respiratory difficulties if they were not induced by the defendant's wrongdoing, and at the same time, would prove the identity of defendant as the wrongdoer. Indeed, the evidence is so persuasive and so necessary in case of infanticide or other child abuse by suffocation if the wrongdoer is to be apprehended, that we think that its relevance clearly outweighs its prejudicial effect on the jury.[10] We reject defendant's argument that the proof was not so clear and

---

[10] Although the average juror, when confronted with such evidence, could have little doubt of defendant's guilt, it is not unlikely that, in view of the abundant evidence of defendant's emotional distress at the loss or illness of each child, he would recognize that there was a pitiable absence of some factor in defendant's personality which would permit her to engage in such repeated conduct.

convincing that its admissibility should not be sustained. If the evidence with regard to each child is considered separately, it is true that some of the incidents are less conclusive than others; but we think the incidents must be considered collectively, and when they are, an unmistakable pattern emerges. That pattern overwhelmingly establishes defendant's guilt.

Admissibility of Evidence to Prove Corpus Delicti. For the reasons stated, the sufficiency of the evidence of (a) what happened to the other children, (b) proof of the fact of Paul's death, and (c) the government's expert testimony of the probable cause of death, to prove the corpus delicti was apparent. Defendant argues strenuously, however, that even if admissible for other purposes, the law does not permit evidence of prior acts to be employed to prove the corpus delicti . . . . [The authorities on which defendant relies] were either cases in which there was a total lack of any evidence of corpus delicti, or mere dictum that corpus delicti might not be proved by evidence of prior acts.

Counsel have not cited, nor have we found, any case which considers whether or not prior acts can be used to establish the corpus delicti of murder, but the law seems clear that prior acts can be proved to establish the corpus delicti of arson,[13] and also that a confession may be relied upon to prove the corpus delicti if there is other corroborating evidence, short of independent proof of the corpus delicti, to prove the reliability of the confession. The rule in cases of arson would seem equally applicable in cases of murder, and the rule with regard to confessions bears a close analogy to the use of other acts to prove murder. We therefore hold that in the instant case proof of the incidents involving other children was admissible to prove the corpus delicti of murder and other acts of child abuse.

NOTES AND PROBLEMS

1. Some critics have attacked the independent logical relevance doctrine on the ground that the distinction between character and noncharacter theories is illusory. These critics contend that even the accepted theories of "independent" relevance involve propensity inferences. Kuhns, *The Propensity to Misunderstand the Character of Specific Acts Evidence*, 66 Iowa L. Rev. 777 (1981). For example, Professor Kuhns critiques the case law admitting evidence of the defendant's commission of an uncharged crime with the same distinctive *modus operandi* as the charged offense. It is clear that in either an exclusionary or inclusionary jurisdiction, a court would routinely admit such evidence. However, Professor Kuhns argues that admitting this evidence to establish the defendant's identity:

> necessarily requires a generalized propensity inference. The only factor that makes commission of the other crime relevant to identify the perpetrator of the charged crime is the assumption that some individual has a propensity to commit both crimes, and this assumption is dependent upon the inference that people generally have a propensity

---

[13] *State v. Schleigh*, 210 Or. 155, 310 P.2d 341, 348 (1957) (repeated fires by spontaneous combustion unlikely; eight fires along one country road immediately after defendant, his father and other drove by show "a deliberate plan to set them"). . . .

not to perpetrate a crime in the same unusual manner in which another person has perpetrated a crime. *Id.* at 787.

The theory of logical relevance sanctioned by the *Woods* case relies on the so–called doctrine of objective chances. 1 E. IMWINKELRIED, UNCHARGED MISCONDUCT EVIDENCE § 4:03 (rev.ed.1999) The theory is that if the defendant suffered a particular type of loss — the death of a spouse or child as in *Woods*— more frequently than the average, innocent citizen would sustain such losses, the defendant's claim of accident is objectively implausible. That theory can be depicted in this fashion:

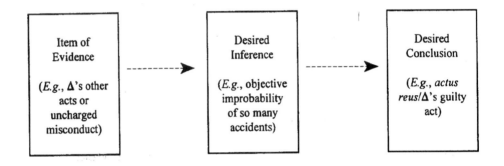

Doesn't the theory of objective chances pose the risk that the jury will be tempted to punish the defendant for past crimes? Isn't that prohibited under Rule 404(a)? Is the theory of objective chances just good, old–fashioned propensity evidence under the guise of pop–statistics? The Supreme Court appeared to endorse the doctrine of objective chances in *Estelle v. McGuire*, 502 U.S. 62 (1991).

2. Problem 14–11. In *Devitt*, the defendant denies the battery and claims that Paterson was mistaken in identifying him. Another man, Anderson, was beaten a week before the alleged battery in this case. He is prepared to identify Devitt as the attacker. Is his testimony admissible under Rule 404(b)? Suppose that Anderson adds that his attack also occurred on Monday, the day of the week Paterson was attacked. His attack occurred at 4:00 in the afternoon, the same time Paterson was beaten. What if, as in the instant case, the assailant wore brown pants and a yellow shirt? What if, as in the instant case, the assailant threatened the victim with a thin, silvery knife? At what point, if any, would you as judge be persuaded to admit the evidence?

3. Problem 14–12. Suppose that Anderson's beating occurred a week after rather than a week before the complainant's attack. The courts sometimes refer to uncharged misconduct as "prior crimes." In principle, should the doctrine be limited to acts occurring before acts alleged in the pleading? *See United States v. Hearst*, 563 F.2d 1331, 1336 (9th Cir. 1977) (evidence of Patty Hearst's participation in a crime a month after the robbery she was tried for); Annot., 88 A.L.R.3d 8, 13–15 (1978). On its face, does Rule 404(b) prescribe a timing requirement?

b. The Balancing Process for Determining the Admissibility of Uncharged Misconduct Evidence

Finding that uncharged misconduct evidence has independent, noncharacter relevance does not end our analysis. That finding satisfies Rule 404(b); but since this evidence is so damaging to the defense, the evidence must still pass muster under Rule 403's legal irrelevance requirements. Under Rule 403, the judge must balance the prosecution's need for the evidence (determined in part by the probative value of the evidence) against its prejudicial character.

1) The Prosecution's Need for the Evidence

The prosecution's need for the evidence depends on four factors: (a) the strength of the evidence that the defendant committed the uncharged act; (b) the extent to which the uncharged act is probative of the fact of consequence the prosecutor offers it to establish; (c) the availability of other, less prejudicial evidence to prove the fact of consequence; and (d) the degree to which that fact of consequence is disputed.

Factor (a). It is not enough that the uncharged misconduct evidence has bare logical relevance; the cases often proclaim that to overcome its prejudicial character, the evidence must have "substantial" relevance. The identification of the defendant as the perpetrator of the uncharged crime should be relatively positive and unequivocal. It was formerly the "clear" majority rule that the prosecution must present clear and convincing evidence that the defendant was the perpetrator. *United States v. Kinney*, 598 F. Supp. 883, 887 (D. Me. 1984). However, in *Huddleston v. United States*, 485 U.S. 681 (1988), the Supreme Court held that the majority view no longer obtains under the Federal Rules. The Court concluded that Rule 104(b) governs the question of the sufficiency of the evidence of the defendant's identity as the actor. However, assume that the identifying evidence was rather vague or indefinite; the witness to the uncharged crime might be prepared to say only that "the defendant looks an awful lot like the guy who I saw commit" that crime. The testimony would probably satisfy Rule 104(b); but given the facial uncertainty of the testimony, the judge might exclude the evidence under Rule 403.

Factor (b). Ideally, there should be only a short time lapse between the two acts. The more remote the uncharged act is in time or place from the charged crime, the less probative the uncharged act is. Unlike Rule 609(b), 404(b) does not contain any general guidelines for evaluating remoteness in time.

Factor (c). The prosecution's need for the uncharged misconduct evidence is certainly bona fide when the prosecution has no other evidence to prove the fact of consequence or the other evidence is "weak and inadequate." *State v. Billstrom*, 276 Minn. 174, 149 N.W.2d 281 (1967); Note, *Developments in Evidence of Other Crimes*, 7 U. MICH. J.L. REFORM 535, 547 (1974). The court must evaluate the need for the evidence in light of the availability of alternative, less prejudicial evidence. *United States v. DiZenso*, 500 F.2d 263 (4th Cir. 1974). If the prosecution has a strong case without the uncharged misconduct evidence, the judge should exclude the evidence. *United States v. Cochran*, 546 F.2d 27 (5th Cir. 1977). The prosecution may not overkill with cumulative testimony; the prosecution should not prove its case to the hilt with uncharged misconduct evidence. *People v. Perez*, 42 Cal. App. 3d 760, 117 Cal. Rptr. 195 (1974).

Factor (d). Lastly, we must factor in the extent to which the fact of consequence is genuinely disputed. In many jurisdictions, if the defendant pleads not guilty, the courts routinely find that the issue is sufficiently disputed to warrant the introduction of uncharged misconduct. *United States v. Roberts*, 619 F.2d 379 (5th Cir. 1980). In these jurisdictions, the defendant must give the prosecution some "enforceable pretrial assurance" that he or she does not intend to dispute the issue to negative the prosecution need. *United States v. Webb*, 625 F.2d 709 (5th Cir. 1980). There is a pertinent passage in the Advisory Committee Note to Rule 401 defining logical relevance:

> The fact to which the evidence is directed need not be disputed. While situations will arise which call for the exclusion of evidence offered to prove a point conceded by the opponent, the ruling should be made on the basis of such considerations as waste of time and undue prejudice (see Rule 403). . . .

PROBLEMS

1. Problem 14–13. Suppose that in *Devitt,* the prosecution offers uncharged misconduct for the stated purpose of proving Devitt's identity as the assailant. Before trial, Devitt offers to stipulate to his identity and defend only on the ground of self–defense. Should the judge in effect force the prosecutor to accept the stipulation, or should the judge nevertheless admit the evidence? *United States v. Coades*, 549 F.2d 1303, 1306 (9th Cir. 1977); *People v. Perez, supra*, at 765–68, 117 Cal. Rptr. at 197–99. *Cf. Old Chief v. United States*, 519 U.S. 172 (1997).

2. Problem 14–14. On direct examination, Devitt frankly admits that he had fought with Paterson but claims self–defense. Does that bar uncharged misconduct on the identity issue? If the issue must be genuinely disputed, what will constitute a sufficient dispute? Is it enough that at a pretrial hearing, the defendant indicates that he will dispute that issue? *United States v. Kirk*, 528 F.2d 1057, 1061 n.3 (5th Cir. 1976). What if the defense counsel suggests the defense in the opening statement? What if the defense counsel vigorously cross–examines the prosecution witnesses who testify to Devitt's identify as the assailant? Or should we require that the prosecutor always defer uncharged misconduct evidence to the rebuttal stage after the defense case–in–chief?

2) The Prejudicial Character of the Evidence

The four factors discussed above determine the probative worth of the uncharged misconduct evidence; but under Rule 403, the judge must balance probative worth against countervailing probative dangers. Almost all uncharged misconduct evidence will be harmful to the defense. Should we recognize degrees of prejudice? It is one thing to admit as uncharged misconduct proof of a petty theft by the defendant. The degree of danger is much greater if we permit the prosecutor to introduce evidence of an uncharged act of child molestation by the defendant—a crime that most jurors would find highly repulsive. *United States v. Cook*, 538 F.2d 1000 (3d Cir. 1976). In the early 1980's, the Bureau of Justice Statistics of the Department of Justice released the findings of its National Survey of Crime Severity. The bureau wanted to determine the public perceptions of the seriousness of various crimes. INSIDE DRUG LAW, Sept. 1984, at 9. Sixty thousand adults were questioned. The participants were asked to rate the gravity of several offenses. The survey resulted in the following ratings, *inter alia*:

72.1—A person plants a bomb in a public building. The bomb explodes, and 20 people are killed.

52.8—A man forcibly rapes a woman. As a result of physical injuries, she dies.

47.8—A parent beats his young child with his fists. As a result, the child dies.

39.1—A factory knowingly gets rid of its waste in a way that pollutes the water supply of a city. As a result, 20 people die.

33.8—A person runs a narcotics ring.

32.7—An armed person skyjacks an airplane and holds the crew and passengers hostage until a ransom is paid.

21.2—A person kidnaps a victim.

20.6—A person sells heroin to others for resale.

20.1—A man forcibly rapes a woman. Her physical injuries require treatment by a doctor but not hospitalization.

19.5—A person smuggles heroin into the country.

19.5—A person kills a victim by recklessly driving an automobile.

17.8—Knowing that a shipment of cooking oil is bad, a store owner decides to sell it anyway. Only one bottle is sold, and the purchaser dies.

16.9—A legislator takes a bribe of $10,000 from a company to vote for a law favoring the company.

12.2—A person pays a witness to give false testimony in a criminal trial.

11.4—A person knowingly lies under oath during a trial.

10.8—A person steals a locked car and sells it.

10.5—A person smuggles marijuana into the country for resale.

10.4—A person intentionally hits a victim with a lead pipe. The victim requires hospitalization.

10.3—A person illegally sells barbiturates, such as prescription sleeping pills, to others for resale.

9.6—A police officer knowingly makes a false arrest.

8.5—A person sells marijuana to others for resale.

6.5—A person uses heroin.

5.4—A person has some heroin for his own use.

4.5—A person cheats on his federal income tax return.

1.6—A person is a customer in a house of prostitution.

1.5—A person takes barbiturates, such as sleeping pills, without a legal prescription.

1.4—A person smokes marijuana.

1.1—A person disturbs the neighborhood with loud, noisy behavior.

NOTES

1. Which of these ratings do you find surprising? As a trial judge, to what extent would you rely on these ratings in administering Rule 403? Do these ratings necessarily establish a significant risk that lay jurors would *misuse* evidence of one of the rated crimes during deliberations?

2. At common law, most courts assumed that the prosecutor has the burden of showing that the probative value of uncharged misconduct evidence outweighs any attendant probative dangers. The courts often declared that the prosecutor's burden was "heavy." *Smith v. State*, 646 S.W.2d 452, 458 (Tex. Crim. App. 1983). Do the Federal Rules continue the common law norm? Rule 404(b) does not even speak to the balancing process. However, the Advisory Committee Note refers the reader to Rule 403. As we noted earlier, on its face, Rule 403 seems to turn the common law norm upside down; the passive voice of the sentence suggests that the opponent has the burden, and the adverb "substantially" indicates that the opponent's burden is now a heavy one. Would it be possible to construe Rule 404(b) as incorporating the factors listed in Rule 403 without adopting the allocation and measure of the burden suggested by Rule 403? *See* Kuhns, *The Propensity to Misunderstand the Character of Specific Acts Evidence*, 66 Iowa L. Rev. 777, 797 n.74 (1981). Is it likely that the drafters intended to do so?

3. It is often assumed that only the prosecutor can employ the uncharged misconduct doctrine. Is that assumption correct? Does the text of Rule 404(b) contain that restriction? Suppose that Devitt's attorney uncovered evidence that a third party had committed other batteries and used exactly the same *modus operandi* as employed in the Paterson attack. Would Rule 404(b) forbid Devitt from offering that evidence to exculpate himself?

3. OTHER ACTS EVIDENCE IN CIVIL ACTIONS

In civil cases, the proponent of other acts evidence cannot offer the evidence simply to (1) increase the probability that the party committed the act alleged in the pleading or (2) support a generalized inference of the party's fault. On those theories of logical relevance, the evidence has minimal probative value— probative value insufficient to overcome the danger of distracting the jury from the central issues in the case. The proponent must offer the evidence for "more sharply refined" purposes. *Britton v. Rogers*, 631 F.2d 572 (8th Cir. 1980). Depending upon the purpose, the court might admit evidence of another contract entered into by a party, another lawsuit filed by that party, or another tort committed by that party.

a. Other Contracts

Suppose that in a contract action, the plaintiff attempts to offer evidence of another contract. The classic discussion of this topic appears in an article by Slough, *Relevancy Unraveled*, 6 U. KAN. L. REV. 38 (1957). Slough noted that when the evidence related to another contract between the same two persons currently litigating a contract dispute, the marked tendency in the cases was to admit the evidence if it shed light on the meaning of the contract or the understanding of the parties regarding the transaction, *so long as* the two agreements were "substantially similar." However, the courts were highly reluctant to admit evidence of another contract between a party to the current suit and a stranger to the litigation. Recently, the absolute rule of exclusion has given way to an occasional exception. For example, in *Firlotte v. Jessee*, 76 Cal. App. 2d 207, 172 P.2d 710 (1946) the question was whether Jessee reserved the right to graze cattle on land he had sold to Firlotte. Firlotte offered testimony by a third party that "Jessee had approached him with an offer to sell . . . the same land and that Jessee had said nothing about reserving the right to pasture his own cattle . . . ." Although the testimony related to Jessee's bargaining with a third party, the evidence was admissible because of its considerable probative worth: "[t]he circumstance of the defendant's offering the identical land to another without reservation afforded a strong probability that the course followed in one instance would be followed in another."

PROBLEMS

1. Problem 14–15. In our torts case, Ms. Hill alleged that at the time the parties signed the written contract, Jefferson's representative made an express oral warranty that the car was "top flight" and "virtually malfunction proof." In its answer, Polecat Motors denies that the warranty was ever made. At trial, could Ms. Hill call as witnesses other customers of Jefferson Motor Co. to elicit their testimony that Jefferson's salespeople made similar representations to them? Does the evidence have "independent" relevance if Ms. Hill offers the evidence to prove that the representation was made as a basis for creating a warranty? Is Ms. Hill simply arguing, "They did it once, therefore they did it again"?

2. Problem 14–16. Would your analysis in the last problem change if Ms. Hill wanted to avoid the contract on the ground of fraud? Ms. Hill has evidence that, two months before her husband's purchase, the same Jefferson salesperson made identical representations to another customer, Mr. Felice. Mr. Felice purchased the identical model of Polecat which Mr. Hill bought. One month later Mr. Felice's car developed severe mechanical problems. Felice brought the car back to the dealership and called the problems to the salesperson's attention. How does the logical relevance of this evidence differ from that of the evidence proffered in Problem 14–15 above? Would this evidence run afoul of the prohibition of using other acts to support a general inference of fault, or does this evidence have "independent" logical relevance?

b. Tort Actions

1) Other Claims by the Plaintiff

Consider the notorious case of *San Antonio Traction Co. v. Cox*, 184 S.W. 722 (Tex. Civ. App. 1916):

> George Cox sued the San Antonio Traction Company for damages in the sum of $950 for personal injuries, which he claimed to have received in alighting from a street car on or about July 23, 1914. He alleged that while he was undertaking to get off the car at the crossing of the San Antonio & Arkansas Pass Railway on the west end car line, the car was carelessly and negligently started too suddenly and without notice or warning before plaintiff had sufficient time to alight, and in so starting the car it was jerked, with the result that plaintiff was thrown or fell from the car and received the injuries described in the petition.
>
> Defendant denied the happening of the accident and the negligence alleged, and further alleged that Cox and some 10 or 11 members of his family have continuously "worked together, conspired, assisted, and abetted each other in propounding false and fraudulent claims against this defendant," and "that this suit and the claim propounded herein is a part and parcel of said co–operation, conspiracy, and abetting of the above–mentioned parties for the purpose of obtaining money from this defendant."
>
> The trial resulted in a verdict and judgment in favor of plaintiff for $250. Appellant complains of the exclusion of certain testimony. . .The testimony excluded shows a remarkable condition of affairs. About 17 claims were propounded by Cox and his relatives, all of which, except 2, were for injuries alleged to have been sustained in alighting from cars. To get off of a street car is a simple thing, and it is inconceivable that all of these people could have been caused to fall by reason of negligence of the operatives of the cars. Surely the company had no desire to willfully inflict injuries upon the members of this family, and surely these people were not all suffering from infirmities such as to prevent them from getting off of a street car without assistance. In spite, however, of the warnings furnished by similar accidents to members of the family, they appear not to have learned caution, but continued taking the risk, a terrible one as to them, of getting off of street cars, with the result that every now and then one of them would be injured just like the others were. We think it so highly improbable that all of these claims could be honest ones, that a jury would be justified in inferring that fraud had been practiced with regard to some of them. The testimony indicates a bad state of affairs, but we do not think, had it been admitted, it would, with the other testimony, have justified a charge on conspiracy. The evidence fails to connect plaintiff with the other claims, except in one instance in which he was with a cousin when he had his fall, and also witnessed the release executed by him to the company. . . .

The issue in this case was whether plaintiff was injured by reason of the negligence of the company as alleged by him, or whether, as is contended by defendant, no such incident as testified to by plaintiff occurred, or if it did, that it was willfully brought about by him, and not caused by negligence of the company. Proof of a conspiracy and of his connection therewith would undoubtedly tend strongly to corroborate the testimony of the employees of defendant that no such incident occurred, or might lead the jury to believe that he willfully permitted himself to be thrown from the steps. But as above pointed out the evidence admitted fails to show any conspiracy between any of the members of the family who propounded claims, and the evidence excluded, considered alone or with that admitted, would not justify a charge on conspiracy, for it merely shows transactions of a similar nature, not connected with each other and not constituting a necessary element in a plan to reach an ulterior object. . . .

NOTES AND PROBLEMS

1. Notice the court's use of such expressions as "conspiracy," "willfully," and "ulterior object." Those passages suggest the court's conception of what would constitute independent relevance. What showing does the court demand in order to tip the legal irrelevance balance in favor of admission?

2. Did the traction company's attorney commit a tactical mistake in alleging that Cox and his family members had entered into a conspiracy to defraud the traction company? The court acknowledges that "it is inconceivable that all of these people could have been caused to fall by reason of negligence of the operatives of the cars." Given that logical relevance, the incidents' striking similarity, and the alleged victims' close family relationships, perhaps the traction company's attorney could have succeeded without alleging a conspiracy. The traction company might argue that, in light of these circumstances, it was objectively unlikely that all of these incidents were bona fide accidents. Would this argument require the jury to draw any inference about the plaintiff's subjective, personal character? If the traction company's attorney had urged that argument on you as trial judge, how would you have ruled? Remember Judge Winter's approval of the doctrine of chances as a noncharacter theory in the *Woods* case excerpted earlier in this chapter.

3. Problem 14–17. How can a defendant prove that the plaintiff is a "claim–minded" individual who files frivolous suits? Suppose that in our torts case there is evidence Ms. Hill filed three unsuccessful products liability cases against other manufacturers in the past 5 years. Would that evidence have sufficient "independent" logical relevance to be admissible? Suppose that the prayer in one of the earlier suits asked for damages for injuries to the plaintiff's back, just as the prayer in the instant case seeks damages for personal injuries to the back. What theory of logical relevance suggests itself now? Would that qualify as "independent" logical relevance?

2) Other Torts by the Defendant

Evidence of another misdeed by a civil defendant can have a dramatic impact on the outcome of the case. In one, well–known empirical study, researchers found that if a civil jury learns that the defendant has a criminal record, the plaintiff can expect a verdict 9% higher than normal. D. HERBERT & R. BARRETT, ATTORNEY'S MASTER GUIDE TO COURTROOM PSYCHOLOGY 321 (1980). More commonly, the plaintiff offers evidence of another tort committed by the defendant. Especially when the defendant is a mass manufacturer as in our torts case, the plaintiff will often be able to find evidence of similar torts committed by the defendant. However, the plaintiff may not offer evidence of the other torts merely to prove that the event alleged in the complaint did, in fact, occur. Nor may the plaintiff offer the evidence to support a general inference that, as in the prior cases, the defendant was at fault. These theories of admissibility fall short of "independent" relevance.

Nowhere in civil actions is the stress on independent logical relevance more explicit. Connolly, *Evidentiary Products in Products Cases*, in PRODUCTS LIABILITY: LAW, PRACTICE, AND SCIENCE 11:46–48 (1967), is illustrative. Connolly lists some of the theories of logical relevance the courts have found acceptable. The theories include, *inter alia*:

- The other accident tended to show the existence of the condition which resulted in the plaintiff's injury. If a third party slipped and fell on the same step the day before the plaintiff's accident, the short time lapse makes it likely that the condition still existed when the plaintiff attempted to use the same stairway.

- The other accident evidenced the instrumentality's potential to cause injury which rendered the instrumentality or condition unsafe. For this purpose, the plaintiff could introduce both prior and subsequent accidents.

- The other accident put the defendant on notice that the instrumentality or condition was unsafe. On this theory of logical relevance, the plaintiff is restricted to prior accidents.

- The other accident involving the defendant's instrumentality or conditions shows that the instrumentality or condition caused the plaintiff's injury.

Connolly notes that when the courts invoked one of these theories, they often declared that only "substantially similar" accidents are admissible. However, he adds that as a practical matter, the courts relax the similarity standard when the plaintiff relied on the notice theory. Citing the original, 1954 edition of the McCormick hornbook, Connolly stated that the other incident need merely "attract the defendant's attention to the dangerous situation." The incident could have a wide "warning radius."

NOTES AND PROBLEMS

1. Connolly refers to "the warning radius of the happening." What does he mean by that expression? Suppose that the prior accident involved a slip and fall on the fourth step on a stairway. The following day the plaintiff is injured in a slip and fall on the fifth step.

2. Problem 14–18. At trial, Polecat Motors calls Dr. Eckert. Eckert is an expert in the design of automobiles. He did his Ph.D. work on the design hazards of gas tanks. Eckert testifies that it would have been physically impossible for Ms. Hill's gas tank to explode as she described merely because Worker's car struck her moving car at the speed Ms. Hill testified to. Eckert adds that the only possible explanation is that Ms. Hill panicked, stepped on the brake rather than the gas, came to an abrupt stop before Worker's car struck hers, and thereby increased the force of the collision. During her rebuttal, Ms. Hill would now like to introduce evidence of four other accidents in which the gas tanks of moving Polecat cars exploded when they were rear–ended. Is the evidence of the other accidents admissible? *Auzene v. Gulf Pub. Serv. Co.*, 188 So. 512, 515 (La. Ct. App. 1939).

3. Problem 14–19. Suppose that Ms. Hill had offered the same evidence during her case–in–chief rather than waiting until her rebuttal. How does that fact change the legal irrelevance analysis?

4. Problem 14–20. In her suit, Ms. Hill alleges a strict products liability cause of action based on a claimed design defect in the Polecat's gas tank. Suppose instead that she had alleged that Polecat negligently manufactured the particular gas tank in her car. How does the inclusion of a design defect allegation in the pleading affect the admissibility of the evidence of the other accidents involving similarly designed products?

5. Problem 14–21. Polecat Motors has evidence of the "safety history" of the model of car that Ms. Hill was driving at the time of the accident. The complaint department's records show that during the three years that Polecat marketed and sold over 300,000 cars of that model, only fifteen complaints were made by customers and none related to the gas tank. Is that evidence admissible in Ms. Hill's products liability suit? *Stark v. Allis Chalmers & Northwest Rds. Inc.*, 2 Wash. App. 399, 467 P.2d 854, 858 (1970).

6. Problem 14–22. Suppose again that instead of invoking a products liability theory. Ms. Hill alleged negligent manufacture. How would that affect the "safety history" evidence? In what sense is a products liability allegation a two–edged sword from the plaintiff's perspective? *See* Morris, *Proof of Safety History in Negligence Cases*, 61 HARV. L. REV. 205 (1948).

4. A COMPARISON OF THE ADMISSIBILITY OF OTHER ACTS EVIDENCE IN CIVIL AND CRIMINAL CASES

The standards for admitting evidence of other acts in civil actions are stricter than those applied to the admissibility of evidence of other crimes in criminal prosecutions. "[I]n many jurisdictions, evidence of a criminal defendant's other homicides is more readily admissible than proof of a civil defendant's other tire failures." Imwinkelried, *Uncharged Misconduct Evidence: Getting It Out Into the Light*, TRIAL, Nov. 1984, at 60. Contrast the trend in criminal cases toward an *inclusionary* approach to uncharged misconduct with the generally *exclusionary* approach taken in the majority of jurisdictions toward the admissibility of evidence of other acts in civil cases. Moreover, even if the evidence of another accident falls within a recognized exception, the courts often demand near identity of circumstances with the pleaded tort. Note, 61 WASH. U. L.Q. 799, 804, 808 (1983). In contrast, the academic commentators have generally been critical of the lax manner in which the courts apply the similarity requirement in prosecutions.

NOTES

1. Initially, consider these divergent approaches as a matter of evidentiary policy. In principle, should the doctrine of legal irrelevance be applied differently in criminal than in civil cases? The stakes are arguably higher in criminal cases. Which species of evidence is more likely to be prejudicial: proof of another tort or evidence of another crime? Consider the ratings in the Bureau of Justice Statistics' National Survey of Crime Severity set forth above. On this analysis isn't the current state of the law dead wrong?

2. Now analyze the problem as one of statutory construction. For civil cases, the doctrine of other acts is largely a creature of common or decisional law. Some commentators assert that the Federal Rules of Evidence leave these rules uncodified and that the courts may continue to enforce them under the general aegis of Rule 403. Langum, *Uncodified Federal Evidence Rules Applicable to Civil Trials*, 19 WILLAMETTE L. REV. 513, 519 (1983). Do you agree? Consider the wording of the first sentence of Rule 404(b). What significance do the words, "wrongs . . . or acts," have if the Rule applies only to evidence of other crimes? *See* 2A N. SINGER, SUTHERLAND STATUTORY CONSTRUCTION § 46.06 (5th ed. 1992). If we assume *arguendo* that the words, "wrongs . . . or acts," are expansive enough to include evidence of other contracts, torts, accidents, lawsuits, etc. — is admissibility governed by the general statute Rule 403 or the more specific provisions of Rule 404(b)? *Busic v. United States*, 446 U.S. 398, 406 (1980) ("a more specific statute will be given precedence over a more general one . . . ."). If Rule 404(b) governs, perhaps a tougher standard for civil actions is appropriate. Doesn't that depend on whether the bias in favor of admission of logically relevant evidence in Rule 403 extends to its adjacent neighbor Rule 404(b)?

3. The number of citations to Rule 404(b) in civil cases is growing rapidly. In the past decade, civil practitioners have come to realize that uncharged misconduct evidence can be highly useful for such purposes as proving discriminatory intent (*Robinson v. Runyon*, 149 F. 3d 507, 513 (6th Cir. 1998)) and proving the malice necessary to permit a recovery of punitive damages. In many states, there is an enhanced burden of proof when the plaintiff seeks punitive damages. A large number of jurisdictions require clear and convincing evidence (*Photias v. Graham*, 14 F. Supp. 2d 126 (D.Me. 1998)(Maine law); *McDermott v. Party City Corp.*, 11 F. Supp.2d 612 (E.D.Pa. 1998)(Pennsylvania law)), and one state has gone to the length of prescribing proof beyond a reasonable doubt as the standard. *Karnes v. SCI Colorado Funeral Services, Inc.*, 162 F.3d 1077, 1982 (10th Cir. 1998). Evidence of the defendant's other, similar intentional misconduct can help the plaintiff meet that heavy burden.

Chapter 15

CREDIBILITY EVIDENCE: BOLSTERING AND IMPEACHING

Read Federal Rules of Evidence 607, 608(a), 801(d)(1)(C) and 806.

A. INTRODUCTION

Although credibility evidence is indisputably material and relevant, that does not guarantee its admission. Credibility evidence can be extremely prejudicial, distracting or likely to pose other probative dangers. Courts have evolved a complex body of law governing credibility evidence. To grasp this body of law, it is important to realize that there are three types of credibility evidence. The first is bolstering evidence. A party bolsters her own witness' credibility when she presents evidence designed to increase the witness' credibility in the jurors' eyes even before the opposing party has attacked that credibility. Second, is attacking evidence. Impeachment is the generic term for an attack on a witness' credibility. Such attacks are designed to convince the jury that a witness is unworthy of belief. Finally, there is rehabilitating evidence. Rehabilitation is the generic term for evidence designed to rebuild or restore a witness' credibility after it has been attacked.

B. THE EVIDENTIARY STATUS OF CREDIBILITY EVIDENCE

For the most part, evidence offered on a credibility theory is admissible only for that purpose and will not be admitted "substantively," that is, to prove or disprove an historical fact or substantive issue in the case. The reason for its substantive inadmissibility may be simply that it is irrelevant. For example, the fact that Jones was once convicted of perjury usually has no bearing on the substantive issues. Jones' conviction neither increases nor decreases the probability that Paterson was assaulted or that Devitt was the attacker. Or it may be inadmissible because it violates some other rule of evidence. Thus, a prior inconsistent statement may violate the rule against hearsay. Suppose that on cross–examination, Devitt impeaches Jones by showing that Jones told his neighbor Wilson that he, Jones, did not think it was Devitt he saw near Paterson's apartment. Devitt may certainly use this prior inconsistent statement to impeach Jones. The fact that Jones made a prior inconsistent statement reduces his credibility, and the judge will admit the statement as credibility evidence. However, if Devitt attempted to use Jones' statement as substantive proof that Devitt was not near Paterson's apartment, an objection on hearsay grounds would be sustained.

PROBLEM

Problem 15–1. In *Devitt*, after the defense impeaches Jones with the prior inconsistent statement, the prosecutor asks for a "limiting" instruction under Rule 105. You are the trial judge. Should you give such an instruction? If so, how should the instruction be worded?

C. BOLSTERING BEFORE IMPEACHMENT

As soon as Jones testifies for the prosecution in *Devitt*, his credibility becomes one of the material facts in the case. Consequently, it would be logically relevant for the prosecution to bolster Jones' believability even before any attack is made upon it. However, the common law generally forbade bolstering. The common law rule is followed in modern cases. *United States v. Perez*, 30 F.3d 1407 (11th Cir. 1994).

The legal irrelevance doctrine furnishes the rationale for the general ban on bolstering evidence. At the point at which the prosecutor attempts bolstering, before Devitt's cross–examination of Jones, we do not know whether Devitt will attack Jones' believability. Devitt may think that Jones' testimony is so innocuous that Devitt waives cross–examination. In that event, the court time devoted to the bolstering evidence has essentially been wasted; the prosecutor spent court time building up the credibility of a witness who was never attacked. On this reasoning, most jurisdictions force the witness' proponent, the party calling the witness to the stand, to wait until redirect to offer evidence designed to enhance the jurors' impression of the witness' credibility. If the opposing party does not attack, we have saved precious court time. If the opposing party attacks, the proponent can offer the evidence as rehabilitation. In the words of Rule 403, until the opposing party sharpens the issue of the witness' credibility by attempted impeachment, devoting court time to bolstering evidence would be a "waste of time."

Notwithstanding the general ban on bolstering evidence, the courts occasionally permit bolstering. Many jurisdictions recognize the "fresh complaint" doctrine. 4 J. WIGMORE, EVIDENCE §§ 1134–40 (Chadbourn rev. 1972); 6 J. WIGMORE, EVIDENCE §§ 1160, 1171 (3d ed. 1940). Hence, during a rape victim's direct examination, the victim could testify that she phoned in a report to the police an hour after the alleged attack. Some jurisdictions admit evidence of a witness' pretrial identification to bolster the witness' in–court identification. *State v. Draughn*, 121 N.J. Super. 64, 296 A.2d 79 (1972); *People v. Nival*, 33 N.Y.2d 391, 353 N.Y.S.2d 409, 308 N.E.2d 883 (1974). Suppose that during his direct examination, Paterson pointed to Devitt and identified him as his assailant. Under this exception to the bolstering prohibition, before concluding his direct, Paterson could add that he also singled Devitt out at a lineup the day after the alleged battery.

There are a couple of reasons for these exceptions. In prior cases, juries often found sexual assault prosecutions hard to decide, especially where the trial became a swearing contest between the complainant and the defendant. There was a special need in these situations for additional credibility evidence. Courts assumed that lay jurors would be troubled by the absence of a fresh complaint to the authorities. Accordingly, this exception to the bolstering rules was formulated. If evidence of a fresh complaint existed, most courts considered it to be admissible. The pretrial identification exception proceeded on different reasoning. A pretrial identification of the suspect by the victim is always closer in time to the actual events in the case than an identification made at trial. Usually it comes a few days or perhaps even hours after the crime. Proximity in time to the litigated events decreases concerns about the quality of the victim's memory.

NOTES AND PROBLEMS

1. Problem 15–2. In *Devitt*, the prosecutor calls Jones as the first government witness. Jones testifies that he saw Devitt "hanging around near Mr. Paterson's apartment." Suppose Devitt waives any cross–examination of Jones, and Jones is excused from the stand. The prosecutor next calls Paterson and seeks to have him testify that he had known Jones "for years" and that in his opinion, he is "an honest, truthful individual." The defense counsel objects on bolstering grounds. What ruling?

2. Problem 15–3. Suppose that in the last problem Ms. Garfield is called as a witness for the prosecution. She is a neighbor of Jones. Ms. Garfield attempts to testify that a couple of days after the assault Jones told her that "I am sure it was Devitt who was casing the Paterson apartment." The defense objects. What ruling? *See Woodard v. State*, 269 Ga. 317, 496 S.E.2d 896 (1998) ("Unless a witness' veracity has affirmatively been placed in issue, the witness' prior consistent statement is pure hearsay evidence, which cannot be admitted merely to corroborate the witness, or to *bolster the witness' credibility in the eyes of the jury.*") (*emphasis added*).

3. Consider the impact of the adoption of the Federal Rules on the common law prohibition of bolstering. In one respect, the rules codify the prohibition; in pertinent part, Rule 608(a) reads:

> The credibility of a witness may be . . . supported by evidence in the form of opinion or reputation, but subject to [this] limitation: . . . evidence of truthful character is admissible only after the character of the witness for truthfulness has been attacked by opinion or reputation evidence or otherwise.

At first blush, Rule 608(a) might seem to preserve the common law rule. However, look more closely. Is it not arguable that Rule 608(a) regulates only one type of bolstering evidence, namely, opinion or reputation testimony about the witness' truthfulness? Is that type of evidence the only conceivable method of bolstering? However, look even more closely. What about the words "or otherwise"?

4. Problem 15–4. In *Devitt*, the defense counsel knows that the prosecutor intends to call Jones. During his opening statement, defense counsel states, "During this trial, you'll hear evidence that only a few short months ago, this witness Jones was convicted of perjury— perjury, ladies and gentlemen." The prosecutor calls Jones as her first witness. On direct examination of Jones, the prosecutor elicits the fact that Jones pleaded guilty to the perjury charge pursuant to a plea bargain. The prosecutor next attempts to elicit the fact that, in the bargain, Jones agreed to testify truthfully in *Devitt*. At that point, the defense counsel objects that the prosecutor is "improperly bolstering Jones' credibility." The prosecutor responds that she is "merely rehabilitating the witness from the attack the defense has already mounted." What ruling? *See United States v. Maniego*, 710 F.2d 24, 27 (2d Cir. 1983). Note the court's construction of the expression, "or otherwise," in Rule 608(a). Is the defense counsel's assertion during opening statement a sufficient attack to allow bolstering of the witness? The judge typically instructs the jury that an attorney's assertions during opening are not evidence in the case.

5. In *United States v. Santiago*, 46 F.3d 885 (9th Cir. 1995) the government showed by direct examination questions that witnesses had little incentive to lie. The court held that the attempt to bolster the witnesses was permissible because the defense had attacked their credibility in opening statement.

D. IMPEACHMENT

1. AN OVERVIEW

While most jurisdictions are hostile to bolstering evidence, they liberally receive impeaching evidence. There are numerous methods of attacking credibility, but basically they all boil down to a charge that the witness is mistaken or lying. California Evidence Code § 780 lists some of the many recognized focal points for impeachment techniques:

> Except as otherwise provided by statute, the court or jury may consider in determining the credibility of a witness any matter that has any tendency in reason to . . . disprove the truthfulness of his testimony at the hearing, including but not limited to any of the following:
>
> (a) His demeanor while testifying and the manner in which he testifies.
>
> (b) The character of his testimony.
>
> (c) The extent of his capacity to perceive, to recollect, or to communicate any matter about which he testifies.
>
> (d) The extent of his opportunity to perceive any matter about which he testifies.
>
> (e) His character for honesty or veracity or their opposites.
>
> (f) The existence of a bias, interest, or other motive.
>
> . . .
>
> (h) A statement made by him that is inconsistent with any part of his testimony at the hearing.
>
> (i) The nonexistence of any fact testified to by him.
>
> (j) His attitude toward the action in which he testifies or toward the giving of testimony.
>
> (k) His admission of untruthfulness.

Some impeachment techniques focus on the witness' testimony in the present case:

Prior inconsistent statements. On some prior occasion, the witness made a statement which is inconsistent with the testimony he has just given in court.

Interest, bias, prejudice, or motive to fabricate. The witness has (a) a personal stake in the outcome of this lawsuit, (b) a bias in favor of one of the parties, (c) a prejudice against one of the parties, or (d) a motive to fabricate (e.g., his testimony has been purchased).

Some impeachment techniques have a much broader focus. Consider subsections of the California Evidence Code § 780 which authorize wide–ranging *ad hominem* attacks:

Character impeachment. The witness' character is defective in a way that affects the believability of his or her testimony. Evidence of character usually consists of proof that the witness (a) has been convicted of a certain type of crime, (b) has engaged in conduct that evidences dishonesty, or (c) is known or reputed to be a dishonest person.

Perception, memory, or narration. The witness did not have sufficient capacity or opportunity to perceive that about which he or she is now testifying; the witness cannot inadequately remember; or the witness cannot articulate his or her testimony in an understandable form.

In sum, impeachment can take a narrow focus suggesting that the witness' testimony is unreliable for case–specified reasons (*e.g.,* a stake in the outcome of this lawsuit) or can be a broadside attack on the witness' general believability. In some forms, the attack can be inoffensive. Devitt could impeach Jones' testimony by calling Dr. Shultz, Jones' optometrist, to testify about Jones' poor eyesight. At the other end of the spectrum, the attack can be insulting in the extreme. Devitt might call Ms. Fulton, one of Jones' acquaintances, to testify that in her opinion Jones "is a liar—the truth is not in the man."

NOTES

1. Earlier, we noted the split of authority over whether a witness' demeanor qualifies as evidence. Evidence Code § 780(a) lists witness demeanor as the very first type of credibility evidence. Empirical research indicates that, when persons communicate, they attach a good deal of significance to the nonverbal conduct accompanying each other's verbal statements. In particular, the results of the Cleveland Jury Project suggest that in "swearing contests"— trials in which witnesses give diametrically opposed testimony—many jurors decide the case by focusing on the witnesses' demeanor. Judge Frank, one of the leading Legal Realist jurists, shared that assessment of the practical importance of demeanor:

The liar's story may seem uncontradicted by one who merely reads it, yet it may be "contradicted" in the trial court by his manner, his intonation, his grimaces, his gestures, and the like—all matters which "cold print could not preserve". . . . the witness' demeanor, not apparent in the record, may alone have "impeached" him.

Broadcast Music, Inc. v. Havana Madrid Restaurant Corp., 175 F.2d 77, 80 (2d Cir. 1949).

2. Does Judge Frank's assessment of the importance of demeanor help explain why appellate courts ordinarily refuse to redetermine the credibility of the witnesses who testify in the trial court? Are there methods for overcoming the practical difficulties in transmitting demeanor evidence to appellate judges?

2. WHOM MAY YOU IMPEACH

By now, we should have a sense of the *how* of impeachment: the methods of attacking a witness' credibility. The next question is whom: *whom* may we impeach?

The most obviously permissible object of impeachment is a witness who has been called by the opposing party. While there can be various aims of cross–examination—one is to impeach. Indeed, the right to impeach has constitutional dimension. *Davis v. Alaska*, 415 U.S. 308 (1974); *Smith v. Illinois*, 390 U.S. 129 (1968). Every jurisdiction would agree that after Jones testifies for the prosecution, Devitt has a right to cross–examine Jones to impeach his credibility. Suppose alternatively that Jones was unavailable at trial but the trial judge allowed another witness, Garner, to testify to Jones' statement placing Devitt near the crime scene. In this variation of the hypothetical, Devitt has two proper targets for impeachment: Garner and Jones, the hearsay declarant. Federal Rule of Evidence 806 declares that like an in–court witness, the credibility of a hearsay declarant is also subject to impeachment. In *United States v. Lawson*, 608 F.2d 1129 (6th Cir. 1979), the court held that the defendant placed his credibility in issue although he never testified; the defense attorney cross–examined a prosecution witness to elicit the fact that the defendant had denied involvement in the crime. That cross–examination allowed the prosecution to attack the defendant's credibility.

The law is less well–settled when you attempt to impeach your own witness rather than a witness called by the other side in the case. Suppose that the prosecutor called Jones but, to the prosecutor's surprise, Jones testified that he was fairly certain that the man standing outside Paterson's apartment was not Devitt. Could the prosecutor attack Jones' credibility?

At early common law, the answer was an emphatic *No.* 3 D. Louisell & C. Mueller, Federal Evidence § 297 (1979). The courts assumed that by calling the witness, the prosecutor "vouched" for the witness' credibility. If the party chose to call the person as a witness and offer the witness' testimony, the courts inferred that the party impliedly warranted the person's believability. Working from that inference, the courts forbade the party from attacking the credibility of his own witnesses. Various inroads and exceptions developed—the primary one being that a party could impeach her own witness if, to the party's surprise, the witness gave testimony affirmatively damaging to the party's case. *St. Clair v. United States*, 154 U.S. 134, 150 (1893). Before resorting to this exception, the party had to satisfy two requirements. First, the witness' testimony must have come as a surprise to the party. *Twyman v. Johnson*, 655 A.2d 850 (D.C. App. 1995). Second, the testimony must have been affirmatively harmful to the party's case. *State v. Anderson*, 304 S.C.

551, 406 S.E.2d 152 (1991). It was not enough that the testimony was merely disappointing to the party.

Even the inroads made by the surprise doctrine, however, did not satisfy the critics of the voucher rule. Their basic complaint was that the historic assumption for the rule (namely, that since parties are free to select their own witnesses, they are therefore somehow accountable for them) has "no application in a modern adversary system: Seldom does a party have a choice among witnesses. . . ." 3 D. LOUISELL & C. MUELLER, FEDERAL EVIDENCE § 297 (1979). Critics of the rule argue that, as a practical matter, a party has little freedom of choice on whom to call as witnesses. Ms. Hill had little role in selecting the eyewitnesses to her accident, and similarly the prosecutor could not determine who happened to witness Devitt's entry to and exit from Paterson's apartment. In light of that reality, the critics view the voucher rule as a silly anachronism. That view has led to the adoption of statutory reforms such as Federal Rule of Evidence 607: "The credibility of a witness may be attacked by any party, including the party calling him." Even in many jurisdictions without the Federal Rules of Evidence, the voucher rule has fallen into disuse. *See Speed v. State*, 512 S.E.2d 896 (Ga. 1999) (a party may impeach his or her own witness without a showing of surprise, notwithstanding a state statute which by its terms embraced the old rule and suggested that there should be no such impeachment unless the impeaching party can show that he "has been entrapped by said witness"). This line of cases demonstrates how modern court decisions sometimes override antiquated statutes like OCGA 24–9–81.

Chambers v. Mississippi, 410 U.S. 284 (1973), which we shall discuss in greater detail later, gave constitutional impetus to the movement to reform the voucher rule. In *Chambers*, the defendant was charged with murdering a policeman named Liberty. The defendant's theory of the case was that the real murderer was one Gable McDonald. McDonald had confessed to several persons that he was the culprit. However, before trial, McDonald repudiated his confession. Both before and during trial, Chambers requested permission to call McDonald and treat him as an adverse witness. In essence, Chambers wanted to cross–examine and impeach McDonald. The trial judge denied Chambers permission to lead or impeach. The Supreme Court held that in doing so, the judge committed constitutional error. Writing for the Court, Justice Powell observed that under primitive English trial practice "oath–takers" or "compurgators" were called to stand behind a particular party's position in any controversy. "Their assertions were strictly partisan and, quite unlike witnesses in criminal trials today, their role bore little relation to the impartial ascertainment of the facts." He ruled that the "voucher" doctrine was out of date:

> . . . It might have been logical for the early common law to require a party to vouch for the credibility of witnesses he brought before the jury to affirm his veracity. Having selected them especially for that purpose, the party might reasonably be expected to stand firmly behind their testimony. But in modern criminal trials, defendants are rarely able to select their witnesses: they must take them where they find them. Moreover, as applied in this case, the "voucher" rule's

impact was doubly harmful to Chambers' efforts to develop his defense. Not only was he precluded from cross–examining McDonald, but, as the State conceded at oral argument, he was also restricted in the scope of his direct examination by the rule's corollary requirement that the party calling the witness is bound by anything he might say. He was, therefore, effectively prevented from exploring the circumstances of McDonald's three prior oral confessions and from challenging the renunciation of the written confession.

NOTES AND PROBLEMS

1. Problem 15–5. Assume that Morena recognizes the surprise exception to the voucher rule. A month before trial, a police officer questioned Jones. Jones told the officer that the man outside Paterson's apartment "might have been Devitt." However, the officer told the prosecutor that "Jones will deliver on the stand—he'll finger Devitt and put him right outside Paterson's door." At trial, the prosecutor calls Jones and on direct examination, Jones testifies:

A. To be honest, I think it probably wasn't that man at the table (Devitt), but then again it might have been.

The prosecutor excuses Jones and calls Waterford. The prosecutor now wants to elicit Waterford's testimony that a week before trial, Jones told him that "it's a good bet that it was Devitt that I saw." The defense counsel objects that there is insufficient proof of surprise. The prosecutor admits that he never spoke with Jones before trial. What ruling? *See Lewis v. State*, 593 S.W. 2d 704, 706 (Tex. Crim. App. 1980). Under the surprise doctrine, should the standard be the prosecutor's subjective good faith, or should the judge evaluate the prosecutor's belief by a standard of objective reasonableness?

2. Assume that there has been an adequate showing of surprise. Should that showing entitle the witness' proponent to use any type of impeachment to attack the witness? Is there a distinction between allowing the proponent to impeach with prior inconsistent statements versus a character trait for untruthfulness or commission of a crime? If the content of the witness' testimony surprises the proponent, should the proponent be restricted to impeachment techniques attacking the specific testimony in the case? Should a showing of surprise or inconsistency be a prerequisite to impeaching by other methods? *See Jones v. State*, 270 Ga. 25, 505 S.E.2d 749 (1998) (law requires that the witness' trial testimony be shown to be inconsistent with his prior statements, and absent this fact, no impeachment may be made by prior conviction or other means.) Even if the proponent is surprised at trial, before trial the proponent had an opportunity to investigate the witness' background. Should that opportunity preclude the proponent from attacking by the technique of character trait or crime?

3. The Advisory Committee Note to Rule 607 states that "[t]he traditional rule against impeaching one's own witness is abandoned as based on false premises. A party does not hold out his witnesses as worthy of belief, since he rarely has a free choice in selecting them." However, despite that Note, some commentators continue to assert that the judge may require a showing of surprise under Rule 607. Is the abolition of the surprise requirement clear from the text of the statute?

4. Problem 15–6. It is often good trial advocacy to anticipate the impeachment of your own witness and preempt it. Suppose, for example, that the prosecutor intends to call Jones but knows that Jones told Waterford that he, Jones, "has real doubts whether the guy by Paterson's door was Devitt." The prosecutor could disregard the prior inconsistent statement and allow the defense counsel to mention the statement for the first time on cross–examination. However, the jurors may infer that the prosecutor was trying to hide something; furthermore, the statement may be elicited in a less damning way or with milder effect if the prosecutor beats defense counsel to the punch and elicits the statement during Jones' direct examination. *United States v. Mobile Materials, Inc.*, 881 F.2d 866 (10th Cir. 1989) (entirely proper for government to disclose immunity agreements with witnesses in opening statements for the purpose of minimizing damage to the witness' credibility). Consider this tactic again when studying impeachment by prior conviction. Does the proponent of the witness need to resort to Rule 607 in order to take the "sting" out of expected prior conviction impeachment of a witness?

5. In *Hill*, the plaintiff produced testimony from a police officer that a bystander had been hit by flying debris and was seriously injured. Before being taken to the hospital, the bystander related that he saw the accident and told the officer "the truck blew the red light." The bystander later died, but the officer's oral report of this exchange was admitted against Roe under a hearsay exception. Now Roe wants to impeach the bystander by proof that the man was convicted of perjury three years ago. What result? See Rule 806.

Chapter 16

CREDIBILITY: IMPEACHMENT TECHNIQUES

Read Federal Rules of Evidence 608, 609, 610 and 613.

A. ATTACKS ON COMPETENCY

1. INTRODUCTION

Earlier we studied the elements of witness competency: (1) moral capacity–sincerity (2) capacity to observe–perception (3) capacity to remember–memory (4) capacity to relate–narration. We saw that as a general proposition, the former grounds for disqualification have evolved into grounds for impeachment.

2. THE TESTIMONIAL QUALITY OF SINCERITY

Atheism was once grounds for disqualification. Correspondingly, courts permitted direct attacks on the witness' sincerity. Courts allowed the cross–examiner to inquire whether the witness believed in a God who punishes perjury. Swancara, *Impeachment of Non–Religious Witnesses*, 13 ROCKY MTN. L. REV. 336 (1941). Theism was considered an important incentive for truthful testimony.

Over the years, judicial attitude toward this type of impeachment changed radically. The prevailing modern view is that religious belief is no longer required to be a competent witness. Nor is the witness' religious belief admissible on the witness' credibility. In almost all jurisdictions and under Federal Rule of Evidence 610, evidence of the witness' religious opinions is inadmissible to enhance or detract from his character for truthfulness. The Note to Rule 610 explains:

> While the rule forecloses inquiry into the religious beliefs or opinions of a witness for the purpose of showing that his character for truthfulness is affected by their nature, an inquiry for the purpose of showing interest or bias because of them is not within the prohibition. Thus disclosure of affiliation with a church which is a party to the litigation would be allowable under the rule.

Rule 610 implements the policy embodied in the First Amendment. That amendment protects the free exercise of religion, and the Supreme Court has been vigilant in protecting freedom of conscience. *Wallace v. Jaffree*, 472 U.S. 38 (1985). In *United States v. Sampol*, 636 F.2d 621, 666 (D.C. Cir. 1980), the court asserted that "[t]he purpose of [Rule 610] is to guard against the prejudice which may result from disclosure of a witness' faith. The scope of the prohibition includes unconventional or unusual religions." In *Government of the Virgin Islands v. Petersen*, 553 F.2d 324 (3d Cir. 1977), the court invoked Rule 610 to bar evidence that a witness was a member of the Rastafarian sect. Questions which amounted to an attack on the tenets of the Jehovah's Witnesses were deemed improper in *Redman v. Watch Tower Bible and Tract Society*, 630 N.E.2d 676 (Oh. 1994). Over repeated objections in *Malek v. Federal Ins. Co.*, 994 F.2d 49 (2d Cir. 1993), the defense was allowed to ask the plaintiff's accountant about whether he had other Hasidic clients and whether his teaching position was part of the Yeshiva University system. This was error.

In *People v. Wood*, 66 N.Y.2d 374, 497 N.Y.S.2d 340, 488 N.E.2d 86 (1985), out of scruple, the witness affirmed rather than swore. The court held that it was error to question the witness about the fact that he refused to swear. Courts are alert to this problem when a witness affirms, rather than taking an oath. In *State v. Rodriguez–Garcia*, 23 Kan. App. 2d 847, 937 P.2d 446 (1997), a state statute provided that "every person has a privilege to refuse to disclose his or her theological opinion or religious belief." When the prosecutor quizzed a witness about affirming and later argued that in her trial testimony "she didn't swear to God, she affirmed," this was error.

NOTES AND PROBLEMS

1. While Rule 610 is a general rule of exclusion, exceptions exist. A person's affiliation with a religious group is properly admissible where probative of an issue in a criminal prosecution. The government inquired into religious practices and beliefs in *United States v. Beasley*, 72 F.3d 1518 (11th Cir. 1996), and the court of appeals approved the inquiries against a Rule 403 challenge.

2. Problem 16–1. In *Hill*, Polecat calls an accident reconstructionist, Wentworth. On direct examination, Wentworth testifies favorably to Polecat. On cross–examination, Ms. Hill would like to elicit that Wentworth is a member of the New Church of the Holy Deity and that the church owns $10,000 of stock in Polecat. Does Rule 610 preclude the cross–examination? *See Firemen's Fund Ins. Co. v. Thien*, 63 F.3d 754, 761 (8th Cir. 1995). Note the last sentence in the Advisory Committee's Note quoted above.

3. Will the examination by the direct examiner sometimes authorize cross–examination in the otherwise forbidden area of religious beliefs? In a rape case, for example, if the prosecution introduces evidence of the victim's religious beliefs pertaining to sexual intercourse outside of marriage, can the defendant confront and impeach the victim on this issue? In *Postell v. State*, 407 S.E.2d 412 (Ga. App. 1991), the defendant claimed consent. The state argued that because of the victim's religious beliefs, she would not have had consensual intercourse with him. "[O]n cross–examination by the defense, the victim testified that on an occasion prior to the rape, she willingly performed oral sex at the defendant's request, and admitted that this was contrary to the teachings of her church."

To what extent should scientific evidence relating to sincerity – most notably, polygraph examinations and statements made under the influence of "truth sera"–be admissible? Here, the fundamental issue is the test's scientific validity. However, there is an additional, often unstated, consideration–our reluctance to admit expert evidence that directly infringes on the lay jury's traditional role of independently evaluating sincerity. The courts often balk at allowing scientific evidence to interfere with that role.

A leading illustration of this problem is the controversy over polygraph or "lie detector" evidence. The courts are split. Some allow it, but with various limitations and conditions. Other courts give the trial judge discretion to evaluate the proponent's foundation–a discretion ordinarily exercised to exclude the evidence. The majority of courts have announced a categorical rule that polygraph evidence is inadmissible. The following case advocates the latter view.

PEOPLE v. GARD

158 Ill. 2d 191, 632 N.E.2d 1026 (1994)

Harrison, Justice.

[A jury found the defendant guilty of two counts of arson. The intermediate appellate court affirmed, but the Illinois Supreme Court reversed because of the introduction of evidence regarding polygraph examinations. Two witnesses, Diana King and John Clutter, testified about lie detector tests and their results.]

This court has consistently held evidence pertaining to polygraph examination of a defendant generally inadmissible, declaring unequivocally in *People v. Baynes*, 88 Ill. 2d 225, 244, 58 Ill. Dec. 819, 430 N.E.2d 1070 (1981), that such evidence is inadmissible in Illinois because it is insufficiently reliable. Moreover, the court observed, "[n]o other form of evidence is as likely to be considered as completely determinative of guilt or innocence as a polygraph examination." (*Baynes*, 88 Ill. 2d at 244, 58 Ill. Dec. 819, 430 N.E.2d 1070). Because the results of polygraph examinations appear to be quasi–scientific, jurors are likely to give such results undue weight. *People v. Taylor*, 101 Ill. 2d 377, 391–92, 78 Ill. Dec. 359, 462 N.E.2d 478 (1984). As a consequence, the prejudicial effects of polygraph evidence substantially outweigh its probative value.

Shortly after its decision in *Baynes*, this court found the guidance provided there controlling in *People v. Yarbrough*, 93 Ill. 2d 421, 426, 67 Ill. Dec. 257, 444 N.E.2d 493 (1982). In *Baynes* the court had held polygraph evidence inadmissible in a criminal trial despite the defendant's stipulation prior to the polygraph examination that the results of the test would be admissible: stipulation cannot and does not render unreliable evidence reliable.

* * *

As the quotations from the record reveal, polygraph evidence was very much a part of this defendant's trial. It would serve no useful purpose to catalogue all of the references to polygraph testing that abound in this record. Suffice it to say that at defendant's trial such references were casual and common-place, virtually ubiquitous. Testimony concerning the polygraph examinations of both Diana King and John Clutter permeates the transcript of proceedings at trial. Indeed, during the course of defendant's trial the polygraph examination of John Clutter became the lodestar by which the jury was invited to measure truth: that which Clutter spoke until and during his polygraph examination was false; that which he spoke once advised by police that he had failed the polygraph examination was true. Clutter's testimony at trial was true. Clutter's testimony at trial was consistent with the latter; ergo, by implication, Clutter's testimony at trial was true. By further implication, other witnesses' testimony consistent with that of Clutter was necessarily true.

For the same reasons that this court has held evidence of polygraph examination of defendant inadmissible at trial, we hold evidence of polygraph examination of a witness inadmissible at trial. Evidence of polygraph testing is rendered no more reliable, and jurors deem it no less worthy of belief, because the person tested was a witness rather than a defendant. Whether the examination is of defendant or witness, evidence of polygraph testing is equally unreliable and likely to be accorded undue weight with the result that its prejudicial effect far exceeds its probative value. As this record amply demonstrates, the use of polygraph evidence at a defendant's trial is no less repugnant and no less an affront to the integrity of the judicial process when the examination has been given to a witness at the defendant's trial than it is when the examination has been given to the defendant himself.

It is a familiar rule that an objection to the introduction of evidence not made at the time of admission and an error not raised in a post–trial motion will be deemed waived for review. (*Baynes, supra* at 230). However, this court may notice error rising to the level of plain error in spite of the defendant's failure to record objections and to preserve properly the record for review. (*Baynes, supra* at 230). If the admission of evidence constitutes plain error that causes a miscarriage of justice upon a defendant or a tainting of the integrity and reputation of the judicial process, the error is considered although it was not brought to the attention of the trial court. (*Baynes, supra* at 231). While one purpose of the plain error rule is to afford certain protections to the accused, the other is to protect and to preserve the integrity and the reputation of the judicial process. (*Baynes, supra* at 230–31). As it was in *Baynes*, the latter purpose is the focus of our concern here. Like the evidence in *Baynes*, the evidence here is not so closely balanced that the defendant may be said to have been prejudiced by the introduction of the polygraph evidence and thereby prevented from receiving a fair trial. Like the defendant in *Baynes* this defendant himself caused, in part, the admission of polygraph evidence. Nevertheless, in *Baynes* this court determined that the stipulated admission of polygraph evidence rose to the level of plain error because it was error impinging upon the integrity of our judicial system. So, too, do we today rule that the admission of evidence of polygraph testing of witnesses at defendant's trial constituted plain error because it was error compromising the integrity and tarnishing the reputation of the judicial process itself.

Accordingly, we reverse the judgments of the appellate and circuit courts and remand the cause for a new trial. In light of our disposition concerning this issue, we need not consider the other point upon which defendant relies for reversal.

Judgments reversed; cause remanded.

NOTES

Gard probably speaks for most courts when it voices the fear that polygraph evidence will overwhelm the jury. That fear is an unstated premise in many cases excluding polygraph evidence. However, the courts' bias against polygraphy is arguably overblown. Empirical studies and simulations of jury evaluations of polygraph testimony suggest that polygraph evidence may not unduly influence the trier's assessment of evidence.

The academic debate has spilled over into the courts. Contrary to *Gard*, the United States Court of Appeals in *United States v. Posado*, 57 F.3d 428 (5th Cir. 1995), held that polygraph test results are not automatically inadmissible. "After *Daubert*, a per se rule [of exclusion] is not viable." *Id.* at 433. The court noted that "tremendous advances have been made in polygraph instrumentation and technique in the years since *Frye*." The Ninth Circuit has issued a similar holding. *United States v. Cordoba*, 104 F.3d 225, 229 (9th Cir. 1997). The *Daubert* decision also had an impact in *United States v. Galbreath*, 908 F. Supp. 877 (D.N.M. 1995). The court noted that although polygraph evidence had been repeatedly rejected, this was prior to *Daubert*. The court ruled that a polygraph expert's testimony is based on scientific knowledge that will assist the trier of fact.

Much of the debate over the admissibility of polygraph in federal courts has been stilled by the following decision.

UNITED STATES v. SCHEFFER

523 U.S. 303 (1998)

JUSTICE THOMAS announced the judgment of the Court.

[The Air Force accused an airman of using an illegal drug. He submitted to a polygraph test given by the Air Force and passed. At trial, admission was denied the polygraph results, and the Supreme Court approved exclusion of the evidence. The Court found no consensus that polygraph results are reliable, and also held that the jury is the lie detector.]

Respondent sought to introduce the polygraph evidence in support of his testimony that he did not knowingly use drugs. The military judge denied the motion, relying on Military Rule of Evidence 707, which provides in relevant part:

"(a)Notwithstanding any other provision of law, the results of a polygraph examination, the opinion of a polygraph examiner, or any reference to an offer to take, failure to take, or taking of a polygraph examination shall not be admitted into evidence.

The military judge determined that Rule 707 was constitutional because "the President may, through the Rules of Evidence, determine that credibility is not an area in which a fact finder needs help, and the polygraph is not a proces that has sufficient scientific acceptability to be relevant." He further reasoned that the factfinder might give undue weight to the polygraph examiner's testimony, and that collateral arguments about such evidence could consume "an inordinate amount of time and expense."

Respondent was convicted on all counts and was sentenced to a bad–conduct discharge, confinement for 30 months, total forfeiture of all pay and allowances, and reduction to the lowest enlisted grade. The Air Force Court of Criminal Appeals affirmed in all material respects, explaining that Rule 707 "does not arbitrarily limit the accused's ability to present reliable evidence."

    . . .

By a 3–to–2 vote, the United States Court of Appeals for the Armed Forces reversed. . . .

Rule 707 serves several legitimate interests in the criminal trial process. These interests include ensuring that only reliable evidence is introduced at trial, preserving the jury's role in determining credibility, and avoiding litigation that is collateral to the primary purpose of the trial. The rule is neither arbitrary nor disproportionate in promoting these ends. Nor does it implicate a sufficiently weighty interest of the defendant to raise a constitutional concern under our precedents.

A

State and federal governments unquestionably have a legitimate interest in ensuring that reliable evidence is presented to the trier of fact in a criminal trial. Indeed, the exclusion of unreliable evidence is a principal objective of many evidentiary rules.

The contentions of respondent and the dissent notwithstanding, there is simply no consensus that polygraphic evidence is reliable. To this day, the scientific community remains extremely polarized about the reliability of polygraph techniques. 1 D. Faigman, D. Kaye, M. Saks, & J. Sanders, Modern Scientific Evidence 565 §§ 14–2.0–3.0 (1997); *see also* 1 P. Giannelli & E. Imwinkelried, Scientific Evidence § 8–2(C), pp. 225–227 (2d ed. 1993); 1 J. Strong, McCormick on Evidence § 206, p. 909 (4th ed. 1992). Some studies have concluded that polygraph tests overall are accurate and reliable. *See e.g.* S. Abrams, The Complete Polygraph Handbook 190–191 (1968) (reporting the overall accuracy rate from laboratory studies involving the common "control question technique" polygraph to be "in the range of 87 percent"). Others have found that polygraph tests assess truthfulness significantly less accurately— that scientific field studies suggest the accuracy rate of the "control question technique" polygraph is "little better than could be obtained by the toss of a coin," that is, 50 percent. *See* Iacono & Lykken, The Scientific Status of Research on Polygraph Techniques: The Case Against Polygraph Tests, in 1 Modern Scientific Evidence, *above*, § 14–5.3, p. 629 (hereinafter Iacono & Lykken).

This lack of scientific consensus is reflected in the disagreement among state and federal courts concerning both the admissibility and the reliability of polygraphic evidence. Although some Federal Courts of Appeal have abandoned the *per se* rule excluding polygraph evidence, leaving its admission or exclusion to the discretion of district courts under *Daubert*, see e.g., *United States v. Posado*, 57 F.3d 428, 434 (C.A.5 1995); *United States v. Cordoba*, 104 F.3d 225, 228 (C.A.9 1997), at least one Federal Circuit has recently reaffirmed its *per se* ban, see *United States v. Sanchez*, 118 F.3d 192, 197 (C.A.4 1997), and another recently noted that it has "not decided whether polygraphy has reached a sufficient state of reliability to be admissible." *United States v. Messian*, 131 F.3d 36, 42 (C.A.2 1997). Most states maintain *per se* rules excluding polygraph evidence. New Mexico is unique in making polygraph evidence generally admissible without the prior stipulation of the parties and without significant restriction. *See* N.M. Rule Evid. § 11– 707. Whatever their approach, state and federal courts continue to express doubt about whether such evidence is reliable.

The approach taken by the President in adopting Rule 707—excluding polygraph evidence in all military trials—is a rational and proportional means of advancing the legitimate interest in barring unreliable evidence. Although the degree of reliability of polygraph evidence may depend upon a variety of identifiable factors, there is simply no way to know in a particular case whether a polygraph examiner's conclusion is accurate, because certain doubts and uncertainties plague even the best polygraph exams. Individual jurisdictions therefore may reasonably reach differing conclusions as to whether polygraph evidence should be admitted. We cannot say, then, that presented with such widespread uncertainty, the President acted arbitrarily or disproportionately in promulgating a *per se* rule excluding all polygraph evidence.
. . .

For the foregoing reasons, Military Rule of Evidence 707 does not unconstitutionally abridge the right to present a defense. The judgment of the Court of Appeals is reversed.

[Footnotes omitted. Opinion of Justice Kennedy, with whom Justices O'Connor, Ginsburg and Breyer joined, concurring in part and concurring in the judgment, omitted in reprinting.]

NOTE

Polygraph examination results were rejected in *United States v. Campos,* 217 F.3d 707 (9th Cir. 2000). Prior to her trial for transporting marijuana, Campos underwent a polygraph test. During the examination, the examiner asked Campos whether she knew there were drugs in the van which she drove into the United States from Mexico. When she answered no, the polygraph examiner concluded Campos was answering truthfully. Campos sought admission at her trial of this polygraph evidence, but the district court precluded its admission and the Court of Appeals affirmed. Applying the rule that no expert may state an opinion that the defendant lacked the mental state to commit the crime, the court held that the examiner's proposed testimony improperly attempted to relate the defendant's mental state.

Courts which apply a different scientific evidence test than the *Daubert* standard often reach the same result as *Scheffer* on polygraph proof. *Robertson v. State*, 268 Ga. 772, 493 S.E.2d 697 (1997) (absent a stipulation of admissibility from the state, exclusion of polygraph results is the rule). *Frye* jurisdictions are inclined to reject polygraph evidence on grounds that it has not gained general acceptance among relevant experts, *See McKensie v. Florida*, 653 So. 2d 395 (Fla. App. 1995); *Commonwealth v. Mendes*, 547 N.E. 2d 35 (Mass. 1989).

3. THE TESTIMONIAL QUALITIES OF PERCEPTION, MEMORY, AND NARRATION

In contrast to the area of sincerity, courts have been fairly receptive to evidence attacking the other elements of the witness' competency. We shall see later that according to the best available empirical evidence, the most common cause of erroneous testimony is misperception or misrecollection rather than deliberate perjury. Moreover, a claim that the witness is mistaken is certainly less insulting to the witness than a claim that she is lying. Both factors– the relative frequency of the different causes of erroneous testimony and the more offensive nature of sincerity attacks–cut in favor of the more liberal admissibility of evidence attacking the other testimonial qualities. That happens to be the case. As an illustration, at common law the courts do not apply the collateral fact rule to this evidence. In 3 D. LOUISELL & C. MUELLER, FEDERAL EVIDENCE § 342 (1979), the authors state:

> Like proof of bias, proof of any kind of incapacity on the part of a witness is always relevant. While cross–examination is the usual vehicle for demonstrating incapacity, extrinsic evidence of many kinds is admissible, and should not be rejected as merely "collateral." However, when the attacking party has had a reasonable opportunity to make his basic points, the trial court may curtail cross–examination or exclude extrinsic evidence pursuant to the general directives of Rules 403 and 611.

Many kinds of information about a "normal" person are relevant to the witness' ability to observe, remember, and narrate. These include her education, intelligence, and interests. This information may be brought out as part of routine cross–examination. However, the trial judge has considerable discretion to protect the witness from harassment.

The cross–examiner may test sight, hearing, or memory by asking questions about the events in question or even unrelated events. The examiner may also conduct an in–court demonstration to test the witness' ability to observe, remember, or relate. Courtroom demonstrations are dangerous; they can backfire if the witness performs well. A demonstration should not be undertaken without careful planning and preparation. If the examiner resorts to the "hop, skip, and jump" technique of cross–examination—questioning the witness about events out of chronological sequence and rapidly shifting from one event to another the cross–examiner may succeed in confusing the witness. However, the likelihood is that the jurors will also be confused and dismiss the witness' mistake as innocent, excusable misrecollection.

Memory and perception can be affected by drugs or alcohol. The attacking party may show that the witness was intoxicated or under the influence of drugs at the time of the events to which she testifies. *United States v. Leonard*, 494 F.2d 955, 971 (D.C. Cir. 1974). Similarly, it may be shown that the witness is under the influence at the time of testifying. *United States v. Banks*, 520 F.2d 627, 631 (7th Cir. 1975). Courts sometimes instruct the jury that the testimony of such a witness should be considered with caution and great care. *United States v. Yarbrough*, 55 F.3d 280 (7th Cir. 1995).

Proof that the witness is a chronic alcoholic is another matter. Most courts exclude evidence of chronic drunkenness unless the evidence shows that the witness was intoxicated at the time of the relevant historical event. *Springer v. Reimers*, 4 Cal. App. 3d 325, 84 Cal. Rptr. 486 (1970). In *United States v. DiPaolo*, 804 F.2d 225 (2d Cir. 1986), the court held that it is within the proper scope of cross–examination to determine whether a witness was under the influence of alcohol or narcotics at the time of observation of events in dispute, or at the time of testifying. Then the court added: "As Wigmore points out, however, 'a general habit of intemperance tells us nothing of the witness' testimonial incapacity [unless it involves] actual intoxication at the time of the event observed or at the time of testifying.' "

There is a variation on this theme in some courts where drug addiction is the issue, not alcoholism. Although the view is not universal, some courts admit proof of a witness' drug use to show the witness' general lack of credibility. Annot., 65 A.L.R.3d 705, 725, 728 (1975). *See Furlong v. Circle Line Statue of Liberty Ferry, Inc.*, 902 F. Supp. 65 (S.D.N.Y. 1995) (if it is shown that a witness was a drug user at the time of a litigated event, the drug use may be relevant to credibility since it can affect perception).

NOTES AND PROBLEMS

1. Is the differential treatment of chronic alcoholism and drug addiction justified? Dean McCormick contended that at least in part, the discrimination reflects the "social odium . . . attached" to drug abuse. C. MCCORMICK, HANDBOOK OF THE LAW OF EVIDENCE § 44, at 163 (4th ed. 1992). Is that the only basis? Suppose that the drug in question is contraband. Is drug abuse logically relevant to credibility on more than one theory?

2. Problem 16–2. In *Hill*, during her case–in–chief the plaintiff calls Mr. Menlow, who claims to have witnessed the collision. During its case–in–chief, Polecat calls Mr. Jensen. Jensen is prepared to testify that he was with Menlow shortly before the collision and saw Menlow swallow two white capsules. Ms. Hill objects that "the witness can't identify the contents of the capsule." What ruling? What if Jensen were also prepared to testify that soon after swallowing the pills, Menlow's speech became slurred and he had "a sort of dazed appearance"?

As we have seen, most jurisdictions liberally admit evidence of deficiencies in the witness' perceptual, retentive, and narrative capacities. Some commentators urge courts to go further and to authorize widespread psychological evaluation of trial witnesses; however, this raises significant issues. Can the party attacking the witness' credibility ask that the witness be tested or observed in the courtroom by a psychiatrist or psychologist, and then have that expert testify about the witness' ability to perceive, remember, or relate? What about psychological testimony evaluating the motives of a witness?

3 J. WEINSTEIN & M. BERGER, WEINSTEIN'S EVIDENCE ¶ 607[04] (Matthew Bender & Co., Inc., 1995)

At first glance, the promise of such expert aid is appealing. Juries, after all, though the final arbiters of fact, have always been allowed the help of experts in evaluating facts whose significance laymen could not be expected to understand. Certainly psychiatrists or psychologists are more cognizant of the complexities of the human mind than the average juror or judge. Accordingly, there are those who argue that the expert—particularly the psychiatrist—should be used in evaluating the credibility of a witness as "the policy of admitting any relevant material demands that he be heard." To such advocates, rejection of psychiatric testimony is an example of rigid adherence to outmoded ideas and a refusal to acknowledge that psychiatry is a science.

But the writings of other commentators and judges suggest that psychiatric testimony often confuses rather than enlightens. Experts often disagree with each other, are unclear and contradictory in their terminology, and do not relate their diagnosis of the witness to his ability to give credible testimony since they are not geared to answering the questions in which a court is interested.

The consequence is that although there is undoubtedly a national tendency toward admitting psychiatric testimony, the federal courts have been hesitant about moving in this direction. In accordance with most other jurisdictions, they have refused to admit the results of lie detector tests and truth–serum interviews where they have not generally recognized the trustworthiness and reliability of such tests as being sufficiently well–established to accord the results the status of competent evidence. The federal courts have also been reluctant to order psychiatric examinations of witnesses. At least one judge has concluded that courts lack inherent power to order such an examination of a witness in a criminal case.

The current hesitation of the federal judiciary is particularly striking because federal courts pioneered the use of a psychiatrist to evaluate the testimony of a witness. In *United States v. Hiss*, 88 F. Supp. 559 (D.C.N.Y. 1950), a prosecution for perjury, the defendant attempted to impeach the cardinal government witness, Whittaker Chambers, with psychiatric testimony that Chambers was a psychopathic personality disposed to making false accusations. Defendant's psychiatrist witness was permitted to state his diagnosis on the basis of a twenty–three page hypothetical question embody-ing facts testified to in court by Chambers, his in–court observations of Chambers, and his study of Chambers' writings. But although all discussions of the use of psychiatric testimony dwell at length on the Hiss trial, and the case has been hailed as the dawn of a new era, in the twenty years that have elapsed, *United States v. Hiss* has been cited more frequently in the federal courts in distinguishing the case at hand than as a precedent.

What then should a federal judge do when counsel wishes to use psychiatric testimony to impeach the credibility of a witness? Probably the most that can be said is that he should maintain a flexible attitude so that he can tailor his decision to the individual facts and accommodate himself to new medical developments. One commentator has suggested that the court should know:

> (1) the method or technique of psychiatric evaluation upon which an opinion as to credibility is based;

> (2) the mode of classification implicit in the opinion; and

> (3) the theory relating to the effect of the mental condition upon credibility.

NOTES

1. In McCord, *Syndromes, Profiles, and Other Mental Exotica: A New Approach to the Admissibility of Nontraditional Psychological Evidence in Criminal Cases*, 66 OR. L. REV. 19, 47 (1987), the author observes that "[w]hile several cases suggest support for . . . *Hiss*, only one court seems to follow it." There is a plausible argument that a psychiatric opinion based on a pretrial examination would be far more probative than the Hiss testimony based on in–court observations.

2. Do you think that the real reason for the courts' reluctance to admit expert testimony on credibility is a doubt about the validity of the scientific techniques? Or is it an intuitive belief that the jurors are generally capable of assessing witnesses' credibility without expert testimony?

One commentator notes that in a small but growing minority of jurisdic-tions, courts have permitted expert psychological witnesses to educate jurors about the credibility of witnesses. Friedland, *On Common Sense and the Evaluation of Witness Credibility*, 40 CASE W. RES. L. REV. 165 (1989–1990). He attributes this to an increased awareness of the inaccuracy of juror credi-bility assessments based exclusively on common sense. Psychological studies call into question the judicial system's reliance on common sense to assess credibility. On the current state of psychological testimony generally, see Com-ment, *Admissibility of Expert Psychological Evidence in the Federal Courts*, 27 ARIZ. ST. L.J. 1315 (1995).

B. PRIOR INCONSISTENT STATEMENTS AND SPECIFIC CONTRADICTION

1. PRIOR INCONSISTENT STATEMENTS AND ACTS

The logical relevance of prior inconsistent statement impeachment is obvious. If on a prior occasion the witness made a statement inconsistent with his testimony at trial, the inconsistency *at least* calls into question the quality of the witness' memory — and maybe more. This mode of impeachment is quite common in civil cases because of the availability of deposition transcripts. The transcript is an ideal source for inconsistent statements. The following text explains and illustrates the effective impeaching use of a deposition transcript.

A. MORRILL, TRIAL DIPLOMACY § 4.29 (2d ed. 1972)

A definite style and technique should be adopted by every trial lawyer in using a deposition to impeach a witness. The following is one of the techniques used to impeach a witness:

Q: You testified in court today that when you first saw Mr. White's automobile, it was traveling about 40 M.P.H.

A: That's correct.

Q: Now, Mr. Smith, do you recall giving your deposition about six months ago?

A: Yes.

Q: That deposition was taken in your lawyer's office, was it not?

A: Yes.

Q: And your lawyer was present the entire time I was asking you those questions?

A: Yes.

Q: There was a court stenographer present at that time, just as there is one here in court today?

A: Yes.

Q: And that court stenographer was taking down all of the questions I asked of you and all of the answers that you gave?

A: Yes.

Q: Before you testified, were you sworn to tell the truth?

A: Yes.

Q: Before I proceeded to ask you any questions, I asked you to listen carefully to my questions and told you I would be happy to repeat any questions you did not understand; is that correct?

A: That is correct.

Q: Do you remember this question being asked of you and this answer being given by you?

[At this juncture, the examining attorney turns to opposing counsel and gives the page reference in the deposition from which he is about to read.]

Q: "Can you estimate the speed of Mr. White's automobile when you first saw it?"

A: "Yes. It was traveling about 25 M.P.H."

Q: Do you recall that question being asked of you and that answer being given by you while you were under oath?

A: Yes.

At this point, the witness has been impeached. There are several possible questions to ask next in following up the impeachment in order to highlight the inconsistencies. Some of the more commonly used are as follows:

Q: Were you lying then or are you lying now?

Q: At the time you gave your deposition, less time had gone by and you undoubtedly remembered the facts more clearly at that time, is that not so?

Q: Mr. Smith, would you like to change your testimony at this time?

I feel it is usually preferable to say nothing at all. If the point has been properly made by the cross–examiner, it is not necessary to give the witness a slap in the face. I do not feel such a slap adds any emphasis to the point already made, and it is always possible that the jurors may sympathize with the witness and dislike the examiner for what they may feel is an unnecessary affront.

NOTES AND PROBLEMS

1. Problem 16–3. In *Hill*, Polecat cross–examines Mr. Menlow, who witnessed the collision. Polecat produces a pretrial statement from Menlow wherein he says he really did not see the whole thing, and attempts to impeach him by referring to the statement. There is an objection: "Beyond the scope. We said nothing about any pretrial statement during our direct, your honor." What ruling? See Rule 611(b). Remember the provision for matters of credibility contained in the federal rule and mentioned earlier in the material on scope of cross–examination.

2. After review of the foregoing passage, it is apparent why Wigmore characterized cross–examination as "the 'greatest legal engine ever invented for the discovery of truth.'" *California v. Green*, 399 U.S. 149, 158, 90 S. Ct. 1930, 1935, 26 L. Ed. 2d 489, 497 (1970) (quoting 5 WIGMORE ON EVIDENCE § 1367, at 32 (Chadbourn rev. 1974)). In *State v. Silva*, 621 A.2d 17 (N.J. 1993), the court listed modes of impeachment, and the prominent place of contradiction by prior statement is noteworthy: "[T]he law recognizes five acceptable modes of attack upon the credibility of a witness: (1) prior inconsistent statements, (2) partiality, (3) defect of character, (4) defect of capacity of the witness to observe, remember, or recount matters, and (5) proof by others that material facts are otherwise than as testified to by the witness under attack. Wigmore (Chadbourn rev. 1974), § 33, at 111–12."

3. In addition to depositions, prior inconsistent statements emanate from a number of other sources. One of these sources is the opponent's own documents. If an opposing witness refreshes his recollection on the witness stand from a writing, the cross–examiner can demand to see the document and impeach the witness from it. *See* FED. R. EVID. 612. The proponent of the witness frequently attempts to block impeachment by objecting to disclosure on privilege grounds, but many cases sweep aside the objection and allow the impeachment to proceed. Floyd, A *"Delicate and Difficult Task": Balancing* *the Competing Interests of Federal Rule of Evidence 612, the Work Product Doctrine, and the Attorney–Client Privilege*, 44 BUFF. L. REV. 101 (1996).

4. As noted, sometimes prior inconsistent statements which are used to impeach come from the opponent's own documents, such as business files in *Travelers Ins. Co. v. Smith*, 991 S.W.2d 591 (Ark. 1999), an insurance company was sued over the conduct of one of its claim adjusters. At trial, a company supervisor swore that the adjuster did not have a history of misconduct. The plaintiff then put in evidence an investigative report drawn from another case wherein a claims department manager for the defendant insurance company concluded that the adjuster who was sued in the *Smith* case had misrepresented facts. The supervisor's trial testimony denying that the company had ever previously thought that the adjuster misrepresented his actions opened the door to this form of impeachment under Rule 613.

5. Prior inconsistent statements can also be found in declarations made by one's opponent during settlement negotiations. If a party testifies at trial, a statement of fact made earlier by that party during settlement negotiations or mediation proceedings may be brought up by the opponent. But will the opponent be able to impeach with such statements? The situation is complicated by policy considerations that bar mention of settlement, as explained in Chapter 27. The freedom of expression which often marks settlement negotiations or mediation discussions will be inhibited, it is argued, if statements made there are later used to impeach the declarant. However, rules of evidence should not be a shield to commit perjury. One commentator argues for more liberal impeachment use of factual representations made during settlement negotiations when the declarant contradicts himself at trial. Rambo, *Impeaching Lying Parties With Their Statements During Negotiation: Demysticizing the Public Policy Rationale Behind Evidence Rule 408 and the Mediation Privilege Statutes*, 75 Wash. L. Rev. 1037 (2000). To the contrary and rejecting impeachment by settlement statements, *see EEOC v. Gear Petroleum, Inc.*, 948 F.2d 1542 (10th Cir. 1991).

a. Cross–Examination about a Prior Inconsistent Statement or Act

In most cases, the inconsistent statement is an assertion about factual data. Here is an easy example. In *Hill*, assume that Mr. Worker testifies on direct examination that Roe ordered him to deliver a package across town but told him to "take your time cause there's no rush." At his deposition, Worker stated that Roe instructed him "to hustle—it's a rush order."

What if the inconsistency stems from opinion rather than factual data? Suppose on direct, Worker merely described his conduct in terms suggesting that he was driving carefully. Could Ms. Hill impeach Worker with a pretrial statement to a friend that he, Worker, was "at fault" in the accident? At common law, the answer was no; the inconsistency had to be a factual statement rather than an opinion. G. LILLY, AN INTRODUCTION TO THE LAW OF EVIDENCE § 83 (1978). Both Wigmore and McCormick attacked the limitation. Responding to the argument, most courts now permit impeachment by prior statements in opinion form.

More fundamentally, does the evidence even have to take the form of a statement? Can a nonverbal act qualify? Common sense suggests an affirmative answer. On impeachment by inconsistent acts, *see Brandt v. Vulcan, Inc.*, 30 F.3d 752 (7th Cir. 1994). In some contexts, courts have accepted scientific testimony about the inconsistencies of conduct. For example, suppose that, in a child sexual abuse prosecution, the defendant is the father of the alleged victim. On cross–examination of the alleged victim, the defense counsel attempts to elicit the fact that she delayed reporting the alleged offense to anyone, including her mother. This is inconsistency by conduct. The prosecutor objects and proffers that he can submit testimony by a child psychologist that in cases of intra–family child abuse, it is "common and quite normal" for the victim to be too afraid to report the abuse. Should the judge preclude the cross–examination? Or should the judge permit the cross–examination but allow the prosecutor to introduce the expert's testimony later in the trial? Most jurisdictions have opted for the latter solution, allowing the "inconsistent act" impeachment to proceed. 2 G. Joseph & S. Saltzburg, Evidence in America: The Federal Rules in the States § 51.3, at 94–97 (Supp. 1992).

Sometimes a witness makes an extensive explanation of a point at trial, even though he was silent on the point earlier when he gave a pretrial statement. Can the impeaching attorney confront the witness with his prior omission or silence as an inconsistent statement or an inconsistent act? The following excerpt addresses that question:

3 J. WEINSTEIN & M. BERGER, WEINSTEIN'S EVIDENCE ¶ 607[06] (Matthew Bender & Co., Inc., 1981) (some citations omitted)

[A] perplexing point is whether a failure to assert a fact it would have been natural to affirm amounts to an assertion of the nonexistence of the fact which can be used to impeach testimony in which the witness admitted the fact's existence. According to Wigmore such a failure to make an assertion should be admitted as a prior inconsistent statement, and the federal cases are in accord.

The Supreme Court in *Jenkins v. Anderson*[29] cited Wigmore with approval in holding that a defendant's failure to tell police authorities that he had killed in self–defense could be used to impeach him after he testified that he had acted solely in self–defense. Distinguishing its decision in *Doyle v. Ohio*[30] on the ground that defendant's silence in that case had been induced by the government through *Miranda* warnings informing the defendant of his right to silence, the majority of the court held that impeachment by use of prearrest silence does not violate the Fourteenth Amendment."[31] This is not to say that

---

[29] 447 U.S. 231, 100 S. Ct. 2124, 65 L. Ed.2d 86 (1986).

[30] 426 U.S. 610, 96 S. Ct. 2240, 49 L. Ed. 2d 91 (1976).

[31] 447 U.S. at 240, 100 S. Ct. at 2130, 65 L. Ed. 2d 96.

prearrest silence will be usable in every instance: it "cannot be used for impeachment where silence is not probative of a defendant's credibility and where prejudice to the defendant might result." Except for silence induced by governmental action, the Supreme Court's decision in *Jenkins* leaves impeachment by silence an evidential rather than a constitutional matter. . . .

Jenkins's distinction between pre–and post–*Miranda* silence seems unsound. *Miranda* was designed to equalize the position of the uninformed defendant with the person who knows his rights. *Jenkins* puts at a disadvantage the defendant who knew enough to remain silent without a warning. On its facts, however, *Jenkins* is not particularly objectionable. After allegedly killing in self–defense, the defendant disappeared for two weeks. Arguably, a reasonable person would have remained to tell the police of the presence of the cadaver. "Hit–and–run" tactics are arguably evidence of a guilty mind, although defendant, then apparently on probation, might well have run out of fear of an unfair and unfavorable impression on his probation officer and other law enforcement officials even if he were guiltless. Had defendant remained on the scene and said to the police before *Miranda* warnings, "I know my rights and I am going to remain silent," use of this refusal to talk would have been shocking on both reasonable inference and constitutional grounds. On Rule 403 grounds the technique used by the prosecutor seems particularly unfortunate since it brought clearly to the jury's attention the defendant's prior criminal history. *Jenkins* puts an added burden on trial courts to weigh carefully Rule 403 implications of this form of impeachment. Prohibiting cross–examination based on silence in *Jenkins*, had the proper objection been made, would have been desirable.

The most unsettled aspect of determining what amounts to an inconsistency is presented when a witness denies all recollection of a matter about which he had formerly made a statement. Can this former statement be regarded as inconsistent? The common law practice—still probably followed in most jurisdictions—would not consider such statements inconsistent and would not, therefore, permit their use even for impeachment purposes. Wigmore objected to a rule of blanket exclusion noting that

> the unwilling witness often takes refuge in a failure to remember, and the astute liar is sometimes impregnable unless this flank can be exposed to an attack of this sort. An absolute rule of prohibition would do more harm than good, and the trial Court should have discretion.

NOTES AND PROBLEMS

1. The foregoing passage suggests two separate scenarios. It is important to keep the competing patterns in mind. In the first, the witness testifies fully at trial about facts he did not mention when he was initially interviewed or deposed. The second situation is one where the witness gave a full pretrial statement, but then claims at trial he cannot remember the events at issue. The latter situation raises some special questions. Counsel may not need to rely exclusively upon an impeachment theory where the trial witness claims he cannot remember. The details of the earlier statement may be elicited under a "refreshing recollection" theory. Dean Ladd's article in the next subsection suggests the technique.

2. How directly must a prior statement conflict with the witness' trial testimony in order to impeach with it? One standard for the requirement of inconsistency in prior statements used for impeachment allows the cross–examiner to impeach when there is "any material variance" between the testimony of the witness and the witness' previous statement. *State v Johanesen*, 873 P.2d 1065, 1069 n.6 (Ore. 1994). "The prior statement 'need only bend in a different direction'" than the trial testimony. J. MCNAUGHT & H. FLANNERY, MASSACHUSETTS EVIDENCE: A COURTROOM REFERENCE 13–5 (1988). Who decides whether an "inconsistency" exists? Is it governed by Rule 104 (a) or (b)? *See United States v. Bonnett*, 877 F.2d 1450, 1463 (10th Cir. 1989) ("the determination as to whether the prior testimony is truly inconsistent is a matter within the discretion of the trial judge").

3. Courts are sometimes called upon to make a "meticulous" examination of the inconsistency issue. *United States v. Higa*, 55 F.3d 448 (9th Cir. 1995). *See Lentomyntioy v. Medivac, Inc.*, 997 F.2d 364 (7th Cir. 1993) (two pretrial statements of an expert seemed to be inconsistent).

4. Problem 16–4. In *Hill*, prior to trial the plaintiff deposes Mr. Worker. During the deposition, Worker states that there were two reasons for his trip the day of the accident. First, Mr. Roe had instructed him to deliver a package across town. Second, there is a gas station on the other side of town with the cheapest diesel gas, and Roe had instructed Worker "to fill up the tank there to keep expenses down." At trial on direct examination, Worker testifies that "my purpose in driving cross town was to drop off that package, as the boss told me." On cross–examination, may Ms. Hill use the deposition transcript to impeach Worker? Is Worker's failure to mention the other purpose "inconsistent"? *Erickson v. Erickson & Co.*, 212 Minn. 119, 2 N.W.2d 824, 827 (1942).

5. Rule 613(a) expressly states that, when cross–examining a witness about a prior inconsistent statement, "the statement need not be shown nor its contents disclosed to the witness at that time. . . ." As we shall see in the excerpt from Dean Ladd's article in the next subsection, at common law when the prior inconsistent statement was in writing, "the writing [had to] be shown to the witness before . . . interrogation upon its content. . . ." Rule 613(a) seems to abolish that requirement. However, Judge Posner has ruled that the trial judge has discretion to require the cross–examination to follow the common law practice. *United States v. Marks*, 816 F.2d 1207, 1211 (7th Cir. 1987) ("If defense counsel had been reading from a transcript of a previous trial or deposition, there would have been no justification for the district judge's procedure. But since a statement appearing in an interview report could easily be garbled, yet seem authoritative when read from a paper that the jury would infer was an official FBI document, the judge was reasonable in insisting that the witness be allowed to examine his purported statement before being impeached by it").

b. Extrinsic Evidence of a Prior Inconsistent Statement or Act

The witness you cross–examined has recently left the stand. You want to impeach him further. The party which originally called the witness has now rested its case. May you call a witness during your part of the case to testify about prior inconsistent statements or acts by the earlier witness? Cross–examining witness #1 about his or her own statement is sometimes referred to as intrinsic impeachment while calling witness #2 to establish witness #1's statement is styled extrinsic impeachment. In the case of prior inconsistent statements, you may present the extrinsic evidence if you satisfy three conditions.

First, at common law, you must lay a foundation during the initial witness' cross–examination. Dean Ladd analyzes the foundational requirement. The Rule of The Queen's Case, mentioned in Dean Ladd's article, is the rule announced in 1820 in an English decision: *Queen Caroline's Case*: "If it be intended to bring the credit of a witness into question by proof of anything he may have said or declared touching the case, the witness is first asked, upon cross–examination, whether or not he has said or declared that which is intended to be proved." In the case of written prior inconsistent statements, many trial judges construed the rule to mean that the cross–examiner had to show the writing to the witness before questioning the witness about the inconsistent statement in writing.

LADD, SOME OBSERVATIONS ON CREDIBILITY: IMPEACHMENT OF WITNESSES, 52 Cornell Law Quarterly 239, 245 (1967)

The Rule of The Queen's Case required that the writing be shown to the witness before permitting interrogation upon its content, thus eliminating what may be an effective part of the impeachment. Likewise, in reference to an oral statement made out of court, counsel on cross–examination may prefer, for the purpose of impeachment, first to ask the witness what he had said, if anything, rather than confront him initially with the statement. In the situation either of a writing or of an oral statement, if the witness were asked what he said before being confronted with the statement, he might give a different story, thus disclosing his desire to evade the effect of what he had said previously. . . . [The issue is the timing of when a contradictory declaration should be made known to the declarant. In most jurisdictions the modern rule is that, before extrinsic proof is made of the statement or the writing,] the statement must be made known or the writing shown to the declarant so that he will have the opportunity to identify and explain or deny it. . . .

A common practice is to proceed as though attempting to refresh the recollection of the witness, making the content of the statement known to him; then, if he denies making the statement, proof by extrinsic evidence may be offered. The detailed steps for impeachment by proof of prior statements of a witness contradictory to the testimony given in court fit into a simple formula. A foundation should be laid, identifying the time, place, occasion, and the person to whom it is claimed the declaration in question was made. The witness should then be informed of the statement and asked if he made it. Only if he denies making the statement may those to whom the statement was made be called to present the impeaching testimony. They, too, will be examined in a similar manner to establish the making of the statement. If the alleged statement was in writing, it would be shown to the declarant with opportunity to admit or deny it as his. In event of denial, the writing should be authenticated and offered in evidence. Some courts permit only the reading of the statement to the jury.

A significant exception applies when the witness is a party and has made an out–of–court declaration inconsistent with his testimony. The statement would be used by the adverse party only if deserving to the declarant and, therefore, is admissible as an admission. It is substantive evidence requiring no foundation other than proof of the fact that the statement was made by the party against whom it is offered.

———

Modern practice is decidedly more flexible. Federal Rule of Evidence 613(b) is in point. Rule 613(b), borrowing heavily from California Evidence Code §§ 768 and 770 provides:

> (b) Extrinsic evidence of prior inconsistent statement of witness. Extrinsic evidence of a prior inconsistent statement by a witness is not admissible unless the witness is afforded an opportunity to explain or deny the same and the opposite party is afforded an opportunity to interrogate the witness thereon, or the interests of justice otherwise require. This provision does not apply to admissions of a party–opponent as defined in Rule 801(d)(2).

PROBLEM

Problem 16–5. In *Devitt*, the defense learns that Paterson told a friend, Ms. Garret, that "I made the whole thing up, and those stupid cops are buying it hook, line, and sinker." At trial, Paterson becomes faint and claims shortness of breath at the end of the direct examination, and the defense counsel is reluctant to confront him directly with his statements to Ms. Garret. Moreover, the defense counsel believes that the later in the trial Ms. Garret testifies, the more surprising and dramatic her testimony will be. As Paterson begins to leave the witness stand, the defense counsel requests that he "be excused subject to recall." The judge grants the request. During the defense case–in–chief, the defense calls Ms. Garret. When it becomes clear to the prosecutor that Ms. Garret is going to testify about Mr. Paterson's statement, the prosecutor objects:

> O. Your Honor, I must object. This is obviously extrinsic evidence to impeach the victim, and there was absolutely no foundation during cross.

What ruling? Morena has adopted Federal Rule of Evidence 613(b). *See In the Matter of Nautilus Motor Tanker Co., Ltd.*, 862 F. Supp. 1251 (D.N.J. 1994) (while witness must be afforded opportunity to address statement, no particular sequence or timing is necessary).

———

If the court insists upon a foundation during cross–examination, the second condition for introducing extrinsic evidence is that the witness' answer must ordinarily be a denial or evasion. This condition is a corollary of the legal irrelevance doctrine. If the witness fully admits the inconsistent statement, there is no need to present cumulative, extrinsic evidence of the statement. Rule 403 would dictate the exclusion of the extrinsic evidence as a "waste of time." In contrast, the witness' flat denial of the statement creates the most compelling need for the extrinsic evidence. Modernly, most courts are lax in enforcing this condition and admit evidence of the prior statement even if the witness' answer falls short of a flat denial. C. McCORMICK, HANDBOOK OF THE LAW OF EVIDENCE § 37, at 20 (4th ed. 1992). The third condition is the collateral fact rule, below.

NOTE AND PROBLEMS

1. Problem 16–6. Assume a variation of the facts in Problem 16–5. When Paterson is on the stand he is asked about his statement to Ms. Garret. He answers: "I don't remember saying that to her," or is evasive, "I could have, but I doubt it." Defense counsel argues that Paterson's evasions and claims of memory lapse amount to implied denials of the facts he earlier admitted to Ms. Garret. What ruling? *See United States v. Insana*, 423 F.2d 1165 (2d Cir.), *cert. denied*, 400 U.S. 841 (1970).

2. Problem 16–7. Assume that when confronted by the defense counsel, Paterson fully admits the statement to Ms. Garret, and simply adds, "I don't know why I said that to her, it was wrong to do so." Now the defense counsel seeks to call Ms. Garret "to further prove Paterson's improper statement." The prosecution objects on the ground that since Paterson admitted the prior statement, further evidence is not needed. What ruling?

3. Some variation in approach may be encountered with respect to the last problem, depending upon the court. Lax enforcement of Rule 403 prompts some judges to permit extrinsic evidence. However, in federal practice a strict approach is often encountered. *See Bank Atlantic v. Paine Webber, Inc.*, 955 F.2d 1467 (11th Cir. 1992) ("when a witness admits making a prior inconsistent statement, extrinsic proof of the statement is excludable"); *United States v. Soundingsides*, 825 F.2d 1468 (10th Cir. 1987) (when witness admits prior statement, witness is adequately impeached and further evidence is not needed). *Compare United States v. Lashmett*, 965 F.2d 179 (7th Cir. 1992). State courts sometimes allow introduction of the statement itself, even in the face of an acknowledgment of it by the declarant. *See, e.g., Duckworth v. State*, 268 Ga. 566, 492 S.E.2d 201 (1997) (cross–examiner does not have to offer prior written statement into evidence before impeaching witness; however, whether witness admits or denies making statement, written statement may be admissible).

2. SPECIFIC CONTRADICTION

This impeachment technique is closely related to, and often confused with impeachment by prior inconsistent statement. To illustrate the difference, suppose that in *Hill*, witness A testified for the plaintiff that "[W]orker was going at least fifty miles an hour just before impact." If Polecat's attorney employed prior inconsistent statement impeachment, the attorney could call witness B to testify that witness A told her that "the car was really going only abut 35—tops." However, Polecat's attorney might specifically contradict witness A by presenting witness B's testimony that she also observed the accident and that in her opinion, "The car was really going only about 35—tops."

The impeaching effect of specific contradiction is indirect. The second witness does not charge that the first witness is a liar or even describe an inconsistent statement by the first witness. The second witness merely gives a contrary version of the facts on the merits of the case. However, inferentially, the specific contradiction is logically relevant to the first witness' credibility; if the second witness is correct, the first witness must be lying or mistaken. In short, specific contradiction evidence has dual logical relevance; on its face, it purports to relate to the historical merits, but it also indirectly attacks the credibility of the opposing witnesses.

Like the prior inconsistent statement technique, this technique raises legal irrelevance problems. We want the jury to concentrate on the historical merits of the case. Cross–examining a witness about his or her credibility may distract a jury somewhat from the merits, but calling a second witness for the purpose of impeaching another witness' credibility arguably poses the danger of distraction to an even greater degree. For that reason, the common law placed restrictions on the use of extrinsic evidence such as calling a secondary witness: Impeachment by prior inconsistent statement and specific contradiction are both subject to the Collateral Fact Rule. Accordingly, that is our next subject.

NOTE

It is clear from the decided cases that, under the Federal Rules, courts continue to permit impeaching attorneys to use the specific contradiction technique. *E.g., United States v. Tarantino*, 846 F.2d 1384, 1409 (D.C. Cir.), *cert. denied*, 488 U.S. 840 (1988). In *United States v. Castillo*, 181 F.3d 1129 (9th Cir. 1999), after a defendant in a drug transporting case took the stand and described himself as an anti–drug crusader who never used drugs, the prosecution was allowed to call a rebuttal witness to tell about the defendant's 1997 arrest for possession of cocaine. This specific contradiction impeachment was approved on appeal.

3. THE COLLATERAL FACT RULE

The collateral fact rule can be stated simply: The attorney may not use extrinsic evidence to impeach a witness on a collateral matter. The rule's phrasing poses two obvious definitional problems: What is "extrinsic evidence"? What is a "collateral" matter?

There is a general agreement on the first definition. All courts concur that evidence is extrinsic if it is presented after the judge has excused the witness to be impeached. For example, after the judge excuses Paterson from the witness stand in *Devitt*, the defense counsel might attempt to (1) introduce a certified copy of the grand jury transcript of Paterson's testimony, reflecting prior inconsistent statements or (2) call another witness, Garret, to whom

Paterson made an inconsistent statement. Both items of evidence would be "extrinsic" to the testimony of Paterson, the witness the defense is attempting to impeach.

The only remaining dispute over the meaning of "extrinsic" is the extent to which the attorney may introduce impeaching documentary evidence during Paterson's cross–examination. The trend in the decided cases is to hold that the attorney may do so as long as the witness willingly authenticates the document. *See e.g., Carter v. Hewitt*, 617 F.2d 961, 970–71 (3d Cir. 1980). Introducing the documentary evidence during the cross–examination may slightly prolong the examination and, to that extent, raise the probative danger of time consumption. However, in the words of the *Carter* court:

> When . . . the extrinsic evidence is obtained from and through examination of the very witness whose credibility is under attack, . . . we must recognize that the rule's core concerns are not implicated.

Id. at 970. Thus, for all practical purposes, you must worry about the collateral fact rule only when you are presenting extrinsic evidence after the excuse of the witness you are attacking.

Even then the rule may be inapplicable. At common law, the rule is not a general limitation on all impeachment techniques. Quite to the contrary, the rule applies to less than a handful of the recognized impeachment techniques. For example, it is well–established that the rule is inapplicable to impeachment for bias. The witness' bias is "always independently provable" by extrinsic evidence. *United States v. Harvey*, 547 F.2d 720 (2d Cir. 1976). The admissibility of extrinsic bias evidence reflects the courts' judgment that bias is so probative of credibility that it is always worth the court's time to hear extrinsic evidence on that issue. In other cases, the rule is inapplicable because the very nature of the impeachment technique necessitates extrinsic proof. For example, under Federal Rule of Evidence 608(b)(2), the attorney may call witness B to testify that witness A has a character trait of untruthfulness. The character witness' testimony will always be extrinsic to the testimony of the witness to be impeached. Once we have made the policy decision to recognize the 608(b)(2) method of impeachment, we must permit extrinsic evidence; and the collateral fact rule cannot be applied.

In truth, the rule applies to only three impeachment techniques: prior inconsistent statement and specific contradiction as well as specific instances of misconduct under Rule 608(b). When the attorney employs one of these techniques, the second definitional problem immediately rears its ugly head: Is the fact "collateral," barring extrinsic evidence?

It is easy to answer the question in the context of Rule 608(b). The statute specifically provides that the attorney may cross–examine the witness about specific instances of conduct "if probative of . . . untruthfulness. . . ." FED. R. EVID. 608(b). Thus, if Paterson had attempted to file a fraudulent welfare application, Devitt's attorney could question about it. A fraudulent grant or employment application is logically relevant to show untruthfulness. However, the statute adds that the act "may not be proved by extrinsic evidence." *Id.* In that sense, the cross–examiner must "take the answer." That expression is a colorful way of saying that the act is a "collateral" fact. The misdeed is relevant only to the witness' credibility and has no bearing on the case's historical merits. Given its minimal probative value, the courts allow inquiry on cross–examination, but cut off the questioning at that point.

It is more difficult to define "collateral" in the context of specific contradiction or prior inconsistent statement impeachment. The problem is that sometimes the inconsistent statements and contradictory testimony relate to collateral facts and sometimes they relate to noncollateral facts. Fortunately, there is an excellent, succinct statement of the definition of "collateral" fact.

C. McCORMICK, HANDBOOK OF THE LAW OF EVIDENCE § 47 (West Publishing Co., Cleary ed. 1984)

[There are several types of facts that are not collateral and hence allow the introduction of extrinsic evidence.]

The first kind are facts that are relevant to the substantive issues in the case. It may seem strained to label this proof of relevant facts with the terms "contradiction" or "impeachment." But it does have the dual aspect of relevant proof and of reflecting on the credibility of contrary witnesses. Here the "contradiction" theory has at least one practical consequence, namely, it permits contradicting proof, which without the contradiction would be confined to the case in chief, to be brought out in rebuttal.

[Another] kind of fact must be considered. Suppose a witness has told a story of a transaction crucial to the controversy. To prove him wrong in some trivial detail of time, place or circumstance is "collateral." But to prove untrue some fact recited by the witness that if he were really there and saw what he claims to have seen, he could not have been mistaken about, is a convincing kind of impeachment that the courts must make place for, although the contradiction evidence is otherwise inadmissible because it is collateral under the tests mentioned above. To disprove such a fact is to pull out the linchpin of the story. so we may recognize this type of allowable contradiction, namely, the contradiction of any part of the witness' account of the background and circumstances of a material transaction, which as a matter of human experience he would not have been mistaken about if his story were true. This test is of necessity a vague one because it must meet an indefinite variety of situations, and consequently in its application a reasonable latitude of discretionary judgment must be accorded to the trial judge.

––––––––––

The expression "facts relevant to the substantive issues in the case" means evidence "logically relevant to the historical issues in the case." If evidence falls into this category, it is not only relevant to credibility, it has dual relevance, and the quantum of probative value justifies the additional expenditure of time necessary to introduce the extrinsic evidence.

A similar analysis obtains in the second category mentioned. If the fact is so fundamental that "he could not have been mistaken about [it] if he were really there and saw what he claims to have seen," the fact is not just relevant to credibility. Disproving the fact also creates the inference that the witness' testimony about the historical merits is necessarily untruthful or mistaken.

The characterization of the test as "a vague one" is certainly accurate. In *United States v. Higa*, 55 F.3d 448 (9th Cir. 1995), the court remarked that the test "is easy to state and difficult to apply." To get a feel for the test, consider the following notes and problems.

NOTES AND PROBLEMS

1. Problem 16–8. In *Devitt*, Paterson is testifying. The defense attorney begins cross–examination. During the cross–examination, she asks Paterson whether he ever filed a false unemployment compensation claim. Paterson denies doing so. The examination continues:

Q: Mr. Paterson, let me remind you of the penalties for perjury in this state.

A: Your Honor, I object. This is collateral impeachment, and the defense counsel knows that she must take the witness' answer.

Q: Your Honor, I have the right to press for an answer.

What ruling? *See* J. WEINSTEIN & M. BERGER, WEINSTEIN'S EVIDENCE ¶ 608[05] (1996).

2. Problem 16–9. The next prosecution witness is Mr. Store, one of Paterson's neighbors. He testified at the grand jury hearing that he saw the defendant exit the Paterson apartment shortly after the time of the alleged battery. He testified, "I was standing in front of a store across the street and talking with three of my friends when I see this guy run out the door to Paterson's apartment." At trial, on direct examination Mr. Store testified that he was talking with two friends. On cross–examination, Store insisted that the correct number was two. After Store leaves the witness stand, may the defense counsel introduce a certified copy of the grand jury transcript containing Store's statement about three friends? *See People v. Dice*, 120 Cal. 189, 201, 52 P. 477, 482 (1898).

3. Problem 16–10. Westra is prepared to testify that on the opposite side of the street from Paterson's apartment, there is only one place that affords a view of the door to Paterson's apartment; Westra was standing there with some friends at the time Store referred to during his direct testimony; but Store was not there at the time. Again the prosecutor objects, calling the testimony "collateral and clearly inadmissible." What ruling? *See East Tenn., Va. & Ga. Ry. v. Daniel*, 91 Ga. 768, 18 S.E. 22, (1893). *See also Orjias v Stevenson*, 31 F.3d 995 (10th Cir. 1994).

4. That courts continue to apply the collateral fact rule is evident in modern cases. *United States v. Higa*, 55 F.3d 448 (9th Cir. 1995).

C. BIAS

1. INTRODUCTION

At early common law, the parties and their spouses were incompetent to testify; these persons had a motive for perjury, and the common law's response was to disqualify these potential witnesses as a means of preventing perjury. Modernly, the former grounds for disqualification serve as grounds for impeachment. Hence, a party may now testify in his own behalf, but the judge may instruct the jury that "[i]n weighing his testimony, . . . you may consider the fact that the [party] has a vital interest in the outcome of this trial." *United States v. Hill*, 470 F.2d 361 (D.C. Cir. 1972).

Bias is not only one of the routine bases for impeachment; in the minds of many courts, it is the most probative impeachment technique. Schmertz & Czapanskiy, *Bias Impeachment and the Proposed Federal Rules of Evidence*, 61 GEO. L.J. 257, 264 (1972).

2. BIAS IMPEACHMENT IN GENERAL

The late John Kaplan of Stanford Law School thought that the case for bias impeachment should be rested squarely on the psychological research documenting the potentially distorting effect of a witness' bias. To prove his point, he often gave friends a copy of the following study. On November 23, 1951, the Dartmouth and Princeton football teams played in the last game of the season for both teams. The game was highly publicized even before kickoff. The game proved to be a rough one; there were serious injuries and numerous penalties against both teams. After the game, the two student newspapers ran strongly worded editorials, each accusing the other team of dirty play. The researchers obtained a film of the game. They showed the same film to a group of Dartmouth undergraduates and another group of Princeton undergraduates. After the undergraduates viewed the film, the researchers questioned them about their perceptions of the film.

HASTORF & CANTRIL, THEY SAW A GAME: A CASE STUDY, 49 Journal of Abnormal and Social Psychology 129 (1954)

Nearly all Princeton students judged the game as "rough and dirty"—not one of them thought it "clean and fair." And almost nine–tenths of them thought the other side started the rough play.

When Princeton students looked at the movie of the game, they saw the Dartmouth team make over twice as many infractions as their own team made. And they saw the Dartmouth team make over twice as many infractions as were seen by Dartmouth students. When Princeton students judged these infractions as "flagrant" or "mild," the ratio was about two "flagrant" to one "mild" on the Dartmouth team, and about one "flagrant" to three "mild" on the Princeton team.

As for the Dartmouth students, while the plurality of answers fell in the "rough and dirty" category, over one–tenth thought the same was "clean and fair" and over a third introduced their own category of "rough and fair" to describe the action. Although a third of the Dartmouth students felt that Dartmouth was to blame for starting the rough play, the majority of Dartmouth students thought both sides were to blame.

When Dartmouth students looked at the movie of the game they saw both teams make about the same number of infractions. And they saw their own team make only half the number of infractions the Princeton students saw them make. The ratio of "flagrant" to "mild" infractions was about one to one when Dartmouth students judged the Dartmouth team, and about one "flagrant" to two "mild" when Dartmouth students judged infractions made by the Princeton team.

Interpretation: The Nature of a Social Event

It seems clear that the "game" actually was many different games and that each version of the events that transpired was just as "real" to a particular person as other versions were to other people. A consideration of the experiential phenomena that constitute a "football game" for the spectator may help us both to account for the results obtained and illustrate something of the nature of any social event.

Of crucial importance is the fact that an "occurrence" on the football field or in any other social situation does not become an experiential "event" unless and until some significance is given to it: an "occurrence" becomes an "event" only when the happening has significance. And a happening generally has significance only if it reactivates learned significances already registered in what we have called a person's assumptive form–world.

Hence the particular occurrences that different people experienced in the football game were a limited series of events from the total matrix of events potentially available to them. People experienced those occurrences that reactivated significances they brought to the occasion; they failed to experience those occurrences which did not reactivate past significances.

NOTES AND PROBLEMS

1. It is a matter of common knowledge that a person's bias can affect her testimony. However, do laypersons fully appreciate the extent of the potential impact of bias? Should courts admit expert testimony on the causes and extent of bias?

2. Problem 16–11. In *Devitt*, the defense calls Mr. Anzalone as a witness. On direct examination, Anzalone testifies that one week after the alleged assault, he was standing at the bar in a local saloon. He adds that Mr. Paterson was standing a few feet away. He testifies that he overheard Paterson say that he had "framed" Devitt. On cross–examination, the prosecutor asks:

Q: Mr. Anzalone, isn't it true that until a few months ago, you were a member of a gang called the Survivors?

A: Yes.

Q: And Mr. Devitt was a member of the same gang? Wasn't he?

A: Yes.

Q: To join the gang, you take an oath. Right?

A: Yes.

Q: An oath you promise you'll keep for your entire life?

A: Yes.

Q: Doesn't that oath include a promise to lie for other gang members?

A: Yes.

The defense objects to the entire line of questioning. The defense attorney adds: "Even if this has some minimal probative value on bias, it's inadmissible. This jurisdiction has adopted the Federal Rules of Evidence, and those rules make no mention of bias impeachment." Before ruling on the defense's objection, consider the Supreme Court's decision in the following case.

UNITED STATES v. ABEL

469 U.S. 45 (1984)

JUSTICE REHNQUIST delivered the opinion of the Court.

[T]he Federal Rules of Evidence . . . do not by their terms deal with impeachment for "bias," although they do expressly treat impeachment by character evidence and conduct, Rule 608, by evidence of conviction of a crime, Rule 609, and by showing of religious beliefs or opinion, Rule 610. Neither party has suggested what significance we should attribute to this fact. Although we are nominally the promulgators of the Rules, and should in theory need only to consult our collective memories to analyze the situation properly, we are in truth merely a conduit when we deal with an undertaking as substantial as the preparation of the Federal Rules of Evidence. In the case of these Rules, too, it must be remembered that Congress extensively reviewed our submission, and considerably revised it. *See* 28 U.S.C. § 2076; 4 J. Bailey III & O. Trelles II, Federal Rules of Evidence: Legislative Histories and Related Documents (1980).

Before the present Rules were promulgated, the admissibility of evidence in the federal courts was governed in part by statutes or Rules, and in part by case law. *See*, e.g., Fed. Rule Civ. Proc. 43(a) (prior to 1975 amendment); Fed. Rule Crim. Proc. 26 (prior to 1975 amendment); *Palmer v. Hoffman*, 318 U.S. 109 (1943); *Funk v. United States*, 290 U.S. 371 (1933); *Shepard v. United States*, 290 U.S. 96 (1933). This Court had held in *Alford v. United States*, 282 U.S. 687 (1931), that a trial court must allow some cross–examination of a witness to show bias. This holding was in accord with the overwhelming weight of authority in the state courts as reflected in Wigmore's classic treatise on the law of evidence. *See Id.*, at 691, citing 3 J. Wigmore, Evidence § 1368 (2d ed. 1923).

With this state of unanimity confronting the drafters of the Federal Rules of Evidence, we think it unlikely that they intended to scuttle entirely the evidentiary availability of cross–examination for bias. One commentator, recognizing the omission of any express treatment of impeachment for bias, prejudice, or corruption, observes that the Rules "clearly contemplate the use of the above–mentioned grounds of impeachment." E. Cleary, MCCORMICK ON EVIDENCE § 40, p. 85 (3d 1984). Other commentators, without mentioning the omission, treat bias as a permissible and established basis of impeachment under the Rules. 3 D. LOUISELL & C. MUELLER, FEDERAL EVIDENCE § 341, p. 470 (1979); 3 J. WEINSTEIN & M. BERGER, WEINSTEIN'S EVIDENCE ¶ 607[03] (1981).

We think this conclusion is obviously correct. Rule 401 defines as "relevant evidence" evidence having any tendency to make the existence of any fact that is of consequence to the determination of the action more probable or less probable than it would be without the evidence. Rule 402 provides that all relevant evidence is admissible, except as otherwise provided by the United States Constitution, by Act of Congress, or by applicable rule. A successful showing of bias on the part of a witness would have a tendency to make the facts to which he testified less probable in the eyes of the jury than it would be without such testimony.

The correctness of the conclusion that the Rules contemplate impeachment by showing of bias is confined by the references to bias in the Advisory Committee Notes to Rules 608 and 610, and by the provisions allowing any party to attack credibility in Rule 607, and allowing cross–examination on "matters affecting the credibility of the witness" in Rule 611(b). The Court of Appeals have upheld use of extrinsic evidence to show bias both before and after the adoption of the Federal Rules of Evidence.

We think the lesson to be drawn from all of this is that it is permissible to impeach a witness by showing his bias under the Federal Rules of Evidence just as it was permissible to do so before their adoption.

NOTES

1. The Court asserts that the Federal Rules "do not by their terms deal with impeachment" for bias. Is that true? Read Rule 411. Can Rule 411 be considered part of the context of Article VI?

2. The *Abel* decision is undeniably important because it clarifies the status of bias impeachment under the Federal Rules and reveals at least part of the Court's conception of the statutory scheme of the Federal Rules. How does Rule 402 figure into that scheme, according to *Abel*?

3. THE TWO STAGES OF BIAS IMPEACHMENT

A party attempting to show a witness' bias may do so in two ways. One way is to cross–examine the witness himself or herself to expose the bias. The other possibility is calling a second witness to establish the first witness' bias. The courts usually employ the expression "extrinsic evidence" to describe the testimony of the second witness.

a. Cross–Examination to Prove Bias

1) Logical Relevance

An attorney may cross–examine a witness to show the witness' bias against the attorney's side of the case or in favor of the opposing side. The scope of cross–examination about bias is quite broad. The courts allow the attorney to inquire about such diverse matters as family ties, *Adams v. State*, 280 Ala. 678, 198 So. 2d 255 (1967); romantic involvement, *People v. Jones*, 7 Cal. App. 3d 48, 86 Cal. Rptr. 717 (1970); and financial ties, *United States v. Kerr*, 464 F.2d 1367 (6th Cir. 1972). The courts tolerate a wide–ranging inquiry about bias. For example, the defense can cross–examine a prosecution witness to elicit the witness' admission that he has been granted immunity, *United States v. Musgrave*, 483 F.2d 327, 328 (5th Cir. 1972); is bargaining for a reduced sentence, *Gordon v. United States*, 344 U.S. 414 (1953); or is a paid informant, *Wheeler v. United States*, 351 F.2d 946 (1st Cir. 1965). Efforts of the witness to avoid the consequences of his own crimes, and the incentive for him to slant his testimony may be shown. *United States v. Cooks*, 52 F.3d 101 (5th Cir. 1995) (jury should have been informed of all pertinent facts surrounding witness' motivation).

Further, the courts even allow attorneys to invoke bias impeachment theories to circumvent other evidentiary rules. Two illustrations will suffice. Federal Rule of Evidence 404(b) limits the admissibility of the defendant's other acts of misconduct. The statute specifically provides that the prosecutor may not introduce evidence of the other acts "to prove the character of [the defendant] to show that he acted in conformity therewith." However, suppose that the defendant calls a witness who has been involved in other crimes with the defendant. There is respectable case authority that the prosecutor may cross–examine the defense witness about other crimes the defendant and witness perpetrated together; the witness' prior criminal association with the defendant is evidence of bias in the defendant's favor. *United States v. Robinson*, 530 F.2d 1076 (D.C. Cir. 1976). *See also Gilbert v. United States*, 366 F.2d 923 (9th Cir. 1966), *cert. denied*, 388 U.S. 922 (1967). In a cocaine prosecution the trial court excluded all cross–examination about internal DEA incentives for agents to obtain convictions of drug traffickers. "This testimony would have revealed the specific benefits that would accrue to the agents should [defendant] be convicted. . . ." By excluding the DEA agent's motives favoring the prosecution, the trial judge violated the defendant's Confrontation Clause rights. *Vega v. Colorado*, 893 P.2d 107 (Colo. 1995) (error, but not reversible deprivation of rights; harmless error rule).

The courts are so impressed with the probative value of bias evidence that they have even allowed attorneys to override evidentiary rules that seemingly block the introduction of bias evidence. In *Davis v. Alaska*, 415 U.S. 308 (1974), which we shall discuss at length in the materials on the Confrontation Clause, the accused was charged with a burglary. The star prosecution witness was Richard Green. Earlier, Green had been adjudged a juvenile delinquent for burglarizing two cabins. Green was on probation for those offenses at the time of the accused's trial. An Alaska statute and court rule generally cloaked juvenile court proceedings with confidentiality. Based on the statute and court rule, the prosecutor obtained an *in limine* order forbidding the defense counsel from questioning Green about the prior juvenile offense. Writing for the majority, Chief Justice Burger concluded that the order violated the accused's confrontation rights. In the course of his opinion, the Chief Justice explained the logical relevance of the excluded evidence.

> [P]etitioner's counsel made it clear that he would not introduce Green's juvenile adjudication as a general impeachment of Green's character as a truthful person but, rather, to show specifically that at the same time Green was assisting the police in identifying petitioner he was on probation for burglary. From this petitioner would seek to show

that Green acted out of fear or concern of possible jeopardy to his probation. Not only might Green have made a hasty and faulty identification of petitioner to shift suspicion away from himself as one who robbed the Polar Bar, but Green might have been subject to undue pressure from the police and made his identifications under fear of possible probation revocation. Green's record would be revealed only as necessary to probe Green for his bias and prejudice and not generally to call Green's good character into question.

More recently, the Supreme Court confirmed the approach of *Davis*. In *Olden v. Kentucky*, 488 U.S. 227 (1988), the defendant claimed that the trial court's refusal to allow him to impeach the complaining witness' testimony by introducing evidence supporting a motive to lie deprived him of his Sixth Amendment right to confront witnesses against him. When the complainant claimed rape, the defendant attempted to cross–examine her as to whether she "concocted the rape story to protect her relationship with [another man.]" The Supreme Court ruled, pursuant to *Davis* and *Delaware v. Van Arsdall*, 475 U.S. 673 (1986), that there is a constitutionally protected right to impeach a witness for bias. *See also Daniels v. State*, 767 P.2d 1163 (Alaska Ct. App. 1989); *State v. Finley*, 300 S.C. 196, 387 S.E.2d 88 (1989).

Courts continue to follow this approach. *United States v. Manske*, 186 F.3d 770 (7th Cir. 1999) (conviction reversed where accused was denied opportunity to question government witnesses about their bias in favor of an accomplice who had already pleaded guilty; the Court of Appeals felt this was a "quint-essentially appropriate topic for cross–examination" and should have been allowed because the bias of a witness is always probative).

PROBLEMS

1. Problem 16–12. A defendant is charged with rape. Police pulled into a parking building late at night and a woman leaped from the defendant's car when the police came into view. She claimed defendant was attacking her, while the defendant claims she had taken $100 for sexual intercourse, which the police interrupted. At trial, the defendant offers evidence that on two prior occasions the complaining witness had been arrested in the same parking building for acts of prostitution. The jurisdiction has a rape shield law like Federal Evidence Rule 412. When the defendant attempts to cross–examine the complainant about whether she was attempting to avoid arrest this time and fabricated the claim of rape, the prosecutor objects, relying upon Rule 412. The defendant responds: "Bias, your honor." What ruling? Is there an analogy to *Davis v. Alaska? See Commonwealth v. Joyce*, 415 N.E.2d 181, 186–87 (Mass. 1981); *State v. Jalo*, 27 Or. App. 845, 557 P.2d 1359, 1362 (1976); *Commonwealth v. Black*, 487 A.2d 396, 401 (Pa. Super. Ct. 1985) (Pennsylvania's Rape Shield Law may not be used to exclude relevant evidence showing a witness' bias).

2. Problem 16–13. In *Devitt*, the prosecution calls Mr. Larson as a witness. On direct examination, Larson testifies that he sometimes works with Devitt. Larson adds that the day before the alleged assault, he had a conversation with Devitt. Larson states that during the conversation, Devitt said that: He,

Devitt, had seen "some fine stuff in that apartment that would look great on me." On cross–examination, the defense counsel attempts to elicit Larson's admission that one month before his alleged conversation with Devitt, he was arrested for selling marijuana. The prosecutor objects that "Mr. Larson's arrests are absolutely irrelevant." *See Commonwealth v. Schand*, 420 Mass. 783, 653 N.E.2d 566 (1995) (defendant has constitutional right to cross–examine witness to inquire whether witness expects more favorable treatment from the government on pending charges in exchange for his testimony in defendant's prosecution). What if the charge was dismissed before trial? Or dismissed before Larson ever mentioned the supposed conversation to the police? On the propriety of prosecutor's granting favorable deals in exchange for testimony, see Note, *Leniency in Exchange for Testimony: Bribery or Effective Prosecution?* 33 Ind. L. Rev. 957 (2000).

3. Problem 16–14. Larson is asked by Devitt's lawyer on cross–examination whether he would like to see Devitt out of the way because "you are both competing for the same girl." When the prosecutor objected and demanded to know the factual basis for the question, the defense attorney responded that "this is bias impeachment, and I do not have to reveal a good faith basis for my questions." What result? *Newman v. United States,* 705 A.2d 246 (D.C. App. 1997).

2)   Legal Irrelevance

Although the courts ascribe great probative value to bias impeachment, the legal irrelevance doctrine often accounts for the exclusion of evidence logically relevant to prove bias.

In *Hafner v. Brown*, 983 F.2d 570, 576 (4th Cir. 1992), the defendants in a civil rights action were police officers. The court ruled that the trial judge "acted well within his discretion" in precluding cross–examination of a plaintiff's witness about the witness' past arrests; the defendants unsuccessfully argued that the arrests were relevant to show the witness' "bias against the police." However, in *United States v. Spencer*, 25 F.3d 1105 (D.C. Cir. 1994), a contrary result occurred. The court found a prior charge admissible as a possible source of a witness' hostility to law enforcement.

Even if the legal irrelevance doctrine does not completely foreclose a topic, the doctrine may restrict the extent of inquiry. *Thornton v. Vonallmon*, 456 S.W.2d 795 (Mo. Ct. App. 1970), exemplifies the restrictive effect. In Thornton, the defendant attempted to impeach a plaintiff's witness by showing that he, the witness, had an intimate, sexual relationship with the plaintiff. On the one hand, the court held that the trial judge erred by precluding all inquiry about the witness' sexual relations with the plaintiff. However, the court added that "specific occasions or particular acts may not be inquired into." The court attempted to strike a legal irrelevance balance by permitting a limited inquiry about the biasing relationship. The lurid details of the relationship may shed little additional light on the magnitude of the bias, and the details may be highly distracting to the jurors.

NOTES AND PROBLEMS

1. Is it material that the bias is directed against a class of persons (the police) rather than a particular individual? How does that affect the probative value of the bias evidence? Schmertz & Czapanskiy, Bias Impeachment and the Proposed Federal Rules of Evidence, 61 GEO. L.J. 257, 262 (1972).

Proof of personal bias is routinely allowed. If a witness strongly dislikes one of the parties to the case, it is clear that such fact is showable to demonstrate the witness' bias. What if the witness does not personally know any of the parties, but instead hates the racial or ethnic group to which the plaintiff or defendant belong? Are the witness' prior expressions of bias against an ethnic group or class admissible? *State v. Loyd*, 459 So.2d 498, 508 (La. 1984) (personal bias vs. general bias). Compare *Simmons v. Collins*, 655 So.2d 330 (La. 1995). What if, in an employment discrimination case, a supervisor is sought to be cross–examined about whether he harbors "a bad attitude against women?"

2. Problem 16–15. In *Hill*, Polecat calls Professor Sjostrom as an expert witness. On direct examination, Professor Sjostrom testifies that the placement of the gas tank was "in full compliance with modern safety standards." On cross–examination, Ms. *Hill* would like to force Sjostrom to admit that:

- During the past five years, he has testified on twenty occasions for automobile manufacturers in suits against the manufacturers.

- During that time, he earned a total of $83,000 as compensation for appearing as a witness for automobile manufacturers.

- The $83,000 represents thirty–six percent of his total income for the period.

- He has testified at the request of Polecat's defense attorney on two other occasions, and collected $4,000 and $5,000 respectively for those two court appearances.

Is this evidence logically relevant? Is it legally relevant? Why? *See* Graham, *Impeaching the Professional Expert by a Showing of Financial Interest*, 53 IND. L.J. 35, 50 (1977). *See also Collins v. Wayne Corp.*, 621 F.2d 777 (5th Cir. 1980); *United States v. Edwardo–Franco*, 885 F.2d 1002, 1009–10 (2d Cir. 1989) (cross–examination of government's handwriting expert as to whether expert received several thousand dollars each time he testified for government was relevant to show potential bias).

3. Problem 16–16. On further cross–examination of Professor Sjostrom, Ms. Hill attempts to elicit his admission that earlier this year he sent an advertisement of his services as an expert witness to every member of a national organization of defense attorneys, including Polecat's firm. *Weatherly v. Miskle*, 655 S.W.2d 842, 844 (Mo. Ct. App. 1983). *See Johnson v. Family Health Plan*, 473 N.W.2d 609 (Wis. App. 1991).

b. Extrinsic Evidence to Prove Bias

The attorney attempting to impeach the witness may not be content with cross–examination. The attorney may press the attack even after that witness has left the stand. To continue the attack, the attorney will have to resort to extrinsic evidence. What are the evidentiary restrictions on the use of such evidence to prove bias?

The most important point to make is that the collateral fact rule is not a restriction. The inapplicability of the rule further reflects the courts' belief that bias is highly probative on the issue of credibility. *United States v. Dunson*, 142 F.3d 1213 (10th Cir. 1998) (bias is never classified as a collateral matter which lies beyond the scope of inquiry).

However, do not leap to the conclusion that extrinsic evidence is always admissible to prove bias. Although the collateral fact rule is inapplicable, in many jurisdictions there is a foundational requirement. The attorney must lay a proper foundation on cross–examination as a condition precedent to introducing the extrinsic proof. C. McCormick, Handbook of the Law of Evidence § 39, at 134–35 (4th ed. 1992). *See also United States v. Weiss*, 930 F.2d 185 (2d Cir. 1991), noting that extrinsic evidence of bias is allowed "although a foundation in the form of a preliminary question is often required."

D. PROOF OF A CHARACTER TRAIT OF UNTRUTHFULNESS AND SPECIFIC UNTRUTHFUL ACTS

1. INTRODUCTION

There are several conceivable ways of proving that a witness is a liar. The opposing attorney could prove that the witness has the reputation of being a liar. Next, the attorney could introduce the testimony of an acquaintance of the witness that in the acquaintance's opinion, the witness is a liar. Finally, we could allow the attorney to prove specific acts of untruthfulness by the witness. In some jurisdictions, only reputation evidence is permissible; in other jurisdictions, reputation and specific acts; and in still other states, all three types of proof are acceptable.

All three types of evidence are undeniably logically relevant on the issue of the witness' credibility. The question is the legal irrelevance of the evidence. Evidence of a witness' untruthful character poses thorny problems. You can understand part of the difficulty if you imagine that your reputation were on public trial. It is a hard issue to try and fraught with potential for abuse and prejudice. As we progress through this chapter, balance the probative value of each type of evidence (reputation, opinion, and specific acts) against the attendant probative dangers.

2. THE GENERAL PERMISSIBILITY OF INTRODUCING EVIDENCE OF THE CHARACTER TRAIT OF A WITNESS FOR UNTRUTHFULNESS

Unfortunately, the expression "character evidence" is often used ambiguously. It is critical to differentiate among the different uses of "character evidence." There are a number of ways in which character evidence can be logically relevant:

a. Character in Issue

Although it is rare, a person's character trait can be an element of the substantive claim or defense. For example, in the *Hill* case one of the charges

of negligence might be that Roe negligently entrusted the motor vehicle to
Worker. To plead a negligent entrustment cause of action, Ms. Hill would have
to allege that Worker is a careless driver, Roe knew or should have known
that Worker is a careless driver, and Roe nevertheless entrusted the motor
vehicle to Worker. Under these pleadings, Worker's character trait would be
logically relevant to the historical merits of the case. Indeed, Worker's
character is one of the ultimate issues.

b. Character as Circumstantial Evidence of Historical Facts of the Merits

If the issue is whether a person performed a particular act, would it be
helpful to the trier of fact to know something about that person's character
trait? If you answer yes, you probably believe that people have a general
propensity to act consistently with their character. Therefore, if you know the
person's pertinent character trait, you will infer that he is more or less likely
to have done the act in question. For example, in the *Devitt* case, if you know
the defendant is or is not a peaceful, law–abiding person, his character makes
it less or more likely that he attacked Paterson. The following diagram depicts
this use of character as circumstantial evidence of the historical facts of the
merits:

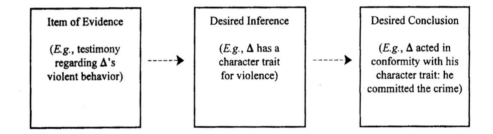

c. Character as Circumstantial Evidence of Credibility

By parity of reasoning, a person's character with respect to truthfulness or
mendacity is relevant to his credibility when he testifies as a witness. If the
person is an habitual liar, that character trait increases the likelihood that
his testimony is perjurious. This diagram depicts the underlying theory of
logical relevance:

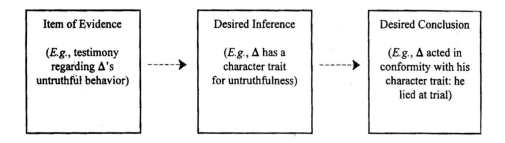

There is a striking similarity between the two diagrams. Under both theories of logical relevance, the proponent of the evidence employs the character evidence as circumstantial proof of a person's conduct on a specific occasion. In one instance, the prosecutor argues that Devitt's character trait for violence increases the likelihood that he committed the crime. In the other instance, the proponent argues that the untruthful witness acted "in character" while testifying and consequently perjured himself. In both cases, the proponent of the evidence invites the jury to draw an inference of specific conduct from the person's character trait.

Despite the essential similarity between the two uses of character evidence, the common law and the Federal Rules treat the two uses very differently. As we shall see in this chapter, both at common law and under the Federal Rules, character evidence is routinely admissible on a credibility theory. In sharp contrast, as we have already seen, the common law and the Federal Rules severely restrict the use of character evidence as circumstantial proof of the historical merits. However, as we saw, the recent adoption of Federal Rules of Evidence 413–15 eliminated some of the asymmetry between the two bodies of law.

What light does the available empirical research shed on the probative value of character evidence? Professor Mendez' survey of the psychological literature on the predictive value of character, based largely on Mischel's research, concludes that the general construct of character is a poor predictor of conduct in specific situations. Other commentators agree. *See* Lawson, *Credibility and Character: A Different Look at an Interminable Problem*, 50 NOTRE DAME L. REV. 758, 779–85 (1975) (one leading study of the degree of consistence between a character trait of truthfulness and conduct on specific occasions reported that "the most striking thing . . . is the amount of inconsistency exhibited"); Munday, *Stepping Beyond the Bounds of Credibility: The Application of Section I(f)(ii) of the Criminal Evidence Act 1898*, 1986 CRIM. L. REV. 511, 513–14; Spector, *Rule 609: A Last Plea for Its Withdrawal*, 32 OKLA. L. REV. 334, 351–53 (1979) ("For example, a prior conviction for perjury will generally say nothing about the willingness of a person to lie on this occasion"). In short, there appears to be little scientific basis for the differential treatment of the two circumstantial uses of character.

Might the difference be justified in terms of the doctrine of legal irrelevance?

3. SPECIFIC METHODS OF PROVING THE CHARACTER TRAIT OF A WITNESS FOR UNTRUTHFULNESS

There are four types of evidence which the impeaching attorney may offer to prove a witness' character trait for untruthfulness: the witness' reputation for untruthfulness, another person's opinion that the witness is untruthful, an untruthful act by the witness (which has not yet resulted in a conviction), or a conviction for such an act. The last type of evidence poses special problems and will be covered in detail at the end of this chapter.

a. Reputation and Opinion Testimony

If the impeaching attorney decides to offer reputation or opinion evidence of a witness' untruthfulness, the evidence usually takes the form of testimony by a second, character witness. The witness to be impeached has already left the stand, and a later witness is now prepared to testify that the earlier witness is reputed to be untruthful or that, in her opinion, the earlier witness is untruthful. There are restrictions on the direct and cross–examination of such character witnesses.

1) Direct Examination

It is generally agreed that the character witness may testify only to the principal witness' specific character trait for truthfulness or veracity. The principal witness' general immoral character may not be shown (on the credibility issue). Prior to the Federal Rules of Evidence, some courts permitted a sightly broader scope: the character trait of "honesty." However, Rule 608(a)(1) expressly confines the scope of the testimony to the "character for truthfulness or untruthfulness."

At common law most jurisdictions limited the form of this proof to testimony by the character witness regarding the reputation of the principal witness for truthfulness. The courts excluded the character witness' personal opinion about the principal witness' veracity. Nor could the character witness bolster her testimony with specific illustrations of the principal witness' truthful conduct.

It might seem anomalous that we not only allow but require proof in the form of reputation—gossip. The stated rationale is that reputation is the most reliable form of evidence because it is based upon collective knowledge acquired over a period of time by those who would know best. Opinion, it was thought, would be too much influenced by the character witness' friendship with the principal witness. Thus, the traditional form of the questions and answers would be as follows. After establishing the extent of the character witness' experience with the relevant community, the questioner asks:

Q: Does X have a general reputation in El Dorado regarding her truthfulness?

A: Yes, she does.

Q: Do you know what that reputation is?

A: Yes, I do.

Q: Please tell the jury what the reputation is.

A: It is bad.

Under Federal Rule 608(a), testimony in the form of reputation or opinion is permissible:

> (a) Opinion and reputation evidence of character. The credibility of a witness may be attacked or supported by evidence in the form of opinion or reputation, but subject to these limitations: (1) The evidence may refer only to character for truthfulness or untruthfulness, and (2) evidence of truthful character is admissible only after the character of the witness for truthfulness has been attacked by opinion or reputation evidence or otherwise.

NOTES AND PROBLEMS

1. As previously stated, most jurisdictions now exclude evidence of the principal witness' general, moral, law–abiding character when it is offered to prove the witness' credibility. Is that evidence logically irrelevant? Or should the evidence be barred under the legal irrelevance doctrine?

2. Problem 16–17. In *Hill*, Mr. Worker testifies for Mr. Roe for three hours. Ms. Hill hired Doctor Schultz, a physician, to attend the trial and observe Worker's testimony. Schultz observed all of Worker's testimony. During her rebuttal, Ms. Hill calls Schultz as a witness. After stating his qualifications and a definition of "pathological liar," Schultz' direct examination continues:

Q: Where were you earlier today, Doctor?

A: Right here in this courtroom.

Q: What were you doing?

A: At your request, I was observing and studying Mr. Worker's behavior and demeanor on the witness stand.

Q: What sort of conduct did you observe?

A: I noted that he repeatedly refused to meet the gaze of the questioner, frequently placed his hand over his mouth while answering, and often changed his position in his chair before beginning an answer.

Q: Doctor, do you have an opinion whether Mr. Worker is a pathological liar, as you previously defined the term.

O: Objection, Your Honor. This question calls for clearly improper matter.

You are the trial judge. What ruling? Does Rule 608(a) bar this testimony? On its face, does Rule 608(a) limit the impeaching attorney to lay opinions? Compare the phrasing of Rule 608(a) with, first, Rule 405(a) and then with Rules 701–702. Rules 701 and 702 draw an explicit distinction between lay and expert opinion testimony. What contextual light do Rules 405, 701, and 702 shed on the meaning of Rule 608(a)? The general consensus is that Rule 405(a) permits the receipt of expert opinion testimony. 22 C. WRIGHT & K. GRAHAM, FEDERAL PRACTICE AND PROCEDURE: EVIDENCE § 5265, at 588–91 (1978).

3. Assume *arguendo* that Rule 608(a) sanctions the introduction of otherwise admissible expert opinions. Is there nevertheless a ground for objecting to Dr. Shultz' testimony? There is a general rule against any witness stating that another lied when he gave his sworn trial testimony. But is that what Schultz is doing? Rather, is he describing a general psychological condition? Would it make a difference if Shultz had examined Worker for five hours at Shultz' clinic before trial? *See United States v. Hiss*, 88 F. Supp. 559, 559–60 (D.C.N.Y. 1950). In a more recent case, a forensic psychiatrist concluded that plaintiff's record indicated that he had lied about himself and fabricated psychiatric symptoms. The expert opinion was excluded as unfairly prejudicial. *Hodges v. Keane*, 886 F. Supp. 352 (S.D.N.Y. 1995).

4. Problem 16–18. After Dr. Shultz leaves the stand, *Hill* calls Mr. Bartosic. Bartosic testifies that, in addition to working for Mr. Roe, Worker is employed part–time at his company. Bartosic testifies that he is familiar with Worker's reputation for truthfulness at his company. *Hill* then asks, "What is that reputation?" As soon as the question is asked, Roe's attorney objects and requests permission to take the witness on *voir dire* before the judge rules on the objection. Does the opposing attorney have a right to *voir dire*? Does this issue fall under Federal Rule 104(a) or Rule 104(b)? Suppose that Roe's attorney conducts a *voir dire* and forces Bartosic to admit that there are only four employees at his company and that he has known Worker for only six months. What ruling? *See Wisinski v. State*, 508 So.2d 504, 505–06 (Fla. App. 1987). For a case excluding reputation drawn from a few people at a skating rink, *see People v. Erickson*, 883 P.2d 511 (Colo. App. 1994).

5. Defendants testified on their own behalf in a federal drug trial. A government informant was from Mexico. That fact alone did not give the defendants, also from Mexico, the right to testify to the informant's bad reputation for truthfulness. *United States v. Ruiz–Castro*, 92 F.3d 1519 (10th Cir. 1996). In order to establish a foundation for reputation testimony, a witness should show acquaintance with the person under attack, "the community in which he has lived and the circles in which he has moved" in order to speak with authority about the manner in which the attacked person is regarded.

2) Cross–Examination

Federal Evidence Rule 608(b) permits a character witness to be cross–examined about specific instances of the principal witness' conduct inconsistent with the reputation or opinion to which the character witness testified.

(b) Specific instances of conduct. Specific instances of the conduct of a witness, for the purpose of attacking or supporting the witness' credibility, other than conviction of crime as provided in rule 609, may not be proved by extrinsic evidence. They may, however, in the discretion of the court, if probative of truthfulness or untruthfulness, be inquired into on cross–examination of the witness (1) concerning the witness' character for truthfulness or untruthfulness, or (2) concerning the character for truthfulness or untruthfulness of another witness as to which character the witness being cross–examined has testified.

Suppose, for instance, that during rebuttal, the prosecutor called a witness who attacked Devitt's character trait of truthfulness. During surrebuttal Devitt called his cousin, Mr. Frontiero, to vouch for his truthfulness. On cross–examination of Frontiero, the prosecutor may ask whether Frontiero has heard that two years ago Devitt testified falsely in a drunk driving prosecution. The ostensible purpose of this question is to show that Frontiero's testimony is not credible. If Frontiero has not heard of the incident, his knowledge of Devitt's reputation is suspect. If Frontiero knows of the incident but still believes that Devitt is a truthful person, the jury may question Frontiero's standard for assessing credibility. (Of course, an illegitimate purpose may also be present—to get otherwise inadmissible evidence of Devitt's alleged perjury and drunk driving before the jury.)

Since we are now getting pretty far afield, this evidence is treated as collateral; the question may be asked, but the cross–examiner must "take the witness' answer." If the witness disputes the specific instance or denies knowledge of the instance inquired about, that is the end of the matter. The cross–examiner cannot later introduce extrinsic evidence of the specific instance to disprove the denial.

NOTES AND PROBLEMS

1. Problem 16–19. In *Devitt*, after the defendant testifies, the prosecutor calls Mr. Lang as a rebuttal witness. Lang testifies that Devitt has "a bad reputation in El Dorado for lying all the time." In surrebuttal, Devitt calls Ms. Wilson, another El Dorado resident, who contradicts Lang. A week before trial, a police officer told the prosecutor that "there's a rumor floating round that Devitt cheated on his last year's income tax." During his cross–examination of Ms. Wilson, the prosecutor asks: Ms. Wilson, have you heard a report that the defendant cheated on his taxes last year?

O: Your Honor, may we approach the bench?

J: Yes.

O: I'd like to know the basis for that question. In fact, I demand to know it.

J: Ms. Prosecutor, what is the basis?

Is a police officer's report a satisfactory basis? What if Devitt had been arrested for tax evasion? What if the local federal grand jury had already indicted Devitt for tax evasion? If a final conviction is unnecessary, at what point should we draw the line? *See* Graham, *Evidence and Trial Advocacy Workshop*, 21 Crim. L. Bull. 495, 510–11 (1985).

2. Courts require a good faith basis before permitting a party to cross–examine about prior bad acts. Earlier, we touched upon this requirement in connection with bias impeachment. This general requirement of an evidentiary basis for cross–examination underlies other impeachment techniques as well, such as prior conviction impeachment.

b.   Specific Untruthful Acts (Which Have Not Resulted in a Conviction)

As we will study next, one method of establishing a mendacious character is proving that the witness has been convicted of certain crimes. Another technique permits proof of specific instances of the witness' untruthful conduct even if that conduct has not led to a judgment of conviction. The issue of the admissibility of this type of evidence has badly divided the courts. Younger,

Three Essays on Character and Credibility Under the Federal Rules of Evidence, 5 HOFSTRA L. REV. 7, 12–13 (1976). The courts have split into three schools of thought.

One group of courts excludes this evidence altogether. In essence, this school deems the evidence worth the court's time only if there is highly reliable proof of the act's commission, namely, a conviction.

At the other extreme, many courts purport to allow the cross–examiner to inquire beyond acts of untruthfulness—into any bad, illegal or immoral act by the witness. These courts might permit the prosecutor to cross–examine a rape defendant about another alleged rape for the purpose of impeaching defendant's credibility. *State v. Caruthers*, 676 S.W.2d 935 (Tenn. 1984). In sex offense prosecutions some of these jurisdictions even go to the length of allowing the cross–examiner to question the victim about her prior sexual misconduct on a credibility theory. Annot. 97 A.L.R.3d 967 (1980); Annot., 94 A.L.R.3d 257 (1979); Ordover, *Admissibility of Patterns of Similar Sexual Misconduct: The Unlamented Death of Character for Chastity*, 63 CORNELL L. REV. 90, 120 (1977). As we have seen, under Federal Rule 412 and in many states, the trend is toward limiting the admission of sexual misconduct whether it is offered to prove the complainant's consent or to attack her credibility. *Stephens v. Miller*, 13 F.3d 998 (7th Cir. 1994); *Slater v. State*, 310 Ark. 73, 832 S.W.2d 846 (1992). One of the reasons for this trend is that we have come to question the connection between sexual morality and credibility. Ordover, *supra*, at 120–26. This same, questioning attitude accounts for the emergence of the third, majority view on the admissibility of specific acts of misconduct.

The majority of jurisdictions permit cross–examination concerning specific acts of misconduct, but only if the acts relate directly to veracity. Rule 608(b) requires that they be "probative of untruthfulness." Deceitful acts, including forgery, bribery, tax fraud, bankruptcy fraud, false statements, false swearing, cheating, embezzlement, swindling, false advertising, issuing bad checks, unlawful use of credit cards, criminal impersonation, and unlawfully concealing a will ordinarily qualify. *United States v. Amahia*, 825 F.2d 177 (8th Cir. 1987) (perjury, subornation of perjury, false statement, and false pretenses). Borderline cases such as smuggling are left to the trial judge's discretion. Acts primarily involving force or intimidation are excluded. The definite trend is toward this majority view, limiting the cross–examiner to acts "probative of . . . untruthfulness." Note the parallel between the evolution of this body of law and character evidence, discussed in section B of this chapter. In that section, we observed a trend toward limiting the opposing attorney to the character trait of untruthfulness rather than general moral character. The law governing specific acts impeachment is moving in the same direction.

One commentator, Professor Friedman, has proposed still another, compromise view. Friedman, *Character Impeachment Evidence: Psycho–Bayesian [!?] Analysis and a Proposal Overhaul*, 38 U.C.L.A. L. REV. 637 (1991). On the one hand, he would absolutely preclude the use of this technique to impeach a criminal accused. On the other hand, subject to the trial judge's discretionary balancing, he would permit the use of the technique to impeach any other type of witness. *See* Friedman, *Character and Impeachment Evidence: The Asymmetrical Interaction Between Personality and Situation*, 43 DUKE L. J. 816 (1994).

The limitations on extrinsic evidence of the act are even more severe than the restrictions on cross–examination. Evidence of specific acts of misconduct is deemed collateral. If the witness denies the misconduct, the cross–examiner must "take the answer" and cannot introduce extrinsic evidence to disprove the denial. *Shipman v. State*, 604 S.W.2d 182 (Tex. Crim. App. 1980). Federal Rule of Evidence 608(b) codifies this rule. *Nicholas v. Pennsylvania State Univ.*, 227 F.3d 133 (3d Cir. 2000); *Becker v. ARCO Chemical Co.*, 207 F.3d 176 (3d Cir. 2000); Note, 4 NEW ENG. L. REV. 133, 139 (1981). Under Rule 608(b), the courts have excluded conviction records, arrest records, Internal Revenue Service reports, and other documents when offered as "extrinsic evidence" of the untruthful act. Annot., 36 A.L.R. Fed. 564, 578–81 (1978). Thus, the collateral fact rule applies to this mode of impeachment. Yet some courts allow extrinsic evidence when the witness admits the misconduct. *United States v. Zandi*, 769 F.2d 229, 236–37 (4th Cir. 1985); *United States v. Jackson*, 876 F. Supp. 1188, 1197–98 (D. Kan. 1994). Many commentators, though, take the position that properly construed, Rule 608(b) bars the introduction of extrinsic evidence whether the witness admits or denies the misconduct. R. CARLSON, 3 CRIMINAL LAW ADVOCACY: TRIAL PROOF ¶ 12.29 (1994).

NOTES AND PROBLEMS

1. How broadly should Rule 608(b) be construed? The crucial language in the rule is "probative of truthfulness or untruthfulness. . . ." Compare that language with the wording of Rule 609(a)(2), "dishonesty or false statement." When a legislature uses different words, the courts typically presume that the legislature meant different things. *Kuhs v. Superior Court*, 201 Cal. App. 3d 966, 974, 247 Cal. Rptr. 544, 549 (1988). *See Robinson v. Shell Oil Co.*, 70 F.3d 325 (4th Cir. 1995). Which language is broader?

In *United States v. Cudlitz*, 72 F.3d 992 (1st Cir. 1996), the prosecutor cross–examined Cudlitz about whether he had solicited a man to burn down a building. The defendant denied doing so. The court held that Cudlitz might have been questioned under Rule 608(b) as to prior instances of forgery or perjury; but soliciting arson is not "probative of untruthfulness."

Similarly, a physician witness for the plaintiff in *Unmack v. Deaconess Medical Center*, 967 P.2d 783 (Mont. 1998) was cross–examined about the fact that at a prior time he had been disciplined by a professional association for misconduct. Using the disciplinary action against him during cross–examination was improper, said the Montana Supreme Court. The disciplinary action was not probative of untruthfulness; and it also carried with it the baggage of extreme prejudice under Evidence Rule 403.

2. Problem 16–20. In *Devitt*, two months before trial, the defendant was playing poker with an acquaintance, Mr. Belville. Devitt drank to excess and leaped to the conclusion that Belville was cheating him. Devitt struck Belville, grabbed all the money on the card table, and fled. Under Morena law, Devitt's conduct amounted to the statutory offense of theft by violence. If Devitt testifies, may the prosecutor cross–examine him about the theft?

3. Problem 16–21. Before trial, Devitt's attorney learns that Mr. Paterson's employer recently fired him because he misstated facts on his original job application. One part of the job application asked applicants to list all prior convictions. Although Paterson had a prior conviction for marijuana possession, he omitted any mention of the conviction. When the defense attorney begins questioning him about the job application, the following conversation occurs at sidebar:

> P. Your Honor, I have reason to believe that the defense counsel is trying to elicit the fact that on his job application, Mr. Paterson lied about a prior for marijuana possession.

> J. Is that true?

> DC. Yes.

> J. What's your theory of admissibility?

> DC. Rule 608(b), Your Honor.

> P. If that's the case, Your Honor, it's clearly inadmissible. Rule 608(b) is limited to acts relevant to "truthfulness or untruthfulness," and marijuana possession had nothing to do with that.

> DC. That misses the point, Your Honor. It's the lie I'm going after.

What ruling? *See United States v. Owens*, 21 M.J. 117, 123 (C.M.A. 1985).

4. A frequently repeated generalization is that mere arrests cannot be asked about on cross–examination. While that may be literally true in many instances, what about the conduct which led to the arrest? In *United States v. Robertson*, 39 M.J. 211 (C.M.A. 1994), the court held that an arrest alone is not probative of credibility; but where the underlying facts which gave rise to the arrest relate to untruthfulness, they may form the basis for questions under Rule 608(b).

5. The law of impeachment by prior conviction, the next topic in the text, bars use of convictions which are remote in time, *i.e.*, stale convictions. Does the same bar apply under Rule 608(b)? Not always. Some decisions have favored admission of old incidents which occurred a long time prior to current trial. *See Hampton v. Dillard Dept. Stores, Inc.*, 18 F.Supp. 2d 1256 (D. Kan. 1998) (evidence of incidents of untruthfulness, one of which was over 20 years old, was admissible to impeach credibility).

E.   CONVICTION OF A CRIME

1.   AN OVERVIEW OF IMPEACHMENT BY PROOF OF A CONVICTION

a.   Logical Relevance

The logical relevance of a witness' criminal conviction is undeniable. The fact of the conviction is some evidence of the witness' willingness to disregard social norms. The theory of logical relevance of the prior conviction is that it increases the probability that at the time of trial, the witness will violate another social norm and testify untruthfully. The conviction is circumstantial proof of the perjurious nature of the witness' trial testimony. As the Advisory

Committee explained, a "demonstrated instance of willingness to engage in conduct in disregard of accepted patterns is translated into willingness to give false testimony." 45 F.R.D. 161, 297.

However, there are grave doubts about the reliability of that translation. Unlike Rule 608(b), conviction impeachment is not limited to conviction for offenses which are directly germane to credibility. By way of example, under Rule 609(a)(1), the impeaching attorney can prove that the witness suffered a prior conviction for voluntary manslaughter or felony drunk driving. Dean Ladd was particularly critical of the probative value of the courts' willingness to admit evidence of convictions for "crimes–at–large." Ladd, *Credibility Tests—Current Trends*, 89 U. PA. L. REV. 166, 177–78 (1940). The courts' willingness to stretch the impeachment that far compounds the doubts raised by the psychological studies. *Id.* In this light, is it sensible to treat conviction impeachment more liberally than Rule 608(b) impeachment?

There is, though, a counter–argument that the bare fact of the conviction raises the probative value of this type of impeachment evidence. The conviction is seemingly trustworthy proof that the witness in fact committed the underlying act. Some courts have asserted that the conviction is "the strongest proof" that the witness committed the act. Note, *Evidence of Other Crimes in Montana*, 30 MONT. L. REV. 235, 238 (1969). When there has been no conviction, it can be highly debatable whether the witness committed the untruthful act. The conviction thus heightens the probative worth of the impeaching evidence.

PROBLEMS

1. Problem 16–22. In *Devitt*, on direct examination the defendant testifies that "I've never been in trouble with the law before." The prosecutor has a certified copy of a judgment of a conviction of Devitt in 19YR. Does the prosecutor have to resort to Rule 609 to justify the admission of the conviction?

2. Problem 16–23. The prosecutor calls Mr. Melrose as a witness against Devitt. Melrose testifies on direct examination that he "happened to be near" Paterson's apartment at the time of the alleged battery and that he saw Devitt running from the apartment. The defense counsel has evidence that in 19YR, Melrose was convicted of sexual assault in Morena and that he is still on probation for the assault. Does the defense counsel have to resort to Rule 609 to justify the admission of the conviction? *See Davis v. Alaska*, 415 U.S. 308, 316–18 (1974).

b.   Legal Irrelevance

There are not only questions about the quantum of probative value of conviction impeachment. The problem is intensified because evidence of a conviction raises a number of Rule 403 concerns. The evidence carries with it a substantial risk of unfair prejudice.

The fact that the witness is a "criminal" or an "ex–con" may induce an emotional reaction by the trier of fact against the witness. Even if he is merely a witness, the judge or jury may discredit his testimony solely because they dislike him. If he is a party, a close case may go against him because of the jury's dislike.

The prejudice becomes acute when the witness is the criminal defendant. When in doubt, the jury may decide to resolve the doubts against him; the jury may be more willing to convict a "criminal." This danger reaches its zenith when the crime for which he was convicted is the same as or similar to the crime now charged. In H. KALVEN & H. ZEISEL, THE AMERICAN JURY 160 (1966), the researchers found that when the strength of the evidence was constant, sixty–five percent of the defendants without a record were acquitted but only thirty–eight percent of the defendants whom the jury knew or suspected had a criminal record. If the jury learns of the defendant's criminal record, they may use a "different . . . calculus of probabilities" in deciding whether to convict. *Id.* at 179.

The advocates of this method of impeachment argue that the opponent is entitled to a limiting instruction and the instruction protects the opponent against misuse of the evidence. Others counter that limiting instructions are notoriously ineffective. Note the comments of one trial judge:

> The defendant is a dead duck once he is on trial before a jury and you present a record that he was convicted . . . twenty–five years ago. . . . If it's any way close, the jury is going to hang him on that record, not on the evidence.

People v. Montgomery, 47 Ill. 2d 510, 514, 268 N.E.2d 695, 697 (1971). On appeal, Justice Shaefer referred to these remarks in discussing the effectiveness of a limiting instruction:

> The remarks of the trial judge reflect his disbelief in the effectiveness of that safeguard. That same disbelief was expressed in more scholarly terms by Dean Griswold: "We accept much self–deception on this. We say that the evidence of the prior conviction is admissible only to impeach the defendant's testimony, and not as evidence of the prior crimes themselves. Juries are solemnly instructed to this effect. Is there anyone who doubts what the effect of this evidence in fact is on the jury? If we know so clearly what we are actually doing, why do we pretend that we are not doing what we clearly are doing?" Griswold, *The Long View* (1965), 51 A.B.A. J. 1017, 1021. *Id.*

Note, 4 COLUM. J.L. & SOC. PROBS. 3, 218 (1968), reports the results of a survey of judges' and attorneys' attitudes toward limiting instructions. Ninety–eight percent of the attorneys surveyed and forty–three percent of the judges surveyed believe that juries are unable to follow such limiting instructions.

The more recent empirical research supports this widespread belief. In a Boston College study, 160 randomly chosen subjects received written descriptions of the evidence in a criminal case, a prosecution for either murder or auto theft. Wissler & Saks, *On the Inefficacy of Limiting Instructions—When Jurors Use Prior Conviction Evidence to Decide Guilt*, 9 LAW & HUM. BEHAV. 37 (1985). The only variation in each case was the impeachment evidence; some jurors were told the defendant had a prior conviction for murder, others auto theft, and still others perjury. All jurors were instructed to limit their consideration of the conviction to the defendant's credibility. Sixty percent of the jurors voted to convict when the impeaching conviction was perjury. However, seventy–five percent voted to convict when the charged crime and the impeaching conviction were identical. In short, the jurors were inclined to use the impeaching conviction as character evidence on the merits rather than confining it to credibility. In addition, "[a]s part of the University of Chicago Jury Project, Dale Broeder interviewed jurors after they had . . . rendered verdicts in criminal trials. Broeder asserted that the 'jurors almost universally used defendant's record to conclude that he was a bad man and hence was more likely than not guilty of the crime for which he was then standing trial.' " Beaver & Marques, *A Proposal to Modify the Rule on Criminal Conviction Impeachment*, 58 TEMP. L.Q. 585, 602 (1985).

Other commentators agree with the prejudice analysis. In Dodson, *What Went Wrong With Federal Rule of Evidence 609: A Look at How Jurors Really Misuse Prior Conviction Evidence*, 48 Drake L. Rev. 1, 45 (1999), this observation appears:

> The current version of Rule 609 sacrifices individual rights and turns traditional notions of American criminal law on its head. The goal has been to increase convictions and get criminals off the street, but what has been forgotten are the underlying social goals and policies behind American criminal law. It has long been recognized that a person should not suffer criminal sanctions because he is a bad person or has done bad things in the past. Criminal justice in this country is premised on the assumption that we should only punish specific acts which the state can prove beyond a reasonable doubt.

NOTES

1. Courts continue to place great confidence in limiting instructions. *United States v. Buchanan*, 70 F.3d 818 (5th Cir. 1995): "Although the danger of prejudice associated with prior conviction evidence is often great, the district court in this case substantially reduced the possibility of prejudice to Bonner by carefully instructing the jury on how they could consider the evidence." The holding in *United States v. Lopez*, 979 F.2d 1024 (5th Cir. 1992), is in accord. In view of the foregoing survey results, is this confidence justified?

2. Is the more liberal admissibility of conviction evidence justifiable? Are the probative dangers less? Are the two types of impeachment distinguishable in another respect under the legal irrelevance doctrine? Suppose that, on cross–examination, the impeaching attorney attempts to force the witness to admit that she committed an untruthful act, provable under Rule 608(b). In response to the cross–examination question, the witness denies committing the act. On redirect, the witness may elaborate on the denial or on any extenuating circumstances. If there has been no conviction, is there a possibility of a distracting dispute over the question of whether the witness engaged in the alleged conduct? How likely is a time–consuming dispute over that issue when the impeaching attorney has a certified copy of the judgment of conviction in hand?

2. CROSS–EXAMINATION OF A WITNESS ABOUT A PRIOR CONVICTION

First consider the restrictions on cross–examining a witness about a prior conviction. There are several points of agreement among the courts. When the attorney is relying on Rule 609 rather than Rule 608(b), the evidence must take the form of a conviction. In most jurisdictions, a judgment of conviction is necessary and sufficient. However, Rule 609 does not explicitly refer to a judgment. The Rule's wording has led some courts to conclude that a verdict of guilty is sufficient. *E.g., United States v. Smith*, 623 F.2d 627 (9th Cir. 1980). So is a conviction resulting from a plea of guilty, even though the sentence is suspended. *United States v. Jackson*, 863 F. Supp. 1462 (D. Kan. 1994).

Even before sentencing and formal entry of judgment, the verdict is persuasive evidence of guilt. In *United States v. Mitchell*, 886 F.2d 667 (4th Cir. 1989), although the defendant had been convicted but not yet sentenced, the court's acceptance of the jury's verdict was a sufficient predicate for the use of the verdict for impeachment in a subsequent trial. A related problem is the effect of a pending new trial motion or appeal on the admissibility of the conviction. Almost all courts agree that the judgment is nevertheless admissible. *McGee v. State*, 206 Tenn. 230, 332 S.W.2d 507 (1960). For example, Rule 609(e) provides that "[t]he pendency of an appeal . . . does not render evidence of a conviction inadmissible." FED. R. EVID. 609(e).

There is also a consensus that the conviction must be valid. The Supreme Court has announced that the conviction is inadmissible if it was obtained in violation of a criminal defendant's Sixth Amendment counsel right. *Loper v. Beto*, 405 U.S. 473 (1972). The prosecution may not use a conviction resulting from a trial at which the right to counsel attached but the defendant neither waived nor was afforded counsel.

There is also general agreement that there are only certain details which the cross–examiner may inquire about—typically, nature of the crime, the date of the offense and the disposition. *Gora v. Costa*, 971 F.2d 1325 (7th Cir. 1992); *Hodges v. State*, 229 Ga. App. 475, 494 S.E.2d 223 (1997); *State v. Higgins*, 422 N.W.2d 277 (Minn. App. 1988). Those details are ordinarily reflected on the face of any copy of the judgment of conviction. As previously stated, one of the rationales for the liberal treatment of conviction impeachment is that the availability of the documentary evidence of the judgment reduces the likelihood that the evidence will distract the jury; it is improbable that the jurors will have to devote an inordinate amount of time to the question of whether the witness committed the act. To some extent that time saving would be lost if the cross–examiner could inquire about aggravating details which are not stated on the face of the document. That inquiry might trigger the very type of lengthy dispute which the availability of the document supposedly precludes. *See Cummings v. Malone*, 995 F.2d 817, 826 (8th Cir. 1993).

The consensus over conviction impeachment ends abruptly at this point. The two questions that have divided the courts relate to the fundamental logical and legal relevance concerns that we mentioned in the previous section. Must the underlying crime involve fraud or dishonesty? And even if the conviction satisfies the normal foundational requirements, should the trial judge have a residual power to balance the conviction's probative value against incidental probative dangers?

a. The Types of Crimes

Before the Federal Rules of Evidence, support could be found in federal cases "for each of the following propositions: a witness may be impeached by inquiry about any conviction of crime, whether felony or misdemeanor; felonies may be shown but misdemeanors may not; only crimes involving moral turpitude may be shown; any felony may be shown but misdemeanors only if they involve moral turpitude; felonies and misdemeanors amounting to *crimen falsi*; or that only crimes resting on dishonest conduct may be shown." 2 C. WRIGHT, FEDERAL PRACTICE AND PROCEDURE: CRIMINAL § 416 (1969). The state cases were also in disarray. California Evidence Code § 788 allowed all felonies to be shown. A respectable number followed the Model Code (Rule 106(b)) and the 1954 Uniform Rules (Rules 20–22) and admitted only crimes involving dishonesty or false statement. However, the majority of courts seemed to allow the proponent to use any felony "without regard to the nature of the particular offense" and crimen falsi offenses "without regard to the grade of the offense." Adv. Comm. Note, FED. R. EVID. 609.

If the Advisory Committee's description of the majority view is accurate, Rule 609(a) should be characterized as a relatively conservative provision; the Rule reflects that view. Rule 609(a) presents several statutory construction issues, and you should read its text carefully. The Conference Report gives us some aid in interpreting the text. The Report explains that the expression, "dishonesty and false statement," includes crimes "such as perjury, subornation of perjury, false statement, criminal fraud, embezzlement, or false pretense, or any other offense in the nature of *crimen falsi*, the commission of which involves some element of deceit, untruthfulness, or falsification. . . ." *Quoted in* 3 J. WEINSTEIN & M. BERGER, WEINSTEIN'S EVIDENCE 609–81 (1985).

NOTES AND PROBLEMS

1. Concentrate on a comparison between the scope of Rules 609(a)(1) and (a)(2). Are the two provisions mutually exclusive, or is there a possibility of overlap? If so, be prepared to give an example of a crime falling in the area of overlap.

2. Problem 16–24. In *Devitt*, the prosecution calls Mr. Melrose. In 1995, Melrose was convicted of shoplifting. The maximum imposable punishment was six months' imprisonment. Morena has adopted Federal Rule 609(a). Can the defense rely on Rule 609(a)(2) as the basis for cross–examining Melrose about the conviction? The defense argues that any theft "inherently involves an element of dishonesty." What ruling? *See* 3 J. WEINSTEIN & M. BERGER, WEINSTEIN'S EVIDENCE 609—72–73 (1985). Remember Professor Cleary's comment on this problem in his article quoted in Chapter 2. Professor Cleary marshalls the legislative history indicating that Congress intended to confine

Rule 609(a)(2) to crimes involving an element of false statement. He argues that, in the collision "between legislative history and the seemingly unmistakable meaning" of the text of Rule 609(a)(2), the legislative history should prevail. *Cleary, Preliminary Notes on Reading the Rules of Evidence*, 57 NEB. L. REV. 908, 917 (1978). Do you agree with Cleary's argument? Under the traditional doctrine of *ut res magis valeat quam pereat*, courts presume that every provision in a statute is intended to have independent effect. *DeSisto College, Inc. v. Town of Howey–in–the–Hills*, 706 F. Supp. 1479, 1485 (M.D. Fla.), *aff'd*, 888 F.2d 766 (11th Cir. 1989). Courts prefer to avoid constructions which render even part of a statute surplusage. *People v. Wesley*, 198 Cal. App. 3d 519, 523, 243 Cal. Rptr. 785, 786 (1988). What effect does Professor Cleary's position have on the meaning of "dishonesty or" in Rule 609(a)(2)? Would Judge Easterbrook favor Professor Cleary's position? Is this one of those instances in which the court's philosophy of statutory construction is outcome–determinative?

3. Misdemeanors which lack dishonesty or false statement characteristics are frequently excluded. See *Daniels v. Loizzo*, 986 F. Supp. 245 (S.D.N.Y. 1997), excluding misdemeanor convictions for unauthorized use of a vehicle, resisting arrest and disorderly conduct. The case also illustrates the use of a motion *in limine* to exclude proof of prior offenses.

Substantial dispute attends the issue of whether a particular crime falls within Rule 609 (a)(2). Perjury, false statement offenses, criminal fraud, embezzlement and false pretenses all come under the rule. *S.E.C. v. Sargent*, 229 F. 3d 68 (1st Cir. 2000). So does criminal impersonation. *Brundige v. City of Buffalo*, 79 F. Supp. 219 (W.D.N.Y. 1999). Whether shoplifting fits the formula has been the subject of debate. One point of view is expressed in *United States v. Dunson*, 142 F.3d 1213 (10th Cir. 1998) (no).

4. Some jurisdictions limit impeaching convictions to those involving "moral turpitude." For an example of a court applying a "moral turpitude " formula, *see Sapp v. State*, 271 Ga. 446, 520 S.E.2d 462 (1999). Questions of interpretation frequently involve the issue of whether a past offense involved this element. Should a judge receive extrinsic evidence respecting the circumstances of the crime in order to determine whether moral depravity was involved? While some courts may proceed in this manner, a competing approach bars the court from taking evidence and going behind the conviction. The latter courts restrict the trial judge to an inspection of the statutory definition of the crime. *People v. Bautista*, 217 Cal. App. 3d 1, 265 Cal. Rptr. 661 (1990).

5. Problem 16–25. In *Hill*, the plaintiff calls Mr. Garfield as a witness to the accident. In 1999, in Wyoming, Garfield was convicted for the third time of drunken driving. Under Wyoming law, as a recidivist, Garfield faced a potential maximum punishment of two years' imprisonment. In fact, he was sentenced to only three months' confinement in the county jail. Under Morena law, even for a third offense, Garfield would have faced a maximum prison term of six months. Morena has adopted Federal Rule 609(a)(1). Is the conviction admissible against Garfield? Would it affect your analysis if the Wyoming Penal Code included the following provision: "When a crime, punishable by imprisonment for more than one year under this code, is punished by imprisonment for less than that period or no imprisonment at all, it shall be deemed a misdemeanor"?

b. The Judge's Discretion to Exclude an Otherwise Admissible Conviction

Since conviction evidence poses severe probative dangers, it would have been only natural if the appellate courts had early given the trial judge discretion to balance the conviction's probative value against any dangers the evidence might generate. Surprisingly, that was not the case. The traditional attitude was that if the evidence satisfied all the routine foundational requirements (*i.e.*, the evidence was a valid final conviction for the right type of crime), the conviction was automatically admissible.

This state of the law was dramatically unsettled when the Court of Appeals for the District of Columbia decided *Luck v. United States*, 348 F.2d 763 (D.C. Cir. 1965). In *Luck*, Judge McGowan proclaimed that the trial judge should have discretion to exclude a conviction if she concluded that "the prejudicial effect of impeachment far outweighs the probative relevance of the prior conviction on the issue of credibility." *Id.* at 768. The *Luck* rule authorized the trial judge to engage in the sort of balancing analysis that is the core of the legal irrelevance doctrine. The case law following *Luck* elaborated the kinds of factors the judge should consider. Among them were:

— the nature of the conduct underlying the conviction

— the similarity or dissimilarity between that conduct and the conduct charged

— the importance of the testimony given by the witness whose credibility is sought to be impeached by the conviction

For example, suppose that the charged offense is murder, the witness is the accused, and the prior conviction is for murder. Suppose the witness is not the accused, but is nevertheless the "star" witness for the defense. In both these examples, the probative danger of allowing impeachment by the conviction would probably be considered high.

The *Luck* approach generated a lot of criticism—which surfaced again during the congressional debate over Federal Rule 609. The 1975 version of that Rule originally specified that the judge must balance the prejudicial effect of the evidence "to the defendant." However, the ambiguity of the Rule generated even further controversy. The Supreme Court attempted to clarify some of the uncertainty in *Green v. Bock Laundry Mach. Co.*, 490 U.S. 504 (1989). The plaintiff in *Green* was a prisoner on work release who was severely injured on the job. He filed a products liability action against the manufacturer of the machine that caused his injury. At trial, the defense was permitted over objection to impeach the plaintiff with his prior convictions for burglary and conspiracy to commit burglary. On appeal, the Supreme Court examined whether or not the trial judge had discretion to exclude otherwise admissible convictions in civil actions:

> . . . We next must decide whether Rule 609(a)(1) governs all prior felonies impeachment, so that no discretion may be exercised to benefit civil parties, or whether Rule 609(a)(1)'s specific reference to the criminal defendant leaves Rule 403 balancing available in the civil context.

Several courts, often with scant analysis of the interrelation between Rule 403 and Rule 609(a)(1), have turned to Rule 403 to weigh prejudice and probativeness of impeaching testimony in civil cases. . . Prodigious scholarship highlighting the irrationality and unfairness of impeaching credibility with evidence of felonies unrelated to veracity indicates that judicial exercise of discretion is in order. If Congress intended otherwise, however, judges must adhere to its decision.

A general statutory rule usually does not govern unless there is no more specific rule. *See D. Ginsburg & Sons, Inc. v. Popkin*, 285 U.S. 204, 208 (1932). Rule 403, the more general provision, thus comes into play only if Rule 609, though specific regarding criminal defendants, does not pertain to civil witnesses. *See* Advisory Committee's Note to Proposed Rule 403, 56 F.R.D., at 218. The legislative history evinces some confusion about Rule 403's applicability to a version of Rule 609 that included no balancing language. That confusion is not an obstacle because the structure of the Rules as enacted resolves the question.

Rule 609(a) states that impeaching convictions evidence "shall be admitted." With regard to subpart (2), which governs impeachment by *crimen falsi* convictions, it is widely agreed that this imperative, coupled with the absence of any balancing language, bars exercise of judicial discretion pursuant to Rule 403. Subpart (1), concerning felonies, is subject to the same mandatory language; accordingly, Rule 403 balancing should not pertain to this subsection either.

Any argument that Rule 403 overrides Rule 609 loses force when one considers that the rule contains its own weighing language, not only in subsection (a)(1), but also in sections (b), pertaining to older convictions, and (d), to juvenile adjudications. These later balances, like Rule 609 in general, apply to both civil and criminal witnesses. *See* Fed. Rule Evid. 1101(b). Earlier drafts of subpart (a)(1) also contained balancing provisions that comprehended both types of witnesses; these, as we have shown, deliberately were eliminated by advocates of an automatic admissibility rule. The absence of balances within only two aspects of the rule—*crimen falsi* convictions and felony convictions of witnesses other than those whose impeachment would prejudice a criminal defendant—must be given its proper effect. Thus Rule 609(a)(1)'s exclusion of civil witnesses from its weighing language is a specific command the impeachment of such witnesses be admitted, which overrides a judge's general discretionary authority under Rule 403. Courts relying on Rule 403 to balance probative value against prejudice to civil witnesses depart from the mandatory language of Rule 609.

In summary, we hold that Federal Rule of Evidence 609(a)(1) requires a judge to permit impeachment of a civil witness with evidence of prior felony convictions regardless of ensuant unfair prejudice to the witness or the party offering the testimony. Thus no error occurred when the jury in this product liability suit learned through impeaching cross–examination that plaintiff Green was a convicted felon. The judgment of the Court of Appeals is *Affirmed*.
(footnotes omitted)

NOTE

What does *Green* tell us about the Court's view of Rule 403? Professor Rothstein suggested that Rule 403 "apparently cuts across the entire body of the [Federal] Rules." Rothstein, *Some Themes in the Proposed Federal Rules of Evidence*, 33 FED. B.J. 21, 29 (1974). In light of *Green*, is that generalization universally true? Why does the majority attach so much significance to Congress' use of the verb "shall" in Rule 609(a)?

———

After *Green*, the Supreme Court proposed amendment of Rule 609—which is now the present version:

Federal Rule of Evidence 609. Impeachment by Evidence of Conviction of Crime. (a) General rule. For the purpose of attacking the credibility of a witness, (1) evidence that a witness other than an accused has been convicted of a crime shall be admitted, subject to Rule 403, if the crime was punishable by death or imprisonment in excess of one year under the law under which the witness was convicted, and evidence that an accused has been convicted of such a crime shall be admitted if the court determines that the probative value of admitting this evidence outweighs its prejudicial effect to the accused; and (2) evidence that any witness has been convicted of a crime shall be admitted if it involved dishonesty or false statement, regardless of the punishment.

(b) Time limit. Evidence of a conviction under this rule is not admissible if a period of more than ten years has elapsed since the date of the conviction or of the release of the witness from the confinement imposed for that conviction, whichever is the later date, unless the court determines, in the interests of justice, that the probative value of the conviction supported by specific facts and circumstances substantially outweighs its prejudicial effect. However, evidence of a conviction more than ten years old as calculated herein, is not admissible unless the proponent gives to the adverse party sufficient advance written notice of intent to use such evidence to provide the adverse party with a fair opportunity to contest the use of such evidence. . . .

NOTES

1. It might seem anomalous that the same Supreme Court which decided *Green* proposed the amendment to overrule *Green*. A significant disadvantage of codifying a body of law is that codification makes it more difficult to correct an erroneous policy choice. If *Green* had been a common law case, the Court could have reevaluated the policy considerations, overruled contrary prior precedents, and simply announced a new decisional rule. However, since the Federal Rules governed, the Court's function was limited to construing the statute. Under Federal Rule 1102, when the Court wants to amend a provision of the Rules, the Court must comply with 28 U.S.C. § 2074, which reads:

(a) The Supreme Court shall transmit to the Congress not later than May 1 of the year in which a rule prescribed under section 2072 is to become effective a copy of the proposed rule. Such rule shall take effect no earlier than December 1 of the year in which such rule is so transmitted unless otherwise provided by law. The Supreme Court may fix the extent such rule shall apply to proceedings then pending, except that the Supreme Court shall not require the application of such rule to further proceedings then pending to the extent that, in the opinion of the court in which such proceedings are pending, the application of such rule in such proceedings would not be feasible or would work injustice, in which event the former rule applies.

(b) Any such rule creating, abolishing, or modifying an evidentiary privilege shall have no force or effect unless approved by Congress.

2. Opponents of codification have argued that once Congress reduced the Rules to statutory form, evidence law would tend to stagnate. Jonakait, *The Supreme Court, Plain Meaning, and the Changed Rules of Evidence*, 68 TEX. L. REV. 745, 784–85 (1990). In large part, the validity of this criticism turns on the difficulty of invoking this amendment procedure. How onerous is this procedure? In most instances, before taking effect, does an amendment require the express approval of Congress?

The certainty which the Court sought to infuse into prior conviction impeachment law by the amendment of Rule 609 seems to have been effective. Cases decided after the amendment uniformly apply the balancing test to the use of prior convictions in civil cases. *Wilson v. Groaning*, 25 F.3d 581 (7th Cir. 1994) ("It is well settled that evidence of prior convictions is admissible in a civil case to impeach the credibility of the plaintiff—subject to the constraints of Rule 403."); *Wilson v. Union P.R. Co.* , 56 F.3d 1226, 1231 (10th Cir. 1995) (excluding evidence of a drug conviction against a party in a civil case because "such evidence can be highly prejudicial and arouse jury sentiment against a party–witness").

Some federal circuits employ a five–part test for determining when the probative value of a prior conviction outweighs its prejudicial effect:

(1)   The impeachment value of the prior crime.

(2)   The point in time of the conviction and the witness' subsequent history.

(3)   The similarity between the past crime and the charged crime.

(4)   The importance of the defendant's testimony.

(5)   The centrality of the credibility issue.

United States v. NurUrdin, 8 F.3d 1187, 1191 (7th Cir. 1993); *United States v. Alexander*, 48 F.3d 1477, 1488 (9th Cir. 1995). In addition to weighing the probative value of the individual conviction, courts sometimes invoke a quantitative factor. In *Wilson v. Groaning*, 25 F.3d 581 (7th Cir. 1994) the court balanced the prejudice of admitting the plaintiff's six convictions against the defendant's right to impeach. The judge decided that allowing admission of three convictions did not pose a danger of unfair prejudice. The court of appeals approved, holding that this was not a case where the defendants were permitted to "harp on the plaintiff's crime, parade it lovingly before the jury in all its gruesome details, and thereby shift the focus of attention from the events at issue to the plaintiff's conviction in the prior case." *Id.* at 586.

NOTES AND PROBLEMS

1. In *Wilson v. Groaning*, the plaintiff's counsel opted to soften the impact of the prior conviction evidence by eliciting Wilson's convictions during his direct examination. Is this a good tactic? What psychological effect is taken away from the opponent when the direct examiner employs this technique? *United States v. DeLoach*, 34 F.3d 1001, 1004 (11 Cir. 1994) (to blunt expected attacks on credibility, defense may elicit evidence of defendant's conviction). Moreover, there is authority that when a direct examiner fully brings out his witness' prior convictions, cross–examination on the same point is disallowed. *Nicholas v. State*, 49 Wis.2d 683, 183 N.W.2d 11 (1971) ("[t]his tactic is permissible; and the matter may not be pursued on cross–examination— provided the answers on direct are truthful and accurate"). The cross–examiner can elicit specific information if not elicited on direct; *e.g.*, the date and place of the conviction, the sentence imposed—but that is about all.

2. While softening the impact of the conviction by bringing it out on direct is often a favorable strategy, there are dangers. If defense counsel goes beyond the name, date, location and punishment for the crime and explores factual nuances, the cross–examiner can also go into details. In addition, the decision in *Ohler v. United States*, 529 U.S. 753 (2000), poses a hazard for criminal case defendants who testify and bring out their prior offenses on direct. The decision holds that defendants who preemptively introduce evidence of prior convictions during direct testimony may not claim on appeal that admission of such evidence was error. This case should be considered in connection with *Luce v. United States*, 469 U.S. 38 (1984), discussed earlier in this text.

3. Suppose the prior convictions are not brought out on direct. Can a cross–examiner inquire by dropping a long sheet of computer paper on the floor, suggesting it to be a printout of the witness' prior convictions, when the fact is that the witness has been convicted only once or twice? How does such a display impact the rule that there must be a good faith basis for cross–examination questions? Will misimpressions created by examiners sometimes rise to the level of reversible error? *See Sanders–El v. Wencewicz*, 987 F.2d 483 (8th Cir. 1993) ("computer printout fiasco").

4. On the general rule that a cross–examiner must have a good faith basis for her questions, see *Medlock v. State*, 263 Ga. 246, 430 S.E.2d 754 (1993). There has been specific application of this rule to prior conviction impeachment. In *United States v. Ruiz–Castro*, 92 F. 3d 1519 (10th Cir. 1996), the defense wanted to cross–examine a government witness about alleged prior convictions in Mexico for drug offenses. However, the court found the defendants failed to present any evidence supporting the alleged convictions, and barred cross–examination on the point. The appellate court observed that the basis for impeachment "cannot be speculation and innuendo with no evidentiary foundation".

5. Problem 16–26. In *Devitt*, the defense introduces the signed statement of Walter Clarkston. He is a friend of Devitt, and in the statement says that Devitt could not have attacked Paterson because Clarkston and Devitt were out on the town looking for prostitutes at the time of the assault. The trial judge found the statement sufficiently "self–denigrating" to permit its admission into evidence. Clarkston has disappeared and cannot be found for the trial. The prosecutor seeks to impeach Clarkston's testimony by showing he was convicted of lying to a federal agent two years ago. The defense objects. What result? Rule 806 allows hearsay declarants to be attacked by a number of forms of impeachment. *United States v. Saada*, 212 F. 3d 210 (3d Cir. 2000) (the credibility of a hearsay declarant may be impeached, among other means, by evidence of criminal convictions under Rule 609).

6. A final procedural point involves the respective burdens of proof when a criminal defendant is impeached by prior convictions as opposed to impeachment of other witnesses. Rule 609(a) establishes its own balancing provision for criminal defendants, and mandates Rule 403 for other witnesses. While Rule 403 is in the passive voice—suggesting that the opponent of the evidence has the burden of persuasion— the criminal defendant provision in Rule 609(a)(1) is in the active voice. In construing it, courts have made clear that the burden is with the government to prove that the probative value of the prior conviction for impeachment purposes outweighs its prejudicial effect to the criminal accused. *United States v. Jackson*, 863 F. Supp. 1462, 1467 (D. Kan. 1994).

3. EXTRINSIC EVIDENCE OF A PRIOR CONVICTION

The attorney attacking the witness' credibility is not limited to cross–examining the witness about a conviction. The collateral fact rule is inapplicable to this impeachment technique, and the attorney may resort to extrinsic evidence of the conviction. *Montgomery v. State*, 277 Ark. 95, 100–01, 640 S.W.2d 108, 112 (Ark. 1982). The Illinois statute is illustrative. Illinois Comp. Stat. Ann. ch. 735 § 5/8–101 (1993) provides:

> 8–101. Interested witness
>
> > (A) conviction may be shown for the purpose of affecting the credibility of [a] witness; and the fact of [a] conviction may be proven like any fact not of record, either by the witness himself or herself (who shall be compelled to testify thereto) . . . or by any other competent evidence.

This does not mean that extrinsic evidence of the conviction is always admissible. Suppose that during direct or cross–examination, the witness admits the prior conviction. In a similar situation, when a witness fully admits a prior inconsistent statement, most courts exclude cumulative extrinsic evidence as a waste of time. By parity of reasoning, the judge can exclude extrinsic evidence of any conviction to which the witness admits. However, if the witness equivocates or denies the conviction, she may be deemed to have invited the presentation of extrinsic evidence, such as a certified copy of the conviction.

NOTES AND PROBLEMS

1. The factor of remoteness in time has generated much litigation. Federal Rule 609(b) attempts to clarify the state of the law governing stale convictions. Under the final version of Rule 609(b), a prior conviction ordinarily will not be usable if more than ten years have expired since the witness was convicted and "served his time." *United States v. Orlando–Figueroa*, 229 F.3d 33 (1st Cir. 2000) (exclusion by trial court of more–than–ten–year old conviction of government witness for mail fraud.) In any case, in order to offer proof of a conviction more than 10 years old, the proponent must give advance written notice.

2. Problem 16–27. In the *Devitt* case, the trial takes place on September 15, 19YR. Devitt has four prior convictions:

Crime	Date of Conviction	Maximum Sentence	Disposition
Computer theft	5 yrs. ago May 5	Supervision* for 1 year	Supervision* completed successfully
Contributing to the delinquency of a child	13 yrs. ago June 6	3 years	Suspended sentence, probation
Unlawful firearms possession	12 yrs. ago April 1	4 years	Served 2 years: 2 years parole
Attempted Murder	8 yrs. ago Sept. 9	5 years	Served 6 months, conviction set aside on habeas corpus for violation of right to counsel; guilty plea to assault, sentenced to time served

*In this jurisdiction, "supervision" does not involve incarceration.

For the prosecution, argue for the admission of these convictions. For the defendant, argue against their admission.

Chapter 17

CREDIBILITY: REHABILITATION

Read Federal Rule of Evidence 801(d)(1)(B).

A. INTRODUCTION

There are three stages of credibility analysis. A previous chapter covered the first stage: bolstering the witness' credibility before attempted impeachment. We then turned our attention to the second stage—impeachment techniques. We analyzed the methods of attacking both the witness and the witness' testimony. This chapter covers the last stage of credibility analysis: rehabilitating the witness' credibility after impeachment.

We shall examine five methods of rehabilitation: (1) the use of redirect examination to deny or explain the impeaching fact; (2) prior consistent statements by the witness; (3) the corroboration of the witness' testimony by other witnesses; (4) proof of the witness' character trait of truthfulness; and (5) expert testimony.

B. THE USE OF REDIRECT EXAMINATION FOR REHABILITATION

We have observed that as the examination proceeds through its various stages of direct and cross, the scope narrows. By the time we reach redirect examination, the only questions the examiner may ask as of right are questions aimed at issues raised for the first time during cross–examination. In most cases, the new issues raised on cross are the impeaching facts that the cross–examiner elicits to attack the witness' credibility. These will be addressed upon redirect, and the examiner frequently uses the opportunity to cover ground which is highly favorable to the examiner.

The most challenging part of conducting a good redirect is finding an effective or persuasive way to deny or explain the impeaching facts that the cross–examiner elicited. T. MAUET, FUNDAMENTALS OF TRIAL TECHNIQUES § 4.14 (4th ed. 1996). Suppose, for example, that in *Hill*, during Mr. Roe's direct examination, he testified that he considered Worker a careful driver and had no hesitation entrusting the car to Worker. On cross–examination, Mr. Hill's attorney asks:

Q: Isn't it true that a month before the accident in this case, you told your secretary that you knew that Worker had been involved in a serious traffic accident in 1993?

A: Yes.

On redirect, the defense attorney can invite Roe to explain away the seemingly impeaching fact elicited on cross:

Q: What else did you tell your secretary in that conversation?

A: I told her that I had spoken with the police officer who investigated the 1993 accident.

Q: What did you tell her about the accident?

A: I mentioned that the police officer assured me that the accident was entirely the fault of the other driver.

PROBLEMS

1. Problem 17–1. In *Devitt*, the prosecution calls Mr. Thompson as a witness. On direct, Thompson testifies that he saw Devitt emerge from Paterson's apartment at the time of the alleged assault. On cross-examination, Thompson admits that a week later, he told the police that the man he saw was definitely not Devitt. On redirect, may the prosecutor elicit Thompson's testimony that he made the inconsistent statement because Devitt had confronted and physically assaulted Thompson prior to his subsequent inconsistent statement to the police? May the prosecutor introduce extrinsic evidence of the assault and Thompson's fear of future reprisal from Devitt, in order to rehabilitate Thompson? *See People v. Hawkins*, 10 Cal. 4th 920, 897 P.2d 574, 42 Cal. Rptr. 2d 636 (1995), *cert. denied*, 116 S. Ct. 1685 (1996).

2. Problem 17–2. During the cross-examination of Mr. Paterson, he admits that he did not report the assault for several hours. On redirect examination, may the prosecutor elicit his testimony that he knew that Devitt had previously been convicted of a violent crime and that Paterson initially feared his reprisal? *State v. Parris*, 592 A.2d 943, 947 (Conn. 1991).

3. Problem 17–3. Suppose Devitt is cross–examined with a prior conviction. On redirect, may he be rehabilitated by his own explanation of the prior conviction? *See United States v. Boyer*, 150 F.2d 595 (D.C. App. 1945) (witness should be able to proceed with any reasonably brief protestations on his own behalf which he may wish to make). However, consider all of the consequences. Some courts apply the rule that a witness who has rehabilitated himself by explaining the circumstances of a previous conviction can be cross–examined concerning the facts surrounding the conviction. *Vincent v. State*, 264 Ga. 234, 442 S.E.2d 748 (1994). Presumably this might come during recross, in the case of witness who has used redirect examination to provide favorable details which mitigate a former conviction.

C.   PRIOR CONSISTENT STATEMENTS

Another use of redirect examination is to prove the witness' prior consistent statements. Just as a prior inconsistent statement detracts from the witness' credibility, a previous consistent statement may enhance the credibility. However, the simplicity and symmetry of that sentence can be misleading. In fact, the body of law governing the admissibility of prior consistent statements is rather complex. To master that body of law, we must grapple with two questions: What must occur on cross-examination to trigger the admissibility of prior consistent statements? Are there any special timing requirements for the statement elicited on redirect?

1. What Triggers Admissibility of Prior Consistent Statements

Not every form of impeachment enables the proponent of a witness to rehabilitate by use of the prior consistent statement method. *Gaines v. Waller*, 986 F.2d 1438 (D.C. App. 1993). California Evidence Code § 791 typifies the approach of many jurisdictions to consistent statements:

> § 791. Prior consistent statement of witness.
>
> Evidence of a statement previously made by a witness that is consistent with his testimony at the hearing is inadmissible to support his credibility unless it is offered after:
>
> (a) Evidence of a statement made by him that is inconsistent with any part of his testimony at the hearing has been admitted for the purpose of attacking his credibility, and the statement was made before the alleged inconsistent statement; or
>
> (b) An express or implied charge has been made that his testimony at the hearing is recently fabricated or is influenced by bias or other improper motive, and the statement was made before the bias, motive for fabrication, or other improper motive is alleged to have arisen.

The only mention of prior consistent statements in the text of the Federal Rules of Evidence appears in Rule 801(d)(1)(B):

> "A statement is not hearsay if . . . [t]he declarant testifies at the trial or hearing and is subject to cross-examination concerning the statement, and the statement is . . . consistent with his testimony and is offered to rebut an express or implied charge against him of recent fabrication or improper influence or motive. . . ."

Professor Graham explains the admission of prior consistent statements in *Prior Consistent Statements: Rule 801(d)(1)(B) of the Federal Rules of Evidence, Critique and Proposal*, 30 HASTINGS L.J. 575, 584 (1979):

> Rule 801(d)(1)(B), in conformity with the common law, recognizes that when during cross-examination an express or implied charge is made that the witness' in-court testimony is false as a result of an improper influence or motive, a consistent statement made prior to the alleged existence of the improper influence or motive is admissible to rebut the charge. Unfortunately, neither term, "improper influence" or "motive," as incorporated into Rule 801(d)(1)(B) is specifically defined in the rule nor clearly defined in the authorities. Under generally accepted definitions of these terms, motive may be said to be an emotional state of an individual, such as racial prejudice, greed, love, or revenge, that may have prompted the individual to falsify his testimony. An influence, on the other hand, may be defined as an outside force such as a bribe that induces an individual to testify in a particular manner.
>
> If the foregoing definitions are employed, an influence may be said to produce a motive to falsify. Thus "motive" is the thrust of our concern. An "improper" motive is any motive that tends to induce the witness to do anything but tell the whole truth.

Wigmore categorizes the kinds of emotions to which Rule 801(d)(1)(B) refers as "untrustworthy partiality." Such partiality has the following components:

> *Bias*, in common acceptance, covers all varieties of hostility or prejudice against the opponent *personally* or of favor to the proponent personally.

> *Interest* signifies the specific inclination which is apt to be produced by the relation between the witness and the *cause at issue* in the litigation.

> *Corruption* is here to be understood as the *conscious false intent* which is inferrible [sic] from giving or taking a bribe or from expressions of a general unscrupulousness for the case in hand.

In order to complete the definition of partiality this author suggests the inclusion of [another] category: *Coercion*, intended to include any form of mental, emotional, or physical duress or compulsion that overcomes a witness' duty to tell the truth. . . .

To illustrate the distinction between an express and an implied charge of partiality, assume that, on cross–examination of the witness, counsel inquires, "You are the mother of the defendant, aren't you?" Counsel has made an implied charge of partiality. Although the question is a direct inquiry as to a fact, it does not inquire as to the natural inference the cross–examiner hopes the trier of fact will draw. Now assume that counsel continues on cross–examination, "You would do anything you could to help your son, wouldn't you?" This is an express charge because the inference previously left to be inferred is now asserted.[39]

NOTES AND PROBLEMS

1. The United States Supreme Court, in *Tome v. United States*, 115 S. Ct. 696 (1995), pointed out that prior consistent statements may not be admitted to counter all forms of impeachment or to bolster the witness merely because she has been discredited. Admissibility is confined to statements which rebut charges of fabrication or improper influence. When the attack on the witness is impeachment of her character, proof of bad reputation, prior convictions or past dishonest acts, the Court endorsed the view that "there is no color for sustaining [the witness] by consistent statements." *See also Woodard v. State*, 269 Ga. 317, 496 S.E.2d 896 (1998), following the view that veracity

---

[39] Note that should the examiner go a step further and question, "Isn't it true that you made up this story to protect your son?," the question would probably be objectionable as argumentative. Heafey states that "a question is argumentative and therefore objectionable if it: (1) Is asked for the purpose of persuading the trier of fact, rather than to elicit information or; (2) Calls for an argument in answer to an argument contained in the question or; (3) Calls for no new facts, but merely asks the witness to assent to inferences drawn by the examiner from proved or assumed facts." HEAFEY, CALIFORNIA TRIAL OBJECTIONS § 14.1, at 67 (1967). In asking the witness whether he has made up his testimony, the cross-examiner is not attempting to elicit information; the real purpose of the question is to persuade the trier of fact. The question merely asks the witness to assent to the inference that counsel has drawn from the witness' testimony. Thus, the cross–examiner's question is subject to the objection that it is argumentative.

is placed in issue so as to permit the introduction of prior consistent statements only when there has been a charge of recent fabrication, improper influence, or improper motive.

2. Problem 17–4. In the *Hill* case, the following occurred during the cross–examination of Mr. Worker:

> Q: Mr. Worker, you testified on direct examination that you lost control of your vehicle because another car suddenly cut in front of you. Didn't you?
>
> A: Yes.
>
> Q: You did speak with a police officer right after the collision. Isn't that true?
>
> A: Yes.
>
> Q: But you didn't mention the other car to the police officer.
>
> A: That's right.

On redirect, would the defense attorney be allowed to elicit Worker's prior consistent statements? *See United States v. Castillo*, 14 F.3d 802, 806 (2d Cir. 1994).

3. Problem 17–5. In the previous problem, the following occurred:

> Q. But you didn't mention the other car to the police officer.
>
> A. Well, ——
>
> Q. Your Honor, I'm sorry. I'd like to withdraw that question.
>
> J. Very well.

Would the defense attorney still be able to elicit prior consistent statements on redirect? *See People v. Williams*, 274 Ill. App. 598, 653 N.E.2d 899, 907 (1995). For a discussion of withdrawn questions, *see United States v. Coleman*, 631 F.2d 908, 914 (D.C. Cir. 1980).

4. Prior consistent statements used to rehabilitate a witness constitute substantive evidence, not simply credibility support. The Advisory Committee Note to Rule 801 concluded that prior consistent statements "are substantive evidence." But the weight to be attached to Advisory Committee Notes remained uncertain until *Tome v. United States, supra.* The Supreme Court relied upon the Notes to decide the case, calling them a "useful guide in ascertaining the meaning of the Rules." Their sometimes compelling import derived from the fact that the "Notes are also a respected source of scholarly commentary." Thus, the Supreme Court held that the Advisory Committee Notes were both persuasive commentary as well as a guide to legislative intent. Taslitz, *Interpretive Method and the Federal Rules of Evidence: A Call for a Politically Realistic Hermeneutics,* 32 HARV. J. ON LEGIS. 329 (1995).

2.   Timing Requirements for Prior Consistent Statements

Once the opposing counsel initiates one of the three types of impeachment on cross–examination, either charges of fabrication, improper influence, or inconsistent statement, rehabilitation by consistent statement may follow. A few jurisdictions allow the witness' proponent on redirect to elicit any prior consistent statements by the witness, whenever the statement was made.

Kizziar v. State, 628 S.W.2d 243 (Tex. Ct. App. 1982). However, under California Evidence Code § 791(a), if the impeachment takes the form of a prior inconsistent statement, the consistent statement must have been "made before the alleged inconsistent statement." Similarly, under subsection (b), when the cross–examiner alleges recent fabrication or improper motive the consistent statement must have been "made before the bias, motive for fabrication, or other improper motive is alleged to have arisen." This restrictive view is the prevailing rule in the United States. *Tome v. United States*, 115 S. Ct. 696 (1995); 1 C. MCCORMICK, HANDBOOK OF THE LAW OF EVIDENCE § 47 (4th ed. 1992).

Even the jurisdictions subscribing to the majority view sometimes differ over the rationale. In some cases, they declare that the consistent statement is logically irrelevant unless the statement is prior: "Only then [is] the . . . consistent statement 'relevant' on the issue of credibility." *United States v. Quinto*, 582 F.2d 224, 232-33 (2d Cir. 1978). These courts argue that if the charge is improper motive, the consistent statement rebuts the charge only when the statement antedates the improper motive. Otherwise, the consistent statement is subject to the same charge as the trial testimony. *Patterson v. State*, 907 P.2d 984, 988 (Nev. 1995). However, other courts rationalize the prevailing view on legal irrelevance grounds. They would probably concede bare materiality under Federal Rule of Evidence 401, but they contend that a subsequent statement "does not have significant force." *United States v. Payne*, 944 F.2d 1458 (9th Cir. 1991). A subsequent statement may also be subject to a charge of improper motive, but the motive reduces the weight of the statement without destroying its materiality. These courts exclude subsequent statements because they demand a greater quantum of probative value on redirect than on cross–examination.

The United States Supreme Court entered the fray in 1995 when it decided:

TOME v. UNITED STATES

115 S. Ct. 696 (1995)

JUSTICE KENNEDY.

[The first witness for the Government in a sexual assault case was cross-examined for two days. The cross–examiner implicitly charged that the witness had a motive to falsify. Thereafter seven pretrial statements of the witness were produced which fortified the direct. On appeal the Court of Appeals affirmed defendant's conviction, holding the out-of-court statements to be admissible even though they had been made after the witness' alleged motive to fabricate arose. The Court of Appeals refused to follow the rule which required the statements to predate the time of fabrication, rejecting the so–called pre–motive requirement. The Supreme Court reversed, aligning its view with the common law and the Federal Rules Advisory Committee.]

The prevailing common-law rule for more than a century before adoption of the Federal Rules of Evidence was that a prior consistent statement introduced to rebut a charge of recent fabrication or improper influence or motive was admissible if the statement had been made before the alleged fabrication, influence, or motive came into being, but it was inadmissible if made after-wards. As Justice Story explained: "[W]here the testimony is assailed as a fabrication of a recent date. . . in order to repel such imputation, proof of the antecedent declaration of the party may be admitted." *Ellicott v. Pearl*, 35 U.S. (10 Pet.) 412, 439, 9 L. Ed. 475 (1836). *See also People v. Singer*, 300 N.Y. 120, 124–125, 89 N.E.2d 710, 712 (1949).

The underlying theory of the Government's position is that an out–of–court consistent statement, whenever it was made, tends to bolster the testimony and so tends also to rebut an express or implied charge that the testimony has been the product of an improper influence. Congress could have adopted that rule with ease, providing, for instance, that "a witness' prior consistent statements are admissible whenever relevant to assess the witness' truthful-ness or accuracy." The theory would be that, in a broad sense, any prior statement by a witness concerning the disputed issues at trial would have some relevance in assessing the accuracy or truthfulness of the witness' in–court testimony on the same subject. The narrow Rule enacted by Congress, however, cannot be understood to incorporate the Government's theory.

Our analysis is strengthened by the observation that the somewhat peculiar language of the Rule bears close similarity to the language used in many of the common law cases that describe the premotive requirement. "Rule 801(d)(1)(B) employs the precise language—'rebut[ting] . . . charge[s] . . . of recent fabrication or improper influence or motive'—consistently used in the panoply of pre-1975 decisions." E.O. Ohlbaum, *The Hobgoblin of the Federal Rules of Evidence: An Analysis of Rule 801(d)(1)(B), Prior Consistent State-ments and a New Proposal*, 1987 B.Y.U. L. Rev. 231, 245. *See, e.g., Ellicott v. Pearl*, 35 U.S. (10 Pet.) 412, 439, 9 L. Ed. 475 (1836); *Hanger v. United States*, 398 F.2d 91, 104 (CA8 1968); *People v. Singer*, 300 N.Y. 120, 89 N.E.2d 710 (1949).

The language of the Rule, in its concentration on rebutting charges of recent fabrication, improper influence and motive to the exclusion of other forms of impeachment, as well as in its use of wording which follows the language of the common–law cases, suggests that it was intended to carry over the common–law pre–motive rule.

NOTES AND PROBLEMS

1. *Tome* accepts statements made prior to a biasing event but rejects subsequent statements. Which view do you prefer: the minority view or the majority doctrine embraced by *Tome*? Why?

2. Problem 17-6. In *Hill*, before trial, Worker has a conversation with the police officer who investigated the accident scene. Early in the interview Worker states, "I feel sorta guilty about the whole thing. I can't help thinking that there was something that I could have done to have avoided the accident." Five minutes later during the same conversation, Worker said, "But I guess when I look at it objectively, there really wasn't anything I could have done. I honestly don't think I was at fault." During Worker's cross–examination, Ms. Hill's attorney forces Worker to admit the statement he made early in his interview with the police officer. On redirect, Roe's attorney elicits the statement Worker made later in the conversation. Worker testifies to the statement and then adds that although he was in an uncertain mood when he made the earlier statement, he had "real conviction in my voice" when he made the later statement. As his next witness, Roe calls the police officer to whom Worker made the statement. The officer is prepared to testify that Worker "seemed much more positive" when he made the second statement. As soon as Roe's attorney begins questioning the officer about his conversation with Worker, Ms. Hill's attorney objects "to all this extrinsic evidence about Worker's credibility. Besides, prior consistent statements cannot be proved through the testimony of third parties, like this officer." Should the collateral fact rule apply to the officer's testimony? Should extrinsic evidence of prior consistent statements be admissible? *See United States v. Montague*, 958 F.2d 1094, 1099 (D.C. Cir. 1992).

3. Trial transcript testimony in Tome, including that of the first witness as well as corroborative statements reported by other witnesses, is reported in Burns, *Bright Lines and Hard Edges: Anatomy of a Criminal Evidence Decision*, 85 J. CRIM. L. & CRIMINOLOGY 843 (1995).

D. CORROBORATION

By definition, corroborating testimony is extrinsic evidence—extrinsic to the testimony of the first witness who is being corroborated. Under the corroboration doctrine, the court is not admitting prior consistent statements by the witness; rather, the court is admitting consistent testimony by another witness. This is a key distinction. The corroborating witness testifies to a relevant event, for example, and the description of it may coincide with that supplied by the main witness. However, when the corroborating witness seeks to testify about the main witness' out–of–court statements, special rules operate. The *Tome* case makes this clear.

Corroboration is the converse of specific contradiction. Courts freely and routinely admit corroborating evidence at numerous places in the trial—not merely on redirect. How does corroboration support the main witness? Does the mere coincidence between the two witnesses' testimony give the supported witness' testimony superior credibility?

E. PROOF OF THE CHARACTER TRAIT OF A WITNESS FOR TRUTHFULNESS

Another type of extrinsic rehabilitating evidence is evidence of the witness' character trait of truthfulness. Like evidence of a witness' prior consistent statement, proof of the witness' truthfulness raises two questions: What types of impeachment trigger the proponent's right to prove the witness' truthfulness? What form must the proof of truthfulness take?

The second question can be answered readily. If a court allows the unfavorable character witness to testify to reputation within a business circle rather than a residential community, the court will accept favorable reputation testimony drawn from the same circle. Further, if the jurisdiction accepts unfavorable opinion testimony as well as unfavorable reputation evidence, the witness' proponent may resort to favorable opinion or reputation.

The first question, however, is more troublesome. What impeachment techniques amount to attacks on the witness' character?

Throughout this chapter, we have seen that the courts' rule of thumb on rehabilitation is response in kind. To minimize the danger of distracting the jury, the courts require the rehabilitation to be a response in kind to the impeachment. On that assumption, the courts should certainly admit favorable character evidence when the opposing counsel called a character witness to testify directly to the prior witness' character trait of untruthfulness. Federal Rule of Evidence 608(a)(2) so provides:

> The credibility of a witness may be . . . supported by evidence in the form of opinion or reputation, but subject to these limitations: . . . evidence of truthful character is admissible only after the character of the witness for truthfulness has been attacked by opinion or reputation or otherwise.

In previous materials cataloguing the various impeachment techniques, we distinguished between *ad hominem* attacks versus attacks on the content of the witness' testimony. Common sense suggests that the courts should treat the *ad hominem* attacks as assaults on the witness' character. Impeachment evidence of a witness' conviction or untruthful act "open the door to character support." 1 McCORMICK, HANDBOOK OF THE LAW OF EVIDENCE 174 (4th ed. 1992). Federal Rule of Evidence 608(a)(2) contains the language "or otherwise."

Lesser attacks do not. *People v. Miller*, 890 P.2d 84, 96 (Colo. 1995), held that merely questioning a witness' credibility on cross–examination does not necessarily constitute an attack which opens the door. Even if we apply the *ejusdem generis* maxim of statutory interpretation to the language, the *ad hominem* attacks should fall within Rule 608(a)(2). The statute cannot be limited to unfavorable reputation and opinion evidence; in that event "or otherwise" would be useless surplusage. If "or otherwise" applies to any other impeachment techniques, the language should apply to the *ad hominem* attacks; they are most closely akin to reputation and opinion evidence because they strongly imply that the witness has a character trait of untruthfulness. *People v. Smith*, 282 N.W.2d 227 (Mich. 1979) (a prior lie by the witness).

The point of disagreement among the courts is whether the opponent's use of any of the other impeachment techniques should permit the proponent to introduce favorable character evidence. Some courts have been reluctant to admit favorable character evidence in response, for example, to prior inconsistent statement impeachment. *People v. Wheatley*, 805 P.2d 1148 (Colo. Ct. App. 1990). *Compare State v. Hall*, 390 S.E.2d 169, 173 (N.C.App. 1990). As trial judge, how would you rule in the following problems?

PROBLEMS

1. Problem 17-7. In *Hill*, the plaintiff calls Professor Monsky, an expert on accident reconstruction. During cross–examination, Roe's attorney questions Monsky about his fee in the *Hill* case and the percentage of income he earns every year by testifying in court. *Syken v. Elkins*, 644 So. 2d 539 (Fla. App. 1994). As her next witness, Ms. Hill calls Professor Lawrence. Professor

Lawrence is prepared to testify to Monsky's good reputation for truthfulness among the faculty members at El Dorado State University. Roe's attorney objects under Rule 608(a)(2). *See People v. Ah Fat*, 48 Cal. 61, 64 (1874).

2. Problem 17-8. In *Devitt*, the defendant testifies that he never had any difficulty with Mr. Paterson. On cross–examination, the prosecutor asked: "Isn't it true that a week after this incident you told your friend Dave Clark that you had clobbered Mr. Paterson?" As his next witness, Devitt calls Father Benedetti, a local priest. Father Benedetti is prepared to testify that in El Dorado, Devitt has a reputation as a truthful person. The prosecution objects, citing Rule 608(a)(2). *See State v. Hall*, 390 S.E.2d 169, 173 (N.C. 1990). Would the result be the same if Devitt's inconsistent statement related to the color of the shirt he saw Paterson wearing the day of the alleged assault? Is it significant that Devitt might easily be mistaken about the color of the shirt?

F. EXPERT TESTIMONY

As we saw in the last chapter, *United States v. Hiss*, 88 F. Supp. 559 (D.C.N.Y. 1950), supported the use of expert psychiatric testimony for the purpose of impeachment. More recently, attorneys have begun using scientific evidence as rehabilitation. In rape or child sexual abuse cases, for example, expert psychiatric testimony has been used to explain why a victim sometimes recants her account of the crime, or delays reporting it. *People v. Taylor*, 75 N.Y. 2d 277, 552 N.Y.S.2d 883, 552 N.E.2d 131, 138 (1990) ("the reaction of a rape victim in the hours following her attack is not something within the common understanding of the average lay juror"; rape trauma syndrome evidence can assist jurors in reaching a verdict). In *State v. Hall*, 330 N.C. 808, 412 S.E.2d 883 (1992), evidence that a victim's symptoms are consistent with those of sexual or physical abuse victims was held to be admissible, but only to aid the jury in assessing the complainant's credibility.

A good summary of the posture of the law appears in Risinger, *Navigating Expert Reliability: Are Criminal Standards of Certainty Being Left on the Dock?*, 64 Albany L. Rev. 99, 116–117 (2000). Professor Risinger reports that a minority of jurisdictions allow prosecutors to use syndrome evidence openly, but an expert would generally not be allowed to say explicitly that the victim was truthful. However, the expert could conclude that there had been a child molestation or a rape. The majority of jurisdictions have held that syndrome evidence is not admissible to prove the existence of the crime. On the other hand, the witness could generally educate the jury regarding features of the syndrome, affirm that the characteristics of the victim were consistent with the syndrome, and could explain why there might be a delay in reporting the crime.

In addition, experts on battered women's syndrome have been used to rehabilitate victims in assault cases. However, while a psychiatrist may be permitted to testify that recantation is consistent with the conduct of many women subjected to battering, numerous courts draw the line when the expert is asked if he believed the victim in this case. *State v. Borrelli*, 227 Conn. 153, 629 A.2d 1105 (Conn. 1993). In *Borrelli* the expert, a sociologist, provided a possible explanation for this assault victim's recantation of her account of her husband's abuse, threats and assaults. The court carefully pointed out that the expert did not testify that this victim was in fact battered; rather, the expert supported the state's position that the victim's recantation was a pattern of typical behavior consistent with battered women's syndrome. A similar distinction has been drawn in cases admitting an expert witness' testimony on the general behavioral characteristics of child abuse victims.

These considerations lead us back to the concept of scientific validation. When a scientist states that a theory or technique has been "validated," he or she means that it has been experimentally verified that the technique can accurately perform a certain task. In *State v. Saldana*, 324 N.W.2d 227, 229-31 (Minn. 1982), the court surveyed some of the scientific literature on rape trauma syndrome, including the heralded study by Burgess and Holmstrom. The court concluded that the syndrome had been validated "not [as] a fact-finding tool, but [only as] a therapeutic tool useful in counseling." *Id.* at 230. In *People v. Shirley*, 31 Cal. 3d 18, 641 P.2d 775, 181 Cal. Rptr. 243, *cert. denied*, 459 U.S. 860 (1982), the hypnotic enhancement case excerpted earlier, the California Supreme Court drew a parallel distinction. The court acknowledged that hypnosis has been validated as a therapeutic tool for treating mental patients troubled by repressed memories. However, the court concluded that hypnosis has not been validated as a technique for helping witnesses retrieve accurate memories of prior events. *Id.* at 66, 641 P.2d at 804, 181 Cal. Rptr. at 243.

NOTE

How would you design an experiment to validate the hypothesis that hypnosis is an effective therapeutic tool for patients troubled by repressed memories of child abuse? In contrast, how would you plan an experiment to validate the hypothesis that the memories a patient purports to retrieve through hypnosis are accurate recollections of actual events? A scientific experiment does not validate all possible applications of a theory or technique; it verifies only a particular hypothesis about a particular application. See Note, *"Lies, Damned Lies, and Statistics"? Psychological Syndrome Evidence in the Courtroom After* Daubert, 71 IND. L.J. 753 (1996), pointing out some of the flaws in the Burgess and Holmstrom research.

Chapter 18

THE RULE AGAINST HEARSAY: THE ADMISSIBILITY OF OUT–OF–COURT STATEMENTS

Read Federal Rules of Evidence 801 and 802.

A. THE REASONS FOR THE HEARSAY RULE

Four factors influence the judge's decision whether to include a particular item of evidence within the definition of hearsay. First, hearsay evidence is usually unsworn. The common law and modern statutes require that, before testifying, a prospective witness acknowledge, by oath or affirmation, the obligation to testify truthfully. FED. R. EVID. 603. One purpose of requiring this acknowledgment is to awaken the person's conscience before testifying, with the hope that the effect will be to increase the probability of the sincerity of the testimony. Many statements falling within the definition of hearsay are unsworn; the lack of an oath or affirmation heightens the judge's doubts about the reliability of the statement. 5 J. WIGMORE, EVIDENCE §§ 1362, 1373–77 (3d ed. 1940). On the other hand, the mere fact that a statement is sworn, does not necessarily make it admissible. *Id.* §§ 1362, 1364.

The second factor is the possibility of error in the oral transmission of information. 2 C. McCORMICK, HANDBOOK OF THE LAW OF EVIDENCE § 245 (5th ed. 1999). The person relaying information orally may misspeak, and the person receiving the information (the witness now on the stand) may err in hearing, remembering, or relating. The longer the chain of transmission, the greater the chance of error. On the other hand, merely because a statement is in writing does not necessarily make it admissible. *Id.*

Third is the jury's inability to observe the hearsay declarant's demeanor while speaking. In *Barber v. Page*, 390 U.S. 719, 725 (1968), the Supreme Court underscored the importance of affording "the jury [the occasion] to weigh the demeanor of the witness." We commonly assume that the person's nonverbal behavior is an important clue to the person's credibility. If a witness fidgets on the stand, perspires, and refuses to look the attorney in the eye, we sometimes suspect the witness' truthfulness. On the other hand, depositions are routinely admissible, even though the deponent's demeanor cannot be assessed.

Finally, we come to what is widely regarded as the preeminent rationale for the rule against hearsay: the admission of a declarant's hearsay statement denies the opposing party an opportunity to cross–examine the declarant about the statement. We exclude hearsay to ensure that as a general rule, the opposing party has an opportunity to challenge the statement by cross–examination.

It is important to realize that the hearsay rule crystallized during a rather romantic era in trial advocacy. One Victorian writer on trial technique declared that "[t]here is never a cause contested, the result of which is not mainly dependent upon the skill with which the advocate conducts his cross–examination." Cox, THE ADVOCATE 434, *in* REED, CONDUCT OF LAWSUITS 277 (2d ed. 1912). Many of the paeans written to the hearsay rule assume that it is all in a day's work for a brilliantly intuitive cross–examiner to unmask even the cleverest perjurer. Wigmore characterized cross–examination as the "greatest legal engine ever invented for the discovery of truth." 5 J. WIGMORE, EVIDENCE § 1367 (3d ed. 1940).

The modern view of the value of cross–examination is more realistic. *See* Goldstein, *The Cardinal Principles of Cross–Examination.* 1959 TRIAL LAW. GUIDE 331. We know now that: Most cases are won by methodically prepared direct examination rather than by divinely inspired cross–examination. Overly aggressive cross–examination can be counterproductive–to put it bluntly, you sometimes slit your own throat when you go for the witness' jugular. The best use of cross–examination is usually to elicit a few favorable admissions from the witness rather than to attempt to browbeat the witness into tears or confession. *Id.* at 338. In the contemporary view, cross–examination has more limited effectiveness than the Victorians assumed; and we consequently have been willing to recognize more hearsay exceptions.

Nevertheless, we regard cross–examination as a valuable right. In our criminal jurisprudence, the right has constitutional status. *Davis v. Alaska,* 415 U.S. 308 (1974); *Alford v. United States,* 282 U.S. 687 (1931). Think back to our discussion of the general elements of competency. To qualify as a witness, a person must have moral capacity and the mental capacities to observe, remember, and relate. These capacities correspond with the testimonial qualities of sincerity, perception, memory, and narration. Cross–examination enables the opposing attorney to test these qualities. It enables the attorney to probe for and expose deficiencies in the elements of competency. Modern courts are lax in enforcing the competency standards; as a matter of course, they allow persons with questionable sincerity or mental capacity to testify. The more liberal the competency standards, the more often persons of suspect credibility can testify, and the more compelling the need to subject the testimony of these persons to the safeguard of cross–examination.

B.   THE DEFINITION OF HEARSAY

As important and entrenched as the hearsay rule is, one might expect a clear definition of hearsay. It would be ideal if hearsay were easily recognizable. Unfortunately, this is not the case. M. LADD & R. CARLSON, CASES AND MATERIALS ON EVIDENCE 802 (1972); McCormick, *The Borderland of Hearsay,* 39 YALE L. J. 489 (1930). The rule is beset with numerous splits of authority, and some of the most important disagreements relate to the definition of hearsay.

The layperson's conception of the rule's scope is very broad. Most laypersons think that the rule forbids any in–court testimony about out–of–court statements. Quite to the contrary, the rule's scope is narrow. We can tentatively define the hearsay rule in this fashion: *an assertion by an out–of–court declarant, offered to prove the truth of the assertion. Cf.* FED. R. EVID. 801(c). To understand the definition, we must examine three aspects of the rule: (1) What types of statements fall within the rule? What sorts of statements are meaningfully testable by cross–examination? (2) For what purpose is the statement offered? Which uses of the statement realistically necessitate that the statement be tested by cross–examination? (3) Which persons should be regarded as out–of–court declarants? Does the declarant's present availability in the courtroom satisfy the need for cross–examination?

1. "AN ASSERTION" — THE TYPES OF STATEMENTS TESTABLE BY CROSS–EXAMINATION

In most jurisdictions, the hearsay rule applies to only assertive statements. Federal Rule of Evidence 801(c) limits the scope of the rule to "statement[s]," and subsection 801(a) then supplies a definition of "statement": "A statement is (1) an oral or written assertion or (2) nonverbal conduct of a person, if it is intended by him as an assertion." If the declaration is an assertive statement, it satisfies this element of the hearsay definition whether it is made in a private, oral conversation or a public newspaper article. *McAllister v. New York City Police Dept.*, 49 F.Supp.2d 688, 705 n.12 (S.D.N.Y. 1999).

The rule's limitation to assertions is a corollary of the primary rationale for the rule. The justification for the rule is guaranteeing the opposing party an opportunity to cross–examine to expose latent weaknesses in sincerity, perception, memory, or narration. Certain types of sentences are usually immune to such weaknesses. For example, if upon observing the collision in *Hill* a bystander utters the exclamation "My God!", there is little reason to be concerned about latent weaknesses in testimonial qualities. Realistically, this type of statement is not testable by cross–examination; there is ordinarily no serious question about the person's perception or memory when the testimony takes the form of an exclamatory, imperative, or interrogatory sentence. *E.g., Servants of Paraclete v. Great American Ins. Co.*, 866 F. Supp. 1560, 1567 (D.N.M. 1994) ("inquiries are not hearsay because . . . they are not assertive"). The conventional wisdom is that the need for cross–examination to unmask weaknesses arises only in connection with assertive statements–sentences that make assertions about facts and events. Park, *"I Didn't Tell Them Anything About You": Implied Assertions as Hearsay Under the Federal Rules of Evidence*, 74 MINN. L. REV. 783 (1990). The sentence must declare or assert a fact susceptible of being true or false. *Craig v. State*, 630 N.E.2d 207 (Ind. 1994).

Given this reasoning, all the courts agree that the definition of assertion includes statements that are in the form of declarative sentences. Again, there is little need for cross–examination if the bystander to the collision in *Hill* utters the exclamation "My God!" However, if the same person adds, "That car (Worker's car) was going at least 40 miles an hour," there is an obvious need to cross–examine the bystander to gauge her testimonial qualities before admitting the sentence as proof of the car's speed. Did she correctly estimate the speed? Does she accurately remember the incident?

It is also necessary to look beyond the sentence's facial appearance and ask whether functionally, the proponent is using it as a declarative assertion. Suppose that before the accident in *Hill,* Polecat's president, Mr. Famiglietti, had a conversation with the chief of safety engineering, Ms. Baker. The conversation occurred in the presence of a witness, Mr. Wright. During the conversation, Wright heard Famiglietti tell Baker, "Baker, I'm not asking you; I'm flat out ordering you to figure out some way to move that gas tank out of the dangerous position we've got it in now." On its face, this sentence is imperative rather than declarative. However, if Hill's attorney offers Wright's testimony to prove that the gas tank is dangerous, that part of Famiglietti's statement is being used as a declarative sentence. For that purpose, most judges would treat the sentence as hearsay.

There is also agreement among the jurisdictions that assertive conduct falls within the hearsay definition. Assume that Mr. Paterson attends a lineup of battery suspects, including Devitt. After he has viewed the lineup, an officer asks Paterson, "Do you see the assailant up there?" Rather than verbalizing an answer, Paterson points at Devitt. The declarant, Mr. Paterson, has not uttered a word; but his act of pointing at Devitt is the functional equivalent of saying, "That man there is the attacker." Paterson subjectively intended his act to be a true substitute for speech. Devitt has the same need to cross–examine to probe Paterson's testimonial qualities that he would have if Paterson had spoken rather than pointed. Suppose alternatively that, as a result of the injuries he sustained in the attack, Paterson has been rendered mute and partially paralyzed; he can neither speak nor use his hands. However, he is conscious and evidently in possession of his mental faculties. A police officer tells him to blink twice if the assailant was the man in the middle of the lineup, Devitt. He does so. Again, Devitt would need to cross–examine him, just as surely as if Paterson had said that the man in the middle was the assailant. *People v. Zollbrecht,* 145 Misc. 2d 880, 548 N.Y.S.2d 380 (Co. Ct. 1989). *See also United States v. Katsougrakis,* 715 F.2d 769 (2d Cir. 1983) (a nod in response to a question is an assertive statement). That need dictates the conclusion reached by Federal Rule 801(a); the definition of hearsay should include "nonverbal conduct of a person, if it is intended by him as an assertion." The trial judge resolves the question of the declarant's intent under Federal Rule 104(a).

In all the above cases–explicitly declarative sentences, sentences used as declarations, and assertive conduct–the need for cross–examination is evident. In each case, the opposing party may have justifiable doubts about the declarant's testimonial qualities. The need is less clear in the case of the last and most controversial category, nonassertive conduct or "Morgan hearsay." The leading authority for extending the hearsay definition to include this last category is a famous English precedent.

WRIGHT v. DOE D. TATHAM

7 Ad. & El. 313, 112 Eng. Rep. 488 (Ex. 1837)

[Action by the heirs of John Marsden to eject the devisee under a will of Marsden from certain manors that he owned at the time of his death. The issue was the sanity of Marsden when the will was executed. To prove that Marsden was mentally competent the defendant offered in evidence certain letters written to the testator by acquaintances who were deceased at the time of the trial. One of the letters involved a matter of business in which Marsden was asked to direct his attorney to submit terms of settlement of a dispute so as to avoid trouble and expense to both parties. The other letters were correspondence of friendship, narrative in character, and of a type that would not be written to a person regarded to be insane. For the exclusion of the letters error is assigned on appeal.]

PARKE, B. The question for us to decide is, whether all or any of the three rejected letters were admissible evidence, on the issue raised in this case, for the purpose of showing that Mr. Marsden was, from his majority in 1779 to and at the time of the making of the alleged will and codicil in 1822 and 1825, a person of sane mind and memory, and capable of making a will?

First, then, were all or any of these letters admissible on the issue in the cause as acts done by the writers, assuming, for the sake of argument, that there was no proof of any act done by the testator upon or relating to these letters or any of them, –that is, would such letters or any of them be evidence of the testator's competence at the time of writing them, if sent to the testator's house and not opened or read by him? Indeed this question is just the same as if the letters had been intercepted before their arrival at his house; for, in so far as the writing and sending the letters by their respective writers were acts done by them towards the testator, those acts would in the two supposed cases be actually complete. It is argued, that the letters would be admissible because they are evidence of the treatment of the testator as a competent person by individuals acquainted with his habits and personal character, not using the word treatment in a sense involving any conduct of the testator himself; that they are more than mere statements to a third person indicating an opinion of his competence by those persons; they are acts done towards the testator by them, which would not have been done if he had been incompetent, and from which, therefore, a legitimate inference may, it is argued, be derived that he was so.

Each of the three letters, no doubt, indicates that in the opinion of the writer the testator was a rational person. He is spoken of in respectful terms in all. Dr. Ellershaw described him as possessing hospitality and benevolent politeness; and Mr. Marton addresses him as competent to do business to the limited extent to which his letter calls upon him to act; and there is no question but that, if any one of those writers had been living, his evidence, founded on personal observation, that the testator possessed the qualities which justified the opinion expressed or implied in his letters, would be admissible on this issue. But the point to be determined is, whether these letters are admissible as proof that he did possess these qualities?

I am of opinion that, according to the established principles of the law of evidence, the letters are all inadmissible for such a purpose. One great principle in this law is, that all facts which are relevant to the issue may be proved; another is, that all such facts as have not been admitted by the party against whom they are offered, or some one under whom he claims, ought to be proved under the sanction of an oath (or its equivalent, a solemn affirmation), either on the trial of the issue or some other issue involving the same question between the same parties or those to whom they are privy.

That the three letters were each of them written by the persons whose names they bear, and sent, at some time before they were found, to the testator's house, no doubt are facts, and those facts are proved on oath; and the letters are without doubt admissible on an issue in which the fact of sending such letters by those persons is relevant to the matter in dispute; as, for instance, of a feigned issue to try the question whether such letters were sent to the testator's house, or on any issue in which it is the material question whether such letters or any of them had been sent.

But the question is, whether the contents of these letters are evidence of the fact to be proved upon this issue, –that is, the actual existence of the qualities which the testator is, in those letters, by implication, stated to possess: and those letters may be considered in this respect to be on the same footing as if they had contained a direct and positive statement that he was competent. For this purpose they are mere hearsay evidence, statements of the writers, not an oath, of the truth of the matter in question, with this addition, that they have acted upon the statements on the faith of their being true, by their sending the letters to the testator. That the so acting cannot give a sufficient sanction for the truth of the statement is perfectly plain; for it is clear that, if the same statements had been made by parol or in writing to a third person, that would have been insufficient. Yet in both cases there has been an acting on the belief of the truth, by making the statement, or writing and sending a letter to a third person; and what difference can it possibly make that this is an acting of the same nature by writing and sending the letter to the testator? It is admitted that you have no right to use in evidence the fact of writing and sending a letter to a third person containing a statement of competence, on the ground that it affords an inference that such an act would not have been done unless the statement was true, or believed to be true, although such an inference no doubt would be raised in the conduct of the ordinary affairs of life, if the statement were made by a man of veracity. But it cannot be raised in a judicial inquiry; and, if such an argument were admissible, it would lead to the indiscriminate admission of hearsay evidence of all manner of facts.

Further, it is clear that an acting to a much greater extent and degree upon such statements to a third person would not make the statements admissible. For example, if a wager to a large amount had been made as to the matter in issue by two third persons, the payment of that wager, however large the sum, would not be admissible to prove the truth of the matter in issue. You would not have had any right to present it to the jury as raising an inference of the truth of the fact, on the ground that otherwise the bet would not have been paid. It is, after all, nothing but the mere statement of that fact, with strong evidence of the belief of it by the party making it. Could it make any difference that the wager was between the third person and one of the parties to the suit? Certainly not. The payment by other underwriters on the same policy to the plaintiff could not be given in evidence to prove that the subject insured had been lost. Yet there is an act done, a payment strongly attesting the truth of the statement, which it implies, that there had been a loss. To illustrate this point still further, let us suppose a third person had betted a wager with Mr. Marsden that he could not solve some mathematical problem, the solution of which required a high degree of capacity; would payment of that wager to Mr. Marsden's banker be admissible evidence that he possessed that capacity? The answer is certain; it would not. It would be evidence of the fact of competence given by a third party not upon oath.

Let us suppose the parties who wrote these letters to have stated the matter therein contained, that is, their knowledge of his personal qualities and capacity for business, on oath before a magistrate, or in some judicial proceedings to which the plaintiff and defendant were not parties. No one could contend that such statement would be admissible on this issue; and yet there would have been an act done on the faith of the statement being true, and a very solemn one, which would raise in the ordinary conduct of affairs a strong belief in the truth of the statement, if the writers were faithworthy. The acting in this case is of much less importance, and certainly is not equal to the sanction of an extra–judicial oath.

The conclusion at which I have arrived is, that proof of a particular fact, which is not of itself a matter in issue, but which is relevant only as implying a statement or opinion of a third person on the matter in issue, is inadmissible in all cases where such a statement or opinion not on oath would be of itself inadmissible; and, therefore, in this case the letters which are offered only to prove the competence of the testator, that is the truth of the implied statements therein contained, were properly rejected, as the mere statement or opinion of the writer would certainly have been inadmissible. It is true that evidence of this description has been received in the Ecclesiastical Courts. But their rules of evidence are not the same in all respects as ours. Some greater laxity may be permitted in a Court which adjudicates both on the law and on the fact, and may be more safely trusted with the consideration of such evidence than a jury; and I would observe, also, that in no instance has the propriety of the reception of it even in the Spiritual Courts been confirmed by the Court of Delegates. I do not think, therefore, that we are bound by the authority of the cases referred to in the Ecclesiastical Courts.

(Judgment affirmed, the judges being equally divided.)

NOTES AND PROBLEMS

1. The English House of Lords recently affirmed the continuing precedential value of *Wright. Regina v. Kearley*, [1992] 2 App.Cas. 228, [1992] 2 All. E.R. 345, [1992] 2 W.L.R. 656, 95 Crim. App. 88. *See* Symposium on Hearsay and Implied Assertions: *How Would (or Should) the Supreme Court Decide the Kearley Case?*, 16 Miss. C. L. Rev. 1 (1995).

2. Although English case law provides the most famous example of non-assertive conduct, American cinema furnishes one of the most delightful illustrations. Think back to the climactic courtroom scene in *Miracle on 34th Street*. As you will recall, the district attorney is attempting to have Kris Kringle committed because Kris says that he is the real Santa Claus. The trial judge demands that the defense attorney produce some evidence that Kris is the real Santa. In the meantime, the local post office has decided to relieve itself of its mountain of mail addressed to Santa by delivering the mail to Kris. The defense attorney offers evidence that the post office delivered the mail to Kris and uses the evidence as proof that Kris is the real Santa Claus. The postal employees march into the courtroom and deliver the envelopes to Kris– without speaking a word. Should the district attorney have objected on hearsay grounds? Kris' attorney argued that the delivery was obviously actuated by a belief that Kris was Santa; and he contended that since the post office was an efficient government entity, its belief was some evidence that Kris was in fact Santa.

3. The Federal Rules Advisory Committee noted that in the case of almost all nonassertive conduct, the declarant is willing to act on his or her belief. The declarant's willingness to do so is certainly some evidence of sincerity. But is the declarant's presumable sincerity sufficient to remove the evidence from the hearsay definition? Professor Morgan argued that the opposing party still has a legitimate need to test the declarant's other testimonial qualities: perception, memory, and narration. Morgan, *Hearsay Dangers and the Application of the Hearsay Concept*, 62 HARV. L. REV. 177, 214, 217 (1948). Modernly, the type of evidence involved in *Wright* is sometimes referred to as "Morgan hearsay."

Most witness psychologists believe that errors in perception and memory cause far more erroneous testimony than insincerity. Stewart, *Perception, Memory, and Hearsay: A Criticism of Present Law and the Proposed Federal Rules of Evidence*, 1970 UTAH L. REV. 1, 9–10. The available empirical data indicate that perjury is relatively rare. Kubie, *Implications for Legal Procedure of the Fallibility of Human Memory*, 108 U. PA. L. REV. 59 (1959). "Witnesses are more often . . . mistaken than committing perjury." Ladd, *The Hearsay We Admit*, 5 OKLA. L. REV. 271, 286 (1952). Psychologists generally agree that the emphasis on deliberate perjury in evidence law is excessive. Stewart, *supra*, at 8–9. Shifting the emphasis to errors in perception and memory would cut in favor of Professor Morgan's position.

4. Problem 18–1. Ms. Hill would like to prove that a week after she filed suit against Roe, Roe began transferring title to all his assets to his brother. Is this evidence logically relevant? Is it hearsay? *See Chaufty v. De Vries*, 41 R.I. 1, 102 A. 612, 616–17 (1918).

5. Problem 18–2. At trial, Polecat Motors calls Mr. Schultz. Schultz testifies that he has been the head of Polecat's Customer Complaint Department for the past fifteen years. May Schultz testify over a hearsay objection that during that time there have been no other customer complaints about the gas tank on the Polecat model that Ms. Hill was driving at the time of the accident? Can silence be considered a statement? *See Howe v. Hull*, 873 F. Supp. 70, 72 (N.D. Ohio 1994).

6. Problem 18–3. In *Devitt,* the prosecutor believes that the defendant may claim that someone else attacked Mr. Paterson. The prosecutor attempts to elicit Police Officer Gravelle's testimony that he interviewed all the occupants of the apartment complex the day of the incident; he asked them whether they had seen any prowlers around the complex that day; and he "ascertained that there were no other strange men around the apartment building that day." Devitt objects on hearsay grounds. Be on the alert when the opposing witness says that she "ascertained," "learned," "determined," or "discovered" something.

7. Problem 18–4. At trial, Devitt in fact claims that the attack was committed by someone else. The defense counsel's theory is that the assailant was a Gene Fulbright. Devitt calls as a witness Robert Montgomery. Montgomery testifies that he was Fulbright's roommate; the day after the alleged attack he saw Fulbright reading the newspaper article about the incident; as soon as he finished reading the article, Fulbright became "nervous"; and that night, Fulbright "got out of town without telling me where he was goin' or even taking any of his stuff with him." The prosecutor objects to Montgomery's testimony on hearsay grounds. *See State v. Minella,* 177 Iowa 283, 158 N.W. 645, 655 (1916).

2. "OFFERED TO PROVE THE TRUTH OF THE ASSERTION" —THE NEED TO TEST THE STATEMENT BY CROSS–EXAMINATION

The assertive character of a statement only establishes that the statement can potentially be tested by cross–examination in a meaningful fashion. That alone is not enough to make it hearsay. There must also be the need for cross–examination. An acute need for cross–examination arises only when the proponent of the evidence offers it for "a hearsay purpose," that is, to prove the assertion. In that circumstance, the opposing attorney should generally be allowed to test the out–of–court declarant's testimonial qualities since the probative value of the evidence depends upon the declarant's sincerity, perception, memory, and narration.

Professor Tribe has proposed visualizing the hearsay analysis as a process of triangulation. Tribe, *Triangulating Hearsay*, 87 HARV. L. REV. 957, 958–61 (1974). He developed a diagram which he called "the testimonial triangle" to help us visualize the flow of the analysis:

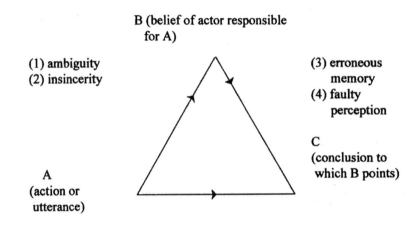

One side of the triangle is the link between A, the out–of–court declarant's utterance or action, and B, the declarant's belief prompting the utterance or action. That link raises two distinct hearsay dangers. One risk is ambiguity. The declarant might have chosen the wrong term to include in the utterance or have used the term in peculiar, idiosyncratic sense. Another hearsay danger is insincerity; the declarant might not have the belief that the utterance or conduct points to.

To complete the path from A to C, the reasoning process adds the next link, B to C. Now the question is the truth of the fact which the declarant evidently believed. Traversing this side of the triangle raises a third and fourth probative danger. The third is erroneous memory. Even when the declarant subjectively entertains the sincere belief at point B of the triangle, the belief may be mistaken; the declarant might misrecollect a fact earlier correctly perceived. The final danger is faulty perception. Again, even if the declarant subjectively entertains the belief, the belief could be mistaken; in this variation of the problem, the declarant might have misperceived the fact or event from the outset.

Professor Tribe argues that evidence is being put to a hearsay use – and, thus there is a compelling need for cross–examination – only when the proponent's theory of logical relevance requires the trier of fact to go from A <u>through</u> <u>B</u> to C. In his view, "when the trier's inference can proceed from A directly to C, the infirmities of hearsay do not arise." *Id.* He gives the following example. Suppose that the only issue is whether the declarant is capable of speech. A witness testifies that the declarant said, "I can speak." The trier can go straight from A (the declarant's statement) to C (the conclusion that the declarant can speak). This inferential process moots any doubts about the declarant's ambiguity or insincerity and consequently cuts against imposing a requirement for cross–examination.

As Professor Tribe's article suggests, if the proponent of the evidence can put the statement to a logically relevant, nonhearsay use, the need for cross–examination decreases. When the evidence is offered for a nonhearsay purpose, the primary need is usually to cross–examine the witness on the stand rather than the out–of–court declarant. When the testimony is offered for a nonhearsay purpose, the fact <u>of</u> the statement is logically relevant even if the facts asserted <u>in</u> the statement are false.

a. Verbal Act or Operative Fact

One common nonhearsay use of evidence is to prove a verbal act or operative fact. The statement itself has significance in the case. *State v. Meadows*, 635 S.W.2d 400 (Tenn. Crim. App. 1982). Professor Tribe's example above is an illustration of a verbal act. The question is whether the declarant can speak, and the declaration is the act of speaking.

Or suppose that in the *Hill* case, Mr. Hill attempted to testify about oral warranties by the salesman of the car. The warranties, describing the car's condition, might be declarative sentences. The salesman was out of court when he made the statement, and he might be unavailable at the time of trial. However, Ms. Hill is not offering the salesman's assertions to prove their truth. Quite to the contrary, she will want to prove that the assertions were untrue, thereby establishing a breach of warranty cause of action. If she establishes that the assertions are true, she proves herself out of court! Under warranty law, it is logically relevant that the salesman made the statements; the statements have direct legal consequences because they are the warranties. For this purpose, we are primarily interested in <u>Mr. Hill's</u> (rather than the salesman's) testimonial qualities: Is he lying about the salesman's representations? Did he hear the salesman correctly? Does he remember the statements accurately? Polecat's opportunity to cross–examine Mr. Hill satisfies the policy concerns underlying the hearsay rule.

There are numerous examples of verbal acts. Although the *Hill* hypothetical focuses on a specific type of statement constituting part of a contract, a warranty representation, more broadly under the objective theory of mutual assent all the statements forming a contract are verbal acts. *Kepner–Tregoe, Inc. v. Leadership Software, Inc.*, 12 F.3d 527 (5th Cir.), *cert. denied*, 513 U.S. 820 (1994). Likewise, in a defamation act, the allegedly libelous statement is admissible as a verbal act. "The making of the defamatory statement is itself of legal significance." *Hickey v. Settlemier*, 318 Ore. 196, 864 P.2d 372, 376–77 (1993). Truth is a defense in libel actions. When the plaintiff offers evidence of the defendant's allegedly defamatory statement, the farthest thing from plaintiff's mind is offering that statement for its truth. In all these cases, the statement is "performative" – "a change in legal rights, duties, powers, privileges, or disabilities" is "wrought by the utterance itself." Park, *The Definition of Hearsay: To Each Its Own*, 16 Miss. C. L. Rev. 125, 133 (1995).

Or suppose that in order to prove that a piece of luggage belonged to a particular person, the proponent offers testimony that a tag stating the person's name and address was attached to the piece of luggage. There is substantial authority that such testimony is admissible as nonhearsay to "link" or "trace" the property to the person. *E.g.*, *United States v. Snow*, 517 F.2d 441, 443–45 (9th Cir. 1975). Ranchers brand their cattle to lay claim to them. The act of affixing the brand is an act of ownedrship. By the same token, the act of affixing the tag lays claim to the attached luggage.

b. Mental Input

Another accepted nonhearsay use of evidence is showing the effect of the statement on the hearer's or reader's state of mind–sometimes referred to as a mental input theory of logical relevance. *Fred Harvey Corp. v. Mateas*, 170 F.2d 612 (9th Cir. 1948). Suppose that Ms. Hill seeks punitive damages on the theory that Polecat knew that the placement of the gas tank was hazardous but nevertheless recklessly failed to make corrective repairs. Ms. Hill calls Mr. Miles as a witness. Miles was present at a conversation between Famiglietti, the president of Polecat, and Mr. Winslow, a consultant from a safety engineering firm. The conversation occurred one year before Ms. Hill's accident. During the conversation, Miles heard Winslow tell Famiglietti that "the way you've placed the tank on that model creates a horrendous risk of explosion and fire on impact." The consultant's statement puts the president on notice of the hazardous condition. When offered for this purpose, the statement is not hearsay. Again, our primary focus is cross–examining Miles, the witness on the stand. Is Miles lying? Was he close enough to hear exactly what Winslow said? Has he confused this conversation with another conversation he overheard? Ms. Hill's attorney will have to present other, independent evidence that the placement of the tank was an unreasonably dangerous design defect, but she can put Miles' testimony to a nonhearsay use. Suppose that as trial judge, you agreed to admit Miles' testimony for the nonhearsay purpose of establishing Famiglietti's notice of the hazardous condition. As trial judge, how would you word the limiting instruction identifying the proper and improper uses of the testimony? Also, in closing argument, the attorney may not treat the statement as proof of the asserted facts; she must walk the tightrope and use the statement only for the nonhearsay purpose for which it was admitted.

As we will cover in detail later, out–of–court reports used as the basis for an expert's opinion under Rule 703 are admitted on this theory. The reports are not admitted to establish the truth of the report, but rather to show the basis for the expert opinion–on what he or she relied in forming that opinion. It is logically relevant that the expert received and read the report. *Wilner v. United States*, 994 F.2d 783, 786 (Fed. Cir. 1993).

Suppose that in a wrongful discharge case, the question is whether the employer acted in good faith in firing the employee. For that purpose, complaints about the employee by customers (*Blanks v. Waste Management of Arkansas, Inc.*, 31 F.Supp.2d 673 (E.D.Ark. 1998)) and co–workers (*Vallabhapurapu v. First Nat'l Bank of Chicago*, 998 F. Supp. 906 (N.D.Ill. 1998)) are admissible as non-hearsay. Even if the complaints are in error, their receipt could give the employer reason to form a bona fide belief that the employee should be terminated.

c. Mental Output

One other nonhearsay use of evidence deserves mention: circumstantial proof of state of mind of the speaker or writer. This use is sometimes referred to as a mental output theory of logical relevance. Assume that Devitt makes a pretrial motion for change of venue. In the motion, the defense counsel argues that there has been such pervasive unfavorable publicity for the case that Devitt cannot obtain a fair trial in El Dorado. At the hearing on the motion, the defense counsel calls Ms. Porter, a professional pollster. Ms. Porter is prepared to testify that she questioned five hundred El Dorado residents and that eighty–five percent indicated that "Devitt is guilty as charged." Just as Ms. Hill would not want to offer the salesman's statements to prove the truth of the representations about the car, Devitt's counsel obviously does not want to prove the truth of the respondents' declarations that Devitt is guilty. (If the defense counsel "succeeds" in proving that, the counsel will be guilty of malpractice and ineffective representation.) Rather, the defense counsel offers the evidence as proof of the respondents' state of mind; the fact that so many made the statement in the public opinion poll proves the bias that necessitates the change of venue.

At first, the hearsay status of public opinion polls troubled the courts. Sherman, *Use of Public Opinion Polls in Continuance and Venue Hearings*, 50 A.B.A. J. 357 (1964); Zeisel, *The Uniqueness of Survey Evidence*, 45 CORNELL L.Q. 322 (1960). However, under the modern view, the responses are admissible as nonhearsay. *See, e.g., Zippo Mfg. Co. v. Rogers Imports, Inc.*, 216 F. Supp. 670 (S.D.N.Y. 1963). The modern view represents sounder hearsay analysis. The real need is to cross–examine Ms. Porter. Is she lying? Did she correctly record the responses? Is her recollection of the responses accurate? It is true that in such cases, there is some concern about the credibility of the respondents. They may have lied to Ms. Porter; and if they did, the poll is not as probative of bias against Devitt. *See generally* Park, *McCormick on Evidence and the Concept of Hearsay: A Critical Analysis Followed by Suggestions to Law Teachers*, 65 MINN. L. REV. 423 (1981). However, the primary focus is on Porter's credibility; and an opportunity to question her will satisfy the essential need for cross–examination.

Prior inconsistent statements, used for impeachment purposes, are admitted on a mental output theory. Suppose that before trial, a witness in the *Devitt* case tells the police that he saw Devitt lurking around Paterson's apartment at 4:00 P.M. the day of the alleged battery. At trial, he testifies that he recalls seeing Devitt near his apartment at 10:00 A.M. that day. Both statements might be false; the truth of the matter might be that Devitt was standing outside the apartment at 1:00 P.M. However, irrespective of the statement's truth, the fact that the witness made the prior statement is logically relevant. The fact *of* the inconsistent statement is relevant even if the fact asserted *in* the statement is false. The fact that the witness made a pretrial statement inconsistent with his trial testimony is circumstantial proof that the witness is at least uncertain. Thus, the evidence gives the trier of fact an insight into the witness' state of mind.

Suppose that the trial judge admitted this evidence for the limited purpose of establishing an impeaching prior inconsistent statement by the witness, Gault. In a limiting instruction, the trial judge could instruct the jurors that they "may consider this evidence only for the limited purpose of deciding Mr. Gault's credibility. You must decide whether Mr. Gault made the statement before trial and, if so, whether the statement is inconsistent with his testimony during this trial. The fact that a person makes inconsistent statements about the same subject can raise questions about his credibility." In closing argument, the defense counsel might tell the jury that "you just can't trust Gault's testimony that Devitt was around the apartment complex at 10:00 a.m. the morning of the alleged attack. Gault blows hot and cold. On the stand you heard him testify that Mr. Devitt was there at 1:00 p.m.. But remember what he was forced to admit during my cross–examination. Right after the incident he spoke with the police. He told them that he saw Mr. Devitt around the complex that day–but not at 10:00 a.m. Instead, he told the police that Mr. Devitt was there at 4:00 p.m.–six hours later. Her Honor has instructed you that '[t]he fact that a person makes inconsistent statements about the same subject can raise questions about his credibility.' Mr. Gault is so inconsistent that there are big questions about his credibility; and since the prosecution never gave you satisfactory answers to those questions, you simply can't accept Gault's testimony."

Or assume that in a trademark infringement case, the issue is whether the defendant's tradename is so similar to that of the plaintiff that consumers are confused over the source of the goods they are purchasing. In that case, testimony about customer phone calls evidencing confusion would be admissible over a hearsay objection. *Medic Alert Foundation U.S., Inc. v. Corel Corp.*, 43 F.Supp.2d 933 (N.D.Ill. 1999).

NOTES AND PROBLEMS

1. This section has highlighted the interface between the logical relevance and hearsay doctrines. Before analyzing the hearsay aspect of any item of evidence, you must identify all the theories on which the item is logically relevant under Federal Rule of Evidence 401. Test the theories one by one, and ask: does the theory require that the evidence be put to a hearsay use? As in so many other areas of evidence law, the premium is on the imaginative development of alternative theories of logical relevance. There is a concise overview of nonhearsay theories in Garland, *An Overview of Relevance and Hearsay: A Nine Step Analytical Guide*, 22 Sw.U. L. Rev. 1039, 1051–62 (1993).

2. Problem 18–5. Assume that Devitt's defense is insanity. At trial, Devitt calls Ms. Solomon as a witness. Ms. Solomon is prepared to testify that she saw Devitt two hours after the incident and that at the time Devitt told her that a Martian invasion was imminent. The prosecutor objects that the testimony is "nothing more than self–serving hearsay." Is the statement "an assertion." Even if it is, is it offered for a hearsay purpose?

3. Problem 18–6. In the *Hill* case, the plaintiff calls Dr. Gartner to testify about the extent of her injuries. Dr. Gartner was a member of a team of three treating physicians. The plaintiff wants to elicit Gartner's final opinion that many of Ms. Hill's injuries will be permanent. Before eliciting the ultimate opinion, Ms. Hill asks Gartner to relate the two other physicians' opinions of the severity and probable duration of her injuries. Polecat objects on hearsay grounds. Consider the relevance of Federal Rule of Evidence 703.

4. Problem 18–7. Polecat contends that the real cause of the accident was that the brakes on Worker's car were in disrepair. Polecat alleges that Roe took the car in to an auto brake shop three days before the accident, obtained an estimate of the cost of repairs, and then decided against the repairs when he learned that the repair bill would be over $800. At trial, Polecat calls Jake Beroni, a repairman at the brake shop. Polecat has Beroni authenticate the repair estimate given Roe and offers the estimate into evidence. Roe objects on hearsay grounds.

5. Problem 18–8. Devitt moves to suppress a statement he gave the police on the ground that the statement is the product of an illegal arrest. *Wong Sun v. United States*, 371 U.S. 471 (1963). He contends that the police lacked probable cause to arrest him. At the hearing on the motion, the prosecutor calls Police Officer Gravelle. Gravelle attempts to testify that two occupants of the apartment complex saw Devitt running from Mr. Paterson's apartment shortly after the alleged battery. Devitt's attorney objects on hearsay grounds. Are the occupants' statements hearsay when offered to establish probable cause? *See Draper v. United States*, 358 U.S. 307, 311–14 (1959).

6. Problem 18–9. Assume that the evidence of the occupants' statements should be admitted at the suppression hearing. The judge denies the motion, and the case goes to trial. Would the police officer's testimony about the statements be equally admissible at the trial on the merits? *See* McElhaney, *It's Not for Its Truth*, 77 A.B.A. J. 80, 82 (Oct. 1991) ("Judge, if this evidence is no good for its truth, then what is it good for?").

7. Problem 18–10. The prosecutor wants to prove that immediately after his arrest, Devitt gave the police a false alibi. Devitt claimed that at the time of the battery he was with his uncle, Josh Devitt, at a nearby lake. Devitt's uncle denies that he was with Devitt at that time. The prosecutor calls Officer Franklin, the police officer who initially interrogated Devitt. Franklin attempts to testify that Devitt said he was with his uncle. Is Franklin's testimony hearsay? (Disregard any argument that the testimony qualifies as the admission of a party–opponent.)

3. "BY AN OUT–OF–COURT DECLARANT" —SATISFYING THE NEED FOR CROSS–EXAMINATION

We have seen that if the statement is assertive and its proponent offers it as proof of the assertion, the opposing party has a need for cross–examination. The remaining question is whether the need for cross–examination has been satisfied. The traditional view is that the only way to meet the need is to subject the statement to cross–examination when it is made. Simply stated, the traditional view is that "once an out–of–court declarant, always an out–of–court declarant." Under this view, the person remains an out–of–court declarant even when she subsequently becomes a witness at trial; if she was not testifying in this case at the time she made the statement, the statement is hearsay. *Comer v. State*, 222 Ark. 156, 257 S.W.2d 564 (1953). The declarant's assertion is hearsay if it was an "out–of–this–court statement." *United States v. Barrett*, 937 F.2d 1346 (8th Cir.), *cert. denied*, 502 U.S. 916 (1991). The orthodox courts adhere to this view even when the same statement is admissible at trial for a nonhearsay purpose. For example, suppose that in *Hill,* an eyewitness to the accident gave the police a statement shortly after the collision. At trial the eyewitness testifies inconsistently with her statement to the police. Her prior statement to the police would qualify as a prior inconsistent statement, and the judge would admit it on a mental output theory for the limited purpose of impeaching her credibility. However, even though the eyewitness is now available for cross–examination and the statement is indisputably admissible on a credibility theory, the traditional view would prevent the use of the statement as substantive evidence.

The traditional view reflects the great value that the early courts attached to the opportunity for cross–examination. These courts reason that the statement must be included within the hearsay definition if the opposing attorney did not have a chance to cross–examine a declarant when the statement was made. Perhaps the most emphatic statement of this reasoning appears in the California Supreme Court's opinion in *People v. Johnson,* 68 Cal. 2d 646, 441 P.2d 111, 68 Cal. Rptr. 599 (1968), *cert. denied,* 393 U.S. 1051 (1969) (some citations omitted):

> The declarant is a witness available for cross–examination at the subsequent trial. Indeed, it is because of this availability that academic writers have long urged that prior inconsistent statements of a witness could be admitted for the truth of the matters therein asserted without violating the hearsay rule. (*see, e.g.,* McCormick, Evidence (1954) § 39; 3 Wigmore, Evidence (3d ed. 1940) § 1018. Adopting this viewpoint, the draftsmen of (California Evidence Code) § 1235 justify their new rule on the ground that it "admits inconsistent statements of witnesses because the dangers against which the hearsay rule is designed to protect are largely nonexistent. The declarant is in court and may be examined and cross–examined in regard to his statements and their subject matter . . . The trier of fact has the declarant before it and can observe his demeanor and the nature of his testimony as he denies or tries to explain away the inconsistency. Hence, it is in as good a position to determine the truth or falsity of the prior statement as it is to determine the truth or falsity of the inconsistent testimony given in court." (Evid. Code, § 1235, comment of Law Revision Com.)

> We cannot share the optimism of this reasoning. As Maguire has candidly admitted, "many trial lawyers will have none of this. They say it is a professorial pipe–dream. They have in mind considerations of practical policy. . . ." (Maguire, Evidence: Common Sense and Common Law (1947) p. 59) Perhaps the foremost practical objection to the academic approach is that it grossly underestimates the value of one of the characteristics which make cross–examination "the greatest legal engine ever invented for the discovery of truth." (5 Wigmore, op. cit. *supra,* at p. 29.) To assert that the dangers of hearsay are "largely nonexistent" when the declarant can be cross–examined at some later date, or to urge that such a cross–examination puts the later trier of fact in "as

good a position" to judge the truth of the out–of–court statement as it is to judge contemporary trial testimony, is to disregard the critical importance of *timely* cross–examination. . . .

. . . In the leading case of *State v. Saporen* (1939) 205 Minn. 358, 285 N.W. 898, 900–901, . . .after observing that the witness' oath does not solemnize his prior extrajudicial statement, the opinion turns to the alleged adequacy of the belated cross–examination of the witness: "The chief merit of cross–examination is not that at some *future* time it gives the party opponent the right to dissect adverse testimony. Its principal virtue is in its *immediate* application of the testing process. Its strokes fall while the iron is hot. False testimony is apt to harden and become unyielding to the blows of truth in proportion as the witness has opportunity for reconsideration and influence by the suggestion of others, whose interest may be, and often is, to maintain falsehood rather than truth." (Italics added.)

––––––––––

Although *Johnson* represents the traditional view at common law, there are competing views. The most extreme competing view is that the person ceases to be an out–of–court declarant as soon as he becomes a witness at trial; the person's availability for questioning at trial satisfies the need for cross–examination and removes his prior statements from the definition of hearsay. Uniform Rule of Evidence 63(1) and Model Code of Evidence 503(b) opted for this position. To date, Kansas is the only jurisdiction firmly committed to this view. KAN. CODE CIV. P. § 60–460(a). One passage in the Advisory Committee Note to Rule 801 indicates sympathy with this view:

Considerable controversy has attended the question of whether a prior out–of–court statement by a person now available for cross–examination concerning it, under oath and in the presence of the trier of fact, should be classified as hearsay. If the witness admits on the stand that he made the statement and that it was true, he adopts the statement and there is no hearsay problem.

Moreover, an occasional federal case seizes upon this passage as support for the ruling that the hearsay objection disappears when the declarant makes the prior statement "part of his oath–supported, court–given testimony subject to cross–examination." *Amarin Plastics, Inc. v. Maryland Cup Corp.*, 946 F.2d 147, 153 (1st Cir. 1991).

Like the traditional position, this view rests on assumptions about the value of cross–examination. Revising his earlier view, Wigmore argued that when the witness was available for cross–examination, "[t]he whole purpose of the hearsay rule has been . . . satisfied" even with respect to the witness' prior statements. 3A J. WIGMORE, EVIDENCE § 1018, p. 996 (Chadbourn rev.). Judge Learned Hand amplified on Wigmore's reasoning. In *Di Carlo v. United States*, 6 F.2d 364 (2d Cir. 1925), Judge Hand explained that when the witness is available at trial, the jury may use the witness' present demeanor to evaluate the credibility of even prior statements: "If from all that the jury sees of the witness, they conclude that what he says now is not the truth, but what he said before, they are none the less deciding from what they see and hear of that person and in court." *Id.* at 368.

Finally, there is a compromise view. Federal Rule 801 is illustrative. At first glance, Rule 801 seems to embrace the traditional view. Rule 801(b) broadly defines "declarant" as any "person who makes a statement." If that subsection stood alone, any person would be an out–of–court declarant even when she subsequently became a witness at trial. However, Rule 801(d)(1) narrows the definition of "declarant" by removing certain prior statements by the witness from the hearsay definition:

> (d) Statements which are not hearsay. A statement is not hearsay if —
>
>> (1) Prior statement by witness. The declarant testifies at the trial or hearing and is subject to cross–examination concerning the statement, and the statement is (A) inconsistent with his testimony, and was given under oath subject to the penalty of perjury at a trial, hearing, or other proceeding, or in a deposition, or (B) consistent with his testimony and is offered to rebut an express or implied charge against him of recent fabrication or improper influence or motive, or (C) one of identification of a person made after perceiving him.

To an extent, Rule 801(d)(1) adopts Hand's reasoning whenever the prior statement would be otherwise admissible for a nonhearsay purpose. If the statement is admissible as a prior identification to bolster credibility (801(d)(1)(C)), a prior inconsistent statement to impeach credibility (801(d)(1)(A)), or a prior consistent statement to rehabilitate credibility (801(d)(1)(B)), the Rules allow the statement's admission as substantive evidence. The Rule embraces Hand's reasoning grudgingly. If the prior statement would be admitted in any event, the jury will be forced to evaluate the statement's credibility and weight in part on the basis of the witness' present demeanor. The drafters reasoned that in this situation, they might as well admit the statement as both substantive proof and credibility evidence. Unfortunately, as we shall now see, the drafters left the courts with several, difficult issues of statutory construction to resolve.

NOTES AND PROBLEMS

1. As we have seen, the traditional doctrine and Hand's view embody opposing assumptions about the need for cross–examination. Which view is sounder? Does *Johnson* overestimate the need for cross–examination? Or does Hand underestimate the danger that the witness will retreat behind the claim, "I know that the statement was correct when I said it, but I'm a little hazy now about the accident itself."? When the witness retreats in that fashion, how effectively can the cross–examiner cross–examine the witness? On the other hand, it is arguable that the answers themselves impeach the witness. During closing argument, the cross–examiner can simply point to the tenor of the answers and invite the jury to disbelieve the witness on that basis.

2. In most jurisdictions following the compromise view, the analysis proceeds in two steps. You initially decide whether the prior statement is admissible for a nonhearsay purpose such as a credibility theory of impeaching or rehabilitating. If the statement is admissible for such a purpose, the proponent then invokes Hand's reasoning and urges its admission as substantive proof.

3. The application of the federal version of the compromise view is a bit more complex. Under the federal version, it is not enough that a prior inconsistent statement satisfies Rule 613; Federal Rule 801(d)(1)(A) allows the admission of prior inconsistent statements only when the statement is given "under oath subject to penalty of perjury at a trial, hearing, or other proceeding." There is no such requirement under (B) or (C). Nineteen states admit prior inconsistent statements as substantive evidence even when the statement was not made under oath. Goldman, *Guilt by Intuition: The Insufficiency of Prior Inconsistent Statements to Convict*, 65 N.C. L. REV. 1, 46 (1986).

4. Problem 18–11. In *Devitt*, Paterson picked the defendant out in a pretrial lineup. The prosecutor wants to elicit Officer Gravelle's testimony that he stood next to Mr. Paterson during the lineup and that Paterson identified Devitt as the assailant. Over Devitt's hearsay objection, may the prosecutor elicit this testimony even before calling Paterson as a witness?

5. Problem 18–12. The prosecutor has Officer Gravelle authenticate a photograph of Devitt's car, including the license plate number. As her next witness, the prosecutor calls Mr. Riley. Riley lives in the same apartment complex as Paterson. Riley identifies the car in the photo as a car that he saw parked near Paterson's apartment the day of the incident. Over Devitt's hearsay objection, may Riley testify that he also identified Devitt's car at the police parking lot the day after the incident? *See Harley v. United States*, 471 A.2d 1013, 1015–16 (D.C. App. 1984). Rule 801(d)(1)(C) refers only to an "identification of a person." Can that language reasonably bear the meaning ascribed to it by *Harley*?

6. Earlier, we discussed rehabilitation after impeachment, noting that under the prevailing view at common law, a consistent statement may be used to rehabilitate the witness' credibility only if the statement predates the impeaching event or influence. Does Rule 801(d)(1)(B) codify the temporal priority doctrine? The Supreme Court confronted that issue in the following case. Tome had been charged with sexual abuse of a child A.T., his own daughter. At the time of the operative facts, Tome was engaged in a custody dispute for the child with his former wife. At trial during A.T.'s cross-examination, the defense suggested that the allegations of sexual abuse had been "concocted so the child would not be returned to her father," the defendant. After A.T.'s testimony, the prosecution called several witnesses to testify about prior statements by A.T. about sexual abuse. The trial judge admitted the statements even though they were made after A.T.'s alleged motive to fabricate arose, and the Court of Appeals for the Tenth Circuit upheld the trial court ruling. The Supreme Court granted *certiorari*.

TOME v. UNITED STATES

513 U.S. 150 (1995)

JUSTICE KENNEDY delivered the opinion of the Court, except as to Part IIB.

II

The prevailing common–law rule for more than a century before adoption of the Federal Rules of Evidence was that a prior consistent statement introduced to rebut a charge of recent fabrication or improper influence or motive was admissible if the statement had been made before the alleged fabrication, influence, or motive came into being, but it was inadmissible if made afterwards. McCormick and Wigmore stated the rule in a . . . categorical manner: "[T]he applicable principle is that the prior consistent statement has no relevancy to refute the charge unless the consistent statement was made before the source of the bias, interest, influence or incapacity originated." E. Cleary, McCormick on Evidence § 49 (2d ed. 1972). *See also* J. Wigmore, Evidence § 1128 (J. Chadbourn rev. 1972). The question is whether Rule 801(d)(1)(B) embodies this temporal requirement. We hold that it does.

A

Rule 801 defines prior consistent statements as nonhearsay only if they are offered to rebut a charge of "recent fabrication or improper influence or motive." Fed. Rule Evid. 801(d)(1)(B). [T]he Advisory Committee decided to treat those consistent statements . . . as nonhearsay and admissible as substantive evidence, not just to rebut an attack on the witness's credibility.

The Rules do not accord this weighty, nonhearsay status to all prior consistent statements. To the contrary, admissibility under the Rules is confined to those statements offered to rebut a charge of "recent fabrication or improper influence or motive," the same phrase used by the Advisory Committee in its description of the "traditiona[l]" common law of evidence . . . . Prior consistent statements may not be admitted to counter all forms of impeachment or to bolster the witness merely because she has been discredited. In the present context, the question is whether A.T.'s out–of–court statements rebutted the alleged link between her desire to be with her mother and her testimony, not whether they suggested that A.T.'s in–court testimony was true. The Rule speaks of a party rebutting an alleged motive, not bolstering the veracity of the story told.

This limitation is instructive, not only to establish the preconditions of admissibility but also to reinforce the significance of the requirement that the consistent statements had been made before the alleged influence, or motive to fabricate arose. That is to say, the forms of impeachment within the Rule's coverage are the ones in which the temporal requirement makes the most sense. Impeachment by charging that the testimony is a recent fabrication or results from an improper influence or motive is, as a general matter, capable of direct and forceful refutation through introduction of out–of–court consistent statements that predate the alleged fabrication, influence, or motive. A consistent statement that predates the motive is a square rebuttal of the charge that the testimony was contrived as a consequence of that motive. By contrast, prior consistent statements carry little rebuttal force when most other types of impeachment are involved. McCormick § 49 ("The defense does not meet the assault").

There may arise instances when out–of–court statements that postdate the alleged fabrication have some probative force in rebutting a charge of fabrication or improper influence or motive, but those statements refute the charged fabrication in a less direct and forceful way. Evidence that a witness made consistent statements after the alleged motive to fabricate arose may suggest in some degree that the in–court testimony is truthful, and thus suggest in some degree that testimony did not result from some improper influence; but if the drafters of Rule 801(d)(1)(B) intended to countenance rebuttal along that indirect inferential chain, the purpose of confining the types of impeachment that open the door to rebuttal by introducing consistent statements becomes unclear. If consistent statements are admissible without reference to the time frame we find imbedded in the Rule, there appears no sound reason not to admit consistent statements to rebut other forms of impeachment as well.

Our analysis is strengthened by the observation that the somewhat peculiar language of the Rule bears close similarity to the language used in many of the common law cases that describe the premotive requirement. "Rule 801(d)(1)(B) employs the precise language . . . consistently used in the panoply of pre–1975 decisions." E. O. Ohlbaum, *Evidence: An Analysis of Rule 801(d)(1)(B), Prior Consistent Statements and a New Proposal*, 1987 B.Y.U. L. Rev. 231, 245. The language of the Rule, . . . which follows the language of the common–law cases, suggests that it was intended to carry over the common–law premotive rule.

B

Our conclusion that Rule 801(d)(1)(B) embodies the common–law premotive requirement is confirmed by an examination of the Advisory Committee Notes to the Federal Rules of Evidence. We have relied on these well–considered Notes as a useful guide in ascertaining the meaning of the Rules. The Notes are a respected source of scholarly commentary. Professor Cleary was a distinguished commentator on the law of evidence, and he and members of the Committee consulted and considered the views, criticisms, and suggestions of the academic community in preparing the Notes.

The Notes disclose a purpose to adhere to the common law in the application of evidentiary principles, absent express provisions to the contrary. Where the Rules did depart from their common–law antecedents, in general the Committee said so. The Notes give no indication . . . that Rule 801(d)(1)(B) abandoned the premotive requirement. Throughout their discussion of the Rules, the Advisory Committee Notes rely on Wigmore and McCormick as authority . . . . In light of the categorical manner in which those authors state the premotive requirement, . . . it is difficult to imagine that the drafters . . . would have remained silent if they intended to modify the premotive requirement. Here, we do not think the drafters of the Rule intended to scuttle the whole premotive requirement and rationale without so much as a whisper of explanation.

"A party contending that legislative action changed settled law has the burden of showing that the legislature intended such a change." *Green v. Bock Laundry Machine Co.*, 490 U.S. 504, 521 (1989). Nothing in the Advisory Committee's Notes suggests that it intended to alter the common–law premotive requirement.

* * *

III

We intimate no view . . . concerning the admissibility of any of A.T.'s out–of–court statements under [Rule 803(24)], or any other evidentiary principles. These matters . . . are for the Court of Appeals to decide . . . . Our holding is confined to the requirements for admission under Rule 801(d)(1)(B). The Rule permits the introduction of a declarant's consistent out–of–court statements to rebut a charge of recent fabrication or improper influence or motive only when those statements were made before the charged fabrication or improper influence or motive. These conditions of admissibility were not established here.

JUSTICE SCALIA, concurring in part and concurring in the judgment.

I concur in the judgment of the Court, and join in its opinion except for Part II–B. That Part, which is devoted entirely to a discussion of the Advisory Committee's Notes pertinent to Rule 801(d)(1)(B), gives effect to those Notes not only because they are "a respected source of scholarly commentary" . . . but also because they display the "purpose" . . . of the draftsmen.

I have previously acquiesced in, *see, e.g., Beech Aircraft Corp. v. Rainey*, 488 U.S. 153 (1988) and indeed myself engaged in, *see United States v. Owens*, 484 U.S. 554, 562 (1988), similar use of the Advisory Committee Notes. More mature reflection has persuaded me that is wrong. Having been prepared by a body of experts, the Notes are assuredly persuasive scholarly commentaries–ordinarily the most persuasive–concerning the meaning of the Rules. But they bear no special authoritativeness as the work of the draftsmen, any more than the views of Alexander Hamilton (a draftsman) bear more authority than the views of Thomas Jefferson (not a draftsman) with regard to the meaning of the Constitution. It is the words of the Rules that have been authoritatively adopted . . . by Congress . . . . Like a . . . statute, the promulgated Rule says what is says, regardless of the intent of its drafters. [T]he Notes cannot, by some power inherent in the draftsmen, change the meaning that the Rules would otherwise bear.

In the present case, the merely persuasive force of the Advisory Committee Notes suffices. Indeed, in my view, the case can be adequately resolved without resort to the Advisory Committee at all. It is well established that "the body of common law knowledge" must be "a source of guidance" in our interpretation of the Rules. *Daubert v. Merrell Dow Pharmaceuticals, Inc.*, 509 U.S. 579 (1993). Rule 801(d)(1)(B) uses language that tracks common–law cases and prescribes a result that makes no sense except on the assumption that that language indeed adopts the common–law rule.

JUSTICE BREYER, with whom THE CHIEF JUSTICE, JUSTICE O'CONNOR and JUSTICE THOMAS join, dissenting.

[In the initial part of this dissent, Justice Breyer argues that the fact that a consistent statement postdates the allegedly impeaching fact "has nothing to do with relevance" and "does not diminish [the] reliability" of the statement. Justice Breyer states:

> A postmotive statement is relevant to rebut . . . . a charge of recent fabrication based on improper motive, . . . when the speaker made the statement while affected by a far more powerful motive to tell the truth. A speaker might be moved to lie to help an acquaintance. But, suppose the circumstances also make clear to the speaker that only the truth will save his child's life. Or, suppose the postmotive statement was made spontaneously, or when the speaker's motive to lie was much weaker than it was at trial.

Moreover, he argues that "the common law premotive rule was not as uniform as the majority suggests." Rather, a minority of courts permitted the admission of postmotive statements. The opinion then continues.]

This Court has acknowledged that the Federal Rules of Evidence worked a change in common–law relevancy rules in the direction of flexibility. *See Daubert v. Merrell Dow Pharmaceuticals, Inc.*, 509 U.S. 579 (1993). In *Daubert*, this Court considered the rule of *Frye v. United States*, 293 F. 1013 (CADC 1923), which had excluded scientific evidence that had not gained general acceptance in the relevant field. Like the premotive rule here at issue, the *Frye* rule was "rigid," setting forth an "absolute prerequisite to admissibility," which the Court said was "at odds with the 'liberal thrust' of the Federal Rules." *Daubert* suggests that the liberalized relevancy provisions of the Federal Rules can supersede a pre–existing rule of relevance, at least where no compelling practical or logical support can be found for the pre–existing rule. It is difficult to find any strong practical or logical considerations for making the premotive rule an absolute condition of admissibility here. Thus, considered purely as a matter of relevancy (and as though Rule 801(d)(1)(B) had not been written), I would conclude that the premotive rule did not survive the adoption of the Rules.

Irrespective of these arguments, one might claim that, nonetheless, the drafters, in writing Rule 801(d)(1)(B), relied on the continued existence of the common–law relevancy rule, and that Rule 801(d)(1)(B) therefore reflects a belief that the common–law relevancy rule would survive. But, I would reject that argument. For one thing, if the drafters had wanted to insulate the common–law from the Rules' liberalizing effect, this would have been a remarkably indirect (and therefore odd) way of doing so–both because Rule 801(d)(1)(B) is utterly silent about the premotive rule and because Rule 801(d)(1)(B) is a rule of hearsay, not relevancy.

Accordingly, I would hold that the Federal Rules authorize a district court to allow (where probative in respect to rehabilitation) the use of postmotive prior consistent statements to rebut a charge of recent fabrication, improper influence, or motive (subject of course to, for example, Rule 403). Where such statements are admissible for this rehabilitative purpose, Rule 801(d)(1)(B) . . . makes them admissible as substantive evidence as well . . . . In most cases, this approach will not yield a different result from a strict adherence to the premotive rule for, in most cases, postmotive statements will not be significantly probative.

QUESTIONS

1. What is the scope of the holding in *Tome*? Does *Tome* govern if the proponent is content to offer the prior statement for the limited purpose of rehabilitating a witness' credibility? Does *Tome* control the admissibility of the statement under Article VI as well as under Article VIII? Note the last paragraph of Justice Kennedy's opinion.

2. Under the majority opinion, what precisely must the statement antedate? Suppose that in the *Hill* case, a passenger in Ms. Hill's car settled with Polecat prior to trial and appeared as a defense witness at trial. Under the terms of the settlement agreement, Polecat paid the witness $20,000. During cross–examination, to impeach the witness for bias, the plaintiff's attorney forces the witness to admit that he has entered into a settlement agreement with Polecat. When would "the improper influence or motive" arise: when the possibility of a settlement between the witness and Polecat was first broached, when they signed the settlement contract, or when Polecat made the first settlement payment to the witness?

3. Can the result in *Tome* be squared with the textualist approach to statutory construction which the Court had followed in previous cases? Note that the leading textualist, Justice Scalia, concurs in this case. He does so in part to protest Justice Kennedy's reliance on the Advisory Committee Note to Rule 801. Does Scalia's concurrence signal that he is shifting to a more extreme textualist position? Or does the fact that he finds it necessary to write a separate opinion on this issue signal that the majority may be retreating from its previous commitment to textualism? As we shall see *infra*, several commentators believe that Justice Kennedy's dissent in an earlier 1994 case, *Williamson*, marked his emergence as an opponent of Justice Scalia's brand of textualism. Scallen, *Classical Rhetoric, Practical Reasoning and the Law of Evidence*, 44 AMER. U. L. REV.1717 (1995); Taslitz, Daubert's *Guide to the Federal Rules of Evidence: A Not–So–Plain–Meaning Jurisprudence*, 32 HARV. J. ON LEGIS. 3, 71–73 (1995). They view his dissent as a call for a more "flexible, pragmatic approach" to statutory construction. *Id.* at 76. If so, the fact that Kennedy writes the lead opinion in *Tome* and that Scalia feels compelled to file a separate concurrence may be significant.

C. CONCLUSION

The analysis outlined in this chapter yields four basic methods of defeating a hearsay objection. The proponent may argue that: The statement is not assertive; the statement, albeit assertive, is being offered for a nonhearsay purpose; the speaker is no longer considered an out–of–court declarant; or the statement falls within the scope of some hearsay exemption or exception. Note the differing procedural consequences that flow from these theories:

- If the theory for defeating the objection is that the statement is nonassertive, the judge will admit the statement only for the purpose of showing that the statement was made. Rule 801(a)

- If the theory is that the statement is offered for a nonhearsay purpose, again the statement will not be admitted as substantive evidence. The trial judge will admit the statement for a specified, nonhearsay purpose but give a limiting instruction identifying that purpose and forbidding the jurors from using the statement for a hearsay purpose. Rules 105, 801(c)

- If the theory is that the speaker is no longer an out–of–court declarant, the statement is admitted as substantive proof without a limiting instruction. Rule 801(d)(1)

- Similarly, if the theory is that the statement is admissible because it falls within an exception or the exemption for admissions, the statement will qualify as substantive evidence; and the judge will not give a limiting instruction. Rules 801(d)(2), 803–04

D. HEARSAY DRILL

In part, the ability to recognize hearsay in the courtroom is an experiential skill. To give the student more realistic practice with the hearsay definition, we have included the following drill, raising the three aspects of the hearsay definition at random.

1. Problem 18–13. The following evidence is offered in the *Devitt* prosecution. Is the evidence hearsay? (At this stage, please disregard the question of whether the evidence might be admissible within a hearsay exemption or exception.)

Pretrial

(a) The prosecution charged Greg Martin with being an accessory before the fact to the battery. Martin confessed. Devitt also gave the police a confession. However, before trial, Devitt moves to suppress his confession on the ground that the confession is involuntary. Specifically, Devitt contends that the police coerced him into making a confession imitating Martin's. At the suppression hearing, the prosecution calls Officer Gomez as a witness. Gomez took the confessions from both Martin and Devitt. The prosecution attempts to elicit Gomez' testimony about the two confessions to show that Devitt's confession does not imitate Martin's; the prosecution points to the differences between the two confessions. The defense counsel objects that Gomez' testimony is hearsay. (Assume that the evidentiary rules, including the hearsay rules, apply at the suppression hearing.) *See Tennessee v. Street*, 471 U.S. 409 (1985).

Trial–Prosecution Case–in–Chief

(b) At trial, the prosecution calls Mr. Paterson as a witness. He testifies that before trial, he met with a police artist. Using an Identikit, the artist helped him prepare a sketch of the assailant's face. At that point, the prosecution marks a sketch as Prosecution Exhibit #1 for identification. Paterson identifies the sketch as the one he prepared with the police artist's help. When the prosecutor offers the exhibit into evidence, the defense counsel objects on hearsay grounds. *See State v. Motta*, 659 P.2d 745, 749–50 (Hawaii 1983).

(c) Assume that a victim has been kidnapped and taken to the kidnapper's apartment. On direct examination, victim seeks to testify that shortly after the alleged incident, he gave the police a description of the kidnapper's apartment; he seeks to testify that he told the police that the apartment had a moosehead on one wall, a triangle–shaped mirror on another wall, and a picture of the Empire State Building on a third wall. The defense counsel objects that such testimony would be hearsay. The prosecutor is prepared to call the victim's landlord to describe the defendant's apartment. *See Bridges v. State*, 247 Wis. 350, 19 N.W.2d 529, 534–36 (1945).

(d) On cross–examination by the defense counsel, Paterson admits that when he was initially interviewed by the police, he said, "At first, I thought the assailant was that guy Devitt I hired to do the carpentry work, but the more I thought about it the more uncertain I became." The prosecutor requests a limiting instruction that the jury may consider the statement only insofar as it reflects on Paterson's credibility. The defense counsel objects and argues that since Paterson is on the witness stand, the statement "can come in as substantive evidence." What result under Federal Rule of Evidence 801(d)(1)(A)? *See United States v. Livingston*, 661 F.2d 239, 242–43 (D.C. Cir. 1981).

(e) In (d), suppose that Mr. Paterson made an inconsistent statement in a sworn battery complaint against Devitt rather than in his interview with the police. *See State v. Smith*, 651 P.2d 207, 209–10 (Wash. 1982).

(f) As its next witness, the prosecution calls Officer Gomez. He testifies that shortly after Paterson's battery report, he conducted a photographic display to help him identify the assailant. He testifies that he included a photograph of the defendant in the photo spread. When he attempts to testify that Paterson selected the defendant's photograph from the stack of photographs, the defense counsel objects on hearsay grounds. *See Jones v. State*, 300 A.2d 424, 425–26 (Md. Ct. App. 1973).

(g) Assume that the trial judge overrules the hearsay objection in (f). Suppose further that the prosecutor next attempts to offer the photograph Paterson selected into evidence. He marks the photograph as Prosecution Exhibit #2 for identification. When he shows it to the opposing counsel, the defense attorney notes that the back of the photograph bears the notation, "Chosen by victim Paterson. Officer Gomez." The prosecutor then offers the exhibit into evidence. The defense counsel objects to "the hearsay writing on the photo." *See State v. Walker*, 654 S.W.2d 129, 131 (Mo. Ct. App. 1983). The prosecutor responds, "Hearsay! Your Honor, the so–called statement isn't even a complete sentence. How can it be hearsay?"

(h) Officer Gomez next attempts to testify that Paterson told him that Devitt was the assailant. The defense counsel objects that "the officer's testimony about Paterson's statements is inadmissible hearsay." Assume that: In Morena, the bolstering rules permit proof of a victim's pretrial identification even before attempted impeachment; when the identification is offered as bolstering evidence, only the victim may testify to the identification; and Morena has enacted Federal Rule of Evidence 801(d)(1)(C). *See People v. Gardner*, 265 N.W.2d 1, 12–16 (Mich. 1978).

(i) Later, on direct examination, Gomez adds that as part of his investigation, he collected physical evidence to send to the crime laboratory for scientific analysis. He testifies that when he asked Paterson for the clothing he wore during the incident, Paterson handed him a shirt and jeans. The defense attorney objects that the testimony about Paterson's conduct amounts to hearsay. *See Stevenson v. Commonwealth*, 237 S.E.2d 779, 781 (Va. 1977). Or suppose that after Gomez asked for the clothing, and without saying a word, Paterson walked over to a dresser and pulled open a drawer containing a shirt and jeans. In Paterson's presence, Gomez reached into the drawer, removed the clothing, and took the clothing with him. Does this conduct amount to hearsay? *See State v. Satterfield*, 316 N.C. 55, 340 S.E.2d 52, 53–54 (1986).

(j) Gomez then testifies that after interviewing Paterson, he went to Devitt's apartment to arrest him. During a lawful search incident to the arrest, Gomez found a slip of paper bearing Paterson's name and address. (It is stipulated that the notations are in Devitt's handwriting.) The defense counsel objects that the notations are hearsay. *See United States v. Anello*, 765 F.2d 253, 261 (1st Cir. 1985).

(k) In (j), assume that there was no stipulation or evidence that the notations were in Devitt's handwriting. However, there are stipulations that the slip of paper was found in Devitt's apartment and that Devitt was the sole tenant of the apartment.

(l) On continued cross–examination of Officer Gomez, the defense counsel asked, "Isn't it true, Officer, that you put my client's photo in that stack of photographs because you and several of the other officers at the station have a grudge against my client?" On redirect examination, the prosecutor attempts to elicit Gomez' testimony that shortly after the alleged battery, he received an anonymous telephone tip that Devitt was the assailant. The defense counsel objects that the testimony would "be the worst sort of hearsay." *See State v. Perez*, 638 P.2d 335, 336–37 (Hawaii 1981).

(m) On cross–examination of Officer Gomez, the defense counsel asked, "In fact, isn't it true that you wanted to get Mr. Devitt so badly that after arresting him, you didn't bother to investigate any other men who might have been around the apartment that day?" On redirect examination, the prosecutor attempts to elicit Gomez' testimony that after Devitt's arrest, Paterson viewed Devitt in a lineup, pointed out Devitt, and said he was "absolutely, 100% positive" that Devitt was the assailant. Again the defense counsel objects on hearsay grounds. *See State v. Giannini*, 606 S.W.2d 780, 781 (Mo. Ct. App. 1980).

(n) As its next witness, the prosecution calls Greg Martin. Martin initially testifies that at one time, he was charged with being an accessory before the fact to Devitt's battery of Paterson. When the prosecutor asks, "How did you plead to that charge?" the defense counsel makes a hearsay objection. (Martin entered a guilty plea.) *See United States v. Melton*, 739 F.2d 576, 578–79 (11th Cir. 1984).

(o) Later in Martin's direct examination, the prosecutor attempts to elicit Martin's admission that after the battery but before his plea, he made an attempt on Paterson's life "to eliminate the key witness." The defense counsel objects that the testimony about Martin's conduct "would constitute implied hearsay."

Trial–Defense Case–in–Chief

(p) During the defense case–in–chief, the defense calls Mr. Andrew Peltier as a witness. Peltier testifies that he is a bartender at a saloon near Paterson's apartment. Peltier testifies that earlier the day of the alleged attack, Paterson visited the bar and had a few drinks. He attempts to testify that before leaving the bar, Paterson requested that the bartender arrange a buy of illegal drugs, including marijuana, for him. The prosecutor objects that "this man's testimony about Paterson's statements is plainly hearsay." *See Harrison v. State*, 686 S.W.2d 220, 222 (Tex. Ct. App. 1984).

(q) During his own direct testimony, Devitt states that after the alleged battery and before his arrest, he had a conversation with Mr. Bart Lawson, a neighbor who happens to be a police officer. Devitt attempts to testify that during the conversation, he told Lawson that he had been at Paterson's apartment. The prosecutor objects that "any testimony about the conversation with Lawson is self–serving hearsay." The defense counsel responds that the testimony is critical to the defense case: "Since my client knew that Lawson was a policeman, he would never have made the statement to Lawson if he hadn't believed that he was not guilty of any crime." *See United States v. Webster*, 750 F.2d 307, 330–31 (5th Cir. 1984).

(r) On cross–examination by the prosecutor, the prosecutor initially attempts to elicit Devitt's admission that when the police tried to arrest him, he gave the name Michael Dunning. The defense counsel objects that "my client was out of court at the time, and so his statements would be hearsay." *See United States v. Bankston*, 603 F.2d 528, 531 n.1 (5th Cir. 1979).

(s) Later on cross–examination, Devitt admits that he has a cousin named Andrea Gertz. The prosecutor next asks, "Later the same day (the day of the alleged battery), didn't you phone her and order her to give false alibi testimony that she was with you at the time of the attack?" The defense counsel objects that "whatever my client said to Ms. Gertz is blatant hearsay." *See United States v. Coven*, 662 F.2d 162, 174 (2d Cir. 1981).

(t) As the next defense witness, the defense counsel calls Ms. Gertz. On the one hand, she admits the telephone call mentioned in (s). On the other hand, when the defense counsel asks what occurred during the call, Ms. Gertz says, "As I've said all along, we just talked about family matters. Dan didn't say anything about an attack or an alibi or anything like that." The prosecutor moves to strike the reference, "As I've said all along" on the ground that it amounts to a description of the content of earlier out–of–court statements and is therefore hearsay. *See United States v. McLennan*, 563 F.2d 943, 952–53 (9th Cir. 1977). Pay special attention to n.5 on page 953 of the opinion.

Trial–Prosecution Rebuttal

(**u**) During the prosecution rebuttal, the prosecutor calls Officer Welsh. Welsh testifies that he is the custodian of records for the El Dorado Police Department. He attempts to testify that he learned from the department's computer that Ms. Gertz has a prior conviction for false statement. The defense counsel objects that the testimony is hearsay. *United States v. Escobar*, 674 F.2d 469, 473–74 (5th Cir. 1982).

(**v**) Later during direct examination, Officer Welsh testifies that he interviewed Ms. Gertz a week after the alleged battery. Welsh testifies without objection that at that time, Ms. Gertz initially said that she was with Devitt at the time of the alleged battery. Over defense hearsay objections, Welsh testifies that: He next told Gertz that the police had already found eyewitnesses to disprove the alibi; he then told Gertz that she could be sentenced to 25 years in jail for perjury; and Gertz responded by saying, "Oh, my God! How can I throw away 25 years of my life?"

(**w**) Assume that, during her direct examination, Ms. Gertz had testified to an alibi for Devitt; she testified that they spent the entire day of March 15, 19YR together at a music festival in a nearby town. As its next rebuttal witness, the prosecution calls Nicole Stewart. Ms. Stewart testifies that she is a good friend of Ms. Gertz. She adds that, in March of 19YR, she received a postcard from Ms. Gertz. She states that she kept the postcard, because the face of the postcard is a particularly beautiful view of an Hawaiian sunset. She identifies the handwriting on the postcard as Ms. Gertz'. The prosecutor then offers the postcard into evidence. The postcard bears a purported postmark reading: "Honolulu, Hawaii 15 Mar 19YR." The defense objects that the postmark is hearsay. The prosecutor replies, "How can it be hearsay? A machine made that mark! You can't cross–examine a machine; a machine can't be a hearsay declarant." What ruling? *United States v. Cowley*, 720 F.2d 1037, 1044–45 (9th Cir. 1983), *cert. denied*, 465 U.S. 1029 (1984). Do you see a distinction between records stored in a machine such as a computer and records generated by a machine such as the digital output of a breathalyzer machine? *Ly v. State*, 908 S.W.2d 598, 600 (Tex.App. 1995) (electronic monitoring system); Schlueter, *Hearsay–When Machines Talk*, 53 Tex.B.J. 1135 (Oct. 1990).

Chapter 19

HEARSAY: THE EXEMPTION FOR ADMISSIONS

Read Federal Rule of Evidence 801(d)(2).

A. INTRODUCTION

In the last chapter, we studied the general rule excluding hearsay evidence. This chapter begins our discussion of the exemptions from and exceptions to that rule. Most of these exemptions and exceptions rest on considerations of reliability and necessity.

This chapter is devoted to the subject of admissions by a party–opponent. We have given admissions singular treatment for several reasons. One is that trial attorneys probably use this doctrine more frequently than any other hearsay exception. Moreover, the admissions exemption stands alone because it has a peculiar rationale. As we pointed out in the previous chapter, the courts ordinarily will not permit the introduction of hearsay unless the circumstances create a strong inference of the statement's trustworthiness. However, an opponent's admissions may be introduced even if they are not based on personal knowledge and, worse still, were self–serving when made. McCormick suggests that "the most satisfactory justification of the admissibility of admissions is that they are the product of the adversary system . . . ." 2 C. McCormick, Handbook of the Law of Evidence § 254, at 136 (5th ed. 1999). Professor Morgan concurs but adds that the doctrine squares with the cross–examination rationale for the hearsay rule: "A party can hardly object that he had no opportunity to cross–examine himself . . . ." E. Morgan, Basic Problems of Evidence 266 (1962).

The unique rationale for the admissibility of admissions led some commentators to urge that admissions be classified as nonhearsay. Hetland, *Admissions in the Uniform Rules: Are They Necessary?*, 46 Iowa L. Rev. 307 (1961). These commentators, including Professor Morgan, reasoned that the hearsay definition should not include admissions, since the cross–examination policy underlying the hearsay definition does not extend to admissions. This reasoning appealed to the drafters of the Federal Rules and influenced the language of Rule 801(d)(2):

> (d) Statements which are not hearsay. A statement is not hearsay if
>
> (2) Admission by party–opponent. The statement is offered against a party and is (A) his own statement, in either his individual or a representative capacity or (B) a statement of which he has manifested his adoption or belief in its truth, or (C) a statement by a person authorized by him to make a statement

concerning the subject, or (D) a statement by his agent or servant concerning a matter within the scope of his agency or employment, made during the existence of the relationship, or (E) a statement by a coconspirator of a party during the course and in furtherance of the conspiracy.

Consequently, in federal parlance and practice, the admissions doctrine constitutes an exemption rather than an exception. However, in federal practice admissions "function as exceptions to the hearsay rule for most purposes." *Macuba v. DeBoer*, 193 F.3d 1316, 1323 n. 14 (11th Cir. 1999).

B. PERSONAL ADMISSIONS

The common law has long assumed that a person must accept the consequences of her own voluntary acts. That assumption is reflected in hearsay doctrine as well as in criminal and tort law. Federal Rule of Evidence 801(d)(2)(A) recognizes the admissibility of a person's "own statement, in either his individual or a representative capacity . . . ." The requirements for a personal admission are minimal: the evidence must be a statement or act of the party–opponent.

The statement can take myriad forms. At one extreme, the statement could be a casual, offhand remark made to a neighbor over a backyard fence. At the other extreme, the statement could be a formal pleading or stipulation filed in another lawsuit. *Dolinar v. Pedone*, 63 Cal. App. 2d 169, 146 P.2d 237 (1944); *Krajewski v. Western & S. Life Ins. Co.*, 241 Mich. 396, 217 N.W. 62 (1928). Even pleadings in prior suits and pleadings which were later amended in this suit are usable as evidentiary admissions. 2 C. McCORMICK, HANDBOOK OF THE LAW OF EVIDENCE § 257 (5th ed. 1999). A minority of courts balk at this, reasoning that treating ancillary or amended pleadings as admissions could interfere with the policies underlying the liberal pleading and amendment provisions of the Federal Rules of Civil Procedure. *Computer Associates Intern. v. American Fundware*, 831 F. Supp. 1516, 1529 (D. Colo. 1993). For other policy reasons, *nolo contendere* pleas are inadmissible in subsequent civil actions. FED. R. EVID. 410(2); *Moser v. Bascelli*, 879 F. Supp. 489, 492 (E.D. Pa. 1995).

The admission can even take the form of conduct. If a police officer confronted a crowd and asked, "Who did this?", the defendant's act of raising his hand would be hearsay (an assertive act) and an admission. Many courts also refer to acts such as a defendant's escape from custody as "an admission of guilt." *See* Annot., 3 A.L.R.4th 1085 (1981). Is that terminology precise? Is this assertive conduct or "Morgan hearsay"?

Whatever form the statement takes, it must be relevant to the issues in the case. Some authorities go farther and require that the statement be inconsistent with the position the party–opponent takes at trial. Does Federal Rule 801(d)(2) expressly incorporate this requirement? Even if it does not, as a practical matter, unless the statement is in some respect unfavorable or disserving to the party–opponent's position at trial, why would the adversary seek to admit it? *See* 1 E. CONRAD, MODERN TRIAL EVIDENCE § 452 (1956). In federal practice, it may be more useful to conceive of the test affirmatively:

Is this item of evidence logically relevant under Federal Rule 401 to prove some fact that the proponent has a right to prove under the pleadings and substantive law? If the test is phrased in this fashion, there is no "need of inquiry as to the disserving aspect of . . . [the] statement . . . ." M. LADD & R. CARLSON, CASES AND MATERIALS ON EVIDENCE 859 (1972). The crux is relevance, not disservice.

NOTES AND PROBLEMS

1. Compare Rule 613(b) on prior inconsistent statements with admissions under Rule 801(d)(2)(A). Is a foundation needed to introduce extrinsic evidence of an admission?

2. At common law, a statement is admissible as an admission even when the speaker does not have personal knowledge of the statement's subject–matter. *Ohlendorf v. Feinstein*, 636 S.W.2d 687 (Mo. Ct. App. 1982). Thus, in *Hill*, if Roe told Ms. Hill in the hospital that "it seems that the person who was driving my car was speeding," Roe's statement would be admissible even though Roe was not with Worker who was driving at the time of the collision. Does Federal Rule 801(d)(2) constitute an implied exception to Rule 602? Does Rule 602 apply to hearsay declarants? The Advisory Committee Note to Rule 801 refers to "[t]he freedom which admissions have [traditionally] enjoyed from . . . the rule requiring firsthand knowledge . . . ."

3. Problem 19–1. Under Morena law, Worker is liable to Roe for the damage to Roe's vehicle if Worker's negligence caused the collision with Ms. Hill. A month after the collision, a customer, Mr. Quartz, heard Worker and Roe arguing in an office at Roe's plant. During the argument, Roe told Worker, "You know that you were at fault in that accident. And your carelessness cost me almost $1400 in repairs to the damn vehicle." In Ms. Hill's suit against him, Roe files an answer denying Worker's negligence. At trial, Ms. Hill calls Quartz as a witness and attempts to elicit his testimony about Roe's statement to Worker. Roe's attorney objects that the question "calls for unreliable hearsay. It was clearly self–serving when made." What ruling? *Compare* Federal Rule of Evidence 801(d) (2) *with* Rule 804(b)(3). *State v. Walls*, 637 S.W.2d 812, 813 (Mo. Ct. App. 1982). *See Jewel v. CSX Transp., Inc.,* 135 F.3d 361, 365 (6th Cir. 1998) ("Trustworthiness is not a separate requirement for admission under Rule 801(d)(2)(A)").

4. Problem 19–2. Suppose that in Problem 19–1, Roe's attorney moved to strike the answer on the ground that "at fault" is obviously an inadmissible opinion. What ruling now? *Compare Wells v. Burton Lines*, 228 N.C. 422, 45 S.E.2d 569, 572 (1947) with *Kellner v. Whaley*, 148 Neb. 259, 27 N.W.2d 183, 189 (1947), and *Eagleston v. Guido*, 41 F.3d 865, 874 (2d Cir. 1994) ("In any event, his views on that subject would be inadmissible because they are legal conclusions concerning an ultimate issue in the case").

C.   ADOPTIVE ADMISSIONS

Adoptive admissions differ radically from personal admissions. In the case of personal admissions, we have the best possible justification for imputing a statement to the party–opponent: The party–opponent made the statement or committed the act constituting the admission. Not so in the case of adoptive admissions. In this setting, some third party–perhaps even a complete stranger–makes the statement; but in the words of Federal Rule of Evidence 801(d)(2) (B), the party–opponent "manifest[s] his adoption or belief in its truth." The pivotal question is whether the surrounding circumstances support an inference of assent. The party–opponent can manifest assent affirmatively or negatively.

1. AFFIRMATIVE ADOPTION

Suppose that in *Hill,* the plaintiff sued to collect for a knee injury that she claims was caused by her collision with Worker. Two years before, when applying for a job with Acme Corporation, Ms. Hill was required to submit a medical report. Ms. Hill visited Dr. Ferguson's office, obtained a report from him, and submitted the report to Acme's Personnel Office. Polecat and Roe could use the report against Ms. Hill at trial as evidence that her knee injury was preexisting. By voluntarily tendering the report to Acme, Ms. Hill affirmatively manifested assent to its contents. *Russo v. Metropolitan Life Ins. Co.*, 125 Conn. 132, 3 A.2d 844 (1939). The adoption can be made by an entity as well as a natural person. If someone submits a report to a corporation, there is an adequate inference of adoption when the entity acts on and implements the report. *Wright–Simmons v. City of Oklahoma City*, 155 F.3d 1264, 1268–69 (10th Cir. 1998); *Pilgrim v. Trustees of Tufts College*, 118 F.3d 864, 869–70 (1st Cir. 1997).

Who decides whether there is a sufficiently strong inference of assent? Think back to our discussion of preliminary fact–finding procedures. In their comments to California Evidence Code § 403 (the California counterpart of Federal Rule 104(b)), the Assembly Committee stated:

> Under existing law, both authorized admissions (by an agent of the party) and adoptive admissions are admitted upon the intro-duction of evidence sufficient to sustain a finding of the founda-tional fact.

Thus, the judge decides only whether the jury could rationally infer that the party–opponent was manifesting assent by performing the act. The jury makes the final decision whether to draw the inference.

PROBLEMS

1. Problem 19–3. Suppose that Acme Corporation had Dr. Ferguson on retainer and required that Ms. Hill go to Ferguson for her preemployment physical examination. Would Ferguson's report still be admissible against Hill as an adoptive admission? Is Ferguson's report less reliable now? Is the reliability of Ferguson's report even relevant on an adoptive admission theory?

2. Problem 19–4. In *Hill*, the trial judge decided to sever Ms. Hill's suit against Roe from her suit against Polecat. Ms. Hill's suit against Roe goes to trial first. At the trial, Ms. Hill calls Mr. Laroby, an eyewitness to the accident. Laroby's testimony is generally favorable to Ms. Hill, but he does say that he detected a slight odor of alcohol on her breath immediately after the collision. Later Ms. Hill's suit against Polecat comes to trial. May Polecat offer Laroby's testimony about the alcoholic breath against Ms. Hill?

3. Problem 19–5. Change one fact in Problem 19–4. Assume that Ms. Hill had deposed Laroby before the first trial and offered Laroby's deposition transcript at the trial because of Laroby's unavailability. Does that fact strengthen or weaken Polecat's argument?

2. NEGATIVE ADOPTION — TACIT ADMISSIONS

In some cases, it is rational to infer a person's assent to a statement from the person's silence in the face of the statement. Since the person's silence is the key to creating the inference, this type of adoption is sometimes called a "tacit admission." In most cases in which the courts find tacit admissions, the following facts are present:

- A third party made a statement.
- The third party made the statement in the party–opponent's hearing and presence.
- The party–opponent understood the statement.
- The party–opponent was physically and mentally capable of replying to the statement.
- The party–opponent made no reply or an evasive response.
- The statement accused the party–opponent of some misconduct.
- In similar circumstances, a reasonable innocent person would have immediately disputed the statement.

Note, *Tacit Criminal Admissions*, 112 U.Pa.L.Rev. 210 (1963). In these circumstances, there is a common sense inference that the party–opponent agreed with the substantive content of the third party's statement if the party–opponent did not "demur." *People v. Rodrigues*, 8 Cal. 4th 1060, 885 P.2d 1, 36 Cal. Rptr.2d 235, 276 (1994), *modified*, 9 Cal. 4th 579A (1995), *cert denied*, 516 U.S. 851 (1995).

Focus for a moment just on the third party's statement. Suppose that in *Hill*, immediately after the accident, Mr. Laroby walked up to Ms. Hill and said, "There's alcohol on your breath. You've pretty clearly been drinking." The third party's statement is admitted for a nonhearsay purpose. The statement is accepted on a mental input theory of logical relevance. The statement is admitted only to show its effect on the party–opponent's state of mind. On request, the trial judge would give the jury a limiting instruction about the evidentiary status of the third party's statement. Furthermore, in closing it would be error for the proponent to treat the third party's statement as substantive evidence of any facts asserted in the statement.

Commentators have increasingly questioned the psychological validity of the underlying assumption that, in these circumstances, the most reasonable explanation for the person's silence is the person's realization of the truth of the accusation. Gamble, *The Tacit Admission Rule: Unreliable and Unconstitutional–A Doctrine Ripe for Abandonment*, 14 Ga. L. Rev. 27 (1979). One commentator charges that the assumption is "no more than a[n unproven] scientific hypothesis." *Id.* at 32. Former Chief Justice Burger himself noted that "there is not a scintilla of empirical data to support" the assumption. *United States v. Hale*, 422 U.S. 171, 181 (1975). In the *Miller* case excerpted in Chapter 3, Judge Bazelon pointed out that a person's neurosis may prompt the person to "react . . . as though he were guilty even though he is innocent . . . ." *Miller v. United States*, 320 F.2d 767, 772 (D.C. Cir. 1963) (citing 2 S. Freud, Collected Papers 13 (1959)). The continued recognition of the tacit admission doctrine may be another instance of the courts' reliance on "common sense psychology"–at odds with the psychological reality. Gamble, *supra*, at 34.

NOTES

1. Is the proper solution the abolition of the tacit admission doctrine or the admission of expert testimony explaining the person's seemingly guilty conduct? Consider this example. In the trial of a defendant accused of murdering his ex–wife, the prosecution offers evidence that upon learning of her death, the brutal circumstances thereof, and that he was the prime suspect, defendant denied any involvement, attempted to flee from the police and threatened to kill himself. The defense counters with expert testimony that the defendant's behavior was typical of the normal denial response of an innocent layperson caught up in the horrifying experience of the murder of a loved one. Common sense psychology?

2. The commentators' criticisms of the tacit admission doctrine are slowly winning some converts among the courts. In 1989, the Alabama Supreme Court severely limited the use of the doctrine in criminal cases. *Ex parte Marek*, 556 So. 2d 375 (Ala. 1989). The court rejected the "underlying premises . . . that an innocent person always objects when confronted with a baseless accusation . . . ." *Id.* at 381. The court specifically cited the Gamble article. *Id.* at 381 n.1.

3. Courts apply the tacit admission doctrine in criminal as well as civil cases. The criminal context poses special problems. To begin with, *Griffin v. California*, 380 U.S. 609 (1965), forbids a prosecutor from commenting on the defendant's invocation of the privilege against self–incrimination, and *Miranda v. Arizona*, 384 U.S. 436 (1966), tells us that the defendant may invoke the privilege simply by falling silent. Further, there is a widespread belief in the United States that an arrestee's wisest course of action is to claim the Fifth Amendment and demand to see an attorney. *Griffin* calls into question the constitutional propriety of inferring assent from a criminal defendant's silence, and the belief weakens the inference of assent from silence. The Supreme Court ventured into this thicket to clarify the state of the law in the following case.

DOYLE v. OHIO

426 U.S. 610 (1976)

Justice Powell delivered the opinion of the Court.

The question is whether a state prosecutor may seek to impeach a defendant's exculpatory story, told for the first time at trial, by cross–examining the defendant about his failure to have told the story after receiving *Miranda* warnings at the time of his arrest. We conclude that use of the defendant's post–arrest silence in this manner violates due process.

Petitioners Doyle and Wood were arrested together and charged with selling 10 pounds of marihuana to a local narcotics bureau informant. They were convicted in separate trials held about one week apart. The evidence at their trials was identical in all material respects.

The State's witnesses sketched a picture of a routine marihuana transaction. William Bonnell, a well–known "street person" with a long criminal record, offered to assist the local narcotics investigation unit in setting up drug "pushers" in return for support in his efforts to receive lenient treatment in his latest legal problems. The narcotics agents agreed. A short time later, Bonnell advised the unit that he had arranged a "buy" of 10 pounds of marihuana and needed $1,750 to pay for it. Since the banks were closed and time was short, the agents were able to collect only $1,320. Bonnell took this money and left for the rendezvous, under surveillance by four narcotics agents in two cars. As planned, he met petitioners in a bar in Dover, Ohio. From there, he and petitioner Wood drove in Bonnell's pickup truck to the nearby town of New Philadelphia, Ohio, while petitioner Doyle drove off to obtain the marihuana and then meet them at a prearranged location in New Philadelphia. The narcotics agents followed the Bonnell truck. When Doyle arrived at Bonnell's waiting truck in New Philadelphia, the two vehicles proceeded to a parking lot where the transaction took place. Bonnell left in his truck, and Doyle and Wood departed in Doyle's car. They quickly discovered that they had been paid $430 less than the agreed–upon price, and began circling the neighborhood looking for Bonnell. They were stopped within minutes by New Philadelphia police acting on radioed instructions from the narcotics agents. One of those agents, Kenneth Beamer, arrived on the scene promptly, arrested the petitioners, and gave them *Miranda* warnings. A search of the car, authorized by warrant, uncovered the $1,320.

Each petitioner took the stand at his trial and admitted practically everything about the State's case except the most crucial point: who was selling marihuana to whom. According to petitioners, Bonnell had framed them. The arrangement had been for Bonnell to sell Doyle 10 pounds of marihuana. Doyle had left the Dover bar for the purpose of borrowing the necessary money, but while driving by himself had decided that he only wanted one or two pounds instead of the agreed–upon 10 pounds. When Bonnell reached Doyle's car in the New Philadelphia parking lot, with the marihuana under his arm, Doyle tried to explain his change of mind. Bonnell grew angry, threw the $1,320 into Doyle's car, and took all 10 pounds of the marihuana back to his truck. The ensuing chase was the effort of Wood and Doyle to catch Bonnell to find out what the $1,320 was all about.

Petitioner's explanation of the events presented some difficulty for the prosecution, as it was not entirely implausible and there was little if any direct evidence to contradict it. In an effort to undercut the explanation, the prosecutor asked each petitioner why he had not told the frame up story to

Agent Beamer when he arrested petitioners. In the first trial, that of petitioner Wood, the following colloquy occurred:

> Q. [By the prosecutor.] Mr. Beamer did arrive on the scene?
>
> A. [By Wood.] Yes, he did.
>
> Q. And I assume you told him all about what happened to you?
>
> . . . .
>
> A. No.
>
> Q. You didn't tell Mr. Beamer?
>
> . . . .
>
> A. No.
>
> Q. And we can't understand any reason why anyone would put money in your car and you were chasing him around town and trying to give it back?
>
> A. I didn't understand that.
>
> Q. You mean you didn't tell him that?
>
> . . . .
>
> A. Tell him what?
>
> . . . .
>
> Q. Mr. Wood, if that is all you had to do with this and you are innocent, when Mr. Beamer arrived on the scene why didn't you tell him?
>
> . . . .
>
> Q. But in any event you didn't bother to tell Mr. Beamer anything about this?
>
> A. No, sir.

Defense counsel's timely objections to the above questions of the prosecutor were overruled. The cross–examination of petitioner Doyle at his trial contained a similar exchange, and again defense counsel's timely objections were overruled.

The State pleads necessity as justification for the prosecutor's action in these cases. It argues that the discrepancy between an exculpatory story at trial and silence at time of arrest gives rise to an inference that the story was fabricated somewhere along the way, perhaps to fit within the seams of the State's case as it was developed at pretrial hearings. Noting that the prosecution usually has little else with which to counter such an exculpatory story, the State seeks only the right to cross–examine a defendant as to post–arrest silence for the limited purpose of impeachment. In support of its position the State relies upon those cases in which this Court has permitted use for impeachment purposes of post–arrest statements that were inadmissible as evidence of guilt because of an officer's failure to follow *Miranda's* dictates. *Harris v. New York*, 401 U.S. 222 (1971); *Oregon v. Hass*, 420 U.S. 714 (1975); *see also Walder v. United States*, 347 U.S. 62 (1954). Thus, although the State does not suggest petitioners' silence could be used as evidence of guilt, it contends that the need to present to the jury all information relevant to the truth of petitioners' exculpatory story fully justifies the cross–examination that is at issue.

The *Miranda* decision compels rejection of the State's position. The warnings mandated by that case, as a prophylactic means of safeguarding Fifth Amendment rights, require that a person taken into custody be advised immediately that he has the right to remain silent, that anything he says may be used against him, and that he has a right to retain or appoint counsel before submitting to interrogation. Silence in the wake of these warnings may be nothing more than the arrestee's exercise of these *Miranda* rights. Thus, every post–arrest silence is insolubly ambiguous because of what the State is required to advise the person arrested. Moreover, while it is true that the *Miranda* warnings contain no express assurance that silence will carry no penalty, such assurance is implicit to any person who receives the warnings. In such circumstances, it would be fundamentally unfair and a deprivation of due process to allow the arrested person's silence to be used to impeach an explanation subsequently offered at trial. MR. JUSTICE WHITE, concurring in the judgment in *United States v. Hale, supra,* at 182–183, put it very well:

> [W]hen a person under arrest is informed, as *Miranda* requires, that he may remain silent, that anything he says may be used against him, and that he may have an attorney if he wishes, it seems to me that it does not comport with due process to permit the prosecution during the trial to call attention to his silence at the time of arrest and to insist that because he did not speak about the facts of the case at that time, as he was told he need not do, an unfavorable inference might be drawn as to the truth of his trial testimony. . . .

We hold that the use for impeachment purposes of petitioners' silence, at the time of arrest and after receiving *Miranda* warnings, violated the Due Process Clause of the Fourteenth Amendment.[11]

NOTES AND PROBLEMS

1. Since rendering the *Doyle* decision, the Supreme Court has revisited the issue. In *Jenkins v. Anderson*, 447 U.S. 231, 238–40 (1980), the Court held that a prosecutor may cross–examine a defendant about prearrest silence. In *Fletcher v. Weir*, 455 U.S. 603 (1982), the Court further limited *Doyle* by announcing that a prosecutor may use post–arrest silence for impeachment if the defendant had not yet been given *Miranda* warnings.

2. Problem 19–6. In *Devitt*, at trial the defendant takes the stand. During direct examination, the following occurs:

Q: What did you do after the police took you to the station?

---

[11] It goes almost without saying that the fact of post–arrest silence could be used by the prosecution to contradict a defendant who testifies to an exculpatory version of events and claims to have told the police the same version upon arrest. In that situation the fact of earlier silence would not be used to impeach the exculpatory story, but rather to challenge the defendant's testimony as to his behavior following arrest. *Cf. United States v. Fairchild*, 505 F.2d 1378, 1383 (CA5 1975).

A: I cooperated fully with the police.

Q: What do you mean by "cooperated"?

A: As best I could, I told them everything they wanted to know about where I had been and what I'd done that day.

In light of this direct testimony, would the prosecutor be able to prove that when first interrogated, Devitt claimed the Fifth Amendment? Note footnote 11 in *Doyle*. Would the prosecutor be able to use Devitt's silence as substantive evidence of guilt or merely as impeachment?

3. Problem 19–7. In *Hill*, Laroby confronts the plaintiff immediately after the collision and accuses her of being drunk. She remains silent. Is her silence automatically admissible? What would you like to know about Ms. Hill's condition at the time Laroby spoke with her? *Klever v. Elliott*, 212 Or. 490, 320 P.2d 263, 264–65 (1958).

4. Problem 19–8. Suppose that after the accident, Mr. Hill wrote a letter to the president of the manufacturer Polecat, and in the letter he asserted that "you should be ashamed of yourself for marketing such a dangerous product." Neither Polecat's president nor any other officer of Polecat responded to the letter. At trial, can Ms. Hill argue that Polecat's failure to respond is an adoptive admission that its gas tank was "dangerous"? Assume alternatively that the president of the Jefferson Motor Cars dealership wrote to the president of Polecat and included a similar assertion in the letter. Jefferson Motor Cars and Polecat have dealt with each other for 15 years. In that light, would Polecat's failure to respond be an adoptive admission? *See* 2 C. McCORMICK, EVIDENCE § 262, at 170–71 (5th ed. 1999).

D. VICARIOUS ADMISSIONS

The last type of admission is the most controversial. In the case of personal and adoptive admissions, there may be some basis for inferring assent. In the case of a vicarious admission, there may be no evidence of assent or agreement. We impute vicarious admissions to the party–opponent solely on the basis of the opponent's legal relationship with the declarant. The statement may be admissible against the opponent even when, in all probability, the opponent would never have made the same statement. The question then becomes: When is the relationship strong and close enough to justify burdening the opponent with the third party's statement?

1. CIVIL CASES

At first, the courts virtually equated the vicarious admission standard with the agency law test for authority to serve as a spokesperson. Even if the third party speaker was indisputably an employee of the party–opponent, the courts refused to admit the speaker's statements as the opponent's vicarious admission unless there was an affirmative showing of "authority to speak for the principal." *Rudzinski v. Warner*, 16 Wis. 2d 241, 114 N.W.2d 466 (1962). Opinions were even replete with references to the RESTATEMENT OF THE LAW OF AGENCY. *Id.* Under this view, statements by Famiglietti, Polecat's president, would qualify as vicarious admissions against Polecat; but assertions by Worker, Roe's employee, would probably be inadmissible against Roe. If Worker were Roe's partner, the result might be different. *Filesi v. United States*, 352 F.2d 339 (4th Cir. 1965). To justify the difference in result, the court would distinguish an employee's authority from a partner's authority under "the substantive laws of Agency." *Id.*

Eventually the courts came to question the facile equation between the agency and evidentiary issues. The nagging issue was whether the limit of authority is necessarily the same as the limit of reliability. More and more courts began to think that the issues were distinguishable and that the evidentiary standard should be more liberal than the agency test. The courts often expressed their dissatisfaction with the test by circumventing the vicarious admission doctrine; they strained to admit employees' statements against employers on alternative theories such as "res gestae" or declarations against interest. *Martin v. Savage Truck Line*, 121 F. Supp. 417 (D.D.C. 1954).

Finally, at the commentators' urging, a number of courts boldly repudiated the traditional view and explicitly adopted a broader standard for the vicarious admissions of agents and employees. The drafters of the Federal Rules embraced that view in Rule 801(d)(2)(C)–(D):

> (d) . . . A statement is not hearsay if—
>
> > (2) Admission by party–opponent. The statement is offered against a party and is . . . (C) a statement by a person authorized by him to make a statement concerning the subject, or (D) a statement by his agent or servant concerning a matter within the scope of his agency or employment, made during the existence of the relationship.

Subsection (C) preserves the traditional route for admitting agents' statements, but (D) supplements (C) and adds a more liberal, alternative tack. Under (D), the declarant need not be a speaking agent (*Hill v. F.R. Tripler & Co., Inc.*, 868 F. Supp. 593, 597 (S.D.N.Y. 1994)); "authorization to speak need not be shown." *Precision Piping & Instruments, Inc. v. E.I. du Pont de Nemours & Co.*, 951 F.2d 613, 619 (4th Cir. 1991). The declarant's statement need only "concern" matters within the scope of the agency. *In re Sunset Bay Associates*, 944 F.2d 1503 (9th Cir. 1991).

NOTES AND PROBLEMS

1. Although Federal Rule 801(d)(2)(D) breaks down the equation between the evidentiary admissibility of the agent's statements against the principal and the principal's *respondeat superior* liability in tort, agency principles are still pertinent to the interpretation of the Rule. The Rule uses the expression "agent or servant" and the courts continue to look to common law principles to determine whether the declarant is "an agent or servant." In *Boren v. Sable*, 887 F.2d 1032, 1038 (10th Cir. 1989), the court observed:

> The use of the terms "agent" or "servant" without definition evidences Congress' intent to describe the traditional master–servant relationship as understood by common law agency doctrine. Use of the term "scope of employment" in Rule 801(d)(2)(D) is

additional evidence of Congress' intent that common law agency principles be used in applying Rule 801.

Likewise, in *Rivera–Lopez v. Dorado*, 979 F.2d 885, 887 (1st Cir. 1992), the court remarked that "this is a recital of, not a change in, the law of agency." As we have seen in the past, when a statute employs a term which has acquired a fixed meaning at common law, the courts ordinarily presume that the legislature used the term in the common law sense. Based on this reasoning, the courts ordinarily refuse to treat a party's expert witnesses as agents. *Kirk v. Raymark Industries, Inc.*, 51 F.3d 1206, 1213–14 (3d Cir. 1995); *Koch v. Koch Industries, Inc.*, 37 F.Supp.2d 1231, 1244–45 (D.Kan.1998). For similar reasons, an outside independent contractor usually does not qualify as an agent for purposes of the statute. *Condus v. Howard Savings Bank*, 986 F.Supp. 914 (D.N.J. 1997).

2. Recall *Bourjaily v. United States*, 483 U.S. 171 (1987), where the Court noted that before the adoption of the Federal Rules of Evidence, the "bootstrapping doctrine" was in effect. By virtue of that doctrine, a prosecutor attempting to lay the foundation for a coconspirator's hearsay declaration had to present independent evidence of such foundational facts as the existence of the conspiracy and the declarant's membership in the conspiracy; the prosecutor could not rely even in part on the content of the declaration itself, since doing so would amount to forbidden "bootstrapping." The *Bourjaily* Court ruled that the doctrine did not survive the enactment of Federal Rule 104(a). Like the pre–Rules criminal cases, some post–Rules civil cases assert that "the statement to be introduced may not be relied upon to establish the alleged agency relationship . . . ." *Pappas v. Middle Earth Condominium Ass'n*, 963 F.2d 534, 548 (2d Cir. 1992). Is that assertion sound? In 1997, Rule 801 (d)(2) was amended to clarify:

> The contents of the statement shall be considered but are not alone sufficient to establish the declarant's authority under subdivision (C), the agency or employment relationship and the scope thereof under subdivision (D), or the existence of the conspiracy and the participation therein of the declarant and the party against whom the statement is offered under subdivision (E).

3. Problem 19–9. After the collision in *Hill*, Worker told a bystander, Ms. Karl, "I guess I just wasn't paying attention to the traffic." Ms. Hill wants to offer Worker's statement, through the testimony of Ms. Karl, as a vicarious admission under Rule 801(d)(2)(D). How could she prove the fact of Worker's agency? Suppose that Ms. Karl also heard Worker say, "Mr. Roe sent me to rush a package cross town, and he's going to be mad as hell when he finds out that I got into this accident on the way."

4. At common law, some courts adopted a strict approach to the agency rationale for vicarious admissions. 2 C. McCORMICK, HANDBOOK OF THE LAW OF EVIDENCE § 259, at 152–53 (5th ed. 1999). Since the courts usually applied the agency doctrines only when some third party sued the principal, the courts refused to admit an agent's statements to another agent or even to the principal as vicarious admissions. *Id.* Did that limitation survive the adoption of Federal Rule 801(d)(2)? The Advisory Committee Note states that "[t]he rule is phrased broadly so as to encompass both" statements to outsiders and statements to insiders.

5. We saw earlier in this chapter that at common law, personal admissions are admissible even if not based on the declarant's personal knowledge. Should the same rule apply to vicarious admissions by agents? Since vicarious admissions are one step removed from the party–opponent himself or herself, there is an additional concern about the probative value of the evidence. What should be the result under Federal Rule 801(d)(2)(D)? *See Brookover v. Mary Hitchcock Mem. Hosp.*, 893 F.2d 411, 415–17 (1st Cir. 1990) ("Commentators and the courts differ on whether personal knowledge is a prerequisite for a vicarious admission under the Rule"). As previously stated, the Advisory Committee Note to Rule 801(d)(2) contains a general reference to "[t]he freedom which admissions have enjoyed . . . from . . . the rule requiring firsthand knowledge . . . ." The trend is to hold that even vicarious admissions need not be based on personal knowlege. *Blackburn v. United Parcel Service, Inc.*, 179 F.3d 81, 96–97 (3d Cir. 1999); *Stagman v. Ryan*, 176 F.3d 986, 996 (7th Cir.) *cert.denied,* 528 U.S. 986 (1999).

6. At common law, the vicarious admission doctrine extended to statements by privies or predecessors in interest. 2 C. McCORMICK, HANDBOOK OF THE LAW OF EVIDENCE § 260 (5th ed. 1999). Georgia Code Annotated § 24–3–32 expressly refers to admissions by "privies in blood, . . .estate, and . . .law." For example, if a previous owner of the fee made a statement about the extent of his title to the property, the statement might be admissible against a subsequent owner. *Id.* Similarly, in many jurisdictions, if a decedent made a statement, the statement would be admissible against the decedent's personal representative or heirs in a survival or wrongful death action brought by the representative or heirs. *Id.* Thus, if Ms. Hill had died in the collision and her heirs had sued Polecat for wrongful death, her antemortem statements would be admissible against her heirs. Should such statements be admissible under Federal Rule 801(d)(2)? *See* Langum, *Uncodified Federal Evidence Rules Applicable to Civil Trials*, 19 WILLAMETTE L. REV. 513, 521–522 (1983).

2.　CRIMINAL CASES

The criminal counterpart of the admission of agents' statements is the doctrine allowing the prosecution to use coconspirators' statements against each other. Levie, *Hearsay and Conspiracy: A Reexamination of the Co–Conspirators' Exception to the Hearsay Rule*, 52 MICH. L. REV. 1159 (1954). The statements may be oral or written. For example, a calendar/ledger maintained by one drug trafficker may be admitted as substantive evidence against her coconspirator. *United States v. Smith*, 893 F.2d 1573 (9th Cir. 1990). Like its civil analogue, the early common law version of this exception looked to substantive law to define the limits of admissibility–in this instance, the vicarious responsibility of coconspirators under criminal law.

R. PERKINS, CRIMINAL LAW 632–35 (2d ed. 1969), sets forth the substantive law in a nutshell: When individuals enter into a criminal conspiracy, each of them "is liable for every act, and is bound by the act and declaration of each and all of the conspirators" done in furtherance of the conspiracy. That liability attaches even if the accused coconspirator was absent when the act was performed or the declaration voiced. When one conspirator commits an act to achieve the main objective of the criminal plan, the act is imputed to every other conspirator. The latter conspirator escapes criminal responsibility only if the former "unexpectedly goes entirely outside the purpose . . . to commit [the] crime . . . ." *Id.* However, once the conspiracy comes to an end, "whether by accomplishment or abandonment" of the criminal objective, the conspirators' vicarious liability also terminates.

The courts' evidentiary rulings on the admissibility of coconspirators' statements parallel the substantive criminal law. The statement qualifies under the evidentiary doctrine only if the declarant actually joined the conspiracy; if the declarant was an undercover agent who would not incur criminal responsibility, the declaration is inadmissible. *United States v. Williamson*, 450 F.2d 585 (5th Cir. 1971), *cert. denied*, 405 U.S. 1026 (1972). Moreover, applying the substantive criminal law rule, the courts usually conclude that the conspiracy terminates when the conspirators either achieve or abandon their main objective. The conspiracy ordinarily ends before individual conspirators begin their personal efforts to conceal the conspiracy and avoid arrest and conviction. Most courts do not imply a subsidiary conspiracy to continue to work in concert after the crime's commission and the division of the fruits of the crime. *Grunewald v. United States*, 353 U.S. 391 (1957); *Lutwak v. United States*, 344 U.S. 604 (1953); *Krulewitch v. United States*, 336 U.S. 440 (1949). To justify the admission of later statements, the prosecution must prove the formation of a *further* conspiracy to continue to act in concert.

Against the backdrop of the common law, consider Federal Rule of Evidence 801(d)(2)(E):

> (d) . . . A statement is not hearsay if—
>
> (2) Admission by Party–Opponent. The statement is offered against a party and is . . . (E) a statement by a coconspirator of a party during the course and in furtherance of the conspiracy.

The Advisory Committee described Rule (d)(2)(E) as being "in the accepted pattern."

NOTES AND PROBLEMS

1. The evolution of the coconspirator doctrine has lagged behind the development of the exception for agents' statements. As we have seen, courts and legislatures in many jurisdictions have liberalized the admissibility of agents' statements and have broken down the equation between agency law and evidence. The equation between criminal law and evidence has proven to be more durable. The courts still require that the statement be "in furtherance" of the conspiracy. *United States v. James*, 510 F.2d 546, 549 (5th Cir. 1975). The proponent need not show that the statement actually had the effect of advancing the goals of the conspiracy, but the proponent must establish that the declarant intended the statement to have that effect. *United States v. Zavala–Serra*, 853 F.2d 1512, 1516 (9th Cir. 1988).

2. Reformers have also urged the courts to expand the duration of the conspiracy for evidentiary purposes. Under the prevailing view, the prosecutor must establish an express agreement to extend the conspiracy into the concealment phase. *Grunewald v. United States*, 353 U.S. 391, 399–406 (1957). The critics of the prevailing view recommend implying an agreement. Although the Georgia legislature adopted this recommendation, most jurisdictions adhere to the traditional view. *Dutton v. Evans*, 400 U.S. 74, 81 (1970). Is the duration limitation more or less defensible than the "in furtherance" requirement?

3. Problem 19–10. In *Devitt*, the prosecution claims that the defendant conspired with and planned the battery with a friend, Mert Bloomington. The prosecution alleges that Bloomington had worked for Paterson and that when Paterson fired him, Bloomington developed a hatred for him. At trial, the prosecutor calls Mr. Kranston as a witness. Kranston was present at several meetings between Devitt and Bloomington, and he testifies that he heard the two men discuss "getting Paterson and paying him back for what he (Paterson) had done to Bloomington." Ultimately, the prosecutor wants to elicit Kranston's testimony that Bloomington said that "Danny (Devitt) is going to nail him good." As soon as the prosecutor asks the question to elicit that testimony, Devitt's attorney objects and requests permission to *voir dire* Kranston and present extrinsic testimony that there was no conspiracy between Bloomington and Devitt.

Should the judge grant the defense request? Does the judge or jury decide whether there was a conspiracy, authorizing the introduction of Bloomington's statement as a vicarious admission? Reread the Supreme Court's decision in *Bourjaily* (excerpted earlier) and compare *Bourjaily* with this passage from the Assembly Committee's Comment to California Evidence Code § 403 (the California analogue to Federal Rule 104(b)): "The admission of a co–conspirator is another form of an authorized admission. Hence, the proffered evidence is admissible upon the introduction of evidence sufficient to sustain a finding of the conspiracy."

4. Problem 19–11. Assume the first trial in *Devitt* resulted in a hung jury and a mistrial. Before the first trial, Devitt's defense attorney anticipated that the prosecution would call Mr. Manville, who lived in the same apartment complex as Paterson. Based on his informal conversations with Manville, the defense attorney expected Manville to testify that he had had a conversation with Devitt just outside the Paterson apartment and that during that conversation Devitt had made a remark that was a veiled threat toward Mr. Paterson. Devitt's attorney tries to preempt Manville's testimony, by conceding, during opening statement, that Devitt made such remarks, but adds: "Ladies and gentlemen, there's a world of difference between casually making a vague threat and actually attacking that person." Manville dies unexpectedly before trial, and his testimony is never presented during the first trial. During the second trial, the prosecutor attempts to offer the defense counsel's opening statement acknowledging that Devitt made the remarks shortly before the alleged attack. Devitt has a new attorney at the second trial, and she objects that the former counsel's statement is "rank hearsay." The prosecutor argues that the defense counsel's statement is a vicarious admission. The prosecutor does not argue that the attorney is a coconspirator under

(E) but contends that the attorney is an "agent" under (C) or (D). Does it make a difference that Devitt has retained new counsel for the second trial? *See United States v. McKeon*, 738 F.2d 26, 30–34 (2d Cir. 1984). In some respects, an attorney is unquestionably the client's agent; and on its face, Rule 801(d)(2) does not carve out any exception for attorneys. *United States v. McClellan*, 868 F.2d 210 (7th Cir. 1989); Humble, *Evidentiary Admissions of Defense Counsel in Federal Criminal Cases*, 24 AM. CRIM. L. REV. 93 (1986). However, "the routine use of attorney statements against a criminal defendant risks impairment of the privilege against self–incrimination, the right to counsel of one's choice, and the right to the effective assistance of counsel." *United States v. Valencia*, 826 F.2d 169, 172 (2d Cir. 1987) (a defense counsel's statement during bail discussions with the prosecutor did not qualify as a vicarious admission).

5. More broadly, in a criminal case, when must the prosecution rely on Rule 801(d)(2)(E)? Or can the prosecution invoke other theories recognized in Rule 801(d)(2)? If the prosecution can resort to other provisions such as Rule 801(d)(2)(D), is Rule 801(d)(2)(E) reduced to mere surplusage? Rule 801(d)(2)(D) is arguably so broad that it might never be necessary for the prosecution to resort to–and comply with–Rule 801(d)(2)(E). The courts ordinarily favor statutory interpretations that give independent effect to each provision in a statute. *See United States v. Weisz*, 718 F.2d 413, 433 (D.C. Cir. 1983).

———

Thus far, we have discussed the prosecution's attempts to use the various admission doctrines against the defendant. Can the defendant turn the tables on the prosecution? Suppose, for example, that, during the pretrial investigation of the case, a police officer or prosecutor makes a statement which tends to exculpate Devitt? May Devitt introduce the statement as evidence against the prosecuting sovereign? The following case, in which the late Professor Irving Younger was the appointed defense counsel, addresses that question:

UNITED STATES v. SANTOS

372 F.2d 177 (2d Cir. 1967)

WATERMAN, CIRCUIT JUDGE.

This is an appeal from a judgment of conviction entered in the United States District Court for the Southern District of New York on April 22, 1965 after a two–day trial before the Honorable Thomas F. Murphy and a jury.

The indictment upon which appellant was tried was filed May 23, 1962. In it he and two others, John Burgos and Mario Reveron, were charged with having violated 18 U.S.C. § 111 in that they on May 7, 1962 assaulted a federal officer, an agent of the Bureau of Narcotics, with a deadly weapon.

Appellant was arrested in Philadelphia on June 15, 1962. When apprehended he was possessing heroin, was promptly arraigned on a state narcotics charge, was convicted thereon on August 14, 1962, and was sentenced to a term of 21/2 to 5 years imprisonment. On December 15, 1964, appellant was released from the Pennsylvania prison, was arrested to answer to the federal May 23, 1962 indictment, was removed to the Southern District of New York, and was first tried on the assault charge on March 10, 1965. The jury disagreeing, he was promptly retried. The second jury returned a verdict of guilty on April 1, 1965, and the judgment of conviction from which the within appeal is taken was entered April 22, 1965.

Appellant maintains that the case should be remanded for a new trial in that it was improper and prejudicial to exclude from evidence a sworn affidavit to an officer's complaint by a narcotics agent, agent Edward R. Dower, who had witnessed the assault, in which agent Dower named another than appellant as one of the three assailants, and which sworn affidavit defendant offered at trial during the defense case as an admission against the Government. We find no merit and affirm the conviction below.

The claim of reversible error may be shortly answered by stating that inconsistent out–of–court statements or actions of a government agent said or done in the course of his employment take on quite a different probative character in a government criminal case from that which inconsistent out–of–court acts of agents acting within the scope of their employment generally take on at a trial. Though a government prosecution is an exemplification of the adversary process, nevertheless, when the Government prosecutes, it prosecutes on behalf of all the people of the United States; therefore all persons, whether law enforcement agents, government investigators, complaining prosecuting witnesses, or the like, who testify on behalf of the prosecution, and who, because of an employment relation or other personal interest in the outcome of the prosecution, may happen to be inseparably connected with the government side of the adversary process, stand in relation to the United States and in relation to the defendant no differently from persons unconnected with the effective development of or furtherance of the success of, the prosecution.

Therefore, the inconsistent out–of–court statements of a government agent made in the course of the exercise of his authority and within the scope of that authority, which statements would be admissions binding upon an agent's principal in civil cases, are not so admissible here as "evidence of the fact."

To be sure, if the defense had adopted different trial tactics and had confronted Dower with this statement of his when cross–examining him the statement would have been admissible as evidence tending to impeach his credibility. This course the defendant elected not to adopt. The course defendant did adopt would have been successful if it had been attempted other than in a criminal prosecution. This limitation upon the use the defendant may make of a government agent's out–of–court inconsistent statement seems grossly unfair to defendants, for the prosecution may introduce against the defendant similar damaging statements by defendants' agents if made in the course of the exercise of the agent's authority and within the scope thereof and the agents' admissions have the same testimonial value as if the inconsistent statements had been made by the defendant himself. As was said by Justice Story in *United States v. Gooding*, 12 Wheaton 460 (1827) at page 469, 6 L. Ed. 693:

In general, the rules of evidence in criminal and civil cases are the same. Whatever the agent does, within the scope of his authority, binds his principal, and is deemed his act. It must, indeed, be shown that the agent has the authority, and that the act is within its scope; but these being conceded or proved, either by the course of business or by express authorization, the same conclusion arises, in point of law, in both cases. Nor is there any authority for confining the rule to civil cases. On the contrary, it is the known and familiar principle of criminal jurisprudence, that he who commands or procures a crime to be done, if it is done, is guilty of the crime, and the act is his act.

This apparent discrimination is explained by the peculiar posture of the parties in a criminal prosecution–the only party on the government side being the Government itself whose many agents and actors are supposedly uninterested personally in the outcome of the trial and are historically unable to bind the sovereign. Apparently recognizing the seeming unfairness of this peculiar relationship Congress by enacting 18 U.S.C. § 3500 has made it a requirement that the prosecution turn over to the defense any inconsistent statements of government witnesses relating to the testimony given by those witnesses at trial so that the defense upon cross–examination can interrogate the witnesses about the inconsistent statements. But these statements are not admissible against the Government as evidentiary proof of the matter therein stated.

Judgment affirmed.

NOTES

1. Professor Younger continued his attack on the *Santos* decision after the decision in the case. Younger, *Sovereign Admissions: A Comment on United States v. Santos*, 43 N.Y.U. L. REV. 108 (1968). Notwithstanding the court's decision, he insisted that when a defendant "confront[s] the sovereign in court, the rules of the game [should] be the same for both." *Id.* at 108. However, both before and after the adoption of the Federal Rules, the courts have tended to follow *Santos. E.g., United States v. Durrani*, 659 F. Supp. 1183, 1185–86 (D. Conn.), *aff'd*, 835 F.2d 410 (2d Cir. 1987).

2. Do you find Judge Waterman's reasoning persuasive? When the sovereign is a party to a civil lawsuit, the courts apply the normal vicarious admission doctrine against the sovereign. *United States v. A. T. & T. Co.*, 524 F. Supp. 1331, 1333–34 (D.D.C. 1981); *Burkey v. Ellis*, 483 F. Supp. 897, 911 n.13 (N.D. Ala. 1979).

3. Which type of statement is more likely to be reliable – a statement by a coconspirator or a statement by a government agent? Conspirators are often inveterate liars. Levie, *Hearsay and Conspiracy: A Reexamination of the Co–Conspirators' Exception to the Hearsay Rule*, 52 MICH. L. REV. 1159, 1166 (1954). It may well be in the conspirator's self–interest to misrepresent the membership or aims of the conspiracy. *Id.* at 1165–66. Professor Mueller put the matter bluntly when he wrote that the coconspirator exception is "an embarrassment." Mueller, *The Federal Coconspirator Exception: Action, Assertion, and Hearsay*, 12 HOFSTRA L. REV. 323, 324 (1984). In contrast, the government has presumably exercised some care in hiring its employees.

4. Consider the problem as an issue of statutory interpretation. Is the wording of Rule 801(d)(2)(D) broad enough to apply to statements by government agents? Given Rule 402, may a court continue to enforce *Santos* on the theory that if Congress had intended to overrule such a well–settled doctrine, Congress "surely" would have done so explicitly? Think back to the Supreme Court's treatment of Rule 402 in *Daubert*, 509 U.S. 579 (1993), discussed in Chapter 12. When Congress wanted to apply different rules to the prosecution and defense, it did so explicitly in the text of the Federal Rules. *E.g.*, FED. R. EVID. 804(b)(3) (the corroboration requirements for defense declarations against interest). Judge Bazelon has questioned whether *Santos* is good law under the Federal Rules. *United States v. Morgan*, 581 F.2d 933, 938 n.14 (D.C. Cir. 1978). So too, the commentators. *See e.g.*, Jonakait, *The Supreme Court, Plain Meaning, and the Changed Rules of Evidence*, 68 TEX. L. REV. 745, 774–78 (1990) ("The plain–meaning standard discards the *Santos* doctrine"). There appears to be some recent movement away from *Santos. E.g.*, *United States v. Zizzo*, 120 F.3d 1338, 1351 n. 5 (7th Cir.) (although this court generally "decline[s] to apply Rule 801(d)(2) to statements made by government employees in criminal cases," the court acknowledged that "a number of courts have rejected that approach when dealing with statements by government attorneys"), *cert.denied*, 522 U.S. 998 (1997); *United States v. Salerno*, 937 F.2d 797, 810–12 (2d Cir.1991) (the government's earlier closing argument); *United States v. GAF Corp.*, 928 F.2d 1253 (2d Cir. 1991) (the government's earlier bill of particulars could be introduced against the prosecution as the admission of a party–opponent); *State v. Cardenas–Hernandez*, 579 N.W. 2d 678, 685 (Wis. 1998) ("We. . .refuse to adopt a per se prohibition on the use of prior statements of prosecutors as admissions of a party–opponent").

Chapter 20

HEARSAY: EXCEPTIONS THAT DO NOT REQUIRE A SHOWING OF UNAVAILABILITY

Read Federal Rule of Evidence 803, subdivisions (1–4, 6–12, 14 and 18).

A. INTRODUCTION

This chapter deals with many of the exceptions listed in Federal Rule of Evidence 803. The Rule is entitled "Hearsay Exceptions: Availability of Declarant Immaterial." (The next chapter deals with exceptions requiring proof of declarant's unavailability.) Courts recognized the exceptions in this chapter because they concluded that the hearsay evidence is likely to be more reliable than any testimony the declarant would now give from the witness stand. Hutchins & Slesinger, *Some Observations on the Law of Evidence: State of Mind in Issue*, 29 U. COLO. L. REV. 147, 149 (1929). In short, the key to these exceptions is the inference of the statement's reliability. That inference supplies both the circumstantial guarantee of trustworthiness (eliminating the need for cross–examination) and the element of necessity – justifying the resort to hearsay. These exceptions fall into two major categories. In one, the inference of reliability arises from circumstances strongly suggesting the declarant's sincerity–the so–called *res gestae* theory. In the other, the statement takes the form of a writing and the care with which the writing was prepared creates the inference of reliability.

B. EXCEPTIONS DERIVED FROM THE "RES GESTAE" THEORY

Although the phrase "res gestae," as the title of a hearsay exception, has been taboo for some time, res gestae nevertheless flourishes as a convenient "catch–all" to ease the courts' conscience in escaping the hearsay rule when they feel certain evidence ought to be admitted.[*] In the trial court, an attorney who may be carefully explaining the reason for admitting certain evidence may find her task simplified when the judge says, "What you are really talking about is res gestae, isn't it?"

Although some trial judges are fond of the res gestae theory, the theory has been a target of criticism for many appellate judges and scholars. The dislike for the phrase "res gestae" has been expressed by great names in the law. In Judge Learned Hand's words, res gestae "is a phrase which has been accountable for so much confusion that it had best be denied any place whatever in legal terminology; if it means anything but an unwillingness to

---

[*] This introductory material is based on M. LADD & R. CARLSON, CASES AND MATERIALS ON EVIDENCE 899–903 (1972).

think at all, what it covers cannot be put in less intelligible terms." *United States v. Matot*, 146 F.2d 197, 198 (2d Cir. 1944). For his part, Dean Wigmore remarked, "This phrase is inexact and indefinite in its scope . . .. The phrase 'res gestae' has long been not only entirely useless but even positively harmful." 6 J. WIGMORE, EVIDENCE § 1767, at 180, 182–83 (3d ed. 1940).

However, no other legal outcast has shown such vitality and recuperative power as res gestae. To this day, the expression "res gestae" is still codified in the Georgia statutes. GA. CODE ANN. § 24–3–3. Many courts continue to use the expression res gestae. *E.g.*, *Williams v. Melton*, 733 F.2d 1492 (11th Cir.), *cert denied*, 469 U.S. 1073 (1984). Professor Morgan employed Res Gestae as a category followed by the statement: "Courts and lawyers constantly use res gestae to describe: (a) part of a relevant transaction which has no hearsay aspect, (b) declarations of presently existing subjective symptoms, offered to prove the existence of those symptoms, (c) declarations of a presently existing mental condition offered to prove that condition and to prove conduct in accord with that mental condition, (d) declarations of a past mental condition or symptom, and (e) spontaneous statements or statements made contemporaneously with a relevant transaction or condition, to prove the truth of the matter stated." Morgan, *The Law of Evidence, 1941–45*, 59 HARV. L. REV. 481, 568 (1946).

Following Professor Morgan's example, in the following four subsections we shall identify the major specific hearsay exceptions spawned by the res gestae theory: excited utterances, contemporaneous statements, declarations of bodily condition, and finally declarations of state of mind.

1. EXCITED OR STARTLED UTTERANCES

The first offspring of the res gestae theory was the excited or startled utterance exception which was based on the rationale that when an observer makes a statement about a startling event that he or she has just witnessed, the statement is probably reliable. In reality, it is the event speaking through the person. Moylan, *Res Gestae, or Why Is That Event Speaking and What Is It Doing in This Courtroom?*, 63 A.B.A. J. 968 (1977). In his lectures for the National Institute on Trial Advocacy, the late Professor Younger pointed out that it is quite easy to recognize excited utterances: They usually begin with "My God" and end with an exclamation mark. Federal Rule of Evidence 803(2) states a modern version of the doctrine:

> The following are not excluded by the hearsay rule, even though the declarant is available as a witness:
>
>> (2) Excited utterance. A statement relating to a startling event or condition made while the declarant was under the stress of excitement caused by the event or condition.

The foundation for an excited utterance attempts to ensure the reliability of the statement by requiring indicia of both perception and sincerity. The foundation ensures perception in two respects. First, the statement must at least purport to describe an event that the declarant personally observed. The troublesome question is whether the proponent must present independent evidence that the event occurred. In *People v. Leonard*, 400 N.E.2d 568 (Ill.

App. Ct. 1980), the court demanded independent proof. The court reasoned that independent evidence is necessary to avoid bootstrapping. The startling event ensures the reliability of the statement, and it would be illicit to take the statement itself at face value as proof of the event's occurrence. Some courts have construed the text of Rule 803(2) as codifying the *Leonard* view and requiring independent proof. *E.g., People v. Burton*, 433 Mich. 268, 445 N.W.2d 133 (1989) (analogizing to *Bourjaily v. United States*, 483 U.S. 171 (1987), strongly suggesting that, under Rule 104, the proponent of a coconspirator's declaration must present some independent evidence of the underlying conspiracy). However, in their Note to Rule 803(2), the Advisory Committee indicated that it intended the Rule to follow "the prevailing practice" dispensing with independent evidence. This is one instance in which the available extrinsic legislative history material furnishes a relatively clear answer to a question of statutory construction. So long as the court believes that it is legitimate to consider the Advisory Committee Note, that Note provides clear guidance.

The second requirement tending to ensure perception is that the statement must relate to the event the observer witnessed. The statute prescribes that the statement "relat[e] to" the startling event. The idea is that this limitation enhances perception and memory as well as sincerity. If the statement could relate to other, earlier events, there would be much more substantial questions about the caliber of the declarant's recollection of the prior events. However, the Committee made it clear that it does not favor rigid enforcement of the limitation. See its comparison of Exceptions 1 and 2 to Rule 803 (contemporaneous statements vs. excited utterances). FED. R. EVID. 803(2), Advisory Committee Note. Suppose that in *Devitt*, Paterson was hospitalized for several days after the alleged battery. When the police arrest Devitt, the local paper carries his photograph on the front page. When the nurse delivers breakfast and the paper to Paterson that morning, Paterson sees the photograph and screams, "That's the man. That's the guy who attacked me." Does his statement qualify as an excited utterance?

UNITED STATES v. NAPIER

518 F.2d 316 (9th Cir. 1975)

SNEED, CIRCUIT JUDGE.

Defendant Napier was indicted on four counts of interstate transportation of a stolen motor vehicle in violation of 18 U.S.C. § 2312 ("Dyer Act") and one count of interstate kidnapping in violation of 18 U.S.C. § 1201 ("Lindbergh Act"). Defendant was convicted by a jury on all counts.

Counts IV and V of the indictment alleged that defendant kidnapped Mrs. Caruso in Oregon, transported her to Washington, and then drove her stolen car back to Oregon. There was very strong circumstantial evidence of defendant's involvement in the incident. Mrs. Caruso, a resident of Portland, Oregon, was found unconscious, with severe head injuries, near Vancouver, Washington. A broken rifle lay by her body. Blood and hair on the hammer of the weapon matched those of Mrs. Caruso; the barrel of the gun bore the fingerprints of the defendant. Tire tracks nearby corresponded to those of the Caruso car, which was later recovered in Oregon. Defendant's fingerprints were found on the car (including the steering wheel) and his personal papers and effects were discovered therein with Mrs. Caruso's purse.

Defendant argues that the court erred in admitting, as a "spontaneous exclamation", an out–of–court statement made by Mrs. Caruso. We find defendant's contention without merit and affirm the conviction.

Caruso was hospitalized for seven weeks following the assault, during which time she underwent two brain operations. There was testimony that she suffered brain damage which rendered her unable to comprehend the significance of an oath and therefore incapable of testifying at trial. It was also testified, although her memory was intact, that her communication with others was restricted to isolated words and simple phrases, often precipitated by situations of stress and strain. Approximately one week after Caruso returned home from the hospital, her sister, Eileen Moore, showed her a newspaper article containing a photograph of the defendant. Moore testified that Caruso looked at the photograph (but did not read the accompanying article), and her "immediate reaction was one of great distress and horror and upset," and that Caruso "pointed to it and she said very clearly, 'He killed me, he killed me.'" Moore also testified that no member of the family had attempted to discuss the incident with Caruso prior to the display of the photograph. The court admitted the statement, over defendant's objection that it was inadmissible hearsay, as a "spontaneous exclamation." We hold that the statement was properly admitted.

Although the government insists that the statement is a "verbal act" and thus not hearsay at all, we do not pass on this contention because it is our view that even if the statement is hearsay it falls within the exception for "spontaneous exclamation" or "excited utterances." Fed. R. Evid. 803(2) provides: "A statement relating to a startling event or condition made while the declarant was under the stress of excitement caused by the event or condition [is not excluded by the hearsay rule]." Appellant disputes the applicability of the "spontaneous exclamation" exception. He argues that since the statement "he killed me" refers to the assault, that event constitutes the "startling" event. Because the statement was not made under the stress of excitement caused by the assault, appellant insists that the statement is not within the exception. We reject appellant's analysis. The display of the photograph qualifies as a sufficiently "startling" event to render the statement made in response thereto admissible.

Although in most cases the "startling" events which prompt "spontaneous exclamations" are accidents, assaults, and the like, *cf.* McCormick, Evidence § 297 at 705 (2d ed. 1972), there is no reason to restrict the exception to those situations. Wigmore, in the classic statement of the admissibility of spontaneous exclamations, writes:

> This general principle is based on the experience that, under certain external circumstances of physical shock, a stress of nervous excitement may be produced which stills the reflective faculties and removes their control, so that the utterance which then occurs is a spontaneous and sincere response to the actual

sensations and perceptions already produced by the external shock. Since this utterance is made under the immediate and uncontrolled domination of the senses, and during the brief period when considerations of self–interest could not have been brought fully to bear by reasoned reflection, the utterance may be taken as particularly trustworthy (or, at least, as lacking the usual grounds of untrustworthiness), and thus as expressing the real tenor of the speaker's belief as to the facts just observed by him; and may therefore be received as testimony to those facts. The ordinary situation presenting these conditions is an affray or a railroad accident. But the principle itself is a broad one.

6 Wigmore, Evidence § 1747, at 135 (3d ed. 1940). And McCormick writes of the nature of the event which underlies the exception: "The courts seem to look primarily to the effect upon the declarant and, if satisfied that the event was such as to cause adequate excitement, the inquiry is ended." McCormick, Evidence § 297, at 705 (2d ed. 1972). In the instant case where Caruso, having never discussed the assault with her family, was suddenly and unexpectedly confronted with a photograph of her alleged assailant, there can be no doubt that the event was sufficiently "startling" to provide adequate safeguards against reflection and fabrication.

NOTES AND PROBLEMS

1. Is *Napier* correctly decided? Does *Napier* interpret "relating to" sensibly? The court treats Mrs. Caruso's viewing of the photograph as the startling event. In the final analysis, though, what was the event Mrs. Caruso was purporting to remember?

2. Assume *arguendo* that the *Napier* court should have treated the earlier crime as the pivotal element. The court focuses on the sincerity factor. However, did the court slight the memory factor? Numerous experiments have demonstrated the alarmingly fast rate at which people forget. Gardner, *The Perception and Memory of Witnesses*, 18 CORNELL L.Q. 391, 393 (1933). In one study testing recollection of words, the typical subject forgot 90% of the information within a week. *Id.* By the time weeks have passed, memory decay is extensive. Stewart, *Perception, Memory, and Hearsay: A Criticism of Present Law and The Proposed Federal Rules of Evidence*, 1970 UTAH L. REV. 1, 24. As we have seen, the *raison d'etre* of the "relating to" requirement is a concern about the quality of the declarant's memory.

3. Problem 20–1. In *Hill*, the plaintiff calls as a witness Mr. Bernstein. Bernstein testifies that he was at the intersection where the collision occurred. A few moments after the crash, he saw a man walking towards him. Mr. Bernstein is prepared to testify that the man said, "Did you see it? It was terrible. That guy must have been going at least 50. What an idiot!" Roe objects on the ground that the man Bernstein is quoting is unidentified. What ruling? *Powers v. Temple*, 250 S.C. 149, 156 S.E.2d 759, 765 (1967). There is substantial authority supporting *Powers. New York, C. & St. L. R.R v. Kovatch*, 120 Ohio St. 532, 166 N.E. 682–84 (1929). However, there are contrary authorities. *Louisville Ry. v. Johnson's Adm'r*, 131 Ky. 277, 115 S.W. 207, 209 (1909).

4. Problem 20–2. In Problem 20–1, suppose that Roe had objected on the ground that there was insufficient proof that the man had personally observed the collision. Would the result be different if Bernstein had not noticed the man until five minutes after the collision? *Beck v. Dye*, 200 Wash. 1, 92 P.2d 1113, 1116–17 (1940). In *Cummiskey v. Chandris, S.A.*, 719 F. Supp. 1183, 1187 (S.D.N.Y. 1989), *aff'd*, 895 F.2d 107 (2d Cir. 1990), the court commented that "[i]n a case where the witness is both unidentified and unavailable, the burden [of showing personal knowledge] is greater." *Accord, Shinners v. K– Mart Corp.*, 847 F.Supp. 31, 34 (D.Del. 1994) ("a heavier burden").

————

Although the two preceding foundational requirements help assure the declarant's perception and memory, the central focus of this exception is the declarant's sincerity. The objective indicator of sincerity is that the event observed must be "startling,"–the type of incident that could generate nervous excitement. In *Lira v. Albert Einstein Medical Center*, 384 Pa. Super. 503, 559 A.2d 550 (1989), the court excluded a statement made by an attending physician during a physical examination of a patient after an operation: "Who's the butcher who [did] this?" The court held that the examination was not the type of shocking occurrence which can prompt a startled utterance. The subjective guarantee is proof that the declarant in fact was in a state of nervous excitement when he or she made the statement. Typically, the courts place great stress on the time interval between the event and the statement. Annot., 89 A.L.R.3d 102 (1979). It is ideal if the declarant makes the statement "a few minutes" after the event. *Peavey v. State*, 631 S.W.2d 821 (Tex. Crim. App. 1982). The courts are relatively tolerant; they have admitted statements made fifteen minutes (*United States v. Golden*, 671 F.2d 369 (10th Cir. 1982)), forty minutes (*State v. Rogers*, 585 S.W.2d 498 (Mo. Ct. App. 1979)), and even seventy–five minutes after the event (*United States v. Iron Shell*, 633 F.2d 77 (8th Cir. 1980), *cert. denied*, 450 U.S. 1001 (1981)). In addition to the timing, the courts consider such factors as the declarant's location at the time of the statement, the declarant's intervening conduct, the declarant's condition at the time of the statement, and whether the statement was a response to a question. *United States v. Merrill*, 484 F.2d 168 (8th Cir.), *cert. denied*, 414 U.S. 1077 (1973); *Jones v. Greer*, 627 F. Supp. 1481, 1492 (C.D. Ill. 1986). The fact that a declarant resorted to curse words is also supposedly an indication of the declarant's excited state. Slovenko, *The Impact of Profanity on Hearsay Evidence*, 1 MED. & LAW 397, 398 (1982).

PROBLEMS

1. Problem 20–3. In *Devitt*, Paterson is beaten so brutally that he goes into an immediate coma. Two weeks pass. Paterson is lying in a hospital bed ten miles from his house when he finally regains consciousness. At that instant, he jumps up in bed and blurts out, "Devitt — is he still here? He just attacked me. Please protect me." The prosecutor offers Nurse Holmstrom's testimony about Paterson's first words after regaining consciousness. Does the statement qualify as an excited utterance? *See Foster v. Thornton*, 125 Fla. 699, 170 So.

459, 463 (1936); *Mills v. State*, 626 S.W.2d 583, 585 (Tex. Crim. App. 1981) ("The time element . . . is not the controlling factor").

2. Problem 20–4. In *Hill*, the plaintiff calls Kathryn Manning as a witness. Ms. Manning testifies that she has a five–year–old daughter, Elise. Elise was three years old at the time she observed the collision. Ms. Manning will testify that when she ran up to the scene of the collision two minutes after impact, Elise screamed, "Mommy, the man in the car was going so fast." It is well–settled in Morena that to be a competent witness, a person must be five years old at the time of the relevant event. Roe objects on the grounds of "the clear incompetency of the hearsay declarant." What ruling? *See* Annot., 15 A.L.R.4th 1043, 1047–54 (1982). Remember the mystical theory that the event is speaking through the person.

3. Problem 20–5. Suppose that the judge overrules the objection in Problem 20–4. You are Ms. Hill's attorney. The judge states, "You can proceed so long as you show that the little girl was in a state of nervous excitement at the time." You must now conduct the direct examination to lay that element of the foundation. What facts would you elicit about Elise's facial expression, tone of voice, the volume of voice, the pace and coherency of speech, and gestures? Be prepared to conduct this part of the direct examination in class. Notice the tightrope you need to walk as a direct examiner laying this foundation. On the one hand, the event needs to be startling enough to attract and hold the declarant's attention. On the other hand, you do not want the jury to think that the declarant was absolutely hysterical at the time of the statement.

———

It should be evident by now that as in the case of admissions, the courts are quite liberal in admitting excited utterances. In some jurisdictions, the statement is admissible even though the declarant is unavailable, was unidentified, and would have been incompetent if called to the witness stand. The courts thus place tremendous faith in the power of sincerity to ensure the reliability of the statement. Is that faith well–placed? In one commentator's view, in the past the courts have naively overestimated the length of time during which a startling event can suppress a person's ability to reflect and fabricate. Even a startled person can come to his or her senses and regain that ability in a matter of seconds. The . . . exception, which tolerates more than a thirty minute gap between the event and the utterance, allows sufficient time for mendacity and calculation of false reports. It does not take much time to lie . . . . Orenstein, *"My God!": A Feminist Critique of the Excited Utterance Exception to the Hearsay Rule*, 85 Cal. L. Rev. 159 (1997). Moreover, even assuming that the event induces a lengthy, truthful frame of mind, witness psychologists have been critical of the excited utterance exception. The following article argues that the excited statement may lose more in accuracy of perception and memory than it gains in sincerity.

HUTCHINS & SLESINGER, SOME OBSERVATIONS ON THE LAW OF EVIDENCE, 28 Columbia Law Review 432, 437–39 (1928) (some citations omitted)

One need not be a psychologist to distrust an observation made under emotional stress; everybody accepts such statements with mental reservation. M. Gorphe cites the case of an excited witness to a horrible accident who erroneously declared that the coachman deliberately and vindictively ran down a helpless woman. Fiore tells of an emotionally upset man who testified that hundreds were killed in an accident; that he had seen their heads rolling from their bodies. In reality only one man was killed, and five others injured. Another excited gentleman took a pipe for a pistol. Besides these stories from real life, there are psychological experiments which point to the same conclusion. After a battle in a classroom, prearranged by the experimenter but a surprise to the students, each one was asked to write an account of the incident. The testimony of the most upset students was practically worthless, while those who were only slightly stimulated emotionally scored better than those left cold by the incident. Miss Hyde of Nebraska tells of an unpublished experiment, the results of which differed only in the general inaccuracy of all accounts, regardless of the amount of emotion generated.[32] The conclusion drawn from these, and other similar experiments, is that "emotion may virtually hold connected perception in abeyance so that the subject has only isolated sensations to remember instead of a logically connected unit perception."

That participants, as well as bystanders,[35] have their perceptions clouded by strong emotions will not be doubted. When a carriage containing the inevitable psychologist upset, that worthy gentleman amused himself and his companions by taking depositions while they awaited assistance. He had no known reality to check their stories against, but it was obvious that if any one was right, all the rest were wrong. That even trained observers are fallible is well brought out in an editorial in the *New York World* in which several accounts of newspaper reports of the striking of Kerensky on his recent visit to America are printed. Though the reporters were all experts, and sitting close to the platform, each one told a different story of what must have been a fairly simple event.[37]

---

[32] The amount, or presence of any emotion at all presents another interesting problem. Syz, *Observations on the Unreliability of Subjective Reports of Emotional Reactions[,]* (1920) 17 BRIT. JOUR. PSYCH. Gen. Sect. 119–26 reports the following. His subjects were hooked up to a psycho–galvanometer capable of recording the electrical change which takes place in one under emotional stress. Then a list of words was given, and they were asked to report those words which caused in them an emotional feeling. Their reports and the galvanometer readings were not in accord. They reported emotion to conventional words like mother, father, etc., whereas they registered emotion with entirely different ones.

[35] It will be remembered that some courts make a distinction between the two.

[37] These are descriptions of the manner in which the young woman struck her blow:

WORLD: "Slashed him viciously across the cheek with her gloves."

NEWS: "Struck him on the left cheek with the bouquet."

AMERICAN: "Dropped her flowers and slapped him in the face with her gloves."

TIMES: "Slapped his face vigorously with her gloves three times."

HERALD TRIBUNE: "Beat him on the face and head . . . a half–dozen blows."

The result of these observations is a dilemma. From the point of view of subjective veracity, the speed the courts demand does not necessarily guarantee truth. And from the standpoint of objective accuracy, emotion is little better. If a speedy reaction means nothing without the aid of a stopwatch, an emotional reaction means nothing without eliminating the emotion. What the emotion gains by way of overcoming the desire to lie, it loses by impairing the declarant's power of observation. On the one hand, if reflective self–interest has not had a chance to operate because of emotional stress, then the statement should be excluded because of the probable inaccuracy of observation. On the other, if little emotion is involved, clearly a very short time is sufficient to allow reflective self–interest to assume full sway. On that basis there would seem to be no reason for this hearsay exception. In fact, the emphasis should be all the other way. On psychological grounds, the rule might very well read: Hearsay is inadmissible, especially (not except) if it be a spontaneous exclamation.

NOTES

1. More modern commentators generally concur with Hutchins and Slesinger. *See* Levine & Tapp, *The Psychology of Criminal Identification: The Gap From* Wade *to* Kirby, 121 U. PA. L. REV. 1079 (1973). Witnesses to traumatic, startling events are particularly unreliable. *Id.* Although hearsay exceptions such as this doctrine have "stressed the element of sincerity, . . . [i]t is believed to be the common experience of attorneys in the trial of cases, when facts are not accurately reported, that witnesses are more often found to be mistaken than committing perjury." Ladd, *The Hearsay We Admit*, 5 OKLA. L. REV. 271, 286 (1952).

Professors Levine and Tapp point out that it is a mistake to generalize that excitement distorts perception. Levine & Tapp, *supra*, at 1098. Although great excitement tends to produce hysteria and distortion, moderate stress seems to improve the witness' attention without great distortion. *Id.* Would it be judicially manageable for the courts to administer a hearsay exception purporting to admit only statements made under "moderate" stress?

2. The Hutchins and Slesinger article is not only the leading secondary authority on this topic, but also happens to be one of the very first authorities

---

EVENING WORLD: Struck him across the face "several times."

MIRROR: Struck him a single time.

POST: "Vigorously and accurately slapped him."

And this is what happened next:

AMERICAN: Kerensky "reeled back."

EVENING WORLD: "He stood unmoved."

NEWS: "He stepped back, maintaining a calm pose."

WORLD: He stood still, but used his arms to "wave back his friends."

HERALD TRIBUNE: He stood still, with his arms "thrown back."

JOURNAL: "He reeled."

POST: "He remained unmoved."

MIRROR: "He reeled from the blow. His supporters were stemmed by a handful of royalists. Fists flew; noses ran red; shirts and collars were torn."

cited in the Advisory Committee Note to Rule 803. Moreover, as previously stated, the Committee opted for the more conservative view restricting this hearsay exception to statements "relating to" the startling event. Some commentators have criticized the Federal Rules provisions on the res gestae exceptions on the ground that the provisions leave intact the common law misconceptions about the relative importance of the memory and sincerity factors. Stewart, *Perception, Memory, and Hearsay: A Criticism of Present Law and the Proposed Federal Rules of Evidence*, 1970 UTAH L. REV. 1. However, the text of Rule 803(2) and the accompanying Note suggests that "the statutory framework of Article VIII . . . directs courts to" place greater stress in the memory factor in deciding whether to admit hearsay. Imwinkelried, *The Importance of the Memory Factor in Analyzing the Reliability of Hearsay Testimony: A Lesson Slowly Learnt – and Quickly Forgotten*, 41 FLA. L. REV. 215, 229 (1989). Prepare to argue for and against this construction of Article VIII.

2. CONTEMPORANEOUS STATEMENTS OR PRESENT SENSE IMPRESSIONS

Like the excited utterance exception, the present doctrine is traceable to the res gestae concept. In the case of excited utterances, the event inspires spontaneity, guaranteeing sincerity. Under the present exception, contemporaneity substitutes for spontaneity. Professor Thayer argued that the courts should treat contemporaneity and spontaneity as alternative methods of demonstrating reliability. Thayer, *Bedingfield's Case–Declarations as a Part of the Res Gestae*, 15 AM. L. REV. 1 (1881). In contrast, Wigmore stressed spontaneity to the virtual exclusion of contemporaneity. Following Wigmore's lead, the courts long ignored contemporaneity. The contemporaneity of the statement eliminated the doubts about the quality of the hearsay declarant's memory. However, as we have seen, the conventional wisdom at common law was that the sincerity factor was far more important than the memory factor. Since there appeared to be no affirmative guarantee of the sincerity of a contemporaneous statement, the overwhelming majority of courts refused to admit such statements. Comment, *The Present Sense Impression Exception to the Hearsay Rule: Federal Rule of Evidence 803(1)*, 81 DICK. L. REV. 347, 351 (1977).

It was left to Professor Morgan to resurrect Thayer's theory. The theory first persuaded a few jurisdictions to adopt contemporaneous statements as a common law exception. *See, e.g., Houston Oxygen Co. v. Davis*, 139 Tex. 1, 161 S.W.2d 474 (1942). These cases eventually led to the Advisory Committee's decision to include the exception in Federal Rule of Evidence 803. The committee stated its decision emphatically by making the exception the very first provision in the rule:

> The following are not excluded by the hearsay rule, even though the declarant is available as a witness:
>
> (1) Present sense impression. A statement describing or explaining an event or condition made while the declarant was perceiving the event or condition, or immediately thereafter.

Citing the Hutchins and Slesinger article, the Committee deliberately opted for what was undeniably a minority view at common law. Congress decided to confirm the Committee's decision, although both the Association of Trial Lawyers of America and the American Bar Association voiced opposition to proposed Rule 803(1). *Rules of Evidence (Supplement): Hearings on Proposed Federal Rules of Evidence Before the Subcomm. on Criminal Justice of the House Comm. on the Judiciary*, 93d Cong., 1st Sess. 116, 119–20, 212–14 (1973).

As in the case of the excited utterance doctrine, the foundation is designed to create an inference of reliability: perception, memory, and sincerity.

The statement must be based on firsthand knowledge. *Bemis v. Edwards*, 45 F.3d 1369, 1373 (9th Cir. 1995). If the declarant has that basis, under Rule 803(1) the declarant may describe "an[y] event or condition." The language of California Evidence Code § 1241 is much more restrictive. That statute limits admissible declarations to statements about the "conduct of the declarant." To be sure, the restriction strengthens the inference of accurate perception; the declarant is less likely to be mistaken about her own conduct than about the acts of other persons and objects caught up in the same event. But is that incremental increase in the trustworthiness of inference worth the cost?

The doctrine also contains a rigorous guarantee of the quality of the declarant's memory. In other words, "immediately thereafter" in Exception (1) is much more vigorously enforced than the time requirement under the excited utterance doctrine. On this timing issue, the California Evidence Code takes an even more conservative position, requiring that the declarant speak "while the declarant was engaged in such conduct." In sum, although the outer limit for excited utterances is usually a matter of hours, contemporaneous statements must ordinarily be made within a matter of minutes after the event. *E.g., Miller v. Crown Amusements, Inc.*, 821 F. Supp. 703 (S.D. Ga. 1993) (two minutes); *Hynes v. Couglin*, 79 F.3d 285, 294 (2d Cir. 1996) ("delay of 15 to 45 minutes 'hardly qualifies as immediately' "). 911 telephone calls frequently qualify when the caller phones immediately after an event occurs. *Bemis v. Edwards*, 45 F.3d 1369 (9th Cir. 1995); *Miller v. Crown Amusements, Inc.*, 821 F. Supp. 703 (S.D.Ga. 1993).

As a doublecheck on the declarant's perception and a guarantee of sincerity, Thayer argued that one of the conditions of admissibility should be that the witness on the stand also observed the event. Thayer, *supra,* at 83, 107 (1881). Subsequent commentators concurred. Comment, *Spontaneous Exclamations in the Absence of a Startling Event*, 46 U. Colo. L. Rev. 430, 439 (1946). At common law, many, if not most, courts regarded the witness' observer status as an element of the foundation. Waltz, *The Present Sense Impression Exception to the Rule Against Hearsay: Origins and Attributes*, 66 Iowa L. Rev. 869, 883 (1981). The courts thought it wise to add that element as a check against any misstatements by the declarant. *Houston Oxygen Co. v. Davis*, 139 Tex. 1, 8, 161 S.W.2d 474, 476–77 (1942). Some courts, however, were contra. Waltz, *supra,* at 888. Rule 803(1) makes no mention of any requirement for a corroborating witness. Did the requirement survive the adoption of the Federal Rules?

PROBLEMS

1. Problem 20–6. In *Hill*, three blocks before colliding with the plaintiff's car, Worker passed Mr. Grimm's car. As Worker's car passed, Grimm swerved to the right and said to his passenger, Ms. Fowler, "That jerk isn't looking where he's driving. He's goin' too fast, and he's not even all the way in his lane." At the time of his statement, Grimm was speaking in a matter–of–fact tone although he seemed a bit angry. At trial, could Ms. Fowler testify to Grimm's statement? *See Houston Oxygen Co. v. Davis*, 139 Tex. 1, 161 S.W.2d 474, 476–77 (1942). Could she do so in California under Evidence Code § 1241:

> Evidence of a statement is not made inadmissible by the hearsay rule if the statement:
>
> (a) Is offered to explain, qualify, or make understandable conduct of the declarant; and
>
> (b) Was made while the declarant was engaged in such conduct.

Roe objects that Grimm's statement refers to "Worker's conduct, not his own." Suppose that at the end of his statement, Grimm added, "If I hadn't swerved, that jerk would have hit us."

2. Problem 20–7. In Problem 20–6, suppose that Ms. Fowler was not in Grimm's car when Worker's car passed. However, Grimm has a car telephone. He was on the phone with Ms. Fowler; and when Worker passed, he made the comment to Ms. Fowler over the phone. He also stated the car's license number and description. Can Grimm's remark qualify as a present sense impression? *See Commonwealth v. Coleman*, 458 Pa. 112, 326 A.2d 387, 389–91 (1974). What would be the result under Federal Rule of Evidence 803(1)? *Miller v. Crown Amusements, Inc.*, 821 F. Supp. 703 (S.D. Ga. 1993) (911 call).

3. Problem 20–8. Suppose that Mr. Hill also sues Roe for the damage his car sustained in the collision. At trial, he is attempting to prove the extent of his property damage. He testifies that he took the car to a local mechanic. Mr. Hill stood by while the mechanic inspected the car. Immediately after the inspection, the mechanic told Mr. Hill that it would cost $3,325 to repair the damage. Roe's attorney objects that the mechanic's statement is inadmissible hearsay. What ruling? Does Rule 803(1) apply to opinionated statements? *See Mekuc v. American Honda Motor Co.*, 835 F.2d 389, 392 (1st Cir. 1987). Would it make a difference if the mechanic reduced the statement to writing and handed it to Roe? Is Rule 803(1) limited to verbal statements? *Phoenix Mut. Life Ins. Co. v. Adams*, 828 F Supp. 379, 389 (D.S.C. 1993), *aff'd*, 30 F.3d 554 (4th Cir. 1994).

3. DECLARATIONS OF BODILY CONDITION

The next two exceptions also derive from the res gestae theory, but they differ from excited utterances and present sense impression statements. Unlike the former (which relate to external reality), these next two exceptions, declarations of bodily and mental condition, relate to an internal reality, a sensation or state of mind that the declarant experiences.

Once again, in deciding whether to admit evidence under a hearsay exception, the basic policy question is whether we need personal cross–examination in the courtroom to assess the declarant's testimonial qualities of perception, memory, narration, and sincerity. In the case of statements of bodily condition, especially present condition, there is rarely any doubt about perception, memory, or narration. The declarant is usually in the best possible position to "perceive" whether she is experiencing pain. When the declaration relates to present bodily condition, there is no serious question about the quality of memory. Moreover, the concepts of physical conditions such as pain are so elementary that there is little concern about the declarant's narrative ability.

However, there can be grave doubts about the declarant's testimonial quality of sincerity. More often than not, this exception is invoked in personal injury litigation; and the plaintiff injured party had already begun a personal injury lawsuit or could at least foresee filing an action. There is a present or potential temptation to lie. Evidence law deals with this danger by limiting the admission of these declarations to circumstances in which the risk of insincerity is the lowest. To identify those circumstances, the courts carefully scrutinize two related factors: (1) the purpose for which the declarant made the statement; and (2) the declarant's addressee. We shall analyze several types of statements in terms of these two factors: declarations of present bodily condition, statements of past bodily condition, and assertions about the cause of the bodily condition.

a. Declarations of Present Bodily Condition

Common sense indicates that our concerns about perception, memory, and narration are relatively insubstantial when the declarant purports to describe a physical condition he is then experiencing. For that reason, the common law courts early fashioned a hearsay exception for such declarations. *Aveson v. Kinnaird*, 6 East 188, 102 Eng. Rep. 1258 (K.B. 1805); *Claspermeyer v. Florsheim Shoe Store Co.*, 313 S.W.2d 198 (Mo. Ct. App. 1958). The Federal Rules of Evidence codify the exception in Rule 803(3):

> The following are not excluded by the hearsay rule, even though the declarant is available as a witness:
>
> (3) Then existing . . . physical condition. A statement of the declarant's then existing . . . sensation or physical condition (such as . . . pain and bodily health). . .

However, at some point, the risk of uncertainty can become intolerably high. Suppose that in the *Hill* case, the plaintiff submitted to a physical examination by a physician whom her attorney hired solely for the purpose of testifying at trial. The purpose of this examination prompts much more serious doubts about the declarant's sincerity. In this situation, at common law many courts drew the line and refused to admit the declaration as substantive evidence. *United States v. Calvey*, 110 F.2d 327 (3d Cir. 1940); *United States v. Roberts*, 62 F.2d 594 (10th Cir. 1932). At least until recently, this attitude has been the prevailing view in the United States.

NOTES AND PROBLEMS

1. Problem 20–9. In *Hill*, two weeks after the collision the plaintiff suffered a spontaneous miscarriage. There was so little tissue that the pathologist could not determine the age of the fetus. Ms. Hill claims that she was pregnant before the accident and that the accident caused the miscarriage. At trial, she calls Ms. Windsong, a neighbor. Ms. Windsong is prepared to testify that one week before the accident Ms. Hill told her that she felt pregnant. Roe objects on the ground that the testimony is inadmissible hearsay. What ruling? *See People v. Wright*, 167 Cal. 1, 8, 138 P. 349, 352 (1914). Note that by its terms, Rule 803(3) refers to "sensation, or physical condition" in the alternative.

2. Problem 20–10. Ms. Hill calls Dr. Nordstrom as a witness. Nordstrom is prepared to testify that during a physical examination one month after the accident Ms. Hill said she was still experiencing "excruciating pain." Before the judge allows Nordstrom to give this testimony, Roe takes Nordstrom on *voir dire* examination:

> Q: Doctor, isn't it true that you did not prescribe any pain–killing drugs for Ms. Hill?
>
> A: Yes.
>
> Q: Or any medication at all for that matter?
>
> A: Yes.
>
> Q: Did you order her to take physical therapy at any local hospital?
>
> A: No.
>
> Q: Did you require her to do physical therapy at your office?
>
> A: No. I suggested some exercises to her when she asked, but I didn't order her.
>
> Q: Your Honor, I renew my objection on the ground that the plaintiff consulted this witness solely for trial preparation.

Morena subscribes to the majority, common law view that statements made to physicians consulted only for testimony fall outside the hearsay exception. What ruling?

b. Past Bodily Condition

Statements of the patient's past symptoms are usually styled "case history." Traditionally most courts balked at introducing these statements as substantive proof. *Martin v. P. H. Hanes Knitting Co.*, 189 N.C. 644, 127 S.E. 688 (1925); Younger, *Statements of Past Physical Condition as an Exception to the Rule Against Hearsay*, 19 N.Y.L.F. 777 (1974). The courts' reluctance to admit these statements is understandable. The risks of misrecollection and insincerity are higher here; the declarant is no longer speaking about a condition she is then experiencing, and the addressee cannot immediately doublecheck the declarant's claimed symptoms.

However, in limited circumstances, some courts carved out a common law exception to the general rule of exclusion. One of the landmark cases in this line of authority is the following opinion.

MEANEY v. UNITED STATES

112 F.2d 538 (2d Cir. 1940)

L. HAND, CIRCUIT JUDGE.

This is an appeal from a judgment, entered upon the verdict of a jury, dismissing a petition in an action to recover upon a policy of war risk insurance. The insured was mustered out on December 31, 1918, and the policy lapsed on January 30, 1919; he died of pulmonary tuberculosis on July 6, 1922, and the question was whether he was permanently and totally disabled when the policy lapsed. He had consulted one physician at some time, not definitely fixed in 1919, and another in December 1920, who found that he had contracted tuberculosis, and that it was already "moderately advanced." By April of 1921 the disease had so far developed that he had to go to a sanatorium, where he stayed till January 1922, only six months before his death. The only error we need consider was a ruling, made during the examination of the physician who had first examined him in December, 1920. This witness said that he had taken care of the insured both at that time and after he came back from the sanatorium; and he was allowed to testify as to what he found on his several examinations, but the judge refused to let him say what the insured had told him of the "history of the case."

The insured's declarations seem to have been offered as a narrative of his condition; so far as appears they were no part of the basis of the physician's opinion as to his condition; at least they were not offered as such. They were therefore hearsay, and moreover, they did not fall within the generally accepted exception in favor of spontaneous expressions of pain. It is quite true that this exception includes narrative statements as well as mere ejaculations, and that it has been extended to a declaration of present symptoms told by a patient to a physician. The utterances of a patient in the course of his examination, so far as they are spontaneous, may be merely ejaculatory–as when he emits a cry upon palpation–or they may be truly narrative; and it will often be impossible to distinguish rationally between the two; between an inarticulate cry, for example, and a statement such as: "That hurts." The warrant for the admission of both is the same: the lack of opportunity or motive for fabrication upon an unexpected occasion to which the declarant responds immediately, and without reflection. But most of what he tells will not ordinarily be of this kind at all; there may be, and there is in fact, good reason to receive it, but it is a very different reason. A man goes to his physician expecting to recount all that he feels, and often he has with some care searched his consciousness to be sure that he will leave out nothing. If his narrative of present symptoms is to be received as evidence of the facts, as distinguished from mere support for the physician's opinion, these parts of it can only rest upon his motive to disclose the truth because his treatment will in part depend upon what he says. That justification is not necessary in the case of his spontaneous declarations; but it is necessary for those we are now considering.

The same reasoning applies with exactly the same force to a narrative of past symptoms, and so the Supreme Court of Massachusetts, declared obiter in *Roosa v. Boston Loan Co.*, 132 Mass. 439. A patient has an equal motive to speak the truth; what he has felt in the past is as apt to be important in his treatment as what he feels at the moment. Thus, in spite of the dicta in *Northern Pacific R. E. v. Urlin, supra* (158 U.S. 271) and *Boston & Albany R. R. v. O'Reilly, supra* (158 U.S. 334) that only declarations of present symptoms are competent, several federal courts have seemed not to take the distinction between declarations of present and past symptoms, provided the patient is consulting the physician for treatment, and Professor Wigmore appears to assent. Wigmore, § 1722. It is true that this body of authority is not impressive as such, but it appears to us that if there is to be any consistency in doctrine, either declarations of all symptoms, present or past, should be competent, or only those which fall within the exception for spontaneous utterances. Nobody would choose the second, particularly as the substance of the declarations can usually be got before the jury as parts of the basis on which the physician's opinion was formed. It is indeed always possible that a patient may not really consult his physician for treatment; the consultation may be colorable. The judge has power to prevent an abuse in such cases, and here as elsewhere, when the competency of evidence depends upon a question of fact, his conclusion is final. He must decide before admitting the declarations whether the patient was consulting the physician for treatment and for that alone. Unless he is so satisfied, he must exclude them, though it is true that if he admits them, the defendant may still argue that they are untrustworthy. They will be evidence, but in estimating their truth the jury may have to decide for themselves the very issue on which the judge himself passed before he admitted them; the competency of evidence is always independent of its weight.

We hold that the insured's "history of the case" as narrated to the physician was competent and that its exclusion was error.

Judgment reversed; new trial ordered.

In the case of declarations of present bodily condition, the addressee and the purpose of the statement can have a negative effect. Although such declarations are ordinarily admissible, statements made to a physician consulted solely for purposes of litigation are often excluded. In this situation, the same factors–the addressee and the purpose of the statement–cut differently and have an affirmative impact. Even after *Meaney* most courts excluded statements of past bodily condition, but some courts admitted the statements when made to a physician for purposes of treatment. Like Judge Hand, these courts reasoned that when the declarant knows that his description of past symptoms will affect his treatment, his realization is a strong motive for sincerity. The patient realizes that "otherwise, [he] may mislead the physician, with disastrous results" to the patient's own health. *Mackey v. Greenview Hosp.*, 587 S.W.2d 249, 254 (Ky. Ct. App. 1979). The motive largely removes the doubts we typically entertain about the declarant's sincerity. The "patient's self–interest in promoting the cure of his own medical ailments guarantees" the truthfulness of the declaration. *Gong v. Hirsch*, 913 F.2d 1269, 1273 (7th Cir. 1990).

This reasoning underlies Federal Rule of Evidence 803(4):

> The following are not excluded by the hearsay rule, even though the declarant is available as a witness:
>
> (4) Statements for purposes of medical diagnosis or treatment. Statements made for purposes of medical diagnosis or treatment and describing medical history, or past or present symptoms, pain, or sensations, or the inception or general character of the cause or external source thereof insofar as reasonably pertinent to diagnosis or treatment.

PROBLEMS

1. Problem 20–11. In *Hill*, the plaintiff rode in an ambulance to the hospital immediately after the collision. Just before the end of the ride, she had a brief conversation with the ambulance attendant, Mr. Sullivan. Sullivan asked her to "tell [him] about the accident, so that I get the info to the docs just as soon as we get to the hospital." In response, Ms. Hill told Sullivan that immediately after the collision, she experienced a sharp pain in her abdomen. An abdominal injury is one of the elements of damage she now claims at trial. When Ms. Hill attempts to elicit Sullivan's testimony about her statement, Roe cites *Meaney* as authority that to qualify as a hearsay exception, the statement "must be made directly, personally to a licensed physician." Does *Meaney* support Roe's argument? Would the argument be tenable under Federal Rule of Evidence 803(4)? In their Note to the Rule, the Advisory Committee commented that "[s]tatements to hospital attendants, ambulance drivers, or even members of the family might be included." *See* Annot., 55 A.L.R. Fed. 689, 695 (1981).

2. Problem 20–12. Would the result in Problem 20–11 be the same if Sullivan had *not* said, "so that I can get the info to the docs . . . ."? Under *Meaney?* Under Federal Rule 803(4)?

3. Problem 20–13. After Ms. Hill arrives at the hospital and receives treatment, she hires an attorney and the attorney immediately employs a physician, Dr. Stewart, to visit Ms. Hill in the hospital. The attorney tells Dr. Stewart, "I want you to examine her thoroughly with a view to testifying at trial." Ms. Hill tells Dr. Stewart about the abdominal pain she described to the ambulance attendant. At trial, Ms. Hill calls Dr. Stewart to testify about her statement. Roe cites *Meaney* for the proposition that the hearsay exception applies only if the patient consulted physicians for treatment. What is the significance of "diagnosis or" in Rule 803(4)? *United States v. Iron Shell*, 633 F.2d 77, 82–85 (8th Cir. 1980), *cert. denied*, 450 U.S. 1001 (1981).

c. Statements Describing the Cause of the Declarant's Physical Condition

While the physician is initially questioning the patient, the physician usually inquires about the cause of the condition as well as the condition's existence. Determining the cause is often the key in diagnosing and prescribing treatment. However, the orthodox view is that the declarant's description of the cause is inadmissible hearsay. Even if the jurisdiction admits case history statements, the courts may exclude statements about causation. *Pinter v. Parsekian*, 92 N.J. Super. 392, 223 A.2d 635 (1966); Theis, *The Doctor as Witness: Statements for Purposes of Medical Diagnosis or Treatment*, 10 Loy. U. Chi. L.J. 363, 369 (1979).

The courts' exclusion of these statements is at least defensible. These statements pose numerous probative dangers. First, the quality of the perception is suspect. The declarant is no longer speaking about an internal reality such as pain; the reference to cause is usually an allusion to an external event such as the collision in *Hill*, and we may have neither the spontaneity demanded by Rule 803(2) nor the contemporaneity required by Rule 803(1). If the reference is to a past event, there is also a concern about the exactitude of the declarant's memory. There is similarly doubt about the declarant's narrative ability. When the declarant said that the event "caused" his injuries, did he mean factual cause in the tort sense, or did his words carry the common law connotation of fault? Finally, if litigation was foreseeable, we would like to question the declarant about his sincerity. For all these reasons, until recently the courts have steadfastly adhered to the view excluding statements about causation. *Hassell v. State*, 607 S.W.2d 529 (Tex. Crim. App. 1980); *Illinois Cent. R.R. v. Sutton*, 42 Ill. 438 (1867).

However, the drafters of Federal Rule of Evidence 803(4) thought otherwise. Note the textual reference to "the inception or general character of the cause or external source." Their reasoning is similar to the reasoning supporting the extension of the hearsay exception to case history declarations; if the patient realizes that the physician wants the information, the patient's realization is a sufficient motive for sincerity.

NOTES AND PROBLEMS

1. Do you agree with the Advisory Committee that the inference of sincerity outweighs the need to cross–examine the declarant about perception, memory, and narration? Remember that statements about causation raise concerns about perception and narration that are absent from case history statements. In *White v. Illinois*, 502 U.S. 346 (1992), writing for the majority, Chief Justice Rehnquist declared: "a statement made in the course of procuring medical services, where the declarant knows that a false statement may cause misdiagnosis or mistreatment, carries special guarantees of credibility that a trier of fact may not think replicated by courtroom testimony." In footnote 8 of his opinion, the Chief Justice remarked that the exception is "widely accepted among the States." *White* involved statements by a very young child to a doctor and an emergency room nurse. Many courts have invoked this exception to justify the introduction of the alleged victim's statements in child abuse prosecutions. Mosteller, *Child Sexual Abuse Statements for the Purpose of Medical Diagnosis or Treatment*, 67 N.C.L.Rev. 257 (1989). Several courts have gone to the length of admitting the child's statement identifying the assailant when the assailant's identity was diagnostically relevant. *United States v. George*, 960 F.2d 97, 99–100 (9th Cir. 1992) ("the exact nature and extent of " the victim's psychological injuries "often depend on the identity of the abuser"). When the alleged abuser is a member of the victim's household, the assailant's identity is relevant at least in the sense that the requisite treatment might include the child's removal from that household. In *State v. Moen*, 309 Or. 45, 786 P.2d 111 (1990), the court extended the same exception to a statement by an adult victim. The defendant was charged with murder. Before her death, the victim consulted a physician for depression and despondency. The victim told the physician that she feared that the defendant would kill her. The court admitted the statement under that state's version of Rule 803(4).

2. Does Rule 803(4) adequately ensure the statement's sincerity? Revisit the last three words in the statute. What is the significance of the expression, "diagnosis or"?

3. Problem 20–14. When Ms. Hill arrived at the emergency room, she was treated by Dr. Farnsworth. Farnsworth told her, "I can see that you have some first–degree burns on your left foot, Ms. Hill. I'm going to apply some salve immediately." Ms. Hill responded, "Please do it as fast as you can. It hurts like hell. The gas tank exploded, and there were flames everywhere." Would Ms. Hill's reference to the explosion fall within Rule 803(4)? Does it satisfy the last eight words of the statute?

4. Problem 20–15. In addition to her statement in Problem 20–14, Ms. Hill told Dr. Farnsworth, "That idiot driver was going so fast that I never had a chance to avoid the accident. He was going way too fast." What additional difficulties does this statement present under Rule 803(4)? *United States v. Narciso*, 446 F. Supp. 252, 284–85, 288–89 (E.D. Mich. 1977).

4.   DECLARATIONS OF STATE OF MIND

To begin with, an utterance evidencing state of mind may not be hearsay; the utterance might be an exclamation falling outside the scope of Rule 801(a). If the utterance is hearsay it may fall within the next doctrine, the exception admitting declarations of state of mind, which is also an offshoot of the res gestae theory. *Trostle v. State*, 588 S.W.2d 925, 930 (Tex. Crim. App. 1980). Like the last exception, this doctrine admits assertions about internal realities such as the declarant's thoughts and emotions. The case for admitting these assertions appears at least as strong as the case for allowing statements about bodily condition. When the declarant purports to describe his present state of mind, we have few doubts about the declarant's perception, memory, or narration. It is true that there may be grounds to suspect the declarant's sincerity. However, in this setting, the suspicions probably carry even less weight than they do when they relate to the sincerity of a statement about bodily condition. There is a greater need to admit statements of mental condition because we have more limited means of corroborating the existence of the conditions than we do physical sensations. A physician may be able to determine whether the patient has the physical symptoms to account for the pain the patient claims to be experiencing, but the psychiatrist has less reliable means of testing the genuineness of a claim of depression. The greater need for the evidence generally justifies running the risk of the declarant's insincerity.

As in the case of statements of bodily condition, the courts differentiate among several uses of statements of mental condition. The probative danger—and consequently the hearsay analysis—varies depending on the type of assertion and its use. We shall now consider the four major situations the courts have encountered.

a.   Declarations of Present State of Mind Used to Prove State of Mind

There is virtually unanimous agreement that if the declarant's state of mind is logically relevant, the declarant's assertion of her then existing state of mind is admissible. *United States v. Dellinger*, 472 F.2d 340 (7th Cir. 1972), *cert. denied*, 410 U.S. 970 (1973). The courts recognized the admissibility of such statements at common law, and many legislatures have sanctioned the admissibility. In the words of California Evidence Code § 1250(a)(1), an assertion of present state of mind is admissible when state of mind is "itself an issue." Federal Rule of Evidence 803(3) sets out the federal version of the doctrine:

> The following are not excluded by the hearsay rule, even though the declarant is available as a witness.
>
> (3) Then existing mental, emotional, or physical condition. A statement of the declarant's then existing state of mind, [or] emotion (such as intent, plan, motive, design, mental feeling . . .), but not including a statement of memory or belief to prove the fact remembered or believed unless it relates to the execution, revocation, identification, or terms of declarant's will.

In this situation, there is little need for an opportunity for cross-examination at trial. The declarant is speaking about present state of mind, removing any doubt about perception or memory. Further, if the declarant is referring to a simple concept such as joy or depression, there is rarely any reason to suspect the declarant's narrative ability. Further, since the declarant is referring to present state of mind, the hearer has at least one check on the declarant's sincerity; the hearer can determine whether the declarant's nonverbal conduct matches the asserted state of mind. If the declarant professes depression while striking a broad smile and the hearer subsequently becomes a witness, questioning the witness about the declarant's behavior will sufficiently impeach the profession of depression.

Given this reasoning, most courts admit declarations of present state of mind if declarant's state of mind is relevant under the substantive law. For example, in *Hill*, one of the issues conditioning Roe's liability is whether Worker was driving in the scope of employment at the time of the accident. Under substantive agency law, in deciding whether Worker was acting within the course of employment, the court can consider the factor of Worker's subjective intention: At the time of the collision, was Worker engaged in conduct subjectively intended to further Roe's business? W. SEAVEY, HANDBOOK OF THE LAW OF AGENCY 150 (1964). Suppose that a few blocks before reaching the scene of the collision, Mr. Worker picked up a hitchhiker, Ms. Randall. A few moments before the collision, Worker told Randall, "I've really got to move it out. See that package in the back seat? Orders from the boss–I've got to get that package 'cross town within the next hour or else." Worker makes the statement almost simultaneously with the collision, and Ms. Hill would have little difficulty persuading the trial judge to admit the statement to prove Worker's intention at the time of the accident.

NOTES AND PROBLEMS

1. Problem 20–16. Suppose that Worker picked up Ms. Randall an hour before the time of the collision. He makes the statement to her that he made in the original hypothetical. Does the timing of the statement preclude its admission? How does Federal Rule of Evidence 401 figure into your analysis of this problem? See the discussion of the concept of continuity of state of mind in 2 C. McCormick, Handbook of the Law of Evidence § 274, at 219–20 (5th ed. 1999).

2. Problem 20–17. An hour after the accident, Worker is speaking with Ms. Randall. He says, "I'm in such trouble. The boss is going to kill me for getting involved in that terrible accident, and he's also going to jump all over me because of the package. Remember that package on the back seat? I've still got to get that to the print shop before the close of business today, or I'll be in big time trouble with my boss." Ms. Hill calls Randall to testify to Worker's statement, but Roe objects that the statement is inadmissible "because it came after the collision." *See Casey v. Casey*, 97 Cal. App. 2d 875, 878–82, 218 P.2d 842, 845–47 (1950).

3. In applying the concept of continuity of state of mind, what factors should you consider in addition to the time lapse? Suppose that the police questioned Worker before he had his conversation with Ms. Randall in Problem 20–17. Would it make a difference if the police officer suggested to Worker that Roe's insurance policy would cover the accident only if Worker were driving in the scope of employment? What role would Federal Rule of Evidence 403 play in the analysis? *See Colasanto v. Life Ins. Co. of North America*, 100 F.3d 203, 212–13 (1st Cir. 1996) (there was an intervening, bitter fight between the event and the letter describing the event).

b.   Declarations of Present State of Mind Used to Prove Subsequent Conduct

A declaration of present state of mind can give rise to more than one inference. As we have seen, under the substantive law our focus may be on the declarant's state of mind at the time. If so, we can use the declaration to establish that state of mind. However, if the asserted state of mind is a plan or intention to engage in future conduct, we can also use the assertion as some evidence that the declarant later carried out the plan or intention. Under Federal Rule of Evidence 401, the asserted intention is logically relevant for that purpose; the fact that a person plans to perform an act slightly increases the likelihood that she subsequently performed the act. Notice that Federal Rule of Evidence 803(3) expressly refers to "[a] statement of the declarant's then existing state of mind . . . such as intent [and] plan . . . ." The California Evidence Code is even more explicit; section 1250(a)(2) announces that an assertion of plan is admissible as evidence to "prove or explain [the subsequent] acts or conduct of the declarant." Whether we are attempting to prove state of mind or subsequent conduct, we invoke the same hearsay exception. In both situations, the immediate inference from the declaration is the existence of the state of mind. The difference is that in the instant case, we draw a further inference as to conduct.

The permissibility of the inference was apparent to the courts at common law. It became well–settled early that statements of present intention can be used as circumstantial proof of subsequent conduct. One of the leading cases in this line of authority is a famous decision by the Supreme Court.

MUTUAL LIFE INSURANCE CO. v. HILLMON

145 U.S. 285 (1892)

JUSTICE GRAY delivered the opinion of the Court.

[Actions by Sallie E. Hillmon to recover on policies of insurance on life of her husband, John W. Hillmon. The question involved was the identity of the deceased. Walters had disappeared, and strong evidence had been introduced showing that the body alleged to have been Hillmon's was in fact the body of Walters and that he had been killed by Hillmon with a view of enabling his wife to recover upon the policies that had been recently issued. To show the probability that the body alleged to be Hillmon's was Walters's, letters were introduced from Walters to his sister and sweetheart, which expressed the intention of leaving Wichita with Hillmon for a trip to "Colorado or parts unknown." After pointing out a procedural error which required reversal, the opinion continues:]

There is, however, one question of evidence so important and so likely to arise upon another trial, that it is proper to express an opinion upon it.

This question is of the admissibility of the letters written by Walters on the first days of March, 1879, which were offered in evidence by the defendants, and excluded by the court. In order to determine the competency of these letters, it is important to consider the state of the case when they were offered to be read.

The matter chiefly contested at the trial was the death of John W. Hillmon, the insured; and that depended upon the question whether the body found at Crooked Creek on the night of March 18, 1879, was his body, or the body of Walters.

Much conflicting evidence had been introduced as to the identity of the body. The plaintiff had also introduced evidence that Hillmon and one Brown left Wichita in Kansas on or about March 5, 1879, and traveled together through Southern Kansas in search of a site for a cattle ranch, and that on the night of March 18 while they were in camp at Crooked Creek, Hillmon was accidentally killed, and that his body was taken thence and buried. The defendants had introduced evidence, without objection, that Walters left his home and his betrothed in Iowa in March, 1878, and was afterwards in Kansas until March, 1879; that during that time he corresponded regularly with his family and his betrothed; that the letters received from him were one received by his betrothed on March 3, and postmarked at Wichita March 2, and one received by his sister about March 4 or 5, and dated at Wichita a day or two before; and that he had not been heard from since.

The evidence that Walters was at Wichita on or before March 5, and had not been heard from since, together with the evidence to identify as his the body found at Crooked Creek on March 18, tended to show that he went from Wichita to Crooked Creek between those dates. Evidence that just before March 5 he had the intention of leaving Wichita with Hillmon would tend to corroborate the evidence already admitted, and to show that he went from Wichita to Crooked Creek with Hillmon. Letters from him to his family and his betrothed were the natural, if not the only attainable evidence of his intention.

The letters should have been admitted. A man's state of mind or feeling can only be manifested to others by countenance, attitude or gesture, or by sounds or words, spoken or written. The nature of the fact to be proved is the same, and evidence of its proper tokens is equally competent to prove it, whether expressed by aspect or conduct, by voice or pen. When the intention to be proved is important only as qualifying an act, its connection with that act must be shown, in order to warrant the admission of declarations of the intention. But whenever the intention is of itself a distinct and material fact in a chain of circumstances, it may be proved by contemporaneous oral or written declarations of the party.

The existence of a particular intention in a certain person at a certain time being a material fact to be proved, evidence that he expressed that intention at that time is as direct evidence of the fact, as his own testimony that he then had that intention would be. After his death, there can hardly be any other way of proving it; and while he is still alive, his own memory of his state of mind at a former time is no more likely to be clear and true than a bystander's recollection of what he then said, and is less trustworthy than letters written by him at the very time and under circumstances precluding a suspicion of misrepresentation.

The letters in question were competent, not as narratives of facts communicated to the writer by another, nor yet as proof that he actually went away from Wichita, but as evidence that, shortly before the time when other evidence tended to show that he went away he had the intention of going, and of going with Hillmon, which made it more probable both that he did go and that he went with Hillmon, than if there had been no proof of such intention. In view of the mass of conflicting testimony introduced upon the question whether it was the body of Walters that was found in Hillmon's camp, this evidence might properly influence the jury in determining that question.

The rule applicable to this case has been thus stated by this court: "Wherever the bodily or mental feelings of an individual are material to be proved, the usual expressions of such feelings are original and competent evidence. Those expressions are the natural reflexes of what it might be impossible to show by other testimony, this may be necessary to set the facts thus developed in their true light, and to give them their proper effect. As independent, explanatory or corroborative evidence, it is often indispensable to the due administration of justice. Such declarations are regarded as verbal acts, and are as competent as any other testimony, when relevant to the issue. Their truth or falsity is an inquiry for the jury." *Ins. Co. v. Mosley*, 75 U.S. 8 Wall 397, 404, 405.

In accordance with this rule, a bankrupt's declarations, at or before the time of leaving or staying away from home, as to his reason for going abroad, have always been held by the English courts to be competent, in an action by his assignees against a creditor, as evidence that his departure was with intent to defraud his creditors, and therefore an act of bankruptcy. *Bateman v. Bailey*, 5 TR 512.

Upon an indictment of one Hunter for the murder of one Armstrong at Camden, the Court of Errors and Appeals of New Jersey unanimously held that Armstrong's oral declarations to his son at Philadelphia, on the afternoon before the night of the murder, as well as a letter written by him at the same time and place to his wife, each stating that he was going with Hunter to Camden on business, were rightly admitted in evidence. Chief Justice Beasley said: "In the ordinary course of things, it was the usual information that a man about leaving home would communicate, for the convenience of his family, the information of his friends, or the regulation of his business. At the time it was given, such declarations could, in the nature of things, mean harm to no one, he who uttered them was bent on no expedition of mischief or wrong, and the attitude of affairs at the time entirely explodes the idea that such utterances were intended to serve any purpose but that of which they were obviously designed. If it be said that such notice of an intention of leaving home could have been given without introducing it in the name of Mr. Hunter, the obvious answer to the suggestion, I think, is that a reference to the companion who is to accompany the person leaving is as natural a part of the transaction as is any other incident or quality of it. If it is legitimate to show by a man's own declarations that he left his home to be gone a week, or for a certain destination, which seems incontestible, why may it not be proved in the same way that a designated person was to bear him company? At the time the words were uttered or written, they imported no wrong doing to any one, and the reference to the companion who was to go with him was nothing more, as matters then stood, than an indication of an additional circumstance of his going. If it was in the ordinary train of events for this man to leave word or to state where he was going, it seems to me it was equally so for him to say with whom he was going." *Hunter v. State,* 40 N.J.L. 495, 534, 536–538.

Upon principle and authority, therefore, we are of opinion that the two letters were competent evidence of the intention of Walters at the time of writing them, which was a material fact bearing upon the question in controversy; and that for the exclusion of these letters, as well as for the undue restriction of the defendants' challenges, the verdicts must be set aside, and a new trial had.

Judgment reversed, and case remanded to the Circuit Court, with directions to set aside the verdict and to order a new trial.

At first blush, *Hillmon* seems innocuous enough. We are interested in the declarant's subsequent conduct, he had earlier professed an intention to engage in the conduct, and the profession certainly passes logical relevance muster under Rule 401. *People v. Alcalde*, 24 Cal. 2d 177, 148 P.2d 627 (1944). But note the Court's statement that the letters were admissible evidence both that he did go and that he went with Hillmon. The language suggests that the insurer could use Walters' declaration as evidence of the conduct of both Walters and Hillmon.

That suggestion has triggered a burning controversy. In one commentary on *Hillmon,* Professor Maguire condemned the suggestion:

> Even if Walters was planning to travel with Hillmon, how would we prove that Hillmon was willing to and did accept him as a companion? By Walters' hearsay declaration? Hardly, unless we drill a new and unusually deep hole in the hearsay rule. It is not customary to accept one man's extra–judicial assertions as evidence of another's mental state.

Maguire, *The Hillmon Case–Thirty–Three Years After*, 38 Harv. L. Rev. 709, 717 (1925). In his dissent in *People v. Alcalde*, 24 Cal. 2d 177, 148 P.2d 627 (1944), Justice Traynor echoed Professor Maguire's view. Justice Traynor argued that "[a] declaration as to what one person intended to do, however, cannot safely be accepted as evidence of what another probably did." *Id.* at 189–90, 148 P.2d at 633. When one person on the stand attempts to testify directly to another person's state of mind, in the view of many judges the testimony is objectionable as improper lay speculation (Rule 701) and lacking in personal knowledge. Fed.R.Evid. 602.

Unfortunately, the adoption of the Federal Rules of Evidence has not laid this controversy to rest. As in the case of the dispute over the existence of a corroboration requirement under Rule 803(1), the root of the problem is ambiguous legislative history material. In *United States v. Phaester*, 544 F.2d 353 (9th Cir. 1976), *cert. denied* sub nom. *Incisco v. United States*, 429 U.S. 1099 (1977), the court stated that Justice Traynor's position "is definitely the minority view, stated primarily in dicta and dissent." *Id.* at 380 n.18. According to the court, most jurisdictions interpret *Hillmon* as permitting the use of the declarant's statement as proof of the third party's subsequent conduct. The court points out that, in its note to Rule 803(3), the Advisory Committee asserted that "[t]he rule of . . . *Hillmon* . . . is . . . left undisturbed." *Id.* at 379. The court construed the note as approving "the prevailing common law position" that *Hillmon* allows the statement to be used to prove the third party's conduct as well as the conduct of the declarant. *Id.* at 379–80. However, the court conceded that the report of the House Committee on the Judiciary takes a "significantly different" approach to *Hillmon. Id.* at 380. That report states:

> [T]he Committee intends that the Rule be construed to limit the doctrine of . . . *Hillmon* . . . so as to render statements of intent

by a declarant admissible only to prove his future conduct, not the future conduct of another person. H.R. REP. No. 93–650.

Id. at 379.

NOTES AND PROBLEMS

1. How would you resolve the seeming conflict between the Advisory Committee Note and the House Report? The House Committee is an agency of Congress. However, the Advisory Committee Notes were widely circulated with the text of the proposed rules. Jurists such as Justice Scalia and Judge Easterbrook have questioned the assumption that most legislators take the time to familiarize themselves with the contents of committee reports. Paradoxically, is the Note better evidence of congressional intent than the Report?

The House Report specifically addresses the question of the propriety of using the declarant's statement to prove the third party's subsequent conduct. Is the Advisory Committee Note as explicit?

2. As a matter of evidentiary policy, which view do you prefer? Was Walters' plan absolutely irrelevant to prove Hillmon's conduct and, therefore, inadmissible under Rule 401? Or when Justice Traynor remarked that Walters' declaration "cannot safely be treated as evidence" of Hillmon's conduct, was he voicing another concern? Is the inference directly from Walters' declaration to Hillmon's conduct, or is there an implicit, intermediate inference about Hillmon's state of mind and intention? If Walters mounted the witness stand, would we allow him to opine about Hillmon's state of mind? If so, under what circumstances? Reread Federal Rule 701. In the past, the courts have focused on the hearsay issue, but perhaps the decisive doctrine is the lay opinion rule.

3. Suppose that the jurisdiction in question subscribes to Justice Traynor's view that the declarant's avowed plan is admissible only for the limited purpose of proving the declarant's subsequent conduct. If you were the trial judge, what kind of limiting instruction would you give the jury about the testimony describing the declarant's statement? During closing argument, what could the proponent of the testimony say about the declarant's statement?

4. Problem 20–18. In *Devitt*, the prosecutor calls Mr. Sharman, who testifies that he knows the defendant; he had a conversation with the defendant a few days before the alleged battery, and the defendant told him that "I'm working for a guy named Paterson. He's been bugging me and whining about every little slip–up I make. The next time he gives me some lip, I'm just gonna slug the jerk." The defense counsel objects that the statement is "clearly inadmissible hearsay and too vague as well." What ruling? *United States v. Curtis*, 568 F.2d 643, 645–46 (9th Cir. 1978). Does the prosecutor have to resort to the admission exemption?

c. Declarations of Present Memory to Prove Past, Remembered Events

Federal Rule of Evidence 803(3) excludes "statement[s] of memory or belief to prove the fact remembered or believed unless it relates to the execution, revocation, identification, or terms of the declarant's will." This part of the Rule also codifies the prevailing common law view. *Welch v. Texas Employers' Ins. Ass'n,* 636 S.W.2d 450 (Tex. Civ. App. 1982). That view bans statements of memory to prove the remembered fact for two reasons.

First, the use of such statements as evidence of prior, remembered facts raises a grave concern about the testimonial quality of memory. Suppose that in *Hill,* the police found an eyewitness, Mr. Bellows, the day after the collision. At that time Mr. Bellows stated that "I distinctly remember that the guy driving the other vehicle wasn't looking at the road ahead. When he passed me, he seemed to be looking at something in a store window to the side." Bellows' statement is a declaration of present state of mind in the sense of present memory. However, if we use the statement as evidence of the remembered fact, the statement's evidentiary value obviously depends upon the accuracy of Bellows' memory. Absent an opportunity to cross–examine Bellows and test the quality of Bellows' memory, we cannot be assured of the statement's reliability. *United States v. Mandel,* 437 F. Supp. 262 (D. Md. 1977).

The second reason for barring this use of declarations of memory is well–stated in the Assembly Committee's Comment to California Evidence Code § 1250(b), setting out the same limitation included in Rule 803(3):

> This limitation is necessary to preserve the hearsay rule. Any statement of a past event is, of course, a statement of the declarant's then existing state of mind–memory or belief–concerning the past event. If the evidence of that . . . memory . . . were admissible to show that the fact remembered or believed actually occurred, any statement narrating a past event would be, by a process of circuitous reasoning, admissible to prove that the event occurred.

These two reasons account for the general norm that statements of memory are inadmissible as proof of the recollected events and facts. M. LADD & R. CARLSON, CASES AND MATERIALS ON EVIDENCE 943–44 (1972). However, in one situation, the courts have deviated from the norm. A famous English precedent, *Sugden v. St. Leonards,* 1 Prob. Div. 154 (1876), admitted a testator's declarations made before and after a will's execution to prove the contents of the lost will. Some American jurisdictions have rejected *Sugden* (*see, e.g., In re Will of Bonner,* 17 N.Y.2d 9, 266 N.Y.S.2d 971, 214 N.E.2d 154 (1966)), while others admit the testator's declarations only when there is independent evidence raising a presumption of the revocation of the will. *Payne v. Payne,* 229 Ga. 822, 194 S.E.2d 458 (1972). However, at common law perhaps a numerical majority of American jurisdictions follow *Sugden* on the ground that there is a special need for the testator's declarations. *Lewis v. Lewis*, 241 Miss. 83, 129 So. 2d 353 (1961). It is normally difficult to prove a person's state of mind; and the proponent usually resorts to this hearsay exception when the declarant, the testator or testatrix, is already deceased. The declarant's death creates an especially compelling justification for resorting to hearsay evidence. There may be doubts about the declarant's memory and sincerity, but most jurisdictions have concluded that the need for the evidence outweighs the doubts. That conclusion explains the concluding clause in Federal Rule 803(3).

d. Declarations of Past State of Mind

Although Rule 803(3) sometimes sanctions the admission of statements of present memory to prove prior events, the Rule refuses to allow the admission of declarations of past state of mind. The doctrine "faces backward and not forward." *United States v. Cosentino*, 581 F. Supp. 600, 602 (E.D.N.Y. 1984) (quoting Justice Cardozo). In *Hill*, suppose that while talking with his wife one week after the collision, Mr. Worker stated, "I feel so bad about the accident. I was rushing across town on the boss's orders to get something delivered, and I wonder if I just rushed too fast." At trial, Ms. Hill calls Mrs. Worker to testify to the first clause in her husband's second sentence. If Ms. Hill offered the testimony under Rule 803(3), the trial judge would probably sustain Mr. Roe's objection.

Why sustain the objection and exclude the evidence? The rationale for the general norm banning such statements is the same justification underlying the exclusion of most statements of present memory: the need for an opportunity to test the quality of the declarant's memory and sincerity. The declarant is not referring to a thought or emotion that he is currently entertaining. The declarant is referring to a past state of mind, and her current statement could be a product of innocent misrecollection.

Most jurisdictions follow the pattern of the Federal Rules and categorically exclude declarations of past state of mind. California is one of the few jurisdictions admitting these declarations. California Evidence Code §§ 1251–52 are in point.

> § 1251. Prior State of Mind.
>
> Subject to Section 1252, evidence of a statement of the declarant's state of mind, emotion, or physical sensation (including a statement of intent, plan, motive, design, mental feeling, pain, or bodily health) at a time prior to the statement is not made inadmissible by the hearsay rule if
>
> (a) The declarant is unavailable as a witness; and
>
> (b) The evidence is offered to prove such prior state of mind or emotion, when it is itself an issue in the action and the evidence is not offered to prove any fact other than such state of mind or emotion.

§ 1252. Statement Under Circumstances Showing Lack of Trustworthiness.

Evidence of a statement is inadmissible under this article if the statement was made under circumstances such as to indicate its lack of trustworthiness.

In its commentary at §§ 1251–52, the California Law Revision Commission frankly acknowledged that the new statutes changed the prior state of the law. However, the Commission argued that when the proponent of the evidence can satisfy § 1251(b), the especial need for the evidence overrides the doubts about the declarant's memory. When § 1251(b) is inapplicable, that is "[i]f the past mental . . . state is to be used merely as circumstantial evidence of some other fact, . . . the statement of the past mental state is inadmissible hearsay."

NOTES AND PROBLEMS

1. How do California Evidence Code §§ 1251–52 relate to the concept of continuity of state of mind for declarations of present state of mind? Should the continuity concept be applied only to declarations of then existing intent? Or should §§ 1251–52 and the continuity concept be treated as alternative methods of admitting declarations of past intent? *See Kelly v. Bank of America*, 112 Cal. App. 2d 388, 394–95, 246 P.2d 92, 96–97 (1952).

2. While most jurisdictions allow statements of present memory to prove past events in estate litigation, the majority exclude declarations of past state of mind. Are these positions consistent? Compare the two types of statements in terms of (a) the concern for cross–examining the declarant about perception, memory and narration, and (b) the need for the evidence. There is arguably greater need to cross–examine the declarant about perception in case of statements of present memory; the declarant is referring to an external event such as a fire that destroyed the will rather than the internal reality of an intention. In both situations, the declarant must be unavailable. Is there such a unique need in estate litigation that it is justifiable to single out that type of case? The need seems debatable, for only a handful of California cases have even discussed § 1251.

3. Problem 20–19. Ms. Hill now offers Mrs. Worker's testimony about Worker's statement that he was "rushing across town on the boss's orders" to prove that Worker acted within the scope of his employment. Would the statement be admissible under the Federal Rules? Would it be admissible under the California Evidence Code? Would it make a difference if Worker himself died before trial?

C. EXCEPTIONS FOR WRITTEN STATEMENTS

1. BUSINESS ENTRIES

The business entry doctrine is the most frequently employed documentary exception. The frequency of the doctrine's use reflects the significant role that businesses–sole proprietorships, partnerships, and corporations–play in American society. Businesses' records are the depositories of a staggering amount of data, and we must devise a convenient means of making that data accessible to the judicial system. Earlier, we saw that the courts have facilitated access by recognizing a special means of authenticating business records. The same impulse helps account for the existence of this hearsay exception, codified in Federal Rules of Evidence 803(6), (7), and (11):

> The following are not excluded by the hearsay rule, even though the declarant is available as a witness:

> (6) Records of regularly conducted activity. A memorandum, report, record, or data compilation, in any form, of acts, events, conditions, opinions, or diagnoses, made at or near the time by, or from information transmitted by, a person with knowledge, if kept in the course of a regularly conducted business activity, and if it was the regular practice of that business activity to make the memorandum, report, or data compilation, all as shown by the testimony of the custodian or other qualified witness, or by certification that complies with Rule 902(11), 902(12), or a statute permitting certification, unless the source of information or the method or circumstances of preparation indicate lack of trustworthiness. The term "business" as used in this paragraph includes business, institution, association, profession, occupation, and calling of every kind, whether or not conducted for profit.

> (7) Absence of entry in records kept in accordance with the provisions of paragraph (6). Evidence that a matter is not included in the memoranda, reports, records, or data compilations in any form, kept in accordance with the provisions of paragraph (6), to prove the nonoccurrence or nonexistence of the matter, if the matter was a kind of which a memorandum, report, record, or data compilation was regularly made and preserved, unless the sources of information or other circumstances indicate lack of trustworthiness.

> (11) Records of religious organizations. Statements of births, marriages, divorces, deaths, legitimacy, ancestry, relationship by blood or marriage, or other similar facts of personal or family history, contained in a regularly kept record of a religious organization.

The Rules represent a fairly traditional version of the business entry doctrine. Initially, Rule 803(6) attempts to ensure that the business entry is based on firsthand perception. Personal knowledge is an element of the common law doctrine. *Lord v. Moore,* 37 Me. 208, 220 (1854). Rule 803(6) expressly refers to "a person with knowledge." Although the Rule is in accord with the majority view, a few jurisdictions have dispensed with the personal knowledge requirement. These jurisdictions have adopted statutes similar to the Model Act for Proof of Business Transactions. The Act was the prototype for 28 U.S.C. § 1732, Rule 803(6)'s predecessor. The Act declared that "all other circumstances, including the lack of personal knowledge by the entrant or maker," affect the weight but not the admissibility of the entry.

Another guarantee of the quality of the declarant's perception is the element of the doctrine that the report must be routine. In the words of Rule 803(6), "it was the regular practice of that business activity to make the memorandum, report, record or data compilation . . . ." The routine nature of the report increases the likelihood that the business' employees have developed a habit of precision in gathering the type of data reflected in the report. However, before the adoption of the Federal Rules, some common law courts had begun to relax this element of the doctrine; they occasionally admitted special business reports about nonrecurring events. JONES, EVIDENCE § 12.5 (6th ed. 1972); 2 B. WITKIN, CALIFORNIA EVIDENCE § 231 (4th ed. 2000). As in the case of the personal knowledge requirement, Congress opted for the orthodox view. Congress amended draft Rule 803(6) to insert the restriction to routine reports. Under the Rule, "[m]iscellaneous jottings" in a desk calendar are inadmissible, since there is no "demonstrable pattern of inclusion or exclusion." *United States v. Ramsey*, 785 F.2d 184, 192 (7th Cir.), *cert. denied*, 476 U.S. 1186 (1986); *Willco Kuwait Trading S.A.K. v. deSavary*, 843 F.2d 618, 628 (1st Cir. 1988) (excluding evidence of a non–routine business telex).

NOTE

How do these guarantees of perception apply to computerized business records? Businesses large enough to resort to computers typically have millions of business entries. Even if the handwriting style of the original slip of paper would have permitted the identification of the author, when the computer operator feeds the entry into the memory element, the entry often becomes an essentially anonymous report. Suppose that in the *Hill* case, Polecat wanted to offer some of its computer records as evidence. How would Polecat's attorney satisfy these elements of the foundation? *See King v. State ex rel. Murdock Acceptance Corp.*, 222 So. 2d 393, 398–99 (Miss. 1969). How could Polecat's attorney use Federal Rule of Evidence 406 in laying these elements of the foundation?

The common law doctrine attempted to ensure the declarant's memory as well as her perception. The doctrine's limitation to routine reports strengthened the inference of the quality of the witness' recollection. If the report were habitual, the declarant would presumably have acquired a habit of precisely recording the data in addition to gathering it accurately. Another indicium of memory is the doctrine's mandate that the entry be prepared at or near the time of the event memorialized. At common law, the courts were fairly tolerant of time lapses and sometimes allowed the introduction of reports prepared months after the event. *Standard Oil Co. v. Moore*, 251 F.2d 188, 223 (9th Cir. 1957), *cert. denied*, 356 U.S. 975 (1958). Despite the liberality of the common law decisions, Congress was unwilling to take the next step and eliminate the timing requirement. Rule 803(6) incorporates the requirement; notice the language, "made at or near the time." *See Carrie Contractors, Inc. v. Blount Construction Group of Blount, Inc.*, 968 F. Supp. 662 (M.D.Ala.

1997)(a delay of 17 months was fatal to the admissibility of accounting records).

Likewise, the doctrine endeavors to eliminate concerns about the declarant's narrative ability. The common law addressed this concern by restricting admissible entries to recitations of observed fact. 2 C. McCORMICK, HANDBOOK OF THE LAW OF EVIDENCE § 287 (5th ed. 1999). If the declarant used lay diction to describe a perceived event, there was little danger that the jury would misunderstand the statement. Thus, the courts readily admit business entries that are "objective observations of occurrences." Garland, *Hospital Records: Legal Requirements of Proof*, 59 ILL. B.J. 312, 313–14 (1970). However, if the declarant makes an opinionated statement such as characterizing a mental patient's condition as "psychotic," there is a much graver risk that the jurors will mistake the declarant's meaning. For that reason, when a hospital record contains a debatable diagnosis involving "judgment or discretion on complex" data, at early common law the trial judge often refused to treat the record as a business entry. Note, 56 GEO. L.J. 939, 945 (1968); Powell, *Admissibility of Hospital Records into Evidence*, 21 MD. L. REV. 22, 43 (1961); Dunsmore, *Hospital Records as Evidence*, 8 CLEV.–MAR. L. REV. 459, 462–63 (1959).

But in this context as well, the courts started to relax the restrictions on the admission of business entries. *Weis v. Weis*, 147 Ohio St. 416, 72 N.E.2d 245 (1947), collected numerous authorities documenting the courts' willingness to accept opinionated entries:

> Types of hospital or physician's office records, which have been held admissible in evidence by the courts, are as follows: Record of examination of a patient on admission to a hospital, stating that he had no external injuries and observation that there was a deviation of the nasal septum . . .; laboratory tests and history sheet . . .; observation that a patient was well under the influence of alcohol . . .; record of admission to hospital including observation, "odor of lcohol on the breath" . . .; diagnosis of cerebral hemorrhage . . .; report to effect patient had ulcer, chronic prostatitis and seminal vesiculitis . . .; pathological record to show that death resulted from venereal disease . . .; record that an insured was delirious four hours before an accident . . . ; record that patient had a fractured right clavicle . . . ; record that patient was suffering from "nephritis" . . . ; record of "moderately advanced tuberculosis" . . . ; record that patient's vomitus had odor of whiskey . . . ; record showing unruly behavior of patient and his disobedience of orders of surgeons and nurses . . . ; and record of treatment prescribed and statements made by patient concerning his symptoms . . . .

NOTES AND PROBLEMS

1. What limits, if any, should there be on the admissibility of opinions in business entries? Is hearsay policy satisfied whenever we are confident that if the expert had been present in the courtroom, the expert could have voiced the opinion stated in the report? *Thomas v. Hogan*, 308 F.2d 355, 358–61 (4th Cir. 1962). Is there a difference between a diagnosis of ulcer (mentioned in

Weis) and a psychiatrist's evaluation of "post–traumatic stress disorder"? *Philips v. Neil*, 452 F.2d 337, 343–47 (6th Cir. 1971), *cert. denied*, 409 U.S. 884 (1972). Are the opinions distinguishable in terms of hearsay policy? *Texas Employers' Ins. Ass'n v. Sauceda*, 636 S.W.2d 494, 499 (Tex. Ct. App. 1982).

2. Regardless of your own policy preference, what position does Rule 803(6) take on the question of whether the business entry must be a recitation of observed fact? Do you think that the Advisory Committee intended that the courts always apply the language literally?

3. Problem 20–20. In *Devitt*, the prosecutor calls Officer Dorsey as a witness. Dorsey testifies that he is the chief of the local police crime laboratory. The prosecutor hands Dorsey an exhibit. Dorsey identifies the exhibit as a report of a comparative chemical and microscopic analysis of hair strands found at the crime scene and strands taken from the defendant. The report concludes with the sentence that the two sets of hair strands "are microscopically identical and indistinguishable." The prosecutor offers the report into evidence. The defense counsel objects on the ground that the entry is "insufficiently factual." What ruling? *See State v. Merritt*, 591 S.W.2d 107, 111–14 (Mo. 1980).

4. Problem 20–21. In Problem 20–20, suppose that Devitt's attorney objected on the ground that there must be a specific showing of the expertise of the analyst who prepared the report. The defense attorney claims that "you can't admit the opinion until we know that if the guy had been in the courtroom, he could have given that opinion from the witness stand." *See State v. Rhone*, 555 S.W.2d 839, 841–42 (Mo. 1977).

———

Lastly, the courts attempted to fashion circumstantial guarantees of the declarant's sincerity. One such guarantee is that the declarant had a business duty to gather and record the data. The accuracy of the records is a matter of paramount concern to the typical business. If they bill too much, they will anger–and lose–clients; but if they bill too little, they will go bankrupt. The declarant is usually an employee of the business. The declarant realizes that his continued employment, his livelihood, depends on the quality of his job performance; and part of that job is collecting and recording business data. This realization is a powerful incentive for accurate perception and memory. An employee's personal notes do not qualify. *Skaletsky v. Board of Trustees Community College*, 75 Supp.2d 885, 888–89 (N.D.Ill. 1999). The following case, which is expressly mentioned in the Advisory Committee Note to Rule 803(6), is the leading authority on the requirement of a business duty.

JOHNSON v. LUTZ

253 N.Y. 124, 170 N.E. 517 (N.Y. 1930)

HUBBS, J.

This action is to recover damages for the wrongful death of the plaintiff's intestate, who was killed when his motorcycle came into collision with the defendants' truck at a street intersection. There was a sharp conflict in the testimony in regard to the circumstances under which the collision took place. A policeman's report of the accident filed by him in the station house was offered in evidence by the defendants under section 374–a of the Civil Practice Act, and was excluded. The sole ground for reversal urged by the appellants is that said report was erroneously excluded. That section reads: "Any writing or record, whether in the form of an entry in a book or otherwise, made as a memorandum or record of any act, transaction, occurrence or event, shall be admissible in evidence in proof of said act, transaction, occurrence or event, if the trial judge shall find that it was made in the regular course of any business, and that it was the regular course of such business to make such memorandum or record at the time of such act, transaction, occurrence or event, or within a reasonable time thereafter. All other circumstances of the making of such writing or record, including lack of personal knowledge by the entrant or maker, may be shown to affect its weight, but they shall not affect its admissibility. The term business shall include business, profession, occupation and calling of every kind."

Prior to the decision in the well–known case of *Vosburgh v. Thayer*, 12 Johns, 461, decided in 1815, shopbooks could not be introduced in evidence to prove an account. The decision in that case established that they were admissible where preliminary proof could be made that there were regular dealings between the parties; that the plaintiff kept honest and fair books; that some of the articles charged had been delivered; and that the plaintiff kept no clerk. At that time it may not have been a hardship to require a shopkeeper who sued to recover an account to furnish the preliminary proof required by that decision. Business was transacted in a comparatively small way, with few, if any, clerks. Since the decision in that case, it has remained the substantial basis of all decisions upon the question in this jurisdiction prior to the enactment in 1928 of section 374–a, Civil Practice Act.

Under modern conditions, the limitations upon the right to use books of account, memoranda, or records, made in the regular course of business, often resulted in a denial of justice, and usually in annoyance, expense, and waste of time and energy. A rule of evidence that was practical a century ago had become obsolete. The situation was appreciated, and attention was called to it by the courts and text–writers. Woods Practice Evidence (2d Ed.) 377; 3 Wigmore on Evidence (1923) § 1530.

The report of the Legal Research Committee of the Commonwealth Fund, published in 1927 under the title, "The Law of Evidence—Some Proposals for Its Reform," dealt with the question under the heading, "Proof of Business Transactions to Harmonize with Current Business Practice." That report, based upon extensive research, pointed out the confusion existing in decisions in different jurisdictions. It explained and illustrated the great need of a more practical, workable, and uniform rule, adapted to modern business conditions and practices. The chapter is devoted to a discussion of the pressing need of a rule of evidence which would "give evidential credit to the books upon which the mercantile and industrial world relies in the conduct of business." At the close of the chapter, the committee proposed a statute to be enacted in all jurisdictions. In compliance with such proposal, the Legislature enacted section 374–a of the Civil Practice Act in the very words used by the committee.

It is apparent that the Legislature enacted section 374–a to carry out the purpose announced in the report of the committee. That purpose was to secure the enactment of a statute which would afford a more workable rule of evidence in the proof of business conditions.

In view of the history of section 374–a and the purpose for which it was enacted, it is apparent that it was never intended to apply to a situation like that in the case at bar. The memorandum in question was not made in the regular course of any business, profession, occupation, or calling. The policeman who made it was not present at the time of the accident. The memorandum was made from hearsay statements of third persons who happened to be present at the scene of the accident when he arrived. It does not appear whether they saw the accident and stated to him what they knew, or stated what some other persons had told them.

The purpose of the Legislature in enacting section 374–a was to permit a writing or record, made in the regular course of business, to be received in evidence, without the necessity of calling as witnesses all of the persons who had any part in making it, provided the record was made as a part of the duty of the person making it, or on information imparted by persons who were under a duty to impart such information. The amendment permits the introduction of shopbooks without the necessity of calling all clerks who may have sold different items of account. It was not intended to permit the receipt in evidence of entries based upon voluntary hearsay statements made by third parties not engaged in the business or under any duty in relation thereto. It was said, in *Mayor, etc., of New York City v. Second Ave. R. Co.*, 102 N.Y. 582, at page 581, 7 N.E. 905, 909, 55 Am. Rep. 839: "It is a proper qualification of the rule admitting such evidence that the account must have been made in the ordinary course of business, and that it should not be extended so as to admit a mere private memorandum, not made in pursuance of any duty owing by the person making it, or when made upon information derived from another who made the communication casually and voluntarily, and not under the sanction of duty or other obligation."

An important consideration leading to the amendment was the fact that in the business world credit is given to records made in the course of business by persons who are engaged in the business upon information given by others engaged in the same business as part of their duty.

"Such entries are dealt with in that way in the most important undertakings of mercantile and industrial life. They are the ultimate basis of calculation, investment, and general confidence in every business enterprise. Nor does the practical impossibility of obtaining constantly and permanently the verification of every employee affect the trust that is given to such books. It would seem that expedients which the entire commercial world recognizes as safe could be sanctioned, and not discredited, by courts of justice. When it is a mere question of whether provisional confidence can be placed in a certain class of statements, there cannot profitably and sensibly be one rule for the business world and another for the court–room. The merchant and the manufacturer must not be turned away remediless because the methods in which the entire community places a just confidence are a little difficult to reconcile with technical scruples on the part of the same persons who as attorneys have already employed and relied upon the same methods. In short, courts must here cease to be pedantic and endeavor to be practical." 3 Wigmore on Evidence (1923) § 1530, p. 278.

The Legislature has sought by the amendment to make the courts practical. It would be unfortunate not to give the amendment a construction which will enable it to cure the evil complained of and accomplish the purpose for which it was enacted. In construing it, we should not, however, permit it to be applied in a case for which it was never intended.

Judgment affirmed.

NOTES AND PROBLEMS

1. It is critical to appreciate the limited nature of the holding in *Johnson*. The court holds only that the proponent may not use the business entry exception to justify the substantive use of bystanders' statements quoted in the police report. *Johnson* does not foreclose developing a nonhearsay use for the statement or invoking another hearsay exception. *See* FED. R. EVID. 805.

2. The commentators use various expressions to describe this problem: double hearsay, multiple hearsay, hearsay within hearsay, or "tacking" hearsay exceptions. For each "link in the hearsay chain," the proponent must develop a nonhearsay theory or invoke an exemption or exception. *Romano v. Howarth*, 998 F.2d 101, 108 (2d Cir. 1993) ("Because the Progress Notes contain [an] additional level of hearsay, another link in the hearsay chain is necessary to usher into evidence the officer's statements to the nurse").

3. Problem 20–22 (a–c). Consider these variations of the *Johnson* fact situation:

(a) In the *Hill* case, a bystander told the investigating police officer that, in her opinion, Worker was driving at least 45 miles an hour. The officer recorded that statement in his report, and Ms. Hill read that statement before she filed suit. In part because of that statement, she agreed that her attorney should allege speeding in her complaint. At trial, Roe calls an accident reconstruction expert who analyzes the physical evidence at the accident scene and convincingly demonstrates that Worker was not speeding. The trial results in a defense verdict. After this trial, Roe sues Ms. Hill for the tort of malicious civil proceeding. In that suit, one issue is whether Ms. Hill had a good faith belief in the allegations she included in her complaint. At the trial of this suit, Ms. Hill attempts to testify to the contents of the police report, including the bystander's statement about Worker's speed. Does *Johnson* preclude Ms. Hill from doing so? Consider Rule 801(c) as well as Rule 803(6).

(b) Suppose that the bystander in question became a defense witness at trial. At trial, she testifies that after carefully reconstructing the accident in her mind, she believes that Worker was driving "at most 25 miles an hour." On cross–examination, Ms. Hill attempts to confront the witness with the passage in the police report. Does *Johnson* preclude Ms. Hill from doing so? Consider Rule 613 as well as Rule 803(6).

(c) Assume that the bystander is unavailable at trial but that, on its face, the police report recites enough facts to bring the bystander's statement within the excited utterance exception under Rule 803(2). During her case–in–chief, Ms. Hill produces a properly attested copy of the police report. She attempts to offer into evidence the passage quoting the bystander. Does *Johnson* bar Ms. Hill from doing so?

Johnson gives one layer of meaning to the expression, "in the regular course of business." *Johnson* requires an affirmative showing that the declarant has a business motivation for gathering and recording the data. However, the *Johnson* doctrine does not exhaust the meaning of "in the regular course of business." The next case, which is also mentioned in the Advisory Committee Note to Rule 803(6), probes even deeper into the significance of that language.

PALMER v. HOFFMAN

318 U.S. 109 (1943)

JUSTICE DOUGLAS delivered the opinion of the Court.

This case arose out of a grade crossing accident which occurred in Massachusetts. Diversity of citizenship brought it to the federal District Court in New York. There were several causes of action. The first two were on behalf of respondent individually, one being brought under a Massachusetts statute, the other at common law. The third and fourth were brought by respondent as administrator of the estate of his wife and alleged the same common law and statutory negligence as the first two counts. On the question of negligence the trial court submitted three issues to the jury–failure to ring a bell, to blow a whistle, to have a light burning in the front of the train. The jury returned a verdict in favor of respondent individually for some $25,000 and in favor of respondent as administrator for $9,000. The District Court of Appeals affirmed, one judge dissenting. The case is here on a petition for a writ of certiorari which presents three points.

The accident occurred on the night of December 25, 1940. On December 27, 1940, the engineer of the train, who died before the trial, made a statement at a freight office of petitioners where he was interviewed by an assistant superintendent of the road and by a representative of the Massachusetts Public Utilities Commission. This statement was offered in evidence by petitioners under the Act of June 20, 1936, 28 U.S.C.A. § 695.[1] They offered

---

[1] "In any court of the United States and in any court established by Act of Congress, any writing or record, whether in the form of an entry in a book or otherwise, made as a memorandum or record of any act, transaction, occurrence, or event, shall be admissible as evidence of said act, transaction, occurrence, or event, if it shall appear that it was made in the regular course of any business, and that it was the regular course of such business to make such memorandum or record at the time of such act, transaction, occurrence, or event or within a reasonable time thereafter. All other circumstances of the making of such writing or record, including lack of personal knowledge by the entrant or maker, may be shown to affect its weight, but they shall not affect its admissibility. The term 'business' shall include business, profession, occupation, and calling of every kind."

to prove that the statement was signed in the regular course of business, it being the regular course of such business to make such a statement. Respondent's objection to its introduction was sustained.

We agree with the majority view below that it was properly excluded.

We may assume that if the statement was made "in the regular course" of business, it would satisfy the other provisions of the Act. But we do not think that it was made "in the regular course" of business within the meaning of the Act. The business of the petitioners is the railroad business. That business like other enterprises entails the keeping of numerous books and records essential to its conduct or useful in its efficient operation. Though such books and records were considered reliable and trustworthy for major decisions in the industrial and business world, their use in litigation was greatly circumscribed or hedged about by the hearsay rule–restrictions which greatly increased the time and cost of making the proof where those who made the records were numerous.[2] 5 Wigmore, Evidence, 3d Ed. 1940, § 1530. It was that problem which started the movement towards adoption of legislation embodying the principles of the present Act. *See* Morgan et al., The Law of Evidence, Some Proposals for its Reform (1927) c V. And the legislative history of the Act indicates the same purpose.[3]

The engineer's statement which was held inadmissible in this case falls into quite a different category. It is not a record made for the systematic conduct of the business as a business. An accident report may affect that business in the sense that it affords information on which the management may act. It is not, however, typical of entries made systematically or as a matter of routine to record events or occurrences, to reflect transactions with others, or to provide internal controls. The conduct of a business commonly entails the payment of tort claims by the negligence of its employees. But the fact that a company makes a business out of recording its employees' versions of their accidents does not put those statements in the class of records made "in the regular course" of the business within the meaning of the Act. If it did, then any law office in the land could follow the same course, since business as

---

[2] The problem was well stated by Judge Learned Hand in *Massachusetts Bonding & Ins. Co. v. Norwich Pharmacal Co.* (CCA 2, 1927) 18 F.2d 934, 937: "The routine of modern affairs, mercantile, financial and industrial, is conducted with so extreme a division of labor that the transactions cannot be proved at first hand without the concurrence of persons, each of whom can contribute no more than a slight part, and that part not dependent on his memory of the event. Records, and records alone, are their adequate repository, and are in practice accepted as accurate upon the faith of the routine itself, and of the self–consistency of their contents. Unless they can be used in court without the task of calling those who at all stages had a part in the transactions recorded, nobody need ever pay a debt, if only his creditor does a large enough business."

[3] Thus the report of the Senate Committee on the Judiciary incorporates the recommendation of the Attorney General who stated in support of the legislation, "The old common–law rule requires that every book entry be identified by the person making it. This is exceedingly difficult, if not impossible, in the case of an institution employing a large bookkeeping staff, particularly when the entries are made by machine. In a recent criminal case the Government was prevented from making out a prima facie case by a ruling that entries in the books of a bank, made in the regular course of business, were not admissible in evidence unless the specific bookkeeper who made the entry could identify it. Since the bank employed 18 bookkeepers, and the entries were made by bookkeeping machines, this was impossible." S. Rep. No. 1965, 74th Cong. 2d Sess., pp. 1, 2.

defined in the Act includes the professions. We would then have a real perversion of a rule designed to facilitate admission of records which experience has shown to be quite trustworthy. Any business by installing a regular system for recording and preserving its version of accidents for which it was potentially liable could qualify those reports under the Act. The result would be that the Act would cover any system of recording events or occurrences provided it was "regular" and though it had little or nothing to do with the management or operation of the business as such. Preparation of cases for trial by virtue of being a "business" or incidental thereto would obtain the benefits of this liberalized version of the early shop book rule. The probability of trustworthiness of records because they were routine reflections of the day to day operations of a business would be forgotten as the basis of the rule. *See Conner v. Seattle, R. & S. R. Co.,* 56 Wash. 310, 312, 313, 105 P. 634. Regularity of preparation would become the test rather than the character of the records and their earmarks of reliability (*Chesapeake & D. Canal Co. v. United States,* 250 U.S. 123, 128, 129) acquired from their source and origin and the nature of their compilation. We cannot so completely empty the words of the Act of their historic meaning. If the Act is to be extended to apply not only to a "regular course" of a business but also to any business, Congress not this Court must extend it. Such a major change which opens wide the door to avoidance of cross–examination should not be left to implication. Nor is it any answer to say that Congress has provided in the Act that the various circumstances of the making of the record should affect its weight, not its admissibility. That provision comes into play only in case the other requirements of the Act are met.

In short, it is manifest that in this case those reports are not for the systematic conduct of the enterprise as a railroad business. Unlike payrolls, accounts receivable, accounts payable, bills of lading and the like, these reports are calculated for use essentially in the court, not in the business. Their primary utility is in litigating, not in railroading.

It is, of course, not for us to take these reports out of the Act if Congress has put them in. But there is nothing in the background of the law on which this Act was built or in its legislative history which suggests for a moment that the business of preparing cases for trial should be included. In this connection it should be noted that the Act of May 6, 1910, 45 U.S.C.A. § 38, requires officers of common carriers by rail to make under oath monthly reports of railroad accidents to the Interstate Commerce Commission, setting forth the nature and causes of the accidents and the circumstances connected therewith. And the same Act (45 U.S.C.A. § 40) gives the Commission authority to investigate and to make reports upon such accidents. It is provided, however, that "Neither the reports required by § 38 of this title nor any report of the investigation provided for in § 40 of this title nor any part thereof shall be admitted as evidence or used for any purpose in any suit or action for damages growing out of any matter mentioned in said report or investigation." 45 U.S.C.A. § 41. A similar provision, 45 U.S.C.A. § 33, bars the use in litigation of reports concerning accidents resulting from the failure of a locomotive boiler or its appurtenances. That legislation reveals an explicit congressional policy to rule out reports of accidents which certainly have as great a claim to objectivity as the statement sought to be admitted in the present case. We can hardly suppose that Congress modified or qualified by implication these long standing statutes when it permitted records made "in the regular course" of business to be introduced. Nor can we assume that Congress having expressly prohibited the use of the company's reports on its accidents impliedly altered that policy when it came to reports by its employees to their superiors. The inference is wholly the other way.

The several hundred years of history behind the Act indicate the nature of the reforms which it was designed to effect. It should of course be liberally interpreted so as to do away with the anachronistic rules which gave rise to its need and at which it was aimed. But "regular course" of business must find its meaning in the inherent nature of the business in question and in the methods systematically employed for the conduct of the business as a business. . . .

PROBLEMS

1. Problem 20–23. In *Hill*, Polecat offers records of safety tests of the Polecat model that the plaintiff was driving at the time of the accident. To lay the foundation for the records, Polecat calls Mr. Granger, the head of the safety department. Granger testifies that the tests were actually conducted by Future Motors, Inc., a wholly owned subsidiary of Polecat. Future Motors' safety personnel conducted the tests, prepared the reports, and sent the reports directly to Polecat. Ms. Hill cites *Johnson* and argues that the reports are inadmissible because the declarants were not employees of Polecat. What result? *United States v. Flom*, 558 F.2d 1179, 1182–83 (5th Cir. 1977). Is the declarant's formal employment status dispositive?

2. Problem 20–24. In *Hill*, the plaintiff offers a hospital record into evidence. The hospital record states that "patient complained that she was experiencing sharp pain in her right side today." Ms. Hill offers the hospital records custodian's testimony to identify the record. Polecat's attorney objects and cites *Johnson*. Is *Johnson* controlling? What is the relevance of Federal Rule of Evidence 805? Think back to our discussion of the res gestae exceptions.

3. Problem 20–25. Suppose that Polecat offered a hospital record stating "patient indicated that her pain was much less severe today." Now Ms. Hill cites *Johnson* to block the introduction of the record. Consider Federal Rule of Evidence 801(d)(2).

4. Problem 20–26. In *Devitt*, as in Problem 20–20, the prosecutor offers the report of the analysis of the hair strands. Now Devitt's attorney cites *Palmer* in support of the objection to the report's admission. What result? *Compare State v. Henderson*, 554 S.W.2d 117, 120 (Tenn. 1977) with *United States v. Evans*, 21 C.M.A. 579, 582, 45 C.M.R. 353, 356 (1972). Assume that Morena has not adopted the Federal Rules of Evidence.

2.   OFFICIAL RECORDS

A doctrine closely related to the business entry exception is the official record exception. Like corporations, government agencies have become a major depository of data in our society. The parallel continues because, as in the case of business records, the courts have recognized extraordinary means of authenticating official documents. To complete the parallel, the courts have fashioned a special doctrine to facilitate the admission of official records as substantive evidence. The courts have invoked the doctrine to justify the admission of a wide variety of documents, including military records, weather reports, tax returns, ships' papers, and hospital reports. Annot., 50 A.L.R.2d 1187 (1956).

The Federal Rules of Evidence include several provisions in Rule 803, based on the official record theory:

> The following are not excluded by the hearsay rule, even though the declarant is available as a witness:
>
> (8) Public records and reports. Records, reports, statements, or data compilations, in any form, of public offices or agencies, setting forth (A) the activities of the office or agency, or (B) matters observed pursuant to duty imposed by law as to which matters there was a duty to report, excluding, however, in criminal cases matters observed by police officers and other law enforcement personnel, or (C) in civil actions and proceedings and against the Government in criminal cases, factual findings resulting from an investigation made pursuant to authority granted by law, unless the sources of information or other circumstances indicate lack of trustworthiness.
>
> (9) Records of vital statistics. Records or data compilations, in any form, of births, fetal deaths, or marriages, if the report thereof was made to a public office pursuant to requirements of law.
>
> (10) Absence of public record or entry. To prove the absence of a record, report, statement, or data compilation, in any form, or the nonoccurrence or nonexistence of a matter of which a record, report, statement, or data compilation, in any form, was regularly made and preserved by a public office or agency, evidence in the form of certification in accordance with rule 902, or testimony, that diligent search failed to disclose the record, report, statement, or data compilation, or entry.
>
> (12) Marriage, baptismal, and similar certificates. Statements of fact contained in a certificate that the maker performed a marriage or other ceremony or administered a sacrament, made by a clergyman, public official, or other person authorized by the rules or practices of a religious organization or by law to perform the act certified, and purporting to have been issued at the time of the act or within a reasonable time thereafter.
>
> (14) Records of documents affecting an interest in property. The record of a document purporting to establish or affect an interest in property, as proof of the content of the original recorded document and its execution and delivery by each person by whom it purports to have been executed, if the record is a record of a

public office and an applicable statute authorizes the recording of documents of that kind in that office.

Once again, we begin our analysis of the exception by pointing to the circumstantial guarantees of the quality of perception. One common denominator with the business entry doctrine is that at common law, an official record must be based on the declarant's firsthand knowledge. *Wetherill v. University of Chicago*, 518 F. Supp. 1387 (N.D. Ill. 1981). Further, if a statute or regulation prescribes a particular procedure for preparing the record, the declarant must substantially comply with the procedure. Annot., 28 A.L.R.2d 1434 (1953). A major irregularity or omission may create an intolerably high risk of the record's inaccuracy. *Id.* at 1445.

The courts and legislatures have also attempted to guard against the declarant's misrecollection. For example, California Evidence Code § 1280(b) limits official records to writings "made at or near the time of the act, condition, or event" recorded. Does Federal Rule of Evidence 803(8) include any comparable language? Contrast Rule 803(8) with Rule 803(6).

To minimize the risks of narration, the common law courts limited official records to recitations of observed fact. The courts routinely excluded statements of medical causation or legal responsibility. *People v. Holder*, 230 Cal. App. 2d 50, 40 Cal. Rptr. 655 (1964). Note that unlike Rule 803(6), Rule 803(8) does not contain an express reference to "opinions, or diagnoses." However, modernly the courts no longer categorically exclude all opinionated statements in official records. In many jurisdictions, statute requires that the medical examiner or coroner state the cause and manner of death in the death certificate. D. BINDER, THE HEARSAY HANDBOOK § 11.02 (2d ed. 1983). Although the view is not universal, many jurisdictions now admit the conclusory statement of cause of death as substantive evidence. *Id.*

Lastly, the courts have tried to ensure the declarant's sincerity. The English courts drew the inference of sincerity from the declarant's realization that the report would be subjected to public scrutiny. M. LADD & R. CARLSON, CASES AND MATERIALS ON EVIDENCE 976 (1972). Their authorities place greater emphasis upon the publicity of the record and the possible discovery of any error as the bases for an exception to the hearsay rule. Lord Blackburn expanded and more clearly enunciated the idea in *Sturla v. Freccia*, [1880] 5 App. Cas. 623, 643, 644: "I understand a public document . . . to mean a document that is made for the purpose of the public making use of it, and being able to refer to it . . . . I think the very object of it must be that it should be made for the purpose of being kept public, so that the persons concerned in it may have access to it afterwards." In *Mercer v. Denne*, [1904] 2 Ch. D. 534, Judge Farwell stated: "The test of publicity as put by Lord Blackburn is that the public are interested in it, and entitled to go and see it, so that if there is anything wrong in it they would be entitled to protest. In that sense it becomes a statement that would be open to the public to challenge or dispute."

The American authorities invoke a different theory as the basis for inferring sincerity: the declarant's official duty to gather and record the data. That duty serves as a motivation for sincerity, just as it provides the declarant with an incentive for accurate perception and memory. As Federal Rules of Evidence 803(9) and (12) imply, the duty can exist even if the declarant is a private person. For instance, under Rule 803(12), when a member of the clergy executes a marriage certificate, that person functions as a *de facto* public official. The courts have likewise been willing to treat foreign governmental documents as official records. *United States v. Grady*, 544 F.2d 598, 604 (2d Cir. 1976) (records of Royal Ulster Constabulary); *United States v. Rodriguez*, 534 F.2d 7 (1st Cir. 1976) (Dominican identification card, military records, and death certificate); *United States v. Wing*, 450 F.2d 806, 810–12 (9th Cir. 1971), *cert. denied,* 405 U.S. 994 (1972) (Mexican government border documents); *United States v. Ghaloub*, 385 F.2d 567, 571 (2d Cir. 1966) (Syrian census records).

The key factor in deciding whether to treat the document as an official record is the document's nature rather than the declarant's identity. The classic analysis of that problem appears in Dean Wigmore's treatise. 5 J. WIGMORE, EVIDENCE § 1636 (3d ed. 1940). Dean Wigmore describes several basic types of official records admitted at common law. One type is a register. Registers record events of which public officials have firsthand knowledge and which typically occur on their premises. For example, in a deed registry, a clerk records that a citizen gave the official a deed to be included in the registry. Another type is a return. As in the case of a registry, the official executing a return ordinarily has personal knowledge; but in the case of a return, the record relates to an act which the official performed off the premises. An illustration would be a police officer's return on a search warrant; the officer executes the warrant away from the police station and files a return, detailing his or her acts, with the court. A third type is a certificate. In the case of a certificate, the official usually gives the record to a private citizen. When a notary public certifies a person's acknowledgment of his or her authorship of a document such as a deed, the notary is acting as a public official; and rather than retaining the certificate, the notary hands the certificate to the person who appeared before them. Lastly, a report generally summarizes an investigation which the official conducted. As in the case of a return, a report of investigation (ROI) relates to the official's conduct away from the official's business premises. However, at least in part the report collects hearsay statements relating to events of which the official lacks personal knowledge. Since the findings in most ROIs rest in part on hearsay, at common law the courts were highly reluctant to admit such findings as substantive evidence.

Although Rule 803(6) essentially codifies the common law business entry exception, Rule 803(8) is innovative. Admittedly, Rule 803(8)(A) is unexceptional, permitting the admission of records reflecting "the activities of the office or agency." However, 803(8)(B) and (8)(C) deviate from the common law. Rule (8)(B) purports to exclude some records that were admissible at common law. The rule states that an admissible record may document "matters observed pursuant to duty imposed by law as to which there was a duty to report, excluding, however, in criminal cases matters observed by police officers and other law enforcement personnel . . . ." How broad is this exclusionary provision? The Court of Appeals for the Second Circuit struggled with that question in the following case.

UNITED STATES v. OATES

560 F.2d 45 (2d Cir. 1977)

[A jury convicted the defendant of possessing heroin with intent to distribute and of conspiracy to commit that substantive offense. One of the alleged coconspirators was Isaac Daniels.]

Appellant claims that the trial court committed error by admitting into evidence at trial two documentary exhibits purporting to be the official report and accompanying worksheet of the United States Customs Service chemist who analyzed the white powdery substance seized from Daniels. The documents, the crucial nature of which is beyond cavil, concluded that the powder examined was heroin. Appellant contends, first of all, that under the new Federal Rules of Evidence the documents should have been excluded as hearsay. Before discussing the merits of these contentions, which raise difficult and important issues of evidential law, it will be helpful to describe briefly the circumstances surrounding the admission of the report and the worksheet.

At trial the government had planned upon calling as one of its final witnesses a Mr. Milton Weinberg, a retired United States Customs Service chemist who allegedly had analyzed the white powder seized from Daniels. It seems that Mr. Weinberg had been present on the day the trial had been scheduled to commence but he was not able to testify then because of a delay occasioned by the unexpected length of the pretrial suppression hearing. The government claims that by the time Weinberg was rescheduled to testify he had become "unavailable" [due to a medical condition].

Before the onset of Weinberg's condition, the prosecutor has planned to call Weinberg for the purpose of eliciting from him testimony that Weinberg had analyzed the powder seized from Daniels and found it to be heroin. When Weinberg became "unavailable," the government decided to call another Customs chemist, Shirley Harrington, who, although she did not know Weinberg personally, was able to testify concerning the regular practices and procedures used by Customs Service chemists in analyzing unknown substances. Through Mrs. Harrington the government was successful in introducing Exhibits 13 and 12 which purported to be, respectively, the handwritten worksheet used by the chemist analyzing the substance seized from Daniels and the official typewritten report of the chemical analysis. When the defense voiced vigorous objection to the attempt to introduce the documents through Mrs. Harrington, the government relied upon [several] different hearsay exceptions contained in the new Federal Rules of Evidence to support its position that the documents were admissible.

[W]e believe that, on balance, appellant's emphasis on the importance of FRE 803(8) is well-founded. That the chemist's report and worksheet could not satisfy the requirements of the "public records and reports" exception seems evident merely from examining, on its face, the language of FRE 803(8). While there may be no sharp demarcation between the records covered by exception 8(B) and those referenced in exception 8(C), and there may in some cases be actual overlap, we conclude without hesitation that surely the language of item (C) is applicable to render the chemist's documents inadmissible as evidence in this case, and they might also be within the ambit of the terminology of item (B), a claim appellant argues to us persuasively.

It is manifest from the face of item (C) that "factual findings resulting from an investigation made pursuant to authority granted by law" are not shielded from the exclusionary effect of the hearsay rule by "the public records exception" if the government seeks to have those "factual findings" admitted *against* the accused in a criminal case. It seems indisputable to us that the chemist's official report and worksheet in the case at bar can be characterized as reports of "factual findings resulting from an investigation made pursuant to authority granted by law." The "factual finding" in each instance, the conclusion of the chemist that the substance analyzed was heroin, obviously is the product of an "investigation,"[19] *see, e.g., Martin v. Reynolds Metal Corp.,* 297 F.2d 49, 57 (9th Cir. 1961) (" 'investigation', when liberally construed, includes the sampling and *testing* here contemplated") (emphasis supplied), supposedly involving on the part of the chemist employment of various techniques of scientific analysis. Furthermore, in view of its reliance on the chemist's report at trial and its representation to the district court that "chemical analys[e]s of unidentified substances are indeed a regularly conducted activity of the Customs laboratory of Customs chemists," the government here is surely in no position to dispute the fact that the analyses regularly performed by United States Customs Service chemists on substances lawfully seized by Customs officers are performed pursuant to authority granted by law.

Though with less confidence, we believe that the chemist's documents might also fail to achieve status as public records under FRE 803(8)(B) because they are records of "matters observed by police officers and other law enforcement personnel." Although in characterizing the chemist's report and worksheet here it is quite accurate to designate those reports as the reports of factual findings made pursuant to an investigation, the reports in this case conceivably could also be susceptible of the characterization that they are "reports . . . setting forth . . . (B) matters observed pursuant to duty imposed by law as to which matters there was a duty to report." If this characterization is justified, the difficult question would be whether the chemists making the observations could be regarded as "other law enforcement personnel." We think this phraseology must be read broadly enough to make its prohibitions against the use of government–generated reports in criminal cases coterminous with the analogous prohibitions contained in FRE 803(8)(C). *See United States v. Smith, supra,* 521 F.2d at 968–69, n.24. We would thus construe "other law enforcement personnel" to include, at the least, any officer or employee of a governmental agency which has law enforcement responsibilities. Applying such a standard to the case at bar, we easily conclude that full–time

---

[19] That "investigation" can encompass scientific testing is clearly shown by the Advisory Committee's Notes which, while noting "the variety of situations encountered" by courts deciding the admissibility of reports of this nature, *see* Advisory Committee's Notes, Note to Paragraph (8) of Rule 803, 56 F.R.D. at 312, characterize as "evaluative reports" certificates issued pursuant to 18 U.S.C. § 4245 and findings made pursuant to 7 U.S.C. § 78.

Certificates under 18 U.S.C. § 4245 are based on psychiatric and psychological examinations while findings made pursuant to the former 7 U.S.C. § 78 could be based on testing of grain.

chemists of the United States Customs Service are "law enforcement person-nel." The chemist in this case was employed by the Customs Service, a governmental agency which had clearly defined law enforcement authority in the field of illegal narcotics trafficking; the officers who actually seized the suspected contraband were employed by the Customs Service, and the uniden-tified substance was delivered by them to a laboratory operated by the Cus-toms Service. The unidentified substance was then subjected to analysis by a chemist, one of whose regular functions is to test substances seized from suspected narcotics violators. Chemists at the laboratory are, without ques-tion, important participants in the prosecutorial effort. As well as analyzing substances for the express purpose of ascertaining whether the substances are contraband, and if so, participating in eventual prosecution of narcotics offenders, the chemists are also expected to be familiar with the need for establishing the whereabouts of confiscated drugs at all times from seizure until trial. Moreover, the role of the chemist typically does not terminate upon completion of the chemical analysis and submission of the resulting report but participation continues until the chemist has testified as an important prosecution witness at trial.

In short, these reports are not "made by persons and for purposes uncon-nected with a criminal case [but rather they are a direct] result of a test made for the specific purpose of convicting the defendant and conducted by agents of the executive branch, the very department of government which seeks defendant's conviction." *State v. Larochelle*, 112 N.H. 392, 400, 297 A.2d 223, 228 (1972) (dissenting opinion). It would therefore seem that if the chemist's report and worksheet here can be deemed to set forth "matters observed," the documents would fail to satisfy the requirements of exception FRE 803(8) for the chemist must be included within the category of "other law enforcement personnel."

The reason why such a restrictive approach was adopted can be established by referring to the Advisory Committee's Notes and by examining the way in which Congress revised the draft legislation proposed by the Advisory Com-mittee and which the Supreme Court submitted to Congress. [A]n overriding concern of the Advisory Committee was that the rules be formulated so as to avoid impinging upon a criminal defendant's right to confront the witnesses against him. . . .

> In one respect, however, the rule with respect to evaluative reports under FRE 803(8)(C) is very specific: they are admissible only in civil cases and against the government in criminal cases in view of the *almost certain collision with confrontation rights which would result from their use against an accused in a criminal case.*

Advisory Committee's Notes, Note to Paragraph (8) of Rule 803, 56 F.R.D. at 313 (emphasis supplied). This preoccupation with preserving the confrontation rights of criminal defendants was shared by a Congress which established enhanced protection for those rights by substantially amending the proposed language of FRE 803(8)(B). An amendment offered by Representative David Dennis added important qualifying language to item (B) which before the amendment deemed as "public records" under FRE 803(8) "matters observed pursuant to duty imposed by law as to which matters there was a duty to report." *See* 120 Cong. Rec. 2387 (1974). The amendment qualified the foregoing language by adding "excluding, however, in criminal cases matters observed by police officers and other law enforcement personnel." *Id.* In the debate that followed the offer of this amendment, the accused's right to confront the witnesses against him was advanced as the impetus for the proposal. . . . Representative Dennis, the sponsor of the proposal,[25] confirmed that this was the intent of the amendment by emphasizing that the amendment pertained to "criminal cases, and in a criminal case the defendant should be confronted with the accuser to give him the chance to cross examine." *Id.* Following the addition of this language excluding reports reciting matters observed by law enforcement personnel, *see* 120 Cong. Rec. 2389 (1974), the Senate added to the pending legislation a proposed FRE 804(b)(5) which would have rendered the exclusion of such reports from the scope of FRE 803(8)(B) ineffective in the event the author of the report was "unavailable" to testify. *See* S. Rep. No. 1277, 93d Cong., 2d Sess. 17 (1974). This attempt to emasculate the Dennis amendment proved to be abortive, however, for the Committee of Conference removed it from the pending legislation. *See* H.R. Rep. No. 1597, 93d Cong., 2d Sess. 12 (1974) (Joint Explanatory Statement of the Committee of Conference).

The discussion in the preceding paragraphs describes *why* Congress decided to take the approach it did with regard to the use of "evaluative" reports under FRE 803(8)(C) and reports of law enforcement personnel under FRE 803(8)(B). The *result* Congress intended was the absolute inadmissibility of records of this nature, and that this was, indeed, the result which Congress believed it had achieved by Rules 803(8)(B) and (C), could not have been articulated with any more clarity than it was by Representative William L. Hungate. As Chairman of the House Judiciary Subcommittee on Criminal Justice, Representative Hungate had been responsible for presiding over extensive hearings on the proposed Federal Rules of Evidence and must be regarded as one of the legislators most knowledgeable about the then pending legislation. . . . [H]e informed the House that the Committee of Conference had rejected the Senate's attempt to create a new hearsay exception which would have permitted admission of police reports authored by officers unavailable to testify. He explained the meaning of the remaining related provisions:

> As the rules of evidence now stand, police and law enforcement reports are not admissible against defendants in criminal cases. This is made quite clear by the provisions of rule 803(8)(B) and (C).

120 Cong. Rec. H12254 (daily ed. Dec. 18, 1974). This unequivocal language shows that it was Representative Hungate's understanding, and he was as familiar with the legislation as anyone else in Congress,[26] that the language

---

[25] It is, of course, well–established that the sponsor's interpretation of his proposal, when expressed prior to adoption of the legislation, is entitled to great weight. (citations omitted)

[26] It is clear that "[r]esort may be had to the statements of such an *authoritative* person," *Ideal Farms, Inc. v. Benson*, 288 F.2d 608, 616 (3d Cir. 1961) (emphasis supplied), *cert. denied,* 372 U.S. 965, 83 S. Ct. 1087, 10 L. Ed. 2d 128 (1963), as Representative Hungate. What persons may be regarded as "authoritative" is equally well–established by numerous cases which have

retained in FRE 803(8)(B) and (C) meant that those provisions had the *effect* of rendering absolutely inadmissible against defendants in criminal cases the "police reports" of item (B) and the "evaluative reports" of item (C).

* * *

[At this point, the court analyzed the substantiality of the defendant's contention that the admission of the report and worksheet violated his rights under the Confrontation Clause. The court stressed that "we do not decide whether appellant's right of confrontation was violated here." However, the court concluded that the defendant's constitutional argument raised sufficiently "serious doubts" to mandate the narrower interpretation of Rule 803(8). Concomitantly, the court ruled that the legislative history was so clear that the prosecution could not even rely on the alternative theory that the chemist's documents qualified as business entries under Rule 803(6).]

[W]e hold here, that in criminal cases reports of public agencies setting forth matters observed by police officers and other law enforcement personnel and reports of public agencies setting forth factual findings resulting from investigations made pursuant to authority granted by law cannot satisfy the standards of any hearsay exception if those reports are sought to be introduced against the accused. Inasmuch as the chemist's documents here can be characterized as governmental reports which set forth matters observed by law enforcement personnel or which set forth factual findings resulting from an authorized investigation, they were incapable of qualifying under any of the exceptions to the hearsay rule specified in FRE 803 and 804.

NOTES

1. Even assuming that you accept the court's interpretation of Rule 803(8), as a matter of statutory construction must you read the same limitation into Rule 803(6)? Most courts have rejected the *Oates* approach. 1 P. GIANNELLI & E. IMWINKELRIED, SCIENTIFIC EVIDENCE § 6–2(A) (3d ed. 1999). Most courts exclude only arrest and lineup reports–documents describing adversarial

---

addressed this question. The sponsor of the legislation would surely be regarded as such a person. *See* note 25, *supra*. So, too, the floor managers, *see, e.g.*, *City of New York v. Train*, *supra*, 494 F.2d at 1039 n.16; the members of the congressional committee which holds hearings on the proposed legislation, *See City of New York v. Train*, *supra*, 494 F.2d at 1039, n.16; and particularly the chairman of such a committee, *See Department of Water & Power v. Allis–Chalmers Mfg. Co.*, *supra* at 351; and the members of the conference committee, *see, e.g.*, *City of New York v. Train*, *supra*, 494 F.2d at 1039 n.16; are regarded as persons whose views, when expressed in the floor debates prior to passage of the legislation, are entitled to particular deference.

The weight to which views of any particular congressman is entitled will vary, of course, with the legislator's familiarity with, and participation in the shaping of, the legislation. It would be difficult to imagine anyone more qualified to comment on the legislation in this case than was Representative Hungate who, as member and Chairman of the House Judiciary Subcommittee on Criminal Justice, and as floor manager and as conference committee member probably had more contact with the proposed rules than any other single legislator. When such impressive credentials exist, we believe that the congressman's "statements in explaining the bill to the House, and the answers made by him to questions asked by members may be considered in construing the bill as it was subsequently enacted into law. These statements are in the nature of supplemental committee reports and are entitled to the same weight accorded to formal committee reports." *Department of Water & Power v. Allis–Chalmers Mfg. Co.*, supra at 351.

confrontations which are most likely to be colored by the officer's subjective evaluation. *United States v. Enterline*, 894 F.2d 287 (8th Cir. 1990). These courts read "law enforcement personnel" more narrowly than the *Oates* court, and they generally refuse to read (8)(C)'s exclusionary provision into Rule 803(6). *United States v. Sokolow*, 81 F.3d 397, 405 (3d Cir. 1996)("many courts" have criticized *Oates*).

2. In some respects, as an exercise in statutory interpretation, the *Oates* opinion is exemplary. The court not only marshalls the extrinsic legislative history materials in detail; the court also critically evaluates the weight of the materials–pausing, for example, to determine whether the source of a statement was a sponsor of the legislative and therefore entitled to greater weight. Nevertheless, the court's conclusions are debatable.

The *Oates* court concedes that it reaches its conclusion about the meaning of "law enforcement personnel" with "less [than complete] confidence." Why? What is the source of the court's uncertainty? The court relies heavily on the constructional maxim that an interpretation mooting concerns about a statute's constitutionality is preferable. Near the end of the opinion, the court brushes aside the government's contention "that the constitutional issue in this case is devoid of merit." In fact, most courts have agreed with the government's position in *Oates* that the admission of laboratory reports such as chemical analyses against a defendant is constitutionally permissible. Imwinkelried, *The Constitutionality of Introducing Evaluative Laboratory Reports Against Criminal Defendants*, 30 HASTINGS L.J. 621 (1979). If the court's assumption about the substantiality of the constitutional issue is erroneous, is the court's reading of 803(8)(B) also wrong?

The court reads "an implied exception into FRE 803(6) . . . ." The proponent of a hearsay statement may ordinarily invoke the various provisions of Rules 803 and 804 as alternative theories for admissibility. For example, the proponent may argue that the statement qualifies as either a present sense impression under Rule 803(1) or a startled utterance under 803(2). Does any of the legislative history cited in *Oates* manifest a clear intention to extend (8)(B)'s exclusionary rule to 803(6)? Absent a clear manifestation of that intent, is the implied exception consistent with Rule 402? However, does the court need to resort to this "implied exception" theory? In a sense, Rule 803(8)(B) applies *Palmer v. Hoffman* to official records; when the prosecution offers police reports against a defendant, the reports can arguably be viewed as suspect, litigation reports. The Advisory Committee Note to Rule 803(6) expressly cites *Palmer*.

While Rule 803(8)(B) departs from the common law by fashioning a new exclusionary provision, (8)(C) deviates from the common law in the opposite direction by expanding the admissibility of certain types of official records. As Wigmore noted, at common law, one of the most controversial issues surrounding the official record doctrine was the admissibility of statements in reports of investigation. This type of official record poses the gravest concerns about the hearsay declarant's testimonial qualities: Is the declarant relating personal knowledge or second–level hearsay from a third party? When the report states conclusions and opinions, are we confident that we understand the meaning the declarant intended to convey by her conclusory, opinionated language? If the trigger for the investigation was an event likely to lead to litigation, was the declarant's sincerity suspect? Given those concerns, the traditional common law view was that reports of investigation did not qualify as official records. Wigmore stressed that "few officers, if any, are found vested by implication with . . . authority" to prepare reports of investigation worthy of admission at trial. 5 J. WIGMORE, EVIDENCE § 1636 (2d ed. 1940). However, McCormick urged more liberal admission of reports. McCormick, *Can the Courts Make Wider Use of Reports of Official Investigations?*, 42 IOWA L. REV. 363, 364–68 (1957).

McCormick's article influenced the Advisory Committee, and in turn the committee persuaded the Supreme Court and Congress to include (8)(C) in Rule 803. Rule 803(8)(C) provides that the official records exception now authorizes the admission "in civil actions and proceedings and against the Government in criminal cases, factual findings resulting from an investigation made pursuant to authority granted by law, unless the sources of information or other circumstances indicate lack of trustworthiness." Like the expression "law enforcement personnel" in (8)(B), the language "factual findings" in (8)(C) divided the lower courts. How broadly did Congress intend the courts to construe this new inclusionary provision? As in the case of the interpretation of (8)(B), when the courts attempted to resolve the interpretation of (8)(C), they had to struggle with "equivocal legislative history." Reid & Nettleton, *Trial by Administrative Ambush*, 16 TRIAL, Fall 1989, at 16. Fortunately, the Supreme Court provided some guidance in the following decision:

BEECH AIRCRAFT CORPORATION v. RAINEY

488 U.S. 153 (1988)

JUSTICE BRENNAN delivered the opinion of the Court.

In this case we address a longstanding conflict among the federal courts of appeal over whether Federal Rule of Evidence 803(8)(C), which provides an exception to the hearsay rule for public investigatory reports containing "factual findings," extends to conclusions and opinions contained in such reports. We also consider whether, on the facts of this case, the trial court abused its discretion in refusing to admit, on cross–examination, testimony intended to provide a more complete picture of a document about which the witness had testified on direct.

This litigation stems from the crash of a Navy training aircraft at Middleton Field, Alabama, on July 13, 1982, which took the lives of both pilots on board, Lieutenant Commander Barbara Ann Rainey and Ensign Donald Bruce Knowlton. The accident took place while Rainey, a Navy flight instructor, and Knowlton, her student, were flying "touch–and–go" exercises in a T–34C Turbo–Mentor aircraft, number 3E955. Their aircraft and several others flew in an oval pattern, each plane making successive landing/takeoff maneuvers on the runway. Following its fourth pass at the runway, 3E955 appeared to make a left turn prematurely, cutting out the aircraft ahead of it in the pattern and threatening a collision. After radio warnings from two other pilots, the plane banked sharply to the right in order to avoid the other aircraft. At that point it lost altitude rapidly, crashed, and burned.

Because of the damage to the plane and the lack of any survivors, the cause of the accident could not be determined with certainty. The two pilots' surviving spouses brought a product liability suit against petitioners Beech Aircraft Corporation, the plane's manufacturer, and Beech Aerospace Services, which serviced the plane under contract with the Navy.[1] The plaintiffs alleged that the crash had been caused by a loss of engine power, known as "rollback," due to some defect in the aircraft's fuel control system. The defendants, on the other hand, advanced the theory of pilot error, suggesting that the plane has stalled during the abrupt avoidance maneuver.

At trial, the only seriously disputed question was whether pilot error or equipment malfunction had caused the crash. Both sides relied primarily on expert testimony. One piece of evidence presented by the defense was an investigative report prepared by Lieutenant Commander William Morgan on order of the training squadron's commanding officer and pursuant to authority granted in the Manual of the Judge Advocate General. This "JAG Report," completed during the six weeks following the accident, was organized into sections labeled "finding of fact," "opinions," and "recommendations," and was supported by some 60 attachments. The "finding of fact" included statements like the following:

> "13. At approximately 1020, while turning crosswind without proper interval, 3E955 crashed, immediately caught fire and burned. . . .
>
> "27. At the time of impact, the engine of 3E955 was operating but was operating at reduced power." App. 10–12.

Among his "opinions" Lieutenant Commander Morgan stated, in paragraph five, that due to the deaths of the two pilots and the destruction of the aircraft "it is almost impossible to determine exactly what happened to Navy 3E955 from the time it left the runway on its last touch and go until it impacted the ground." He nonetheless continued with a detailed reconstruction of a possible set of events, based on pilot error, that could have caused the accident. The next two paragraphs stated a caveat and a conclusion:

> "6. Although the above sequence of events is the most likely to have occurred, it does not change the possibility that a 'rollback' did occur.
>
> "7. The most probable cause of the accident was the pilots [*sic*] failure to maintain proper interval." *Id.,* at 15.

The trial judge initially determined, at a pretrial conference, that the JAG Report was sufficiently trustworthy to be admissible, but that it "would be admissible only on its factual findings and would not be admissible insofar as any opinions or conclusions are concerned." *Id.,* at 35. The day before trial,

---

[1] The manufacturer of the plane's engine was also a defendant, but it subsequently settled with respondents and is no longer a party to this action.

however, the court reversed itself and ruled, over the plaintiffs' objection, that certain of the conclusions would be admitted. *Id.*, at 40–41. Accordingly, the court admitted most of the report's "opinions," including the first sentence of paragraph five about the impossibility of determining exactly what happened, and paragraph seven, which opined about failure to maintain proper interval as "[t]he most probable cause of the accident." *Id.*, at 97. On the other hand, the remainder of paragraph five was barred as "nothing but a possible scenario," *id.*, at 40, and paragraph six, in which investigator Morgan refused to rule out rollback, was deleted as well.

[T]he jury returned a verdict for the petitioners. A panel of the Eleventh Circuit reversed and remanded for a new trial. . . .[holding that] the "conclusions" contained in the JAG Report should have been excluded. . . .

Federal Rule of Evidence 803 provides that certain types of hearsay statements are not made excludable by the hearsay rule, whether or not the declarant is available to testify. Rule 803(8) defines the "public records and reports" which are not excludable, as follows:

> "Records, reports, statements, or data compilations, in any form, of public offices or agencies, setting forth (A) the activities of the office or agency, or (B) matters observed pursuant to duty imposed by law as to which matters there was a duty to report, . . . or (C) in civil actions and proceedings and against the Government in criminal cases, factual findings resulting from an investigation made pursuant to authority granted by law, unless the sources of information or other circumstances indicate lack of trustworthiness."

* * *

Because the Federal Rules of Evidence are a legislative enactment, we turn to the "traditional tools of statutory construction," *INS v. Cardoza–Fonseca*, 480 U.S. 421, 446 (1987), in order to construe their provisions. We begin with the language of the Rule itself. Proponents of the narrow view have generally relied heavily on a perceived dichotomy between "fact" and "opinion" in arguing for the limited scope of the phrase "factual findings." *Smith v. Ithaca Corp.*, [612 F.2d 215 (5th Cir. 1980)] contrasted the term "factual findings" in Rule 803(8)(C) with the language of Rule 803(6) (records of regularly conducted activity), which expressly refers to "opinions" and "diagnoses." "Factual findings," the court opined, must be something other than opinions. *Smith, supra,* at 221–222.[8]

---

[8] The court in *Smith* found it significant that different language was used in Rules 803(6) and 803(8)(C): "Since these terms are used in similar context within the same Rule, it is logical to assume that Congress intended that the terms have different and distinct meanings." 612 F.2d, at 222. The Advisory Committee notes to Rule 803(6) make clear, however, that the Committee was motivated by a particular concern in drafting the language of that Rule. While opinions were rarely found in traditional "business records," the expansion of that category to encompass documents such as medical diagnoses and test results brought with it some uncertainty in earlier versions of the Rule as to whether diagnoses and the like were admissible. "In order to make clear its adherence to the [position favoring admissibility]," the Committee stated, "the rule specifically includes both diagnoses and opinions, in addition to acts, events, and conditions, as proper subjects of admissible entries." Advisory Committee's Notes on Fed. Rule Evid. 803(6),

For several reasons, we do not agree. In the first place, it is not apparent that the term "factual findings" should be read to mean simply "facts" (as opposed to "opinions" or "conclusions"). A common definition of "finding of fact" is, for example, "[a] conclusion by way of reasonable inference from the evidence." Black's Law Dictionary 569 (5th ed. 1979). To say the least, the language of the Rule does not compel us to reject the interpretation that "factual findings" includes conclusions or opinions that flow from a factual investigation. Second, we note that, contrary to what is often assumed, the language of the Rule does not state that "factual findings" are admissible, but that "*reports* . . . setting forth . . . factual findings" (emphasis added) are admissible. On this reading, the language of the Rule does not create a distinction between "fact" and "opinion" contained in such reports.

Turning next to the legislative history of Rule 803(8)(C), we find no clear answer to the question of how the Rule's language should be interpreted. Indeed, in this case the legislative history may well be at the origin of the dispute. Rather than the more usual situation where a court must attempt to glean meaning from ambiguous comments of legislators who did not focus directly on the problem at hand, here the Committees in both Houses of Congress clearly recognized and expressed their opinions on the precise question at issue. Unfortunately, however, they took diametrically opposite positions. Moreover, the two Houses made no effort to reconcile their views, either through changes in the Rule's language or through a statement in the Report of the Conference Committee.

*   *   *

Clearly this legislative history reveals a difference of view between the Senate and the House that affords no definitive guide to the congressional under-standing. It seems clear however that the Senate understanding is more in accord with the wording of the Rule and with the comments of the Advisory Committee. [9]

The Advisory Committee's comments are notable, first, in that they contain no mention of any dichotomy between statements of "fact" and "opinions" or "conclusions." What was on the Committee's mind was simply whether what it called "evaluative reports" should be admissible. Illustrating the previous division among the courts on this subject, the Committee cited numerous cases in which the admissibility of such reports had been both sustained and denied. It also took note of various federal statutes that made certain kinds of

---

28 U.S.C. App., p. 723. Since that specific concern was not present in the context of Rule 803(8)(C), the absence of identical language should not be accorded much significance. See *Rainey v. Beech Aircraft Corp.,* 827 F.2d 1498–1512 (CA11 1987) (en banc) (Tjoflat, J., concurring). What is more, the Committee's report on Rule 803(8)(C) strongly suggests that that Rule has the same scope of admissibility as does Rule 803(6): "Hence the rule, *as in Exception [paragraph] (6),* assumes admissibility in the first instance but with ample provision for escape if sufficient negative factors are present." Advisory Committee's Notes on Fed. Rule Evid. 803(8), 28 U.S.C. App., p. 725 (emphasis added).

[9] See Advisory Committee's Notes on Fed. Rule Evid. 803(8), 28 U.S.C. App., pp. 724–725. As Congress did not amend the Advisory Committee's draft in any way that touches on the question before us, the Committee's commentary is particularly relevant in determining the meaning of the document Congress enacted.

evaluative reports admissible in evidence. What is striking about all of these examples is that these were *reports that stated conclusions. E.g., Moran v. Pittsburgh–Des Moines Steel Co.*, 183 F.2d 467–473 (CA3 1950) (report of Bureau of Mines concerning the cause of a gas tank explosion inadmissible); *Franklin v. Skelly Oil Co.*, 141 F.2d 568–572 (CA10 1944) (report of state fire marshal on the cause of a gas explosion admissible); 42 U.S.C. § 269(b) (bill of health by appropriate official admissible as prima facie evidence of vessel's sanitary history and condition). The Committee's concern was clearly whether reports of this kind should be admissible. Nowhere in its comments is there the slightest indication that it even considered the solution of admitting only "factual" statements from such reports. Rather, the Committee referred throughout to "reports," without any such differentiation regarding the statements they contained. What the Committee referred to in the Rule's language as "reports . . . setting forth . . . factual findings" is surely nothing more or less than what in its commentary it called "evaluative reports." Its solution as to their admissibility is clearly stated in the final paragraph of its report on this Rule. That solution consists of two principles: First, "the rule . . . assumes admissibility in the first instance. . . ." Second, it provides "ample provision for escape if sufficient negative factors are present."

That "provision for escape" is contained in the final clause of the Rule: evaluative reports are admissible "unless the sources of information or other circumstances indicate lack of trustworthiness." This trustworthiness inquiry–and not an arbitrary distinction between "fact" and "opinion"–was the Committee's primary safeguard against the admission of unreliable evidence, and it is important to note that it applies to all elements of the report. Thus, a trial judge has the discretion, and indeed the obligation, to exclude an entire report or portions thereof–whether narrow "factual" statements or broader "conclusions" –that she determines to be untrustworthy.[11] Moreover, safeguards built in to other portions of the Federal Rules, such as those dealing with relevance and prejudice, provide the court with additional means of scrutinizing and, where appropriate, excluding evaluative reports or portions of them. And of course it goes without saying that the admission of a report containing "conclusions" is subject to the ultimate safeguard–the opponent's right to present evidence tending to contradict or diminish the weight of those conclusions.

Our conclusion that neither the language of the Rule nor the intent of its framers calls for a distinction between "fact" and "opinion" is strengthened

---

[11] The Advisory Committee proposed a nonexclusive list of four factors it thought would be helpful in passing on this question: (1) the timeliness of the investigation; (2) the investigator's skill or experience; (3) whether a hearing was held; and (4) possible bias when reports are prepared with a view to possible litigation *(citing Palmer v. Hoffman*, 318 U.S. 109, 63 S. Ct. 477, 87 L. Ed. 645 (1943)). Advisory Committee's Notes on Fed. Rule Evid. 803(8), 28 U.S.C. App., p. 725; *see* Note, The Trustworthiness of Government Evaluative Reports under Federal Rule of Evidence 803(8)(C), 96 Harv. L. Rev. 492 (1982).

In a case similar in many respects to this one, the trial court applied the trustworthiness requirement to hold inadmissible a JAG Report on the causes of a Navy airplane accident; it found the report untrustworthy because it "was prepared by an inexperienced investigator in a highly complex field of investigation." *Fraley v. Rockwell Int'l Corp.*, 470 F. Supp. 1264, 1267 (S.D. Ohio 1979). In the present case, the District Court found the JAG Report to be trustworthy. App. 35. As no party has challenged that finding, we have no occasion to express an opinion on it.

by the analytical difficulty of drawing such a line. It has frequently been remarked that the distinction between statements of fact and opinion is, at best, one of degree:

> "All statements in language are statements of opinion, i.e., statements of mental processes or perceptions. So–called 'statements of fact' are only more specific statements of opinion. What the judge means to say, when he asks the witness to state the facts, is: 'The nature of this case requires that you be more specific, if you can, in your description of what you saw.' " W. King & D. Pillinger, Opinion Evidence in Illinois 4 (1942) (footnote omitted).

See also E. Cleary, McCormick on Evidence 27 (3d ed. 1984) ("There is no conceivable statement however specific, detailed and 'factual,' that is not in some measure the product of inference and reflection as well as observation and memory"); R. Lempert & S. Saltzburg, A Modern Approach to Evidence 449 (2d ed. 1982) ("A factual finding, unless it is a simple report of something observed, is an opinion as to what more basic facts imply").

In the present case, the trial court had no difficulty in admitting as a factual finding the statement in the JAG Report that "[a]t the time of impact, the engine of 3E955 was operating but was operating at reduced power." Surely this "factual finding" could also be characterized as an opinion, which the investigator presumably arrived at on the basis of clues contained in the airplane wreckage. Rather than requiring that we draw some inevitably arbitrary line between the various shades of fact/opinion that invariably will be present in investigatory reports, we believe the Rule instructs us–as its plain language states–to admit "reports . . . setting forth . . . factual findings." The Rule's limitations and safeguards lie elsewhere: First, the requirement that reports contain factual findings bars the admission of statements not based on factual investigation. Second, the trustworthiness provision requires the court to make a determination as to whether the report, or any portion thereof, is sufficiently trustworthy to be admitted.

A broad approach to admissibility under Rule 803(8)(C), as we have outlined it, is also consistent with the Federal Rules' general approach of relaxing the traditional barriers to "opinion" testimony. Rules 702–705 permit experts to testify in the form of an opinion, and without any exclusion of opinions on "ultimate issues." And Rule 701 permits even a lay witness to testify in the form of opinions or inferences drawn from her observations when testimony in that form will be helpful to the trier of fact. We see no reason to strain to reach an interpretation of Rule 803(8)(C) that is contrary to the liberal thrust of the Federal Rules.

We hold, therefore, that portions of investigatory reports otherwise admissible under Rule 803(8)(C) are not inadmissible merely because they state a conclusion or opinion. As long as the conclusion is based on a factual investigation and satisfies the Rule's trustworthiness requirement, it should be admissible along with other portions of the report.[13] As the trial judge in this

---

[13] We emphasize that the issue in this case is whether Rule 803(8)(C) recognizes any difference between statements of "fact" and "opinion." There is no question in this case of any distinction between "fact" and "law." We thus express no opinion on whether legal conclusions contained in an official report are admissible as "findings of fact" under Rule 803(8)(C).

case determined that certain of the JAG Report's conclusions were trustworthy, he rightly allowed them to be admitted into evidence. We therefore reverse the judgment of the Court of Appeals in respect of the Rule 803(8)(C) issue.

NOTES AND PROBLEMS

1. What questions about Rule 803(8)(C) does *Rainey* settle? What questions does the opinion leave unresolved? Does (8)(C) authorize the admission of conclusions of law set out in otherwise admissible official reports? *Hines v. Brandon Steel Decks, Inc.*, 886 F.2d 299, 302–03 (11th Cir. 1989). Read footnote 13 in the Supreme Court's opinion. How liberally should the courts invoke the "unless" clause in (8)(C)? *See Anderson v. City of New York*, 657 F. Supp. 1571, 1577–90 (S.D.N.Y. 1987) (report of the Criminal Justice Subcommittee of the House Judiciary Committee); *United States v. Durrani*, 659 F. Supp. 1183 (D. Conn.) (report of the President's Special Review Board, the Tower report, on the Iran–Contra scandal), *aff'd*, 835 F.2d 410 (2d Cir. 1987). The opponent has the burden of coming forward with proof of facts to trigger the "unless" clause. *Johnson v. City of Pleasanton*, 982 F.2d 350, 352 (9th Cir. 1992). In effect, proof of the normal foundational elements creates a rebuttable presumption of admissibility. *Moss v. Ole South Real Estate, Inc.*, 933 F.2d 1300, 1305 (5th Cir. 1991).

2. According to Justice Brennan, what was the better evidence of legislative intent: the Advisory Note or the House Judiciary Report? Why?

3. As we have noted in the past, one of the maxims of interpretation is that, if the legislature uses different terms, the legislature presumptively intended different meanings. *Smith v. Ithaca Corporation*, cited *supra* in *Beech*, relied heavily on that maxim in championing the "narrow" interpretation of Rule 803(8)(C). The *Smith* court noted that unlike Rule 803(6), Rule 803(8) contained no reference to "opinions." Justice Brennan expressly rejects both that interpretation and the *Smith* court's reasoning. Why does Brennan attach so little weight to the maxim in *Rainey*?

4. Problem 20–27. In *Hill*, before the accident, Polecat exchanged correspondence with the National Highway Traffic Safety Administration. The NHTSA recommended that Polecat recall the model that Ms. Hill drove. Specifically, NHTSA urged that Polecat strengthen the gas tank "because of its hazardous placement." At trial, Ms. Hill calls an NHTSA official to authenticate the letter. Polecat's attorney objects that "a mere letter can't qualify under Rule 803(8)." What ruling? *Tveraas v. Coffey*, 818 F. Supp. 75, 77–78 (D. Vt. 1993) (official letter of reprimand); *In re Multi–Piece Rims Prods. Liability Litig.*, 545 F. Supp. 149, 150–52 (W.D. Mo. 1982).

5. Problem 20–28. The NHTSA conducted safety tests on the Polecat model. The test inspector was Mr. Blumoff. The day after the tests, Blumoff dictated his report to his government secretary, Ms. Chernoff. During the dictation, he said, "In this inspector's opinion, the placement of the gas tank is hazardous." Ms. Chernoff was not listening closely; and when she typed the final report, she inserted the word "not" before "hazardous." Blumoff signed the report without reading it carefully. As soon as he signed it, he placed it in the NHTSA's permanent files. A year later, while browsing through the files on an unrelated case, he came across the report and noticed the error. He immediately dictated a "Corrected Final Report" and inserted it in the file. At trial, Ms. Hill calls Blumoff to offer the "Corrected Final Report." Would the report be admissible under Rule 803(8)? Under California Evidence Code § 1280(b) ("the writing was made at or near the time of the act, condition, or event")? *See Apollo Fuel Oil v. United States*, 73 F.Supp. 2d 254 (E.D.N.Y.) (the inspector later changed the date on a work history sheet when he realized that it was off by one day), *aff'd*, 195 F.3d 74 (2d Cir. 1999).

6. Problem 20–29. In *Devitt*, the prosecutor again offers the crime laboratory report of the hair analysis. Assume that the judge accepted Devitt's argument that *Palmer* precludes admitting the report as a business entry. The prosecutor now remarks, "Well, if that's the case, Your Honor, I'll just offer it as an official record rather than a business entry. *Palmer* deals only with the business entry exception." Is there any language in Rule 803(8) that Devitt can rely on? *See* Annot., 56 A.L.R. Fed. 168, 171–72 (1982).

7. The courts generally limit the scope of Rule 803(8) to final reports approved by the government entity. Neither drafts (*Figures v. Bd. of Public Utilities*, 967 F.2d 357 (10th Cir. 1992)) nor preliminary staff reports (*Kemper Architects v. McFall, Konkel & Kimball Consulting Engineers, Inc.*, 843 P.2d 1178 (Wyo. 1992)) qualify.

Although the courts recognize that limitation on the scope of (8)(C), they otherwise have applied the hearsay exception fairly liberally to administrative reports and investigations. *Guild v. General Motors Corp.*, 53 F. Supp.2d 363 (W.D.N.Y. 1999); *Livingston v. Isuzo Motors, Ltd.*, 910 F.Supp.1473, 1497 (D.Mont. 1995). Yet, given Rule 803(22), most courts have balked at extending (8)(C) to judicial findings of fact. *Hairston v. Washington Metropolitan Area Transit Auth.*, 1997 U.S. Dist. LEXIS 5188, 1997 WL 411946 (D.D.C. Apr. 10, 1997).

8. By this time, you should be conversant with the business entry and official record exceptions. It should be evident that the doctrines are so closely akin that it is easy to confuse them. Be prepared to list all the differences between the two hearsay exceptions.

3. LEARNED TREATISES

At the outset of our discussion of this hearsay exception, we must differentiate it from the preceding documentary hearsay exceptions and a credibility doctrine. The prior hearsay exceptions are distinguishable because under those exceptions, we normally admit writings reflecting specific events such as the delivery of merchandise or the service of a search warrant. In contrast, under the learned treatise exception, we typically introduce texts and articles discussing general principles in subject areas such as science, geography, and history. Thus, the content of a learned treatise differs from that of a routine business entry or official record.

To distinguish this hearsay exception from the related credibility doctrine, though, we must focus on the use of the treatise rather than its content. In a later chapter, we will see that on direct examination, an expert customarily states a principle or theory that serves as the major premise in the expert's syllogistic reasoning. On cross–examination in most jurisdictions, the opposing counsel may confront the expert with passages from learned treatises that contradict the principle on which the expert is relying. 2 C. McCORMICK, HANDBOOK OF THE LAW OF EVIDENCE § 321 (5th ed. 1999). Jurisdictions disagree on the extent to which you may use learned treatises to impeach the witness' testimony about the principle or theory. Some states limit the cross–examiner to texts on which the expert admits relying in forming her opinion. Other states follow the "recognition" test that the cross–examiner may resort to any text that the expert acknowledges as a standard authority in the field. C. HIRSCH, R. MORRIS & A. MORITZ, HANDBOOK OF LEGAL MEDICINE 274 (5th ed. 1979). At the extreme, some jurisdictions allow the cross–examiner to quote any contradictory passage to the witness without a preliminary identification of the text or its authoritative status. R. HABUSH, CROSS EXAMINATION OF NON–MEDICAL EXPERTS 20–9–10 (1981). All jurisdictions agree, however, that on this theory, the passage may not be treated as substantive evidence during summation, and the attorney may not use it as substantive proof to support any finding of fact on appeal. On request, the trial judge gives the jurors a limiting instruction stating that they are not to treat the passage as substantive proof.

In contrast, when a judge invokes the learned treatise hearsay exception, the passage is introduced as substantive proof. There is no limiting instruction, the attorney may invite the jury to accept the passage as substantive evidence, and on appeal the attorney may use the passage to support a judgment in her client's favor. Those are the procedural consequences when the attorney persuades the judge that the proffered text falls within Federal Rule of Evidence 803(18):

> The following are not excluded by the hearsay rule, even though the declarant is available as a witness:

> (18) Learned treatises. To the extent called to the attention of an expert witness upon cross–examination or relied upon by him in direct examination, statements contained in published treatises, periodicals, or pamphlets on a subject of history, medicine, or other science or art, established as a reliable authority by the testimony or admission of the witness or by other expert testimony or by judicial notice. If admitted, the statements may be read into evidence but may not be received as exhibits.

The justification for recognizing this hearsay exception is relatively straightforward. In the case of scholarly texts, there is rarely any question about the quality of the declarant's perception or memory. The declarant, the author, may be describing the results of a long–term research project. The declarant had substantial time to collect the raw data, record it, refine the record into a manuscript, and publish the manuscript after painstaking proofreading. Objectively, there is far less reason to question the perception or memory of the treatise author than that of a startled declarant or a bookkeeper hurriedly dashing off an invoice.

Furthermore, there is good reason to assume the declarant's sincerity. The author is not writing with a view to litigation. The *Palmer* reasoning works in reverse here; the absence of any litigation motivation supports the inference that the author wrote impartially and truthfully. Moreover, the author knows that his work will be subjected to close scrutiny by colleagues—and critics. The author will be writing in journals such as *Clinics of North America, American Medical Association Journal, Journal of Industrial Medicine, New England Journal of Medicine*, and *Mayo Clinics*. Comment, *Learned Treatises as Direct Evidence: The Alabama Experience*, 1967 DUKE L.J. 1169, 1182 n.53. Given the journal's knowledgeable readership, the author can expect an immediate attack on any unsound statements in the article. The author knows that his professional reputation is at risk.

However, while the factors of perception, memory, and sincerity cut in favor of recognizing a hearsay exception for learned treatises, the testimonial quality of narration cuts strongly in the opposite direction. 6 J. WIGMORE EVIDENCE § 1690 (3d ed. 1940). When the author uses a technical term of art in the text, what meaning did she ascribe to the term? Did the author intend that the statement be construed literally and categorically, or would the author concede any exceptions or qualifications? At the time of trial, in the light of more recent research, would the author revise any statements in the text?

These narrative concerns are so weighty that until recently only a few jurisdictions recognized the learned treatise exception. Before the adoption of the Federal Rules, only a distinct minority of courts, including such jurisdictions as Alabama, California, Iowa, and Wisconsin, had accepted the exception. *Bowers v. Garfield*, 382 F. Supp. 503, 507 (E.D. Pa. 1974). With the adoption of the Federal Rules by thirty–nine states, a majority of the jurisdictions now employ the learned treatise exception.

However, even now there is disagreement over the appropriate scope of the exception. Some jurisdictions have traditionally limited the exception to texts relating to the hard, exact sciences such as physics, chemistry, and mathematics. W. REYNOLDS, TRIAL EVIDENCE 50 (1912). These jurisdictions reason that texts relating to these disciplines are much more reliable; in the exact sciences, there often is only one correct answer to the question, and there is less need to bring the declarant into the courtroom. These jurisdictions balk at admitting texts in fields such as medicine, psychiatry, and surgery. *Allison v. State*, 203 Md. 1, 98 A.2d 273 (1953); *Moore v. State*, 184 Ark. 682, 43 S.W.2d 228 (1931); *Eggart v. State*, 40 Fla. 527, 25 So. 144 (1898). California Evidence Code § 1341 is markedly broader. That statute permits the admission of "books of science or art."

NOTES AND PROBLEMS

1. The Advisory Committee conceived of Rule 803(18) as a compromise view. In what sense is it a compromise? Note the introductory phrase in the first sentence of the Rule. In its Note on Rule 803(18), the Committee commented that "[t]he rule avoids the danger of misunderstanding and misapplication by limiting the use of treatises as substantive evidence to situations in which an expert is on the stand and available to explain and assist in the application of the treatise if desired." Does this compromise adequately address the narrative dangers that originally accounted for the courts' reluctance to admit treatises as substantive proof?

2. Problem 20–30. In *Devitt*, the prosecutor calls Dr. Norris as a witness. Dr. Norris identifies himself as a licensed psychiatrist. The prosecutor then marks a text as an exhibit. The text is entitled *The Assault Victim—A Profile* by Chang and Holguin, two practicing psychiatrists. After stating that the text is the most widely read authority on the psychiatric disorders caused by assaults, Norris reads into the record the part of the text describing post–traumatic stress disorder–the symptomatology of a person subjected to an assault. Norris then asserts that he examined Mr. Paterson and concluded that he displayed all the symptoms described by Chang and Holguin. During closing argument, the prosecutor states, "You heard the description of post–traumatic stress disorder, ladies and gentlemen. You know that Mr. Paterson matches that description perfectly." At this point, the defense objects, "Your Honor, there is no substantive proof of the nature of that syndrome. The prosecutor never offered his text into evidence." What ruling? Note the last sentence in Rule 803(18). What do "admitted" and "received" mean? How do they differ? *See Maggipinto v. Reichman*, 607 F.2d 621, 622 (3d Cir. 1979).

3. Problem 20–31. In *Hill*, the plaintiff attempts to introduce a Model Code of Safe Automotive Engineering, prepared by the National Highway Traffic Safety Administration. The Code contains a provision on gas tank placement, and the Polecat model involved was designed in violation of the provision. The NHTSA promulgated the Code as an advisory guide; the federal government never enacted the Code. Can Ms. Hill offer the Code under Rule 803(18)? Suppose that the Code had been promulgated by the National Association of Automotive Safety Engineers, a voluntary private organization. *See Johnson v. Ellis & Sons Iron Works, Inc.*, 604 F.2d 950, 957 (5th Cir. 1979); Annot., 58 A.L.R.3d 148, 153–55 (1974).

4. Does the treatise have to take the form of a conventional book or article? Does Rule 803(18) require that? In *Constantino v. Herzog*, 203 F.3d 164 (2d Cir. 2000), the court applied the exception to a videotape intended to educate physicians on the proper technique for conducting a particular medical procedure.

D. CONCLUSION

As you studied this chapter, you undoubtedly noted the general trend toward the expansion of the exceptions recognized in Rule 803. It is useful at this juncture to pause and assess the wisdom of that trend.

The Undervaluation of Demeanor: Some critics have argued whether the trend overlooks the importance of demeanor evidence to the trier of fact. One of the factors originally accounting for the emergence of the hearsay doctrine is the belief that the admission of hearsay deprives the trier of fact of the opportunity to assess the declarant's demeanor while he or she is speaking. The Rule 803 exceptions arguably depreciate the importance of demeanor by admitting hearsay evidence even when there is no necessity to dispense with demeanor evidence–that is, there is no showing of the declarant's unavailability.

Some modern legal psychologists disagree with the manner in which the courts routinely downplay the importance of demeanor evidence. In the Cleveland Jury Project, the researchers concluded that when the witnesses disagree, jurors often decide the case by focusing on the witnesses' demeanor rather than the substance of their testimony. Austin, *Why Jurors Don't Heed the Trial*, NAT'L L.J., Aug. 12, 1985, at 18. Communications experts commonly assert that when one person speaks to another, the speaker's nonverbal conduct accounts for more than 50% of the information communicated. J. KESTLER, QUESTIONING TECHNIQUES AND TACTICS § 2.49 (1982). If the speaker's statement is laden with emotion, more than 90% of the message may be communicated nonverbally. K. TAYLOR, R. BUCHANAN & D. STRAWN, COMMUNICATION STRATEGIES FOR TRIAL ATTORNEYS 49 (1984). Further, when the listener perceives a conflict between the speaker's statement and the accompanying metacommunication cues, the listener usually opts to disbelieve the statement. J. KESTLER, *supra,* at § 3.34; Peskin, *Non–Verbal Communication in the Courtroom*, 3 TRIAL DIPL. J. 8 (Wint. 1980). In light of these findings, should the courts be so ready to admit hearsay and dispense with demeanor?

The counterpoint to this criticism, though, is that although laypersons might attach significant weight to demeanor in evaluating a witness' credibility, there is mounting evidence that demeanor is a poor indicator of the witness' subjective truthfulness, much less the objective trustworthiness of the witness' testimony. Wellborn, *Demeanor*, 76 CORNELL L. REV. 1075 (1991). As Professor Wellborn has written:

> If ordinary people in fact possess the capacity to detect falsehood or error on the part of others by observing their nonverbal behavior, then it should be possible . . . to demonstrate such a capacity under controlled conditions. Over the past twenty–five years, a large number of experiments involving thousands of subjects have searched for this capacity. With remarkable consistency, the experiments have shown that it simply does not exist.

Id. at 1104. Other commentators concur. Blumenthal, *A Wipe of the Hands, a Lick of the Lips: The Validity of Demeanor Evidence in Assessing Witness Credibility*, 72 NEB. L. REV. 1157 (1994).

The Overvaluation of Sincerity: A second criticism has been leveled against the current state of law on the Rule 803 exceptions–a criticism that seemingly has more merit than the first. By now, it should be obvious that in deciding whether to admit a type of hearsay, the common law attached great, often decisive, significance to an inference of the declarant's sincerity. If the declarant's nervous excitement or business duty strongly suggested that her subjective motivation was truthful, the courts were inclined to characterize the statement as sufficiently reliable to be admitted.

The early common law stress on sincerity is understandable, given its virtual obsession with the prevention of perjury. The preamble to the original English Statute of Frauds referred to the "fraudulent practices which are commonly endeavored to be upheld by perjury and subornation." 6 HOLDSWORTH, HISTORY OF ENGLISH LAW 379–97 (1924). One of the reasons for the emergence of the authentication requirement (the courts' refusal to follow the practice of "everyday affairs of business and social life" of taking documents at face value) was that the courts believed that the requirement would be "a necessary check on the perpetration of fraud." 2 C. MCCORMICK, EVIDENCE § 219 (5th ed. 1999).

It is to be expected that courts so intent on preventing perjury would be readily impressed by an inference of subjective sincerity. However, the question is whether the courts have been overly impressed—whether their focus on sincerity has led them to neglect serious doubts about the declarant's perception, memory, or narration. E. MORGAN, SOME PROBLEMS OF PROOF UNDER THE ANGLO–AMERICAN SYSTEM OF LITIGATION 139–40 (1956). The inference of sincerity may be an adequate substitute for the oath; but when there are substantial questions about the declarant's other testimonial qualities, it is doubtful whether it is wise to waive the opportunity for cross–examination. *Id.* at 164–66.

Trial attorneys' experience and witness psychologists' research suggest the need for a rethinking of the stress on sincerity. Although most hearsay exceptions "stress the element of sincerity . . ., [i]t is believed to be the common experience of attorneys in the trial of cases, when facts are not accurately reported, that witnesses are more often found to be mistaken than committing perjury." Ladd, *The Hearsay We Admit*, 5 OKLA. L. REV. 271, 286 (1952). The traditional exceptions sanction the admission of many types of hearsay that witness psychology tells us are likely to be inaccurate. Stewart, *Perception, Memory, and Hearsay: A Criticism of Present Law and the Proposed Federal Rules of Evidence*, 1970 UTAH L. REV. 1, 9–10, 28. The excited utterance doctrine is particularly suspect. Psychologists have charged that excited utterances are "[t]he most unreliable type of evidence admitted under hearsay exceptions." *Id.* at 28.

NOTE

As a matter of policy, is it time for a wholesale revision of the hearsay exceptions discussed in this chapter? If so, what form should the revision take: (a) the abolition of exceptions such as excited utterance? (b) the revision of the exceptions to require more extensive foundations? or (c) a general directive to the trial judges administering the hearsay rule to make a more searching inquiry into the declarant's perception, memory, and narration?

Chapter 21

HEARSAY: EXCEPTIONS THAT REQUIRE A SHOWING OF UNAVAILABILITY

Read Federal Rules of Evidence 803(5) and 804. Reread Federal Rule of Evidence 612.

A. INTRODUCTION

As we proceed through this chapter, compare the Rule 804 doctrines and exceptions with those we studied in Rule 803. Are the statements admitted under Rule 804 more or less reliable than those under Rule 803? If there is a weaker inference of trustworthiness, is that weakness outweighed by more powerful showing of necessity required under Rule 804? How stringent is that showing requirement?

B. PROOF OF THE DECLARANT'S UNAVAILABILITY

The Supreme Court's 1980 decision in *Ohio v. Roberts*, 448 U.S. 56 (1980) suggested that in criminal cases the prosecution must normally demonstrate the unavailability of its hearsay declarants. That suggestion raised the question of whether the Sixth Amendment confrontation clause requires that we read an unavailability requirement into all the Rule 803 exceptions when they are employed against a criminal defendant. Adding an unavailability requirement would have dramatically changed many of those exceptions. In its 1986 decision in *United States v. Inadi*, 475 U.S. 387 (1986), the majority of the Court disavowed that suggestion in *Roberts*. In 1992, *White v. Illinois*, 502 U.S. 346 (1992), citing *Inadi*, made it clear that the confrontation clause does not impose a general constitutional requirement for proof of unavailability. By statute, the exceptions discussed in this chapter include a requirement for proof of the declarant's unavailability. Thus, the issue is not whether we should require unavailability; the only question is the standard for assessing unavailability.

The hearsay exceptions mentioned in this chapter emerged one by one. As a by–product of that historical accident, the courts developed differing standards for judging unavailability under the various exceptions. C. McCORMICK, HANDBOOK OF THE LAW OF EVIDENCE 608 (2d ed. 1972). The strictness of the standard varies tremendously. In the case of dying declarations, the traditional view recognized the declarant's death as the only acceptable showing of unavailability. *State v. Carden*, 209 N.C. 404, 183 S.E. 898, *cert. denied*, 292 U.S. 682 (1936). The standard under the past recollection recorded doctrine is in marked contrast. Under the doctrine, the witness' prior statement can be admitted even if the witness is both alive and physically present in the courtroom; the only requisite unavailability is the witness' lack of memory about the previous fact or event. *Cohen v. Berry*, 188 A.2d 302 (D.C. App. 1963).

In theory, it is justifiable to have a different unavailability standard for each hearsay exception. The decision whether to recognize an exception depends upon the strength of the proof of reliability and necessity. The stronger the showing of reliability, the less the need for proof of unavailability, and vice versa. However, in practice, using a different unavailability standard for each exception "has little to commend it." C. McCORMICK, HANDBOOK OF THE LAW OF EVIDENCE 608 (2d ed. 1972). The differing standards generate confusion in the application of the hearsay rule.

To eliminate that confusion, most jurisdictions have now opted for a uniform unavailability standard for all exceptions requiring proof of unavailability. Federal Rule of Evidence 804 illustrates that trend:

(a) Definition of unavailability. "Unavailability as a witness" includes situations in which the declarant—

(1) is exempted by ruling of the court on the ground of privilege from testifying concerning the subject matter of his statement; or

(2) persists in refusing to testify concerning the subject matter of his statement despite an order of the court to do so; or

(3) testifies to a lack of memory of the subject matter of his statement; or

(4) is unable to be present or to testify at the hearing because of death or then existing physical or mental illness or infirmity; or

(5) is absent from the hearing and the proponent of his statement has been unable to procure his attendance (or in the case of a hearsay exception under subdivision (b)(2), (3), or (4), his attendance or testimony) by process or other reasonable means.

A declarant is not unavailable as a witness if his exemption, refusal, claim of lack of memory, inability, or absence is due to the procurement or wrongdoing of the proponent of his statement for the purpose of preventing the witness from attending or testifying.

(b) Hearsay exceptions. The following are not excluded by the hearsay rule if the declarant is unavailable as a witness:

* * *

(6) Forfeiture by wrongdoing. A statement offered against a party that has engaged or acquiesced in wrongdoing that was intended to, and did, procure the unavailability of the declarant as a witness.

Rule 804 states a rather liberal definition of unavailability. Subsection (2) treats a witness' "refusing to testify" as a species of unavailability. That was not the common law view in some jurisdictions. *Pleau v. State*, 255 Wis. 362, 38 N.W.2d 496, 498 (1949). Some critics argue that characterizing refusal as unavailability gives the witness' proponent an incentive to encourage the witness to refuse; the proponent gets the benefit of the favorable hearsay, and the opponent cannot effectively cross–examine the witness on the stand. Does the last sentence in Rule 804(a) adequately protect the opponent against that danger?

Subsection (3) recognizes a witness' lack of memory as adequate unavailability. Like subsection (2), this provision departs from the common law in a number of states. *See, e.g., A. T. Stearns Lumber Co. v. Howlett*, 239 Mass. 59, 131 N.E. 217, 218 (1921). The courts rejecting lack of memory argue that recognizing forgetfulness as unavailability encourages perjured claims of loss of memory. Will the trial judge be able to make a reliable finding whether the witness' forgetfulness is genuine or feigned? Some courts have made such findings under Rule 613 in deciding that a witness' claimed forgetfulness was in reality an evasion of a question about a prior statement.

Subsection 804 (b)(6) was added in 1997. The accompanying Advisory Committee Note acknowledges that prior to the amendment, the courts of appeal differed over the proper measure of the burden of proving the facts effecting the forfeiture. Since the conduct waives the constitutional right to confrontation as well as the statutory hearsay rule, some courts had insisted that the prosecution prove the foundational facts by clear and convincing evidence. *E.g., United States v. Thevis*, 665 F.2d 616, 631 (5th Cir.), *cert.denied*, 459 U.S. 825 (1982). However, the Note cited a large number of cases taking the contra view that the applicable standard is a mere preponderance of the evidence. The concluding sentence of the Note specifies that "[t]he usual Rule 104(a) preponderance of the evidence standard has been adopted. . ."

NOTES AND PROBLEMS

1. As noted above, in most respects Rule 804(a) represents a liberal admissibility standard. However, notice the peculiar—and rather awkward—language of 804(a)(5). What is the significance of the disjunctive "or" in the parenthetical statement? Suppose that a declarant's statement would otherwise qualify as a declaration against interest under 804(b)(3), the declarant is in fact unavailable for trial, but the declarant was deposed before trial. *See Campbell by Campbell v. Coleman*, 786 F.2d 892, 895–96 (8th Cir. 1986). Does the answer depend on whether the party offering the declaration at trial is also the party who took the pretrial deposition?

Now read the part of Rule 804(a)(5) after the parenthetical statement. What is the significance of the four concluding words "or other reasonable means"? Does it suffice for the proponent of the witness' former testimony to show that the witness is beyond the reach of compulsory process?

2. Problem 21–1. Morena allows depositions in criminal cases. Morena also permits the introduction of the deposition transcript as substantive evidence at trial if the deponent is then unavailable. Before trial in *Devitt*, the prosecution deposes Mr. Prentiss. At the deposition, Prentiss claims that he and Devitt planned the attack on Paterson. At the time of trial, Prentiss is incarcerated in a state prison in Missouri. The prosecutor argues that Prentiss' imprisonment automatically makes him unavailable. Both Morena and Missouri have adopted the Uniform Act to Secure the Attendance of Witnesses from Without a State in Criminal Proceedings. 9 U.L.A. 50 (1967 Supp.). Devitt's attorney argues that the admission of Prentiss' deposition would "violate both Rule 804 and the Constitution." What ruling? *See Barber v. Page*, 390 U.S. 719, 722–25 (1968).

3. Problem 21–2. Suppose that at the time of trial Prentiss had moved to Australia. Prentiss is still an American citizen, but he has become a permanent resident of Australia. Is this sufficient proof of unavailability? *See Mancusi v. Stubbs*, 408 U.S. 204, 209–13 (1972) (The witness became unavailable when he took up permanent residence in Sweden). The *Mancusi* Court relied on 28 U.S.C. § 1783(a). When the facts in *Mancusi* arose, the statute read: "A court of the United States may subpoena, for appearance before it, a citizen or resident of the United States who . . . is beyond the jurisdiction of the United States and whose testimony in a criminal proceeding is desired by the Attorney General . . . ." (1958 ed.). Section 1783 now provides that "[a] court of the United States may order the issuance of a subpoena requiring the appearance as a witness before it, or before a person or body designated by it, of a national or resident of the United States who is in a foreign country . . . ." Unlike the earlier version of the statute, the amendment authorizes federal process to return an American citizen for a state trial. Would the amendment of § 1783 affect the result in *Mancusi* and this problem?

4. Problem 21–3. Assume that *Mancusi* is still good law. The prosecutor does not have any testimony that Prentiss is in fact a resident of Australia. However, the prosecutor calls Ms. Ferguson, a friend of Prentiss. Ferguson testifies that a month before trial, Prentiss told her that he was "moving to Australia in two weeks at the latest." Is Ferguson's testimony sufficient proof of Prentiss' unavailability? *See United States v. Arthur*, 22 C.M.R. 482, 484 (A.C.M.R. 1958). Distinguish between the question of whether the law recognizes a particular ground as an acceptable form of unavailability and the question of whether there has been sufficient proof of the ground.

C. EXCEPTIONS REQUIRING PROOF OF UNAVAILABILITY

1. FORMER OR PRIOR TESTIMONY

If one party is involved in two or more hearings, several legal doctrines might come into play. Under civil procedure law, decisions rendered in the first proceeding may have issue or claim preclusive effects in the second case. *McNulty v. Copp*, 125 Cal. App. 2d 697, 271 P.2d 90 (1954) (res judicata); *Shell Oil Co. v. Texas Gas Transmission Corp.*, 176 So. 2d 692 (La. Ct. App. 1965). Alternatively, under Federal Rule of Evidence 803(22), the judgment in the prior case may be admissible as evidence in the second case. Or under Rule 804(b)(1), testimony in trial one may be admissible as evidence in trial two:

(b) Hearsay exceptions. The following are not excluded by the hearsay rule if the declarant is unavailable as a witness:

(1) Former testimony. Testimony given as a witness at another hearing of the same or a different proceeding, or in a deposition taken in compliance with law in the course of the same or another proceeding, if the party against whom the testimony is now offered, or, in a civil action or

proceeding, a predecessor in interest, had an opportunity and similar motive to develop the testimony by direct, cross, or redirect examination.

The evolution of the law of former testimony parallels that of the vicarious admission doctrine. As we saw earlier, the vicarious admission doctrine was at first dominated by the substantive law of agency and criminal imputability. The courts gradually de–emphasized those substantive law considerations, focused squarely on the reliability of the statements admitted, and liberalized the standards for admitting vicarious admissions. For its part, the early law of former testimony was dominated by related civil procedure rules. The courts are slowly freeing the former testimony doctrine from the grip of those rules and relaxing the admissibility of prior testimony. As in the case of vicarious admissions, the focus is shifting to the reliability of the proffered evidence. What are the guarantees of reliability in the case of former testimony? The basic foundation includes proof of: the presentation of the testimony at an earlier fair hearing, the earlier witness' unavailability at the present hearing, and identity of both issues and parties between the two hearings.

The first guarantee is that *the witness gave the prior testimony at a fair adversary hearing.* The testimony must have been given under oath; and if the hearing was a critical stage in a criminal prosecution, the state must have afforded the defendant a right to counsel. *Pointer v. Texas*, 380 U.S. 400 (1965) (testimony given at preliminary hearing at which the accused was denied counsel). However, the most important procedural safeguard is the procedure central to hearsay policy, the opportunity for cross–examination. If the party had an opportunity for cross–examination, the testimony can qualify under Rule 804(b)(1). It is well–settled that if the party had no opportunity to cross–examine, the evidence cannot be admitted as former testimony. *Edgerley v. Appleyard*, 110 Me. 337, 86 A. 244 (1913). In *California v. Green*, 399 U.S. 149 (1970), the Court sustained the admission of a witness' preliminary hearing testimony. The Court stressed that the previous opportunity for cross–examination at the preliminary hearing served to satisfy the mandates of both the hearsay rule and the confrontation clause. The opportunity is the essential requirement. So long as that opportunity is afforded, even a deposition conducted under foreign law can qualify; the deposition can be admitted even if the foreign deposition procedure differs radically from American procedure. *United States v. Kelly*, 892 F.2d 255 (3d Cir.) (Belgian deposition), *cert. denied*, 497 U.S. 1006 (1989); *United States v. Salim*, 664 F. Supp. 682 (E.D.N.Y. 1987), *aff'd*, 855 F.2d 944 (2d Cir. 1988) (under French law, the attorneys' only participation was the ability to submit written interrogatories, and all questions were asked by the judge); *United States v. Casamento*, 887 F.2d 1141, 1174 (2d Cir. 1989) (Swiss depositions), *cert. denied*, 493 U.S. 1081 (1990).

PROBLEMS

1. Problem 21–4. In *Devitt*, one witness, Ms. Farrell, testified before the grand jury that returned the indictment against the defendant. Farrell testified that she saw Devitt leave Paterson's apartment at the time of the alleged battery and that at the time Devitt appeared to be upset and in a rush. Farrell died before trial. Can the prosecutor introduce Farrell's grand jury testimony at the trial? *Young v. United States*, 406 F.2d 960, 962 n.2 (D.C. Cir. 1968).

2. Problem 21–5. In *Hill*, the state of Morena brought an administrative action against Worker to suspend his license. At the license revocation hearing, Ms. Pepperidge testified that in her opinion Worker was driving at least fifteen miles an hour in excess of the speed limit. Pepperidge dies before trial. Can Ms. Hill introduce Pepperidge's testimony under Rule 804(b)(1)? Is it controlling that the hearing was "administrative" rather than "judicial"? 2 C. McCormick, Handbook of the Law of Evidence § 305 (5th ed. 1999). Would Ms. Hill have to name Worker as a defendant before invoking 804(b)(1)?

———

The second traditional guarantee of reliability is that ***there must be "identity" of parties between the two hearings.*** It is true that the early common law admitted evidence as former testimony even if there were additional parties in one of the lawsuits. *Philadelphia, W. & B.R. Co. v. Howard*, 54 U.S. (13 How.) 307 (1951). However, civil procedure came to dominate evidence law to such an extent that the parties to suit two had to be parties to suit one or there had to be technical privity. *Bryan v. Malloy*, 90 N.C. 508 (1883). The question, of course, was whether it was sound to equate the civil procedure and evidentiary issues.

One of the most famous former testimony cases, *United States v. Aluminum Co. of America*, 1 F.R.D. 48 (S.D.N.Y. 1938), illustrates the equation. Prior to the case, the Federal Trade Commission had brought an administrative proceeding against Alcoa. In that proceeding, a witness, now deceased, was called by the F.T.C. In the second case, the case that produced the opinion, the United States sought to use that witness' former testimony against Alcoa. The court held that the testimony was inadmissible: "in order for testimony to be admissible in the second case when offered by one party, there must exist a reciprocal right in the other party to introduce it." In other words, in the instant case the United States could not introduce the testimony against Alcoa unless, had the tables been turned, Alcoa could have introduced it against the United States.

Then, the court went on to point out that had the tables been turned, Alcoa could not have introduced the testimony against the United States. The court characterized the United States as "the dominant party" and the F.T.C. as "subordinate." According to the court's strict conception of the privity doctrine, the dominant party must be a party to the first proceeding. The court posed the rhetorical question: "Just think of what would be the situation if a litigation conducted by a subordinate party should lead to binding the dominant party with respect to the admissibility of testimony." In this case, since the party to the first proceeding was the subordinate party, the F.T.C., Alcoa could not have introduced the evidence against the United States in the second case. Since Alcoa could not have introduced the evidence against the United States, the court's reasoning dictated the inadmissibility of the testimony against Alcoa.

NOTE

The *Alcoa* case represents the zenith of the application of the technical requirements for the admission of former testimony. The case not only requires privity; the court also insists upon reciprocity. The United States called the witness at hearing #2, but the court inquired whether Alcoa could have called the witness against the United States at that hearing. The reciprocity requirement for former testimony parallels the traditional mutuality of estoppel requirement for issue preclusion. F. JAMES, G. HAZARD & J. LEUBSDORF, CIVIL PROCEDURE § 11.25 (4th ed. 1992). Adherence to the mutuality requirement "has been steadily eroding." J. FRIEDENTHAL, M. KANE & A. MILLER, CIVIL PROCEDURE § 14.14, at 687–88 (1985). Modernly, the courts have abandoned the reciprocity requirement for former testimony.

The *Alcoa* court plainly missed the point. M. LADD & R. CARLSON, CASES AND MATERIALS ON EVIDENCE 1005 (1972). As Wigmore noted, the limit of privity is not the extent of reliability. The logic of Wigmore's position eventually prevailed. *Mid–City Bank & Trust Co. v. Reading Co.*, 3 F.R.D. 320 (C.D.N.J. 1944). The first step in implementing Wigmore's position was to recognize that cross–examination policy is satisfied when the party in trial two whom the testimony is offered against was a party to trial one. If that party had an opportunity to cross–examine in trial one, there is a sufficient guarantee of reliability. Notice Rule 804(b)(1)'s explicit reference to "the party against whom the testimony is now offered."

Requiring that the person against whom the former testimony is offered have been a party to the former proceeding makes eminent good sense (not to mention, being required by Due Process) if the consequence is preclusive effect. However, the only effect of the hearsay exception for former testimony is that the former testimony is admissible evidence. Given the more limited effect of the evidentiary doctrine, it was urged that the testimony be admitted in trial two if the party it was offered against in trial one was similarly situated—that is, possessed a similar interest and motive to develop the testimony. If that party had the necessary interest and motive, that party would have cross–examined and probed the prior testimony to ensure that it was trustworthy. Hence, there would be an inference of reliability even if the party the testimony is now offered against was not a party or in technical privity with a party in trial one. The California legislature accepted this reasoning for civil cases in Evidence Code § 1292(a):

Evidence of former testimony is not made inadmissible by the hearsay rule if:

(1) The declarant is unavailable as a witness;

(2) The former testimony is offered in a civil action; and

(3) The issue is such that the party to the action or proceeding in which the former testimony was given had the right and opportunity to cross–examine the declarant with an interest and motive similar to that which the party against whom the testimony is offered has at the hearing.

NOTES AND PROBLEMS

1. Problem 12–6. Before the *Hill* case came to trial, Roe sued Worker for indemnification for the property damage to Roe's truck. At the trial, Roe called Ms. Pepperidge as a witness. She testified that she believed that Worker was speeding. Pepperidge dies before the trial in *Hill.* In *Hill,* the plaintiff offers the transcript of Pepperidge's testimony against Roe. Disregard the possibility of introducing the testimony as an admission by Roe. Does the evidence qualify under the former testimony exception? Did Roe have an opportunity to "cross–examine" Pepperidge in the prior trial? *See* FED. R. EVID. 804(b) (1) and CAL. EVID. CODE § 1291(a)(1). Section 1291(a)(1) reads: "Evidence of former testimony is not made inadmissible by the hearsay rule if the declarant is unavailable as a witness and . . . [t]he former testimony is offered against a person who offered it in evidence in his own behalf on the former occasion or against the successor in interest of such person . . . ."

2. Problem 21–7. Before *Hill* comes to trial, Ms. Oppenheimer brought a similar lawsuit against Polecat to trial. At that trial, Oppenheimer called Professor Vincent as an expert witness on safety design. He testified that in his opinion, the placement of the gas tank was hazardous. Professor Vincent dies before the trial in *Hill.* May Ms. Hill offer evidence of Vincent's testimony against Polecat in the present trial?

3. The courts construing Rule 804(b)(1) have found the expression, "predecessor in interest," troublesome. *New England Life Ins. Co. v. Anderson,* 888 F.2d 646, 651–52 (10th Cir. 1989) (distinguishing between "realistic . . ." and "formalistic . . ." interpretations of "predecessor in interest"); Turner, *Federal Rule of Evidence 804: Will the Real Predecessor–in–Interest Please Stand Up,* 19 AKRON L. REV. 251 (1985). Three different interpretations emerge from the cases. Some courts construe the expression in the narrow property sense of privity. *Id.* at 261. Other courts go to the polar extreme and find a predecessor in interest whenever there is similarity of motive between the earlier litigant and the party in the instant suit. *Id.* at 262; *Supermarket of Marlinton v. Meadow Gold Dairies,* 875 F. Supp. 340, 344–45 (W.D. Va. 1994). Still other courts have embraced a compromise position and insist on a unique relationship between the two parties that ensures similarity of interest and motive. Turner, *supra,* at 264. The current Reporter for the Federal Rules of Evidence Advisory Committee, Professor Daniel Capra, touched upon this issue in ADVISORY COMMITTEE NOTES TO THE FEDERAL RULES OF EVIDENCE THAT MAY REQUIRE CLARIFICATION (Fed. Jud. Center 1998). On the one hand, he points out that given the way the expression, "predecessor in interest, " "is ordinarily used," the statute appears to require proof of "some kind of [technical] privity relationship." *Id.* at 20–21. On the other hand, he observes that the Advisory Committee Note uses broader language. Further, as he reads the cases, the courts "have generally opted. . . for the Advisory Committee approach" and permitted the Note to "supersede" the statutory text. *Id.* at 21–22. The most recent decision, *New Jersey Turnpike Authority v. PPG Industries,* 197 F.3d 96, 110 n. 21 (3d Cir. 1999) bears out Professor Capra's observation. Does this phenomenon indicate that many lower courts still adhere to the legal process theory of statutory construction?

Which view do you prefer? By its terms, in addition to requiring that the party to the prior hearing was "a predecessor in interest," Rule 804(b)(1) imposes a separate requirement that the party "had a . . . similar motive to develop the testimony . . . ." Does that express requirement strengthen or weaken the argument for an expansive construction of "predecessor in interest"? When a legislature uses different terms—"interest" as opposed to "motive"—the courts normally presume that the legislature meant different things. The extrinsic legislative history material is of little help. 2 McCormick, Evidence § 303, at 294 (5th ed. 1999) ("the House Subcommittee that drafted this [language] intended it to require a 'formal relationship' between the parties. [But h]ow much weight to give such obscure indications of legislative intent is . . . uncertain, particularly since even the Senate Judiciary Committee did not appear to understand the significance of the language").

The last guarantee of reliability takes the form of a requirement that ***there be identity of issues between the two hearings***. Although the courts usually refer to "issues," it would be more precise to focus on the issue in the singular—a comparison between the fact that the testimony was offered to prove in trial one and the fact that it is now offered to establish.

The modern understanding of the requirements for identity of parties and issues is that the requirements are merely means to an end—the objective of ensuring that at the prior hearing, the testimony was probed with roughly the same vigor that it would have been challenged with in the current trial. 2 C. McCormick, Handbook of the Law of Evidence § 304 (5th ed. 1999). In a civil case, that necessitates inquiring whether the stakes in the prior hearing were roughly equivalent to the stakes in the current trial. If Ms. Oppenheimer's prior suit against Polecat had been a claim for only $2,000 in property damage to her car, we cannot be confident that Professor Vincent's testimony was tested as rigorously as it would be in *Hill* with hundreds of thousands of dollars in issue. The motive and incentive to cross–examine would be much greater in *Hill*. As the Assembly Committee's Comment to California Evidence Code § 1291 states, "[t]he determination of similarity of interest and motive in cross–examination should be based on practical considerations and not merely on the similarity of the party's position in the two cases. For example, testimony contained in a deposition that was taken, but not offered in evidence at the trial, in a different action should be excluded if the judge determines that the deposition was taken for discovery purposes and that the party did not subject the witness to a thorough cross–examination because he sought to avoid a premature revelation of the weakness in the testimony of the witness or in the adverse party's case."

NOTE

It is generally understood that criminal defense counsel use preliminary hearings for discovery. Unlike Perry Mason, who wins all his cases at the preliminary hearing, most defense counsel do not present a full case at the hearing; rather, they sit back and discover the case the police have amassed against their client. Given that common practice, is there sufficient practical identity of issues between the preliminary hearing and the trial? *Compare California v. Green*, 399 U.S. 149, 166 (1970) *with Ohio v. Roberts*, 448 U.S. 56, 61–62, 69–72 (1980).

Just as the defense's motivation might change from the preliminary hearing to trial, the prosecution's motivation can change from the grand jury to trial. In *United States v. Salerno*, 937 F.2d 797 (2d Cir. 1991), the defendants, alleged Cosa Nostra members, were charged with rigging bids on Manhattan construction projects. The indictment averred that the defendants did so by allocating contracts among a "Club" of six concrete companies. Two witnesses, DeMatteis and Bruno, testified before a grand jury but invoked their privilege against self–incrimination at trial. The witnesses owned Cedar Park Concrete Construction, one of the firms in the "Club." Before the grand jury, the witnesses stated that neither they nor the firm participated in the Club. At trial, the defense offered their grand jury testimony against the government. The government objected on the ground that there was insufficient similarity of issues between the two proceedings. The court noted that although the witnesses' trial testimony was unavailable to the defendant, as a practical matter it was available to the prosecution. The lower court held that "since these witnesses were available to the government at trial through a grant of immunity, the government's motive in examining the witnesses at the grand jury was irrelevant." The government prosecuted an appeal to the Supreme Court:

UNITED STATES v. SALERNO

505 U.S. 317 (1992)

Justice Thomas delivered the opinion of the Court.

The District Court refused to admit the grand jury testimony. It observed that Rule 804(b)(1) permits admission of former testimony against a party at trial only when that party had a "similar motive to develop the testimony by direct, cross, or redirect examination." The District Court held that the United States did not have this motive, stating that the "motive of a prosecutor in questioning a witness before the grand jury in the investigatory stages of a case is far different from the motive of a prosecutor in conducting the trial." A jury subsequently convicted the respondents of the RICO counts and other federal offenses.

The United States Court of Appeals for the Second Circuit reversed, holding that the District Court had erred in excluding DeMatteis and Bruno's grand jury testimony. Although the Court of Appeals recognized that "the government may have had no motive . . . to impeach Bruno or DeMatteis" before the grand jury, it concluded that "the government's motive in examining the witnesses . . . was irrelevant." The Court of Appeals decided that, in order to maintain "adversarial fairness," Rule 804(b)(1)'s similar motive element should "evaporat[e]" when the government obtains immunized testimony in a grand jury proceeding from a witness who refuses to testify at trial. We granted certiorari, and now reverse and remand.

The parties acknowledge that the hearsay rule, standing by itself, would have blocked the introduction at trial of DeMatteis and Bruno's grand jury testimony. Rule 804(b)(1), however, establishes an exception to the hearsay rule for former testimony. This exception provides: "The following are not excluded by the hearsay rule if the declarant is unavailable as a witness: Former Testimony. Testimony given as a witness at another hearing . . . if the party against whom the testimony is now offered . . . had an opportunity and similar motive to develop the testimony by direct, cross, or redirect examination." We must decide whether the Court of Appeals properly interpreted Rule 804(b)(1) in this case.

Nothing in the language of Rule 804(b)(1) suggests that a court may admit former testimony absent satisfaction of each of the Rule's elements. The United States thus asserts that, unless it had a "similar motive," we must conclude that the District Court properly excluded DeMatteis and Bruno's testimony as hearsay. The respondents, in contrast, urge us not to read Rule 804(b)(1) in a "slavishly literal fashion." They contend that "adversarial fairness" prevents the United States from relying on the similar motive requirement in this case. We agree with the United States.

When Congress enacted the prohibition against admission of hearsay in Rule 802, it placed 24 exceptions in Rule 803 and 5 additional exceptions in Rule 804. Congress thus presumably made a careful judgment as to what hearsay may come into evidence and what may not. To respect its determination, we must enforce the words that it enacted. The respondents, as a result, have no right to introduce DeMatteis and Bruno's former testimony under Rule 804(b)(1) without showing a "similar motive." This Court cannot alter evidentiary rules merely because litigants might prefer different rules in a particular class of cases.

The respondents' argument for a different result takes several forms. They first assert that adversarial fairness requires us to infer that Rule 804(b)(1) contains implicit limitations. They observe, for example, that the Advisory Committee Note to Rule 804 makes clear that the former testimony exception applies only to statements made under oath or affirmation, even though the Rule does not state this restriction explicitly. The respondents maintain that we likewise may hold that Rule 804(b)(1) does not require a showing of similar motive in all instances.

The respondents' example does not persuade us to change our reading of Rule 804(b)(1). If the Rule applies only to sworn statements, it does so not because adversarial fairness implies a limitation, but simply because the word "testimony" refers only to statements made under oath or affirmation. *See* BLACK'S LAW DICTIONARY 1476 (6th ed. 1990). We see no way to interpret the text of Rule 804(b)(1) to mean that defendants sometimes do not have to show "similar motive."

The respondents also assert that courts often depart from the Rules of Evidence to prevent litigants from presenting only part of the truth. For example, citing *United States v. Miller*, 600 F.2d 498 (CA5 1979), the respondents maintain that, although parties may enjoy various testimonial privileges, they can forfeit these privileges by "opening the door" to certain subjects. In the respondents' view, the United States is attempting to use the hearsay rule like a privilege to keep DeMatteis and Bruno's grand jury testimony away from the jury. They contend . . . that adversarial fairness requires us to conclude that the United States forfeited its right to object to admission of the testimony when it introduced contradictory evidence about Cedar Park.

This argument also fails. Even assuming that we should treat the hearsay rule like the rules governing testimonial privileges, we would not conclude that a forfeiture occurred here. Parties may forfeit a privilege by exposing privileged evidence, but do not forfeit one merely by taking a position that the evidence might contradict. *See* 8 J. WIGMORE, EVIDENCE § 2327, at 636 (McNaughton rev. 1961). . . . In *Miller*, for example, the court held that a litigant, "after giving the jury his version of a privileged communication, [could not] prevent the cross–examiner from utilizing the communication itself to get at the truth." 600 F.2d at 501. . . . In this case, by contrast, the United States never presented to the jury any version of what DeMatteis and Bruno had said in the grand jury proceedings. Instead, it attempted to show Cedar Park's participation in the Club solely through other evidence available to the respondents. The United States never exposed to the jury anything analogous to a "privileged communication."

The question remains whether the United States had a "similar motive" in this case. The United States asserts that the District Court specifically found that it did not and that we should not review its factual determinations. It also argues that a prosecutor generally will not have the same motive to develop testimony in grand jury proceedings as he does at trial. A prosecutor, it explains, must maintain secrecy during the investigatory stages of the criminal process and therefore may not desire to confront grand jury witnesses with contradictory evidence. It further states that a prosecutor may not know, prior to indictment, which issues will have importance at trial and accordingly may fail to develop grand jury testimony effectively.

The respondents disagree with both of the United States' arguments. They characterize the District Court's ruling as one of law, rather than fact, because the District Court essentially ruled that a prosecutor's motives at trial always differ from his motives in grand jury proceedings. The respondents contend further that the grand jury transcripts in this case show that the United States thoroughly attempted to impeach DeMatteis and Bruno. They add that, despite the United States' stated concern about maintaining secrecy, the United States revealed to DeMatteis and Bruno the identity of the major witnesses who testified against them at trial.

The Court of Appeals . . . erroneously concluded that the respondents did not have to demonstrate a similar motive in this case to make use of Rule 804(b)(1). It therefore declined to consider fully the arguments now presented by the parties about whether the United States had such a motive. Rather than address this issue here in the first instance, we think it prudent to remand the case for further consideration.

NOTES

1. To appreciate the importance of *Salerno*, we must preview a bit of constitutional law on the accused's constitutional right to introduce exculpatory testimony even when the testimony is technically inadmissible. When potential defense witnesses in possession of exculpatory information refused to testify due to fear of incrimination, defendants have argued that the prosecution is obliged to grant the witness immunity in order to make the exculpatory testimony available. For the most part, the courts have rejected these arguments. *United States v. Khan*, 728 F.2d 676 (5th Cir. 1984). Given the failure of the constitutional argument, defendants have turned to non-constitutional theories such as the argument advanced in *Salerno*.

2. The starting point of Justice Thomas' opinion is predictable—the text of the statute. The defense urges the Court not to adopt a "slavishly literal" reading of Rule 804(b)(1). Did the Court do so? The defense's proposed statutory interpretation was rather novel. In effect, the defense conceded that Rule 804(b)(1) controlled, but the defense contended that it did not have to comply with one of the requirements set out on the face of 804(b)(1). Did the defense articulate any convincing justification for singling out the motive requirement and obviating the need to satisfy it? Did the defense commit a strategic error by conceding that 804(b)(1) was in point? Should the defense have relied on 804(b)(5) instead?

3. What "extrinsic" source did Justice Thomas consult to determine the meaning of the word "testimony" in Rule 804(b)(1). According to some commentators, reliance on dictionaries can be treacherous. Cunningham *et al.*, *Plain Meaning and Hard Cases*, 103 YALE L. J. 1561, 1615 (1994). "[T]here are a wide variety of dictionaries from which to choose, and all of them usually provide several entries for each word. The selection of a particular dictionary and a particular definition is not obvious and must be defended on some other grounds of suitability." Note, *Looking It Up: Dictionaries and Statutory Interpretation*, 107 HARV. L. REV. 1437, 1445 (1994).

4. As previously stated, the McCormick treatise argues that the motive requirement should be viewed as a means to the end of safeguarding the opponent's opportunity to question the declarant. 2 MCCORMICK, EVIDENCE § 304 (5th ed. 1999). Should the defense have argued that there was no need to enforce that requirement in *Salerno* because the prosecution had other means of attaining the same end? The defense might have urged that as a more purposive construction of the statute.

5. Assume that the motive requirement is applicable. On the facts, who has the better of the argument that the defense satisfied the requirement? In dissent in *Salerno*, Justice Stevens argued that the defense complied with the requirement. On remand, a panel of the lower court agreed. 974 F.2d 231 (2d Cir. 1992). However, the *en banc* Second Circuit reheard the case, vacated the panel decision, and held that the government did not have a sufficiently similar motive. 8 F.3d 909, 915 (2d Cir. 1993).

2. DECLARATIONS AGAINST INTEREST

In the case of former testimony, the circumstantial guarantee of trustworthiness is the prior opportunity to test the declarant's perception, memory, narration, and sincerity by cross–examination. There is a different basis for inferring reliability in the case of declarations against interest. Here the inference arises from the disserving quality of the statement—the fact that it is against the person's rational self–interest to make the statement. The statement must be based on firsthand perception. *United States v. Lang*, 589 F.2d 92 (2d Cir. 1978). However, the real rationale for admitting the statement is its presumed sincerity. At common law, when the declarant makes the statement, she must realize that the statement is disserving to her interest. The Federal Rules codify the doctrine in Rule 804(b)(3):

> (b) Hearsay exceptions. The following are not excluded by the hearsay rule if the declarant is unavailable as a witness:
>
> > (3) Statement against interest. A statement which was at the time of its making so far contrary to the declarant's pecuniary or proprietary interest, or so far tended to subject him to civil or criminal liability, or to render invalid a claim by him against another, that a reasonable man in his position would not have made the statement unless he believed it to be true. A statement tending to expose the declarant to criminal liability and offered to exculpate the accused is not admissible unless corroborating circumstances clearly indicate the trustworthiness of the statement.

Again, the key circumstantial guarantee of sincerity is the declarant's realization that the statement is contrary to his or her interests. The realization must exist when the declarant makes the statement. The timing requirement is a fundamental distinction between admissions and declarations against interest. Earlier we noted that in a sense, an admission must be inconsistent with the party's position at trial; if it is, it is admissible even if the admission was self–serving when made. The converse is true for declarations against interest. The declaration theory rests on an inference of sincerity rather than the peculiar justification of the admissions doctrine, and inferring sincerity requires a finding that the statement was disserving when made.

In principle, the sincerity must exist in the declarant's mind. Morgan, *Declarations Against Interest*, 5 VAND. L. REV. 451, 477 (1952); Jefferson, *Declarations Against Interest: An Exception to the Hearsay Rule*, 58 HARV. L. REV. 1, 18, 23 (1944). Of course, the state of mind of the hypothetical reasonable person is relevant; if a reasonable person would have thought that the statement was disserving, that is some evidence that the actual declarant entertained that thought. "[I]f a reasonable man would have had the belief, the declaration will be received unless there is a finding that the declarant did not believe the declaration to be against interest." *Id.* at 22–23. The reasonable person's hypothetical belief is circumstantial evidence of the declarant's actual belief. Does Rule 804(b)(3) treat the reasonable person's state of mind as mere circumstantial evidence, or does it accord that state of mind greater weight? Is the language of (b)(3) simply inartful or positively wrong–minded? The federal courts seem to interpret (b)(3) literally. They have declared that the test is "objective" (*United States v. Turner*, 475 F. Supp. 194 (E.D. Mich. 1978)), based on the perception of a reasonable person in the declarant's position rather than the declarant herself. *United States v. Satterfield*, 572 F.2d 687 (9th Cir.), *cert. denied*, 439 U.S. 840 (1978).

According to the text of Rule 804(b)(3), the declarant's perception must be a consciousness that the "statement" is contrary to interest. As the following case demonstrates, in determining the declarant's state of mind, the judge may encounter a number of thorny problems.

WILLIAMSON v. UNITED STATES

512 U.S. 594 (1994)

JUSTICE O'CONNOR delivered the opinion of the Court, except as to Part II–C.

In this case we clarify the scope of the hearsay exception for statements against penal interest. Fed. Rule Evid. 804(b)(3).

I

A deputy sheriff stopped the rental car driven by Reginald Harris for weaving on the highway. Harris consented to a search of the car, which revealed 19 kilograms of cocaine in two suitcases in the trunk. Harris was promptly arrested.

Shortly after Harris' arrest, Special Agent Donald Walton of the Drug Enforcement Administration (DEA) interviewed him by telephone. During that conversation, Harris said that he got the cocaine from an unidentified Cuban in Fort Lauderdale; that the cocaine belonged to petitioner Williamson; and that it was to be delivered that night to a particular dumpster. Williamson was also connected to Harris by physical evidence: The luggage bore the initials of Williamson's sister, Williamson was listed as an additional driver on the car rental agreement, and an envelope addressed to Williamson and a receipt with Williamson's girlfriend's address were found in the glove compartment.

Several hours later, agent Walton spoke to Harris in person. During that interview, Harris said that he had rented the car a few days earlier and had driven it to Fort Lauderdale to meet Williamson. According to Harris, he had gotten the cocaine from a Cuban who was Williamson's acquaintance, and the Cuban had put the cocaine in the car with a note telling Harris how to deliver the drugs. Harris repeated that he had been instructed to leave the drugs in a certain dumpster, to return to his car, and to leave without waiting for anyone to pick up the drugs.

Agent Walton then took steps to arrange a controlled delivery of the cocaine. But as Walton was preparing to leave the interview room, Harris "got out of [his] chair . . . and . . . took a half step toward [Walton] . . . and said, 'I can't let you do that,' threw his hands up and said, 'that's not true, I can't let you go up there for no reason.'" Harris told Walton that he had lied about the Cuban, the note, and the dumpster. The real story, Harris said, was that he was transporting the cocaine to Atlanta for Williamson, and that Williamson was traveling in front of him in another rental car. Harris added that after his car was stopped, Williamson turned around and drove past the location of the stop, where he could see Harris' car with its trunk open. Because Williamson had apparently seen the police searching the car, Harris explained that it would be impossible to make a controlled delivery.

Harris told Walton that he had lied about the source of the drugs because he was afraid of Williamson. Though Harris freely implicated himself, he did not want his story to be recorded, and he refused to sign a written version of the statement. Walton testified that he had promised to report any cooperation by Harris to the Assistant United States Attorney. Walton said Harris was not promised any reward or other benefit for cooperating.

Williamson was eventually convicted of possessing cocaine with intent to distribute, conspiring to possess cocaine with intent to distribute, and traveling interstate to promote the distribution of cocaine. When called to testify at Williamson's trial, Harris refused, even though the prosecution gave him use immunity and the court ordered him to testify. The District Court then ruled that, under Rule 804(b)(3), Agent Walton could relate what Harris had said to him:

> The ruling of the Court is that the statements . . . are admissible under [Rule 804(b)(3)], which deals with statements against interest. First, defendant Harris' statements clearly implicated himself, and therefore, are against his penal interest. Second, defendant Harris, the declarant, is unavailable. And third . . ., there are sufficient corroborating circumstances in this case to ensure the trustworthiness of his testimony. Therefore . . ., these statements by defendant Harris implicating [Williamson] are admissible.

Williamson appealed his conviction, claiming that the admission of Harris' statements violated Rule 804(b)(3) and the Confrontation Clause of the Sixth Amendment. The Court of Appeals for the Eleventh Circuit affirmed . . ., and we granted certiorari.

II

A

The hearsay rule, Fed. Rule Evid. 802, is premised on the theory that out–of–court statements are subject to particular hazards. The declarant might be lying; he might have misperceived the events which he relates; he might have faulty memory; his words might be misunderstood or taken out of context by the listener. And the ways in which these dangers are minimized for in–court statements—the oath, the witness' awareness of the gravity of the proceedings, the jury's ability to observe the witness' demeanor, and, most importantly, the right of the opponent to cross–examine—are generally absent for things said out of court.

Nonetheless, the Federal Rules of Evidence also recognize that some kinds of out–of–court statements are less subject to these hearsay dangers, and therefore except them from the general rule that hearsay is inadmissible. One such category covers statements that are against the declarant's interest . . . . Fed. Rule Evid. 804(b)(3).

To decide whether Harris' confession is made admissible under Rule 804(b)(3), we must first decide what the Rule means by "statement," which Federal Rule of Evidence 801(a)(1) defines as "an oral or written assertion."

One possible meaning, "a report or narrative," WEBSTER'S THIRD NEW INTERNATIONAL DICTIONARY 2229, defn. 2(a) (1961), connotes an extended declaration. Under this reading, Harris' entire confession — even if it contains both self–inculpatory and non–self–inculpatory parts—would be admissible so long as in the aggregate the confession sufficiently inculpates him. Another meaning of "statement," "a single declaration or remark," *ibid.*, defn. 2(b), would make Rule 804(b)(3) cover only those declarations or remarks within the confession that are individually self–inculpatory.

Although the text of the Rule does not directly resolve the matter, the principle behind the Rule, so far as it is discernible from the text, points clearly to the narrower reading. Rule 804(b)(3) is founded on the commonsense notion that reasonable people, even reasonable people who are not especially honest, tend not to make self–inculpatory statements unless they believe them to be true. This notion simply does not extend to the broader definition of "statement." The fact that a person is making a broadly self–inculpatory confession does not make more credible the confession's non–self–inculpatory parts. One of the most effective ways to lie is to mix falsehood with truth, especially truth that seems particularly persuasive because of its self–inculpatory nature.

. . . In our view, the most faithful reading of Rule 804(b)(3) is that it does not allow admission of non–self–inculpatory statements, even if they are made within a broader narrative that is generally self–inculpatory. The district court may not just assume for purposes of Rule 804(b)(3) that a statement is self–inculpatory because it is part of a fuller confession, and this is especially true when the statement implicates someone else. "[T]he arrest statements of a codefendant have traditionally been viewed with special suspicion. Due to his strong motivation to implicate the defendant and to exonerate himself, a codefendant's statements about what the defendant said or did are less credible than ordinary hearsay evidence." *Lee v. Illinois*, 476 U.S. 530, 541 (1986).

*   *   *

C

In this case, . . . we cannot conclude that all that Harris said was properly admitted. Some of Harris' confession would clearly have been admissible under Rule 804(b)(3); for instance, when he said he knew there was cocaine in the suitcase, he essentially forfeited his only possible defense to a charge of cocaine possession, lack of knowledge. But other parts of his confession, especially the parts that implicated Williamson, did little to subject Harris himself to criminal liability. A reasonable person in Harris' position might even think that implicating someone else would decrease his practical exposure to criminal liability, at least so far as sentencing goes. Small fish in a big conspiracy often get shorter sentences than people who are running the whole show . . ., especially if the small fish are willing to help the authorities catch the big ones . . . .

Nothing in this record shows that the District Court or the Court of Appeals inquired whether each of the statements in Harris' confession was truly self–inculpatory. [T]his can be a fact–intensive inquiry, which would require careful examination of all the circumstances surrounding the criminal activity; we therefore remand to the Court of Appeals to conduct this inquiry in the first instance.

JUSTICE SCALIA, concurring.

I quite agree with the Court that a reading of the term "statement" to connote an extended declaration (and which would allow both self–inculpatory and non–self–inculpatory parts of a declaration to be admitted so long as the declaration in the aggregate was sufficiently inculpatory) is unsupportable.

[A] declarant's statement is not magically transformed from a statement against penal interest into one that is inadmissible merely because the declarant names another person . . . . For example, if a lieutenant in an organized crime operation described the inner workings of an extortion and protection racket, naming some of the other actors and thereby inculpating himself on racketeering and/or conspiracy charges, I have no doubt that some of those remarks could be admitted as statements against penal interest. Of course, naming another person, if done . . . in a context where the declarant is minimizing culpability or criminal exposure, can bear on whether the statement meets the Rule 804(b)(3) standard. The relevant inquiry, however—and one that is not furthered by clouding the waters with manufactured categories such as "collateral neutral" and "collateral self–serving" . . . —must always be whether the particular remark at issue (and not the extended narrative) meets the standard set forth in the rule.

JUSTICE GINSBURG, with whom JUSTICE BLACKMUN, JUSTICE STEVENS, and JUSTICE SOUTER join, concurring in part and concurring in the judgment.

[These justices would have gone farther and ruled that "Harris' statements . . . do not fit, even in part, within" Rule 804(b)(3). Harris had been "caught red-handed with 19 kilos of cocaine." The self-inculpatory parts of his statements "provided only marginal or cumulative evidence of his guilt." Overall, the circumstances "project an image of a person acting not against his penal interest, but striving mightily to shift personal responsibility to someone else." In that light, "none of Harris' hearsay statements were admissible under Rule 804(b)(3)."]

JUSTICE KENNEDY, with whom THE CHIEF JUSTICE and JUSTICE THOMAS join, concurring in the judgment.

The rationale of the hearsay exception for statements against interest is that people seldom "make statements which are damaging to themselves unless satisfied for good reason that they are true." Advisory Committee Notes on Fed. Rule Evid. 804 . . . . Of course, the declarant may make his statement against interest (such as "I shot the bank teller") together with collateral but related declarations (such as "John Doe drove the getaway car"). The admissibility of those collateral statements under Rule 804(b)(3) is the issue we must decide here.

There has been a long–running debate among commentators over the admissibility of collateral statements. Dean Wigmore took the strongest position in favor of admissibility, arguing that "the statement may be accepted, not merely as to the specific fact against interest, but also as to every fact contained in the same statement." 5 J. WIGMORE, EVIDENCE § 1465 (3d ed.

1940). According to Wigmore, because "the statement is made under circumstances fairly indicating the declarant's sincerity and accuracy," the entire statement should be admitted. Dean McCormick's approach regarding collateral statements was more guarded. He argued for the admissibility of collateral statements of a neutral character; and for the exclusion of collateral statements of a self–serving character. For example, in the statement "John and I robbed the bank," the words "John and" are neutral (save for the possibility of conspiracy charges). On the other hand, the statement, "John, not I, shot the bank teller" is to some extent self–serving and therefore might be inadmissible. *See* C. MCCORMICK, LAW OF EVIDENCE § 256 (1954). Professor Jefferson took the narrowest approach, arguing that the reliability of a statement against interest stems only from the disserving fact stated and so should be confined "to the proof of the fact which is against interest." Jefferson, *Declarations Against Interest: An Exception to the Hearsay Rule*, 58 HARV. L. REV. 1 (1944). Under the Jefferson approach, neither collateral neutral nor collateral self–serving statements would be admissible.

The text of Rule [804(b)(3)] does not tell us whether collateral statements are admissible . . . . The Court resolves the issue . . . by adopting the extreme position that no collateral statements are admissible under Rule 804(b)(3). The Court reaches that conclusion by relying on the "principle behind the Rule" . . . and reasons that this policy "expressed in the statutory text" . . . does not extend to collateral statements. I disagree with this analysis.

II

Because the text of Rule 804(b)(3) expresses no position regarding the admissibility of collateral statements, we must determine whether there are other authoritative guides on the question. In my view, three sources demonstrate that Rule 804(b)(3) allows the admission of some collateral statements: the Advisory Committee Note, the common law . . . , and the general presumption that Congress did not enact statutes that have almost no effect.

First, the Advisory Committee Note establishes that some collateral statements are admissible. In fact, it refers in specific terms to the issue we here confront: "[o]rdinarily the third–party confession is thought of in terms of exculpating the accused, but this is by no means always or necessarily the case; it may include statements implicating him, and under the general theory of declarations against interest they would be admissible as related statements." This language seems a forthright statement that collateral statements are admissible under Rule 804(b)(3). [T]he text of the Rule does not answer the question whether collateral statements are admissible. When as here the text of a Rule of Evidence does not answer a question that must be answered in order to apply the Rule, and when the Advisory Committee Note does answer the question, our practice indicates that we should pay attention to the Advisory Committee Note. We have referred often to those Notes in interpreting the Rules of Evidence, and I see no reason to jettison that well–established practice here. *See Huddleston v. United States*, 485 U.S. 681 (1988); *United States v. Owens*, 484 U.S. 554 (1988); *Bourjaily v. United States*, 483 U.S. 171 (1987); *United States v. Abel*, 469 U.S. 45 (1984).

Second, even if the Advisory Committee Note were silent about collateral statements, I would not adopt a rule excluding all statements collateral or related to the specific words against penal interest. Absent contrary indications, we can presume that Congress intended the principles and terms used in the Federal Rules of Evidence to be applied as they were at common law. *See Daubert v. Merrell Dow Pharmaceuticals, Inc.*, 509 U.S. 579 (1993); *Green v. Bock Laundry Machine Co.*, 490 U.S. 504 (1989) . . . . Application of that interpretive principle indicates that collateral statements should be admissible. "From the very beginning of this exception, it has been held that a declaration against interest is admissible, not only to prove the disserving fact but also to prove other facts contained in collateral statements connected with the disserving statement." Jefferson, 58 Harv. L. Rev. at 57 . . . . Congress legislated against the common law background allowing the admission of some collateral statements, and I would not assume that Congress gave the common law rule a silent burial in Rule 804(b)(3).

There is yet a third reason weighing against the Court's interpretation . . . . [W]e should assume that Congress intended the penal interest exception for inculpatory statements to have some meaningful effect. That counsels against adopting a rule excluding collateral statements. As commentators have recognized, "the exclusion of collateral statements would cause the exclusion of almost all inculpatory statements." Comment, 66 Calif. L. Rev. at 1207. To be sure, under the approach adopted by the court, there are some situations where the Rule would still apply. For example, if the declarant said that he stole certain goods, the statement could be admitted in a prosecution of the accused for receipt of stolen goods in order to show that the goods were stolen. But . . . it is likely to be the rare case where the precise self–inculpatory words of the declarant, without more, also inculpate the defendant. I would not presume that Congress intended the penal interest exception . . . to have so little effect with respect to statements that inculpate the accused.

* * *

In sum, I would adhere to the following approach with respect to statements against penal interest that inculpate the accused. A court first should determine whether the declarant made a statement that contained a fact against penal interest. If so, the court should admit all statements related to the precise statement against penal interest, subject to two limits. Consistent with the Advisory Committee Note, the court should exclude a collateral statement that is so self–serving as to render it unreliable (if, for example, it shifts blame to someone else for a crime the defendant could have committed). In addition, in cases where the statement was made under circumstances where it is likely that the declarant had a significant motivation to obtain favorable treatment, as when the government made an explicit offer of leniency in exchange for the declarant's admission of guilt, the entire statement should be inadmissible.

A ruling on the admissibility of evidence under Rule 804(b)(3) is a preliminary question to be determined by the District Judge under Rule 104(a). That determination of necessity calls for an inquiry that depends to a large extent on the circumstances of a particular case. For this reason, application of the general principles here outlined to a particular narrative statement often will require a difficult, factbound determination. District Judges, who are close to the facts and far better able to evaluate the various circumstances than an appellate court, therefore must be given wide discretion to examine a particular statement to determine whether all or part of it should be admitted.

NOTES

1. What was the very first source Justice O'Connor considered when she attempted to ascertain the meaning of "statement" in Rule 804(b)(3)? Remember Justice Thomas' analysis of the word "testimony" in Rule 804(b)(1) in *Salerno* and the commentators' criticism of heavy reliance on dictionaries.

2. Did Justice O'Connor pay sufficient attention to the context, namely, the statutory definition of "statement" in Rule 801(a)? Under Rule 801(a), what is the unit of analysis—the individual assertion or the larger declaration or writing including the assertion? *United States v. Canan*, 48 F.3d 954 (6th Cir. 1995), *cert. denied*, 516 U.S. 1050 (1996), reads *Williamson* as requiring "sentence by sentence" analysis. In *United States v. Sims*, 879 F. Supp. 828, 832, 835 (N.D. Ill. 1995), the court declares that *Williamson* mandates that the trial judge engage in "a segmented, not aggregate, analysis" to determine whether "each part of a proffered statement is . . . against . . . interest." Would it be more precise to say that the analysis must proceed assertion by assertion? Remember that like Rule 801(a), the text of Rule 804(b)(3) purports to refer to a "statement" in the singular.

3. Some commentators claim that the key issue in modern "legisprudence" is not *whether* to consult extrinsic legislative history material but rather *how much* extrinsic material such as a drafter's or Advisory Committee Note should "count" in a court's interpretive decision. W. ESKRIDGE & P. FRICKEY, CASES AND MATERIALS ON LEGISLATION: STATUTES AND THE CREATION OF PUBLIC POLICY 698 (1988). Does the disagreement between Justices O'Connor and Kennedy bear out that claim? Some contemporary students of statutory construction view *Williamson* as a turning point away from a strict textualist approach. Taslitz, Daubert's *Guide to the Federal Rules of Evidence: A Not–So–Plain–Meaning Jurisprudence*, 32 HARV. J. ON LEGIS. 3, 71–73 (1995). Think back on the *Tome* case (also by Justice Kennedy later in 1994) which also relied heavily on Advisory Committee Notes.

4. The opinions in *Williamson* use the categories: self–inculpatory, disserving, non–self–inculpatory, self–serving, and neutral. How would you characterize the following statements:

(a) Suppose that Harris stated: "Williamson and I arranged the drug delivery." At the time of the statement Harris was on probation, one of the probation conditions was that he not associate with convicted felons, and Williamson was a convicted felon. Is Harris' reference to Williamson disserving to Harris' interest? Admitting involvement in the drug buy exposes Harris to the risk of prosecution for the drug offense. What else does the reference to Williamson expose Harris to?

(b) Again, Harris said: "Williamson and I arranged the drug delivery." Before Harris made the statement, he had been arrested. The police made it clear to Harris that they knew Williamson was a "big fish" in the drug ring and that Harris would receive more lenient treatment if he helped them build a case against Williamson.

(c) Again, Harris said: "Williamson and I arranged the drug delivery." However, as far as Harris can tell at the time he makes the statement, it is a matter of indifference to the police whether he names Williamson rather than C, D, or anybody else.

5. While *Williamson* is based on the Court's statutory construction of the Federal Rules of Evidence, in *Lilly v. Virginia*, 527 U.S. 116 (1999) the Court reached the question of the confrontation clause limitations on the admission of statements which qualify as declarations against interest under state law. In that case, a state court had held that the defendant's brother's custodial statement to the police was admissible against the defendant as a declaration against interest. Initially, the lead opinion, authored by Justice Stevens, concluded that federal law governs the question of whether a hearsay exception is firmly rooted for purposes of confrontation clause analysis. The lead opinion then ruled that the application of the exception to an accomplice's confession to the police is not firmly rooted. For that reason, the admission of the confession would comport with the confrontation clause only if the record contained particularized indicia of the confession's reliability. The lead opinion found such indicia lacking in *Lilly*. The brother's confession tended to shift blame to the defendant. Neither the fact that the statement was partially against the declarant's interest, nor the absence of any promise of leniency, nor the declarant's receipt of *Miranda* warnings sufficed.

Another controversy surrounding the declaration against interest doctrine centers on the type of interest to which the statement must be contrary. As a question of first impression, it would seem that there should be no limitation on the type of interest that is disserved. The only questions should be the magnitude of the interest and the degree to which the statement is contrary to the interest. Whatever the type of interest, the declarant's realization that the statement is directly contrary to a weighty interest supplies an inference of sincerity. However, rejecting common sense, the common law sharply differentiated among various types of interest. The early common law adopted a narrow view and recognized only pecuniary and proprietary interest. If Mr. Hill admitted that he owed Jefferson Motor Car Co. $100 on a late installment payment on the car, that statement would be admissible. Similarly, if he confessed that he did not have full title to the car and that Jefferson retained a security interest, that statement would be sufficiently disserving. The American cases strained to broaden the categories of pecuniary and proprietary interest to include statements that exposed the declarant to civil liability. *E.g., Weber v. Chicago, R.I. & P. Ry.*, 175 Iowa 358, 151 N.W. 852 (1915). However, in its 1844 decision in the *Sussex Peerage Case*, 11 Cl. & F. 85, 8 Eng. Rep. 1034 (1844), the House of Lords drew the line at pecuniary and proprietary interest and refused to recognize penal interest. The acceptance of penal interest in the United States has come grudgingly.

In *People v. Spriggs*, 60 Cal. 2d 868, 389 P.2d 377, 36 Cal. Rptr. 841 (1964), Justice Roger Traynor presented a persuasive argument that the doctrine should extend to penal interest. In time, the soundness of Justice Traynor's argument won over the Supreme Court. Even before the adoption of the Federal Rules of Evidence, the Court converted to the view that a statement against penal interest can be trustworthy precisely because of its disserving character. *United States v. Matlock*, 415 U.S. 164 (1974); *Chambers v. Mississippi*, 410 U.S. 284 (1973); *United States v. Harris*, 403 U.S. 573 (1971).

Rule 804(b)(3) not only specifically mentions statements "subject[ing] the declarant to . . . criminal liability" as being exceptionally admissible; the Rule also arguably adopts a broad version of the exception. Since Rule 804(b)(3) uses the expression "tended to subject," some courts have held that the Rule is not even limited to direct confessions of criminal responsibility. *United States v. Slaughter*, 891 F.2d 691 (9th Cir. 1989).

The modern state of the law is a three–way split of authority. As at early common law, there are still occasional judicial opinions declaring that penal interest does not qualify. *E.g.*, *State v. Turner*, 623 S.W.2d 4 (Mo. 1981), *cert. denied*, 456 U.S. 931 (1982); *State v. Hill*, 614 S.W.2d 744, 752 (Mo. Ct. App. 1981) ("[I]t has consistently been held that declarations against penal interest are not admissible"). Although most courts now accept penal interest, they balk at social interest. California extended the doctrine to statements disserving social interest. Under California Evidence Code § 1230, a statement is admissible if the declarant realized that the statement would make "him an object of hatred, ridicule, or social disgrace in the community." Congress decided against including social interest in Rule 804(b)(3). However, eleven states have decided to follow California's lead and have adopted a version of Rule 804(b)(3) recognizing social interest. Note, *Sin, Suffering, and "Social Interest": Exception for Statements Subjecting the Hearsay Declarant to "Hatred, Ridicule, or Disgrace,"* 4 REV. LITIG. 367 (1985). In these jurisdictions, the courts often treat statements on the following topics as declarations against social interest: sexual impropriety, illegitimacy, criminal activity, suicide, insanity, or professional business incompetence, malpractice, or misconduct. *Id.* at 392. Is Congress' decision defensible on the ground that it is more difficult to determine whether a statement will make a person "an object of . . . social disgrace" than to decide whether the statement might subject him to prosecution?

NOTES AND PROBLEMS

1. Problem 21–8. In *Devitt*, the defense counsel calls Mr. Napier as a witness. Napier is prepared to testify that he knows a Mr. Johnson and that Johnson confided in him that he had attacked Paterson. Johnson died a month before trial. The prosecutor objects on hearsay grounds. The defense counsel responds that the statement qualifies as a declaration against interest. What result? *See Harris v. State*, 387 A.2d 1152, 1155–56 (Md. Ct. Spec. App. 1978). Suppose that Johnson had said that he "alone had attacked Paterson." *Commonwealth v. Colon*, 461 Pa. 577, 584, 337 A.2d 554, 558 (1975), *cert. denied*, 423 U.S. 1056 (1976).

2. Note the last sentence in Rule 804(b)(3). The courts enforce the corroboration requirement and bar defense evidence of third–party confessions absent corroboration. *United States v. Annese*, 631 F.2d 1041, 1044 (1st Cir. 1980). Many jurisdictions impose the corroboration requirement as a matter of decisional law. *Smith v. State*, 587 S.W.2d 659, 661 (Tenn. 1979), *cert. denied*, 446 U.S. 920 (1980). The argument is that unless corroboration is required, it would be too easy for the defendant to obtain perjured testimony about third–party confessions. Is the declaration theory the only exception that presents that danger? Is it justifiable to single out declarations against penal interest?

3. Does Rule 804(b)(3) impose the same requirement on prosecution evidence? If not, is the statute constitutional? *See* Tague, *Perils of the Rulemaking Process: The Development, Application, and Unconstitutionality of Rule 804(b)(3)'s Penal Interest Exception*, 69 GEO. L.J. 851, 978–1011 (1981). To moot the constitutional issue, should the court read a corroboration requirement for prosecution evidence into the statute? *American Automotive Accessories, Inc. v. Fishman*, 175 F.3d 534, 541 (7th Cir. 1999)("We believe it best to . . .utilize a unitary standard for applying Rule 804(b)(3) to statements offered both to exculpate and to inculpate a third party"); *United States v. Candoli*, 870 F.2d 496, 509 (9th Cir. 1989) (citing Second, Third, Fifth, and Eighth Circuit cases imposing a corroboration requirement). As a matter of statutory interpretation, it seems strained to read in the requirement. May a court go to that length to moot the constitutional issue? *See* 2A N. SINGER, SUTHERLAND STATUTORY CONSTRUCTION § 45.11, at 48 (5th ed. 1992). Given the separation of powers doctrine, the courts cannot simply rewrite statutes to eliminate conceivable constitutional infirmities in the statutes. *People's Advocate, Inc. v. Superior Court*, 181 Cal. App. 3d 316, 330 n.15, 226 Cal. Rptr. 640, 648 n.15 (1986). Should the answer turn on the question of whether the constitutional attack on the statute is strong or merely plausible? Even when the potential constitutional attack is strong, may the court adopt the narrower interpretation when it is relatively clear that the legislature contemplated the broader construction? *U.S. Dept. of Air Force v. F.L.R.A.*, 952 F.2d 446, 452 n. 5 (D.C. Cir. 1991) ("a court does not have the 'prerogative to ignore the legislative will . . . so as to save [a statute] against constitutional attack, it must not . . . carry out this [canon of construction] to the point of perverting the purpose of a statute and judicially rewriting it' "); *United States v. Harvey*, 814 F.2d 905, 917–18 (4th Cir. 1987).

3. DYING DECLARATIONS

One of the more mystical hearsay exceptions is the dying declaration doctrine. This doctrine allows the admission of dramatic evidence of deathbed statements on the assumption that the declarant would not want to meet her Maker with a lie on her lips. Quick, *Some Reflections on Dying Declarations*, 6 HOW. L.J. 109, 111 (1960). As the Quick article explains, at common law, the foundation for this exception required proof of the following foundational facts: (1) At the time of the statement, the declarant had "a settled hopeless expectation of immediately impending death." The declarant had to believe that death was both certain and imminent. That belief is the circumstantial guarantee of the declarant's sincerity. (2) The declarant had personal knowledge of the facts recited in the statement. That showing is insurance of the testimonial quality of perception. (3) The declaration had to relate to "the circumstances directly leading up to the declarant's death." (4) The accusatory pleading had to charge the accused with the declarant's murder. (5) At the time of trial, the declarant had to be dead. Death was the only acceptable showing of the declarant's unavailability. Which of these restrictions make sense?

The first requirement is obviously defensible. Throughout the history of this exception, the courts have stressed the declarant's evident sincerity as the basis for inferring reliability. The inference arises from the declarant's belief that imminent death is certain. At one time, the courts were exceedingly strict in demanding proof of the declarant's belief. Modernly, they accept numerous types of circumstantial evidence of that belief, including the condition or severity of the wound, *Territory of New Mexico v. Eagle*, 15 N.M. 609, 110 P. 862 (1910); *People v. Gorman*, 252 Mich. 603, 233 N.W. 430 (1930); *Emmett v. State*, 195 Ga. 517, 25 S.E.2d 9, *cert. denied*, 320 U.S. 774 (1943); the administration of the last rites to the declarant, and the declarant's own statements. *Satterfield v. State*, 68 Ga. App. 7, 21 S.E.2d 861 (1942); *Allen v. Commonwealth*, 302 Ky. 546, 195 S.W.2d 96 (1946).

The second and third requirements pass muster. Two of the key hearsay dangers are misperception and misrecollection. These requirements are calculated to reduce those dangers. Like the "relating to" restriction in Rule 803(2) governing excited utterances, the third limitation evidences concern about the quality of the declarant's memory. When the declarant refers to preceding events such as earlier arguments with the alleged killer, there is a much substantial risk of misrecollection.

In contrast, some of the other requirements enforced at common law made little or no sense. For instance, at early common law, the courts limited the doctrine to statements by deceased declarants, named as the victim in homicide prosecutions. The courts reasoned that the most compelling need was for the declarations of homicide victims. If the declarant recovered, or the declarant was not the named victim, or the case was not a homicide prosecution, the courts barred the evidence. These restrictions were subjected to pointed criticism. 5 J. WIGMORE EVIDENCE § 1433 (3d ed. 1940). Under Federal Rule of Evidence 804, it is no longer necessary that the declarant be dead at the time of trial. The only requirements are that the declarant meet the general unavailability test announced in Rule 804(a) and that the declarant make the statement "while believing that his death was imminent." FED. R. EVID. 804(b)(2), Advisory Committee Note.

The exception's limitation to declarants named as victims in the pleading was also assailed. The limitation led to seemingly absurd results: If the defendant killed two persons by the same blow but the indictment named only one as the victim, the other victim's statements were excluded. *Westberry v. State*, 175 Ga. 115, 164 S.E. 905 (1932). McCormick concurred with Wigmore's remark, "Could one's imagination devise a more senseless rule of exclusion . . .?" 2 C. MCCORMICK, HANDBOOK OF THE LAW OF EVIDENCE § 311 (5th ed. 1999) (citing 5 J. WIGMORE EVIDENCE § 1433 (3d ed. 1940)). The Advisory Committee also agreed and impliedly abolished the restriction in Rule 804(b)(3).

Like the prior restriction, the exception's limitation to homicide prosecution came under attack. Even before the adoption of the Federal Rules, several state legislatures had made inroads on this aspect of the orthodox rule. After much debate, Congress adopted a compromise position in Rule 804(b)(2):

(b) Hearsay exceptions. The following are not excluded by the hearsay rule if the declarant is unavailable as a witness:

(2) Statement under belief of impending death. In a prosecution for homicide or in a civil action or proceeding, a statement made by a declarant while believing that his death was imminent, concerning the cause or circumstances of what he believed to be his impending death.

NOTES AND PROBLEMS

1. Problem 21–9. In *Devitt*, Paterson died after the attack. Devitt is now charged with murder. The prosecutor calls Patrolman Winslow as a witness. Winslow is prepared to testify that just before Paterson died at the scene, he said, "That bastard Devitt did this to me. I'll get him for this. I'll pay him back. He never would have . . . ." The defense counsel objects that the statement does not fall within Rule 804(b)(2). What ruling?

2. Problem 21–10. Paterson told Winslow, "That bastard Devitt did this to me. He did it on purpose." The defense objects that the second sentence is irrelevant and incompetent hearsay because "it is too highly conclusory and opinionated." *See Pippin v. Commonwealth*, 117 Va. 919, 86 S.E. 152, 154–55 (1915).

3. Problem 21–11. Paterson told Winslow, "That bastard Devitt did this to me. He said before that if I pushed him too far, something bad would happen. He lived up to his word." Does this testimony relate to "the cause and circumstances" of Paterson's death?

4. Although dying declarations have long been admissible, there has always been a strain of skepticism about them. 2 McCormick, Evidence § 314 (5th ed. 1999). Several jurisdictions require that the judge give the jury a cautionary instruction about dying declarations. Kliks, *Impeachment of Dying Declarations*, 19 Or. L. Rev. 265 (1940). Some jurisdictions demand that the judge tell the jury that a dying declaration is entitled to less weight than other evidence in the case. *Id.* at 286. Other jurisdictions insist that both the judge and jury pass on the admissibility of the declaration. Quick, *supra*, at 6 How. L.J. 109, 128.

Is this skepticism about dying declarations warranted? The skepticism might reflect a growing realization of the common law's overemphasis on the sincerity factor. Or is the fear that the evidence is so dramatic that the jury will attach too much weight to it?

5. Be prepared to list in class all the differences between the excited utterance and dying declaration doctrines.

4. PAST RECOLLECTION RECORDED

In the last section, we considered the Rule 804 hearsay exception requiring the most extreme showing of necessity, the declarant's death. The next exception, past recollection recorded, is the polar extreme. Although this exception also requires a showing of necessity, this doctrine accepts a minimal showing of necessity: the witness' present inability to remember. In part because there is such a lax standard of unavailability for this exception, the exception is codified in Rule 803 rather than Rule 804.

a. Contrasted with Present Recollection Refreshed

Before considering the past recollection recorded exception in detail, we should distinguish the exception from a related doctrine—often confused with past recollection recorded—present recollection refreshed or revived. By virtue of this doctrine, if the witness on the stand temporarily forgets a fact, the attorney may present the witness with an object such as a prior writing to revive the witness' memory. The object serves as a memory jogger for the witness, and the actual evidence is the oral testimony from the witness' refreshed recollection. The doctrine thus rests on the psychological phenomenon of association. The witness associates the memory of a fact with a certain writing or object, and permitting the witness to inspect the writing or object will hopefully help the witness retrieve the associated memory. Gardner, *The Perception and Memory of Witnesses*, 18 CORNELL L.Q. 390, 392 (1933).

Like past recollection recorded, the present recollection refreshed doctrine requires a showing of necessity before the attorney may resort to the document. On the record, the witness professes that he or she cannot remember the fact or event. "Most jurisdictions require a foundation that the witness cannot now recall all the facts about an event, or that the witness' memory is exhausted." Tanford, *An Introduction to Trial Law*, 51 MO. L. REV. 623, 667 (1986). Once the witness asserts a lack of memory, the attorney ordinarily inquires: "Is there anything—any writing, for example—that might help you remember?" The witness then identifies the document. The attorney marks the document as an exhibit for identification and presents it to the witness. The witness reads the document silently to himself. The attorney next asks: "Having read plaintiff's exhibit number three for identification, can you now recall the license number?" If the witness answers yes, the witness proceeds to testify unaided by the exhibit. Since the real evidence is the witness' testimony, the exhibit is not formally admitted into evidence; it remains an exhibit for identification. *United States v. Faulkner*, 538 F.2d 724 (6th Cir.), *cert. denied*, 429 U.S. 1023 (1976).

The present recollection refreshed procedure raises several questions. To begin with, what types of documents may the witness use to refresh his memory? When we consider past recollection recorded, we shall see a number of restrictions on the documents usable under that theory. Some jurisdictions apply the same restrictions to writings employed to refresh recollection. 1 C. MCCORMICK, EVIDENCE § 9 (5th ed. 1999). However, "the wiser practice" and prevailing view is that "any memorandum . . . without restriction . . . as to authorship, guaranty of correctness, or time of making" can be used. *Id.* at 19. For example, there is substantial case authority that the witness may use documents prepared by third parties. *United States v. Conley*, 503 F.2d 520 (8th Cir. 1974); 4 JONES ON EVIDENCE § 27:5 (Gard ed. 1972).

What mechanics should the witness' proponent use to refresh the witness' recollection? As previously stated, in many jurisdictions the proponent instructs the witness to read the document silently to himself. If the witness cannot read, the judge usually allows the witness to retire with counsel and have the memorandum read to him outside the jury's hearing. *Id.* § 27:8. The jury should not hear the document's contents. *Id.* The thrust of the present recollection refreshed doctrine is that the substantive evidence is the witness' oral testimony rather than the document. If the jury heard the document read, the jury would be tempted to treat the document as evidence.

Finally, consider the doctrine from the perspective of the opposing counsel. May the opponent inspect the document that the witness uses to refresh his memory? The courts concur on the proposition that the opponent has a right to inspect any document that the witness uses while on the witness stand. The more difficult question is whether the opponent has a right to inspect documents that the witness uses before trial. This question has divided the courts into three schools of thought.

The traditional view was that these documents are nondiscoverable. *Goldman v. United States*, 316 U.S. 129, 132 (1942); Annot., 82 A.L.R.2d 473 (1962). These courts realized that it is a common practice among trial attorneys to prepare their witnesses by reviewing the witnesses' statements with the witnesses before trial. The courts regarded this as a legitimate practice that has the advantage of expediting the trial. The courts feared that recognizing the discoverability of writings used before trial would create a disincentive for adequate pretrial preparation of the witnesses; the attorneys would realize that they were rendering the document discoverable by showing it to the witness during the pretrial conference.

Other jurisdictions repudiated the traditional view and declared that the opponent has a right to discover documents reviewed prior to trial. They asserted that the distinction between documents used at the trial and those reviewed pretrial is "artificial." *Commonwealth v. Marsh*, 354 Mass. 713, 242 N.E.2d 545 (1968). In their minds, a document used before trial is the "functional equivalent" of one used on the witness stand. *Ballew v. State*, 640 S.W.2d 237, 244 (Tex. Crim. App. 1982).

The trend in the case law and statutes is toward a third view, according the trial judge discretion to order the production of documents used before trial. Federal Rule of Evidence 612 is illustrative. Rule 612(2) states that the opponent may examine a document used "before testifying, if the court in its discretion determines it is necessary in the interests of justice." FED. R. EVID. 612. The early cases in this line of authority were criminal decisions (*State v. Deslovers*, 40 R.I. 89, 100 A. 64 (1917)), but the trend soon spread to civil cases as well. On its face, Rule 612 applies to both types of proceedings. The boldest cases not only hold that the document is generally discoverable, but also announce that, by using the document before trial to refresh the witness' recollection, the party waives any privilege that would otherwise attach to the document. Belcour, *Use It and Lose It—Privileged Documents, Preparing Witnesses, and Rule 612 of the Federal Rules of Evidence*, 31 FED. B. NEWS & J. 171, 172 (1984). The more "cautious" cases hold that Rule 612 comes into play only when the record shows both that the witness consulted the document and that the witness did so for the specific purpose of refreshing memory to testify. *United States v. Sheffield*, 55 F.3d 341 (8th Cir. 1995); Applegate, *Preparing for Rule 612*, 19 LITIGATION, Spr. 1993, at 17, 20.

Under this third view, the pivotal question is identifying the factors that should inform the exercise of the judge's discretion. The two most obviously relevant factors are the importance of the topic the document relates to and the time lapse between the incident and trial. The more central the topic, the greater the opponent's need to challenge the witness' testimony. Further, the longer the time lapse, the stronger the inference that the witness is relying heavily on the document. 4 JONES ON EVIDENCE § 27:7 (Gard ed. 1972). Can you think of any other factors that the judge should weigh?

NOTES

1. Assume that your jurisdiction follows the view that the foundation for present recollection refreshed must include the witness' statement on the record that he or she cannot remember the data. During a witness' direct examination, she misstates a fact. Realizing the error, the direct examiner asks her point blank whether she is certain of that fact. The witness adamantly insists that she testified correctly. The direct examiner has a prior statement by the witness which correctly states the facts. May the direct examiner show the statement to the witness to try to correct the mistaken statement? Tanford, *An Introduction to Trial Law*, 51 MO. L. REV. 623, 667 (1986).

2. Why require a showing of necessity before permitting the witness to resort to a document to refresh her memory? Some have argued that liberally permitting witnesses to consult documents would probably improve the accuracy of courtroom testimony. Suppose that the witness prepared the notes with a view to using them while she was on the witness stand. Assume further that the attorney helped the witness prepare the notes. *See NLRB v. Federal Dairy Co.*, 297 F.2d 487, 489 (1st Cir. 1962).

3. Are documents the only objects that the witness should be permitted to use to revive her memory? What if the witness stated that seeing a photograph or listening to a recording might refresh her memory? 4 JONES ON EVIDENCE § 27:2 (Gard ed. 1972). As previously stated, the present recollection refreshed theory rests on the psychological phenomenon of association. Is it sound to limit the present recollection refreshed theory to documents? *Baker v. State*, 35 Md. App. 593, 371 A.2d 699 (1977), contains the following colorful passage:

> It may be a line from Kipling or the dolorous strain of "The Tennessee Waltz"; a whiff of hickory smoke; the running of the fingers across a swatch of corduroy; the sweet carbonation of a chocolate soda; the sight of a faded snapshot in a long–neglected album. All that is required is that it may trigger the Proustian moment. It may be anything that produces the desired testimonial prelude, "It all comes back to me now."

Recent Decision, *Evidence—Refreshed Recollection Testimony—Witness Must Refresh Memory by a Writing or Some Tangible Evidence*, 62 MISS. L.J. 245

(1992), criticizes a case precluding a witness from refreshing his memory by talking to another witness.

b. Past Recollection Recorded

Unlike present recollection refreshed, past recollection recorded is a full–fledged hearsay exception. Under the traditional view of this theory, an exhibit representing past recollection recorded is formally admitted because the writing is the actual evidence. What showing of reliability and necessity must the proponent make to justify the admission of the exhibit as past recollection recorded? Federal Rule of Evidence 803(5) addresses that question:

> The following are not excluded by the hearsay rule, even though the declarant is available as a witness:
>
> (5) Recorded recollection. A memorandum or record concerning a matter about which a witness once had knowledge but now has insufficient recollection to enable him to testify fully and accurately, shown to have been made or adopted by the witness when the matter was fresh in his memory and to reflect that knowledge correctly. If admitted, the memorandum or record may be read into evidence but may not itself be received as an exhibit unless offered by an adverse party.

At common law and under the Federal Rule, a complete foundation for past recollection recorded entails proof of the writing's reliability and the necessity for resorting to the writing. The foundational requirements relate to three distinct points in time: the time of the recorded event, the time of the preparation of the record, and the time of trial.

The initial requirement relates to the time of the event which is recorded. As one mark of reliability, the writing must be based on personal knowledge of the fact or event recorded. When Rule 803(5) refers to "knowledge," the term means firsthand or personal knowledge.

The next two requirements relate to the time of the preparation of the record. One requirement speaks to the question of *who* prepares the record. The doctrine demands that the firsthand observer participate in preparing the writing. It is ideal if the observer herself prepared the writing. In *Devitt*, suppose that another tenant saw a car race away from Paterson's apartment and had the sense to note the car's license number, but she cannot remember the number at trial. Every jurisdiction would treat the note as past recollection recorded if the tenant herself wrote the note. Likewise, every jurisdiction will accept the note if the observer dictated the information to a third–party writer and personally checks the note for accuracy. One tenant, the wife, is standing by the window and sees the car race away. She immediately relays the license number to her husband sitting at the kitchen table. He records the number on a note pad, and his wife immediately walks over, picks up the note pad, and ensures that her husband correctly recorded the number.

It is more troublesome if the observer neglects to verify the writing at the time of the event. Suppose that the wife did not bother to walk across the room to check the number her husband recorded on the note pad. At common law, the courts dubbed this problem a "cooperative report." 2 C. McCormick,

HANDBOOK OF THE LAW OF EVIDENCE § 283 (5th ed. 1999). The courts admitted these records only if both witnesses testified at trial; the wife testified that she observed the car and relayed the license number to her husband, and the husband testified that he accurately recorded the number his wife gave him. *Rathbun v. Brancatella*, 93 N.J.L. 222, 107 A. 279 (1919).

NOTES

1. Note the language of Rule 803(5): "made or adopted by the witness when the evidence was fresh in his memory." Is that language broad enough to include cooperative records? In fact, the lower courts continue to accept such records, as they did at common law. *Boehmer v. LeBoeuf*, 650 A.2d 1336 (Maine 1994). The Advisory Committee Note reads: "Multiple person involvement in the process of observing and recording, as in *Rathbun v. Brancatella*, 93 N.J.L. 222, 107 A. 279, 280 (1919), is entirely consistent with the exception." Is the statutory language at least ambiguous enough to permit resort to this legislative history material? Does the court have to find an ambiguity on the face of the statute before the court may legitimately resort to extrinsic legislative history materials such as the Note? *See* 2A N. SINGER, SUTHERLAND STATUTORY CONSTRUCTION § 48.01, at 301 (5th ed.1992). In his article on the interpretation of the Federal Rules, Professor Cleary stated that sometimes, when there is a "collision . . . between legislative history and the seemingly unmistakable meaning of [the text] of a Rule," the *text* must yield. Would Judge Easterbrook agree? Given the phrasing of Rule 803(5) and the Advisory Committee Note, would Easterbrook construe the Rule as admitting cooperative reports? This may be another instance in which the court's construction of the statute turns on the court's philosophy of statutory interpretation.

2. Do the courts need to stretch the language of Rule 803(5) to continue employing the common law cooperative record doctrine? Consider the significance of Rule 803(1), the exception for present sense impressions. Does Rule 803(1) apply when, after observing the car race away, the wife turns and immediately tells the license number to her husband? Given Rule 803(1), will both the wife and the husband need to testify at trial to permit the introduction of the note recording the license number? *Cf. Cargill, Inc. v. Boag Cold Storage Warehouse, Inc.*, 71 F.3d 545, 554–55 (6th Cir. 1995).

The doctrine requires assurances of accurate memory as well as indications of firsthand knowledge; thus, a further requirement relates to *when* the record is prepared. The required assurance is that the writer prepared the document while the observer had a good memory of the data. Like the preceding requirement, this foundational requirement applies at the time of the preparation of the record. The strict, early common law was that the writer had to draft the document at or near the time of the event. *Gigliotti v. United Illuminating Co.*, 151 Conn. 114, 193 A.2d 718 (1963). The courts' intention was to require that the writer draft the document within a few hours after the event. The modern common law view is more liberal. Under this standard, the courts tolerate delays of a few days in preparing the writing. Their tolerance is in accord with the state of modern witness psychology research. The data indicate that the psychological curve of memory declines rapidly after one or two days. E. LOFTUS, EYEWITNESS TESTIMONY 53 (1979); Stewart, *Perception, Memory, and Hearsay: A Criticism of Present Law and the Proposed Federal Rules of Evidence*, 1970 UTAH L. REV. 1. However, when the time lapse is longer—for example, approaching a week — the memory decay becomes extensive. *Id.* at 16; Gardner, *The Perception and Memory of Witnesses*, 18 CORNELL L.Q. 391, 393 (1933) (in a study of word recollection, the typical subject forgot 90% of the information within a week).

PROBLEM

Problem 21–12. In *Devitt*, the tenant, Mrs. Murchison, saw the license plate number of Devitt's car as he drove away from Paterson's apartment. Mrs. Murchison prides herself on her memory and felt no need to write the number down. However, there were delays in bringing Devitt to trial, and when ten months had elapsed, Mrs. Murchison became concerned that she might forget. At that point, she sat down and wrote the license number on a note pad. She is prepared to testify that when she wrote on the pad she still "distinctly recalled" the license number she had seen. Can her notation qualify under Rule 803(5) ("when the matter was fresh in his memory")? *See United States v. Patterson*, 678 F.2d 774, 778–80 (9th Cir.), *cert. denied*, 459 U.S. 911 (1982). Professor Schmertz has roundly criticized *Patterson*. In his view, "it would seem preferable to rely upon a more objective test of memory freshness on accepted psychological findings on the general patterns of human forgetting rather than rely to a large degree on the credibility of the witness as to the state of his memory . . . months before . . . ." 7 FED. RULES EVID. NEWS 82–95 (1982).

The past recollection recorded doctrine demands still another guarantee of the quality of memory; at the time of trial, the witness must vouch that the document was accurate when prepared. In the words of Rule 803(5), the document must be "shown to have been made or adopted by the witness when the matter was fresh in his memory *and* to reflect that knowledge correctly" (emphasis added). It is certainly sufficient if the witness testifies that she recalls recording the data and recognizing the recorded data as correct. The proponent may also use habit evidence to lay this element of the foundation. If the writer had been a police officer entering the license number in his notebook, the officer could vouch that he is aware of the importance of this sort of entry and habitually doublechecks such entries in his notebook. Some jurisdictions have even permitted the witness to vouch for himself; they admit the document even when the witness says only that he recognizes his handwriting and is positive that he would not have recorded the information if it had not been true. *Walker v. Larson*, 284 Minn. 99, 169 N.W.2d 737 (1969).

Even the above marks of reliability are insufficient to establish the admissibility of the writing. At the time of trial, the proponent must also establish the necessity for introducing the writing. At early common law, the witness virtually had to say that he had drawn a complete blank; even after reviewing the writing on the witness stand, he could not remember any of the recorded data. *Bennefield v. State*, 281 Ala. 283, 202 So. 2d 55 (1967). However, in some cases, it was clearly absurd to require that the witness lack any current memory. If the writing listed several hundred items, it was altogether plausible that an honest witness would remember some items but forget others. *Shea v. Fridley*, 123 A.2d 358, 362 (D.C. Mun. App. 1956). The next step in liberalizing the standard was the adoption of the test codified in Rule 803(5): Even after reviewing the document, the witness has "insufficient recollection to enable him to testify fully and accurately."

NOTES

1. How does the unavailability standard for past recollection recorded differ from the unavailability for the other exceptions covered in this chapter? *Compare* Federal Rule 803(5) *with* Rule 804(a)(3). Does it make sense to require a stronger showing of unavailability in the case of former testimony that has already been subjected to cross–examination? Do the witness' physical presence and availability for cross–examination justify a more relaxed standard of unavailability in the case of past recollection recorded?

2. The traditional view is that once the proponent lays a complete foundation of reliability and necessity, the writing itself is admitted as substantive evidence. *Fisher v. Swartz*, 333 Mass. 265, 130 N.E.2d 575, 579 (1965). Does Rule 803(5) codify the traditional view? Like Rule 803(18) on learned treatises, Rule 803(5) uses the expressions "admitted" and "received." In *Maggipinto v. Reichman*, 607 F.2d 621, 622 (3d Cir. 1979), construing Rule 803(18), the court interpreted "admitted" as meaning formally introduced into evidence and "received" as referring to physical receipt of the exhibit by the trier of fact. When a legislature repeats the same words in different sections of the same statutory scheme, the courts ordinarily presume that the legislature intended the words to bear the same meaning in both sections. *Barnson v. United States*, 816 F.2d 549, 554 (10th Cir.), *cert. denied*, 484 U.S. 896 (1987). Under the Rule, how do the mechanics of handling a past recollection recorded document differ from those for a document used to revive recollection?

3. Rule 803(5) accords "an adverse party" the right to offer the document into evidence. Why might the adverse party want to offer the document? How might the document's contents impeach the witness' testimony?

D.   CONCLUSION

A comparison between the exceptions in Rules 803 and 804 suggests a major inconsistency in hearsay jurisprudence. To invoke the 803 exceptions, the proponent does not have to establish any absolute necessity. At most, the proponent must show relative necessity: the hearsay evidence is likely to be more reliable than testimony now given on the witness stand. However, to trigger the 804 exceptions, the proponent must prove some species of absolute unavailability: death, presence beyond the territorial reach of compulsory process, or lack of present memory. At least when the proponent can establish the declarant's unavailability, there is a genuine need for dispensing with otherwise valuable demeanor.

Common sense suggests an inverse relationship between the factors of reliability and necessity; the greater the necessity, the less demanding we should be regarding proof of reliability. If that were the case, since the 804 exceptions require proof of absolute necessity, we would ordinarily assume that they rest on a weaker inference of reliability than the exceptions in 803. Is that true?

Compare the strength of the inference of reliability underlying the former testimony exception with that of the exceptions in Rule 803. Morgan proclaimed that the restrictions on former testimony are so severe that "[w]ere the same strictness applied to all hearsay, evidence of reported testimony would constitute the only exception to the hearsay rule." Morgan, *The Law of Evidence, 1941–45*, 59 HARV. L. REV. 481, 552 (1946). If the inference of reliability is so strong in the case of former testimony, does it make sense to require the additional hurdle of proof of unavailability?

If the law of hearsay is inconsistent in this respect, what should we do to harmonize it? Would the best solution be to liberalize Rule 804 by dispensing with proof of unavailability? In *People v. Spriggs*, 60 Cal. 2d 868, 875–76, 389 P.2d 377, 381–82, 36 Cal. Rptr. 841, 845–46 (1964), the California court struck that requirement from the foundation for declarations against interest. Or would it be better to tighten up Rule 803 to require much greater reliability?

Which path do you think that the law of hearsay should take to eliminate the inconsistency? That question serves as a natural segue to the subject of the next chapter: the future of the hearsay doctrine.

Chapter 22

THE FUTURE OF THE RULE AGAINST HEARSAY: RESIDUAL EXCEPTION

Read Federal Rule of Evidence 807.

A. INTRODUCTION

In our review of hearsay, we have highlighted the leading exceptions; however, we confess that there are other hearsay exceptions that we have omitted. For example, Federal Rule of Evidence 803(20) allows the admission of community reputation about "boundaries of and customs affecting land" as well as "events of general history important to the community." Furthermore, when a matter of "general history or boundaries . . . would be provable by . . . reputation," Rule 803(23) authorizes the use of a prior judgment to prove the matter. A whole host of exceptions– Rules 803(13), 803(19), 803(23), and 804(b)(4)–feature in estate litigation to help litigants prove family relationships. Moreover, because of the special reliability of judgments, Rule 803(22) broadly permits the introduction of:

> [e]vidence of a final judgment . . .., adjudging a person guilty of a crime punishable by death or imprisonment in excess of one year, to prove any fact essential to sustain the judgment, but not including, when offered by the Government in a criminal prosecution for purposes other than impeachment, judgments against persons other than the accused.

Rather than attempt to cover all exceptions, including those infrequently encountered, it is more useful to focus now on the future of the rule against hearsay. The contours of the rule have changed during the past two decades, and we can expect still more change in the future. One of the most thoughtful statements by the drafters of the Federal Rules appears in the Committee's Note to Rule 803(24), one of the predecessors to the current Rule 807:

> The preceding . . . exceptions . . . are designed to take full advantage of the accumulated wisdom and experience of the past in dealing with hearsay. It would, however, be presumptuous to assume that all possible desirable exceptions to the hearsay rule have been catalogued and to pass the hearsay rule to oncoming generations as a closed system. [R]oom is left for growth and development of the law of evidence in the hearsay area . . . .

FED. R. EVID. 803(24), Advisory Committee Note. Based on that reasoning, the Advisory Committee added residual hearsay exceptions at the end of both Rule 803 and Rule 804. To invoke either exception, the proponent had to affirmatively show both that the statement is reliable and that there is an element of necessity for resorting to the hearsay statement. The residual exceptions were particularly important because they created a window to common law process.

The two exceptions have now been consolidated into a single statutory provision, Rule 807, which reads:

> A statement not specifically covered by Rule 803 or Rule 804 but having equivalent circumstantial guarantees of trustworthiness, is not excluded by the hearsay rule, if the court determines that (A) the statement is offered as evidence of a material fact; (B) the statement is more probative on the point for which it is offered than any other evidence which the proponent can procure through reasonable efforts; and (C) the general purposes of these rules and the interests of justice will be best served by admission of the statement into evidence. However, a statement may not be admitted under this exception unless the proponent of it makes known to the adverse party sufficiently in advance of the trial or hearing to provide the adverse party with a fair opportunity to prepare to meet it, the proponent's intention to offer the statement and the particulars of it, including the name and address of the declarant.

The accompanying Advisory Committee Note states simply that, although Rules 803(24) and 804(b)(5) were repealed, "No change in meaning is intended."

The future of the hearsay doctrine will be shaped in part by the statutory construction of the residual exceptions. As we shall see, the courts are badly divided over the proper interpretation of the residual exceptions. The future of the doctrine is also likely to be impacted by empirical research. One of the most heated hearsay debates is whether there should be a special exception for statements by the alleged victims in child abuse prosecutions. The outcome of that debate may depend on the ultimate findings of the ongoing psychological research into the trustworthiness of such statements.

B. FUTURE LEGISLATIVE CHANGES

1. ABOLITION OF THE HEARSAY EXCLUSION

Although the hearsay doctrine is a creature of common law, most of the major recent changes have been effected by legislation. What legislative changes could occur in the near future?

The most drastic possible change would be the abolition of the hearsay rule. In this century, the English Parliament has taken major steps toward legislating the hearsay rule out of existence in civil cases. 2 C. McCormick, Handbook of the Law of Evidence § 326 (5th ed. 1999). The English Civil Evidence Acts of 1995 and 1968 and their predecessor, the Evidence Act of 1938, have dramatically relaxed the barriers to admitting hearsay evidence. Law on Civil Hearsay, Herbert Smith Briefing 5–6 (Mar. 1996); St. 1968, c. 64, Civil Evidence; St. 1938, c. 28, Evidence. Di Birch, *The Evidence Provisions*, 1989 Crim. L. Rev. 15; Clark, *The Changing Face of the Rule*

Against Hearsay in English Law, 21 AKRON L. REV. 67 (1987). England's relaxation of the hearsay rule "seem[s] obviously to have been inspired by the virtual disappearance in that country of jury trial in civil cases." 2 C. MCCORMICK, HANDBOOK OF THE LAW OF EVIDENCE § 327, at 378 (4th ed. 1992). "[J]uries in Britain today decide only 1 percent of the civil trials and 5 percent of the criminal trials." Kimel, *Does the Jury System Need Repair?*, LEGAL TIMES, Jan. 30, 1995, at p. 58. In the United States, the debate over proposals to abolish the hearsay rule is also tied to the issue of the future of the jury system. Thayer claimed that the hearsay rule was "the child of the jury," the product of our fears that lay jurors would not be skeptical enough of hearsay testimony. J. THAYER, PRELIMINARY TREATISE ON EVIDENCE 47 (1898). In the words of one of the leading modern commentators, our continued adherence to the hearsay rule reflects a fear of the "danger of jury overvaluation of hearsay . . . ." Park, *A Subject Matter Approach to Hearsay Reform*, 86 MICH. L. REV. 51, 122 (1987).

Concerns regarding the limited competence of lay jurors are certainly alive today. Former Chief Justice Warren Burger long advocated the study of alternatives to the current jury system. *Alternatives to Complex Jury Cases?*, CAL. LAW., Apr. 1982, at 35. Speaking before the Conference of Chief Justices, Justice Burger declared that "when the framers of the Constitution were engaged in the practice of law in the colonies, they were not dealing with the kinds of complex cases that are the daily fare of the courts in the second half of the 20th century." Sylvester, *Jury's Still Out on Jury Trials*, NAT'L L.J., Mar. 1, 1982, at 1. The concern about jurors' competence has been compounded by the belief that jury trials aggravate the problem of crowded dockets. At an annual meeting of the American Bar Association, Justice Stevens stated that court time is a "scarce resource" in the United States. Corboy, *The Right to Trial by Jury*, TRIAL, May 1980, at 17. The Justice added that given the backlog of cases, the right to jury trial is "a luxury that perhaps we may not be able to afford to the extent we have over the years." *Id.*

On the other hand, there is a growing body of research data indicating that the doubts about jurors' competence to critically evaluate hearsay evidence are overstated. Kovera, Park & Penrod, *Jurors' Perceptions of Eyewitness and Hearsay Evidence*, 76 MINN. L. REV. 703, 722 (1992) ("this study's results suggest that in general, jurors are skeptical of the quality and usefulness of hearsay testimony. More specifically, jurors in this study were able to differentiate among accurate and inaccurate hearsay witnesses"); Landsman & Rakos, *Research Essay: A Preliminary Empirical Enquiry Concerning the Prohibition of Hearsay Evidence in American Courts*, 15 LAW & PSYCH. REV. 65, 66 (1991) ("preliminary empirical data . . . suggest the incompetence [thesis] is open to doubt"); Miene, Park & Borgida, *Juror Decision Making and the Evaluation of Hearsay Evidence*, 76 MINN. L. REV. 683, 699 (1992) ("the data from this study suggest that hearsay as a form of testimony is not overvalued by jurors . . . . [S]ubjects in this study did not give much weight to hearsay evidence . . . .").

Occasional high–profile jury verdict debacles aside, there probably is still solid, widespread support for the present jury system–especially among federal and state trial judges. Guinther, *The Jury in America*, *in* THE

AMERICAN CIVIL JURY 44, 53 (1987) ("In one national survey, nearly 90% of the responding judges expressed faith in the jury system"). Given such support, the jury system in America is likely to survive relatively intact for the short term at least. Hence, rather than focus on abolition of the hearsay rule, it is more realistic to look at other proposed reforms.

2.   RECOGNITION OF NEW SPECIFIC HEARSAY EXCEPTIONS

The least controversial step toward reforming the hearsay rule would be recognizing new specific hearsay exceptions.* Two exceptions in particular warrant discussion.

a.   Child Hearsay Statements

The nationwide campaign against child abuse has wrought numerous changes in American evidence law. Raeder, *Navigating Between Scylla and Charybdis: Ohio's Efforts to Protect Children Without Eviscerating the Rights of Criminal Defendants–Evidentiary Considerations and the Rebirth of Confrontation Clause Analysis in Child Abuse Cases*, 25 U. TOL. L. REV. 44 (1993–94). As noted earlier, the campaign has led to relaxed competency standards for prospective child witnesses, special procedures such as the use of videotaping or closed–circuit television to make the experience of testifying less traumatic for children, and novel types of expert testimony such as child sexual abuse accommodation syndrome (CSAAS).

In addition, the campaign created pressure on state legislatures and courts to facilitate the more liberal admission of hearsay statements by young victims of alleged sexual abuse. Graham, *Indicia of Reliability and Face to Face Confrontation: Emerging Issues in Child Sexual Abuse Prosecutions*, 40 U. MIAMI L. REV. 19 (1985). In some cases, the courts have liberally applied existing hearsay exceptions to achieve that result. In *White v. Illinois*, 502 U.S. 346 (1992), the prosecution employed the excited utterance exception and the exception covering statements made for medical purposes. In *Idaho v. Wright*, 497 U.S. 805 (1990), the prosecution attempted to invoke the residual hearsay exception discussed later in this chapter. The Advisory Committee for the Federal Rules of Criminal Procedure has proposed adapting Rule 804(b)(5) (one of the predecessors to the current Rule 807) for that very purpose.

However, many jurisdictions took the next step and recognized a new hearsay exception for statements made by alleged child victims. In some jurisdictions, the courts fashioned a new exception as a matter of case law. *E.g.*, *State v. Boston*, 46 Ohio St.3d 108, 545 N.E.2d 1220 (1989). Special statutes are in effect in roughly half the states. Mosteller, *Remaking Confrontation Clause and Hearsay Doctrine Under the Challenge of Child Sexual Abuse Prosecutions*, 1993 U. ILL. L. REV. 691, 697. The statutes vary in detail, but typically they admit statements of children below a certain age (*e.g.*, under

---

* This section is based in part on M. LADD & R. CARLSON, CASES AND MATERIALS ON EVIDENCE 1023–28 (1972).

ten) who have been the victims of specified crimes, usually sexual abuse. The Pennsylvania statute is illustrative; section 5985.1(a)(1) of title 42 reads:

> An out–of–court statement made by a child victim or witness, who at the time the statement was made was 12 years of age or younger, describing indecent contact, sexual intercourse or deviate sexual intercourse performed with or on the child by another, not otherwise admissible by statute or rule of evidence, is admissible in evidence in any criminal proceeding if . . . [t]he court finds . . . that the time, content and circumstances of the statement provide sufficient indicia of reliability.

In addition to mandating some showing of the statement's reliability, the statutes typically speak to the subject of the child's availability as a witness. Most statutes "require that the child either testify or be found unavailable." Mosteller, *supra*, at 699. Again, the Pennsylvania statute fits the mold; section 5985.1(b)(2) conditions the admission of the statement on a showing that "[t]he child either (i) testifies at the proceeding; or (ii) is unavailable as a witness and there is corroborative evidence of the act."

Some jurisdictions have expanded the unavailability standard in child abuse cases, to authorize admission at trial of pretrial videotaping of the child victim's testimony in lieu of live testimony, if the prosecution can show that the experience of live testimony in the defendant's presence would traumatize the child. *E.g.*, *Miller v. State*, 517 N.E.2d 64 (Ind. 1987) (construing the Indiana statute and describing legislation in other jurisdictions); Graham, *The Confrontation Clause, the Hearsay Rule, and Child Sexual Abuse Prosecutions: The State of the Relationship*, 72 MINN. L. REV. 523, 558–62 (1988).

The Criminal Rules Advisory Committee thought that a clarifying amendment regarding availability would be useful. That Committee proposed adding the following language at the very end of 804(a)(4): "or there is substantial likelihood that the testifying would result in serious physical, psychological, or emotional trauma to a declarant of tender years."

NOTES

1. In *Maryland v. Craig*, 497 U.S. 836 (1990), the Court announced that a trial judge may deny a defendant face–to–face confrontation with a child accuser only when the judge makes a case–specific finding that "the child witness would be traumatized, not by the courtroom generally, but by the presence of the defendant." In deciding whether there is an adequate showing of unavailability under the special statutory hearsay exceptions for child statements, many courts analogize to *Craig*. Does the state of the psychological art permit the trial judge to make the sort of case–specific finding contemplated by *Craig*? For a skeptical analysis, see Crump, *Child Victim Testimony, Psychological Trauma, and the Confrontation Clause: What Can the Scientific Literature Tell Us?*, 8 ST. JOHN'S J. LEGAL COMMENT. 83, 95–96 (1992) ("it is scientifically unsound to imagine that a judge, psychotherapist, or anyone else can predict the long–term effects, into adulthood, of vigorously cross–examining an abused child"). *See also* Montoya, *Something Not So*

Funny Happened on the Way to Conviction: The Pretrial Interrogation of Child Witnesses, 35 ARIZ. L. REV. 927 (1993).

2. Although the results of recent research seem to reflect favorably on the general trustworthiness of child witnesses, there is an ongoing debate over the specific factors which the courts should consider in deciding whether a particular child hearsay statement is sufficiently reliable to be admissible. Some commentators are optimistic that aided by expert testimony, the courts can identify the factors pertinent to the decision. Honts, *Assessing Children's Credibility: Scientific and Legal Issues in 1994*, 70 N.D. L. REV. 879 (1994) (discussing the use of the Statement Validity Assessment technique); Comment, *The Admissibility of Expert Testimony in Intrafamily Child Sexual Abuse Cases*, 34 U.C.L.A. L. REV. 175 (1986). Other commentators are more guarded. In numerous cases, the courts have asserted that the child's consistent repetition of the statement and the lack of leading questions are indicia of trustworthiness. Note, *Determining the Reliability Factors in Child Hearsay Statements:* Wright *and Its Progeny Confront the Psychological Research*, 79 IOWA L. REV. 1149, 1166, 1177 (1994). These commentators believe that those assertions are "unsupported by empirical findings." *Id.* at 1177. *See also* Montoya, *Lessons from* Akiki *and* Michaels *on Shielding Child Witnesses*, 1 PSYCHOL., PUB. POL'Y & L. 340 (1995).

b. Declarations of Recent Perception

Another new specific exception has been proposed on the theory that the type of statement in question is presumptively trustworthy: a declaration of recent perception. What is a declaration of recent perception? Suppose that a Mr. Fowler observed the collision in the *Hill* case. About a week after the accident, Fowler was visiting Ms. Halston and told her a detailed account of the accident. Fowler could have testified at trial about what he personally perceived, but at the time of trial he is dead or otherwise unavailable. In his stead, Ms. Hill calls Ms. Halston to relate Fowler's statement. Fowler's statement to Halston was not excited; nor was it against his interest. Fowler's statement does not fall within any recognized hearsay exception.

Thayer recommended a new hearsay exception for such statements. In 1898, the Massachusetts legislature adopted Thayer's suggestion:

> A declaration of a deceased person shall not be inadmissible in evidence as hearsay if the Court finds that it was made in good faith before the commencement of the action and upon the personal knowledge of the declarant.

Chapter 535. Amended in 1941 and 1943, MASS. GEN. LAWS (Ter Ed.) ch. 233 § 65.

The success of the statute led the drafters of the Uniform Rules to recognize statements of recent perception as a hearsay exception. Although the Uniform Rules received a cool reception in most states, the Advisory Committee decided to resurrect the recent perception exception. Their draft of the Federal Rules of Evidence included the following provision as Rule 804(b)(2):

> Statement of Recent Perception. A statement, not in response to the instigation of a person engaged in investigating, litigating, or

settling a claim, which narrates, describes, or explains an event
or condition recently perceived by the declarant, made in good
faith, not in contemplation of pending or anticipated litigation in
which he was interested, and while his recollection was clear.

While Congress ultimately balked at recognizing what it considered to be a
novel exception and decided against including this exception in the Federal
Rules of Evidence, several states included the proposed exception in their
versions of the federal rules of evidence. Comment, *The Recent Perception
Exception to the Hearsay Rule: A Justifiable Track Record*, 1985 WIS. L. REV.
1525, 1527.

NOTES

1. One of the arguments against an exception for recent perception is that
it makes possible the admission of witness statements, carefully prepared by
claim adjusters, investigators, or lawyers with a view to litigation. The
language of the proposed Federal Rule attempted to obviate this risk. Did it
succeed?

2. Why did Congress enact Rule 803(1)'s exception for present sense impressions but refuse to enact the proposed exception for declarations of recent
perception? Are the two types of statements distinguishable in terms of the
magnitude of the risk of defective memory? Under the present sense impression doctrine, the courts tend to admit only statements made within seconds,
minutes, or at most an hour or so after the observed event. Imwinkelried, *The
Importance of the Memory Factor in Analyzing the Reliability of Hearsay Testimony: A Lesson Slowly Learnt—And Quickly Forgotten*, 41 FLA. L. REV. 215,
237 (1989). Under this exception, the strict enforcement of the contemporaneity requirement reduces the risk of misrecollection to a negligible possibility.
However, under the recent perception exception, the courts could admit statements made the day after the event. *Id.* at 238.

3. CREATING BROAD EXCEPTIONS TO THE HEARSAY RULE

Some critics of the present hearsay rule have not been content to urge new,
narrow exceptions. Rather, they favor wholesale exceptions that would
markedly increase the admissibility of hearsay. The critics are especially fond
of Model Code of Evidence Rule 503:

Evidence of a hearsay declaration is admissible if the judge finds
that the declarant:

(a) is unavailable as a witness, or

(b) is present and subject to cross–examination.

The brevity and simplicity of the statute should not mislead you. If adopted,
the statute would virtually revolutionize hearsay law. Moreover, it could pose
major constitutional problems if applied against the accused in a criminal
prosecution. We shall return to this question later when we cover constitutional overrides to the rules of evidence. For now, suffice it to say, that any

broad exception to the hearsay rule requires serious, constitutional analysis if it is sought to be applied against the criminal defendant.

An alternative to the statutory codification approach (*e.g.*, Model Code 503) is resort to common law. During the 1950's, the New Hampshire courts explicitly recognized the existence of a residual hearsay exception, based on the factors of reliability and necessity. In cases such as *Gagnon v. Pronovost*, 97 N.H. 500, 92 A.2d 904 (1952), and *Perry v. Parker*, 101 N.H. 295, 141 A.2d 883 (1958), the New Hampshire courts admitted reliable, necessary hearsay that did not fall within any recognized exception.

The most famous case adopting this approach is the Fifth Circuit's decision in *Dallas County v. Commercial Union Assurance Co.*, 286 F.2d 388 (5th Cir. 1961). In that case, the county sued its insurer when the county courthouse collapsed. The county claimed that lightning had struck the courthouse. The policy's coverage included lightning as a risk. The county offered evidence that the debris included charred timbers. However, the insurer denied liability, claiming that the collapse was due to the building's structural weakness. To explain away the charred timbers, the insurer attempted to introduce a copy of the June 9, 1901, SELMA MORNING TIMES. The paper carried an article referring to a fire during the construction of the courthouse. The judge admitted the newspaper, and the county attacked the ruling on appeal. Judge Wisdom began the opinion by noting that there is no legal "canon against the exercise of common sense in deciding the admissibility of hearsay evidence." *Id.* at 397. The judge stressed that the newspaper reporter had no motive to lie and that the community was so small that any lie would have been immediately unmasked. *Id.* In the judge's mind, it was sufficient justification for the admission of the newspaper article that the article was "necessary and trustworthy." *Id.* at 398. Even before the adoption of the Federal Rules, in *United States v. Barbati*, 284 F. Supp. 409 (E.D.N.Y. 1968), Judge Weinstein remarked that "the current clear tendency" at federal common law was to admit "necessary and trustworthy hearsay." *Id.* at 412.

In the process leading to adoption of the Federal Rules of Evidence, there was extensive congressional discussion regarding the wisdom of explicitly conferring discretion on trial judges to admit hearsay that did not fall within a specific exception. *See* Imwinkelried, *The Scope of the Residual Hearsay Exceptions in the Federal Rules of Evidence*, 15 SAN DIEGO L. REV. 239, 247–52 (1978). The idea of a "residual hearsay exception" engendered vigorous debate. The Senate Judiciary Committee cautioned against granting trial judges "broad license" or "unbridled discretion," stating that "The Committee . . . agrees . . . that an overly broad residual hearsay exception could emasculate the hearsay rule and the recognized exceptions or vitiate the rationale behind codification of the rules." S. Rep. No. 1277, 93rd Cong. 2d Sess. 6 (1974), *quoted in* ALI–ABA Comm. on Cont. Prof. Ed., Resource Matls. –Fed. Rules of Evid. at 339 (1975). The Senate Report stated that *Dallas County* "illustrates" the quantum of discretion the trial judge needs. *Id.*

The enactment of the residual hearsay exceptions in the Federal Rules (now Rule 807) did not end the debate. In the 1970's, there was a sharp split of authority in the courts. *Lowery v. Maryland*, 401 F. Supp. 604 (D. Md. 1975), is illustrative of the courts' early approach to the interpretation of the residual exceptions. In *Lowery*, a habeas proceeding, the court declared that the residual exception should be used sparingly. In that case, the defendant offered evidence of a statement by Dixon, the chief prosecution witness against him at trial. In his later statement, Dixon admitted giving perjured testimony against the defendant. Dixon did not appear at the hearing in the habeas proceeding. The court held that the witness' statement did not qualify as a declaration against interest under Rule 804(b)(3). The court then announced that "[s]ince statements such as Dixon's are covered by Rule 804(b)(3), the admissibility cannot be considered under Rule 804(b)(5)." In a similar spirit, in *United States v. Mathis*, 559 F.2d 294, 299 (5th Cir. 1977), the court asserted that "tight reins must be held" over the residual exception. Until recently, many courts followed the "near miss" theory: If a statement seemed to be covered by a specific hearsay exception but nearly missed satisfying the exception's requirements, the statement could not be admitted under a residual exception. *United States v. Popenas*, 780 F.2d 545 (6th Cir. 1985).

In contrast, another 1970's decision, *United States v. American Cyanamid Co.*, 427 F. Supp. 859 (S.D.N.Y. 1977), rejected the narrow construction of the residual exceptions. The court stressed that on its face, the statute is not limited to exceptional cases or evidence with extraordinary probative value. The court considered Rule 102, encouraging liberal construction of the Rules, as part of the context of the residual exceptions. The court believed that implying a limitation of the exceptions to extraordinary cases would "negate the requirement of Rule 102." *Id.* at 866.

In the 1980's there was a marked trend toward a more expansive construction of the residual exceptions. The trend was particularly noticeable in cases admitting grand jury testimony under the exceptions. Jonakait, *The Subversion of the Hearsay Rule: The Residual Hearsay Exceptions, Circumstantial Guarantees of Trustworthiness, and Grand Jury Testimony*, 36 CASE W. RES. L. REV. 431 (1985–86). Moreover, several jurisdictions relied on the residual exceptions as the basis for admitting hearsay statements by child sex abuse victims. *State v. Dollinger*, 20 Conn. App. 530, 568 A.2d 530 (1990).

The liberal trend persisted into the 1990's. At the outset of the decade, the First Circuit handed down one of the most liberal applications of the exception, *United States v. Zannino*, 895 F.2d 1 (1st Cir.), *cert. denied*, 494 U.S. 1082 (1990). In *Zannino*, a witness had testified at a codefendant's trial. The prosecution realized that the testimony could not be admitted against the defendant under the former testimony exception; the codefendant was not a "predecessor in interest" of the defendant. However, the prosecutor offered the evidence on the alternative theory that the testimony satisfied the residual exception, and the court sustained its admission on that theory. At the earlier trial, the codefendant's counsel had vigorously cross–examined the witness, and the testimony consequently "bore . . . staunch hallmarks of reliability . . . ." *Id.* at 7. Cole, *The Federal Hearsay Rule and Its Exceptions*, 19 LITIGATION, Sum. 1993, at 17, 23, catalogues 14 different types of hearsay statements that the courts have admitted under the residual exceptions, including accomplices' grand jury testimony, statements by sexually abused children, newspaper articles, diary entries, affidavits, bystander's accounts, and telexes from government agencies. The author concludes that as of the mid–1990's, there is a discernible trend to "expand . . ." the residual exceptions. *Id.*

Although the expansive interpretation of the residual exception (present Rule 807) is now ascendant, it would be an overstatement to assert that that view is universal. Some courts continue to apply the exception cautiously. *E.g.*, *Coyle v. Kristjan Palusalu Maritime Co., Ltd.*, 83 F.Supp.2d 535, 545–46 (E.D. Pa. 2000) (stating that Rule 807 should be applied rarely only in exceptional circumstances and noting that the Third Circuit has "required some degree of rigor attendant to its invocation"); *In re Cypress Semiconductor Securities Litigation*, 891 F. Supp. 1369 (N.D. Cal. 1995) (ruling 803(24) inapplicable to certain magazine articles when the proponent did not attempt to depose the authors of the articles); *Parsons v. Honeywell, Inc.*, 929 F.2d 901, 907 (2d Cir. 1991); *Brookover v. Mary Hitchcock Mem. Hosp.*, 893 F.2d 411 (1st Cir. 1990); *United States v. Fernandez*, 892 F.2d 976 (11th Cir. 1989) (refusing to admit grand jury testimony under the residual exception). For that matter, the "near miss" theory still has adherents. *Acme Printing Ink Co. v. Menard*, 812 F. Supp. 1498 (E.D. Wis. 1992); *United States v. Vigoa*, 656 F. Supp. 1499 (D.N.J. 1987), *aff'd*, 857 F.2d 1467 (3d Cir. 1988). To date, the Supreme Court has not visited the question of the proper interpretation of the residual exception.

NOTES AND PROBLEMS

1. Approach the problem as one of statutory construction. Does the statutory language lend itself to the interpretation given it in the 1970's by *Lowery* and *Mathis*? Is the language ambiguous enough to allow a court to resort to extrinsic legislative materials such as the Senate Report? How much weight is the Report entitled to? The problem of the legislative history of the residual exception is a case study in the danger of taking isolated statements in a statute's legislative history at face value. There are passages in the congressional hearings that both sides of the dispute can seize upon. When legislative history materials "lend great comfort to both sides," the legislative history materials are "of no real assistance in interpreting the statute." *American Chicle Co. v. United States*, 41 F. Supp. 537, 543 (Ct. Cl. 1941), *aff'd*, 316 U.S. 450 (1942). Has the Congress in reality delegated the policy choice to the courts?

2. It is true that on its face, the residual exception neither requires a showing of extraordinary probative value nor is limited in its scope to unusual situations. However, there is a plausible statutory construction argument for the "near miss" theory. The statutes refer to "[a] statement not specifically covered by any of the foregoing exceptions." In *United States v. Dent*, 984 F.2d 1453, 1465–66 (7th Cir.), *cert. denied*, 510 U.S. 858 (1993), the court argued that the jurisdictions liberally reading the residual exceptions "treat Rule 804(b)(5) as if it began: 'A statement not specifically admissible under any of the foregoing exceptions . . . .' Rule 804(b)(5) reads more naturally if we understand that evidence of a kind specifically addressed ('covered') by one of the four other subsections must satisfy the conditions laid down for its admission." Since Rule 807 uses the same language as Rule 804(b)(5), the *Dent* court's argument is still viable.

3. Problem 22–1. In *Hill*, the plaintiff offers a private memorandum book that one of the Polecat test drivers kept as a personal record at home. The test driver was an independent contractor rather than a Polecat employee. There was no company policy requiring him to keep the record, but he wanted a daily diary of his professional work. One entry in the diary indicates that one of the designers of the Polecat model Ms. Hill was driving told him to be especially careful in collisions in the test because "God knows what will happen if you crack the rear end near that damn gas tank." Assume that the trial judge rules that the memorandum book cannot qualify under Rule 803(6). *See Gagnon v. Pronovost*, 97 N.H. 500, 92 A.2d 904, 905–06 (1952). Analyze the problem in terms of the fundamental probative dangers–perception, memory, narration, and sincerity.

4. Problem 22–2. In *Devitt*, the prosecutor calls Mr. Carmody as a witness. Carmody testifies that he owns a small hardware store near Paterson's apartment. Carmody says that he was closing his shop to go home when he heard someone scream, "I've been attacked," and the sound of a car racing away. At that instant, Carmody saw two people standing just outside his closed glass entrance door. A lady was standing next to the door. The lady was a customer, but Carmody cannot remember her name. Carmody also saw a young man looking off in the direction of the car speeding away. Carmody could not hear the young man, but he saw the man's lips move. The lady turned to Carmody and told him that the young man had "gotten the car's license plate number." She immediately told Carmody the number. The number is Devitt's license plate. Neither the lady nor the young man is available at trial. Devitt objects to Carmody's testimony as incompetent hearsay. *United States v. Medico*, 557 F.2d 309, 314–16 (2d Cir. 1977), *cert. denied*, 434 U.S. 986 (1977).

Chapter 23

OPINION EVIDENCE: LAY AND EXPERT

Read Federal Rules of Evidence 701 through 706.

A. THE NORM EXCLUDING LAY OPINION TESTIMONY

1. THE RATIONALE FOR EXCLUSION

In the typical case, the fact–finding process can operate in the following fashion. Because of the requirement of personal knowledge, the witness bases all of his or her testimony on facts and events personally observed. Further, because of the opinion prohibition, the witness limits the testimony to recitation of observed facts. Finally, the trier of fact decides which inferences and conclusions to draw from the facts testified to. In the typical case, the witness is capable of verbalizing the observed facts, and the lay jurors are competent to draw the necessary inferences. In the typical situation, hence, the model works well.

However, in some situations, the model breaks down. Those situations highlight the underlying rationale for admitting lay opinion testimony. The following case sheds some light on that rationale.

GOVERNMENT OF THE VIRGIN ISLANDS v. KNIGHT

989 F.2d 619 (3d Cir. 1993)

COWEN, CIRCUIT JUDGE.

[Henry Knight repeatedly struck the head of Andreas Miller with a pistol. The gun eventually discharged and killed Miller. In Knight's trial for second degree murder, proof was adduced that Miller had allegedly stolen property from Knight, and Knight was confronting Miller about this when the fatal encounter occurred. Defense counsel proffered eyewitness testimony that Knight never threatened to shoot Miller or pointed the gun at him. The district court permitted this factual testimony, but precluded the eyewitness as well as an investigating police officer from supplying their opinions that the firing of the gun was an accident. Our focus hereafter is upon the rule barring opinion testimony.]

Federal Rule of Evidence 701 states:

> If the witness is not testifying as an expert, the witness' testimony in the form of opinions or inferences is limited to those opinions or inferences which are (a) rationally based on the perception of the witness and (b) helpful to a clear understanding of the witness' testimony or the determination of a fact in issue.

The requirement that a lay opinion be rationally based on the witness' perception requires that the witness have firsthand knowledge of the factual predicates that form the basis for the opinion. Fed. R. Evid. 701(a) advisory committee's note. The district court properly excluded the investigating police officer's opinion because he did not observe the assault. In contrast, the eyewitness obviously had first-hand knowledge of the facts from which his opinion was formed.

Having met the firsthand knowledge requirement of Rule 701(a), the eyewitness' opinion was admissible if it would help the jury to resolve a disputed fact. The "modern trend favors admissibility of opinion testimony." *Leo*, 941 F.2d at 193 (quoting *Teen-Ed Inc. v. Kimball Int'l, Inc.*, 620 F.2d 399, 403 (3d Cir. 1980)). The relaxation of the standards governing the admissibility of opinion testimony relies on cross-examination to reveal any weaknesses in the witness' conclusions. Fed. R. Evid 701(b) advisory committee's note. If circumstances can be presented with greater clarity by stating an opinion, then that opinion is helpful to the trier of fact. *See United States v. Skeet*, 665 F.2d 983, 985 (9th Cir. 1982). Allowing witnesses to state their opinions instead of describing all of their observations has the further benefit of leaving witnesses free to speak in ordinary language. *See Stone v. United States*, 385 F.2d 713, 716 (10th Cir. 1967), *cert. denied*, 391 U.S. 966, 88 S. Ct. 2038, 20 L. Ed. 2d 880 (1968).

In this case, an eyewitness' testimony that Knight fired the gun accidentally would be helpful to the jury. The eyewitness described the circumstances that led to his opinion. It is difficult, however, to articulate all of the factors that lead one to conclude a person did not intend to fire a gun. Therefore, the witness' opinion that the gunshot was accidental would have permitted him to relate the facts with greater clarity, and hence would have aided the jury. Based on an assessment of the witness' credibility, the jury then could attach an appropriate weight to this lay opinion.

Although the district court should not have excluded this opinion, the exclusion of the opinion was harmless error as it did not prejudice Knight.

NOTES

1. Why does the *Knight* court sanction the admission of the opinion testimony? Are there two distinct justifications, clarity as well as difficulty in articulating all the factors that lead to a conclusion? How close was Shakespeare to the latter rationale when he alluded to our "poor, poor power of speech"? Other courts have used slightly different formulations. For example, in *Baltimore & O. R.R. v. Schultz*, 43 Ohio St. 270, 282, 1 N.E. 324, 332 (1885), the court stated that lay opinions are admissible "where it is not practicable to place before the jury all the primary facts upon which they are founded. . . ." *Id.* at 332.

2. At common law, the lay witness' inability to articulate the underlying primary sensory data creates an element of necessity for resorting to the witness' opinionated testimony. Does Rule 701 liberalize the admissibility of lay opinion testimony by eliminating the requirement for showing such necessity? Consider Rule 701(b). The Advisory Committee Note to Rule 701(b) states that "[w]itnesses often find difficulty in expressing themselves in language which is not that of an opinion or conclusion." Is it significant that Rule 701(b) uses the expression "helpful" rather than "necessary"?

2. THE ACCEPTABLE TYPES OF LAY OPINION TESTIMONY

Focus on the language of Rule 701:

> If the witness is not testifying as an expert, the witness' testimony in the form of opinions or inferences is limited to those opinions or inferences which are (a) rationally based on the perception of the witness, (b) helpful to a clear understanding of the witness' testimony or the determination of a fact in issue, and (c) not based on scientific, technical, or other specialized knowledge within the scope of Rule 702.

The language would lead the reader to believe that admissible, lay opinion testimony comes in some unified format. In fact, there are at least two distinct types of lay opinion testimony; and there is a fundamental difference between the two types. In both types of lay opinion, there is an element of necessity for resorting to opinionated testimony; the witness is likely to have difficulty verbalizing the underlying data. However, the foundational requirements for the two types of lay opinion differ. The foundational requirements are designed to ensure that both types of the lay opinion are reliable as well as necessary.

These foundational requirements are particularly important because the empirical studies indicate that lay opinion is error prone. Previously, we mentioned studies documenting the unreliability of lay opinions about handwriting identification (Inbau, *Lay Witness Identification of Handwriting*, 34 ILL. L. REV. 433 (1939)) and lay opinions identifying voices (McGehee, *The Reliability of the Identification of the Human Voice*, 17 J. GEN. PSYCHOLOGY 249 (1937)). In both studies, the researchers concluded that the reliability of a lay opinion was quite low.

a. Collective Fact, Composite Fact or Shorthand Rendition Lay Opinions

Under this first doctrine, a lay witness may express an opinion on such subjects as whether a person was drunk (*Singletary v. Secretary of Health, Education & Welfare*, 623 F.2d 217 (2d Cir. 1980); *State v. Palmer*, 606 S.W.2d 207 (Mo. Ct. App. 1980); *People v. Garcia*, 27 Cal. App. 3d 639, 104 Cal. Rptr. 69 (1972); or as in *Knight*, whether a killing was accidental (*Mathis v. State*, 591 S.W.2d 679 (Ark. Ct. App. 1980)). The courts usually refer to this doctrine as the collective fact, composite fact (*Giller Industries v. Consolidated Casting*, 590 S.W.2d 818, 820 (Tex. Civ. App. 1979)), or shorthand rendition doctrine. *United States v. McClintic*, 570 F.2d 685 (8th Cir. 1978). For example, in *Government of the Virgin Islands v. Knight, supra*, at 629 n.4, this note appears:

> Lay opinion sometimes has been referred to as a shorthand statement of the facts. *See, e.g. Kerry Coal Co. v. United Mine Workers*, 637 F.2d

957, 967 (3d Cir.) ("testimony was merely a shorthand report of his observations"), *cert. denied*, 454 U.S. 823, 102 S. Ct. 109, 70 L. Ed. 2d 95 (1981); 3 J. WEINSTEIN & M. BERGER, WEINSTEIN'S EVIDENCE § 701[02] at 701–23 (Matthew Bender 1990) ("One commentator calls this type of opinion testimony 'permissible shorthand rendering of the facts.' ") (quoting M. McCormick, *Opinion Evidence in Iowa*, 19 DRAKE L. REV. 245, 248 (1970)).

Delaware Rule of Evidence 701 states the principle in an interesting format: "If a witness is not testifying as an expert, his testimony about what he perceived may be in the form of inference and opinion, when: . . . The witness cannot readily, and with equal accuracy and adequacy, communicate what he has perceived to the trier of fact without testifying in terms of inferences or opinions. . . ." The doctrine permits lay persons to opine on such varied subjects as relative darkness, speed, sound, size, age, weight, and distance. Concerning speed of vehicles, *See Gust v. Jones*, 162 F.2d 587 (10th Cir. 1998).

PROBLEM

23–1. In *Hill*, an eyewitness seeks to testify that worker was driving the truck "real fast." There is an objection by Roe that "the witness must testify in the form of estimated m.p.h., not simply 'fast' or 'real fast.' " What result?

To trigger the collective fact doctrine, the proponent must lay a foundation proving two elements:

The witness' opinion is based on personally observed facts. As we previously noted, Federal Rule of Evidence 701(a) requires that the inference be "rationally based on the perception of the witness. . . ." Proof of perception should precede the question eliciting the opinion. *State v. Palmer*, 606 S.W.2d 207 (Mo. Ct. App. 1980). This requirement is as much a product of Rule 602 as it is of Rule 701.

By adding the adverb "rationally," the drafters suggest that the judge must not merely inquire whether the opinion has some underlying factual basis; rather, the judge must also assess the sufficiency or adequacy of the basis. This suggestion parallels the law governing expert opinion testimony that we shall study in the next chapter. There, too, the judge must not only examine the quality of the bases of the expert's opinion—that is, inquire whether each basis is proper; but the judge must also assess the quantity of the bases and determine that cumulatively, they are sufficient to support a rational opinion on the subject.

A number of courts have vigorously enforced this foundation requirement. In *Gross v. Burggraf Constr. Co.*, 53 F.3d 1531, 1544 (10th Cir. 1995), the defendant was charged with sexual harassment. The plaintiff, a female truck driver, complained about the attitude of Anderson, supervisor of the construction project where plaintiff worked. Plaintiff offered a witness' alleged statement that "Anderson had a problem with women who were not between the ages of 19 and 25 and who weighed more than 115 pounds." The court rejected the conclusion: "[The witness'] opinion regarding Anderson's idiosyncratic impression about female beauty was inadmissible under Rule 701(a) of the Federal Rules of Evidence because it was not based on his personal knowledge of any statement Anderson may have made about his preferences concerning a woman's appearance." Emphasizing the personal knowledge requirement, *See Hart v. O'Brien*, 127 F.3d 424 (5th Cir. 1997) (rejecting opinion); *Stagman v. Ryan*, 176 F.3d 986 (7th Cir. 1999) (excluding opinion).

In *Alexis v. McDonald's Restaurants of Massachusetts*, 67 F.3d 341 (1st Cir. 1995), an African-American restaurant customer was arrested by a police officer for allegedly causing a disturbance at a fast food restaurant. At issue was the testimony of an eyewitness to the events who opined that "had Alexis been 'a rich white woman' she would not have been treated in the same manner." In Alexis' civil rights action against the restaurant and the police officer, exclusion of the lay opinion was approved on appeal. The court stated: "[T]here simply is no foundation for an inference that [the restaurant manager] harbored a racial animus toward Alexis or anyone else. . . ." As *Alexis* illustrates, courts demand an evidentiary foundation for an inference of racial animus or other conclusory lay opinions. Rule 701 does not authorize the admission of "flights of fancy, speculations, hunches, intuitions, or rumors. . . ." *Visser v. Packer Engineering Associates, Inc.*, 924 F.2d 655, 659 (7th Cir. 1991).

PROBLEMS

1. Problem 23-2. In *Devitt*, you are the defense counsel ultimately desiring to elicit the witness' testimony that Devitt was drunk. What foundation must you lay?

The witness' bare assertion that he "saw" Devitt?

The witness' testimony that he saw Devitt in a bar?

Testimony that he saw Devitt consume four drinks?

Testimony that Devitt's speech was slurred and his eyes hazy?

Testimony that he has seen drunks on previous occasions?

How extensive a foundation does the collective fact doctrine require?

2. Problem 23-3. Like intoxication, identity is a common subject of collective fact lay opinion. Suppose that in *Devitt* the prosecutor called Mr. Marshall as a witness. Marshall happened to be walking near the door to Paterson's apartment at the time of the alleged attack. He is prepared to testify that the apartment door burst open and a man exited, running toward the parking area. The prosecutor would ultimately like to elicit Marshall's opinion that the man he saw was Devitt. Marshall gives the following testimony:

Q. How well could you see the man?

A. Not too well.

Q. Could you be more specific?

A. I was viewing him through a line of bushes along the path to the parking area.

Q. How much of the man's face could you see?

A. I got a good look at the peculiar shape of his nose and a pretty good view of his right ear. I could see the guy's right side as he ran down the path to the parking lot.

Q. Who was that man?

O. Your Honor, I must object. May we approach the bench?

J. Yes.

O. (At sidebar) Your Honor, this is certainly not proper opinion.

Q. I must disagree, Your Honor. The case law clearly establishes that identity is a proper subject for lay opinion under Rule 701.

O. That's true as far as it goes, Your Honor. But 701 also says that the opinion must be "rationally based on . . . perception . . . ." Mr. Marshall didn't see enough to form any worthwhile opinion.

Q. Your Honor, that goes to weight rather than admissibility. I urge you to overrule the objection.

As trial judge, how would you rule?

3. Problem 23-4. In the last problem, in addition to urging her objection, the defense counsel requests permission to take the witness on *voir dire* before the judge rules finally on her objection. She states, "Your Honor, I think a short *voir dire* will show exactly how scanty the basis for any opinion is here." The prosecutor opposes any defense *voir dire*. Should the judge permit the *voir dire*?

4. Problem 23-5. In the *Hill* case, the witness is Ms. Hill herself. After testifying about the accident, she begins describing her damages. May she testify about her current medical condition? How detailed may she be? May she testify in terms of her "diagnosis"? What may she say about her treatment? *Miracle v. State*, 604 S.W.2d 120, 127 (Tex. Crim. App. 1980); *Rogers v. State of Ala. Dept. of Mental Health*, 825 F. Supp. 986 (M.D. Ala. 1993) (patient's testimony about status of her mental health allowed under Rule 701).

The opinion is the type of inference that lay persons commonly and reasonably draw. As we shall see, there are some inferences that only an expert can draw; the expert's knowledge or skill enables the expert to draw conclusions beyond the capacity of laypersons. Thus, this element of the foundation is the dividing line between lay and expert opinion testimony. If expert knowledge or skill is necessary to draw a particular inference, laypersons cannot commonly draw the inference; and, hence, lay opinion on that subject would be inadmissible. The dividing line has become increasingly blurred because the courts are now quite receptive to lay opinion testimony. *Teen-Ed, Inc. v. Kimball Intern, Inc.*, 620 F.2d 399, 403 n.4 (3d Cir. 1980). However, trial courts must continue to exercise some care. Improvident admission of lay opinion can lead to reversible error. *Hester v. BIC Corp.*, 225 F.3d 178 (2d Cir. 2000).

The following problems test the limits of the liberality of admitting lay opinion testimony.

PROBLEMS

1. **Problem 23-6.** In our torts case, an eyewitness to the accident saw the plaintiff's car being operated by Ms. Hill just before the collision and is ready to testify "she was driving recklessly." The defense lawyer will also ask this witness: "Did she seem to be driving in disregard of human life?" Will you admit these opinions? *United States v. Sheffey*, 57 F.3d 1419 (6th Cir. 1995) (lay witnesses permitted to answer such questions because they do not embrace "specialized legal terms"), *cert. denied*, 116 S. Ct. 749 (1996). In contrast, courts usually prevent witnesses (lay or expert) from opining that an actor's conduct was "negligent" or "legally negligent."

2. **Problem 23-7.** In the same case, Silverstein, who lived near the accident scene and observed the accident, was prepared to testify that "any car that would behave that way has to be just plain unsafe." Would you admit that opinion? *Randolph v. Collectramatic, Inc.*, 590 F.2d 844, 847–48 (10th Cir. 1979).

3. **Problem 23-8.** In the *Devitt* prosecution, defendant wanted to testify that as far as he could tell, Paterson "seemed to have trouble on his mind" after he finished his beer. In the past, many judges routinely excluded such opinions on the ground that the question calls for improper "speculation" or "conjecture" about another person's state of mind. Some courts continue to bar such opinions under Rule 701. *United States v. Guzzino*, 810 F.2d 687, 699 n.15 (7th Cir.) (collecting cases excluding proffered lay opinions about another person's intention, meaning, or reason), *cert. denied*, 481 U.S. 1030 (1987). However, under Rule 701, many courts have been surprisingly liberal in admitting lay opinions about the state of mind of third persons. *United States v. Hoffner*, 777 F.2d 1423, 1425 (10th Cir. 1985) ("[C]ourts have been liberal in admitting witnesses' testimony as to another's state of mind . . . ."); *John Hancock Mut. Life Ins. Co. v. Dutton*, 585 F.2d 1289, 1294 (5th Cir. 1978) (testimony of decedent's daughter that she did not believe that the decedent's wife would ever shoot him); *United States v. McClintic, supra* (third party was aware of a fact); *United States v. Smith*, 550 F.2d 277, 281 (5th Cir.), *cert. denied*, 434 U.S. 841 (1977) (third party "knew and understood" certain requirements). How would you rule as trial judge?

Consider a case in which the trial court allowed a rape complainant to testify that the defendants "knew that I was trying to get away." Sometimes such testimony is excluded as speculation; on the other hand, it may be deemed to be admissible as a firsthand impression. The latter approach was followed in *State v. Ayala*, 178 Ariz. 385, 873 P.2d 1307, 1994 Ariz. App. LEXIS 9, 156 Ariz. Adv. Rep. 66 (Ct. App. 1994). In similar fashion in a business litigation context, See *Winant v. Bostic*, 5 F.3d 767 (4th Cir. 1993) (witness concluded that land developers never intended to do what they had promised).

4. **Problem 23-9.** No witness, lay or expert, is allowed to state directly that another witness who testified earlier in the case lied when he gave his testimony. *United States v. Akitoye*, 923 F.2d 221 (1st Cir. 1991). How far removed from this is it when a witness opines that a criminal defendant "feigned grief" over his wife's death? In *United States v. Meling*, 47 F.3d 1546 (9th Cir.), *cert. denied*, 116 S. Ct. 130 (1995), a paramedic was allowed to give

his impression that the defendant was feigning grief when the paramedic was treating defendant's wife. One potential distinction is that the witness is not characterizing the accused's demeanor and truthfulness *at trial*.

Just as a witness cannot tell the trial jury that a witness who previously testified was lying, affirmations that another witness gave honest testimony are barred. "Vouching testimony" came in the form of opinion testimony by lay witnesses that a rape complainant was sincere when she told them about the crime in *Maurer v. Minnesota*, 32 F.3d 1286 (8th Cir. 1994). Admission of the vouching testimony was held to have denied the defendant due process of law.

b. Skilled Lay Observer Testimony

There is a second type of opinion that lay persons are often permitted to express on the witness stand. The courts sometimes use the label, "skilled lay observer" testimony. The courts admit this type of opinion on such subjects as the identification of a defendant as the person in a surveillance photograph (*United States v. Borrelli*, 621 F.2d 1092 (10th Cir.), *cert. denied*, 449 U.S. 956 (1980)); sanity (*Spillman v. Estate of Spillman*, 587 S.W.2d 170 (Tex. Civ. App. 1979)); *Estate of Clegg v. Wiebe*, 87 Cal. App. 3d 594, 151 Cal. Rptr. 158 (1978)), the identification of handwriting style, or the recognition of a voice.

In one key respect, collective fact opinion and skilled lay observer opinion are alike. The reliability model breaks down here as it does in the case of collective fact opinion testimony. Remember that if the witness wants to give skilled lay observer testimony identifying Devitt's handwriting style on a letter containing a relevant admission, under Evidence Rule 901(b)(2) the witness must have "familiarity" with Devitt's handwriting. Just as it is practically impossible for a lay witness to verbalize all the primary sensory data leading to the conclusion that a color was red, it seems virtually impossible for a lay witness to describe the bases for the familiarity in complete detail. The witness may have observed the purported author's hand-writing style on hundreds of prior occasions. It would be ridiculous to expect the witness to articulate every prior observation, and it hardly seems worth the effort so long as the witness has some substantial basis for familiarity.

If we make the threshold policy decision to admit skilled lay observer opinions, two questions then naturally arise. The first is how do we distinguish between collective fact and skilled lay observer opinions. If a lay witness is going to express a collective fact opinion on a subject such as color or speed, the foundation need not include the witness' explicit testimony that on prior occasions, he or she has seen red objects or observed passing automobiles. We assume that most normal persons have had such observations; given that assumption, in most cases, requiring proof of prior observation would be a waste of time.

NOTES AND PROBLEMS

1. Contrast the practice for collective fact opinion with the practice for skilled lay observer testimony. If a lay person is going to express an opinion on a subject such as handwriting style or sanity, the opinion must be preceded by testimony about the witness' familiarity with the person whose handwriting or sanity is in issue. *Avery v. State*, 609 S.W.2d 52, 53 (Ark. 1980). Do you think that it is sound to treat the two types of lay opinion differently in this respect? Is this an argument for deleting the foundational requirement for skilled lay observer opinion—or for at least occasionally adding that requirement for collective fact opinion?

2. Problem 23-10. In the *Devitt* case, Ms. Mussio, a prosecution witness, is prepared to testify that shortly after the alleged assault on Paterson, she saw Devitt and observed "bloodstains" on his shirt. Would you classify that opinion as collective fact or skilled lay observer? What foundation would you lay before eliciting the final opinion? *See State v. Boucher*, 376 A.2d 478, 480–81 (Me. 1977).

3. Problem 23-11. In the last problem, assume that the judge rules that "you need a foundation, counselor." What foundation would be adequate?

Ms. Mussio's statement that "I am familiar with blood"?

Her testimony that "I've seen blood before"?

Her statement that "I've seen blood on tens of occasions"?

Her testimony that she served as a Red Cross aide in a combat zone in Vietnam in 1972?

Her testimony that she presently works as a technician in a medical clinic?

How does Rule 701's language, "rationally based on the perception of the witness," apply to skilled lay observer testimony?

The second question that should occur to you is how do we distinguish between skilled lay observer and expert opinions. Sometimes, the law permits us to use both types of opinion on the same subject. For example, a friend of Devitt's could give skilled lay observer testimony on the subject of whether Devitt appeared insane or irrational shortly after the alleged attack but we would also permit a psychiatrist who had evaluated Devitt to testify on the subject of Devitt's sanity.

NOTES

1. A number of cases allow lay witnesses to state that an accused person "seemed irrational" on the day of a crime. Other related opinions have been allowed as well. *United States v. Rea*, 958 F.2d 1206, 1215 (2d Cir. 1992) ("there is no theoretical prohibition against allowing lay witnesses to give their opinions as to the mental states of others. Accordingly, these Rules do not, in principle, bar a lay witness from testifying as to whether a defendant in a criminal prosecution had the requisite knowledge").

2. In one respect, lay opinion testimony may be more liberally admissible than expert opinion. Federal Rule of Evidence 704(b) prohibits an expert in a criminal case from testifying "as to whether the defendant did or did not have the mental state or condition constituting an element of the crime charged or of a defense thereto. Such ultimate issues are matters for the trier of fact alone." Some courts have held that this prohibition is inapplicable to lay opinion testimony and that consequently, otherwise admissible lay opinions may directly address those questions. *United States v. Rea, supra*, at 1215. The *Rea* court conceded that "the last sentence [of 704(b)], if read literally, could be understood to bar even opinions of lay witnesses on the ultimate issue of the state of mind of a defendant in a criminal case . . . ." However, the court argued that "there would have been no need to include the word 'expert' in the first sentence" if 704(b) applied to lay opinion testimony.

c. Other "Lay" Opinion Testimony

At common law, the courts often allowed owners to testify about the value of their personal or real property. Some courts extended the practice and permitted persons to testify about the value of their services. *General Aggregate Corp. v. Labrayere*, 666 S.W.2d 901 (Mo. App. 1994). The courts admitted these opinions liberally. The witness' status as owner was the only required foundation. *Arkansas Okla. Gas Corp. v. Burton*, 10 Ark. App. 419, 664 S.W.2d 894 (1984). The witness' proponent did not have to establish the witness' qualification as an expert. *Citizens Elec. Corp. v. Amberger*, 591 S.W.2d 736 (Mo. App. 1979). The witness could opine even though he was ignorant of market values in the general area. *Arkansas La. Gas Co. v. Cates*, 10 Ark. App. 426, 664 S.W.2d 897 (1984). The witness could testify about the value of his own property even though it was perfectly clear that he would not be permitted to express a similar opinion about the value of other persons' property in the same area. *Bower v. Processor and Chem. Serv.*, 672 S.W.2d 30 (Tex. App. 1984); *Southwest Craft Center v. Heilner*, 670 S.W.2d 651 (Tex. App. 1984).

NOTE

Federal tribunals continue to admit these valuation opinions. *Gregg v. United States Industries*, 887 F.2d 1462 (11th Cir. 1989); *United States v. 215.7 Acres of Land in Kent Cty., Del.*, 719 F. Supp. 273 (D. Del. 1989). So do state courts. *Great Plains Equip. v. Koch Gathering Systems*, 45 F.3d 962 (5th Cir. 1995). The general rule is that an owner may testify as to the value of his or her own land. *Hidden Oaks Ltd. v. City of Austin*, 138 F.3d 1036 (5th Cir. 1998).

3. SUMMARY AND PREVIEW

To better understand these rules and contrast them with the next section on expert opinion, it may be helpful to visualize the rules in this fashion:

Lay Opinion Testimony

The lay witness can verbalize all the primary data underlying the inference	The lay witness cannot verbalize all the underlying data; but he or she can draw a reliable inference from the data	Only an expert can draw a reliable inference from the data
(Therefore, lay opinion testimony is excluded as unnecessary)	(Therefore, lay opinion testimony is admitted as necessary and trustworthy)	(Therefore, lay opinion testimony is excluded as untrustworthy)

At common law, the preference for factual testimony by lay witnesses yields when the lay opinion is both necessary and reliable. On the one hand, when the lay witness can readily verbalize the underlying factual data, the courts exclude the witness' opinion as unnecessary. On the other hand, when the subject is so arcane that only an expert can draw a trustworthy inference, the courts exclude lay opinions as unreliable. In the parlance of Rule 701, to be admissible, a lay opinion must be both "helpful" and reliable in the sense that it is "rationally based on the perception of the witness."

B. EXPERT OPINION TESTIMONY

1. INTRODUCTION

Expert opinion testimony has become one of the most important types of evidence. In criminal cases, lay jurors have come to expect scientific proof of guilt in such forms as fingerprints. In the words of one prosecutor, scientific proof has become "the backbone of every circumstantial evidence case." Clark, *Scientific Evidence, in* THE PROSECUTOR'S DESKBOOK 542 (1971). In major civil cases, expert testimony has become virtually indispensable, especially on the issues of causation and damages.

The presence of experts has become so commonplace that commentators have suggested that the American judicial hearing is becoming trial by expert. Pizzi, *Expert Testimony in the US*, 145 NEW L.J. 82 (Jan. 27, 1995). As recently as 1974, the Jury Verdict Reporter for Cook County, Illinois, listed only 188 regularly testifying experts. Blum, *Experts: How Good Are They?*, NAT'L L.J., Aug. 24, 1989, at 1. "Today, there are more than 3,100—a 1,540% increase." *Id.* In the late 1980's, the Cook County state courts averaged one expert per trial. *Id.* In some areas, the trend is even more pronounced. In the early 1980's, the Rand Corporation released a study of the use of experts in trials in California courts of general jurisdiction. Gross, *Expert Evidence*, 1991 WIS.

L. REV. 1113, 1118–19. Expert witnesses appeared in 86% of the trials studied, and on average there were 3.3 experts per trial. *Id.* at 1119.

There has been concern over the quality of the testimony presented as well as its sheer quantity. In particular, some critics have argued that the admissibility standards for expert opinions are so lax that the courts routinely permit the introduction of spurious testimony. In his 1991 text, GALILEO'S REVENGE, Peter Huber of the Manhattan Institute leveled the charge that much of this expert testimony is "junk science." HUBER, GALILEO'S REVENGE: JUNK SCIENCE IN THE COURTROOM (1991). The debate over that charge was spirited and sometimes bitter. *See* Chesebro, *Galileo's Retort: Peter Huber's Junk Scholarship*, 42 AM. U. L. REV. 1637 (1993); Nolan & Ursin, *Tort Law and Science*, 254 SCIENCE MAG. 1663 (1991).

While an expert can occupy a number of roles—advisor to the attorney, teacher of abstract scientific principles, lecturer to the jury about the technical processes—clearly the most common role for the expert in the courtroom is the complex role of evaluator. The expert not only describes the pertinent theories but also applies those theories to the facts and draws a conclusion. This is the role on which this material focuses.

When the expert functions in this role, the expert voices an opinion and, in that respect, deviates from the trustworthiness model that we discussed earlier. As we have seen, the common law's preference is that witnesses restrict their testimony to recitations of observed fact; the common law assumes that the lay jurors are competent to draw their own inferences from the underlying sensory data. In the preceding materials, we saw one deviation from this norm: the common law accepts lay opinion testimony when the lay witness cannot verbalize the underlying data. This material deals with another deviation from the norm. And the first question we must ask is why evidence law admits expert opinions. The following section explains why the trustworthiness model breaks down in the case of expert opinion testimony.

2. THE RATIONALE FOR ADMITTING EXPERT OPINION

Federal Rule of Evidence 702 states:

> If scientific, technical, or other specialized knowledge will assist the trier of fact to understand the evidence or to determine a fact in issue, a witness qualified as an expert by knowledge, skill, experience, training, or education, may testify thereto in the form of an opinion or otherwise, if (1) the testimony is based upon sufficient facts or data, (2) the testimony is the product of reliable principles and methods, and (3) the witness has applied the principles and methods reliably to the facts of the case.

How does the expert "assist the trier of fact"? In this context, the underlying data can be verbalized; for example, the physician can list all the symptoms he or she observed. However, are the lay jurors equally competent to draw reliable inferences from the data? The expert's unique ability is drawing conclusions from the data. The cases traditionally announced that expert opinion testimony is admissible only when it is strictly necessary, that is, when the subject-matter is within their comprehension, an expert opinion is superfluous. *Bartak v. Bell-Galyardt & Wells, Inc.*, 629 F.2d 523 (8th Cir. 1980). As in the case of collective fact and skilled lay observer testimony, the model breaks down here, but it fails at a different step in the inferential process.

On the whole, the courts have been quite liberal in finding that a topic is proper subject-matter for expert opinion testimony. As *Dunn v. Hovic*, 1 F.3d 1362 (3d Cir. 1993), notes, "even when jurors are well equipped to make judgments on the basis of their common knowledge and experience, experts may have specialized knowledge to bring to bear on the same issue which would be helpful." In personal injury actions, the courts increasingly allow testimony by human factors engineers who may testify, for example, that yellow paint on a curb would make a defect in the curb inconspicuous to the average person. *Scott v. Sears, Roebuck & Co.*, 789 F.2d 1052, 1054–56 (5th Cir. 1986). In medical and legal malpractice cases, the courts are not only receptive to expert opinion testimony; in most cases, for the plaintiff to make out a submissible case, the courts demand that the plaintiff present expert opinion that the defendant professional's conduct violates the pertinent standard of care. These cases illustrate the courts' liberality. However, the reader should not be misled: There are limits to the courts' receptivity to expert opinion testimony.

UNITED STATES v. AMARAL

488 F.2d 1148 (9th Cir. 1973)

TURRENTINE, DISTRICT JUDGE, sitting by designation.

On May 14, 1973, a two count indictment was filed against appellate Amaral and co-defendant Nordfelt. Count one charged Nordfelt with the January 23, 1973, robbery of a national bank in violation of 18 U.S.C. § 2113(a). Count two charged appellant Amaral with the February 12, 1973, robbery of a national bank, and Nordfelt with aiding and abetting in violation of 18 U.S.C. § 2. A motion to sever was granted. On April 6, 1973, Nordfelt was tried by a jury and convicted on both counts. Defendant Amaral pleaded not guilty. The case was tried by a jury on April 4–6, 1973 and the defendant was found guilty.

Defendant Amaral appeals his conviction. Appellant maintains that the trial court abused its discretion in refusing to allow the defense to present testimony by an alleged expert witness regarding the reliability of eye-witness testimony. We find that these contentions are without merit, and we accordingly affirm the conviction.

The basic purpose of any proffered evidence is to facilitate the acquisition of knowledge by the triers of fact, thus enabling them to reach a final determination. As often stated, our system of evidence rests on two axioms: only facts having rational probative value are admissible and all facts having rational probative value are admissible unless some specific policy forbids. 1 Wigmore, Evidence §§ 9, 10 (3d ed., 1940). Evidence which has any tendency in reason to prove any material fact has rational probative value.

The general test regarding the admissibility of expert testimony is whether the jury can receive "appreciable help" from such testimony. 7 Wigmore, Evidence § 1923 (3d ed., 1940). The balancing of the probative value of the tendered expert testimony evidence against its prejudicial effect is committed to the "broad discretion" of the trial judge and his action will not be disturbed unless manifestly erroneous. *Salem v. United States Lines Co.*, 370 U.S. 31 (1962).

The countervailing considerations most often noted to exclude what is relevant and material evidence are the risk that admission will 1) require undue consumption of time, 2) create a substantial danger of undue prejudice or of confusing the issues or of misleading the jury, 3) or unfairly and harmfully surprise a party who has not had a reasonable opportunity to anticipate the evidence submitted. Scientific or expert testimony particularly courts the second danger because of its aura of special reliability and trustworthiness.

Because of the peculiar risks of expert testimony, courts have imposed an additional test, *i.e.* that the testimony be in accordance with a generally accepted explanatory theory. *Frye v. United States*, 293 F. 1013 (1923). "The theory upon which expert testimony is excepted from the opinion evidence rule is that such testimony serves to inform the court [and jury] about affairs not within the full understanding of the average man." *Farris v. Interstate Circuit*, 116 F.2d 409, 412 (5th Cir. 1941) . Therefore, expert testimony must also be in regards to a proper subject. Finally, expert testimony is admissible only when the witness is in fact an expert and is accepted as such by the trial court.

[Because the defense had a full opportunity to cross-examine eyewitnesses, the court held that any deficiencies in the witness' perceptions could be spotted by jurors who did not require expert assistance to evaluate the testimony.]

NOTES AND PROBLEMS

1. *Amaral* is the leading case on the subject of the admissibility of expert testimony on the unreliability of eyewitness identification. A few courts have admitted such testimony, but most of the reported appellate opinions are cases affirming a trial judge's exclusion of the evidence. *E.g.*, *People v. Campbell*, 785 P.2d 153 (Colo. App. 1989); *State v. Bell*, 788 P.2d 1109 (Wash. App. 1990). Do you agree with this result? It is true that lay jurors realize that eyewitnesses can be mistaken, but does that dictate the conclusion that an expert witness' testimony would not be helpful to the lay jurors? Do the lay jurors fully appreciate the extent or causes of the unreliability? Levine & Tapp, *The Psychology of Criminal Identification: The Gap from* Wade *to* Kirby, 121 U. Pa. L. Rev. 1079 (1973). Some experimental data indicate that lay jurors are more willing to convict on the basis of fallible eyewitness testimony than on the basis of high caliber scientific evidence such as fingerprints. N.Y. Times, March 17, 1981, at Y16.

2. The experimental data mentioned above was gathered by Dr. Elizabeth Loftus of the University of Washington. Dr. Loftus not only favors admitting psychological testimony to apprise the jurors of the weaknesses of lay witness testimony; she has testified as an expert in such cases. Loftus, *Silence Is Not Golden*, 38 Amer. Psychologist 564 (1983). However, other witness psychologists oppose the admission of such testimony. Egeth & McCloskey, *Eyewitness*

Identification—What Can a Psychologist Tell a Jury?, 38 AMER. PSYCHOLOGIST 550 (1983).

3. Problem 23-12. In most of the appellate opinions affirming the exclusion of expert testimony on the unreliability of eyewitness identification, the courts stop short of announcing a categorical rule that such testimony is inadmissible; rather, the courts hold that the trial judge did not abuse his or her discretion in excluding the evidence. If the standard is abuse of discretion, when, if ever, will the appellate courts find the exclusion to be error? Suppose that Paterson had never seen Devitt before the alleged assault and that he first identified him in a photographic lineup more than a year after the crime. Would expert evidence on behalf of *Devitt* be admissible then? Assume further that there were significant differences between Devitt's facial features and the initial description that Paterson gave the police of the attacker's face. *See State v. Chapple*, 660 P.2d 1208, 1217–24 (Ariz. 1983).

In the 1990's, new decisions receptive to scientific proof and expert opinions caused some commentators to forecast that courts would be widely opened to eyewitness experts. As the following case demonstrates, a trend in that direction is not discernible.

UNITED STATES v. SMITH

122 F. 3d 1355 (11th Cir. 1997)

PER CURIAM. On January 11, 1993, after 10:00 a.m., a lone individual entered and robbed the Buckhead branch of Merchant Bank of Atlanta. The robber approached the window of teller Diane Hansek, asked for some change, and then pulled out a gun and asked for all her money. Hansek and two other witnesses to the robbery described the robber as a black male with a clean–shaven face wearing a white, snap–brim cap. Hansek described the gun as a revolver with a brown handle and silver barrel, while the other two witnesses described it as a silver–plated automatic. After the robber exited the building, one of the other witnesses ran out the back door and saw the robber drive off rapidly in a reddish–orange car that looked like a Mustang.

To assist in apprehending the bank robber, law enforcement officials sent photographs from the video surveillance camera to Atlanta television stations. The next day, the local FBI office received a phone call from Robert Lun, an inmate in the Atlanta Federal Penitentiary. Lun, who is black, had seen the televised photographs and identified the defendant Fred Smith as the perpetrator of the Merchant Bank robbery.

* * *

Defendant Smith offered as his first witness Dr. Brian Cutler, an expert witness in eyewitness identification. Smith made an extensive offer of proof outside the presence of the jury with regard to Dr. Cutler. Dr. Cutler's proposed testimony involved scientific research that showed eyewitness identification could be unreliable under certain circumstances. Dr. Cutler further proposed to testify that several of those circumstances were present in the Merchant Bank robbery: disguise, cross–racial identification, weapons focus, presentation bias in law enforcement lineup, delay between the event and the time of identification, stress, and eyewitness certainty as a predictor of accurate identification.

The district court excluded Dr. Cutler's proposed testimony in its entirety, holding that although the proposed testimony was relevant, it would not assist the trier of fact. Alternatively, the district court held that the probative value of the testimony was outweighed by the possible danger of misleading or confusing the jury.

The jury convicted Smith on both the bank robbery count and the use of a firearm count. The court sentenced Smith to 336 months' imprisonment, and Smith appealed.

* * *

Smith relies upon an emerging body of case law that he claims looks more favorably on expert testimony regarding eyewitness reliability. As an initial matter, we note that in none of the decisions Smith relies upon has any court embraced the position that expert testimony regarding eyewitness reliability ought to be admitted wholesale in every case. Instead, some courts have held that such evidence would be admissible under "narrow" or "certain" circumstances. *United States v. Harris*, 995 F.2d 532, 535 (4th Cir. 1993); *United States v. Stevens*, 935 F.2d 1380, 1400 (3d Cir. 1991). Moreover, we have found only one case where a district court was reversed for excluding expert testimony regarding eyewitness reliability. *Stevens*, 935 F.2d at 1401. In that one case, the district court had admitted some of the expert's testimony, but the court of appeals reversed because it had not admited all of the relevant expert testimony. *Id.* at 1400–01.

[The court affirmed Smith's conviction, holding that the problems of an eyewitness' perception can be adequately addressed on cross–examination. Further, the jury can adequately weigh these problems through common–sense evaluation, the court held.]

NOTE

State courts continue to reject eyewitness experts. *See, e.g., Johnson v. State*, 511 S.E.2d 603 (Ga. App. 1999). Criticizing this approach, *see* Gross, *The Unfortunate Faith: A Solution to the Unwarranted Reliance Upon Eyewitness Testimony*, 5 Tex. Wesleyan L. Rev. 307 (1999).

In most instances, the proponent offers expert testimony to prove a factual proposition. As we shall see, this century has witnessed a dramatic liberalization of the rules governing the admissibility of expert testimony on factual issues. However, notwithstanding that liberalization "it remains black–letter law that expert legal testimony is not permissible." Note, *Expert Legal*

Testimony, 97 HARV. L. REV. 797 (1984). The rationale for the black–letter rule harks back to the traditional view that expert testimony is admissible only when it is necessary. One commentator has condemned expert testimony when it is given in open court on the state of the law of the forum jurisdiction in which the court is sitting, or the state of federal law. Baker, *The Impropriety of Expert Witness Testimony on the Law*, 40 U. KAN. L. REV. 325 (1992). *See United States v. Weitzenhoff*, 1 F.3d 1523 (9th Cir. 1993) (court's admission of expert testimony on contested issues of law in lieu of instructing the jury was manifestly erroneous, but error held harmless).

NOTES AND PROBLEMS

1. Does Federal Rule of Evidence 702 bar the admission of expert legal testimony? What is the significance of the expression, "to determine a fact in issue," in Rule 702?

2. Problem 23-13. During the investigation in the *Devitt* case, the police seized some incriminating physical evidence from Devitt's apartment the day after the arrest. Devitt files a pretrial motion to suppress the evidence on the ground that the police lacked probable cause to believe that any relevant objects would be found in his apartment. Assume that in Morena, the evidentiary rules apply at the hearing on the motion to suppress. At the hearing, the prosecutor calls an attorney from the Morena Attorney General's Appellate Department. She is prepared to testify that she is the Deputy Attorney General with primary responsibility for litigating Fourth Amendment issues and that in her expert opinion, there was probable cause for the search in the Devitt case. The defense attorney objects that "this would amount to grossly improper opinion on a question of law." As the judge presiding at the hearing, how would you rule? *See DiBella v. County of Suffolk*, 574 F. Supp. 151, 152–54 (E.D.N.Y. 1983).

3. Problem 23-14. At trial in the *Hill* case, Ms. Hill calls Professor Bertram Oakley, who teaches Contemporary Ethics in the University of Morena Philosophy Department. He is prepared to testify that he has studied contemporary American social ethics and that in his opinion, marketing a product as dangerous as the Polecat model Mr. Hill purchased is "the sort of socially irresponsible act that almost all Americans would regard as misconduct richly deserving punishment and censure." Ms. Hill offers to accept a limiting instruction that the jurors may consider Professor Oakley's testimony only on the punitive damages issue. Polecat's attorney objects that "like opinion testimony on the law, opinions about morality have no place in the courtroom." As trial judge, how would you rule? *See* Delgado & McAllen, *The Moralist as Expert Witness*, 62 B.U. L. REV. 869, 881–85, 923–24 (1982).

4. What other topics lend themselves to expert opinion? Do words and terms used in contracts merit expert explanation? What about the question of whether particular remarks are libelous? Urging expert assistance in these situations, *see* Solan, *Can the Legal System Use Experts on Meaning?*, 66 Tenn. L. Rev. 1167 (1999) (lawyers have been consulting with linguists and language experts in a diverse array of legal cases).

3. THE FOUNDATION FOR AN OPINION EVALUATING OR INTERPRETING UNDERLYING DATA

a. The Statement of the Expert's Qualifications

A proper foundation must be laid for expert opinion. The first part of the foundation is proof of the witness' expertise. We have seen that the expert witness draws inferences beyond the capability of the lay jurors. Federal Evidence Rule 702 attempts to explain how the expert does so. That Rule provides that a witness may qualify as an expert "by knowledge, skill, experience, training, or education." Unfortunately, that provision is drafted inartfully. The provision arguably mixes apples and oranges. On the one hand, experience, training, and education seem to be methods of gaining the expert's unique ability to draw inferences. On the other hand, knowledge and skill are the end products of experience, training, and education.

Notice the disjunctive wording, "or education." The wording suggests that a person may qualify as an expert on the basis of education, or experience, or a combination of both. The case law bears out that suggestion. In some contexts, experience standing alone will qualify a person as an expert. Based on their law enforcement experience, police officers have often been permitted to testify as experts on criminal *modus operandi*. Schofield, *Criteria for Admissibility of Expert Opinion Testimony on Criminal Modus Operandi*, 3 UTAH L. REV. 547 (1978). In one case, a retired burglar was permitted to give expert testimony that implements found in the defendant's possession (crowbar, flashlight, gloves, and wire) were typical burglar tools. *State v. Briner*, 255 N.W.2d 422 (Neb. 1977). In a large number of cases, drug addicts and users have been qualified as experts on the identification of drugs. *See, e.g.*, *People v. Boyd*, 236 N.W.2d 744 (Mich. Ct. App. 1976); *White v. Commonwealth*, 499 S.W.2d 285 (Ky. 1973). However, sometimes courts insist upon a depth of experience in order for an expert of this sort to testify. In one case, for example, the court rejected the testimony of a drug user that the defendant was smoking marijuana, where the drug user had smoked marijuana only three times previously. *People v. Kenny*, 320 N.Y.S.2d 972 (1971). In *Thomas v. Newton Int'l Enterprises*, 42 F.3d 1266 (9th Cir. 1994), a longshore worker with 29 years of experience testified about the dangers of unguarded, uncovered manholes. In *United States v. Williams*, 81 F.3d 1434 (7th Cir. 1996), a former gang member was deemed to be properly designated an expert witness for purposes of translating a gang's street code.

In other situations, the witness can qualify as an expert on the basis of academic education alone. For example, in *State v. Chatham*, 153 N.J. Super. 35, 383 A.2d 440 (1978), the defense attempted to attack the prosecution expert's flameless atomic absorption analysis of suspected gunshot residue on the defendant's hands. The defense offered a witness as an expert. The witness admitted that he had never conducted an AA test, but he added that he was familiar with the theory because he had read extensively on the subject. The trial judge ruled that the witness did not qualify as an expert, but the appellate court overturned the ruling. The court stressed that often academic credentials alone are enough.

It is ideal, of course, if the witness has both academic education and practical experience in the field. Such a witness testified in *Moss v. Swann Oil, Inc.*, 423 F. Supp. 1280 (E.D. Pa.), *aff'd*, 566 F.2d 1170 (3d Cir. 1977). The expert was a professor of civil engineering, held a doctor of philosophy degree in engineering, and had worked for one and a half years on bridge construction.

In the end, it is the trial judge who makes the determination regarding whether a proposed expert is properly qualified to supply opinions. "The trial court, exercising its gatekeeping function, must examine (among other things) the expert's qualifications, the methodologies she used, and the relevance of the final results to the questions before the jury." *Adams v. Ameritech Services, Inc.*, 231 F.3d 414 (7th Cir. 2000). While the trial court has authority to exclude expert testimony, it must exercise it carefully. *Smith v. Ford Motor Co.*, 215 F.3d 713 (7th Cir. 2000) (district court erroneously determined that witnesses did not qualify as experts; "we conclude that the district court abused its discretion when it excluded plaintiff's proposed experts").

NOTES AND PROBLEMS

1. Problem 23-15. Devitt raises an insanity defense. He calls Dr. Miguel, a general practitioner physician. By happenstance, the physician saw Devitt a few days before the alleged offense, and Dr. Miguel is prepared to testify that in her opinion, Devitt was "mentally disturbed." The witness testifies that she had some formal psychiatric training during medical school. On *voir dire* by the prosecutor, she admits:

Q: Isn't it true that psychiatry is a recognized specialty within the medical profession?

A: Yes.

Q: And you are not a specialist in that field. Are you?

A: No.

Q: Moreover, you can be certified as a specialist in that field by a special board. Isn't that true?

A: Yes.

Q: Isn't it true that you are not board certified in the field of psychiatry?

A: Yes.

Q: Isn't it also a fact that as a general proposition, the opinion of a board certified psychiatrist would be more expert than the opinion of a general practitioner on a psychiatric issue?

A: I guess so, as a general proposition.

Would you sustain the prosecutor's objection to the witness' proposed testimony? *See Alvarado v. Weinberger*, 511 F.2d 1046, 1048–49 (2d Cir. 1975).

2. Courts often assert that the expert witness need not be a specialist. For example, in a case where medical opinion is relevant to a party's personal injuries, testimony by a specialist in the sort of medical condition involved in the case is not invariably required. However, the rule often changes in disputes where professional misconduct is at issue. In medical malpractice cases, for example, experts who testify regarding whether due care was used in completing a medical procedure are often required to be members of the branch of the profession to which the defendant belongs.

3. State statutes sometimes provide that when a witness proposes to testify on a medical question, the witness must be a currently licensed physician in the jurisdiction. Several jurisdictions impose that requirement for witnesses who propose to testify to the standard of care in medical malpractice actions. *Dawsey v. Olin Corp.*, 782 F.2d 1254, 1262 (5th Cir. 1986) (discussing the Louisiana statute). However, licensure in the forum is usually unnecessary to qualify as an expert witness. *Mulholland v. DEC Int'l Corp.*, 432 Mich. 395, 405 n.4, 443 N.W.2d 340, 345 n.4 (1989) ("Michigan has no statute prohibiting unlicensed professionals from testifying as experts. States which prohibit such testimony continue to constitute a small minority of the jurisdictions in this country").

4. Lawyers who wish to challenge the qualifications of an expert sometimes do so immediately upon the completion of the expert's background information. The voir dire examination by opposing counsel probes the expert's qualifications, seeking to exclude the expert by showing he is unqualified. *Dimambro Northend Associates v. Williams*, 169 Ga. App. 219, 312 S.E. 2d 386, 389–90 (1983) (opposing party must be afforded the opportunity, if he so requests it, to cross–examine the witness on the question of his qualifications *before* the discretionary determination of admissibility is made by the trial court). Often this request for an out–of–order cross examination regarding credentials comes right after the expert is tendered by the proponent of the witness, a procedure which is discussed next.

5. In some jurisdictions, after eliciting the witness' description of her qualifications, the proponent expressly tenders the witness as an expert or moves that the judge accept the witness as an expert—even if the opponent does not voice an objection. *United States v. Vastola*, 899 F.2d 211, 234 (3d Cir.) ("the usual trial practice"), *vacated*, 497 U.S. 1001 (1990). Does Federal Rule 702 or 104(a) require a formal tender or motion? If not, why would the proponent make such a tender or motion? In *United States v. Bartley*, 855 F.2d 547, 552 (8th Cir. 1988), the court warned that "[s]uch an offer and finding by the court might influence the jury in its evaluation of the expert. . . ." The court stated that "the better procedure [for the judge] is to avoid an acknowledgment of the witnesses' expertise. . . ." The official commentary to Kentucky Rule 702 similarly recommends that "the practice of tendering a witness [as an expert] should be discontinued," since the judge's "anointing" or "approbation" of the witness improperly conveys the impression "that the witness' testimony is especially believable." On the other hand, a formal tender serves the practical end of signaling to court and counsel that qualifications are completed and the direct examiner is about to proceed to the merits of the litigated case. That is why a number of courts express a preference for a formal tender by the proponent of the witness. They say it lends order to the proceedings and provides a valuable line of demarcation. Consider this in connection with the voir dire procedure discussed in Note 4, *supra*.

b. The Principles and Theories to Be Applied to Evaluate the Facts in the Case

Rules 703 and 705 must now also be analyzed:

Rule 703. Bases of Opinion Testimony by Experts.

The facts or data in the particular case upon which an expert bases an opinion or inference may be those perceived by or made known to the expert at or before the hearing. If of a type reasonably relied upon by experts in the particular field in forming opinions or inferences upon the subject, the facts or data need not be admissible in evidence in order for the opinion or inference to be admitted. Facts or data that are otherwise inadmissible shall not be disclosed to the jury by the proponent of the opinion or inference unless the court determines that their probative value in assisting the jury to evaluate the expert's opinion substantially outweighs their prejudicial effect.

Rule 705. Disclosure of Facts or Data Underlying Expert Opinion.

The expert may testify in terms of opinion or inference and give reasons therefor without prior disclosure of the underlying facts or data, unless the court requires otherwise. The expert may in any event be required to disclose the underlying facts or data on cross-examination.

After the proponent qualifies the expert, the proponent can present the balance of the expert's testimony in syllogistic fashion: major premise, minor premise, and conclusion. The major premise is usually the principle or theory that the expert proposes to use to evaluate the data in the case. For example, in our torts case, after qualifying a witness as a safety expert in the automobile industry, Ms. Hill's attorney could have the witness describe the safety standards recognized within the industry. Maslow, *Products Liability Comes of Age*, JURIS. DR., Feb. 1975, at 23–25.

In some cases, the expert derives the general principle from practical experience. For example, a veteran D.E.A. agent may testify about the general operational procedures of narcotics dealers. *United States v. Mang Sun Wong*, 884 F.2d 1537 (2d Cir. 1989), *cert. denied*, 493 U.S. 1082 (1990). In other cases, the expert will rely on a principle or theory derived by scientific experimentation.

NOTES AND PROBLEMS

1. Suppose that the expert is premising her testimony on a scientific principle. In addition to describing the theory and its experimental verification, to what else should the witness testify? Think back to our previous study of the validation of scientific evidence. Do *Frye* and *Daubert* apply here?

2. Problem 23-16 In the last problem, Devitt wants to elicit Dr. Miguel's testimony that even though she is only a general practitioner, the psychiatric theory she applied in Devitt's case is widely accepted by specialists. Dr. Miguel is prepared to refer to four articles and two texts (all written by board-certified psychiatrists) that subscribe to the same theory. When she attempts to do so, the prosecutor objects on hearsay grounds. As trial judge, would you sustain the objection? Consider Federal Rules of Evidence 703 and 803(18). *Compare Chorzelewski v. Druker*, 546 So. 2d 1118 (Fla. App. 1989) (on direct examination, an expert could not read from a medical treatise to "bolster his own opinion testimony") *with* Imwinkelried, *The "Bases" of Expert Testimony: The Syllogistic Structure of Scientific Testimony*, 67 N.C. L. REV. 1, 9 (1988) ("Would we require a modern accident reconstruction expert to replicate Newton's seventeenth century experiments to derive the laws of motion? Suppose that a physicist is testifying about the safety of a nuclear power plant. If the physicist contemplates relying on the words of Fermi or Oppenheimer, would we require that the physicist duplicate their research?"). Should the hearsay rule apply when the witness attempts to refer to another researcher's work to establish the validity of the theory the witness contemplates relying on?

3. Previously, we attempted to visualize the restrictions on lay opinion testimony. We can similarly depict the limitations on the expert's major premise:

Expert Opinion Testimony

Even a layperson could draw a reliable inference	Only an expert can draw a reliable inference	Even an expert cannot draw a reliable inference
(Therefore, expert testimony is excluded as unnecessary under the introductory clause in Rule 702)	(Therefore, expert testimony is admitted as necessary and trustworthy)	(Therefore, expert testimony is excluded as untrustworthy under *Frye* or *Daubert*)

As in the case of lay opinion testimony, the preferential rule excluding opinions yields when the proponent can demonstrate that the opinion is necessary as well as reliable. Although the common law required that expert opinions be strictly necessary, Rule 702 now provides that the expert need only be helpful and "assist the trier of fact." The split of authority over *Daubert* and *Frye* relates to the second component of the required showing by the proponent. Jurisdictions following *Frye* demand that the expert vouch that her theory is generally accepted, while *Daubert* jurisdictions require only that the expert establish that the theory has been experimentally verified.

4. The expert's theories will come under increasing courtroom scrutiny as the rules for scientific evidence tighten. In *Kumho Tire Co. v. Carmichael*, 526 U.S. 137 (1999) the general *Daubert* reliability test was extended to nonscientific expert testimony.

Writing for the majority, Justice Breyer ruled that like scientific expert testimony, non–scientific expertise must satisfy a reliability standard. He emphasized that the trial judge need not accept the *ipse dixit* of the practicioners of an assertedly expert discipline. He cautioned that "the discipline itself [might] lack reliability, as for example, do theories grounded in any so–called generally accepted principles of astrology and necromancy."

Then Justice Breyer took up the question of the manner in which the trial judge is to assess the reliability of non–scientific expert testimony. After noting the list of factors enumerated in *Daubert*, Justice Breyer opined that in a given case, one or more of those factors might be relevant to the judge's assessment. He added that "we can neither rule out, nor rule in, for all cases and for all times the applicability of the factors mentioned in *Daubert*, nor can we do so for subsets of cases categorized by category of expert or by kind of evidence. Too much depends on the particular circumstances of the particular case at issue." The justice stated that "the trial judge must have considerable leeway in deciding in a particular case how to go about determining whether particular expert testimony is reliable. That is to say, a trial court should consider the specific factors identified in *Daubert* where they are reasonable measures of the reliability of expert testimony."

Does *Kumho* provide a workable approach for the trial judge? In light of *Kumho*, as a trial judge how would you approach the task of evaluating the reliability of the testimony of a musician in a copyright infringement action or of an economist in an antitrust case? *See* Imwinkelried, *Evaluating the Reliability of Nonscientific Expert Testimony: A Partial Answer to the Questions Left Unresolved by Kumho Tire Co. v. Carmichael*, 52 Maine L. Rev. 19 (2000). The author suggests that in the following situations, a trial judge could find non–scientific expertise sufficiently reliable:

- A well–designed empirical study demonstrates that the practitioners of the discipline can generally arrive at more accurate opinions than laypersons. For example, there is some research indicating that professional questioned document examiners can perform indentification tasks much more accurately than laypersons.

- In the real world, there is substantial reliance on the opinions of the members of the discipline. For example, for decades, motorists have turned to auto mechanics when their cars malfunction. Motorists generally accept their opinions and find their services useful. Is there a sufficiently strong inference of the reliability of the non–scientific expertise in those situations? What other circumstances would give rise to an adequate inference of the reliability of the expertise?

The Advisory Committee Note to Rule 702 (revised in 2000 in response to *Daubert* and *Kumho*) lists other factors courts have found relevant in assessing reliability:

- Whether experts are "proposing to testify about matters growing naturally and directly out of research they have conducted independent of the litigation or whether they have developed their opinions expressly for purposes of testifying." *Daubert v. Merrell Dow Pharmaceuticals, Inc.*, 43 F.3d 1311, 1317 (9th Cir. 1995).

• Whether the expert has unjustifiably extrapolated from an accepted premise to an unfounded conclusion. *See General Elec. Co. v. Joiner*, 522 U.S. 136, 146 (1997) (noting that in some cases a trial court "may conclude that there is simply too great an analytical gap between data and the opinion proffered.")

•Whether the expert has adequately accounted for obvious alternative explanations. *See Claar v. Burlington N.R.R.*, 29 F.3d 499 (9th Cir. 1994) (testimony excluded where the expert failed to consider other obvious causes for the plaintiff's condition). *Compare Ambrosini v. Labarraque*, 101 F.3d 129 (D.C.Cir. 1996) (the possibility of some uneliminated causes presents a question of weight, so long as the most obvious causes have been considered and reasonably ruled out by the expert).

On the topic of scientific evidence, *see Goodwin, The Hidden Significance of Kumho Tire Co. v. Carmichael*, 2000 Baylor L. Rev. 603; Caudill and Redding, *Junk Philosophy of Science?: The Paradox of Expertise and Interdisciplinarity in Federal Courts*, 57 Wash. & Lee L. Rev. 685 (2000); Swift, *One Hundred Years of Evidence Law Reform: Thayer's Triumph*, 88 Cal. L. Rev. 2437, 2466 (2000); Risinger, *Defining the "Task at Hand": Non–Science Forensic Science After Kumho Tire v. Carmichael*, 57 Wash. & Lee L. Rev. 767 (2000); Capra, *The Daubert Puzzle*, 32 Ga. L. Rev. 699 (1998).

5. The Advisory Committee Note to revised Rule 702 also attempts to clarify the procedural burden attached to the court's gatekeeping function regarding the reliability of expert testimony. Noting that the applicable standard in applying the 2000 amendment is Rule 104(a), the committee cautioned that "[a ruling] that an expert's testimony is reliable, does not necessarily mean that contradictory expert testimony is unreliable:

As the court stated in *In re Paoli R.R. Yard PCB Litigation*, 35 F.3d 717, 744 (3d Cir. 1994), proponents "do not have to demonstrate to the judge by a preponderance of the evidence that the assessments of their experts are correct, they only have to demonstrate by a preponderance of evidence that their opinions are reliable. . . .The evidentiary requirement of reliability is lower than the merits standard of correctness." *See also Daubert v. Merrell Dow Pharmaceuticals, Inc.*, 43 F. 3d 1311, 1318 (9th Cir. 1995) (scientific experts might be permitted to testify if they could show that the methods they used were also employed by a "recognized minority of scientists in their field."); *Ruiz–Troche v. Pepsi Cola*, 161 F.3d 77, 85 (1st Cir. 1988) ("*Daubert* neither requires nor empowers trial courts to determine which of several competing scientific theories has the best provenance.")"

6. In Giannelli & Imwinkelried, *Scientific Evidence: The Fallout from the Supreme Court's Decision in Kumho Tire*, Criminal Justice 13 (Winter 2000), the authors note that *Kumho* is generating fresh courtroom tests of the acceptability of a number of processes, such as hair sample analysis, ballistics identification, bite–mark comparisons, and handwriting analysis. On handwriting analysis, *See United States v. Van Wyk*, 83 F. Supp. 2d 515 (D. N.J. 2000).

7. While federal courts are controlled by *Daubert* and *Kumho*, other jurisdictions are free to follow different standards. *Gilkey v. Schweitzer*, 983 P.2d 869 (Mont. 1999).

c. The Factual Bases or Data to which the Expert Will Apply the Theory

The next step in our syllogistically structured foundation is the minor premise, the factual data, commonly referred to as "the bases of the opinion." At this juncture, the expert specifies the case-specific information which she will evaluate by applying the general principle or theory. For example, after stating the diagnostic criteria for a particular mental illness (her major premise), the expert would describe the case history of the patient in question. Unless an appropriate foundation is laid for the expert's opinion, it will be excluded. *Concord Boat Corp. v. Brunswick Corp.*, 207 F. 3d 1039 (8th Cir. 2000) (expert opinion should not have been admitted because it did not incorporate all of the needed underlying data; because of deficiencies in foundation, the expert's conclusions were deemed to be "mere speculation").

There are three permissible bases or sources for data the expert factors into her conclusions: her own personal observation, the trial attorney's hypothesis, or a third party's hearsay report:

Facts the expert personally observed. Even at early common law, there was universal agreement that an expert could properly base an opinion on factual data he or she had personally observed. The example that comes most readily to mind is the physician describing the nature and extent of personal injuries the physician has personally examined and diagnosed. Personal observation is obviously a trustworthy source of factual data to support an opinion, and the acceptance of this basis is consistent with the common law reliability model. Revisit Federal Rule of Evidence 703. The Rule's language, "those [facts] perceived by . . . him," continues the common law view.

Facts the proponent asks the expert to assume hypothetically. The following is a familiar courtroom litany:

> Q: Doctor, please assume the following facts: One, in the accident, the plaintiff sustained a cut four inches in length and one-quarter inch in depth on the right front part of his head. Two, the plaintiff bled profusely from the cut. Three, immediately after the accident, the plaintiff began experiencing sharp, painful headaches in the right front of his head.
>
> A: Yes.
>
> Q: On the basis of those facts, do you have an opinion about the nature of the plaintiff's illness?
>
> A: Yes.
>
> Q: Doctor, what is that opinion?

This litany is the hypothetical question technique.

The initial question that should occur to you is whether we should permit hypothetical questions at all. Bear in mind the policy considerations which dictate such usage. If we restrict expert opinions to conclusions based on personally observed facts, we would thereby restrict the parties' access to experts. If the expert is too busy to personally study the facts before trial or if the party could not afford that expense, requiring personal knowledge would effectively keep that expert off the witness stand. Thus, it can be argued that restricting the bases of experts' opinions to observed facts is neither desirable nor necessary. The expert can contribute to the fact–finding process even when he or she has not personally observed the underlying data before trial. So long as the proponent presents admissible, independent evidence of the data, the hypothetical question techniques seem useful.

On the other hand, the technique's critics have indicted the technique because of the practical problems related to the use of hypothetical questions. To begin with, the proponent can virtually deliver a closing argument under the guise of asking a question. Wellman cites the following example:

> To illustrate the lengths to which the hypothetical question has gone, I may mention a contested will case recently tried in New York, in which a hypothetical question was propounded to three experts on each side. The two questions together consisted of about 36,000 words, that is, about 36 columns of newspaper print, and occupied more than four hours in the reading.

F. Wellman, THE ART OF CROSS-EXAMINATION 109 (4th ed. 1936).

Consider the effect of such a lengthy hypothesis on the jurors. It is unrealistic to assume that the jurors can properly evaluate the weight of an opinion resting on such a gargantuan hypothesis. Worse still, some jurisdictions permit the proponent to ask an expert witness who has been sitting in the courtroom during the prior testimony to assume the truth of "the prior testimony" or the testimony of a particular witness. That form of hypothetical question increases the danger of jury confusion. The danger is especially acute if the number of witnesses who have already testified is large or if there were some discrepancies between the testimony of the prior witnesses. The Advisory Committee attempted, in drafting Rule 705, to remedy the weaknesses of the hypothetical question. The Committee explained:

> The hypothetical question has been the target of a great deal of criticism as encouraging partisan bias, affording an opportunity to sum up in the middle of the case, and as complex and time consuming. While the rule allows counsel to make disclosure of the underlying facts or data as a preliminary to the giving of an expert opinion, if he chooses, the instances in which he is required to do so are reduced. This is true whether the expert bases his opinion on data furnished him at secondhand or observed by him at firsthand.

NOTE

A technique which is related to use of the hypothetical question is that of allowing the expert to remain in the courtroom to hear other witnesses. Thereafter, she may give her opinion based on their testimony. For example, highly qualified Dr. X is consulted by the plaintiff in an injury case and remains in the courtroom during testimony of the plaintiff and the plaintiff's attending physician. Based on what she hears, Dr. X testifies that the injuries are permanent. Note that this tactic requires creative use of Federal Evidence Rule 615(3).

Hearsay reports of third parties. The traditional view limits experts to the first two types of bases for their opinions: facts the experts have personally observed and facts to which other witnesses testify from personal knowledge and that the expert is asked to assume hypothetically. At common law, the expert could not base an opinion, even in part, on hearsay reports from third parties if the report was not within a hearsay exception and hence independently admissible.

The traditional view has been subjected to searching criticism. That criticism led to the adoption of Federal Evidence Rule 703. If the practitioners within a specialty customarily consider a particular type of hearsay data in forming their opinions, that very practice furnishes an argument for relaxing the traditional view. The Advisory Committee explained:

> [T]he rule is designed . . . to bring the judicial practice into line with the practice of the experts themselves when not in court. Thus a physician in his own practice bases his diagnosis on information from numerous sources and of considerable variety, including statements by patients and relatives, reports and opinions from nurses, technicians, and other doctors, hospital records, and x–rays. The physician makes life–and–death decisions in reliance upon them. His validation, expertly performed and subject to cross–examination, ought to suffice for judicial purposes.

The fundamental question is to what extent evidence law should defer to the practice within the expert's own specialty. That question is highly debatable. Although there are arguments in favor of the Advisory Committee's view, there are counterarguments:

NOTE, HEARSAY BASES OF PSYCHIATRIC OPINION TESTIMONY: A CRITIQUE OF FEDERAL RULE OF EVIDENCE 703, 51 Southern California Law Review 129 (1977)

Potential Problems of Unreliability in Hearsay Bases of Psychiatric Opinion Testimony

The diagnoses and predictions that psychiatrists make in court are often based on a variety of information. In some cases the opinion is the result of extensive interviews with the patient and direct observations of his behavior. In other cases, however, the opinion will be based partly or primarily on the reports of others.

These secondhand reports are provided to the testifying psychiatrist either by other experts or by lay third parties. For example, the testifying psychiatrist might rely on such expert sources as observations by other psychiatrists, observations of patient behavior by nurses and other hospital attendants, and psychological test reports contained in hospital records. In addition, he might rely on lay third–party sources, including statements by the patient's family, neighbors, and friends; and reports by community agencies, such as the police, schools, and the armed services. Each of these reports may be contained in the patient's psychiatric hospital record.

The source of hearsay information provided to the psychiatrist and the influences that act upon that source in reporting or recording the information may affect the reliability of the information that forms the basis of the psychiatrist's opinion.

[This Note urges that observations of other psychiatrists may be biased, and information provided by lay third-party sources to testifying psychiatrists may be unreliable for reasons similar to those that make expert hearsay sources potentially unreliable. Lay reports, like expert reports, concern the behavior of a particular individual, and human behavior is subject to varying interpretation even by experts. Untrained persons might be expected to give even less accurate accounts of behavior than experts.

Thus, because of the ambiguity of human behavior and possible biases of the observer, expert and lay hearsay bases of a psychiatrist's opinion testimony may be unreliable. The suggestion is that unless it is hedged with controls and restrictions, Rule 703 may expose the jurors to hearsay of highly suspect reliability.]

NOTES AND PROBLEMS

1. As previously stated, one underlying policy question is the extent to which the courts should defer to experts' selection of information to be included in the data supporting her opinion. Assume *arguendo* that the question arises in a *Frye* jurisdiction. *Frye* rests on a judgment that the courts should defer to experts' judgment on the validity of scientific theories; the courts should admit testimony based on a theory only if the theory has gained the status of general acceptance. Does that judgment dictate the conclusion that the courts should also defer to the experts' judgment as to the proper type of case-specific information to rely on?

There is much less reason to defer to the scientist's choice of the information functioning as her minor premise. An expert's willingness to rely on a report about the facts in the instant case is no guarantee of the report's trustworthiness. As an expert in medicine, a physician is in a better position than the judge or jury to determine that the presence of symptoms A, B, and C is the distinctive symptomatology for disease D. That determination is an exercise in scientific analysis. Suppose, however, that symptom A is nausea, and the patient tells the physician that she experienced nausea the day before visiting the doctor's office. The patient is the plaintiff in a personal injury action, and the question is whether plaintiff truthfully described her symptoms. Does the physician's medical degree make the physician a better judge of character than the judge or jury? A physician's medical school coursework does not include any specialized training in determining credibility. The determination of the content of expert's minor premise is predominantly an exercise in factual analysis rather than true scientific analysis. To make that determination, the expert temporarily "step[s] into the shoes of the factfinder" at trial. We do not assign that final determination to experts because the determination amounts to "factfinding, not the application of expertise." Empowering experts to finally decide the facts constituting the minor premise would "usurp . . . and derogate . . . the function of the factfinder."

Imwinkelried, *supra*, at 67 N.C. L. REV. 1, 10–11.

2. What is the relationship between Rules 702 and 703? The Advisory Committee Note to revised Rule 703 sought to clarify the issue:

> There has been some confusion over the relationship between Rules 702 and 703. The amendment makes clear that the sufficiency of the basis of an expert's testimony is to be decided under Rule 702. Rule 702 sets forth the overarching requirement of reliability, and an analysis of the sufficiency of the expert's basis cannot be divorced from the ultimate reliability of the expert's opinion. In contrast, the "reasonable reliance" requirement of Rule 703 is a relatively narrow inquiry. When an expert relies on inadmissible information, Rule 703 requires the trial court to determine whether that information is of a type reasonably relied on by other experts in the field. If so, the expert can rely on the information in reaching an opinion. However, the question whether the expert is relying on a *sufficient* basis of information— whether admissible information or not—is governed by the requirements of Rule 702.

3. We turn now from the question of evidentiary policy to the problem of statutory construction. Does the use of "reasonably" in Rule 703 give the trial judge the power to second guess the customary practice of the specialty? *Compare In re Japanese Elec. Prods. Antitrust Litig.*, 723 F.2d 238, 275–79 (3d Cir. 1983) *with In re "Agent Orange" Prod. Liab. Litig.*, 611 F. Supp. 1223, 1243–45 (E.D.N.Y. 1985) (citing Carlson, *Collision Course in Expert Testimony: Limitations on Affirmative Introduction of Underlying Data*, 36 U. FLA. L. REV. 234 (1984)). *See also* Carlson, *Policing the Bases of Modern Expert Testimony*, 39 VAND. L. REV. 577 (1986); *In re Paoli R.R. Yard PCB Litigation*, 35 F.3d 717, 748 (3d Cir. 1994), *cert. denied*, 115 S. Ct. 1253 (1995) (empowering the trial judge to rule that the specialty's customary practice is unreasonable).

4. Problem 23-17. In our torts case, Dr. Knopf is prepared to testify about the extent of Ms. Hill's injuries. He has personally examined her, but before trial the doctor told you frankly that his diagnosis rests in significant part on the records of the hospital where Ms. Hill was first treated and a report from Dr. Mason, the consulting burn expert. The records and reports themselves are inadmissible for some reason such as the hearsay doctrine. Under Rule 703, what foundation must the plaintiff lay if the plaintiff nevertheless wants the doctor to base an opinion on the reports? *People v. Ward*, 61 Ill. 2d 559, 338 N.E.2d 171, 176–77 (1975). Be prepared to conduct a short direct examination of Dr. Knopf in class to lay this foundation.

5. Assume that in the last problem, the plaintiff laid a proper foundation to permit the use of the reports for the limited purpose of establishing the bases of the expert's opinion. Should the written records be formally admitted into evidence and shown to the jurors? Some trial judges apparently construe Rule 703 as permitting both the formal admission of the reports and their submission to the jury. Carlson, *Collision Course in Expert Testimony: Limitations on Affirmative Introduction of Underlying Data*, 36 U. FLA. L. REV. 234, 235, 242–43 (1984). Is that interpretation sound? What light does the wording of Rules 612 and 803(18) shed on the proper construction of Rule 703? Citing Professor Carlson, the Minnesota drafting committee revised that state's version of Rule 703 to add this provision:

> (b) Underlying expert data must be independently admissible in order to be received upon direct examination; provided that when good cause is shown in civil cases and the underlying data is particularly trust-worthy, the court may admit the data under this rule for the limited purpose of showing the basis for the expert's opinion.

However, at least one commentator feels strongly that the jury must learn the full basis for the expert's opinion. Rice, *Inadmissible Evidence as a Basis for Expert Opinion Testimony: A Response to Professor Carlson*, 40 VAND. L. REV. 583 (1987).

6. The debate continues. *See* Epps, *Clarifying the Meaning of Federal Rule of Evidence 703*, 36 B.C. L. REV. 53 (1994); Allen & Miller, *The Common Law Theory of Experts: Deference or Education?*, 87 NW. U. L. REV. 1131 (1993). A modern study underlines the advisability of enactments like the Minnesota rule set forth in the prior section. *See* Schuller, *Expert Evidence and Hearsay: The Influence of "Secondhand" Information on Jurors' Decisions*, 19 LAW & HUM. BEHAV. 345 (1995). Participants in an experiment were exposed to unsubstantiated and secondhand information conveyed by means of an expert relating her background investigations to the jury. Mock juror simulations indicated that expert background hearsay was used to reach verdict decisions, despite judicial instructions to ignore the substantive facts asserted in the hearsay statements. The results underline the danger in allowing experts to freely relate otherwise inadmissible hearsay.

7. Cases allowing the expert to give her opinion but barring wide-open introduction of the expert's underlying data include *People v. Campos*, 32 Cal. App. 4th 304, 38 Cal. Rptr. 2d 113 (1995); *State v. Williams*, 549 So. 2d 1071 (Fla. Dist. Ct. App. 1989); *First Southwest Lloyds Ins. Co. v. MacDowell*, 769 S.W.2d 954 (Tex. Ct. App. 1989). For federal courts, the matter appears to be settled. A December 1, 2000 amendment to Rule 703 "provides a presump-tion against disclosure to the jury of otherwise inadmissible information used as the basis of an expert's opinion or inference, where that information is offered by the proponent of the expert." Advisory Committee Note to Rule 703. The revised rule provides that if facts or data are otherwise inadmissible, they "shall not be disclosed to the jury by the proponent of the opinion or inference unless. . .their probative value . . .substantially outweighs their prejudicial effect." This new dimension to Rule 703 is discussed in Carlson, *Is Revised Expert Witness Rule 703 a Critical Modernization for the New Century?*, 52 Fla. L. Rev. 715 (2000).

8. Assume that your jurisdiction subscribes to the federal and Minnesota positions that the data the expert relies on cannot be formally received into evidence unless it is independently admissible. In a hypothetical case, the expert intends to rely on a medical report which is not independently admissible. May the expert at least state that she is relying on the report? May she generally describe its contents? May she go into detail and quote key passages of the report? *Continental Airlines v. McDonnell Douglas Corp.*, 216 Cal. App. 3d 388, 411, 264 Cal. Rptr. 779, 791–94 (1989).

d. The Statement of the Ultimate Opinion

There are two limitations on the phrasing of the ultimate opinion with which we should be familiar.

The first is that in many jurisdictions, the expert must be prepared to vouch for the opinion as a "reasonable medical certainty" or "reasonable scientific certainty." Do you see any justification for imposing that limitation? At first, the limitations may seem arbitrary, but there is a connection between this limitation and the *Frye* rule. As we have seen, in part *Frye* rests on the fear that the lay jurors will assume that virtually all scientific testimony is infallible. If we work from that premise, it makes sense to limit expert testimony to opinions that merit the weight we think the jurors will accord the opinions. If jurors are likely to give scientific evidence certain or conclusive weight, it is arguable that only scientific opinions of that degree of certitude should be admitted. On the other hand, if we abandon the traditional rule and permit experts to express probabilities and even possibilities, that shift would seem to diminish the danger that the jury will attach undue weight to the evidence. Forcing the expert to characterize every courtroom opinion as a certainty may heighten the very danger on which *Frye* rests. The trend is toward abandoning the traditional view and permitting the expert to specify whatever degree of certitude with which he or she feels comfortable. *State v. Jarrell*, 608 P.2d 218 (Utah 1980) (reasonable probability); *Holtkamp v. State*, 588 S.W.2d 183 (Mo. Ct. App. 1979); *State v. Williams*, 388 A.2d 500 (Me. 1978).

The second limitation is the orthodox view that even an expert may not express an opinion on an "ultimate fact." This view is related to the trustworthiness model to which we continually refer: The witnesses supply the evidentiary data, and the jurors are then supposed to draw the inferences as to the ultimate facts in the case. Viewed as an adjunct to the trustworthiness model, the ultimate fact rule makes some sense if it is conceived as a norm or working guide rather than a categorical prohibition.

The problem is that the early common law courts tended to overstate the rule and phrase it categorically. As a categorical rule, the prohibition proved undesirable. The enforcement of an absolute rule would deprive the jury of the benefit of many valuable opinions. For example, in personal injury cases, the courts had the sense to realize that the medical expert must be permitted to testify on the issue of causation although causation is by any standard one of the ultimate facts. *Norland v. Washington Gen. Hosp.*, 461 F.2d 694 (8th Cir. 1972). The drafters of the Federal Rule took the dramatic step of jettisoning the ultimate fact rule in Rule 704(a). Rule 704 reads:

> (a) Except as provided in subdivision (b), testimony in the form of an opinion or inference otherwise admissible is not objectionable because it embraces an ultimate issue to be decided by the trier of fact.

(b) No expert witness testifying with respect to the mental state or condition of a defendant in a criminal case may state an opinion or inference as to whether the defendant did or did not have the mental state or condition constituting an element of the crime charged or of a defense thereto. Such ultimate issues are matters for the trier of fact alone.

Subsection (b) was added in 1984 as part of the Comprehensive Crime Control Act, primarily in reaction to several high–profile insanity defense cases, including Hinckley's attempted assassination of President Reagan. The subsection purports to resurrect the ultimate fact prohibition in a specific context. The legislative history indicates that in enacting the subsection, Congress intended to "eliminate the confusing spectacle of competing expert witnesses testifying to directly contradictory conclusions as to the ultimate legal issue to be found by the trier of fact." S. Rep. No. 225, 98th Cong., 1st. Sess. 230 (1983). The rationale for subsection (b) is that "insanity involves a legal (moral), not a medical issue, and therefore, no matter how the test for insanity is phrased, a psychiatrist or psychologist is no more qualified than any other person to give an opinion whether a particular defendant's mental condition satisfies the legal test for insanity." P. GIANNELLI & E. IMWINKEL-RIED, SCIENTIFIC EVIDENCE § 9-3(B), at 286 (1986).

NOTES

1. After Rule 704(a), what, if anything, remains of the ultimate fact rule? While there is support for the view that an expert may voice limited opinions on mixed questions of law and fact where such opinions form part of the vocabulary in the expert's field, there are boundaries. Consider this excerpt from the Advisory Committee Note on Rule 704:

> The abolition of the ultimate issue rule does not lower the bars so as to admit all opinions. Under Rules 701 and 702, opinions must be helpful to the trier of fact, and Rule 403 provides for exclusion of evidence which wastes time. These provisions afford ample assurances against the admission of opinions which would merely tell the jury what result to reach, somewhat in the manner of the oath–helpers of an earlier day. They also stand ready to exclude opinions phrased in terms of inadequately explored legal criteria. Thus the question, "Did T have capacity to make a will?" would be excluded, while the question, "Did T have sufficient mental capacity to know the nature and extent of his property and the natural objects of his bounty and to formulate a rational scheme of distribution?" would be allowed. McCormick § 12.

2. It is clear that some opinions are off-limits. Even an expert may not tell the trier of fact that the conduct of one of the parties in a case was "criminally negligent." Nor may an expert in criminology tell the jury that a defendant's conduct was in violation of the state criminal code, the very issue the jury was to decide. Legal opinions remain barred. *See* Ehrhardt, *The Conflict Concerning Expert Witnesses and Legal Conclusions*, 92 W.VA. L. REV. 645 (1990), citing *Torres v. County of Oakland*, 758 F.2d 147 (6th Cir. 1985).

3. Does the expression, "ultimate issue," in 704(a) mean "ultimate factual issue"? Does 704(a) authorize the admission of opinions on mixed questions of law and fact? *Compare Carol Barnhart Inc. v. Economy Cover Corp.*, 773 F.2d 411 (2d Cir. 1985) *with Bammerlin v. Navistar Int'l Transportation Corp.*, 30 F.3d 898, 900–01 (7th Cir. 1994). Judge Easterbrook's view on the law speaks volumes:

> [Plaintiff] wants Professor Lloyd Weinreb to testify as an expert witness about the copyright process in general, and the copyrightability of mannequin heads in particular. . .[It] objects to what it sees as undue restrictions on Professor Weinreb's testimony. . . . Professor Weinreb is a distinguished scholar, but he will not be allowed to testify in this case.
>
> Whether mannequin heads in general, or these mannequin heads in particular, are copyrightable is a question of law, which the court will decide (perhaps in response to dispositive motions soon to be filed). A jury has nothing to do with this subject. . . . If the court determines that mannequin heads are copyrightable subject matter, the jury will be so instructed. Similarly, the court will provide the jury with any necessary general information about the operation of the copyright system. There is no need for expert testimony on this subject; in a trial there is only one legal expert—the judge. *Pivot Point International, Inc. v. Charlene Products, Inc.*, 932 F. Supp. 220, 225 (N.D. Ill. 1996).

4. How broad is the prohibition in Rule 704(b)? To be sure, the Rule prohibits at least "opinions incorporating the statutory language of the insanity standard." Note, *Resurrection of the Ultimate Issue Rule: Federal Rule of Evidence 704(b) and the Insanity Defense*, 72 CORNELL L. REV. 620, 639 (1987). However, it remains to be seen whether the courts will extend the prohibition to opinions that "go to the very brink," that is, opinions so closely related to the ultimate issue that they indirectly communicate to the jury the expert's opinion on the ultimate issue. *Id.* Suppose that Devitt raised an insanity defense. Would Rule 704(b) prohibit an expert from testifying that, at the time of the assault, Devitt believed that he was merely dreaming? Or assume that the expert was willing to testify that Devitt did not understand that he was actually beating Paterson. Could the expert testify that Devitt did not understand the nature of the act? *Id.* at 638. In *United States v. Masat*, 896 F.2d 88, 93 (5th Cir. 1990), the court indicated that Rule 704(b) applies to "only a direct statement on the issue of intent." Testimony that the accused did not possess the requisite mens rea was excluded in *United States v. Campos*, 217 F.3d 708 (9th Cir. 2000).

4. THE FUTURE OF EXPERT OPINION TESTIMONY

The net effect of the adoption of Article VII of the Federal Rules of Evidence is to liberalize the admission of expert opinion testimony. In sum, we are likely to encounter "the battle of the experts" in the courtroom more frequently in the future. The basic policy question is whether that battle belongs in the courtroom. To some degree, we continue to adhere to the view that expert testimony is admissible only if the subject matter is beyond the comprehension or ken of the jurors. But if that is true, are the jurors capable of evaluating the proper weight to assign to the evidence and resolving a dispute between two experts?

One of the recurring criticisms of expert opinion testimony is that each side finds a partisan expert and presents the expert most willing to slant his or her testimony in favor of the party calling—and paying—the expert. Many commentators, including McCormick, suggested that this problem could be remedied by a more liberal use of the courts' power to appoint impartial experts. The drafters of the Federal Rules attempted to implement that suggestion in Rule 706. The Rule provides that the court may appoint expert witnesses agreed upon by the parties or of its own selection. Witnesses so appointed must advise the parties of their findings and be available to be deposed by any party. They may be called to testify by the court or any party and shall be subject to cross–examination by any party, including the proponent of such witnesses.

Courts have been hesitant to use their power to appoint experts; consequently Rule 706 is underused. This is in contrast to most of the countries in Europe where the judge makes the final selection of the experts to be called as witnesses. "The experts [in civil-law jurisdictions] are formally appointed as the court's own witnesses and compensated for their services with public funds. . . .The pattern is radically different in most common–law jurisdictions like the United States and the United Kingdom." Imwinkelried, *The Court Appointment of Expert Witnesses in the United States: A Failed Experiment*, 8 MED. & LAW 601 (1989).

NOTE

Should American judges be eager or reluctant to appoint experts under Rule 706? In countries where expert testimony has been largely privatized like the United States, the attorneys representing private parties play the major role in selecting experts. Is this preferable to the approach in most civil law countries? While considerations such as ensuring a witness' scientific objectivity may be aided by the European practice, does it introduce a larger measure of judicial bias into the dispute?

Are there other concerns which may account for the infrequency of use? *See* Diamond, *The Fallacy of the Impartial Expert*, 3 ARCHIVES OF CRIM. PSYCHODYNAMICS 221 (1959). Which approach is more in keeping with an adversary model of adjudication?

Chapter 24

THE BEST EVIDENCE RULE: THE ADMISSIBILITY OF COPIES, SUMMARIES, ETC.

Read Federal Rules of Evidence 1001 through 1007.

A. INTRODUCTION

The best evidence rule rests on the assumption that one type of evidence, the original document, has superior trustworthiness. The common law implements that assumption by demanding that the proponent produce or account for the original document when the document's terms are in issue. However, courts realize that sometimes, through no fault of the proponent's, the original will be unavailable at trial. In this situation, the common law relents and accepts secondary evidence. To ensure that the secondary evidence is both necessary and reliable, the common law defines both the acceptable types of excuses for the nonproduction of the original and the kinds of admissible secondary evidence. In short, the best evidence rule operates as a preferential doctrine rather than as a categorical exclusionary rule.

The doctrine is codified in Rule 1002:

> Rule 1002. Requirement of Original.
>
> To prove the content of a writing, recording, or photograph, the original writing, recording, or photograph is required, except as otherwise provided in these rules or by Act of Congress.

The federal approach can be restated as follows: When the terms of a document are in issue, the proponent must: either produce an original or duplicate, <u>or</u> both establish an excuse for the nonproduction of the document and offer a satisfactory type of secondary evidence.

To understand the doctrine, we must analyze five questions: What is a "document" for purposes of the best evidence rule? When are the terms of a document "in issue"? How should we define an "original" or "duplicate"? What are adequate excuses for the nonproduction of the original? And, finally, what are the acceptable types of secondary evidence?

As we trace the evolution of the answers to those questions from the common law to the Federal Rules of Evidence, we shall note the gradual, but steady, liberalization of the admissibility of secondary evidence of a document's contents. To a large extent, scientific advances have driven the liberalization. The conservative, common law best evidence rule "has its roots in a time before word processors, copier machines, typewriters or even carbon paper." McElhaney, *The Best Evidence*, 75 A.B.A. J. 72 (Jan. 1989).

As many commentators have noted, the expression "the best evidence *rule*" is a misnomer and, worse still, misleading. The title of the doctrine suggests that there is a general requirement that the proponent always produce the most trustworthy evidence. Again, such a broad requirement exists only in the form of the principle that the opponent may comment on the proponent's failure to produce more reliable evidence presumably within the proponent's possession. There is no general rule excluding the proponent's evidence simply because more trustworthy evidence may be available.

B.   WHAT IS A "DOCUMENT" FOR PURPOSES OF THE BEST EVIDENCE RULE?

The modern doctrine traces its origins to a statement by Chief Justice Holt in *Ford v. Hopkins*, 1 Salk 283, 91 Eng. Rep. 250 (K.B. 1700): "the best proof that the nature of the thing will afford is only required." Although Holt's language is broad enough to apply to non–documentary evidence, in the 19th century Professor Thayer's writings persuaded most courts that the rule proper should be confined to documents. Comment, *Authentication and the Best Evidence Rule Under the Federal Rules of Evidence*, 16 Wayne L. Rev. 195, 218–19 (1969).

The rationale for the rule is twofold: preventing copying mistakes and fraud, particularly given the law's "special regard" for the importance of the written word. When a contracts or property case turns on the exact wording of an agreement or deed, it is vital to minimize the risk of mistransmission or misdescription of the document's contents. The primacy of this rationale helps account for the liberalization of the rule, since science has generated better and better mechanical means of reproduction "which virtually eliminate the possibility of unintentional mistransmission." 2 C. McCormick, Evidence § 231, at 63 (5th ed. 1999). The other concern—prevention of fraud—originally stemmed from suspicion that a litigant who failed to produce an original might be trying to hide something or deceive the court. In an era before pretrial discovery, it would have been difficult to detect fraudulent copies or fabricated secondary evidence. The advent of modern discovery has also had a liberalizing effect on the rule. Yet, as the courtroom scenes in the movie *The Verdict* suggest, there can still be pitched best evidence rule battles over the admissibility of copies of allegedly altered records in medical malpractice actions. Liability can turn on whether a sentence includes the word "not" or whether the passage reads "4" rather than "1."

The following paragraphs list the four types of evidence most commonly subsumed in the definition of a document.

1.   CONVENTIONAL WRITINGS

The most obvious candidate for inclusion within the rule's scope is a conventional writing. Federal Rule of Evidence 1001(1) states a broad definition of the term. In our torts case, if Ms. Hill's attorney wanted to introduce the written contract of purchase, the best evidence rule would unquestionably apply. In the *Devitt* case, if the prosecutor offered a laboratory report to establish the presence of bloodstains on Paterson's shirt, again the rule would certainly apply. Or suppose that, with the help of a police artist, Paterson prepared an Identikit drawing of the assailant's face. The prosecutor might want to introduce the drawing to show a striking similarity between the features in the drawing and Devitt's facial features. The drawing would be a writing, triggering the rule. *Seiler v. Lucasfilm, Ltd.*, 808 F.2d 1316 (9th Cir.), *cert. denied*, 454 U.S. 26 (1987).

2. TAPE RECORDINGS

The traditional common law definition of "document" emerged before tape recordings even existed. When tape recordings developed, the question naturally arose whether the best evidence rule should be extended to audiotapes. Suppose that in the *Devitt* case, the police had a tape recording of a threatening call the attacker made anonymously to Paterson the week before the incident. The prosecutor wants to have a police officer testify about the tape recording. The best evidence rule would require the prosecutor to produce the audiotape recording itself. We would reach the same result under Federal Evidence Rule 1001(1). *See People v. Kirk*, 43 Cal. App. 3d 921, 117 Cal. Rptr. 345 (1974).

3. PHOTOGRAPHS

Another technological innovation that affected the scope of the best evidence rule is the development of the photographic process. Assume that in the *Devitt* case, shortly after Devitt's arrest the police searched Devitt's apartment. During the search, the officers found several photographs of Paterson's apartment and the vicinity—suggesting that Devitt had been "casing" the apartment for some time. The prosecutor wants one of the searching officers to testify to this discovery. At common law, many courts balked at extending the best evidence rule to photographs. It is true that a photograph is not a conventional writing, but some of the same policy considerations do come into play. The Federal Rules of Evidence change the state of the law. Carefully study both Rule 1001(1) and Rule 1001(2). Which subdivision is apposite to this hypothetical?

4. INSCRIBED CHATTELS

Suppose that in *Devitt*, Mr. Paterson testifies that the assailant brandished a knife and the police find a knife on Devitt's person at the time of arrest. Without producing the knife, the prosecutor could elicit the arresting officer's testimony about the knife on Devitt's person. *Redman v. State*, 580 S.W.2d 945 (Ark. 1979). Or in our torts case, Ms. Hill might have a testing laboratory subject the metal from which the gas tank is made to a thin layer chromatography (TLC) test to determine its chemical composition. The test is run on plates; the length and color of the streaks of the unknown developed on the plate indicate the chemical composition of the unknown. It is clear that the chemist may testify to describe the TLC test result without producing the plates. *United States v. Gavic*, 520 F.2d 1346 (8th Cir. 1975).

Although we begin with the assumption that a chattel is not a document for purposes of the best evidence rule, there are circumstances in which a chattel should functionally be treated as a document. Change the *Devitt* hypothetical just a bit. Suppose that Paterson adds that when the assailant brandished the knife, he saw the inscription "Buck Knives" on the blade. The police officer might attempt to testify that Devitt's knife bore that inscription without producing the knife in the courtroom. Even in this situation, a few jurisdictions refuse to apply the best evidence rule. Their refusal reflects a hostility to rules limiting the admissibility of logically relevant evidence. Others invoke the rule whenever the focus shifts to an inscription on a chattel. These jurisdictions reason that the concern for detail that inspires the best evidence rule applies equally to an inscription on a chattel and the writing in a conventional document. These courts argue that limiting the rule's scope to documents in the orthodox sense is arbitrary. Still others, probably the numerical majority at common law, give the trial judge discretion to decide whether to treat the chattels the same as documents.

NOTES AND PROBLEMS

1. In exercising that discretion, what factors should the judge consider? What is the significance of the fact that the inscription is relatively short? Suppose that the knife could easily be brought into the courtroom. How does that factor cut? Would it affect your ruling if the issue of Devitt's identification as the assailant were a close one?

2. In almost all jurisdictions, inscribed chattels represent the outer limit of the definition of "document." For that reason, the courts have refused to hold that in drug prosecutions, the government must produce the drugs themselves; the drugs are not inscribed in any sense. However, suppose the defense argued that the drugs are such vital evidence in these prosecutions that the best evidence rule should be extended? What policy arguments might the defense make? *See G.E.G. v. State*, 417 So. 2d 975, 977–78 (Fla. 1982).

3. Federal Rule 1001 contains these definitions:

For purposes of this article the following definitions are applicable:

(1) Writings and recordings. "Writings" and "recordings" consists of letters, words, or numbers, or their equivalent, set down by handwriting, typewriting, printing, photostating, photographing, magnetic impulse, mechanical or electronic recording, or other form of data compilation.

(2) Photographs. "Photographs" include still photographs, X–ray films, video tapes, and motion pictures.

4. Problem 24–1. Suppose that in the *Devitt* hypothetical, the Morena legislature had adopted Federal Evidence Rules 1001–08. As trial judge, how would you rule on the defense counsel's objection? Be prepared to point to the statutory language that you think is dispositive. Under Rule 1001(1), does the judge have discretion whether to treat the inscription as a writing, or is the application of the definition to inscriptions mandatory? *Compare United States v. Yamin*, 868 F.2d 130, 134 (5th Cir.) (the judge has discretion whether to treat the Rolex inscription on allegedly counterfeit watches as a writing), *cert. denied*, 492 U.S. 924 (1989), *with* 2 B. JEFFERSON, CALIFORNIA EVIDENCE BENCHBOOK § 31.12, at 647 (3d ed. 1997) (arguing that under the very similar California statute, the application is mandatory).

C. WHEN ARE THE DOCUMENT'S TERMS "IN ISSUE"?

Even if the object in question qualifies as a document, the best evidence rule does not come into play unless the document's terms are in issue. In the words of Federal Rule of Evidence 1002, the rule applies only when the proponent is attempting "[t]o prove the content of a writing, recording, or photograph." That requirement is directly related to the rationale for the best evidence rule. When the document's terms are in issue, the concern for accuracy underlying the best evidence rule mandates the application of the rule. The courts customarily find that a document's terms are in issue in three situations.

1. WHEN THE MATERIAL FACTS OF CONSEQUENCE AUTOMATICALLY PLACE THE DOCUMENT'S TERMS IN ISSUE

In our torts case, Ms. Hill's complaint specifically alleges that her husband purchased a Polecat automobile from Jefferson Motor Car Company by a written contract. That allegation places the contract's contents squarely within the range of issues in the case. (Indeed, in most jurisdictions, a copy of the writing will be attached to the complaint as an exhibit, and the complaint will purport to incorporate the terms of the writing by reference.) Given that allegation, Ms. Hill may not testify orally to the content of the written contract between her husband and Jefferson Motor Car.

Distinguish the above situation from the deceptively similar, but utterly different, situation in which both non–documentary and documentary evidence of the same fact exists independently of each other. If an eyewitness could have observed the fact or event without relying upon the document, the fact or event exists "independently" of the document; and oral testimony about the fact or event, if based on personal knowledge, is admissible. For example, to recover, Ms. Hill must prove that her husband fulfilled his obligations under the contract with Jefferson Motor Car Company. May she orally testify that she paid his monthly installments, or must she produce the written receipts Jefferson gave him? The best evidence rule is not triggered merely because the witness is testifying to facts which also happen to be "contained in a writing." *Moschale v. Mock*, 591 S.W.2d 415, 419 (Mo. Ct. App. 1979). The rule does not "prohibit a witness from testifying to a fact simply because the fact can be supported by written documentation." *McKeown v. Woods Hole*, 9 F.Supp.2d 32, 40 (D.Mass. 1998).

PROBLEMS

1. Problem 24–2. Suppose that in *Devitt*, it became relevant to show that Paterson reported the battery to the police shortly after the alleged incident. During cross–examination of Paterson, the defense implied that there was no attack; the defense counsel suggested that Paterson did not report the incident promptly, and at sidebar the defense counsel explains to the judge that during closing, he intends to treat Paterson's alleged failure as prior inconsistent conduct impeaching his trial testimony. To rehabilitate Paterson's credibility, the prosecutor would like a police officer to testify that shortly after the alleged battery, Paterson phoned and reported that he had just been attacked. A few minutes after receiving the telephone call, the officer recorded the report in a police log. Could the officer testify to the report without bringing the log into the courtroom? *See State v. Cameron*, 604 S.W.2d 653, 660 (Mo. Ct. App. 1980). Or suppose that the police department routinely tape–records all incoming calls. Could the officer testify to the report without producing the audiotape? *United States v. Fagan*, 821 F.2d 1002, 1009 n.1 (5th Cir. 1987), *cert. denied*, 484 U.S. 1005 (1988).

2. Problem 24–3. In our torts case, it so happened that Mr. Michelson, who was vacationing in town on May 15, was standing at the intersection where Ms. Hill's and Mr. Worker's cars collided. He was using his motion picture camera to film some footage of his wife standing in front of the old courthouse near the intersection. While he was attempting to film this footage, he happened to see the collision occur. He not only saw the collision; he filmed it and has had the film developed. At trial, Ms. Hill calls Michelson as a witness. During pretrial discovery, Polecat Motors learned of Michelson's identity and of the existence of the film. Polecat Motors' attorney objects that Michelson may not testify without first accounting for the film. As trial judge, would you sustain the objection? *Cf. United States v. Gonzales–Benitez*, 537 F.2d 1051, 1053–54 (9th Cir. 1976), *cert. denied*, 429 U.S. 923.

2. WHEN THE PROFFERED TESTIMONY CONTAINS AN EXPRESS OR IMPLIED REFERENCE TO THE CONTENTS OF A DOCUMENT

Sometimes, even when the material facts of consequence do not require the proponent to resort to documentary proof, the proponent does so. For example, it is well–settled that the proponent can prove the fact of a marriage ceremony without producing the marriage certificate. The marriage ceremony occurs independently of the certificate, and an eyewitness can observe the entire ceremony without ever seeing the certificate. However, at the time of trial, the proponent may be unable to locate an eyewitness to the marriage ceremony. The unavailability of eyewitnesses might force the proponent to resort to the certificate, and in that situation the proponent would have to comply with the best evidence rule.

PROBLEMS

1. Problem 24–4. As we have seen, to make out a prima facie case, Ms. Hill must prove not only that her husband formed a contract to purchase the Polecat automobile but also that he fulfilled all of his conditions under the contract, including the down payment of the purchase price. When he made the down payment, a Jefferson employee gave him a receipt. Ms. Hill witnessed the delivery of the receipt. As trial judge, would you permit Ms. Hill to testify, "And I've got a receipt to prove it," to corroborate her testimony?

2. Problem 24–5. In *Devitt*, the officer who originally received the complaint of the battery cannot presently recall the report. On direct examination, the officer purports to recall Paterson's report. However, on cross–examination, the officer admits that he has received so many reports of batteries and other crimes in his years of service as an officer that he cannot presently recall that particular telephone call. The officer admits that he is relying on his entry in the log book. At that point, what should the defense attorney do? Assuming that the log book is not in the courtroom, how should the trial judge rule?

3.   STATUTORY EXTENSIONS OF THE BEST EVIDENCE RULE

The best evidence rule is a creation of the common law. Like other common law doctrines, the rule can be modified by legislation. The Federal Rules of Evidence represent such a modification. As previously noted, at common law, it is well– settled that the proponent can prove the fact of a marriage without introducing the marriage certificate. However, add the fact that the pertinent state statute provides that the marriage certificate is "legal proof" of the marriage. *See* Comment, *Contents of Writings, Recordings, and Photographs*, 27 ARK. L. REV. 357, 362–65 (1973). Note also, that by the terms of Rule 1002, federal statutes can work exceptions or modifications.

NOTE

As a matter of statutory construction, what is the meaning of "legal proof"? Does it mean merely that the certificate is admissible proof of the marriage? If so, does the statute serve any purpose? The certificate be would be admissible even absent the statute. Or does it mean that the best evidence rule applies and that secondary evidence is inadmissible until the proponent accounts for the certificate? Does it mean that the certificate is the only admissible evidence of the fact of the marriage? Do you think that it is likely that the legislature intended that result? That result represents a step beyond the best evidence rule, which is a preferential rule rather than a categorical exclusionary rule.

D.   THE DEFINITIONS OF "ORIGINAL" AND "DUPLICATE"

If the item involved is a document and the document's terms are in issue, the best evidence rule applies. When the best evidence rule applies, the common law prefers that the proponent introduce primary evidence. Evidence is primary if it constitutes either the original or a duplicate (sometimes called a counterpart). At common law, originals and duplicates are equally admissible; if the proponent can persuade the trial judge that the evidence qualifies as either an original or duplicate, the evidence is admissible—and there is no necessity to account for or produce any other document. Thus, it is critical to understand the definitions of "original" and "duplicate."

1.   THE DEFINITION OF "ORIGINAL"

The common law knew only a single "original" writing, which in most cases, was the document produced first in point of time. That observation must be qualified by the additional concept that the definition of "original" is legal rather than chronological. The original is the document that has legal significance under the substantive law.

To illustrate that point, consider this hypothetical. Suppose that in our torts case, Mr. Hill and Jefferson Motor Car entered into the contract for the purchase of the automobile by correspondence. Mr. Hill types an offer to buy the car, makes a photocopy of the offer, and mails the photocopy to the Jefferson Motor Car Company. The typed document was prepared first in point of time. However, that document is not the "original." To identify the original, we must resort to the governing substantive law. Under contract law, a document does not become legally effective as an offer until the offeree receives the document. The upshot is that the document created second in point of time is the original.

Federal Rule of Evidence 1001(3) adds its own definition of "original":

> An "original" of a writing or recording is the writing or recording itself or any counterpart intended to have the same effect by a person executing or issuing it. An "original" of a photograph includes the negative or any print therefrom. If data are stored in a computer or similar device, any printout or other output readable by sight, shown to reflect the data accurately, is an "original."

NOTE

Does this statute simply codify the common law definition of "original"? If not, how does the statute differ from the common law? Is the definition broader or narrower? To what extent do the scientific advances in reproduction technology help to explain the changes? Under this definition, will there necessarily be only one "original" writing? Are multiple "originals" possible?

2. THE DEFINITION OF "DUPLICATE" OR "COUNTERPART"

At common law, the term "duplicate" is short for "duplicate original." To qualify a document as a "duplicate original"—admissible without accounting for the absence of any other "original"—the proponent had to demonstrate that:

a) The document is an exact copy of the original;

b) The parties made the copy at the same time as the original;

c) The parties intended the copy to have the same legal effect as the original; and

d) The parties executed the copy with roughly the same formalities as the original.

In other words, a "duplicate original" is simply one of two or more originals. Perhaps it would have been better to call these "multiple originals," since the word "duplicate" (apart from implying two items) has other connotations today because of duplicating machines and, now, because of Federal Rule of Evidence 1001(4).

Until recently, all subsequently prepared copies were treated as secondary evidence, since:

> "a Bob Cratchit, fingers numbed by cold in the counting house and fraught with anxiety over the health of Tiny Tim, might distractedly

misplace a decimal point, invert a pair of digits or drop a line. A Xerox machine, by way of contrast, does not worry about Tiny Tim and does not, therefore, misplace decimal points, invert digits, drop lines, or suffer any of the mental lapses that flesh is heir to."

Equitable Life Assur. Soc'y v. Starr, 241 Neb. 609, 489 N.W.2d 857, 863 (1992). Thus, as modern science spawned superior technologies for document reproduction, the common law's timing requirement became correspondingly less important as a means of assuring the copy's accuracy. The issue became *how* the document was prepared—not *when* it was prepared.

To bring the best evidence rule in line with common business practice and modern technology, many jurisdictions adopted the Uniform Photographic Copies of Business Records as Evidence Act. For instance, that Act is now in effect in California as Evidence Code § 1550:

> A photostatic, microfilm, microcard, miniature photographic or other photographic copy or reproduction, or an enlargement thereof, of a writing is admissible as the writing itself if such copy or reproduction was made and preserved as a part of the records of business . . . in the regular course of such business.

The Act in effect created a new, unnamed category. The Act not only eliminated the timing requirement; it also abolished the requirement that the parties intended the document to be the functional equivalent of an original. On the other hand, the new document had to be generated by one of the specified mechanical processes, and "made and preserved as a part of the records of [a] business in the regular course of such business." Although the Uniform Act effected some liberalization, the question arose whether the Act went far enough.

The drafters of the Federal Rules of Evidence obviously decided that it did not. Federal Rule 1001(4) creates a new category of document called a "duplicate," defined as follows:

> A "duplicate" is a counterpart by the same impression as the original, or from the same matrix, or by means of photography, including enlargements and miniatures, or by mechanical or electronic rerecording, or by chemical reproduction, or by other equivalent technique which accurately reproduces the original.

A "duplicate" under the Federal Rules is quite different from the common law "duplicate original,"—the most important difference being that the parties do not need to *intend* the duplicate to be the functional equivalent of an original. The Federal Rule also dispenses with the timing requirement. In common parlance, it is a copy. In modern federal practice, to minimize the potential confusion, it would probably be preferable to restrict the term "duplicate" to documents that qualify under Rule 1001(4), and to refer to documents that would have been "duplicate originals" at common law as "multiple originals."

NOTES AND PROBLEMS

1. Apply the four–part common law definition to a variation of our torts case. Assume that rather than finalizing the contract by correspondence, Mr. Hill visited Jefferson Motor Car's showroom to sign the contract of purchase. Jefferson's representative handed Mr. Hill a carbon manifold: an original form on top, a sheet of carbon paper, and an exact copy on the bottom. When Mr. Hill and Jefferson's sales manager signed the original form on top, the signatures were impressed through the carbon paper and onto the copy on the bottom. Would the carbon copy qualify as a duplicate? Under the common law? Under the Uniform Act? Under Rule 1001(4)? In what respects do the three definitions differ?

2. Note one peculiarity of the Federal Rules. At common law, a duplicate is just as admissible as an original. If a document qualifies as either an original or a duplicate, the document is admissible; and there is no necessity for the proponent to account for the original or other duplicates. Is that true under the Federal Rules? Read Rule 1003 carefully:

> A duplicate is admissible to the same extent as an original unless (1) a genuine question is raised as to the authenticity of the original or (2) in the circumstances it would be unfair to admit the duplicate in lieu of the original.

Does Rule 1003 reflect the continuing vitality of the secondary rationale for the original document rule, namely, fraud prevention?

Consider also the accompanying Advisory Committee Note to Rule 1003:

> Therefore, if no genuine issue exists as to authenticity and no other reason exists for requiring the original, a duplicate is admissible under the rule. This position finds support in the decisions, *Myrick v. United States*, 332 F.2d 279 (5th Cir. 1964), no error in admitting photostatic copies of checks instead of original microfilm in absence of suggestion to trial judge that photostats were incorrect; *Johns v. United States*, 323 F.2d 421 (5th Cir. 1963), not error to admit concededly accurate tape recording made from original wire recording; *Sauget v. Johnston*, 315 F.2d 816 (9th Cir. 1963), not error to admit copy of agreement when opponent had original and did not on appeal claim any discrepancy. Other reasons for requiring the original may be present when only a part of the original is reproduced and the remainder is needed for cross–examination or may disclose matters qualifying the part offered or otherwise useful to the opposing party. *United States v. Alexander*, 326 F.2d 736 (4th Cir. 1964). *And see Toho Bussan Kaisha, Ltd. v. American President Lines, Ltd.*, 265 F.2d 418, 76 A.L.R.2d 1344 (2d Cir. 1959).

3. The Advisory Committee Note attempts to illustrate the exceptions in Rules 1003(1) and 1003(2). Do you find the note sufficiently explanatory? What must the opposing attorney do to invoke Rule 1003(1)? Is it sufficient for the opposing attorney to assert that there is a question about the authenticity of the original, or must the opponent have available, admissible evidence calling the original's authenticity into question? *United States v. Leight*, 818 F.2d 1297, 1305 (7th Cir.), *cert. denied*, 484 U.S. 958 (1987).

4. Problem 24–6. In our torts case, when Mr. Hill and Jefferson's sales manager signed the contract, they both signed one document, but there was no carbon copy in existence at the time of signature. However, before Mr. Hill left, Jefferson's sales manager made a Xerox copy of the signed document and handed the copy to Mr. Hill. Under the Federal Rules, would the Xerox copy qualify as either an original or a duplicate?

5. Problem 24–7. Assume *arguendo* that in Problem 24–6, the copy at least qualifies as a duplicate. At trial, Jefferson's attorney proffers the copy into evidence. The Xerox copy shows marks lining out many of the warranty provisions of the contract. Suppose that Mr. Hill testifies that the copy is "just plain wrong—there were no marks lining out the warranty provisions" in the contract. Would the copy be automatically admissible in the face of that testimony? What else would Jefferson have to prove? Suppose that Mr. Hill's testimony was somewhat less definite; he said only that he "cannot recall" marks lining out the warranty provisions.

6. Problem 24–8. Suppose that Ms. Hill is attempting to prove that her husband fulfilled all of his conditions under the contract with Jefferson Motor Car Company. Unfortunately, he cannot distinctly remember making the monthly installment payments. However, he has the cancelled checks he wrote to make the payments. Rather than bring the checks to trial, he photographs them. Are the photographs admissible? *United States v. Patten*, 826 F.2d 198 (2d Cir.), *cert. denied*, 484 U.S. 968 (1987).

E. ADEQUATE EXCUSES FOR THE NONPRODUCTION OF THE ORIGINAL

As we have stressed, the best evidence rule is a preferential doctrine rather than an absolute exclusionary rule. The marked preference is for an original or duplicate; but in an appropriate case, the common law will reluctantly accept secondary evidence. However, in some jurisdictions, before a common law judge will allow the introduction of secondary evidence, the proponent must persuade the trial judge that there is some necessity for resorting to secondary evidence; the judge will demand that the proponent establish an adequate excuse for the nonproduction of the original and *all* duplicate originals. Over the years, the courts have recognized numerous situations as cases in which the proponent may dispense with production of the original or a duplicate original.

The Federal Rules' stance on excuses for nonproduction is a bit ambivalent. In one respect, the Federal Rules liberalize admissibility standards. Under Rule 1004, the proponent must establish excuses only for the nonproduction of "originals"—there is no duty to excuse the nonproduction of duplicates. However, in other respects the Federal Rules merely codify the received orthodoxy. The Federal Rules catalogue most of the recognized excuses. The Rules take a relatively conservative position and effect few, if any, major changes from the predominant views in the United States.

Federal Rule 1004 lists four different excuses that are generally accepted throughout the United States:

The original is not required, and other evidence of the contents of a writing, recording, or photograph is admissible if—

(1) *Originals lost or destroyed.* All originals are lost or have been destroyed, unless the proponent lost or destroyed them in bad faith; or

(2) *Original not obtainable.* No original can be obtained by any available judicial process or procedure; or

(3) *Original in possession of opponent.* At a time when an original was under the control of the party against whom offered, he was put on notice, by the pleadings or otherwise, that the contents would be a subject of proof at the hearing, and he does not produce the original at the hearing; or

(4) *Collateral matters.* The writing, recording, or photograph is not closely related to a controlling issue.

While in large part Rule 1004 is a straightforward codification of the common law excuses, there are some differences worth noting. At common law, if the excuse is that the original has been lost, the proponent must demonstrate that he or she·made a recent, diligent search for the original. Some jurisdictions have even laid down a hard and fast rule that the proponent must personally contact the last known custodian. Does the Federal Rule require proof of a diligent search? What is the standard?

Similarly, most jurisdictions concur that there is an adequate excuse when the original is beyond the territorial reach of compulsory process. Some of those jurisdictions limit the doctrine to their own compulsory process. Thus, a California proponent must show only that the original is beyond the reach of California's compulsory process. Even if it is clear that the original is in Nevada, the proponent need not investigate the possibility that Nevada courts would give some extraterritorial effect to California process. Is that true under the Federal Rule? Consider the pertinent Advisory Committee Note:

> When the original is in the possession of a third person, inability to procure it from him by resort to process or other judicial procedure is a sufficient explanation of nonproduction. Judicial procedure includes subpoena duces tecum as an incident to the taking of a deposition in another jurisdiction. No further showing is required. See McCormick § 202.

In some jurisdictions, even when the document is in the possession of a third party beyond the reach of compulsory process, the proponent must either attempt to contact that person to induce that person to voluntarily return the document to the site of trial or show that any contact would be futile because, for example, of the person's hostility to the proponent. Does the Federal Rule incorporate that requirement?

Rule 1004(3) reflects a frequently used excuse. The opponent in possession of the original can be put "on notice" in a variety of ways. If the complaint specifically refers to the written contract, that will put the defendant on notice that the original will be needed at trial. What other means can the proponent use to give the opponent notice? Compulsory process, such as a motion to produce, can suffice; however, even an informal notice or demand can put the opponent on notice that "the contents (of the original) will be a subject of proof at the hearing"? It should be understood that special problems can arise in applying this excuse in criminal cases, due to the defendant's Fifth Amendment privilege.

With respect to Rule 1004(4), some jurisdictions define "collateral" in a technical sense. As we saw earlier, a fact is collateral (and therefore cannot be proven by extrinsic evidence) if its only logical relevance is to a witness' credibility. Using that technical definition, these courts permit the use of copies of prior written inconsistent statements. Rule 1004(4) rejects that technical definition. The Rule's definition is more practical in character. The drafters of the Rules reasoned that the concern for detail is an acute consideration only when, as a practical matter, the document plays a central role in the case. If the document's role is practically collateral, we can relax the best evidence rule.

Rule 1005 codifies another, frequently used excuse for nonproduction relative to Public Records:

> The contents of an official record, or of a document authorized to be recorded or filed and actually recorded or filed, including data compilations in any form, if otherwise admissible, may be proved by copy, certified as correct in accordance with rule 902 or testified to be correct by a witness who has compared it with the original. If a copy which complies with the foregoing cannot be obtained by the exercise of reasonable diligence, then other evidence of the contents may be given.

At first glance, Rule 1005 does not even appear to deal with the question of excuses for nonproduction. However, by affirmatively authorizing the admission of a certified copy, Rule 1005 impliedly dispenses with the production of the original. Here, too, the Federal Rules differ slightly from the common law. At early common law, some jurisdictions limited this excuse to documents, the removal of which from official custody was forbidden by statute or regulation. Rule 1005 is not so limited. Many jurisdictions still limit the excuse to official records, that is, documents created by government agencies and remaining in official custody; these jurisdictions do not extend the doctrine to private documents that have found their way into official custody. What position does Rule 1005 take on this issue?

Rule 1006 is another element of the federal statutory scheme regulating excuses for nonproduction. The Rule also incorporates an often invoked excuse for nonproduction:

Rule 1006. Summaries.

> The contents of voluminous writings, recordings, or photographs which cannot conveniently be examined in court may be presented in the form of a chart, summary, or calculation. The originals, or duplicates, shall be made available for examination or copying, or both, by other parties at reasonable time and place. The court may order that they be produced in court.

Note that by its terms, Rule 1006 does not require that the underlying records actually be introduced into evidence. *Herman v. Davis Acoustical Corp.*, 21 F. Supp.2d 130, 135 (N.D.N.Y. 1998)

PROBLEM

Problem 24–9. Suppose that in our torts case, before marketing the model Mr. Hill purchased, Polecat Motors ran extensive safety tests. The results of the tests are compiled in a 5,000 page report. During discovery, Ms. Hill obtained the report and submitted the report for analysis by her safety expert, Dr. D'Antoni. At trial, the doctor wants to testify to express his opinion of the model's safety. The doctor could testify to that opinion over a best evidence objection by the defendant. *See Nichols v. Upjohn Co.*, 610 F.2d 293 (5th Cir. 1980). May the doctor present an oral summary or prepare a written "chart, summary, or calculation"? What is the meaning of the expression "conveniently examined in court" in Rule 1006? *United States v. Stephens*, 779 F.2d 232, 238–39 (5th Cir. 1985). A written summary can be a potent weapon at trial. In most jurisdictions, unlike purely illustrative exhibits admitted solely for pedagogic purposes, Rule 1006 summaries are treated as substantive evidence and can be sent to the jury during deliberations.

Lastly, Rule 1007 supplies another excuse for nonproduction.

Rule 1007. Testimony or Written Admission of Party.

Contents of writings, recordings, or photographs may be proved by the testimony or deposition of the party against whom offered or by his written admission, without accounting for the nonproduction of the original.

Rule 1007 represents a moderate view between polar extreme positions taken at common law. On the one hand, at common law some jurisdictions do not recognize any admission excuse. On the other hand, some jurisdictions treat any alleged admission as an adequate excuse. These jurisdictions have been known to apply the excuse even when the alleged admission was oral and the opponent flatly—and convincingly— denied making the admission. In this situation, there is a risk that the opponent in fact never made the admission; the testimony about the oral admission may be fabricated.

NOTES

1. In what sense is Rule 1007 a compromise between these two views? Note that Rule 1007 is only a partial excuse. In the case of most excuses for nonproduction, once the excuse is proven, any type of secondary evidence is admissible. However, in the case of Rules 1005–1007, even after the excuse is established, only certain, specified types of secondary evidence are admissible.

2. Before we close on this topic, consider one last issue of statutory construction. In common law jurisdictions, the trial judge has the normal power to be creative and recognize new excuses for nonproduction. For example, some jurisdictions permit the proponent to introduce secondary evidence as the exhibit so long as the proponent makes the original available in the courtroom. The original's availability enables the opponent to compare it with the formal exhibit and point out any discrepancies. Does the trial judge retain that power under the Federal Rules? Or is the list of excuses in Rules 1004–1007 exhaustive? Do Rules 1004–1007 answer that question, or must we look elsewhere in the Rules? Contrast the wording of Rule 1002 with that of Rules 404(b) ("such as") and 901(b) ("illustrations"). Does Article X recognize any window to the common law? Consider Rule 1004(4). Substantively, Article X is a relatively conservative statutory scheme which, for the most part, merely tinkers with the common law excuses for nonproduction. However, like Rule 402, Article X can be construed as lending strong support to the radical conception of the Federal Rules as a civil law code. Rule 1004(4) is the only real safety valve in Article X.

F.   IF THERE IS AN ADEQUATE EXCUSE FOR NONPRODUCTION, WHAT TYPES OF SECONDARY EVIDENCE ARE ADMISSIBLE?

If the proponent adequately excuses the nonproduction of the primary evidence, the proponent may resort to secondary evidence. However, there are limitations on the admission of secondary evidence. These limitations ensure that the secondary evidence admitted is not only necessary but also reliable.

1.   THE TYPES OF SECONDARY EVIDENCE

There are two types of secondary evidence of a document's contents. The first type is oral recollection testimony. A witness testifies that he or she once read the original and can presently recall the content of the document. The cases are quite liberal and permit the witness to testify so long as the witness claims that he or she can presently recall the substance of the document. The requirement for proof that the witness has previously read the document is not a product of the best evidence rule itself; rather, the personal knowledge doctrine codified in Rule 602 is the basis for the requirement. That doctrine is one aspect of the common law's insistence on a showing of underlying logical relevance.

The other type of secondary evidence is a written copy, not qualifying as a "duplicate." The courts ordinarily insist that the copy be complete and verbatim. In some jurisdictions, the judge may admit an abstract of an official record. The requisite foundation includes proof of the exhibit's authenticity. Again, that foundation is not a product of the best evidence rule; its basis is the independent requirement for underlying probative value, embodied in Article IX of the Federal Rules of Evidence.

2.   THE DEGREES OF SECONDARY EVIDENCE

By now you should be wondering: Given the logic of the best evidence rule, should we not also prefer a written copy over oral recollection testimony? And if that is the case, ought we not require the proponent to excuse the nonproduction of any written copies before resorting to oral recollection testimony? The argument runs that the hierarchy should be primary evidence, secondary copies, and finally oral recollection testimony. In fact, that was the majority view in the United States at the common law—the so–called American rule. Indeed, some jurisdictions such as Georgia have codified the majority view. Ga. Code Annot. § 24–5–5.

Logical symmetry supports the American rule: If the trustworthiness model mandates the use of primary evidence rather than secondary evidence, it is a very short next step to differentiating between the two types of secondary evidence. The American rule is undeniably consistent with the policy underlying the best evidence rule.

But can we reach a point of diminishing returns? The less controversial application of the American rule is to prefer a written copy over oral recollection testimony. But some courts have gone even further; they prefer a firsthand copy (a copy made from an original or duplicate) over a secondhand copy (a copy made from a copy). Those courts take the logic of the best evidence rule far indeed.

Sensing the necessity for drawing a line to identify the point of diminishing returns, even at common law a minority of courts rejected the proposition that there are degrees of secondary evidence. This is the so–called English view. Under this view, with one exception, there are no degrees of secondary evidence; the proponent can introduce oral recollection testimony without any necessity for accounting for written copies. The exception is a preference for a certified copy of official records.

NOTES AND PROBLEMS

1. Which view do the Federal Rules adopt? Consider the following excerpts from the Advisory Committee Notes to Rules 1004–5:

(Rule 1004)

The rule recognizes no "degrees" of secondary evidence. While strict logic might call for extending the principle of preference beyond simply preferring the original, the formulation of a hierarchy of preferences and a procedure for making it effective is believed to involve unwarranted complexities. Most, if not all, that would be accomplished by an extended scheme of preferences will, in any event, be achieved through the normal motivation of a party to present the most convincing evidence possible and the arguments and procedures available to his opponent if he does not. Compare McCormick § 207.

(Rule 1005)

Public records call for somewhat different treatment. Removing them from their usual place of keeping would be attended by serious inconvenience to the public and to the custodian. As a consequence judicial decisions and statutes commonly hold that no explanation need be given for failure to produce the original of a public record. McCormick § 204; 4 Wigmore §§ 1215–1228. This blanket dispensation from producing or accounting for the original would open the door to the introduction of every kind of secondary evidence of contents of public records were it not for the preference given certified or compared copies. Recognition of degrees of secondary evidence in this situation is an appropriate *quid pro quo* for not applying the requirement of producing the original.

2. As we have seen, a best evidence objection can raise several issues: whether there was a document, whether its terms are in issue, etc. Which issues does the judge finally decide, and which issues are reserved for the jury? *See* Federal Rules of Evidence 104(a)–(b) and 1008.

Rule 1008. Functions of Court and Jury. When the admissibility of other evidence of contents of writings, recordings, or photographs under these rules depends upon the fulfillment of a condition of fact, the question whether the condition has been fulfilled is ordinarily for the court to determine in accordance with the provisions of Rule 104. However, when an issue is raised (a) whether the asserted writing ever existed, or (b) whether another writing, recording, or photograph produced at the trial is the original, or (c) whether other evidence of contents correctly reflects the contents, the issue is for the trier of fact to determine as in the case of other issues of fact.

3. Problem 24–10. In the *Hill* case, the Chief of Polecat's Safety Design Department, Mr. Balboa, is still on the stand. Earlier in his direct examination, Polecat's attorney introduced a number of the Department's records. The judge admitted the records. Now the following occurs:

Def. Mr. Balboa, I hand you what has been marked and admitted as Defense Exhibit L. What is it?

A. It's one of the Safety Design Department records I described earlier.

Def. All right. I'd like to focus your attention on the third paragraph of the second page. Please read that paragraph aloud to the jury.

Pl. Objection, Your Honor. The document is the best evidence and speaks for itself. His testimony would violate Rule 1002.

What ruling? When the best evidence rule applies, does the document's production in court preclude oral testimony about its contents? What about oral quotations of the document? Consider Federal Rules of Evidence 611(a), and 1002. W. BROCKETT & J. KEKER, EFFECTIVE DIRECT & CROSS–EXAMINATION § 11.11, at 248–49 (1986). Although the best evidence rule requires the production of the writing in court, what rule governs the permissible courtroom uses of the produced writing?

G.   RECENT LEGISLATIVE REFORMS

Effective January 1, 1999, the California legislature repealed its version of the traditional best evidence rule, substituting a new statutory scheme entitled the "Secondary Evidence Rule." The legislature acted on the recommendation of the California Law Revision Commission:

The Best Evidence Rule is an anachronism. In yesterday's world of manual copying and limited pretrial discovery, it served as a safeguard against misleading use of secondary evidence. Under contemporary circumstances, in which high quality photocopies are standard and litigants have broad opportunities for pretrial inspection of original documents, the Best Evidence Rule is no longer necessary to protect against unreliable secondary evidence. Because the rule's costs now outweigh its benefits, the Law Revision Commission recommends that it be repealed.

26 CAL. LAW REVISION COMM'N, *Best Evidence Rule* 389 (1996).

The new legislative scheme includes the following statutes:

§1520. Content of writing; proof

The content of a writing may be proved by an otherwise admissible original.

§1521. Secondary evidence rule

(a) The content of a writing may be proved by otherwise admissible secondary evidence. The court shall exclude secondary evidence of the content of writing if the court determines either of the following:

(1) A genuine dispute exists concerning material terms of the writing and justice requires the exclusion.

(2) Admission of the secondary evidence would be unfair.

(b) Nothing in this section makes admissible oral testimony to prove the content of a writing if the testimony is inadmissible under Section 1523 (oral testimony of the content of a writing).

(c) Nothing in this section excuses compliance with Section 1401 (authentication).

(d) This section shall be known as the "Secondary Evidence Rule."

§1522. Additional grounds for exclusion of secondary evidence.

(a) In addition to the grounds for exclusion authorized by Section 1521, in a criminal action the court shall exclude secondary evidence of the content of a writing if the court determines that the original is in the proponent's possession, custody or control, and the proponent has not made the original reasonably available for inspection at or before trial. This section does not apply to any of the following:

(1) A duplicate as defined in Section 260.

(2) A writing that is not closely related to the controlling issues in the action.

(3) A copy of a writing in the custody of a public entity.

(4) A copy of a writing that is recorded in the public records, if the record or a certified copy of it is made evidence of the writing by statute.

(b) In a criminal action, a request to exclude secondary evidence of the content of a writing, under this section or any other law, shall not be made in the presence of the jury.

§1523. Oral testimony of the content of a writing; admissibility

(a) Except as otherwise provided by statute, oral testimony is not admissible to prove the content of a writing.

(b) Oral testimony of the content of a writing is not made inadmissible by subdivision (a) if the proponent does not have possession or control of a copy of the writing and the original is lost or has been destroyed without fraudulent intent on the part of the proponent of the evidence.

(c) Oral testimony of the content of a writing is not made inadmissible by subdivision (a) if the proponent does not have possession or control of the original or a copy of the writing and either of the following conditions is satisfied:

(1) Neither the writing nor a copy of the writing was reasonably procurable by the proponent by use of the court's process or by other available means.

(2) The writing is not closely related to the controlling issues and it would be inexpedient to require its production.

(d) Oral testimony of the content of a writing is not made inadmissible by subdivision (a) if the writing consists of numerous accounts or other writings that cannot be examined in court without great loss of time, and the evidence sought from them is only the general result of the whole.

QUESTIONS

1. How do these statutes differ from their federal counterparts? What types of written evidence are now presumptively admissible?

2. Do you think that there was a need to further liberalize the best evidence doctrine? It was a widespread perception that best evidence objections were rarely sustained. Moreover, any experienced litigator realizes that it is usually best to submit the most original evidence to the jury. Doing so enhances the persuasiveness of the trial presentation. Simply stated, presenting the best evidence is ordinarily good trial advocacy.

3. Do you favor administering different sets of rules in criminal and civil cases? Does the Sixth Amendment Confrontation Clause mandate a more stringent set of rules in prosecutions?

Part 4

ADMISSIBILITY RULES BASED ON SOCIAL POLICY

Chapter 25

PRIVILEGE: A GENERAL ANALYTICAL APPROACH

A. INTRODUCTION

In contrast to our preceding study of admissibility doctrines which focused on the supposed unreliability of certain types of evidence, we shift now to a much different focus: evidence rules based on extrinsic social policy. For example, in the case of privileged information, the concern is not unreliability. Quite to the contrary, the privileges often exclude patently trustworthy and critical evidence. Rather, when privileged information is excluded, it is done to promote social policy, such as the protection of the attorney–client relationship.

We must carefully distinguish privilege doctrine from the legal irrelevance doctrine. In two respects, the doctrines are alike and, hence, easy to confuse. Both doctrines lead to the exclusion of logically relevant evidence, and both rest on policy. The pivotal difference is the nature of the policy underlying the doctrine. The legal irrelevance concept rests on such policy considerations as preventing the distraction of the jury and the waste of court time. We previously described these policies as "intrinsic to trial administration." These policies bear on the way trials should be conducted. In contrast, the policies supporting the privileges are "extrinsic" in the sense that they are calculated to affect the behavior of persons outside the courtroom. More specifically, the policy is designed to encourage free communication between persons who stand in certain confidential relationships, such as spouses and physician and patient.

We must be frank about the effect of applying privileges. At least if we consider only the particular case in which the privilege is invoked, the privilege can exact a high cost by suppressing the truth and obstructing the factual inquiry. The proponents of privileges argue that the suppression of truth is a small cost to pay to protect certain vital relationships such as that between a client and attorney. However, as our review progresses, the empirical research to date calls into question the assumption that the recognition of an evidentiary privilege promotes these relationships to any significant degree. Given the cost of privileges and doubt about their benefits, many courts are hostile to privileges. They are reluctant to recognize new privileges (*In re Sealed Case*, 676 F.2d 793 (D.C. Cir. 1982)) and, whenever possible, will narrow the scope of existing privileges. *Miller v. Transamerican Press, Inc.*, 621 F.2d 721, 725 (5th Cir. 1980). In *Herbert v. Lando*, 441 U.S. 153 (1979), the Supreme Court voiced the sentiment of most American courts when it remarked that "[e]videntiary privileges in litigation are not favored . . . ."

Although there is substantial hostility to the recognition of privileges and their obstructive effect, there is a surprisingly large number of privileges, especially statutory, in the various jurisdictions. For example, many jurisdictions recognize privileges for clients of social workers, crime victims who receive counseling at rape crisis centers, bank depositors, and customers of accountants. *See, e.g.*, Annot., 50 A.L.R.3d 563 (1973); Annot., 38 A.L.R.2d 670 (1954). In a text of this size, it would be impossible to cover all the extant privileges. This text takes a different tack. This chapter is designed to highlight the basic structure of a privilege. The succeeding material deals with the privileges most often encountered in practice, and underscores the unique features of those privileges.

When the Advisory Committee drafted the Federal Rules, the Committee included 12 detailed statutes in Article V devoted to privilege. However, Congress balked at enacting those statutes. Instead, Congress enacted a solitary statute, Rule 501, which stated:

> Except as otherwise required by the Constitution of the United States or provided by Act of Congress or in the rules prescribed by the Supreme Court pursuant to statutory authority, the privilege of a witness, person, government, State, or political subdivision thereof shall be governed by the principles of the common law as they may be interpreted by the courts of the United States in the light of reason and experience. However, in civil actions and proceedings, with respect to an element of a claim or defense as to which State law supplies the rule of decision, the privilege of a witness, person, government, State, or political subdivision thereof shall be determined in accordance with State law.

Rule 501 is the most explicit window to the common law in the Federal Rules of Evidence; the rule empowers the courts to continue to evolve privilege doctrine by common law process. Nonetheless, issues of statutory construction will still arise. In shaping privilege doctrine, what inferences should the courts draw from Congress' refusal to enact the statutes proposed by the Advisory Committee? One of the murkiest problems in statutory interpretation is the significance of legislative action such as a legislature's refusal to enact a proposed bill. W. ESKRIDGE & P. FRICKEY, CASES AND MATERIALS ON LEGISLATION: STATUTES AND THE CREATION OF PUBLIC POLICY 772–74 (1988). As we shall see, several of the statutes proposed by the Committee would have effected innovative changes in privilege law. Notwithstanding Congress' refusal to enact those statutes, are the courts free to embrace those changes under Rule 501? A legislature's failure to act is often equivocal, and the courts must be especially careful in analyzing the significance of the failure. *Id.* at 772–73.

The Court has attached significance to the draft Federal Rule of Evidence provisions on privilege. In *United States v. Gillock*, 445 U.S. 360 (1980), the Court cited the draft provisions in support of its decision not to recognize a privilege for state legislators. The draft provisions did not contain any such privilege. In *Jaffee v. Redmond*, 518 U.S. 1 (1996), the Court cited the draft provisions in support of its decision to recognize a psychotherapist privilege. Draft Fed. R. Evid. 504 provided for such a privilege. In *Tennenbaum v. Deloitte & Touche*, 77 F.3d 337, 340 (9th Cir. 1996), the court described the draft rules as "a convenient comprehensive guide to the federal law of privilege as it now stands."

B.   THE CRITERIA FOR DETERMINING WHETHER TO RECOGNIZE A PRIVILEGE

Some commentators, such as the late Professor David Louisell of Berkeley, attempted to ground privilege doctrine on the theory that privileges serve as protections for personal autonomy and privacy. C. MUELLER & L. KIRKPAT-RICK, FEDERAL EVIDENCE § 170 (2d ed. 1994). Kinports, *Evidence Engendered*, 1991 U. ILL. L. REV. 413, argues in favor of the "humanistic rationale . . . that certain relationships are entitled to protection by their very private nature . . . ," pointing out that this rationale is more consistent with "[a] feminist approach to evidence . . . ." *Id.* Privilege doctrine relates to the question "at the center of the contemporary debate about the foundation of a liberal [democratic] society"—namely, the definition of the boundary between the public sphere and the private sphere for the exercise of personal autonomy. Levinson, *Testimonial Privileges and the Preferences of Friendship*, 1984 DUKE L.J. 631, 662.

However, the dominant view has been Wigmore's utilitarian approach. As we shall see, in both *Jaffee v. Redmond*, 518 U.S. 1 (1996) and *Swidler & Berlin v. United States*, 524 U.S. 399 (1998), although the lower courts relied in part on a humanistic approach, the Supreme Court eschewed that approach and chose to rely exclusively on instrumental reasoning in the Wigmorean tradition. Wigmore viewed privileges in an instrumental fashion: The courts should treat privileges as a means to the end of promoting certain, valued social relationships. Given his instrumental conception of privileges, Wigmore prescribed the following criteria for recognizing a privilege:

General Principle of Privileged Communications

Looking back upon the principle of privilege, as an exception to the general liability of every person to give testimony upon all facts inquired of in a court of justice, and keeping in view that preponderance of extrinsic policy which alone can justify the recognition of any such exception, four fundamental conditions are recognized as necessary to the establishment of a privilege against the disclosure of communications:

(1) The communications must originate in a *confidence* that they will not be disclosed.

(2) This element of *confidentiality must be essential* to the full and satisfactory maintenance of the relation between the parties.

(3) The *relation* must be one which in the opinion of the community ought to be sedulously *fostered*.

(4) The *injury* that would inure to the relation by the disclosure of the communications must be *greater than the benefit* thereby gained for the correct disposal of litigation.

Only if these four conditions are present should a privilege be recognized.

That they are present in most of the recognized privileges is plain enough; and the absence of one or more of them serves to explain why certain privileges have failed to obtain the recognition sometimes demanded for them. In the privilege for communications between attorney and client, for example, all four are present, the only condition open to any dispute being the fourth. In the privilege for communications between husband and wife, the first three conditions are again clearly present, with only the fourth in any doubt; and the chief variance of judicial opinion in defining the privilege (some extending it to all communications while others to confidential communications only) is due to a question as to the fulfillment of the first condition. In the privileges for communications between jurors and between informer and government, the four conditions are clearly present. In the privilege (denied at common law) for communications between physician and patient, the fallacy of recognizing it lies in the incorrect assumption that the second and fourth conditions are generally present. In the privilege (also denied at common law) for communications between priest and penitent, the objection to its recognition has probably lain in a tacit denial of the third condition. In the privilege (sometimes urged) for communications sent by telegraph or like methods, the reluctance to recognize it has apparently been due to the recognition that no one of the four conditions is thoroughly fulfilled.

These four conditions must serve as the foundation of policy for determining all such privileges, whether claimed or established.

8 J. WIGMORE, EVIDENCE § 2285 (McNaughton rev. 1961). (Emphasis added.)

C. AN ANALYTICAL OUTLINE

The law of privilege can be capsulized very simply. In certain types of proceedings, the holder has certain privileges with respect to certain types of information unless (1) the holder has waived the privilege or (2) there is a special exception to the privilege's scope. 8 J. WIGMORE, EVIDENCE § 2292 (McNaughton rev. 1961). Almost all privilege issues are thus reducible to one of these seven questions:

- To what types of proceedings does the privilege apply?
- Who is the holder of the privilege?
- What is the nature of the privilege?
- What type of information is privileged?
- Has there been a waiver of the privilege?
- Is there any pertinent special exception?
- Is the privilege absolute or qualified?

1. TO WHAT TYPES OF PROCEEDINGS DOES THE PRIVILEGE APPLY?

The courts usually say that the rationale for creating privileges is that privileges encourage full, free communication between persons standing in such relationships as wife and husband, and penitent and clergy. The courts assume that it would affect that freedom of communication if privileges did not exist. The courts' assumption is debatable. Would the persons standing in these special relationships communicate less freely if there were no privilege? To what extent? Is the supposed decrease in the flow of information great enough to justify the obstructive effect the privileges have on the search for truth?

For purposes of argument, make the courts' assumption. On that assumption, the courts quite correctly have decided to apply privileges to a wide variety of legal proceedings: criminal cases such as the *Devitt* prosecution, civil actions such as our torts case, and even administrative proceedings. From the perspective of the communicating parties, the nature of the proceeding in which disclosure occurs makes no difference; the thing that will chill their communication is disclosure, in whatever context it occurs. California Evidence Code § 901 represents the emerging view in the United States. That statute applies most privileges in all "proceedings" and defines "proceeding" as:

> any action, hearing, investigation, inquest, or inquiry (whether conducted by a court, administrative agency, hearing officer, administrator, legislative body, or any other person authorized by law) in which, pursuant to law, testimony can be compelled to be given.

Currently, the only major dispute seems to be whether the privileges apply as a matter of right to legislative hearings. Hamilton, *Attorney–Client Privilege in Congress*, 12 LITIGATION, Winter 1986, at 3. In some instances, congressional committees have asserted their prerogative to disregard claims of evidentiary privilege. Note, *The Attorney–Client Privilege in Congressional Investigations*, 88 COLUM. L. REV. 145, 146 (1988).

————————

While most privileges apply in all types of proceedings, the statutes creating privileges sometimes specifically provide that the privilege is inapplicable to certain types of proceedings. For instance, in most jurisdictions, the statutory physician–patient privilege does not apply to criminal cases; and under California Evidence Code § 986, the spousal privilege is inapplicable to juvenile court proceedings. These restrictions are founded on the judgment that those types of proceedings trigger special, countervailing policies that override the policy supporting the privilege. These restrictions can be analyzed under this issue, or they can be rationalized as special exceptions to the scope of the privilege. It would be dishonest to contend that disclosure in these proceedings does not tend to chill the freedom of communication between the parties, but the courts and legislatures believe that there are policies weightier than freedom of communication.

2. WHO IS THE HOLDER OF THE PRIVILEGE?

This aspect of privilege law is one of the most important distinctions between privileges, on the one hand, and both legal relevance and competence rules resting on trustworthiness, on the other hand. If legally irrelevant evidence or incompetent opinion is offered at trial, the opposing party automatically has a right to object. The opposing party does not have the same automatic right to object on privilege grounds.

To begin with, the party is not necessarily a holder. Suppose that in the *Devitt* case, the prosecutor calls Paterson's doctor as a witness. The doctor is describing the results of his examination of Paterson immediately after the battery, and the prosecutor next asks the doctor to relate what Paterson told him about the battery. Devitt may be able to object successfully on hearsay grounds. However, Devitt cannot properly object on the ground of Paterson's doctor–patient privilege. He cannot assert the privilege because he is not the holder.

Further, the holder is not necessarily a party. Although Paterson is not a formal party to the prosecution, he could appear and invoke the physician–patient privilege. A person claiming a privilege can intervene in a proceeding specially for the purpose of asserting a privilege. *United States v. Feeney*, 641 F.2d 821 (10th Cir. 1981).

a. The Original Holder

We have seen that we cannot routinely equate the holder with a party to the lawsuit. In the case of the professional privileges such as the one protecting attorney–client communications, the holder is the person seeking professional services. In the case of the spousal privilege, at least the communicating spouse will be treated as a holder. We can phrase the test more broadly and inquire who is the intended beneficiary of the protection the privilege confers.

The penitent–clergy privilege is unique. In the case of most professional privileges, the layperson seeking services is the only holder. Although the courts' bias in favor of professionals has led them to give "top billing" to the professional (hence, the "attorney–client" privilege rather than the "client–attorney" privilege), the client is the holder. However, many of the jurisdictions recognizing the clergy–penitent privilege treat it differently. For example, California Evidence Code § 1033 grants a normal privilege to the penitent, but § 1034 then confers a separate privilege on the clergyperson. The clergyperson can assert the privilege even after the penitent has waived the regular privilege. If Devitt confesses to a priest and then publicly acknowledges guilt, the priest nevertheless can refuse to disclose the confession. The Virginia Code is to the same effect. *Seidman v. Fishburne–Hudgins Educ. Found., Inc.*, 724 F.2d 413, 415–16 (4th Cir. 1984) (construing Va. Code § 8.01–400).

NOTE

As we have seen, in the case of most privileges, the policy is protecting the confidentiality the layperson reposes in the professional and thereby encouraging free communication. In the case of the clergy–penitent privilege, does another policy come into play? If so, how important is that policy? Can you construct an argument that the policy has constitutional stature? *See* Ponder,

Will Your Pastor Tell?, LIBERTY, May/June 1978, at 3. Suppose that out of religious scruple, the priest refuses to divulge the content of a confession. If the priest has no privilege to refuse, the tribunal could imprison him for contempt until he discloses.

b.   Successor Holders

Suppose that in our torts case, Ms. Hill's attorney discovered that another person has been killed in a strikingly similar accident involving one of the defendant's cars, manufactured on the very same day as the car which injured Ms. Hill. The plaintiff's attorney believes that evidence of the third party's accident might be admissible against Polecat Motors in this trial on an issue such as causation. Ms. Hill serves a subpoena duces tecum on the decedent's physician to obtain a copy of all the records of the injury and subsequent treatment. The decedent's surviving son moves to quash the subpoena on the ground of the physician–patient privilege. The motion poses the question of whether the privilege survives the decedent's death.

The jurisdictions are badly divided on this issue. In some, the privilege terminates when the original holder dies. In others, the privilege lasts until the formal discharge of the decedent's personal representative, that is, the administrator or executor. *In re John Doe Grand Jury Investigation*, 408 Mass. 480, 562 N.E.2d 69 (1990). In still others, the privilege lasts indefinitely and passes like intestate property—a type of property to which the rule against perpetuities does not apply. *United States v. King*, 536 F. Supp. 253, 263 n.17 (C.D. Cal. 1982).

NOTE

Which view do you prefer? The trend seems to be toward the second view. For example, before the adoption of the California Evidence Code, the third view was apparently the law in California. *See Collette v. Sarrasin*, 184 Cal. 283, 289, 193 P. 571, 573 (1920). In provisions such as § 953 defining the holder of the attorney–client privilege, the new Code opted for the second view.

c.   Agents of the Original Holder

In the case of most professions bound by confidentiality, the profession's own code of ethics requires the professional to claim the privilege in the holder's absence. For example, an attorney has an ethical duty to assert the privilege on behalf of a client.

However, the rules of professional ethics are not coextensive with evidentiary rules. Some jurisdictions have bridged the gap and, in some circumstances, make the lawyer's ethical duty also a legal obligation. For example, California gives the lawyer implied–in–law authority to make a legally effective privilege claim in the holder's absence. California Evidence Code § 954 is illustrative:

> Subject to Section 912 and except as otherwise provided in this article, the client, whether or not a party, has a privilege to refuse to disclose, and to prevent another from disclosing, a confidential communication between client and lawyer if the privilege is claimed by:

(a) The holder of the privilege;

(b) A person who is authorized to claim the privilege by the holder of the privilege; or

(c) The person who was the lawyer at the time of the confidential communication, but such person may not claim the privilege if there is no holder of the privilege in existence or if he is otherwise instructed by a person authorized to permit disclosure.

Section 955 is even more emphatic:

The lawyer who received or made a communication subject to the privilege under this article shall claim the privilege whenever he is present when the communication is sought to be disclosed and is authorized to claim the privilege under subdivision (c) of Section 954.

In *Swidler & Berlin v. United States,* 524 U.S. 399 (1998), *infra*, while the Supreme Court did not go as far as § 955, the Court permitted an attorney to assert the privilege on behalf of his deceased client.

3.   WHAT IS THE NATURE OF A PRIVILEGE?

We ordinarily refer to the attorney–client or spousal "privilege" in the singular. In truth, that expression is inaccurate. The expression really subsumes three different rights.

a.   The Right Personally to Refuse to Disclose the Privileged Information

When we use the expression "privilege," we ordinarily mean the holder's right personally to refuse to disclose certain information. For example, assume that the prosecutor were cross–examining Devitt, and the following occurred:

Q: Mr. Devitt, isn't it a fact that you admitted to your attorney that you committed this battery?

A: I refuse to answer the question. I'm claiming my attorney–client privilege.

If the trial judge sustains the privilege claim, Devitt cannot be held in contempt for refusing to answer. A privilege gives the person refusing to answer protection from contempt.

NOTES AND PROBLEMS

1. Problem 25–1. Is impunity from contempt the full extent of the privilege? Suppose that in our torts case, Ms. Hill sought a copy of a memorandum from the president of Polecat Motors to the corporation's chief counsel. Ms. Hill made a pretrial motion for production of the memo, and the defendant opposed discovery on the ground of the attorney–client privilege. Is the memo protected, or would you grant the motion and impose discovery sanctions if the defendant disobeyed the order? Is Federal Rule of Civil Procedure 26 helpful in answering this question?

General Provisions Governing Discovery

*   *   *

(b) Scope of Discovery. Unless otherwise limited by order of the court in accordance with these rules, the scope of discovery is as follows:

(1) *In General.* Parties may obtain discovery regarding any matter, not privileged, which is relevant to the subject matter involved in the pending action, whether it relates to the claim or defense of the party seeking discovery or to the claim or defense of any other party, including the existence, description, nature, custody, condition and location of any books, documents, or other tangible things and the identity and location of persons having knowledge of any discoverable matter. It is not ground for objection that the information sought will be inadmissible at the trial if the information sought appears reasonably calculated to lead to the discovery of admissible evidence.

2. The pivotal language in FRCP 26 is obviously "not privileged." How should we construe that language? Does the reference contemplate that the courts will apply the privilege law in effect when the Rule was originally promulgated, or does the Rule permit the court to apply later changes in privilege law? If the latter is the case, should the court apply the privilege law in effect at the time it must decide the privilege issue or that in effect when the parties engaged in the allegedly privileged communication?

b.   The Right to Prevent a Third Party From Making an Unauthorized Disclosure of the Privileged Communication

A holder such as a client not only has a right personally to refuse to disclose privileged information. The holder can also prevent the intended recipient of the communication such as the attorney from making disclosure. If the attorney–client privilege precludes the prosecutor from forcing Devitt from disclosing an attorney–client communication, the privilege also bars the prosecutor from eliciting the information from the attorney over Devitt's privilege claim. The extension of the privilege to silence Devitt's addressee is certainly defensible.

Other types of third parties have proven more troublesome for the courts. Thus, the traditional view has been that at least inadvertent eavesdroppers and interceptors are not bound by the privilege. If a third party accidentally overhears the damning part of Devitt's consultation with his attorney, most courts permit the eavesdropper to testify to the communication. The courts opting for the traditional view will grant the holder protection only when the intended recipient "connives with" the third party. For example, suppose that the attorney secretly harbored a hatred for Devitt and told a third party exactly where and when to station himself with a parabolic microphone to overhear the conversation.

The recent trend in both the case law and the statutes has evidenced more sensitivity to the interest in privacy. Some courts now silence the third party if the third party intentionally overheard or intercepted. A few jurisdictions now silence all third parties, even inadvertent eavesdroppers.

NOTES AND PROBLEMS

1. The trend toward silencing third parties may strike you as anomalous. Previously, we saw that most jurisdictions are now liberalizing competence rules based on trustworthiness; it is becoming easier to introduce opinions, secondary evidence, and hearsay. Given that trend, how can we explain that at least in this respect the privileges are being toughened? Is there any necessary inconsistency between these trends?

2. Problem 25–2. Suppose that Devitt's attorney breached his duty of confidentiality by informing the police that Devitt had told him (the attorney) that he (Devitt) had confessed the battery to his brother. The police follow up on the investigative lead and confront Devitt's brother. Devitt's brother reluctantly agrees to testify against his brother. At trial, can Devitt object to his brother's testimony on the ground that the testimony is derived from a breach of Devitt's attorney–client privilege? *See State v. Sandini*, 395 So. 2d 1178, 1180–81 (Fla. Dist. Ct. App. 1981); *United States v. Seiber*, 12 U.S.C.M.A. 520, 31 C.M.R. 106, 107–10 (1961).

Under the Fourth Amendment exclusionary rule, the courts exclude derivative evidence ("the fruit of the poisonous tree"). *Wong Sun v. United States*, 371 U.S. 471, 484–93 (1963). Should they treat evidence derived from a breach of a common law privilege in the same fashion? Less than a handful of courts have expressed a willingness to exclude evidence derived from a violation of a non–constitutional privilege. Comment, *Evidentiary Privileges and the Exclusion of Derivative Evidence: Commentary and Analysis*, 26 SAN DIEGO L. REV. 625 (1989); *United States v. Ankeny*, 30 M.J. 10 (U.S.C.M.A. 1990). The majority view is understandable. In a technical sense, the derivative evidence is not the product of a violation of any evidentiary privilege. As we have seen, in contrast to ethical and tort duties of confidentiality, privileges apply only in legal proceedings in which the tribunal has a power of compulsory process. Thus, when an attorney discloses confidential information out of court, as in Problem 25–2, the disclosure can amount to a breach of an ethical or tort duty; but it does not violate an evidentiary privilege.

c. The Right to Prevent Trial Comment on the Invocation of the Privilege

In the Fifth Amendment context, it is well–settled that neither the judge nor the prosecutor can comment on a defendant's invocation of the privilege. The Supreme Court pronounced that doctrine in *Griffin v. California*, 380 U.S. 609 (1965). The Court reasoned that it would be inconsistent to grant the Fifth Amendment privilege and yet make its assertion at trial "costly." There is no such constitutional prohibition in civil cases.

Roughly half the jurisdictions in the United States apply the same "no comment" rule to all privileges: Neither the judge nor the opposing party may invite the jury to draw an adverse inference from the invocation of the privilege at trial. In those jurisdictions permitting such comment, there may be a two or three–fold deterrent to invoking the privilege in the first place. For example, in our torts case, if Polecat Motors invoked the attorney–client privilege in order not to disclose the memorandum the corporate president sent the corporate counsel, these jurisdictions would permit Ms. Hill to elicit that fact during cross–examination of the president. They would additionally permit her attorney to argue during summation:

> Remember, ladies and gentlemen, that the defendant's president admitted that they refused to show us that memo about the accident. Why? I think we all know the answer. They're hiding something from us; they're afraid to let us see what's in that memo. For all we know, that memo could say, "There's no question; we're at fault in this accident."

Some would even permit the court to instruct the jury on permissible adverse inferences.

Proposed Federal Rule of Evidence 513 would have forbidden such argument:

Comment Upon or Inference from Claim of Privilege; Instruction

[Not enacted.]

(a) *Comment or inference not permitted.* The claim of a privilege, whether in the present proceeding or upon a prior occasion, is not a proper subject of comment by judge or counsel. No inference may be drawn therefrom.

(b) *Claiming privilege without knowledge of jury.* In jury cases, proceedings shall be conducted, to the extent practicable, so as to facilitate the making of claims of privilege without the knowledge of the jury.

(c) *Jury instructions.* Upon request, any party against whom the jury might draw an adverse inference from a claim of privilege is entitled to an instruction that no inference may be drawn therefrom.

NOTE

Which view do you prefer? To be sure, there is an element of inconsistency if we grant the privilege and then permit adverse comment on its invocation. Yet the adverse inference is perfectly reasonable; in fact, the common sense inference is that the memorandum contains harmful admissions. Moreover, even if we permit comment, we have given the holder a valuable privilege. So long as we grant the holder the right to personally withhold the information, the holder can win a directed verdict; the holder may be able to withhold information the opponent needs to sustain the burden of going forward. It is certainly an overstatement to argue that permitting comment makes the privilege meaningless or deprives the privilege of all substance. How should the balance be struck?

4. WHAT TYPE OF INFORMATION IS PRIVILEGED?

In most cases, this question can be answered with misleading simplicity: "Privileged information" is a confidential communication occurring between properly related parties and incident to the relationship. In the case of professional privileges, the policy applies to both the statements by the client or patient and the statements by the professional. *Gonzalez Crespo v. Wella Corp.*, 774 F. Supp. 688 (D.P.R. 1991). The simplicity is misleading because this concept poses four issues—any one of which could lead to the defeat of the privilege in a particular case.

a. A "Communication"

We have repeatedly noted that the policy underlying the creation of privileges is the promotion of communication between persons standing in certain relations. Given that policy and the belief that the search for truth should be obstructed only to the extent necessary, privileges protect only information in the nature of communication.

PROBLEM

Problem 25–3. In most cases, the courts construe "communication" according to the ordinary usage of the term. With that usage in mind, decide whether the following items would qualify as "communications" for purposes of privilege law.

(a) An oral statement Devitt made to his attorney during the initial interview.

(b) The fact that Devitt nodded when the attorney asked, "Did you actually do it?"

(c) The fact that Devitt said nothing and glanced down when the attorney asked, "Did you actually do it?"

(d) A letter Devitt wrote his attorney about the case.

(e) A copy of a threatening letter Devitt had previously sent Paterson and decided to send to the attorney to help the attorney prepare for trial. Can you distinguish this letter from the previous letter? In terms of the policy underlying the privilege, is it significant that the second letter did not come into existence as an attorney–client communication? If Devitt retained the second letter, could he refuse to comply with compulsory process demanding the production of the letter? *See Fisher v. United States*, 425 U.S. 391, 403–04 (1976).

(f) Suppose that Devitt verbally told his attorney where he hid the clothes he wore during the battery. Could the prosecutor force the attorney to disclose his knowledge of the whereabouts of the fabric evidence?

––––––––––

We shall see that certain privileges, notably the spousal and medical privileges, use an expanded definition of "communication." However, we can see at this point that even under the conventional usage of the term, the court can be faced with difficult questions of determining whether the information sought qualifies for protection under privilege law.

b. A "Confidential" Communication

It is not enough that the information qualifies as a communication; to be protected, the communication must have been confidential. It is true that it would maximally promote freedom of communication to protect all communications. But not all types of communication need the protection of a privilege. If the communicating parties did not manifest an intent to maintain secrecy at the time of communication, the court will not confer confidentiality later in the courtroom.

If we decide to impose a confidentiality requirement as all jurisdictions do, we must then decide what the party claiming the privilege must prove to establish confidentiality. Ordinarily, a showing of confidentiality requires proof of two things.

First, at the time of communication, the parties had physical privacy. Assume that Devitt is talking with his attorney in the presence of a third party—and that Devitt realizes that the third party is present. The common sense inference negates confidentiality. *United States v. Cochran*, 546 F.2d 27 (5th Cir. 1977); *State v. Shafer*, 609 S.W.2d 153 (Mo. 1980). Distinguish this rule from the traditional eavesdropper rule we previously discussed. If an eavesdropper overheard without Devitt's realization, the eavesdropper can testify in most jurisdictions, but the attorney is still bound by the privilege. However, if Devitt realizes that the third party is present, normally no one is bound by a privilege.

In addition to showing physical privacy, the party claiming the privilege must show that at the time of communication there was an intent to maintain secrecy in the future. *United States v. Bump*, 605 F.2d 548 (10th Cir. 1979). The courts often say that "the parties" must have this intent.

NOTES AND PROBLEMS

1. Problem 25–4. The courts and legislatures have recognized numerous exceptions to the norm that the third party's presence negates confidentiality. Suppose Devitt were deaf or not fluent in English, and the attorney hired an interpreter. Should the interpreter's presence preclude the privilege from attaching? *Duckett v. Touhey*, 36 Md. App. 238, 373 A.2d 323 (1977).

2. Can you think of any other situations in which a third party's presence is realistically necessary for effective communication? In the context of professional privileges such as the attorney–client privilege, the courts permit the presence or intervention of "secretaries, file clerks, telephone operators, messengers, clerks not yet admitted to the bar, and aides of other sorts." *von Bulow v. von Bulow*, 811 F.2d 136, 146 (2d Cir.), *cert. denied*, 481 U.S. 1015 (1987). California has taken the most liberal position on this issue. Under Cal. Evid. Code § 952, the third party's presence does not negate confidentiality so long as the third party was "present to further the interest of the client in the consultation." Does that provision go too far? Should we draw the line at the fact situation at which there is some degree of necessity for the third party's presence? Does the California view depreciate the interest in finding the truth, or does the view merely reflect the way in which attorneys practice their profession and business?

3. Problem 25–5. Does the intent of both "parties" govern the intent to maintain secrecy? Is that the most precise way of expressing the requirement? Whose intent is critical? *See Apex Mun. Fund v. N–Group Securities*, 841 F. Supp. 1423, 1426–27 (S.D. Tex. 1993). Suppose that at the initial attorney–client interview in our torts case, Ms. Hill's attorney told her that he needed some information for "the complaint I'll put on file with the court." How would that statement affect your confidentiality analysis? If you were the attorney, how would you have phrased the statement? *See In re Grand Jury Proceedings*, 727 F.2d 1352, 1356–58 (4th Cir. 1984) (the preparation of a securities prospectus); *In re Grand Jury Investigation*, 842 F.2d 1223 (11th Cir. 1987) (the preparation of a tax return); *United States v. Bohonnon*, 628 F. Supp. 1026 (D. Conn.) (the preparation of a tax return), *aff'd*, 795 F.2d 79 (2d Cir. 1985). Has Ms. Hill in effect delegated to her attorney the choice of the information to include in the complaint? Has Ms. Hill agreed to disclose "only so much of the information . . . as the attorney concludes should be . . . ." included in the complaint? *Schenet v. Anderson*, 678 F. Supp. 1280, 1283 (E.D. Mich. 1988).

c. A Confidential Communication Between "Properly Related Parties"

As you review the subject of privilege, ask yourself these questions. Are these relationships sufficiently important to warrant this extraordinary legal protection? Can we justify protecting those relationships while simultaneously denying protection to relationships such as student–teacher and parent–child in most jurisdictions? Some commentators have suggested that in all too many cases, the existence of professional privileges represents successful lobbying by a special interest group for a prestigious trapping of professional status, rather than a principled legislative judgment that a particular social relation both needs and warrants privilege protection. However, the attorney–client relationship arguably warrants the protection. Clients often speak to their attorneys against the backdrop of imminent or pending litigation. In the litigation context, there is an opponent with a motive to put the information to adverse use.

d. A Confidential Communication that Occurs Between Properly Related Parties and "Incident to the Relationship"

It is not enough that the client consult his or her attorney. The cases tell us that the privilege comes into play only when the client is consulting the attorney *qua* attorney, in the person's unique capacity as a lawyer. This expression is another way of saying that the purpose of the client's communication must somehow be related to obtaining legal advice. Some authorities go further and assert that the privilege attaches only if the client consults the attorney "primarily" to obtain legal advice. *Resolution Trust Corp. v. Diamond*, 773 F. Supp. 597 (S.D.N.Y. 1991).

The question arises whether we should limit the privilege to communications incident to the relationship. Perhaps we can defend the limitation on the theory that we are attempting to balance the courts' truth–seeking function against protection of these social relations. The protected relations weigh more heavily in the balance when the communication is directly related to the relation. Moreover, the courts suspect that if the communication were not incident or germane to the relation, the holder would have made the statement even absent the privilege. If, in our torts case, we conclude that Polecat Motors' president was consulting the corporate counsel *qua* business advisor, we can assume that the president would have made the statement even without an attorney–client privilege. *See Hercules, Inc. v. Exxon Corp.*, 434 F. Supp. 136 (D. Del. 1977).

NOTES

Once we have decided to impose the incidence requirement, we face the task of defining when a communication is incident to the particular relationship. When would a communication be "incident" to the attorney–client relation? The physician–patient relation? The penitent–clergy relation? Review the following California statutes and isolate the specific language phrasing the incidence requirement for the various privileges:

§ 951. Client Defined.

As used in this article, "client" means a person who, directly or through an authorized representative, consults a lawyer for the purpose of retaining the lawyer or securing legal service or advice from him in his professional capacity, and includes an incompetent (a) who himself so consults the lawyer or (b) whose guardian or conservator so consults the lawyer in behalf of the incompetent.

§ 991. Patient Defined.

As used in this article, "patient" means a person who consults a physician or submits to an examination by a physician for the purpose of securing a diagnosis or preventive, palliative, or curative treatment of his physical or mental or emotional condition.

§ 1011. Patient Defined.

As used in this article, "patient" means a person who consults a psychotherapist or submits to an examination by a psychotherapist for the purpose of securing a diagnosis or preventive, palliative, or curative treatment of his mental or emotional condition or who submits to an examination of his mental or emotional condition for the purpose of scientific research on mental or emotional problems.

§ 1031. Penitent Defined.

As used in this article, "penitent" means a person who has made a penitential communication to a clergyman.

§ 1032. Penitential Communication Defined.

As used in this article, "penitential communication" means a communication made in confidence, in the presence of no third person so far as the penitent is aware, to a clergyman who, in the course of the discipline or practice of his church, denomination, or organization, is authorized or accustomed to hear such communications and, under the discipline or tenets of his church, denomination, or organization, has a duty to keep such communications secret.

Consider the wording of § 1032. Should the privilege be confined to required confessional statements? In the Catholic faith, a penitent must confess to a priest who must be male. Suppose that Devitt were Catholic and had a good friend, Sister Dominic, a nun, he frequently consulted as a spiritual consultant. After his encounter with Paterson, Devitt experiences a deep sense of guilt and goes to talk to Sister Dominic. Should the privilege be rejected simply because she is a nun rather than a priest? *See Eckmann v. Board of Educ.*, 106 F.R.D. 70, 72–73 (E.D. Mo. 1985).

5. HAS THERE BEEN A WAIVER OF THE PRIVILEGE?

Under Federal Rule of Evidence 104(a), the person claiming a privilege has the burden of proving the first four elements of a privilege. If that person persuades the judge that the right type of holder is claiming the right type of privilege for the right type of information in an appropriate proceeding, there is a prima facie case for sustaining the privilege claim. However, that is not the end of the analysis. Even if there is a prima facie case for upholding the privilege, the party opposing the claim can defeat the privilege by showing either a waiver or a special exception. The proposed Federal Rules of Evidence contained two provisions on the waiver of privileges:

Rule 511.

Waiver of Privilege by Voluntary Disclosure

[Not enacted.]

A person upon whom these rules confer a privilege against disclosure of the confidential matter or communication waives the privilege if he or his predecessor while holder of the privilege voluntarily discloses or consents to disclosure of any significant part of the matter or communication. This rule does not apply if the disclosure is itself a privileged communication.

Rule 512.

Privileged Matter Disclosed Under Compulsion or Without Opportunity to Claim Privilege

[Not enacted.]

Evidence of a statement or other disclosure of privileged matter is not admissible against the holder of the privilege if the disclosure was (a) compelled erroneously or (b) made without opportunity to claim the privilege.

The waiver doctrine presents us with two issues.

a. Whether There Has Been a Waiver

The holder may either assert or waive the privilege. As the reader might expect, since most courts are generally hostile to the privileges, they are eager to find waivers. The courts will usually find a waiver whenever the holder discloses a substantial part of the privileged information. *Champion Int'l Corp. v. International Paper Co.*, 486 F. Supp. 1328 (N.D. Ga. 1980). Proposed Rule 512 restates the common law when the rule indicates that, to effect a waiver, a disclosure must be voluntary. *Id.* The case law is less clear on whether the holder must subjectively intend a waiver. Modernly, there is a three–way split of authority over inadvertent waiver. *Farm Credit Bank of St. Paul v. Huether*, 454 N.W.2d 710 (N.D. 1990); Meese, *Inadvertent Waiver of the Attorney–Client Privilege by Disclosure of Documents: An Economic Analysis*, 23 CREIGHTON L. REV. 513 (1990). Some courts treat inadvertent disclosure as an automatic waiver, others refuse to do so, and still others examine the surrounding circumstances such as whether the disclosing party had taken reasonable steps to prevent unintended disclosures.

Professor Richard Marcus has argued that it is a mistake to analyze the waiver issue in terms of the holder's subjective intent. Marcus, *The Perils of Privilege: Waiver and the Litigator*, 84 MICH. L. REV. 1605 (1986). He emphasizes that the primary objection to privileges is that they obstruct the search for truth. In that light, he contends that, in waiver analysis, "the focus should be on unfairness flowing from . . . selective use of privileged materials to garble the truth . . . . [T]he opponent [should have] access to related material to set the record straight." *Id.* at 1607. His position seems to be gaining judicial adherents. *In re von Bulow*, 828 F.2d 94 (2d Cir. 1987); *In re Southern and Eastern Dist. Asbestos Litig.*, 730 F. Supp. 582 (S.D.N.Y. 1990) (a party may not use privilege doctrine to "distort" the search for truth); *McLaughlin v. Lunde Truck Sales, Inc.*, 714 F. Supp. 916, 918 (N.D. Ill. 1989) (privileges "may not be manipulated to the advantage of the party asserting the privilege"); *In re Consolidated Litig. Concerning Int'l Harvester's Disposition of Wis. Steel*, 666 F. Supp. 1148 (N.D. Ill. 1987).

PROBLEMS

1. Problem 25–6. Would you find a waiver in the following variations of our torts case?

(a) Polecat Motors calls Ms. Hill's physician. On direct examination, the defense attorney asks, "Isn't it true that three days after the accident, the plaintiff told you that she was feeling 'fairly well'?" Ms. Hill's attorney fails to object.

(b) Ms. Hill takes the witness stand. On direct examination, she refers to the treatment she received and adds that "I had several conversations with Dr. Tyler."

(c) Assume *arguendo* that you found a waiver in the last variation. Should the result be the same if Ms. Hill made the reference during cross–examination by the defense attorney? In some jurisdictions, the holder's responses during cross–examination do not effect a waiver. Is that view sound?

(d) Assume *arguendo* that you did not find a waiver in (b). Would your answer be the same if Ms. Hill said, "I had several conversations about the accident with Dr. Tyler"? If she said, "I had several conversations about the accident with Dr. Tyler, and I told him how Worker's car injured me"? How specific must the reference be before there is a waiver? Does the answer depend upon whether the privilege at stake is the attorney–client or physician–patient privilege? As we shall see, the definition of "communication" is much broader under the physician–patient privilege. Do you see a connection between the breadth of the concept of "communication" and the ease with which a court can find a waiver? Perhaps the breadth of the definition of "communication" is a two–edged sword; it can make it easier to find both a communication and a waiver.

(e) Ms. Hill tells her husband what she told her doctor. A waiver can occur outside the courtroom. Can we infer from this particular disclosure that the plaintiff intended to abandon secrecy?

(f) At the first trial of her lawsuit, Ms. Hill recovers a huge verdict. The verdict is so highly publicized that a publisher approaches Ms. Hill's attorney and asks him to write a book about the trial. He does so. In one passage, he refers to a privileged conversation with Ms. Hill. The attorney gives Ms. Hill a copy of the manuscript to review before he mails it to the publisher. She browses through the manuscript and vaguely notices that the manuscript refers to her conversation with the attorney. She makes no objection to the release of the book. *In re von Bulow*, 828 F.2d 94, 100 (2d Cir. 1987) (discussing Professor Alan Dershowitz' book, REVERSAL OF FORTUNE—INSIDE THE VON BULOW CASE (1986)).

In which of these problems, if any, would it make a difference whether the court employed the traditional analysis, based on the holder's subjective intent, or the fairness analysis urged by Professor Marcus? What is your view about the fairness of "selective disclosure"? Is the philosophy, if not the text, of Rule 106 relevant?

b. The Extent of the Waiver

Even if there has been a waiver, we should not leap to the conclusion that the privilege is lost in its entirety. In the following situations, how might you limit the waiver? In most cases finding a waiver, the courts rationalize the result on the theory that the holder has consented to surrendering the protection of the privilege. If we begin with that theory as the premise, there is a strong argument that the holder can exercise some control over the scope of the waiver. If waiver doctrine is grounded in consent, should not the holder be able to influence—if not determine —the extent to which he or she loses the protection of the privilege?

PROBLEMS

1. Problem 25–7.

(a) Ms. Hill and Mr. Grant hired the same attorney. The court concludes that by failing to claim the privilege during pretrial discovery, Grant waived the privilege. Can Ms. Hill still claim it?

(b) Ms. Hill consulted two doctors, Dr. Tyler and Dr. Gibson. At trial, Ms. Hill called Dr. Tyler as a witness to testify about the extent and permanency of the plaintiff's injuries. Can she still claim a privilege for Dr. Gibson? *Helman v. Murray's Steaks, Inc.*, 728 F. Supp. 1099, 1103 (D. Del. 1990). Should it make a difference whether the plaintiff consulted the doctors individually or jointly?

(c) After Ms. Hill sues Polecat Motors, she sues Turner Company, the defendant's parts supplier who furnished the gas tank on the defendant's car. Ms. Hill called Dr. Tyler as a witness in the first suit. Can the plaintiff still assert the physician–patient privilege for Dr. Tyler's testimony in the second suit?

(d) A year after Ms. Hill sues Polecat Motors, she sues a cosmetic company for scalp injuries she sustained when she used a cold cream the company manufactured. Dr. Tyler also treated the plaintiff for the scalp injuries. If the plaintiff waives the physician–patient privilege by calling Tyler in the first suit, can she still assert the privilege as against the cosmetic company?

(e) Before the trial in Ms. Hill's lawsuit against Polecat Motors, Dr. Tyler submitted two reports to Ms. Hill's attorney. Both reports dealt with Ms. Hill's injuries that allegedly resulted from the collision. During her case–in–chief, Ms. Hill introduced the first report. Does her introduction of the report waive any privilege for the second report? Suppose that the first report dealt with Ms. Hill's burn injuries but the second report related to bone fractures caused by the accident. Would it make a difference that the second report addressed both the cause and the extent of the bone fractures? *See Helman, supra*, at 1103–04; *Central Soya Co. v. Geo. A. Hormel & Co.*, 581 F. Supp. 51, 53–54 (W.D. Okla. 1982).

2. In *Zenith Radio Corp. v. United States*, 588 F. Supp. 1443 (U.S. Ct. Int'l Trade 1984), the court discussed the sharp split of authority over the extent to which a civil plaintiff waives privileges pertaining to information relevant to the lawsuit. According to the court, several courts have "adopted the automatic waiver rule . . . on the theory that when a party seeks judicial relief, he waives whatever privilege he has." *Id.* at 1445. Most courts reject this rule. It seems arbitrary to forfeit a person's privileges simply because he or she happens to be the plaintiff in a legal action; under modern civil procedure including the availability of declaratory actions, a person's normal role as plaintiff or defendant can be reversed. Other courts follow a balancing approach "in which the need for discovery is weighed against the need for secrecy." *Id.* Still other courts hold that there is a waiver only when three criteria are met:

(1) assertion of the privilege was a result of some affirmative act, such as filing suit, by the asserting party; (2) through this affirmative act, the asserting party put the protected information at issue by making it relevant to the case; and (3) application of the privilege would have denied the opposing party access to information vital to his defense. *Id.* at 1446, citing *Hearn v. Rhay*, 68 F.R.D. 574 (E.D. Wash. 1975).

See also In re Geothermal Resources International, Inc., 93 F.3d 648, 653 (9th Cir. 1996); *Zenith Radio Corp. v. United States*, 764 F.2d 1577, 1580 (Fed. Cir. 1985).

6. IS THERE A PERTINENT SPECIAL EXCEPTION TO THE SCOPE OF THE PRIVILEGE?

The special exceptions to the various privileges are far too numerous to list exhaustively here. However, there are several recurring themes that run through the exceptions.

One theme is the interpretative intent of the holder. Interpretative intent is a concept borrowed from Scholastic philosophy: It is the intent a person probably would have had if a person had foreseen a problem that materialized later. For example, after the death of a client, an attorney is often permitted to disclose the client's otherwise privileged statements about dispositive instruments the attorney drafted for the client. The assumption is that if the decedent had foreseen the dispute that arose after his or her death, the decedent would want full disclosure to ensure that the court effectuates his or her actual intent.

Another motif is fairness. When we consider the legal and medical privileges, we shall see that there is a "crime or tort" exception. There is no privilege if the services of the professional were sought or obtained in order to commit a crime, fraud or tort.

Although Wigmore acknowledged that in some exceptional cases privileges had to yield, he insisted that any exceptions be phrased in crystal clear terms. His instrumental theory places a premium on bright line standards. The basic premise of the theory is that at the time they are deciding whether to communicate and reveal sensitive information, the parties must be able to predict with relative confidence whether a privilege will attach and protect their communication. That ability would be undermined if the privileges were subject to vague exceptions.

7. IS THE PRIVILEGE ABSOLUTE OR QUALIFIED

Some privileges, such as attorney–client, are considered "true" or "absolute" privileges. They are not absolute in the broad sense that they do not admit of any exceptions; rather, they are absolute in the technical sense that they cannot be surmounted by an *ad hoc* showing of necessity. In other words, if the party claiming the privilege establishes the requisite foundation, the opposing party cannot defeat the privilege claim by showing a compelling, case–specific need for the privileged information. *Admiral Ins. Co. v. United States Dist. Ct. for the Dist. of Ariz.*, 881 F.2d 1486 (9th Cir. 1989). In such cases, normally the only way to defeat the privilege is by proving waiver or special exception. The absolute character of these privileges is another corollary of Wigmore's instrumental theory. As previously stated, under the theory, it is essential that at the time of communication the parties be able to predict whether their communication will be protected; but for the assurance of confidentiality furnished by the privilege, the parties would supposedly be deterred from communicating. If a judge had the power to later override the privilege on the basis of an ad hoc showing of need, the parties could not predict the applicability of the privilege.

Some privileges on the other hand, such as attorney work product, are qualified. Even if the privilege attaches, the party seeking discovery can obtain the privileged information by demonstrating an overriding need for the information. Qualified privileges allow the court the discretion to weigh the importance of confidentiality against countervailing social policies. For example, many jurisdictions grant reporters a privilege to withhold the identity of confidential sources of information. However, that privilege will yield when the source of information possesses information vital to the disposition of criminal charges. The privilege rests on a legitimate extrinsic policy; but in this circumstance, the policy collides with another, weightier extrinsic policy, the criminal defendant's right to a fair trial. (As we shall see in Chapter 32, recent cases have recognized that civil litigants have a similar procedural due process right which sometimes overrides evidentiary privileges.)

Chapter 26
PRIVILEGE: SPECIALIZED ASPECTS

A. CONFIDENTIAL FAMILY COMMUNICATIONS

Looking broadly at the subject of marital testimonial protections or "privileges," there are several concepts to keep separate. Jurisdictions vary widely in their approaches. Earlier we dealt with the question of spousal *incompetency*—now abolished everywhere. Next is the doctrine of husband–wife or spousal *disqualification*. In some jurisdictions this enables the party spouse to prevent the witness spouse from testifying against her; or it entitles the witness spouse to refuse to testify against the party spouse; or both. Finally, there is a related, but radically different, *privilege* protecting confidential communications between spouses.

Although disqualification and privilege rest on the policy of protecting the marital relationship, there are significant procedural differences. Unlike the disqualification, the privilege does not keep the witness entirely off the stand; rather, the privilege comes into play after the witness takes the stand and merely prevents the witness spouse from answering questions calling for the substance of conversations with the other spouse. The privilege differs from the disqualification in another respect; the disqualification can be invoked only during the marriage, but the privilege survives the marriage's termination and can be asserted later. *Pereira v. United States*, 347 U.S. 1, 6 (1954).

The drafters of the Federal Rules of Evidence proposed a marked departure from the common law; they would have retained the disqualification but abolished the privilege.

Draft Rule 505—Husband–Wife Privilege

[Not enacted.]

(a) General rule of privilege. An accused in a criminal proceeding has a privilege to prevent his spouse from testifying against him.

(b) Who may claim the privilege. The privilege may be claimed by the accused or by the spouse on his behalf. The authority of the spouse to do so is presumed in the absence of evidence to the contrary.

(c) Exceptions. There is no privilege under this rule (1) in proceedings in which one spouse is charged with a crime against the person or property of the other or of a child of either, or with a crime against the person or property of a third person committed in the course of committing a crime against the other, or (2) as to matters occurring prior to the marriage, or (3) in proceedings in which a spouse is charged with importing an alien for prostitution or other immoral purpose in violation of 8 U.S.C. § 1328, with transporting a female in interstate commerce for immoral purposes or other offense in violation of 18 U.S.C. §§ 2421–2424, or with violation of other similar statutes.

The Note to proposed Rule 505 declared:

> While some 10 jurisdictions recognize a privilege not to testify against one's spouse in a criminal case, and a much smaller number do so in civil cases, the great majority recognize no privilege on the part of the testifying spouse and this is the position taken by the rule.

* * *

> The rule recognizes no privilege . . . . The traditional justifications for privileges . . . have been the prevention of marital dissension and the repugnancy of requiring a person to condemn or be condemned by his spouse. These considerations bear no relevancy to marital communications. Nor can it be assumed that marital conduct will be affected by a privilege . . . of whose existence the parties in all likelihood are unaware. The other communication privileges, by way of contrast, have as one party a professional person who can be expected to inform the other of the existence of the privilege. Moreover, the relationships from which those privileges arise are essentially and almost exclusively verbal in nature, quite unlike marriage.

However, the Committee did not persuade Congress. Proposed Rule 505 was another of the privilege provisions Congress balked at enacting. Nonetheless, as a matter of case law, the Supreme Court has adopted a testimonial privilege that differs from proposed Rule 505 and most state court privileges.

TRAMMEL v. UNITED STATES

445 U.S. 40 (1980)

CHIEF JUSTICE BURGER delivered the opinion of the Court.

We granted certiorari to consider whether an accused may invoke the privilege against adverse spousal testimony so as to exclude the voluntary testimony of his wife. This calls for a re–examination of *Hawkins v. United States*, 358 U.S. 74 (1958).

On March 10, 1976, petitioner Otis Trammel was indicted with two others, Roberts and Freeman, for importing heroin into the United States from Thailand and the Philippine Islands and for conspiracy to import heroin. The indictment named six unindicted co–conspirators, including petitioner's wife Elizabeth Ann Trammel.

According to the indictment, petitioner and his wife flew from the Philippines to California in August 1975, carrying with them a quantity of heroin. Freeman and Roberts assisted them in its distribution. Elizabeth Trammel then travelled to Thailand where she purchased another supply of the drug. On November 3, 1975, with four ounces of heroin on her person, she boarded a plane for the United States. During a routine customs search in Hawaii, she was searched, the heroin was discovered, and she was arrested. After discussions with Drug Enforcement Administration agents, she agreed to cooperate with the Government.

Prior to trial on this indictment, petitioner moved to sever his case from that of Roberts and Freeman. He advised the court that the Government intended to call his wife as an adverse witness and asserted his claim to a privilege to prevent her from testifying against him. At a hearing on the motion, Mrs. Trammel was called as a Government witness under a grant of use immunity. She testified that she and petitioner were married in May 1975 and that they remained married. She explained that her cooperation with the Government was based on assurances that she would be given lenient treatment. She then described her role and that of her husband in the heroin distribution conspiracy.

After hearing this testimony, the District Court ruled that Mrs. Trammel could testify in support of the Government's case to any act she observed during the marriage and to any communication "made in the presence of a third person"; however, confidential communications between petitioner and his wife were held to be privileged and inadmissible. The motion to sever was denied.

At trial, Elizabeth Trammel testified within the limits of the court's pretrial ruling; her testimony constituted virtually its entire case against petitioner. He was found guilty on both the substantive and conspiracy charges.

In the Court of Appeals petitioner's only claim of error was that the admission of the adverse testimony of his wife, over his objection, contravened this Court's teaching in *Hawkins v. United States, supra*, and therefore constituted reversible error. The Court of Appeals rejected this contention. It concluded that *Hawkins* did not prohibit "the voluntary testimony of a spouse who appears as an unindicted co–conspirator under grant of immunity from the Government in return for her testimony."

The privilege claimed by petitioner has ancient roots. Despite its medieval origins, this rule of spousal disqualification remained intact in most common–law jurisdictions well into the 19th century. It was applied by this Court in *Stein v. Bowman*, 13 Pet. 209, 220–23 (1839) and again in *Jin Fuey Moy v. United States*, 254 U.S. 189, 195 (1920). Indeed, it was not until 1933, in *Funk v. United States*, 290 U.S. 371, that this Court abolished the testimonial disqualification in the federal courts to permit the spouse of a defendant to testify in the defendant's behalf. *Funk*, however, left undisturbed the rule that either spouse could prevent the other from giving adverse testimony. *Id.*, at 373. The rule thus evolved into one of privilege rather than one of absolute disqualification. *See* J. Maguire, Evidence, Common Sense and Common Law 78–92 (1947).

The modern justification for this privilege against adverse spousal testimony is its perceived role in fostering the harmony and sanctity of the marriage relationship. Notwithstanding this benign purpose, the rule was sharply criticized. Professor Wigmore termed it "the merest anachronism in legal theory and an indefensible obstruction to truth in practice." 8 Wigmore § 2228, at 221. In its place, Wigmore suggested a privilege protecting only private marital communications, modeled on the privilege between attorney and client. *See* 8 Wigmore § 2332 *et seq.*

* * *

In *Hawkins v. United States*, 358 U.S. 74 (1958), this Court considered the continued vitality of the privilege against adverse spousal testimony in the federal courts. There the District Court had permitted petitioner's wife, over his objection, to testify against him. With one questioning concurring opinion, the Court held the wife's testimony inadmissible; it took note of the critical comments that the common–law rule had engendered but chose not to abandon it. Also rejected was the Government's suggestion that the Court modify the privilege by vesting it in the witness spouse, with freedom to testify or not independent of the defendant's control. The Court viewed this proposed modification as antithetical to the widespread belief, evidenced in the rules then in effect in a majority of the States and in England, "that the law should not force or encourage testimony which might alienate husband and wife, or further inflame existing domestic differences."

* * *

Since 1958, when *Hawkins* was decided, support for the privilege against adverse spousal testimony has been corroded further. Thirty–one jurisdictions then allowed an accused a privilege to prevent adverse spousal testimony. The number has now declined to 24. . . .The trend in state law toward divesting the accused of the privilege to bar adverse spousal testimony[10] has special relevance because the law of marriage and domestic relations are concerns traditionally reserved to the states. Scholarly criticism of the *Hawkins* rule has also continued unabated. . . .

It is essential to remember that the *Hawkins* privilege is not needed to protect information privately disclosed between husband and wife in the confidence of the marital relationship—once described by this Court as "the best solace of human existence." *Stein v. Bowman*, 13 Pet., at 223. Those confidences are privileged under the independent rule protecting confidential marital communications. *Blau v. United States*, 340 U.S. 332 (1951). The *Hawkins* privilege is invoked, not to exclude private marital communications, but rather to exclude evidence of criminal acts and of communications made in the presence of third persons.

No other testimonial privilege sweeps so broadly. The privileges between priest and penitent, attorney and client, and physician and patient limit protection to private communications. The *Hawkins* rule stands in marked contrast to these three privileges. Its protection is not limited to confidential communications; rather it permits an accused to exclude all adverse spousal testimony. As Jeremy Bentham observed, such a privilege goes far beyond making "every man's house his castle," and permits a person to convert his house into "a den of thieves." 5 Rationale of Judicial Evidence 340 (1827).

---

[10] In 1965, California took the privilege from the defendant–spouse and vested it in the witness–spouse, accepting a study commission recommendation that the "latter [was] more likely than the former to determine whether or not to claim the privilege on the basis of the probable effect on the marital relationship." *See* Cal. Evid. Code Ann. §§ 970–973 (West 1966 and Supp. 1979) and 1 California Law Revision Commission, Recommendation and Study relating to the Marital "For and Against" Testimonial Privilege, at F–5 (1956).

The ancient foundations for so sweeping a privilege have long since disappeared. Nowhere in the common law world—indeed in any modern society—is a woman regarded as chattel or demeaned by denial of a separate legal identity. The contemporary justification for affording an accused such a privilege is also unpersuasive. When one spouse is willing to testify against the other in a criminal proceeding—whatever the motivation—their relationship is almost certainly in disrepair; there is probably little in the way of marital harmony for the privilege to preserve. In these circumstances, a rule of evidence that permits an accused to prevent adverse spousal testimony seems far more likely to frustrate justice than to foster family peace.[12] Indeed, there is reason to believe that vesting the privilege in the accused could actually undermine the marital relationship. For example, in a case such as this, the Government is unlikely to offer a wife immunity and lenient treatment if it knows that her husband can prevent her from giving adverse testimony. If the Government is dissuaded from making such an offer, the privilege can have the untoward effect of permitting one spouse to escape justice at the expense of the other. It hardly seems conducive to the preservation of the marital relation to place a wife in jeopardy solely by virtue of her husband's control over her testimony.

"Reason and experience" no longer justify so sweeping a rule as that found in *Hawkins*. We conclude that the existing rule should be modified so that the witness spouse alone has a privilege to refuse to testify adversely; the witness may be neither compelled to testify nor foreclosed from testifying. This modification—vesting the privilege in the witness spouse—furthers the important public interest in marital harmony without unduly burdening legitimate law enforcement needs.

NOTES AND PROBLEMS

1. Both *Trammel* and the case it overruled, *Hawkins*, made certain sociological assumptions about the general state of the institution of marriage in the United States. Those assumptions "were hardly indisputable." 2 McCORMICK ON EVIDENCE § 328, at 386 (J. Strong ed., 4th ed. 1992). Are the *Trammel* Court's assumptions nevertheless justifiable? Or is *Trammel* simply another illustration of the courts' unfortunate tendency to confuse *a priori* conjecture with empirical fact? *See* 2 K. DAVIS & R. PIERCE, ADMINISTRATIVE LAW TREATISE § 10.6 (3d ed. 1994). How does the Court know that those assumptions are true? Before indulging in those assumptions, should the Court demand empirical verification of the assumptions?

2. Do you agree with the Court's reasoning in *Trammel*? At least one respected authority, Professor Lempert, does not. Lempert, *A Right to Every Woman's Evidence*, 66 IOWA L. REV. 725 (1981). Professor Lempert points out that the government can pressure a wife into "consenting" to testify against her husband. *Id.* at 733–34. He points out that while the *Hawkins* case was

---

[12] It is argued that abolishing the privilege will permit the Government to come between husband and wife, pitting one against the other. That, too, misses the mark. Neither *Hawkins,* nor any other privilege, prevents the Government from enlisting one spouse to give information concerning the other or to aid in the other's apprehension. It is only the spouse's testimony in the courtroom that is prohibited.

pending before the Court, the Court discovered that "Hawkins' wife had been imprisoned as a material witness and released only after giving a three thousand dollar bond conditioned upon her appearance in court as a witness for the United States." *Id.* at 733. *Hawkins* illustrates how the prosecution can obtain "apparently voluntary testimony" from an unwilling spouse. *Id.*

Would Professor Lempert's argument still have merit if, in applying *Trammel*, the courts allowed the defendant to challenge the voluntariness of his spouse's consent to testifying? Should the defendant have standing to raise the question of the voluntariness of the spouse's consent?

1. SPOUSAL PRIVILEGE

a. The Types of Information Protected by the Spousal Privilege

1) The Definition of "Confidential Communication"

In the last chapter we examined the conventional definition of the word "communication." We saw that in the context of most privileges, "communication" has the ordinary lay usage of information conveyed orally or in writing from one person to another. The issue is whether that definition obtains here. To answer that question, initially consider the following case.

BLAU v. UNITED STATES

340 U.S. 332 (1951)

JUSTICE BLACK delivered the opinion of the Court.

Petitioner was summoned to appear before a federal district grand jury in Colorado. Both before that body and before the district judge where he was later taken, petitioner declined to answer questions concerning the activities and records of the Communist Party of Colorado, claiming his constitutional privilege against self–incrimination. He also refused to reveal the whereabouts of his wife, who was wanted by the grand jury as a witness in connection with the same investigation. As to this refusal to testify, petitioner asserted his privilege against disclosing confidential communications between husband and wife. The district judge overruled both claims of privilege and sentenced petitioner to six months in prison for contempt of court. The Court of Appeals for the Tenth Circuit affirmed.

For the reasons set out in our recent opinion in *Patricia Blau v. United States*, 340 U.S. 159, we hold it was error to fail to sustain the claim of privilege against self–incrimination.

This leaves for consideration the validity of the sentence insofar as it rests on the failure of petitioner to disclose the whereabouts of his wife. In *Wolfle v. United States*, 291 U.S. 7, this Court recognized that a confidential communication between husband and wife was privileged. It is not disputed in the present case that petitioner obtained his knowledge as to where his wife was by communication from her. Nevertheless, the Government insists that he should be denied the benefit of the privilege because he failed to prove that the information was privately conveyed. This contention ignores the rule that marital communications are presumptively confidential. *Wolfle v. United States, supra,* at 14; Wigmore, Evidence, § 2336. The Government made no effort to overcome the presumption. In this case, moreover, the communication to petitioner was of the kind likely to be confidential. Petitioner's wife, according to the district judge, knew that she and a number of others were "wanted" as witnesses by the grand jury but she "hid out, apparently so that the process . . . could not be served upon her." Several of the witnesses who appeared were put in jail for contempt of court. Under such circumstances, it seems highly probable that Mrs. Blau secretly told her husband where she could be found. Petitioner's refusal to betray his wife's trust therefore was both understandable and lawful. We have no doubt that he was entitled to claim his privilege.

Reversed.

Justice Black speculates that "it seems highly probable that Mrs. Blau secretly told her husband where she could be found." Under the federal statutory scheme, the trial judge should assess that probability under Rule 104(a). Justice Black's statement raises two issues. The first issue is procedural: Who has the burden of proving the basis of Blau's knowledge of his wife's whereabouts? Since the person invoking the privilege knows the basis of his or her knowledge, that party usually assumes the burden. But note the presumption Justice Black mentions. Many lower courts have construed Justice Black's statement as creating a presumption that "communications between spouses are . . . confidential." *Proctor & Gamble Co. v. Bankers Trust Co.,* 909 F. Supp. 525, 527 (S.D. Ohio 1995). The second issue is substantive: As a matter of policy, should information standing alone be protected? Certainly, it would have been objectionable if the questioner had asked what his wife told Blau about her whereabouts. On its face, that question calls for the revelation of spousal communications. But the questioner was not quite so blatant in *Blau.* Would we reach the same result if Blau's knowledge of his wife's whereabouts rested only partially on her communication? Suppose that after speaking with her, Blau had visited her. Should that fact change the result in *Blau?*

Blau raises the question of when the normal definition of "communication" should be expanded to include information. Moreover, the courts have taken another step in expanding the definition of communication for purpose of the spousal privilege. The following article discusses the expansion.

COMMENT, THE HUSBAND–WIFE PRIVILEGES OF TESTIMONIAL NON–DISCLOSURE, 56 Northwestern University Law Review 208, 220–22 (1961)

There is a wide variance in the decisions purporting to define communication, though they may be categorized in one of five areas, *viz.,* (1) verbal exchanges whether oral or written, (2) acts performed with manifest intent to convey information, (3) acts performed with intent to convey information, the intent being implied from the propinquity of the marital relation, (4) acts performed with knowledge that they might convey information, but apparently lacking in intent to so convey, and (5) any act or effect observed by the actor's spouse accidentally, but consequent upon the marital relation.

Most of the cases adhere to the first definition, though an increasing number of courts seem prone to privilege acts which are manifestly intended to impart information, such as displaying stolen goods to one's wife.

The third category may be illustrated by the husband who develops a mental problem or disease. Though he may seek to conceal it, the very closeness of a normal marital relation will cause its revelation; and in the event that his wife's knowledge may constitute prejudicial testimony at a later date, the courts should look to the circumstances inducing his attempted concealment, and imply intent to communicate by virtue of propinquity, thus preserving the privilege where it would be manifestly against the policy of inducing and protecting marital confidence to deny it, and likewise offensive to society. The lack of overt intent to convey information results from false pride or shame, and should not prevent the application of the privilege to the knowledge acquired by the partner spouse. Some courts have been willing to extend the privilege to the knowledge acquired by the partner spouse. Some courts have been willing to extend the privilege to this third category and the opinions seem well reasoned.

Though some courts have extended the privilege in the fourth category, they seem to torture the policy by disallowing disclosure of actions performed without express or implied intent to convey information, simply because such actions are fortuitously observed by the actor's spouse. No privilege should be allowed ostensibly to protect and foster communication when, in fact, the communicator had no intent to impart knowledge. Like considerations apply also to the fifth category, which is illustrated by the situation wherein a husband places papers in his desk knowing and relying on his knowledge that his wife is not wont to look into his desk, but she chances to see them.

NOTES AND PROBLEMS

1. Problem 26–1. In *Devitt*, assume Devitt was married at the time of the battery. That evening, Mrs. Devitt hears a noise in the backyard. She walks into the backyard to find Devitt digging a hole to bury property he had stolen from Paterson's apartment. Could she testify over the defense objection that she would be testifying to a spousal communication from Devitt?

2. Problem 26–2. Later Devitt divorces his wife. May Devitt's former wife testify about Devitt's action over a defense objection that she is revealing a spousal communication?

3. Is there something about the nature of the marital relationship that necessitates broadening the concept of communication? Remember the Advisory Committee's Note to proposed Rule 505: "[T]he relationships for which those [professional] privileges arise are essentially and almost exclusively verbal in nature, quite unlike marriage." The Note may argue against a privilege; but once the decision is made to recognize a privilege, the argument cuts in favor of a broad privilege. What rationale do you find most appealing?

2) The Requirement that the Communication Occur Between Properly Related Parties

At first glance, the application of this requirement to the spousal privilege seems to be a simple matter: We apply the privilege only if the parties were "married" at the time of the communication. However, on closer scrutiny, it develops that the issue is not as clear–cut as we might first suppose.

The initial question is whether we should limit the evidentiary privilege to persons who are formally married. In the past three decades, we have witnessed a revolution in society's attitude toward the cohabitation of unmarried persons. We now extend many of the legal protections formerly reserved for married persons to cohabiting persons. If we begin to treat cohabitation as the functional legal equivalent of marriage in some respects, why not this respect as well? Suppose that Devitt were cohabiting with the woman in the last hypothetical rather than being married to her. If they had been cohabiting for a substantial period of time and had bought personal and real property together, why deny them the protection of the evidentiary privilege? The received orthodoxy is that they are not entitled to any privilege (*In re Grand Jury Proceedings*, 562 F. Supp. 486 (N.D. Cal. 1983)). Do you agree? What problems or issues do you see in extending the privilege to cohabiting parties?

Additionally, even when the marriage is technically valid, the marriage may be a "sham" in another sense. In *Lutwak v. United States*, 344 U.S. 604 (1953), the defendants had been convicted of conspiring to defraud the United States by obtaining illegal entry under the War Brides Act. Writing for the majority, Justice Minton specifically stated that "[w]e do not believe that the validity of the marriages is material," *id.* at 611, and sustained the testimony of the purported wives against their defendant husbands.

NOTES AND PROBLEMS

1. Now consider the last step in analysis. Even assuming that the marriage was valid at the time of the ceremony, the marriage may not be viable at the time of the communication. Should that affect the application of the spousal privilege? The traditional view is that even here we must mechanically apply the privilege. Annot., 98 A.L.R.3d 1285 (1980). However, some courts have been willing to rethink the assumptions underlying a mechanical application of the privilege. *People v. D'Amato*, 105 Misc. 2d 1048, 430 N.Y.S.2d 521, 522–24 (Sup. Ct. 1980).

2. Problem 26–3. The stated justification for the spousal privilege is protecting the marital relationship. If Devitt's marriage had been in shambles, would it make any sense to apply the privilege at the expense of suppressing the truth? Remember the Supreme Court's reasoning in *Trammel v. United States*, 445 U.S. 40 (1980). Does the answer depend on whether the deterioration occurred by the time of (a) the communication or (b) the trial? Even if Devitt's marriage had been in shambles, would a refusal to apply the privilege chill the candor between other spouses? For that matter, can the courts frame judicially manageable standards to determine when a marriage is in such disarray that it no longer merits the protection of the evidentiary privilege? Even if the courts are generally unwilling to inquire whether a marriage has deteriorated, should the courts recognize a privilege when the spouses are permanently separated? *United States v. Byrd*, 750 F.2d 585, 591–94 (7th Cir. 1984).

3) The Requirement that the Communication Be Incident to the Relationship

Even a confidential communication between properly related persons is unprotected unless the communication occurs incident to the relationship. In the case of the professional privileges, it is rather easy for the courts to administer that requirement.

It is especially difficult to apply such a requirement to spousal communications. The marital relationship is so broad, encompassing such a wide range of human activities, that it is difficult to find a subject that spouses would not discuss with each other in the normal course of their marital relation. As a practical matter, the spousal privilege is the most difficult privilege to defeat on the theory that the communication was not incident to the relationship.

While it is difficult to do so, it is not impossible. The party resisting the privilege claim usually attempts to prove that there was another relationship between the spouses and that the communication occurred incident to that relationship.

PROBLEMS

1. Problem 26–4. Suppose that in our torts case, Ms. Hill and her husband were partners in a landscaping and gardening business. It was a small business, and both Ms. Hill and her husband did a good deal of manual labor involved in the landscaping and gardening. Approximately one month before trial, Ms. Hill and her husband had a long, detailed discussion of the extent of her physical injuries. Polecat Motors' attorney believes that during the discussion, Ms. Hill told her husband that her injuries are not as severe as she claims in her complaint. At trial, Polecat Motors' attorney calls Ms. Hill's husband as an adverse witness. The following occurs:

Q: And both of you do some of the manual work in this business?

A: Yes.

Q: So your wife's physical condition is of interest to you as her business partner. Isn't that correct?

A: Right.

Q: How much money you make as her partner depends in part on how much landscaping she is capable of doing?

A: Yes.

Q: Isn't it true that during that conversation you admitted you had with your wife, she told you that she expected to be back at work and "right as rain" within three months?

> A: Your Honor, I object to that question on the ground that it calls for privileged information.

> Q: Your Honor, it's clear that Ms. Hill gave the witness this information because he is her business partner. This wasn't a husband–wife communication.

As trial judge, how would you rule on the objection? Must Polecat Motors' attorney convince you that the statement related only to the business partnership, or is it enough that you conclude that Ms. Hill would have made the statement to the witness even if they had not been married? Which standard is more appropriate?

2. Problem 26–5. Suppose that Devitt's wife hated Paterson and had helped Devitt plan an assault on the complainant. Mrs. Devitt would then be chargeable as a coconspirator. Should her status as a coconspirator defeat the privilege? *See United States v. Picciandra*, 788 F.2d 39, 43 (1st Cir. 1986); *People v. Watkins*, 89 Misc. 2d 870, 393 N.Y.S.2d 283, 285–86 (1977), *aff'd*, 63 A.D.2d 1033, 406 N.Y.S.2d 343, *cert. denied*, 439 U.S. 984 (1978). The case for overriding the privilege seems especially strong when the other relationship between the spouses is one of criminal agency.

b. Special Exceptions to the Spousal Privilege

Compared to the other privileges, the spousal privilege has relatively few exceptions. Though the exceptions are few in number, the exceptions are important inroads on the privilege's protective scope. In some cases, the exceptions are common to most privileges. For example, California Evidence Code § 984 provides:

There is no privilege under this article in

(a) A proceeding brought by or on behalf of one spouse against the other spouse.

(b) A proceeding between a surviving spouse and a person who claims through the deceased spouse, regardless of whether such claim is by testate or intestate succession or by inter vivos transaction.

Section 981 reads:

> There is no privilege under this article if the communication was made, in whole or in part, to enable or aid anyone to commit or plan to commit a crime or a fraud.

We shall see that most privileges yield when the purpose of the communication was "to enable or aid anyone to commit or plan to commit a crime or a fraud." It is important, though, to understand the limited scope of this exception. Would this exception come into play if Devitt disclosed the battery to his wife the day after the battery? Suppose that the day before the battery, he suggested to his wife that he was planning on committing the battery. What facts must you add before the exception comes into play?

In other cases, the exceptions are unique to the spousal privilege. Just as there is an injured spouse exception to the spousal disqualification, most jurisdictions recognize an injured spouse exception to the privilege. California Evidence Code § 985 codifies the exception in this fashion:

There is no privilege under this article in a criminal proceeding in which one spouse is charged with:

(a) A crime committed at any time against the person or property of the other spouse or of a child of either.

(b) A crime committed at any time against the person or property of a third person committed in the course of committing a crime against the person or property of the other spouse.

(c) Bigamy.

(d) A crime defined by Section 270 [child neglect] or 270a [non-support of wife] of the Penal Code.

There is an element of inconsistency and unfairness when the defendant commits "offenses against the marital relation" while simultaneously invoking the spousal privilege and attempting to "hide the truth behind" the same marital relation.

Finally, consider California Evidence Code § 987:

There is no privilege under this article in a criminal proceeding in which the communication is offered in evidence by a defendant who is one of the spouses between whom the communication was made.

In the case of most of the other exceptions, the rationale is a variation of the theme that society has countervailing interests that override the interests of the holder of the privilege. In this case, the focus is different; the party seeking disclosure is the defendant spouse. Not all jurisdictions would agree that the correct balance favors disclosure. *See, e.g., Steeley v. State*, 17 Okla. Crim. App. 252, 187 P. 821 (1920). In your judgment, how should the balance be struck?

NOTES AND PROBLEMS

1. Problem 26–6. Suppose that Devitt's battery of Paterson was part of a rampage that afternoon. The rampage began with a violent attack on his wife an hour before his attack on Paterson. Devitt and his wife had quarreled violently, and the quarrel triggered both attacks. Could the prosecutor call Devitt's wife as a witness to the quarrel and Devitt's battery on her to prove the motive for the subsequent battery? *See People v. Love*, 339 N.W.2d 493, 496–97 (Mich. Ct. App. 1983).

Add the fact that Paterson and Devitt's wife were acquaintances and that Mrs. Devitt had referred to Paterson during the quarrel immediately before Devitt's attack on his wife. Do these facts change the result?

2. Courts have divided over whether there should be a "joint participants" exception—that is, whenever both spouses conspired or participated in committing the charged crime—to the disqualification and/or the privilege. For example, in the *Devitt* case, assume that Devitt's wife helped him plan the crime. Assume also that Morena follows the *Trammel* decision. At trial, she asserts her right under *Trammel* to refuse to testify against her husband. Should she be compelled to testify over Devitt's objection? (Assume there is no self–incrimination problem; ordinarily, the witness will be given immunity or some sort of "deal.") To date, the majority of federal circuits that have passed on the exception have adopted it. *See, e.g., United States v. Keck*, 773 F.2d 759, 766 (7th Cir. 1985). However, the courts of appeal for the Second and Third Circuits have rejected the exception. *In re Koecher*, 755 F.2d 1022 (2d Cir. 1985), *cert. granted*, 474 U.S. 815 (1985), *vacated as moot*, 475 U.S. 133, (1986); *Appeal of Malfitano*, 633 F.2d 276, 279 (3d Cir. 1980). With respect to such an exception for the marital privilege, compare *United States v. Clark*, 712 F.2d 299, 300–01 (7th Cir. 1983) with *In re Koecher, supra*, at 1025.

2. A PARENT–CHILD PRIVILEGE?

Once we accept the proposition that the spousal relation warrants the protection of an evidentiary privilege, the question naturally arises whether we should grant similar protection to other family relationships such as the parent–child relationship. The analogy is certainly appealing. Even if we should not allow a child to disqualify a parent as a potential witness against the child, the analogy suggests that we ought to give the child or the parent the more limited protection of an evidentiary privilege for confidential communications. For their part, most commentators favor recognizing a parent–child privilege. *See, e.g.*, Comment, 16 SAN DIEGO L. REV. 811 (1979); Comment, 47 FORDHAM L. REV. 771 (1979); Comment, 1978 B.Y.U. L. REV. 1002. Commentators point out that other legal traditions recognize a parent–child privilege. Note, *Parent–Child Loyalty and Testimonial Privilege*, 100 HARV. L. REV. 910, 912 (1987). "[T]he prevailing view in the civil law countries of Western Europe is that no person will be forced to divulge confidences between him or herself and another family member." Watts, *The Parent–Child Privilege: Hardly a New or Revolutionary Concept*, 28 WM. & MARY L. REV. 583, 593 (1987). The American Bar Association's Criminal Justice Section has proposed a model statute generally providing that "[n]either a parent nor the parent's child may be compelled to answer a question concerning confidential communications [between them]." *Id.* at 619–31. Three states (Idaho, Massachusetts, and Minnesota) have enacted statutes recognizing some form of familial privilege. Watts, *Do We Need a Parent–Child Privilege? Yes*, 2 CRIM. JUST. 11, 34 (Summer 1987). However, at common law the courts have balked. Annot., 6 A.L.R.4th 544 (1981). With the exception of New York and one federal district court, most jurisdictions addressing the commentators' argument have rejected it. *In re Agosto*, 553 F. Supp. 1298 (D. Nev. 1983).

In analogizing to *Trammel*, Chief Judge Clairborne, in *Agosto*, recognized a child's right to refuse to testify adversely to a parent:

> Applying this rationale to the case at bar, it is reasonable to hold that Charles Agosto may claim the parent–child privilege not only for confidential communications which transpired between his father and himself, but he may likewise claim the privilege for protection against being compelled to be a witness and testify adversely against his father in any criminal proceeding.

Id. at 1325. However, other courts have refused to recognize a new disqualification for the parent–child relationship (*In re Doe*, 842 F.2d 244 (10th Cir.), *cert. denied*, 488 U.S. 894 (1988); *In re Santarelli*, 740 F.2d 816, 816–17 (11th

Cir. 1984)) at least when the child is emancipated. *United States v. Ismail*, 756 F.2d 1253, 1258 (6th Cir. 1985).

Is the parent–child relationship sufficiently analogous to the spousal relation to justify a privilege? In *People v. Doe*, 61 A.D. 2d 426, 403 N.Y.S.2d 375 (1978), the court answered in the affirmative:

> Witnesses appearing before the grand jury placed a 16–year–old boy near the scene of the fire. The district attorney issued subpoenas to the youth's parents, allegedly seeking admissions thought to have been made by the boy to his parents. The issue, which this court believes to be one of first impression, is: can the state, in seeking criminal evidence, compel parents of a minor child to testify before a grand jury concerning confidential admissions by the child?

Some commentators have opposed the privilege and argued that the analogy to the spousal relation is specious. Comment, 3 U. PUGET SOUND 177 (1979); Note, 45 ALB. L. REV. 142 (1980). What weaknesses, if any, do you see in the analogy?

B. LEGAL PRIVILEGE: ATTORNEY–CLIENT PRIVILEGE AND THE WORK PRODUCT DOCTRINE

1. THE ATTORNEY–CLIENT PRIVILEGE: AN OVERVIEW

The Advisory Committee's proposed Rule 503 was as follows:

Lawyer–Client Privilege

[Not enacted.]

(a) Definitions. As used in this rule:

(1) A "client" is a person, public officer, or corporation, association, or other organization or entity, either public or private, who is rendered professional legal services by a lawyer, or who consults a lawyer with a view to obtaining professional legal services from him.

(2) A "lawyer" is a person authorized, or reasonably believed by the client to be authorized, to practice law in any state or nation.

(3) A "representative of the lawyer" is one employed to assist the lawyer in the rendition of professional legal services.

(4) A communication is "confidential" if not intended to be disclosed to third persons other than those to whom disclosure is in furtherance of the rendition of professional legal services to the client or those reasonably necessary for the transmission of the communication.

(b) General rule of privilege. A client has a privilege to refuse to disclose and to prevent any other person from disclosing confidential communications made for the purpose of facilitating the rendition of professional legal services to the client, (1) between himself or his representative and his lawyer or his lawyer's representative, or (2) between his lawyer and the lawyer's representative, or (3) by him or his lawyer to a lawyer representing another in a matter of common interest, or (4) between representatives of the client or between the client and a representative of the client, or (5) between lawyers representing the client.

(c) Who may claim the privilege. The privilege may be claimed by the client, his guardian or conservator, the personal representative of a deceased client, or the successor, trustee, or similar representative of a corporation, association, or other organization, whether or not in existence. The person who was the lawyer at the time of the communication may claim the privilege but only on behalf of the client. His authority to do so is presumed in the absence of evidence to the contrary.

(d) Exceptions. There is no privilege under this rule:

(1) Furtherance of crime or fraud. If the services of the lawyer were sought or obtained to enable or aid anyone to commit or plan to commit what the client knew or reasonably should have known to be a crime or fraud; or

(2) Claimants through same deceased client. As to a communication relevant to an issue between parties who claim through the same deceased client, regardless of whether the claims are by testate or intestate succession or by *inter vivos* transaction; or

(3) Breach of duty by lawyer or client. As to a communication relevant to an issue of breach of duty by the lawyer to his client or by the client to his lawyer; or

(4) Document attested by lawyer. As to a communication relevant to an issue concerning an attested document to which the lawyer is an attesting witness: or

(5) Joint clients. As to a communication relevant to a matter of common interest between two or more clients if the communication was made by any of them to a lawyer retained or consulted in common, when offered in an action between any of the clients.

a. The Threshold Question of the Wisdom of Recognizing the Privilege

Since the time of Jeremy Bentham, the critics of privileges have underscored the cost of recognizing privileges: the suppression of relevant, often highly reliable, evidence. What benefits allegedly offset the cost and justify recognizing a privilege? In large part, the benefit argument is that, without the assurance of the privilege, clients would be reluctant to disclose sensitive information to their attorneys. There have been some empirical investigations of that argument:

ZACHARIAS, RETHINKING CONFIDENTIALITY, 74 Iowa Law Review 351, 377–81, 383–86, 389–90, 394–95, 409–11 (1989)
(excerpted and some citations omitted)

The Yale Study on Attorney–Client Privilege

In 1962, the *Yale Law Journal* conducted a study of the importance and effect of attorney–client privilege rules. Its primary mission was to compare the privilege accorded the bar to that granted other professions. The *Journal* distributed questionnaires and accumulated responses from 108 laypersons, 125 lawyers, and between 12 and 51 members of several other professions, including psychology, psychiatry, social work, marriage counseling, and accounting.[119]

The survey revealed widespread misinformation concerning privileges, particularly the attorney–client privilege. Interestingly, "[l]awyers, significantly more than laymen, believe the privilege encourages free disclosure to them." Seventy–one of 108 laypersons surveyed understood that, as a general matter, attorneys would not disclose confidential matter. But a significant percentage of the laypersons thought that lawyers, if questioned in court, would have an obligation to reveal confidences.

* * *

Several aspects of the survey are telling. First, the figures on lay perceptions of attorneys suggest that, while a preference for nondisclosure rules exists, a substantial majority of laypersons would continue to use lawyers even if secrecy were limited. Indeed, many of the subjects believed that the privilege rules should be confined. Second, the comparative figures suggest that laypersons do not perceive any dramatic contrast in the way different professionals will protect their communications. What makes these results particularly significant is that most of the nonlegal professions are *not* governed by the same highly protective privilege that is applicable to the legal profession. That the professions continue to thrive despite the "theoretical" lay hesitation to disclose absent confidentiality suggests that either consumer ignorance or a simple need for professional services is what really controls the marketplace.[134]

---

[119] Note, *Functional Overlap Between the Lawyer and Other Professionals: Its Implications for the Privileged Communications Doctrine,* 71 YALE L.J. 1226, 1227 (1962). There are several reasons to caution against too much reliance on the Yale study. First, the number of subjects was limited. Second, subjects were not chosen with sufficient randomness to assure the significance of the results. *See id.* at 1227 n.6. Third, the study was conducted by a legal periodical, without statistical rigor. Still, the study contains the only available empirical data. The results provide valuable food for thought.

[134] *See* Moore, *Limits to Attorney–Client Confidentiality: A "Philosophically Informed" and Comparative Approach to Legal and Medical Ethics,* 36 CASE W. RES. 177, 196–211 (1985) (comparing confidentiality in medical and legal professions).

The Tompkins County Study on Confidentiality

In connection with this Article, I conducted a survey of attorneys and laypersons in Tompkins County, New York. All practicing attorneys in Tompkins County received a questionnaire. Sixty–three attorneys completed the questionnaire.

Simultaneously, a pool of laypersons from Tompkins County received a questionnaire. A total of 105 completed the survey. The seventy–three subjects who had consulted lawyers in the past (hereinafter referred to as "clients") were asked about their experiences. The entire pool (hereinafter referred to as "laypersons") responded to questions regarding their understanding of confidentiality.

Neither subject pool was large or diverse enough to represent the country as a whole. Although the sixty–three responding lawyers probably make up a majority of active Tompkins County practitioners, the community in which they practice is rural and university oriented. Their clientele may be more personal and their subject matter less complex than, for example, large–firm urban lawyers. Similarly, the lay and client pool consisted of self–selected Tompkins County residents who had volunteered to serve as jurors in mock trials at Cornell Law School. By volunteering, all had exhibited an interest in legal issues. One might therefore surmise that the surveyed laypersons were more legally sophisticated than typical individual clients, but not so educated as business clients one would find in commercial urban litigation.

Several responses support the proposition that some form of confidentiality rule serves confidentiality's basic rationales. Approximately half of the lay respondents predicted that they would withhold information from attorneys if no firm obligation of confidentiality existed. A substantial number of the surveyed clients claimed to have relied upon confidentiality; nearly 30% stated that they gave information to their attorneys that "they would not have given without a guarantee of confidentiality."

Extent of clients' confidence in lawyer discretion. The extent to which confidentially rules induce full disclosure depends in part on whether clients believe lawyers follow the rules. Over 42% of the surveyed clients understood confidentiality to be absolute. Yet only 19.7% believed that "attorneys as a matter of practice [always] keep information confidential." Of those clients who believed in absolute confidentiality, 14.3% stated that in practice a lawyer will disclose "depending on the lawyer's personal sense of what should be kept confidential."

As in the Yale study, a comparison of lawyers with other professionals proved enlightening on the subject of the significance of secrecy rules to clients. [A] large majority of clients responded that lawyers are no more obligated to preserve confidences than doctors, psychologists, and psychiatrists; a healthy minority believed the same held true for accountants and social workers. A similar pattern appeared when clients were asked whether "attorneys in fact guard client confidences more carefully than" the other professionals.

* * *

Even more interesting were client responses to the question, "Assuming you needed the assistance of each of the following professionals, would you be more likely to give information to attorneys than to [blank]?" On the whole, the clients accepted that lawyers have a higher legal obligation to preserve confidences than accountants and social workers. Yet only half of the clients were more likely to give information to attorneys. Few were prepared to trust lawyers over priests, doctors, psychologists, or psychiatrists.

* * *

Confidentiality's effect in inducing client communication. Most lawyers surveyed believed that they would get the same information from clients even if they never informed the clients about confidentiality.[172] A higher percentage, 85.9%, believed they would get enough information to represent clients competently.[173] The answers at least suggest that strict rules are not essential to maintaining an adversary system.

The client survey further supports this conclusion. It shows that clients never told of confidentiality may be as ready to provide information as clients who were informed. The layperson survey, however, is perhaps most informative on the question of what encourages client trust: the general notion of the lawyer as a discreet professional, or the strictness of confidentiality rules. The survey asked whether the subjects would withhold information from their attorney "if [the] attorney told you that he/she could not guarantee confidentiality but that, except in unusual cases, he/she would keep information secret." A majority of laypersons answered that they would withhold information. But when the same respondents were asked whether they would still withhold information if the lawyer "promised confidentiality except for specific types of information which he/she described in advance," only 15.1% said they would withhold. That is not significantly different from the 11.3% of the surveyed clients who admitted to withholding information from their attorneys under current confidentiality rules. These results suggest that the general sense of trust in attorneys as professionals—rather than particularly strict confidentiality rules—is what fosters client candor.

---

[172] T.C. Table L1, at 5 (71.9%). This figure might be explained on the basis that lawyers assume clients know about confidentiality without being told. To some extent, the survey supports that conclusion. A large majority of clients whose lawyers never explained confidentiality, 91.1%, believed confidentiality exists, though 41.2% believed it exists to a greater extent than the law actually requires. T.C. Table J4A, at 86–87. On the other hand, a significant number of clients believed similar confidentiality guarantees exist for dealings with priests, doctors, psychologists and psychiatrists, accountants, and social workers. *See* T.C. Table J3A, at 12–17. It is probably fair to conclude that, in the absence of an explanation of what attorney–client confidentiality means, clients are at least somewhat confused.

[173] T.C. Table L1, at 5. Similarly, lawyers do not seem to share the code drafters' concern with client lies or withholding of information. Few of the lawyers surveyed believed their clients lied in more than a quarter of their cases. T.C. Table L1, at 10 (23.4%). When, however, lawyers thought their clients lied or withheld information, only 19.3% of the lawyers believed the failure to disclose significantly affected more than 25% of the cases. T.C. Table L1, at 10.

b. The Scope of the Privilege

1) The Definition of "Confidential Communication"

Suppose that after the battery and before any arrest, Devitt contacts an attorney. Devitt describes the crime to the attorney and hires the attorney to defend him against any charge that might be filed against him. The attorney, Larson, decides to check on Paterson's status. The attorney learns that he is in the hospital. Larson visits the hospital, identifies himself to the floor nurse, and learns that Paterson is still in serious condition. The nurse reports to the police that Larson, an attorney, has stopped by. The police then contact Larson and demand that he divulge the identity of his client. When he refuses to do so, the police persuade the district attorney to initiate a grand jury investigation. Larson is subpoenaed before the grand jury. The grand jury demands that Larson identify his client. At this point, can Larson still refuse to divulge Devitt's identity?

On the one hand, it is a well–established general rule that the identity of a client is <u>not</u> within the privilege. *Frank v. Tomlinson*, 351 F.2d 384 (5th Cir. 1965), *cert. denied*, 382 U.S. 1028 (1966). However, on infrequent occasions, the courts have held that the client's identity is protected. *See, e.g., Matter of Kozlov*, 398 A.2d 882 (N.J. 1979). In the leading case, *United States v. Hodge & Zweig*, 548 F.2d 1347 (9th Cir. 1977), the court announced this test:

> As a general rule, where a party demonstrates that there is a legitimate need for a court to require disclosure of such matters, the identity of an attorney's clients and the nature of his fee arrangements with his clients are not confidential communications protected by the attorney–client privilege. The general rule, however, is qualified by an important exception: A client's identity and the nature of that client's fee arrangements may be privileged where the person invoking the privilege can show that a strong probability exists that disclosure of such information would implicate that client in the very criminal activity for which legal advice was sought.

Id. at 1353. This doctrine is sometimes referred to as the "legal advice" exception to the general rule. Przypyszny, *Public Assault on the Attorney–Client Privilege: Ramifications of Baltes v. Doe*, 3 Geo. J. Legal Ethics 351, 358 (1989). Note the verb "implicate" in the last sentence quoted from *Hodge & Zweig*. Rather than resting exclusively on the attorney–client privilege, this exception is based on the interplay between that privilege and the Fifth Amendment privilege against self–incrimination.

Although the "legal advice" exception has some judicial support, other courts have adopted the "last link" exception. In *Baird v. Koerner*, 279 F.2d 623 (9th Cir. 1960), the court declared that:

> The name of the client will be considered privileged matter where the circumstances of the case are such that the name of the client is material only for the purpose of showing an acknowledgment of guilt

on the part of such client of the very offenses on account of which the attorney was employed.

Id. at 633. Following *Baird,* some courts apply the privilege when the revelation of the client's identity would furnish "the last link in an existing chain of incriminating evidence likely to lead to the client's indictment." Przypyszny, *supra,* at 356. Like the "legal advice" exception, this doctrine also has a hybrid rationale, resting on Fifth Amendment concerns as well as the attorney–client privilege.

However, there is a third doctrine based squarely on the privilege— "confidential communication" exception. *Id.* at 359. *United States v. Liebman,* 742 F.2d 807 (3d Cir. 1984) is illustrative. In *Liebman,* the Internal Revenue Service asked a law firm to identify all its clients whom the firm had erroneously advised that certain fees in connection with a particular real estate transaction were deductible. The court held that, in these limited circumstances, the clients' identities were privileged; by revealing the clients' identities, the firm would implicitly simultaneously disclose the substance of the communication between the firm and the client. In cases such as *Liebman,* the courts expand the protection of the privilege to cloak the client's identity as a means to the end of protecting the privileged communications themselves.

NOTES AND PROBLEMS

1. The application of the Fifth Amendment and the attorney–client privilege to the client's identity and fee information is of more than theoretical interest. Section 60501 of the Internal Revenue Code requires attorneys receiving a cash fee exceeding $10,000 to disclose the receipt of the fee and the identity of the fee's source to the I.R.S. Many criminal defense attorneys have filed forms, disclosing the receipt of the fee but refusing to divulge the identity of the source. The government is said to have more than 15,000 partially completed forms on file. In late 1989, the I.R.S. sent 950 attorneys letters threatening enforcement actions against them if they did not supply the omitted information. 46 CRIM. L. REP. 1503 (Mar. 14, 1990). The Justice Department filed suit for enforcement against two New York firms.

2. Note that in the case of the attorney–client privilege, as with other professional privileges, the privilege is a two–way street, protecting both what the client tells the professional and the advice the professional gives the client. *Sackman v. Liggett Group, Inc.,* 920 F. Supp. 357, 364 (E.D.N.Y. 1996).

2) The Requirement that the Confidential Communication Occur Between Properly Related Parties

In most fact patterns, the courts have had little difficulty deciding whether to treat the communication as occurring between properly related parties. One of the most interesting recent developments has been the extension of the privilege to allied party exchanges of information. Kopta, *Applying the Attorney–Client and Work Product Privileges to Allied Party Exchange of Information in California,* 36 U.C.L.A. L. REV. 151 (1988). Suppose, for instance, that Devitt was being tried with a codefendant and that they contemplated a joint defense. The court would probably apply the privilege to cloak exchanges of information between the defense counsel. Or assume that, in the *Hill* case, Ms. Hill's attorney decided to share information with the attorney representing another plaintiff pressing a similar product liability claim against Polecat. Again, the court would likely apply the privilege to protect the information exchanged. *Id.* at 168 (noting that it is misleading to refer to this doctrine as the joint "defense" privilege). Under this "common interest" doctrine, the privilege protects the exchanged information, so long as the interests of the parties are "substantially identical." *In re Regents of the University of California*, 101 F.3d 1386 (Fed. Cir. 1996) The theory is that by facilitating the pooling of information by litigants, this extension of the privilege promotes the efficiency of the operation of the litigation system. However, in two fact situations, the courts have experienced difficulty determining whether a communication occurred between an attorney and client.

Communications with corporate employees. Suppose that in our torts case, soon after Ms. Hill files her complaint, the in–house counsel for Polecat Motors begins a factual investigation to prepare for trial. The counsel wants to be able to persuade the judge that the defendant corporation is intensely concerned about quality control of safety features. Consequently, the counsel interviews both executive officers such as the president and assembly line workers, compiling the interviews into a single report. The in–house counsel retains one copy of the report and sends the only other copy to the outside firm defending the litigation. Subsequently, in response to an interrogatory, the defendant discloses the existence of the report. Ms. Hill's attorney then moves for the production of the report. Can the defendant successfully resist production of the entire report or any part of it on the ground of the attorney–client privilege?

The threshold question, of course, is whether, like a natural person, a corporate entity can qualify as a client. On the one hand, given the size of many corporations, the extension of the privilege to corporations has a greater potential for obstructing the search for truth than the application of the privilege to individual natural persons. A tremendous volume of data could be secreted in the millions of corporate file cabinets. On the other hand, a corporate entity has the same legitimate need for legal counsel as do individuals.

Beyond the question whether the privilege should apply to other than natural persons, there is the much more complex question of scope of protection afforded to entities. The Supreme Court, in a case of first impression at the High Court level, struggled with the split of authority that existed in this regard:

UPJOHN CO. v. UNITED STATES

449 U.S. 383 (1981)

JUSTICE REHNQUIST delivered the opinion of the Court.

We granted certiorari in this case to address important questions concerning the scope of the attorney–client privilege in the corporate context. With respect to the privilege question the parties and various *amici* have described our task as one of choosing between two "tests" which have gained adherents in the courts of appeals. We are acutely aware, however, that we sit to decide concrete cases and not abstract propositions of law. We decline to lay down a broad rule or series of rules to govern all conceivable future questions in this area, even were we able to do so. We can and do, however, conclude that the attorney–client privilege protects the communications involved in this case from compelled disclosure.

Petitioner Upjohn manufactures and sells pharmaceuticals here and abroad. In January 1976 independent accountants conducting an audit of one of petitioner's foreign subsidiaries discovered that the subsidiary made payments to or for the benefit of foreign government officials in order to secure government business. The accountants so informed Mr. Gerard Thomas, petitioner's Vice–President, Secretary, and General Counsel. He consulted with outside counsel and R.T. Parfet, Jr., petitioner's Chairman of the Board. It was decided that the company would conduct an internal investigation of what were termed "questionable payments." As part of this investigation the attorneys prepared a letter containing a questionnaire which was sent to "all foreign general and area managers" over the Chairman's signature. The letter began by noting recent disclosures that several American companies made "possibly illegal" payments to foreign government officials and emphasized that the management needed full information concerning any such payments made by Upjohn. The letter indicated that the Chairman had asked Thomas, identified as "the company's General Counsel," "to conduct an investigation for the purpose of determining the nature and magnitude of any payments made by the Upjohn Company or any of its subsidiaries to any employee or official of a foreign government." The questionnaire sought detailed information concerning such payments. Managers were instructed to treat the investigation as "highly confidential" and not to discuss it with anyone other than Upjohn employees who might be helpful in providing the requested information. Responses were to be sent directly to Thomas. Thomas and outside counsel also interviewed the recipients of the questionnaire and some 33 other Upjohn officers or employees as part of the investigation.

On March 26, 1976, the company voluntarily submitted a preliminary report to the Securities and Exchange Commission on Form 8–K disclosing certain questionable payments. A copy of the report was simultaneously submitted to the Internal Revenue Service, which immediately began an investigation to determine the tax consequences of the payments. Special agents conducting the investigation were given lists by Upjohn of all those interviewed and all who had responded to the questionnaire. On November 23, 1976, the Service issued a summons demanding production of . . .[all files, responses of questionnaires, and memoranda or notes of interviews relative to the investigation conducted under the supervision of Gerard Thomas to identify payments to employees of foreign governments made by the Upjohn Company or any of its affiliates.] The company declined to produce the documents . . . on the grounds that they were protected from disclosure by the attorney–client privilege. . . .

The Court of Appeals, however, considered the application of the privilege in the corporate context to present a "different problem," since the client was an inanimate entity and "only the senior management, guiding and integrating the several operations, . . . can be said to possess an identity analogous to the corporation as a whole." 600 F.2d at 1226. The first case to articulate the so–called "control group test" adopted by the court below, *City of Philadelphia v. Westinghouse Electric Corp.*, 210 F. Supp. 483, 485 (E.D. Pa.), petition for mandamus and prohibition denied, 312 F.2d 742 (CA3 1962), cert. denied, 372 U.S. 943 (1963), reflected a similar conceptual approach:

> Keeping in mind that the question is, Is it the corporation which is seeking the lawyer's advice when the asserted privileged communication is made?, the most satisfactory solution, I think, is that if the employee making the communication, of whatever rank he may be, is in a position to control or even to take a substantial part in a decision about any action which the corporation may take upon the advice of the attorney, . . . then, in effect, *he is (or personifies) the corporation* when he makes his disclosure to the lawyer and the privilege would apply. (Emphasis supplied.)

Such a view, we think, overlooks the fact that the privilege exists to protect not only the giving of professional advice to those who can act on it but also the giving of information to the lawyer to enable him to give sound and informed advice. *See Trammel*, 445 U.S., at 51. The first step in the resolution of any legal problem is ascertaining the factual background and sifting through the facts with an eye to the legally relevant. *See* ABA Code of Professional Responsibility, Ethical Consideration 4–1:

> A lawyer should be fully informed of all the facts of the matter he is handling in order for his client to obtain the full advantage of our legal system. It is for the lawyer in the exercise of his independent professional judgment to separate the relevant and important from the irrelevant and unimportant. The observance of the ethical obligation of a lawyer to hold inviolate the confidences and secrets of his client not only facilitates the full development of facts essential to proper representation of the client but also encourages laymen to seek early legal assistance.

In the case of the individual client, the provider of information and the person who acts on the lawyer's advice are one and the same. In the corporate context, however, it will frequently be employees beyond the control group as defined by the court below—"officers and agents . . . responsible for directing [the company's] actions in response to legal advice"—who will possess the information needed by the corporation's lawyers. Middle–level—and indeed lower–level—employees can, by actions within the scope of their employment, embroil the corporation in serious legal difficulties, and it is only natural that these employees would have the relevant information needed by corporate counsel if he is adequately to advise the client with respect to such actual or potential difficulties. This fact was noted in *Diversified Industries, Inc. v. Meredith*, 572 F.2d 596 (CA8 1978) (en banc):

> In a corporation, it may be necessary to glean information relevant to a legal problem from middle management or non–management personnel as well as from top executives. The attorney dealing with

a complex legal problem "is thus faced with a 'Hobson's choice.' If he interviews employees not having 'the very highest authority' their communications to him will not be privileged. If, on the other hand, he interviews *only* those employees with the 'very highest authority,' he may find it extremely difficult, if not impossible, to determine what happened." *Id.,* at 608–609.

The control group test . . . not only makes it difficult for corporate attorneys to formulate sound advice when their client is faced with a specific legal problem but also threatens to limit the valuable efforts of corporate counsel to ensure their client's compliance with the law. In light of the vast and complicated array of regulatory legislation confronting the modern corporation, corporations, unlike most individuals, "constantly go to lawyers to find out how to obey the law," Burnham, The Attorney–Client Privilege in the Corporate Arena, 24 Bus. Law, 901, 913 (1969), particularly since compliance with the law in this area is hardly an instinctive matter, *see, e.g., United States v. United States Gypsum Co.,* 438 U.S. 422, 440–441 (1978). . . .

The communications at issue were made by Upjohn employees to counsel for Upjohn acting as such, at the direction of corporate superiors in order to secure legal advice from counsel. As the magistrate found, "Mr. Thomas consulted with the Chairman of the Board and outside counsel and thereafter conducted a factual investigation to determine the nature and extent of the questionable payments *and to be in a position to give legal advice to the company with respect to the payments.*" (Emphasis supplied.) Pet. App. 13a. Information, not available from upper–echelon management, was needed to supply a basis for legal advice concerning compliance with securities and tax laws, foreign laws, currency regulations, duties to shareholders, and potential litigation in each of these areas. The communications concerned matters within the scope of the employees' corporate duties, and the employees themselves were sufficiently aware that they were being questioned in order that the corporation could obtain legal advice. The questionnaire identified Thomas as "the company's General Counsel" and referred in its opening sentence to the possible illegality of payments such as the ones on which information was sought. App. 48a. A statement of policy accompanying the questionnaire clearly indicated the legal implications of the investigation. The policy statement was issued "in order that there be no uncertainty in the future as to the policy with respect to the practices which are the subject of this investigation." It began "Upjohn will comply with all laws and regulations," and stated that commissions or payments "will not be used as a subterfuge for bribes or illegal payments" and that all payments must be "proper and legal." Any future agreements with foreign distributors or agents were to be approved "by a company attorney" and any questions concerning the policy were to be referred "to the company's General Counsel." App. 165a– 166a. This statement was issued to Upjohn employees worldwide, so that even those interviewees not receiving a questionnaire were aware of the legal implications of the interviews. Pursuant to explicit instructions from the Chairman of the Board, the communications were considered "highly confidential" when made, and have been kept confidential by the company. Consistent with the underlying purposes of the attorney–client privilege, these communications must be protected against compelled disclosure.

The Court of Appeals declined to extend the attorney–client privilege beyond the limits of the control group test for fear that doing so would entail severe burdens on discovery and create a broad "zone of silence" over corporate affairs. Application of the attorney–client privilege to communications such as those involved here, however, puts the adversary in no worse position than if the communications had never taken place. The privilege only protects disclosure of communications; it does not protect disclosure of the underlying facts by those who communicated with the attorney:

> The protection of the privilege extends only to *communications* and not to facts. A fact is one thing and a communication concerning that fact is an entirely different thing. The client cannot be compelled to answer the question "What did you say or write to the attorney?" but may not refuse to disclose any relevant fact within his knowledge merely because he incorporated a statement of such fact into his communication to his attorney. *City of Philadelphia v. Westinghouse Electric Corp.*, 205 F. Supp. 830, 831 (E.D. Pa. 1962).

Here the Government was free to question the employees who communicated with Thomas and outside counsel. Upjohn has provided the IRS with a list of such employees, and the IRS has already interviewed some 25 of them. While it would probably be more convenient for the Government to secure the results of petitioner's internal investigation by simply subpoenaing the questionnaires and notes taken by petitioner's attorneys, such considerations of convenience do not overcome the policies served by the attorney–client privilege. As Justice Jackson noted in his concurring opinion in *Hickman v. Taylor*, 329 U.S., at 516: "Discovery was hardly intended to enable a learned profession to perform its functions . . . on wits borrowed from the adversary."

Needless to say, we decide only the case before us, and do not undertake to draft a set of rules which should govern challenges to investigatory subpoenas. Any such approach would violate the spirit of F.R.E. 501. While such a "case–by–case" basis may to some slight extent undermine desirable certainty in the boundaries of the attorney–client privilege, it obeys the spirit of the Rules. At the same time we conclude that the narrow "control group test" sanctioned by the Court of Appeals in this case cannot, consistent with "the principles of the common law as . . . interpreted . . . in light of reason and experience," F.R.E. 501, govern the development of the law in this area.

Accordingly, the judgment of the Court of Appeals is reversed, and the case remanded for further proceedings.

CHIEF JUSTICE BURGER, concurring in part and concurring in the judgment.

I agree fully with the Court's rejection of the so–called "control group" test, its reasons for doing so, and its ultimate holding that the communications at issue are privileged. As the Court states, however, "if the purpose of the attorney–client privilege is to be served, the attorney and the client must be able to predict with some degree of certainty whether particular discussions will be protected." *Ante,* at 8. For this very reason, I believe that we should articulate a standard that will govern similar cases and afford guidance to corporations, counsel advising them, and federal courts.

* * *

[T]o say we should not reach all facets of the privilege does not mean that we should neglect our duty to provide guidance in a case that squarely presents the question in a traditional adversary context. Indeed, because Federal Rule of Evidence 501 provides that the law of privileges "shall be governed by the principles of the common law as they may be interpreted by the courts of the United States in light of reason and experience," this Court has a special duty to clarify aspects of the law of privileges properly before us. Simply asserting that this failure "may to some slight extent undermine desirable certainty" neither minimizes the consequences of continuing uncertainty and confusion nor harmonizes the inherent dissonance of acknowledging that uncertainty while declining to clarify it within the frame of issues presented.

NOTE

Do you agree with the *Upjohn* Court? Are the communications of the lower echelon employees (outside the control group) as likely to be affected by the existence *vel non* of a privilege as the communications of control group members? Is it not safe to assume that lower echelon employees will normally report data to their superiors out of a general sense of business duty—rather than because of any motivation to obtain legal advice?

Unlike a natural person, an entity cannot represent itself in court. *In re Bigelow*, 179 F.3d 1164, 1165 (9th Cir. 1999),. Thus, whenever there is a realistic possibility of litigation, the entity must turn to counsel. Further, the turnover rate in the American workforce is quite high. "According to a BNA survey, one in seven permanent employees switched jobs in 1999.. . ." Semmes, *Rising Employee Turnover Rate Puts Spotlight on Agreements to Protect Trade Secrets*, 69 U.S.L.W. (BNA) 2211 (Oct. 17, 2000). Hence, an entity would take a huge legal risk if it did not order its employees to disclose relevant information to counsel immediately.

The involvement of an intermediary. Normally the client and attorney communicate directly. However, direct communication is sometimes impossible. Suppose, for example, that Devitt were not fluent in English. Common sense would move the attorney to have an interpreter present during the interview of Devitt. In this situation, the interpreter's presence would not negate the privilege. *See Federal Trade Comm'n v. TRW, Inc.*, 479 F. Supp. 160, 163 n.7 (D.C.C. 1979). We can go further. Suppose that Devitt were charged with a tax offense. Devitt brings to the attorney–client interview not only his voluminous records but also an accountant to help him interpret the records for the attorney. There is authority that even here the accountant's presence does not negate the privilege. *See United States v. Kovel*, 296 F.2d 918 (2d Cir. 1961); *In re Consolidated Litig. Concerning Int'l Harvester's Disposition of Wis. Steel*, 666 F. Supp. 1148, 1157 (N.D. Ill. 1987) (collecting the most recent cases following *Kovel,* including decisions rendered after the adoption of the Federal Rules of Evidence). The extension of the attorney–client privilege to communications with experts now appears to be the majority view. *Miller v. District Court*, 737 P.2d 834 (Colo. 1987); *Haynes v. State*, 103 Nev. 309, 739 P.2d 497 (1987).

In these fact situations, some courts have been willing to treat the expert as a necessary intermediary between the attorney and client. The information being interpreted emanates from the client, but the client lacks the expertise to effectively interpret the information for the attorney. The expert's intervention is either absolutely or relatively necessary for effective communication between attorney and client. When this doctrine comes into play, the courts have extended the privilege to (a) the client's disclosures to the expert (*People v. Goldbach*, 27 Cal. App. 3d 563, 103 Cal. Rptr. 800 (1972); *contra Granviel v. Estelle*, 655 F.2d 673 (5th Cir. 1981)); (b) the knowledge the expert acquires and the opinion the expert forms (*San Francisco v. Superior Court*, 37 Cal. 2d 227, 231 P.2d 26 (1951)); and (c) any written report the expert submits to the attorney. (*Jones v. Superior Court*, 58 Cal. 2d 56, 372 P.2d 919, 22 Cal. Rptr. 879 (1962).)

PROBLEMS

1. Problem 26–10. In *Devitt*, the defense decides to raise an insanity defense. To prepare for trial, the defense attorney sends Devitt to a psychiatrist for an evaluation. Will the attorney–client privilege attach? *State v. Pratt*, 284 Md. 516, 398 A.2d 421, 423–24 (1979); Casenote, 9 U. Balt. L. Rev. 99 (1979). *But see State v. Carter*, 641 S.W.2d 54, 57 (Mo. 1982).

2. Problem 26–11. In our torts case, attorney for Polecat Motors hires a safety engineer and sends the engineer to the site of the accident to identify any features of the section of road that might have caused the accident. Will the privilege attach to the report the expert prepares on that subject? *See Grand Lake Drive–In v. Superior Court*, 179 Cal. App. 2d 122, 125–28, 3 Cal. Rptr. 621, 624–27 (1960).

3)   Special Exceptions to the Attorney–Client Privilege

The California statutes list most of the recognized exceptions to this privilege:

§ 956. Lawyer Obtained to Aid in Planning, Committing Crime.

There is no privilege under this article if the services of the lawyers were sought or obtained to enable or aid anyone to commit or plan to commit a crime or a fraud.

§ 957. Communication Between Parties Claiming Under Deceased Client.

There is no privilege under this article as to a communication relevant to an issue between parties all of whom claim through a deceased client, regardless of whether the claims are by testate or intestate succession or by inter vivos transaction.

§ 958. Communications of Issue of Breach of Duty—Lawyer–Client.

There is no privilege under this article as to a communication relevant to an issue of breach, by the lawyer or by the client, of a duty arising out of the lawyer–client relationship.

§ 959. Communication of Intention or Competence of Client Executing Attested Document.

There is no privilege under this article as to a communication relevant to an issue concerning the intention or competence of a client executing an attested document of which the lawyer is an attesting witness, or concerning the execution.

§ 960. Communication of Intention of Deceased Client with Respect to Writing Affecting Property Interest.

There is no privilege under this article as to a communication relevant to an issue concerning the intention of a client, now deceased, with respect to a deed of conveyance, will, or other writing, executed by the client, purporting to affect an interest in property.

§ 961. Validity of Writing by Deceased Client Affecting Interest in Property.

There is no privilege under this article as to a communication relevant to an issue concerning the validity of a deed of conveyance, will, or other writing, executed by a client, now deceased, purporting to affect an interest in property.

§ 962. Communication Made Where Two or More Clients Retain Same Lawyer *in Matter of Common Interest.*

Where two or more clients have retained or consulted a lawyer upon a matter of common interest, none of them, nor one successor in interest of any of them, may claim a privilege under this article as to a communication made in the course of that relationship when such communication is offered in a civil proceeding between one of such clients (or his successor in interest) and another of such clients (or his successor in interest).

NOTES AND PROBLEMS

1. Consider the situation in which a client tells her lawyer that she plans to commit fraud, robbery or assault. Must or may the lawyer disclose the client's plan to the authorities? The answer can depend upon whether the jurisdiction follows the Model Code of Professional Responsibility, Model Rules of Professional Conduct, or special state law. *See generally*, Zacharias, *Federalizing Legal Ethics*, 73 TEX. L. REV. 335 (1994). Despite the language of § 956, California takes a very strict approach to requiring lawyers to preserve client confidentiality. *Id.* at 359. *See also* Mosteller, *Child Abuse Reporting Laws and Attorney–Client Confidences: The Reality and Specter of Lawyer as Informant*, 42 DUKE L. J. 203 (1992).

2. Problem 26–12. If Devitt subsequently accuses his attorney of ineffective representation or if the products liability plaintiff later sues her attorney for malpractice, should the attorney be permitted to use otherwise privileged communications to respond? Suppose that the ethics committee of the State Bar leveled that charge. Should the result be the same? What result under California Evidence Code § 958?

———

Although California courts have the benefit of a statute codifying the crime–fraud exception, there is no corresponding statute in federal practice.

However, the federal courts recognized the exception as a matter of common law before the adoption of the Federal Rules. In the following case, the Supreme Court confronted two questions, *inter alia:* (1) whether the exception survived the passage of the Federal Rules; and (2) if so, whether, in deciding whether to invoke the exception, the trial judge may order the party claiming the privilege to submit the allegedly privileged material to the judge for *in camera* examination. Think back to the discussion of preliminary fact–finding procedures under Rule 104. Remember that the last sentence of Rule 104(a) reads: "In making its determination [the court] is not bound by the rules of evidence except those with respect to privileges."

The catalyst for this case was a protracted, high–profile Internal Revenue Service investigation of the Church of Scientology and its founder, L. Ron Hubbard. In an earlier California state case, the church had sued a former member, Gerald Armstrong, who had allegedly illegally taken documents belonging to the church. The parties to the state case filed several documents, including some tapes about the church's activities, with the clerk of the court, Mr. Zolin, under seal. The I.R.S. then served a summons on Zolin to produce the tapes. The I.R.S. filed a petition to enforce the summons. In support of its petition, the I.R.S. filed with the federal district court partial transcripts of the tapes. The I.R.S. claimed that it lawfully obtained the transcripts from a confidential source. The church opposed enforcement of the summons on the ground that the tapes were attorney–client communications, and the I.R.S. countered that the tapes were subject to the crime or fraud exception to the privilege.

UNITED STATES v. ZOLIN

491 U.S. 554 (1989)

JUSTICE BLACKMUN delivered the opinion of the Court.

[This case arose out of an I.R.S. investigation of L. Ron Hubbard, founder of the Church of Scientology.]

* * *

Questions of privilege that arise in the course of the adjudication of federal rights are "governed by the principles of the common law as they may be interpreted by the courts of the United States in the light of reason and experience." Fed. Rule Evid. 501. We have recognized the attorney–client privilege under federal law, as "the oldest of the privileges for confidential communications known to the common law." *Upjohn Co. v. United States*, 449 U.S. 383, 389 (1981). . . .

The attorney–client privilege is not without its costs. Cf. *Trammel v. United States*, 445 U.S. 40, 50, (1980). "[S]ince the privilege has the effect of withholding relevant information from the factfinder, it applies only where necessary to achieve its purpose." *Fisher*, 425 U.S., at 403. The attorney–client privilege must necessarily protect the confidences of wrongdoers, but the reason for that protection—the centrality of open client and attorney communication to the proper functioning of our adversary system of justice—"ceas[es] to operate at a certain point, namely, where the desired advice refers *not to prior wrongdoing,* but to *future wrongdoing.*" 8 Wigmore, § 2298, p. 573 (emphasis in original). . . . It is the purpose of the crime–fraud exception to the attorney–client privilege to assure that the "seal of secrecy," *ibid.,* between lawyer and client does not extend to communications "made for the purpose of getting advice for the commission of a fraud" or crime. *O'Rourke v. Darbishire,* [1920] A.C. 581, 604.

The District Court and the Court of Appeals found that the tapes at issue in this case recorded attorney–client communications. [That] finding [is] not at issue here. Thus, the remaining obstacle to respondents' successful assertion of the privilege is the IRS' contention that the recorded attorney–client communications were made in furtherance of a future crime or fraud.

A variety of questions may arise when a party raises the crime–fraud exception. The parties to this case have not been in complete agreement as to which of these questions are presented here. In an effort to clarify the matter, we observe, first, that we need not decide the quantum of proof necessary ultimately to establish the applicability of the crime–fraud exception. *Cf. Clark,* 289 U.S., at 15, quoting O'Rourke, S. Stone & R. Liebman, Testimonial Privileges § 1.65, p. 107 (1983).[7] Rather, we are concerned here with the *type* of evidence that may be used to make that ultimate showing. Within that general area of inquiry, the initial question in this case is whether a district court, at the request of the party opposing the privilege, may review the allegedly privileged communications *in camera* to determine whether the crime–fraud exception applies. If such *in camera* review is permitted, the second question we must consider is whether some threshold evidentiary showing is needed before the district court may undertake the requested review. Finally, if a threshold showing is required, we must consider the type of evidence the opposing party may use to meet it: *i.e.,* in this case, whether the partial transcripts the IRS possessed may be used for that purpose.

We consider the question whether a district court may *ever* honor the request of the party opposing the privilege to conduct an *in camera* review

---

[7] We note, however, that this Court's use in *Clark v. United States,* 289 U.S. 1, 14 (1933), of the phrase "*prima facie* case" to describe the showing needed to defeat the privilege, has caused some confusion. *See* Gardner, The Crime or Fraud Exception to the Attorney–Client Privilege, 47 A.B.A.J. 708, 710–711 (1961); Note, 51 Brooklyn L. Rev. 913, 918–919 (1985) ("The *prima facie* standard is commonly used by courts in civil litigation to *shift* the burden of proof from one party to the other. In the context of the fraud exception, however, the standard is used to dispel the privilege altogether *without* affording the client an opportunity to rebut the *prima facie* showing" (emphasis in original)). *See also In re Grand Jury Subpoena Duces Tecum Dated September 15, 1983,* 731 F.2d 1032, 1039 (CA2 1984). In using the phrase in *Clark,* the Court was aware of scholarly controversy concerning the role of the judge in the decision of such preliminary questions of fact. *See* 289 U.S., at 14, n. *. The quantum of proof needed to establish admissibility was then, and remains, subject to question. *See, e.g.,* Maguire & Epstein, Preliminary Questions of Fact in Determining the Admissibility of Evidence, 40 Harv. L. Rev. 392, 400 (criticizing courts insofar as they "have allowed themselves to be led into holding that only a superficial, one–sided showing is allowable on any admissibility controversy"), 414–424 (exploring alternative rules) (1927); 21 C. Wright & K. Graham, Federal Practice and Procedure: Evidence § 5052, p. 248 (1977) (suggesting, with respect to the process of proving preliminary questions of fact, that "[p]erhaps it is a task, like riding a bicycle, that is easier to do if you do not think too much about what you are doing"). In light of the narrow question presented here for review, this case is not the proper occasion to visit these questions.

of allegedly privileged communications to determine whether those communications fall within the crime–fraud exception. We conclude that no express provision of the Federal Rules of Evidence bars such use of *in camera* review, and that it would be unwise to prohibit it in all instances as a matter of federal common law.

At first blush, two provisions of the Federal Rules of Evidence would appear to be relevant. Rule 104(a) provides: "Preliminary questions concerning the qualification of a person to be a witness, *the existence of a privilege,* or the admissibility of evidence shall be determined by the court. . . . In making its determination it is not bound by rules of evidence *except those with respect to privileges*" (emphasis added). Rule 1101(c) provides: "The rule with respect to privileges applies at all stages of all actions, cases, and proceedings." Taken together, these Rules might be read to establish that in a summons–enforcement proceeding, attorney–client communications cannot be considered by the district court in making its crime–fraud ruling: to do otherwise, under this view, would be to make the crime–fraud determination without due regard to the existence of the privilege.

Even those scholars who support this reading of Rule 104(a) acknowledge that it leads to an absurd result.

> "Because the judge must honor claims of privilege made during his preliminary fact determinations, many exceptions to the rules of privilege will become 'dead letters,' since the preliminary facts that give rise to these exceptions can never be proved. For example, an exception to the attorney–client privilege provides that there is no privilege if the communication was made to enable anyone to commit a crime or fraud. There is virtually no way in which the exception can ever be proved, save by compelling disclosure of the contents of the communication; Rule 104(a) provides that this cannot be done." 21 C. Wright & K. Graham, Federal Practice & Procedure: Evidence § 5055, p. 276 (1977) (footnote omitted).

We find this Draconian interpretation of Rule 104(a) inconsistent with the Rule's plain language. The Rule does not provide by its terms that all materials as to which a "clai[m] of privilege" is made must be excluded from consideration. In that critical respect, the language of Rule 104(a) is markedly different from the comparable California evidence rule, which provides that "the presiding officer may not require disclosure of information *claimed to be privileged* under this division in order to rule on the claim of privilege." Cal. Evidence Code § 915(a) (West 1966 & Supp. 1989) (emphasis added).[10] There

---

[10] A good example of the effect of the California rule is provided by the record in this case. While the disputed matters were being briefed in Federal District Court, the state Superior Court held a hearing on a motion by Government attorneys seeking access to materials in the Armstrong case for ongoing litigation in Washington, D.C. The transcript of the hearing was made part of the record before the District Court in this case. Regarding the tapes, the Government argued to the Superior Court that the attorney–client conversations on the tapes reflect the planning or commission of a crime or fraud. Transcripts of Hearing of February 11, 1985, p. 52. That claim was supported by several declarations and other extrinsic evidence. The Government noted, however, that "the tape recordings themselves would . . . be the best evidence of exactly what was going on." *Id.,* at 53. The intervenors stressed that, as a *matter of California* law, "you can't show the tapes are not privileged by the contents." *Id.,* 58; *see also Id.,* at 68. The Superior Court acknowledged the premise that "you can't look at the conversation itself to make [the crime-fraud] determination," *Id.,* at 74, and concluded that the extrinsic evidence was not sufficient to make out a prima facie case that the crime–fraud exception applies. *Id.,* at 75–76.

is no reason to read Rule 104(a) as if its text were identical to that of the California rule.

* * *

In fashioning a standard for determining when *in camera* review is appropriate, we begin with the observation that "*in camera* inspection. . .is a smaller intrusion upon the confidentiality of the attorney–client relationship than is public disclosure." Fried, Too High a Price for Truth: The Exception to the Attorney–Client Privilege for Contemplated Crimes and Frauds, 64 N.C.L.Rev. 443, 467 (1986). We therefore conclude that a lesser evidentiary showing is needed to trigger *in camera* review than is required ultimately to overcome the privilege. *Ibid.* The threshold we set, in other words, need not be a stringent one.

We think that the following standard strikes the correct balance. Before engaging in *in camera* review to determine the applicability of the crime–fraud exception, "the judge should require a showing of a factual basis adequate to support a good faith belief by a reasonable person," *Caldwell v. District Court*, 644 P. 2d 26, 33 (Colo. 1982), that *in camera* review of the materials may reveal evidence to establish the claim that the crime–fraud exception applies. . .

The question remains as to what kind of evidence a district court may consider in determining whether it has the discretion to undertake an *in camera* review of an allegedly privileged communcation at the behest of the party opposing the privilege. Here the issue is whether the partial transcripts may be used by the IRS in support of its request for *in camera* review of the tapes. The answer to that question. . .must be found in Rule 104(a), which establishes that materials that have been determined to be privileged may not be considered in making the preliminary determination of the existence of a privilege. Neither the District Court nor the Court of Appeals made factual findings as to the privileged nature of the partial transcripts, so we cannot determine on this record whether Rule 104(a) would bar their consideration. Assuming for the moment, however, that no rule of privilege bars the IRS' use of the partial transcripts, we fail to see what purpose would be served by excluding the transcripts from the District Court's consideration.. . .Permitting district courts to consider this type of evidence would aid them substantially in rapidly and reliably determining whether *in camera* review is appropriate. . . .We conclude that the party opposing the privilege may use any nonprivileged evidence in support of its request for *in camera* review, even if its evidence is not "independent" of the contested communications. . . .

We. . .hold. . .that before a district court may engage in *in camera* review at the request of the party opposing the privilege, that party must present evidence sufficient to support a reasonable belief that *in camera* review may yield evidence that establishes the exception's applicability. [Further], we hold that the threshold showing to obtain *in camera* review may be met by using any relevant evidence, lawfully obtained, that has not been adjudicated to be privileged.. . .

NOTES

1. How broad is the scope of the Court's ruling in *Zolin*? Does the Court settle the issue of the measure of the final burden of proof on the question of the applicability of the crime–fraud exception? What precisely is the holding in *Zolin*? *Zolin* seems to contemplate a two–step procedure, a preliminary judicial examination of the allegedly privileged records and a final ruling by the judge.

2. Prior to the adoption of the Federal Rules, federal judges had asserted common law power to require *in camera* examinations. The Court concludes that the common law practice is still good law under Rule 104(a). Is the Court's reasoning persuasive? Justice Blackmun asserts that a contrary interpretation of Rule 104(a) would "lead . . . to an absurd result." It is an ancient maxim of statutory interpretation that, whenever possible, the court should reject a construction which would lead to an absurd result. *Lovely v. Cunningham*, 796 F.2d 1, 5 (1st Cir. 1986). However, the maxim is a dangerous one; a judge may attempt to conceal a debatable policy judgment by mongering the label "absurd." Has Justice Blackmun in effect said that California Evidence Code § 915 is "absurd"? Do you think that the Court would be willing to invalidate § 915 as a violation of due process?

3. On remand in *Zolin*, the court found that the crime–fraud exception applied to the tapes in question. 905 F.2d 1344 (9th Cir. 1990), *cert. denied*, 499 U.S. 920 (1991).

4)   The Duration of the Privilege

SWIDLER & BERLIN v. UNITED STATES

524 U.S. 399 (1998)

Chief Justice REHNQUIST delivered the opinion of the Court.

* * *

This dispute arises out of an investigation conducted by the Office of the Independent Counsel into whether various individuals made false statements, obstructed justice, or committed other crimes during investigations of the 1993 dismissal of employees from the White House Travel Office. Vincent W. Foster, Jr., was Deputy White House Counsel when the firings occurred. In July, 1993, Foster met with petitioner James Hamilton, an attorney at petitioner Swidler & Berlin, to seek legal representation concerning possible congressional or other investigations of the firings. During a 2–hour meeting, Hamilton took three pages of handwritten notes. One of the first entries in the notes is the word "Privileged." Nine days later, Foster committed suicide.

In December 1995, a federal grand jury, at the request of the Independent Counsel, issued subpoenas to petitioners Hamilton and Swidler & Berlin for, *inter alia*, Hamilton's handwritten notes of his meeting with Foster. Petitioners filed a motion to quash, arguing that the notes were protected by the attorney client privilege and by the work product privilege. The District Court, after examining the notes in camera, concluded they were protected from disclosure by both doctrines and denied enforcement of the subpoenas. The Court of Appeals for the District of Columbia Circuit reversed. *In re Sealed Case*, 124 F.3d 230 (1997). While recognizing that most courts assume the privilege survives death, the Court of Appeals noted that holdings actually manifesting the posthumous force of the privilege are rare. Instead, most judicial references to the privilege's posthumous application occur in the context of a well recognized exception allowing disclosure for disputes among the client's heirs. Id., at 231–232. It further noted that most commentators support some measure of posthumous curtailment of the privilege. Id., at 232. The Court of Appeals thought that the risk of posthumous revelation, when confined to the criminal context, would have little to no chilling effect on client communication, but that the costs of protecting communications after death were high. It therefore concluded that the privilege was not absolute in such circumstances, and that instead, a balancing test should apply. Id., at 233–234. It thus held that there is a posthumous exception to the privilege for communications whose relative importance to particular criminal litigation is substantial. Id., at 235. While acknowledging that uncertain privileges are disfavored, *Jaffe v. Redmond*, 518 U.S. 1, 17–18 (1996), the Court of Appeals determined that the uncertainty introduced by its balancing test was insignificant in light of existing exceptions to the privilege. 124 F.3d, at 235. The Court of Appeals also held that the notes were not protected by the work product privilege.

* * *

The Independent Counsel argues that the attorney–client privilege should not prevent disclosure of confidential communications where the client has died and the information is relevant to a criminal proceeding. There is some authority for this position. One state appellate court, *Cohen v. Jenkintown Cab. Co.*, 238 Pa.Super. 456, 357 A.2d 689 (1976), and the Court of Appeals below have held the privilege may be subject to posthumous exceptions in certain circumstances. In *Cohen*, a civil case, the court recognized that the privilege generally survives death, but concluded that it could make an exception where the interest of justice was compelling and the interest of the client in preserving the confidence was insignificant. Id., 462–464, 357 A.2d, at 692–693.

But other than these two decisions, cases addressing the existence of the privilege after death—most involving the testamentary exception–uniformly presume the privilege survives even if they do not so hold. See, e.g., *Mayberry v. Indiana*, 670 N.E.2d 1262 (Ind.1996); *Morris v. Cain*, 39 La. Ann. 712, 1 So. 797 (1887); *People v. Podzelewski*, 611 N.Y.S.2d 22, 203 A.D.2d 594 (1994). Several State Supreme Court decisions expressly hold that the attorney–client privilege extends beyond the death of the client, even in the criminal context. See *In re John Doe Grand Jury Investigation*, 408 Mass. 480, 481–483, 562 N.E.2d 69, 70 (1990); *State v. Doster*, 276 S.C. 647, 650–651, 284 S.E.2d 218, 219 (1981); *State v. Macumber*, 112 Ariz. 569, 571, 544 P.2d 1084, 1086 (1976). . . .

. . . .Undoubtedly, as the Independent Counsel emphasizes, various commentators have criticized this rule, urging that the privilege should be abrogated after the client's death where extreme injustice would result, as long as disclosure would not seriously undermine the privilege by deterring client communication. See, e.g., C. Mueller & L. Kirkpatrick, 2 Federal Evidence § 199, at 380–381 (2d ed. 1994); Restatement (Third) of the Law Governing Lawyers § 127, Comment (Proposed Final Draft No. 1, Mar. 29, 1996). But even these critics clearly recognize that established law supports the continuation of the privilege and that a contrary rule would be a modification of the common law. See, e.g., Mueller & Kirkpatrick, supra, at 379; Restatement of the Law Governing Lawyers, supra, § 127, Comment c; 24 C. Wright & K. Graham, Federal Practice and Procedure §5498, p. 483 (1986).

Despite the scholarly criticism, we think there are weighty reasons that counsel in favor of posthumous application. Knowing that communications will remain confidential even after death encourages the client to communicate fully and frankly with counsel. While the fear of disclosure, and the consequent withholding of information from counsel, may be reduced if disclosure is limited to posthumous disclosure in a criminal context, it seems unreasonable to assume that it vanishes altogether. Clients may be concerned about reputation, civil liability, or possible harm to friends or family. Posthumous disclosure of such communications may be as feared as disclosure during the client's lifetime.

* * *

The Independent Counsel suggests that his proposed exception would have minimal impact if confined to criminal cases, or, as the Court of Appeals suggests, if it is limited to information of substantial importance to a particular criminal case. However, there is no case authority for the proposition that the privilege applies differently in criminal and civil cases, and only one commentator ventures such a suggestion, See Mueller & Kirkpatrick, supra, at 380–381. In any event, a client may not know at the time he discloses information to his attorney whether it will later be relevant to a civil or a criminal matter, let alone whether it will be of substantial importance. Balancing ex post the importance of the information against client interests, even limited to criminal cases, introduces substantial uncertainty into the privilege's application. For just that reason, we have rejected use of a balancing test in defining the contours of the privilege. See *Upjohn*, 449 U.S., at 393; *Jaffe*, supra, at 17–18.

In a similar vein, the Independent Counsel argues that existing exceptions to the privilege, such as the crime–fraud exception and the testamentary exception, make the impact of one more exception marginal. However, these exceptions do not demonstrate that the impact of a posthumous exception would be insignificant, and there is little empirical evidence on this point.[4]

---

[4] Empirical evidence on the privilege is limited. Three studies do not reach firm conclusions on whether limiting the privilege would discourage full and frank communication. Alexander, The Corporate Attorney Client Privilege: A Study of the Participants, 63 St. John's L.Rev. 191 (1989); Zacharias, Rethinking Confidentiality, 74 Iowa L.Rev. 352 (1989); Comment, Functional Overlap Between the Lawyer and Other Professionals: Its Implications for the Privileged Communications Doctrine, 71 Yale L.J. 1226 (1962). These articles note that clients are often uninformed or mistaken about the privilege, but suggest that a substantial number of clients and attorneys think the privilege encourages candor. Two of the articles conclude that a substantial number of clients

The established exceptions are consistent with the purposes of the privilege, see *Glover*, 165 U.S., at 407–408; *United States v. Zolin*, 491 U.S. 554, 562–563 (1989), while a posthumous exception in criminal cases appears at odds with the goals of encouraging full and frank communication and of protecting the client's interests. A "no harm in one more exception" rationale could contribute to the general erosion of the privilege, without reference to common law principles or "reason and experience."

Finally, the Independent Counsel, relying on cases such as *United States v. Nixon*, 418 U.S. 683, 710 (1974), and *Branzburg v. Hayes*, 408 U.S. 665 (1972), urges that privileges be strictly construed because they are inconsistent with the paramount judicial goal of truth seeking. But both *Nixon* and *Branzburg* dealt with the creation of privileges not recognized by the common law, whereas here we deal with one of the oldest recognized privileges in the law. And we are asked not simply to "construe" the privilege, but to narrow it, contrary to the weight of the existing body of caselaw.

* * *

Reversed.

Justice O'CONNOR, with whom Justice SCALIA and Justice THOMAS join, dissenting.

Although the attorney–client privilege ordinarily will survive the death of the client, I do not agree with the Court that it inevitably precludes disclosure of a deceased client's communications in criminal proceedings. In my view, a criminal defendant's right to exculpatory evidence or a compelling law enforcement need for information may, where the testimony is not available from other sources, override a client's posthumous interest in confidentiality.

* * *

I agree that a deceased client may retain a personal, reputational, and economic interest in confidentiality. But, after death, the potential that disclosure will harm the client's interest has been greatly diminished, and the risk that the client will be held criminally liable has abated altogether. Thus, some commentators suggest that terminating the privilege upon the client's death "could not to any substantial degree lessen the encourgement for free disclosure which is [its] purpose." 1 J. Strong, McCormick on Evidence § 94, p. 350 (4th ed. 1992); see also Restatement (Third) of the Law Governing Lawyers § 127, Comment d (Proposed Final Draft No. 1, Mar. 29, 1996). This diminished risk is coupled with a heightened urgency for discovery of a deceased client's communications in the criminal context. The privilege does not "protect [ ] disclosure of the underlying facts by those who communicated with the attorney," Upjohn, supra, at 395, 101 S.Ct., at 685, and were the client living, prosecutors could grant immunity and compel the relevant testimony.

---

and attorneys think the privilege enhances open communication, Alexander, supra, at 244–246, 261, and that the absence of a privilege would be detrimental to such communication, Comment, 71 Yale L.J., supra, at 1236. The third article suggests instead that while the privilege is perceived as important to open communication, limited exceptions to the privilege might not discourage such communication, Zacharias, supra, at 382, 386.

After a client's death, however, if the privilege precludes an attorney from testifying in the client's stead, a complete "loss of crucial information" will often result, see 24 C. Wright & K. Graham, Federal Practice and Procedure § 5498, p. 484 (1986).

As the Court of Appeals observed, the costs of recognizing an absolute posthumous privilege can be inordinately high. *See In re Sealed Case*, 124 F.3d 230, 233–234 (C.A.D.C.1997). Extreme injustice may occur, for example, where a criminal defendant seeks disclosure of a deceased client's confession to the offense. See *State v. Macumber*, 112 Ariz. 569, 571, 544 P.2d 1084, 1086 (1976); cf. *In the Matter of John Doe Grand Jury Investigation*, 408 Mass. 480, 486, 562 N.E.2d 69, 72 (1990) (Nolan, J., dissenting). In my view, the paramount value that our criminal justice system places on protecting an innocent defendant should outweigh a deceased client's interest in preserving confidences. See, e.g., *Schlup v. Delo*, 513 U.S. 298, 324–325 (1995); *In re Winship*, 397 U.S. 358, 371 (1970) (Harlan, J., concurring).. . .

Moreover, as the Court concedes, there is some authority for the proposition that a deceased client's communications may be revealed, even in circumstances outside of the testamentary context. California's Evidence Code, for example, provides that the attorney–client privilege continues only until the deceased client's estate is finally distributed, noting that "there is little reason to preserve secrecy at the expense of excluding relevant evidence after the estate is wound up and the representative is discharged." Cal. Evid. Code Ann. § 954, and comment, p. 232, § 952 (West 1995). And a state appellate court has admitted an attorney's testimony concerning a deceased client's communications after "balanc[ing] the necessity for revealing the substance of the [attorney–client conversation] against the unlikelihood of any cognizable injury to the rights, interests, estate or memory of [the client]." See Cohen, supra, at 464, 357 A.2d, at 693. The American Law Institute, moreover, has recently recommended withholding the privilege when the communication "bears on a litigated issue of pivotal significance" and has suggested that courts "balance the interest in confidentiality against any exceptional need for the communication." Restatement (Third) of the Law Governing Lawyers § 127, at 431, Comment d; see also 2 C. Mueller & L. Kirkpatrick, Federal Evidence, § 199, p.380 (2d ed. 1994) ("[I]f a deceased client has confessed to criminal acts that are later charged to another, surely the latter's need for evidence sometimes outweighs the interest in preserving the confidences").

Where the exoneraton of an innocent criminal defendant or a compelling law enforcement interest is at stake, the harm of precluding critical evidence that is unavailable by any other means outweighs the potential disincentive to forthright communication. In my view, the cost of silence warrants a narrow exception to the rule that the attorney–client privilege survives the death of the client. . . .

NOTES AND QUESTIONS

1. There are several parallels between *Swidler & Berlin* and *Jaffee v. Redmond*, 518 U.S. 1 (1996), the case announcing the existence of a federal psychotherapist privilege. As in *Jaffee*, although the lower court cited both instrumental and humanistic rationales for the privilege, the Supreme Court chose to rely exclusively on instrumental reasoning.

2. A further parallel is that as in *Jaffee*, in footnote the lead opinion in *Swidler & Berlin* appeals to empirical research to justify its decision. The Court's decision to rely on the instrumental theory helps explain why the Court felt obliged to point to any empirical evidence supporting the behavioral assumption that clients would not consult attorneys or make necessary revelations but for the existence of a privilege. However as we shall see in Section C.2 *infra*, on close scrutiny, the studies cited in *Jaffee* did not bear out the generalization that in the typical case, the patient would either not consult a therapist or divulge essential information but for the assurance of confidentiality furnished by an evidentiary privilege. Other commentators have reached the same conclusion about the attorney–client studies in *Swidler & Berlin*. Wydick, *The Attorney–Client Privilege: Does It Really Have Life Everlasting?*, 87 K.Y.L.J. 1165, 1173–74 (1999).

3. Does the *Swidler & Berlin* decision signal that in the future, the Court will be more receptive to novel privilege claims? In a sense, is *Swidler & Berlin* a status quo decision? The Court pointed out that the weight of authority favored the view that even after the client's death, the privilege both survived and remained absolute in character. In the Court's mind, the Independent Counsel was proposing a novel exception to the scope of an existing privilege.

2. THE WORK PRODUCT DOCTRINE

When the attorney–client privilege applies, it provides absolute protection, unless there is some exception or waiver. That is, barring exception or waiver, no showing of need for the evidence—no matter how compelling—can breach the privilege. It is in this sense that the attorney–client privilege is regarded as an "absolute privilege."

Other evidentiary protections also apply to legal service providers. The other major one protects attorney's work product. Some consider work product protection as a qualified privilege. Others regard it not as a privilege at all; just as a doctrine that provides presumptive protection to certain types of legal work products, <u>unless</u> those seeking disclosure make a sufficient showing of need for the information. The latter is probably a more illuminating perspective.

HICKMAN v. TAYLOR

329 U.S. 495 (1947)

JUSTICE MURPHY delivered the opinion of the Court.

This case presents an important problem under the Federal Rules of Civil Procedure as to the extent to which a party may inquire into oral and written statements of witnesses, or other information, secured by an adverse party's counsel in the course of preparation for possible litigation after a claim has arisen. Examination into a person's files and records, including those resulting from the professional activities of an attorney, must be judged with care. It is not without reason that various safeguards have been established to preclude unwarranted excursions into the privacy of a man's work. At the same time, public policy supports reasonable and necessary inquiries. Properly to balance these competing interests is a delicate and difficult task.

[A tug boat sank while helping to tow a car float of the Baltimore & Ohio Railroad across the Delaware River. The cause of the accident was unknown. Five of the nine crew members were drowned. Three days later the tug owners and the underwriters employed a law firm, of which attorney Fortenbaugh was a member, to defend them against potential suits by representatives of the deceased crew members and to sue the railroad for damages to the tug. After a public administrative hearing at which four survivors testified (such testimony was recorded and made available to all interested parties), Fortenbaugh interviewed and obtained signed statements from the survivors. He also interviewed other persons, sometimes making notes or "memoranda." One year after the filing of the claim, plaintiff filed interrogatories directed to the tug owners, asking for copies of the statements of any survivors and "if oral, set forth in detail the exact provisions of any such oral statements or reports." Upon refusal to make disclosure, Fortenbaugh and his clients were held in contempt.]

* * *

We also agree that the memoranda, statements and mental impressions at issue in this case fall outside the scope of the attorney–client privilege and hence are not protected from discovery on that basis. It is unnecessary here to delineate the content and scope of that privilege as recognized in the federal courts. For present purposes, it suffices to note that the protective cloak of this privilege does not extend to information which an attorney secures from a witness while acting for his client in anticipation of litigation. Nor does this privilege concern the memoranda, briefs, communications and other writings prepared by counsel for his own use in prosecuting his client's case; and it is equally unrelated to writings which reflect an attorney's mental impressions, conclusions, opinions or legal theories.

But the impropriety of invoking that privilege does not provide an answer to the problem before us. Petitioner has made more than an ordinary request for relevant, non–privileged facts in the possession of his adversaries or their counsel. He has sought discovery as of right of oral and written statements of witnesses whose identity is well known and whose availability to petitioner appears unimpaired. He has sought production of these matters after making the most searching inquiries of his opponents as to the circumstances surrounding the fatal accident, which inquiries were sworn to have been answered to the best of their information and belief. Interrogatories were directed toward all the events prior to, during and subsequent to the sinking of the tug. Full and honest answers to such broad inquiries would necessarily have included all pertinent information gleaned by Fortenbaugh through his interviews with the witnesses. Petitioner makes no suggestion, and we cannot assume, that the tug owners or Fortenbaugh were incomplete or dishonest in the framing of their answers. In addition, petitioner was free to examine the public testimony of the witnesses taken before the United States Steamboat Inspectors. We are thus dealing with an attempt to secure the production of written statements and mental impressions contained in the files and the mind of the attorney Fortenbaugh without any showing of necessity or any indication or claim that denial of such production would unduly prejudice the preparation of petitioner's case or cause him any hardship or injustice. For aught that appears, the essence of what petitioner seeks either has been revealed to him already through the interrogatories or is readily available to him direct from the witnesses for the asking.

The District Court, after hearing objections to petitioner's request, commanded Fortenbaugh to produce all written statements of witnesses and to state in substance any facts learned through oral statements of witnesses to him. Fortenbaugh was to submit any memoranda he had made of the oral statements so that the court might determine what portions should be revealed to petitioner. All of this was ordered without any showing by petitioner, or any requirement that he make a proper showing, of the necessity for the production of any of this material or any demonstration that denial of production would cause hardship or injustice. The court simply ordered production on the theory that the facts sought were material and were not privileged as constituting attorney–client communications.

In our opinion, neither Rule 26 nor any other rule dealing with discovery contemplates production under such circumstances. That is not because the subject matter is privileged or irrelevant, as those concepts are used in these rules. Here is simply an attempt, without purported necessity or justification, to secure written statements, private memoranda and personal recollections prepared or formed by an adverse party's counsel in the course of his legal duties. As such, it falls outside the arena of discovery and contravenes the public policy underlying the orderly prosecution and defense of legal claims. Not even the most liberal of discovery theories can justify unwarranted inquiries into the files and the mental impressions of an attorney.

In performing his various duties, it is essential that a lawyer work with a certain degree of privacy, free from unnecessary intrusion by opposing parties and their counsel. Proper preparation of a client's case demands that he assemble information, sift what he considers to be the relevant from the irrelevant facts, prepare his legal theories and plan his strategy without undue and needless interference. That is the historical and the necessary way in which lawyers act within the framework of our system of jurisprudence to promote justice and to protect their clients' interests. This work is reflected, of course, in interviews, statements, memoranda, correspondence, briefs, mental impressions, personal beliefs, and countless other tangible and intangible ways—aptly though roughly termed by the Circuit Court of Appeals in this case as the "work product of the lawyer." Were such materials open to opposing counsel on mere demand, much of what is now put down in writing would remain unwritten. An attorney's thoughts, heretofore inviolate, would not be his own. Inefficiency, unfairness and sharp practices would inevitably develop in the giving of legal advice and in the preparation of cases for trial. The effect on the legal profession would be demoralizing. And the interests of the clients and the cause of justice would be poorly served.

We do not mean to say that all written materials obtained or prepared by an adversary's counsel with an eye toward litigation are necessarily free from discovery in all cases. Where relevant and non–privileged facts remain hidden in an attorney's file and where production of those facts is essential to the preparation of one's case, discovery may properly be had. Such written statements and documents might, under certain circumstances, be admissible in evidence or give clues as to the existence or location of relevant facts. Or they might be useful for purposes of impeachment or corroboration. And production might be justified where the witnesses are no longer available or can be reached only with difficulty. . . .

But as to oral statements made by witnesses to Fortenbaugh, whether presently in the form of his mental impressions or memoranda, we do not believe that any showing of necessity can be made under the circumstances of this case so as to justify production. Under ordinary conditions, forcing an attorney to repeat or write out all that witnesses have told him and to deliver the account to his adversary gives rise to grave dangers of inaccuracy and untrustworthiness. No legitimate purpose is served by such production. The practice forces the attorney to testify as to what he remembers or what he saw fit to write down regarding witnesses' remarks. Such testimony could not qualify as evidence; and to use it for impeachment or corroborative purposes would make the attorney much less an officer of the court and much more an ordinary witness. The standards of the profession would thereby suffer.

Denial of production of this nature does not mean that any material, non–privileged facts can be hidden from the petitioner in this case. He need not be unduly hindered in the preparation of his case, in the discovery of facts or in his anticipation of his opponents' position. Searching interrogatories directed to Fortenbaugh and the tug owners, production of written documents and statements upon a proper showing and direct interviews with the witnesses themselves all serve to reveal the facts in Fortenbaugh's possession to the fullest possible extent consistent with public policy. Petitioner's counsel frankly admits that he wants the oral statements only to help prepare himself to examine witnesses and to make sure that he has overlooked nothing. That is insufficient under the circumstances to permit him an exception to the policy underlying the privacy of Fortenbaugh's professional activities. If there should be a rare situation justifying production of these matters, petitioner's case is not of that type.

* * *

The work product doctrine has been extended to criminal cases. *E.g.*, *People v. Municipal Court*, 89 Cal. App. 3d 739, 153 Cal. Rptr. 69 (1979); *Goldberg v. United States*, 425 U.S. 94 (1976); *In re Grand Jury Investigation*, 412 F. Supp. 943 (E.D. Pa. 1976); Feldman, *The Work Product Rule in Criminal Practice and Procedure*, 50 U. Cin. L. Rev. 495 (1981).

Most courts read *Hickman* narrowly; however, they are willing to grant an attorney's mental impressions and trial strategy formed in preparation for litigation more protection than other types of work product information. *E.g.*, *Escalante v. Sentry Ins.*, 49 Wash. App. 375, 743 P.2d 832 (1987). The concept "in preparation for litigation" has engendered endless litigation and academic debate. For a recent recap of the controversy, *See In Re Sealed Case*, 146 F.3d 881 (D.C.Cir. 1998).

NOTES AND PROBLEMS

1. Problem 26–13. In our torts case, Ms. Hill's attorney interviews an eyewitness to the accident before trial. The witness dictates and signs a statement about the accident. Is that statement entitled to work product protection? Suppose that after the witness left the attorney's office, the attorney dictated a memorandum for file, summarizing what the witness told the attorney about the accident in the interview. Protected? Suppose the attorney's summarization is not merely a recap of the interview but also contains hints of how he intends to conduct the witness' direct examination and lists areas where the witness may prove vulnerable to cross–examination. Absolutely protected?

2. Courts and commentators have fashioned a distinction between "ordinary" and "opinion" work product—the latter being accorded much more protection usually. *Compare Duplan Corp. v. Moulinage et Retorderie de Chavanoz*, 509 F.2d 730 (4th Cir. 1974) *with Holmgren v. State Farm Mut. Auto. Ins. Co.*, 976 F.2d 573 (9th Cir. 1992).

3. Problem 26–14. In our torts case, suppose counsel for Polecat Motors tells the company president: "Someday we're going to get sued on this safety issue. Have your people start gathering and compiling data on all accidents or problems that come to their attention. Send everything (including all copies) to me marked '**Privileged—attorney–client/work–product**'." Is the information in the attorney's possession discoverable?

C. MEDICAL PRIVILEGE: PHYSICIAN, PSYCHOTHERAPIST, ETC.

1. AN OVERVIEW

The American Medical Association imposed a confidentiality duty on its members in its first code of ethics in 1847. D. SHUMAN & M. WEINER, THE PSYCHOTHERAPIST–PATIENT PRIVILEGE: A CRITICAL EXAMINATION (1987). The A.M.A. still prescribes that duty:

> A physician may not reveal the confidence entrusted to him in the course of medical attendance, or the deficiencies he may observe in the character of patients, unless he is required to do so by law or unless it becomes necessary in order to protect the welfare of the individual or of the community.

AMERICAN MEDICAL ASSOCIATION, PRINCIPLES OF MEDICAL ETHICS § 9 (1957).

Although the medical privileges did not exist at common law (unlike attorney–client), they were nonetheless among the first to be codified. The first such statute was enacted in New York in 1928:

> No person duly authorized to practice physic or surgery shall be allowed to disclose any information which he may have acquired in

attending any patient, in a professional character, and which information was necessary to enable him to prescribe for such patient as a physician, or to do any act for him as a surgeon.

Statutes creating medical privileges exist in 40 of the 50 states. Shuman & Weiner, *The Privilege Study: An Empirical Examination of the Psychotherapist–Patient Privilege*, 60 N.C. L. REV. 893, 907–911 n.100 (1982). The very existence of these statutes evidences the common law courts' reluctance to recognize a medical privilege as a matter of decisional law. Indeed, courts routinely declare that there is no common law medical privilege. *Whalen v. Roe*, 429 U.S. 589, 602 n.28 (1977); *Patterson v. Caterpillar, Inc.*, 70 F.3d 503, 506–07 (7th Cir. 1995); *Perkins v. United States*, 877 F. Supp. 330, 332 (E.D. Tex. 1995).

What accounts for that reluctance? Is the medical relationship somehow less important than the legal relationship? Is there less need for a medical privilege? Given the stakes in medical care—the preservation of life and the prevention of pain, how likely is it that the absence of a privilege will deter the patient from making full disclosure to the physician? Shuman & Weiner, *supra*.

When it drafted the new Federal Rules of Evidence, the Advisory Committee decided to omit a general physician–patient privilege, opting instead for only a psychotherapist–patient privilege. In the Note accompanying proposed Rule 504 on the psychotherapist–patient privilege, the Committee asserted that the courts and legislatures have recognized so many exceptions to the physician–patient privilege that "little if any basis for the privilege" remains. Even the advocates of medical privileges ordinarily concede than the case for a psychotherapist privilege is stronger than the case for a general physician–patient privilege.

NOTES AND PROBLEMS

1. Suppose that in the *Devitt* case, the defendant consulted a physician the day after the alleged battery. If Devitt told the physician: "I've got some bruises on my chest where a guy punched me," that statement would fall within the orthodox definition of "communication" and be protected by the privilege. However, assume that rather than making that statement, Devitt took off his shirt, displayed the bruises and scratches to the physician, and winced painfully when touched. The physician could not testify to his or her observation of the injuries over Devitt's objection. Comment, 56 Nw. U.L. REV. 263, 270–71 (1961).

2. Problem 26–15. Suppose that the physician orders a blood test of Devitt and the technician informs the physician that Devitt's blood type is A. Can Devitt preclude the physician from revealing that fact?

———————

Treatment vs. forensic purposes. Earlier we studied the hearsay exception for statements made for medical purposes. As we saw, in most jurisdictions that exception is limited to statements the patient makes with a view to treatment or diagnosis. The medical privilege is similarly limited. In *Devitt,* assume that as part of pretrial preparation, defense counsel sends Devitt to a serologist for a blood grouping test. The medical privilege would not attach, since the purpose is legal rather than medical. However, what if defense counsel sends Devitt to a psychotherapist and Devitt discloses his inner–most thoughts?

NOTES AND PROBLEMS

1. Problem 26–16. To prepare for trial, Ms. Hill's attorney sends her to Dr. Legomsky for a physical evaluation. Prior to this, Ms. Hill had never consulted Dr. Legomsky. As she walks into Legomsky's examination room, Ms. Hill tells the doctor, "My attorney sent me. I'm here for that exam to get ready for trial." Legomsky says, "Fine. I'll get all the facts and send the report straight to your lawyer." Dr. Legomsky spends an hour examining Ms. Hill. Just before she leaves, Legomsky says, "You know it wouldn't be a bad idea if you started using a salve on those real bad burns on your ankles. In addition, twice–a–day baths with oil might help restore some of that skin tissue." Within a week, Legomsky sends his report to Ms. Hill's attorney. Is the report protected by the physician–patient privilege? What if, as Ms. Hill walks into the examination room, she tells Dr. Legomsky, "I'm here for that exam to get ready for trial. In addition, Doc, the burnt skin around my ankles has been very sensitive lately; it hurts all the time. I'd really appreciate it if you could advise me." Protected?

2. A growing number of jurisdictions recognize a special exception to the medical privilege in child abuse cases. These jurisdictions have enacted statutes requiring physicians to report suspected child abuse to the authorities and eliminating any privilege precluding the physician from testifying about the child's injuries at a subsequent prosecution. *E.g.*, Minn. Stat. § 626.556 (the Minnesota Maltreatment of Minors Reporting Act), *construed in State v. Andring*, 342 N.W.2d 128 (Minn. 1984). As with the attorney–client relationship, the duty of confidentiality can present agonizing conflicts for medical professionals, particularly when revealing a patient's confidences could prevent physical harm to others. *See* Fleming & Maximov, *The Patient or His Victim: The Therapist's Dilemma*, 62 Cal. L. Rev. 1025 (1974) *cited in Tarasoff v. Regents of University of California*, 17 Cal. 3d 425, 131 Cal. Rptr. 14, 551 P.2d 334 (1976).

2. SPECIALIZED ASPECTS: THE PSYCHOTHERAPIST PRIVILEGE

At first, there was no separate psychotherapist–patient privilege. The only available protection was the traditional physician–patient privilege. If the psychotherapist were a licensed physician practicing psychiatry, the traditional privilege applied; otherwise, there was no protection. Understandably, as society came to accept—and expect—the services of non–physician psychotherapists, a tension was generated. Psychotherapists argued that confidentiality is even more essential to their profession than it is to the practice of medicine. They have been persuasive in stating their separate case. In its commentary on the California statutory privilege, the Report of the California Senate Committee on the Judiciary explained:

> A broad privilege should apply to both psychiatrists and certified psychologists. Psychoanalysis and psychotherapy are dependent upon the fullest revelation of the most intimate and embarrassing details of the patient's life. Research on mental or emotional problems requires similar disclosure. Unless a patient or research subject is assured that such information can and will be held in utmost confidence, he will be reluctant to make the full disclosure upon which diagnosis and treatment or complete and accurate research depends.

> The Law Revision Commission has received several reliable reports that persons in need of treatment sometimes refuse such treatment from psychiatrists because the confidentiality of their communications cannot be assured under existing law. Many of these persons are seriously disturbed and constitute threats to other persons in the community. Accordingly, this article establishes a new privilege that grants to patients of psychiatrists a privilege much broader in scope than the ordinary physician–patient privilege. Although it is recognized that the granting of the privilege may operate in particular cases to withhold relevant information, the interests of society will be better served if psychiatrists are able to assure patients that their confidences will be protected.

> The Commission has also been informed that adequate research cannot be carried on in this field unless persons examined in connection therewith can be guaranteed that their disclosures will be kept confidential.

The same Federal Rules Advisory Committee that rejected a general physician–patient privilege was willing to codify a psychotherapist–patient privilege. The committee alluded to the psychotherapist's "special need to maintain confidentiality." Given that special need, the Committee proposed Rule 504:

Psychotherapist–Patient Privilege

[Not enacted.]

(a) Definitions.

(1) A "patient" is a person who consults or is examined or interviewed by a psychotherapist.

(2) A "psychotherapist" is (A) a person authorized to practice medicine in any state or nation, or reasonably believed by the patient so to be, while engaged in the diagnosis or treatment of a mental or emotional condition, including drug addiction, or (B) a person licensed or certified as a psychologist under the laws of any state or nation, while similarly engaged.

(3) A communication is "confidential" if not intended to be disclosed to third persons other than those present to further the interest of the patient in the consultation, examination, or interview, or persons reasonably

necessary for the transmission of the communication, or persons who are participating in the diagnosis and treatment under the direction of the psychotherapist, including members of the patient's family.

(b) General rule of privilege. A patient has a privilege to refuse to disclose and to prevent any other person from disclosing confidential communications, made for the purposes of diagnosis or treatment of his mental or emotional condition, including drug addiction, among himself, his psychotherapist, or persons who are participating in the diagnosis or treatment under the direction of the psychotherapist, including members of the patient's family.

(c) Who may claim the privilege. The privilege may be claimed by the patient, by his guardian or conservator, or by the personal representative of a deceased patient. The person who was the psychotherapist may claim the privilege but only on behalf of the patient. His authority so to do is presumed in the absence of evidence to the contrary.

(d) Exceptions.

(1) Proceedings for hospitalization. There is no privilege under this rule for communications relevant to an issue in proceedings to hospitalize the patient for mental illness, if the psychotherapist in the course of diagnosis or treatment has determined that the patient is in need of hospitalization.

(2) Examination by order of judge. If the judge orders an examination of the mental or emotional condition of the patient, communications made in the course thereof are not privileged under this rule with respect to the particular purpose for which the examination is ordered unless the judge orders otherwise.

(3) Condition an element of claim or defense. There is no privilege under this rule as to communications relevant to an issue of the mental or emotional condition of the patient in any proceeding in which he relies upon the condition as an element of his claim or defense, or, after the patient's death, in any proceeding in which any party relies upon the condition as an element of his claim or defense.

JAFFEE v. REDMOND

518 U.S. 1 (1996)

JUSTICE STEVENS delivered the opinion of the Court.

After a traumatic incident in which she shot and killed a man, a police officer received extensive counseling from a licensed clinical social worker. The question we address is whether statements the officer made to her therapist during the counseling sessions are protected from compelled disclosure in a federal civil action brought by the family of the deceased. Stated otherwise, the question is whether it is appropriate for federal courts to recognize a "psychotherapist privilege" under Rule 501 of the Federal Rules of Evidence.

* * *

Rule 501 of the Federal Rules of Evidence authorizes federal courts to define new privileges by interpreting "common law principles . . . in the light of reason and experience." The authors of the Rule borrowed this phrase from our opinion in *Wolfle v. United States*, 291 U.S. 7, 12, 78 L. Ed. 617, 54 S. Ct. 279 (1934), which in turn referred to the oft–repeated observation that "the common law is not immutable but flexible, and by its own principles adapts itself to varying conditions." *Funk v. United States*, 290 U.S. 371, 383, 78 L. Ed. 369, 54 S. Ct. 212 (1933). *See also Hawkins v. United States*, 358 U.S. 74, 79, 3 L. Ed. 2d 125, 79 S. Ct. 136 (1958) (changes in privileges may be "dictated by 'reason and experience' "). The Senate Report accompanying the 1975 adoption of the Rules indicates that Rule 501 "should be understood as reflecting the view that the recognition of a privilege based on a confidential relationship . . . should be determined on a case–by–case basis." S. Rep. No. 93–1277, p. 13 (1974). . . . The Rule thus did not freeze the law governing the privileges of witnesses in federal trials at a particular point in our history, but rather directed federal courts to "continue the evolutionary development of testimonial privileges." *Trammel v. United States*, 445 U.S. 40, 47, 63 L. Ed. 2d 186, 100 S. Ct. 906 (1980); *see also University of Pennsylvania v. E.E.O.C.*, 493 U.S. 182, 189, 107 L. Ed. 2d 571, 110 S. Ct. 577 (1990).

The common–law principles underlying the recognition of testimonial privileges can be stated simply. " 'For more than three centuries it has now been recognized as a fundamental maxim that the public . . . has a right to every man's evidence. When we come to examine the various claims of exemption, we start with the primary assumption that there is a general duty to give what testimony one is capable of giving, and that any exemptions which may exist are distinctly exceptional, being so many derogations from a positive general rule.' " . . . Exceptions from the general rule disfavoring testimonial privileges may be justified, however, by a " 'public good transcending the normally predominant principle of utilizing all rational means for ascertaining the truth.'

III

Like the spousal and attorney–client privileges, the psychotherapist–patient privilege is "rooted in the imperative need for confidence and trust." *Trammel*, 445 U.S. at 51. Treatment by a physician for physical ailments can often proceed successfully on the basis of a physical examination, objective information supplied by the patient, and the results of diagnostic tests. Effective psychotherapy, by contrast, depends upon an atmosphere of confidence and trust in which the patient is willing to make a frank and complete disclosure of facts, emotions, memories, and fears. Because of the sensitive nature of the problems for which individuals consult psychotherapists, disclosure of confidential communications made during counseling sessions may cause embarrassment or disgrace. For this reason, the mere possibility of disclosure may impede development of the confidential relationship necessary for successful treatment. . .

. . . The psychotherapist privilege serves the public interest by facilitating the provision of appropriate treatment for individuals suffering the effects of a mental or emotional problem. The mental health of our citizenry, no less than its physical health, is a public good of transcendent importance.[10]

In contrast to the significant public and private interests supporting recognition of the privilege, the likely evidentiary benefit that would result from the denial of the privilege is modest. If the privilege were rejected, confidential conversations between psychotherapists and their patients would surely be chilled, particularly when it is obvious that the circumstances that give rise to the need for treatment will probably result in litigation. Without a privilege, much of the desirable evidence to which litigants such as petitioner seek access—for example, admissions against interest by a party—is unlikely to come into being. This unspoken "evidence" will therefore serve no greater truth–seeking function than if it had been spoken and privileged.

That it is appropriate for the federal courts to recognize a psychotherapist privilege under Rule 501 is confirmed by the fact that all 50 States and the District of Columbia have enacted into law some form of psychotherapist privilege. We have previously observed that the policy decisions of the States bear on the question whether federal courts should recognize a new privilege or amend the coverage of an existing one. . . . Because state legislatures are fully aware of the need to protect the integrity of the factfinding functions of their courts, the existence of a consensus among the States indicates that "reason and experience" support recognition of the privilege. In addition, given the importance of the patient's understanding that her communications with her therapist will not be publicly disclosed, any State's promise of confidentiality would have little value if the patient were aware that the privilege would not be honored in a federal court. Denial of the federal privilege therefore would frustrate the purposes of the state legislation that was enacted to foster these confidential communications. . . .

[W]e hold that confidential communications between a licensed psychotherapist and her patients in the course of diagnosis or treatment are protected from compelled disclosure under Rule 501 of the Federal Rules of Evidence.

IV

All agree that a psychotherapist privilege covers confidential communications made to licensed psychiatrists and psychologists. We have no hesitation in concluding in this case that the federal privilege should also extend to confidential communications made to licensed social workers in the course of psychotherapy. . . . Today, social workers provide a significant amount of mental health treatment. . . . Their clients often include the poor and those of modest means who could not afford the assistance of a psychiatrist or psychologist, . . . but whose counseling sessions serve the same public goals.

---

[10] This case amply demonstrates the importance of allowing individuals to receive confidential counseling. Police officers engaged in the dangerous and difficult tasks associated with protecting the safety of our communities not only confront the risk of physical harm but also face stressful circumstances that may give rise to anxiety, depression, fear, or anger. The entire community may suffer if police officers are not able to receive effective counseling and treatment after traumatic incidents, either because trained officers leave the profession prematurely or because those in need of treatment remain on the job.

Perhaps in recognition of these circumstances, the vast majority of States explicitly extend a testimonial privilege to licensed social workers. . . .

JUSTICE SCALIA, with whom THE CHIEF JUSTICE joins as to Part III, dissenting.

The Court has discussed at some length the benefit that will be purchased by creation of the evidentiary privilege in this case: the encouragement of psychoanalytic counseling. It has not mentioned the purchase price: occasional injustice. That is the cost of every rule which excludes reliable and probative evidence—or at least every one categorical enough to achieve its announced policy objective. . . .

[E]ffective psychotherapy undoubtedly is beneficial to individuals with mental problems, and surely serves some larger social interest in maintaining a mentally stable society. But merely mentioning these values does not answer the critical question: are they of such importance, and is the contribution of psychotherapy to them so distinctive, and is the application of normal evidentiary rules so destructive to psychotherapy, as to justify making our federal courts occasional instruments of injustice? On that central question I find the Court's analysis insufficiently convincing to satisfy the high standard we have set for rules that "are in derogation of the search for truth.". . .

When is it, one must wonder, that the psychotherapist came to play such an indispensable role in the maintenance of the citizenry's mental health? For most of history, men and women have worked out their difficulties by talking to, inter alios, parents, siblings, best friends and bartenders—none of whom was awarded a privilege against testifying in court. Ask the average citizen: Would your mental health be more significantly impaired by preventing you from seeing a psychotherapist, or by preventing you from getting advice from your mom? I have little doubt what the answer would be. Yet there is no mother–child privilege. . . . The Court's failure to put forward a convincing justification of its own could perhaps be excused if it were relying upon the unanimous conclusion of state courts in the reasoned development of their common law. It cannot do that, since no State has such a privilege apart from legislation. What it relies upon, instead, is "the fact that all 50 States and the District of Columbia have [1] enacted into law [2] some form of psychotherapist privilege." Ante, at 10 (emphasis added). Let us consider both the verb and its object: The fact [1] that all 50 States have enacted this privilege argues not for, but against, our adopting the privilege judicially. At best it suggests that the matter has been found not to lend itself to judicial treatment— perhaps because the pros and cons of adopting the privilege, or of giving it one or another shape, are not that clear; or perhaps because the rapidly evolving uses of psychotherapy demand a flexibility that only legislation can provide. At worst it suggests that the privilege commends itself only to decisionmaking bodies in which reason is tempered, so to speak, by political pressure from organized interest groups (such as psychologists and social workers), and decisionmaking bodies that are not overwhelmingly concerned (as courts of law are and should be) with justice.

* * *

NOTES

1. In this case, the lower court, the Court of Appeals for the Seventh Circuit, cited both instrumental and humanistic justifications for recognizing a psychotherapist privilege. *Jaffee v. Redmond*, 51 F.3d 1346 (7th Cir. 1995). In its opinion, did the Supreme Court rely at all on humanistic reasoning?

2. What light does *Jaffee* shed on the meaning of "experience" in Rule 501? Justice Scalia seems inclined to limit the term to judicial experience. In contrast, the majority appears to construe the term more expansively to include either legal or social experience.

3. If either more expansive interpretation of "experience" is appropriate, how hard was it for the Court to decide that it is appropriate to recognize a psychotherapist privilege? After all, all 50 states and D.C. concurred. That fact alone distinguishes *Jaffee* from all the prior cases in which the Court has balked at recognizing an uncodified privilege or in the situation where the states are split over the wisdom of fashioning a particular privilege.

4. Distinguish the majority's threshold decision to recognize a privilege from the majority's choice to extend the privilege to communications with social workers. That choice is the most debatable aspect of the majority's opinion. The majority's stated justification is egalitarian: Since rich people who consult psychiatrists enjoy a privilege, poor people who resort to social workers should have one as well. We might inquire about the meaning of "reason" in Rule 501. Once a court has decided that "experience" counsels recognizing a privilege, what role does "reason" play in defining the contours of the privilege?

5. In a footnote of its opinion, the *Jaffee* Court pointed to a number of "authorities" which supposedly substantiated the generalization that in the typical case, a patient would either not consult a mental health expert or not make necessary disclosures without the assurance of confidentiality furnished by an evidentiary privilege. Some commenators dispute that characterization of the studies arrayed in the footnote. Imwinkelried, *The Rivalry Between Truth and Privilege: The Weakness of the Supreme Court's Instrumental Reasoning in* Jaffee v. Redmond, 518 U.S. 1, 49 HASTINGS L.J. 969 (1996). In some cases, the studies turn out to be surveys of mental health experts rather than actual and prospective patients. In other cases, the surveys indicate that the patients are far more concerned about unsupervised, out–of–court disclosure to employers than judicially supervised disclosure. If the typical patient would refrain from either consulting or disclosing absent a privilege, the recognition of a privilege, would come relatively cost free; the suppressed evidence would not have come into existence but for the privilege. However, a close examination of the studies indicates that the *Jaffee* Court understated the social cost of the privilege.

6. Once a separate psychotherapist–patient privilege is recognized, the problem becomes one of relating the specific contours of the privilege to that of the physician privilege, if any, recognized in the jurisdiction. Often the psychotherapist privilege is broader. Many jurisdictions do not recognize the physician privilege in criminal cases. Thus, if Devitt attempted to prevent his treating physician from testifying to bruises the physician observed on Devitt's chest, the trial judge would routinely overrule the objection. In contrast, suppose that after the battery, Devitt began experiencing guilt and suicidal tendencies. He consults a psychotherapist rather than a physician. During the consultation, Devitt describes what he believes to be the cause of his mental problems: his revulsion at the realization that he attacked Paterson. The trial judge would not permit the psychotherapist to testify to Devitt's admissions.

Another way in which the privileges can differ relates to the "professional" patient consults. California Evidence Code § 990 simply defines "physician" as "a person authorized, or reasonably believed by the patient to be authorized, to practice medicine in any state or nation." The California Evidence Code defines psychotherapist to include the foregoing but also:

> (b) A [state] licensed psychologist

> (c) A [state] licensed clinical social worker when he is engaged in applied psychotherapy of a nonmedical nature

> (d) A person who is serving as a school psychologist and holds a credential authorizing such service issued by the state

> (e) A [state] licensed marriage, family and child counselor

D.   GOVERNMENT SECRETS

1.   AN OVERVIEW

Most of the privileges considered to date are communications privileges. They shield confidential communications about facts, but not the facts themselves. Thus, at a deposition, a client who has been involved in a traffic accident can refuse to answer questions about her communications about the accident with her attorney; but she cannot refuse to answer otherwise proper questions about the accident itself. However, some privileges are topical in nature and directly protect facts. For example, the original draft of Article V would have recognized topical privileges for trade secrets and the tenor of a person's vote. More commonly, though, there are the topical privileges for certain types of government information.

There are a large number of privileges for various sorts of government information in various jurisdictions. Comment, 7 U.S.F. L. Rev. 282 (1973). One court has fashioned a privilege for complaints made to a state ombudsman office. *Shabazz v. Scurr*, 662 F. Supp. 90 (S.D. Iowa 1987). The courts have even derived evidentiary privileges for governmental actors from such constitutional provisions as the speech and debate clause. *United States v. Gillock*, 445 U.S. 360 (1980); *Gravel v. United States*, 408 U.S. 606, *reh'g denied,* 409 U.S. 902 (1972); Annot., 60 L. Ed. 2d 1166 (1980). Another court has recognized a privilege for confidential communications between a judge and his or her law clerks. *In re Certain Complaints Under Investigation by an Investigating Comm. of Judicial Council of Eleventh Circuit*, 783 F.2d 1488, 1518–20 (11th Cir. 1986). In a short text such as this, we can only highlight the government privileges encountered most frequently in practice.

2. MILITARY AND STATE SECRETS

UNITED STATES v. REYNOLDS

345 U.S. 1 (1953)

CHIEF JUSTICE VINSON delivered the opinion of the Court.

These suits under the Tort Claims Act arise from the death of three civilians in the crash of a B–29 aircraft at Waycross, Georgia, on October 6, 1948. Because an important question of the Government's privilege to resist discovery is involved, we granted certiorari.

The aircraft had taken flight for the purpose of testing secret electronic equipment, with four civilian observers aboard. While aloft, fire broke out in one of the bomber's engines. Six of the nine crew members and three of the four civilian observers were killed in the crash.

The widows of the three deceased civilians observers brought consolidated suits against the United States. In the pretrial stages the plaintiffs moved, under Rule 34 of the Federal Rules of Civil Procedure, for production of the Air Force's official accident investigation report and the statements of the three surviving crew members, taken in connection with the official investigation. The Government moved to quash the motion, claiming that these matters were privileged against disclosure pursuant to Air Force regulations promulgated under R.S. § 161. The District Judge sustained plaintiffs' motion, holding that good cause for production had been shown. . . . [The claim of privilege under R.S. § 161 was rejected on the premise that the Tort Claims Act, in making the Government liable "in the same manner" as a private individual, had waived any privilege based upon executive control over governmental documents.]

Shortly after this decision, the District Court received a letter from the Secretary of the Air Force, stating that "it has been determined that it would not be in the public interest to furnish this report. . . ." The court allowed a rehearing on its earlier order, and at the rehearing the Secretary of the Air Force filed a formal "Claim of Privilege." This document repeated the prior claim based generally on R.S. § 161, and then stated that the Government further objected to production of the documents "for the reason that the aircraft in question, together with the personnel on board, were engaged in a highly secret mission of the Air Force." An affidavit of the Judge Advocate General, United States Air Force, was also filed with the court, which asserted that the demanded material could not be furnished "without seriously hampering national security, flying safety and the development of highly technical and secret military equipment." The same affidavit offered to produce the three surviving crew members, without cost, for examination by the plaintiffs. The witnesses would be allowed to refresh their memories from any statement made by them to the Air Force, and authorized to testify as to all matters except those of a "classified nature."

The District Court ordered the Government to produce the documents in order that the court might determine whether they contained privileged matter. The Government declined, so the court entered an order, under Rule

37(b)(2)(I), that the facts on the issue of negligence would be taken as established in plaintiffs' favor. After a hearing to determine damages, final judgment was entered for the plaintiffs. The Court of Appeals affirmed, both as to the showing of good cause for production of the documents, and as to the ultimate disposition of the case as a consequence of the Government's refusal to produce the documents.

* * *

Judicial experience with the privilege which protects military and state secrets has been limited in this country. English experience has been more extensive, but still relatively slight compared with other evidentiary privileges. Nevertheless, the principles which control the application of the privilege emerge quite clearly from the available precedents. The privilege belongs to the Government and must be asserted by it; it can neither be claimed nor waived by a private party. It is not to be lightly invoked. There must be a formal claim of privilege, lodged by the head of the department which has control over the matter, after actual personal consideration by that officer. The court itself must determine whether the circumstances are appropriate for the claim of privilege, and yet do so without forcing a disclosure of the very thing the privilege is designed to protect. The latter requirement is the only one which presents real difficulty. As to it, we find it helpful to draw upon judicial experience in dealing with an analogous privilege, the privilege against self–incrimination.

The privilege against self–incrimination presented the courts with a similar sort of problem. Too much judicial inquiry into the claim of privilege would force disclosure of the thing the privilege was meant to protect, while a complete abandonment of judicial control would lead to intolerable abuses. Indeed, in the earlier stages of judicial experience with the problem, both extremes were advocated, some saying that the bare assertion by the witness must be taken as conclusive, and others saying that the witness should be required to reveal the matter behind his claim of privilege to the judge for verification. Neither extreme prevailed, and a sound formula of compromise was developed. This formula received authoritative expression in this country as early as the Burr trial. There are differences in phraseology, but in substance it is agreed that the court must be satisfied from all the evidence and circumstances and "from the implications of the question, in the setting in which it is asked, that a responsive answer to the question or an explanation of why it cannot be answered might be dangerous because injurious disclosure could result." *Hoffman v. United States*, 341 U.S. 479, 486–487 (1951). If the court is so satisfied, the claim of the privilege will be accepted without requiring further disclosure.

Regardless of how it is articulated, some like formula of compromise must be applied here. Judicial control over the evidence in a case cannot be abdicated to the caprice of executive officers. Yet we will not go so far as to say that the court may automatically require a complete disclosure to the judge before the claim of privilege will be accepted in any case. It may be possible to satisfy the court, from all the circumstances of the case, that there is a reasonable danger that compulsion of the evidence will expose military matters which, in the interest of national security, should not be divulged. When this is the case, the occasion for the privilege is appropriate, and the court should not jeopardize the security which the privilege is meant to protect by insisting upon an examination of the evidence, even by the judge alone, in chambers.

In the instant case we cannot escape judicial notice that this is a time of vigorous preparation for national defense. Experience in the past war has made it common knowledge that air power is one of the most potent weapons in our scheme of defense, and that newly developing electronic devices have greatly enhanced the effective use of air power. It is equally apparent that these electronic devices must be kept secret if their full military advantage is to be exploited in the national interests. On the record before the trial court it appeared that this accident occurred to a military plane which had gone aloft to test secret electronic equipment. Certainly there was a reasonable danger that the accident investigation report would contain references to the secret electronic equipment which was the primary concern of the mission.

*   *   *

In each case, the showing of necessity which is made will determine how far the court should probe in satisfying itself that the occasion for invoking the privilege is appropriate. Where there is a strong showing of necessity, the claim of privilege should not be lightly accepted, but even the most compelling necessity cannot overcome the claim of privilege if the court is ultimately satisfied that military secrets are at stake. *A fortiori*, where necessity is dubious, a formal claim of privilege, made under the circumstances of this case, will have to prevail. Here, necessity was greatly minimized by an available alternative, which might have given respondents the evidence to make out their case without forcing a showdown on the claim of privilege. By their failure to pursue that alternative, respondents have posed the privilege question for decision with the formal claim of privilege set against a dubious showing of necessity.

There is nothing to suggest that the electronic equipment, in this case, had any causal connection with the accident. Therefore, it should be possible for respondents to adduce the essential facts as to causation without resort to material touching upon military secrets. Respondents were given a reasonable opportunity to do just that when petitioner formally offered to make the surviving crew members available for examination. We think that offer should have been accepted.

Reversed and remanded.

NOTES

1. Given the absolute nature of the privilege, it is important to develop a manageable definition of military and state secrets. The statutes recognizing the privilege often attempt to define its scope in terms of the effect of disclosing the information: "exceptionally grave damage to the Nation" or "detrimental to the national security." Zagel, *The State Secrets Privilege*, 50 MINN. L. REV. 875, 881 (1966). The Advisory Committee proposed a rule, Federal Rule of

Evidence 509, on government secrets, including state secrets. The proposed rule would have defined a state secret as "a governmental secret relating to the national defense or the international relations of the United States." Commentators have tried their hand at fashioning a definition:

(a) the plans and capabilities of specific combat operations; (b) the official estimates of the military plans and capabilities of potential enemy nations; (c) the existence, design, and production of new weapons or equipment or the existence and results of research programs specifically directed toward producing new weapons and equipment; (d) the existence and nature of special ways and means of organizing combat operations; (e) the identity and location of vulnerable areas such as production facilities, critical supply depots, or weapons installations; (f) the existence and nature of clandestine intelligence operations, special plans, or data; (g) the keys to communication codes; (h) the existence and nature of international agreements relative to military plans and capabilities and the exchange of intelligence.

Zagel, *supra,* at 884–5. *See also* PROPOSED FED. R. EVID. 509.

2. Does Judge Zagel's definition explain the scope of the privilege for "state" secrets as opposed to "military" secrets? The courts have encountered more difficulty defining the scope of the protection for state secrets concerning the country's foreign relations. What possiblities of abuse arise?

3. CONFIDENTIAL GOVERNMENT INFORMATION

Besides national security information, the government has an array of other protections for its confidential information. One frequently encountered in criminal work, is the qualified privilege for an informant's identity. In short, there may be secrecy for the identity of persons who furnish information regarding violations of law to enforcement agents such as police and prosecutor. Even when the privilege attaches, it is qualified: the discovering party can defeat the privilege by showing substantial need for disclosure of the information. *See, Roviaro v. United States*, 353 U.S. 53 (1957) and PROPOSED FED. R. EVID. 510.

Another major area of qualified governmental privilege is executive privilege, agency deliberative privilege, or law enforcement investigative information privilege. *See, e.g., United States v. Nixon*, 418 U.S. 683 (1974). The federal courts often refer to their doctrine as the consultative (*United States v. Winner*, 641 F.2d 825 (10th Cir. 1981)), predecisional (*Falcone v. Internal Revenue Serv.*, 479 F. Supp. 985 (E.D. Mich. 1979)), or deliberative (*id.*) privilege. The privilege is closely akin to the exemption for intra–agency memoranda under the Freedom of Information Act. *Conoco v. United States Dep't of Justice*, 521 F. Supp. 1301 (D. Del. 1981). The purpose of the privilege is to encourage candor in government decisionmaking. The premise is that if government decisionmakers have an assurance of confidentiality, their internal discussions will be franker, and the end product, the final government decision, should be of higher quality. To accomplish this objective, the courts cloak with a privilege advisory opinions, recommendations, and deliberations that are an integral part of the decisionmaking process. *Armstrong Bros. Tool Co. v. United States*, 463 F. Supp. 1316 (Cust. Ct. 1979). Such materials reflect the thought processes of government decisionmakers. *New York City Managerial Employee Ass'n v. Dinkins*, 807 F. Supp. 955 (S.D.N.Y. 1992). To be protected, a document must be *both* predecisional and deliberative; that is, the document must be generated as part of a decisionmaking process resulting in a final government action, and the document must reflect the "give–and–take" of opinions in the decisionmaking process. *Dow, Lohnes & Albertson v. Presidential Comm'n on Broadcasting to Cuba*, 624 F. Supp. 572 (D.D.C. 1984). The document "must bear on the formulation or exercise of policy–oriented judgment." *Ethyl Corp. v. U.S.E.P.A.*, 25 F.3d 1241, 1248 (4th Cir. 1994). The privilege protects the government's internal working papers. *Brinton v. United States Dep't of State*, 476 F. Supp. 535 (D.D.C. 1979). The protection is especially strong at the higher levels of government decisionmaking. *United States v. American Tel. & Tel. Co.*, 524 F. Supp. 1381, 1387 n.18 (D.D.C. 1981).

Note the two limitations on this privilege. First, it generally does not protect raw, factual data the government gathers during decisionmaking. Weaver & Jones, *The Deliberative Process Privilege*, 54 Mo. L. Rev. 279, 297 (1989). Further, the privilege does not protect the final opinion adopted by the agency. *Falcone v. Internal Revenue Serv., supra*. Second, the privilege can be overcome by a showing of compelling need. *United States v. Farley*, 11 F.3d 1385, 1389 (7th Cir. 1993). In deciding whether to uphold the privilege, the courts consider the following factors, *inter alia:* the relevance of the information sought, the availability of alternative evidence, the seriousness of the litigation, the role of the government in the litigation, and the possibility of future timidity by government employees who will realize that their secrets are violable. *In re Franklin Nat'l Bank Securities Litig.*, 478 F. Supp. 577 (E.D.N.Y. 1979).

E. THE FUTURE OF PRIVILEGE

1. INTRODUCTION

By now, you should sense that the basic trend in American evidence law since World War II has been toward a liberalization of the standards of admissibility—a gradual triumph of logical relevance over both legal irrelevance and competence restrictions. The common law courts began the trend, and the advent of the Federal Rules of Evidence accelerated it. However, the major privileges—spousal, attorney–client, physician–patient, and the like—have proved remarkably resistant to the trend. Indeed, since the enactment of the Federal Rules, the courts have recognized several new privileges.

At first blush, the most recent Supreme Court privilege decisions seem to suggest that the Court has adopted a more receptive attitude toward claims of novel privileges. However, it would be a mistake to read too much into either *Jaffee v. Redmond*, 518 U.S. 1 (1996) or *Swidler & Berlin v. United States*, 524 U.S. 399 (1998). In both cases, the Court approvingly cited its prior precedents stating that it is reluctant to fashion new privileges or expand old privileges. In *Jaffee*, the case for recognizing the psychotherapist privilege was exceptionally strong. Not only had the draft Federal Rules included the privilege; moreover, as the Court noted at several points in in its opinion, all

50 states had opted to recognize the privilege. In *Swidler* the Court was not extending the attorney–client privilege; rather, it was rejecting the Independent Counsel's attempt to contract the common law scope of the doctrine. In short, it is still true that a litigant urging a court to recognize a new privilege faces an uphill battle. For example, during the Independent Counsel's investigation of the Clinton administration, the courts refused to create a new privilege for Secret Service agents' observations of and communications with the President. *In re Sealed Case*, 146 F.3d 1031 (D.C.Cir.), *cert. denied sub nom. Rubin v. United States, 525 U.S. 990 (1998); Comment, How Secret Is the Service?: Exploring the Validity and Legality of a Secret Service Testimonial Privilege. 104 Dick.L.Rev. 227 (1999).*

2. RECENT DEVELOPMENTS

Financial Secrets: The financial community has not been content with the attorney–client privilege; it has sought other privileges as well. State legislatures have frequently responded favorably to the community's entreaties. For example, in some jurisdictions, there is a banker–depositor privilege. *United States v. Prevatt*, 526 F.2d 400 (5th Cir. 1976). Many jurisdictions have created an evidentiary privilege for trade secrets. Cal. Evid. Code § 1060. The accounting profession has argued that it performs services analogous to those of lawyers and is, therefore, entitled to similar protection. Bowing to the lobbying, statutory accountant–client privileges have become quite common, *see* 3 Jones on Evidence—Civil and Criminal § 21.42 (S. Gard ed. 1972) especially in the industrial states. *See, e.g., Western Employers Ins. Co. v. Merit Ins. Co.*, 492 F. Supp. 53 (N.D. Ill. 1979).

First Amendment Based Privileges: Reporters claim that without a privilege protecting their information gathering activities, freedom of the press will be impaired. Courts have struggled with the concept of First Amendment privileges. The process has been long and tortuous; even today, the area is not well–established except in a few states. *See Herbert v. Lando*, 441 U.S. 153 (1979); *Branzburg v. Hayes*, 408 U.S. 665 (1972); *Knight–Ridder Broadcasting v. Greenberg*, 70 N.Y.2d 151, 511 N.E.2d 1116, 518 N.Y.S.2d 595 (1987); *State v. Rinaldo*, 36 Wash. App. 86, 673 P.2d 614 (1983), *aff'd*, 102 Wash.2d 749, 689 P.2d 392 (1984).

The academic profession has also sought the refuge of privilege via the First Amendment, claiming the need for protection for research and peer review in academic personnel evaluation. *See University of Pennsylvania v. E.E.O.C.*, 493 U.S. 182 (1990); *In re R.J. Reynolds Tobacco Co.*, 136 Misc.2d 282, 518 N.Y.S.2d 729 (Sup. Ct. 1987); Note, University of Pennsylvania v. E.E.O.C. *and* Dixon v. Rutgers: *Two Supreme Courts Speak on the Academic Freedom Privilege*, 42 Rutgers L. Rev. 1089 (1990); Comment, 14 San Diego L. Rev. 876 (1977).

Pressing Social Problems: Juvenile crime is a major challenge facing our nation. The juvenile court system often employs confidential proceedings. The system operates on the assumption that the child may reform and that it is unwise to subject the child to publicity that may stigmatize the child during her adult life. Based on that assumption, a number of jurisdictions, such as

New York and California, have fashioned an evidentiary privilege for the child's testimony at juvenile court hearings. *In re Luis R.*, 414 N.Y.S.2d 997 (N.Y. Fam. Ct. 1978); *Bryan v. Superior Court*, 7 Cal. 3d 575, 498 P.2d 1079, 102 Cal. Rptr. 831 (1972).

Another major social problem is drug abuse. We want to encourage users to seek treatment, and many would not do so unless assured confidentiality. Ehrhardt, *Privileged Communications by the Drug User in Federal Court*, J. Drug Issues, Summer 1973, at 258. The federal government has adopted regulations to guarantee confidentiality at its drug rehabilitation facilities. Weissman, *Law Enforcement and the New Federal Alcohol and Drug Abuse Confidentiality Regulations*, 5 J. Police Sci. & Admin. 299 (1977). Several states have adopted similar legislation. *See, e.g.*, Cal. Welf. & Inst. Code § 5328. Several courts have construed these statutes and regulations as creating evidentiary privileges. *E.g.*, *United States v. Eide*, 875 F.2d 1429 (9th Cir. 1989); *Whyte v. Connecticut Mut. Life Ins. Co.*, 818 F.2d 1005, 1008–10 (1st Cir. 1987) (Wisdom, J.); *United States v. Cresta*, 825 F.2d 538, 551–52 (1st Cir. 1987), *cert. denied*, 486 U.S. 1042 (1988).

Concern over rape prevention accounts for the adoption of the rape shield laws discussed earlier, and has also led some states to create a qualified privilege for statements by rape victims to rape crisis counselors. Note, *The Constitutionality of an Absolute Privilege for Rape Crisis Counseling*, 30 B.C. L. Rev. 411 (1989).

Concern over corporate responsibility has led some courts to fashion new privileges for aspects of corporate operations. By way of example, one court has recognized a privilege for statements made by the entity's employees to corporate ombudsmen. *Kientzy v. McDonnell Douglas Corp.*, 133 F.R.D. 570 (E.D. Mo. 1991). *See* Note, *Privileged Communication Extended to the Corporate Ombudsmen–Employee Relationship Via Federal Rule of Evidence 501*, 1991 J. Dispute Resol. 367. The court reasoned that a privilege would facilitate the ombudsman's work and that "[h]aving an ombudsman detached from the political control of management leads to increased corporate integrity . . . ." *Id.* at 371. In addition, although there is contrary authority (Flanagan, *Rejecting a General Privilege for Self–Critical Analysis*, 51 Geo. Wash. L. Rev. 551 (1983)), a number of courts have fashioned a qualified privilege of "self–critical analysis for corporations. *In re Air Crash near Cali, Columbia on Dec. 20, 1995*, 959 F.Supp. 1529 (S.D.Fla. 1997); *Dowling v. American Hawaii Cruises, Inc.*, 971 F.2d 423, 425–27 (9th Cir. 1992); *In re Crazy Eddie Securities Litigation*, 792 F. Supp. 197, 205–06 (E.D.N.Y. 1992); Comment, *Stimulating Corporate Self-Regulation—The Corporate Self-Evaluative Privilege: Paradigmatic Preferentialism or Pragmatic Panacea*, 87 Nw. U. L. Rev. 597 (1993). Their rationale is that the existence of a privilege will encourage intensive internal corporate investigations and self–policing. *Id.* at 598–99. The hope is that "aggressive corporate self–monitoring" will lead to "self–correction." *Id.* at 600. Compare the similarity of reasoning here and in Rule 407 and the discussion in Chapter 28.

Roughly half the states have enacted statutes protecting environmental self–audits. Fildes, *Statutory Privileges and Immunities for Voluntarily Performed Environmental Audits: Should New York Join the Race?*, 5

BUFF.ENVT'L L.J. 257, 258 (1998). The argument runs that governmental environmental agencies have limited enforcement resources and that it is therefore vital to encourage businesses to monitor and police their own practices which can affect the quality of the environment. Mostek, *Limited Privilege and Immunity for Self-Evaluative Audits in Nebraska: Moving Environmental Performance to the Next Level*, 32 CREIGHTON L.REV. 545 (1998); Manta & Brock, *Protecting the Confidentiality of Corporate Internal Investigations and Compliance Audits*, 12 CORPORATE COUNSEL'S QUARTERLY 1–23 (Jan. 1996).

3. THE TWIN THEMES: CODIFICATION AND THE IMPORTANCE OF EMPIRICAL RESEARCH

Many of the disputes over privilege doctrine highlight the need for additional empirical research into the assumptions underlying evidence law. Privilege doctrines are largely designed to affect behavior outside the courtroom, and many of the controversies over privilege doctrine are reducible to the question of whether the doctrine will have the intended effect. Further social science research can help the courts resolve that question. To what extent would the lack of a privilege deter mental patients from either seeking assistance or disclosing sensitive information to treating experts? Will forced testimony by children against their parents inflict psychological harm on the children? These questions cannot be answered by abstract reasoning. They can be intelligently resolved only on the basis of additional experimentation and investigation. The answers to these questions have profound implications for the future of privilege doctrine. As we have seen, the empirical studies conducted to date call into question Wigmore's assumption that in the typical case, laypersons are so concerned about evidence law that they would not exchange confidential information but for the existence of a formal evidentiary privilege. If additional research further undermines Wigmore's assumption, in the future, the courts may depreciate the instrumental theory and rely more heavily on a humanistic rationale. If that development comes to pass, in the future, it may be more difficult to defend the conventional wisdom that communications privileges must be "absolute" in character. Significantly, in both *Jaffee v. Redmond*, 518 U.S. 1 (1996) and *Swidler & Berlin v. United States*, 524 U.S. 399 (1998), the lower courts not only relied on humanistic reasoning but also treated the privileges in question as qualified.

The preceding material also forces us to reflect on the codification of evidence law. Congress refused to enact the specific privilege statutes proposed by the Advisory Committee. However, most of the states which have enacted a version of the Federal Rules decided to adopt specific statutes. 1 G. JOSEPH & S. SALTZBURG, EVIDENCE IN AMERICA: THE FEDERAL RULES IN THE STATES § 23.2 (1987). In fact, most of those statutes went to the extreme of closing the window to the common law which Federal Rule 501 opens; their statutory schemes "foreclose . . . common law development and restrict . . . privileges to those specifically provided for by constitution, statute or court rule." *Id.* § 23.2.

At a theoretical level, there is a strong case for formal codification of privilege law. As we have emphasized, there is an especial need for predictability in the privilege area. To achieve the desired effect on out–of–court behavior, privilege rules must be relatively predictable; the person deciding whether to communicate delicate information arguably needs a firm assurance of confidentiality.

Moreover, to a greater extent than any other area of evidence law, the formulation of privilege doctrine necessitates gathering a wealth of information about society at large. Compared to the judicial branch, the legislature has vastly superior fact–finding capability; it can assemble the complex information needed to assess the probable social impact of a proposed privilege much more efficiently and effectively. However, serious, practical problems arise when a legislature undertakes to formulate privilege rules. It may be very difficult to develop the political consensus needed to enact such legislation. Precisely because privilege rules affect society at large, they are likely to divide legislators along political lines. Should we extend a privilege to the counselors of victims of rape and domestic violence? The affirmative arguments on these issues are essentially anti–crime arguments, while the negative arguments rest on privacy considerations dear to civil libertarians.

Chapter 27

COMPROMISE

Rules of Evidence 408–10.

A. INTRODUCTION

It would be difficult to overestimate the importance of settlement and settlement negotiations in the dispute resolution process. Roughly ninety-seven percent of all civil claims that come into attorneys' offices are settled prior to trial. Kelner, *Settlement Techniques—Part One*, TRIAL, Feb. 1980, at 46. Most civil claims are settled before suit is even filed. Of the claims that are filed, over ninety percent are settled before trial. Plea bargaining plays an equally vital role in criminal proceedings. Approximately ninety-six percent of the arrestees who are booked plead guilty, and in most instances the plea is negotiated. Beall, *Negotiating the Disposition of Criminal Charges*, TRIAL, Oct. 1980, at 46; *Gannett Co. v. De Pasquale*, 443 U.S. 368, 389 (1979) (Burger, C.J., concurring).

Thus, only a tiny percentage of all cases are tried. Even this small percentage strains our judicial system. REPORT OF THE FEDERAL COURTS STUDY COMMITTEE 4–10 (1990). In many major metropolitan areas, even after the complaint has been filed, the litigants can expect to wait 1 to 3 years before disposition; in some very crowded dockets it is not unheard of to wait five years for a trial date. In the words of one commentator, "[e]xisting court calendar backlogs and prosecutors' and public defenders' case loads make the social costs of an even larger number of trials unacceptable, especially in view of the longer delays in civil dockets that would also inevitably result." Welch, *Settling Criminal Cases*, 6 LITIGATION, Winter 1980, at 32. More and more jurisdictions are experimenting with alternative dispute resolution techniques, such as arbitration and mediation, to uncrowd court dockets and expedite the processing of cases.

Given the burden of the judicial system, it is understandable that the courts not only depend upon the out-of-court settlement of cases, they are also interested in encouraging settlement. One method is an exclusionary rule for statements the parties make in the process of bargaining. The courts reason that the exclusionary rule will encourage a candid exchange during bargaining. Better informed parties, the courts believe, can better evaluate their case and settle it. In short, the rationale for the exclusionary rule is to "encourage nonlitigious solutions to disputes." *Reichenbach v. Smith*, 528 F.2d 1072 (5th Cir. 1976).

Some critics question whether an exclusionary rule is needed. After all, there are already numerous powerful factors pressuring the parties to settle—caseloads, economics, and the desirability of avoiding exposure to higher damages awards and sentences. Given these pressures, it seems unlikely that an exclusionary rule will have an appreciable impact on the parties' willingness to negotiate. When we studied privileges, we questioned whether laypersons were aware of (and, therefore, affected by) the availability of a privilege. To whatever extent they are, it is probably a safe assumption that they are less likely to know that there is an evidentiary doctrine protecting statements made during settlement negotiations. The critics therefore argue that it is fanciful to assume that the doctrine is an important facilitator for negotiations. These critics believe that the courts have overestimated the impact of the evidentiary rules on the parties' negotiating behavior outside the court. Notwithstanding this criticism, the courts and many legislatures have steadfastly adhered to the exclusionary rule. Unfortunately, there has been little empirical research into the question of the impact of the exclusionary rule on parties' behavior during negotiation.

B. THE RULE EXCLUDING THE PARTIES' CONDUCT DURING AN ATTEMPT TO COMPROMISE A CIVIL CLAIM

1. STATEMENTS MADE DURING COMPROMISE NEGOTIATIONS

With some changes that we shall highlight later, Federal Evidence Rule 408 codifies the common law standards:

> Rule 408. Compromise and Offers to Compromise.
>
> Evidence of (1) furnishing or offering or promising to furnish, or (2) accepting or offering or promising to accept, a valuable consideration in compromising or attempting to compromise a claim which was disputed as to either validity or amount, is not admissible to prove liability for or invalidity of the claim or its amount. Evidence of conduct or statements made in compromise negotiations is likewise not admissible. This rule does not require the exclusion of any evidence otherwise discoverable merely because it is presented in the course of compromise negotiations. This rule also does not require exclusion when the evidence is offered for another purpose, such as proving bias or prejudice of a witness, negativing a contention of undue delay, or proving an effort to obstruct a criminal investigation or prosecution.
>
> We will cover the three primary issues raised under Rule 408: the meaning of compromise negotiations, the types of statements protected, and the exceptions.

a. "Compromise" Negotiations

Rule 408 states the scope of the exclusionary rule. Notice that the statute repeatedly uses the expression, "compromise." The policy underlying Rule 408 certainly warrants extending its protection to negotiations in which the parties attempt to resolve a bona fide dispute over liability or the amount of damages. Those are the types of disputes that would otherwise require judicial resolution. By applying Rule 408 to statements made during such negotiations, it is to be hoped that we encourage the pretrial settlement of those disputes and ease the burden on the courts. The issue is whether the rule applies to other types of disputes.

NOTES AND PROBLEMS

1. Problem 27–1. In our torts case, Polecat Motors learns that Ms. Hill is desperate for cash. The plaintiff's medical bills were mounting, and she was in imminent danger of losing her house because of delinquent mortgage payments. Sensing the possibility of a "cheap" settlement, Polecat's agent approaches Ms. Hill. In the course of the meeting, Polecat's agent says, "We'll admit that your claim is valid. We're even willing to concede that the amount of your claim is fair; we've checked out the damages you claim and everything seems to be on the up and up. But face facts: You need cash right now. We're prepared to pay you $15,000 cash—right now, on the barrelhead—to settle this claim." The plaintiff rejects the settlement offer, and the case goes to trial. Does the exclusionary rule prevent the plaintiff from proving the statements of the defendant's agent? *See* Michaels, *Rule 408: A Litigation Mine Field*, 19 LITIGATION, Fall 1992, at 36 ("The statement by a debtor, 'Of course I owe you the money, but unless you are willing to settle for less you will have to sue me for it' is, according to Weinstein, admissible. [T]here is no policy reason to exclude evidence when a debtor merely tries to induce a creditor to settle an admittedly due amount for a lesser sum".)

2. By its terms, Rule 408 is limited to claims "disputed as to either validity or amount." The courts have divided over the interpretation of that expression. *See* Michaels, *supra*, at 35 ("The Federal Circuit has held . . . that an acknowledged 'probability' of an eventual court battle is not sufficient . . . if the claim has not yet been contested. [T]he Tenth Circuit reached a similar result; [i]t held that 'threatened litigation' is a clear point for invoking Rule 408 protection. Statements made before threatened litigation are . . . not within the purview of the Rule.") However, in *Affiliated Manufacturers, Inc. v. Aluminum Co. of America*, 56 F.3d 521 (3d Cir. 1995), the court ruled that a clear difference of opinion between the parties is sufficient to bring 408 into play even though the disagreement had not yet crystallized to the stage of threatened litigation. On the other hand, *Kraemer v. Franklin and Marshall College*, 909 F. Supp. 267, 268 (E.D. Pa. 1995), asserts that while litigation " 'need not have commenced for Rule 408 to apply,' there must be some dispute which the parties are attempting to resolve through discussion." In that case, the court found that "[a]lthough there is a difference of view between the parties as to the validity of Plaintiff's claim, no compromise negotiations or offers to settle occurred." *See also Walsh v. First Unum Life Ins. Co.*, 982 F.Supp. 929 (W.D.N.Y. 1997). In *S.A. Healey Co. v. Milwaukee Metropolitan Sewerage*, 50 F.3d 476, 480 (7th Cir. 1995), Chief Judge Posner writes: "A dispute arises only when a claim is rejected at the initial or some subsequent level." The court found that no dispute had arisen "until the rejection of th[e] claim." *See generally*, Brazil, *Protecting the Confidentiality of Settlement Negotiations*, 39 HASTINGS L.J. 955, 961 (1988). Which interpretation is sounder? Which interpretation is more likely to help "creat[e] the kinds of feelings between the parties that are . . . conducive to reaching agreement"? *Id.* at 965.

b. Protected Statements

If the exchange between the parties constitutes compromise negotiations and thereby triggers Rule 408, the next question that arises is what types of statements are protected. That question has long been disputed:

WALTZ & HUSTON, THE RULES OF EVIDENCE IN SETTLEMENT, 5 LITIGATION, Fall 1978, at 11 [excerpted]

Courts at common law consistently ruled that offers to settle a disputed claim by compromise were inadmissible when offered at a later trial to substantiate the plaintiff's claim. Inconsistence set in, however, when courts considered the admissibility of subsidiary or collateral conversations occurring during settlement talks. The rationale relied upon by a court in excluding evidence of the actual compromise offer usually dictated its approach to independent statements of fact accompanying the offer. Most courts excluded offer evidence on a sometimes strained theory of evidentiary relevance. Others adopted theories of contract or privilege.

Prior to Rule 408's advent, all federal and most state courts excluded offers of compromise as irrelevant to the substantive issues; such offers, they said, implied merely a desire for peace, not a concession of a wrong done. The result was different when an offer of compromise was extended before any dispute had hardened. *E.g.*, *Perzinski v. Chevron Chemical Company*, 503 F.2d 654 (7th Cir. 1974). If the driver of a vehicle that struck and injured a pedestrian dropped by the victim's hospital room on the day after the accident to offer payment of his medical bills, his words would rise to haunt him at a subsequent trial since they preceded any negotiations to dispose of an actual dispute.

Once a dispute arose, the only true offer of compromise was "an offer to pay an amount conditioned on the denial of liability." *Factor v. C.I.R.*, 281 F.2d 100, 128 (9th Cir. 1960), *cert. denied*, 364 U.S. 933 (1961). (That's not what you have when one side concedes liability for an undisputed amount but nonetheless tries, on a sort of reverse nuisance basis, to chisel down the amount to be paid.) If unqualified, independent fact statements surrounded the offer, they would not be shielded at a later trial if the parties' settlement efforts broke down. *E.g.*, *Brown v. Hyslop*, 153 Neb. 669, 45 N.W.2d 743 (1951). [I]t often was difficult to separate the collateral evidence, which was admissible, from the offer of compromise itself, which was inadmissible.

A few courts excluded compromise offers on a contract theory. *E.g.*, *White v. Old Dominion S.S. Co.*, 102 N.Y. 550, 6 N.E. 289 (1886). Anything said or done during compromise negotiations was later admissible unless it had been accompanied by an express or presumed "without prejudice" reservation. The offer itself was presumed to have been made without prejudice to future denials of liability but the collateral conversation was not. If an offer of compromise was not accepted, the courts reasoned, there was no contract between the parties and the defendant's offer was stripped of its evidentiary impact, but the force of unqualified fact admissions lingered on.

If the contract theory was excessively conceptualistic, the relevance theory was excessively unrealistic. The offer of $500.00 in a disputed lawsuit with a million dollar prayer is either a nuisance offer aimed at avoiding costly combat or a bad case of whistling in the dark. An offer of $500,000 in the same suit is a definite straw in the wind. [S]o substantial an offer of compromise reflected a sense of pessimism by defendant on the liability issue. Pessimism of that magnitude was surely probative.

Faced with two flawed theories, some courts faced up to realities and frankly excluded offers of compromise because to do otherwise would inhibit free discourse during bargaining and frustrate the public policy favoring the extrajudicial disposition of disputes. This policy-based version of the exclusionary rule sounded very much like a privilege.

As we have already suggested, a crucial flaw in both the relevance and the contract theories at common law was that they required courts to draw a distinction between the actual offer and the words or conduct surrounding it. One test, Dean Wigmore's, emphasized the form of the proffered statement. 4 J. WIGMORE, EVIDENCE IN TRIALS AT COMMON LAW § 1061 at 41 (Chadbourne Rev. 1972). Wigmore thought the speaker's intention was the key and the form of his statement was the best indicator of that intent. If the offeror did not intend his fact statement to be an assertion of his actual belief about the facts, he would phrase it hypothetically or conditionally. ("Fred, we don't believe it for a minute but just for the sake of argument let's assume that we've got a defective product here. What would you say to $150,000?") Conversely, if the offeror intended his comment as an assertion of belief—that is, as an admission—he would probably speak in explicit, unconditional terms, or so Dean Wigmore thought. ("Let's face it, Fred, we put out a defective gear box on this motorbike and we know we're going to have to pay for it.") Under Wigmore's test, only unconditional collateral assertions were admissible if settlement negotiations aborted. Thus counsel's first remark to Fred would not be admissible later; the second comment, an unqualified admission, would be.

A second test tried to focus on the relationship of the proffered collateral evidence and the offer of compromise or the subject matter of the discussions. *See, e.g., M'Neil v. Holbrook*, 37 U.S. 84 (1838). The closer, the more intimately intertwined the relationship, the more likely it was that the collateral evidence would be held inadmissible at trial. The most commonly encountered litmus was whether the proffered words had been "in furtherance" of compromise.

It has been said that Wigmore's test victimized the unsophisticated, who might fail to tack endless conditions and disclaimers onto their settlement offers. The relationship or "in furtherance" test was so unpredictable it left everyone vulnerable. These difficulties made the privilege theory look good: since collateral fact assertions could be as hurtful as proof of an outright offer when introduced later, the policy-based privilege theory excluded the collateral evidence along with the offer. The workability of this approach helps to explain the form given to Federal Rule of Evidence 408 by the U.S. Supreme Court's Advisory Committee, and ultimately, by the Congress.

The Advisory Committee was dissatisfied with the common law rule that excluded offers of compromise on a theory of irrelevance. It preferred to base the rule on the public policy favoring the compromise and settlement of meritorious disputes; in other words, it opted for the privilege approach. Advisory Committee Note to Court, Rule 408, 56 F.R.D. 183, 227–228 (1972).

Consistent with its privilege approach, the Advisory Committee fashioned a rule that made collateral evidence, as well as offers of compromise, inadmissible to prove liability for, or the amount of, a disputed claim. One can see Rule 408 as it appeared in the preliminary draft by withdrawing the third sentence and the word "also," from the fourth sentence of the present Rule 408. Rule 408 was unchanged after three revisions of the rules by the Advisory Committee, the scrutiny of the Supreme Court, and the first series of hearings before the Subcommittee on Criminal Justice of the House Committee on the Judiciary. It went almost completely unnoticed in those hearings and the Subcommittee adopted intact the Supreme Court's version of Rule 408 in its Committee Print of June 28, 1973. When that print was circulated among bench and bar, Rule 408 drew the concerned attention of three government agencies. They warned that Rule 408 would permit parties to immunize information essential to proving violations of law by the simple tactic of presenting the information in the course of compromise negotiations. The Equal Employment Opportunity Commission was concerned primarily with preserving the admissibility of factual material, documents, compilations and the like that are essential to prove a violation.

PROBLEMS

1. Problem 27–2. In our torts case, you represent Polecat Motors. You have completed most of your pretrial discovery, and you are ready to make a serious settlement offer to Ms. Hill. On the one hand, you want to go into enough detail about the facts of the case to enable Ms. Hill's attorney to appreciate your case evaluation. On the other hand, you want to be certain that none of your factual statements in the letter will come back to haunt you at trial. How would you word the settlement letter to ensure that you will be able to invoke Rule 408 if Ms. Hill's attorney attempts to offer the letter against you at trial?

2. Problem 27–3. Shortly after the accident, Ms. Hill's attorney spoke with Mr. Flesher, the head of Polecat Motors' Claims Department. A week before the meeting, Ms. Hill's attorney had sent a demand letter to Flesher. The demand was for $250,000. During their meeting, Flesher made a counteroffer for $50,000. Flesher told Ms. Hill's attorney that Ms. Hill had "a pretty good case." Flesher also stated that "our preliminary investigation uncovered no evidence that your client was guilty of any contrib." At common law, would Flesher's last statement be admissible against Polecat Motors? Under Rule 408?

3. A number of recent decisions have extended the scope of Rule 408 to exclude evidence of consent decrees entered in administrative or judicial proceedings. *New Jersey Turnpike Authority v. PPG Industries*, 16 F.Supp.2d 460 (D.N.J. 1998)(a civil consent decree with a state environmental agency),*aff'd*, 197 F.3d 96 (3d Cir. 1999); *Option Resource Group v. Chambers Development Company, Inc.*, 967 F. Supp. 846 (W.D.Pa.1996)(consent judgment in civil proceeding and compromise settlement in Securities and Exchange Commission proceeding).

c. The Permissible Uses of Compromise Statements

Finally, even if the evidence the opponent objects to is a protected type of statement that was made during "compromise" negotiations, note the last sentence in Rule 408. The structure of the exclusionary rule is very similar to that of the uncharged misconduct doctrine. The last sentence makes it clear that the proponent may introduce the evidence so long as the proponent can articulate a theory of logical relevance other than the forbidden purposes specified in the Rule's first sentence. *See Coakley & Williams Constr., Inc. v. Structural Concrete Equip., Inc.*, 973 F.2d 349 (4th Cir. 1992) (Rule 408's exclusionary rule renders settlement offers inadmissible "only" if offered to prove liability or damages); Michaels, *Rule 408: A Litigation Mine Field*, 19 LITIGATION, Fall 1992, at 37 ("Settlement evidence has been admitted for the following purposes: to show notice; to rebut a contention of failure to mitigate damages; to show that the incident in question was not the result of accident or mistake; to show a course of reckless and outrageous conduct; to explain the absence of settling defendants who were previously in court; to assist the jury in understanding why certain individuals were not litigants; and to show the intent to commit fraud"). *See also Board of Trustees of Knox County Hosp. v. Shalala*, 135 F.3d 493 (7th Cir. 1998) (impeachment); *Towerridge, Inc. v. T.A.O., Inc.*, 111 F.3d 758 (10th Cir. 1997) (bad faith); *United States v. J.R. LaPointe & Sons, Inc.*, 950 F.Supp. 21 (D.Me. 1996)(acknowledgment of debt sufficient to restart statute of limitations).

The last sentence in Rule 408 is often applied in cases arising from traffic accidents. Suppose that the defendant's truck injured both the driver and the guest in a passenger car. Before trial, the defendant settles with the guest. At trial, the guest appears as a defense witness and testifies that the plaintiff was inattentive and, hence, guilty of contributory negligence. Under the first sentence of Rule 408, the plaintiff may not prove the witness' settlement with the defendant to show the defendant's fault directly or to prove the defendant's consciousness of fault. However, under the last sentence of Rule 408, there is a perfectly sound alternative theory of logical relevance: bias. If the proponent relies on that theory, the judge would give the jury a limiting instruction permitting the jurors to treat the evidence as proof of bias but forbidding them from inferring antecedent fault from the settlement. The proponent would have to observe a similar limitation during his or her closing argument.

NOTES AND PROBLEM

1. Problem 27–4. In our torts case, Ms. Hill settles with Roe before trial, and Roe agrees to testify for Ms. Hill at trial. The settlement between Hill and Roe is a so–called "Mary Carter" agreement. Ms. Hill not only releases her claim against Roe; Ms. Hill also promises to pay or credit Roe a portion of any recovery obtained against Polecat Motors. *Clayton v. Volkswagenwerk A.G.*, 606 S.W.2d 15, 17 (Tex. Civ. App. 1980). A "Mary Carter" agreement gives the settling defendant a direct financial interest in the plaintiff's recovery. *Lubbock Mfg. Co. v. Perez*, 591 S.W.2d 907, 919 (Tex. Civ. App. 1979). May Polecat use evidence of the settlement to impeach any trial testimony by Roe that seems to aid Hill? *Houston v. Sam P. Wallace & Co.*, 585 S.W.2d 669, 673–74 (Tex. 1979).

2. Another theory of independent relevance is the use of evidence of compromise negotiations to rebut a contract defendant's claim that the plaintiff failed to mitigate damages. For example, if a defendant contractor walked off a construction project, in a subsequent suit by the landowner the contractor might allege that the landowner failed to mitigate damages by delaying hiring a new contractor. The landowner can rejoin by explaining that there were pending compromise negotiations and that he delayed hiring a new contractor because he thought the defendant might "come to his senses" and finish the construction project.

3. If the statement amounts to an independent violation of law and the proponent offers the statement to prove that violation, the exclusionary rule is inapplicable. *Carney v. American University*, 151 F.3d 1090 (D.C. 1998). In the words of one court, "Rule 408 is . . .inapplicable when the claim is based upon some wrong that was committed in the course of settlement negotiations; e.g. libel, assault, breach of contract, unfair labor practices, and the like. . ." *Uforma/Shelby Business Forms, Inc. v. National Labor Relations Board*, 111 F.3d 1284 (6th Cir. 1997). Thus, when it is relevant for the proponent to show that the opponent threatened to retaliate against the proponent, Rule 408 would not bar proof of the threat even if the threat was made during compromise negotiations. *Dimino v. New York City Transit Authority*, 64 F.Supp. 2d 136, 163 (E.D.N.Y. 1999). *See also Starter Corp. v. Converse, Inc.* 170 F.3d 286 (2d Cir. 1999)(to prove estoppel).

2. PAYMENTS BY THE POTENTIAL DEFENDANT TO THE POTENTIAL PLAINTIFF

While Rule 408 governs the admissibility of the parties' statements during compromise negotiations, Rule 409 reads:

> Evidence of furnishing or offering or promising to pay medical, hospital, or similar expenses occasioned by an injury is not admissible to prove liability for the injury.

The scope of this exclusionary rule is broader and more absolute than Rule 408. The differences between Rules 408 and 409 would certainly be indefensible if, like Rule 408, Rule 409 rested solely on the same policy of encouraging compromise negotiations. However, another policy comes into play when we shift from statement to payments. In *Ferguson v. Graddy*, 565 S.W.2d 600 (Ark. 1978), the Arkansas Supreme Court discussed Arkansas Evidence Rule 409, modeled after the federal statute. The court asserted that Rule 409 is also designed to encourage Good Samaritans: "It is in the best interest of society and in keeping with the mores of the community that humanitarian and benevolent instincts not be hobbled by the hazard that assistance to an injured person be taken as an admission of liability."

NOTES

1. Compare and contrast the two statutes. Does Rule 409 apply only to payments made in an attempt to compromise a disputed claim? Rule 408 explicitly limits its scope to statements incident to negotiation over "a claim which was disputed as to either validity or amount . . . ." Does Rule 409 contain a similar limitation?

2. Does Rule 409 exclude evidence of payments only when offered for certain forbidden purposes? The proponent can defeat a Rule 408 objection by articulating a theory of independent logical relevance. Can the proponent overcome a Rule 409 objection by the same tactic? Is the text of Rule 409, "to prove liability for the injury," more or less restrictive than the language of Rule 408?

At this point, students familiar with alternative dispute resolution may wonder why Rule 408 seems to be confined to cases in which the parties are formally litigating their dispute. The simple answer is that the Rule developed before the recent growth in interest in non-judicial dispute resolution mechanisms. The American Bar Association Standing Committee on Dispute Resolution has proposed a model statute endorsing confidentiality for mediation proceedings. Prigoff, *Toward Candor or Chaos: The Case of Confidentiality in Mediation*, 12 SETON HALL LEGIS. J. 1, 65–70 (1988). Some of the federal civil rights statutes, notably Title VII, explicitly exclude conciliation materials. *E.E.O.C. v. Gear Petroleum, Inc.*, 948 F.2d 1542 (10th Cir. 1991) (distinguishing Title VII from the Age Discrimination Employment Act). A number of states have already enacted legislation creating a limited evidentiary privilege for statements made during mediation. *Id.* at 11 n.42; Levin, *Protecting Settlement Negotiations*, 46 J. Mo. BAR 355 (July–Aug. 1990).

Although there has been widespread support for the creation of a privilege for some alternative dispute resolution proceedings, there have been critics. *E.g.*, Green, *A Heretical View of the Mediation Privilege*, 2 OHIO ST. J. ON DISP. RESOL. 1 (1986). The critics argue in part that "no empirical data exists to" establish a need for a privilege for their informal ADR proceedings. Prigoff, *supra*, at 14. Are these proceedings distinguishable from negotiations contemplating formal judicial proceedings? In the latter proceedings, attorneys are likely to exercise substantial control over the course of the negotiations. Knowing evidence law, the attorneys will realize that there is a quasi-privilege for concessions made during the negotiations. However, in the majority of cases, the parties in ADR proceedings are not represented by attorneys. On the other hand, a mediator could make it a routine practice to inform the lay participants that there is a legal rule cloaking their statements during the proceeding with a privilege.

C.   THE RULE EXCLUDING STATEMENTS MADE DURING CRIMINAL PLEA BARGAINING

At the outset, we must delimit the scope of this section. This section does not address the question whether a defendant's final guilty or *nolo* plea in another case qualifies as the admission of a party opponent. That question relates to the admission exemption to the hearsay rule which we took up earlier. Rather, our present focus is evidence falling short of the final plea:

offers to plead or accept a plea, statements related to the offer, and withdrawn pleas.

As in the case of the analogous civil rule, there has been virtually no empirical investigation of the impact of the existence of the criminal exclusionary rule on plea bargaining behavior. There have been numerous studies of the question of the impact of the abolition of plea bargaining. *E.g.*, M. RUBINSTEIN, S. CLARKE & T. WHITE, ALASKA BANS PLEA BARGAINING (1980); Callan, *An Experience in Justice Without Plea Negotiation*, 13 LAW & SOC'Y REV. 327 (1979). However, our concern now is a radically different question: Assuming, as a matter of policy, that it is preferable to retain a plea bargaining system, can the system operate effectively without an exclusionary rule for plea offers, related statements, and withdrawn pleas?

At first, it may seem strange that there is another exclusionary rule for a defendant's admissions during plea bargaining. After all, the prosecution already has to surmount several formidable hurdles to introduce a confession: corroboration requirements, the voluntariness doctrine, the *McNabb–Mallory* rule, *Miranda,* and *Massiah. See* C. McCORMICK, HANDBOOK OF THE LAW OF EVIDENCE Ch. 14 (3d ed. 1984).

However, this evidentiary exclusionary rule rests on a different policy foundation than the above criminal procedure rules. In part, those rules reflect a concern for the unreliability of evidence obtained in violation of a suspect's Fifth or Sixth Amendment rights. The rules are calculated to insulate the suspect from certain types of pressure that might prompt the suspect to make a false confession or admission. The present exclusionary rule is more analogous to the doctrine considered earlier in this chapter, the rule excluding statements made during negotiations to compromise a civil claim. Like civil settlement negotiations, plea bargaining is recognized as a legitimate part of our litigation process. *Santobello v. New York*, 404 U.S. 257 (1971). In the words of one California court:

> Exclusion of admissions made in the course of plea negotiations is equally important to the proper functioning of the criminal justice system. In deciding whether a settlement in a criminal case is in the public interest, a district attorney must be influenced by his assessment of the defendant's culpability. Indeed, one of the advantages of plea bargaining is that it allows a fine adjustment of the criminal charge to the facts of the particular offense. (*See People v. West*, 3 Cal. 3d 595, 605, 91 Cal. Rptr. 385, 477 P.2d 409.) Accordingly, if we wish to encourage negotiated pleas, defendant's actual guilt should not be a forbidden topic of discussion. That exclusion of admissions will promote this form of candor and thus facilitate settlements seems beyond dispute. Failure to exclude such admissions would not only hamper efforts to reach an agreement but also, by discouraging plain speaking, would perpetuate the deviousness in the plea negotiation procedure so much condemned by our Supreme Court.

People v. Tanner, 45 Cal. App. 3d 345, 119 Cal. Rptr. 407 (1975). In *United States v. Verdoorn*, 528 F.2d 103, 107 (8th Cir. 1976), the Eighth Circuit echoed the sentiments of the California court: "[I]t is essential that plea negotiations remain confidential to the parties if they are unsuccessful.

Meaningful dialogue between the parties would, as a practical matter, be impossible if either party has to assume the risk that plea offers would be admissible in evidence." That belief led to the enactment of Federal Rule of Evidence 410:

> Rule 410. Inadmissibility of Pleas, Plea Discussions, and Related Statements.
>
> Except as otherwise provided in this rule, evidence of the following is not, in any civil or criminal proceeding, admissible against the defendant who made the plea or was a participant in the plea discussions:
>
> (1) a plea of guilty which was later withdrawn;
>
> (2) a plea of nolo contendere;
>
> (3) any statement made in the course of any proceedings under Rule 11 of the Federal Rules of Criminal Procedure or comparable state procedure regarding either of the foregoing pleas; or
>
> (4) any statement made in the course of plea discussions with an attorney for the prosecuting authority which do not result in a plea of guilty or which result in a plea of guilty later withdrawn.
>
> However, such a statement is admissible (i) in any proceeding wherein another statement made in the course of the same plea or plea discussions has been introduced and the statement ought in fairness be considered contemporaneously with it, or (ii) in a criminal proceeding for perjury or false statement if the statement was made by the defendant under oath, on the record and in the presence of counsel.

For all practical purposes, Rule 410 is identical to Federal Rule of Criminal Procedure 11(e)(6). The balance of this section dissects Rule 410.

1. OFFERS AND STATEMENTS

a. "Plea bargaining"

Rule 410 governs criminal plea bargaining just as Rule 408 controls civil compromise negotiation. Moreover, just as the civil exclusionary rule does not apply to all communications between potential plaintiffs and potential defendants, this doctrine does not apply to all discussions between the defendant and law enforcement authorities. In one respect, Rule 410 is certainly broader than Rule 408; Rule 410 does *not* require a bona fide dispute over guilt, as we require a bona fide dispute over liability or damages. In the overwhelming majority of cases, both sides realize the defendant's guilt of some crime. The points of dispute are (1) the precise charge the defendant will plead to and (2) the sentence concessions the defendant can obtain. "Sentence concessions" should be understood in a broad sense, including negotiations over immunity, forfeiture, and civil penalties. *United States v. Boltz*, 663 F. Supp. 956 (D. Alaska 1987). The courts apply the exclusionary rule not only to statements made after the beginning of discussions over sentence concessions but also to "statements made in an effort to initiate plea bargaining.. . ." *United States v. Bridges*, 46 F.Supp.2d 462, 465 (E.D.Va. 1999).

As in contract law, the definition of "plea bargaining" seems tied to the concept of one party seeking a *quid pro quo. United States v. Geders*, 566 F.2d 1227 (5th Cir. 1978), *cert. denied*, 441 U.S. 922 (1979). The case law has limited the scope of the expression "plea discussions" in Rule 410(4) by attempting to define both the state of mind of the accused participating in the discussions and the identity of the person with whom the accused is negotiating. The following case focuses on the question of the requisite state of mind of the accused:

UNITED STATES v. ROBERTSON

582 F.2d 1356 (5th Cir. 1978)

JAMES C. HILL, CIRCUIT JUDGE.

Plea negotiations are inadmissible, but surely not every discussion between an accused and agents for the government is a plea negotiation. Suppressing evidence of such negotiations serves the policy of insuring a free dialogue only when the accused and the government actually engage in plea negotiations: "discussions in advance of the time for pleading with a view to an agreement whereby the defendant will enter a plea in the hope of receiving certain charge or sentence concessions." ABA Standards, Introduction at 3. *See Bordenkircher v. Hayes*, 434 U.S. 357, 362 (1978); *Santobello v. New York*, 404 U.S. at 260; *United States v. Herman*, 544 F.2d at 797 ("Statements are inadmissible if made at any point during a discussion in which the defendant seeks to obtain concessions from the government in return for a plea."). Thus plea negotiations contemplate a bargaining process, a "mutuality of advantage," and a mutuality of disadvantage. That is, the government and the accused both seek a concession for a concession, a *quid pro quo. United States v. Geders*, 566 F.2d at 1231. The accused contemplates entering a plea to obtain a concession from the government. The government contemplates making some concession to obtain the accused's plea.

To determine whether a discussion should be characterized as a plea negotiation and as inadmissible, the trial court should carefully consider the totality of the circumstances. Thus, each case must turn on its own facts. However, the policy underlying Fed. R. Crim. P. 11(e)(6) and Fed. R. Evid. 410 provides the basic orientation toward this characterization. In essence, the rule of inadmissibility is designed to serve both as an incentive and as a prophylactic; the rule both encourages and protects a free plea dialogue between the accused and the government. Given this essential purpose, the trial court's initial inquiry must be focused on the accused's perceptions of the discussion, in context.

Obviously, then, the accused's assertions concerning his state of mind are critical in determining whether a discussion should be characterized a plea negotiation. However, under a totality of the circumstances approach, an accused's subsequent account of his prior subjective mental impressions cannot be considered the sole determinative factor. Otherwise, every confession would be vulnerable to such subsequent challenge. *See United States v. Geders*, 556 F.2d at 1231. The trial court must apply a two-tiered analysis and determine, first, whether the accused exhibited an actual subjective expectation to negotiate a plea at the time of the discussion, and, second, whether the accused's expectation was reasonable given the totality of the objective circumstances. *Cf. Toler v. Wyrick*, 563 F.2d 372 (8th Cir. 1977).

The initial inquiry into the accused's subjective state of mind must be made with care to distinguish between those discussions in which the accused was merely making an admission and those discussions in which the accused was seeking to negotiate a plea agreement. The trial court must appreciate the tenor of the conversation. *See United States v. Smith*, 525 F.2d 1017, 1020 (10th Cir. 1975). In those situations in which the accused's subjective intent is clear and the objective circumstances show that a plea bargain expectation was reasonable, the inquiry may end. For example, if the accused unilaterally offers to "plead guilty," *United States v. Herman*, 544 F.2d at 793, or to "take the blame," *United States v. Ross*, 493 F.2d at 774, in exchange for a government concession, then the policy underlying Fed. R. Crim. P. 11(e)(6) and Fed. R. Evid. 410 is served only if the discussions are held inadmissible. That is not to say that we *require* a "preamble explicitly demarcating the beginning of plea discussions," *United States v. Herman*, 544 F.2d at 797. Yet, when such a preamble *is* delivered, it cannot be ignored. Indeed, even when such nascent overtures are completely ignored by the government, such express unilateral offers ought to be held inadmissible, if the context is consistent. *See United States v. Brooks*, 536 F.2d 1137, 1138 n. 1, 1139 (6th Cir. 1976) and cases cited. In those situations, such as the present case, in which the record does not disclose a clear expression of a subjective intent on the part of the accused to pursue plea negotiations, the accused's after the fact expressions of his intent must be more carefully evaluated. The trial court must focus searchingly on the record to determine whether the accused reasonably had such a subjective intent, examining all of the objective circumstances.

Somewhat analogous to this two-tiered inquiry is the judicial skepticism accorded after the fact assertions by an accused who claims to have misunderstood the specific terms of a plea agreement. *See generally* Note, *Withdrawal of Guilty Pleas Under Rule 32(d)*, 64 Yale L.J. 590 (1955). Courts have been very reluctant to allow an accused to withdraw a guilty plea merely on allegations of a misunderstanding resulting from an accused's purely subjective beliefs. Yet, when there is objective evidence that the accused had been reasonably and justifiably confused concerning the terms of the plea agreement during plea negotiations, withdrawal is usually permitted as a matter of course. *See, e.g., United States v. Pihakis*, 545 F.2d 973 (5th Cir. 1977). So too with an accused's after the fact assertions that he intended to negotiate a plea, the objective record must establish that the accused's statements were made in a reasonable belief that he was negotiating a plea agreement. *Johnson v. Beto*, 466 F.2d 478–80 (5th Cir. 1972).

With this analysis, a distinction will be drawn between offers to do something in furtherance of a negotiated plea, which are inadmissible, and independent admissions of fact, which may be admitted. *See United States v. Shotwell Manufacturing Co.*, 287 F.2d 667, 673 (7th Cir. 1961), *aff'd*, 371 U.S. 341 (1963). "A plea of guilty differs in purpose and effect from a mere admission or an extra judicial confession; it is itself a conviction." *Kercheval v. United States*, 274 U.S. 220, 223 (1927). A confession only relates a set of facts and, therefore, requires only a knowledge of the factual situation. A guilty plea is something more; it is an admission of all the elements of the crime charged. *See* ABA Standards § 1.4(a). While all guilty pleas are confessions, not all confessions are guilty pleas. Therefore, it follows that not all confessions are plea negotiations.

We are not suggesting that confessions or admissions made in the course of plea negotiations are admissible under the law of confessions. Such an approach would eviscerate Fed. R. Crim. P. 11(e)(6) and Fed. R. Evid. 410. *Cf. Christian v. United States*, 8 F.2d 732 (5th Cir. 1925). However, confessions or admissions which are either made in the absence of plea negotiations or which are wholly independent from any plea negotiations are still admissible. *See Hutto v. Ross*, 429 U.S. 28, 30 (1976). Generally, a person who has been fully advised of his rights may make a full or partial admission to the arresting officers. Such a statement, if otherwise admissible under the general law of confessions, still is admissible despite the fact that the accused makes some request of those in charge. Such a request, without more, does not transform a confession into a plea negotiation. Today, we eschew a simplistic *per se* approach in favor of requiring a wholistic examination of the circumstances surrounding the discussion. Unlike the rule set forth in *Miranda*, Fed. R. Crim. P. 11(e)(6) and Fed. R. Evid. 410 do not have as their purpose the protection of criminal defendants from unwise or uninformed confessions. Moreover, application of Fed. R. Crim. P. 11(e)(6) and Fed. R. Evid. 410 to circumstances such as those presented in this case would have a substantial adverse effect on important law enforcement interests. It is reasonable to assume that the cooperation of an arrested person often is prompted by a desire for leniency for himself or others. Statements or confessions made in such circumstances, if they are voluntary and made with full awareness of the person's rights, are reliable, probative and constitutionally admissible evidence. *See* 18 U.S.C.A. § 3501. We do not believe that Fed. R. Crim. P. 11(e)(6) and Fed. R. Evid. 410 require otherwise.

NOTES

1. Is the *Robertson* test sufficiently protective of the defendant? *Miranda* teaches us that the atmosphere of custodial interrogation is inherently compulsive. Given the nature of the setting, is it fair to demand that the defendant's belief be objectively reasonable, judged in hindsight? Or do you think that it is sufficient to factor the nature of the setting into "the totality of the circumstances," as the Fifth Circuit does?

2. Apart from the merits of the policy dispute, is *Robertson* still good law under the current version of Rule 410? Note the date of the decision. The Fifth Circuit formulated its two-tiered analysis under the earlier version of Rule 410:

Inadmissibility of Pleas, Offers of Pleas, and Related Statements

Except as otherwise provided in this rule, evidence of a plea of guilty, later withdrawn, or a plea of nolo contendere, or of an offer to plead guilty or nolo contendere to the crime charged or any other crime, or of statements made in connection with, and relevant to, any of the foregoing pleas or offers, is not admissible in any civil or criminal proceeding against the person who made the plea or offer. However, evidence of a statement made in connection with, and relevant to, a plea of guilty, later withdrawn, a plea of nolo contendere, or an offer to plead guilty or nolo contendere to the crime charged or any other crime, is admissible in a criminal proceeding for perjury or false statement if the statement was made by the defendant under oath, on the record, and in the presence of counsel.

Many courts simply assume that the two-tiered approach is still good law under revised Rule 410. *United States v. Kearns*, 109 F.Supp. 2d 1309, 1315 (D.Kan.2000); *United States v. Leon Guerrero*, 847 F.2d 1363, 1367 (9th Cir. 1988); *United States v. Swidan*, 689 F. Supp. 726 (E.D. Mich. 1988). However, other courts no longer enforce the requirement that the defendant's beliefs have been reasonable. *State v. Fox*, 760 P.2d 670, 674–75 (Haw. 1988). These courts point out that Rule 410 now purports to apply broadly to any "statement made in the course of plea discussions . . . ."

The language of current Rule 410 differs significantly from the wording of the earlier version. When a drafter materially changes the wording of a statute, we ordinarily assume that the drafter intended materially to change the meaning of the statute. *Smith v. Board of Supvrs. of San Francisco*, 216 Cal. App. 3d 862, 872, 265 Cal. Rptr. 466, 472 (1989). However, as we shall see, the one change which revised Rule 410 indisputably makes is narrowing the class of persons the accused can engage in "plea discussions" with. Narrowing the class of persons contracts the scope of Rule 410 and consequently benefits the prosecutor. Is it plausible that the drafter would relax the test for the accused's state of mind while simultaneously tightening the class of persons the accused may negotiate with? Perhaps the revised Rule represents an even-handed package of reforms, one reform benefitting the prosecution and one benefitting the defense.

We turn now to the class of persons the accused may engage in "plea discussions." Contrast the current wording of Rule 410 and the language of its earlier version.

PROBLEMS

1. Problem 27–5. While in jail, Devitt tells the jailer that he would like to speak with the detectives assigned to the case. The detectives come to Devitt's cell. He tells them that he wants "to cop a plea and strike a deal." The detectives assure him only that they will bring his cooperation to the prosecutor's attention. At that point, Devitt makes an admission that complies with all the pertinent criminal procedure rules. Does Rule 410 bar the statement's admission? *See United States v. Posey,* 611 F.2d 1389, 1390–91 (5th Cir. 1980). In analyzing this problem, use the former version of Rule 410.

2. Problem 27–6. In this problem, the police initiate the discussion with Devitt. Under Morena law, they lack actual authority to grant or offer Devitt any concessions. However, they not only do not make that clear to Devitt; they suggest to him that they are so "tight with the DA" that they "can probably deliver" if Devitt has "the right sort of story to tell." Devitt does not formally offer to plead guilty during this meeting; but in response to the police officers' urgings, he makes several damaging admissions. Would the former version of Rule 410 have barred the introduction of these admissions? *United States v. Geders,* 566 F.2d 1227, 1229–32 (5th Cir. 1978), *cert. denied,* 441 U.S. 922 (1979); *United States v. Herman,* 544 F.2d 791, 795–99 (5th Cir. 1977).

3. Problem 27–7. Now analyze Problem 27-5 under the current version of Rule 410. Focus on subsection (4). *See United States v. Perez-Franco,* 873 F.2d 455, 461 (1st Cir. 1989) ("This rule has been consistently interpreted by the courts to protect only those statements made by a defendant to the prosecuting attorney himself"). *But See United States v. Millard,* 139 F.3d 1200, 1205 n. 4 (8th Cir.)("Agent Hein represented to the Millards that he was working directly with Assistant United States Attorney Lester Paff. Furthermore, during the course of these conversations, Hein telephoned Paff and discussed with Paff what deal they could offer the Millards"), *cert.denied,* 525 U.S. 949 (1998); *State v. Smallwood,* 594 N.W.2d 144 (Minn. 1999)(here the police acted as agents of the prosecutor in bringing the offer to the prosecutor's attention and relaying information back to the defendant).

4. Problem 27–8. Also analyze Problem 27–6 under the current version of Rule 410. Did Congress intend subsection (4) to apply even when the police misrepresent their authority? Is it conscionable to apply the statute literally here?

b. Protected Statements

If the contact between the suspect and the law enforcement officers constitutes plea bargaining within Rule 410, the next question is what types of statements are excluded. The offer itself is certainly excludable. What about accompanying statements of fact? We have seen that in the civil context, the traditional rule was that the statements of fact were excludable only if they were expressly made hypothetical, *e.g.,* "arguendo" or "without prejudice." The courts have not applied the same standard to criminal plea bargaining. This may reflect the courts' assumption that the typical arrestee engaged in plea bargaining lacks the sophistication of the typical businessperson attempting to compromise a civil claim. In *People v. Tanner, supra,* the California court extended protection to accompanying statements of fact, although on its face, the California statute referred only to offers. Rule 410 as originally enacted expressly mentioned "statements made in connection with, and relevant to, any of the foregoing pleas or offers." The current version of the Rule refers to "any statement."

Suppose that the negotiations lead to a cooperation agreement between the suspect and the prosecution. Pursuant to the agreement, the suspect makes certain statements to the prosecutor. The suspect later breaches the cooperation agreement. Rule 410 may still bar the admission of the suspect's statements made in the negotiations culminating in the cooperation agreement. However, does the expression "any statement" in Rule 410 extend to statements the suspect makes after striking the cooperation deal with the prosecution? *United States v. Tarrant*, 730 F. Supp. 30, 34–35 (N.D. Tex. 1990).

c. The Permissible Uses of Plea Bargaining Statements

We have learned that the rule governing evidence of payments by a potential defendant is an absolute ban on the introduction of the evidence. In contrast, the proponent may offer evidence of compromise offers and statements if the proponent can develop any theory of independent logical relevance. The configuration of Rule 410 differs from both the rule controlling civil payments and the rule governing compromise statements; the Rule does not create an absolute ban, but the Rule recognizes only a limited number of specified exceptions. Reread the last sentence of Rule 410 very carefully.

NOTES AND PROBLEMS

1. Problem 27–9. Devitt made a statement during plea bargaining, the bargain "fell through," and at the subsequent trial Devitt gave testimony contradicting his plea bargaining statement. Would Rule 410 permit the prosecutor to use the plea bargaining statement as a prior inconsistent statement? At one time, the Rule expressly allowed the prosecution to use plea bargaining statements to impeach the suspect's subsequent testimony. *United States v. Mathis,* 550 F.2d 180, 182 (4th Cir. 1976), *cert. denied sub nom. Moore v. United States*, 429 U.S. 1107 (1977). Congress later amended the Rule to delete the general exception for impeachment. *United States v. Martinez*, 536 F.2d 1107, 1108 (5th Cir.), *cert. denied*, 429 U.S. 985 (1976).

2. As a matter of policy, which version of Rule 410 do you prefer? The prosecutor will undoubtedly analogize to *Harris v. New York*, 401 U.S. 222, 223–25 (1971), allowing the impeachment use of statements obtained in violation of *Miranda*. Recently the Court has read this impeachment exception very expansively. *See United States v. Havens*, 446 U.S. 620, 624–28 (1980). How strong is the analogy between this situation and *Harris*? *State v. Vargas*, 618 P.2d 229, 230–31 (Ariz. 1980). Is the policy underlying Rule 410 strong enough to override the law's abhorrence for perjury? *People v. Benniefield*, 88 Ill. App. 3d 150, 410 N.E.2d 455, 458 (1980).

3. Suppose that the defense attempts to offer a statement made by the prosecutor during plea bargaining. (Disregard any hearsay objection.) May the prosecution invoke Rule 410 to exclude the statement? *See United States v. Verdoorn*, 528 F.2d 103, 107 (8th Cir. 1976). Does *Verdoorn* reach the correct result as a matter of statutory construction? What is the relevance of Federal Rule of Evidence 402? Consider this sentence in the last paragraph of the Criminal Advisory Committee's Note on the latest version of Rule 410: "[N]o disapproval is intended of such decisions as *United States v. Verdoorn*." Does this legislative history justify a court in allowing the government to use Rule 410 against the defense? Does the government have to rely on Rule 410? Might the government cite Rule 408? *See* 2 C. MUELLER & L. KIRKPATRICK, FEDERAL EVIDENCE § 149 (2d ed. 1994).

2. WITHDRAWN PLEAS

A related problem that Rule 410 addresses is the admissibility of withdrawn pleas. If the defendant has entered a plea but obtained a court's permission to withdraw the plea, the withdrawn plea is normally inadmissible at trial. To be sure, the exclusion of even withdrawn pleas furthers the policy of encouraging plea bargaining. However, in the leading precedent, *Kercheval v. United States*, 274 U.S. 220, 224 (1927), Justice Butler added another justification for the norm of inadmissibility:

> [O]n timely application, the court will vacate a plea of guilty shown to have been unfairly obtained or given through ignorance, fear or inadvertence. Such an application does not involve any question of guilt or innocence. *Commonwealth v. Crapo,* 212 Mass. 209. The court in exercise of its discretion will permit one accused to substitute a plea of not guilty and have a trial if for any reason the granting of the privilege seems fair and just. *Swang v. State,* 2 Coldw. (Tenn.) 212.

> The effect of the court's order permitting the withdrawal was to adjudge that the plea of guilty be held for naught. Its subsequent use as evidence against petitioner was in direct conflict with that determination. When the plea was annulled it ceased to be evidence. By permitting it to be given weight the court reinstated it *pro tanto*. The conflict was not avoided by the court's charge. Giving to the withdrawn plea any weight is in principle quite as inconsistent with the prior order as it would be to hold the plea conclusive.

While *Kercheval* is a well respected precedent, it has come under some criticism:

> The *Kercheval* rationale is based upon the mistaken assumption that pleas of guilt are permitted to be withdrawn only when the court has some reason to believe the plea was unfairly obtained and is therefore unreliable. This is not the case. Federal trial judges will often permit a plea of guilt to be withdrawn at any time up to sentence if the attorney for the defendant wishes it withdrawn, unless the court is convinced that there is no possibility of a defense and that the plea and its withdrawal were part of a scheme to obtain delay or to prejudice the government—as by a loss of key evidence in reliance on the plea. The defendant may truly believe himself guilty and he may have been fully advised when he pleaded. Yet this does not mean he will be found guilty. He has a constitutional right to be proved guilty beyond a reasonable doubt and courts are reluctant to hold a defendant to a waiver of this fundamental right.

> Since Rule 11(e)(6) of the Rules of Criminal Procedure which supersedes Rule 410 excludes evidence of any withdrawn plea in any proceeding regardless of knowledge and willingness of the pleader the line of cases permitting withdrawn pleas to be used if withdrawal was

not approved by the court is overruled. The *Kercheval* rationale is no longer adequate.

A franker rationale for exclusion is that permitting use of the withdrawn plea would make the granting of a trial meaningless. Cases which permitted the withdrawn plea to be admitted into evidence were based upon the assumption that proper instructions to the jury would insure that it would use the plea merely as evidence of conduct inconsistent with the defendant's claim of innocence. Courts have increasingly doubted the efficacy of such cautionary instructions.

2 J. WEINSTEIN & M. BERGER, WEINSTEIN'S EVIDENCE ¶ 410[03] 410-36 to 410-37 (1986). The same criticisms are reiterated in 2 WEINSTEIN'S FEDERAL EVIDENCE § 410.02[2] (2d ed. 1997).

NOTE

Which justification do you find more persuasive? If the second rationale proposed by Weinstein and Berger is sounder, does the exclusion of withdrawn pleas rest on extrinsic policy or legal irrelevance considerations?

3. WAIVER

In *United States v. Mezzanatto*, 513 U.S. 196 (1995), the Supreme Court held that a suspect may waive the protection of Rule 410. Some prosecutors demand that the suspect execute a written waiver as a precondition to entering into plea bargaining discussions. Rogers & Silverman, *Before Your Client Talks, Read the Fine Print in the Prosecutor's Proffer Agreement*, LEGAL TIMES, Sep. 20, 1999, at p. S29. Depending on the wording of the proffer agreement, the agreement might not only allow the prosecution to use the statements for impeachment during rebuttal; the agreement could even permit the prosecution to offer the statements as substantive proof during its case–in–chief. *United States v. Krilich*, 159 F.3d 1020, 1024–25 (7th Cir. 1998), *cert.denied*, 526 U.S. 810 (1999); *United States v. Burch*, 156 F.3d 1315 (D.C.Cir. 1998), *cert.denied*, 526 U.S. 1011 (1999). Of course, even if the wording of the agreement is broad, the suspect might later be able to establish that the waiver was unknowing and therefore ineffective. *E.g, United States v. Young*, 73 F. Supp.2d 1014 (N.D. Iowa 1999)(the defendent was not advised of the nature or existence of a right to have the statements excluded).

Chapter 28

REPAIRS

Read Federal Rule of Evidence 407.

A. INTRODUCTION

Modern American society is extremely safety–conscious. Accordingly, our courts are committed to promoting the social policy of encouraging remedial or safety measures. A reflection of that policy is one of the most controversial evidentiary rules, the so–called "subsequent remedial measures" doctrine. The doctrine excludes evidence of repair measures the defendant implements after an accident.

Federal Rule of Evidence 407 on Subsequent Remedial Measures codifies this exclusionary rule:

> When, after an injury or harm allegedly caused by an event, measures are taken that, if taken previously, would have made the injury or harm less likely to occur, evidence of the subsequent measures is not admissible to prove negligence, culpable conduct, a defect in a product, a defect in a product's design, or a need for a warning or instruction. This rule does not require the exclusion of evidence of subsequent measures when offered for another purpose, such as proving owner-ship, control, or feasibility of precautionary measures, if controverted, or impeachment.

The courts differ over the policy justification for this rule. Some of the courts exclude the evidence on the theory that it is immaterial and irrelevant. Others take the position that such evidence should be excluded as a matter of social policy, since such subsequent repairs, alterations, or precautions are to be encouraged in order to prevent future accidents; and if such improvements could be introduced as evidence of prior negligence of the person who made the repairs, it would deter or discourage repair of the place or thing that caused the injury. *Johns v. Pomtree*, 240 Ark. 234, 398 S.W.2d 674 (1966). *See generally*, Slough, *Relevancy Unraveled, Part III*, 5 KANS. L. REV. 675 (1957).

B. THE CURRENT STATUS OF THE EXCLUSIONARY RULE

1. THE EXCLUSIONARY RULE

Our analysis must begin with a discussion of some definitional problems.

First, **whose** subsequent remedial measures are covered? The threshold question is whether Rule 407 applies only when the person taking the remedial action is a litigant. This question relates to the very purpose of the doctrine. If the focus is on the relevance rationale for this doctrine, it should not make any difference whether the person is a litigant or a non–party. However, if the focus is the policy rationale, it makes sense to limit the exclusionary rule to changes effected by parties to the litigation. When that person is not joined as a litigant, the litigants lack standing to invoke the exclusionary rule. *See TLT–Babcock, Inc. v. Emerson Elec. Co.*, 33 F.3d 397 (4th Cir. 1994); *Brandt v. Vulcan, Inc.*, 30 F.3d 752, 759 (7th Cir. 1994).

Second, what does **subsequent** mean in this context? The doctrine certainly applies when the defendant makes the repairs after the accident in which the plaintiff is injured. "Subsequent" thus can mean after the accident. A second possible meaning would be subsequent to the sale of the product to the plaintiff.

In *Shatz v. TEC Technical Adhesives*, 415 A.2d 1188 (N.J. Super. Ct. App. Div. 1980), the plaintiff was having some workers install a slate floor in a windowless room of his house. The workers were using TEC 21F mastic cement manufactured by the defendant. The defendant's container warned only against using the cement near flame. In *Shatz*, the workers used the cement near electrical wires, and one worker knocked a wire onto the floor. The wire then ignited vapors from the cement. The ignition started a fire that destroyed the plaintiff's house. At trial, the plaintiff proffered evidence that sometime before the fire, the plaintiff added a warning to the container label to use its cement with cross–ventilation to prevent a vapor build–up. The defendant objected that the evidence amounted to proof of a subsequent remedial measure. In this situation, the New Jersey court refused to apply the doctrine to exclude the evidence. The court reasoned that it was fanciful to believe that a manufacturer would forego safety improvements to avoid adverse inferences in cases arising from accidents that have not as yet occurred. When the defendant added the new warning to its label, the fire at the plaintiff's house had not yet occurred; and realistically, the defendant would much more likely be deterred from making a repair by fear of proof of the repair in a suit over a claim that had already arisen. The defendant is much less likely to be concerned about possible future claims such as the plaintiff's. The court hence rejected the second meaning of "subsequent."

NOTES

1. The definition of "subsequent" has divided the courts. A number of courts had extended Rule 407 to safety improvements implemented after the date of the sale but before the accident. *Petree v. Victor Fluid Power, Inc.*, 831 F.2d 1191 (3d Cir. 1987). *Compare Kelly v. Crown Equipment Co.*, 970 F.2d 1273, 1277 (3d Cir. 1992) ("the Rule can properly be applied to pre–accident conduct . . . .") *with U.S. Fidelity & Guarantee v. Baker Material Handling Corp.*, 62 F.3d 24, 27 (1st Cir. 1995); *Cates v. Sears, Roebuck & Co.*, 928 F.2d 679, 686 (5th Cir. 1991) ("The 'event' to which Rule 407 speaks is the accident, not the sale"), *McWhorter v. Birmingham*, 906 F.2d 674 (11th Cir. 1990), *and Roberts v. Harnischfeger Corp.*, 901 F.2d 42 (5th Cir. 1989). The extension also had scholarly support. Note, *Excluding Subsequent Design Modifications in Product Liability Litigation: The Propriety of a Post–Sale Versus a Post–Accident Exclusion*, 29 Ariz. L. Rev. 621 (1987).

2. Which view is sounder? Is it fanciful to think that a manufacturer would be concerned about the admissibility of the design modification? Given the incidence of product liability suits, it would seem that the manufacturer well might consider the admissibility of the evidence even before any accidents have occurred. Further, is there an element of "Catch–22" reasoning to the *Shatz* view? Which manufacturer is more responsible–the one which makes changes only after accidents or the one which implements changes even before accidents? Under *Shatz*, which manufacturer enjoys the protection of Rule 407?

3. Effective December 1, 1997, Rule 407 was amended, to include the phrase: "after an injury or harm allegedly caused by an event." The Advisory Committee Note specifically states that the amendment was "added to clarify that the rule applies only to changes made after the occurrence that produced the damages giving rise to the action. Evidence of measures taken by the defendant prior to the 'event' causing 'injury or harm' does not fall within the exclusionary scope of Rule 407 even if they occurred after the manufacture or design of the product." The amendment has thus settled the 407 issue in federal practice. *Trull v. Volkswagen of America, Inc.*, 187 F.3d 88, 96 (1st Cir. 1999)(pre–accident measures not within Rule 407; however, court has discretion to exclude under Rule 403).

Although the courts have narrowed the meaning of "subsequent," they have tended to construe **remedial measure** very broadly. In *Vander Missen v. Kellogg–Citizens Nat'l Bank*, 481 F. Supp. 742 (E.D. Wis. 1979), the plaintiff sued the defendant bank under the Equal Credit Opportunity Act and alleged that the defendant unlawfully denied her credit because of her husband's unfavorable credit rating. On a motion to compel an answer to an interrogatory, the plaintiff argued that she was entitled to discover whether the bank had taken any steps to ensure that future credit applicants would not be discriminated against on the basis of sex. The court invoked Rule 407 and sustained the defendant's objection to the interrogatory. (Arguably, the court should have permitted pretrial discovery of the information but excluded the evidence at trial.)

Ford v. Schmidt, 577 F.2d 408 (7th Cir.), *cert. denied*, 439 U.S. 870 (1978), was decided in a similar vein. Prison inmates sued to challenge a state prison policy forbidding possession of negotiable items within the prison. At trial, to show the prison officials' realization that their policy was invalid, the inmates offered evidence that after the incident triggering the suit, the officials adopted a new policy allowing the possession of some negotiable items. Again, the court cited Rule 407 as the basis for excluding the evidence. On the same rationale, many courts routinely exclude evidence that after an alleged tort, the defendant employer fired the employees who were personally involved in the incident. *Wanke v. Lynn's Transp. Co.*, 836 F. Supp. 587, 595 (N.D. Ind. 1993) (post-event dismissal or discipline of an employee responsible for the event); *World Boxing Council v. Cosell*, 715 F. Supp. 1259, 1267 (S.D.N.Y. 1989) ("Courts have applied the broad language of this rule 'to exclude evidence of . . . installation of safety devices, changes in company rules, and discharge of employees.' ").

NOTES AND PROBLEMS

1. How would you define "remedial measure" or "repair"? Would "precautionary measure" be a more precise expression? Revisit the first clause in Rule 407. Does that clause contain a working definition? Some courts and commentators refer to this rule as the subsequent "repair" doctrine. Is that description accurate? When is a repair merely a replacement, in the sense of merely returning something to its previous, undamaged condition. Suppose, for example, that the tires to Worker's truck were damaged in the accident, and Roe had them replaced with the identical product. Is that the type of remedial measure to which Rule 407 applies? Would that repair even be relevant in the suit between Roe and Ms. Hill? The real question is: What type of "measure" could support an inference of antecedent negligence?

2. Apply that definition to the fact situation in *Patrick v. South Cent. Bell Tel. Co.*, 641 F.2d 1192, 1195–97 (6th Cir. 1980). The plaintiff's decedent was killed in an industrial accident; he was electrocuted. He was in a repair truck that came into contact with a tree-damaged power line. Before the accident, the defendant had strung the line thirteen feet above the ground. Immediately after the accident, the defendant restored the cable to its original thirteen feet. Later the defendant elevated the cable another ten feet. Does Rule 407 exclude proof of the defendant's restoring of the cable to thirteen–foot height? What about the later height increase? Can you distinguish these two "remedial measures" in terms of the policy underlying Rule 407?

3. Problem 28–1. A related issue, the admissibility of a defendant's recall letters and campaigns, raises intriguing questions about the relationship between the relevance doctrine and the extrinsic policy considerations underlying Rule 407.

Suppose that Polecat Motors had sent out a recall letter, mentioning the position of the gas tank as a defect and proposing a bumper modification to increase the protection of the gas tank. Could Ms. Hill's attorney offer a copy of the recall letter at trial? At first, Rule 407 seems to govern this problem and bar the admission of the recall evidence. *Gauche v. Ford Motor Co.*, 226 So. 2d 198, 210–11 (La. Ct. App. 1969). But does the deterrence rationale apply here? *Kociemba v. G. D. Searle & Co.*, 683 F. Supp. 1579, 1580–81 (D. Minn. 1988). Remember that the National Traffic and Motor Vehicle Safety Act of 1966, 15 U.S.C. § 1411, requires automobile manufacturers to issue recall letters when they discover defects. On the one hand, given that legislation, will the admissibility of the recall letter discourage the repair? *Barry v. Manglass*, 55 A.D. 2d 1, 389 N.Y.S.2d 870, 874–77 (1976). Maine Evidence Rule 407(b) explicitly sanctions proof of recall letters. *See O'Dell v. Hercules, Inc.*, 904 F.2d 1194, 1204 (8th Cir. 1990) ("An exception to Rule 407 is recognized for evidence of remedial action mandated by superior governmental authority . . .").

On the other hand, while the legislation may undercut the Rule 407 objection, does the legislation give rise to another possible objection? *See*

Vockie v. General Motors Corp., Chevrolet Div., 66 F.R.D. 57, 60–62 (E.D. Pa.), *aff'd without op.*, 523 F.2d 1052 (3d Cir. 1975).

4. Problem 28–2. Suppose that, in Problem 28-1, there was no statute or regulation compelling the recall; Polecat issued the recall letter voluntarily as a safety measure, and the judge decides to apply Rule 407 to the letter itself. Before deciding to issue the recall letter, Polecat conducted a study of the crashworthiness of the design of the gas tank. Polecat initiated the study with a view to deciding whether to issue a recall letter. Does Rule 407 bar the admission of the study? *Compare Martel v. Mass. Bay Transp. Auth.*, 403 Mass. 1, 525 N.E.2d 662 (1988) *with Rocky Mountain Helicopters v. Bell Helicopters*, 805 F.2d 907, 918 (10th Cir. 1986). The question is whether the Rule applies not only to "the actual remedial measures" but also to "the initial steps toward ascertaining whether any remedial measures are called for." *In re Aircrash in Bali, Indonesia*, 871 F.2d 812, 816 n.2 (9th Cir.), *cert. denied*, 110 S. Ct. 277 (1989); *Prentiss & Carlisle Co. v. Koehring–Waterous Div. of Timberjack, Inc.*, 972 F.2d 6, 10 (1st Cir. 1992) (after an accident, the defendant conducted an internal investigation of the incident; while Rule 407 required redacting the parts of the report of investigation discussing possible remedial measures, the "analysis" section of the report was admissible).

5. Is the language of Rule 407 broad enough to apply to a study? Does it effectuate the purpose of Rule 407 to extend the language that far? At one time, these questions were not as critical as they are today. During the 1970's and 1980's there was a strong trend toward recognizing a "self–critical analysis" privilege. Note, *The Privilege of Self–Critical Analysis: Encouraging Recognition of the Misunderstood Privilege*, 8 KAN.J.L. & PUB. POL'Y 221, 225 (1999)(collecting cases). For example, if a corporation conducted an internal investigation into its compliance with environmental laws, the conditional self–critical analysis privilege might attach to the report documenting the investigation. Thus, even if Rule 407 did not cloak a study, this privilege might. However, in 1990, the Supreme Court handed down its decision in *University of Pennsylvania v. Equal Employment Opportunity Commission*, 493 U.S. 182 (1990). In that decision, the Court in effect rejected a self–critical privilege for university tenure reviews. Since the rendition of that decision, most federal courts have rejected claims of the self–critical privilege. *Dowling v. America Hawaii Cruises, Inc.*, 971 F.2d 423 (9th Cir. 1992); Pollard, *Unconscious Bias and Self–Critical Analysis: The Case for a Qualified Evidentiary Equal Employment Opportunity Privilege*, 74 WASH.L.REV. 913, 989, 993 (1999). Indeed, some courts which previously recognized the privilege have done an aboutface and overruled their earlier precedents. Note, *What's Good for the Goose. . .Differential Treatment of the Deliberative Process and Self–Critical Analysis Privileges*, 52 WASH.U.J. URBAN & CONTEMP. L. 255, 269 n.82 (1997). The court's retrenchment on the self–critical privilege has increased the importance of the question of the scope of Federal Rule 407.

2. THE "EXCEPTIONS" TO THE EXCLUSIONARY RULE

The configuration of the subsequent remedial measures doctrine is strikingly similar to the structure of the uncharged misconduct doctrine, discussed earlier. We noted the two formulations of that doctrine–the exclusionary and

inclusionary views–and that the exclusionary view is gradually giving way
to the inclusionary approach.

Traditional commentators often suggest that there is a general exclusionary
rule regarding subsequent remedial measures, with a list of recognized
exceptions. That suggestion is inconsistent with the language of the second
sentence of Rule 407. Here, too, an inclusionary formulation is more precise.
Consider these comments:

> The exclusionary rule against subsequent remedial conduct loses much
> of its vitality in light of the several recognized exceptions. Courts have
> admitted evidence of subsequent repairs or corrective measures to establish
> notice of a prior defect; the cause of the accident, condition at the time of
> the accident; control of the premises in question; the duty of the defendant
> to repair; the feasibility of avoiding the accident; for purposes of rebuttal
> and impeachment, and when repair or changes are effected by a third per-
> son. One commentator has noted that the rule is no longer one of general
> exclusion, but rather a positive rule of admissibility subject only to the
> exception where the evidence is used as an admission of negligence. Such
> a swallowing of the exclusionary rule by its exceptions has not always been
> lauded in light of the policy behind the rule.

Comment, *Ault v. International Harvester Co.–Death Knell to the Exclusionary
Rule Against Subsequent Remedial Conduct in Strict Products Liability*, 13
SAN DIEGO L. REV. 208 (1975).

When the judge finds that an "exception" applies, the judge overrules the
objection and admits the evidence. However, the evidence still cannot be used
for the purpose of inferring antecedent negligence or fault. Consequently,
when Federal Evidence Rule 105 applies, the judge will have to give a limiting
instruction. Rule 105 reads: "When evidence which is admissible . . . for one
purpose but not admissible . . . for another purpose is admitted, the court,
upon request, shall restrict the evidence to its proper scope and instruct the
jury accordingly." The instruction will specify the permissible and impermissible uses of the subsequent remedial measures evidence. Of course, the limiting
instruction will restrict what the proponent of the evidence may say about
the testimony during closing argument.

NOTES AND PROBLEMS

1. Problem 28–3. In our torts case, Ms. Hill has sued Roe on a *respondeat
superior* theory. However, in his answer, Roe denies that Worker was acting
within the course and scope of his employment. Would it be permissible for
Ms. Hill's attorney to prove at trial that after the accident, one of Roe's tow
trucks picked up Worker's damaged car and brought it back to the Roe
motorpool for repairs? Is there any language in Rule 407 that controls this
situation?

2. Problem 28–4. Seven months after Mr. Hill bought the Polecat, six
months after the accident but before trial, Polecat Motors' Safety engineers
redesigned the rear of the Polecat model Ms. Hill was driving at the time of
the accident. The new design positioned the gas tank farther toward the front
of the car and strengthened the bumper to give the gas tank additional

protection. At trial, Ms. Hill calls Mr. Foster, the head of Polecat Motors' Production Design Division, as an adverse witness. Ms. Hill's attorney attempts to elicit Foster's admission that the rear of that model of Polecat was redesigned after the accident. The following occurs at sidebar:

O. Your Honor, I must object to that question. It patently calls for evidence in violation of Rule 407.

Q. Your Honor, I'm not offering this to prove fault in general. I have a much more specific purpose in mind.

J. Namely?

Q. I'm offering this to prove that it would have been feasible for Polecat to have designed a safer car. This is a products liability case, and I think I'm entitled to show that, Your Honor.

What ruling?

3. Problem 28-5. Would the result in the last problem be the same if the defendant had presented expert testimony about the "state of the art"? Assume that during the defense case-in-chief, Polecat had called Ms. Judd, a safety engineer, who had testified that "when it rolled off the assembly line, that model not only had the safest gas tank on any model car, domestic or foreign; its gas tank had every protective feature we safety engineers were familiar with at the time." *See Cech v. State*, 598 P.2d 584, 587–89 (Mont.), *rev'd on other grounds*, 604 P.2d 97 (Mont. 1979); *Blythe v. Sears, Roebuck & Co.*, 586 So.2d 861 (Ala. 1991) (the safety expert testifies either in superlatives or in a false, misleading manner). Note the precise wording of the second sentence in Rule 407. Why did the drafters add the requirement mentioned in that sentence? Does the drafter's motivation relate to the danger mentioned in the last sentence of the law review article quoted above? *Complaint of Consolidation Coal Co.*, 123 F.3d 126, 136 (3d Cir. 1997)("a court must interpret the impeachment exception to Rule 407 circumspectly because 'any evidence of subsequent remedial measures might be thought to contradict and so in a sense impeach [a party's] testimony. . .' Accordingly, the evidence offered for impeachment must contradict the witness's testimony directly"), *cert.denied*, 523 U.S. 1054 (1998); *Harrison v. Sears, Roebuck & Co.*, 981 F.2d 25, 31 (1st Cir. 1992) ("cases which have admitted subsequent remedial measures for impeachment purposes tend to involve a greater nexus between the statement sought to be impeached and the remedial measure . . . . Rule 407's impeachment exception must not be used as a subterfuge to prove negligence or culpability").

4. What degree of dispute is necessary to satisfy the "if controverted" requirement in Rule 407? In *Grenada Steel Indus. v. Alabama Oxygen Co.*, 695 F.2d 883, 888–89 (5th Cir. 1983), the court rejected the plaintiff's contention that feasibility is inherently in issue in any design defect case. In a similar spirit, *Werner v. Upjohn Co.*, 628 F.2d 848, 855 (4th Cir. 1980), *cert. denied*, 449 U.S. 1080 (1981), brushed aside a plaintiff's contention that the defendant must admit the issue to remove the issue from controversy. *Cf. Tuer v. McDonald*, 347 Md. 507, 701 A.2d 1101 (1997) (discussing a more expansive view as to when feasibility is controverted).

C. THE CURRENT CONTROVERSY OVER THE SCOPE OF THE EXCLUSIONARY RULE

The subsequent remedial measures doctrine crystallized long before strict products liability became a common basis for imposing tort damages. Thus, it initially was unnecessary for the courts to answer the question whether evidence of subsequent remedial measures was inadmissible in products liability cases to the same extent that it was excluded in negligence actions. However, as products liability became a more popular basis for tort liability, it became inevitable that the courts would have to address the question. When they did, the courts at first made the easy assumption that the doctrine was equally applicable. However, that assumption quickly came under serious attack. Just as the California Supreme Court's tort decisions were instrumental in expanding strict products liability, it was that court that vigorously attacked the assumption in the following case. The following decision construes the expression "culpable conduct" in California Evidence Code § 1151 and succinctly explains the controversy over application of the exclusionary rule to strict liability cases.

AULT v. INTERNATIONAL HARVESTER CO.

13 Cal. 3d 113, 528 P.2d 1148, 117 Cal. Rptr. 812 (1974)

MOSK, JUSTICE.

Plaintiff was injured in an accident involving a motor vehicle known as a "Scout," manufactured by defendant. He brought an action alleging that the accident was caused by a defect in the design of the vehicle, asserting that he was entitled to recovery under theories of strict liability, breach of warranty, and negligence.

The gear box of the Scout involved in the accident was manufactured of aluminum 380, a material which plaintiff asserts was defective for that purpose. At the trial evidence established that after the accident defendant changed from aluminum 380 to malleable iron in the production of the gear box. A jury returned a verdict of $700,000 in plaintiff's favor. On the appeal from the ensuing judgment, defendant maintains that the trial court erred in several rulings regarding the admission and exclusion of evidence. It places primary reliance upon the admission into evidence of the change to malleable iron in the manufacture of the gear box, contending that the receipt of this evidence violates the prohibition contained in section 1151 of the Evidence Code.[1]

* * *

Defendant asserts that the admission of the evidence it changed from aluminum 380 to malleable iron after the accident violated the proscription

[1] Section 1151 provides, "When, after the occurrence of an event, remedial or precautionary measures are taken, which, if taken previously, would have tended to make the event less likely to occur, evidence of such subsequent measures is inadmissible to prove negligence or culpable conduct in connection with the event." All statutory references will be to the Evidence Code, unless otherwise noted.

of section 1151. In our view, however, the language and the legislative history of section 1151 demonstrate that the section is designed for cases involving negligence or culpable conduct on the part of the defendant, rather than to those circumstances in which a manufacturer is alleged to be strictly liable for placing a defective product on the market. Furthermore, we are not persuaded that the rationale which impelled the Legislature to adopt the rule set forth in the section for cases involving negligence is applicable to suits founded upon strict liability, and we therefore decline to judicially extend the application of the section to litigation founded upon that theory.

Section 1151 by its own terms excludes evidence of subsequent remedial or precautionary measures only when such evidence is offered to prove negligence or culpable conduct. In an action based upon strict liability against a manufacturer, negligence or culpability is not a necessary ingredient. The plaintiff may recover if he establishes that the product was defective, and he need not show that the defendants breached a duty of due care. (*Greenman v. Yuba Power Products, Inc.* (1963) 59 Cal. 2d 57, 62–63.)[2]

Defendant maintains that the phrase "culpable conduct" in section 1151 is sufficiently broad to encompass strict liability. It concedes that the term "culpable" implies blameworthiness, and that a manufacturer in a strict liability action may not be blameworthy in a legal sense. However, asserts defendant, a manufacturer who has placed a defective product on the market is blameworthy in a moral sense, and is therefore guilty of "culpable conduct" within the meaning of section 1151. We are unpersuaded by this tenuous construction. It is difficult to escape a contrary conclusion: if the Legislature had intended to encompass cases involving strict liability within the ambit of section 1151, it would have used an expression less related to and consistent with affirmative fault than "culpable conduct" –a term which, under defendant's theory, would embrace a moral rather than a legal duty.[3]

* * *

[C]ourts and legislatures. . .retained the exclusionary rule in negligence cases as a matter of "public policy," reasoning that the exclusion of such evidence may be necessary to avoid deterring individuals from making improvements or repairs after an accident has occurred. Section 1151 rests explicitly on this "public policy" rationale. In explaining the purpose of the section, the draftsmen's comment states: "The admission of evidence of subsequent repair *to prove negligence* would substantially discourage persons from making repairs after the occurrence of an accident." (Emphasis added.) (Law Revision Com. comment to Evid. Code § 1151.)

---

[2] The clear theoretical distinction between these two bases of recovery impelled this court in a recent decision to hold that contrary to the Restatement (Rest. 2d Torts, § 402a), a plaintiff is not required, in order to prevail on the theory of strict liability, to show that a product is unreasonably dangerous to the use, and that it is sufficient if he demonstrates that it contained a defect which caused him injury. *Cronin v. J. B. E. Olson Corp.* (1972) 8 Cal. 3d 121, 135.

[3] Another argument of defendant is that unless "culpable conduct" is interpreted to include strict liability, the phrase has no meaning in section 1151 because it would then be synonymous with "negligence." However, there are types of faulty conduct other than negligence which are encompassed within "culpable conduct," such as wanton and reckless misconduct. *Donnelly v. Southern Pac. Co.* (1941) 18 Cal. 2d 863, 869; Rest. 2d Torts, § 500.

While the provisions of section 1151 may fulfill this anti–deterrent function in the typical negligence action, the provision plays no comparable role in the products liability field. Historically, the common law rule codified in section 1151 was developed with reference to the usual negligence action, in which a pedestrian fell into a hole in a sidewalk (*see, e.g.*, *City of Miami Beach v. Wolfe* (Fla. 1955) 83 So. 2d 774) or a plaintiff was injured on unstable stairs (*see, e.g.*, *Hadges v. New York Rapid Transit Corporation* (1940), 18 N.Y.S.2d 304); in such circumstances, it may be realistic to assume that a landowner or potential defendant might be deterred from making repairs if such repairs could be used against him in determining liability for the initial accident.

When the context is transformed from a typical negligence setting to the modern products liability field, however, the "public policy" assumptions justifying this evidentiary rule are no longer valid. The contemporary corporate mass producer of goods, the normal products liability defendant, manufactures tens of thousands of units of goods; it is manifestly unrealistic to suggest that such a producer will forego [sic] making improvements in its product, and risk innumerable additional lawsuits and the attendant adverse effect upon its public image, simply because evidence of adoption of such improvement may be admitted in an action founded on strict liability for recovery on an injury that preceded the improvement. In the products liability area, the exclusionary rule of section 1151 does not affect the primary conduct of the mass producer of goods, but serves merely as a shield against potential liability. In short, the purpose of section 1151 is not applicable to a strict liability case and hence its exclusionary rule should not be gratuitously extended to that field.

This view has been advanced by others. It has been pointed out that not only is the policy of encouraging repairs and improvements of doubtful validity in an action for strict liability since it is in the economic self interest of a manufacturer to improve and repair defective products, but that the application of the rule would be contrary to the public policy of encouraging the distributor of mass-produced goods to market safer products. (Note, *Products Liability and Evidence of Subsequent Repairs*, 1972 DUKE L.J. 837, 845–852.)[4]

---

[4] In a cogent analysis of the policy considerations underlying the admission of evidence of post-occurrence changes in a products liability context, the author states, "The assumption that the admission of evidence of subsequent repairs discourages defendants from making required repairs may be erroneous. Manufacturers and distributors of mass–produced products may not be so callous to the safety of the consumer as the general exclusionary rule presumes. Furthermore, to the extent that admission of such evidence results in recovery by injured plaintiffs, it can be argued that evidence of subsequent repairs *encourages* future remedial action. A distributor of mass-produced goods may have thousands of goods on the market. If his products are defective, the distributor would probably face greater total liability by allowing such defective products to remain on the market or by continuing to put more defective products on the market than he would by being adjudged liable in one particular case where evidence of subsequent repairs was introduced. Also, concern on the part of the distributors for consumer protection is promoted by consumer organizations, federal agencies, and mass media exposure of product defects. To some extent, the economic self–interest of product distributors requires that they repair and improve defective products to avoid adverse publicity which might result from future litigation. Since a prior jury finding of product defectiveness is admissible in a subsequent suit when the product causing the second injury is substantially similar to the first, distributors of defective products are under pressure to repair or alter their products to insulate themselves from a finding of defectiveness which may be used against them in subsequent litigation.

* * *

The judgment is affirmed.

WRIGHT, C. J., and MCCOMB, TOBRINER, SULLIVAN and BURKE, JJ., concur.

CLARK, JUSTICE (dissenting).

I dissent.

* * *

Lack of probative value is the basis for the exclusionary rule according to Professor Wigmore, although he recognizes that some courts have also relied on public policy to avoid discouraging persons from making repairs following an accident. 2 Wigmore on Evidence (3d ed. 1940) pp. 151–159. There is even less probative value when evidence of subsequent change is offered to prove an admission in product liability cases. Change in a product is frequently made for reasons unrelated to the remedial nature of the change. Among the motivations for change are the desires to decrease production cost or to increase efficiency or salability. The most striking illustration of lack of probative value is supplied by the automobile industry. Each year hundreds of changes are made in a new model. It is absurd to suggest that each change reflects an admission the modification was made to remedy a defect.

Notwithstanding the lack of probative value, juries, in the heat of negligence or product liability trials–learning only of a single change–may conclude the change reflects an admission of negligence or defect and may give great and decisive weight to the perceived admission. The danger of such misuse of evidence is at least as great in product liability cases as in negligence cases.

* * *

The record reveals that improper introduction of the subsequent modification was highly prejudicial to defendant. The evidence on the critical issue— whether the aluminum steering gear box *actually caused* the injury—was closely balanced. In the first trial, the jury was unable to reach a verdict. During the second trial, plaintiff's trial tactics included constant emphasis of the subsequent change in the steering gear box, resulting in a plaintiff's verdict. Under these circumstances, it must be concluded the improper admission of evidence substantially affected the verdict, constituting reversible error.

There is a sharp division of authority over the proper scope of the subsequent remedial measures doctrine. Annot., 50 A.L.R. Fed. 935 (1980). Several jurisdictions, including New York and South Dakota, have followed *Ault* as

---

"In conclusion, excluding evidence of subsequent repairs to encourage future remedial action may preclude recovery under theories of products liability which are themselves designed to ensure safety in marketed products. Relevant evidence should not be excluded from a products liability case by an obsolete evidentiary rule when modern legal theories, accompanied by economic and political pressures, will achieve the desired policy goals." (*Id.* at pp. 848–850.)

a matter of decisional law. *Caprara v. Chrysler Corp.*, 52 N.Y.2d 114, 436 N.Y.S.2d 251, 417 N.E.2d 545 (N.Y. Ct. App. 1981); *Shaffer v. Honeywell, Inc.*, 249 N.W.2d 251 (S.D. 1976). In Colorado, the official comment to that state's version of Rule 407 declares that the exclusionary rule does not apply to strict liability design defect cases. *See Forma Scientific, Inc. v. BioSera, Inc.*, 960 P.2d 108 (Colo. 1998); *Chart v. General Motors Corp.*, 258 N.W.2d 680 (Wis. 1977). A number of jurisdictions, including Maine, Oklahoma, and Wyoming, have even amended their version of the rule to expressly allow the admission of subsequent repair evidence in strict products liability cases.

However, numerous jurisdictions were adamant and continued to apply the exclusionary doctrine in products liability actions. *E.g.*, *Werner v. Upjohn Co.*, 628 F.2d 848 (4th Cir. 1980), *cert. denied*, 101 S. Ct. 862 (1981). In *Gauthier v. AMF, Inc.*, 788 F.2d 634, 637 (9th Cir. 1986), the court stated that "[t]he overwhelming trend in the federal courts has been to exclude evidence of subsequent remedial measures in products liability cases." *Traylor v. Husqvarna Motor*, 988 F.2d 729, 733 (7th Cir. 1993) ("We have understood 'culpable conduct' to include the creation of a product defect"); *Prentiss & Carlisle Co. v. Koehring-Waterous Div. of Timberjack, Inc.*, 972 F.2d 6, 10 (1st Cir. 1992) ("Like the majority of circuits, this court has held that Rule 407 applies to strict product liability actions"); *Raymond v. Raymond Corp.*, 938 F.2d 1518 (1st Cir. 1991).

Effective December 1, 1997, Federal Rule 407 was amended to extend the exclusionary rule to proffers of subsequent repair evidence to prove "a defect in a product, a defect in a product's design, or a need for a warning or instruction." The accompanying Advisory Committee Note acknowledges the prior split of authority. However, the Note specifically states that the amendment is intended to codify the "view of a majority of the circuits that have interpreted Rule 407 to apply to product liability actions."

NOTES

1. Does Justice Mosk cite any empirical support for his assertion that the threat of tort exposure will counteract the repair disincentive created by limiting the subsequent remedial measures doctrine? Some courts seem to think that Justice Mosk's assertion is a self-evident proposition. *Shaffer v. Honeywell, Inc.*, 249 N.W.2d 251, 257, n.7 (S.D. 1976) ("In an age of mass production it is not reasonable to assume that manufacturers would forego improvements in a product and subject themselves to mass liability for a defect just because evidence of an improvement is admissible in a pre-improvement liability case. The pure economics of the situation dictate otherwise.") Justice Mosk relies heavily on the 1972 DUKE LAW JOURNAL Note–rather than an article from an economics journal. In turn, the cited pages of the DUKE Note rely on cases and law review articles–rather than economic research. The justice describes the Note's analysis as "cogent." The analysis may be both cogent and plausible. But has it been validated and proven?

2. Does Justice Mosk's position go far enough? The drafters of the new Maine Rules of Evidence pursued what they thought to be the internal logic of the *Ault* decision in enacting Maine Rule 407(a):

(a) Subsequent Remedial Measures. When, after an event, measures are taken which, if taken previously, would have made the event less likely to occur, evidence of the subsequent measures is admissible.

The note accompanying the new rule declares: "The public policy behind the rule against admissibility was that it would deter repairs. This rationale is unpersuasive today." The Maine drafters saw the real issue posed by *Ault:* Is it time to abolish the subsequent remedial measures doctrine even in negligence cases involving mass producer defendants?

Chapter 29

LIABILITY INSURANCE

Read Federal Rule of Evidence 411.

A. THE RULE PRECLUDING ANY MENTION OF LIABILITY INSURANCE

Suppose in our torts case, Ms. Hill learns during discovery that Polecat Motors carries a public liability policy with a limit of $25,000,000 per incident. The existence of the liability policy is logically relevant to a material fact of consequence. The existence of the policy makes it slightly more likely that the defendant would be careless. For instance, the defendant's agents might think that any judgment against their employer will come "out of the insurer's pocket" rather than out of the corporate funds used to pay their wages. The inference is admittedly weak, for it depends on the awareness of insurance by defendant's agents. Moreover, there is an obvious contrary inference; we normally assume that uninsured persons are less careful than the average person.

Even though the evidence has some logical relevance, there is an available legal irrelevance objection. The evidence is "prejudicial" in the technical sense in which we use that expression in legal irrelevance analysis. If the jury hears the evidence of the defendant's liability insurance, the evidence may tempt the jury to decide the case on an improper basis. They may find for the plaintiff–not because they believe that the defendant was careless but rather because they feel that the insurer is better able to absorb the loss. *See Pride Transport Co. v. Hughes*, 591 S.W.2d 631 (Tex. Civ. App. 1979). The fear that the jury may succumb to the temptation underlies the common law exclusionary rule barring mention of the defendant's insurance. Federal Rule of Evidence 411 codifies the rule:

> Rule 411. Liability Insurance.
>
> Evidence that a person was or was not insured against liability is not admissible upon the issue whether the person acted negligently or otherwise wrongfully. This rule does not require the exclusion of evidence of insurance against liability when offered for another purpose, such as proof of agency, ownership, or control, or bias or prejudice of a witness.

There has been little research to validate the existence of the fear underlying the exclusionary rule. The following article reports some research on the subject.

KALVEN, THE JURY, THE LAW, AND THE PERSONAL INJURY DAMAGE AWARD, 19 Ohio State Law Journal 158, 170–72 (1958)

A word about the jury and insurance. Of all the points of "jury law" this has long been the most widely recognized. There is familiar law on the propriety of insurance questions on *voir dire* and on admissibility of evidence of insurance for limited purposes during trial. In states like Texas and Tennessee there are even precedents that the mention of insurance in jury deliberations may impeach a verdict. Certainly the prevalence of insurance has affected the thinking of everyone about tort. Thus there is evidence suggesting that the lawyer strategy on *voir dire* does not work; most of the jury do not understand the point of the insurance questions. But they think there is insurance anyway. There are interesting suggestions that some jurors, echoing as it were Professor Ehrenzweig, see a kind of negligence in the failure to insure. There is evidence that the silent instruction on insurance leaves the jury in the dark as to the propriety of considering it. There is the appearance from time to time of the juror who is explicitly concerned with the level of insurance premiums.

But the points I should like to underscore here are three. First that liability insurance, at least in auto cases and for the business enterprise defendant, is now so frequent that its impact on the jury is probably reduced. Second that it may have a somewhat different relevance for jury thinking on damages than for their thinking about liability. There is the arresting suggestion in some of our data that the effect of insurance may be not so much to inflate damages as it is to persuade the jury that the full loss be placed on the defendant. That is, doubts as to insurance are likely to cause the jury to award less than what it regards as the adequate award, out of regard to the burden it places on the defendant. And finally there is the underlying premise which an occasional juror puts into words. Insurance and ability to pay are relevant only in the case of real doubt. There is no simple jury rule that the insured defendant cannot win. Rather it is that where there is doubt and consequently the risk of injustice and error in deciding the case either way, it is better to risk error against the insurance fund than against the injured plaintiff. The result therefore is a subtle shift of the burden of proof, particularly on damage issues, to the insurance fund.

This last observation invites a strong note of caution as to what has been said in this section. I have been reporting primarily on what the jury talks about when confronted with the various damage issues. For several reasons such data although relevant must not be taken too literally as prediction of jury decision. On many points we have at most suggestive anecdotes, not systematic data. Again what has been reported is almost always the reactions of some individual jurors, not the consensus of the jury as a whole and it is the jury as a whole that makes the decision. The give and take of the deliberation process and the requirement of a group decision operates to limit greatly extreme tendencies to do equity as one or two jurors may see it. The jury is likely to be more conventional and in accord with the law than is the individual juror. Jury discussion is highly fluid, arguments are frequently rationalizations or rhetoric or face saving gestures making possible changes in position and there may be a wide gulf between the way the jury talks and how it finally decides.

NOTES

1. Consider the note of caution which Professor Kalven sounds at the end of the excerpt. Throughout this text we have cited empirical "jury" studies as a basis for critiquing evidentiary doctrine. Some commentators are highly skeptical of the value of these studies. What problems arise when the researchers use mock jurors–persons who know that their decision will not in fact deprive an accused of his liberty or a civil defendant of her money? According to Professor Kalven, what problems are present even when the researchers interview actual jurors? Do these problems raise concerns about the internal or external validity of the studies?

2. For purposes of argument, accept Professor Kalven's tentative findings at face value. How should this research data affect: (a) the scope of the exclusionary rule, and (b) the courts' attitude toward the enforcement of the rule? In the past, the courts have enforced this rule with remarkable vigor. Annot., 40 A.L.R. Fed. 541 (1978). The rule's violation has led to many a sustained objection and reversed judgment. Moreover, in the past trial judges often enforced the rule by mistrying a case in which there was any mention of the defendant's insurance. *Id.* However, as the following case illustrates, more recently judges have seemed less willing to grant the drastic relief of a mistrial declaration.

EDE v. ATRIUM SOUTH OB-GYN, INC.

71 Ohio St.3d 124; 642 N.E.2d 365 (1994)

This is a medical malpractice/wrongful death action brought by the plaintiff-appellant, Charles Ede, as administrator of the estate of his wife, Sheri Ede, who died on August 28, 1989. The defendants-appellees are George R. Dakoske, M.D., and the corporation of which he is the president, Atrium South OB-GYN, Inc. Dr. Dakoske performed surgery on Sheri Ede on August 24, 1989. Sheri had been scheduled to undergo an abdominal hysterectomy, but during that procedure Dakoske discovered a cancerous tumor on Sheri's right ovary which required further surgery. Sheri died four days later. Appellant alleges that Dakoske's negligent post-operative care caused Sheri's death.

The focus of this appeal is whether the trial court properly precluded appellant from eliciting testimony at trial regarding the commonality of insurance interests between Dakoske and other physicians testifying as experts on Dakoske's behalf. Before trial, Dakoske's counsel had filed a motion *in limine*, seeking to exclude from the trial any mention of liability insurance, including reference to the fact that Dakoske and other testifying physicians are insured by Physicians' Mutual Insurance Company ("PIE"). Appellant argued that since PIE is a mutual insurance company, each insured's policy is evidence of some fractional part ownership in PIE. Appellant argued that PIE-insured medical experts have a built-in bias -fewer successful malpractice claims means lower premiums charged for malpractice insurance.

. . . During oral argument on the motion, the trial judge asked Dakoske's counsel whether PIE's insurance rates were related to whether an insured agreed to testify on behalf of another insured. Dakoske's counsel, reminding the court that he was "a lawyer, not an insurance man," stated that they were not. The trial judge did not, however, seek to determine whether insurance rates for a particular classification of doctor might be affected by the outcome of a particular case.

At trial, Dr. Martin Schneider, an obstetrician/gynecologist, testified on behalf of Dakoske. Appellant's cross–examination included questioning regarding Schneider's possible bias. Appellant established that Dakoske's counsel, Jacobson, Maynard, Tuschman & Kalur, previously had defended Schneider in his own malpractice case, and that Schneider had also testified as an expert in cases defended by the same firm.

Appellant's counsel then sought to establish that Schneider and Dakoske were insured by the same malpractice insurer, PIE, and asked Schneider the following question:

> "Have you ever entered into any contractual relationship with any Ohio corporation for which the law firm of Jacobson, Maynard, Tuschman & Kalur provided legal services?"

Dakoske's counsel objected, which objection the trial judge sustained, "for the same reason I grant[ed] the [motion *in*] *limine* at the start of the trial." Appellant's counsel again argued that Schneider had a potential bias and financial interest in the outcome of the case due to the terms of his insurance contract with PIE, and that the matter of insurance may be brought up pursuant to Evid. R. 411 if used to show bias. The trial judge responded:

> "I think that insurance always has some tendency to show certain relevant factors.
>
> "The issue is more appropriately dealt with under Rule 403, as to whether or not the prejudice substantially outweighs the probative value.
>
> "And I, and just so the record is clear on the thing, we had inquiry before and I was told and it was represented that the premium rates for each of those physicians are determined according to their classification and practice and that they would not be affected by whether or not a physician, ah, determined to testify on behalf of the insurance company or didn't."

The trial judge thus precluded appellant from embarking on any questioning relevant to insurance. A jury returned a verdict in favor of Dakoske and Atrium South, and Ede appealed. The appellate court affirmed, finding that the trial court's exclusion of the insurance evidence did not amount to an abuse of discretion. The appellate court did make clear, however, that admission of the evidence, coupled with a limiting instruction, would likewise not have amounted to an abuse of discretion. The appellate court noted that "[d]epending upon the directness and scope of the potential pecuniary impact of an adverse award upon the expert witness, admission of this type of evidence upon cross-examination, coupled with the limiting instruction as to its permitted use, would seem to be the preferred choice."

* * *

The trial court in this case pointed to Evid. R. 403 in determining that the issue of the commonality of interests between Drs. Dakoske and Schneider could not be demonstrated through evidence of a common insurance carrier. The trial court ruled that the danger of prejudice outweighed the probative value of such testimony. We find that determination to be unreasonable, and therefore reversible error, for two reasons.

First, the trial court did not appreciate the probative value of establishing that Dakoske and Schneider were both insured by PIE. The trial court focused its inquiry on only one thing–whether a doctor's premiums could be raised by PIE if the doctor refused to testify on behalf of another PIE-insured doctor. Thus, the trial court sought to determine whether PIE coerced Schneider's testimony, but did not seem to consider Schneider's personal bias resulting from his insurance relationship. Satisfied by Dakoske's attorney's assurance that Schneider was not being coerced by PIE, the trial court failed to consider other possible biases created by Schneider's relationship with PIE. The trial court was not responsive to appellant's argument that as a fractional part-owner of PIE, Schneider's own premiums might fluctuate due to the result of the case. Such testimony would have been probative of bias.

Second, the trial court erred by grossly overestimating to what extent testimony that Dakoske was insured would prejudice the jury. The second sentence of Evid. R. 411 exists for a reason–it recognizes that testimony regarding insurance is not always prejudicial. However, too often courts have a Pavlovian response to insurance testimony–immediately assuming prejudice. It is naive to believe that today's jurors, bombarded for years with information about health care insurance, do not already assume in a malpractice case that the defendant doctor is covered by insurance. The legal charade protecting juries from information they already know keeps hidden from them relevant information that could assist them in making their determinations. Our Rules of Evidence are designed with truth and fairness in mind; they do not require that courts should be blind to reality. . . .

Given the sophistication of our juries, the first sentence of Evid. R. 411 ("[e]vidence that a person was or was not insured against liability is not admissible upon the issue [of] whether he acted negligently or otherwise wrongfully") does not merit the enhanced importance it has been given. Instead of juries knowing the truth about the existence and extent of coverage, they are forced to make assumptions which may have more prejudicial effect than the truth.

Thus, the second sentence of Evid. R. 411, which allows courts to operate in a world free from truth-stifling legal fictions, ought to be embraced. In such instances as the case at hand, truth should win out over a naively inspired fear of prejudice.

Therefore, we hold that in a medical malpractice action, evidence of a commonality of insurance interests between a defendant and an expert witness is sufficiently probative of the expert's bias as to clearly outweigh any potential prejudice evidence of insurance might cause. Thus, in the present case, the trial court acted unreasonably in excluding evidence regarding the commonality of insurance interests of Drs. Dakoske and Schneider. The judgment of the court of appeals is reversed and the cause is remanded to the trial court for a new trial.

Judgment reversed and cause remanded.

NOTES

1. Perhaps it is time to substitute an instruction to the jury in place of the old exclusionary rule. Many jurors will simply assume that the defendant has insurance; we fear that this assumption will influence the jurors' evaluation of the evidence of liability. In cases in which the defendant lacks insurance, why not deal with the problem in an honest, straightforward fashion and tell the jury that the defendant lacks insurance? Or why not tell them in every case that whether the defendant carries insurance is irrelevant? To use Professor Kalven's words, why "leave . . . the jury in the dark"?

2. Diamond, Casper, & Ostergren, three psychology researchers, attack the practice of "blindfolding the jury." *Blindfolding the Jury*, 52 LAW & CONT. PROBLEMS 247 (1989). They argue:

> Jurors hold expectations that influence their perceptions and judgments. Not all of those expectations are accurate, and when the inaccuracies go uncorrected at trial because of blindfolding, such false expectations may influence jury verdicts. For example, jurors may generally expect defendants to carry insurance that will cover the total cost of a damage award, but the general rule is that the jury cannot be told whether or to what extent the parties are insured against liability. Faced with an injured plaintiff, the jury will presumably by overgenerous if it thinks that an insurance company will pay.

Id. at 252. The authors attack "the . . . fiction that the jury operates on a blank slate, influenced only by what it hears and sees in court, and uninfluenced by . . . expectations . . . ." *Id.* at 251.

B. THE "EXCEPTIONS" TO THE RULE

Reread the last sentence in Federal Rule of Evidence 411. The structure of the Rule is similar to the configuration of the uncharged misconduct doctrine stated in Rule 404(b). As in the case of that doctrine, there is one purpose for which the evidence may not be offered: in the words of Rule 411, "upon the issue whether he acted negligently or otherwise wrongfully." To defeat an objection based on the exclusionary rule, the proponent need not fit the evidence within a pigeonhole exception. The proponent need only articulate a theory of independent logical relevance: "when offered for another purpose, such as . . . ." There are several well–accepted theories of independent logical relevance. The following problems exemplify some of the theories.

NOTES AND PROBLEMS

1. Problem 29–1. In our torts case, after the accident, Polecat Motors' president told Ms. Hill, "Don't worry. We carry over $25,000,000 in liability insurance." What inference does the plaintiff want the jury to draw from this statement? Does the judge have to construe this statement as an admission of liability by the defendant? *Brainard v. Cotner*, 59 Cal. App. 3d 790, 795–96, 130 Cal. Rptr. 915, 918 (1976). Assume that the judge interprets the statement in that fashion. Should the admission drag the mention of insurance into evidence with it? *See Keown v. Monks*, 491 So. 2d 914, 915–16 (Ala. 1986) ("I've got insurance and I'm just real sorry.").

2. Problem 29–2. Would the result be different if the statement read: "Don't worry. We're at fault, but we're good for it. We carry over $25,000,000 in liability insurance." Is the difference purely linguistic?

3. Problem 29–3. Ms. Hill has added Roe, Mr. Worker's employer, as a defendant. In his answer, Roe denies that Worker was one of his agents. Would it be permissible for Ms. Hill to prove that at the time of the accident, Roe's liability insurance policy included Worker on Schedule B, the list of employees whose acts were covered by the policy? *See Cherry v. Stockton*, 75 N.M. 488, 406 P.2d 358, 360 (1965).

4. Problem 29–4. In his answer, Roe denies owning the truck involved in the accident. Could Ms. Hill prove that Schedule C, the list of covered instrumentalities, mentioned the car? *See Dobbins v. Crain Bros.*, 432 F. Supp. 1060, 1069–70 (W.D. Pa. 1976), *modified*, 567 F.2d 559 (3d Cir. 1977). Does the language of Rule 411 support your conclusion?

5. Problem 29–5. During its case-in-chief, Polecat Motors calls Dr. Vaughn, who testifies that in his opinion Ms. Hill's injuries are not permanent in character and that the prognosis is a complete recovery. Vaughn is being paid by the defendant's liability insurer, Allstate. In fact, in the past three years, Allstate has hired Vaughn to give similar testimony in ten other cases. What is the logical relevance of the evidence of defendant's liability insurance? Does this theory qualify as a theory of independent relevance? *Charter v. Chleborad*, 551 F.2d 246, 248 (8th Cir.), *cert. denied*, 434 U.S. 856 (1977). Again, is there any textual support for your conclusion in Rule 411?

6. Note the contrast between Rules 411 and 407, dealing with evidence of subsequent remedial measures. Rule 407 specifically requires that the fact the evidence is offered to prove be "controverted." Rule 411 omits that language. Can the judge nevertheless exclude insurance evidence under Rule 403 if the evidence is offered to prove an issue that is only technically in dispute? 23 C. WRIGHT & K. GRAHAM, FEDERAL PRACTICE AND PROCEDURE: EVIDENCE § 5365, at 455 (1980). Assume that, in a fact situation like Problem 29–3 or 29–4, the issue which Ms. Hill offered the evidence to prove was undisputed. For example, Roe's attorney might offer to stipulate that Worker was one of Roe's employees or that Roe owned the truck involved in the accident. May the judge exclude the evidence under Rule 403?

May the court read the requirement for a bona fide dispute into Rule 411 on the theory that the omission was inadvertent? One commentator has characterized the omission as an "oversight" by the drafters. Schmertz, *Relevance and Its Policy Counterweights: A Brief Excursion Through Article IV of the Proposed Federal Rules of Evidence*, 33 FED. B.J. 1, 20 (1974). Some students of legislation believe that "scrivener's errors" are relatively common.

Eskridge, *The New Textualism*, 37 U.C.L.A. L. REV. 621, 687 (1990). Courts often assert the power to effectively insert words into a statute to correct legislative drafting "mistakes." However, that power must be exercised cautiously due to separation of power considerations. W. ESKRIDGE & P. FRICKEY, CASES AND MATERIALS ON LEGISLATION: STATUTES AND THE CREATION OF PUBLIC POLICY 633 (1988).

Is there an alternative statutory construction argument? Perhaps, rather than justifying an addition to Rule 411, the courts should inquire whether they may in effect delete "controverted" from Rule 407 on the theory that the term is surplusage. In some states, including Michigan and Texas, the drafters added an adjective, either "controverted" or "disputed," to Rule 411 to moot this issue of statutory interpretation. 23 C. WRIGHT & K. GRAHAM, FEDERAL PRACTICE AND PROCEDURE: EVIDENCE § 5365 (1980).

A closely related issue can arise much earlier–during the *voir dire* examination of the prospective jurors. If the defendant has an insurer, one of the insurer's stockholders or employees may be a venireperson. The venireperson may even be challengeable for cause on that very ground. During *voir dire*, many jurisdictions permit counsel to ask prospective jurors whether there are any "policyholders, stockholders, present employees, past employees, or claims adjusters" of an insurance company among them. *George v. Howard Constr. Co.*, 604 S.W.2d 685 (Mo. Ct. App. 1980). *But see Parento v. Palumbo*, 677 F.2d 3, 4–5 (1st Cir. 1982) (noting the split of authority); *Morrow v. Zigaitis*, 608 S.W.2d 427 (Mo. Ct. App. 1980); *Imparato v. Rooney*, 95 Ill. App. 3d 11, 419 N.E.2d 620 (1981).

NOTE

Although this inquiry is logically relevant to a ground for challenge, the inquiry also serves as a transparent device for suggesting the presence of insurance to the jury. If, as judge, you permitted the attorney to question prospective jurors regarding the "insurance question," what type of instruction would you give the jury? Does our toleration of this *voir dire* practice mean that it is time to abandon the exclusionary rule?

Part 5

SUFFICIENCY OF THE EVIDENCE

Chapter 30

THE INITIAL BURDEN OF GOING FORWARD

Federal Rule of Evidence 301. Presumptions in General in Civil Actions and Proceedings:

In all civil actions and proceedings not otherwise provided for by Act of Congress or by these rules, a presumption imposes on the party against whom it is directed the burden of going forward with evidence to rebut or meet the presumption, but does not shift to such party the burden of proof in the sense of the risk of nonpersuasion, which remains throughout the trial upon the party on whom it was originally cast.

Federal Rule of Evidence 302. Applicability of State Law in Civil Actions and Proceedings:

In civil actions and proceedings, the effect of a presumption respecting a fact which is an element of a claim or defense as to which State law supplies the rule of decision is determined in accordance with State law.

A. INTRODUCTION

Previously, in Parts 3 and 4 of this text, we examined questions of admissibility of various types of evidence. In this Part we shift our focus to a broader perspective: evaluating the cumulative sufficiency of all the evidence to prove the facts in question. Even if the plaintiff or prosecutor wins the battle over the admission of an item of evidence, she may lose the war. The judge may conclude that the cumulative probative value of all the admitted items of evidence is insufficient to establish a fact the plaintiff or prosecutor must prove and, on that ground, direct a defense verdict.

There are several ways of establishing a fact during a trial. As we saw at the beginning, some facts are so well known or easily verifiable that the judge can judicially notice their existence. Or the parties may establish the fact by stipulating to the fact's existence. However, in most instances, neither of these shortcuts is available. Usually, one of the parties must bear the burden of attempting to introduce enough evidence to persuade the judge and jury that the fact exists.

Two actors evaluate the sufficiency of the evidence to prove the disputed facts. The judge performs the first evaluation; the judge assesses the legal sufficiency of the evidence. As a method of controlling the rationality of the jury's findings, the judge scrutinizes the evidence to determine whether it has sufficient probative value to permit a rational trier of fact to conclude that the fact exists. In other words, the judge inquires whether the proponent has sustained the initial burden of going forward (sometimes this is also called "the burden of production"). If the proponent fails to sustain the burden, the judge makes a peremptory ruling against the proponent; the judge takes the issue away from the jury and announces that the opponent has prevailed on the issue "as a matter of law."

However, if the proponent sustains the initial burden, the proponent has still another major hurdle: persuading the trier of fact (the jury or, in a bench trial, the judge). In ruling on the burden of going forward, the judge decides only the question of law whether a rational trier of fact could decide that the fact exists. For example, in *Devitt* the prosecutor must persuade the judge that Paterson's identification of Devitt as the assailant is definite enough to permit a rational juror to find that Devitt committed the battery. Next, the trier of fact assesses the factual sufficiency of the evidence. The trier evaluates the evidence to decide whether the fact exists: the prosecutor now faces the heavier burden of convincing the jury, beyond a reasonable doubt, that Devitt in fact attacked Paterson.

At the outset, you should be struck by the fact that, in our law, the number of rules governing the admissibility of evidence dwarfs the number governing the sufficiency of evidence. In many civil law countries, there are detailed rules to determine the sufficiency of the evidence. For example, two witnesses or a witness' testimony corroborated by documentary evidence may be necessary to establish a proposition. In contrast, in Anglo–American evidence, largely due to the influence of Jeremy Bentham, "[t]here are few formal rules governing questions of" the sufficiency of evidence. Twining, *The Rationalist Tradition of Evidence Scholarship*, in WELL AND TRULY TRIED 211, 221 (E. Campbell & L. Waller, eds. 1982). Rather than fashioning "artificial legal rules," our system relies primarily on "the natural processes of the mind" to determine the legal sufficiency of evidence. J. WIGMORE, 1 THE SCIENCE OF JUDICIAL PROOF 5 (3d ed. 1937). Occasionally, common law jurisdictions recognize numerical rules. For example, Pennsylvania follows a "two witness" rule in contract reformation cases. *Giant Eagle, Inc. v. Federal Ins. Co.*, 92 F.3d 205, 212 (3d Cir. 1996). As a general proposition, though, the testimony of a single witness is sufficient to support any finding of fact. CAL.EVID. CODE § 411; GA. CODE ANNOT. § 24–4–8.

B. THE INITIAL BURDEN OF GOING FORWARD: AN OVERVIEW

Before analyzing the operation of the burden of production, we must consider the definition and allocation of the burden. The steps the proponent and opponent progress through become meaningful only after we understand what the burden is and how the proponent becomes saddled with the burden.

The burden is a duty owed the trial judge. The duty is the obligation of convincing the judge that the proponent's evidence is strong enough to allow a rational trier of fact to return a verdict in the proponent's favor. There are various verbal formulae: The proponent's evidence must be sufficient to make out a "submissible" case, a case strong enough to submit to a rational jury. The issue must be "trial–worthy." *Colantuoni v. Alfred Calcagni & Sons, Inc.*, 44 F.3d 1 (1st Cir. 1994). In deciding whether the evidence would support a logical inference by a rational jury, "[t]he key . . . is the reasonable probability that the conclusion flows from the evidentiary datum because of past experience in human affairs." *Levendos v. Stern Entertainment Co.*, 909 F.2d 747,

753 (3d Cir. 1990) (quoting R. Aldisert, Logic for Lawyers: A Guide to Clear Legal Thinking 29 (1989)).

Suppose, for example, that at the close of Ms. Hill's case–in–chief, Polecat Motors' attorney does not believe that Ms. Hill has presented sufficient evidence of negligent manufacture or an unreasonably dangerous defect. Polecat's attorney should move for a nonsuit or judgment as a matter of law. If the judge agrees that Ms. Hill has presented insufficient proof of negligence or defect, the judge would grant the motion and proclaim a defense victory. For purposes of ruling on this motion, the judge accepts, *arguendo*, the truth of all Ms. Hill's evidence. In order to grant the motion and declare a defense victory, the judge must conclude that even if the jury chose to believe all of Ms. Hill's evidence, the evidence is insufficiently probative of negligence or a defect to support a rational plaintiff's verdict. To shield Polecat Motors from an irrational verdict, the judge takes the case away from the jury and enters a judgment for the defense. The title of the judge's ruling varies from jurisdiction to jurisdiction: nonsuit, directed verdict, judgment as a matter of law, finding of not guilty, or judgment of acquittal. However, the common denominator is the judge's decision to preclude the possibility of an irrational decision by taking the case from the jury and announcing the result "as a matter of law."

How does the judge decide to whom to allocate the burden on the various factual issues in the case? We shall consider the allocation of the ultimate burden of persuasion in detail in the next chapter. At this point, it suffices to suggest that you begin with the rule of thumb that the party with the ultimate burden will have the initial burden. In *Hill,* the plaintiff has both the initial and ultimate burdens on the factual issues of negligent manufacture and the existence of an unreasonably dangerous design defect. However, it would be wasteful and unduly burdensome to assign to plaintiff the initial burden to negate all possible affirmative defenses. In most jurisdictions, for example, if Roe wants to raise the issue of Ms. Hill's contributory negligence, Roe must assume the initial and ultimate burdens on the issue.

1. THE GENERAL MECHANICS OF THE BURDEN

2 E. IMWINKELRIED, P. GIANNELLI, F. GILLIGAN & F. LEDERER, CRIMINAL EVIDENCE 1089–1100 (3d ed. 1998)
(citations omitted)

Attempting to Sustain the Burden

Many evidence students have complained that this area of law is abstract to the point of being metaphysical. At the outset, diagramming the steps the proponent and opponent progress through is helpful. The following is a discussion of the most important steps depicted on the diagram.

The Proponent Fails to Sustain the Burden. In the first step, the proponent's evidence is insufficient to sustain the burden. The older view is that a mere scintilla of evidence is sufficient to sustain the burden. More recently, the prevailing view is that the evidence must have sufficient probative value to permit the jurors to rationally infer that the disputed fact exists.

. . . [By virtue of *Jackson v. Virginia*, 443 U.S. 307 (1979), a] stricter standard applies in criminal cases. This view is that the test in criminal cases is whether the evidence is so weak that the jurors must have a remaining lingering reasonable doubt; even if there is a permissive inference of the fact's existence, the evidence is insufficient if it would necessarily leave rational jurors with a lingering doubt about the defendant's guilt.

Proponent

→

1	2	3	4
absolute peremptory ruling against	permissive inference	true presumption	absolute peremptory ruling in favor

Opponent

←

9	8	7	6	5
absolute peremptory ruling in favor	counter-presumption	rebuts presumed fact	rebuts foundational fact	rebuts neither foundational nor presumed fact

Suppose that the defendant attempts to raise the defense of insanity. The judge allocates the defendant the initial burden of going forward on that issue. Suppose further that the defendant's only evidence of insanity is the testimony of a lay witness to the crime. That witness gives conclusory testimony that several hours before the crime, the defendant was acting "a bit peculiar." At the instructions conference, the defense attorney requests an instruction on insanity. The judge will undoubtedly deny the request, for logically, the evidence lacks sufficient probative value to support an inference of insanity. Thus to control the rationality of the jury's findings, the judge will withdraw the issue from the jury. This ruling can be restated symbolically. The proponent, the defense, has presented credible evidence of fact A, the defendant's slightly peculiar behavior before the offense. The ultimate material fact in dispute is E, the defendant's sanity. In effect, the judge has ruled that *even if the jurors believe the evidence of A, they may not infer E*. A is the foundational or basic fact. E is the presumed fact. In this case, the foundational or basic fact does not have sufficient probative worth to permit an inference that E exists.

What is the procedural consequence if the proponent reaches only this step? As a matter of law, the judge will make an absolute peremptory ruling against the proponent. If the prosecution has the burden on an issue and prosecution reaches only step #1, the judge will grant a motion for directed verdict, judgment of acquittal, or finding of not guilty. When the defense has the burden on a defense and reaches only step #1, the judge will not instruct the jury on the defense. The proponent suffers an absolute defeat on the issue.

The Proponent Barely Sustains the Burden. In the second step, the proponent barely sustains the burden of going forward. The proponent ordinarily reaches this step by presenting sufficient evidence to support a rational jury finding of the existence of the fact in dispute. Under *Jackson v. Virginia*, when the prosecution has the burden, the evidence must be sufficient to permit a hypothetical juror to infer guilt beyond a reasonable doubt. The judge assesses the probative value of the proponent's evidence and concludes that the value is sufficient to sustain the burden. Alternatively, for policy reasons the legislature can declare that if the proponent proves specified foundational facts, the jury may infer the fact in dispute. [T]he creation of an inference by legislative fiat poses serious constitutional questions in criminal cases.

Returning to the original hypothetical, suppose that the defense attorney now presents more extensive lay testimony. The lay witness states that he or she has known the defendant intimately for several years; at the time of the offense, the defendant was absolutely incoherent, lacked muscular control, and had a dazed appearance; and in the witness' opinion, the defendant was insane. Once again, the defense attorney requests an instruction on insanity. Now the judge will probably grant the request. The proponent defense has presented evidence of fact B, detailed testimony about bizarre behavior on the part of the defendant whom the witness knew well. The judge rules that *if the jurors believe the evidence of B, they may infer E*.

At this stage, the proponent has created a permissive inference or presumption of fact. The procedural consequence is that the judge will submit the issue to the jury. If the proponent reaches only step #2, neither party will be subject to a peremptory ruling by the judge.

The Proponent Creates a True Presumption. In the third step, the proponent goes beyond barely sustaining the burden, presenting sufficient evidence to create a true presumption or mandatory inference. In the second step, the proponent creates a mere permissive inference; the jury may infer the existence of the fact in dispute from the foundational evidence. The third step is qualitatively different. There is such a necessary or highly probable connection between the foundational fact and the fact in dispute that the inference is mandatory; if the jurors believe the foundational evidence, they must infer the existence of the fact in dispute. The California statutes clearly draw the distinction. California Evidence Code § 600(b) defines an inference as "a deduction of fact that may logically and reasonably be drawn from another fact or group of facts." In contrast, Evidence Code § 600 (a) declares that a presumption is "an assumption of fact that the law requires to be made from another or group of facts." Ordinarily the proponent must rely upon the evidence's sheer probative value to carry the proponent to the third step. Of course, as in the second step, a legislature may create a presumption by fiat, declaring that if the jury finds that specified foundational facts exist, they must infer the fact in dispute. Here again, in criminal cases, such legislative declarations pose constitutional issues.

Revisiting the hypothetical, suppose that the defense attorney presents a properly authenticated copy of a judgment showing that shortly before the alleged offense, a court of competent jurisdiction adjudged the defendant permanently insane. If the defendant suffered from a relatively permanent mental disorder such a short time before the offense, he or she was probably insane at the time of the alleged *actus reus*. The foundational evidence is so powerful that it creates a mandatory inference or true presumption of insanity. The foundational evidence, fact C, gives rise to a mandatory inference of the existence of the fact in dispute. The judge would rule that *if the jurors believe the evidence of C, they must infer E.*

The proponent has now created a mandatory inference or presumption of law or prima facie case. A true presumption has one and sometimes two procedural consequences. The first is that if the presumption does not disappear from the case, it will entitle the proponent to a conditional peremptory ruling which takes the form of a favorable instruction to the jury. Because the presumption does not entitle the proponent to an absolute peremptory ruling, the judge will not instruct the jury that E, the fact in dispute, exists. Rather, the ruling is conditional, and the condition is the jury's belief of the foundational evidence. Thus the judge instructs the jury that they must infer E if they believe the evidence of C. The conditional ruling is peremptory because the judge has withdrawn from the jury the issue of the connection between C and E, telling the jury that a necessary connection exists between the two facts. However, the jury must nevertheless decide whether to believe the evidence of C.

In some jurisdictions, a second procedural consequence flowing from the creation of a presumption is a shift of the ultimate burden of proof. This consequence could conceivably operate against a criminal defendant. In a homicide case, the prosecution must prove the death of the alleged victim. Some jurisdictions recognize a burden–shifting presumption that a person is dead if he or she has not been heard from in seven years. In a bigamy case, the prosecution must establish the validity of the first marriage. Several jurisdictions recognize a burden–shifting presumption that a ceremonial marriage is valid. Some statutes creating burden–shifting presumptions expressly provide that the presumption may not operate against a criminal defendant.

The Proponent Obtains an Absolute Peremptory Ruling. In the first step, the judge makes an absolute peremptory ruling against the proponent; the judge withdraws the issue from the jury and announces the proponent's loss. In the fourth step, the judge makes an absolute peremptory ruling in the proponent's favor; the judge withdraws the issue from the jury and announces the proponent's victory. In this situation the proponent presents such overwhelming evidence and the opponent presents such meager evidence that the jury's finding against the proponent would be irrational.

Understandably, a proponent rarely reaches the fourth step. The fifth and fourteenth amendments preclude absolute peremptory rulings against the defendant on essential elements of the charged offense. However, occasionally, some defendants have won absolute peremptory ruling. In the original hypothetical, suppose that the defense presented extensive expert psychiatric testimony of schizophrenia, and the prosecution did not present even lay rebuttal testimony. Under these circumstances, some defendants have won absolute peremptory rulings which dismiss the charges against them. There is also authority that if the defendant presents uncontradicted evidence of entrapment, the defendant is entitled to dismissal. Such cases share several common elements. First, the proponent presents extensive, credible evidence of the foundational facts. Second, the opponent presents no or very meager rebuttal evidence. Third, the opponent usually has the ultimate burden of proof on the issue. In the insanity cases, although the defense has the initial burden of going forward on the insanity issue, in most jurisdictions the prosecution has the ultimate burden of proof. If all three elements are present, an absolute peremptory ruling in the proponent's favor is appropriate.

Here the foundational evidence is D. The judge rules that *(1) the jury must believe the evidence of D and (2) the jury must infer E from D.* In the third step, the judge makes only the second ruling—the conditional peremptory ruling that a necessary connection exists between C and E. However, the judge does not direct the jury to believe the evidence of C. In the fourth step, the judge concludes that the jury's disbelieving the evidence of D would be irrational. Therefore, the judge removes the condition and makes an absolute ruling. For example, if several reputable psychiatrists testify that the defendant was suffering from a psychosis and the prosecution presents no rebuttal, the defense is entitled to an absolute peremptory ruling. The ruling for the defense takes the form of a directed verdict, judgment of acquittal, or finding of not guilty.

Attempting to Rebut the Evidence

Assume that the proponent reaches either step #2 or #3. If the proponent reaches step #2, the proponent has barely sustained the burden; if the proponent reaches step #3, the proponent creates a true presumption. In both cases, the proponent has satisfied the burden of going forward. However, so long as the proponent does not reach step #4, the opponent escapes an absolute peremptory ruling. Moreover, the opponent usually has the opportunity to present rebuttal evidence to demonstrate that the presumed fact does not exist, for most presumptions are rebuttable. Although the proponent gains the benefit of a permissive or mandatory inference that E exists, the opponent may introduce evidence that E does not exist.[22]

[22] There are conclusive or irrebuttable presumptions. Such presumptions are in this form: If the jurors believe the evidence of C, they must infer E. That statement is elliptical; to state the

The Opponent Does Not Present Sufficient Evidence to Rebut Either the Foundational or the Presumed Fact. In the fifth step, the opponent fails to present sufficient evidence to rebut either the foundational fact or the presumed fact. The form of the instruction the jury hears depends upon whether the proponent attained the second or the third step. If the proponent reached the second step, the instruction is that *if the jurors believe the evidence of B, they may infer E.* If the proponent attained the third step, the instruction is that *if the jurors believe the evidence of C, they must infer E.*

The Opponent Presents Sufficient Evidence to Rebut the Foundational Fact. In the sixth step, the opponent still fails to present sufficient evidence to rebut the ultimate fact in dispute, E. However, the opponent does succeed in presenting sufficient evidence to rebut the foundational fact. With one exception, the jury instructions are the same as they are in the fifth step. This exception is that judge must call the jury's attention to the fact that the parties have presented conflicting evidence on the foundational fact. There is now a disputed question of fact over whether the foundational fact exists. The judge instructs that *the jurors must resolve the conflict in the evidence over whether the foundational fact, B or C, exists.* The judge then delivers the instructions previously outlined.

The Opponent Presents Sufficient Evidence to Rebut the Presumed Fact. In the seventh step, the opponent mounts a sufficient rebuttal against E itself, the ultimate fact in dispute. Two questions arise. The first is the standard for determining when the opponent has presented sufficient rebuttal evidence. The second is the procedural effect of the opponent's presentation of sufficient rebuttal evidence.

The Sufficiency of the Rebuttal Evidence. The courts have unfortunately articulated numerous conflicting standards for testing the sufficiency of the opponent's rebuttal evidence, including "substantial evidence to the contrary, any contradictory evidence, some evidence to the contrary, competent evidence, evidence of equal weight, evidence legally sufficient to overcome the presumption, and testimony that outweighs the presumption." Nevertheless, the wealth of verbal formulae is reducible to five primary standards: the

---

matter more starkly, if the jurors believe the evidence of C, they must infer E even if the opponent has credible evidence that E does not exist. The truth of the matter is that a conclusive presumption is a substantive rule of law rather than an evidentiary rule. 9 WIGMORE, EVIDENCE § 2492 (3d ed. 1940). The legal consequence flows from the foundational facts, and the existence or non–existence of the presumed fact is immaterial.

Consider this statutory presumption for criminal nonsupport actions. A child born while a husband and wife are cohabiting is conclusively presumed to be the husband's natural offspring. In a nonsupport action, the defendant husband could attack the foundational facts. The husband could introduce evidence that the woman was not his lawful wife or that they were not cohabiting when the child was born. However, the husband could not attack the presumed fact, the child's legitimacy. The husband could not introduce another man's admission that he considered himself the father. In reality, the child's legitimacy is immaterial in the nonsupport action. By enacting the statutory evidentiary presumption, the legislature has effectively promulgated a substantive rule of law that a husband has a legal duty to support a child born of his wife while they are cohabiting. *Brian C. v. Ginger K.*, 77 Cal.App.4th 1198, 92 Cal.Rptr.2d 294, 298 (2000)("While nominally a rule of evidence, there is no doubt that the conclusive presumption is a substantive rule of law . . .").

Model Code standard of "any evidence contrary thereto, regardless of whether it is credible or substantial"; substantial evidence to the contrary; evidence sufficient, standing alone, to support a finding that the material fact in dispute does not exist; evidence sufficient to leave the issue in equipoise; and finally, evidence which makes the fact's non–existence more likely than its existence.

The Effect of the Presentation of Sufficient Rebuttal Evidence. Suppose that under the prevailing standard in the jurisdiction, the judge decides that the opponent has presented sufficient rebuttal evidence. What is the procedural consequence? There are two schools of thought on this question.

The first is the majority view, the "bursting bubble" theory, advocated by Thayer, Wigmore, and the drafters of the Model Code. Their view is that the presumption disappears or self–destructs as soon as the opponent presents sufficient rebuttal evidence. If the opponent presents such evidence, the judge will not mention a mandatory inference or even the word presumption in the final jury charge. This school theorizes that presumptions are merely procedural devices for allocating the burden of going forward during the trial. If the judge has decided that the case should be submitted to the jury, the presumption has already spent its force and fulfilled its function.

Only the presumption has disappeared; the proponent is no longer at step #3. Usually a permissive inference remains, for the evidence of the foundational facts is still in the record, and that evidence ordinarily has sufficient probative value to keep the proponent at step #2, thus preventing an absolute peremptory ruling against the proponent. Conceivably, when the presumption disappears, the proponent could revert back to step #1. This possibility arises because, as previously stated, a legislature may create a presumption by fiat. If the foundational facts specified in the statute do not have sufficient probative value to support a permissive inference of the existence of the ultimate fact, E, the presentation of sufficient rebuttal evidence is fatal to the proponent's case. The immediate effect is the disappearance of the presumption; the proponent is no longer at step #3. More importantly, because the foundational facts do not support a permissive inference of E, the proponent reverts to step #1 and suffers an unfavorable absolute peremptory ruling.

The second school of thought asserts that the presumption remains in the case even after opponent presents sufficient rebuttal evidence. The adherents of this view include Morgan, McCormick, Bohlen, and the drafters of the Uniform Rules. This view has significant procedural consequences. First, even after the opponent reaches step #7, the proponent remains at step #3. Hence, it is impossible for the proponent to revert to step #1 and suffer an unfavorable absolute peremptory ruling. Second, regardless of the rebuttal evidence, the proponent obtains a favorable jury instruction. However, even the courts subscribing to the second school of thought disagree over the instruction's wording.

Some courts prefer merely to inform the jury that the presumption exists and do not even attempt to explain the presumption's operation to the jury. Other courts inform the jury of the presumption's existence and then describe the presumption itself as evidence. Still other courts use the term, presumption, but describe the presumption as a permissive inference. The final group of courts urge that the presumption not only remains in the case but also shifts the ultimate burden of proof to the opponent. They instruct the jury *if the jurors believe the evidence of C, they must infer E unless the opponent proves by a certain measure of proof that E does not exist*—for example, by a preponderance of the evidence. Morgan and McCormick would apply this view to all true presumptions.

NOTES AND PROBLEMS

1. Note the similarity in mode of analysis between Rule 104(b) admissibility determinations and sufficiency decisions under the initial burden of going forward. Under 104(b), the judge accepts the foundational testimony at face value to determine whether the proffered item of evidence is admissible and may be presented to the jury. Under the initial burden, the judge accepts the testimony on the historical merits at face value and decides whether the proponent's case may be submitted to the jury.

2. Problem 30–1. In *Hill*, the Morena legislature enacts a statute creating a presumption that when an injury results from an automobile accident, the manufacturer's negligence in manufacturing the auto was one of the causes of the accident. At trial, Ms. Hill requests the judge to give the jury an instruction based on the statutory presumption. Polecat Motors' attorney opposes the request and assails the statute's constitutionality.

(a) Do the underlying facts, the accident and resulting injury, support a permissive inference of negligence on the manufacturer's part?

(b) If not, what argument should Ms. Hill make to support the statute? Assume that as a matter of substantive due process, it would be constitutional for the Morena legislature to impose strict liability on automobile manufacturers for deaths resulting from the use of their products.

See Ferry v. Ramsey, 277 U.S. 88, 94–95 (1928).

3. Problem 30–2. In Morena, the plaintiff in a negligence action has the ultimate burden of proving freedom from contributory negligence to recover. However, the Morena legislature has enacted a statutory "presumption" that persons injured in automobile accidents exercised due care in attempting to avoid the accident. During their defense case–in–chief, Polecat Motors attempts to rebut the charge of design defect and Roe attempts to disprove the allegation of negligent operation; but neither presents affirmative evidence of Ms. Hill's negligence. At the close of all the evidence, Ms. Hill requests an instruction based on the presumption. As trial judge, would you give an instruction? If so, how would you word it? Should the instruction include the word "must"? Should the instruction include the word "presume" or "presumption"?

4. Is the presumption of innocence a true presumption? Does the defendant have to prove any foundational facts to avail himself of the "presumption"? *See Carr v. State*, 192 Miss. 152, 156, 4 So. 2d 887, 888 (1941). It might be more accurate to refer to the doctrine as an "assumption."

5. Problem 30–3. During her cross–examination, Ms. Hill gives the following testimony:

Q: Were you watching the road at the time of the collision?

A: No.

Q: Isn't it true that you were searching through your purse for a cigarette lighter?

A: Maybe.

Q: Yes or no, Ms. Hill.

A: Yes.

Q: And you were doing that for five or six seconds before the collision. Weren't you?

A: Yes.

Q: With your eyes off the road?

A: Yes.

At the close of the plaintiff's case–in–chief, Mr. Roe's attorney moves for a directed verdict on the ground of contributory negligence. What ruling? *Fidelity & Guar. Ins. Underwriters, Inc. v. Mendoza*, 588 S.W.2d 612, 615–16 (Tex. Civ. App. 1979); Note, *Directing a Verdict in Favor of the Party with the Burden of Proof*, 16 WAKE FOREST L. REV. 607, 612 (1980).

6. Problem 30–4. Suppose that rather than giving the testimony in Problem 30–3, Ms. Hill had admitted that she was driving "about 10–12 miles over the speed limit." Should the trial judge direct a defense verdict on the basis of that testimony? Is the testimony in this variation of the hypothetical distinguishable from that in Problem 30–3? *Smith v. Secrist*, 590 S.W.2d 386, 389–90 (Mo. Ct. App. 1979).

7. Problem 30–5. Revisit Problem 30–2. During his defense case–in–chief, Mr. Roe calls Mr. Taylor as a witness. Taylor states that he observed Ms. Hill "for about five or six seconds before impact, and she didn't seem to be watching the road at all." As in Problem 30–2, Ms. Hill requests an instruction based on the statute. In a jurisdiction following the Morgan–McCormick view, how would you phrase the instruction?

8. Which view is sounder? The proponents of the Morgan–McCormick view point out that lay jurors are unaccustomed to working with the formal rules of logic and circumstantial evidence. In his classic article on the subject, Dean McCormick asserted that lay "[p]ersons unaccustomed to weighing evidence . . . are notoriously suspicious of circumstantial inferences." McCormick, *What Shall the Trial Judge Tell the Jury About Presumptions?*, 13 WASH. L. REV. 185, 188 (1938). They argue that the presumption instruction gives the jury needed guidance in evaluating the circumstantial evidence. Does that argument really lead to the conclusion that the judge should instruct on a presumption? Could the judge give the jury sufficient guidance by informing them that a certain configuration of circumstantial evidence would sustain a permissive inference? Is there any need to resort to the words "must" or "presume"?

9. Which view does Federal Rule of Evidence 301 adopt? *See Texas Dept. of Community Affairs v. Burdine*, 450 U.S. 248, 254–5 (1981); *Usery v. Turner Elkhorn Mining Co.*, 428 U.S. 1, 27 (1976). When the Supreme Court submitted proposed Article III of the Federal Rules of Congress, that article suffered a fate similar to proposed Article V. The Court's proposal included draft Rule 3–03(b), reading that "[a] presumption imposes on the party against whom it is directed the burden of proving that the nonexistence of the presumed fact is more probable than its existence." Congress refused to enact the proposed rule. Instead, Congress adopted the current Rule 301. The Conference Report states that, under Rule 301, "[i]f the adverse party . . . offer[s] evidence contradicting the presumed fact, the court cannot instruct the jury that it may presume the existence of the presumed fact from proof of the basic fact." Thus, unless there is a contrary statute, the federal courts generally apply the "bursting bubble" theory. *Nunley v. City of Los Angeles*, 52 F.3d 792 (9th Cir. 1995). The single notable exception to this general rule is maritime law. There, even without the benefit of a statute, the courts sometimes recognize presumptions shifting the ultimate burden of proof. Admiralty law tends to "stand . . . apart from other areas of federal law." *Hood v. Knappton Corp., Inc.*, 986 F.2d 329 (9th Cir. 1993); *Kelly v. Armstrong*, 141 F.3d 799, 802 (8th Cir. 1998)("th[e] inference or presumption of negligence [on an admiralty law issue]. . .is not governed by Rule 301. . .[but] is determined as a matter or substantive law. . .").

10. Note the eighth step on the diagram, the opponent's creation of a counter–presumption. The step can arise in a case in which conflicting presumptions could conceivably apply. Suppose, for example, that there is a contest over a decedent's estate. Ms. Hill died in the collision, and two men—Arthur and Gilbert—both claim to be her surviving husband and heir–at–law. Gilbert has evidence that he married the decedent in 1973. Morena has a presumption that, once created, a condition or status such as marriage continues. However, Arthur has evidence of a ceremonial marriage with the decedent in 1978. Morena also has a presumption of the validity of ceremonial marriages. *See* Cal. Evid. Code § 663. This problem has divided the courts into four different schools of thought.

One school of thought is the double bursting bubble—the presumptions negate each other, and both presumptions disappear from the case. The judge calls the jurors' attention to the evidence on both sides of the issue, allocates the ultimate burden of proof, and tells the jury nothing more.

Another view is that the judge should identify the "weightier" presumption and instruct on that presumption. *Rader v. Thrasher*, 57 Cal. 2d 244, 252, 368 P.2d 360, 364–65, 18 Cal. Rptr. 736, 740–41 (1962). In weighing the presumption, the judge considers such factors as the probative value of the foundational facts and the magnitude of any social policy the presumption implements.

A third position—Wigmore's view—denies that there are "conflicting" presumptions. Wigmore argued that there are successive presumptions rather than conflicting presumptions. The first presumption arises when Gilbert presents his evidence of the 1973 marriage, but that bubble bursts as soon as Arthur proves the 1978 marriage. The only remaining presumption is the presumption of the validity of the 1978 ceremonial marriage. *Montpelier v. Calais*, 114 Vt. 5, 39 A.2d 350, 356 (1944).

The fourth approach is to tailor a third presumption for the case to resolve the conflict between the first two presumptions. For example, the court might mediate the conflict in our hypothetical by fashioning a presumption that the first marriage terminated by divorce. *Hewitt v. Firestone Tire & Rubber Co.*, 490 F. Supp. 1358, 1362 (E.D. Va. 1980); *Vargas v. Superior Ct.*, 9 Cal. App. 3d 470, 473, 88 Cal. Rptr. 281, 283 (1970).

2. THE SUFFICIENCY OF "NAKED" STATISTICAL EVIDENCE TO SATISFY THE BURDEN

Earlier, we saw that there is a heated controversy over the admissibility of statistical evidence. On the issue of admissibility, the trend appears to be toward the more liberal admission of that type of evidence. The admissibility question, though, is by no means the end of the controversy over statistical evidence. Suppose that the plaintiff or prosecutor presents only overtly statistical evidence; she does not present any individualized or particularistic evidence about the parties in the case. Is a case consisting of naked statistical evidence sufficient to go to the jury? The following case represents the traditional answer to that question.

SMITH v. RAPID TRANSIT, INC.

58 N.E.2d 754 (Mass. 1945)

SPALDING, JUSTICE.

The decisive question in this case is whether there was evidence for the jury that the plaintiff was injured by a bus of the defendant that was operated by one of its employees in the course of his employment. If there was, the defendant concedes that the evidence warranted the submission to the jury of the question of the operator's negligence in the management of the bus. The case is here on the plaintiff's exception to the direction of a verdict for the defendant.

These facts could have been found: While the plaintiff at about 1:00 A. M. on February 6, 1941, was driving an automobile on Main Street, Winthrop, in an easterly direction toward Winthrop Highlands, she observed a bus coming toward her which she described as a "great big, long, wide affair." The bus, which was proceeding at about forty miles an hour, "forced her to turn to the right," and her automobile collided with a "parked car." The plaintiff was coming from Dorchester. The department of public utilities had issued a certificate of public convenience or necessity to the defendant for three routes in Winthrop, one of which included Main Street,[1] and this was in effect in February, 1941. "There was another bus line in operation in Winthrop at that time but not on Main Street." According to the defendant's time–table, buses were scheduled to leave Winthrop Highlands for Maverick Square via Main Street at 12:10 A. M., 12:45 A. M., 1:15 A. M., and 2:15 A. M. The running time for this trip at that time of night was thirty minutes.

The direction of a verdict for the defendant was right. The ownership of the bus was a matter of conjecture. While the defendant had the sole franchise

---

[1] The defendant in its brief concedes that this route included the place where the accident occurred.

for operating a bus line on Main Street, Winthrop, this did not preclude private or chartered buses from using this street; the bus in question could very well have been one operated by someone other than the defendant. It was said in *Sargent v. Massachusetts Accident Co.*, 307 Mass. 246, at page 250, 29 N.E.2d 825, at page 827, that it is "not enough that mathematically the chances somewhat favor a proposition to be proved; for example, the fact that colored automobiles made in the current year outnumber black ones would not warrant a finding that an undescribed automobile of the current year is colored and not black, nor would the fact that only a minority of men die of cancer warrant a finding that a particular man did not die of cancer." The most that can be said of the evidence in the instant case is that perhaps the mathematical chances somewhat favor the proposition that a bus of the defendant caused the accident. This was not enough. A "proposition is proved by a preponderance of the evidence if it is made to appear more likely or probable in the sense that actual belief in its truth, derived from the evidence, exists in the mind or minds of the tribunal notwithstanding any doubts that may still linger there." *Sargent v. Massachusetts Accident Co.*, 307 Mass. 246, at page 250, 29 N.E.2d 825 at page 827.

In cases where it has been held that a vehicle was sufficiently identified so as to warrant a finding that it was owned by the defendant, the evidence was considerably stronger than that in the case at bar. *See,* for example, *Kelly v. Railway Express Agency, Inc.*, 315 Mass. 301, 52 N.E.2d 411; *Gallagher v. R. E. Cunniff, Inc.*, 314 Mass. 7, 8, 9, 49 N.E.2d 448; *Breen v. Dedham Water Co.*, 241 Mass. 217, 135 N. E. 130; *Heywood v. Ogasapian*, 224 Mass. 203, 112 N.E. 619; *Hopwood v. Pokrass*, 219 Mass. 263, 106 N.E. 997.

The evidence in the instant case is no stronger for the plaintiff than that in *Atlas v. Silsbury–Gamble Motors Co.*, 278 Mass. 279, 180 N.E. 127, or in *Cochrane v. Great Atlantic & Pacific Tea Co.*, 281 Mass. 386, 183 N.E. 757, where it was held that a finding that the vehicle in question was owned by the defendant was not warranted.

Exceptions overruled.

NOTES

1. The orthodox view has been that if a party relied on naked statistical evidence, as a matter of law the party's case was legally insufficient; "the evidence would never reach the jury." Nesson, *The Evidence or the Event? On Judicial Proof and the Acceptability of Verdicts*, 98 HARV. L. REV. 1357, 1380 (1985). Professor Nesson cites *Smith* as authority for that proposition. However, other commentators argue that "the support for the proposition that courts are reluctant to let cases be decided on 'statistical evidence' is greatly exaggerated in the literature." Allen, *A Reconceptualization of Civil Trials*, 66 B.U. L. REV. 401, 429 n.67 (1986). There are signs that the courts are more inclined to uphold the sufficiency of cases consisting of statistical evidence. *Kaminsky v. Hertz Corp.*, 94 Mich. App. 356, 288 N.W.2d 426, 427 (1979).

2. Professor Allen disputes the characterization of *Smith* as a case involving naked statistical evidence. The plaintiff "did not rely on any such evidence. She merely asserted that she was forced off the road by a bus and in addition proved that Rapid Transit, Inc., was the only bus line operating regularly on the road where the accident occurred." Allen, *supra.* In *Smith,* did the plaintiff establish that more than 50% of the buses on that road belonged to the defendant?

3. Why not uphold a case based on statistical evidence? If statistical evidence generates a 51% probability of all the relevant events and the normal test for the sufficiency of the evidence is whether a rational juror could find a 51% probability, why take the case away from the jury? To use Dean Wigmore's expression, if "the natural processes of the mind" would lead a juror to conclude that the test has been satisfied, why create an "artificial legal rule" that the evidence is insufficient? In the final analysis, like the traditional support for the *Frye* test, the reluctance of some courts to uphold cases based on statistical evidence may bespeak the courts' fear that the jurors will overvalue the scientific testimony. However, several empirical studies indicate that, rather than being overwhelmed by statistical evidence, jurors tend to underutilize statistical evidence during their deliberations. Kaye & Koehler, *Can Jurors Understand Probabilistic Evidence?*, 154 J.ROYAL STAT.SOC. 75, 79–80 (1991)("[t]he clearest and most consistent finding"); Thompson & Shumann, *Interpretation of Statistical Evidence in Criminal Trials: The Prosecutor's Fallacy and the Defense Attorney's Fallacy*, 11 LAW & HUM. BEHAV. 167, 183 (1987) ("[F]inal judgments of guilt . . . tended to be significantly lower than a Bayesian analysis suggests they should have been"); Faigman & Baglioni, *Bayes' Theorem in the Trial Process: Instructing Jurors on the Value of Statistical Evidence*, 12 LAW & HUM. BEHAV. 1, 13–16 (1988). There is a natural distrust of the unfamiliar, and that distrust may be operative here.

4. Students of the application of probability theory to jury trials have developed several hypotheticals illustrating some of the dangers of upholding cases resting on naked statistical evidence.

One is the hypothetical of the blue bus, based on *Smith.* Kaye, *The Laws of Probability and the Law of the Land*, 47 U. CHI. L. REV. 34, 40 (1979). The evidence establishes that the plaintiff was negligently run over by a blue bus and that the defendant operates four–fifths of all the blue buses in town. Kaye, *Paradoxes, Gedanken Experiments and The Burden of Proof: A Response to Dr. Cohen's Reply*, 1981 ARIZ. ST. L.J. 635, 636–37.

Another is the hypothetical of the gatecrasher. L. COHEN, THE PROBABLE AND THE PROVABLE 49–120 (1977); Cohen, *Subjective Probability and the Paradox of the Gatecrasher*, 1981 ARIZ. ST. L.J. 627. The management of a rodeo sold 499 tickets. When they take attendance, they discover that there are 1,000 people in the seats—and a hole in the fence. There are 499 legal entrants, and 501 trespassers. They pick one attendee at random and sue him for the cost of admission. Of course, there is a better than 50% probability that he is a trespasser.

Are the two hypotheticals distinguishable? The argument against recovery in the gatecrasher hypothetical is a species of argument *reductio ad absurdum*; the management could present the same case against all 1,000 attendees and could possibly recover then even from the 499 legal entrants.

Does permitting recovery in the blue bus hypothetical lead to the same absurd consequences?

It is not only arguable that the blue bus hypothetical is distinguishable. Professor Kaye has advanced a further argument for resolving the supposed paradox of the blue bus hypothetical: When more particularized evidence is readily available, a rational juror would find naked statistical evidence insufficient. Should jurors consider not only the evidence the parties have furnished but also data that conspicuously has been not supplied? Should jurors consider the completeness of the evidence? It may be helpful to remember that the various burdens of proof express "degree[s] of the jury's belief." 2 C. McCormick, HANDBOOK OF THE LAW OF EVIDENCE § 339, at 438 (4th ed. 1992).

Professor Shaviro goes further. *Statistical–Probability Evidence and the Appearance of Justice*, 103 HARV. L. REV. 530 (1989). He notes that all testimony involves uncertainty. *Id.* at 536. Eyewitness identification testimony is unquestionably prone to error, and "the exact error rate" has not been quantified. Yet the courts routinely sustain criminal guilty verdicts on the basis of such testimony. He concedes that statistical evidence is more overtly uncertain and probabilistic. *Id.* at 546. Although in the past courts have been squeamish about relying on statistical evidence, Professor Shaviro argues that the admission of such testimony can improve the accuracy of fact–finding and thereby strengthen society's commitment to minimize injustice. *Id.* at 548.

5. We saw that given *Jackson v. Virginia*, 443 U.S. 307, 318 (1979), there is a higher standard for the burden of going forward in criminal cases. The prosecution evidence must not only create a permissive inference of the existence of every element of the charged crime; the evidence must be capable of banishing every reasonable doubt from the mind of the hypothetical juror. Since the test is more rigorous in criminal trials, it would be consistent to hold that a naked statistical evidence case is sufficient in civil practice but not in a prosecution. Does Professor Kaye's argument in the blue bus hypothetical show that there is less than a 50% probability or that the hypothetical juror should have a lingering, reasonable doubt about the defendant's liability?

6. In sum, there are at least four positions a court can take on this controversy: A case consisting of naked statistical evidence is sufficient; the case is sufficient unless, as in the gatecrasher hypothetical, upholding the sufficiency of the evidence leads to absurd consequences; the case is legally insufficient; and the case is legally insufficient in a criminal trial. Which view do you prefer? Why?

C. THE INITIAL BURDEN IN CRIMINAL CASES

Peculiar problems arise when we attempt to analyze the operation of the initial burden in criminal cases. The burden's primary function is to regulate the rationality of jury findings. However, in criminal cases, the solicitude for the defendant's liberty interest is so strong that we tolerate some irrational jury behavior in the defendant's favor. For example, because of the use of a general verdict and the secrecy of jury deliberations, the jury has the power to nullify the substantive law by acquitting an obviously guilty defendant.

Comment, 13 WASHBURN L.J. 129 (1974). The Supreme Court itself has recognized the power. *Spark & Hanson v. United States*, 156 U.S. 51 (1895). To protect defendants from oppressive laws, the courts have acknowledged "the undisputed power of the jury to acquit, even if its verdict is contrary to the law . . . and the evidence." *United States v. Moylan*, 417 F.2d 1002, 1006 (4th Cir. 1969), *cert. denied*, 397 U.S. 910 (1970). Moreover, due process mandates that the judge instruct the jury that they cannot convict the defendant unless they are convinced of the existence of all the crime's elements beyond a reasonable doubt. *In re Winship*, 397 U.S. 358 (1970). To be frank, this standard of proof can and does lead to erroneous acquittals of guilty persons, but we tolerate those errors as the cost of society's decision to minimize the risk of the wrongful conviction of the innocent.

It is understandable then that the initial burden must be modified to adapt it to criminal cases. To some extent, the adaptation is reflected in the interpretation of statutes purporting to create "presumptions." As previously stated, the term "presumption" is often used in a vague, imprecise manner. In the technical, common law sense, a presumption is a mandatory inference. When a statute uses a term which has acquired a technical meaning at common law, the courts ordinarily presume that the legislature intended the term in its common law sense. However, when a "presumption" is designed to operate against a criminal accused, there is a countervailing consideration: the rule of lenity. *Busic v. United States*, 446 U.S. 398, 406 (1980). When a criminal statute is ambiguous, the rule operates in the accused's favor and counsels the court to strictly construe the statute. *United States v. Gray*, 633 F. Supp. 1311 (D. Mont. 1986), *aff'd*, 809 F.2d 579 (9th Cir.), *vacated on other grounds*, 484 U.S. 807 (1987). Hence, despite the fact that the statute uses the term "presumption," the court might interpret the statute as recognizing only a permissive inference.

As the preceding paragraph indicates, constitutional considerations indirectly influence the construction of statutes relating to presumption law. However, those considerations do not merely affect statutory interpretation; they can also directly restrict the operative effect of the presumptions.

1. BARELY SUSTAINING THE BURDEN

To begin with, the Constitution demands that the initial burden be applied in a modified fashion in criminal cases. One constitutional modification affects the standard for determining whether the proponent, the prosecutor, has sustained the burden. Until 1979, many jurisdictions applied the same standard in civil and criminal cases; whether the standard was a scintilla of evidence or substantial evidence, the same test governed both types of cases. However, in *Jackson v. Virginia*, 443 U.S. 307 (1979), the Supreme Court shattered the equation. In *Jackson*, Justice Stewart drew heavily on *Winship*. *Id.* at 314–16. Although on its face *Winship* deals with only the measure of the ultimate burden of proof, Justice Stewart treated *Winship* as evidence of the preeminent value attached to the liberty interest—a value that warrants toughening the initial burden as well as the ultimate burden in criminal cases. On that reasoning, Justice Stewart announced that due process requires a directed verdict when the judge concludes "that upon the record evidence adduced at trial, no rational trier of fact could have found proof of guilt beyond a reasonable doubt." *Id.* at 324. The justice thus incorporated the expression, "beyond a reasonable doubt," into the test for sustaining the initial burden. *Id.* at 316.

NOTES AND PROBLEMS

1. Problem 30–6. In *Devitt*, the attacker covered his face with a handkerchief. Paterson had a clear view of only the assailant's eyes and the bridge of his nose. At trial, Paterson admits that he had a "very limited" view of the attacker's face but nevertheless expresses "complete confidence that that man (pointing to Devitt) is the attacker." At the close of the prosecution case–in–chief, the defense attorney moves for a directed verdict. The defense attorney asserts that "although there might be barely a permissive inference of my client's identity as the assailant, that's not enough under *Jackson*, Your Honor. In a case as flimsy as this, any reasonable juror would necessarily have a lingering doubt about my client's innocence." What ruling? *See United States v. Sears*, 332 F.2d 199, 200–01 (7th Cir. 1964) (antedating *Jackson v. Virginia*).

2. Problem 30–7. Before trial, Paterson picked out Devitt's picture in a photograph spread at the police station. However, at trial, he could not identify Devitt; he testified, "It sorta looks like him, but I just can't be sure. I don't wanta guess." The trial judge admitted Paterson's pretrial identification of Devitt and treated it as substantive evidence of Devitt's identity as the assailant under Rule 801(d)(1)(C). At the close of the prosecution case–in–chief, the defense attorney again moves for a directed verdict. What ruling? Is Paterson's out–of–court statement entitled to as much weight as in–court testimony? *See People v. Valenzuela*, 175 Cal. App. 3d 381, 222 Cal. Rptr. 405, 410–11 (1985). Would it make a difference if the pretrial identification has been a corporeal lineup rather than a photographic spread? *See* Annot., 29 A.L.R.4th 104, 130–33 (1984).

3. Problem 30–8. Vary the facts in Problem 30–7. At a preliminary hearing, Paterson identifies Devitt as the attacker. However, at trial he is uncertain of the identification. On the witness stand, he states that Devitt "sorta looks like the guy. However, I've got to be honest with you, and I can't truthfully say that that's even probably the guy who attacked me. If I'm forced to say, I don't think it's him." At that point, the trial judge permits the prosecution to introduce Paterson's preliminary hearing identification as substantive evidence under Federal Rule 801(d)(1)(A). The prosecution rests without presenting further evidence of Devitt's identity as the attacker. The defense moves for a directed verdict. What ruling? *See People v. Gould*, 54 Cal. 2d 621, 631, 354 P.2d 865, 870, 7 Cal. Rptr. 273, 278 (1960) (en banc); Goldman, *Guilt by Intuition: The Insufficiency of Prior Inconsistent Statements to Convict*, 65 N.C. L. Rev. 1, 40 (1986).

4. The British courts have taken a different approach to the problem of the sufficiency of eyewitness identification testimony; they have been more impressed by the scientific evidence of the unreliability of eyewitness testimony. The Court of Appeal, Criminal Division, has announced corroboration requirements. Theresby, *A Turnaround in the Use of Identification Evidence*, 62 A.B.A. J. 1343–44 (1976). The trial judge assesses the quality of the eyewitness testimony by considering such factors as the lighting conditions and the length of the opportunity for observation. If the caliber of the testimony is high, the judge submits the case to the jury with a cautionary instruction. "But if the quality was poor, as for instance if it depended solely on a fleeting glance, then the judge should withdraw the case from the jury and direct an acquittal, unless there was other evidence to support the correctness of the identification." *Id.*

2. CREATING A TRUE PRESUMPTION

The next modification is a constitutionally mandatory test for determining the validity of presumptions in criminal cases. The Court first addressed the issue in *Tot v. United States*, 319 U.S. 463 (1943). In *Tot,* the Court invalidated a statutory presumption that a firearm found in an ex–convict's possession had been received in interstate commerce. The Court rejected the "greater includes the lesser" theory applicable in civil cases. The Court declared that in a criminal case, "a statutory presumption cannot be sustained if there be no rational connection between the fact proved and the ultimate fact presumed, if the inference of the one from proof of the other is arbitrary because of lack of connection between the two in common experience." *Id.* at 467.

The *Tot* Court did not define "rational connection." Did the term mean logical relevance or sufficiency? Was it enough that the foundational fact was relevant to the presumed fact under Federal Rule of Evidence 401, or did the foundational fact have to have at least sufficient probative value to support an inference that the presumed fact exists? The Court embraced the second interpretation in 1969 in *Leary v. United States*, 395 U.S. 6 (1969). Speaking for the Court, Justice Harlan stated that "a criminal statutory presumption must be regarded as 'irrational' or 'arbitrary' and hence unconstitutional, unless it can at least be said with substantial assurance that the presumed fact is more likely than not to flow from the proved fact on which it is made to depend." *Id.* at 36.

However, even *Leary* did not satisfy the most ardent advocates of extending *Winship*'s protection to criminal defendants. For example, in *Turner v. United States*, 396 U.S. 398 (1970), the defense invited the Court to adopt "the more exacting reasonable doubt standard normally applicable in criminal cases." *Id.* at 416. Do the foundational facts have to have enough probative value to establish the presumed fact beyond a reasonable doubt? The Court declined the invitation in *Turner;* and three years later in *Barnes v. United States*, 412 U.S. 837, 843 (1973), the Court confessed that "the teaching" of its prior precedents was "not altogether clear." The Court did not bring needed clarity to this area of law until 1979. In that year, in *Ulster County Ct. v. Allen,* 442 U.S. 140 (1979), the Court passed on New York's statutory presumption that a firearm's presence in an automobile is evidence of its illegal possession by all the occupants. In the course of upholding the presumption, Justice Stevens wrote:

> Inferences and presumptions are a staple of our adversarial system of factfinding. It is often necessary for the trier of fact to determine

the existence of an element of the crime—that is, an "ultimate" or "elemental" fact—from the existence of one or more "evidentiary" or "basic" facts. *E.g.*, *Barnes v. United States*, 412 U.S. 837, 843–844; *Tot v. United States*, 319 U.S. 463, 467. The value of these evidentiary devices, and their validity under the Due Process Clause, vary from case to case, however, depending on the strength of the connection between the particular basic and elemental facts involved and on the degree to which the device curtails the factfinder's freedom to assess the evidence independently. Nonetheless, in criminal cases, the ultimate test of any device's constitutional validity in a given case remains constant: the device must not undermine the factfinder's responsibility at trial, based on evidence adduced by the State, to find the ultimate facts beyond a reasonable doubt. *See In re Winship*, 397 U.S. 358, 364.

The most common evidentiary device is the entirely permissive inference or presumption, which allows—but does not require—the trier of fact to infer the elemental fact from proof by the prosecutor of the basic one and that places no burden of any kind on the defendant. *See, e.g.*, *Barnes v. United States*, *supra*, at 840 n.3. In that situation the basic fact may constitute prima facie evidence of the elemental fact. *See, e.g.*, *Turner v. United States*, 396 U.S. 398, 402 n.2. When reviewing this type of device, the Court has required the party challenging it to demonstrate its invalidity as applied to him. *E.g.*, *Barnes v. United States*, *supra*, at 845; *Turner v. United States*, *supra*, at 419–424. Because this permissive presumption leaves the trier of fact free to credit or reject the inference and does not shift the burden of proof, it affects the application of the "beyond a reasonable doubt" standard only if, under the facts of the case, there is no rational way the trier could make the connection permitted by the inference. For only in that situation is there any risk that an explanation of the permissible inference to a jury, or its use by a jury, has caused the presumptively rational factfinder to make an erroneous factual determination.

A mandatory presumption is a far more troublesome evidentiary device. For it may affect not only the strength of the "no reasonable doubt" burden but also the placement of that burden; it tells the trier that he or they must find the elemental fact upon proof of the basic fact, at least unless the defendant has come forward with some evidence to rebut the presumed connection between the two facts. *E.g.*, *Turner v. United States*, *supra*, at 401–402, and n.1; *Leary v. United States*, 395 U.S. 6, 30; *United States v. Romano*, 382 U.S. 136, 137, and n.4, 138, 143; *Tot v. United States*, *supra*, at 469.[16] In this

---

[16] This class of more or less mandatory presumptions can be subdivided into two parts: presumptions that merely shift the burden of production to the defendant, following the satisfaction of which the ultimate burden of persuasion returns to the prosecution; and presumptions that entirely shift the burden of proof to the defendant. The mandatory presumptions examined by our cases have almost uniformly fit into the former subclass, in that they never totally removed the ultimate burden of proof beyond a reasonable doubt from the prosecution. *E.g.*, *Tot v. United States*, *supra*, at 469.

To the extent that a presumption imposes an extremely low burden of production — *e.g.*, being

situation, the Court has generally examined the presumption on its face to determine the extent to which the basic and elemental facts coincide. *E.g., Turner v. United States, supra,* at 408–418; *United States v. Romano, supra,* at 140–141; *Tot v. United States, supra,* at 468. To the extent that the trier of fact is forced to abide by the presumption, and may not reject it based on an independent evaluation of the particular facts presented by the State, the analysis of the presumption's constitutional validity is logically divorced from those facts and based on the presumption's accuracy in the run of cases.[17] It is for

---

satisfied by "any" evidence — it may well be that its impact is no greater than that of a permissive inference and it may be proper to analyze it as such. *See generally Mullaney v. Wilbur, supra,* 421 U.S., at 703 n.31.

In deciding what type of inference or presumption is involved in a case, the jury instructions will generally be controlling, although their interpretation may require recourse to the statute involved and the cases decided under it. *Turner v. United States, supra,* provides a useful illustration of the different types of presumptions. It analyzes the constitutionality of two different presumption statutes (one mandatory and one permissive) as they apply to the basic fact of possession of both heroin and cocaine, and the presumed facts of importation and distribution of narcotic drugs. The jury was charged essentially in the terms of the two statutes.

The importance of focusing attention on the precise presentation of the presumption to the jury and the scope of that presumption is illustrated by a comparison of *United States v. Gainey,* 380 U.S. 63 with *United States v. Romano,* 382 U.S. 130. Both cases involved statutory presumptions based on proof that the defendant was present at the site of an illegal still. In *Gainey* the Court sustained a conviction "for carrying on" the business of the distillery in violation of 26 U.S.C. § 5601(a)(4), whereas in *Romano,* the Court set aside a conviction for being in "possession, custody, and control" of such a distillery in violation of § 5601(a)(1). The difference in outcome was attributable to two important differences between the cases. Because the statute involved in *Gainey* was a sweeping prohibition of almost any activity associated with the still, whereas the *Romano* statute involved only one narrow aspect of the total undertaking, there was a much higher probability that mere presence could support an inference of guilt in the former case than in the latter.

Of perhaps greater importance, however, was the difference between the trial judge's instructions to the jury in the two cases. In *Gainey* the judge had explained that the presumption was permissive; it did not require the jury to convict the defendant even if it was convinced that he was present at the site. On the contrary, the instructions made it clear that presence was only "a circumstance to be considered along with all the other circumstances in the case." As we emphasized, the "jury was thus specifically told that the statutory [presumption] was not conclusive." 380 U.S., at 69–70. In *Romano* the trial judge told the jury that the defendant's presence at the still "shall be deemed sufficient evidence to authorize conviction." 382 U.S., at 182. Although there was other evidence of guilt, that instruction authorized conviction even if the jury disbelieved all of the testimony except the proof of presence at the site. This Court's holding that the statutory presumption could not support the *Romano* conviction was thus dependent, in part, on the specific instructions given by the trial judge. Under those instructions it was necessary to decide whether, regardless of the specific circumstances of the particular case, the statutory presumption adequately supported the guilty verdict.

[17] In addition to the discussion of *Romano* in n. 16, *supra,* this point is illustrated by *Leary v. United States, supra.* In that case, Dr. Timothy Leary, a professor at Harvard University was stopped by customs inspectors in Laredo, Texas as he was returning from the Mexican side of the international border. Marihuana seeds and a silver snuff box filled with semirefined marihuana and three partially smoked marihuana cigarettes were discovered in his car. He was convicted of having knowingly transported marihuana which he knew had been illegally imported into this country in violation of 21 U.S.C. § 176a. That statute includes a mandatory presumption: "possession shall be deemed sufficient evidence to authorize conviction [for importation] unless the defendant explains his possession to the satisfaction of the jury." Leary admitted possession of the marihuana and claimed that he had carried it from New York to Mexico and then back.

Justice Harlan for the Court noted that under one theory of the case, the jury could have found

this reason that the Court has held it irrelevant in analyzing a mandatory presumption, but not in analyzing a purely permissive one, that there is ample evidence in the record other than the presumption to support a conviction. *E.g.*, *Turner v. United States, supra*, at 407; *Leary v. United States, supra*, at 31–32, *United States v. Romano, supra*, at 138–139.

Without determining whether the presumption in this case was mandatory, the Court of Appeals analyzed it on its face as if it were. In fact, it was not, as the New York Court of Appeals had earlier pointed out.

The trial judge's instructions make it clear that the presumption was merely a part of the prosecution's case, that it gave rise to a permissive inference available only in certain circumstances, rather than a mandatory conclusion of possession, and that it could be ignored by the jury even if there was no affirmative proof offered by defendants in rebuttal. The judge explained that possession could be actual or constructive, but that constructive possession could not exist without the intent and ability to exercise control or dominion over the weapons. He also carefully instructed the jury that there is a mandatory presumption of innocence in favor of the defendants that controls unless it, as the exclusive trier of fact, is satisfied beyond a reasonable doubt that the defendant possessed the handguns in the manner described by the judge. In short, the instructions plainly directed the jury to consider all the circumstances tending to support or contradict the inference that all four occupants of the car had possession of the two loaded handguns and to decide the matter for itself without regard to how much evidence the defendants introduced. Our cases considering the validity of permissive statutory presumptions such as the one involved here have rested on an evaluation of the presumption as applied to the record before the Court. None suggests that a court should pass on the constitutionality of this kind of statute "on its face." It was error for the Court of Appeals to make such a determination in this case.

NOTES AND PROBLEMS

1. Under *Ulster County, supra*, the substantive test for and the mode of analyzing the constitutionality of mandatory inferences differ from those for

---

direct proof of all of the necessary elements of the offense without recourse to the presumption. But he deemed that insufficient reason to affirm the conviction because under another theory the jury might have found knowledge of importation on the basis of either direct evidence or the presumption, and there was accordingly no certainty that the jury had not relied on the presumption. 395 U.S., at 31–32. The Court therefore found it necessary to test the presumption against the Due Process Clause. Its analysis was facial. Despite the fact that the defendant was well educated and had recently traveled to a country that is a major exporter of marihuana to this country, the Court found the presumption of knowledge of importation from possession irrational. It did so not because Dr. Leary was unlikely to know the source of the marihuana but instead because "a majority of possessors" were unlikely to have such knowledge. *Id.* at 53. Because the jury had been instructed to rely on the presumption even if it did not believe the Government's direct evidence of knowledge of importation (unless, of course, the defendant met his burden of "satisfying" the jury to the contrary), the Court reversed the conviction.

permissive inferences. Be prepared to state the test and mode of analysis for each type of inference.

2. Problem 30–9. In *Devitt*, Paterson tells the prosecutor that although he had not seen Devitt in the week before the attack, during that week he had mailed Devitt a letter, firing him and stating that Devitt had done such shoddy carpentry work that he would not pay him anything for the work Devitt had already done. The prosecution contends that the contents of the letter gave Devitt a motive to attack Paterson. Morena normally presumes the addressee's receipt of a properly addressed, stamped, and mailed letter. 2 McCormick, Evidence § 343, at 439 (5th ed. 1999). At trial, Paterson testifies that he properly addressed, stamped, and mailed the letter to Devitt. Devitt does not take the stand. The prosecutor requests that the judge instruct the jury that "if you believe Mr. Paterson's testimony, you must conclude that Devitt received his letter." Devitt's attorney objects that "the instruction would violate *Ulster County*." What result? Does *Ulster County* apply to this instruction? Is the presumed fact ultimate or evidentiary? *United States v. Waldemer*, 50 F.3d 1379, 1386 (7th Cir. 1995) ("A mandatory presumption occurs where an instruction requires the jury to presume the existence of an ultimate fact, that is an element of the offense charged"); Hug, *Presumptions and Inferences in Criminal Law*, 56 Mil. L. Rev. 81, 91, 105 (1972).

3. OBTAINING AN ABSOLUTE PEREMPTORY RULING

Still another modification peculiar to criminal cases is that the prosecutor cannot reach step four and obtain a peremptory ruling. *People v. Mayberry*, 15 Cal. 3d 143, 542 P.2d 1337, 125 Cal. Rptr. 745 (1975). The judge may not direct a verdict of guilty, in whole or in part. *United States v. Bosch*, 505 F.2d 78 (5th Cir. 1974). The judge may not do so even if the prosecution's evidence is overwhelming (*People v. Mayberry*, *supra*) or seemingly conclusive. *Connecticut v. Johnson*, 460 U.S. 73, 83 (1983) (plurality opinion).

4. REBUTTING THE PRESUMED FACT

Winship has also necessitated modifications relating to the stages in which the opponent attempts to overcome a presumption. May a conclusive presumption operate against a defendant? May a presumption shift the ultimate burden to the defendant? The Court reached those questions in the following case, in which the trial judge gave a homicide jury the seemingly innocuous instruction that "the law presumes that a person intends the ordinary consequences of his voluntary acts."

SANDSTROM v. MONTANA

442 U.S. 510 (1979)

Justice Brennan delivered the opinion of the Court.

The threshold inquiry in ascertaining the constitutional analysis applicable to this kind of jury instruction is to determine the nature of the presumption it describes. *See Ulster County Court v. Allen*, . . . 99 S. Ct. 2213 (1979). That determination requires careful attention to the words actually spoken to the jury, *see id.,* at _____ n. 16, for whether a defendant has been accorded his constitutional rights depends upon the way in which a reasonable juror could have interpreted the instruction.

Respondent argues, first, that the instruction merely described a permissive inference—that is, it allowed but did not require the jury to draw conclusions about defendant's intent from his actions—and that such inferences are constitutional. These arguments need not detain us long, for even respondent admits that "it's possible" that the jury believed they were required to apply the presumption. Sandstrom's jurors were told that "the law presumes that a person intends the ordinary consequences of his voluntary acts." They were not told that they had a choice, or that they might infer that conclusion; they were told only that the law presumed it. It is clear that a reasonable juror could easily have viewed such an instruction as mandatory. *See generally* Montana Rules of Evidence 301(a).[4]

In the alternative, respondent urges that even if viewed as a mandatory presumption rather than as a permissive inference, the presumption did not conclusively establish intent but rather could be rebutted. On this view, the instruction required the jury, if satisfied as to the facts which trigger the presumption, to find intent unless the defendant offered evidence to the contrary. Moreover, according to the State, all the defendant had to do to rebut the presumption was produce "some" contrary evidence; he did not have to "prove" that he lacked the required mental state. Thus, "[a]t most, it placed a burden of production on the petitioner," but "did not shift to petitioner the burden of persuasion with respect to any element of the offense. . . ." Brief for Respondent 3. Again, respondent contends that presumptions with this limited effect pass constitutional muster.

We need not review respondent's constitutional argument on this point either, however, for we reject this characterization of the presumption as well. Respondent concedes there is a "risk" that the jury, once having found petitioner's act voluntary, would interpret the instruction as automatically directing a finding of intent. Tr. of Oral Arg. 29. Moreover, the State also concedes that numerous courts "have differed as to the effect of the presumption when given as a jury instruction without further explanation as to its use by the jury," and that some have found it to shift more than the burden of production, and even to have conclusive effect. Brief for Respondent 17. Nonetheless, the State contends that the only authoritative reading of the effect of the presumption resides in the Supreme Court of Montana. And the State argues that by holding that "[d]efendant's sole burden under instruction No. 5 was to produce some evidence that he did not intend the ordinary consequences of his voluntary acts, not to disprove that he acted 'purposely' or 'knowingly,' " 580 P.2d, at 109, the Montana Supreme Court decisively established that the presumption at most affected only the burden of going forward with evidence of intent—that is, the burden of production.

---

[4] "Rule 301 (a) Presumption defined. A presumption is an assumption of fact that the law requires to be made from another fact or group of facts found or otherwise established in the action or proceeding."

The Supreme Court of Montana is, of course, the final authority on the legal weight to be given a presumption under Montana law, but it is not the final authority on the interpretation which a jury could have given the instruction. If Montana intended its presumption to have only the effect described by its Supreme Court, then we are convinced that a reasonable juror could well have been misled by the instruction given, and could have believed that the presumption was not limited to requiring the defendant to satisfy only a burden of production. Petitioner's jury was told that "the law presumes that a person intends the ordinary consequences of his voluntary acts." They were not told that the presumption could be rebutted, as the Montana Supreme Court held, by the defendant's simple presentation of "some" evidence; nor even that it could be rebutted at all. Given the common definition of "presume" as "to suppose to be true without proof," Webster's New Collegiate Dictionary 911 (1974), and given the lack of qualifying instructions as to the legal effect of the presumption, we cannot discount the possibility that the jury may have interpreted the instruction in either of two more stringent ways.

First, a reasonable jury could well have interpreted the presumption as "conclusive," that is, not technically as a presumption at all, but rather, as an irrebuttable direction by the court to find intent once convinced of the facts triggering the presumption. Alternatively, the jury may have interpreted the instruction as a direction to find intent upon proof of the defendant's voluntary actions (and their "ordinary" consequences), unless the defendant proved the contrary by some quantum of proof which may well have been considerably greater than "some" evidence—thus effectively shifting the burden of persuasion on the element of intent. Numerous federal and state courts have warned that instructions of the type given here can be interpreted in just these ways. *See generally United States v. Wharton*, 139 U.S. App. D.C. 293, 433 F.2d 451 (1970); *State v. Roberts*, 88 Wash. 337, 341–42, 562 P.2d 1259, 1261–1262 (1977). And although the Montana Supreme Court held to the contrary in this case, Montana's own Rules of Evidence expressly state that the presumption at issue here may be overcome only "by a preponderance of evidence contrary to the presumption." Montana Rules of Evidence 301 (b)(2). Such a requirement shifts not only the burden of production, but also the ultimate burden of persuasion on the issue of intent.

We do not reject the possibility that some jurors may have interpreted the challenged instruction as permissive, or, if mandatory, as requiring only that the defendant come forward with "some" evidence in rebuttal. However, the fact that a reasonable juror could have given the presumption conclusive or persuasion–shifting effect means that we cannot discount the possibility that Sandstrom's jurors actually did proceed upon one or the other of these latter interpretations. And that means that unless these kinds of presumptions are constitutional, the instruction cannot be adjudged valid. *Ulster County Court v. Allen,* _____ U.S., at _____ n. 17, 60 L. Ed. 2d 777, 99 S. Ct. 2213. It is the line of cases urged by petitioner, and exemplified by *In re Winship*, 397 U.S. 358 (1970), that provides the appropriate mode of constitutional analysis for these kinds of presumptions.

We consider first the validity of a conclusive presumption. This Court has considered such a presumption on at least two prior occasions. In *Morissette v. United States*, 342 U.S. 246 (1952), the defendant was charged with willful and knowing theft of government property. Although his attorney argued that for his client to be found guilty, "the taking must have been with felonious intent," the trial judge ruled that "[t]hat is presumed by his own act." *Id.*, at 249. After first concluding that intent was in fact an element of the crime charged, and after declaring that "[w]here intent of the accused is an ingredient of the crime charged, its existence is a . . . jury issue," *Morissette* held:

> It follows that the trial court may not withdraw or prejudge the issue by instruction that the law raises a presumption of intent from an act. It often is tempting to cast in terms of a "presumption" a conclusion which a court thinks probable from given facts. . . . [But] [we] think presumptive intent has no place in this case. A conclusive presumption which testimony could not overthrow would effectively eliminate intent as an ingredient of the offense. A presumption which would permit but not require the jury to assume intent from an isolated fact would prejudge a conclusion which the jury should reach of its own volition. A presumption which would permit the jury to make an assumption which all the evidence considered together does not logically establish would give to a proven fact an artificial and fictional effect. In either case, this presumption would conflict with the overriding presumption of innocence with which the law endows the accused and which extends to every element of the crime. 342 U.S., at 274–275.

Just last Term, in *United States v. United States Gypsum*, 438 U.S. 422 (1978), we reaffirmed the holding of *Morissette*. In that case defendants, who were charged with criminal violations of the Sherman Act, challenged the following jury instruction:

> The law presumes that a person intends the necessary and natural consequences of his acts. Therefore, if the effect of the exchanges of pricing information was to raise, fix, maintain, and stabilize prices, then the parties to them are presumed, as a matter of law, to have intended that result. 438 U.S., at 430.

After again determining that the offense included the element of intent, we held

> [A] defendant's state of mind or intent is an element of a criminal antitrust offense which . . . cannot be taken from the trier of fact through reliance on a legal presumption of wrongful intent from proof of effect on prices. "Although an effect on prices may well support an inference that the defendant had knowledge of the probability of such a consequence at the time he acted, the jury must remain free to consider additional evidence before accepting or rejecting the inference . . . . [U]ltimately, the decision on the issue of intent must be left to the trier of fact alone. The instruction given invaded this factfinding function. *Id..*, at 435, 446.

As in *Morissette* and *United States Gypsum*, a conclusive presumption in this case would "conflict with the overriding presumption of innocence with which the law endows the accused and which extends to every element of the crime," and would "invade [the] factfinding function" which in a criminal case the law assigns solely to the jury. The instruction announced to David Sandstrom's jury may well have had exactly these consequences. Upon finding proof of one element of the crime (causing death), and of facts insufficient to establish the second (the voluntariness and "ordinary consequences" of defendant's action), Sandstrom's jurors could reasonably have concluded that they were directed to find against defendant on the element of intent. The State was thus not forced to prove "beyond a reasonable doubt . . . every fact necessary to constitute the crime . . . charged," 397 U.S., at 364, and defendant was deprived of his constitutional rights as explicated in *Winship*.

A presumption which, although not conclusive, had the effect of shifting the burden of persuasion to the defendant, would have suffered from similar infirmities. If Sandstrom's jury interpreted the presumption in that manner, it could have concluded that upon proof by the State of the slaying, and of additional facts not themselves establishing the element of intent, the burden was shifted to the defendant to prove that he lacked the requisite mental state. Such a presumption was found constitutionally deficient in *Mullaney v. Wilbur*, 421 U.S. 684 (1975). In *Mullaney* the charge was murder, which under Maine law required proof not only of intent but of malice. The trial court charged the jury that " 'malice aforethought is an essential and indispensable element of the crime of murder.' " *Id.*, at 686. However, it also instructed that if the prosecution established that the homicide was both intentional and unlawful, malice aforethought was to be implied unless the defendant proved by a fair preponderance of the evidence that he acted in the heat of passion on sudden provocation. *Mullaney v. Wilbur*, 421 U.S., at 686. As we recounted just two Terms ago in *Patterson v. New York*, "[t]his Court . . . unanimously agreed with the Court of Appeals that Wilbur's due process rights had been invaded by the presumption casting upon him the burden of proving by a preponderance of the evidence that he had acted in the heat of passion upon sudden provocation." 432 U.S., at 214. And *Patterson* reaffirmed that "a State must prove every ingredient of an offense beyond a reasonable doubt, and . . . may not shift the burden of proof to the defendant" by means of such a presumption. *Id.*, a

Because David Sandstrom's jury may have interpreted the judge's instruction as constituting either a burden–shifting presumption like that in *Mullaney*, or a conclusive presumption like those in *Morissette* and *United States Gypsum*, and because either interpretation would have deprived defendant of his right to the due process of law, we hold the instruction given in this case unconstitutional.

NOTES

1. In light of *Sandstrom*, you should be able to answer the questions posed earlier. May the state erect a conclusive presumption of the existence of an element of the charged crime?

2. In 1985, the Supreme Court revisited this topic in *Francis v. Franklin*, 471 U.S. 307 (1985). In large part, *Francis* reaffirmed *Sandstrom*. Several courts have interpreted *Francis* as announcing a categorical rule that a mandatory inference may not operate against a criminal defendant on an ultimate fact in issue. For example, in *Coleman v. Butler*, 816 F.2d 1046, 1048 (5th Cir. 1987), the court stated that "[a] mandatory presumption, one that instructs a criminal jury that it must infer a presumed fact if the state proves the predicate facts or fact, is unconstitutional." *Potts v. Kemp*, 814 F.2d 1512 (11th Cir. 1987), reaches the same conclusion.

3. The lower courts' broad reading of *Sandstrom* and *Francis* is debatable. In both cases, the defense presented a case–in–chief and attempted to rebut the presumed fact. In terms of the diagram found in section B.1. of this chapter, the defense was at step #7. At that step, under the second school of thought, the presumption remains in the case but shifts the burden of proof. The proponents of the second school would want the trial judge to instruct the jury: "If you believe the prosecution's evidence of C (the foundational fact), you must infer E (the presumed fact) unless the defense convinces you of non–E." Of course, the "unless" clause is the language shifting the burden of proof to the defense.

In *Francis*, the majority commented that "[w]e are not required to decide in this case whether a mandatory presumption that shifts only a burden of production to the defendant is consistent with the Due Process Clause, and we express no opinion on that question." *Francis, supra,* at 314 n.3. Suppose that, in *Francis*, the defense had not presented any evidence rebutting the presumed fact. Or suppose that the defense did not present any case–in–chief. The final step of the record would then be step #3 on the diagram. At that step, under the common law conception of a presumption, the judge would direct the jury: "If you believe the prosecution's evidence of C, you must infer E." Since there is no defense rebuttal evidence, there would be no need for the judge to add the "unless" clause at the end of the instruction. Thus, strictly speaking, there is no necessity to even reach the question of shifting the ultimate burden of proof. Would this instruction violate *Francis*?

4. Lastly, the Court decided *Carella v. California*, 491 U.S. 263 (1989). In that case, unlike *Sandstrom* and *Francis*, the defendant did not attempt to rebut the presumed fact. The trial judge directed the jury that, if they believed the prosecution evidence of the foundational facts, the fact in issue "shall be presumed." Since the defense had not offered any rebuttal evidence, there was no need for the trial judge to add an "unless" clause at the end of the instruction. Nevertheless, the Court held that the instruction ran afoul of *Francis*. *Carella* strengthens the case for the lower courts' broad interpretation of *Sandstrom* and *Francis*.

Chapter 31

THE ULTIMATE BURDEN OF PERSUASION

Federal Rule of Evidence 301. Presumptions in General in Civil Actions and Proceedings:

In all civil actions and proceedings not otherwise provided for by Act of Congress or by these rules, a presumption imposes on the party against whom it is directed the burden of going forward with evidence to rebut or meet the presumption, but does not shift to such party the burden of proof in the sense of the risk of nonpersuasion, which remains throughout the trial upon the party on whom it was originally cast.

Federal Rule of Evidence 302. Applicability of State Law in Civil Actions and Proceedings:

In civil actions and proceedings, the effect of a presumption respecting a fact which is an element of a claim or defense as to which State law supplies the rule of decision is determined in accordance with State law.

A. INTRODUCTION

In the preceding chapter, we examined the burden of producing evidence in support of each issue of fact. Now we encounter the second aspect, the burden of persuading the trier of fact that a given fact in issue is proved by the applicable standard of proof (preponderance of the evidence, clear and convincing evidence, or beyond a reasonable doubt). The burden is sometimes referred to as the "risk of nonpersuasion" because it allocates the loss to the party who fails to persuade the trier of fact that the evidence meets the requisite standard. In the words of the Supreme Court, the burden embodies "the notion that if the evidence is evenly balanced, the party that bears the burden of persuasion must lose." *Director, Office of Workers' Compensation Programs, Dep't of Labor v. Greenwich Collieries*, 512 U.S. 267 (1994). The concept of a risk of nonpersuasion is critical in decisionmaking both within and outside the judicial system. R. GASKINS, BURDENS OF PROOF IN MODERN DISCOURSE (1993). If we need to reach closure on a question on which knowledge is incomplete and truth uncertain, the allocation of the risk can determine the outcome.

The burden of persuasion differs from the burden of going forward in several respects.

First, the burden of persuasion is a duty owed to the trier of fact.[*] The burden of going forward is owed to the judge. Once the parties have satisfied all burdens of going forward on various facts, the remaining fact issues are for the jury.

---

[*] The term "trier of fact" includes the judge sitting as trier of fact in a bench trial.

Second, whether a party has satisfied his burden of persuasion on a given issue is a question of fact. The status of the burden of going forward is an issue of law for the judge (although it often requires the judge to evaluate the factual evidence). In passing on the legal sufficiency of the evidence, the judge accepts the evidence at face value without evaluating the witnesses' credibility; in this respect, the judge's ruling on the sufficiency of the evidence is similar to the judge's ruling on the admissibility of evidence under Federal Rule of Evidence 104(b). The judge must draw every permissive inference favoring the fact the proponent is attempting to establish. In contrast, the jury may choose to disbelieve a witness; and the jury may select what it believes to be the most realistic of the competing permissive inferences from the evidence.

Third, the penalty for failing to sustain the burden of persuasion is an adverse finding by the jury. The penalty for failing to satisfy the burden of going forward is a peremptory ruling by the judge, except that in a criminal case, the judge cannot direct a verdict against the defendant.

Fourth, the burden of persuasion is allocated by a rule of law, and once allocated, it usually never shifts from one party to the other. The exception is the unusual case of a Morgan–McCormick–type presumption, as we saw earlier. In contrast, the burden of going forward on an issue may shift back and forth during the trial, as first one party and then the other introduces evidence relevant to that issue.

B. THE ALLOCATION OF THE BURDEN OF PERSUASION

1. THE COMMON LAW

The common law (and occasionally some statute) allocates the burden of persuasion of each issue of fact to one of the parties. Usually (but not invariably) this is the party who must plead the existence of the fact. How does the law allocate this burden between the parties?

F. JAMES & G. HAZARD, CIVIL PROCEDURE § 7.8 (3d ed. 1985)

There is no satisfactory test for allocating the burden of proof in either sense on any given issue. The allocation is made on the basis of one or more of several variable factors. Before considering these, however, we should note three formal tests which have some currency but are not very helpful.

(1) It is often said that the party who must establish the affirmative proposition has the burden of proof on the issue. But language can be manipulated so as to state most propositions either negatively or affirmatively. Breach of a promise may be called nonfulfillment. Negligence is often described as the lack of or failure to exercise due care. An action in which plaintiff seeks a declaration of nonliability is just as truly one seeking a declaration that good defenses exist to the claim asserted by the defendant.

(2) It is sometimes said that the burden of proof is upon the party to whose case the fact in question is essential, and so it is, but this test simply poses

another question: to which party's case is the fact essential? And the second question is no easier to answer than the first; indeed it is but a restatement of the same question.

(3) It is often said that the party who has the burden of pleading a fact must prove it. This is in large part true and where there is clear authority on the pleading rule this is a fairly good, though not infallible, indication that the rule of burden of proof will parallel it. Three things should, however, be noted. The burden of proof does not follow the burden of pleading in all cases. Many jurisdictions, for example, require a plaintiff to plead nonpayment of an obligation sued upon but do not require him to prove it. In federal courts defendant must plead contributory negligence as an affirmative defense to an action for injuries negligently caused, but federal courts in diversity of citizenship cases will follow a local rule which puts on plaintiff the burden of proving his freedom from contributory negligence. The second difficulty with the suggested test is that there is often no clear authority upon the pleading rule. The burden of pleading is itself allocated on the basis of pragmatic considerations of fairness, convenience, and policy, rather than on any general principle of pleading. Since the burden of proof is allocated on very much the same basis, an inquiry to determine the pleading rule (where there is no clear authority) would be similar to the inquiry needed to determine the burden of proof rule in the first instance. This fact, incidentally, suggests why burden of pleading and burden of proof are usually parallel; they are both manifestations of the same or similar considerations. A third difficulty with the proposed rule is that under modern systems pleadings are cut off with the answer, so that issues often have to be tried that do not appear in the pleadings at all.

Another rule for allocating the burden of proof would put it on the party having the readier access to knowledge about the fact in question. This, it will be noted, is not merely a formal rule. It refers rather to one of the considerations which should and do in fact influence the allocation of the burden of proof. But it is not the only consideration and it is by no means always controlling. It is an everyday occurrence in litigation that a party has the burden to prove what his opponent's conduct was. Examples are negligence, contributory negligence, and breach of contract, in many common situations. In these instances the consideration arising from greater access to evidence is overcome by a feeling that a charge of wrongdoing should in fairness be proven by the party making it.

Another factor to be considered is the extent to which a party's contention departs from what would be expected in the light of ordinary human experience. It is a matter of convenience to assume that things occurred as they usually do and to make the party who asserts the uncommon occurrence prove that it did happen as he claims. Thus where services are performed for another in an ordinary business or professional context, it is unlikely that they were understood to be gratuitous. It is not surprising, therefore, to find that the burden of proving such an understanding is on the one who claims it. By way of contrast, where services are performed for other members of the immediate family, living together, the likelihood of an agreement to pay for them is not so great and must be proved by him who claims the right to be paid.

Substantive considerations may also be influential. For real or supposed reasons of policy the law sometimes disfavors claims and defenses which it nevertheless allows. Where that is the case, procedural devices like burden of proof are often used as handicaps, to use Judge Clark's felicitous phrase, against the disfavored contention. Thus whoever charges his adversary with fraud, be he plaintiff or defendant, must prove it. And although falsity is often included in the definitions of defamatory statements (and hence must be pleaded by the plaintiff), the defendant in libel or slander until recently had to plead and prove the truth of the objectionable words if he would escape liability on that basis. In many of the older states, plaintiff, in a negligence action, had to prove his own due care, but as the defense of contributory negligence became increasingly unpopular with courts and legislatures, the tendency has been increasingly to make defendants plead and prove it.

The degree of persuasion required is also sometimes manipulated as a handicap against disfavored contentions. Thus if a claim is presented that a written contract was orally modified, the party claiming the modification must in some jurisdictions prove his contention by clear and convincing evidence.

NOTES

1. In the excerpt from CIVIL PROCEDURE, Professors James and Hazard mention several factors that the courts consider in allocating the burden of proof. In your opinion, which factor is the most important? Which factor is the least important? Why?

2. If a statute creates a cause of action or crime, the courts search for manifestations of a legislative intention on the allocation of the burden. *United States v. Moore*, 613 F.2d 1029, 1044 (D.C. Cir. 1979). "It is a basic principle of statutory construction that the party wishing to come within [a] statutory exception bears the burden of proof." *In re Asuschnet River & New Bedford Harbor*, 722 F. Supp. 893, 901 n.21 (D. Mass. 1989). The rub is determining whether the legislature intended a particular provision in a statute to function as a "statutory exception." In making the determination, many courts rely heavily on matters of form. If the statute describes the cause of action or crime and, in a separate clause or sentence, refers to grounds for avoiding responsibility, the courts tend to treat the reference as an affirmative defense and allocate the burden to the defendant. *Id.* The tendency is especially pronounced if the reference includes such language as "exception, excuse, proviso, or exemption." *Walker v. Commonwealth*, 212 Va. 289, 290, 183 S.E.2d 739, 740 (1971). In many, if not most, cases, the legislature did not consciously advert to the procedural issue of allocating the burden; the legislature's primary concern was simply announcing a new substantive law rule. How ambiguous must the statute be before the court considers itself free to make its own allocation of the burden by independently evaluating the factors listed by James and Hazard?

2. CONSTITUTIONAL LIMITATIONS ON THE ALLOCATION OF THE ULTIMATE BURDEN

As we noted earlier, the legislature is not free to allocate the burden of persuasion in criminal cases as it wishes. The first in a line of decisions on this topic, *In re Winship*, 397 U.S. 358 (1970), held that in a criminal case, due process requires the government to prove beyond a reasonable doubt every fact necessary to constitute the crime charged. This requirement is deceptively simple. What elements are "necessary" to the crime charged?

In *Mullaney v. Wilbur*, 421 U.S. 684 (1975), the defendant was convicted of murder in a Maine state court. Maine's statute defined murder as the unlawful killing of a human being "with malice aforethought, either express or implied." Manslaughter was a killing "in the heat of passion, on sudden provocation, without express or implied malice aforethought." Under Maine law, "malice aforethought" was defined as the absence of "heat of passion on sudden provocation." The Maine courts assigned the defendant the burden of proving by a preponderance of the evidence that he had killed in the "heat of passion, on sudden provocation." "Heat of passion" was an affirmative defense by which an accused could reduce murder to manslaughter.

In a unanimous decision, the United States Supreme Court held that the Maine rule unconstitutionally placed this burden on the defendant. The Court reasoned that the absence of "heat of passion on sudden provocation" (*i.e.*, malice aforethought under Maine law) was a necessary element of the crime, and under *Winship* the burden of proof of such an element must rest and remain on the government.

While this may seem reasonably clear on its face, the *Winship/Mullaney* rule introduced a new complexity into sufficiency–of–proof issues in criminal cases. Does *Mullaney* apply only if the fact in question negates an element of the definition of the crime? Or does *Mullaney* mean that whenever defendant raises an issue that would lessen the degree of the offense, the government must disprove the existence of that element? In some cases, the courts had little difficulty deciding the proper allocation. The courts routinely assigned the government the burden on alibi (*Robinson v. State*, 316 A.2d 268 (Md. Ct. Spec. App. 1974)) while requiring the defendant to assume the burden on entrapment. *People v. Long*, 83 Misc. 2d 14, 372 N.Y.S.2d 389 (1975). *See also United States v. Blassingame*, 197 F.3d 271 (7th Cir. 1999)(distinguishing between alibi and entrapment).

Other allocation decisions, such as the burden on complex *mens rea* elements in homicide cases, proved more troublesome. Those decisions prompted disagreements among the courts, and in turn the disagreements forced the Supreme Court to revisit the issue in the following case.

PATTERSON v. NEW YORK

432 U.S. 197 (1977)

Justice White delivered the opinion of the Court.

The question here is the constitutionality under the Fourteenth Amendment's Due Process Clause of burdening the defendant in a New York State murder trial with proving the affirmative defense of extreme emotional disturbance as defined by New York Law.

After a brief and unstable marriage, the appellant, Gordon Patterson, Jr., became estranged from his wife, Roberta. Roberta resumed an association with John Northrup, a neighbor to whom she had been engaged prior to her marriage to appellant. On December 27, 1970, Patterson borrowed a rifle from an acquaintance and went to the residence of his father–in–law. There, he observed his wife through a window in a state of semiundress in the presence of John Northrup. He entered the house and killed Northrup by shooting him twice in the head.

Patterson was charged with second–degree murder. In New York there are two elements of this crime: (1) "intent to cause the death of another person"; and (2) "caus[ing] the death of such person or of a third person." NY Penal Law § 125.25. Malice aforethought is not an element of the crime. In addition, the State permits a person accused of murder to raise an affirmative defense that he "acted under the influence of extreme emotional disturbance for which there was a reasonable explanation or excuse."[2]

New York also recognizes the crime of manslaughter. A person is guilty of manslaughter if he intentionally kills another person "under circumstances which do not constitute murder because he acts under the influence of extreme emotional disturbance."[3] Appellant confessed before trial to killing Northrup, but at trial he raised the defense of extreme emotional disturbance.

The jury was instructed as to the elements of the crime of murder. Focusing on the element of intent, the trial court charged:

> Before you can convict this defendant or anyone of murder, you must believe and decide that the People have established beyond a reasonable doubt that he intended, in firing the gun, to kill either the victim himself or some other human being. . . .

> Always remember that you must not expect or require the defendant to prove to your satisfaction that his acts were done without the intent to kill. Whatever proof he may have attempted, however far he may have gone in an effort to convince you of his innocence or guiltlessness, he is not obligated to prove anything. It is always the People's burden to prove his guilt, and to prove that he intended to kill in this instance beyond a reasonable doubt.

---

[2] Section 125.25 provides in relevant part: "A person is guilty of murder in the second degree when:

"1. With intent to cause the death of another person, he causes the death of such person or of a third person; except that in any prosecution under this subdivision, it is an affirmative defense that:

"(a) The defendant acted under the influence of extreme emotional disturbance for which there was a reasonable explanation or excuse, the reasonableness of which is to be determined from the viewpoint of a person in the defendant's situation under the circumstances as the defendant believed them to be. Nothing contained in this paragraph shall constitute a defense to a prosecution for, or preclude a conviction of, manslaughter in the first degree or any other crime."

[3] Section 125.20(2). NY Penal Law § 125.20(2) provides: "A person is guilty of manslaughter in the first degree when:

"2. With intent to cause the death of another person, he causes the death of such person or of a third person under circumstances which do not constitute murder because he acts under the influence of extreme emotional disturbance, as defined in paragraph (a) of subdivision one of section 125.25. The fact that homicide was committed under the influence of extreme emotional disturbance constitutes a mitigating circumstance reducing murder to manslaughter in the first degree and need not be proved in any prosecution initiated under this subdivision."

The jury was further instructed, consistently with New York law, that the defendant had the burden of proving his affirmative defense by a preponderance of the evidence. The jury was told that if it found beyond a reasonable doubt that appellant had intentionally killed Northrup but that appellant had demonstrated by a preponderance of the evidence that he had acted under the influence of extreme emotional disturbance, it had to find appellant guilty of manslaughter instead of murder.

The jury found appellant guilty of murder. Judgment was entered on the verdict, and the Appellate Division affirmed. While appeal to the New York Court of Appeals was pending, this Court decided *Mullaney v. Wilbur*, 421 U.S. 684 (1975), in which the Court declared Maine's murder statute unconstitutional.

In the Court of Appeals appellant urged that New York's murder statute is functionally equivalent to the one struck down in *Mullaney* and that therefore his conviction should be reversed.

The Court of Appeals rejected appellant's argument. The Court distinguished *Mullaney* on the ground that the New York statute involved no shifting of the burden to the defendant to disprove any fact essential to the offense charged, since the New York affirmative defense of extreme emotional disturbance bears no direct relationship to any element of murder. This appeal ensued. We affirm.

In determining whether New York's allocation to the defendant of proving the mitigating circumstances of severe emotional disturbance is consistent with due process, it is relevant to note that this defense is a considerably expanded version of the common–law defense of heat of passion on sudden provocation and that at common law the burden of proving the latter, as well as other affirmative defenses–indeed, "all . . . circumstances of justification, excuse or alleviation"–rested on the defendant. 4 W. Blackstone, Commentaries *201. This was the rule when the Fifth Amendment was adopted, and it was the American rule when the Fourteenth Amendment was ratified. *Commonwealth v. York*, 50 Mass. 93 (1845).

In 1895 the common–law view was abandoned with respect to the insanity defense in federal prosecutions. *Davis v. United States*, 160 U.S. 469 (1895). This ruling had wide impact on the practice in the federal courts with respect to the burden of proving various affirmative defenses, and the prosecution in a majority of jurisdictions in this country sooner or later came to shoulder the burden of proving the sanity of the accused and of disproving the facts constituting other affirmative defenses, including provocation. *Davis* was not a constitutional ruling, however, as *Leland v. Oregon*, 343 U.S. 790 (1952) made clear.

At issue in *Leland v. Oregon* was the constitutionality under the Due Process Clause of the Oregon Rule that the defense of insanity must be proved by the defendant beyond a reasonable doubt. Noting that *Davis* "obviously establish[ed] no constitutional doctrine," 343 U.S., at 797, the Court refused to strike down the Oregon scheme, saying that the burden of proving all elements of the crime beyond a reasonable doubt, including the elements of premeditation and deliberation, was placed on the State under Oregon procedures and remained there throughout the trial. To convict, the jury was required to find each element of the crime beyond reasonable doubt, based on all the evidence, including the evidence going to the issue of insanity. Only then was the jury "to consider separately the issue of legal sanity per se . . . ." *Id.,* at 795. This practice did not offend the Due Process Clause even though among the 20 States then placing the burden of proving his insanity on the defendant, Oregon was alone in requiring him to convince the jury beyond a reasonable doubt.

In 1970, the Court declared that the Due Process Clause "protects the accused against conviction except upon proof beyond a reasonable doubt of every fact necessary to constitute the crime with which he is charged." *In re Winship,* 397 U.S. 358, 364 (1970). Five years later, in *Mullaney v. Wilbur,* 421 U.S. 684 (1975), the Court further announced that under the Maine law of homicide, the burden could not constitutionally be placed on the defendant of proving by a preponderance of the evidence that the killing had occurred in the heat of passion on sudden provocation. The Chief Justice and Mr. Justice Rehnquist, concurring, expressed their understanding that the *Mullaney* decision did not call into question the ruling in *Leland v. Oregon* with respect to the proof of insanity.

Subsequently, the Court confirmed that it remained constitutional to burden the defendant with proving his insanity defense when it dismissed, as not raising a substantial federal question, a case in which the appellant specifically challenged the continuing validity of *Leland v. Oregon.* This occurred in *Rivera v. Delaware,* 429 U.S. 877 (1976), an appeal from a Delaware conviction which, in reliance on *Leland,* had been affirmed by the Delaware Supreme Court over the claim that the Delaware statute was unconstitutional because it burdened the defendant with proving his affirmative defense of insanity by a preponderance of the evidence. The claim in this Court was that *Leland* had been overruled by *Winship* and *Mullaney.* We dismissed the appeal as not presenting a substantial federal question.

We cannot conclude that Patterson's conviction under the New York law deprived him of due process of law. The crime of murder is defined by the statute, which represents a recent revision of the state criminal code, as causing the death of another person with intent to do so. The death, the intent to kill, and causation are the facts that the State is required to prove beyond a reasonable doubt if a person is to be convicted of murder. No further facts are either presumed or inferred in order to constitute the crime. The statute does provide an affirmative defense—that the defendant acted under the influence of extreme emotional disturbance for which there was a reasonable explanation—which, if proved by a preponderance of the evidence, would reduce the crime to manslaughter, an offense defined in a separate section of the statute. It is plain enough that if the intentional killing is shown, the State intends to deal with the defendant as a murderer unless he demonstrates the mitigating circumstances.

Here, the jury was instructed in accordance with the statute, and the guilty verdict confirms that the State successfully carried its burden of proving the facts of the crime beyond a reasonable doubt. Nothing in the evidence, including any evidence that might have been offered with respect to Patterson's mental state at the time of the crime, raised a reasonable doubt about his guilt as a murderer; and clearly the evidence failed to convince the jury that Patterson's affirmative defense had been made out. It seems to us that the State satisfied the mandate of *Winship* that it prove beyond a reasonable doubt "every fact necessary to constitute the crime with which [Patterson was] charged." 397 U.S., at 364.

In convicting Patterson under its murder statute, New York did no more than *Leland* and *Rivera* permitted it to do without violating the Due Process Clause. Under those cases, once the facts constituting a crime are established beyond a reasonable doubt, based on all the evidence including the evidence of the defendant's mental state, the State may refuse to sustain the affirmative defense of insanity unless demonstrated by a preponderance of the evidence.

The New York law on extreme emotional disturbance follows this pattern. This affirmative defense, which the Court of Appeals described as permitting "the defendant to show that his actions were caused by a mental infirmity not arising to the level of insanity, and that he is less culpable for having committed them," does not serve to negative any facts of the crime which the State is to prove in order to convict of murder. It constitutes a separate issue on which the defendant is required to carry the burden of persuasion; and unless we are to overturn *Leland* and *Rivera,* New York has not violated the Due Process Clause, and Patterson's conviction must be sustained.

We are unwilling to reconsider *Leland* and *Rivera.* But even if we were to hold that a State must prove sanity to convict once that fact is put in issue, it would not necessarily follow that a State must prove beyond a reasonable doubt every fact, the existence or nonexistence of which it is willing to recognize as an exculpatory or mitigating circumstance affecting the degree of culpability or the severity of the punishment. Here, in revising its criminal code, New York provided the affirmative defense of extreme emotional disturbance, a substantially expanded version of the older heat–of–passion concept; but it was willing to do so only if the facts making out the defense were established by the defendant with sufficient certainty. The State was itself unwilling to undertake to establish the absence of those facts beyond a reasonable doubt, perhaps fearing that proof would be too difficult and that too many persons deserving treatment as murderers would escape that punishment if the evidence need merely raise a reasonable doubt about the defendant's emotional state. It has been said that the new criminal code of New York contains some 25 affirmative defenses which exculpate or mitigate but which must be established by the defendant to be operative. The Due Process Clause, as we see it, does not put New York to the choice of abandoning those defenses or undertaking to disprove their existence in order to convict of a crime which otherwise is within its constitutional powers to sanction by substantial punishment.

We decline to adopt as a constitutional imperative, operative countrywide, that a State must disprove beyond a reasonable doubt every fact constituting any and all affirmative defenses related to the culpability of an accused. Traditionally, due process has required that only the most basic procedural safeguards be observed; more subtle balancing of society's interests against those of the accused have been left to the legislative branch. We therefore will not disturb the balance struck in previous cases holding that the Due Process

Clause requires the prosecution to prove beyond a reasonable doubt all of the elements included in the definition of the offense of which the defendant is charged. Proof of the nonexistence of all affirmative defenses has never been constitutionally required; and we perceive no reason to fashion such a rule in this case and apply it to the statutory defense at issue here.

This view may seem to permit state legislatures to reallocate burdens of proof by labeling as affirmative defenses at least some elements of the crimes now defined in their statutes. But there are obviously constitutional limits beyond which the States may not go in this regard. "[I]t is not within the province of a legislature to declare an individual guilty or presumptively guilty of a crime." *McFarland v. American Sugar Rfg. Co.*, 241 U.S. 79, 86 (1916). The legislature cannot "validly command that the finding of an indictment, or mere proof of the identity of the accused, should create a presumption of the existence of all the facts essential to guilt." *Tot v. United States*, 319 U.S. 463, 469 (1943).

It is urged that *Mullaney v. Wilbur* necessarily invalidates Patterson's conviction. In *Mullaney* the charge was murder, which the Maine statute defined as the unlawful killing of a human being "with malice aforethought, either express or implied." The trial court instructed the jury that the words "malice aforethought" were most important because "malice aforethought is an essential and indispensable element of the crime of murder." Malice, as the statute indicated and as the court instructed, could be implied and was to be implied from "any deliberate, cruel act committed by one person against another suddenly . . . or without a considerable provocation," in which event an intentional killing was murder unless by a preponderance of the evidence it was shown that the act was committed "in the heat of passion, on sudden provocation." The instructions emphasized that " 'malice aforethought and heat of passion on sudden provocation are two inconsistent things'; thus, by proving the latter the defendant would negate the former." 421 U.S., at 686–687.

Mullaney's holding, it is argued, is that the State may not permit the blameworthiness of an act or the severity of punishment authorized for its commission to depend on the presence or absence of an identified fact without assuming the burden of proving the presence or absence of that fact, as the case may be, beyond a reasonable doubt.[15] In our view, the *Mullaney* holding

---

[15] There is some language in *Mullaney* that has been understood as perhaps construing the Due Process Clause to require the prosecution to prove beyond a reasonable doubt any fact affecting "the degree of criminal culpability." *See, e.g.,* Note, *Affirmative Defenses After Mullaney v. Wilbur*: New York's Extreme Emotional Disturbance, 43 BROOKLYN L REV. 171 (1976); Note, *Affirmative Defenses in Ohio After Mullaney v. Wilbur,* 36 OHIO ST. L.J. 828 (1975); Comment, *Unburdening the Criminal Defendant: Mullaney v. Wilbur and the Reasonable Doubt Standard,* 11 HARV. CIV. RIGHTS – CIV. LIB. L. REV. 390 (1976). Such a rule would deprive legislatures of any discretion whatsoever in allocating the burden of proof, the practical effect of which might be to undermine legislative reform of our criminal justice system. Carried to its logical extreme, such a reading of *Mullaney* might also, for example, discourage Congress from enacting pending legislation to change the felony–murder rule by permitting the accused to prove by a preponderance of the evidence the affirmative defense that the homicide committed was neither a necessary nor a reasonably foreseeable consequence of the underlying felony. *See* Senate Bill — 1, 94th Cong., 1st Sess., 118 (1975). The Court did not intend *Mullaney* to have such far–reaching effect.

should not be so broadly read. The concurrence of two Justices in *Mullaney* was necessarily contrary to such a reading; and a majority of the Court refused to so understand and apply *Mullaney* when *Rivera* was dismissed for want of a substantial federal question.

Mullaney surely held that a State must prove every ingredient of an offense beyond a reasonable doubt, and that it may not shift the burden of proof to the defendant by presuming that ingredient upon proof of the other elements of the offense. This is true even though the State's practice, as in Maine, had been traditionally to the contrary. Such shifting of the burden of persuasion with respect to a fact which the State deems so important that it must be either proved or presumed is impermissible under the Due Process Clause.

It was unnecessary to go further in *Mullaney*. The Maine Supreme Judicial Court made it clear that malice aforethought, which was mentioned in the statutory definition of the crime, was not equivalent to premeditation and that the presumption of malice traditionally arising in intentional homicide cases carried no factual meaning insofar as premeditation was concerned. Even so, a killing became murder in Maine when it resulted from a deliberate, cruel act committed by one person against another, "suddenly without any, or without a considerable provocation." *State v. Lafferty, supra* at 665. Premeditation was not within the definition of murder; but malice, in the sense of the absence of provocation, was part of the definition of that crime. Yet malice, *i.e.*, lack of provocation, was presumed and could be rebutted by the defendant only by proving by a preponderance of the evidence that he acted with heat of passion upon sudden provocation. In *Mullaney* we held that however traditional this mode of proceeding might have been, it is contrary to the Due Process Clause as construed in *Winship*.

As we have explained, nothing was presumed or implied against Patterson; and his conviction is not invalid under any of our prior cases. The judgment of the New York Court of Appeals is affirmed.

NOTES AND PROBLEMS

1. The dissenters in *Patterson* charged that the distinctions the majority drew between *Patterson* and *Mullaney* were "indefensibly formalistic." Do you agree? Is the majority elevating form over substance?

2. The majority opinion accords the legislature great latitude in defining crimes and allocating burdens, but the majority is quick to add that "there are obviously constitutional limits beyond which the States may not go . . . ." What limits does the majority identify? Allen, *Structuring Jury Decisionmaking in Criminal Cases: A Unified Constitutional Approach to Evidentiary Devices*, 94 HARV. L. REV. 321, 342–48 (1980).

3. The majority argues that the Court should not "put New York to the choice of abandoning those defenses or undertaking to disprove their existence in order to convict of a crime which otherwise is within its constitutional powers to sanction." Would a broad interpretation of *Mullaney* put New York to that choice? If so, which option is New York likely to choose? Would a broad reading of *Mullaney* be counterproductive?

4. One of the most important progeny of *Patterson* is *Martin v. Ohio*, 480 U.S. 228 (1987). In *Martin*, the Court sustained the constitutionality of state legislation, allocating the defendant the burden of proof on self–defense. The Ohio statutes defined murder as "purposely causing the death of another with prior calculation or design." *Id.* at 233. The prosecution had the burden of proof on the elements of the crime. The Court acknowledged that the evidence the defendant offered on self–defense might also be logically relevant to the question of whether the defendant "purposely killed with prior calculation and design." *Id.* "[E]vidence [relevant] to prove [self-defense] will often tend to negate [the elements of aggravated murder]." *Id.* at 234. However, the Court concluded that "when read as a whole," the trial judge's instruction permitted the jury to consider the self–defense evidence on the question of whether there was a reasonable doubt as to any element of the crime. The judge merely charged the jury that, when they turned to the separate issue of self–defense, the defense had the burden of proof by a preponderance of the evidence.

In 1996, in *Montana v. Egelhoff*, 518 U.S. 37 (1996), a majority of the Court indicated that they read *Patterson* and *Martin* as permitting the legislature to go quite far in redefining the *mens rea* elements of offenses. In *Egelhoff*, the question was the constitutionality of a Montana statute providing that in determining whether the defendant had purposely or knowingly caused a death, the jury could not consider any evidence of the defendant's voluntary intoxication. Justices Scalia, Kennedy, and Thomas filed the lead, plurality opinion, joined by the Chief Justice. Justice Ginsburg concurred in the judgment. While the plurality Justices indicated that they were willing to uphold the statute as either an evidentiary rule or a substantive redefinition of *mens rea*, Justice Ginsburg characterized the statue as "a redefinition of the mental–state element of the offense." She wrote that "when a State's power to define criminal conduct is challenged under the Due Process Clause, we inquire only whether the law offends some principle of justice so rooted in the traditions and conscience of our people as to be ranked as fundamental." She emphasized the portion of the plurality opinion noting the English tradition that voluntary intoxication may not serve as an excuse in a criminal case. She also noted that "a significant minority of the States" adhere to the English position even "today." She concluded that "comprehended as a measure redefining mens rea," the statute "encounters no constitutional shoal."

5. Problem 31–1. Suppose that Paterson's daughter had interrupted the burglary in the *Devitt* case and that before fleeing, the perpetrator raped her. Just before the incident, the Morena legislature passed and the governor signed the following Penal Code provision:

> (a) Rape is the carnal knowledge of a woman by a man not her husband without her actual consent.

> (b) Sexual assault [a lesser offense] is the carnal knowledge of a woman by a man not her husband without her actual consent, but with her apparent consent. "Apparent consent" is words or conduct or both that create in another the genuine but unreasonable belief that consent was given.

(c) Apparent consent is an affirmative defense that must be raised by the defendant and proved by him by a preponderance of the evidence.

Is this statute constitutional? In *State v. Camara*, 113 Wash. 2d 631, 781 P.2d 483 (1989), the court upheld state legislation providing that, in a rape case, the victim's consent is an affirmative defense. The court noted that, in the past, it had inquired "whether . . . an element of the defense 'negates' an element of the crime charged." *Id.* at 781 P.2d at 487. However, the court then added:

> In light of [*Martin v. Ohio*], we have substantial doubt about the correctness of the "negates" analysis and thus decline to apply it in this case. In *Martin*.., [a]cknowledging an overlap between self–defense and the elements of purpose and prior calculation and design, the Court nevertheless held that the State's burden to prove the elements of the crime was unrelieved.

Id. The court ruled that "while there is a conceptual overlap between the consent defense and the rape crime's element of forcible compulsion, we cannot hold that for that reason alone the burden of proof on consent must rest with the State." *Id.* In the passage in *Martin* which the *Camara* court alluded to, the Supreme Court stated that "the elements of aggravated murder and self–defense overlap in the sense that evidence to prove the latter will often tend to negate the former." 480 U.S. at 234. Does *Camara* properly interpret *Martin*? There was an evidentiary overlap in *Martin*; there were items of evidence which were logically relevant both to the question of purposeful killing and the issue of self–defense. Was there also a "conceptual overlap" in *Martin*, as there was in *Camara*?

6. Problem 31–2. In the original *Devitt* battery prosecution, Devitt is charged with a specific intent assault, assault with intent to inflict grievous bodily injury. His friend, James Woodley, is prepared to testify that Devitt was "roaring drunk" an hour before the alleged assault. Morena recognizes voluntary intoxication as a defense to specific intent crimes. May Morena assign Devitt the burden of proof on the issue of intoxication? *United States ex rel. Goddard v. Vaughn*, 614 F.2d 929, 936 (3d Cir. 1980).

7. Problem 31–3. Assume that in *Devitt*, Woodley was a codefendant. The prosecution theory is that while they were drinking together, Devitt and Woodley entered into a conspiracy to attack Paterson. Woodley intends to defend on the theory that although he initially "went along" with Devitt, Woodley withdrew from the conspiracy. May Morena require Woodley to assume the burden of proving withdrawal? *United States v. Read*, 658 F.2d 1225, 1232–36 (7th Cir. 1981).

8. Problem 31–4. Devitt is charged with battery, a general intent crime under Morena law. He concedes that he physically touched Paterson, but he claims that the touching was accidental. He testifies that after they argued, he was attempting to leave; and he was passing Paterson in the hallway of the apartment when he tripped on one of his tools and fell into Paterson. May Morena assign Devitt the burden on the issue of accident? *See Fornash v. Marshall*, 686 F.2d 1179, 1183 (6th Cir. 1982).

C. THE MEASURE OF THE BURDEN OF PERSUASION

1. THE COMMON LAW

Different standards for meeting the burden of persuasion have been devised for different types of cases and issues. The following explanation is taken from M. LADD & R. CARLSON, CASES AND MATERIALS ON EVIDENCE 1189–90 (1972):

The standards are designed to control the mental processes of the jury through fixing a measure of the persuasive force required for fulfilling the burden of proof. The tests generally fit into three categories: proof by a preponderance of evidence, proof by clear and convincing evidence, and proof beyond a reasonable doubt.

In principle, the court's choice of a measure for the burden should reflect the stakes in the case; the more important the stakes, the higher the burden should be. Saltzburg, *Standards of Proof and Preliminary Questions of Fact*, 27 STAN. L. REV. 271, 278–80, 304 (1975). The court should weigh the risk of error before selecting a measure. *Motor & Equipment Mfrs. Ass'n v. E.P.A.*, 627 F.2d 1095, 1122 (D.C. Cir. 1979). However, the reader should also realize that to some extent, the particular measure of the burden on an issue depends on the vagaries of historical accident. "The forms of action we have buried, but they still rule us from their graves." F. MAITLAND, THE FORMS OF ACTION AT COMMON LAW 2 (1936 ed.). At the risk of oversimplification, the civil law courts generally used the standard of preponderance of the evidence, the equity courts employed the extraordinary measure of clear and convincing proof, and the criminal courts developed the test of proof beyond a reasonable doubt. Consider each of the three standards.

Preponderance of the evidence. In most civil cases the test requires that there must be a preponderance of evidence in favor of the party who has the burden of proof. Preponderance and greater weight of evidence are synonymous terms. The triers of fact must believe that the existence of a fact is more probable than its nonexistence. The court's instruction usually includes a cautionary statement that the greater weight or preponderance of evidence does not necessarily mean the greater quantity of evidence or the larger number of witnesses but is the greater weight of proof. Some courts have struggled over the meaning of preliminary words in the instruction such as informing the jury that they must be "satisfied" by a preponderance of evidence. Some take the view that satisfaction would require more proof than a preponderance, and others feel that a jury might be satisfied with less than a preponderance. The cases tend to overemphasize the niceties of expression. Such linguistic nuances probably have little or no effect upon the thinking process of the average juror.

In *Livanovitch v. Livanovitch*, 99 Vt. 327, 131 A. 799 (1926), the court emphasized how easily the proponent can establish a preponderance of the evidence:

The slightest preponderance of the evidence in his favor entitle[s] the plaintiff to a verdict. All that is required in a civil case of one who has the burden of proof is that he establish his claim by a preponderance of the evidence. When the equilibrium of proof is destroyed, and the beam inclines toward him who has the burden, however slightly, he has satisfied the requirement of the law, and is entitled to the verdict. "A bare preponderance is sufficient, though the scales drop but a feather's weight."

As ILLINOIS PATTERN JURY INSTRUCTIONS (CIVIL) SECOND § 21.01 (1971) demonstrates, the judge can convey this concept to the jury without using the classical expression, "preponderance":

Meaning of Burden of Proof

When I say that a party has the burden of proof on any proposition, or use the expression "if you find", or "if you decide", I mean you must be persuaded, considering all the evidence in the case, that the proposition on which [he] has the burden of proof is more probably true than not true.

NOTES AND PROBLEMS

1. We should not succumb to the simplistic notion that the preponderance standard applies only in civil cases. Not only do equity courts often use the standard, criminal courts sometimes employ the preponderance measure. In many jurisdictions, preponderance is the measure on the issue of the defendant's competency to stand trial. *United States v. Digilio*, 538 F.2d 972, 988 (3d Cir. 1976). Further, a number of states use preponderance as the test for the sufficiency of the evidence of criminal venue and jurisdiction. Annot., 67 A.L.R.3d 988 (1975). What common denominator do these issues–competency, venue, and jurisdiction–share?

2. Problem 31–5. In *Devitt*, the prosecution attempts to prove that the defendant mailed Mr. Paterson a threatening letter a week before the alleged attack. An acquaintance of the defendant, Mr. McManis, is prepared to identify the letter's handwriting style as Devitt's. However, the defense has a questioned document examiner, Ms. Mussio, who will give contrary testimony. Does the letter's authenticity fall under Federal Rule of Evidence 104(a) or 104(b)? Who finally decides the letter's authenticity–the judge or jury? What standard of proof applies to the question of the letter's genuineness?

Clear and convincing evidence. The second standard of proof requirement lies somewhere between a preponderance of evidence and proof beyond reasonable doubt. The common expression is "clear and convincing evidence." Other similar expressions are used such as "clear, precise, and indubitable," "clear conviction without hesitation," and "clear, satisfactory, and convincing." This higher standard of proof is required in "a limited range" actions in which it is thought that the status quo should not be changed by a mere preponderance of evidence. *In re Marriage of Haines*, 33 Cal. App. 4th 277, 294 n. 9, 39 Cal. Rtpr.2d 673, 84 (1995). *See also Mattco Forge, Inc. v. Arthur Young & Co.*, 52 Cal.App.4th 820 n. 4, 60 Cal.Rptr.2d 780, 800–01 n.4 (1997)(listing 11 different types of actions in which California courts require clear and convincing evidence). Illustrative are actions to reform a written contract because of mutual mistake, to show civil contempt, to establish the existence and content of a lost will or deed, to prove that a deed of land was in fact a mortgage, to impeach a notary's certificate of acknowledgment, to establish the malice required to recover punitive damages, to prove a ground for disbarment of an attorney, to establish the facts triggering promissory estoppel, to show the invalidity of a patent, and to prove fraud.

> This standard was applied in equity and in law where the claimant either sought extraordinary relief or based his claim on disfavored grounds, or where he sought relief which would have serious social consequences or harsh effects on an individual beyond the mere award of money damages.

Comment, 24 EMORY L.J. 105, 114 (1975).

As in the case of the preponderance standard, do not think that the standard is confined to civil actions. To begin with, the Supreme Court has mandated the standard in eyewitness identification cases. In *United States v. Wade*, 388 U.S. 218 (1967), the Court recognized a limited right to counsel at lineups. The Court added that when the pretrial lineup violates the defendant's right to counsel, the eyewitness' in–court identification is admissible only if the government "establish[es] by clear and convincing evidence that the in–court identifications were based upon observations of the suspect other than the lineup identification." *Id.* at 240. In the Fourth Amendment context, if the prosecution relies on the defendant's consent as the basis for a warrantless search, some jurisdictions require the prosecutor to prove consent by clear and positive evidence. *See, e.g., People v. Reynolds*, 55 Cal. App. 3d 357, 127 Cal. Rptr. 561 (1976).

NOTES

1. Who decides the issues of consent and the propriety of an in–court identification–the judge or jury? Does that help explain why the courts apply a more rigorous standard of proof? Remember that the standard originated in equity suits. Is there usually a jury in equity suits?

2. The clear and convincing proof standard now applies in several types of cases tried by juries. 2 C. McCORMICK, HANDBOOK OF THE LAW OF EVIDENCE § 340 (5th ed. 1999). As trial judge, how would you explain the concept of clear and convincing proof to lay jurors? The concept refers to the quality of the evidence rather than any particular quantum of proof. *Nguyen v. IBP, Inc.*, 905 F. Supp. 1471, 1481 n. 2 (D. Kan. 1995) (the court added that "[t]he evidence is clear 'if it is certain, unambiguous, and plan to the understanding. It is convincing if it is reasonable and persuasive enough to cause the trier of facts to believe it' "); *Modern Air Conditioning, Inc. v. Cinderella Homes, Inc.*, 226 Kan. 70, 78, 596 P.2d 816 (1979)("the witness to a fact must be found to be credible; the facts to which the witness testifies must be distinctly remembered; the details in connection with the transaction must be narrated exactly and in order, . . .and the witness must be lacking in confusion as to the facts at issue"). One commentator suggests that the judge merely tell the jury that the truth of the contention must be "highly probable." McBaine, *Burden of Proof: Degrees of Belief*, 32 CAL. L. REV. 242, 246, 253–54 (1944). Following that suggestion, the pattern instruction in California directs the jury that " 'clear and convincing' evidence means evidence of such a convincing force that it demonstrates . . . a high probability of the truth of the fact for which it is offered as proof." BOOK OF APPROVED JURY INSTRUCTIONS § 2.62 (1988

It has been observed that this standard "takes into account the subjective belief of the factfinder as to the validity of the proposition . . . rather than simply weighing [the] evidence . . . ." Comment, 24 EMORY L.J. 105, 114 (1975). The Nebraska Supreme Court has described this quantum of evidence as "that amount . . . which produces in the trier of fact a firm belief or conviction . . . ." *Haines v. Mensen*, 233 Neb. 543, 446 N.W.2d 716, 719 (1989). The following year, the United States Supreme Court elaborated on the concept as evidence which "produces in the mind of the trier of fact a firm belief or conviction as to the truth of the allegations sought to be established, evidence so clear, direct, and weighty and convincing as to enable the fact finder to come to a clear conviction, without hesitancy, of the truth of the precise facts . . . ." *Cruzan v. Director, Missouri Dept. of Health*, 497 U.S. 261, 285 n. 11 (1990).

Proof beyond a reasonable doubt. In *Commonwealth v. Webster*, 59 Mass. (5 Cush.) 295, 320 (1850), Chief Justice Shaw coined the classic definition of a reasonable doubt:

> It is that state of the case, which after the entire comparison and consideration of all the evidence, leaves the minds of the jurors in that condition that they cannot say they feel an abiding conviction, to a moral certainty, of the truth of the charge.

Many states' pattern jury instructions incorporate this precise language, and some jurisdictions have gone to the length of codifying the definition. CAL. PENAL CODE § 1096.

Most trial judges treat Shaw's definition as if it were irreducible; they refuse to amplify on the definition. Their refusal is understandable; in many states, the trial judge risks reversal by the appellate court whenever he or she attempts to explain the concept further.

However, some judges believe that the jury needs additional guidance. In some jurisdictions, the judge may add that the doubt is the kind of doubt that would make a reasonable person hesitate to act. *United States v. Dunmore*, 446 F.2d 1214, 1222 (8th Cir. 1971), *cert. denied*, 404 U.S. 1041 (1972). The judge should stress hesitancy to act rather than willingness to act. The judge can err by telling the jury that proof beyond a reasonable doubt is evidence "of such a convincing character that you would be willing to rely upon it unhesitatingly in the most important of your own affairs." *United States v. Williams*, 505 F.2d 947, 948 n.1 (8th Cir. 1974). Even in jurisdictions allowing the judge to refer to the jury's willingness to act in important affairs, the judge risks reversal if the judge takes the next step and gives the jury examples of important affairs. In *Commonwealth v. Ferreira*, 364 N.E.2d 1264 (Mass. 1977), the judge listed several "important decisions" in the jury charge: whether to get married or stay single, to buy a house or continue renting, to leave school, to get a job, or to move to another community. The appellate court reversed, expressing the fear that the trial judge's examples understated and trivialized the standard in the jury's mind.

NOTES

1. It was once common practice to give the jury a specially refined definition of proof beyond a reasonable doubt when the prosecution relied on circumstantial evidence. Thus, in *State v. DeRaad*, 164 N.W.2d 108, 110 (Iowa 1969), the court directed the trial judge to instruct the jury that:

> [W]here circumstantial evidence alone is relied on . . ., the . . . circumstances must be entirely consistent with defendant's guilt and wholly inconsistent with any rational hypothesis of defendant's innocence . . . .

However, *Holland v. United States*, 348 U.S. 121, 139–40 (1954), is a watershed in the history of that instruction. *Holland* asserted that the instruction probably succeeds only in confusing the jurors. Since the *Holland* decision, all of the federal circuits have abandoned the hypothesis of innocence phraseology. *United States v. Bell*, 678 F.2d 547, 549 n.3 (5th Cir. 1982). The instruction has also fallen into disrepute in most states.

2. Is the analogy to a chain of circumstances leading to a conviction of guilt open to the argument that a chain is no stronger than its weakest link and that the weak link is sufficient to create a reasonable doubt? Is a better analogy to a cable made up of many strands that together give the evidential force to establish guilt beyond reasonable doubt, although each strand alone would be insufficient and the separate strands might vary considerably in their strength? M. LADD & R. CARLSON, CASES AND MATERIALS ON EVIDENCE 1214 (1972).

3. There has been very little research into the jury's understanding of the various measures of the burden. One of the few studies to explore that question was the London School of Economics Jury Project. *Juries and the Rules of Evidence*, 1973 CRIM. L. REV. 208, *cited in Addington, infra*. In the study, the subjects heard several variations of an instruction on the measure. Some were told that they had to be convinced of guilt "beyond reasonable doubt," others were instructed that they had to be "sure and certain" of guilt, and still others were directed that they had to "feel satisfied that it is more likely than not that the accused is guilty." *Id*. at 213–14. In a hypothetical theft case, under the three instructions, the percentage of convictions increased from 31% to 35% to 46%. The results in two other hypothetical cases, though, were more mixed; while the subjects receiving the last instruction convicted more frequently than the subjects receiving the first instruction, the lowest conviction rate was under the "sure and certain" instruction. *Id*. at 216–17. The researchers acknowledged that they had conducted a limited study. *Id*. at 221. However, they added that the results of the study indicated that "jurors are not influenced" by instructions on the measure of the burden to the extent that is commonly assumed. *Id*. at 219.

4. In the vast majority of cases, the proof beyond a reasonable doubt standard is applied in prosecutions rather than civil actions. However, in rare cases, the standard comes into play in civil cases. By way of example, when a litigant seeks rescission of a contract on the ground of unilateral mistake, Mississippi law requires proof of the mistake beyond a reasonable doubt. *Crosby–Mississippi Resources, Ltd. v. Prosper Energy Corp.*, 974 F.2d 612 (5th Cir. 1992). Similarly, by statute, Colorado requires that certain elements of a claim for punitive damages be proven beyond a reasonable doubt. *Karnes v. SCI Colorado Funeral Services, Inc.*, 162 F.3d 1077, 1082 (10th Cir. 1998)(discussing Colo.Rev.Stat. §13–25–127).

2. CONSTITUTIONAL REQUIREMENTS

ADDINGTON v. TEXAS

441 U.S. 418 (1979)

CHIEF JUSTICE BURGER delivered the opinion of the Court.

The question in this case is what standard of proof is required by the Fourteenth Amendment to the Constitution in a civil proceeding brought under state law to commit an individual involuntarily for an indefinite period to a state mental hospital.

On seven occasions between 1969 and 1975, appellant was committed temporarily to various Texas state mental hospitals and was committed for indefinite periods to Austin State Hospital on three different occasions. On December 18, 1975, when appellant was arrested on a misdemeanor charge of "assault by threat" against his mother, the county and state mental health authorities therefore were well aware of his history of mental and emotional difficulties.

Appellant's mother filed a petition for his indefinite commitment in accordance with Texas law. The county psychiatric examiner interviewed appellant while in custody and after the interview issued a Certificate of Medical Examination for Mental Illness. In the certificate, the examiner stated his opinion that appellant was "mentally ill and require[d] hospitalization in a mental hospital."

Appellant retained counsel and a trial was held before a jury to determine in accord with the statute:

(1) whether the proposed patient is mentally ill, and if so

(2) whether he requires hospitalization in a mental hospital for his own welfare and protection or the protection of others, and if so

(3) whether he is mentally incompetent.

Art. 5547–51 (Vernon 1958). The trial on these issues extended over six days.

The State offered evidence that appellant suffered from serious delusions, that he often had threatened to injure both of his parents and others, that he had been involved in several assaultive episodes while hospitalized and that he had caused substantial property damage both at his own apartment and at his parents' home. From these undisputed facts, two psychiatrists, who qualified as experts, expressed opinions that appellant suffered from psychotic schizophrenia and that he had paranoid tendencies. They also expressed medical opinions that appellant was probably dangerous both to himself and to others. They explained that appellant required hospitalization in a closed area to treat his condition because in the past he had refused to attend outpatient treatment programs and had escaped several times from mental hospitals.

Appellant did not contest the factual assertions made by the State's witnesses; indeed, he conceded that he suffered from a mental illness. What appellant attempted to show was that there was no substantial basis for concluding that he was probably dangerous to himself or others.

The trial judge submitted the case to the jury with the instructions in the form of two questions:

1. Based on clear, unequivocal and convincing evidence, is Frank O'Neal Addington mentally ill?

2. Based on clear, unequivocal and convincing evidence, does Frank O'Neal Addington require hospitalization in a mental hospital for his own welfare and protection or the protection of others?

Appellant objected to these instructions on several grounds, including the trial court's refusal to employ the "beyond a reasonable doubt" standard of proof.

The jury found that appellant was mentally ill and that he required hospitalization for his own or others' welfare. The trial court then entered an order committing appellant as a patient to Austin State Hospital for an indefinite period.

Appellant appealed that order to the Texas Court of Civil Appeals, arguing, among other things, that the standards for commitment violated his substantive due process rights and that any standard of proof for commitment less than that required for criminal convictions, i.e., beyond a reasonable doubt, violated his procedural due process rights. The Court of Civil Appeals agreed with appellant on the standard of proof issue and reversed the judgment of the trial court. Because of its treatment of the standard of proof, that court did not consider any of the other issues raised in the appeal.

On appeal, the Texas Supreme Court reversed the Court of Civil Appeals' decision. In so holding, the supreme court relied primarily upon its previous decision in *State v. Turner*, 556 S.W.2d 563 (1977), *cert. denied*, 435 U.S. 929 (1978).

In *Turner*, the Texas Supreme Court held that a "preponderance of the evidence" standard of proof in a civil commitment proceeding satisfied due process. The court declined to adopt the criminal law standard of "beyond a reasonable doubt" primarily because it questioned whether the State could prove by that exacting standard that a particular person would or would not be dangerous in the future. It also distinguished a civil commitment from a criminal conviction by noting that under Texas law the mentally ill patient has the right to treatment, periodic review of his condition, and immediate release when no longer deemed to be a danger to himself or others. Finally, the *Turner* court rejected the "clear and convincing" evidence standard because under Texas rules of procedure juries could be instructed only under a beyond–a–reasonable–doubt or a preponderance standard of proof.

Reaffirming *Turner*, the Texas Supreme Court in this case concluded that the trial court's instruction to the jury, although not in conformity with the legal requirements, had benefited appellant, and hence the error was harmless. Accordingly, the court reinstated the judgment of the trial court.

We noted probable jurisdiction. After oral argument it became clear that no challenge to the constitutionality of any Texas statute was presented. Under 28 U.S.C. § 1257(2) no appeal is authorized; accordingly, construing the papers filed as a petition for a writ of certiorari, we now grant the petition.

The function of a standard of proof, as that concept is embodied in the Due Process Clause and in the realm of factfinding, is to "instruct the factfinder concerning the degree of confidence our society thinks he should have in the correctness of factual conclusions for a particular type of adjudication." *In re Winship*, 397 U.S. 358, 370 (1970). The standard serves to allocate the risk of error between the litigants and to indicate the relative importance attached to the ultimate decision.

Generally speaking, the evolution of this area of the law has produced across a continuum three standards or levels of proof for different types of cases. At one end of the spectrum is the typical civil case involving a monetary dispute between private parties. Since society has a minimal concern with the outcome of such private suits, plaintiff's burden of proof is a mere preponderance of the evidence. The litigants thus share the risk of error in roughly equal fashion.

In a criminal case, on the other hand, the interests of the defendant are of such magnitude that historically and without any explicit constitutional requirement they have been protected by standards of proof designed to exclude as nearly as possible the likelihood of an erroneous judgment. In the administration of criminal justice, our society imposes almost the entire risk of error upon itself. This is accomplished by requiring under the Due Process Clause that the state prove the guilt of an accused beyond a reasonable doubt. *In re Winship, supra*.

The intermediate standard, which usually employs some combination of the words "clear," "cogent," "unequivocal," and "convincing," is less commonly used, but nonetheless "is no stranger to the civil law," *Woodby v. INS*, 385 U.S. 276, 285 (1966). One typical use of the standard is in civil cases involving allegations of fraud or some other quasi–criminal wrongdoing by the defendant. The interests at stake in those cases are deemed to be more substantial than mere loss of money and some jurisdictions accordingly reduce the risk to the defendant of having his reputation tarnished erroneously by increasing the plaintiff's burden of proof. Similarly, this Court has used the "clear, unequivocal and convincing" standard of proof to protect particularly important individual interests in various civil cases. *See, e.g., Woodby v. INS, supra*, at 285 (deportation); *Chaunt v. United States*, 364 U.S. 350, 353 (1960) (denaturalization); *Schneiderman v. United States*, 320 U.S. 118, 125, 159 (1943) (denaturalization).

Candor suggests that, to a degree, efforts to analyze what lay jurors understand concerning the differences among these three tests or the nuances of a judge's instructions on the law may well be largely an academic exercise;

there are no directly relevant empirical studies. Indeed, the ultimate truth as to how the standards of proof affect decisionmaking may well be unknowable, given that factfinding is a process shared by countless thousands of individuals throughout the country. We probably can assume no more than that the difference between a preponderance of the evidence and proof beyond a reasonable doubt probably is better understood than either of them in relation to the intermediate standard of clear and convincing evidence. Nonetheless, even if the particular standard–of–proof catch words do not always make a great difference in a particular case, adopting a "standard of proof is more than an empty semantic exercise." *Tippett v. Maryland*, 436 F.2d 1153, 1166 (CA4 1971), *cert. dismissed sub nom. Murel v. Baltimore City Criminal Court*, 407 U.S. 355 (1972). In cases involving individual rights, whether criminal or civil, "[t]he standard of proof [at a minimum] reflects the value society places on individual liberty." 436 F.2d, at 1166.

In considering what standard should govern in a civil commitment proceeding, we must assess both the extent of the individual's interest in not being involuntarily confined indefinitely and the state's interest in committing the emotionally disturbed under a particular standard of proof.

This Court repeatedly has recognized that civil commitment for any purpose constitutes a significant deprivation of liberty that requires due process protection. *See, e.g., Jackson v. Indiana*, 406 U.S. 715 (1972). Moreover, it is indisputable that involuntary commitment to a mental hospital after a finding of probable dangerousness to self or others can engender adverse social consequences to the individual. Whether we label this phenomena "stigma" or choose to call it something else is less important than that we recognize that it can occur and that it can have a very significant impact on the individual.

The state has a legitimate interest under its parens patriae powers in providing care to its citizens who are unable because of emotional disorders to care for themselves; the state also has authority under its police power to protect the community from the dangerous tendencies of some who are mentally ill. Under the Texas Mental Health Code, however, the State has no interest in confining individuals involuntarily if they are not mentally ill or if they do not pose some danger to themselves or others. Since the preponderance standard creates the risk of increasing the number of individuals erroneously committed, it is at least unclear to what extent, if any, the state's interests are furthered by using a preponderance standard in such commitment proceedings.

The expanding concern of society with problems of mental disorders is reflected in the fact that in recent years many states have enacted statutes designed to protect the rights of the mentally ill. However, only one state by statute permits involuntary commitment by a mere preponderance of the evidence, Miss. Code. Ann. § 41–21–75, and Texas is the only state where a court has concluded that the preponderance of the evidence standard satisfies due process. We attribute this not to any lack of concern in those states, but rather to a belief that the varying standards tend to produce comparable results. As we noted earlier, however, standards of proof are important for their symbolic meaning as well as for their practical effect.

At one time or another every person exhibits some abnormal behavior which might be perceived by some as symptomatic of a mental or emotional disorder, but which is in fact within a range of conduct that is generally acceptable. Obviously, such behavior is no basis for compelled treatment and surely none for confinement. However, there is the possible risk that a factfinder might decide to commit an individual based solely on a few isolated instances of unusual conduct. Loss of liberty calls for a showing that the individual suffers from something more serious than is demonstrated by idiosyncratic behavior. Increasing the burden of proof is one way to impress the factfinder with the importance of the decision and thereby perhaps to reduce the chances that inappropriate commitments will be ordered.

The individual should not be asked to share equally with society the risk of error when the possible injury to the individual is significantly greater than any possible harm to the state. We conclude that the individual's interest in the outcome of a civil commitment proceeding is of such weight and gravity that due process requires the state to justify confinement by proof more substantial than a mere preponderance of the evidence.

Appellant urges the Court to hold that due process requires use of the criminal law's standard of proof—"beyond a reasonable doubt." He argues that the rationale of the *Winship* holding that the criminal law standard of proof was required in a delinquency proceeding applies with equal force to a civil commitment proceeding.

* * *

There are significant reasons why different standards of proof are called for in civil commitment proceedings as opposed to criminal prosecutions. In a civil commitment state power is not exercised in a punitive sense.[4] . . .

In addition, the "beyond a reasonable doubt" standard historically has been reserved for criminal cases. This unique standard of proof, not prescribed or defined in the Constitution, is regarded as a critical part of the "moral force of the criminal law," *In re Winship*, 397 U.S., at 364, and we should hesitate to apply it too broadly or casually in noncriminal cases.

The heavy standard applied in criminal cases manifests our concern that the risk of error to the individual must be minimized even at the risk that some who are guilty might go free. *Patterson v. New York*, 432 U.S. 197, 208 (1977). The full force of that idea does not apply to a civil commitment. It may be true that an erroneous commitment is sometimes as undesirable as an erroneous conviction, 5 J. Wigmore, Evidence § 1400 (Chadbourn rev. 1974). However, even though an erroneous confinement should be avoided in the first instance, the layers of professional review and observation of the patient's condition, and the concern of family and friends generally will provide continuous opportunities for an erroneous commitment to be corrected. Moreover, it is not true that the release of a genuinely mentally ill person

---

[4] The State of Texas confines only for the purpose of providing care designed to treat the individual. As the Texas Supreme Court said in *State v. Turner,* 556 S.W.2d 563, 566 (1977): "The involuntary mental patient is entitled to treatment, to periodic and recurrent review of his mental condition, and to release at such time as he no longer presents a danger to himself or others."

is no worse for the individual than the failure to convict the guilty. One who is suffering from a debilitating mental illness and in need of treatment is neither wholly at liberty nor free of stigma. *See* Chodoff, *The Case for Involuntary Hospitalization of the Mentally Ill*, 133 AM. J. PSYCHIATRY 496, 498 (1976); Schwartz, Myers, & Astrachan, *Psychiatric Labeling and the Rehabilitation of the Mental Patient*, 31 ARCH. GEN. PSYCHIATRY 329, 334 (1974). It cannot be said, therefore, that it is much better for a mentally ill person to "go free" than for a mentally normal person to be committed.

Finally, the initial inquiry in a civil commitment proceeding is very different from the central issue in either a delinquency proceeding or a criminal prosecution. In the latter cases the basic issue is a straightforward factual question–did the accused commit the act alleged? There may be factual issues to resolve in a commitment proceeding, but the factual aspects represent only the beginning of the inquiry. Whether the individual is mentally ill and dangerous to either himself or others and is in need of confined therapy turns on the meaning of the facts which must be interpreted by expert psychiatrists and psychologists. Given the lack of certainty and the fallibility of psychiatric diagnosis, there is a serious question as to whether a state could ever prove beyond a reasonable doubt that an individual is both mentally ill and likely to be dangerous. Note, *Civil Commitment of the Mentally Ill: Theories and Procedures*, 79 HARV. L. REV. 1288, 1291 (1966); Note, *Due Process and the Development of "Criminal" Safeguards in Civil Commitment Adjudications*, 42 FORDHAM L. REV. 611, 624 (1974).

The subtleties and nuances of psychiatric diagnosis render certainties virtually beyond reach in most situations. The reasonable–doubt standard of criminal law functions in its realm because there the standard is addressed to specific, knowable facts. Psychiatric diagnosis, in contrast, is to a large extent based on medical "impressions" drawn from subjective analysis and filtered through the experience of the diagnostician. This process often makes it very difficult for the expert physician to offer definite conclusions about any particular patient. Within the medical discipline, the traditional standard for "factfinding" is a "reasonable medical certainty." If a trained psychiatrist has difficulty with the categorical "beyond a reasonable doubt" standard, the untrained lay juror–or indeed even a trained judge–who is required to rely upon expert opinion could be forced by the criminal law standard of proof to reject commitment for many patients desperately in need of institutionalized psychiatric care. *See ibid.* Such "freedom" for a mentally ill person would be purchased at a high price.

* * *

Having concluded that the preponderance standard falls short of meeting the demands of due process and that the reasonable doubt standard is not required we turn to a middle level of burden of proof that strikes a fair balance between the rights of the individual and the legitimate concerns of the state. We note that 20 states, most by statute, employ the standard of "clear and convincing" evidence; three states use "clear, cogent, and convincing" evidence; and two states require "clear, unequivocal and convincing" evidence.

In *Woodby v. INS*, 385 U.S. 276 (1966), dealing with deportation, and *Schneiderman v. United States*, 320 U.S. at 125, 159, dealing with denaturalization, the Court held that "clear, unequivocal, and convincing" evidence was the appropriate standard of proof. The term "unequivocal," taken by itself, means proof that admits of no doubt, a burden approximating, if not exceeding, that used in criminal cases. The issues in *Schneiderman* and *Woodby* were basically factual and therefore susceptible of objective proof and the consequences to the individual were unusually drastic–loss of citizenship and expulsion from the United States.

We have concluded that the reasonable doubt standard is inappropriate in civil commitment proceedings because, given the uncertainties of psychiatric diagnosis, it may impose a burden the state cannot meet and thereby erect an unreasonable barrier to needed medical treatment. Similarly, we conclude that use of the term "unequivocal" is not constitutionally required, although the states are free to use that standard. To meet due process demands, the standard has to inform the factfinder that the proof must be greater than the preponderance of the evidence standard applicable to other categories of civil cases.

We noted earlier that the trial court employed the standard of "clear, unequivocal and convincing" evidence in appellant's commitment hearing before a jury. That instruction was constitutionally adequate. However, determination of the precise burden equal to or greater than the "clear and convincing" standard which we hold is required to meet due process guarantees is a matter of state law which we leave to the Texas Supreme Court. Accordingly, we remand the case for further proceedings not inconsistent with this opinion.

Vacated and remanded.

NOTES AND PROBLEMS

1. In *Santosky v. Kramer*, 455 U.S. 745, 768–69 (1982), the Court extended *Addington* to proceedings to terminate natural parents' rights in their children. The Court declared that the child and the natural parents share a "vital interest in preventing erroneous termination of their relationship." *Id.* at 760. However, in *Rivera v. Minnich*, 483 U.S. 574 (1987), the Court refused to extend *Santosky* to paternity litigation between private parties. The Court distinguished *Santosky* on several grounds, including the private character of the litigants. The Court noted that, in all the cases in which it has held an enhanced standard of proof to be constitutionally required, "the contestants" have been "the State and an individual." *Id.* at 581. In each case, it was "appropriate for society to impose upon itself a disproportionate share of the risk of error"; "the State has superior resources," and the private individual faced "especially severe consequences." *Id.* However, in paternity litigation between private parties, the competing interests are in relative "equipoise." *Id.*

2. Like *Mullaney*, *Addington* relies on *Winship*. Should *Mullaney*, like *Addington*, now extend to civil cases? Even if you would not apply *Mullaney* in the typical civil action, would you apply it in a termination proceeding as in *Santosky*? Suppose that the government assigned the natural parents the burden of proving that they had not neglected the child.

3. Over the years, the Supreme Court has designated several interests as "fundamental": voting, free speech, and travel. Case Comment, 26 U. FLA. L. REV. 155, 156 (1973). Does *Santosky* augur the application of *Addington* to all proceedings in which a fundamental interest is at stake?

4. In many jurisdictions, the prosecution's burden at pretrial motion hearings is a mere preponderance. *See, e.g., United States v. Tucker*, 495 F. Supp. 607, 613 (E.D.N.Y. 1980). The Supreme Court itself has sanctioned that burden. *Lego v. Twomey*, 404 U.S. 477, 488 (1972). However, in light of *Addington*, is that minimalist burden suspect?

5. In *Addington*, the appellant argued that the clear and convincing evidence standard was too low. In *Cruzan v. Director, Missouri Dept. of Health*, 497 U.S. 261 (1990), the co–guardians of a petitioner presented the converse argument that the standard was too high. In *Cruzan*, the petitioner, Nancy Cruzan, had been rendered incompetent by virtue of injuries sustained in an automobile accident. Her parents were her co–guardians, and they became convinced that she had virtually no chance of recovering her cognitive faculties. They then sought a court order directing the withdrawal of the petitioner's artificial life support equipment. The Missouri Supreme Court denied relief for the stated reason that there was no clear and convincing evidence of the petitioner's desire to have life–sustaining treatment withdrawn. Writing for the majority, Chief Justice Rehnquist stated that Missouri's choice of an enhanced standard was defensible, since "the interests at stake . . . are more substantial, both on an individual and societal level, than those involved in the run–of–the–mine civil dispute." The Chief Justice stated:

> In *Santosky*, one of the factors which led the Court to require proof by clear and convincing evidence in a proceeding to terminate parental rights was that a decision in such a case was final and irrevocable. The same must surely be said of the decision to discontinue hydration and nutrition of a patient such as Nancy Cruzan, which all agree will result in her death.

6. In *Cooper v. Oklahoma*, 517 U.S. 348 (1996), a defendant attacked the constitutionality of a state law requiring him to prove his alleged incompetence to stand trial by clear and convincing evidence. The Supreme Court invalidated the law. Oklahoma had invoked *Addington* in its attempt to persuade the Court to uphold the law. Writing for a unanimous Court, Justice Stevens distinguished *Addington*:

> Our decision today is in complete agreement with the basis for our ruling in *Addington*. Both cases concern the proper protection of fundamental rights in circumstances in which the State proposes to take drastic action against an individual. The requirement that the grounds for civil commitment be shown by clear and convincing evidence protects the individual's fundamental interest in liberty. The prohibition against requiring the criminal defendant to demonstrate incompetence by clear and convincing evidence safeguards the fundamental right not to stand trial while incompetent.

7. Problem 31–6. In *Devitt*, the defendant is convicted. In addition to alleging the battery, the initial indictment charged that Devitt is a "special dangerous violent offender." Under Morena law, once convicted, the defendant faces an enhanced punishment if the prosecution can prove other violent misconduct. During sentencing, the prosecutor intends to offer evidence of three other assaults by Devitt. The defense attorney learns of the prosecutor's intention and objects, citing *Winship*. The defense attorney asserts that "just like the charged battery, these assaults have to be proven beyond a reasonable doubt." You are the judge. What ruling? *Compare Specht v. Patterson*, 386 U.S. 605, 609–11 (1967) *with United States v. Inendino*, 604 F.2d 458, 463 (7th Cir. 1978).

8. Problem 31–7. In *Devitt*, the defendant is acquitted. However, the prosecutor immediately files a new proceeding to have Devitt involuntarily committed as a mentally disordered violent offender (MDVO). The Morena statutes refer to this type of proceeding as "a civil action." The statutes authorize involuntary commitment when on the basis of past violent misconduct, the judge finds that the subject is "predisposed" to commit future violent crimes. During the proceeding, the prosecutor intends to offer the evidence of the battery and three assaults mentioned in Problem 31–6. At a pretrial hearing, the defense attorney argues that the past acts relied on as the basis for the prediction of future violent misconduct must be proved beyond a reasonable doubt. What ruling? *See People v. Burnick*, 14 Cal. 3d 306, 313–26, 535 P.2d 352, 356–64, 121 Cal. Rptr. 488, 492–500 (1975).

CONSTITUTIONAL OVERRIDES TO THE RULES OF EVIDENCE

Chapter 32

COMPULSORY PROCESS, DUE PROCESS AND CONFRONTATION

A. INTRODUCTION

Beginning in 1967, the United States Supreme Court recognized that the accused in a criminal case has a constitutional right to introduce vital, reliable exculpatory evidence. On numerous occasions the Court has permitted the accused to invoke the right to override exclusionary rules of evidence. The jurisprudence may still be evolving.

B. THE CONSTITUTIONAL RIGHT TO PRESENT EVIDENCE IN CRIMINAL CASES

WASHINGTON v. TEXAS

388 U.S. 14 (1967)

MR. CHIEF JUSTICE WARREN delivered the opinion of the Court.

We granted certiorari in this case to determine whether the right of a defendant in a criminal case under the Sixth Amendment[1] to have compulsory process for obtaining witnesses in his favor is applicable to the States through the Fourteenth Amendment, and whether that right was violated by a state procedural statute providing that persons charged as principals, accomplices, or accessories in the same crime cannot be introduced as witnesses for each other.

Petitioner, Jackie Washington, was convicted in Dallas County, Texas, of murder with malice and was sentenced by a jury to 50 years in prison. The prosecution's evidence showed that petitioner, an 18–year–old youth, had dated a girl named Jean Carter until her mother had forbidden her to see him. The girl thereafter began dating another boy, the deceased. Evidently motivated by jealousy, petitioner with several other boys began driving around the City of Dallas on the night of August 29, 1964, looking for a gun. The search eventually led to one Charles Fuller, who joined the group with his shotgun. After obtaining some shells from another source, the group of boys proceeded to Jean Carter's home, where Jean, her family and the deceased were having supper. Some of the boys threw bricks at the house and then ran back to the car, leaving petitioner and Fuller alone in front of the house with the shotgun. At the sound of the bricks the deceased and Jean Carter's mother rushed out on the porch to investigate. The shotgun was fired by either

---

[1] "In all criminal prosecutions, the accused shall enjoy the right . . . to have compulsory process for obtaining witnesses in his favor. . . ."

petitioner or Fuller, and the deceased was fatally wounded. Shortly afterward petitioner and Fuller came running back to the car where the other boys waited, with Fuller carrying the shotgun.

Petitioner testified in his own behalf. He claimed that Fuller, who was intoxicated, had taken the gun from him, and that he had unsuccessfully tried to persuade Fuller to leave before the shooting. Fuller had insisted that he was going to shoot someone, and petitioner had run back to the automobile. He saw the girl's mother come out of the door as he began running, and he subsequently heard the shot. At the time, he had thought that Fuller had shot the woman. In support of his version of the facts, petitioner offered the testimony of Fuller. The record indicates that Fuller would have testified that petitioner pulled at him and tried to persuade him to leave, and that petitioner ran before Fuller fired the fatal shot.

It is undisputed that Fuller's testimony would have been relevant and material, and that it was vital to the defense. Fuller was the only person other than petitioner who knew exactly who had fired the shotgun and whether petitioner had at the last minute attempted to prevent the shooting. Fuller, however, had been previously convicted of the same murder and sentenced to 50 years in prison, and he was confined in the Dallas County jail. Two Texas statutes provided at the time of the trial in this case that persons charged or convicted as coparticipants in the same crime could not testify for one another,[4] although there was no bar to their testifying for the State. On the basis of these statutes the trial judge sustained the State's objection and refused to allow Fuller to testify. Petitioner's conviction followed, and it was upheld on appeal by the Texas Court of Criminal Appeals. We granted certiorari. We reverse.

[In this part of its opinion, the majority ruled that the due process clause of the Fourteenth Amendment incorporates the compulsory process guarantee of the Sixth Amendment and renders the guarantee enforceable against the states.]

Since the right to compulsory process is applicable in this state proceeding, the question remains whether it was violated in the circumstances of this case. The testimony of Charles Fuller was denied to the defense not because the State refused to compel his attendance, but because a state statute made his testimony inadmissible whether he was present in the courtroom or not. We are thus called upon to decide whether the Sixth Amendment guarantees a defendant the right under any circumstances to put his witnesses on the stand, as well as the right to compel their attendance in court. The resolution of this question requires some discussion of the common–law context in which the Sixth Amendment was adopted.

---

[4] "Persons charged as principals, accomplices or accessories, whether in the same or by different indictments, can not be introduced as witnesses for one another, but they may claim a severance, and if one or more be acquitted they may testify in behalf of the others." Tex. Pen. Code, Art. 82.

"Persons charged as principals, accomplices or accessories, whether in the same or different indictments, cannot be introduced as witnesses for one another, but they may claim a severance; and, if any one or more be acquitted, or the prosecution against them be dismissed, they may testify in behalf of the others." Tex. Code Crim. Proc., Art. 711 (1925).

Joseph Story, in his famous Commentaries on the Constitution of the United States, observed that the right to compulsory process was included in the Bill of Rights in reaction to the notorious common–law rule that in cases of treason or felony the accused was not allowed to introduce witnesses in his defense at all. Although the absolute prohibition of witnesses for the defense had been abolished in England by statute before 1787, the Framers of the Constitution felt it necessary specifically to provide that defendants in criminal cases should be provided the means of obtaining witnesses so that their own evidence, as well as the prosecution's, might be evaluated by the jury.

Despite the abolition of the rule generally disqualifying defense witnesses, the common law retained a number of restrictions on witnesses who were physically and mentally capable of testifying. To the extent that they were applicable, they had the same effect of suppressing the truth that the general proscription had had. Defendants and codefendants were among the large class of witnesses disqualified from testifying on the ground of interest. A party to a civil or criminal case was not allowed to testify on his own behalf for fear that he might be tempted to lie. Although originally the disqualification of a codefendant appears to have been based only on his status as a party to the action, and in some jurisdictions co–indictees were allowed to testify for or against each other if granted separate trials, other jurisdictions came to the view that accomplices or co–indictees were incompetent to testify at least in favor of each other even at separate trials, and in spite of statutes making a defendant competent to testify in his own behalf. It was thought that if two persons charged with the same crime were allowed to testify on behalf of each other, "each would try to swear the other out of the charge." This rule, as well as the other disqualifications for interest, rested on the unstated premises that the right to present witnesses was subordinate to the court's interest in preventing perjury, and that erroneous decisions were best avoided by preventing the jury from hearing any testimony that might be perjured, even if it were the only testimony available on a crucial issue.

The federal courts followed the common–law restrictions for a time, despite the Sixth Amendment. In *United States v. Reid*, 12 How. 361 (1852), the question was whether one of two defendants jointly indicted for murder on the high seas could call the other as a witness. Although this Court expressly recognized that the Sixth Amendment was designed to abolish some of the harsh rules of the common law, particularly including the refusal to allow the defendant in a serious criminal case to present witnesses in his defense, it held that the rules of evidence in the federal courts were those in force in the various States at the time of the passage of the Judiciary Act of 1789, including the disqualification of defendants indicted together. The holding in *United States v. Reid* was not satisfactory to later generations, however, and in 1918 this Court expressly overruled it, refusing to be bound by "the dead hand of the common–law rule of 1789," and taking note of "the conviction of our time that the truth is more likely to be arrived at by hearing the testimony of all persons of competent understanding who may seem to have knowledge of the facts involved in a case, leaving the credit and weight of such testimony to be determined by the jury or by the court . . . ." *Rosen v. United States*, 245 U.S. 467, 471.

Although *Rosen v. United States* rested on nonconstitutional grounds, we believe that its reasoning was required by the Sixth Amendment. In light of the common–law history, and in view of the recognition in the *Reid* case that the Sixth Amendment was designed in part to make the testimony of a defendant's witnesses admissible on his behalf in court, it could hardly be argued that a State would not violate the clause if it made all defense testimony inadmissible as a matter of procedural law. It is difficult to see how the Constitution is any less violated by arbitrary rules that prevent whole categories of defense witnesses from testifying on the basis of *a priori* categories that presume them unworthy of belief.

The rule disqualifying an alleged accomplice from testifying on behalf of the defendant cannot even be defended on the ground that it rationally sets apart a group of persons who are particularly likely to commit perjury. The absurdity of the rule is amply demonstrated by the exceptions that have been made to it. For example, the accused accomplice may be called by the prosecution to testify against the defendant. Common sense would suggest that he often has a greater interest in lying in favor of the prosecution rather than against it, especially if he is still awaiting his own trial or sentencing. To think that criminals will lie to save their fellows but not to obtain favors from the prosecution for themselves is indeed to clothe the criminal class with more nobility than one might expect to find in the public at large. Moreover, under the Texas statutes the accused accomplice is no longer disqualified if he is acquitted at his own trial. Presumably, he would then be free to testify on behalf of his comrade, secure in the knowledge that he could incriminate himself as freely as he liked in his testimony, since he could not again be prosecuted for the same offense. The Texas law leaves him free to testify when he has a great incentive to perjury, and bars his testimony in situations where he has a lesser motive to lie.

We hold that the petitioner in this case was denied his right to have compulsory process for obtaining witnesses in his favor because the State arbitrarily denied him the right to put on the stand a witness who was physically and mentally capable of testifying to events that he had personally observed, and whose testimony would have been relevant and material to the defense.[21] The Framers of the Constitution did not intend to commit the futile act of giving to a defendant the right to secure the attendance of witnesses whose testimony he had no right to use. The judgment of conviction must be reversed.

NOTES

1. To justify his conclusion, Chief Justice Warren resorts to *reductio ad absurdum* reasoning: The Chief Justice argues that it would obviously be unconstitutional if "a State . . . made all defense testimony inadmissible as

---

[21] Nothing in this opinion should be construed as disapproving testimonial privileges, such as the privilege against self–incrimination or the lawyer–client or husband–wife privileges, which are based on entirely different considerations from those underlying the common–law disqualifications for interest. Nor do we deal in this case with nonarbitrary state rules that disqualify as witnesses persons who, because of mental infirmity or infancy, are incapable of observing events or testifying about them.

a matter of procedural law." The Chief Justice states that it is equally clear that "the Constitution is . . . violated by arbitrary rules that prevent whole categories of defense witnesses from testifying on the basis of *a priori* categories that presume them unworthy of belief." Assume that such evidentiary rules would be patently unconstitutional. Did the Court have to imply a right to present evidence from the compulsory process clause to find a doctrinal basis for holding those rules unconstitutional? What other doctrinal basis could the Court have invoked to invalidate a truly "arbitrary" rule? Is arbitrariness the sole concern?

2. Did the Chief Justice have to derive the right by implication? Could he have done so by interpretation? One commentator asserts that "[w]ere [the compulsory process clause] intended to merely give subpoena power, the clause would instead have been worded such that an accused shall have 'compulsory process of witnesses in his favor' rather than worded, 'obtaining witnesses in his favor.'" Note, *Compulsory Process vs. The Preclusion Sanction—Taylor v. Illinois, 108 S. Ct. 646 (1988)*, 10 WHITTIER L. REV. 741, 756–57 (1989).

3. What is the significance of footnote 21? Does *Washington* apply only to sweeping incompetency rules which have the effect of altogether barring testimony by a witness? The Illinois Supreme Court construed footnote 21 in that fashion. *People v. Scott*, 52 Ill. 2d 432, 288 N.E.2d 478 (1972). In the *Scott* court's view, the right announced in *Washington* spent its force by requiring the state to put the defense witness on the stand; the right did not regulate the validity of the state evidentiary rules governing the content of the witness' testimony. As the next opinion demonstrates, the Supreme Court ultimately reached a contrary conclusion in the following landmark case:

CHAMBERS v. MISSISSIPPI

410 U.S. 284 (1973)

MR. JUSTICE POWELL delivered the opinion of the Court.

Petitioner, Leon Chambers, was tried by a jury in a Mississippi trial court and convicted of murdering a policeman. The jury assessed punishment at life imprisonment, and the Mississippi Supreme Court affirmed, one justice dissenting. Pending disposition of his application for certiorari to this Court, petitioner was granted bail by order of the Circuit Justice, dated February 1, 1972. Two weeks later, on the State's request for reconsideration, that order was reaffirmed. Subsequently, the petition for certiorari was granted, to consider whether petitioner's trial was conducted in accord with principles of due process under the Fourteenth Amendment. We conclude that it was not.

I

The events that led to petitioner's prosecution for murder occurred in the small town of Woodville in southern Mississippi. On Saturday evening, June 14, 1969, two Woodville policemen, James Forman and Aaron "Sonny" Liberty, entered a local bar and pool hall to execute a warrant for the arrest of a youth named C. C. Jackson. Jackson resisted and a hostile crowd of some 50 or 60 persons gathered. The officers' first attempt to handcuff Jackson was frustrated when 20 or 25 men in the crowd intervened and wrestled him free. Forman then radioed for assistance and Liberty removed his riot gun, a 12–gauge sawed–off shotgun, from the car. Three deputy sheriffs arrived shortly thereafter and the officers again attempted to make their arrest. Once more, the officers were attacked by the onlookers and during the commotion five or six pistol shots were fired. Forman was looking in a different direction when the shooting began, but immediately saw that Liberty had been shot several times in the back. Before Liberty died, he turned around and fired both barrels of his riot gun into an alley in the area from which the shots appeared to have come. The first shot was wild and high and scattered the crowd standing at the face of the alley. Liberty appeared, however, to take more deliberate aim before the second shot and hit one of the men in the crowd in the back of the head and neck as he ran down the alley. That man was Leon Chambers.

Officer Forman could not see from his vantage point who shot Liberty or whether Liberty's shots hit anyone. One of the deputy sheriffs testified at trial that he was standing several feet from Liberty and that he saw Chambers shoot him. Another deputy sheriff stated that, although he could not see whether Chambers had a gun in his hand, he did see Chambers "break his arm down" shortly before the shots were fired. The officers who saw Chambers fall testified that they thought he was dead but they made no effort at that time either to examine him or to search for the murder weapon. Instead, they attended to Liberty, who was placed in the police car and taken to a hospital where he was declared dead on arrival. A subsequent autopsy showed that he had been hit with four bullets from a .22–caliber revolver.

Shortly after the shooting, three of Chambers' friends discovered that he was not yet dead. James Williams, Berkley Turner, and Gable McDonald loaded him into a car and transported him to the same hospital. Later that night, when the county sheriff discovered that Chambers was still alive, a guard was placed outside his room. Chambers was subsequently charged with Liberty's murder. He pleaded not guilty and has asserted his innocence throughout.

The story of Leon Chambers is intertwined with the story of another man, Gable McDonald. McDonald, a lifelong resident of Woodville, was in the crowd on the evening of Liberty's death. Sometime shortly after that day, he left his wife in Woodville and moved to Louisiana and found a job at a sugar mill. In November of that same year, he returned to Woodville when his wife informed him that an acquaintance of his, known as Reverend Stokes, wanted to see him. Stokes owned a gas station in Natchez, Mississippi, several miles north of Woodville, and upon his return McDonald went to see him. After talking to Stokes, McDonald agreed to make a statement to Chambers' attorneys, who maintained offices in Natchez. Two days later, he appeared at the attorneys' offices and gave a sworn confession that he shot Officer Liberty. He also stated that he had already told a friend of his, James Williams, that he shot Liberty. He said that he used his own pistol, a nine–shot .22–caliber revolver, which he had discarded shortly after the shooting. In response to questions from Chambers' attorneys, McDonald affirmed that his confession was voluntary and that no one had compelled him to come to them. Once the confession had been transcribed, signed, and witnessed, McDonald was turned over to the local police authorities and was placed in jail.

One month later, at a preliminary hearing, McDonald repudiated his prior sworn confession. He testified that Stokes had persuaded him to confess that he shot Liberty. He claimed that Stokes had promised that he would not go to jail and that he would share in the proceeds of a lawsuit that Chambers would bring against the town of Woodville. On examination by his own attorney and on cross–examination by the State, McDonald swore that he had not been at the scene when Liberty was shot but had been down the street drinking beer in a cafe with a friend, Berkley Turner. When he and Turner heard the shooting, he testified, they walked up the street and found Chambers lying in the alley. He, Turner, and Williams took Chambers to the hospital. McDonald further testified at the preliminary hearing that he did not know what had happened, that there was no discussion about the shooting either going to or coming back from the hospital, and that it was not until the next day that he learned that Chambers had been felled by a blast from Liberty's riot gun. In addition, McDonald stated that while he once owned a .22–caliber pistol he had lost it many months before the shooting and did not own or possess a weapon at that time. The local justice of the peace accepted McDonald's repudiation and released him from custody. The local authorities undertook no further investigation of his possible involvement.

Chambers' case came on for trial in October of the next year. At trial, he endeavored to develop two grounds of defense. He first attempted to show that he did not shoot Liberty. Only one officer testified that he actually saw Chambers fire the shots. Although three officers saw Liberty shoot Chambers and testified that they assumed he was shooting his attacker, none of them examined Chambers to see whether he was still alive or whether he possessed a gun. Indeed, no weapon was ever recovered from the scene and there was no proof that Chambers had ever owned a .22–caliber pistol. One witness testified that he was standing in the street near where Liberty was shot, that he was looking at Chambers when the shooting began, and that he was sure that Chambers did not fire the shots.

Petitioner's second defense was that Gable McDonald had shot Officer Liberty. He was only partially successful, however, in his efforts to bring before the jury the testimony supporting this defense. Sam Hardin, a lifelong friend of McDonald's, testified that he saw McDonald shoot Liberty. A second witness, one of Liberty's cousins, testified that he saw McDonald immediately after the shooting with a pistol in his hand. In addition to the testimony of these two witnesses, Chambers endeavored to show the jury that McDonald had repeatedly confessed to the crime. Chambers attempted to prove that McDonald had admitted responsibility for the murder on four separate occasions, once when he gave the sworn statement to Chambers' counsel and three other times prior to that occasion in private conversations with friends.

In large measure, he was thwarted in his attempt to present this portion of his defense by the strict application of certain Mississippi rules of evidence. Chambers asserts in this Court, as he did unsuccessfully in his motion for new trial and on appeal to the State Supreme Court, that the application of these evidentiary rules rendered his trial fundamentally unfair and deprived him of due process of law. It is necessary, therefore, to examine carefully the rulings made during the trial.

II

Chambers filed a pretrial motion requesting the court to order McDonald to appear. Chambers also sought a ruling at that time that, if the State itself chose not to call McDonald, he be allowed to call him as an adverse witness. Attached to the motion were copies of McDonald's sworn confession and of the transcript of his preliminary hearing at which he repudiated that confession. The trial court granted the motion requiring McDonald to appear but reserved ruling on the adverse–witness motion. At trial, after the State failed to put McDonald on the stand, Chambers called McDonald, laid a predicate for the introduction of his sworn out–of–court confession, had it admitted into evidence, and read it to the jury. The State, upon cross–examination, elicited from McDonald the fact that he had repudiated his prior confession. McDonald further testified, as he had at the preliminary hearing, that he did not shoot Liberty, and that he confessed to the crime only on the promise of Reverend Stokes that he would not go to jail and would share in a sizable tort recovery from the town. He also told his own story of his actions on the evening of the shooting, including his visit to the cafe down the street, his absence from the scene during the critical period, and his subsequent trip to the hospital with Chambers.

At the conclusion of the State's cross–examination, Chambers renewed his motion to examine McDonald as an adverse witness. The trial court denied the motion, stating: "He may be hostile, but he is not adverse in the sense of the word, so your request will be overruled." On appeal, the State Supreme Court upheld the trial court's ruling, finding that "McDonald's testimony was not adverse to appellant" because "[n]owhere did he point the finger at Chambers." 252 So. 2d, at 220.

Defeated in his attempt to challenge directly McDonald's renunciation of his prior confession, Chambers sought to introduce the testimony of the three witnesses to whom McDonald had admitted that he shot the officer. The first of these, Sam Hardin, would have testified that, on the night of the shooting, he spent the late evening hours with McDonald at a friend's house after their return from the hospital and that, while driving McDonald home later that night, McDonald stated that he shot Liberty. The State objected to the admission of this testimony on the ground that it was hearsay. The trial court sustained the objection.

Berkley Turner, the friend with whom McDonald said he was drinking beer when the shooting occurred, was then called to testify. In the jury's presence, and without objection, he testified that he had not been in the cafe that Saturday and had not had any beers with McDonald. The jury was then excused. In the absence of the jury, Turner recounted his conversations with McDonald while they were riding with James Williams to take Chambers to the hospital. When asked whether McDonald said anything regarding the shooting of Liberty, Turner testified that McDonald told him that he "shot him." Turner further stated that one week later, when he met McDonald at a friend's house, McDonald reminded him of their prior conversation and urged Turner not to "mess him up." Petitioner argued to the court that, especially where there was other proof in the case that was corroborative of these out–of–court statements. Turner's testimony as to McDonald's self–incriminating remarks should have been admitted as an exception to the hearsay rule. Again, the trial court sustained the State's objection.

The third witness, Albert Carter, was McDonald's neighbor. They had been friends for about 25 years. Although Carter had not been in Woodville on the evening of the shooting, he stated that he learned about it the next morning from McDonald. That same day, he and McDonald walked out to a well near McDonald's house and there McDonald told him that he was the one who shot Officer Liberty. Carter testified that McDonald also told him that he had disposed of the .22–caliber revolver later that night. He further testified that several weeks after the shooting, he accompanied McDonald to Natchez where McDonald purchased another .22 pistol to replace the one he had discarded.[5] The jury was not allowed to hear Carter's testimony. Chambers urged that these statements were admissible, the State objected, and the court sustained the objection. On appeal, the State Supreme Court approved the lower court's exclusion of these witnesses' testimony on hearsay grounds. 252 So. 2d, at 220.

In sum, then, this was Chambers' predicament. As a consequence of the combination of Mississippi's "party witness" or "voucher" rule and its hearsay rule, he was unable either to cross–examine McDonald or to present witnesses in his own behalf who would have discredited McDonald's repudiation and demonstrated his complicity. Chambers had, however, chipped away at the fringes of McDonald's story by introducing admissible testimony from other sources indicating that he had not been seen in the cafe where he said he was when the shooting started, that he had not been having beer with Turner, and that he possessed a .22 pistol at the time of the crime. But all that remained from McDonald's own testimony was a single written confession countered by an arguably acceptable renunciation. Chambers' defense was far less persuasive than it might have been had he been given an opportunity to subject McDonald's statements to cross–examination or had the other confessions been admitted.

III

The right of an accused in a criminal trial to due process is, in essence, the right to a fair opportunity to defend against the State's accusations. The rights to confront and cross–examine witnesses and to call witnesses in one's own behalf have long been recognized as essential to due process. Mr. Justice Black, writing for the Court in *In re Oliver*, 333 U.S. 257, 273 (1948), identified these rights as among the minimum essentials of a fair trial:

> "A person's right to reasonable notice of a charge against him, and an opportunity to be heard in his defense–a right to his day in court–are basic in our system of jurisprudence; and these rights include, as

---

[5] A gun dealer from Natchez testified that McDonald had made two purchases. The witness' business records indicated that McDonald purchased a nine–shot .22–caliber revolver about a year prior to the murder. He purchased a different style .22 three weeks after Liberty's death.

a minimum, a right to examine the witnesses against him, to offer testimony, and to be represented by counsel."

See also Jenkins v. McKeithen, 395 U.S. 411, 428–29 (1969). Both of these elements of a fair trial are implicated in the present case.

A

Chambers was denied an opportunity to subject McDonald's damning repudiation and alibi to cross–examination. He was not allowed to test the witness' recollection, to probe into the details of his alibi, or to "sift" his conscience so that the jury might judge for itself whether McDonald's testimony was worthy of belief. *Mattox v. United States*, 156 U.S. 237, 242–243 (1895). The right of cross–examination is more than a desirable rule of trial procedure. It is implicit in the constitutional right of confrontation, and helps assure the "accuracy of the truth–determining process." *Dutton v. Evans*, 400 U.S. 74, 89 (1970). It is, indeed, "an essential and fundamental requirement for the kind of fair trial which is this country's constitutional goal." *Pointer v. Texas*, 380 U.S. 400, 405 (1965). [I]ts denial or significant diminution calls into question the ultimate " 'integrity of the fact–finding process' " and requires that the competing interest be closely examined. *Berger v. California*, 393 U.S. 314, 315 (1969).

In this case, petitioner's request to cross–examine McDonald was denied on the basis of a Mississippi common–law rule that a party may not impeach his own witness. The rule rests on the presumption–without regard to the circumstances of the particular case–that a party who calls a witness "vouches for his credibility." *Clark v. Lansford*, 191 So. 2d 123, 125 (Miss. 1966). Although the historical origins of the "voucher" rule are uncertain, it appears to be a remnant of primitive English trial practice in which "oath–takers" or "compurgators" were called to stand behind a particular party's position in any controversy. Their assertions were strictly partisan and, quite unlike witnesses in criminal trials today, their role bore little relation to the impartial ascertainment of the facts.

Whatever validity the "voucher" rule may have once enjoyed, and apart from whatever usefulness it retains today in the civil trial process, it bears little present relationship to the realities of the criminal process. It might have been logical for the early common law to require a party to vouch for the credibility of witnesses he brought before the jury to affirm his veracity. Having selected them especially for that purpose, the party might reasonably be expected to stand firmly behind their testimony. But in modern criminal trials, defendants are rarely able to select their witnesses: they must take them where they find them. Moreover, as applied in this case, the "voucher" rule's impact was doubly harmful to Chambers' efforts to develop his defense. Not only was he precluded from cross–examining McDonald, but, he was also restricted in the scope of his direct examination by the rule's corollary requirement that the party calling the witness is bound by anything he might say. He was, therefore, effectively prevented from exploring the circumstances of McDonald's three prior oral confessions and from challenging the renunciation of the written confession.

In this Court, Mississippi has not sought to defend the rule or explain its underlying rationale. Nor has it contended that its rule should override the accused's right of confrontation. Instead, it argues that there is no incompatability [sic] between the rule and Chambers' rights because no right of confrontation exists unless the testifying witness is "adverse" to the accused. The State's brief asserts that the "right of confrontation applies to witnesses *against* an accused." Relying on the trial court's determination that McDonald was not "adverse," and on the State Supreme Court's holding that McDonald did not "point the finger at Chambers," the State contends that Chambers' constitutional right was not involved.

The argument that McDonald's testimony was not "adverse" to, or "against," Chambers is not convincing. The State's proof at trial excluded the theory that more than one person participated in the shooting of Liberty. To the extent that McDonald's sworn confession tended to incriminate him, it tended also to exculpate Chambers. And, in the circumstances of this case, McDonald's retraction inculpated Chambers to the same extent that it exculpated McDonald. It can hardly be disputed that McDonald's testimony was in fact seriously adverse to Chambers. The availability of the right to confront and to cross–examine those who give damaging testimony against the accused has never been held to depend on whether the witness was initially put on the stand by the accused or by the State. We reject the notion that a right of such substance in the criminal process may be governed by that technicality or by any narrow and unrealistic definition of the word "against." The "voucher" rule, as applied in this case, plainly interfered with Chambers' right to defend against the State's charges.

B

We need not decide, however, whether this error alone would occasion reversal since Chambers' claimed denial of due process rests on the ultimate impact of that error when viewed in conjunction with the trial court's refusal to permit him to call other witnesses. The trial court refused to allow him to introduce the testimony of Hardin, Turner, and Carter. Each would have testified to the statements purportedly made by McDonald, on three separate occasions shortly after the crime, naming himself as the murderer. The State Supreme Court approved the exclusion of this evidence on the ground that it was hearsay.

The hearsay rule, which has long been recognized and respected by virtually every State, is based on experience and grounded in the notion that untrustworthy evidence should not be presented to the triers of fact. Out–of–court statements are traditionally excluded because they lack the conventional indicia of reliability: they are usually not made under oath or other circumstances that impress the speaker with the solemnity of his statements; the declarant's word is not subject to cross–examination; and he is not available in order that his demeanor and credibility may be assessed by the jury. *California v. Green*, 399 U.S. 149, 158 (1970). A number of exceptions have developed over the years to allow admission of hearsay statements made under circumstances that tend to assure reliability and thereby compensate for the absence of the oath and opportunity for cross–examination. Among the most prevalent of these exceptions is the one applicable to declarations against interest–an exception founded on the assumption that a person is unlikely to fabricate a statement against his own interest at the time it is made. Mississippi recognizes this exception but applies it only to declarations against pecuniary interest. It recognizes no such exception for declarations, like McDonald's in this case, that are against the penal interest of the declarant. *Brown v. State*, 99 Miss. 719, 55 So. 961 (1911).

This materialistic limitation on the declaration–against–interest hearsay exception appears to be accepted by most States in their criminal trial processes, although a number of States have discarded it. Declarations against penal interest have also been excluded in federal courts under the authority of *Donnelly v. United States*, 228 U.S. 243, 272–273 (1913), although exclusion would not be required under the newly proposed Federal Rules of Evidence. Exclusion, where the limitation prevails, is usually premised on the view that admission would lead to the frequent presentation of perjured testimony to the jury. It is believed that confessions of criminal activity are often motivated by extraneous considerations and, therefore, are not as inherently reliable as statements against pecuniary or proprietary interest. While that rationale has been the subject of considerable scholarly criticism, we need not decide in this case whether, under other circumstances, it might serve some valid State purpose by excluding untrustworthy testimony.

The hearsay statements involved in this case were originally made and subsequently offered at trial under circumstances that provided considerable assurance of their reliability. First, each of McDonald's confessions was made spontaneously to a close acquaintance shortly after the murder had occurred. Second, each one was corroborated by some other evidence in the case–McDonald's sworn confession, the testimony of an eyewitness to the shooting, the testimony that McDonald was seen with a gun immediately after the shooting, and proof of his prior ownership of a .22–caliber revolver and subsequent purchase of a new weapon. The sheer number of independent confessions provided additional corroboration for each. Third, whatever may be the parameters of the penal–interest rationale, each confession here was in a very real sense self–incriminatory and unquestionably against interest. *See United States v. Harris*, 403 U.S. 573, 584 (1971); *Dutton v. Evans*, 400 U.S., at 89. McDonald stood to benefit nothing by disclosing his role in the shooting to any of his three friends and he must have been aware of the possibility that disclosure would lead to criminal prosecution. Indeed, after telling Turner of his involvement, he subsequently urged Turner not to "mess him up." Finally, if there was any question about the truthfulness of the extrajudicial statements, McDonald was present in the courtroom and was under oath. He could have been cross–examined by the State, and his demeanor and responses weighed by the jury. *See California v. Green*, 399 U.S. 149 (1970). The availability of McDonald significantly distinguishes this case from the prior Mississippi precedent, *Brown v. State*, *supra*, and from the *Donnelly*–type situation, since in both cases the declarant was unavailable at the time of trial.

Few rights are more fundamental than that of an accused to present witnesses in his own defense. *E.g.*, *Washington v. Texas*, 388 U.S. 14, 19

(1967). In the exercise of this right, the accused, as is required of the State, must comply with established rules of procedure and evidence designed to assure both fairness and reliability in the ascertainment of guilt and innocence. Although perhaps no rule of evidence has been more respected or more frequently applied in jury trials than that applicable to the exclusion of hearsay, exceptions tailored to allow the introduction of evidence which in fact is likely to be trustworthy have long existed. The testimony rejected by the trial court here bore persuasive assurances of trustworthiness and thus was well within the basic rationale of the exception for declarations against interest. That testimony also was critical to Chambers' defense. In these circumstances, where constitutional rights directly affecting the ascertainment of guilt are implicated, the hearsay rule may not be applied mechanistically to defeat the ends of justice.

We conclude that the exclusion of this critical evidence, coupled with the State's refusal to permit Chambers to cross–examine McDonald, denied him a trial in accord with traditional and fundamental standards of due process. In reaching this judgment, we establish no new principles of constitutional law. Nor does our holding signal any diminution in the respect traditionally accorded to the States in the establishment and implementation of their own criminal trial rules and procedures. Rather, we hold quite simply that under the facts and circumstances of this case the rulings of the trial court deprived Chambers of a fair trial.

The judgment is reversed and the case is remanded to the Supreme Court of Mississippi for further proceedings not inconsistent with this opinion.

NOTES

1. *Chambers* establishes that the accused can invoke the constitutional right to surmount essentially procedural rules, such as the restriction on the leading form of questions, as well as substantive evidentiary rules, such as hearsay. Westen, *Confrontation and Compulsory Process: A Unified Theory of Evidence for Criminal Cases*, 91 HARV. L. REV. 567, 609, 612–13 (1978).

2. The commentators typically focus on the Court's holding that McDonald's declaration against his penal interest was so reliable that its exclusion constituted constitutional error. Did the Court also modify the unavailability standard for declarations against penal interest? Was McDonald unavailable within the meaning of that expression in Federal Rule of Evidence 804(a)? *State v. Barts*, 321 N.C. 170, 362 S.E.2d 235 (1987).

3. In *Chambers*, the Court found two constitutional errors which cumulatively denied the defendant a fair trial. Suppose that there had been only one error. Without more, does the exclusion of demonstrably reliable, exculpatory hearsay violate the defendant's constitutional right to present evidence? The Court implicitly answered that question in *Green v. Georgia*, 442 U.S. 95 (1979). In *Green*, the only error was the exclusion of the hearsay. Despite that difference, the *Green* Court treated *Chambers* as dispositive. *Foster v. State*, 297 Md. 191, 464 A.2d 986 (1983), *cert. denied*, 464 U.S. 1073 (1984), characterizes *Green* as clarifying the scope of *Chambers*.

4. Like *Washington*, *Chambers* left significant questions about its scope unanswered. In *Chambers*, the Court had overridden the hearsay rule, an exclusionary doctrine based on doubts about the reliability of uncross–examined testimony. It makes sense to say that that type of exclusionary rule must yield to a strong showing of the trustworthiness of defense evidence. However, as we have seen, there are other types of exclusionary rules. Would they also be subject to constitutional attack? The next noteworthy case is a 1974 decision of the Court.

DAVIS v. ALASKA

415 U.S. 308 (1974)

Mr. Chief Justice Burger delivered the opinion of the Court.

We granted certiorari in this case to consider whether the Confrontation Clause requires that a defendant in a criminal case be allowed to impeach the credibility of a prosecution witness by cross–examination directed at possible bias deriving from the witness' probationary status as a juvenile delinquent when such an impeachment would conflict with a State's asserted interest in preserving the confidentiality of juvenile adjudications of delinquency.

(1)

When the Polar Bar in Anchorage closed in the early morning hours of February 16, 1970, well over a thousand dollars in cash and checks was in the bar's Mosler safe. About midday, February 16, it was discovered that the bar had been broken into and the safe, about two feet square and weighing several hundred pounds, had been removed from the premises.

Later that afternoon the Alaska State Troopers received word that a safe had been discovered about 26 miles outside Anchorage near the home of Jess Straight and his family. The safe, which was subsequently determined to be the one stolen from the Polar Bar, had been pried open and the contents removed. Richard Green, Jess Straight's stepson, told investigating troopers on the scene that at about noon on February 16 he had seen and spoken with two Negro men standing alongside a late–model metallic blue Chevrolet sedan near where the safe was later discovered. The next day Anchorage police investigators brought him to the police station where Green was given six photographs of adult Negro males. After examining the photographs for 30 seconds to a minute, Green identified the photograph of petitioner as that of one of the men he had encountered the day before and described to the police. Petitioner was arrested the next day, February 18. On February 19, Green picked petitioner out of a lineup of seven Negro males.

At trial, evidence was introduced to the effect that paint chips found in the trunk of petitioner's rented blue Chevrolet could have originated from the surface of the stolen safe. Further, the trunk of the car contained particles which were identified as safe insulation characteristic of that found in Mosler safes. The insulation found in the trunk matched that of the stolen safe.

Richard Green was a crucial witness for the prosecution. He testified at trial that while on an errand for his mother he confronted two men standing beside a late–model metallic blue Chevrolet, parked on a road near his family's house. The man standing at the rear of the car spoke to Green asking if Green lived nearby and if his father was home. Green offered the men help, but his offer was rejected. On his return from the errand Green again passed the two men and he saw the man with whom he had had the conversation standing at the rear of the car with "something like a crowbar" in his hands. Green identified petitioner at the trial as the man with the "crowbar." The safe was discovered later that afternoon at the point, according to Green, where the Chevrolet had been parked.

Before testimony was taken at the trial of petitioner, the prosecutor moved for a protective order to prevent any reference to Green's juvenile record by the defense in the course of cross–examination. At the time of the trial and at the time of the events Green testified to, Green was on probation by order of a juvenile court after having been adjudicated a delinquent for burglarizing two cabins. Green was 16 years of age at the time of the Polar Bar burglary, but had turned 17 prior to trial.

In opposing the protective order, petitioner's counsel made it clear that he would not introduce Green's juvenile adjudication as a general impeachment of Green's character as a truthful person but, rather, to show specifically that at the same time Green was assisting the police in identifying petitioner he was on probation for burglary. From this petitioner would seek to show–or at least argue–that Green acted out of fear or concern of possible jeopardy to his probation. Not only might Green have made a hasty and faulty identification of petitioner to shift suspicion away from himself as one who robbed the Polar Bar, but Green might have been subject to undue pressure from the police and made his identifications under fear of possible probation revocation. Green's record would be revealed only as necessary to probe Green for bias and prejudice and not generally to call Green's good character into question.

The trial court granted the motion for a protective order, relying on Alaska Rule of Children's Procedure 23,[1] and Alaska Stat. § 47.10.080 (g) (1971).[2]

Although prevented from revealing that Green had been on probation for the juvenile delinquency adjudication for burglary at the same time that he originally identified petitioner, counsel for petitioner did his best to expose Green's state of mind at the time Green discovered that a stolen safe had been discovered near his home. Green denied that he was upset or uncomfortable about the discovery of the safe. He claimed not to have been worried about

---

[1] Rule 23 provides:

"No adjudication, order, or disposition of a juvenile case shall be admissible in a court not acting in the exercise of juvenile jurisdiction except for use in a presentencing procedure in a criminal case where the superior court, in its discretion, determines that such use is appropriate."

[2] Section 47.10.080 (g) provides in pertinent part:

"The commitment and placement of a child and evidence given in the court are not admissible as evidence against the minor in a subsequent case or proceedings in any other court . . . ."

any suspicions the police might have been expected to harbor against him, though Green did admit that it crossed his mind that the police might have thought he had something to do with the crime.

Defense counsel cross–examined Green in part as follows:

Q: "Were you upset at all by the fact that this safe was found on your property?

A: "No, sir.

Q: "Did you feel that they might in some way suspect you of this?

A: "No.

Q: "Did you feel uncomfortable about this though?

A: "No, not really.

Q: "The fact that a safe was found on your property?

A: "No.

Q: "Did you suspect for a moment that the police might somehow think that you were involved in this?

A: "I thought they might ask a few questions is all.

Q: "Did that thought ever enter your mind that you—that the police might think that you were somehow connected with this?

A: "No, it didn't really bother me, no.

Q: "Well, but . . . .

A: "I mean, you know, it didn't—it didn't come into my mind as worrying me, you know.

Q: "That really wasn't—wasn't my question, Mr. Green. Did you think that—not whether it worried you so much or not, but did you feel that there was a possibility that the police might somehow think that you had something to do with this, that they might have that in their mind, not that you . . . .

A: "That came across my mind, yes, sir.

Q: "That did cross your mind?

A: "Yes.

Q: "So as I understand it you went down to the—you drove in with the police in—in their car from mile 25, Glenn Highway down to the city police station?

A: "Yes, sir.

Q: "And then went into the investigators' room with Investigator Gray and Investigator Weaver?

A: "Yeah.

Q: "And they started asking you questions about—about the incident, is that correct?

A: "Yeah.

Q: "Had you ever been questioned like that before by any law enforcement officers?

A: "No.

"MR. RIPLEY: I'm going to object to this, Your Honor, it's a carry–on–with rehash of the same thing. He's attempting to raise in the jury's mind . . . .

"THE COURT: I'll sustain the objection."

Since defense counsel was prohibited from making inquiry as to the witness' being on probation under a juvenile court adjudication, Green's protestations of unconcern over possible police suspicion that he might have had a part in the Polar Bar burglary and his categorical denial of ever having been the subject of any similar law–enforcement interrogation went unchallenged. The tension between the right of confrontation and the State's policy of protecting the witness with a juvenile record is particularly evident in the final answer given by the witness. Since it is probable that Green underwent some questioning by police when he was arrested for the burglaries on which his juvenile adjudication of delinquency rested, the answer can be regarded as highly suspect at the very least. The witness was in effect asserting, under protection of the trial court's ruling, a right to give a questionably truthful answer to a cross–examiner pursuing a relevant line of inquiry; it is doubtful whether the bold "No" answer would have been given by Green absent a belief that he was shielded from traditional cross–examination. It would be difficult to conceive of a situation more clearly illustrating the need for cross–examination. The remainder of the cross–examination was devoted to an attempt to prove that Green was making his identification at trial on the basis of what he remembered from his earlier identifications at the photographic display and lineup, and not on the basis of his February 16 confrontation with the two men on the road.

The Alaska Supreme Court affirmed petitioner's conviction, concluding that it did not have to resolve the potential conflict in this case between a defendant's right to a meaningful confrontation with adverse witnesses and the State's interest in protecting the anonymity of a juvenile offender since "our reading of the trial transcript convinces us that counsel for the defendant was able adequately to question the youth in considerable detail concerning the possibility of bias or motive." 499 P. 2d 1025, 1036 (1972). Although the court admitted that Green's denials of any sense of anxiety or apprehension upon the safe's being found close to his home were possibly self–serving, "the suggestion was nonetheless brought to the attention of the jury, and that body was afforded the opportunity to observe the demeanor of the youth and pass on his credibility." *Ibid.* The court concluded that, in light of the indirect references permitted, there was no error.

Since we granted certiorari limited to the question of whether petitioner was denied his right under the Confrontation Clause to adequately cross–examine Green, 410 U.S. 925 (1973), the essential question turns on the correctness of the Alaska court's evaluation of the "adequacy" of the scope of cross–examination permitted. We disagree with that court's interpretation of the Confrontation Clause and we reverse.

(2)

The Sixth Amendment to the Constitution guarantees the right of an accused in a criminal prosecution "to be confronted with the witnesses against him." This right is secured for defendants in state as well as federal criminal proceedings under *Pointer v. Texas,* 380 U.S. 400 (1965). Confrontation means more than being allowed to confront the witness physically. "Our cases construing the [confrontation] clause hold that a primary interest secured by it is the right of cross–examination." *Douglas v. Alabama,* 380 U.S. 415, 418 (1965). Professor Wigmore stated:

> "The main and essential purpose of confrontation is *to secure for the opponent the opportunity of cross–examination.* The opponent demands confrontation, not for the idle purpose of gazing upon the witness, or of being gazed upon by him, but for the purpose of cross–examination, which cannot be had except by the direct and personal putting of questions and obtaining immediate answers." 5 J. Wigmore, Evidence § 1395, p. 123 (3d ed. 1940). (Emphasis in original.)

Cross–examination is the principal means by which the believability of a witness and the truth of his testimony are tested. Subject always to the broad discretion of a trial judge to preclude repetitive and unduly harassing interrogation, the cross–examiner is not only permitted to delve into the witness' story to test the witness' perceptions and memory, but the cross–examiner has traditionally been allowed to impeach, *i.e.,* discredit, the witness. One way of discrediting the witness is to introduce evidence of a prior criminal conviction of that witness. By so doing the cross–examiner intends to afford the jury a basis to infer that the witness' character is such that he would be less likely than the average trustworthy citizen to be truthful in his testimony. The introduction of evidence of a prior crime is thus a general attack on the credibility of the witness. A more particular attack on the wit-ness' credibility is effected by means of cross–examination directed toward revealing possible biases, prejudices, or ulterior motives of the witness as they may relate directly to issues or personalities in the case at hand. The partiality of a witness is subject to exploration at trial, and is "always relevant as discrediting the witness and affecting the weight of his testimony." 3A J. Wigmore, Evidence § 940, p. 775 (Chadbourn rev. 1970). We have recognized that the exposure of a witness' motivation in testifying is a proper and important function of the constitutionally protected right of cross–examination. *Greene v. McElroy,* 360 U.S. 474, 496 (1959).

In the instant case, defense counsel sought to show the existence of possible bias and prejudice of Green, causing him to make a faulty initial identification of petitioner, which in turn could have affected his later in–court identification of petitioner.

We cannot speculate as to whether the jury, as sole judge of the credibility of a witness, would have accepted this line of reasoning had counsel been permitted to fully present it. But we do conclude that the jurors were entitled to have the benefit of the defense theory before them so that they could make an informed judgment as to the weight to place on Green's testimony which provided "a crucial link in the proof . . . of petitioner's act." *Douglas v. Alabama,* 380 U.S., at 419. The accuracy and truthfulness of Green's testi-mony were key elements in the State's case against petitioner. The claim of bias which the defense sought to develop was admissible to afford a basis for an inference of undue pressure because of Green's vulnerable status as a probationer, as well as of Green's possible concern that he might be a suspect in the investigation.

We cannot accept the Alaska Supreme Court's conclusion that the cross-examination that was permitted defense counsel was adequate to develop the issue of bias properly to the jury. While counsel was permitted to ask Green *whether* he was biased, counsel was unable to make a record from which to argue *why* Green might have been biased or otherwise lacked that degree of impartiality expected of a witness at trial. On the basis of the limited cross-examination that was permitted, the jury might well have thought that defense counsel was engaged in a speculative and baseless line of attack on the credibility of an apparently blameless witness or, as the prosecutor's objection put it, a "rehash" of prior cross-examination. On these facts it seems clear to us that to make any such inquiry effective, defense counsel should have been permitted to expose to the jury the facts from which jurors, as the sole triers of fact and credibility, could appropriately draw inferences relating to the reliability of the witness. Petitioner was thus denied the right of effective cross-examination which " 'would be constitutional error of the first magnitude and no amount of showing of want of prejudice would cure it.' *Brookhart v. Janis*, 384 U.S. 1, 3." *Smith v. Illinois*, 390 U.S. 129, 131 (1968).

(3)

The claim is made that the State has an important interest in protecting the anonymity of juvenile offenders and that this interest outweighs any competing interest this petitioner might have in cross-examining Green about his being on probation. The State argues that exposure of a juvenile's record of delinquency would likely cause impairment of rehabilitative goals of the juvenile correctional procedures. This exposure, it is argued, might encourage the juvenile offender to commit further acts of delinquency, or cause the juvenile offender to lose employment opportunities or otherwise suffer unnecessarily for his youthful transgression.

We do not and need not challenge the State's interest as a matter of its own policy in the administration of criminal justice to seek to preserve the anonymity of a juvenile offender. *Cf. In re Gault*, 387 U.S. 1, 25 (1967). Here, however, petitioner sought to introduce evidence of Green's probation for the purpose of suggesting that Green was biased and, therefore, that his testimony was either not to be believed in his identification of petitioner or at least very carefully considered in that light. Serious damage to the strength of the State's case would have been a real possibility had petitioner been allowed to pursue this line of inquiry. In this setting we conclude that the right of confrontation is paramount to the State's policy of protecting a juvenile offender. Whatever temporary embarrassment might result to Green or his family by disclosure of his juvenile record–if the prosecution insisted on using him to make its case–is outweighed by petitioner's right to probe into the influence of possible bias in the testimony of a crucial identification witness.

In *Alford v. United States*, 282 U.S. 687 (1931), we upheld the right of defense counsel to impeach a witness by showing that because of the witness' incarceration in federal prison at the time of trial, the witness' testimony was biased as "given under promise or expectation of immunity, or under the coercive effect of his detention by officers of the United States." 282 U.S., at 693. In response to the argument that the witness had a right to be protected from exposure of his criminal record, the Court stated:

> "[N]o obligation is imposed on the court, such as that suggested below, to protect a witness from being discredited on cross–examination, short of an attempted invasion of his constitutional protection from self incrimination, properly invoked. There is a duty to protect him from questions which go beyond the bounds of proper cross–examination merely to harass, annoy or humiliate him." *Id.*, at 694.

As in *Alford*, we conclude that the State's desire that Green fulfill his public duty to testify free from embarrassment and with his reputation unblemished must fall before the right of petitioner to seek out the truth in the process of defending himself.

The State's policy interest in protecting the confidentiality of a juvenile offender's record cannot require yielding of so vital a constitutional right as the effective cross–examination for bias of an adverse witness. The State could have protected Green from exposure of his juvenile adjudication in these circumstances by refraining from using him to make out its case; the State cannot, consistent with the right of confrontation, require the petitioner to bear the full burden of vindicating the State's interest in the secrecy of juvenile criminal records. The judgment affirming petitioner's convictions of burglary and grand larceny is reversed and the case is remanded for further proceedings not inconsistent with this opinion.

NOTES AND PROBLEMS

1. How strong a showing of the reliability of its evidence must the defense make to trigger the constitutional right? The *Chambers* Court stressed that the excluded hearsay statements had "considerable assurance of their reliability"–their spontaneity, the corroboration, their disserving character, and their "sheer number." If *Chambers* is the appropriate benchmark, it may be difficult for an accused to successfully resort to the constitutional right. However, the Court seemingly lowered the threshold showing of reliability in *Rock v. Arkansas*, 483 U.S. 44 (1987). In that case, the defendant was charged with shooting her husband. Before trial, she had difficulty remembering the precise details of the shooting. She underwent hypnosis by a neuropsychologist to revive her memory. Only after hypnosis did she remember that her gun was defective and had accidentally misfired. The prosecutor filed a pretrial motion to bar the defendant's testimony about the events recalled only after hypnosis. The state court adopted the rule that hypnotically enhanced testimony is *per se* inadmissible. On appeal to the Supreme Court, the majority held that the exclusion violated the accused's right under *Washington*. In so holding, the majority acknowledged that "the current medical . . . view" of the reliability of enhanced testimony "is unsettled." *Id.* at 59. *But cf., United States v. Scheffer*, 523 U.S. 303 (1998)(polygraph evidence) and note 6 below.

2. For their part, the lower courts have aggressively enforced the accused's right to present evidence. In some jurisdictions, the courts have relied on the right in according the defense a right to introduce otherwise inadmissible polygraph evidence. 1 P. GIANNELLI & E. IMWINKELRIED, SCIENTIFIC EVIDENCE § 8–3(D) (3d ed. 1999). Many courts have invoked the right to override evidentiary privileges blocking the admission of defense evidence. Note, *Defendant v. Witness: Measuring Confrontation and Compulsory Process Rights Against Statutory Communications Privileges,* 30 STAN. L. REV. 935, 990 (1978); *Doe v. Diamond,* 964 F.2d 1325 (2d Cir. 1992) (the psychotherapist–patient privilege); *People v. Boyette,* 201 Cal. App. 3d 1527, 247 Cal. Rptr. 795 (1988) (possibly surmounting the psychotherapist–patient privilege); *People v. Adamski,* 198 Mich. App. 133, 497 N.W.2d 546 (1993) (overriding the psychologist–patient privilege); *State v. Juarez,* 570 A.2d 1118 (R.I. 1990) (overriding the attorney–client privilege).

3. Problem 32–1. Devitt informs his defense attorney that before Paterson filed battery charges against him, he found him engaged in sexual intercourse with a minor. Devitt had threatened to inform the authorities and have him prosecuted for statutory rape. He tells his defense attorney that he suspects Paterson filed a false battery charge against him "to beat me to the punch." The state rape shield law would otherwise bar cross–examining Paterson about the incident with the minor. The defense cites *Davis* and argues that that application of the statute would deny Devitt his constitutional right to present evidence. What ruling? *See State v. Jalo,* 27 Or. App. 845, 557 P.2d 1359 (1976).

4. When the defense invokes this constitutional right, it can often effectively use empirical evidence to support its argument. To begin with, the defense may rely on scientific evidence to establish the reliability of its exculpatory evidence. In *Patrick v. State,* 295 Ark. 473, 750 S.W.2d 391 (1988), the defense offered the exculpatory result of a portable breathalyzer test. The court had previously ruled that the test was too novel to qualify for admissibility on behalf of the prosecution. At trial, the defense presented a scientist's testimony attesting to the general trustworthiness of PBT tests. Citing *Rock,* the state court held that the evidence was trustworthy enough to trigger the accused's constitutional right. Similarly, the defense may marshal empirical evidence to diminish the magnitude of the countervailing government interest. Suppose that the exclusionary rule in question is an evidentiary privilege. Those doctrines rest on the assumption that laypersons such as clients and patients would be unwilling to communicate with professional counselors without the protection of a privilege; yet the few empirical investigations to date call the validity of the assumption into question.

5. Problem 32–2. Devitt is charged with a specific intent offense, assault with intent to cause serious bodily injury. The defense contemplates offering psychiatric testimony to negate the intent. State law declares that mental health expert testimony is admissible to establish a full–fledged insanity defense but not to disprove specific intent. The defense argues that it violates *Washington* and *Chambers* for the state law to flatly declare expert testimony irrelevant to negate specific intent. What ruling? *See Hughes v. Matthews,* 576 F.2d 1250, 1255–56 (7th Cir. 1978); *People v. Bobo,* 221 Cal. App. 3d 1432, 271 Cal. Rptr. 277, 293 (1990) ("if a crime requires a particular mental state, the Legislature <u>cannot</u> deny a defendant the opportunity to prove that he did not entertain that state") (emphasis in original). *See Montana v. Egelhoff*, 518 U.S. 37 (1996), discussed in the previous chapter.

6. In *Washington, Chambers, and Davis*, the defense succeded in persuading the Supreme Court to override a statutory or common law exclusionary rule of evidence. However, a similar defense argument failed in *United States v. Scheffer*, 523 U.S. 303 (1998), discussed in Chapter 16, *supra*. In that case, the question was the constitutionality of Military Rule of Evidence 707, a blanket prohibition on the admission of polygraph evidence in courts–martial. Justice Thomas authored the lead opinion. *Scheffer* does not purport to over-rule any of the prior precedents in the *Washington* line of cases. However, Justice Thomas' opinion reads those precedents narrowly as standing for the limited proposition that statutory and common law evidentiary rules violate the accused's constitutional right only when they are "arbitrary" or "dispropor-tionate to the purposes they are designed to serve." *Id.* at 308. *Scheffer* may be a "harbinger" that in the future, the Court will be more reluctant to invalidate evidentiary rules. Nagareda, *Reconceiving the Right to Present Witnesses*, 97 MICH.L.REV. 1063, 1098 (1999).

On the other hand, it may be a mistake to read too much into *Scheffer*. While Justice Thomas wrote the lead opinion, Justice Kennedy filed a concurrence, and Justice Stevens filed a dissent. The dissent would have rejected Rule 707 in part because it was an absolute, per se ban on polygraph evidence. 523 U.S. at 321. More importantly, Justice Kennedy's concurrence asserts that "some later case might present a more compelling case for introduction of testimony than this one does." *Id.* at 318. Hence, although Justice Kennedy voted to uphold Rule 707 as applied in the instant case, he was unwilling to sustain it as an absolute ban. Three justices joined in his concurrence. The upshot is that between the concurrence and the dissent, five justices refused to uphold Rule 707 and completely foreclose an as–applied attack on its constitutional-ity.

C.   THE IMPACT OF THE EMERGENCE OF CONSTITUTIONAL OVERRIDES ON EVIDENCE STATUTES

Washington, Chambers, and *Davis* all reach the same outcome: The Consti-tution sometimes mandates the introduction of inadmissible defense evidence. However, while *Washington* and *Chambers* rely on an implication from the compulsory process clause, *Chambers* also relies heavily on due process, and *Davis* premises the decision on the Confrontation Clause. The advent of this new constitutional jurisprudence has had a twofold impact on codified eviden-tiary rules.

One impact is indirect: The existence of the right may give the proponent of evidence at least a colorable argument that a narrow construction of a rule of evidence would be unconstitutional and, thus, enable the proponent to argue for a more expansive interpretation, admitting his or her evidence. *Common-wealth v. Joyce*, 382 Mass. 222, 415 N.E.2d 181 (1981). In that case, the accused was charged with rape. The accused sought to introduce evidence of the victim's alleged prior sexual activity. The prosecutor objected on the

ground that the state rape shield statute barred the evidence. The court refused to adopt the prosecutor's proposed interpretation of the statute. The
defense had argued that, as construed by the prosecutor, the statute abridged
the accused's constitutional right to present evidence. The court found the
defense argument persuasive. The court emphasized that, in that jurisdiction,
it was well–settled that "a 'statute must be construed, if fairly possible so as
to avoid not only the conclusion that it is unconstitutional but also grave
doubts upon that score.' " *Id.* at 185 n.5.

The other impact is direct: If the court concludes that the proponent's
interest in introducing the evidence outweighs the public interest underlying
the exclusionary rule, the court holds that that application of the statute in
a specific case violates the Constitution. Suppose, for example, that in the
Devitt case, a trial judge rules that, although it is technically inadmissible
under the statutory hearsay rules in the jurisdiction, certain defense hearsay
is so demonstrably reliable that the Constitution mandates its admission. The
immediate effect is the creation of a differential standard: the normal statutory standard which the prosecution must satisfy and the relaxed standard
for the criminal defendant under *Chambers*.

D. THE FUTURE

The relationship between constitutional overrides and the hearsay rules is
a fascinating microcosm of Supreme Court jurisprudence. Starting in 1965,
in *Pointer v. Texas*, 380 U.S. 400 (1965), when the Court made the Confrontation Clause obligatory upon the states, the debate has raged from one extreme
to another–in no small part due to the Court's zigs and zags. At one early
point, it appeared that the Court had constitutionalized the rule against
hearsay, potentially rendering unconstitutional many of the exceptions when
applied to a criminal defendant. The Court eventually retreated, but for about
15 years there was great uncertainty.

First consider *California v. Green*, 399 U.S. 149 (1970), in which the Court
sustained the admission of the preliminary hearing testimony of a witness,
Porter, who claimed at trial that he could not remember his prior testimony.
(Under California Evidence Code § 1235 the evidence would have come in both
substantively and for impeachment purposes as a prior inconsistent statement.) The California Supreme Court construed the Confrontation Clause to
require exclusion of Porter's prior testimony because it was not adequately
amenable to cross–examination by defendant. The United States Supreme
Court disagreed, holding that the declarant's presence at trial obviated any
Confrontation Clause problem, because there he was subject to cross–
examination on the prior testimony (although belated and perhaps impaired
by claimed memory loss).

Does the presence of the declarant at trial, without more, satisfy the
Confrontation Clause? Since *Green*, the Court has not had occasion to rest
a holding squarely on the theory that a hearsay declarant's mere presence
at trial automatically satisfies the constitutional requirements. Professor
Mosteller has argued that *Green* should be limited to situations in which, as
a witness, the declarant responds to questions (*i.e.*, cases in which the

opponent has a meaningful opportunity to cross–examine the declarant at trial.) Mosteller, *Remaking Confrontation Clause and Hearsay Doctrine Under the Challenge of Child Sexual Abuse Prosecutions*, 1993 U. ILL. L. REV. 691, 729. However, he acknowledges that some passages in the *Green* opinion support the view that the declarant's mere physical availability suffices. *Id.* at 727. All of the Court's recent citations to *Green* have been reaffirming. *United States v. Owens*, 484 U.S. 554 (1988); *Nelson v. O'Neil*, 402 U.S. 622 (1971).

What if the declarant is not present at trial? In *Ohio v. Roberts*, 448 U.S. 56 (1980), the Court fashioned a new, two–part standard: if the declarant is unavailable, the out of court statement must either (1) fall within a firmly rooted hearsay exception or (2) have particularized guarantees of trustworthiness such that adversarial testing would be expected to add little, if anything, to the statement's reliability. *Id.* at 65–6.

The *Roberts* decision began the shift in focus from availability to reliability. *Roberts* involved former testimony–an exception which has always involved unavailability and a high degree of comfort about trustworthiness.

What about coconspirators spewing forth hearsay inculpating one another? In *United States v. Inadi*, 475 U.S. 387 (1986), the Court found no need to produce or require a showing of unavailability before the hearsay declaration of the coconspirator was admissible against the accused. Then in *Bourjaily v. United States*, 483 U.S. 171 (1987), the Court told us that coconspirators statements were "firmly rooted"– at least, firmly enough rooted that there was no need for an independent inquiry into reliability.

What about non–traditional or evolving exceptions, particularly the residual exception in Rule 807? In *Idaho v. Wright*, 497 U.S. 805 (1990), the trial court admitted the hearsay statements of a child to a doctor under the state's residual hearsay exception which was identical to the federal rule. The Supreme Court held that the Confrontation Clause had been violated, noting that the residual exception is not "firmly rooted." The effect of the *Wright* decision may be to temper the zeal of lower courts to invoke the residual exceptions against the accused.

In the past, in evaluating the trustworthiness of hearsay which did not fall within any enumerated exception, many courts considered the corroboration supplied by extrinsic evidence and events. Some courts took the position that "corroboration of the hearsay by other trial evidence alone satisfies the trustworthiness requirement." Cole, *Residual Exceptions to the Hearsay Rule*, 16 LITIGATION, Fall 1989, at 26, 29–30. However, in *Wright*, Justice O'Connor, writing for the majority, declared that "the relevant circumstances include only those that surround the making of the statement . . . ." The judge must assess the reliability of the statement by "its inherent trustworthiness, not by reference to other evidence at trial." In *Lilly v. Virginia*, 527 U.S. 116 (1999), the Court reaffirmed Justice O'Connor's approach in *Wright, supra*. *Lilly* involved the confession of a non–testifying accomplice. The confession contained some statements against the accomplice's penal interest and other statements which exculpated the accomplice and incriminated the accused. Finding that this kind of "against penal interest" evidence did not come within a firmly rooted hearsay exception, the Court went on to the second prong of the test and reiterated its long–standing view that accomplice confessions implicating the accused are inherently unreliable. In assessing the second prong, the Court focused exclusively on the circumstances surrounding the making of the confession: declarant's strong motive to exculpate himself, the custodial context and "leading" nature of the interrogation, and declarant's inebriated state. The Court rejected any argument that external factors could supply the requisite indicia of reliability (*e.g.*, other evidence at trial corroborated the substance of the confession, declarant had been Mirandized, and there was no express promise of leniency.)

NOTES AND PROBLEMS

1. Problem 32–3. Model Code of Evidence Rule 503 urged a revolutionary reform of the rule against hearsay, with all its exceptions and convolutions. The simplicity of the statute should be again noted:

> Evidence of a hearsay declaration is admissible if the judge finds that the declarant:
>
> (a)   is unavailable as a witness, or
>
> (b)   is present and subject to cross–examination

In *Devitt*, suppose Paterson is unavailable at the time of trial. Morena has enacted Model Code of Evidence Rule 503. The prosecutor attempts to introduce Paterson's grand jury testimony. A partial transcript of the grand jury hearing includes the following passage:

Q: Isn't it true that you were attacked on March 15 of this year?

A: Yes.

Q: And that attack occurred in your apartment?

A: Right.

Q: And the assailant was Daniel Devitt. Wasn't it?

A: Yes.

Q: Do you remember going to the police station on March 17?

A: Sort of.

Q: The police station at First and Elm Streets in El Dorado.

A: Now I remember.

Q: And you witnessed a lineup then. Correct?

A: Yes.

Q: And wasn't Devitt in that lineup?

A: Yes.

Q: And you again picked him out as the attacker. Didn't you?

A: Yes.

Defense counsel objects that the testimony is "insufficiently reliable to comply with the Confrontation Clause." Consider the relevance of Federal Rule of Evidence 611(c). Is the consistently leading nature of the questions sufficient to render the answers unreliable or at least suspect? *See United States v. Gonzalez*, 559 F.2d 1271, 1273–74 (5th Cir. 1977).

2. Problem 32–4. In Problem 32–3, add the fact that between his grand jury testimony and the time of trial, Paterson told Ms. Ferguson, a friend, that "I made the whole thing up. That punk kid gave me all sorts of lip while he was working for me, and I guess I fixed him but good." Should this information preclude the admission of Paterson's grand jury testimony? Or should the judge admit both the grand jury transcript and Ms. Ferguson's testimony? *See United States v. Carlson*, 547 F.2d 1346, 1360 n.14 (8th Cir. 1976).

3. Problem 32–5. Suppose that Paterson is unavailable and his grand jury testimony is the only testimony identifying Devitt as the assailant. Does the lack of other evidence decrease the reliability of Paterson's testimony?

4. Problem 32–6. In *Devitt*, the prosecutor calls Paterson as a witness. Paterson refuses to testify. His responses are "I don't know," "I can't remember," and "I won't answer that." Morena has enacted Model Code of Evidence Rule 503(b). The prosecutor argues that since Paterson is physically present in the courtroom, his prior preliminary hearing testimony is admissible. The prosecutor cites *California v. Green*. Is *Green* distinguishable? Remember Professor Mosteller's proposed reading of the *Green* opinion. If this application of the statute would be unconstitutional, is a saving, narrowing construction possible? *See People v. Newton*, 8 Cal. App. 3d 359, 384–85, 87 Cal. Rptr. 394, 410–11 (1970).

5. Note the divergent treatment for exceptions that are "firmly rooted" and those that are not. The latter require particularized guarantees of trustworthiness inherent in the hearsay statement. In *Lilly v. Virginia*, 527 U.S. 116 (1999), the Court sought to justify the firmly rooted test:

> We now describe a hearsay exception as "firmly rooted" if, in light of "longstanding judicial and legislative experience," *Idaho v. Wright*, 497 U.S. 805 , 817, 110 S.Ct. 3139, 111 L.Ed.2d 638 (1990), it "rest[s] [on] such [a] solid foundatio[n] that admission of virtually any evidence within [it] comports with the 'substance of the constitutional protection.'" *Roberts*, 448 U.S., at 66, 100 S.Ct. 2531 (quoting *Mattox*, 156 U.S., at 244, 15 S.Ct. 337). This standard is designed to allow the introduction of statements falling within a category of hearsay whose conditions have proven over time "to remove all temptation to falsehood, and to enforce as strict an adherence to the truth as would the obligation of an oath" and cross–examination at a trial. *Mattox*, 156 U.S., at 244, 15 S.Ct. 337. In *White*, for instance, we held that the hearsay exception for spontaneous declarations is firmly rooted because it "is at least two centuries old," currently "widely accepted among the States," and carries "substantial guarantees of. . .trustworthiness. . .[that] cannot be recaptured even by later in–court testimony." 502 U.S., at 335–356, and n.8, 112 S.Ct. 736. Established practice, in short, must confirm that statements falling within a category of hearsay inherently "carr[y] special guarantees of credibility" essentially equivalent to, or greater

than, those produced by the Constitution's preference for cross–examined trial testimony. *Id.*, at 356, 112 S.Ct. 736.

Judicial opinions identifying which exceptions are "firmly rooted" are accumulating. *Ohio v. Roberts* suggested several exceptions could be considered "firmly rooted": former testimony, business records, public records, and dying declarations. 448 U.S. at 66 n. 8. *Bourjaily v. United States*, 483 U.S. 171, 183 (1987), classified the coconspirator exemption as "firmly rooted." Professor Goldman collects the exceptions that lower courts have characterized as "firmly rooted": excited utterances, present sense impressions, some admissions, some declarations against interest, and statements for purposes of medical diagnosis or treatment. *See Distorted Vision: Spontaneous Exclamations as a "Firmly Rooted" Exception to the Hearsay Rule*, 23 LOY. L.A. L. REV. 453, 454–55 (1990); *Not So "Firmly Rooted": Exceptions to the Confrontation Clause*, 66 N.C. L. REV. 1, 26–43 (1987).

Summarizing thus far, is it correct to say: Hearsay considered within "firmly rooted" or traditional exceptions poses no Confrontation Clause problem? Moreover, the Court is apparently not inclined to interpret the Confrontation Clause as rendering unconstitutional the current definition of unavailability.

6. *Washington*, *Chambers*, and *Davis* all are criminal cases. The premises for those decisions are constitutional guarantees peculiar to criminal cases, namely, the Sixth Amendment compulsory process and confrontation provisions. It has, however, been argued that under Fifth Amendement procedural due process, *civil* litigants should be accorded a similar constitutional right to introduce demonstrably reliable, critical evidence. Imwinkelried, *The Case for Recognizing a New Constitutional Entitlement: The Right to Present Favorable Evidence in Civil Cases.* 1990 UTAH.L.REV.1. The courts are beginning to recognize such a right.

In *Adams v. St. Francis Regional Medical Center*, 264 Kan. 144, 955 P.2d 1169 (1998), the Kansas Supreme Court held that certain statutory health care privileges, invoked by the providers to shield an investigative review by the state board of nursing and peer review/disciplinary records of the hospital, unconstitutionally abridged the malpractice plaintiff's right to due process:

> In the present case the legislature granted a peer review privilege to health care providers to maintain staff competency by encouraging frank and open discussions and thus improving the quality of medical care in Kansas. We must weigh that privilege against the plaintiffs' right to due process and the judicial need for the fair administration of justice. There can be no question that in granting the privilege, the legislature did not intend to restrict or eliminate a plaintiff's right to bring a medical malpractice action against a health care provider. To allow the hospital here to insulate from discovery the facts and information which go to the heart of the plaintiffs' claim would deny plaintiffs that right.
> . . .
> In the present case, we conclude that although the interest in creating a statutory peer review privilege is strong, it is outweighed by the fundamental right of the plaintiffs to have access to all the

relevant facts. The district court's protective order and order granting other discovery relief denied plaintiffs that access and thus violated plaintiff's right to due process and a fair determination of their malpractice action against the defendants.

QUESTIONS AND NOTES

1. Assume *arguendo* that the courts extend the right to present reliable, critical evidence to civil cases. Is that extension likely to have as much impact as the existence of the parallel right on the criminal side? Consider the difference in the ultimate burden of proof between civil and criminal cases. In a prosecution, to gain an acquittal, an accused need only raise a reasonable doubt about an element of the charged offense. Can a civil defendant gain a defense verdict as easily? Even if other courts decide to follow the lead of the *Adams* decision, the recognition of the constitutional override in the civil arena might have a less dramatic effect.

2. In *Baptist Memorial Hospital–Union County v. Johnson*, 754 So.2d 1165 (Miss. 2000), the Mississippi Supreme Court reached a result in accord with the outcome in *Adams*. In *Baptist Memorial*, the plaintiff mother gave birth to her child at the defendant hospital. A nurse in the defendant's employ misdelivered the child to another woman to be nursed. The latter woman breast–fed the child. When the plaintiff and her husband later discovered the mixup, they sued the hospital for negligence. In order to determine whether the breastfeeding endangered their child's health, they sought discovery of the other woman's identity and medical records. On the one hand, the court ruled that the medical privilege applied to the woman's identity and that the hospital could assert the privilege on behalf of the unidentified woman. On the other hand, the court concluded that the plaintiffs had such a "compelling" need for the information that their constitutional rights surmounted the medical privilege.

E. AND BACK

On the whole, the Supreme Court's more recent jurisprudence leans toward viewing constitutional overrides on the rules of evidence very narrowly–some say "merely procedurally." To be sure, there is still some debate over which exceptions will be deemed "firmly rooted" and which not. But essentially the forces of conservatism appear to have prevailed.

While the practical advantages of this perspective are apparent–at least for the prosecution–the difficulty lies in the obvious tension with much of the legal history surrounding evolution of the right to confrontation. 3 J. STORY, COMMENTARIES ON THE CONSTITUTION OF THE UNITED STATES 662 (1833). *See also* Pollitt, *The Right of Confrontation: Its History and Modern Dress*, 8 J. PUB. L. 381 (1959); 9 WM. HOLDSWORTH, HISTORY OF ENGLISH LAW 216–228 (3d ed. 1944).

Catherine Drinker Bowen, in her majestic work, THE LION AND THE THRONE (Little, Brown and Co. 1956) gives an indelible historical vignette. *Id.* at 190–217, 414–16.

THE TRIAL OF SIR WALTER RALEIGH

State Trials, Vol. 2 (1603)
(Cobbett's Complete Collection, Howell ed. 1809, pp. 1–46)

[The following excerpt is from Waltz & Park, EVIDENCE, (Foundation Press 8th ed. 1995) p. 82–83:] The general rule excluding hearsay statements did not become firmly fixed in England until the latter part of the 17th Century. Thus Sir Walter Raleigh had his problems with hearsay earlier in that century.

Sir Walter Raleigh's Case (J.G. Phillimore, "History and Principles of the Law of Evidence," 1850, p. 157). (1603. Raleigh was tried for a conspiracy of treason to dethrone Elizabeth and to put Arabella Stuart in her place, by the aid of Spanish money and intrigue. Sir Edward Coke, attorney–general, conducted the prosecution. The principal evidence against him was the assertion of Lord Cobham, a supposed fellow–conspirator, who had betrayed Raleigh in a sworn statement made before trial. Cobham himself was in prison, and was not produced on the trial.) . . .

Raleigh. "But it is strange to see how you press me still with my Lord Cobham, and yet will not produce him; it is not for gaining of time or prolonging my life that I urge this; he is in the house hard by, and may soon be brought hither; let him be produced, and if he will yet accuse me or avow this confession of his, it shall convict me and ease you of further proof."

Lord Cecil. "Sir Walter Raleigh presseth often that my Lord Cobham should be brought face to face; if he ask a thing of grace and favour, they must come from him only who can give them; but if he ask a matter of law, then, in order that we, who sit here as commissioners, may be satisfied, I desire to hear the opinions of my Lords, the judges, whether it may be done by law."

The Judges all answered, "that in respect it might be a mean to cover many with treasons, and might be prejudicial to the King, therefore, by the law, it was not sufferable."

Popham, C.J. "There must not such a gap be opened for the destruction of the King as would be if we should grant this; you plead hard for yourself, but the laws plead as hard for the King. Where no circumstances do concur to make a matter probable, then an accuser may be heard; but so many circumstances agreeing and confirming the accusation in this case, the accuser is not to be produced; for, having first confessed against himself voluntarily, and so charged another person, if we shall now hear him again in person, he may, for favour or fear, retract what formerly he hath said, and the jury may, by that mean, be inveigled." . . .

Raleigh.—"I never had intelligence with Cobham since I came to the Tower."

Lord Cecil.—"Sir Walter Raleigh, if my Lord Cobham will now affirm, that you were acquainted with his dealings with Count Aremberg, that you knew of the letter he received, that you were the chief instigator of him, will you then be concluded by it?"

Raleigh.—"Let my Lord Cobham speak before God and the King, and deny God and the King if he speak not truly, and will then say that ever I knew of Arabella's matter, or the money out of Spain, or the Surprising Treason, I will put myself upon it."

Lord Henry Howard.—"But what if my Lord Cobham affirm anything equivalent to this; what then?"

Raleigh.—"My Lord, I put myself upon it."

Attorney–General.—"I shall now produce a witness viva voce:"

He then produced one *Dyer*, a pilot, who, being sworn, said, "Being at Lisbon, there came to me a Portuguese gentleman, who asked me how the King of England did, and whether he was crowned? I answered him, that I hoped our noble king was well, and crowned by this; but the time was not come when I came from the coast of Spain. 'Nay,' said he 'your king shall never be crowned, for Don Cobham and Don Raleigh will cut his throat before he come to be crowned.' And this, in time, was found to spoken in mid July."

Raleigh.—"This is the saying of some wild Jesuit or beggarly priest; but what proof is it against me?"

Attorney–General.—"It must perforce arise out of some preceding intelligence, and shews that your treason had wings." . . .

Thus on the single evidence of Cobham, never confronted with Raleigh, who retracted his confession, and then (according to the advocates of the Crown) recalled his retraction, did an English jury, to the amazement and horror of the bystanders, and the perpetual disgrace of the English name, find the most illustrious of their fellow subjects guilty of high treason.

RALEIGH'S SENTENCING

[Excerpt from Bowen, *supra*, at 216–17:] Raleigh was led to the bar. Chief Justice Popham stood up, bareheaded. In his hand he held the black cap that signified a death sentence. "Sir Walter Raleigh," he said, "I am sorry to see this fallen upon you this day. You have always been taken for a wise man. And I cannot but marvel to see that a man of your wit, as this day you have approved it, could be entangled with so many treasons. I grieve to find that a man of your quality would have sold yourself for a spy to the enemy of your country for 1500 pounds a year. This covetousness is like a canker, that eats the iron place where it lives. . . ."

There was more; to Raleigh it must have been well nigh unendurable. "O God!" he had written to his wife from the Tower, "I cannot live to think how I am derided, the scorns I shall receive, the cruel words of lawyers, the infamous taunts and despites, to be made a wonder and a spectacle! O death, destroy the memory of these and lay me up in dark forgetfulness!"

Of all these cruel taunts, Popham's solemn pronouncement was the worst. Coke had raved but Raleigh could answer him. Now, for Raleigh, denial and affirmation were forever blocked. What the Chief Justice said, the world (or so thought Raleigh) would take as truth. "It now comes to my mind," Popham continued, "why you may not have your accuser brought face to face: for such an one is easily brought to retract when he seeth there is no hope of his own life. . . . It now only remaineth to pronounce the judgment, which I would to

God you had not to receive this day of me. I never saw the like trial, and I hope I shall never see the like again."

Raising both hands with the deliberation of an aged man, Popham set the black cap on his head. "Sir Walter Raleigh," he said, "since you have been found guilty of these horrible treasons, the judgment of this court is, That you shall be had from hence to the place whence you came, there to remain until the day of execution. And from thence you shall be drawn upon a hurdle through the open streets to the place of execution, there to be hanged and cut down alive, and your body shall be opened, your heart and bowels plucked out, and your privy members cut off and thrown into the fire before your eyes. Then your head to be stricken off from your body, and your body shall be divided into four quarters, to be disposed of at the King's pleasure.

"And God have mercy upon your soul."

POSTSCRIPT

Raleigh was condemned in 1603. The death sentence was commuted to imprisonment in the Tower. After 13 years in the Tower, Raleigh was freed (but not pardoned) by James I to embark on a 2–year voyage to Guiana in search of gold. Raleigh was eventually executed in 1621; his last words were to become legend. As Sir Walter knelt by the block, the headsman bade him face east as he lay down. "What matter how the head lie," said Raleigh, "so the heart be right?" *Id.* at 414, 416.

TABLE OF CASES

[References are to pages. Principal cases are capitalized.]

[References are to pages. Principal cases are capitalized.]

[References are to pages. Principal cases are capitalized.]

[References are to pages. Principal cases are capitalized.]

D

[References are to pages. Principal cases are capitalized.]

[References are to pages. Principal cases are capitalized.]

[References are to pages. Principal cases are capitalized.]

[References are to pages. Principal cases are capitalized.]

[References are to pages. Principal cases are capitalized.]

[References are to pages. Principal cases are capitalized.]

[References are to pages. Principal cases are capitalized.]

[References are to pages. Principal cases are capitalized.]

[References are to pages. Principal cases are capitalized.]

[References are to pages. Principal cases are capitalized.]

[References are to pages. Principal cases are capitalized.]

[References are to pages. Principal cases are capitalized.]

X

Y

Z

TABLE OF SECONDARY AUTHORITIES

[References are to page numbers.]

[References are to page numbers.]

C

[References are to page numbers.]

[References are to page numbers.]

[References are to page numbers.]

H

[References are to page numbers.]

I

[References are to page numbers.]

[References are to page numbers.]

M

[References are to page numbers.]

[References are to page numbers.]

[References are to page numbers.]

[References are to page numbers.]

[References are to page numbers.]

[References are to page numbers.]

Y

Z

[References are to page numbers.]

[References are to page numbers.]

INDEX

[References are to pages.]

A

ABSOLUTE PRIVILEGE
Generally . . . 666–67

ADMISSIBILITY
Attorney, role of
  Opponent of item (See subhead: Opponent of item of, role of)
  Proponent of item (See subhead: Proponent of item of, role of)
Civil case, in (See CIVIL CASES)
Competent witness (See COMPETENCY OF WITNESSES)
Criminal case, in (See CRIMINAL CASES)
Curative admissibility doctrine . . . 179–80
Evidence, of (See specific type of Evidence)
Exclusion of evidence (See EVIDENCE, subhead: Exclusion of)
Expert testimony . . . 602–07
Foundational facts, proof of . . . 109–16
Hearsay rule (See HEARSAY RULE)
Instructions to jury . . . 55
Judge, role of (See JUDGES)
Lay person testimony (See TESTIMONY)
Legal relevance doctrine . . . 117–18
Logical relevance requirement (See LOGICAL RELEVANCE)
Offer of proof . . . 90–91
Opponent of item of, role of
  Motion *in limine* . . . 92
  Motion to supress . . . 91–92
  Pretrial motions . . . 91–94
  Trial, at . . . 94–100
Petit jurors, role of (See PETIT JURORS)
Proponent of item of, role of
  Motion *in limine* . . . 87
  Pretrial motions . . . 87–88
  Trial, at . . . 88–91
Rule 103 . . . 90–91
Social policy . . . 118
Sufficiency rules, satisfaction of . . . 119
Testimony, of (See TESTIMONY)
Threshold question, as . . . 117
Uncharged misconduct evidence . . . 345–48
Witness competency (See COMPETENCY OF WITNESSES)

ADMISSIONS
Adoptive admissions, exemption to hearsay rule for . . . 465–72
Judicial admission . . . 42
Personal admissions, exemption to hearsay rule for . . . 464–65

ADMISSIONS—Cont.
Vicarious admissions, exemption to hearsay rule for
  Civil cases . . . 472–75
  Criminal cases . . . 475–81

ADOPTIONS
Adoptive admissions, exemption to hearsay rule for . . . 465–72
Affirmative adoption, exemption to hearsay rule for . . . 466
Negative adoption, exemption to hearsay rule for . . . 467–72

ADVERSARY SYSTEM
Continental Europe legal system, United States distinguished from
  Generally . . . 3–4
  Juries . . . 7
Criticisms of . . . 4
Joint Conference Report
  Generally . . . 5–6
  Intuitive hypothesis of . . . 6
Rationale for . . . 4–6

AFFIRMATIVE ADOPTION
Exemption to hearsay rule for . . . 466

ATTORNEY-CLIENT PRIVILEGE
Generally . . . 682–83
Confidential communication, defined . . 686
Duration of . . . 701–06
Exceptions to, special . . . 695
Properly related parties, requirement that communication occur between . . . 687–95
Recognition of . . . 683–86
Special exceptions to . . . 695–701

ATTORNEYS
Admissibility of evidence, role in
  Opponent of item (See ADMISSIBILITY, subhead: Opponent of item of, role of)
  Proponent of item (See ADMISSIBILITY, subhead: Proponent of item of, role of)
Attorney-client privilege (See ATTORNEY-CLIENT PRIVILEGE)
Competent witness, as . . . 171
Evidence, role in admittance of (See EVIDENCE)
Evidentiary presentation, control over . . . 3–4
Jury trials (See JURY TRIALS)
Pretrial discovery, control over . . . 3–4
Trials (See JURY TRIALS)

AUDIOTAPES
Best evidence rule, defined under . . . 627

[References are to pages.]

[References are to pages.]

[References are to pages.]

[References are to pages.]

[References are to pages.]

F

G

H

[References are to pages.]

[References are to pages.]

[References are to pages.]

[References are to pages.]

X

EVIDENCE:

TEACHING MATERIALS FOR AN AGE OF SCIENCE AND STATUTES

Fifth Edition: 2002
2002 Statutory Appendix—The Federal Rules of Evidence

Ronald L. Carlson
Fuller E. Callaway Professor of Law
University of Georgia

Edward J. Imwinkelried
Professor of Law
University of California at Davis

Edward J. Kionka
Professor of Law
Southern Illinois University

Kristine Strachan
(Retired) Dean and Professor of Law
University of San Diego

Place in pocket of bound volume and recycle previous supplement.

LexisNexis™

Library of Congress Control Number: 2001096164

ISBN#: 0-82055-313-1

Editorial Offices
744 Broad Street, Newark, NJ 07102 (973) 820-2000
201 Mission St., San Francisco, CA 94105-1831 (415) 908-3200
www.lexis.com

APPENDIX

FEDERAL RULES OF EVIDENCE

Effective July 1, 1975
As amended up to December, 2001

Article I. General Provisions

Rule 101. Scope

These rules govern proceedings in the courts of the United States and before United States bankruptcy judges and United States magistrate judges, to the extent and with the exceptions stated in rule 1101.

Rule 102. Purpose and Construction

These rules shall be construed to secure fairness in administration, elimination of unjustifiable expense and delay, and promotion of growth and development of the law of evidence to the end that the truth may be ascertained and proceedings justly determined.

Rule 103. Rulings on Evidence

(a) *Effect of erroneous ruling.*—Error may not be predicated upon a ruling which admits or excludes evidence unless a substantial right of the party is affected, and

(1) Objection. — In case the ruling is one admitting evidence, a timely objection or motion to strike appears of record, stating the specific ground of objection, if the specific ground was not apparent from the context; or

(2) Offer of proof. — In case the ruling is one excluding evidence, the substance of the evidence was made known to the court by offer or was apparent from the context within which questions were asked.

Once the court makes a definitive ruling on the record admitting or excluding evidence, either at or before trial, a party need not renew an objection or offer of proof to preserve a claim of error for appeal.

(b) *Record of offer and ruling.*— The court may add any other or further statement which shows the character of the evidence, the form in which it was offered, the objection made, and the ruling thereon. It may direct the making of an offer in question and answer form.

(c) *Hearing of jury.* — In jury cases, proceedings shall be conducted, to the extent practicable, so as to prevent inadmissible evidence from being suggested to the jury by any means, such as making statements or offers of proof or asking questions in the hearing of the jury.

(d) *Plain error.* — Nothing in this rule precludes taking notice of plain errors affecting substantial rights although they were not brought to the attention of the court.

Rule 104. Preliminary Questions

(a) *Questions of admissibility generally.* — Preliminary questions concerning the qualification of a person to be a witness, the existence of a privilege, or the admissibility of evidence shall be determined by the court, subject to the provisions of subdivision (b). In making its determination it is not bound by the rules of evidence except those with respect to privileges.

(b) *Relevancy conditioned on fact.* — When the relevancy of evidence depends upon the fulfillment of a condition of fact, the court shall admit it upon, or subject to, the introduction of evidence sufficient to support a finding of the fulfillment of the condition.

(c) *Hearing of jury.* — Hearings on the admissibility of confessions shall in all cases be conducted out of the hearing of the jury. Hearings on other preliminary matters shall be so conducted when the interests of justice require, or when an accused is a witness and so requests.

(d) *Testimony by accused.* — The accused does not, by testifying upon a preliminary matter, become subject to cross-examination as to other issues in the case.

(e) *Weight and credibility.* — This rule does not limit the right of a party to introduce before the jury evidence relevant to weight or credibility.

Rule 105. Limited Admissibility

When evidence which is admissible as to one party or for one purpose but not admissible as to another party or for another purpose is admitted, the court, upon request, shall restrict the evidence to its proper scope and instruct the jury accordingly.

Rule 106. Remainder of or Related Writings or Recorded Statements

When a writing or recorded statement or part thereof is introduced by a party, an adverse party may require the introduction at that time of any other part or any other writing or recorded statement which ought in fairness to be considered contemporaneously with it.

Article II. Judicial Notice

Rule 201. Judicial Notice of Adjudicative Facts

(a) Scope of rule

(b) Kinds of facts

(c) When discretionary

(d) When mandatory

(e) Opportunity to be heard

(f) Time of taking notice

(g) Instructing jury

Rule 201. Judicial Notice of Adjudicative Facts

(a) *Scope of rule.* — This rule governs only judicial notice of adjudicative facts.

(b) *Kinds of facts.* — A judicially noticed fact must be one not subject to reasonable dispute in that it is either (1) generally known within the territorial jurisdiction of the trial court or (2) capable of accurate and ready determination by resort to sources whose accuracy cannot reasonably be questioned.

(c) *When discretionary.* — A court may take judicial notice, whether requested or not.

(d) *When mandatory.* — A court shall take judicial notice if requested by a party and supplied with the necessary information.

(e) *Opportunity to be heard.* — A party is entitled upon timely request to an opportunity to be heard as to the propriety of taking judicial notice and the tenor of the matter noticed. In the absence of prior notification, the request may be made after judicial notice has been taken.

(f) *Time of taking notice.* — Judicial notice may be taken at any stage of the proceeding.

(g) *Instructing jury.* — In a civil action or proceeding, the court shall instruct the jury to accept as conclusive any fact judicially noticed. In a criminal case, the court shall instruct the jury that it may, but is not required to, accept as conclusive any fact judicially noticed.

Article III. Presumptions in Civil
Actions and Proceedings

Rule   301. Presumptions in General Civil Actions and Proceedings
Rule   302. Applicability of State Law in Civil Actions and Proceedings

Rule 301.   Presumptions in General Civil Actions and Proceedings

In all civil actions and proceedings not otherwise provided for by Act of Congress or by these rules, a presumption imposes on the party against whom it is directed the burden of going forward with evidence to rebut or meet the presumption, but does not shift to such party the burden of proof in the sense of the risk of nonpersuasion, which remains throughout the trial upon the party on whom it was originally cast.

Rule 302.   Applicability of State Law in Civil Actions and Proceedings

In civil actions and proceedings, the effect of a presumption respecting a fact which is an element of a claim or defense as to which State law supplies the rule of decision is determined in accordance with State law.

Article IV. Relevancy and Its Limits

Rule   401. Definition of "Relevant Evidence"
Rule   402. Relevant Evidence Generally Admissible; Irrelevant Evidence Inadmissible
Rule   403. Exclusion of Relevant Evidence on Grounds of Prejudice, Confusion, or Waste of Time
Rule   404. Character Evidence Note Admissible To Prove Conduct; Exceptions; Other Crimes
   (a)   Character evidence generally
      (1)   Character of accused
      (2)   Character of alleged victim
      (3)   Character of witness
   (b)   Other crimes, wrongs, or acts
Rule   405. Methods of Proving Character
   (a)   Reputation or opinion
   (b)   Specific instances of conduct

Rule 401. Definition of "Relevant Evidence"

"Relevant evidence" means evidence having any tendency to make the existence of any fact that is of consequence to the determination of the action more probable or less probable than it would be without the evidence.

Rule 402. Relevant Evidence Generally Admissible; Irrelevant Evidence Inadmissible

All relevant evidence is admissible, except as otherwise provided by the Constitution of the United States, by Act of Congress, by these rules, or by other rules prescribed by the Supreme Court pursuant to statutory authority. Evidence which is not relevant is not admissible.

Rule 403. Exclusion of Relevant Evidence on Grounds of Prejudice, Confusion, or Waste of Time

Although relevant, evidence may be excluded if its probative value is substantially outweighed by the danger of unfair prejudice, confusion of the issues, or misleading the jury, or by considerations of undue delay, waste of time, or needless presentation of cumulative evidence.

Rule 404. Character Evidence Not Admissible To Prove Conduct; Exceptions; Other Crimes

(a) *Character evidence generally.* — Evidence of a person's character or a trait of character is not admissible for the purpose of proving action in conformity therewith on a particular occasion, except:

(1) Character of accused. — Evidence of a pertinent trait of character offered by an accused, or by the prosecution to rebut the same, or if evidence of a trait of character of the alleged victim of the crime is offered by an accused and admitted under Rule 404 (a)(2), evidence of the same trait of character of the accused offered by the prosecution;

(2) Character of alleged victim. — Evidence of a pertinent trait of character of the alleged victim of the crime offered by an accused, or by the

prosecution to rebut the same, or evidence of a character trait of peacefulness of the alleged victim offered by the prosecution in a homicide case to
rebut evidence that the alleged victim was the first aggressor;

(3) Character of witness. — Evidence of the character of a witness, as
provided in rules 607, 608, and 609.

(b) *Other crimes, wrongs, or acts.* — Evidence of other crimes, wrongs, or
acts is not admissible to prove the character of a person in order to show action
in conformity therewith. It may, however, be admissible for other purposes,
such as proof of motive, opportunity, intent, preparation, plan, knowledge,
identity, or absence of mistake or accident, provided that upon request by the
accused, the prosecution in a criminal case shall provide reasonable notice
in advance of trial, or during trial if the court excuses pretrial notice on good
cause shown, of the general nature of any such evidence it intends to introduce
at trial.

Rule 405. Methods of Proving Character

(a) *Reputation or opinion.* — In all cases in which evidence of character
or a trait of character of a person is admissible, proof may be made by
testimony as to reputation or by testimony in the form of an opinion. On cross-
examination, inquiry is allowable into relevant specific instances of conduct.

(b) *Specific instances of conduct.* — In cases in which character or a trait
of character of a person is an essential element of a charge, claim, or defense,
proof may also be made of specific instances of that person's conduct.

Rule 406. Habit; Routine Practice

Evidence of the habit of a person or of the routine practice of an organization, whether corroborated or not and regardless of the presence of eyewitnesses, is relevant to prove that the conduct of the person or organization on
a particular occasion was in conformity with the habit or routine practice.

Rule 407. Subsequent Remedial Measures

When, after an injury or harm allegedly caused by an event, measures are
taken that, if taken previously, would have made the injury or harm less likely
to occur, evidence of the subsequent measures is not admissible to prove
negligence, culpable conduct, a defect in a product, a defect in a product's
design, or a need for a warning or instruction. This rule does not require the
exclusion of evidence of subsequent measures when offered for another
purpose, such as proving ownership, control, or feasibility of precautionary
measures, if controverted, or impeachment.

Rule 408. Compromise and Offers to Compromise

Evidence of (1) furnishing or offering or promising to furnish, or (2)
accepting or offering or promising to accept, a valuable consideration in
compromising or attempting to compromise a claim which was disputed as

to either validity or amount, is not admissible to prove liability for or invalidity of the claim or its amount. Evidence of conduct or statements made in compromise negotiations is likewise not admissible. This rule does not require the exclusion of any evidence otherwise discoverable merely because it is presented in the course of compromise negotiations. This rule also does not require exclusion when the evidence is offered for another purpose, such as proving bias or prejudice of a witness, negativing a contention of undue delay, or proving an effort to obstruct a criminal investigation or prosecution.

Rule 409. Payment of Medical and Similar Expenses

Evidence of furnishing or offering or promising to pay medical, hospital, or similar expenses occasioned by an injury is not admissible to prove liability for the injury.

Rule 410. Inadmissibility of Pleas, Plea Discussions, and Related Statements

Except as otherwise provided in this rule, evidence of the following is not, in any civil or criminal proceeding, admissible against the defendant who made the plea or was a participant in the plea discussions:

(1) a plea of guilty which was later withdrawn;

(2) a plea of *nolo contendere;*

(3) any statement made in the course of any proceedings under Rule 11 of the Federal Rules of Criminal Procedure or comparable state procedure regarding either of the foregoing pleas; or

(4) any statement made in the course of plea discussions with an attorney for the prosecuting authority which do not result in a plea of guilty or which result in a plea of guilty later withdrawn.

However, such a statement is admissible (i) in any proceeding wherein another statement made in the course of the same plea or plea discussions has been introduced and the statement ought in fairness be considered contemporaneously with it, or (ii) in a criminal proceeding for perjury or false statement if the statement was made by the defendant under oath, on the record and in the presence of counsel.

Rule 411. Liability Insurance

Evidence that a person was or was not insured against liability is not admissible upon the issue whether the person acted negligently or otherwise wrongfully. This rule does not require the exclusion of evidence of insurance against liability when offered for another purpose, such as proof of agency, ownership, or control, or bias or prejudice of a witness.

Rule 412. Sex Offense Cases; Relevance of Alleged Victim's Past Sexual Behavior or Alleged Sexual Predisposition

(a) *Evidence Generally Inadmissible.* — The following evidence is not admissible in any civil or criminal proceeding involving alleged sexual misconduct except as provided in subdivisions (b) and (c):

(1) Evidence offered to prove that any alleged victim engaged in other sexual behavior.

(2) Evidence offered to prove any alleged victim's sexual predisposition.

(b) *Exceptions.*

(1) In a criminal case, the following evidence is admissible, if otherwise admissible under these rules:

(A) evidence of specific instances of sexual behavior by the alleged victim offered to prove that a person other than the accused was the source of semen, injury or other physical evidence;

(B) evidence of specific instances of sexual behavior by the alleged victim with respect to the person accused of the sexual misconduct offered by the accused to prove consent or by the prosecution; and

(C) evidence the exclusion of which would violate the constitutional rights of the defendant.

(2) In a civil case, evidence offered to prove the sexual behavior or sexual predisposition of any alleged victim is admissible if it is otherwise admissible under these rules and its probative value substantially outweighs the danger of harm to any victim and of unfair prejudice to any party. Evidence of an alleged victim's reputation is admissible only if it has been placed in controversy by the alleged victim.

(c) *Procedure to Determine Admissibility.*

(1) A party intending to offer evidence under subdivision (b) must—

(A) file a written motion at least 14 days before trial specifically describing the evidence and stating the purpose for which it is offered unless the court, for good cause requires a different time for filing or permits filing during trial; and

(B) serve the motion on all parties and notify the alleged victim or, when appropriate, the alleged victim's guardian or representative.

(2) Before admitting evidence under this rule the court must conduct a hearing in camera and afford the victim and parties a right to attend and be heard. The motion, related papers, and the record of the hearing must be sealed and remain under seal unless the court orders otherwise.

Rule 413. Evidence of Similar Crimes in Sexual Assault Cases

(a) In a criminal case in which the defendant is accused of an offense of sexual assault, evidence of the defendant's commission of another offense or offenses of sexual assault is admissible, and may be considered for its bearing on any matter to which it is relevant.

(b)   In a case in which the Government intends to offer evidence under this rule, the attorney for the Government shall disclose the evidence to the defendant, including statements of witnesses or a summary of the substance of any testimony that is expected to be offered, at least fifteen days before the scheduled date of trial or at such later time as the court may allow for good cause.

(c)   This rule shall not be construed to limit the admission or consideration of evidence under any other rule.

(d)   For purposes of this rule and Rule 415, "offense of sexual assault" means a crime under Federal law or the law of a State (as defined in section 513 of title 18, United States Code) that involved—

(1)   any conduct proscribed by chapter 109A of title 18, United States Code;

(2)   contact, without consent, between any part of the defendant's body or an object and the genitals or anus of another person;

(3)   contact, without consent, between the genitals or anus of the defendant and any part of another person's body;

(4)   deriving sexual pleasure or gratification from the infliction of death, bodily injury, or physical pain on another person; or

(5)   an attempt or conspiracy to engage in conduct described in paragraphs (1)-(4).

Rule 414.   Evidence of Similar Crimes in Child Molestation Cases

(a)   In a criminal case in which the defendant is accused of an offense of child molestation, evidence of the defendant's commission of another offense or offenses of child molestation is admissible, and may be considered for its bearing on any matter to which it is relevant.

(b)   In a case in which the Government intends to offer evidence under this rule, the attorney for the Government shall disclose the evidence to the defendant, including statements of witnesses or a summary of the substance of any testimony that is expected to be offered, at least fifteen days before the scheduled date of trial or at such later time as the court may allow for good cause.

(c)   This rule shall not be construed to limit the admission or consideration of evidence under any other rule.

(d)   For purposes of this rule and Rule 415, "child" means a person below the age of fourteen, and "offense of child molestation" means a crime under Federal law or the law of a State (as defined in section 513 of title 18, United States Code) that involved—

(1)   any conduct proscribed by chapter 109A of title 18, United States Code, that was committed in relation to a child;

(2)   any conduct proscribed by chapter 110 of title 18, United States Code;

(3)   contact between any part of the defendant's body or an object and the genitals or anus of a child;

(4)   contact between the genitals or anus of the defendant and any part of the body of a child;

(5)   deriving sexual pleasure or gratification from the infliction of death, bodily injury, or physical pain on a child; or

(6)   an attempt or conspiracy to engage in conduct described in paragraphs (1)-(5).

Rule 415.   Evidence of Similar Acts in Civil Cases Concerning Sexual Assault or Child Molestation

(a)   In a civil case in which a claim for damages or other relief is predicated on a party's alleged commission of conduct constituting an offense of sexual assault or child molestation, evidence of that party's commission of another offense or offenses of sexual assault or child molestation is admissible and may be considered as provided in Rule 413 and Rule 414 of these rules.

(b)   A party who intends to offer evidence under this Rule shall disclose the evidence to the party against whom it will be offered, including statements of witnesses or a summary of the substance of any testimony that is expected to be offered, at least fifteen days before the scheduled date of trial or at such later time as the court may allow for good cause.

(c)   This rule shall not be construed to limit the admission or consideration of evidence under any other rule.

Article V. Privileges

Rule   501. General Rule

Rule 501.   General Rule

Except as otherwise required by the Constitution of the United States or provided by Act of Congress or in rules prescribed by the Supreme Court pursuant to statutory authority, the privilege of a witness, person, government, State, or political subdivision thereof shall be governed by the principles of the common law as they may be interpreted by the courts of the United States in the light of reason and experience. However, in civil actions and proceedings, with respect to an element of a claim or defense as to which State law supplies the rule of decision, the privilege of a witness, person, government, State, or political subdivision thereof shall be determined in accordance with State law.

Article VI. Witnesses

Rule   601. General Rule of Competency
Rule   602. Lack of Personal Knowledge
Rule   603. Oath or Affirmation
Rule   604. Interpreters
Rule   605. Competency of Judge as Witness

Rule 601.   General Rule of Competency

Every person is competent to be a witness except as otherwise provided in these rules. However, in civil actions and proceedings, with respect to an element of a claim or defense as to which State law supplies the rule of decision, the competency of a witness shall be determined in accordance with State law.

Rule 602.   Lack of Personal Knowledge

A witness may not testify to a matter unless evidence is introduced sufficient to support a finding that the witness has personal knowledge of the matter. Evidence to prove personal knowledge may, but need not, consist of the witness' own testimony. This rule is subject to the provisions of rule 703, relating to opinion testimony by expert witnesses.

Rule 603. Oath or Affirmation

Before testifying, every witness shall be required to declare that the witness will testify truthfully, by oath or affirmation administered in a form calculated to awaken the witness' conscience and impress the witness' mind with the duty to do so.

Rule 604. Interpreters

An interpreter is subject to the provisions of these rules relating to qualification as an expert and the administration of an oath or affirmation to make a true translation.

Rule 605. Competency of Judge as Witness

The judge presiding at the trial may not testify in that trial as a witness. No objection need be made in order to preserve the point.

Rule 606. Competency of Juror as Witness

(a) *At the trial.* — A member of the jury may not testify as a witness before that jury in the trial of the case in which the juror is sitting. If the juror is called so to testify, the opposing party shall be afforded an opportunity to object out of the presence of the jury.

(b) *Inquiry into validity of verdict or indictment.* — Upon an inquiry into the validity of a verdict or indictment, a juror may not testify as to any matter or statement occurring during the course of the jury's deliberations or to the effect of anything upon that or any other juror's mind or emotions as influencing the juror to assent to or dissent from the verdict or indictment or concerning the juror's mental processes in connection therewith, except that a juror may testify on the question whether extraneous prejudicial information was improperly brought to the jury's attention or whether any outside influence was improperly brought to bear upon any juror. Nor may a juror's affidavit or evidence of any statement by the juror concerning a matter about which the juror would be precluded from testifying be received for these purposes.

Rule 607. Who May Impeach

The credibility of a witness may be attacked by any party, including the party calling the witness.

Rule 608. Evidence of Character and Conduct of Witness

(a) *Opinion and reputation evidence of character.* — The credibility of a witness may be attacked or supported by evidence in the form of opinion or reputation, but subject to these limitations: (1) the evidence may refer only to character for truthfulness or untruthfulness, and (2) evidence of truthful character is admissible only after the character of the witness for truthfulness has been attacked by opinion or reputation evidence or otherwise.

(b) *Specific instances of conduct.* — Specific instances of the conduct of a witness, for the purpose of attacking or supporting the witness' credibility, other than conviction of crime as provided in rule 609, may not be proved by extrinsic evidence. They may, however, in the discretion of the court, if probative of truthfulness or untruthfulness, be inquired into on cross-examination of the witness (1) concerning the witness' character for truthfulness or untruthfulness, or (2) concerning the character for truthfulness or untruthfulness of another witness as to which character the witness being cross-examined has testified.

The giving of testimony, whether by an accused or by any other witness, does not operate as a waiver of the accused's or the witness' privilege against self-incrimination when examined with respect to matters which relate only to credibility.

Rule 609. Impeachment by Evidence of Conviction of Crime

(a) *General rule.* — For the purpose of attacking the credibility of a witness,

(1) evidence that a witness other than an accused has been convicted of a crime shall be admitted, subject to Rule 403, if the crime was punishable by death or imprisonment in excess of one year under the law under which the witness was convicted, and evidence that an accused has been convicted of such a crime shall be admitted if the court determines that the probative value of admitting this evidence outweighs its prejudicial effect to the accused; and

(2) evidence that any witness has been convicted of a crime shall be admitted if it involved dishonestly or false statement, regardless of the punishment.

(b) *Time limit.* — Evidence of a conviction under this rule is not admissible if a period of more than ten years has elapsed since the date of the conviction or of the release of the witness from the confinement imposed for that conviction, whichever is the later date, unless the court determines, in the interests of justice, that the probative value of the conviction supported by specific facts and circumstances substantially outweighs its prejudicial effect. However, evidence of a conviction more than 10 years old as calculated herein, is not admissible unless the proponent gives to the adverse party sufficient advance written notice of intent to use such evidence to provide the adverse party with a fair opportunity to contest the use of such evidence.

(c) *Effect of pardon, annulment, or certificate of rehabilitation.* — Evidence of a conviction is not admissible under this rule if (1) the conviction has been the subject of a pardon, annulment, certificate of rehabilitation, or other equivalent procedure based on a finding of the rehabilitation of the person convicted, and that person has not been convicted of a subsequent crime which was punishable by death or imprisonment in excess of one year, or (2) the conviction has been the subject of a pardon, annulment, or other equivalent procedure based on a finding of innocence.

(d) *Juvenile adjudications.* — Evidence of juvenile adjudications is generally not admissible under this rule. The court may, however, in a criminal case allow evidence of a juvenile adjudication of a witness other than the accused if conviction of the offense would be admissible to attack the credibility of an adult and the court is satisfied that admission in evidence is necessary for a fair determination of the issue of guilt or innocence.

(e) *Pendency of appeal*. — The pendency of an appeal therefrom does not render evidence of a conviction inadmissible. Evidence of the pendency of an appeal is admissible.

Rule 610. Religious Beliefs or Opinions

Evidence of the beliefs or opinions of a witness on matters of religion is not admissible for the purpose of showing that by reason of their nature the witness' credibility is impaired or enhanced.

Rule 611. Mode and Order of Interrogation and Presentation

(a) *Control by court*. — The court shall exercise reasonable control over the mode and order of interrogating witnesses and presenting evidence so as to (1) make the interrogation and presentation effective for the ascertainment of the truth, (2) avoid needless consumption of time, and (3) protect witnesses from harassment or undue embarrassment.

(b) *Scope of cross-examination*. — Cross-examination should be limited to the subject matter of the direct examination and matters affecting the credibility of the witness. The court may, in the exercise of discretion, permit inquiry into additional matters as if on direct examination.

(c) *Leading questions*. — Leading questions should not be used on the direct examination of a witness except as may be necessary to develop the witness' testimony. Ordinarily leading questions should be permitted on cross-examination. When a party calls a hostile witness, an adverse party, or a witness identified with an adverse party, interrogation may be by leading questions.

Rule 612. Writing Used to Refresh Memory

Except as otherwise provided in criminal proceedings by section 3500 of title 18, United States Code, if a witness uses a writing to refresh memory for the purpose of testifying, either—

(1) while testifying, or

(2) before testifying, if the court in its discretion determines it is necessary in the interests of justice, an adverse party is entitled to have the writing produced at the hearing, to inspect it, to cross-examine the witness thereon, and to introduce in evidence those portions which relate to the testimony of the witness. If it is claimed that the writing contains matters not related to the subject matter of the testimony the court shall examine the writing in camera, excise any portions not so related, and order delivery of the remainder to the party entitled thereto. Any portion withheld over objections shall be preserved and made available to the appellate court in the event of an appeal. If a writing is not produced or delivered pursuant to order under this rule,

the court shall make any order justice requires, except that in criminal cases when the prosecution elects not to comply, the order shall be one striking the testimony or, if the court in its discretion determines that the interests of justice so require, declaring a mistrial.

Rule 613. Prior Statements of Witnesses

(a) *Examining witness concerning prior statement.* — In examining a witness concerning a prior statement made by the witness, whether written or not, the statement need not be shown nor its contents disclosed to the witness at that time, but on request the same shall be shown or disclosed to opposing counsel.

(b) *Extrinsic evidence of prior inconsistent statement of witness.* — Extrinsic evidence of a prior inconsistent statement by a witness is not admissible unless the witness is afforded an opportunity to explain or deny the same and the opposite party is afforded an opportunity to interrogate the witness thereon, or the interests of justice otherwise require. This provision does not apply to admissions of a party-opponent as defined in rule 801(d)(2).

Rule 614. Calling and Interrogation of Witnesses by Court

(a) *Calling by court.* — The court may, on its own motion or at the suggestion of a party, call witnesses, and all parties are entitled to cross-examine witnesses thus called.

(b) *Interrogation by court.* — The court may interrogate witnesses, whether called by itself or by a party.

(c) *Objections.* — Objections to the calling of witnesses by the court or to interrogation by it may be made at the time or at the next available opportunity when the jury is not present.

Rule 615. Exclusion of Witnesses

At the request of a party the court shall order witnesses excluded so that they cannot hear the testimony of other witnesses, and it may make the order of its own motion. This rule does not authorize exclusion of (1) a party who is a natural person, or (2) an officer or employee of a party which is not a natural person designated as its representative by its attorney, or (3) a person whose presence is shown by a party to be essential to the presentation of the party's cause, or (4) a person authorized by statute to be present.

Article VII. Opinions and Expert Testimony

Rule   706. Court Appointed Experts

(a)   Appointment

(b)   Compensation

(c)   Disclosure of appointment

(d)   Parties' experts of own selection

Rule 701.   Opinion Testimony by Lay Witnesses

If the witness is not testifying as an expert, the witness' testimony in the form of opinions or inferences is limited to those opinions or inferences which are (a) rationally based on the perception of the witness, and (b) helpful to a clear understanding of the witness' testimony or the determination of a fact in issue, and (c) not based on scientific, technical, or other specialized knowledge within the scope of Rule 702.

Rule 702.   Testimony by Experts

If scientific, technical, or other specialized knowledge will assist the trier of fact to understand the evidence or to determine a fact in issue, a witness qualified as an expert by knowledge, skill, experience, training, or education, may testify thereto in the form of an opinion or otherwise, if (1) the testimony is based upon sufficient facts or data, (2) the testimony is the product of reliable principles and methods, and (3) the witness has applied the principles and methods reliably to the facts of the case.

Rule 703.   Bases of Opinion Testimony by Experts

The facts or data in the particular case upon which an expert bases an opinion or inference may be those perceived by or made known to the expert at or before the hearing. If of a type reasonably relied upon by experts in the particular field in forming opinions or inferences upon the subject, the facts or data need not be admissible in evidence in order for the opinion or inference to be admitted. Facts or data that are otherwise inadmissible shall not be disclosed to the jury by the proponent of the opinion or inference unless the court determines that their probative value in assisting the jury to evaluate the expert's opinion substantially outweighs their prejudicial effect.

Rule 704.   Opinion on Ultimate Issue

(a)   Except as provided in subdivision (b), testimony in the form of an opinion or inference otherwise admissible is not objectionable because it embraces an ultimate issue to be decided by the trier of fact.

(b)   No expert witness testifying with respect to the mental state or condition of a defendant in a criminal case may state an opinion or inference as to whether the defendant did or did not have the mental state or condition constituting an element of the crime charged or of a defense thereto. Such ultimate issues are matters for the trier of fact alone.

Rule 705. Disclosure of Facts or Data Underlying Expert Opinion

The expert may testify in terms of opinion or inference and give reasons therefor without first testifying to the underlying facts or data, unless the court requires otherwise. The expert may in any event be required to disclose the underlying facts or data on cross-examination.

Rule 706. Court Appointed Experts

(a) *Appointment.* — The court may on its own motion or on the motion of any party enter an order to show cause why expert witnesses should not be appointed, and may request the parties to submit nominations. The court may appoint any expert witnesses agreed upon by the parties, and may appoint expert witnesses of its own selection. An expert witness shall not be appointed by the court unless the witness consents to act. A witness so appointed shall be informed of the witness' duties by the court in writing, a copy of which shall be filed with the clerk, or at a conference in which the parties shall have opportunity to participate. A witness so appointed shall advise the parties of the witness' findings, if any; the witness' deposition may be taken by any party; and the witness may be called to testify by the court or any party. The witness shall be subject to cross-examination by each party, including a party calling the witness.

(b) *Compensation.* — Expert witnesses so appointed are entitled to reasonable compensation in whatever sum the court may allow. The compensation thus fixed is payable from funds which may be provided by law in criminal cases and civil actions and proceedings involving just compensation under the fifth amendment. In other civil actions and proceedings the compensation shall be paid by the parties in such proportion and at such time as the court directs, and thereafter charged in like manner as other costs.

(c) *Disclosure of appointment.* — In the exercise of its discretion, the court may authorize disclosure to the jury of the fact that the court appointed the expert witness.

(d) *Parties' experts of own selection.* — Nothing in this rule limits the parties in calling expert witnesses of their own selection.

Article VIII. Hearsay

Rule 801. Definitions

(a) Statement

(b) Declarant

(c) Hearsay

(d) Statements which are not hearsay

    (1) Prior statement by witness

    (2) Admission by party-opponent

Rule 801. Definitions

The following definitions apply under this article:

(a) *Statement.* — A "statement" is (1) an oral or written assertion or (2) nonverbal conduct of a person, if it is intended by the person as an assertion.

(b) *Declarant.* — A "declarant" is a person who makes a statement.

(c) *Hearsay.* — "Hearsay" is a statement, other than one made by the declarant while testifying at the trial or hearing, offered in evidence to prove the truth of the matter asserted.

(d) *Statements which are not hearsay.* — A statement is not hearsay if—

(1) Prior statement by witness. The declarant testifies at the trial or hearing and is subject to cross-examination concerning the statement, and the statement is (A) inconsistent with the declarant's testimony, and was given under oath subject to the penalty of perjury at a trial, hearing, or other proceeding, or in a deposition, or (B) consistent with the declarant's testimony and is offered to rebut an express or implied charge against the declarant of recent fabrication or improper influence or motive, or (C) one of identification of a person made after perceiving the person; or

(2) Admission by party-opponent. The statement is offered against a party and is (A) the party's own statement in either an individual or a representative capacity or (B) a statement of which the party has manifested an adoption or belief in its truth, or (C) a statement by a person authorized by the party to make a statement concerning the subject, or (D) a statement by the party's agent or servant concerning a matter within the scope of the agency or employment, made during the existence of the relationship, or (E) a statement by a co-conspirator of a party during the course and in furtherance of the conspiracy.

The contents of the statement shall be considered but are not alone sufficient to establish the declarant's authority under subdivision (C), the agency or employment relationship and scope thereof under subdivision (D), or the existence of the conspiracy and the participation therein of the declarant and the party against whom the statement is offered under subdivision (E).

Rule 802. Hearsay Rule

Hearsay is not admissible except as provided by these rules or by other rules prescribed by the Supreme Court pursuant to statutory authority or by Act of Congress.

Rule 803. Hearsay Exceptions; Availability of Declarant Immaterial

The following are not excluded by the hearsay rule, even though the declarant is available as a witness:

(1) *Present sense impression.* — A statement describing or explaining an event or condition made while the declarant was perceiving the event or condition, or immediately thereafter.

(2) *Excited utterance.* — A statement relating to a startling event or condition made while the declarant was under the stress of excitement caused by the event or condition.

(3) *Then existing mental, emotional, or physical condition.* — A statement of the declarant's then existing state of mind, emotion, sensation, or physical condition (such as intent, plan, motive, design, mental feeling, pain, and bodily health), but not including a statement of memory or belief to prove the fact remembered or believed unless it relates to the execution, revocation, identification, or terms of declarant's will.

(4) *Statements for purposes of medical diagnosis or treatment.* — Statements made for purposes of medical diagnosis or treatment and describing medical history, or past or present symptoms, pain, or sensations, or the inception or general character of the cause or external source thereof insofar as reasonably pertinent to diagnosis or treatment.

(5) *Recorded recollection.* — A memorandum or record concerning a matter about which a witness once had knowledge but now has insufficient recollection to enable the witness to testify fully and accurately, shown to have been made or adopted by the witness when the matter was fresh in the witness' memory and to reflect that knowledge correctly. If admitted, the memorandum or record may be read into evidence but may not itself be received as an exhibit unless offered by an adverse party.

(6) *Records of regularly conducted activity.* — A memorandum, report, record, or data compilation, in any form, of acts, events, conditions, opinions, or diagnoses, made at or near the time by, or from information transmitted by, a person with knowledge, if kept in the course of a regularly conducted business activity, and if it was the regular practice of that business activity to make the memorandum, report, record or data compilation, all as shown by the testimony of the custodian or other qualified witness, or by certification that complies with Rule 902(11), Rule 902(12), or a statute permitting certification, unless the source of information or the method or circumstances

of preparation indicate lack of trustworthiness. The term "business" as used in this paragraph includes business, institution, association, profession, occupation, and calling of every kind, whether or not conducted for profit.

(7) *Absence of entry in records kept in accordance with the provisions of paragraph (6).* — Evidence that a matter is not included in the memoranda reports, records, or data compilations, in any form, kept in accordance with the provisions of paragraph (6), to prove the nonoccurrence or nonexistence of the matter, if the matter was of a kind of which a memorandum, report, record, or data compilation was regularly made and preserved, unless the sources of information or other circumstances indicate lack of trustworthiness.

(8) *Public records and reports.* — Records, reports, statements, or data compilations, in any form, of public offices or agencies, setting forth (A) the activities of the office or agency, or (B) matters observed pursuant to duty imposed by law as to which matters there was a duty to report, excluding, however, in criminal cases matters observed by police officers and other law enforcement personnel, or (C) in civil actions and proceedings and against the Government in criminal cases, factual findings resulting from an investigation made pursuant to authority granted by law, unless the sources of information or other circumstances indicate lack of trustworthiness.

(9) *Records of vital statistics.* — Records or data compilations, in any form, of births, fetal deaths, deaths, or marriages, if the report thereof was made to a public office pursuant to requirements of law.

(10) *Absence of public record or entry.* — To prove the absence of a record, report, statement, or data compilation, in any form, or the nonoccurrence or nonexistence of a matter of which a record, report, statement, or data compilation, in any form, was regularly made and preserved by a public office or agency, evidence in the form of a certification in accordance with rule 902, or testimony, that diligent search failed to disclose the record, report, statement, or data compilation, or entry.

(11) *Records of religious organizations.* — Statements of births, marriages, divorces, deaths, legitimacy, ancestry, relationship by blood or marriage, or other similar facts of personal or family history, contained in a regularly kept record of a religious organization.

(12) *Marriage, baptismal, and similar certificates.* — Statements of fact contained in a certificate that the maker performed a marriage or other ceremony or administered a sacrament, made by a clergyman, public official, or other person authorized by the rules or practices of a religious organization or by law to perform the act certified, and purporting to have been issued at the time of the act or within a reasonable time thereafter.

(13) *Family records.* — Statements of fact concerning personal or family history contained in family Bibles, genealogies, charts, engravings on rings, inscriptions on family portraits, engravings on urns, crypts, or tombstones, or the like.

(14) *Records of documents affecting an interest in property.* — The record of a document purporting to establish or affect an interest in property, as proof of the content of the original recorded document and its execution and delivery by each person by whom it purports to have been executed, if the record is

a record of a public office and an applicable statute authorizes the recording of documents of that kind in that office.

(15) *Statements in documents affecting an interest in property.* — A statement contained in a document purporting to establish or affect an interest in property if the matter stated was relevant to the purpose of the document, unless dealings with the property since the document was made have been inconsistent with the truth of the statement or the purport of the document.

(16) *Statements in ancient documents.* — Statements in a document in existence twenty years or more the authenticity of which is established.

(17) *Market reports, commercial publications.* — Market quotations, tabulations, lists, directories, or other published compilations, generally used and relied upon by the public or by persons in particular occupations.

(18) *Learned treatises.* — To the extent called to the attention of an expert witness upon cross-examination or relied upon by the expert witness in direct examination, statements contained in published treatises, periodicals, or pamphlets on a subject of history, medicine, or other science or art, established as a reliable authority by the testimony or admission of the witness or by other expert testimony or by judicial notice. If admitted, the statements may be read into evidence but may not be received as exhibits.

(19) *Reputation concerning personal or family history.* — Reputation among members of a person's family by blood, adoption, or marriage, or among a person's associates, or in the community, concerning a person's birth, adoption, marriage, divorce, death, legitimacy, relationship by blood, adoption, or marriage, ancestry, or other similar fact of personal or family history.

(20) *Reputation concerning boundaries or general history.* — Reputation in a community, arising before the controversy, as to boundaries of or customs affecting lands in the community, and reputation as to events of general history important to the community or State or nation in which located.

(21) *Reputation as to character.* — Reputation of a person's character among associates or in the community.

(22) *Judgment of previous conviction.* — Evidence of a final judgment, entered after a trial or upon a plea of guilty (but not upon a plea of *nolo contendere*), adjudging a person guilty of a crime punishable by death or imprisonment in excess of one year, to prove any fact essential to sustain the judgment, but not including, when offered by the Government in a criminal prosecution for purposes other than impeachment, judgments against persons other than the accused. The pendency of an appeal may be shown but does not affect admissibility.

(23) *Judgment as to personal, family, or general history, or boundaries.* — Judgments as proof of matters of personal, family or general history, or boundaries, essential to the judgment, if the same would be provable by evidence of reputation.

(24) [Transferred to Rule 807]

Rule 804. Hearsay Exceptions; Declarant Unavailable

(a) *Definition of unavailability.* — "Unavailability as a witness" includes situations in which the declarant—

(1) is exempted by ruling of the court on the ground of privilege from testifying concerning the subject matter of the declarant's statement; or

(2) persists in refusing to testify concerning the subject matter of the declarant's statement despite an order of the court to do so; or

(3) testifies to a lack of memory of the subject matter of the declarant's statement; or

(4) is unable to be present or to testify at the hearing because of death or then existing physical or mental illness or infirmity; or

(5) is absent from the hearing and the proponent of a statement has been unable to procure the declarant's attendance (or in the case of a hearsay exception under subdivision (b)(2), (3), or (4), the declarant's attendance or testimony) by process or other reasonable means.

A declarant is not unavailable as a witness if exemption, refusal, claim of lack of memory, inability, or absence is due to the procurement or wrongdoing of the proponent of a statement for the purpose of preventing the witness from attending or testifying.

(b) *Hearsay exceptions.* — The following are not excluded by the hearsay rule if the declarant is unavailable as a witness:

(1) Former testimony. — Testimony given as a witness at another hearing of the same or a different proceeding, or in a deposition taken in compliance with law in the course of the same or another proceeding, if the party against whom the testimony is now offered, or, in a civil action or proceeding, a predecessor in interest, had an opportunity and similar motive to develop the testimony by direct, cross, or redirect examination.

(2) Statement under belief of impending death. — In a prosecution for homicide or in a civil action or proceeding, a statement made by a declarant while believing that the declarant's death was imminent, concerning the cause or circumstances of what the declarant believed to be impending death.

(3) Statement against interest. — A statement which was at the time of its making so far contrary to the declarant's pecuniary or proprietary interest, or so far tended to subject the declarant to civil or criminal liability, or to render invalid a claim by the declarant against another, that a reasonable person in the declarant's position would not have made the statement unless believing it to be true. A statement tending to expose the declarant to criminal liability and offered to exculpate the accused is not admissible unless corroborating circumstances clearly indicate the trustworthiness of the statement.

(4) Statement of personal or family history. — (A) A statement concerning the declarant's own birth, adoption, marriage, divorce, legitimacy, relationship by blood, adoption, or marriage, ancestry, or other similar fact of personal or family history, even though declarant had no means of

acquiring personal knowledge of the matter stated; or (B) a statement concerning the foregoing matters, and death also, of another person, if the declarant was related to the other by blood, adoption, or marriage or was so intimately associated with the other's family as to be likely to have accurate information concerning the matter declared.

(5) [Transferred to Rule 807]

(6) Forfeiture by wrongdoing. — A statement offered against a party that has engaged or acquiesced in wrongdoing that was intended to, and did, procure the unavailability of the declarant as a witness.

Rule 805. Hearsay Within Hearsay

Hearsay included within hearsay is not excluded under the hearsay rule if each part of the combined statements conforms with an exception to the hearsay rule provided in these rules.

Rule 806. Attacking and Supporting Credibility of Declarant

When a hearsay statement, or a statement defined in Rule 801(d)(2)(C), (D), or (E), has been admitted in evidence, the credibility of the declarant may be attacked, and if attacked may be supported, by any evidence which would be admissible for those purposes if declarant had testified as a witness. Evidence of a statement or conduct by the declarant at any time, inconsistent with the declarant's hearsay statement, is not subject to any requirement that the declarant may have been afforded an opportunity to deny or explain. If the party against whom a hearsay statement has been admitted calls the declarant as a witness, the party is entitled to examine the declarant on the statement as if under cross-examination.

Rule 807. Residual Exception

A statement not specifically covered by Rule 803 or 804 but having equivalent circumstantial guarantees of trustworthiness, is not excluded by the hearsay rule, if the court determines that (A) the statement is offered as evidence of a material fact; (B) the statement is more probative on the point for which it is offered than any other evidence which the proponent can procure through reasonable efforts; and (C) the general purposes of these rules and the interests of justice will best be served by admission of the statement into evidence. However, a statement may not be admitted under this exception unless the proponent of it makes known to the adverse party sufficiently in advance of the trial or hearing to provide the adverse party with a fair opportunity to prepare to meet it, the proponent's intention to offer the statement and the particulars of it, including the name and address of the declarant.

Article IX. Authentication and Identification

Rule 901. Requirement of Authentication or Identification

(a) General provision

  (b) Illustrations

     (1) Testimony of witness with knowledge

     (2) Nonexpert opinion on handwriting

     (3) Comparison by trier or expert witness

     (4) Distinctive characteristics and the like

     (5) Voice identification

     (6) Telephone conversations

     (7) Public records or reports

     (8) Ancient documents or data compilation

     (9) Process or system

     (10) Methods provided by statute or rule

Rule 902. Self-authentication

Rule 903. Subscribing Witness' Testimony Unnecessary

Rule 901. Requirement of Authentication or Identification

  (a) *General provision.* — The requirement of authentication or identification as a condition precedent to admissibility is satisfied by evidence sufficient to support a finding that the matter in question is what its proponent claims.

  (b) *Illustrations.* — By way of illustration only, and not by way of limitation, the following are examples of authentication or identification conforming with the requirements of this rule:

    (1) Testimony of witness with knowledge. — Testimony that a matter is what it is claimed to be.

    (2) Nonexpert opinion on handwriting. — Nonexpert opinion as to the genuineness of handwriting, based upon familiarity not acquired for purposes of the litigation.

    (3) Comparison by trier or expert witness. — Comparison by the trier of fact or by expert witnesses with specimens which have been authenticated.

    (4) Distinctive characteristics and the like. — Appearance, contents, substance, internal patterns, or other distinctive characteristics, taken in conjunction with circumstances.

    (5) Voice identification. — Identification of a voice, whether heard firsthand or through mechanical or electronic transmission or recording, by opinion based upon hearing the voice at any time under circumstances connecting it with the alleged speaker.

    (6) Telephone conversations. — Telephone conversations, by evidence that a call was made to the number assigned at the time by the telephone company to a particular person or business, if (A) in the case of a person, circumstances, including self-identification, show the person answering to be the one called, or (B) in the case of a business, the call was made to a place of business and the conversation related to business reasonably transacted over the telephone.

(7) Public records or reports. — Evidence that a writing authorized by law to be recorded or filed and in fact recorded or filed in a public office, or a purported public record, report, statement, or data compilation, in any form, is from the public office where items of this nature are kept.

(8) Ancient documents or data compilation. — Evidence that a document or data compilation, in any form, (A) is in such condition as to create no suspicion concerning its authenticity, (B) was in a place where it, if authentic, would likely be, and (C) has been in existence 20 years or more at the time it is offered.

(9) Process or system. — Evidence describing a process or system used to produce a result and showing that the process or system produces an accurate result.

(10) Methods provided by statute or rule. — Any method of authentication or identification provided by Act of Congress or by other rules prescribed by the Supreme Court pursuant to statutory authority.

Rule 902. Self-authentication

Extrinsic evidence of authenticity as a condition precedent to admissibility is not required with respect to the following:

(1) *Domestic public documents under seal.* — A document bearing a seal purporting to be that of the United States, or of any State, district, Commonwealth, territory, or insular possession thereof, or the Panama Canal Zone, or the Trust Territory of the Pacific Islands, or of a political subdivision, department, officer, or agency thereof, and a signature purporting to be an attestation or execution.

(2) *Domestic public documents not under seal.* — A document purporting to bear the signature in the official capacity of an officer or employee of any entity included in paragraph (1) hereof, having no seal, if a public officer having a seal and having official duties in the district or political subdivision of the officer or employee certifies under seal that the signer has the official capacity and that the signature is genuine.

(3) *Foreign public documents.* — A document purporting to be executed or attested in an official capacity by a person authorized by the laws of a foreign country to make the execution or attestation, and accompanied by a final certification as to the genuineness of the signature and official position (A) of the executing or attesting person, or (B) of any foreign official whose certificate of genuineness of signature and official position relates to the execution or attestation or is in a chain of certificates of genuineness of signature and official position relating to the execution or attestation. A final certification may be made by a secretary of an embassy or legation, consul general, consul, vice consul, or consular agent of the United States, or a diplomatic or consular official of the foreign country assigned or accredited to the United States. If reasonable opportunity has been given to all parties to investigate the authenticity and accuracy of official documents, the court may, for good cause shown, order that they be treated as presumptively authentic without final certification or permit them to be evidenced by an attested summary with or without final certification.

(4) *Certified copies of public records.* — A copy of an official record or report or entry therein, or of a document authorized by law to be recorded or filed and actually recorded or filed in a public office, including data compilations in any form, certified as correct by the custodian or other person authorized to make the certification, by certificate complying with paragraph (1), (2), or (3) of this rule or complying with any Act of Congress or rule prescribed by the Supreme Court pursuant to statutory authority.

(5) *Official publications.* — Books, pamphlets, or other publications purporting to be issued by public authority.

(6) *Newspapers and periodicals.* — Printed materials purporting to be newspapers or periodicals.

(7) *Trade inscriptions and the like.* — Inscriptions, signs, tags, or labels purporting to have been affixed in the course of business and indicating ownership, control, or origin.

(8) *Acknowledged documents.* — Documents accompanied by a certificate of acknowledgment executed in the manner provided by law by a notary public or other officer authorized by law to take acknowledgments.

(9) *Commercial paper and related documents.* — Commercial paper, signatures thereon, and documents relating thereto to the extent provided by general commercial law.

(10) *Presumptions under Acts of Congress.* — Any signature, document, or other matter declared by Act of Congress to be presumptively or prima facie genuine or authentic.

(11) *Certified domestic records of regularly conducted activity.* — The original or a duplicate of a domestic record of regularly conducted activity that would be admissible under Rule 803(6) if accompanied by a written declaration of its custodian or other qualified person, in a manner complying with any Act of Congress or rule prescribed by the Supreme Court pursuant to statutory authority, certifying that the record—

(A) was made at or near the time of the occurrence of the matters set forth by, or from information transmitted by, a person with knowledge of those matters;

(B) was kept in the course of the regularly conducted activity; and

(C) was made by the regularly conducted activity as a regular practice.

A party intending to offer a record into evidence under this paragraph must provide written notice of that intention to all adverse parties, and must make the record and declaration available for inspection sufficiently in advance of their offer into evidence to provide an adverse party with a fair opportunity to challenge them.

(12) *Certified foreign records of regularly conducted activity.* — In a civil case, the original or a duplicate of a foreign record of regularly conducted activity that would be admissible under Rule 803(6) if accompanied by a written declaration by its custodian or other qualified person certifying that the record—

(A) was made at or near the time of the occurrence of the matters set forth by, or from information transmitted by, a person with knowledge of those matters;

(B) was kept in the course of the regularly conducted activity; and

(C) was made by the regularly conducted activity as a regular practice.

The declaration must be signed in a manner that, if falsely made, would subject the maker to criminal penalty under the laws of the country where the declaration is signed. A party intending to offer a record into evidence under this paragraph must provide written notice of that intention to all adverse parties, and must make the record and declaration available for inspection sufficiently in advance of their offer into evidence to provide an adverse party with a fair opportunity to challenge them.

Rule 903. Subscribing Witness' Testimony Unnecessary

The testimony of a subscribing witness is not necessary to authenticate a writing unless required by the laws of the jurisdiction whose laws govern the validity of the writing.

Article X. Contents of Writings, Recordings, and Photographs

Rule 1001. Definitions
(1) Writings and recordings
(2) Photographs
(3) Original
(4) Duplicate
Rule 1002. Requirement of Original
Rule 1003. Admissibility of Duplicates
Rule 1004. Admissibility of Other Evidence of Contents
(1) Originals lost or destroyed
(2) Original not obtainable
(3) Original in possession of opponent
(4) Collateral matters
Rule 1005. Public Records
Rule 1006. Summaries
Rule 1007. Testimony or Written Admission of Party
Rule 1008. Functions of Court and Jury

Rule 1001. Definitions

For purposes of this article the following definitions are applicable:

(1) *Writings and recordings.* — "Writings" and "recordings" consist of letters, words, or numbers, or their equivalent, set down by handwriting, typewriting, printing, photostating, photographing, magnetic impulse, mechanical or electronic recording, or other form of data compilation.

(2) *Photographs.* — "Photographs" include still photographs, X-ray films, video tapes, and motion pictures.

(3) *Original.* — An "original" of a writing or recording is the writing or recording itself or any counterpart intended to have the same effect by a person executing or issuing it. An "original" of a photograph includes the negative or any print therefrom. If data are stored in a computer or similar device, any printout or other output readable by sight, shown to reflect the data accurately, is an "original".

(4) *Duplicate.* — A "duplicate" is a counterpart produced by the same impression as the original, or from the same matrix, or by means of photography, including enlargements and miniatures, or by mechanical or electronic re-recording, or by chemical reproduction, or by other equivalent techniques which accurately reproduces the original.

Rule 1002. Requirement of Original

To prove the content of a writing, recording, or photograph, the original writing, recording, or photograph is required, except as otherwise provided in these rules or by Act of Congress.

Rule 1003. Admissibility of Duplicates

A duplicate is admissible to the same extent as an original unless (1) a genuine question is raised as to the authenticity of the original or (2) in the circumstances it would be unfair to admit the duplicate in lieu of the original.

Rule 1004. Admissibility of Other Evidence of Contents

The original is not required, and other evidence of the contents of a writing, recording, or photograph is admissible if—

(1) *Originals lost or destroyed.* — All originals are lost or have been destroyed, unless the proponent lost or destroyed them in bad faith; or

(2) *Original not obtainable.* — No original can be obtained by any available judicial process or procedure; or

(3) *Original in possession of opponent.* — At a time when an original was under the control of the party against whom offered, that party was put on notice, by the pleadings or otherwise, that the contents would be a subject of proof at the hearing, and that party does not produce the original at the hearing; or

(4) *Collateral matters.* — The writing, recording, or photograph is not closely related to a controlling issue.

Rule 1005. Public Records

The contents of an official record, or of a document authorized to be recorded or filed and actually recorded or filed, including data compilations in any form, if otherwise admissible, may be proved by copy, certified as correct in accordance with rule 902 or testified to be correct by a witness who has compared it with the original. If a copy which complies with the foregoing cannot be obtained by the exercise of reasonable diligence, then other evidence of the contents may be given.

Rule 1006. Summaries

The contents of voluminous writings, recordings, or photographs which cannot conveniently be examined in court may be presented in the form of a chart, summary, or calculation. The originals, or duplicates, shall be made available for examination or copying, or both, by other parties at reasonable time and place. The court may order that they be produced in court.

Rule 1007. Testimony or Written Admission of Party

Contents of writings, recordings, or photographs may be proved by the testimony or deposition of the party against whom offered or by that party's written admission, without accounting for the nonproduction of the original.

Rule 1008. Functions of Court and Jury

When the admissibility of other evidence of contents of writings, recordings, or photographs under these rules depends upon the fulfillment of a condition of fact, the question whether the condition has been fulfilled is ordinarily for the court to determine in accordance with the provisions of rule 104. However, when an issue is raised (a) whether the asserted writing ever existed, or (b) whether another writing, recording, or photograph produced at the trial is the original, or (c) whether other evidence of contents correctly reflects the contents, the issue is for the trier of fact to determine as in the case of other issues of fact.

Article XI. Miscellaneous Rules

Rule 1101. Applicability of Rules
- (a) Courts and judges
- (b) Proceedings generally
- (c) Rule of privilege
- (d) Rules inapplicable
  - (1) Preliminary questions of fact
  - (2) Grand jury
  - (3) Miscellaneous proceedings
- (e) Rules applicable in part

Rule   1102. Amendments
Rule   1103. Title

Rule 1101. Applicability of Rules

(a) *Courts and judges.* — These rules apply to the United States district courts, the District Court of Guam, the District Court of the Virgin Islands, the District Court for the Northern Mariana Islands, the United States courts of appeals, the United States Claims Court, and to United States bankruptcy judges and United States magistrate judges, in the actions, cases, and proceedings and to the extent hereinafter set forth. The terms "judge" and "court" in these rules include United States bankruptcy judges and United States magistrate judges.

(b) *Proceedings generally.* — These rules apply generally to civil actions and proceedings, including admiralty and maritime cases, to criminal cases and proceedings, to contempt proceedings except those in which the court may act summarily, and to proceedings and cases under title 11, United States Code.

(c) *Rule of privilege.* — The rule with respect to privileges applies at all stages of all actions, cases, and proceedings.

(d) *Rules inapplicable.* — The rules (other than with respect to privileges) do not apply in the following situations:

(1) Preliminary questions of fact. — The determination of questions of fact preliminary to admissibility of evidence when the issue is to be determined by the court under rule 104.

(2) Grand jury. — Proceedings before grand juries.

(3) Miscellaneous proceedings. — Proceedings for extradition or rendition; preliminary examinations in criminal cases; sentencing, or granting or revoking probation; issuance of warrants for arrest, criminal summonses, and search warrants; and proceedings with respect to release on bail or otherwise.

(e) *Rules applicable in part.* — In the following proceedings these rules apply to the extent that matters of evidence are not provided for in the statutes which govern procedure therein or in other rules prescribed by the Supreme Court pursuant to statutory authority: the trial of misdemeanors and other petty offenses before United States magistrate judges; review of agency actions when the facts are subject to trial *de novo* under section 706(2)(F) of title 5, United States Code; review of orders of the Secretary of Agriculture under section 2 of the Act entitled "An Act to authorize association of producers of agricultural products" approved February 18, 1922 (7 U.S.C. 292), and under sections 6 and 7(c) of the Perishable Agricultural Commodities Act, 1930 (7 U.S.C. 499f, 499g(c)); naturalization and revocation of naturalization under sections 310-318 of the Immigration and Nationality Act (8 U.S.C. 1421-1429); prize proceedings in admiralty under sections 7651-7681 of title 10, United States Code; review of orders of the Secretary of the Interior under section 2 of the Act entitled "An Act authorizing associations of producers of aquatic products" approved June 25, 1934 (15 U.S.C. 522); review of orders of petroleum control boards under section 5 of the Act entitled "An Act to regulate interstate and foreign commerce in petroleum and its products by prohibiting the shipment in such commerce of petroleum and its products produced in violation of State law, and for other purposes", approved February 22, 1935 (15 U.S.C. 715d); actions for fines, penalties, or forfeitures under part V of title IV of the Tariff Act of 1930 (19 U.S.C. 1581-1624), or under the Anti-Smuggling Act (19 U.S.C. 1701-1711); criminal libel for condemnation, exclusion of imports, or other proceedings under the Federal Food, Drug, and Cosmetic Act (21 U.S.C. 301-392); disputes between seamen under sections 4079, 4080, and 4081 of the Revised Statutes (22 U.S.C. 256-258); *habeas corpus* under sections 2241-2254 of title 28, United States Code; motions to vacate, set aside or correct sentence under section 2255 of title 28, United States Code; actions for penalties for refusal to transport destitute seamen under section 4578 of the Revised Statutes (46 U.S.C. 679); actions against the United States under the Act entitled "An Act authorizing suits against the United States in admiralty for damage caused by and salvage service rendered to public vessels belonging to the United States, and for other purposes", approved March 3, 1925 (46 U.S.C. 781-790), as implemented by section 7730 of title 10, United States Code.

Rule 1102. Amendments

Amendments to the Federal Rules of Evidence may be made as provided in section 2072 of title 28 of the United States Code.

Rule 1103. Title

These rules may be known and cited as the Federal Rules of Evidence.